COLLINS

Easy Learning FRENCH DICTIONARY

D0734111

Collins
An Imprint of HarperCollins*Publishers*

first published in this edition 1998

© HarperCollins Publishers 1996, 1998

latest reprint 2000

HarperCollins Publishers
Westerhill Road, Bishopbriggs, Glasgow G64 2QT, Great Britain

The HarperCollins website address is
www.**fire**and**water**.com

Collins® and Bank of English® are registered trademarks
of HarperCollins Publishers Limited

ISBN 0 00 472189-6

---

project management
Ray Carrick, Michela Clari

general editor
Horst Kopleck

editorial coordination
Vivian Marr, Nicola Cooke

editors
Christine Penman
Daphne Day
Chantal Testa
Harry Campbell
Cécile Aubinière-Robb
Gavin Killip
Hélène Bernaërt
Elspeth Anderson
Sabine Citron

computing staff
Ann Rautenbach

our thanks to the following
for their help in researching the project
Maree Airlie, Teresa Alvarez, Phyllis Gautier, Janet Gough, Sharon Hunter, Mary James, Cordelia Lilly, Carol MacLeod, Jill McNair, Janet Chalmers

maps
HarperCollins Cartographic

series editor
Lorna Sinclair Knight

Corpus Acknowledgements

We would like to acknowledge the assistance of the many hundreds of individuals and companies who have kindly given permission for copyright material to be used in The Bank of English. The written sources include many national and regional newspapers in Britain and overseas; magazine and periodical publishers; and book publishers in Britain, the United States and Australia. Extensive spoken data has been provided by radio and television broadcasting companies; research workers at many universities and other institutions; and numerous individual contributors. We are grateful to them all.

All rights reserved

A catalogue record for this book is available from the British Library

Printed and bound in Italy by Rotolito Lombarda S.p.A.

ɔw to use the dictionary 3
ENCH → ENGLISH 11
ames 271
ench verbs 281
umbers 300
me and Date 301
NGLISH → FRENCH 303

INTRODUCTION

llins Easy Learning French Dictionary is an innovative new dictionary designed specifically for yone starting to learn French. We are grateful to all those teachers who have contributed its development by advising us on how to tailor it to the needs of their students. We also atefully acknowledge the help of the Northern Examinations and Assessment Board, whom have consulted throughout this project, and whose word lists and exam papers we refully studied when compiling this dictionary.

HOW TO USE THE DICTIONARY

ing a dictionary is a skill you can improve with practice and by following some basic idelines. This section gives you a detailed explanation of how to use the dictionary to sure you get the most out of it.

e answers to all the questions in this section are on page 10.

AKE SURE YOU LOOK IN THE RIGHT SIDE OF THE DICTIONARY

e French–English side comes first: you look there to find the meaning of a French word. e second part is English–French. That's what you need for translating into French. remind yourself which side is which, you could remember the phrase *French first.*) At the p of every page, you will see either **French ~ English** or **English ~ French**, so you can see mediately if you've got the side you want. The middle pages of the book have a red border that you can see where one side finishes and the other starts.

> **Check:** 1 Which side of the dictionary would you need to look up to translate *le fauteuil?*

NDING THE WORD YOU WANT

hen you are looking for a word, for example *nouveau*, look at the first letter – **n** – and find e **N** section in the French–English side. Look at page 170. At the top of the page, you'll d the words **négatif** → **n'importe**. These are the first and last words on that page. So uveau is not going to be on page 170 because its second letter, **o**, comes after **i**, the second ter of **n'importe**. You have to go past all the words starting with **ne** and all the words rting with **ni** until you get to words starting with **no**. Scan down these until you find the ord you want. Remember that even if a letter has an accent on it, it makes no difference to e alphabetical order.

> **Check:** 2 Which comes first – **nager** or **nécessaire**?
> 3 Does **nouveau** come before or after **Noël**?
> 4 Does **chou-fleur** come before or after **chocolat**?

MAKE SURE YOU LOOK AT THE RIGHT ENTRY

An entry is made up of a **word**, its *translations* and, often, example phrases to show you ho to use the translations. If there is more than one entry for the same word, then there is a warning box to tell you so. Look at the following example entries:

flat ADJECTIVE
see also flat NOUN
1 *plat* ◇ *a flat roof* un toit plat ◇ *flat shoes* des chaussures plates
2 *crevé* (*tyre*) ◇ *I've got a flat tyre.* J'ai un pneu crevé.

flat NOUN
see also flat ADJECTIVE
l' *appartement* MASC ◇ *She lives in a flat.* Elle habite un appartement.

Check: 5 Which of the two entries above will help you translate the phrase *I live in a flat?*

Look for the two clues which are there to help you:
◇ an example similar to what you want to say
◇ the word NOUN

Always pay attention to information boxes – they tell you if there is more than one entry f the same word, give you guidance on grammatical points, and tell you about differences between French and British life.

NOUNS, PRONOUNS, ADJECTIVES, VERBS, ADVERBS, PREPOSITIONS

There are two entries for **flat** because this word can be a noun or an adjective. It helps to choose correctly between entries if you know how to recognise these different types of wor

Nouns and pronouns

Nouns often appear with words like *a, the, this, that, my, your* and *his.* They can be singular (abbreviated to SING in the dictionary):

a friend *the* street *this* year *my* dog *your* car

or plural (abbreviated to PL in the dictionary):

the facts *those* people *his* shoes *our* holidays

They can be the subject of a verb:

Vegetables are good for you

or the object of a verb:

I play *tennis*

Words like *I, me, you, he, she, him, her* and *they* are pronouns. They can be used instead of nouns. You can refer to a person as *he* or *she* or to a thing as *it.*

Check: *I bought my mother a box of chocolates.*

6 Which three words are nouns in this sentence?
7 Which of the nouns is plural?
8 Which word is a pronoun?

French nouns are either masculine or feminine (abbreviated to MASC and FEM). Masculine nouns are shown by **le**:

le bateau *le* chien *le* jardin

eminine nouns are shown by **la**:

la porte *la* robe *la* souris

f a noun starts with a vowel or a vowel sound, then **le** or **la** becomes **l'**:

*l'*ami *l'*eau *l'*orage *l'*histoire

he plural forms of **le, la** and **l'** is **les.** As in English, the plural of most French nouns is made y adding **s:**

les chiens *les* portes *les* tables

f the singular form already ends in **s,** or if it ends in **x,** then you don't have to add anything:

*l'*ananas *les ananas*
la voix *les voix*

ometimes, however, the plural form is irregular and this is shown in the entry:

le **cheval** NOUN
(PL les **chevaux**)
horse

horse NOUN
le *cheval*
(les *chevaux* PL)

Check: *Je me brosse les dents tous les soirs*

9 Two words in this sentence are nouns. Which ones?
10 Are they singular or plural?
11 What is the plural form of *le choix*?
12 Look in the dictionary to find the plural form of *le travail.*

djectives

lat can be an adjective as well as a noun. Adjectives describe nouns: your tyre can be **flat,** ou can have a pair of **flat** shoes.

Check: 13 *dark* is an adjective in one of these sentences and a noun in the other. Which is which?

I'm not afraid of the dark.
She's got dark hair.

rench adjectives can be masculine or feminine, singular or plural, depending on the noun hey describe:

un **petit** garçon (MASC SING)
une **petit***e* fille (FEM SING = masculine singular + **e**)
trois **petit**s garçons (MASC PL = masculine singular + **s**)
trois **petit***es* filles (FEM PL = masculine singular + **es**)

nly the masculine singular form of regular adjectives is shown in the dictionary. So if you vant to find out what sort of shoes **des chaussures plates** are, look under **plat**.

f the feminine or the plural form of an adjective does *not* follow the above rules, then the rregular form is shown in the dictionary:

frais ADJECTIVE
(FEM SING **fraîche**)
see also frais NOUN
fresh

fresh ADJECTIVE
frais MASC
fraîche FEM

bon ADJECTIVE, ADVERB
(FEM SING **bonne**)
see also bon NOUN
good

good ADJECTIVE
1 *bon* MASC
bonne FEM

If the masculine form ends in **s** or **x**, then you don't need to add **s** to make the masculine plural. And if the masculine form ends in **e**, you don't add anything to form the feminine form. But remember – if the adjective ends in **é**, then it behaves like any regular adjective.

MASC SING	FEM SING	MASC PL	FEM PL
gris	grise	gris	grises
anxieux	anxieuse	anxieux	anxieuses
agréable	agréable	agréables	agréables
passé	passée	passés	passées

Some adjectives remain the same whether they're masculine, feminine or plural. This is also shown in the dictionary:

arrière ADJECTIVE (MASC, FEM, PL)
see also arrière NOUN
back

back ADJECTIVE, ADVERB
see also back NOUN, VERB
arrière MASC, FEM, PL

Check: 14 What is the feminine singular form of **vert**?
15 What is the masculine plural form of **aimable**?
16 What is the masculine singular form of **heureux**?
17 What is the masculine plural form of **gras**? And the feminine singular (look in the dictionary for this one)?

Verbs

His time in the race was a new world record.
She's going to record the programme for me.

Record in the first sentence is a noun. In the second, it is a verb.

One way to recognize a verb is that it frequently comes with a pronoun such as **I, you** or **sh** or with somebody's name. Verbs can relate to the present, the past or the future. They have number of different forms to show this: **I'm going** (present), **he will go** (future), and **Nicola went by herself** (past). Often verbs appear with **to: they promised to go**. This basic form of the verb is called the infinitive.

In this dictionary, verbs are preceded by "to", so you can identify them at a glance. No matter which of the four previous examples you want to translate, you should look up to **g** not **going** or **went.** If you want to translate **I thought**, look up to **think**.

Check: 18 What would you look up to translate the verbs in these phrases?

I ***went***	*she's* ***crying***	*he* ***was lying***
I ***did*** *it*	*he's out*	*they've* ***gone***

Verbs have different endings, depending on whether you are talking about **je, tu, nous, ils** etc: **j'aime, tu aimes, nous aimons, ils aiment** etc. They also have different forms for the present, future, past etc. **Nous mangeons** (*we eat* = present), **nous avons mangé** (*we ate* = past). **Manger** is the infinitive and is the form that appears in the dictionary.

Sometimes the verb changes completely between the infinitive form and the **je, tu, ils** etc form. For example, *I go* is **je vais**, but *to go* is **aller**, and **nous faisons** (*we do*) comes from **fair** (*to do*). **J'ai fait** (*I have done* or *I did*) also comes from **faire**.

On pages 284-297 of the dictionary, you will find tables of the most important forms of 14 French verbs. And on pages 298-299, you will find a list of the main forms of other French irregular verbs.

dverbs

n adverb is a word that describes a verb or an adjective:

Write ***soon.*** *They arrived* ***late.***

Check your work ***carefully.*** *The film was* ***very*** *good.*

the sentence *The swimming pool is open daily,* **daily** is an adverb describing the adjective **pen.** In the phrase *my daily routine,* **daily** is an adjective describing the noun **routine.** We use e same word in English but to get the right French translation, it is important to know if 's being used as an adjective or an adverb. When you look up daily you find:

daily ADJECTIVE, ADVERB
1 *quotidien* MASC
quotidienne FEM
◇ *It's part of my daily routine.* Ça fait partie de mes occupations quotidiennes.
2 *tous les jours* ◇ *The pool is open daily from 9 a.m. to 6 p.m.* La piscine est ouverte tous les jours de neuf heures à dix-huit heures.

he examples show you **daily** being used as an adjective and as an adverb and will help you hoose the right French translation.

> **Check:** Take the sentence *The menu changes daily.*
>
> 19 Does **daily** go with the noun **menu** or the verb **changes**?
> 20 Is it an adverb or an adjective?
> 21 How would you translate **daily** in this sentence?

repositions

repositions are words like **for, with** and **across,** which are followed by nouns or pronouns:

I've got a present ***for*** *David.* *Come* ***with*** *me.* *He ran* ***across*** *the road.*

> **Check:** *The party's over.*
> *The shop's just over the road.*
>
> 22 In one of these sentences **over** is an adjective describing a noun, in the other it is a preposition followed by a noun. Which is which?

HOOSING THE RIGHT TRANSLATION

he main translation of a word is shown on a new line in underlined italic to make it stand ut from the rest of the entry. If there is more than one main translation for a word, each ne is numbered. If an entry continues over the page, there is a signpost to indicate this.

ften you will see phrases in *italics,* preceded by a white diamond ◇. These show how the anslation they follow can be used. They also help you choose the translation you want cause they give you examples of the context in which it can be used.

bouillant ADJECTIVE
1 *boiling* ◇ *Faites cuire les pâtes à l'eau bouillante.* Cook the pasta in boiling water.
2 *piping hot* ◇ *La soupe est servie bouillante.* The soup should be served piping hot.

to **overlook** VERB
1 *donner sur* (*have view of*) ◇ *The hotel overlooked the beach.* L'hôtel donnait sur la plage.
2 *négliger* (*forget about*) ◇ *He had overlooked one important problem.* Il avait négligé un problème important.

Check: 23 Use the dictionary to translate *That's a very hard question.*

Words often have more than one meaning and more than one translation: if you don't **get** to the station on time, you don't arrive on time, but if you say "I don't **get** it", you mean you don't understand. When you are translating from English, be careful to choose the French word that has the particular meaning you want. The dictionary offers you a lot of help with this. Look at the following entry:

pool NOUN
1 la *flaque* (*puddle*)
2 l' *étang* MASC (*pond*)
3 la *piscine* (*for swimming*)
4 le *billard américain* (*game*)

A **pool** can be a puddle, a pond or a swimming pool; **pool** can also be a game. The underlined italic highlights all the main translations, the numbers tell you that there is more than one possible translation and the words in brackets in *italics* after the translations help you choose which translation you want.

Check: 24 How would you translate *I like playing pool?*

Never take the first translation you see without looking at the others. Always look to see if there is more than one translation in underlined italic.

Phrases in **bold type** preceded by a black diamond ◆ are phrases which are particularly common or important. Sometimes the phrases have a completely different translation from the main translation; sometimes the translation is the same. For example:

le **dommage** NOUN
damage ◇ *La tempête a causé d'importants dommages.* The storm caused a lot of damage.
◆ **C'est dommage.** It's a shame. ◇ *C'est dommage que tu ne puisses pas venir.* It's a shame you can't come.

to **go out** VERB
1 *sortir* (*person*) ◇ *Are you going out tonight?* Tu sors ce soir?
◆ **to go out with somebody** sortir avec quelqu'un ◇ *Are you going out with him?* Est-ce que tu sors avec lui?
2 *s'éteindre* (*light, fire, candle*) ◇ *Suddenly the lights went out.* Soudain les lumières se sont éteintes.

When you look up a word, make sure you look beyond the main translations to see if the entry includes any **bold phrases**.

Check: 25 In a job advert you read that applicants *doivent tous passer une viste médicale.* What must they all do?

Look up **viste** and find the answer as quickly as possible by skimming down the **bold phrases**.

MAKING USE OF PHRASES IN THE DICTIONARY

Sometimes when you look up a word you will find not only the word, but the exact phrase you want. For example, you might want to say *What's the date today*? Look up **date** and you will find:

date NOUN
1 la *date* ◇ *my date of birth* ma date de naissance
◆ **What's the date today?** Quel jour sommes-nous?

metimes you have to adapt what you find in the dictionary. If you want to say *I play darts* d look up **dart** you will find:

dart NOUN
la *fléchette* ◇ *to play darts* jouer aux fléchettes

u have to substitute *je joue* for the infinitive form *jouer*. You will often have to adapt the finitive in this way, adding the correct ending for **je**, **tu**, **il** etc and choosing the present, ture or past form. For help with this, look at the verb tables. **Jouer** is a verb ending in *–er* it follows the same pattern as **aimer**, which is set out on page 284.

Check: 26 How would you say *We played football?*

rases containing nouns and adjectives also need to be adapted. You may need to make the un plural, or the adjective feminine or plural. Remember that some nouns and adjectives ve irregular feminine or plural forms and that this is shown in the entry.

Check: 27 How would you say *The jewels are beautiful?*

ON'T OVERUSE THE DICTIONARY

takes time to look up words so try to avoid using the dictionary unnecessarily, **especially exams**. Think carefully about what you want to say and see if you can put it another way, ing words you already know. To rephrase things you can:

- ◇ Use a word with a similar meaning. This is particularly easy with adjectives, as there are a lot of words which mean good, bad, big etc and you're sure to know at least one.
- ◇ Use negatives: if the cake you made was a total disaster, you could just say it wasn't very good.
- ◇ Use particular examples instead of general terms. If you are asked to describe the sports facilities in your area, and time is short, don't look up *facilities* - say something like "In our town there is a swimming pool and a football ground."

Check: 28 You want to ask *Have you got any pets?* How could you avoid using the word *pet* if you don't know it?
29 How could you say *The palace of Versailles is huge* without looking up the word *huge?*

ou can also often guess the meaning of a French word by using others to give you a clue. you see the sentence *j'écoute de la musique rap*, you may not know the meaning of the word **oute**, but you do know it's a verb because it's preceded by **j'**. Therefore it must be mething you can do to music: **listen**. So the translation is: *I listen to rap music.*

Check: 30 In a description of a holiday centre you see a picture of bikes and read *On peut louer des vélos: 20F la journée.* You may not know the meaning of *louer*, but you can see that you have to pay 20 francs, which gives you a clue to what it could mean. What can you do – ride bikes, borrow bikes or hire bikes?

Answers

1 the French side
2 **nager**
3 **nouveau** comes after **Noël**
4 **chou–fleur** comes after **chocolat**
5 the second entry (the NOUN entry)
6 **mother, box** and **chocolates** are nouns
7 **chocolates** is plural
8 **I** is a pronoun
9 **dents** and **soirs** are nouns
10 they are both plural
11 **les choix**
12 **les travaux**
13 **dark** in the first sentence is a noun and in the second, it's an adjective
14 **verte**
15 **aimables**
16 **heureux**
17 the masculine plural form is **gras** and the feminine singular form is **grasse**
18 to **go**, to **cry**, to **lie**, to **do**, to **be**, to **go**
19 **daily** goes with the verb **changes**
20 it is an adverb
21 **tous les jours**
22 in the first sentence, **over** is an adjective and in the second, it's a preposition
23 **c'est une question très difficile**
24 **j'aime jouer au billard américain**
25 they must all have a **medical examination**
26 **nous avons joué au football**
27 **les bijoux sont beaux**
28 you could ask, "Have you got a cat or a dog?"
29 you could say, "Very big."
30 you can **hire** bikes

A

a VERB *see* **avoir**

a *should not be confused with the preposition* **à**.

- **Il a beaucoup d'amis.** He has a lot of friends.
- **Il a mangé des frites.** He had some chips.
- **Il a neigé pendant la nuit.** It snowed during the night.
- **il y a (1)** there is ◇ *Il y a un bon film à la télé.* There's a good film on TV.
- **il y a (2)** there are ◇ *Il y a beaucoup de monde.* There are lots of people.

à PREPOSITION

à *should not be confused with the verb form* **a**. *See also* **au (=à+le)** *and* **aux (=à+les)**.

1 *at* ◇ *être à la maison* to be at home ◇ *à trois heures* at 3 o'clock

2 *in* ◇ *être à Paris* to be in Paris ◇ *habiter au Portugal* to live in Portugal ◇ *habiter à la campagne* to live in the country ◇ *au printemps* in the spring ◇ *au mois de juin* in June

3 *to* ◇ *aller à Paris* to go to Paris ◇ *aller au Portugal* to go to Portugal ◇ *aller à la campagne* to go to the country ◇ *donner quelque chose à quelqu'un* to give something to somebody ◇ *Cette veste appartient à Marie.* This jacket belongs to Marie. ◇ *Je n'ai rien à faire.* I've got nothing to do.

- **Ce livre est à Paul.** This book is Paul's.
- **Cette voiture est à nous.** This car is ours.

4 *by* ◇ *à bicyclette* by bicycle ◇ *être payé à l'heure* to be paid by the hour

- **à pied** on foot
- **C'est à côté de chez moi.** It's near my house.
- **C'est à dix kilomètres d'ici.** It's 10 kilometres from here.
- **C'est à dix minutes d'ici.** It's 10 minutes from here.
- **cent kilomètres à l'heure** 100 kilometres an hour
- **À bientôt!** See you soon! ◇ *À demain!* See you tomorrow! ◇ *À samedi!* See you on Saturday! ◇ *À tout à l'heure!* See you later!

abandonner VERB

1 *to abandon* ◇ *Avant les vacances, beaucoup de chiens sont abandonnés par leurs maîtres.* Before the holidays, a lot of dogs are abandoned by their owners.

2 *to give up* ◇ *J'ai décidé d'abandonner la natation.* I've decided to give up swimming.

l'**abeille** FEM NOUN
bee

abîmer VERB
to damage
- **s'abîmer** to get damaged

l'**abonnement** MASC NOUN
1 *season ticket*
2 *subscription* (*to magazine*)

s'**abonner** VERB
- **s'abonner à une revue** to take out a subscription to a magazine

l'**abord** MASC NOUN
- **d'abord** first ◇ *Je vais rentrer chez moi d'abord.* I'll go home first.

aboyer VERB
to bark

l'**abri** MASC NOUN
shelter
- **être à l'abri** to be under cover
- **se mettre à l'abri** to shelter

l'**abricot** MASC NOUN
apricot

s'**abriter** VERB
to shelter

l'**absence** FEM NOUN
absence
- **Il est passé pendant ton absence.** He came while you were away.

absent ADJECTIVE
absent

absolument ADVERB
absolutely

l'**accélérateur** MASC NOUN
accelerator

accélérer VERB
to accelerate

l'**accent** MASC NOUN
accent ◇ *Il a l'accent de Marseille.* He has a Marseilles accent.
- **un accent aigu** an acute accent
- **un accent grave** a grave accent
- **un accent circonflexe** a circumflex

accentuer VERB
to stress

accepter VERB
to accept
- **accepter de faire quelque chose** to agree to do something

l'**accessoire** MASC NOUN
1 *accessory* ◇ *les accessoires de mode* fashion accessories
2 *prop*

l'**accident** MASC NOUN
accident ◇ *un accident de la route* a

PTO

road accident

accompagner VERB
to accompany

l'**accord** MASC NOUN
agreement
- **être d'accord** to agree ◇ *Tu es d'accord avec moi?* Do you agree with me?
- **se mettre d'accord** to come to an agreement
- **D'accord!** OK!

l'**accordéon** MASC NOUN
accordion ◇ *Ray joue de l'accordéon.* Ray plays the accordion.

l'**accoudoir** MASC NOUN
armrest

l'**accrochage** MASC NOUN
collision

accrocher VERB
- **accrocher quelque chose à (1)** to hang something on ◇ *Il a accroché sa veste au portemanteau.* He hung his jacket on the coat rack.
- **accrocher quelque chose à (2)** to hitch something up to ◇ *Ils ont accroché la remorque à leur voiture.* They hitched the trailer up to their car.
- **s'accrocher à quelque chose** to catch on something ◇ *Sa jupe s'est accrochée aux ronces.* Her skirt got caught on the brambles.

s'**accroupir** VERB
to squat down

l'**accueil** MASC NOUN
welcome ◇ *Il nous a remerciés de notre accueil.* He thanked us for our welcome.
- **Elle s'occupe de l'accueil des visiteurs.** She's in charge of looking after visitors.

accueillir VERB
to welcome

accumuler VERB
to accumulate
- **s'accumuler** to pile up

l'**accusé** MASC NOUN
accused ◇ *L'accusé a déclaré que...* The accused stated that...
- **un accusé de réception** an acknowledgement of receipt

l'**accusée** FEM NOUN
accused

accuser VERB
to accuse ◇ *accuser quelqu'un de quelque chose* to accuse somebody of something

l'**achat** MASC NOUN
purchase
- **faire des achats** to do some shopping

acheter VERB
to buy ◇ *J'ai acheté des gâteaux à la pâtisserie.* I bought some cakes at the cake shop.
- **acheter quelque chose à quelqu'un (1)** to buy something for somebody ◇ *Qu'est-ce que tu lui as acheté pour son anniversaire?* What did you buy him for his birthday?
- **acheter quelque chose à quelqu'un (2)** to buy something from somebody ◇ *J'ai acheté des œufs au fermier.* I bought some eggs from the farmer.

acide ADJECTIVE
see also acide NOUN
acid ◇ *Ce pamplemousse est trop acide.* This grapefruit is too acid.

l'**acide** MASC NOUN
see also acide ADJECTIVE
acid

l'**acier** MASC NOUN
steel

l'**acné** FEM NOUN
acne ◇ *Il a de l'acné.* He has acne.

acquérir VERB
to acquire

acquis VERB *see* **acquérir**

acquitter VERB
to acquit ◇ *L'accusé a été acquitté.* The accused was acquitted.

l'**acte** MASC NOUN
act
- **un acte de naissance** a birth certificate

l'**acteur** MASC NOUN
actor ◇ *Il est acteur.* He's an actor. ◇ *un acteur de cinéma* a film actor

actif ADJECTIVE
(FEM SING **active**)
active
- **la population active** the working population

l'**action** FEM NOUN
action
- **une bonne action** a good deed

s'**activer** VERB
1 *to bustle about* ◇ *Elle s'activait à préparer le repas.* She bustled about preparing the meal.
2 *to move oneself* ◇ *Allez! Active-toi!* Come on! Get moving!

l'**activité** FEM NOUN
activity

l'**actrice** FEM NOUN
actress ◇ *Elle est actrice.* She's an actress. ◇ *une actrice de cinéma* a film actress

l'**actualité** FEM NOUN
current events
- **un problème d'actualité** a topical issue

- **les actualités** the news

actuel ADJECTIVE
(FEM SING **actuelle**)
present ◇ *le système actuel* the present system
- **à l'heure actuelle** at the present time

actuellement ADVERB
at present

l'**adaptateur** MASC NOUN
adaptor

l'**addition** FEM NOUN
1 *addition* ◇ *Il a fait une erreur dans son addition.* He made a mistake in his addition.
2 *bill* ◇ *L'addition, s'il vous plaît!* Can we have the bill, please?

additionner VERB
to add up

adhésif ADJECTIVE
(FEM SING **adhésive**)
- **le ruban adhésif** sticky tape

l'**adjectif** MASC NOUN
adjective

admettre VERB
1 *to admit* ◇ *Il refuse d'admettre qu'il s'est trompé.* He won't admit that he made a mistake.
2 *to allow* ◇ *Les chiens ne sont pas admis dans le restaurant.* Dogs are not allowed in the restaurant.

l'**administration** FEM NOUN
administration
- **l'Administration** the Civil Service

admirable ADJECTIVE
wonderful

l'**admirateur** MASC NOUN
admirer

l'**admiratrice** FEM NOUN
admirer

admirer VERB
to admire

admis VERB *see* **admettre**

l'**adolescence** FEM NOUN
adolescence

l'**adolescent** MASC NOUN
teenager

l'**adolescente** FEM NOUN
teenager

adopter VERB
to adopt

adorable ADJECTIVE
lovely

adorer VERB
to love ◇ *Elle adore le chocolat.* She loves chocolate. ◇ *J'adore jouer au tennis.* I love playing tennis.

l'**adresse** FEM NOUN
address

adresser VERB
- **adresser la parole à quelqu'un** to speak to someone
- **s'adresser à quelqu'un (1)** to speak to somebody ◇ *C'est à toi que je m'adresse.* It's you I'm speaking to.
- **s'adresser à quelqu'un (2)** to go and see somebody ◇ *Adressez-vous au patron.* Go and see the boss. ◇ *Adressez-vous aux renseignements.* Ask at the enquiry desk.
- **s'adresser à quelqu'un (3)** to be aimed at somebody ◇ *Ce film s'adresse surtout aux enfants.* This film is aimed mainly at children.

l'**adulte** MASC/FEM NOUN
adult

l'**adverbe** MASC NOUN
adverb

l'**adversaire** MASC/FEM NOUN
opponent

aérien ADJECTIVE
(FEM SING **aérienne**)
- **une compagnie aérienne** an airline

l'**aérobic** MASC NOUN
aerobics ◇ *Teresa fait de l'aérobic.* Teresa does aerobics.

l'**aérogare** FEM NOUN
terminal

l'**aéroglisseur** MASC NOUN
hovercraft

l'**aéroport** MASC NOUN
airport

l'**affaire** FEM NOUN
see also les affaires
1 *case* ◇ *une affaire de drogue* a drugs case
2 *business* ◇ *Son affaire marche bien.* His business is doing well.
- **une bonne affaire** a real bargain
- **Ça fera l'affaire.** This will do nicely.
- **avoir affaire à quelqu'un** to deal with somebody

les **affaires** FEM NOUN
see also l'affaire
1 *things* ◇ *Va chercher tes affaires!* Go and get your things!
2 *business* ◇ *Les affaires marchent bien en ce moment.* Business is good at the moment. ◇ *Mêle-toi de tes affaires.* (*informal*) Mind your own business.
- **un homme d'affaires** a businessman
- **le ministre des Affaires étrangères** the Foreign Secretary

l'**affection** FEM NOUN
affection

affectueux ADJECTIVE
(FEM SING **affectueuse**)
affectionate

l'**affiche** FEM NOUN

PTO

poster

afficher VERB
to put up ◇ *Ils ont affiché les résultats dehors.* They've put the results up outside.
◆ **"Défense d'afficher"** "Stick no bills"

affilée
◆ **d'affilée** ADVERB
at a stretch ◇ *Il a travaillé douze heures d'affilée.* He worked 12 hours at a stretch.

l'**affluence** FEM NOUN
◆ **les heures d'affluence** the rush hour

s'**affoler** VERB
to panic ◇ *Ne t'affole pas!* Don't panic!

affranchir VERB
to stamp

affreux ADJECTIVE
(FEM SING **affreuse**)
awful

affronter VERB
to face ◇ *L'Allemagne affronte l'Italie en finale.* Germany will face Italy in the final.

afin de CONJUNCTION
◆ **afin de faire quelque chose** so as to do something ◇ *Je me suis levé très tôt afin d'être prêt à temps.* I got up very early so as to be ready on time.

afin que CONJUNCTION
so that
afin que *is followed by a verb in the subjunctive.*
◇ *Il m'a téléphoné afin que je sois prêt à temps.* He phoned me so that I'd be ready on time.

africain ADJECTIVE, NOUN
(FEM SING **africaine**)
African
◆ **un Africain** an African (*man*)
◆ **une Africaine** an African (*woman*)

l'**Afrique** FEM NOUN
Africa
◆ **en Afrique (1)** in Africa
◆ **en Afrique (2)** to Africa
◆ **l'Afrique du Sud** South Africa

agacer VERB
to get on somebody's nerves ◇ *Tu m'agaces avec tes questions!* You're getting on my nerves with all your questions!

l'**âge** MASC NOUN
age
◆ **Quel âge as-tu?** How old are you?

âgé ADJECTIVE
old ◇ *Son père est âgé.* His father's old. ◇ *Il est âgé de dix ans.* He's 10 years old.
◆ **les personnes âgées** the elderly

l'**agence** FEM NOUN
1 *agency*
◆ **une agence de voyages** a travel agency
2 *office* ◇ *Nous avons plusieurs agences à Londres.* We have several offices in London.
◆ **une agence immobilière** an estate agent's

l'**agenda** MASC NOUN
diary (*for appointments*)

s'**agenouiller** VERB
to kneel down

l'**agent** MASC NOUN
◆ **un agent de police** a policeman

l'**agglomération** FEM NOUN
town
◆ **l'agglomération parisienne** Greater Paris

aggraver VERB
to make worse
◆ **s'aggraver** to worsen

agir VERB
to act ◇ *Il a agi par vengeance.* He acted out of vengeance.
◆ **Il s'agit de...** It's about... ◇ *Il s'agit du club de sport.* It's about the sports club. ◇ *De quoi s'agit-il?* What is it about?
◆ **Il s'agit de faire attention.** We must be careful.

agité ADJECTIVE
1 *restless* ◇ *Les élèves sont agités.* The pupils are restless.
2 *rough* ◇ *La mer est agitée.* The sea is rough.
◆ **un sommeil agité** broken sleep

agiter VERB
to shake ◇ *Agitez la bouteille.* Shake the bottle.

l'**agneau** MASC NOUN
(PL les **agneaux**)
lamb

l'**agrafe** FEM NOUN
staple (*for papers*)

l'**agrafeuse** FEM NOUN
stapler

agrandir VERB
1 *to enlarge* ◇ *J'ai fait agrandir mes photos.* I've had my photos enlarged.
2 *to extend* ◇ *Ils ont agrandi leur jardin.* They've extended their garden.
◆ **s'agrandir** to expand ◇ *Leur magasin s'est agrandi.* Their shop has expanded.

agréable ADJECTIVE
nice

agréer VERB
◆ **Veuillez agréer, Monsieur, l'expression de mes sentiments les meilleurs. Jean Ormal.** Yours sincerely, Jean Ormal.

agressif ADJECTIVE

(FEM SING **agressive**)
aggressive

agricole ADJECTIVE
agricultural ◇ *le matériel agricole* agricultural machinery
- **une exploitation agricole** a farm

l'**agriculteur** MASC NOUN
farmer
- **Il est agriculteur.** He's a farmer.

l'**agriculture** FEM NOUN
farming

ai VERB *see* **avoir**
- **J'ai deux chats.** I have two cats.
- **J'ai bien dormi.** I slept well.

l'**aide** FEM NOUN
1 *help* ◇ *J'ai besoin de ton aide.* I need your help. ◇ *appeler quelqu'un à l'aide* to call to somebody for help
- **À l'aide!** Help!

2 *aid* ◇ *une aide financière* financial aid
- **à l'aide de** using ◇ *J'ai réussi à ouvrir la boîte à l'aide d'un couteau.* I managed to open the tin using a knife.

aider VERB
to help

l'**aide-soignant** MASC NOUN
(PL les **aides-soignants**)
auxiliary nurse ◇ *Il est aide-soignant.* He's an auxiliary nurse.

l'**aide-soignante** FEM NOUN
(PL les **aides-soignantes**)
auxiliary nurse ◇ *Françoise est aide-soignante.* Françoise is an auxiliary nurse.

aie VERB *see* **avoir**

aïe EXCLAMATION
Ouch!

aigre ADJECTIVE
sour

l'**aiguille** FEM NOUN
needle ◇ *une aiguille à tricoter* a knitting needle
- **les aiguilles d'une montre** the hands of a watch

l'**ail** MASC NOUN
garlic

l'**aile** FEM NOUN
wing

aille VERB *see* **aller**

ailleurs ADVERB
somewhere else
- **partout ailleurs** everywhere else
- **nulle part ailleurs** nowhere else
- **d'ailleurs** besides

aimable ADJECTIVE
kind

l'**aimant** MASC NOUN
magnet

aimer VERB
1 *to love* ◇ *Elle aime ses enfants.* She loves her children.

2 *to like* ◇ *Tu aimes le chocolat?* Do you like chocolate? ◇ *J'aime bien ce garçon.* I like this boy. ◇ *J'aime bien jouer au tennis.* I like playing tennis. ◇ *J'aimerais aller en Grèce.* I'd like to go to Greece.
- **J'aimerais mieux ne pas y aller.** I'd rather not go.

aîné ADJECTIVE
see also **aîné** NOUN
elder ◇ *mon frère aîné* my big brother

l'**aîné** MASC NOUN
see also **aîné** ADJECTIVE
oldest child ◇ *Il est l'aîné.* He's the oldest child.

l'**aînée** FEM NOUN
oldest child ◇ *Elle est l'aînée.* She's the oldest child.

ainsi ADVERB
in this way ◇ *Il faut faire ainsi.* This is the way to do it.
- **C'est ainsi qu'il a réussi.** That's how he succeeded.
- **ainsi que** as well as
- **et ainsi de suite** and so on

l'**air** MASC NOUN
1 *air* ◇ *l'air chaud* warm air
- **prendre l'air** to get some fresh air

2 *tune* ◇ *Elle a joué un air au piano.* She played a tune on the piano.
- **Elle a l'air fatiguée.** She looks tired.
- **Il a l'air d'un clown.** He looks like a clown.

l'**aise** FEM NOUN
- **être à l'aise** to be at ease ◇ *Elle est à l'aise avec tout le monde.* She's at ease with everybody.
- **être mal à l'aise** to be ill at ease
- **se mettre à l'aise** to make oneself comfortable

ait VERB *see* **avoir**

ajouter VERB
to add

l'**alarme** FEM NOUN
alarm ◇ *donner l'alarme* to raise the alarm

l'**Albanie** FEM NOUN
Albania

l'**album** MASC NOUN
album

l'**alcool** MASC NOUN
alcohol ◇ *Je ne bois pas d'alcool.* I don't drink alcohol.
- **les alcools forts** spirits

alcoolisé ADJECTIVE
alcoholic

- **une boisson non alcoolisée** a soft drink

les **alentours** MASC NOUN
- **dans les alentours** in the area
- **aux alentours de Paris** in the Paris area
- **aux alentours de cinq heures** around 5 o'clock

l'**algèbre** FEM NOUN
algebra

Alger NOUN
Algiers

l'**Algérie** FEM NOUN
Algeria

algérien ADJECTIVE, NOUN
(FEM SING **algérienne**)
Algerian
- **un Algérien** an Algerian (*man*)
- **une Algérienne** an Algerian (*woman*)

l'**algue** FEM NOUN
seaweed

l'**aliment** MASC NOUN
food

l'**alimentation** FEM NOUN
1 *groceries* ◇ *le rayon alimentation du supermarché* the grocery department in the supermarket
2 *diet* ◇ *Elle a une alimentation saine.* She has a healthy diet.

l'**allée** FEM NOUN
1 *path* ◇ *les allées du parc* the paths in the park
2 *drive* (*in street names*)
- **les allées et venues** comings and goings

allégé ADJECTIVE
low-fat ◇ *un yaourt allégé* a low-fat yoghurt

l'**Allemagne** FEM NOUN
Germany
- **en Allemagne (1)** in Germany
- **en Allemagne (2)** to Germany

allemand ADJECTIVE, NOUN
German ◇ *Elle parle allemand.* She speaks German.
- **un Allemand** a German (*man*)
- **une Allemande** a German (*woman*)
- **les Allemands** the Germans

aller VERB
see also aller NOUN

Present tense:

je vais	*nous allons*
tu vas	*vous allez*
il/elle va	*ils/elles vont*

Past participle: *allé*

to go ◇ *Je suis allé à Londres.* I went to London. ◇ *Je dois y aller.* I've got to go. ◇ *Elle ira le voir.* She'll go and see him. ◇ *Je vais me fâcher.* I'm going to get angry.
- **s'en aller** to go away ◇ *Je m'en vais demain.* I'm going tomorrow.
- **aller bien à quelqu'un** to suit somebody ◇ *Cette robe te va bien.* This dress suits you.
- **Allez! Dépêche-toi!** Come on! Hurry up!
- **Comment allez-vous? – Je vais bien.** How are you? – I'm fine.
- **Comment ça va? – Ça va bien.** How are you? – I'm fine.
- **aller mieux** to be better

l'**aller** MASC NOUN
see also aller VERB
1 *outward journey* ◇ *L'aller nous a pris trois heures.* The journey there took us three hours.
2 *single* (*ticket*) ◇ *Je voudrais un aller pour Angers.* I'd like a single to Angers.
- **un aller simple** a single
- **un aller retour (1)** a return ticket ◇ *Je voudrais un aller retour pour Londres.* I'd like a return to London.
- **un aller retour (2)** a round trip ◇ *Il a fait l'aller retour en dix heures.* He did the round trip in ten hours.

allergique ADJECTIVE
- **allergique à** allergic to ◇ *Je suis allergique aux poils de chat.* I'm allergic to cat fur.

allô EXCLAMATION
Hello! ◇ *Allô! Je voudrais parler à Monsieur Simon.* Hello! I'd like to speak to Mr Simon.

l'**allocation** FEM NOUN
allowance
- **les allocations chômage** unemployment benefit

s'**allonger** VERB
to lie down ◇ *Il s'est allongé sur son lit.* He lay down on his bed.

allumer VERB
1 *to put on* (*light*) ◇ *Tu peux allumer la lumière?* Can you put the light on?
2 *to light* ◇ *Elle a allumé une cigarette.* She lit a cigarette.
- **s'allumer** (*light*) to come on ◇ *La lumière s'est allumée.* The light came on.

l'**allumette** FEM NOUN
match ◇ *une boîte d'allumettes* a box of matches

l'**allure** FEM NOUN
1 *speed* ◇ *à toute allure* at top speed
2 *look* ◇ *avoir une drôle d'allure* to look odd

l'**allusion** FEM NOUN
reference

alors ADVERB

1 *then* ◇ *Tu as fini? Alors je m'en vais.* Have you finished? I'm going then.
2 *so* ◇ *Alors je lui ai dit de partir.* So I told him to leave.
- **Et alors?** So what?
3 *at that time* ◇ *Il habitait alors à Paris.* He was living in Paris at that time.
- **alors que (1)** as ◇ *Il est arrivé alors que je partais.* He arrived just as I was leaving.
- **alors que (2)** while ◇ *Alors que je travaillais dur, lui se reposait.* While I was working hard, he was resting.

les **Alpes** FEM NOUN
Alps ◇ *dans les Alpes* in the Alps

l'**alphabet** MASC NOUN
alphabet

alphabétique ADJECTIVE
alphabetical ◇ *par ordre alphabétique* in alphabetical order

l'**alpinisme** MASC NOUN
mountaineering

l'**alpiniste** MASC/FEM NOUN
mountaineer

l'**Alsace** FEM NOUN
Alsace

l'**amande** FEM NOUN
almond
- **la pâte d'amandes** marzipan

l'**amant** MASC NOUN
lover

amateur ADJECTIVE
(FEM SING **amateur**)
see also amateur NOUN
amateur ◇ *Elle est pianiste amateur.* She's an amateur pianist.

l'**amateur** MASC NOUN
see also amateur ADJECTIVE
amateur
- **en amateur** as a hobby ◇ *Il fait de la photo en amateur.* He takes photos as a hobby.
- **C'est un amateur de musique.** He's a music lover.

l'**ambassade** FEM NOUN
embassy

l'**ambassadeur** MASC NOUN
ambassador

l'**ambiance** FEM NOUN
atmosphere ◇ *Je n'aime pas l'ambiance ici.* I don't like the atmosphere here. ◇ *Il y a de l'ambiance dans ce café.* This café has a lively atmosphere.
- **la musique d'ambiance** background music

l'**ambulance** FEM NOUN
ambulance

l'**âme** FEM NOUN
soul

améliorer VERB
to improve
- **s'améliorer** to improve ◇ *Le temps s'améliore.* The weather's improving.

l'**amende** FEM NOUN
fine ◇ *une amende de cinq cents francs* a 500 franc fine

amener VERB
to bring ◇ *Qu'est-ce qui t'amène?* What brings you here? ◇ *Est-ce que je peux amener un ami?* Can I bring a friend?

amer ADJECTIVE
(FEM SING **amère**)
bitter

américain ADJECTIVE, NOUN
(FEM SING **américaine**)
American
- **un Américain** an American (*man*)
- **une Américaine** an American (*woman*)

l'**Amérique** FEM NOUN
America
- **en Amérique (1)** in America
- **en Amérique (2)** to America
- **l'Amérique du Nord** North America
- **l'Amérique du Sud** South America

l'**ami** MASC NOUN
friend
- **C'est son petit ami.** He's her boyfriend.

amical ADJECTIVE
(MASC PL **amicaux**)
friendly

l'**amie** FEM NOUN
friend
- **C'est sa petite amie.** She's his girlfriend.

l'**amitié** FEM NOUN
friendship
- **Fais mes amitiés à Paul.** Give my regards to Paul.
- **Amitiés, Christèle.** (*in letter*) Best wishes, Christèle.

l'**amour** MASC NOUN
love
- **faire l'amour** to make love

amoureux ADJECTIVE
(FEM SING **amoureuse**)
in love ◇ *être amoureux de quelqu'un* to be in love with somebody

l'**amour-propre** MASC NOUN
self-esteem

l'**amphithéâtre** MASC NOUN
lecture theatre

amplement ADVERB
- **Nous avons amplement le temps.** We have plenty of time.

l'**ampoule** FEM NOUN

PTO

1 *light bulb*
2 *blister* ◇ *J'ai une ampoule au pied.* I've got a blister on my foot.

amusant ADJECTIVE
amusing

les **amuse-gueule** MASC NOUN
party nibbles

amuser VERB
to amuse
- **s'amuser (1)** to play ◇ *Les enfants s'amusent dehors.* The children are playing outside.
- **s'amuser (2)** to enjoy oneself ◇ *On s'est bien amusés à cette soirée.* We really enjoyed ourselves at that party.

l'**an** MASC NOUN
year
- **le premier de l'an** New Year's Day
- **le nouvel an** New Year

l'**analyse** FEM NOUN
1 *analysis*
2 *test* (*medical*) ◇ *une analyse d'urine* a urine test

l'**ananas** MASC NOUN
pineapple

l'**ancêtre** MASC/FEM NOUN
ancestor

l'**anchois** MASC NOUN
anchovy

ancien ADJECTIVE
(FEM SING **ancienne**)
1 *former* ◇ *C'est une ancienne élève.* She's a former pupil.
2 *old* ◇ *notre ancienne voiture* our old car
3 *antique* ◇ *un fauteuil ancien* an antique chair

l'**ancre** FEM NOUN
anchor

Andorre FEM NOUN
Andorra

l'**âne** MASC NOUN
donkey

l'**ange** MASC NOUN
angel
- **être aux anges** to be over the moon

l'**angine** FEM NOUN
throat infection

anglais ADJECTIVE, NOUN
(FEM SING **anglaise**)
English ◇ *Est-ce que vous parlez anglais?* Do you speak English?
- **un Anglais** an Englishman
- **une Anglaise** an Englishwoman
- **les Anglais** the English

l'**angle** MASC NOUN
1 *angle* ◇ *un angle droit* a right angle
2 *corner* ◇ *à l'angle de la rue* at the corner of the street

l'**Angleterre** FEM NOUN
England
- **en Angleterre (1)** in England ◇ *J'habite en Angleterre.* I live in England.
- **en Angleterre (2)** to England ◇ *Je suis allée en Angleterre le mois dernier.* I went to England last month.

anglo- PREFIX
anglo-
- **les îles Anglo-Normandes** the Channel Islands

anglophone ADJECTIVE
English-speaking

l'**animal** MASC NOUN
(PL **les animaux**)
animal

l'**animateur** MASC NOUN
1 *host* ◇ *Il est animateur à la télé.* He's a TV host.
2 *youth leader* ◇ *Pierre est animateur au centre sportif.* Pierre is a youth leader at the sports centre.

l'**animatrice** FEM NOUN
1 *host* ◇ *Elle est animatrice à la télé.* She's a TV host.
2 *youth leader* ◇ *Cécile est animatrice au centre sportif.* Cécile is a youth leader at the sports centre.

animé ADJECTIVE
lively ◇ *Cette rue est très animée.* This is a very lively street.
- **un dessin animé** a cartoon

l'**anis** MASC NOUN
aniseed

l'**anneau** MASC NOUN
(PL **les anneaux**)
ring

l'**année** FEM NOUN
year ◇ *l'année dernière* last year ◇ *l'année prochaine* next year

l'**anniversaire** MASC NOUN
1 *birthday* ◇ *C'est l'anniversaire de Janet.* It's Janet's birthday.
2 *anniversary* ◇ *un anniversaire de mariage* a wedding anniversary

l'**annonce** FEM NOUN
advert ◇ *J'ai lu votre annonce dans le journal.* I saw your advert in the newspaper. ◇ *passer une annonce* to place an ad
- **les petites annonces** the small ads

annoncer VERB
to announce ◇ *Ils ont annoncé leurs fiançailles.* They've announced their engagement.

l'**annuaire** MASC NOUN
phone book

annuel ADJECTIVE

(FEM SING **annuelle**)
annual

annuler VERB
to cancel

anonyme ADJECTIVE
anonymous

l'**anorak** MASC NOUN
anorak

ANPE ABBREVIATION (= *Agence nationale pour l'emploi*)
national employment agency ◇ *Je suis allé à l'ANPE.* I went to the job centre.

l'**Antarctique** MASC NOUN
Antarctic

l'**antenne** FEM NOUN
1 *aerial*
2 *antenna*
- **être à l'antenne** to be on the air

l'**antibiotique** MASC NOUN
antibiotic

l'**antigel** MASC NOUN
antifreeze

s**Antilles** FEM NOUN
West Indies
- **aux Antilles (1)** in the West Indies
- **aux Antilles (2)** to the West Indies

antipathique ADJECTIVE
unpleasant ◇ *Je le trouve plutôt antipathique.* I find him rather unpleasant.

antipelliculaire ADJECTIVE
anti-dandruff

l'**antiquaire** MASC/FEM NOUN
antique dealer ◇ *Elle est antiquaire.* She's an antique dealer.

l'**antiquité** FEM NOUN
antique ◇ *un magasin d'antiquités* an antique shop
- **pendant l'antiquité** in classical times

antiseptique ADJECTIVE
see also antiseptique NOUN
antiseptic

l'**antiseptique** MASC NOUN
see also antiseptique ADJECTIVE
antiseptic

anxieux ADJECTIVE
(FEM SING **anxieuse**)
anxious ◇ *Il est anxieux de nature.* He's a born worrier.

août MASC NOUN
August
- **en août** in August

apercevoir VERB
to see ◇ *J'aperçois la côte.* I can see the shore.
- **s'apercevoir de quelque chose** to notice something
- **s'apercevoir que...** to notice that...

l'**apéritif** MASC NOUN
aperitif ◇ *Venez donc prendre l'apéritif ce soir!* Come round for drinks this evening!

apparaître VERB
to appear

l'**appareil** MASC NOUN
device
- **un appareil dentaire** a brace (*for teeth*)
- **les appareils ménagers** domestic appliances
- **un appareil photo** a camera
- **Qui est à l'appareil?** Who's speaking? (*on phone*)

apparemment ADVERB
apparently

l'**apparence** FEM NOUN
appearance

l'**apparition** FEM NOUN
appearance ◇ *Il n'a fait qu'une brève apparition.* He only appeared briefly.

l'**appartement** MASC NOUN
flat

appartenir VERB
- **appartenir à quelqu'un** to belong to somebody

apparu VERB *see* **apparaître**

l'**appel** MASC NOUN
1 *cry* ◇ *un appel au secours* a cry for help
2 *phone call*
- **faire appel à quelqu'un** to appeal to somebody
- **faire l'appel** to call the register (*in school*)
- **faire un appel de phares** to flash one's headlights

appeler VERB
to call ◇ *Elle a appelé le médecin.* She called the doctor. ◇ *J'ai appelé Richard à Londres.* I called Richard in London.
- **s'appeler** to be called ◇ *Comment ça s'appelle?* What is it called? ◇ *Elle s'appelle Muriel.* Her name's Muriel. ◇ *Comment tu t'appelles?* What's your name?

l'**appendicite** FEM NOUN
appendicitis

appétissant ADJECTIVE
appetizing

l'**appétit** MASC NOUN
appetite
- **Bon appétit!** Enjoy your meal!

applaudir VERB
to clap (*applaud*)

les **applaudissements** MASC NOUN
applause

appliquer VERB
1 *to apply*

2 *to enforce* ◇ *appliquer la loi* to enforce the law

◆ **s'appliquer** to apply oneself

apporter VERB
to bring

apprécier VERB
to appreciate

appréhender VERB
to dread ◇ *J'appréhende cette réunion.* I'm dreading this meeting.

apprendre VERB
1 *to learn* ◇ *apprendre quelque chose par cœur* to learn something by heart

◆ **apprendre à faire quelque chose** to learn to do something ◇ *J'apprends à faire la cuisine.* I'm learning to cook.

2 *to hear* ◇ *J'ai appris son départ.* I heard that she had left.

◆ **apprendre quelque chose à quelqu'un (1)** to teach somebody something ◇ *Ma mère m'a appris l'anglais.* My mother taught me English. ◇ *Elle lui a appris à conduire.* She taught him to drive.

◆ **apprendre quelque chose à quelqu'un (2)** to tell somebody something ◇ *Jean-Pierre m'a appris la nouvelle.* Jean-Pierre told me the news.

appris VERB *see* **apprendre**

approcher VERB

◆ **approcher de** to approach ◇ *Nous approchons de Paris.* We are approaching Paris.

◆ **s'approcher de** to come closer to ◇ *Ne t'approche pas, j'ai la grippe!* Don't get too close to me, I've got flu!

approuver VERB
to approve of ◇ *Je n'approuve pas ses méthodes.* I don't approve of his methods.

approximatif ADJECTIVE
(FEM SING **approximative**)
1 *approximate* ◇ *un prix approximatif* an approximate price
2 *rough* ◇ *un calcul approximatif* a rough calculation

l'**appui** MASC NOUN
support ◇ *J'ai besoin de votre appui.* I need your support.

appuyer VERB
1 *to press* ◇ *appuyer sur un bouton* to press a button
2 *to lean* ◇ *Elle a appuyé son vélo contre la porte.* She leaned her bike against the door.

◆ **s'appuyer** to lean ◇ *Elle s'est appuyée contre le mur.* She leaned against the wall. ◇ *Il s'est appuyé sur la table.* He leaned on the table.

après PREPOSITION, ADVERB
1 *after* ◇ *après le déjeuner* after lunch ◇ *après son départ* after he had left ◇ *après qu'il est parti* after he had left ◇ *Nous viendrons après avoir fait la vaisselle.* We'll come after we've done the dishes.
2 *afterwards* ◇ *aussitôt après* immediately afterwards

◆ **après coup** afterwards ◇ *J'y ai repensé après coup.* I thought about it again afterwards.

◆ **d'après** according to ◇ *D'après lui, c'est une erreur.* According to him, that's a mistake.

◆ **après tout** after all

après-demain ADVERB
the day after tomorrow

l'**après-midi** MASC OR FEM NOUN
afternoon

l'**aquarium** MASC NOUN
aquarium

arabe ADJECTIVE, NOUN
1 *Arab* ◇ *les pays arabes* the Arab countries
2 *Arabic* ◇ *la littérature arabe* Arabic literature ◇ *Il parle arabe.* He speaks Arabic.

◆ **un Arabe** an Arab (*man*)

◆ **une Arabe** an Arab (*woman*)

l'**Arabie Saoudite** FEM NOUN
Saudi Arabia

l'**araignée** FEM NOUN
spider

l'**arbitre** MASC NOUN
1 *referee*
2 *umpire*

l'**arbre** MASC NOUN
tree

◆ **un arbre généalogique** a family tree

l'**arbuste** MASC NOUN
shrub

l'**arc** MASC NOUN
bow ◇ *son arc et ses flèches* his bow and arrows

l'**arc-en-ciel** MASC NOUN
(PL **les arcs-en-ciel**)
rainbow

l'**archéologie** FEM NOUN
archaeology

l'**archéologue** MASC/FEM NOUN
archaeologist ◇ *Elle est archéologue.* She's an archaeologist.

l'**archipel** MASC NOUN
archipelago

l'**architecte** MASC NOUN
architect ◇ *Il est architecte.* He's an architect.

l'**architecture** FEM NOUN

architecture

l'**Arctique** MASC NOUN
Arctic

l'**ardoise** FEM NOUN
slate

l'**arène** FEM NOUN
bullring
- **des arènes romaines** a Roman amphitheatre
- **l'arène politique** the political arena

l'**arête** FEM NOUN
fish bone

l'**argent** MASC NOUN
1 *silver* ◇ *une bague en argent* a silver ring
2 *money* ◇ *Je n'ai plus d'argent.* I haven't got any more money.
- **l'argent de poche** pocket money
- **l'argent liquide** cash

argentin ADJECTIVE, NOUN
(FEM SING **argentine**)
Argentinian
- **un Argentin** an Argentinian (*man*)
- **une Argentine** an Argentinian (*woman*)

l'**Argentine** FEM NOUN
Argentina

l'**argile** FEM NOUN
clay

l'**argot** MASC NOUN
slang

l'**arme** FEM NOUN
weapon
- **une arme à feu** a firearm

l'**armée** FEM NOUN
army
- **l'armée de l'air** the Air Force

l'**armistice** MASC NOUN
armistice

l'**armoire** FEM NOUN
wardrobe

l'**armure** FEM NOUN
armour ◇ *un chevalier en armure* a knight in armour

arnaquer (*informal*) VERB
to con

aromatisé ADJECTIVE
flavoured

l'**arôme** MASC NOUN
1 *aroma*
2 *flavouring* (*added to food*)

arpenter VERB
to pace up and down ◇ *Il arpentait le couloir.* He was pacing up and down the corridor.

arrache-pied
- **d'arrache-pied** ADVERB
furiously ◇ *travailler d'arrache-pied* to work furiously

arracher VERB
1 *to take out* ◇ *Le dentiste m'a arraché une dent.* The dentist took one of my teeth out.
2 *to tear out* ◇ *Arrachez la page.* Tear the page out.
3 *to pull up* ◇ *Elle a arraché les mauvaises herbes.* She pulled up the weeds.
- **arracher quelque chose à quelqu'un** to snatch something from somebody

arranger VERB
1 *to arrange* ◇ *arranger des fleurs dans un vase* to arrange flowers in a vase
2 *to suit* ◇ *Ça m'arrange de partir plus tôt.* It suits me to leave earlier.
- **s'arranger** to come to an agreement ◇ *Arrangez-vous avec le patron.* You'll have to come to an agreement with the boss.
- **Je vais m'arranger pour venir.** I'll organize things so that I can come.
- **Ça va s'arranger.** Things will work themselves out.

l'**arrestation** FEM NOUN
arrest ◇ *en état d'arrestation* under arrest

l'**arrêt** MASC NOUN
stop ◇ *un arrêt de bus* a bus stop
- **sans arrêt (1)** non-stop ◇ *Elle travaille sans arrêt.* She works non-stop.
- **sans arrêt (2)** continually ◇ *Ils se disputent sans arrêt.* They quarrel continually.

arrêter VERB
1 *to stop*
- **Arrête!** Stop it!
- **arrêter de faire quelque chose** to stop doing something
2 *to switch off* ◇ *Il a arrêté le moteur.* He switched the engine off.
3 *to arrest* ◇ *Mon voisin a été arrêté.* My neighbour's been arrested.
- **s'arrêter** to stop ◇ *Elle s'est arrêtée devant une vitrine.* She stopped in front of a shop window.
- **s'arrêter de faire quelque chose** to stop doing something ◇ *s'arrêter de fumer* to stop smoking

les **arrhes** FEM NOUN
deposit ◇ *verser des arrhes* to pay a deposit

l'**arrière** MASC NOUN
see also **arrière** ADJECTIVE
back ◇ *l'arrière de la maison* the back of the house
- **à l'arrière** at the back
- **en arrière** behind ◇ *Ils sont restés en arrière.* They stayed behind.

arrière ADJECTIVE (MASC, FEM, PL)
see also arrière NOUN
back ◇ *le siège arrière* the back seat ◇ *les roues arrière* the rear wheels

l'**arrière-grand-mère** FEM NOUN
(PL les **arrière-grands-mères**)
great-grandmother

l'**arrière-grand-père** MASC NOUN
(PL les **arrière-grands-pères**)
great-grandfather

l'**arrivée** FEM NOUN
arrival

arriver VERB
1 *to arrive* ◇ *J'arrive à l'école à huit heures.* I arrive at school at 8 o'clock.
2 *to happen* ◇ *Qu'est-ce qui est arrivé à Christian?* What happened to Christian?
◆ **arriver à faire quelque chose** to manage to do something ◇ *J'espère que je vais y arriver.* I hope I'll manage it.
◆ **Il m'arrive de dormir jusqu'à midi.** I sometimes sleep till midday.

arrogant ADJECTIVE
arrogant

l'**arrondissement** MASC NOUN
district
Paris, Lyons and Marseilles are divided into numbered districts called arrondissements.

arroser VERB
to water ◇ *Daphne arrose ses tomates.* Daphne is watering her tomatoes.
◆ **Ils ont arrosé leur victoire.** They had a drink to celebrate their victory.

l'**arrosoir** MASC NOUN
watering can

l'**art** MASC NOUN
art

l'**artère** FEM NOUN
1 *artery*
2 *thoroughfare* ◇ *les grandes artères de Paris* the main roads of Paris

l'**artichaut** MASC NOUN
artichoke

l'**article** MASC NOUN
1 *article* ◇ *un article de journal* a newspaper article
2 *item* ◇ *les articles en promotion* items on special offer

l'**articulation** FEM NOUN
joint ◇ *l'articulation du genou* the knee joint

articuler VERB
to pronounce clearly

artificiel ADJECTIVE
(FEM SING **artificielle**)
artificial

l'**artisan** MASC NOUN
self-employed craftsman

l'**artiste** MASC/FEM NOUN
1 *artist*
2 *performer*

artistique ADJECTIVE
artistic

as VERB *see* **avoir**
see also as NOUN
◆ **Tu as de beaux cheveux.** You've got nice hair.

l'**as** MASC NOUN
see also as VERB
ace ◇ *l'as de trèfle* the ace of clubs

l'**ascenseur** MASC NOUN
lift

l'**Ascension** FEM NOUN
Ascension

asiatique ADJECTIVE
Asiatic ◇ *la cuisine asiatique* Oriental cooking ◇ *le Sud-Est asiatique* South East Asia

l'**Asie** FEM NOUN
Asia
◆ **en Asie (1)** in Asia
◆ **en Asie (2)** to Asia

l'**aspect** MASC NOUN
appearance

l'**asperge** FEM NOUN
asparagus

l'**aspirateur** MASC NOUN
vacuum cleaner
◆ **passer l'aspirateur** to vacuum

l'**aspirine** FEM NOUN
aspirin

assaisonner VERB
to season

l'**assassin** MASC NOUN
murderer

assassiner VERB
to murder

assembler VERB
to assemble
◆ **s'assembler** to gather ◇ *Une foule énorme s'était assemblée.* A huge crowd had gathered.

s'**asseoir** VERB
to sit down ◇ *Asseyez-vous!* Sit down! ◇ *Assieds-toi!* Sit down!

assez ADVERB
1 *enough* ◇ *Nous n'avons pas assez de temps.* We don't have enough time. ◇ *Est-ce qu'il y a assez de pain?* Is there enough bread?
◆ **J'en ai assez!** I've had enough!
2 *quite* ◇ *Il faisait assez beau.* The weather was quite nice.

l'**assiette** FEM NOUN
plate ◇ *une assiette creuse* a soup

plate ◇ *une assiette à dessert* a dessert plate

◆ **une assiette anglaise** assorted cold meats

assis VERB *see* **asseoir**

assis ADJECTIVE
sitting ◇ *Il est assis par terre.* He's sitting on the floor.

l'**assistance** FEM NOUN
1 *audience* ◇ *Y a-t-il un médecin dans l'assistance?* Is there a doctor in the audience?
2 *aid* ◇ *l'assistance humanitaire* humanitarian aid
3 *assistance* ◇ *avec l'assistance de quelqu'un* with the assistance of somebody

l'**assistant** MASC NOUN
assistant ◇ *Il était assistant d'anglais à Tourcoing.* He was an English assistant in Tourcoing.

◆ **un assistant social** a social worker

l'**assistante** FEM NOUN
assistant ◇ *Elle est assistante de français à Oxford.* She's a French assistant in Oxford.

◆ **une assistante sociale** a social worker

assister VERB

◆ **assister à un accident** to witness an accident

◆ **assister à un cours** to attend a class

◆ **assister à un concert** to be at a concert

l'**association** FEM NOUN
association

l'**associé** MASC NOUN
partner (*in business*)

l'**associée** FEM NOUN
partner (*in business*)

s'**associer** VERB
to go into partnership

assommer VERB
to knock out ◇ *Il l'a assommé avec une bouteille.* He knocked him out with a bottle.

l'**Assomption** FEM NOUN
Assumption

assorti ADJECTIVE
1 *matching* ◇ *des couleurs assorties* matching colours
2 *assorted* ◇ *des chocolats assortis* assorted chocolates

◆ **être assorti à quelque chose** to match something ◇ *Son sac est assorti à ses chaussures.* Her bag matches her shoes.

l'**assortiment** MASC NOUN
assortment

l'**assurance** FEM NOUN
1 *insurance* ◇ *une assurance maladie* medical insurance
2 *confidence* ◇ *parler avec assurance* to speak with confidence

assurer VERB
1 *to insure* ◇ *La maison est assurée.* The house is insured. ◇ *être assuré contre quelque chose* to be insured against something
2 *to assure* ◇ *Je t'assure que c'est vrai!* I assure you it's true!

◆ **s'assurer de quelque chose** to make sure of something ◇ *Il s'est assuré que la porte était fermée.* He made sure the door was shut.

l'**asthme** MASC NOUN
asthma ◇ *une crise d'asthme* an asthma attack

l'**astronaute** MASC/FEM NOUN
astronaut

l'**astronomie** FEM NOUN
astronomy

astucieux ADJECTIVE
(FEM SING **astucieuse**)
clever

l'**atelier** MASC NOUN
1 *workshop*
2 *studio* (*artist's*)

Athènes NOUN
Athens

l'**athlète** MASC/FEM NOUN
athlete

l'**athlétisme** MASC NOUN
athletics ◇ *un championnat d'athlétisme* an athletics championship

l'**Atlantique** MASC NOUN
Atlantic

l'**atlas** MASC NOUN
atlas

l'**atmosphère** FEM NOUN
atmosphere

atomique ADJECTIVE
atomic ◇ *la bombe atomique* the atomic bomb

atroce ADJECTIVE
terrible

attachant ADJECTIVE
lovable ◇ *un enfant attachant* a lovable child

attacher VERB
to tie up ◇ *Elle a attaché ses cheveux avec un élastique.* She tied her hair up with an elastic band.

◆ **s'attacher à quelqu'un** to become attached to somebody

◆ **une poêle qui n'attache pas** a non-stick frying pan

attaquer VERB
to attack

atteindre VERB
to reach

attendant
- **en attendant** ADVERB
  in the meantime

attendre VERB
to wait ◇ *attendre quelqu'un* to wait for someone ◇ *J'attends d'avoir un appartement à moi.* I'm waiting until I've got a flat of my own. ◇ *Attends qu'il ne pleuve plus.* Wait until it's stopped raining.
- **attendre un enfant** to be expecting a baby
- **s'attendre à** to expect ◇ *Je m'attends à ce qu'il soit en retard.* I expect he'll be late.

l'**attentat** MASC NOUN
- **un attentat à la bombe** a terrorist bombing

l'**attente** FEM NOUN
wait ◇ *deux heures d'attente* two hours' wait
- **la salle d'attente** the waiting room

attentif ADJECTIVE
(FEM SING **attentive**)
attentive

l'**attention** FEM NOUN
attention ◇ *à l'attention de* for the attention of
- **faire attention** to be careful
- **Attention!** Watch out! ◇ *Attention, tu vas te faire écraser!* Watch out, you'll get run over!

attentionné ADJECTIVE
thoughtful

atterrir VERB
to land

l'**atterrissage** MASC NOUN
landing (*of plane*)

attirant ADJECTIVE
attractive

attirer VERB
to attract ◇ *attirer l'attention de quelqu'un* to attract somebody's attention
- **s'attirer des ennuis** to get into trouble ◇ *Si tu continues, tu vas t'attirer des ennuis.* If you keep on like that, you'll get yourself into trouble.

l'**attitude** FEM NOUN
attitude

l'**attraction** FEM NOUN
- **un parc d'attractions** an amusement park

attraper VERB
to catch

attrayant ADJECTIVE
attractive

attrister VERB
to sadden

au PREPOSITION *see* **à**
au *is the contracted form of* **à** + **le**.
- **au printemps** in the spring

l'**aube** FEM NOUN
dawn ◇ *à l'aube* at dawn

l'**auberge de jeunesse** FEM NOUN
youth hostel

l'**aubergine** FEM NOUN
aubergine

aucun ADJECTIVE, PRONOUN
1 *no* ◇ *Il n'a aucun ami.* He's got no friends. ◇ *Aucun enfant ne pourrait le faire.* No child could do that.
2 *none* ◇ *Aucun d'entre eux n'est venu.* None of them came. ◇ *Aucune de mes amies n'aime le football.* None of my female friends like football. ◇ *Tu aimes ses films?–Je n'en ai vu aucun.* Do you like his films?–I haven't seen any of them.
- **sans aucun doute** without any doubt

au-delà ADVERB
- **au-delà de** beyond ◇ *Votre ticket n'est pas valable au-delà de cette limite.* Your ticket is not valid beyond this point.

au-dessous ADVERB
1 *downstairs* ◇ *Ils habitent au-dessous.* They live downstairs.
2 *underneath*
- **au-dessous de** under ◇ *au-dessous du pont* under the bridge ◇ *dix degrés au-dessous de zéro* ten degrees below zero

au-dessus ADVERB
1 *upstairs* ◇ *J'habite au-dessus.* I live upstairs.
2 *above*
- **au-dessus de** above ◇ *au-dessus de la table* above the table

audiovisuel ADJECTIVE
(FEM SING **audiovisuelle**)
audiovisual

l'**auditeur** MASC NOUN
listener (*to radio*)

l'**auditrice** FEM NOUN
listener (*to radio*)

l'**augmentation** FEM NOUN
rise

augmenter VERB
to increase

aujourd'hui ADVERB
today

auparavant ADVERB
first ◇ *Vous pouvez utiliser l'ordinateur mais auparavant vous devez taper le mot de passe.* You can use the computer but first you have to key in the password.

auquel PRONOUN

(MASC PL **auxquels**, FEM PL **auxquelles**)
auquel *is the contracted form of* **à + lequel**.
◇ *l'homme auquel j'ai parlé* the man I spoke to

aura, aurai, auras, aurez, aurons, auront VERB *see* **avoir**

l'**aurore** FEM NOUN
daybreak

ausculter VERB
◆ **Le médecin l'a ausculté.** The doctor listened to his chest.

aussi ADVERB
1 *too* ◇ *Dors bien. – Toi aussi.* Sleep well. – You too. ◇ *Lui aussi parle espagnol.* He too speaks Spanish.
2 *also* ◇ *J'aimerais aussi que tu achètes le journal.* I'd also like you to get the paper. ◇ *Je parle anglais et aussi allemand.* I speak English and also German.
◆ **aussi...que** as...as ◇ *aussi grand que moi* as big as me

aussitôt ADVERB
straight away ◇ *aussitôt après son retour* straight after his return
◆ **aussitôt que** as soon as ◇ *aussitôt que tu auras fini* as soon as you've finished

l'**Australie** FEM NOUN
Australia
◆ **en Australie (1)** in Australia
◆ **en Australie (2)** to Australia

australien ADJECTIVE, NOUN
(FEM SING **australienne**)
Australian
◆ **un Australien** an Australian (*man*)
◆ **une Australienne** an Australian (*woman*)

autant ADVERB
◆ **autant de (1)** so much ◇ *Je ne veux pas autant de gâteau.* I don't want so much cake.
◆ **autant de (2)** so many ◇ *Je n'ai jamais vu autant de monde.* I've never seen so many people.
◆ **autant...que (1)** as much...as ◇ *J'ai autant d'argent que toi.* I've got as much money as you have.
◆ **autant...que (2)** as many...as ◇ *J'ai autant d'amis que lui.* I've got as many friends as he has.
◆ **d'autant plus que** all the more since ◇ *Elle est d'autant plus déçue qu'il le lui avait promis.* She's all the more disappointed since he had promised her.
◆ **d'autant moins que** even less since ◇ *C'est d'autant moins pratique pour lui qu'il doit changer deux fois de train.* It's even less convenient for him since he has to change trains twice.

l'**auteur** MASC NOUN
author

l'**auto** FEM NOUN
car

l'**autobus** MASC NOUN
bus ◇ *en autobus* by bus

l'**autocar** MASC NOUN
coach ◇ *en autocar* by coach

autocollant ADJECTIVE
see also autocollant NOUN
self-adhesive ◇ *une étiquette autocollante* a self-adhesive label
◆ **une enveloppe autocollante** a self-seal envelope

l'**autocollant** MASC NOUN
see also autocollant ADJECTIVE
sticker

l'**auto-école** FEM NOUN
driving school

automatique ADJECTIVE
automatic

l'**automne** MASC NOUN
autumn
◆ **en automne** in autumn

automobile ADJECTIVE
see also automobile NOUN
◆ **une course automobile** a motor race

l'**automobile** FEM NOUN
see also automobile ADJECTIVE
car

l'**automobiliste** MASC/FEM NOUN
motorist

l'**autoradio** MASC NOUN
car radio

l'**autorisation** FEM NOUN
1 *permission* ◇ *Il m'a donné l'autorisation de sortir ce soir.* He's given me permission to go out tonight.
2 *permit* ◇ *Il faut une autorisation pour camper ici.* You need a permit to camp here.

autoriser VERB
to give permission for ◇ *Il m'a autorisé à en parler.* He's given me permission to talk about it.

autoritaire ADJECTIVE
authoritarian

l'**autorité** FEM NOUN
authority

l'**autoroute** FEM NOUN
motorway

l'**auto-stop** MASC NOUN
◆ **faire de l'auto-stop** to hitchhike

l'**auto-stoppeur** MASC NOUN
hitchhiker

l'**auto-stoppeuse** FEM NOUN
hitchhiker

autour ADVERB

PTO

around ◇ *autour de la maison* around the house

autre ADJECTIVE, PRONOUN
other ◇ *Je viendrai un autre jour.* I'll come some other day. ◇ *J'ai d'autres projets.* I've got other plans.
- **autre chose** something else
- **autre part** somewhere else
- **un autre** another ◇ *Tu veux un autre morceau de gâteau?* Would you like another piece of cake?
- **l'autre** the other ◇ *Non, pas celui-ci, l'autre.* No, not that one, the other one.
- **d'autres** others ◇ *Je t'en apporterai d'autres.* I'll bring you some others.
- **les autres** the others ◇ *Les autres sont arrivés plus tard.* The others arrived later.
- **ni l'un ni l'autre** neither of them
- **entre autres** among other things ◇ *Nous avons parlé, entre autres, de nos projets de vacances.* We talked about our holiday plans, among other things.

autrefois ADVERB
in the old days ◇ *Autrefois Saint-Tropez n'était qu'un village de pêcheurs.* In the old days Saint-Tropez was just a fishing village.

autrement ADVERB
1 *differently* ◇ *Il l'a fait autrement.* He did it differently.
2 *otherwise* ◇ *Je n'ai pas pu faire autrement.* I couldn't do otherwise.
- **autrement dit** in other words

l'**Autriche** FEM NOUN
Austria
- **en Autriche (1)** in Austria
- **en Autriche (2)** to Austria

autrichien ADJECTIVE, NOUN
(FEM SING **autrichienne**)
Austrian
- **un Autrichien** an Austrian (*man*)
- **une Autrichienne** an Austrian (*woman*)

l'**autruche** FEM NOUN
ostrich

aux PREPOSITION *see* **à**
aux *is the contracted form of* **à + les**.
◇ *J'ai dit aux enfants d'aller jouer.* I told the children to go and play.

auxquelles PRONOUN
auxquelles *is the contracted form of* **à + lesquelles**.
◇ *les revues auxquelles il est abonné* the magazines to which he subscribes

auxquels PRONOUN
auxquels *is the contracted form of* **à + lesquels**.
◇ *les enfants auxquels il a parlé* the children he spoke to

l'**avalanche** FEM NOUN
avalanche

avaler VERB
to swallow

l'**avance** FEM NOUN
- **être en avance** to be early
- **à l'avance** beforehand ◇ *réserver longtemps à l'avance* to book well beforehand
- **d'avance** in advance ◇ *payer d'avance* to pay in advance

avancé ADJECTIVE
advanced ◇ *à un niveau avancé* at an advanced level
- **bien avancé** well under way ◇ *Les travaux sont déjà bien avancés.* The work is already well under way.

avancer VERB
1 *to move forward* ◇ *Il avançait prudemment.* He was moving forward cautiously.
2 *to bring forward* ◇ *La date de l'examen a été avancée.* The date of the exam has been brought forward.
3 *to put forward* ◇ *Il a avancé sa montre d'une heure.* He put his watch forward an hour.
4 *to be fast* (*watch*) ◇ *Ma montre avance d'une heure.* My watch is an hour fast.
5 *to lend* ◇ *Peux-tu m'avancer cent francs?* Can you lend me 100 francs?

avant PREPOSITION, ADJECTIVE
see also **avant** NOUN
1 *before* ◇ *avant qu'il ne pleuve* before it rains ◇ *avant de partir* before leaving
2 *front* ◇ *la roue avant* the front wheel ◇ *le siège avant* the front seat

l'**avant** MASC NOUN
see also **avant** PREPOSITION
front ◇ *l'avant de la voiture* the front of the car
- **à l'avant** in front
- **en avant** forward ◇ *Il a fait un pas en avant.* He took a step forward.

l'**avantage** MASC NOUN
advantage

l'**avant-bras** MASC NOUN
(PL les **avant-bras**)
forearm

avant-dernier ADJECTIVE
(FEM **avant-dernière**, MASC PL **avant-derniers**)
last but one ◇ *l'avant-dernière page* the last page but one ◇ *Ils sont arrivés avant-derniers.* They arrived last but one.

avant-hier ADVERB
the day before yesterday ◇ *Il est*

arrivé avant-hier. He arrived the day before yesterday.

avare ADJECTIVE
see also avare NOUN
miserly

l'**avare** MASC/FEM NOUN
see also avare ADJECTIVE
miser

avec PREPOSITION
with ◇ *avec mon père* with my father
◆ **Et avec ça?** Anything else? (*in shop*)

l'**avenir** MASC NOUN
future
◆ **à l'avenir** in future ◇ *À l'avenir, essayez d'être à l'heure.* Try to be on time in future.
◆ **dans un proche avenir** in the near future

l'**aventure** FEM NOUN
adventure

l'**avenue** FEM NOUN
avenue

l'**averse** FEM NOUN
shower (*of rain*)

avertir VERB
to warn
◆ **avertir quelqu'un de quelque chose** to warn somebody about something

l'**avertissement** MASC NOUN
warning

aveugle ADJECTIVE
blind

l'**avion** MASC NOUN
plane
◆ **aller en avion** to go by plane ◇ *Il est allé en Italie en avion.* He flew to Italy.
◆ **par avion** by airmail

l'**aviron** MASC NOUN
rowing

l'**avis** MASC NOUN
1 *opinion* ◇ *J'aimerais avoir ton avis.* I'd like to have your opinion.
◆ **à mon avis** in my opinion
2 *notice* ◇ *jusqu'à nouvel avis* until further notice
◆ **changer d'avis** to change one's mind
◇ *J'ai changé d'avis.* I've changed my mind.

l'**avocat** MASC NOUN
1 *lawyer* ◇ *Il est avocat.* He's a lawyer.
2 *avocado*

l'**avocate** FEM NOUN
lawyer ◇ *Elle est avocate.* She's a lawyer.

l'**avoine** FEM NOUN
oats ◇ *les flocons d'avoine* porridge oats

avoir VERB

Present tense:	
j'ai	*nous avons*
tu as	*vous avez*
il/elle a	*ils/elles ont*
Past participle: *eu*	

1 *to have* ◇ *Ils ont deux enfants.* They have two children. ◇ *Il a les yeux bleus.* He's got blue eyes. ◇ *J'ai déjà mangé.* I've already eaten. ◇ *Est-ce que tu as vu ce film?* Have you seen this film? ◇ *Je lui ai parlé hier.* I spoke to him yesterday.
◆ **On t'a bien eu!** (*informal*) You've been had!
2 *to be* ◇ *Il a trois ans.* He's three. ◇ *J'avais dix ans quand je l'ai rencontré.* I was ten when I met him.
◆ **il y a (1)** there is ◇ *Il y a quelqu'un à la porte.* There's somebody at the door.
◆ **il y a (2)** there are ◇ *Il y a des chocolats sur la table.* There are some chocolates on the table.
◆ **il y a (3)** ago ◇ *Je l'ai rencontré il y a deux ans.* I met him two years ago.
◆ **Qu'est-ce qu'il y a?** What's the matter?
◆ **Il n'y a qu'à partir plus tôt.** We'll just have to leave earlier.

l'**avortement** MASC NOUN
abortion

avril MASC NOUN
April
◆ **en avril** in April

ayez, ayons VERB *see* **avoir**

B

le **baby-foot** NOUN
table football ◇ *jouer au baby-foot* to play table football

le **baby-sitting** NOUN
◆ **faire du baby-sitting** to babysit

le **bac** = **baccalauréat**

le **baccalauréat** NOUN
A levels ◇ *Elle a passé son baccalauréat l'année dernière.* She did her A levels last year.

The French baccalauréat, *or* bac *for short, is taken at the age of 17 or 18. Students have to sit one of a variety of set subject combinations, rather than being able to choose any combination of subjects they want. If you pass you have the right to a place at university.*

bâcler VERB
to botch up ◇ *Je déteste le travail bâclé!* I hate work that's not done properly!

le **bagage** NOUN
luggage
◆ **faire ses bagages** to pack
◆ **les bagages à main** hand luggage ◇ *un bagage à main* a piece of hand luggage

la **bagarre** NOUN
fight ◇ *Une bagarre a éclaté à la fermeture du pub.* A fight broke out when the pub closed.

se **bagarrer** VERB
to fight ◇ *Il s'est encore bagarré avec son frère.* He's been fighting with his brother again.

la **bagnole** NOUN (*informal*)
car

la **bague** NOUN
ring

la **baguette** NOUN
1 *stick of French bread*
2 *chopstick* ◇ *manger avec des baguettes* to eat with chopsticks
◆ **une baguette magique** a magic wand

la **baie** NOUN
bay

se **baigner** VERB
to go swimming ◇ *Si on allait se baigner?* Shall we go swimming?

la **baignoire** NOUN
bath (*bathtub*)

bâiller VERB
to yawn

le **bain** NOUN
bath ◇ *prendre un bain* to take a bath ◇ *prendre un bain de soleil* to sunbathe

le **baiser** NOUN
kiss

baisser VERB
1 *to turn down* ◇ *Il fait moins froid, tu peux baisser le chauffage.* It's not so cold, you can turn down the heating.
2 *to fall* ◇ *Le prix des CD a baissé.* The price of CDs has fallen.
◆ **se baisser** to bend down ◇ *Il s'est baissé pour ramasser son mouchoir.* He bent down to pick up his handkerchief.

le **bal** NOUN
dance ◇ *un bal populaire* a local dance
◆ **un bal costumé** a fancy dress ball

la **balade** NOUN (*informal*)
walk ◇ *faire une balade* to go for a walk

se **balader** VERB (*informal*)
to wander around ◇ *J'adore me balader dans les rues de Paris.* I love to wander around the streets of Paris.

le **baladeur** NOUN
personal stereo

le **balai** NOUN
broom ◇ *Je vais donner un coup de balai dans la cuisine.* I'm going to sweep the kitchen.

la **balance** NOUN
scales PL (*for weighing*)
◆ **la Balance** Libra ◇ *Todd est Balance.* Todd is Libra.

se **balancer** VERB
to swing

la **balançoire** NOUN
swing

balayer VERB
1 *to sweep* ◇ *Jean-Pierre a balayé la cuisine.* Jean-Pierre swept the kitchen.
2 *to sweep up* ◇ *Va balayer les feuilles sur la terrasse.* Go and sweep up the leaves on the terrace.

le **balayeur** NOUN
roadsweeper

balbutier VERB
to stammer

le **balcon** NOUN
balcony

la **baleine** NOUN
whale

la **balle** NOUN
1 *ball* ◇ *une balle de tennis* a tennis ball
2 *bullet*

la **ballerine** NOUN
1 *ballet dancer*
2 *ballet shoe* ◇ *une paire de ballerines rouges* a pair of red ballet

shoes

le **ballet** NOUN
ballet

le **ballon** NOUN
1 *ball* ◇ *lancer le ballon* to throw the ball
◆ **un ballon de football** a football
2 *balloon*

balnéaire ADJECTIVE
◆ **une station balnéaire** a seaside resort

banal ADJECTIVE
(MASC PL **banaux**)
1 *commonplace* ◇ *La violence est devenue banale à la télévision.* Violence has become commonplace on television.
2 *hackneyed* ◇ *L'intrigue du film est très banale.* The plot of the film is very hackneyed.

la **banane** NOUN
banana

le **banc** NOUN
bench

bancaire ADJECTIVE
◆ **une carte bancaire** a bank card

le **bandage** NOUN
bandage

la **bande** NOUN
1 *gang* ◇ *une bande de voyous* a gang of louts
2 *bunch* ◇ *C'est une bande d'idiots!* They are a bunch of idiots!
3 *bandage* ◇ *une bande Velpeau ®* a crepe bandage
◆ **une bande dessinée** a comic strip
Comic strips are very popular in France with people of all ages.
◆ **une bande magnétique** a tape
◆ **la bande sonore** the sound track
◆ **Elle fait toujours bande à part.** She always keeps to herself.

le **bandeau** NOUN
(PL les **bandeaux**)
headband

bander VERB
to bandage ◇ *L'infirmière lui a bandé la jambe.* The nurse bandaged his leg.

le **bandit** NOUN
bandit

la **banlieue** NOUN
suburbs ◇ *Christèle habite en banlieue.* Christèle lives in the suburbs.
◆ **les lignes de banlieue** suburban lines
◆ **les trains de banlieue** commuter trains

la **banque** NOUN
bank

le **banquet** NOUN
dinner ◇ *le banquet annuel de l'association* the club's annual dinner

la **banquette** NOUN
seat ◇ *la banquette arrière de la voiture* the back seat of the car

le **banquier** NOUN
banker

le **baptême** NOUN
christening ◇ *le baptême de notre fille* our daughter's christening
◆ **C'était mon baptême de l'air.** It was the first time I had flown.

le **baquet** NOUN
tub

le **bar** NOUN
bar

la **baraque** NOUN (*informal*)
house ◇ *Elle habite dans une belle baraque.* She lives in a beautiful house.

barbare ADJECTIVE
barbaric

la **barbe** NOUN
beard ◇ *Il porte la barbe.* He's got a beard.
◆ **Quelle barbe!** (*informal*) What a drag!
◆ **la barbe à papa** candyfloss

barbouiller VERB
to daub ◇ *Les murs étaient barbouillés de graffitis.* The walls were daubed with graffiti.
◆ **J'ai l'estomac barbouillé.** (*informal*) I'm feeling queasy.

barbu ADJECTIVE
bearded ◇ *un grand barbu* a big, bearded man

barder VERB (*informal*)
◆ **Ça va barder!** There's going to be trouble!

le **baromètre** NOUN
barometer

la **barque** NOUN
rowing boat ◇ *Ils sont allés faire une promenade en barque.* They've gone for a row.

le **barrage** NOUN
dam
◆ **un barrage de police** a police roadblock

la **barre** NOUN
bar (*metal*) ◇ *une barre de fer* an iron bar

le **barreau** NOUN
(PL les **barreaux**)
bar (*on window*) ◇ *Il s'est retrouvé derrière les barreaux.* He ended up behind bars.

barrer VERB
to block ◇ *Il y a un tronc d'arbre qui barre la route.* There's a tree trunk blocking the road.
◆ **se barrer** (*informal*) to clear off

◇ *Barre-toi!* Clear off!

la **barrette** NOUN
hair slide

la **barrière** NOUN
fence

le **bar-tabac** NOUN
(PL les **bars-tabacs**)

A bar-tabac *is a bar which also sells cigarettes and stamps; you can tell a* bar-tabac *by the red diamond-shaped sign outside it.*

le **bas** NOUN
see also bas ADJECTIVE
1 *bottom* ◇ *en bas de la page* at the bottom of the page ◇ *en bas de l'escalier* at the bottom of the stairs
2 *stocking* ◇ *une paire de bas* a pair of stockings

bas ADJECTIVE, ADVERB
(FEM SING **basse**)
see also bas NOUN
low ◇ *parler à voix basse* to speak in a low voice
◆ **en bas (1)** down ◇ *Ça me donne le vertige de regarder en bas.* I get dizzy if I look down.
◆ **en bas (2)** (down) at the bottom ◇ *Son nom est tout en bas.* His name is down at the bottom. ◇ *Il y a un marchand de journaux en bas de la rue.* There's a newsagent's at the bottom of the street.
◆ **en bas (3)** downstairs ◇ *Elle habite en bas.* She lives downstairs.

le **bas-côté** NOUN
verge ◇ *Il s'est garé sur le bas-côté de la route.* He stopped his car on the verge.

la **bascule** NOUN
◆ **un fauteuil à bascule** a rocking chair

la **base** NOUN
base ◇ *la base de la pyramide* the base of the pyramid
◆ **de base** basic ◇ *Le pain et le lait sont des aliments de base.* Bread and milk are basic foods.
◆ **à base de** made from ◇ *des produits de beauté à base de plantes* cosmetics made from plants
◆ **une base de données** a database

le **basket** NOUN
basketball ◇ *jouer au basket* to play basketball

les **baskets** FEM NOUN
trainers ◇ *une paire de baskets* a pair of trainers

le/la **Basque** NOUN
Basque (*person, language*)

basque ADJECTIVE
Basque

basse ADJECTIVE *see* **bas**

la **basse-cour** NOUN
(PL les **basses-cours**)
farmyard

le **bassin** NOUN
1 *pond* ◇ *Il y a un bassin à poissons rouges dans le parc.* There's a goldfish pond in the park.
2 *pelvis* ◇ *une fracture du bassin* a fractured pelvis

la **bassine** NOUN
bowl (*for washing*)

le **bas-ventre** NOUN
stomach ◇ *Elle se plaint de douleurs dans le bas-ventre.* She is complaining of pains in her stomach.

la **bataille** NOUN
battle

le **bateau** NOUN
(PL les **bateaux**)
boat

le **bateau-mouche** NOUN
(PL les **bateaux-mouches**)
pleasure boat

bâti ADJECTIVE
◆ **bien bâti** well-built

le **bâtiment** NOUN
building

bâtir VERB
to build

le **bâton** NOUN
stick ◇ *un coup de bâton* a blow with a stick

le **battement** NOUN
◆ **J'ai dix minutes de battement.** I've got ten minutes free.

la **batterie** NOUN
1 *battery* ◇ *La batterie est à plat.* The battery is flat.
2 *drums* ◇ *jouer de la batterie* to play drums
◆ **la batterie de cuisine** the pots and pans

le **batteur** NOUN
drummer

battre VERB
to beat ◇ *Quand je le vois, mon cœur bat plus vite.* When I see him, my heart beats faster.
◆ **se battre** to fight ◇ *Je me bats souvent avec mon frère.* I fight a lot with my brother.
◆ **battre son plein** to in be full swing ◇ *A minuit, la fête battait son plein.* At midnight, the party was in full swing.

bavard ADJECTIVE
talkative

bavarder VERB
to chat

baver VERB
to dribble

baveux ADJECTIVE
(FEM SING **baveuse**)
runny ◇ *une omelette baveuse* a runny omelette

la **bavure** NOUN
blunder ◇ *une bavure policière* a police blunder

le **bazar** NOUN
general store
◆ **Quel bazar!** (*informal*) What a mess!

BCBG ADJECTIVE (= *bon chic bon genre*)
posh

la **BD** NOUN (= *bande dessinée*)
comic strip ◇ *Marguerite adore les BD.* Marguerite loves comic strips.

béant ADJECTIVE
gaping ◇ *un trou béant* a gaping hole

beau ADJECTIVE, ADVERB
(MASC SING ALSO **bel**, FEM SING **belle**, MASC PL **beaux**)

beau *changes to* **bel** *before a vowel and most words beginning with "h".*

1 *lovely* ◇ *un bel été* a lovely summer ◇ *une belle journée* a fine day
2 *beautiful* ◇ *C'est une belle femme.* She is a beautiful woman.
3 *good-looking* ◇ *C'est un beau garçon.* He is a good-looking boy.
4 *handsome* ◇ *un bel homme* a handsome man

◆ **Il fait beau aujourd'hui.** It's a nice day today.
◆ **J'ai beau essayer, je n'y arrive pas.** However hard I try, I just can't do it.

beaucoup ADVERB
1 *a lot* ◇ *Il boit beaucoup.* He drinks a lot.
2 *much* ◇ *Elle n'a pas beaucoup d'argent.* She hasn't got much money. ◇ *Janet est beaucoup plus grande que moi.* Janet is much taller than me.

◆ **beaucoup de** a lot of ◇ *Il y avait beaucoup de monde au concert.* There were a lot of people at the concert. ◇ *Elle fait beaucoup de fautes.* She makes a lot of mistakes.
◆ **J'ai eu beaucoup de chance.** I was very lucky.

le **beau-fils** NOUN
(PL les **beaux-fils**)
1 *son-in-law*
2 *stepson*

le **beau-frère** NOUN
(PL les **beaux-frères**)
brother-in-law

le **beau-père** NOUN
(PL les **beaux-pères**)
1 *father-in-law*
2 *stepfather*

la **beauté** NOUN
beauty

les **beaux-arts** MASC NOUN
fine arts

les **beaux-parents** MASC NOUN
in-laws

le **bébé** NOUN
baby

le **bec** NOUN
beak

la **bécane** NOUN (*informal*)
bike

la **bêche** NOUN
spade

bêcher VERB
to dig ◇ *Il bêchait son jardin.* He was digging the garden.

bégayer VERB
to stammer

beige ADJECTIVE
beige

le **beignet** NOUN
fritter ◇ *les beignets aux pommes* apple fritters

bel ADJECTIVE *see* **beau**

le/la **Belge** NOUN
Belgian

belge ADJECTIVE
Belgian

la **Belgique** NOUN
Belgium
◆ **en Belgique (1)** in Belgium
◆ **en Belgique (2)** to Belgium

le **bélier** MASC NOUN
ram
◆ **le Bélier** Aries ◇ *Christine est Bélier.* Christine's Aries.

belle ADJECTIVE *see* **beau**

la **belle-famille** NOUN
in-laws

la **belle-fille** NOUN
(PL les **belles-filles**)
1 *daughter-in-law*
2 *stepdaughter*

la **belle-mère** NOUN
(PL les **belles-mères**)
1 *mother-in-law*
2 *stepmother*

la **belle-sœur** NOUN
(PL les **belles-sœurs**)
sister-in-law

la **bénédiction** NOUN
blessing

le **bénéfice** NOUN
profit ◇ *La société réalise de gros bénéfices.* The company is making big profits.

bénévole ADJECTIVE
voluntary ◇ *du travail bénévole* voluntary work

bénir VERB
to bless

bénit ADJECTIVE
consecrated ◇ *l'eau bénite* holy water

la **béquille** NOUN
crutch ◇ *Il marche avec des béquilles.* He walks on crutches.

le **berceau** NOUN
(PL les **berceaux**)
cradle

bercer VERB
to rock

la **berceuse** NOUN
lullaby

le **béret** NOUN
beret

la **berge** NOUN
bank (*of river*)

le **berger** NOUN
shepherd

la **bergère** NOUN
shepherdess

le **besoin** NOUN
need
◆ **avoir besoin de quelque chose** to need something ◇ *J'ai besoin d'argent.* I need some money. ◇ *J'ai besoin d'y réfléchir.* I need to think about it.
◆ **une famille dans le besoin** a needy family

le **bétail** NOUN
livestock

la **bête** NOUN
see also bête ADJECTIVE
animal

bête ADJECTIVE
see also bête NOUN
stupid

la **bêtise** NOUN
◆ **faire une bêtise** to do something stupid ◇ *Je crois que j'ai fait une bêtise.* I think I've done something stupid.
◆ **dire des bêtises** to talk nonsense ◇ *Tu dis des bêtises!* You're talking nonsense!

le **béton** NOUN
concrete
◆ **un alibi en béton** a cast-iron alibi

la **betterave** NOUN
beetroot ◇ *la salade de betterave* beetroot salad

le/la **beur** NOUN (*informal*)
A beur *is a young person of North African origin born in France.*

le **beurre** NOUN
butter ◇ *une sauce au beurre* a sauce made with butter

beurrer VERB
to butter

Beyrouth NOUN
Beirut

le **bibelot** NOUN
ornament

le **biberon** NOUN
baby's bottle

la **Bible** NOUN
Bible

le/la **bibliothécaire** NOUN
librarian

la **bibliothèque** NOUN
1 *library* ◇ *emprunter un livre à la bibliothèque* to borrow a book from the library
2 *bookcase* ◇ *une bibliothèque en chêne massif* a bookcase made of solid oak

le **bic** ® NOUN
Biro ®

la **biche** NOUN
doe

la **bicyclette** NOUN
bicycle

le **bidet** NOUN
bidet

le **bidon** NOUN
see also bidon ADJECTIVE
can ◇ *un bidon d'essence* a can of petrol

bidon ADJECTIVE (*informal*)
see also bidon NOUN
phoney ◇ *Son histoire est complètement bidon.* His story is a complete load of rubbish.

le **bidonville** NOUN
shanty town

la **Biélorussie** NOUN
Belarus

le **bien** NOUN
see also bien ADJECTIVE
1 *good* ◇ *le bien et le mal* good and evil ◇ *Jean m'a dit beaucoup de bien de toi.* Jean told me a lot of good things about you. ◇ *C'est pour son bien.* It's for his own good.
◆ **faire du bien à quelqu'un** to do somebody good ◇ *Ses vacances lui ont fait beaucoup de bien.* His holiday has done him a lot of good.
2 *possession* ◇ *son bien le plus précieux* his most treasured possession

bien ADJECTIVE, ADVERB
see also bien NOUN
1 *well* ◇ *Daphne travaille bien.* Daphne works well. ◇ *Je me sens bien.* I feel fine. ◇ *Je ne me sens pas bien.* I

don't feel well.
2 *good* ◇ *Ce restaurant est vraiment bien.* This restaurant is really good.
3 *quite* ◇ *bien assez* quite enough
Je veux bien le faire. I'm quite willing to do it.
bien mieux much better
J'espère bien y aller. I very much hope to go.
4 *right* ◇ *Ce n'est pas bien de dire du mal des gens.* It's not right to say nasty things about people. ◇ *Il croyait bien faire.* He thought he was doing the right thing.
C'est bien fait pour lui! It serves him right!

ien-être NOUN
well-being ◇ *une sensation de bien-être* a feeling of well-being

ienfaisance NOUN
charity
une œuvre de bienfaisance a charity

ien que CONJUNCTION
although ◇ *Il fait assez chaud bien qu'il n'y ait pas de soleil.* It's quite warm although there's no sun.

ien sûr ADVERB
of course

ientôt ADVERB
soon ◇ *À bientôt!* See you soon!

ienvenu NOUN
Vous êtes le bienvenu! You're welcome! ◇ *Vous êtes tous les bienvenus!* You're all welcome!

ienvenue NOUN
welcome ◇ *Bienvenue à Paris!* Welcome to Paris! ◇ *Vous êtes la bienvenue!* You're welcome!

ière NOUN
beer
la bière blonde lager
la bière brune brown ale
la bière pression draught beer

ifteck NOUN
steak

igoudi NOUN
roller (*in hair*)

ijou NOUN
(PL les **bijoux**)
jewel

ijouterie NOUN
jeweller's

ijoutier NOUN
jeweller

ijoutière NOUN
jeweller ◇ *Elle est bijoutière.* She's a jeweller.

ilan NOUN
faire le bilan de quelque chose to assess something ◇ *Il faut faire le bilan de la situation.* We need to assess the situation.

bilingue ADJECTIVE
bilingual

le **billard** NOUN
billiards
◆ **le billard américain** pool

la **bille** NOUN
marble (*toy*) ◇ *jouer aux billes* to play marbles

le **billet** NOUN
1 *ticket* ◇ *un billet d'avion* a plane ticket
2 *banknote* ◇ *un billet de cent francs* a 100 franc note

le **billion** NOUN
billion

la **biographie** NOUN
biography

la **biologie** NOUN
biology

biologique ADJECTIVE
1 *organic* ◇ *des légumes biologiques* organic vegetables
2 *biological* ◇ *des armes biologiques* biological weapons

la **Birmanie** NOUN
Burma

bis ADVERB
see also **bis** NOUN
◇ *Il habite au douze bis rue des Fleurs.* He lives at 12A rue des Fleurs.

le **bis** NOUN
see also **bis** ADVERB
encore

la **biscotte** NOUN
toasted bread (*sold in packets*)

le **biscuit** NOUN
biscuit
◆ **un biscuit de Savoie** a sponge cake

la **bise** NOUN
kiss ◇ *Grosses bises de Bretagne.* Love and kisses from Brittany.

bissextile ADJECTIVE
◆ **une année bissextile** a leap year

le **bistrot** NOUN (*informal*)
café
Cafés in France sell both alcoholic and non-alcoholic drinks.

bizarre ADJECTIVE
strange

la **blague** NOUN (*informal*)
1 *joke* ◇ *raconter une blague* to tell a joke
◆ **Sans blague!** No kidding!
2 *trick* ◇ *André nous a encore fait une blague!* André has played a trick on us again!

blaguer VERB (*informal*)
to joke

le **blaireau** NOUN
(PL les **blaireaux**)
shaving brush

blâmer VERB
to blame

blanc ADJECTIVE
(FEM SING **blanche**)
see also blanc NOUN
1 *white* ◇ *un chemisier blanc* a white blouse
2 *blank* ◇ *une page blanche* a blank page

le **blanc** NOUN
see also blanc ADJECTIVE
1 *white* ◇ *Colette est habillée tout en blanc.* Colette is dressed all in white.
2 *white wine* ◇ *un verre de blanc* a glass of white wine
- **un blanc d'œuf** an egg white
- **un blanc de poulet** a chicken breast

le **Blanc** NOUN
white man

la **Blanche** NOUN
white woman

blanche ADJECTIVE *see* **blanc**

la **blanchisserie** NOUN
laundry

le **blé** NOUN
wheat

blessé ADJECTIVE
see also blessé NOUN
injured

le **blessé** NOUN
see also blessé ADJECTIVE
injured person ◇ *L'accident a fait trois blessés.* Three people were injured in the accident.

la **blessée** NOUN
injured person

blesser VERB
1 *to injure* ◇ *Il a été blessé dans un accident de voiture.* He was injured in a car accident.
2 *to hurt* ◇ *Il a fait exprès de le blesser.* He hurt him on purpose.
- **se blesser** to hurt oneself ◇ *Je me suis blessé au pied.* I've hurt my foot.

la **blessure** NOUN
injury

bleu ADJECTIVE
see also bleu NOUN
1 *blue* ◇ *une veste bleue* a blue jacket
- **bleu marine** navy blue
2 *very rare* (*steak*)

le **bleu** NOUN
see also bleu ADJECTIVE
1 *blue* ◇ *Le bleu est ma couleur préférée.* Blue is my favourite colour.
2 *bruise* ◇ *Il a un bleu au front.* He's got a bruise on his forehead.

le **bleuet** NOUN
cornflower

le **bloc** NOUN
pad ◇ *un bloc de papier à lettres* a pad of writing paper
- **le bloc opératoire** the operating theatre

le **bloc-notes** NOUN
(PL les **blocs-notes**)
note pad

blond ADJECTIVE
blond
- **blond cendré** ash blond ◇ *Andrew a les cheveux blond cendré.* Andrew has ash blond hair.

bloquer VERB
to block ◇ *bloquer le passage* to block the way
- **être bloqué dans un embouteillage** to be stuck in a traffic jam

se **blottir** VERB
to huddle ◇ *Ils étaient blottis l'un contre l'autre.* They were huddled together.

la **blouse** NOUN
overall

le **blouson** NOUN
jacket ◇ *un blouson en cuir* a leather jacket

la **bobine** NOUN
reel ◇ *une bobine de fil* a reel of thread

le **bocal** NOUN
(PL les **bocaux**)
jar

le **bœuf** NOUN
1 *ox*
2 *beef* ◇ *un rôti de bœuf* a joint of beef

bof EXCLAMATION (*informal*)
- **Le film t'a plu? – Bof! C'était pas terrible!** Did you like the film? – Well...it wasn't that great!
- **Comment ça va? – Bof! Pas terrible.** How is it going? – Oh...not too well actually.

le **bohémien** NOUN
gipsy

la **bohémienne** NOUN
gipsy

boire VERB
to drink
- **boire un coup** (*informal*) to have a drink

le **bois** NOUN
wood
- **en bois** wooden ◇ *une table en bois* a

wooden table
- **avoir la gueule de bois** (*informal*) to have a hangover

boisson NOUN
drink

boîte NOUN
1 *box* ◇ *une boîte d'allumettes* a box of matches
- **une boîte aux lettres** a letter box
- **une boîte postale** a PO Box

2 *tin* ◇ *une boîte de sardines* a tin of sardines
- **une boîte de conserve** a tin
- **en boîte** tinned ◇ *des petits pois en boîte* tinned peas
- **une boîte de nuit** a night club

boiter VERB
to limp

bol NOUN
bowl
- **en avoir ras le bol** (*informal*) to be fed up ◇ *J'en ai ras le bol de ce boulot.* I'm fed up with this job.

bombarder VERB
to bomb

bombe NOUN
1 *bomb* ◇ *une bombe atomique* an atomic bomb

2 *aerosol* ◇ *du déodorant en bombe aérosol* aerosol deodorant

bon ADJECTIVE, ADVERB
(FEM SING **bonne**)
see also bon NOUN
1 *good* ◇ *un bon restaurant* a good restaurant ◇ *Le tabac n'est pas bon pour la santé.* Smoking isn't good for you.
- **être bon en maths** to be good at maths
- **sentir bon** to smell nice
- **Bon voyage!** Have a good trip!
- **Bon weekend!** Have a nice weekend!
- **Bonne chance!** Good luck!
- **Bonne nuit!** Good night!
- **Bon anniversaire!** Happy birthday!
- **Bonne année!** Happy New Year!

2 *right* ◇ *Il est arrivé au bon moment.* He arrived at the right moment. ◇ *Ce n'est pas la bonne réponse.* That's not the right answer.
- **Il fait bon aujourd'hui.** It's nice today.
- **de bonne heure** early
- **bon marché** cheap ◇ *Les fraises ne sont pas bon marché en hiver.* Strawberries aren't cheap in winter.
- **Ah bon?** Really? ◇ *Je pars aux États-Unis la semaine prochaine.–Ah bon?* I'm going to the States next week.–Really?
- **J'aimerais vraiment que tu viennes!–Bon, d'accord.** I'd really like you to come!–OK then, I will.

le **bon** NOUN
see also bon ADJECTIVE
voucher ◇ *un bon d'achat* a voucher
- **pour de bon** for good ◇ *Cette fois, c'est pour de bon.* This time it's for good.

le **bonbon** NOUN
sweet

bondé ADJECTIVE
crowded

bondir VERB
to leap

le **bonheur** NOUN
happiness
- **porter bonheur** to bring luck

le **bonhomme** NOUN
(PL les **bonshommes**)
- **un bonhomme de neige** a snowman

bonjour EXCLAMATION
1 *Hello!* ◇ *Donne le bonjour à tes parents de ma part.* Say hello to your parents for me.
2 *Good morning!*
3 *Good afternoon!*

bonjour *is used in the morning and afternoon; in the evening* **bonsoir** *is used instead.*
- **C'est simple comme bonjour!** It's easy as pie!

bonne ADJECTIVE *see* **bon**

le **bonnet** NOUN
hat ◇ *un bonnet de laine* a woolly hat
- **un bonnet de bain** a bathing cap

bonsoir EXCLAMATION
Good evening!

la **bonté** NOUN
kindness

le **bord** NOUN
1 *edge* ◇ *le bord de la table* the edge of the table

2 *side* ◇ *Jane a garé sa voiture au bord de la route.* Jane parked her car on the side of the road.
- **au bord de la mer** at the seaside
- **au bord de l'eau** by the water
- **monter à bord** to go on board
- **être au bord des larmes** to be on the verge of tears

le **bordeaux** NOUN
see also bordeaux ADJECTIVE
Bordeaux wine
- **du bordeaux rouge** claret

bordeaux ADJECTIVE
see also bordeaux NOUN
maroon ◇ *une jupe bordeaux* a maroon skirt

le **bordel** NOUN
brothel ◇ *Quel bordel!* (*informal*) What a bloody mess!

border VERB
1 *to line* ◇ *une route bordée d'arbres* a tree-lined street
2 *to trim* ◇ *un col bordé de dentelle* a collar trimmed with lace
3 *to tuck up* ◇ *Sa mère vient la border tous les soirs.* Her mother comes and tucks her up every night.

la **bordure** NOUN
border
➔ **une villa en bordure de mer** a villa right by the sea

la **Bosnie** NOUN
Bosnia
➔ **la Bosnie-Herzégovine** Bosnia-Herzegovina

la **bosse** NOUN
bump ◇ *Jacques a une grosse bosse au front.* Jacques has got a big bump on his forehead. ◇ *La route est pleine de bosses.* The road is very bumpy.

le **bossu** NOUN
hunchback

la **bossue** NOUN
hunchback

botanique ADJECTIVE
see also botanique NOUN
botanic ◇ *les jardins botaniques* the botanic gardens

la **botanique** NOUN
see also botanique ADJECTIVE
botany

la **botte** NOUN
1 *boot* ◇ *une paire de bottes* a pair of boots
➔ **les bottes de caoutchouc** wellington boots
2 *bunch* ◇ *une botte de radis* a bunch of radishes

le **bottin** ® NOUN
phone book

le **bouc** NOUN
1 *goatee beard*
2 *billy goat*
➔ **un bouc émissaire** a scapegoat

la **bouche** NOUN
mouth
➔ **le bouche à bouche** the kiss of life
➔ **une bouche d'égout** a manhole
➔ **une bouche de métro** an entrance to the underground

la **bouchée** NOUN
mouthful
➔ **une bouchée à la reine** a chicken vol-au-vent

boucher VERB
see also boucher NOUN
1 *to fill* ◇ *boucher un trou* to fill a hole
2 *to block* ◇ *L'évier est bouché.* The sink is blocked. ◇ *J'ai le nez bouché.* My nose is blocked.

le **boucher** NOUN
see also boucher VERB
butcher ◇ *Il est boucher.* He's a butcher.

la **bouchère** NOUN
butcher ◇ *Elle est bouchère.* She's a butcher.

la **boucherie** NOUN
butcher's

le **bouchon** NOUN
1 *top* (*of plastic bottle*)
2 *cork* (*of wine bottle*)
3 *hold-up* ◇ *Il y avait beaucoup de bouchons sur l'autoroute.* There were a lot of hold-ups on the motorway.

la **boucle** NOUN
curl (*of hair*)
➔ **une boucle d'oreille** an earring ◇ *une paire de boucles d'oreille* a pair of earrings

bouclé ADJECTIVE
curly

le **bouclier** NOUN
shield

le/la **bouddhiste** NOUN
Buddhist

bouder VERB
to sulk

le **boudin** NOUN
➔ **le boudin noir** black pudding
➔ **le boudin blanc** white pudding

la **boue** NOUN
mud

la **bouée** NOUN
buoy
➔ **une bouée de sauvetage** a life buoy

boueux ADJECTIVE
(FEM SING **boueuse**)
muddy

la **bouffe** NOUN (*informal*)
food ◇ *La bouffe est infecte à la cantine.* The food in the canteen is revolting.

la **bouffée** NOUN
➔ **une bouffée d'air frais** a breath of fresh air

bouffer VERB (*informal*)
to eat

le **bougeoir** NOUN
candlestick

bouger VERB
to move

la **bougie** NOUN
candle

la **bouillabaisse** NOUN
fish soup

bouillant ADJECTIVE

1 *boiling* ◇ *Faites cuire les pâtes à l'eau bouillante.* Cook the pasta in boiling water.
2 *piping hot* ◇ *La soupe est servie bouillante.* The soup should be served piping hot.

ouillir VERB
to boil ◇ *L'eau bout.* The water's boiling.
Je bous d'impatience. I'm bursting with impatience.

ouilloire NOUN
kettle

ouillon NOUN
stock ◇ *du bouillon de légumes* vegetable stock

ouillotte NOUN
hot-water bottle

oulanger NOUN
baker ◇ *Il est boulanger.* He's a baker.

oulangère NOUN
baker ◇ *Elle est boulangère.* She's a baker.

oulangerie NOUN
baker's

oule NOUN
ball ◇ *une boule de cristal* a crystal ball
une boule de neige a snowball
jouer aux boules to play bowls

oulevard NOUN
boulevard

ouleverser VERB
1 *to move deeply* ◇ *Cette histoire déchirante m'a bouleversée.* This heartbreaking story moved me deeply.
2 *to shatter* ◇ *La mort de son ami l'a bouleversé.* He was shattered by the death of his friend.
3 *to turn upside down* ◇ *Cette rencontre a bouleversé sa vie.* This meeting turned his life upside down.

oulot NOUN (*informal*)
1 *job* ◇ *Anita a trouvé du boulot.* Anita has found a job.
2 *work* ◇ *J'ai beaucoup de boulot en ce moment.* I've got a lot of work to do at the moment.

oum NOUN (*informal*)
party

ouquet NOUN
bunch of flowers ◇ *un bouquet de roses* a bunch of roses

ouquin NOUN (*informal*)
book

ouquiner VERB (*informal*)
to read

ourdonner VERB
to buzz

ourg NOUN
small market town

bourgeois ADJECTIVE
middle-class ◇ *un quartier bourgeois* a posh area

le **bourgeon** NOUN
bud

la **Bourgogne** NOUN
Burgundy

bourré ADJECTIVE
◆ **bourré de** stuffed with ◇ *un portefeuille bourré de billets* a wallet stuffed with banknotes
◆ **être bourré** (*informal*) to be plastered ◇ *Il était complètement bourré.* He was completely plastered.

le **bourreau** NOUN
(PL les **bourreaux**)
executioner
◆ **C'est un véritable bourreau de travail.** He's a real workaholic.

bourrer VERB
to stuff ◇ *bourrer une valise de vêtements* to stuff clothes into a case

la **bourse** NOUN
grant
◆ **la Bourse** the Stock Exchange

bous VERB *see* **bouillir**

la **bousculade** NOUN
crush ◇ *la bousculade dans les grands magasins au moment des soldes* the crush in the big stores at sale time

bousculer VERB
1 *to jostle* ◇ *être bousculé par la foule* to be jostled by the crowd
2 *to rush* ◇ *Je n'aime pas qu'on me bouscule.* I don't like to be rushed.

la **boussole** NOUN
compass

bout VERB *see* **bouillir**

le **bout** NOUN
1 *end* ◇ *Elle habite au bout de la rue.* She lives at the end of the street. ◇ *Jane est assise en bout de table.* Jane is sitting at the end of the table.
2 *tip* ◇ *le bout du nez* the tip of the nose
3 *bit* ◇ *un petit bout de fromage* a bit of cheese
◆ **un bout de papier** a scrap of paper
◆ **au bout de** after ◇ *Au bout d'un moment, il s'est endormi.* After a while he fell asleep.
◆ **Elle est à bout.** She's at the end of her tether.

la **bouteille** NOUN
bottle ◇ *une bouteille de vin rouge* a bottle of red wine
◆ **une bouteille de gaz** a gas cylinder

la **boutique** NOUN

PTO

shop

le **bouton** NOUN
1 *button*
2 *spot* (*on skin*) ◇ *J'ai un bouton sur le nez.* I've got a spot on my nose.
3 *bud* ◇ *un bouton de rose* a rosebud
➔ **un bouton d'or** a buttercup

le **bowling** NOUN
1 *tenpin bowling*
2 *bowling alley*

la **boxe** NOUN
boxing

le **boxeur** NOUN
boxer

le **bracelet** NOUN
bracelet

le **bracelet-montre** NOUN
wristwatch

le **brancard** NOUN
stretcher

le **brancardier** NOUN
stretcher-bearer

la **branche** NOUN
branch

branché ADJECTIVE (*informal*)
trendy ◇ *avoir un look branché* to look trendy

brancher VERB
1 *to connect* ◇ *Le téléphone est branché?* Is the phone connected?
2 *to plug in* ◇ *L'aspirateur n'est pas branché.* The hoover isn't plugged in.

le **bras** NOUN
arm

la **brasse** NOUN
breaststroke ◇ *nager la brasse* to do the breaststroke

la **brasserie** NOUN
café-restaurant

brave ADJECTIVE
nice ◇ *C'est un brave type.* He's a nice enough fellow.

bravo EXCLAMATION
Bravo!

le **break** NOUN
estate car

la **brebis** NOUN
ewe
➔ **le fromage de brebis** sheep's cheese

bref ADJECTIVE, ADVERB
(FEM SING **brève**)
short ◇ *Sa lettre était brève.* His letter was short.
➔ **en bref** in brief ◇ *l'actualité en bref* the news in brief
➔ **...bref, ça s'est bien terminé.** ...to cut a long story short, it turned out all right in the end.

le **Brésil** NOUN
Brazil

la **Bretagne** NOUN
Brittany

la **bretelle** NOUN
strap ◇ *La bretelle de son soutien-gorge dépasse.* Her bra strap is showing.
➔ **les bretelles** braces ◇ *Il porte des bretelles.* He's wearing braces.

breton ADJECTIVE, NOUN
(FEM SING **bretonne**)
Breton ◇ *Ils parlent breton.* They speak Breton.
➔ **un Breton** a Breton (*man*)
➔ **une Bretonne** a Breton (*woman*)
➔ **les Bretons** the Bretons

brève ADJECTIVE *see* **bref**

le **brevet** NOUN
certificate

le **bricolage** NOUN
do-it-yourself ◇ *Elle aime le bricolage.* She likes doing DIY. ◇ *un magasin de bricolage* a DIY shop

la **bricole** NOUN (*informal*)
➔ **J'ai acheté une bricole pour le bébé de Sabine.** I've bought a little something for Sabine's baby.
➔ **J'ai encore quelques bricoles à faire avant de partir.** I've still got a few things to do before I go.

bricoler VERB
to do DIY ◇ *Pascal aime bricoler.* Pascal loves doing DIY.

le **bricoleur** NOUN
DIY enthusiast

la **bricoleuse** NOUN
DIY enthusiast

le **bridge** NOUN
bridge (*game*) ◇ *Horst adore jouer au bridge.* Horst loves playing bridge.

brièvement ADVERB
briefly ◇ *Expliquez-moi brièvement ce qui s'est passé.* Tell me briefly what happened.

la **brigade** NOUN
squad (*of police*) ◇ *la brigade des stups* (*informal*) the drugs squad

brillamment ADVERB
brilliantly ◇ *Il a réussi brillamment à son examen.* He did brilliantly in the exam.

brillant ADJECTIVE
1 *brilliant* ◇ *une brillante carrière* a brilliant career ◇ *Ses notes ne sont pas brillantes.* His marks aren't brilliant.
2 *shiny* ◇ *des cheveux brillants* shiny hair

briller VERB
to shine

brin NOUN
- **un brin d'herbe** a blade of grass
- **un brin de muguet** a sprig of lily of the valley

brindille NOUN
twig

brioche NOUN
brioche bun

brique NOUN
brick

briquet NOUN
cigarette lighter

brise NOUN
breeze

briser VERB
to break ◇ *Le vase s'est brisé en mille morceaux.* The vase broke into a thousand pieces.

Britannique NOUN
Briton
- **les Britanniques** the British

britannique ADJECTIVE
British

brocante NOUN
junk ◇ *un magasin de brocante* a junk shop

brocanteur NOUN
dealer in second-hand goods

brocanteuse NOUN
dealer in second-hand goods

broche NOUN
brooch ◇ *une broche en argent* a silver brooch
- **à la broche** spit-roasted ◇ *un poulet à la broche* a spit-roasted chicken

brochette NOUN
skewer
- **les brochettes d'agneau** lamb kebabs

brochure NOUN
brochure

broder VERB
to embroider

broderie NOUN
embroidery

bronchite NOUN
bronchitis ◇ *avoir une bronchite* to have bronchitis

bronze NOUN
bronze ◇ *la médaille de bronze* the bronze medal

bronzer VERB
to get a tan ◇ *Il est bien bronzé.* He's got a good tan.
- **se bronzer** to sunbathe

brosse NOUN
brush
- **une brosse à cheveux** a hairbrush
- **une brosse à dents** a toothbrush
- **Il est coiffé en brosse.** He's got a crew cut.

brosser VERB
to brush
- **se brosser les dents** to brush one's teeth ◇ *Je me brosse les dents tous les soirs.* I brush my teeth every night.

la **brouette** NOUN
wheelbarrow

le **brouillard** NOUN
fog ◇ *Il y a du brouillard.* It's foggy.

le **brouillon** NOUN
first draft ◇ *Ce n'est qu'un brouillon.* It's just a first draft.

les **broussailles** FEM NOUN
undergrowth

brouter VERB
to graze (*animals*)

broyer VERB
to crush
- **broyer du noir** to be down in the dumps

le **brugnon** NOUN
nectarine

le **bruit** NOUN
1 *noise* ◇ *J'ai entendu un bruit.* I heard a noise. ◇ *faire du bruit* to make a noise
- **sans bruit** without a sound

2 *rumour* ◇ *Des bruits circulent à son sujet.* There are rumours going round about him.

brûlant ADJECTIVE
1 *blazing* ◇ *un soleil brûlant* a blazing sun

2 *boiling hot* ◇ *Faith boit son café brûlant.* Faith drinks her coffee boiling hot.

le **brûlé** NOUN
smell of burning ◇ *Ça sent le brûlé.* There's a smell of burning.

brûler VERB
to burn
- **se brûler** to burn oneself

la **brûlure** NOUN
burn
- **des brûlures d'estomac** heartburn

la **brume** NOUN
mist

brun ADJECTIVE
brown
- **Catherine est brune.** Catherine's got dark hair.

le **brushing** NOUN
blow-dry ◇ *une coupe et un brushing* a cut and blow-dry

brusque ADJECTIVE
abrupt
- **d'un ton brusque** brusquely

brusquer VERB

to rush ◇ *Il ne faut pas la brusquer.* You mustn't rush her.

brut ADJECTIVE
- **le champagne brut** dry champagne
- **le pétrole brut** crude oil
- **son salaire brut** his gross salary

brutal ADJECTIVE
(MASC PL **brutaux**)
brutal

brutaliser VERB
to knock about ◇ *Il a été brutalisé par la police.* He was treated roughly by the police.

Bruxelles NOUN
Brussels

bruyamment ADVERB
noisily

bruyant ADJECTIVE
noisy

la **bruyère** NOUN
heather

bu VERB *see* **boire**

la **bûche** NOUN
log
- **la bûche de Noël** the Yule log

This is what is usually eaten in France instead of Christmas pudding.

le **bûcheron** NOUN
woodcutter

le **budget** NOUN
budget

le **buffet** NOUN
1 *sideboard* ◇ *un buffet en chêne* an oak sideboard
2 *buffet* ◇ *un buffet froid* a cold buffet ◇ *un buffet de gare* a station buffet

le **buisson** NOUN
bush

la **Bulgarie** NOUN
Bulgaria

la **bulle** NOUN
bubble ◇ *une bulle de savon* a soap bubble

le **bulletin** NOUN
1 *bulletin*
- **le bulletin d'informations** the news bulletin

2 *report* ◇ *Ton bulletin n'est pas fameux ce mois-ci.* Your school report isn't very good this month.
- **le bulletin météorologique** the weather report
- **le bulletin de salaire** pay slip
- **le bulletin de vote** the ballot paper

le **bureau** NOUN
(PL les **bureaux**)
1 *desk* ◇ *Posez le dossier sur mon bureau.* Put the file on my desk.
2 *office* ◇ *Il vous attend dans son bureau.* He's waiting for you in his office.
- **un bureau de change** a bureau de change
- **le bureau de poste** the post office
- **le bureau de tabac** the tobacconist's
- **le bureau de vote** the polling station

bus VERB *see* **boire**

le **bus** NOUN
bus

le **buste** NOUN
bust

but VERB *see* **boire**

le **but** NOUN
1 *aim* ◇ *Ils n'ont pas de but dans la vie.* They have no aim in life.
- **Quel est le but de votre visite?** What's the reason for your visit?
- **dans le but de** with the intention of ◇ *Je suis venue dans le but de vous aider.* I came to help you.

2 *goal* ◇ *marquer un but* to score a goal

le **butane** NOUN
Calor gas ®

le **butin** NOUN
loot ◇ *Les cambrioleurs se sont partagé le butin.* The burglars shared the stolen goods.

buvais, buvait VERB *see* **boire**

le **buvard** NOUN
blotter

C

c' PRONOUN *see* **ce**

ça PRONOUN

1 *this* ◇ *Est-ce que vous pouvez me donner un peu de ça?* Can you give me a bit of this?

2 *that* ◇ *Est-ce que tu peux prendre ça, là-bas dans le coin?* Can you bring that from over there in the corner?

3 *it* ◇ *Ça ne fait rien.* It doesn't matter.

- **Comment ça va?** How are you?
- **Ça alors!** Well, well!
- **C'est ça.** That's right.
- **Ça y est!** That's it!

çà ADVERB

- **çà et là** here and there

cabane NOUN

hut

cabillaud NOUN

cod

cabine NOUN

cabin (*on a ship*)

- **une cabine d'essayage** a fitting room
- **une cabine téléphonique** a phone box

cabinet NOUN

surgery (*of doctor, of dentist*)

- **une chambre avec cabinet de toilette** a room with washing facilities

cabinets MASC NOUN

toilet

câble NOUN

cable

cabosser VERB

to dent

cacahuète NOUN

peanut

- **le beurre de cacahuète** peanut butter

cacao NOUN

cocoa

- **le beurre de cacao** cocoa butter

cache-cache MASC NOUN

- **jouer à cache-cache** to play hide-and-seek

cachemire NOUN

cashmere ◇ *un pull en cachemire* a cashmere jumper

cache-nez NOUN

(PL les **cache-nez**)

long woollen scarf

cacher VERB

to hide ◇ *J'ai caché les cadeaux sous le lit.* I hid the presents under the bed. ◇ *Tu me caches quelque chose!* You're hiding something!

- **se cacher** to hide ◇ *Elle s'est cachée sous la table.* She's hiding under the table.

le **cachet** NOUN

1 *tablet*

- **un cachet d'aspirine** an aspirin

2 *fee* (*for performer*) ◇ *Il a touché un gros cachet pour ce concert.* He got a big fee for the concert.

- **le cachet de la poste** the postmark

la **cachette** NOUN

hiding place

- **en cachette** on the sly ◇ *Il est sorti en cachette sans réveiller ses parents.* He crept out on the sly without waking his parents.

le **cachot** NOUN

dungeon

le **cactus** NOUN

cactus

le **cadavre** NOUN

corpse

le **Caddie ®** NOUN

supermarket trolley

le **cadeau** NOUN

(PL les **cadeaux**)

present

- **faire un cadeau à quelqu'un** to give somebody a present

le **cadenas** NOUN

padlock

cadet ADJECTIVE

(FEM SING **cadette**)

see also **cadet** NOUN

1 *younger* (*brother, sister*) ◇ *ma sœur cadette* my younger sister

2 *youngest* (*son, daughter*) ◇ *son fils cadet* his youngest son

le **cadet** NOUN

see also **cadet** ADJECTIVE

youngest ◇ *C'est le cadet de la famille.* He's the youngest of the family.

la **cadette** NOUN

youngest ◇ *C'est la cadette de la famille.* She's the youngest of the family.

le **cadre** NOUN

1 *frame* ◇ *un cadre en bois* a wooden frame

2 *surroundings* ◇ *L'hôtel est situé dans un très beau cadre.* The hotel is set in beautiful surroundings.

3 *executive* ◇ *un cadre supérieur* a senior executive

le **cafard** NOUN

cockroach

- **avoir le cafard** (*informal*) to be feeling down ◇ *J'ai le cafard.* I'm feeling down.

le **café** NOUN
1 *coffee* ◇ *un café au lait* a white coffee
2 *café*
Cafés in France sell both alcoholic and non-alcoholic drinks.

le **café-tabac** NOUN
A café-tabac *is a bar which also sells cigarettes and stamps; you can tell a* café-tabac *by the red diamond-shaped sign outside it.*

la **cafetière** NOUN
1 *coffee maker*
2 *coffee pot*

la **cage** NOUN
cage
◆ **la cage d'escalier** the stairwell

la **cagoule** NOUN
balaclava

le **cahier** NOUN
exercise book ◇ *mon cahier de brouillon* my rough book

la **caille** NOUN
quail

le **caillou** NOUN
(PL les **cailloux**)
pebble

la **caisse** NOUN
1 *box* ◇ *une caisse à outils* a tool box
2 *till* ◇ *le ticket de caisse* the till receipt
3 *checkout* ◇ *J'ai dû faire la queue à la caisse.* I had to queue at the checkout.

le **caissier** NOUN
cashier

la **caissière** NOUN
cashier

le **cake** NOUN
fruit cake

le **calcul** NOUN
1 *calculation* ◇ *Je me suis trompé dans mes calculs.* I made a mistake in my calculations.
2 *arithmetic* ◇ *Je ne suis pas très bon en calcul.* I'm not very good at arithmetic.

la **calculatrice** NOUN
calculator

calculer VERB
to work out ◇ *J'ai calculé combien ça allait coûter.* I worked out how much it was going to cost.

la **calculette** NOUN
pocket calculator

la **cale** NOUN
wedge

calé ADJECTIVE (*informal*)
◆ **Elle est calée en histoire.** She's really good at history.

le **caleçon** NOUN
1 *boxer shorts*
2 *leggings*

le **calendrier** NOUN
calendar

le **calepin** NOUN
notebook

caler VERB
to stall ◇ *La voiture a calé dans une côte.* The car stalled on a hill.

câlin ADJECTIVE
see also câlin NOUN
cuddly

le **câlin** NOUN
see also câlin ADJECTIVE
cuddle ◇ *faire un câlin à quelqu'un* to give somebody a cuddle

le **calmant** NOUN
tranquillizer

calme ADJECTIVE
see also calme NOUN
1 *quiet* ◇ *un endroit calme* a quiet place
2 *calm* ◇ *Elle est restée très calme.* She stayed very calm.

le **calme** NOUN
see also calme ADJECTIVE
peace and quiet ◇ *J'ai besoin de calme pour travailler.* I need peace and quiet to work.

calmer VERB
to soothe ◇ *Cette pommade calme les démangeaisons.* This ointment soothes itching.
◆ **se calmer** to calm down ◇ *Calme-toi!* Calm down!

la **calorie** NOUN
calorie

le/la **camarade** NOUN
friend
◆ **un camarade de classe** a school friend

le **cambriolage** NOUN
burglary

cambrioler VERB
to burgle

le **cambrioleur** NOUN
burglar

la **cambrioleuse** NOUN
burglar

la **camelote** NOUN (*informal*)
junk ◇ *C'est vraiment de la camelote.* It's absolute junk.

la **caméra** NOUN
camera (*cinema, TV*)

le **caméscope®** NOUN
camcorder

le **camion** NOUN
lorry

camionnette NOUN
van
camionneur NOUN
lorry driver
camomille NOUN
camomile tea
camp NOUN
camp ◇ *un camp de prisonniers* a prison camp ◇ *un camp de vacances* a holiday camp
campagne NOUN
1 *country*
◆ **à la campagne** in the country ◇ *Nous passons nos vacances à la campagne.* We spend our holidays in the country.
2 *campaign* ◇ *une campagne de marketing* a marketing campaign
camper VERB
to camp
campeur NOUN
camper
campeuse NOUN
camper
camping NOUN
camping ◇ *faire du camping* to go camping
◆ **un terrain de camping** a campsite
Canada NOUN
Canada
◆ **au Canada (1)** in Canada
◆ **au Canada (2)** to Canada
canadien ADJECTIVE, NOUN
(FEM SING **canadienne**)
Canadian
◆ **un Canadien** a Canadian (*man*)
◆ **une Canadienne** a Canadian (*woman*)
canal NOUN
(PL les **canaux**)
canal
canapé NOUN
1 *sofa*
2 *open sandwich*
canard NOUN
duck
canari NOUN
canary
cancer NOUN
cancer ◇ *le cancer du poumon* lung cancer
◆ **le Cancer** Cancer ◇ *Sabine est Cancer.* Sabine's Cancer.
candidat NOUN
1 *candidate* (*in exam, election*)
2 *applicant* (*for job*)
candidate NOUN
1 *candidate* (*in exam, election*)
2 *applicant* (*for job*)
candidature NOUN
◆ **poser sa candidature à un poste** to apply for a job ◇ *Il a posé sa candidature à des dizaines de postes.* He has applied for dozens of jobs.
le **caneton** NOUN
duckling
la **canette** NOUN
◆ **une canette de bière** a small bottle of beer
le **caniche** NOUN
poodle
la **canicule** NOUN
scorching heat
le **canif** NOUN
penknife
le **caniveau** NOUN
(PL les **caniveaux**)
gutter
la **canne** NOUN
walking stick
◆ **une canne à pêche** a fishing rod
la **cannelle** NOUN
cinnamon
le **canoë** NOUN
1 *canoe*
2 *canoeing* ◇ *faire du canoë* to go canoeing
le **canon** NOUN
1 *gun* ◇ *un canon antichar* an anti-tank gun
2 *cannon* ◇ *un boulet de canon* a cannon ball
le **canot** NOUN
dinghy ◇ *un canot pneumatique* a rubber dinghy
◆ **un canot de sauvetage** a lifeboat
la **cantatrice** NOUN
opera singer
la **cantine** NOUN
canteen
le **caoutchouc** NOUN
rubber
◆ **des bottes en caoutchouc** Wellington boots
le **cap** NOUN
cape ◇ *le cap Horn* Cape Horn
capable ADJECTIVE
◆ **Elle est capable de marcher pendant des heures.** She can walk for hours.
◆ **Il est capable de changer d'avis au dernier moment.** He's capable of changing his mind at the last minute.
la **cape** NOUN
cape
le **capitaine** NOUN
captain
la **capitale** NOUN
capital ◇ *la capitale de la France* the capital of France
le **capot** NOUN

PTO

bonnet (*of car*)

la **capote** NOUN (*informal*)
condom

la **câpre** NOUN
caper (*food*)

le **caprice** NOUN
- **faire des caprices** to make a fuss ◇ *Il n'aime pas les enfants qui font des caprices.* He doesn't like children who make a fuss.

capricieux ADJECTIVE
(FEM SING **capricieuse**)
- **un enfant capricieux** an awkward child

le **Capricorne** NOUN
Capricorn ◇ *Helen est Capricorne.* Helen's Capricorn.

captivant ADJECTIVE
fascinating

la **captivité** NOUN
captivity ◇ *en captivité* in captivity

capturer VERB
to capture

la **capuche** NOUN
hood ◇ *un manteau à capuche* a coat with a hood

le **capuchon** NOUN
cap (*of pen*)

la **capucine** NOUN
nasturtium

le **car** NOUN
see also car CONJUNCTION
coach ◇ *un car scolaire* a school bus

car CONJUNCTION
see also car NOUN
because ◇ *Nous sommes inquiets car il n'est pas encore rentré.* We're worried because he isn't back yet.

la **carabine** NOUN
rifle

le **caractère** NOUN
personality ◇ *Il a le même caractère que son père.* He's got the same personality as his father.
- **Il a bon caractère.** He's good-natured.
- **Elle a mauvais caractère.** She's bad-tempered.
- **Il n'a pas un caractère facile.** He isn't easy to get on with.

caractéristique ADJECTIVE
see also caractéristique NOUN
characteristic

la **caractéristique** NOUN
see also caractéristique ADJECTIVE
characteristic

la **carafe** NOUN
jug ◇ *une carafe d'eau* a jug of water

les **Caraïbes** FEM NOUN
Caribbean Islands

le **caramel** NOUN
1 *caramel* ◇ *la crème caramel* crème caramel
2 *toffee*

la **caravane** NOUN
caravan

carbonique ADJECTIVE
- **le gaz carbonique** carbon dioxide

le **carburant** NOUN
fuel

cardiaque ADJECTIVE
- **une crise cardiaque** a heart attack
- **Ma tante est cardiaque.** My aunt has heart trouble.

le **cardigan** NOUN
cardigan

le/la **cardiologue** NOUN
heart specialist

le **carême** NOUN
Lent

la **caresse** NOUN
stroke ◇ *faire des caresses à un chat* to stroke a cat

caresser VERB
to stroke

la **carie** NOUN
tooth decay ◇ *J'ai une carie.* I've got a hole in my tooth.

caritatif ADJECTIVE
(FEM SING **caritative**)
- **une organisation caritative** a charity

le **carnaval** NOUN
carnival

le **carnet** NOUN
1 *notebook*
2 *book* ◇ *un carnet d'adresses* an address book ◇ *un carnet de chèques* a cheque book ◇ *un carnet de timbres* a book of stamps ◇ *un carnet de tickets* a book of tickets

In the Paris metro it is cheaper to buy tickets in a book of ten, known as a carnet.

- **mon carnet de notes** my school report

la **carotte** NOUN
carrot ◇ *les carottes râpées* grated carrots

carré ADJECTIVE
see also carré NOUN
square
- **un mètre carré** a square metre

le **carré** NOUN
see also carré ADJECTIVE
square

le **carreau** NOUN
(PL les **carreaux**)
1 *check* ◇ *une chemise à carreaux* a checked shirt
2 *tile* (*on floor, wall*) ◇ *Je viens de laver les carreaux de la cuisine.* I've just washed the kitchen floor.

3 *pane* ◇ *Il a cassé un carreau.* He broke a windowpane.
4 *diamonds* (*cards*) ◇ *l'as de carreau* the ace of diamonds

carrefour NOUN
junction

carrelage NOUN
tiled floor

carrément ADVERB
1 *completely* ◇ *C'est carrément impossible.* It's completely impossible.
2 *straight out* ◇ *Dis-lui carrément ce que tu penses.* Tell him straight out what you think.

carrière NOUN
career
- **un militaire de carrière** a professional soldier

carrure NOUN
build ◇ *Il a une carrure d'athlète.* He has an athletic build.

cartable NOUN
satchel

carte NOUN
1 *card*
- **une carte d'anniversaire** a birthday card
- **une carte postale** a postcard
- **une carte de vœux** a Christmas card

The French send greetings cards (les cartes de vœux) *in January rather than at Christmas, with best wishes for the New Year.*

- **une carte bancaire** a cash card
- **une carte de crédit** a credit card
- **une carte d'embarquement** a boarding card
- **une carte d'identité** an identity card
- **une carte de séjour** a residence permit
- **une carte téléphonique** a phonecard
- **un jeu de cartes (1)** a pack of cards
- **un jeu de cartes (2)** a card game

2 *map* ◇ *une carte de France* a map of France ◇ *une carte routière* a road map
3 *menu* ◇ *la carte des vins* the wine list
- **manger à la carte** to eat à la carte ◇ *Nous avons décidé de manger à la carte.* We decided to choose from the à la carte menu.

carton NOUN
1 *cardboard* ◇ *un morceau de carton* a piece of cardboard
2 *cardboard box* ◇ *un carton à chaussures* a shoe box

cartouche NOUN
cartridge
- **une cartouche de cigarettes** a carton of cigarettes

le **cas** NOUN
(PL les **cas**)
case ◇ *plusieurs cas* several cases
- **ne faire aucun cas de** to take no notice of ◇ *Il ne fait aucun cas de ce qu'on lui dit.* He takes no notice of what people say to him.
- **en aucun cas** on no account
- **en tout cas** at any rate
- **au cas où** in case ◇ *Prends un sandwich au cas où la cantine serait fermée.* Take a sandwich in case the canteen's closed.
- **en cas de** in case of ◇ *En cas d'incendie, appelez ce numéro.* In case of fire, call this number.

la **cascade** NOUN
waterfall

le **cascadeur** NOUN
stuntman

la **caserne** NOUN
barracks

cash ADVERB
- **payer cash** to pay cash

le **casier** NOUN
locker

le **casque** NOUN
1 *helmet*
2 *headphones*

la **casquette** NOUN
cap

cassant ADJECTIVE
- **Il m'a parlé d'un ton cassant.** He spoke to me curtly.

le **casse-croûte** NOUN
(PL les **casse-croûte**)
snack

le **casse-noix** NOUN
(PL les **casse-noix**)
nutcrackers

casse-pieds ADJECTIVE (MASC, FEM, PL)
(*informal*)
- **Il est vraiment casse-pieds!** He's a real pain in the neck!

casser VERB
to break ◇ *J'ai cassé un verre.* I've broken a glass.
- **se casser** to break ◇ *Il s'est cassé la jambe au ski.* He broke his leg when he was skiing.
- **se casser la tête** (*informal*) to go to a lot of trouble ◇ *Je ne vais pas me casser la tête pour le dîner: je vais ouvrir une boîte de conserve.* I'm not going to go to a whole lot of trouble over dinner: I'll just open a tin.

la **casserole** NOUN
saucepan

le **casse-tête** NOUN

PTO

(PL les **casse-tête**)
- **C'est un vrai casse-tête!** It's a real headache!

la **cassette** NOUN
cassette

le **cassis** NOUN
blackcurrant

le **castor** NOUN
beaver

le **catalogue** NOUN
catalogue

la **catastrophe** NOUN
disaster

le **catch** NOUN
wrestling

le **catéchisme** NOUN
catechism

la **catégorie** NOUN
category

catégorique ADJECTIVE
firm ◇ *un refus catégorique* a flat refusal

la **cathédrale** NOUN
cathedral

catholique ADJECTIVE
see also catholique NOUN
Catholic

le/la **catholique** NOUN
see also catholique ADJECTIVE
Catholic

le **cauchemar** NOUN
nightmare ◇ *faire un cauchemar* to have a nightmare

la **cause** NOUN
cause
- **à cause de** because of ◇ *Nous n'avons pas pu sortir à cause du mauvais temps.* We couldn't go out because of the bad weather.

causer VERB
1 *to cause* ◇ *La tempête a causé beaucoup de dégâts.* The storm caused a lot of damage.
2 *to chat* ◇ *Nous n'avons pas beaucoup eu le temps de causer.* We didn't have much time to chat.

la **caution** NOUN
1 *bail*
2 *deposit*

le **cavalier** NOUN
1 *rider*
2 *partner* (*at dance*)

la **cavalière** NOUN
rider

la **cave** NOUN
cellar

la **caverne** NOUN
cave

le **CD** NOUN
(PL les **CD**)
CD

le **CD-ROM** NOUN
(PL les **CD-ROM**)
CD-ROM

la **CE** NOUN (= *Communauté européenne*)
EC

ce ADJECTIVE
(MASC SING **cet**, FEM SING **cette**, PL **ces**)
see also **ce** PRONOUN
ce *changes to* **cet** *before a vowel and most words beginning with "h".*
1 *this* ◇ *Tu peux prendre ce livre.* You can take this book. ◇ *cet après-midi* this afternoon ◇ *cet hiver* this winter
- **ce livre-ci** this book
- **cette voiture-ci** this car

2 *that* ◇ *Je n'aime pas du tout ce film.* I don't like that film at all.
- **ce livre-là** that book
- **cette voiture-là** that car

ce PRONOUN
see also **ce** ADJECTIVE
ce *changes to* **c'** *before the vowel in* **est**, **était** *and* **étaient**.
it ◇ *Ce n'est pas facile.* It's not easy.
- **c'est (1)** it is ◇ *C'est vraiment trop cher.* It's really too expensive. ◇ *Ouvre, c'est moi!* Open the door, it's me!
- **c'est (2)** he is ◇ *C'est un peintre du début du siècle.* He's a painter from the turn of the century.
- **c'est (3)** she is ◇ *C'est une romancière très célèbre.* She's a very famous novelist.
- **ce sont** they are ◇ *Ce sont des amis à mes parents.* They're friends of my parents'.
- **Qui est-ce?** Who is it?
- **Qu'est-ce que c'est?** What is it?
- **ce qui** what ◇ *C'est ce qui compte.* That's what matters.
- **tout ce qui** everything that ◇ *J'ai rangé tout ce qui traînait par terre.* I've tidied up everything that was on the floor.
- **ce que** what ◇ *Je vais lui dire ce que je pense.* I'm going to tell him what I think.
- **tout ce que** everything ◇ *Tu peux avoir tout ce que tu veux.* You can have everything you want.

ceci PRONOUN
this ◇ *Prends ceci, tu en auras besoin.* Take this, you'll need it.

céder VERB
to give in ◇ *Elle a tellement insisté qu'il a fini par céder.* She went on so much that he eventually gave in.

◆ **céder à** to give in to ◇ *Je ne veux pas céder à ses caprices.* I'm not going to give in to her whims.

cédille NOUN
cedilla

ceinture NOUN
belt ◇ *une ceinture en cuir* a leather belt
◆ **votre ceinture de sécurité** your seatbelt

cela PRONOUN
1 *it* ◇ *Cela dépend.* It depends.
2 *that* ◇ *Je n'aime pas cela.* I don't like that.
◆ **C'est cela.** That's right.
◆ **à part cela** apart from that

célèbre ADJECTIVE
famous

célébrer VERB
to celebrate

céleri NOUN
◆ **le céleri-rave** celeriac
◆ **le céleri en branche** celery

célibataire ADJECTIVE, NOUN
single
◆ **un célibataire** a bachelor
◆ **une célibataire** a single woman

celle PRONOUN *see* **celui**

celles PRONOUN *see* **ceux**

cellule NOUN
cell

celui PRONOUN
(FEM **celle**, MASC PL **ceux**, FEM PL **celles**)
the one ◇ *Prends celui que tu préfères.* Take the one you like best.
◇ *Je n'ai pas d'appareil photo mais je peux emprunter celui de ma sœur.* I haven't got a camera but I can borrow my sister's.
◇ *Je n'ai pas de platine laser mais je peux emprunter celle de mon frère.* I haven't got a CD player but I can borrow my brother's.
◆ **celui-ci** this one
◆ **celle-ci** this one
◆ **celui-là** that one
◆ **celle-là** that one

cendre NOUN
ash

cendrier NOUN
ashtray

censé ADJECTIVE
◆ **être censé faire quelque chose** to be supposed to do something ◇ *Vous êtes censé arriver à l'heure.* You're supposed to get here on time.

cent NUMBER
a hundred ◇ *cent francs* a hundred francs

> **cent** *is spelt with an* **-s** *when there are two or more hundreds, but not when it is followed by another number, as in "a hundred and two".*

◇ *trois cents ans* three hundred years
◇ *cent deux kilomètres* a hundred and two kilometres ◇ *trois cent cinquante kilomètres* three hundred and fifty kilometres ◇ *trois cent mille kilomètres* three hundred thousand kilometres

la **centaine** NOUN
about a hundred ◇ *Il y avait une centaine de personnes dans la salle.* There were about a hundred people in the hall.
◆ **des centaines de** hundreds of ◇ *Des centaines de réfugiés se sont présentés à l'ambassade.* Hundreds of refugees came to the embassy.

le **centenaire** NOUN
centenary

centième ADJECTIVE
hundredth

le **centilitre** NOUN
centilitre

le **centime** NOUN
centime

> *The franc is divided into 100* centimes.

◇ *une pièce de cinquante centimes* a 50-centime coin

le **centimètre** NOUN
centimetre

central ADJECTIVE
(MASC PL **centraux**)
central

la **centrale** NOUN
power station ◇ *une centrale nucléaire* a nuclear power station

le **centre** NOUN
centre
◆ **un centre commercial** a shopping centre

le **centre-ville** NOUN
town centre

cependant ADVERB
however

le **cercle** NOUN
circle ◇ *Entourez d'un cercle la bonne réponse.* Put a circle round the right answer.
◆ **un cercle vicieux** a vicious circle

le **cercueil** NOUN
coffin

la **céréale** NOUN
cereal ◇ *un bol de céréales* a bowl of cereal
◆ **un pain aux cinq céréales** a multigrain loaf

la **cérémonie** NOUN
ceremony

C

le **cerf** NOUN
stag

le **cerf-volant** NOUN
(PL les **cerfs-volants**)
kite

la **cerise** NOUN
cherry

le **cerisier** NOUN
cherry tree

cerné ADJECTIVE
- **avoir les yeux cernés** to have shadows under one's eyes ◇ *Elle avait les yeux cernés.* She had shadows under her eyes.

cerner VERB
- **J'ai du mal à le cerner.** I can't figure him out.

certain ADJECTIVE
1 *certain* ◇ *Je suis certain que je l'ai remis en place.* I'm certain that I put it back. ◇ *Ce n'est pas certain.* It's not certain.
2 *some* ◇ *Certaines personnes n'aiment pas la crème.* Some people don't like cream.
- **un certain temps** quite some time ◇ *J'ai mis un certain temps à comprendre ce qu'elle disait.* It took me quite some time to understand what she was saying.

certainement ADVERB
1 *definitely* ◇ *C'est certainement le meilleur film que j'ai vu cette année.* It's definitely the best film I've seen this year.
2 *of course* ◇ *Est-ce que je peux t'emprunter ton stylo? – Mais certainement!* Can I borrow your pen? – Of course!

certains PRONOUN
1 *some* ◇ *certains de ses amis* some of his friends ◇ *certains d'entre vous* some of you
2 *some people* ◇ *Certains pensent que le film est meilleur que le roman.* Some people think that the film is better than the novel.

certes ADVERB
certainly ◇ *Nous nous connaissons, certes, mais nous ne sommes pas amis.* We know each other, certainly, but we are not friends.

le **certificat** NOUN
certificate

le **cerveau** NOUN
(PL les **cerveaux**)
brain

la **cervelle** NOUN
brain
- **se creuser la cervelle** (*informal*) to rack one's brains

le **CES** NOUN (= *Collège d'enseignement secondaire*)
secondary school

In France pupils go to a CES *between the ages of 11 and 15, and then to a* lycée *until the age of 18.*

ces ADJECTIVE
1 *these* ◇ *Tu peux prendre ces photos si tu veux.* You can have these photos if you like.
- **ces photos-ci** these photos
2 *those* ◇ *Ces montagnes sont dangereuses en hiver.* Those mountains are dangerous in winter.
- **ces livres-là** those books

cesse
- **sans cesse** ADVERB
continually
- **Elle me dérange sans cesse.** She keeps interrupting me.

cesser VERB
to stop ◇ *cesser de faire quelque chose* to stop doing something

le **cessez-le-feu** NOUN
(PL les **cessez-le-feu**)
ceasefire

c'est-à-dire ADVERB
that is ◇ *Est-ce que tu peux venir lundi prochain, c'est-à-dire le quinze?* Can you come next Monday, that's the 15th?

cet ADJECTIVE
(FEM SING **cette**)

ce *changes to* **cet** *before a vowel and most words beginning with "h".*

1 *this* ◇ *cet après-midi* this afternoon ◇ *cet hiver* this winter ◇ *cette année* this year
- **cette semaine-ci** this week
2 *that* ◇ *Est-ce que tu peux me passer cette assiette?* Could you pass me that plate?
- **cet après-midi-là** that afternoon
- **cette nuit (1)** tonight ◇ *On prévoit de l'orage pour cette nuit.* A storm is forecast for tonight.
- **cette nuit (2)** last night ◇ *J'ai très mal dormi cette nuit.* I slept very badly last night.

cette PRONOUN *see* **ce**

ceux PRONOUN
(FEM PL **celles**)
the ones ◇ *Prends ceux que tu préfères.* Take the ones you like best. ◇ *Je n'ai pas de skis mais je peux emprunter ceux de ma sœur.* I haven't got any skis but I can borrow my

sister's. ◇ *Je n'ai pas de jumelles mais je peux emprunter celles de mon frère.* I haven't got any binoculars but I can borrow my brother's.
- **ceux-ci** these ones
- **celles-ci** these ones
- **ceux-là** those ones
- **celles-là** those ones

chacun PRONOUN
1 *each* ◇ *Il nous a donné un cadeau à chacun.* He gave us each a present. ◇ *Nous avons chacun donné dix francs.* We each gave 10 francs.
2 *everyone* ◇ *Chacun fait ce qu'il veut.* Everyone does what they like.

le **chagrin** NOUN
- **avoir du chagrin** to be very upset ◇ *Elle a eu beaucoup de chagrin à la mort de sa tante.* She was terribly upset by the death of her aunt.

le **chahut** NOUN
bedlam ◇ *Il y avait du chahut dans la classe.* There was bedlam in the classroom.

la **chaîne** NOUN
1 *chain* ◇ *une chaîne en or* a gold chain
2 *channel* (*on TV*) ◇ *Le film passe sur quelque chaîne?* Which channel is the film on?
- **une chaîne hi-fi** a hi-fi system
- **une chaîne laser** a CD player
- **une chaîne stéréo** a music centre
- **travailler à la chaîne** to work on an assembly line

la **chair** NOUN
flesh
- **en chair et en os** in the flesh ◇ *J'ai vu Mel Gibson en chair et en os.* I saw Mel Gibson in the flesh.
- **avoir la chair de poule** to have goose pimples

la **chaise** NOUN
chair
- **une chaise longue** a deckchair

le **châle** NOUN
shawl

la **chaleur** NOUN
1 *heat*
2 *warmth*

chaleureux ADJECTIVE
(FEM SING **chaleureuse**)
warm ◇ *un accueil chaleureux* a warm welcome

se **chamailler** VERB (*informal*)
to squabble ◇ *Elle se chamaille sans cesse avec son frère.* She's always squabbling with her brother.

la **chambre** NOUN
room ◇ *C'est la chambre de Camille.* This is Camille's room.
- **une chambre à coucher** a bedroom
- **une chambre d'amis** a spare room
- **une chambre à un lit** a single room
- **une chambre pour deux personnes** a double room

le **chameau** NOUN
(PL les **chameaux**)
camel

le **champ** NOUN
field

le **champagne** NOUN
champagne

le **champignon** NOUN
mushroom ◇ *une omelette aux champignons* a mushroom omelette
- **un champignon de Paris** a button mushroom

le **champion** NOUN
champion

le **championnat** NOUN
championship ◇ *le championnat du monde* the world championship

la **championne** NOUN
champion

la **chance** NOUN
1 *luck*
- **Bonne chance!** Good luck!
- **avoir de la chance** to be lucky ◇ *Tu as de la chance de partir au soleil!* You're lucky, going off to the sun!

2 *chance* ◇ *Il n'a aucune chance.* He's got no chance. ◇ *Il a des chances de réussir.* He's got a good chance of passing.

le **change** NOUN
exchange ◇ *le taux de change* the exchange rate

le **changement** NOUN
change ◇ *Il n'aime pas le changement.* He doesn't like changes.

changer VERB
to change ◇ *Il n'a pas beaucoup changé.* He hasn't changed much. ◇ *J'ai changé les draps ce matin.* I changed the sheets this morning. ◇ *J'ai changé trois cents francs.* I changed 300 francs.
- **se changer** to get changed ◇ *Je vais me changer avant de sortir.* I'm going to get changed before I go out.
- **changer de** to change ◇ *Je change de chaussures et j'arrive!* I'll change my shoes and then I'll be ready!
- **changer d'avis** to change one's mind ◇ *Appelle-moi si tu changes d'avis.* Give me a ring if you change your mind.

la **chanson** NOUN

PTO

song

le **chant** NOUN
singing ◇ *des cours de chant* singing lessons
◆ **un chant de Noël** a Christmas carol

le **chantage** NOUN
blackmail ◇ *faire du chantage à quelqu'un* to blackmail somebody

chanter VERB
to sing

le **chanteur** NOUN
singer

la **chanteuse** NOUN
singer

le **chantier** NOUN
building site

la **Chantilly** NOUN
whipped cream

chantonner VERB
to hum

le **chapeau** NOUN
(PL les **chapeaux**)
hat

la **chapelle** NOUN
chapel

le **chapitre** NOUN
chapter

chaque ADJECTIVE
1 *every* ◇ *chaque année* every year
2 *each* ◇ *Ces verres coûtent cinquante francs chaque.* These glasses cost 50 francs each.

le **char** NOUN
tank (*military*)

le **charabia** NOUN (*informal*)
gibberish ◇ *Je n'y comprends rien: c'est du charabia.* I don't understand any of it: it's gibberish.

la **charade** NOUN
1 *riddle*
2 *charade* ◇ *jouer aux charades* to play charades

le **charbon** NOUN
coal
◆ **le charbon de bois** charcoal

la **charcuterie** NOUN
1 *pork butcher's*
2 *cold meats*

A charcuterie *sells cuts of pork and pork products such as sausages, salami and pâté, as well as various cooked dishes and salads;* charcuterie *served at a meal is an assortment of ham, sausage and pâtés.*

le **charcutier** NOUN
pork butcher

la **charcutière** NOUN
pork butcher

le **chardon** NOUN
thistle

charger VERB
to load
◆ **charger quelqu'un de faire quelque chose** to tell somebody to do something ◇ *Paul m'a chargé de vous dire que la clé est sous le paillasson.* Paul told me to tell you that the key's under the mat.

le **chariot** NOUN
trolley (*at supermarket*)

charmant ADJECTIVE
charming

le **charme** NOUN
charm

charmer VERB
to charm

la **charrue** NOUN
plough

la **chasse** NOUN
1 *hunting* ◇ *un chien de chasse* a hunting dog
2 *shooting* ◇ *la chasse au canard* duck shooting
◆ **tirer la chasse d'eau** to flush the toilet

le **chasse-neige** NOUN
(PL les **chasse-neige**)
snowplough

chasser VERB
1 *to hunt* ◇ *Mon père chasse le lapin.* My father hunts rabbits.
2 *to chase away* ◇ *Ils ont chassé les cambrioleurs.* They chased away the robbers.
3 *to get rid of* ◇ *Ouvre donc la fenêtre pour chasser les odeurs de cuisine.* Open the window to get rid of the cooking smells.

le **chasseur** NOUN
hunter

le **chat** NOUN
cat

la **châtaigne** NOUN
chestnut

le **châtaignier** NOUN
chestnut tree

châtain ADJECTIVE (MASC, FEM, PL)
brown ◇ *J'ai les cheveux châtain.* I've got brown hair.

le **château** NOUN
(PL les **châteaux**)
1 *castle*
◆ **un château fort** a castle
2 *palace* ◇ *le château de Versailles* the palace of Versailles

le **chaton** NOUN
kitten

chatouiller VERB
to tickle

chatouilleux ADJECTIVE

(FEM SING **chatouilleuse**)
ticklish

la **chatte** NOUN
cat (*female*)

chaud ADJECTIVE
1 *warm* ◇ *des vêtements chauds* warm clothes
➔ **avoir chaud** to be warm ◇ *J'ai assez chaud.* I'm warm enough.
2 *hot* ◇ *Il fait chaud aujourd'hui.* It's hot today. ◇ *un plat chaud* a hot dish ◇ *Attention, c'est chaud!* Mind, it's hot! ◇ *J'ai trop chaud!* I'm too hot!

le **chauffage** NOUN
heating ◇ *Le chauffage est en panne.* The heating isn't working.
➔ **le chauffage central** central heating

le **chauffe-eau** NOUN
(PL les **chauffe-eau**)
water heater

chauffer VERB
to warm ◇ *Je vais mettre de l'eau à chauffer pour faire du thé.* I'm going to put some water on to make tea.

le **chauffeur** NOUN
driver

le **chaume** NOUN
➔ **un toit de chaume** a thatched roof

chausser VERB
➔ **Vous chaussez du combien?** What size shoe do you take?

la **chaussette** NOUN
sock

le **chausson** NOUN
slipper
➔ **un chausson aux pommes** an apple turnover

la **chaussure** NOUN
shoe
➔ **les chaussures de ski** ski boots

chauve ADJECTIVE
bald

la **chauve-souris** NOUN
(PL les **chauves-souris**)
bat (*animal*)

le **chef** NOUN
1 *head* ◇ *le chef de famille* the head of the family
➔ **le chef de l'État** the Head of State
2 *boss* ◇ *Je dois demander la permission à mon chef.* I have to get permission from my boss.
➔ **un chef d'entreprise** a company director
3 *chef* ◇ *la spécialité du chef* the chef's speciality
➔ **un chef d'orchestre** a conductor

le **chef-d'œuvre** NOUN
(PL les **chefs-d'œuvre**)
masterpiece

le **chemin** NOUN
1 *path* ◇ *Je suis descendu à la plage par un petit chemin.* I went down a little path to the beach.
2 *way* ◇ *Quel est le chemin le plus court pour aller à l'aéroport?* What's the quickest way to the airport?
➔ **en chemin** on the way ◇ *Je mangerai mon sandwich en chemin.* I'll eat my sandwich on the way.
➔ **les chemins de fer** the railways

la **cheminée** NOUN
1 *chimney*
2 *fireplace*

la **chemise** NOUN
1 *shirt* ◇ *une chemise à carreaux* a checked shirt
➔ **une chemise de nuit** a nightdress
2 *folder* ◇ *J'ai classé mes cours dans des chemises de couleurs différentes.* I've sorted my notes into different coloured folders.

le **chemisier** NOUN
blouse

le **chêne** NOUN
oak ◇ *une armoire en chêne* an oak wardrobe

le **chenil** NOUN
kennels

la **chenille** NOUN
caterpillar

le **chèque** NOUN
cheque
➔ **les chèques de voyage** traveller's cheques

le **chéquier** NOUN
cheque book

cher ADJECTIVE, ADVERB
(FEM SING **chère**)
1 *dear* ◇ *Chère Mélusine...* Dear Mélusine...
2 *expensive* ◇ *C'est trop cher.* It's too expensive. ◇ *coûter cher* to be expensive

chercher VERB
1 *to look for* ◇ *Je cherche mes clés.* I'm looking for my keys.
2 *to look up* ◇ *chercher un mot dans le dictionnaire* to look up a word in the dictionary
➔ **aller chercher (1)** to go to get ◇ *Elle est allée chercher du pain pour ce midi.* She's gone to get some bread for lunch.
➔ **aller chercher (2)** to pick up ◇ *J'irai te chercher à la gare.* I'll pick you up at the station.

le **chercheur** NOUN
scientist

C

la **chercheuse** NOUN
scientist

chère ADJECTIVE *see* **cher**

chéri ADJECTIVE
see also chéri NOUN
darling ◇ *ma petite fille chérie* my darling daughter

le **chéri** NOUN
see also chéri ADJECTIVE
darling
➔ **mon chéri** darling

la **chérie** NOUN
darling
➔ **ma chérie** darling

le **cheval** NOUN
(PL les **chevaux**)
horse ◇ *un cheval de course* a racehorse
➔ **à cheval** on horseback
➔ **faire du cheval** to go riding

le **chevalier** NOUN
knight

la **chevalière** NOUN
signet ring

chevalin ADJECTIVE
➔ **une boucherie chevaline** a horsemeat butcher's

les **chevaux** MASC NOUN *see* **cheval**

le **chevet** NOUN
➔ **une table de chevet** a bedside table
➔ **une lampe de chevet** a bedside lamp

les **cheveux** MASC NOUN
hair ◇ *Elle a les cheveux courts.* She's got short hair.

la **cheville** NOUN
ankle

la **chèvre** NOUN
goat
➔ **le fromage de chèvre** goat's cheese

le **chevreau** NOUN
(PL les **chevreaux**)
kid (*animal, leather*)

le **chèvrefeuille** NOUN
honeysuckle

le **chevreuil** NOUN
1 *roe deer*
2 *venison* ◇ *un rôti de chevreuil* roast venison

le **chewing-gum** NOUN
chewing gum

chez PREPOSITION
➔ **chez Pierre (1)** at Pierre's house
➔ **chez Pierre (2)** to Pierre's house
➔ **chez moi (1)** at my house ◇ *Je suis resté chez moi ce week-end.* I stayed at home this weekend.
➔ **chez moi (2)** to my house ◇ *Je vais rentrer chez moi.* I'm going home.
➔ **chez le dentiste (1)** at the dentist's ◇ *J'ai rendez-vous chez le dentiste demain matin.* I've got an appointment at the dentist's tomorrow morning.
➔ **chez le dentiste (2)** to the dentist's ◇ *Je vais chez le dentiste.* I'm going to the dentist's.

chic ADJECTIVE
1 *smart* ◇ *une tenue chic* a smart outfit
2 *nice* ◇ *C'est chic de ta part de m'avoir invité.* (*informal*) It was nice of you to invite me.

la **chicorée** NOUN
endive

le **chien** NOUN
dog
➔ **"Attention, chien méchant"** "Beware of the dog"

la **chienne** NOUN
bitch (*dog*)

le **chiffon** NOUN
cloth

chiffonner VERB
to crease ◇ *Ma robe est toute chiffonnée.* My dress is all creased.

le **chiffre** NOUN
figure ◇ *en chiffres ronds* in round figures
➔ **les chiffres romains** Roman numerals

le **chignon** NOUN
bun (*in hair*) ◇ *Elle s'est fait un chignon.* She put her hair in a bun.

le **Chili** NOUN
Chile

la **chimie** NOUN
chemistry ◇ *un cours de chimie* a chemistry lesson

chimique ADJECTIVE
chemical ◇ *une réaction chimique* a chemical reaction
➔ **les produits chimiques** chemicals

la **Chine** NOUN
China

chinois ADJECTIVE, NOUN
Chinese ◇ *Il apprend le chinois.* He's learning Chinese.
➔ **un Chinois** a Chinese (*man*)
➔ **une Chinoise** a Chinese (*woman*)
➔ **les Chinois** the Chinese

le **chiot** NOUN
puppy

les **chips** FEM NOUN
crisps ◇ *un paquet de chips* a packet of crisps

chirurgical ADJECTIVE
(MASC PL **chirurgicaux**)
➔ **une intervention chirurgicale** an operation

la **chirurgie** NOUN

surgery
- **la chirurgie esthétique** plastic surgery

le **chirurgien** NOUN
surgeon

le **choc** NOUN
shock ◇ *Ça m'a fait un sacré choc de le voir comme ça.* It gave me a hell of a shock to see him in that state.
- **Elle est encore sous le choc.** She's still in shock.

le **chocolat** NOUN
chocolate
- **un chocolat chaud** a hot chocolate
- **le chocolat à croquer** dark chocolate

le **chœur** NOUN
choir

choisir VERB
to choose

le **choix** NOUN
1 *choice*
- **avoir le choix** to have the choice

2 *selection* ◇ *Il n'y a pas beaucoup de choix dans ce magasin.* There's not a very wide selection of things in this shop.

le **chômage** NOUN
unemployment
- **être au chômage** to be unemployed

le **chômeur** NOUN
unemployed person ◇ *Il est chômeur.* He's unemployed.

la **chômeuse** NOUN
unemployed woman ◇ *Elle est chômeuse.* She's unemployed.

choquer VERB
to shock ◇ *Cette remarque m'a choqué.* I was shocked by that remark.

la **chose** NOUN
thing ◇ *J'ai fait des choses intéressantes pendant les vacances.* I did some interesting things during the holidays.
- **C'est peu de chose.** It's nothing really.

le **chou** NOUN
(PL les **choux**)
cabbage
- **les choux de Bruxelles** Brussels sprouts
- **un chou à la crème** a choux bun

le **chouchou** NOUN (*informal*)
teacher's pet

la **chouchoute** NOUN (*informal*)
teacher's pet

la **choucroute** NOUN
sauerkraut (*with sausages and ham*)

la **chouette** NOUN
see also chouette ADJECTIVE
owl

chouette ADJECTIVE
see also chouette NOUN (*informal*)
brilliant ◇ *Chouette alors!* Brilliant!

le **chou-fleur** NOUN
(PL les **choux-fleurs**)
cauliflower

chrétien ADJECTIVE
(FEM SING **chrétienne**)
Christian ◇ *Il est chrétien.* He's a Christian.

le **Christ** NOUN
Christ

chronologique ADJECTIVE
chronological

le **chronomètre** NOUN
stopwatch

chronométrer VERB
to time

le **chrysanthème** NOUN
chrysanthemum
Chrysanthemums are strongly associated with funerals in France.

chuchoter VERB
to whisper

chut EXCLAMATION
Shh!

la **chute** NOUN
fall
- **faire une chute** to fall
- **une chute d'eau** a waterfall
- **la chute des cheveux** hair loss
- **les chutes de neige** snowfalls

Chypre NOUN
Cyprus

-ci ADVERB
- **ce livre-ci** this book
- **ces bottes-ci** these boots

la **cible** NOUN
target

la **ciboulette** NOUN
chives

la **cicatrice** NOUN
scar

se **cicatriser** VERB
to heal up ◇ *Cette plaie s'est vite cicatrisée.* This wound has healed up quickly.

ci-contre ADVERB
opposite ◇ *la page ci-contre* the opposite page

ci-dessous ADVERB
below ◇ *la photo ci-dessous* the picture below

ci-dessus ADVERB
above

le **cidre** NOUN
cider

le **ciel** NOUN
1 *sky* ◇ *un ciel nuageux* a cloudy sky
2 *heaven* ◇ *être au ciel* to be in heaven

C

le **cierge** NOUN
candle (*in church*)

la **cigale** NOUN
cicada

le **cigare** NOUN
cigar ◇ *Il fume le cigare.* He smokes cigars.

la **cigarette** NOUN
cigarette

la **cigogne** NOUN
stork

ci-joint ADVERB
enclosed ◇ *Veuillez trouver ci-joint mon curriculum vitae.* Please find enclosed my CV.

le **cil** NOUN
eyelash

le **ciment** NOUN
cement

le **cimetière** NOUN
cemetery

le/la **cinéaste** NOUN
film-maker

le **cinéma** NOUN
cinema

cinq NUMBER
five ◇ *Il est cinq heures du matin.* It's five in the morning. ◇ *Il a cinq ans.* He's five.
◆ **le cinq février** the fifth of February

la **cinquantaine** NOUN
about fifty ◇ *Il y avait une cinquantaine de personnes.* There were about fifty people there.
◆ **Il a la cinquantaine.** He's in his fifties.

cinquante NUMBER
fifty ◇ *Il a cinquante ans.* He's fifty.
◆ **cinquante et un** fifty-one
◆ **cinquante-deux** fifty-two

cinquième ADJECTIVE
see also cinquième NOUN
fifth ◇ *au cinquième étage* on the fifth floor

la **cinquième** NOUN
see also cinquième ADJECTIVE
second year
In French secondary schools, years are counted from the sixième *(youngest) to* première *and* terminale *(oldest).*
◇ *Mon frère est en cinquième.* My brother's in second year.

le **cintre** NOUN
coat hanger

le **cirage** NOUN
shoe polish

circonflexe ADJECTIVE
◆ **un accent circonflexe** a circumflex

la **circonstance** NOUN
circumstance ◇ *dans les circonstances actuelles* in the present circumstances

la **circulation** NOUN
1 *traffic* ◇ *Il y avait beaucoup de circulation.* There was a lot of traffic.
2 *circulation* ◇ *Elle a des problèmes de circulation.* She has bad circulation.

circuler VERB
to run ◇ *Il n'y a qu'un bus sur trois qui circule.* Only one bus in three is running.

la **cire** NOUN
wax

le **ciré** NOUN
oilskin jacket

cirer VERB
to polish (*shoes, floor*)

le **cirque** NOUN
circus

les **ciseaux** MASC NOUN
◆ **une paire de ciseaux** a pair of scissors

le **citadin** NOUN
city dweller

la **citation** NOUN
quotation

la **cité** NOUN
estate ◇ *J'habite dans une cité.* I live on an estate.
◆ **une cité universitaire** halls of residence
◆ **une cité-dortoir** a dormitory town

citer VERB
to quote

le **citoyen** NOUN
citizen

la **citoyenne** NOUN
citizen

le **citron** NOUN
lemon
◆ **un citron vert** a lime

la **citronnade** NOUN
still lemonade

la **citrouille** NOUN
pumpkin

le **civet** NOUN
stew ◇ *du civet de lapin* rabbit stew

civil ADJECTIVE
civilian
◆ **en civil** in civilian clothes

la **civilisation** NOUN
civilization

clair ADJECTIVE, ADVERB
1 *light* ◇ *vert clair* light green ◇ *C'est une pièce très claire.* It's a very light room.
2 *clear* (*water*)
◆ **voir clair** to see clearly
◆ **le clair de lune** moonlight

clairement ADVERB
clearly

la **clairière** NOUN
clearing

clandestin ADJECTIVE
➔ **un passager clandestin** a stowaway

la **claque** NOUN
slap ◇ *Elle m'a donné une claque.* She gave me a slap.

claquer VERB
1 *to bang* ◇ *On entend des volets qui claquent.* You can hear shutters banging.
2 *to slam* ◇ *Elle est partie en claquant la porte.* She left, slamming the door behind her.

les **claquettes** FEM NOUN
➔ **faire des claquettes** to tap-dance

la **clarinette** NOUN
clarinet ◇ *Gavin joue de la clarinette.* Gavin plays the clarinet.

la **classe** NOUN
1 *class* ◇ *C'est la meilleure élève de la classe.* She's the best pupil in the class.
◇ *voyager en première classe* to travel first class
2 *classroom*

classer VERB
to arrange ◇ *Les livres sont classés par ordre alphabétique.* The books are arranged in alphabetical order.

le **classeur** NOUN
ring binder

classique ADJECTIVE
1 *classical* ◇ *de la musique classique* classical music
2 *classic* ◇ *un style classique* a classic style

le **clavier** NOUN
keyboard (*of computer, typewriter*)

la **clé** NOUN
1 *key*
2 *clef* ◇ *la clé de sol* the treble clef
◇ *la clé de fa* the bass clef

la **clef** = **clé**

le **client** NOUN
customer

la **cliente** NOUN
customer

la **clientèle** NOUN
customers

cligner VERB
➔ **cligner des yeux** to blink

le **clignotant** NOUN
indicator ◇ *Il a mis son clignotant à gauche.* He's indicating left.

le **climat** NOUN
climate

la **climatisation** NOUN
air conditioning

climatisé ADJECTIVE
air-conditioned ◇ *L'hôtel est climatisé.* The hotel is air-conditioned.

le **clin d'œil** NOUN
(PL les **clins d'œil**)
wink
➔ **en un clin d'œil** in a flash

la **clinique** NOUN
private hospital

le **clochard** NOUN
tramp

la **cloche** NOUN
bell

le **clocher** NOUN
1 *church tower*
2 *steeple*

le **clou** NOUN
nail
➔ **un clou de girofle** a clove

le **clown** NOUN
clown

le **club** NOUN
club

le **cobaye** NOUN
guinea pig

le **coca** NOUN
Coke ®

la **cocaïne** NOUN
cocaine

la **coccinelle** NOUN
ladybird

cocher VERB
to tick ◇ *Cochez la bonne réponse.* Tick the right answer.

le **cochon** NOUN
see also **cochon** ADJECTIVE
pig
➔ **un cochon d'Inde** a guinea pig

cochon ADJECTIVE (*informal*)
see also **cochon** NOUN
dirty ◇ *une histoire cochonne* a dirty story

le **cocktail** NOUN
1 *cocktail*
2 *cocktail party*

le **coco** NOUN
➔ **une noix de coco** a coconut

cocorico EXCLAMATION
1 *Cock-a-doodle-doo!*
2 *Three cheers for France!*
The symbol of France is the cockerel and so cocorico! *is sometimes used as an expression of French national pride.*

la **cocotte** NOUN
casserole (*pan*)
➔ **une cocotte-minute** ® a pressure cooker

le **code** NOUN
code
➔ **le code de la route** the highway code

PTO

◆ **le code postal** the postcode

le **cœur** NOUN
heart
◆ **avoir bon cœur** to be kind-hearted
◆ **la dame de cœur** the queen of hearts
◆ **avoir mal au cœur** to feel sick
◆ **par cœur** by heart ◇ *apprendre quelque chose par cœur* to learn something by heart

le **coffre** NOUN
1 *boot* (*of car*)
2 *chest* (*furniture*)

le **coffre-fort** NOUN
(PL les **coffres-forts**)
safe

le **coffret** NOUN
◆ **un coffret à bijoux** a jewellery box

le **cognac** NOUN
brandy

se **cogner** VERB
◆ **se cogner à quelque chose** to bang into something ◇ *Je me suis cogné à la table.* I banged into the table. ◇ *Je me suis cogné la tête contre la porte du placard.* I banged my head on the cupboard door.

coiffé ADJECTIVE
◆ **Tu es bien coiffée.** Your hair looks nice.

coiffer VERB
◆ **se coiffer** to do one's hair

le **coiffeur** NOUN
hairdresser

la **coiffeuse** NOUN
hairdresser

la **coiffure** NOUN
hairstyle ◇ *Cette coiffure te va bien.* That hairstyle suits you.
◆ **un salon de coiffure** a hairdresser's

le **coin** NOUN
corner
◆ **Tu habites dans le coin?** Do you live near here?
◆ **Je ne suis pas du coin.** I'm not from here.
◆ **le bistrot du coin** the local pub

coincé ADJECTIVE
1 *stuck* ◇ *La clé est coincée dans la serrure.* The key is stuck in the keyhole.
2 *stuffy* ◇ *Il est un peu coincé.* (*informal*) He's a bit stuffy.

coincer VERB
to jam ◇ *La porte est coincée.* The door's jammed.

la **coïncidence** NOUN
coincidence

le **col** NOUN
1 *collar*
2 *pass* (*of mountain*)

la **colère** NOUN
anger
◆ **Je suis en colère.** I'm angry.
◆ **se mettre en colère** to get angry

le **colin** NOUN
hake

la **colique** NOUN
diarrhoea

le **colis** NOUN
parcel

collaborer VERB
to collaborate

collant ADJECTIVE
see also collant NOUN
1 *sticky*
2 *clingy* ◇ *Je le trouve un peu collant.* (*informal*) He's always hanging around me.

le **collant** NOUN
see also collant ADJECTIVE
tights ◇ *un collant en laine* woollen tights

la **colle** NOUN
1 *glue* ◇ *un tube de colle* a tube of glue
2 *detention* ◇ *J'ai une heure de colle samedi prochain.* (*informal*) I've got an hour's detention next Saturday.
◆ **Je n'en sais rien: tu me poses une colle.** (*informal*) I really don't know: you've got me there.

la **collecte** NOUN
collection (*of money*) ◇ *On a fait une collecte au profit des victimes.* There was a collection for the victims.

la **collection** NOUN
collection ◇ *une collection de timbres* a stamp collection

collectionner VERB
to collect

le **collège** NOUN
secondary school
In France pupils go to a collège *between the ages of 11 and 15, and then to a* lycée *until the age of 18.*

le **collégien** NOUN
schoolboy

la **collégienne** NOUN
schoolgirl

le/la **collègue** NOUN
colleague

coller VERB
1 *to stick* ◇ *Il y a un chewing-gum collé sous la chaise.* There's a bit of chewing gum stuck under the chair.
2 *to be sticky* ◇ *Ce timbre ne colle plus.* This stamp won't stick on.
3 *to press* ◇ *J'ai collé mon oreille au mur.* I pressed my ear against the wall.

le **collier** NOUN
1 *necklace* ◇ *un collier de perles* a pearl necklace
2 *collar* (*of dog, cat*)

la **colline** NOUN
hill

la **colombe** NOUN
dove

la **colonie** NOUN
- **aller en colonie de vacances** to go to summer camp

la **colonne** NOUN
column
- **la colonne vertébrale** the spine

le **colorant** NOUN
colouring

le **coloris** NOUN
colour

le **coma** NOUN
coma ◇ *être dans le coma* to be in a coma

le **combat** NOUN
fighting ◇ *Les combats ont repris ce matin.* Fighting started again this morning.
- **un combat de boxe** a boxing match

le **combattant** NOUN
- **un ancien combattant** a war veteran

combattre VERB
to fight

combien ADVERB
1 *how much* ◇ *Vous en voulez combien? Un kilo?* How much do you want? One kilo? ◇ *Combien est-ce que ça coûte?* How much does it cost? ◇ *Combien ça fait?* How much does it come to?
2 *how many* ◇ *Tu en veux combien? Deux?* How many do you want? Two?
- **combien de (1)** how much ◇ *Combien de purée est-ce que je vous sers?* How much mashed potato shall I give you?
- **combien de (2)** how many ◇ *Combien de personnes as-tu invitées?* How many people have you invited?
- **combien de temps** how long ◇ *Combien de temps est-ce que tu seras absente?* How long will you be away?
- **On est le combien aujourd'hui? – On est le vingt.** What's the date today? – It's the 20th.

la **combinaison** NOUN
1 *combination* ◇ *J'ai changé la combinaison de mon antivol.* I've changed the combination on my bike lock.
2 *slip* (*petticoat*)
- **une combinaison de plongée** a wetsuit
- **une combinaison de ski** a ski suit

le **comble** NOUN
- **Alors ça, c'est le comble!** That's the last straw!

la **comédie** NOUN
comedy
- **une comédie musicale** a musical

le **comédien** NOUN
actor

la **comédienne** NOUN
actress

comestible ADJECTIVE
edible

comique ADJECTIVE
see also comique NOUN
comical

le **comique** NOUN
see also comique ADJECTIVE
comedian

le **commandant** NOUN
captain (*of ship, plane*)

la **commande** NOUN
order ◇ *un bon de commande* an order form
- **être aux commandes** to be at the controls

commander VERB
1 *to order* ◇ *J'ai commandé une robe par catalogue.* I've ordered a dress from a catalogue.
2 *to give orders* ◇ *C'est moi qui commande ici, pas vous!* I give the orders here, not you!

comme CONJUNCTION, ADVERB
1 *like* ◇ *Il est comme son père.* He's like his father. ◇ *Je voudrais un manteau comme celui de la photo.* I'd like a coat like the one in the picture.
2 *for* ◇ *Qu'est-ce que tu veux comme dessert?* What would you like for pudding?
3 *as* ◇ *J'ai travaillé comme serveuse cet été.* I worked as a waitress this summer. ◇ *Faites comme vous voulez.* Do as you like.
- **comme ça** like this ◇ *Ça se plie comme ça.* You fold it like this. ◇ *C'était un poisson grand comme ça.* The fish was this big.
- **comme il faut** properly ◇ *Mets le couvert comme il faut!* Set the table properly!
- **Comme tu as grandi!** How you've grown!
- **Regarde comme c'est beau!** Look, isn't it lovely!
- **comme ci comme ça** so-so ◇ *Comment est-ce que tu as trouvé le film? – Comme ci comme ça.* What did you think of the film? – So-so.

le **commencement** NOUN
beginning

commencer VERB
to start ◇ *Les cours commencent à huit heures.* Lessons start at 8 o'clock. ◇ *Il a commencé à pleuvoir.* It started raining. ◇ *J'ai commencé de réviser pour les examens.* I've started revising for the exams.

comment ADVERB
how ◇ *Comment arrives-tu à travailler dans ce bruit?* How can you possibly work with this noise?
- **Comment allez-vous?** How are you?
- **Comment s'appelle-t-il?** What's his name?
- **Comment?** What did you say?

le **commentaire** NOUN
comment

les **commérages** MASC NOUN
gossip

le **commerçant** NOUN
shopkeeper

le **commerce** NOUN
1 *trade* ◇ *le commerce extérieur* foreign trade
2 *business* ◇ *Il fait des études de commerce.* He's studying business.
3 *shop* ◇ *On trouve ça facilement dans le commerce.* You can easily find it in the shops.

commercial ADJECTIVE
(MASC PL **commerciaux**)
- **un centre commercial** a shopping centre

le **commissaire** NOUN
police superintendent

le **commissariat** NOUN
police station

les **commissions** FEM NOUN
shopping ◇ *J'ai quelques commissions à faire.* I've got some shopping to do.

commode ADJECTIVE
see also commode NOUN
handy ◇ *Ce sac est très commode pour les voyages.* This bag is very handy for travelling.
- **Son père n'est pas commode.** His father is a difficult character.

la **commode** NOUN
see also commode ADJECTIVE
chest of drawers

commun ADJECTIVE
shared ◇ *une salle de bain commune* a shared bathroom ◇ *Nous avons des intérêts communs.* We have interests in common.
- **en commun** in common ◇ *Ils n'ont rien en commun.* They've got nothing in common.
- **les transports en commun** public transport
- **mettre quelque chose en commun** to share something ◇ *Nous mettons tous nos livres en commun.* We share all our books.

la **communauté** NOUN
community

la **communication** NOUN
communication
- **une communication téléphonique** a telephone call

la **communion** NOUN
communion ◇ *faire sa première communion* to make one's first communion

communiquer VERB
to communicate

communiste ADJECTIVE
communist ◇ *le Parti communiste* the Communist Party

compact ADJECTIVE
compact
- **un disque compact** a compact disc

la **compagne** NOUN
1 *companion*
2 *partner* (*living together*)

la **compagnie** NOUN
company ◇ *J'aime avoir de la compagnie.* I like to have company. ◇ *Je viendrai te tenir compagnie.* I'll come to keep you company.
- **une compagnie d'assurances** an insurance company
- **une compagnie aérienne** an airline

le **compagnon** NOUN
1 *companion*
2 *partner* (*living together*)

la **comparaison** NOUN
comparison ◇ *en comparaison de* in comparison with

comparer VERB
to compare

le **compartiment** NOUN
compartment (*on train*)

le **compas** NOUN
compass (*for drawing circles*)

compatible ADJECTIVE
compatible

la **compétence** NOUN
competence

compétent ADJECTIVE
competent

la **compétition** NOUN
competition

complet ADJECTIVE
(FEM SING **complète**)
see also complet NOUN

1 *complete* ◇ *les œuvres complètes de Shakespeare* the complete works of Shakespeare
2 *full* ◇ *L'hôtel est complet.* The hotel is full.
- **"complet"** "no vacancies"
- **le pain complet** wholemeal bread

le **complet** NOUN
see also complet ADJECTIVE
suit (*for man*)

complètement ADVERB
completely ◇ *J'avais complètement oublié que tu viendrais.* I'd completely forgotten that you were coming.

compléter VERB
to complete ◇ *Complétez les phrases suivantes.* Complete the following phrases.

complexe ADJECTIVE
complex

complexé ADJECTIVE
screwed-up

la **complication** NOUN
complication

le/la **complice** NOUN
accomplice

les **compliments** MASC NOUN
compliment SING
- **faire des compliments** to compliment ◇ *Il m'a fait des compliments sur ma robe.* He complimented me on my dress.

compliqué ADJECTIVE
complicated ◇ *C'est une histoire compliquée.* It's a complicated story.

le **complot** NOUN
plot

le **comportement** NOUN
behaviour

comporter VERB
1 *to consist of* ◇ *Le château comporte trois parties.* The castle consists of three parts.
2 *to have* ◇ *Ce modèle comporte un écran couleur.* This model has a colour screen.
- **se comporter** to behave ◇ *Il s'est comporté de façon odieuse.* He behaved atrociously.

composer VERB
to compose (*music, text*)
- **composer un numéro** to dial a number
- **se composer de** to consist of ◇ *L'uniforme se compose d'une veste, d'un pantalon et d'une cravate.* The uniform consists of a jacket, trousers and a tie.

le **compositeur** NOUN
composer

la **composition** NOUN
test ◇ *Nous avons une composition de français cet après-midi.* We've got a French test this afternoon.

la **compositrice** NOUN
composer

composter VERB
to punch ◇ *N'oublie pas de composter ton billet avant de monter dans le train.* Remember to punch your ticket before you get on the train.

In France you have to punch your ticket on the platform to validate it before getting onto the train.

la **compote** NOUN
stewed fruit
- **la compote de prunes** stewed plums

compréhensible ADJECTIVE
understandable

compréhensif ADJECTIVE
(FEM SING **compréhensive**)
understanding

comprendre VERB
1 *to understand* ◇ *Je ne comprends pas ce que vous dites.* I don't understand what you're saying.
2 *to include* ◇ *Le forfait ne comprend pas la location des skis.* The price doesn't include ski hire.

le **comprimé** NOUN
tablet ◇ *un comprimé d'aspirine* an aspirin

compris ADJECTIVE
included ◇ *Le service n'est pas compris.* Service is not included.
- **y compris** including ◇ *Ils ont tout vendu, y compris leur voiture.* They sold everything, including their car.
- **non compris** excluding ◇ *un menu à cent francs, vin non compris* a set menu for 100 francs, excluding wine
- **cent francs tout compris** 100 francs all-inclusive

la **comptabilité** NOUN
accounting ◇ *un cours de comptabilité* a course in accounting

le/la **comptable** NOUN
accountant ◇ *Il est comptable.* He's an accountant.

comptant ADVERB
- **payer comptant** to pay cash

le **compte** NOUN
account ◇ *J'ai déposé le chèque sur mon compte.* I've paid the cheque into my account.
- **Le compte est bon.** That's the right amount.
- **tenir compte de (1)** to take into account ◇ *Ils ont tenu compte de mon expérience.* They took my experience

PTO

into account.

- **tenir compte de (2)** to take notice of ◇ *Il n'a pas tenu compte de mes conseils.* He took no notice of my advice.
- **travailler à son compte** to be self-employed
- **en fin de compte** all things considered ◇ *Le voyage ne s'est pas mal passé, en fin de compte.* The journey wasn't bad, all things considered.

compter VERB
to count

le **compte rendu** NOUN
(PL les **comptes rendus**)
report

le **compteur** NOUN
meter

le **comptoir** NOUN
bar ◇ *au comptoir* at the bar

con ADJECTIVE (*rude*)
(FEM SING **conne**)
bloody stupid

se **concentrer** VERB
to concentrate ◇ *J'ai du mal à me concentrer.* I find it hard to concentrate.

la **conception** NOUN
design

concerner VERB
to concern ◇ *en ce qui me concerne* as far as I'm concerned

- **Je ne me sens pas concerné.** I don't feel it's anything to do with me.

le **concert** NOUN
concert

le/la **concierge** NOUN
caretaker

conclure VERB
to conclude

la **conclusion** NOUN
conclusion

le **concombre** NOUN
cucumber

concorder VERB
to tally ◇ *Les dates concordent.* The dates tally.

le **concours** NOUN
1 *competition* ◇ *un concours de chant* a singing competition
2 *competitive exam*

concret ADJECTIVE
(FEM SING **concrète**)
concrete

conçu VERB
designed ◇ *Ces appartements sont très mal conçus.* These flats are very badly designed.

la **concurrence** NOUN
competition ◇ *La concurrence est vive sur ce marché.* There's a lot of competition in this market.

le **concurrent** NOUN
competitor

la **concurrente** NOUN
competitor

condamner VERB
to sentence ◇ *Il a été condamné à deux ans de prison.* He was sentenced to two years in prison. ◇ *condamner à mort* to sentence to death

la **condition** NOUN
condition ◇ *Je le ferai à une condition...* I'll do it, on one condition...

- **à condition que** provided that ◇ *Je viendrai à condition qu'il me le demande.* I'll come provided he asks me to.
- **les conditions de travail** working conditions

le **conditionnel** NOUN
conditional tense

le **conducteur** NOUN
driver

la **conductrice** NOUN
driver

conduire VERB
to drive ◇ *Est-ce que tu sais conduire?* Can you drive? ◇ *Je te conduirai chez le docteur.* I'll drive you to the doctor's.

- **se conduire** to behave ◇ *Il s'est mal conduit.* He behaved badly.

la **conduite** NOUN
behaviour

la **conférence** NOUN
1 *lecture* ◇ *donner une conférence* to give a lecture
2 *conference* ◇ *une conférence internationale* an international conference

se **confesser** VERB
to go to confession

la **confiance** NOUN
1 *trust*

- **avoir confiance en quelqu'un** to trust somebody ◇ *Je n'ai pas confiance en lui.* I don't trust him.

2 *confidence*

- **Tu peux avoir confiance. Il sera à l'heure.** You don't need to worry. He'll be on time.
- **confiance en soi** self-confidence ◇ *Elle manque de confiance en elle.* She lacks self-confidence.

confiant ADJECTIVE
confident

les **confidences** FEM NOUN

- **faire des confidences à quelqu'un** to confide in someone ◇ *Elle me fait quelquefois des confidences.* She sometimes confides in me.

confidentiel ADJECTIVE
(FEM SING **confidentielle**)
confidential

confier VERB
- **se confier à quelqu'un** to confide in somebody ◇ *Elle s'est confiée à sa meilleure amie.* She confided in her best friend.

confirmer VERB
to confirm

la **confiserie** NOUN
sweet shop

confisquer VERB
to confiscate

confit ADJECTIVE
- **des fruits confits** crystallized fruits

la **confiture** NOUN
jam ◇ *la confiture de fraises* strawberry jam
- **la confiture d'oranges** marmalade

le **conflit** NOUN
conflict

confondre VERB
to mix up ◇ *On le confond souvent avec son frère.* People often mix him up with his brother.

le **confort** NOUN
comfort
- **tout confort** with all mod cons ◇ *un appartement tout confort* a flat with all mod cons

confortable ADJECTIVE
comfortable ◇ *des chaussures confortables* comfortable shoes

confus ADJECTIVE
1 *unclear* ◇ *J'ai trouvé ses explications confuses.* I thought his explanation was unclear.
2 *embarrassed* ◇ *Il avait l'air confus.* He looked embarrassed.

la **confusion** NOUN
1 *confusion*
2 *embarrassment* ◇ *rougir de confusion* to go red with embarrassment

le **congé** NOUN
holiday ◇ *une semaine de congé* a week's holiday
- **en congé** on holiday ◇ *Je serai en congé la semaine prochaine.* I'll be on holiday next week.
- **un congé de maladie** sick leave ◇ *Il est en congé de maladie.* He's on sick leave.

le **congélateur** NOUN
freezer

congeler VERB
to freeze

la **conjonctivite** NOUN
conjunctivitis

la **conjugaison** NOUN
conjugation

la **connaissance** NOUN
1 *knowledge* ◇ *...pour approfondir vos connaissances* ...to increase your knowledge
2 *acquaintance* ◇ *Ce n'est pas vraiment une amie, juste une connaissance.* She's not really a friend, just an acquaintance.
- **perdre connaissance** to lose consciousness

connaître VERB
to know ◇ *Je ne connais pas du tout cette région.* I don't know this area at all. ◇ *Je le connais de vue.* I know him by sight.
- **Ils se sont connus à Nantes.** They first met in Nantes.
- **s'y connaître en quelque chose** to know about something ◇ *Je ne m'y connais pas beaucoup en musique classique.* I don't know much about classical music.

la **connerie** NOUN (*rude*)
bloody stupid thing ◇ *faire une connerie* to do something bloody stupid

connu ADJECTIVE
well-known ◇ *C'est un acteur connu.* He's a well-known actor.

conquérir VERB
to conquer

consacrer VERB
to devote ◇ *Il consacre beaucoup de temps à ses enfants.* He devotes a lot of time to his children. ◇ *Je suis désolé, je n'ai pas beaucoup de temps à vous consacrer.* I'm afraid I can't spare much time for you.

la **conscience** NOUN
conscience ◇ *avoir mauvaise conscience* to have a guilty conscience
- **prendre conscience de** to become aware of ◇ *Ils ont fini par prendre conscience de la gravité de la situation.* They eventually became aware of the seriousness of the situation.

consciencieux ADJECTIVE
(FEM SING **consciencieuse**)
conscientious

conscient ADJECTIVE
conscious

consécutif ADJECTIVE
(FEM SING **consécutive**)
consecutive

le **conseil** NOUN

advice ◇ *Est-ce que je peux te demander conseil?* Can I ask you for some advice?

➔ **un conseil** a piece of advice

conseiller VERB

1 *to advise* ◇ *Il a été mal conseillé.* He has been badly advised.

2 *to recommend* ◇ *Il m'a conseillé ce livre.* He recommended this book to me.

le **consentement** NOUN

consent ◇ *le consentement des parents* the parents' consent

consentir VERB

to agree ◇ *consentir à quelque chose* to agree to something

la **conséquence** NOUN

consequence

➔ **en conséquence** consequently

conséquent ADJECTIVE

➔ **par conséquent** consequently

le **conservatoire** NOUN

school of music ◇ *Elle fait du piano au conservatoire.* She's learning the piano at the school of music.

la **conserve** NOUN

tin ◇ *Je vais ouvrir une conserve.* I'll open a tin.

➔ **une boîte de conserve** a tin

➔ **les conserves** tinned food ◇ *Il n'est pas bon de manger tous les jours des conserves.* It's not healthy to eat tinned food every day.

➔ **en conserve** tinned ◇ *des petits pois en conserve* tinned peas

conserver VERB

to keep ◇ *J'ai conservé toutes ses lettres.* I've kept all her letters.

➔ **se conserver** to keep ◇ *Ce pain se conserve plus d'une semaine.* This bread will keep for more than a week.

considérable ADJECTIVE

considerable ◇ *Il a fait des progrès considérables.* He's made considerable progress.

la **considération** NOUN

➔ **prendre quelque chose en considération** to take something into consideration

considérer VERB

➔ **considérer que** to believe that ◇ *Je considère que le gouvernement devrait investir davantage dans l'éducation.* I believe that the government should invest more money in education.

la **consigne** NOUN

left-luggage office

➔ **une consigne automatique** a left-luggage locker

consistant ADJECTIVE

substantial ◇ *un petit déjeuner consistant* a substantial breakfast

consister VERB

➔ **consister à** to consist of ◇ *Mon travail consiste à répondre au téléphone et à recevoir les clients.* My job consists of answering the phone and welcoming the customers. ◇ *En quoi consiste votre travail?* What does your job involve?

consoler VERB

to console

le **consommateur** NOUN

1 *consumer*

2 *customer* (*in café*)

la **consommation** NOUN

1 *consumption* ◇ *la consommation d'électricité* electricity consumption

2 *drink* ◇ *Le billet d'entrée donne droit à une consommation gratuite.* The ticket entitles you to one free drink.

la **consommatrice** NOUN

1 *consumer*

2 *customer* (*in café*)

consommer VERB

1 *to use* ◇ *Ces grosses voitures consomment beaucoup d'essence.* These big cars use a lot of petrol.

2 *to have a drink* ◇ *Est-ce qu'on peut consommer à la terrasse?* Can we have drinks outside?

la **consonne** NOUN

consonant

constamment ADVERB

constantly ◇ *Elle se plaint constamment.* She's constantly complaining.

constant ADJECTIVE

constant

constater VERB

to notice

constipé ADJECTIVE

constipated

constitué ADJECTIVE

➔ **être constitué de** to consist of

constituer VERB

to make up ◇ *les États qui constituent la Fédération russe* the states which make up the Russian Federation

la **construction** NOUN

building ◇ *des matériaux de construction* building materials

➔ **une maison en construction** a house being built

construire VERB

to build ◇ *Ils font construire une maison neuve.* They're having a new house built.

la **consultation** NOUN

- **les heures de consultation** surgery hours

consulter VERB
1 *to consult* ◇ *Tu devrais consulter un médecin.* You should see a doctor.
2 *to see patients* ◇ *Le docteur ne consulte pas le samedi.* The doctor doesn't see patients on Saturdays.

le **contact** NOUN
contact ◇ *les contacts humains* human contact
- **Il a le contact facile.** He's very approachable.
- **garder le contact avec quelqu'un** to keep in touch with somebody

contacter VERB
to get in touch with ◇ *Je te contacterai dès que j'aurai des nouvelles.* I'll get in touch with you as soon as I have some news.

contagieux ADJECTIVE
(FEM SING **contagieuse**)
infectious ◇ *une maladie contagieuse* an infectious disease ◇ *Restez chez vous si vous êtes contagieux.* Stay at home if you've got something infectious.

contaminer VERB
to contaminate

le **conte de fées** NOUN
(PL les **contes de fées**)
fairy tale

contempler VERB
to gaze at

contemporain ADJECTIVE
contemporary
- **un auteur contemporain** a modern writer

contenir VERB
to contain ◇ *un portefeuille contenant de l'argent* a wallet containing money

content ADJECTIVE
glad ◇ *Je suis content que tu sois venu.* I'm glad you've come.
- **content de** pleased with ◇ *Elle m'a dit qu'elle était contente de mon travail.* She told me she was pleased with my work.

contenter VERB
to please ◇ *Il est difficile à contenter.* He's hard to please.
- **Je me contente de peu.** I can make do with very little.

contesté ADJECTIVE
controversial ◇ *Cette décision est très contestée.* This is a very controversial decision.

le **continent** NOUN
continent

continu ADJECTIVE
continuous
- **faire la journée continue** to work without taking a full lunch break

continuellement ADVERB
constantly

continuer VERB
to carry on ◇ *Continuez sans moi!* Carry on without me! ◇ *Il ne veut pas continuer ses études.* He doesn't want to go on studying.
- **continuer à faire quelque chose** to go on doing something ◇ *Ils ont continué à regarder la télé sans me dire bonjour.* They went on watching TV without saying hello to me.
- **continuer de faire quelque chose** to go on doing something ◇ *Il continue de fumer malgré son asthme.* He keeps on smoking, despite his asthma.

contourner VERB
to go round ◇ *La route contourne la ville.* The road goes round the town.

le **contraceptif** NOUN
contraceptive

la **contraception** NOUN
contraception

le **contractuel** NOUN
traffic warden

la **contractuelle** NOUN
traffic warden

la **contradiction** NOUN
contradiction
- **par esprit de contradiction** just to be awkward ◇ *Il a refusé de venir par esprit de contradiction.* He refused to come, just to be awkward.

le **contraire** NOUN
opposite ◇ *Il a fait le contraire de ce que je lui avais demandé.* He did the opposite of what I asked him.
- **au contraire** on the contrary

contrarier VERB
1 *to annoy* ◇ *Il avait l'air contrarié.* He looked annoyed.
2 *to upset* ◇ *Est-ce que tu serais contrariée si je ne venais pas?* Would you be upset if I didn't come?

le **contraste** NOUN
contrast

le **contrat** NOUN
contract ◇ *un contrat de travail* an employment contract

la **contravention** NOUN
parking ticket

contre PREPOSITION
1 *against* ◇ *Ne mets pas ton vélo contre le mur.* Don't put your bike against the wall. ◇ *Tu es pour ou contre ce projet?* Are you for or against this

TO

plan?
2 *for* ◇ *échanger quelque chose contre quelque chose* to swap something for something
◆ **par contre** on the other hand

la **contrebande** NOUN
smuggling
◆ **des produits de contrebande** smuggled goods

la **contrebasse** NOUN
double bass

contrecœur
◆ **à contrecœur** ADVERB
reluctantly ◇ *Il est venu à contrecœur.* He came reluctantly.

contredire VERB
to contradict ◇ *Il ne supporte pas d'être contredit.* He can't stand being contradicted.

la **contre-indication** NOUN
◆ **"Contre-indication en cas d'eczéma"** "Should not be used by people with eczema"

le **contresens** NOUN
mistranslation

le **contretemps** NOUN
◆ **Désolé d'être en retard: j'ai eu un contretemps.** Sorry I'm late: I was held up.

contribuer VERB
◆ **contribuer à** to contribute to ◇ *Est-ce que tu veux contribuer au cadeau pour Marie?* Do you want to contribute to Marie's present?

le **contrôle** NOUN
1 *control* ◇ *le contrôle des passeports* passport control
2 *check*
◆ **un contrôle d'identité** an identity check
◆ **le contrôle des billets** ticket inspection
3 *test* ◇ *un contrôle antidopage* a drugs test
◆ **le contrôle continu** continuous assessment

contrôler VERB
to check ◇ *Personne n'a contrôlé mon billet.* Nobody checked my ticket.

le **contrôleur** NOUN
ticket inspector

la **contrôleuse** NOUN
ticket inspector

controversé ADJECTIVE
controversial

convaincre VERB
1 *to persuade* ◇ *Il a essayé de me convaincre de rester.* He tried to persuade me to stay.
2 *to convince* ◇ *Tu n'as pas l'air convaincu.* You don't look convinced.

la **convalescence** NOUN
convalescence

convenable ADJECTIVE
decent ◇ *un hôtel convenable* a decent hotel
◆ **Ce n'est pas convenable.** It's bad manners.

convenir VERB
◆ **convenir à** to suit ◇ *Est-ce que cette date te convient?* Does this date suit you? ◇ *J'espère que cela vous conviendra.* I hope this will suit you.
◆ **convenir de** to agree on ◇ *Nous avons convenu d'une date.* We've agreed on a date.

conventionné ADJECTIVE
◆ **un médecin conventionné** a Health Service doctor

All doctors in France charge for treatment, but patients of Health Service doctors get their money refunded by the government.

convenu ADJECTIVE
agreed ◇ *au moment convenu* at the agreed time

la **conversation** NOUN
conversation

la **convocation** NOUN
notification

convoquer VERB
◆ **convoquer quelqu'un à une réunion** to invite somebody to a meeting ◇ *Le directeur a convoqué tous les parents à la réunion.* The headmaster has invited all the parents to the meeting.

la **coopération** NOUN
co-operation

coopérer VERB
to co-operate

le **copain** NOUN (*informal*)
1 *friend* ◇ *C'est un bon copain.* He's a good friend.
2 *boyfriend* ◇ *Je l'ai vue avec son copain.* I saw her with her boyfriend.

la **copie** NOUN
1 *copy* ◇ *Ce tableau n'est qu'une copie.* This picture is only a copy.
2 *paper* ◇ *Il a des copies à corriger ce week-end.* He's got some papers to mark this weekend.

copier VERB
to copy

copieux ADJECTIVE
(FEM SING **copieuse**)
hearty ◇ *un repas copieux* a hearty meal

la **copine** NOUN (*informal*)
1 *friend* ◇ *Je sors avec une copine ce soir.* I'm going out with a friend tonight.

2 *girlfriend* ◇ *Je ne savais pas qu'il avait une copine.* I didn't know he had a girlfriend.

oq NOUN
cockerel

oque NOUN
hull (*of boat*)
un œuf à la coque a soft-boiled egg

oquelicot NOUN
poppy

oqueluche NOUN
whooping cough

oquillage NOUN
1 *shellfish*
2 *shell* ◇ *Nous avons ramassé des coquillages sur la plage.* We picked up some shells on the beach.

oquille NOUN
shell
une coquille d'œuf an eggshell
une coquille Saint-Jacques a scallop

oquin ADJECTIVE
cheeky ◇ *Il m'a regardé d'un air coquin.* He gave me a cheeky look.

or NOUN
horn ◇ *Je joue du cor.* I play the horn.

orbeau NOUN
(PL les **corbeaux**)
crow

orbeille NOUN
basket ◇ *une corbeille de fruits* a basket of fruit
une corbeille à papier a wastepaper basket

orde NOUN
1 *rope*
2 *string* (*of violin, tennis racket*)
une corde à linge a clothes line

ordonnerie NOUN
shoe repair shop

ordonnier NOUN
cobbler

oriace ADJECTIVE
tough

orne NOUN
horn

ornemuse NOUN
bagpipes ◇ *jouer de la cornemuse* to play the bagpipes

ornet NOUN
un cornet de frites a bag of chips
un cornet de glace an ice cream cone

ornichon NOUN
gherkin

ornouailles NOUN
Cornwall

orps NOUN
body

correct ADJECTIVE
1 *correct* ◇ *Ce n'est pas tout à fait correct.* That's not quite correct.
2 *reasonable* ◇ *un salaire correct* a reasonable salary ◇ *Le repas était tout à fait correct.* The meal was quite reasonable.

la **correction** NOUN
correction

la **correspondance** NOUN
1 *correspondence*
◆ **un cours par correspondance** a correspondence course
2 *connection* (*train, plane*) ◇ *Il y a une correspondance pour Toulouse à dix heures.* There's a connection for Toulouse at ten o'clock.

le **correspondant** NOUN
penfriend

la **correspondante** NOUN
penfriend

correspondre VERB
to correspond

le **corridor** NOUN
corridor

corriger VERB
to mark ◇ *Le prof n'a pas encore corrigé nos copies.* The teacher hasn't marked our papers yet.

corse ADJECTIVE, NOUN
Corsican
◆ **un Corse** a Corsican (*man*)
◆ **une Corse** a Corsican (*woman*)

la **Corse** NOUN
Corsica

la **corvée** NOUN
chore ◇ *Quelle corvée!* What a chore!

costaud ADJECTIVE
brawny

le **costume** NOUN
1 *suit* (*man's*) ◇ *Tu devrais mettre un costume et une cravate pour l'entretien.* You should wear a suit and tie for the interview.
2 *costume* (*theatre*) ◇ *Nous avons fait nous-mêmes tous les costumes pour la pièce.* We made all the costumes for the play ourselves.

la **côte** NOUN
1 *coastline* ◇ *La route longe la côte.* The road follows the coastline.
◆ **la Côte d'Azur** the French Riviera
2 *hill* ◇ *J'ai grimpé la côte.* I went up the hill.
3 *rib* ◇ *Il s'est cassé une côte en tombant.* He broke a rib when he fell.
4 *chop* ◇ *une côte de porc* a pork chop
◆ **une côte de bœuf** a rib of beef

PTO

- **côte à côte** side by side

le **côté** NOUN
side
- **à côté de (1)** next to ◇ *Le café est à côté du sucre.* The coffee's next to the sugar.
- **à côté de (2)** next door to ◇ *Il habite à côté de chez moi.* He lives next door to me.
- **de l'autre côté** on the other side ◇ *La pharmacie est de l'autre côté de la rue.* The chemist's is on the other side of the street.
- **De quel côté est-il parti?** Which way did he go?
- **mettre quelque chose de côté** to save something ◇ *J'ai mis de l'argent de côté.* I've saved some money.

la **côtelette** NOUN
chop ◇ *une côtelette d'agneau* a lamb chop

le **coton** NOUN
cotton ◇ *une chemise en coton* a cotton shirt
- **le coton hydrophile** cotton wool

le **cou** NOUN
neck

couchant ADJECTIVE
- **le soleil couchant** the setting sun

la **couche** NOUN
1 *layer* ◇ *la couche d'ozone* the ozone layer
2 *coat* (*of paint, varnish*)
3 *nappy*

couché ADJECTIVE
1 *lying down* ◇ *Il était couché sur le tapis.* He was lying on the carpet.
2 *in bed* ◇ *À huit heures, il était déjà couché.* He was already in bed at 8 o'clock.

le **coucher** NOUN
see also coucher VERB
- **un coucher de soleil** a sunset

se **coucher** VERB
see also coucher NOUN
1 *to go to bed* ◇ *Je me suis couché tard hier soir.* I went to bed late last night.
2 *to set* (*sun*)

la **couchette** NOUN
1 *couchette* (*on train*)
2 *bunk* (*on boat*)

le **coude** NOUN
elbow

coudre VERB
1 *to sew* ◇ *J'aime coudre.* I like sewing.
2 *to sew on* ◇ *Il ne sait même pas coudre un bouton.* He can't even sew a button on.

la **couette** NOUN
duvet

les **couettes** FEM NOUN
bunches ◇ *Quand j'étais petite, ma mère me faisait des couettes.* When I was little, my mother put my hair in bunches.

couler VERB
1 *to run* ◇ *Ne laissez pas couler les robinets.* Don't leave the taps running. ◇ *J'ai le nez qui coule.* My nose is running.
2 *to flow* ◇ *La rivière coulait lentement.* The river was flowing slowly.
3 *to leak* ◇ *Mon stylo coule.* My pen's leaking.
4 *to sink* ◇ *Un bateau a coulé pendant la tempête.* A boat sank during the storm.

la **couleur** NOUN
colour ◇ *une pellicule couleur* a colour film
- **Tu as pris des couleurs.** You've got a tan.

la **couleuvre** NOUN
grass snake

les **coulisses** FEM NOUN
wings (*in theatre*)
- **dans les coulisses** behind the scenes

le **couloir** NOUN
corridor

le **coup** NOUN
1 *knock* ◇ *donner un coup à quelque chose* to give something a knock
2 *blow* ◇ *Il m'a donné un coup!* He hit me!
- **un coup de pied** a kick
- **un coup de poing** a punch
3 *shock* ◇ *Ça m'a fait un coup de le voir comme ça!* (*informal*) It gave me a shock to see him like that!
- **un coup de feu** a shot
- **un coup de fil** (*informal*) a ring ◇ *Je te donnerai un coup de fil dans la soirée.* I'll give you a ring this evening.
- **donner un coup de main à quelqu'un** to give somebody a hand ◇ *Je viendrai te donner un coup de main.* I'll come and give you a hand.
- **un coup d'œil** a quick look ◇ *jeter un coup d'œil* to have a quick look
- **attraper un coup de soleil** to get sunburnt
- **un coup de téléphone** a phone call
- **un coup de tonnerre** a clap of thunder
- **boire un coup** (*informal*) to have a drink
- **après coup** afterwards ◇ *Après coup j'ai regretté de m'être mis en colère.*

Afterwards I was sorry I'd got angry.
- **à tous les coups** (*informal*) every time ◇ *Je me trompe de rue à tous les coups.* I get the street wrong every time.
- **du premier coup** first time ◇ *Il a été reçu au permis du premier coup.* He passed his driving test first time.
- **sur le coup** at first ◇ *Sur le coup je ne l'ai pas reconnu.* I didn't recognize him at first.

coupable ADJECTIVE
see also coupable NOUN
guilty

coupable NOUN
see also coupable ADJECTIVE
culprit

coupe NOUN
cup (*sport*) ◇ *Ils ont remporté la coupe du monde.* They won the World Cup.
- **une coupe de cheveux** a haircut
- **une coupe de champagne** a glass of champagne

couper VERB
1 *to cut*
2 *to turn off* ◇ *couper le courant* to turn off the electricity
3 *to take a short-cut* ◇ *On peut couper par la forêt.* There's a short-cut through the woods.
- **couper l'appétit** to spoil one's appetite
- **se couper** to cut oneself ◇ *Je me suis coupé le doigt avec une boîte de conserve.* I cut my finger on a tin.
- **couper la parole à quelqu'un** to interrupt somebody

couple NOUN
couple

couplet NOUN
verse ◇ *le premier couplet* the first verse

coupure NOUN
cut
- **une coupure de courant** a power cut

cour NOUN
1 *yard* ◇ *la cour de l'école* the school yard
2 *court* ◇ *la cour de Louis XIV* the court of Louis XIV ◇ *la cour d'assises* the criminal court

courage NOUN
courage

courageux ADJECTIVE
(FEM SING **courageuse**)
brave

couramment ADVERB
1 *fluently* ◇ *Elle parle couramment japonais.* She speaks Japanese fluently.
2 *commonly* ◇ *C'est une expression que l'on emploie couramment.* It's a commonly used phrase.

courant ADJECTIVE
see also courant NOUN
1 *common* ◇ *C'est une erreur courante.* It's a common mistake.
2 *standard* ◇ *C'est un modèle courant.* It's a standard model.

le **courant** NOUN
see also courant ADJECTIVE
1 *current* (*of river*)
- **un courant d'air** a draught
2 *power* ◇ *une panne de courant* a power cut
- **Je le ferai dans le courant de la semaine.** I'll do it some time during the week.
- **être au courant de quelque chose** to know about something ◇ *Je ne suis pas au courant de ses projets pour l'été.* I don't know about her plans for the summer.
- **mettre quelqu'un au courant de quelque chose** to tell somebody about something
- **Tu es au courant?** Have you heard about it?
- **se tenir au courant de quelque chose** to keep up with something ◇ *J'essaie de me tenir au courant de l'actualité.* I try to keep up with the news.

le **coureur** NOUN
runner
- **un coureur à pied** a runner
- **un coureur cycliste** a racing cyclist
- **un coureur automobile** a racing driver

la **coureuse** NOUN
runner

la **courgette** NOUN
courgette

courir VERB
to run ◇ *Elle a traversé la rue en courant.* She ran across the street.
- **courir un risque** to run a risk

la **couronne** NOUN
crown

courons, courez VERB *see* **courir**

le **courrier** NOUN
post ◇ *Est-ce qu'il y avait du courrier ce matin?* Was there any post this morning? ◇ *N'oublie pas de poster le courrier.* Don't forget to post the letters.
- **le courrier électronique** E-mail

la **courroie** NOUN
- **la courroie du ventilateur** fan belt

le **cours** NOUN
1 *lesson* ◇ *un cours d'espagnol* a Spanish lesson ◇ *des cours particuliers* private lessons
2 *course* ◇ *un cours intensif* a crash

PTO

course
3 *rate* ◇ *le cours du change* the exchange rate
◆ **au cours de** during ◇ *Il a été réveillé trois fois au cours de la nuit.* He was woken up three times during the night.

la **course** NOUN
1 *running* ◇ *la course de fond* long-distance running
2 *race* ◇ *une course hippique* a horse race
3 *shopping* ◇ *J'ai juste une course à faire.* I've just got a bit of shopping to do.
◆ **faire les courses** to go shopping ◇ *Elle est partie faire les courses de la semaine.* She's gone to do her weekly shopping.

court ADJECTIVE
see also **court** NOUN
short

le **court** NOUN
see also **court** ADJECTIVE
◆ **un court de tennis** a tennis court

couru VERB *see* **courir**

le **couscous** NOUN
couscous
couscous *is a spicy North African dish made with meat, vegetables and steamed semolina.*

le **cousin** NOUN
cousin

la **cousine** NOUN
cousin

le **coussin** NOUN
cushion

le **coût** NOUN
cost ◇ *le coût de la vie* the cost of living

le **couteau** NOUN
(PL les **couteaux**)
knife

coûter VERB
to cost ◇ *Est-ce que ça coûte cher?* Does it cost a lot?
◆ **Combien ça coûte?** How much is it?

coûteux ADJECTIVE
(FEM SING **coûteuse**)
expensive

la **coutume** NOUN
custom

la **couture** NOUN
1 *sewing* ◇ *Je n'aime pas la couture.* I don't like sewing.
◆ **faire de la couture** to sew
2 *seam* ◇ *La couture de mon pantalon s'est défaite.* The seam of my trousers has come undone.

le **couturier** NOUN
fashion designer ◇ *un grand couturier* a top designer

la **couturière** NOUN
dressmaker

le **couvercle** NOUN
1 *lid* (*of pan*)
2 *top* (*of tube, jar, spray can*)

couvert VERB *see* **couvrir**

couvert ADJECTIVE
see also **couvert** NOUN
◆ **couvert de** covered with ◇ *Cet arbre est couvert de fleurs au printemps.* This tree is covered with blossom in spring.
overcast (*sky*)

le **couvert** NOUN
see also **couvert** ADJECTIVE
◆ **mettre le couvert** to lay the table

les **couverts** MASC NOUN
cutlery ◇ *Les couverts sont dans le tiroir de gauche.* The cutlery is in the left-hand drawer.

la **couverture** NOUN
blanket

le **couvre-lit** NOUN
bedspread

couvrir VERB
to cover ◇ *Le chien est revenu couvert de boue.* The dog came back covered with mud.
◆ **se couvrir (1)** to wrap up ◇ *Couvre-toi bien: il fait très froid dehors.* Wrap up well: it's very cold outside.
◆ **se couvrir (2)** to cloud over ◇ *Le ciel se couvre.* The sky's clouding over.

le **crabe** NOUN
crab

cracher VERB
to spit

le **crachin** NOUN
drizzle

la **craie** NOUN
chalk

craindre VERB
to fear ◇ *Tu n'as rien à craindre.* You've got nothing to fear.

la **crainte** NOUN
fear
◆ **de crainte de** for fear of ◇ *Il n'ose rien dire de crainte de la vexer.* He daren't say anything for fear of upsetting her.

craintif ADJECTIVE
(FEM SING **craintive**)
timid

la **crampe** NOUN
cramp ◇ *J'ai une crampe au mollet.* I've got a cramp in my calf.

le **cran** NOUN
hole (*in belt*)
◆ **avoir du cran** (*informal*) to have guts

le **crâne** NOUN

skull

crâner VERB (*informal*)
to show off

crapaud NOUN
toad

craquer VERB
1 *to creak* ◇ *Le plancher craque.* The floor creaks.
2 *to burst* ◇ *Ma fermeture éclair a craqué.* My zip's burst.
3 *to crack up* ◇ *Je vais finir par craquer!* (*informal*) I'm going to crack up at this rate!
◆ **Quand j'ai vu cette robe, j'ai craqué!** (*informal*) When I saw that dress, I couldn't resist it!

crasse NOUN
filth

cravate NOUN
tie

crawl NOUN
crawl ◇ *nager le crawl* to do the crawl

crayon NOUN
pencil ◇ *un crayon de couleur* a coloured pencil
◆ **un crayon feutre** a felt-tip pen

création NOUN
creation

crèche NOUN
1 *nursery* ◇ *Elle dépose ses enfants à la crèche à huit heures.* She leaves her children at the nursery at 8 o'clock.
2 *nativity scene*

crédit NOUN
credit

créer VERB
to create

crémaillère NOUN
◆ **pendre la crémaillère** to have a house-warming party

crème NOUN
see also le crème
cream
◆ **la crème Chantilly** whipped cream
◆ **la crème fouettée** whipped cream
◆ **une crème caramel** a crème caramel
◆ **une crème au chocolat** a chocolate dessert

crème NOUN
see also la crème
white coffee ◇ *un grand crème* a large white coffee

crémeux ADJECTIVE
(FEM SING **crémeuse**)
creamy

crêpe NOUN
pancake

crêperie NOUN
pancake restaurant

le **crépuscule** NOUN
dusk

le **cresson** NOUN
watercress

la **Crète** NOUN
Crete

creuser VERB
to dig (*a hole*)
◆ **Ça creuse!** That gives you a real appetite!
◆ **se creuser la cervelle** (*informal*) to rack one's brains

creux ADJECTIVE
(FEM SING **creuse**)
hollow

la **crevaison** NOUN
puncture

crevé ADJECTIVE
1 *punctured* ◇ *un pneu crevé* a puncture
2 *knackered* ◇ *Je suis complètement crevé!* (*informal*) I'm knackered!

crever VERB
1 *to burst* (*balloon*)
2 *to have a puncture* (*motorist*) ◇ *J'ai crevé sur l'autoroute.* I had a puncture on the motorway.
◆ **Je crève de faim!** (*informal*) I'm starving!
◆ **Je crève de froid!** (*informal*) I'm freezing!

la **crevette** NOUN
prawn
◆ **une crevette rose** a prawn
◆ **une crevette grise** a shrimp

le **cri** NOUN
1 *scream* ◇ *J'ai entendu un cri.* I heard a scream. ◇ *pousser des cris de douleur* to scream with pain
2 *call* ◇ *Il sait reconnaître les cris des oiseaux.* He can identify the calls of birds.
◆ **C'est le dernier cri.** It's the latest fashion. ◇ *Ces chaussures sont du dernier cri.* These shoes are the latest fashion.

criard ADJECTIVE
garish (*colours*)

le **cric** NOUN
jack (*for car*)

crier VERB
to shout
◆ **crier de douleur** to scream with pain

le **crime** NOUN
1 *crime* ◇ *un crime de guerre* a war crime
2 *murder* ◇ *Un crime a été commis ici.* There was a murder here.

le **criminel** NOUN

PTO

1 *criminal* ◇ *un criminel de guerre* a war criminal
2 *murderer*

la **criminelle** NOUN
1 *criminal*
2 *murderer*

le **crin** NOUN
horsehair

la **crinière** NOUN
mane

le **criquet** NOUN
grasshopper

la **crise** NOUN
1 *crisis*
◆ **la crise économique** the recession
2 *attack* ◇ *une crise d'asthme* an asthma attack ◇ *une crise cardiaque* a heart attack
◆ **une crise de foie** an upset stomach
◆ **piquer une crise de nerfs** to go hysterical
◆ **avoir une crise de fou rire** to have a fit of the giggles

le **cristal** NOUN
(PL les **cristaux**)
crystal ◇ *un verre en cristal* a crystal glass

le **critère** NOUN
criterion

critique ADJECTIVE
see also critique NOUN
critical

le **critique** NOUN
see also la critique *and* critique ADJECTIVE
critic ◇ *un critique de cinéma* a film critic

la **critique** NOUN
see also le critique *and* critique ADJECTIVE
1 *criticism* ◇ *Elle ne supporte pas les critiques.* She can't stand being criticized.
2 *review* ◇ *Le film a reçu de bonnes critiques.* The film's had good reviews.

critiquer VERB
to criticize

la **Croatie** NOUN
Croatia

le **crochet** NOUN
1 *hook*
2 *detour* ◇ *faire un crochet* to make a detour
3 *crochet* ◇ *un pull au crochet* a crocheted sweater

le **crocodile** NOUN
crocodile

croire VERB
to believe ◇ *Il croit tout ce qu'on lui raconte.* He believes everything he's told.
◆ **croire que** to think that ◇ *Tu crois qu'il fera meilleur demain?* Do you think the weather will be better tomorrow?
◆ **croire à quelque chose** to believe in something
◆ **croire en Dieu** to believe in God

crois VERB *see* **croire**

croîs VERB *see* **croître**

le **croisement** NOUN
crossroads ◇ *Tournez à gauche au croisement.* Turn left at the crossroads.

croiser VERB
◆ **J'ai croisé Anne-Laure dans la rue.** I bumped into Anne-Laure in the street.
◆ **croiser les bras** to fold one's arms
◆ **croiser les jambes** to cross one's legs
◆ **se croiser** to pass each other ◇ *Nous nous croisons dans l'escalier tous les matins.* We pass each other on the stairs every morning.

la **croisière** NOUN
cruise

la **croissance** NOUN
growth

le **croissant** NOUN
croissant ◇ *un croissant au beurre* a butter croissant

croit VERB *see* **croire**

croître VERB
to grow

la **croix** NOUN
cross
◆ **la Croix-Rouge** the Red Cross

le **croque-madame** NOUN
(PL les **croque-madame**)
toasted ham and cheese sandwich with fried egg on top

le **croque-monsieur** NOUN
(PL les **croque-monsieur**)
toasted ham and cheese sandwich

croquer VERB
to munch ◇ *croquer une pomme* to munch an apple
◆ **le chocolat à croquer** plain chocolate

le **croquis** NOUN
sketch

la **crotte** NOUN
◆ **une crotte de chien** dog dirt

le **crottin** NOUN
1 *manure* ◇ *du crottin de cheval* horse manure
2 *small goat's cheese*

croustillant ADJECTIVE
crusty

la **croûte** NOUN
1 *crust* (*of bread*)
◆ **en croûte** in pastry
2 *rind* (*of cheese*)
3 *scab* (*on skin*)

roûton NOUN
1 *crust* (*end of loaf*)
2 *crouton* ◇ *des croûtons frottés d'ail* garlic croutons

royons, croyez VERB *see* **croire**

CRS MASC NOUN
French riot police

cru VERB *see* **croire**

cru ADJECTIVE
raw ◇ *la viande crue* raw meat
◆ **le jambon cru** Parma ham

crû VERB *see* **croître**

cruauté NOUN
cruelty

cruche NOUN
jug

crudités FEM NOUN
assorted raw vegetables

cruel ADJECTIVE
(FEM SING **cruelle**)
cruel

crustacés MASC NOUN
shellfish

cube NOUN
cube
◆ **un mètre cube** a cubic metre

cueillette NOUN
picking ◇ *la cueillette des champignons* mushroom picking

cueillir VERB
to pick (*flowers, fruit*)

cuiller NOUN
spoon
◆ **une cuiller à café** a teaspoon
◆ **une cuiller à soupe** a soup spoon

cuillère NOUN
spoon
◆ **une cuillère à café** a teaspoon
◆ **une cuillère à soupe** a soup spoon

cuillerée NOUN
spoonful

cuir NOUN
leather ◇ *un sac en cuir* a leather bag
◆ **le cuir chevelu** the scalp

cuire VERB
to cook ◇ *cuire quelque chose à feu vif* to cook something on a high heat
◆ **cuire quelque chose au four** to bake something
◆ **cuire quelque chose à la vapeur** to steam something
◆ **bien cuit** well done
◆ **trop cuit** overdone

cuisine NOUN
1 *kitchen*
2 *cooking* ◇ *la cuisine française* French cooking
◆ **faire la cuisine** to cook

cuisiné ADJECTIVE
◆ **un plat cuisiné** a ready-made meal

cuisiner VERB
to cook ◇ *J'aime beaucoup cuisiner.* I love cooking.

le **cuisinier** NOUN
cook

la **cuisinière** NOUN
1 *cook*
2 *cooker* ◇ *une cuisinière à gaz* a gas cooker

la **cuisse** NOUN
thigh
◆ **une cuisse de poulet** a chicken leg

la **cuisson** NOUN
cooking ◇ *"une heure de cuisson"* "cooking time: one hour"

cuit VERB *see* **cuire**

le **cuivre** NOUN
copper

le **cul** NOUN (*rude*)
bum

le **culot** NOUN (*informal*)
cheek ◇ *Quel culot!* What a cheek! ◇ *Il a un sacré culot!* He's got a damn cheek!

la **culotte** NOUN
knickers

la **culpabilité** NOUN
guilt

le **cultivateur** NOUN
farmer

la **cultivatrice** NOUN
farmer

cultivé ADJECTIVE
cultured ◇ *Il est très cultivé.* He's very cultured.

cultiver VERB
to grow ◇ *Il cultive la vigne.* He grows grapes.
◆ **cultiver la terre** to farm the land

la **culture** NOUN
1 *farming* ◇ *les cultures intensives* intensive farming
2 *education* ◇ *Pour cet emploi, on demande une bonne culture générale.* For this job, a good general education is needed.
◆ **la culture physique** physical education

le **culturisme** NOUN
body-building

le **curé** NOUN
parish priest

le **cure-dent** NOUN
toothpick

curieux ADJECTIVE
(FEM SING **curieuse**)
curious

la **curiosité** NOUN
curiosity

la **cuvette** NOUN
bowl ◇ *une cuvette en plastique* a plastic bowl

cyclable ADJECTIVE
◆ **une piste cyclable** a cycle track

le **cycle** NOUN
cycle

le/la **cycliste** NOUN
cyclist

le **cyclomoteur** NOUN
moped

le **cyclone** NOUN
hurricane

le **cygne** NOUN
swan

D

d' PREPOSITION, ARTICLE *see* **de**

dactylo NOUN
1 *typist* ◇ *Elle est dactylo.* She's a typist.
2 *typing* ◇ *Je prends des cours de dactylo.* I'm doing typing lessons.

daim NOUN
suede ◇ *une veste en daim* a suede jacket

dame NOUN
1 *lady*
2 *queen* (*in cards, chess*)

dames FEM NOUN
draughts

Danemark NOUN
Denmark

dangereux ADJECTIVE
(FEM SING **dangereuse**)
dangerous

danois ADJECTIVE, NOUN
(FEM SING **danoise**)
Danish ◇ *Il parle danois.* He speaks Danish.
- **un Danois** a Dane (*man*)
- **une Danoise** a Dane (*woman*)
- **les Danois** the Danish

dans PREPOSITION
1 *in* ◇ *Il est dans sa chambre.* He's in his bedroom. ◇ *dans deux mois* in two months' time
2 *into* ◇ *Il est entré dans mon bureau.* He came into my office.
3 *out of* ◇ *On a bu dans des verres en plastique.* We drank out of plastic glasses.

danse NOUN
1 *dance* ◇ *la danse moderne* modern dance ◇ *des danses folkloriques* folk dances
- **la danse classique** ballet
2 *dancing* ◇ *des cours de danse* dancing lessons

danser VERB
to dance

danseur NOUN
dancer

danseuse NOUN
dancer

date NOUN
date ◇ *votre date de naissance* your date of birth ◇ *la date limite de vente* the sell-by date
- **un ami de longue date** an old friend

dater VERB
- **dater de** to date from ◇ *Cette coutume date du moyen âge.* This custom dates from the Middle Ages.

la **datte** NOUN
date (*fruit*)

le **dauphin** NOUN
dolphin

davantage ADVERB
- **davantage de** more ◇ *Il faudrait davantage de stages de formation.* There should be more training courses.

de PREPOSITION, ARTICLE
see also **du (=de+le)** *and* **des (=de+les). de** *changes to* **d'** *before a vowel and most words beginning with "h"*
1 *of* ◇ *le toit de la maison* the roof of the house ◇ *la voiture de Paul* Paul's car ◇ *la voiture de mes parents* my parents' car ◇ *la voiture d'Hélène* Hélène's car ◇ *deux bouteilles de vin* two bottles of wine ◇ *un litre d'essence* a litre of petrol
- **un bébé d'un an** a one-year-old baby
- **un billet de cinquante francs** a 50-franc note
2 *from* ◇ *de Londres à Paris* from London to Paris ◇ *Il vient de Londres.* He comes from London. ◇ *une lettre de Victor* a letter from Victor
3 *by* ◇ *augmenter de dix francs* to increase by ten francs
You use **de** *to form expressions with the meaning of* **some** *and* **any**.
- **Je voudrais de l'eau.** I'd like some water. ◇ *du pain et de la confiture* bread and jam
- **Il n'a pas de famille.** He hasn't got any family.
- **Il n'y a plus de biscuits.** There aren't any more biscuits.

le **dé** NOUN
1 *dice*
2 *thimble*

le **dealer** NOUN (*informal*)
drug-pusher

déballer VERB
to unpack

le **débardeur** NOUN
tank top

débarquer VERB
to disembark ◇ *Nous avons dû débarquer à Marseille.* We had to disembark at Marseilles.
- **débarquer chez quelqu'un** (*informal*) to descend on somebody ◇ *Ils ont débarqué chez nous à dix heures du soir.* They descended on us at ten o'clock at night.

le **débarras** NOUN
junk room
- **Bon débarras!** Good riddance!

débarrasser VERB
to clear ◇ *Tu peux débarrasser la table, s'il te plaît?* Can you clear the table please?
- **se débarrasser de quelque chose** to get rid of something ◇ *Je me suis débarrassé de mon vieux frigo.* I got rid of my old fridge.

le **débat** NOUN
debate

se **débattre** VERB
to struggle

débile ADJECTIVE
crazy ◇ *C'est complètement débile!* (*informal*) That's totally crazy!

débordé ADJECTIVE
- **être débordé** to be snowed under

déborder VERB
to overflow (*river*)
- **déborder d'énergie** to be full of energy

le **débouché** NOUN
job prospect ◇ *Quels débouchés y a-t-il après ces études?* What sort of job does this course qualify you for?

déboucher VERB
1 *to unblock* (*sink, pipe*)
2 *to open* (*bottle*)
- **déboucher sur** to lead into ◇ *La rue débouche sur une place.* The street leads into a square.

debout ADVERB
1 *standing up* ◇ *Il a mangé ses céréales debout.* He ate his cereal standing up.
2 *upright* ◇ *Mets les livres debout sur l'étagère.* Put the books upright on the shelf.
3 *up* ◇ *Tu es déjà debout?* Are you up already?
- **Debout!** Get up!

déboutonner VERB
to unbutton

débraillé ADJECTIVE
sloppily dressed

débrancher VERB
to unplug

le **débris** NOUN
- **des débris de verre** bits of glass

débrouillard ADJECTIVE
streetwise

se **débrouiller** VERB
to manage ◇ *C'était difficile, mais je ne me suis pas trop mal débrouillé.* It was difficult, but I managed OK.
- **Débrouille-toi tout seul.** Sort things out for yourself.

le **début** NOUN
beginning ◇ *au début* at the beginning
- **début mai** in early May

le **débutant** NOUN
beginner

la **débutante** NOUN
beginner

débuter VERB
to start

décaféiné ADJECTIVE
decaffeinated

le **décalage horaire** NOUN
time difference (*between time zones*) ◇ *Il y a une heure de décalage horaire entre la France et la Grande-Bretagne.* There's an hour's time difference between France and Britain.

décalquer VERB
to trace

décapiter VERB
to behead

décapotable ADJECTIVE
convertible

décapsuler VERB
- **décapsuler une bouteille** to take the top off a bottle

le **décapsuleur** NOUN
bottle-opener

décéder VERB
to die ◇ *Son père est décédé il y a trois ans.* His father died three years ago.

décembre MASC NOUN
December
- **en décembre** in December

décemment ADVERB
decently

décent ADJECTIVE
decent

la **déception** NOUN
disappointment

décerner VERB
to award

le **décès** NOUN
death

décevoir VERB
to disappoint

décharger VERB
to unload

se **déchausser** VERB
to take off one's shoes

les **déchets** MASC NOUN
waste ◇ *les déchets nucléaires* nuclear waste ◇ *les déchets toxiques* toxic waste

déchiffrer VERB
to decipher

déchirant ADJECTIVE
heart-rending

déchirer VERB
1 *to tear* (*clothes*)
2 *to tear up* ◇ *déchirer une lettre* to tear up a letter
3 *to tear out* ◇ *déchirer une page d'un livre* to tear a page out of a book
◆ **se déchirer** to tear ◇ *se déchirer un muscle* to tear a muscle

déchirure NOUN
tear (*rip*)
◆ **une déchirure musculaire** a torn muscle

décidé ADJECTIVE
determined
◆ **C'est décidé.** It's decided.

décidément ADVERB
certainly ◇ *Décidément, je n'ai pas de chance aujourd'hui.* I'm certainly not having much luck today.

décider VERB
to decide
◆ **décider de faire quelque chose** to decide to do something ◇ *Ils ont décidé de passer leurs vacances en Normandie.* They decided to go to Normandy for their holiday.
◆ **se décider** to make up one's mind ◇ *Elle n'arrive pas à se décider.* She can't make up her mind.

décisif ADJECTIVE
(FEM SING **décisive**)
decisive

décision NOUN
decision

déclaration NOUN
statement ◇ *Je n'ai aucune déclaration à faire.* I have no statement to make.
◆ **faire une déclaration de vol** to report something as stolen

déclarer VERB
to declare ◇ *déclarer la guerre à un pays* to declare war on a country
◆ **se déclarer** to break out ◇ *Le feu s'est déclaré dans la cantine.* The fire broke out in the canteen.

déclencher VERB
to set off (*alarm, explosion*)
◆ **se déclencher** to go off

déclic NOUN
click

décoiffé ADJECTIVE
◆ **Elle était toute décoiffée.** Her hair was in a real mess.

décollage NOUN
takeoff (*of plane*)

décollé ADJECTIVE
◆ **avoir les oreilles décollées** to have sticking-out ears

décoller VERB
1 *to unstick* ◇ *décoller une étiquette* to unstick a label
◆ **se décoller** to come unstuck
2 *to take off* ◇ *L'avion a décollé avec dix minutes de retard.* The plane took off ten minutes late.

décolleté ADJECTIVE
see also **décolleté** NOUN
low-cut

le **décolleté** NOUN
see also **décolleté** ADJECTIVE
◆ **un décolleté plongeant** a plunging neckline

se **décolorer** VERB
to fade ◇ *Ce tee-shirt s'est décoloré au lavage.* This T-shirt has faded in the wash.
◆ **se faire décolorer les cheveux** to have one's hair bleached

les **décombres** MASC NOUN
rubble

se **décommander** VERB
to cry off ◇ *Elle devait venir mais elle s'est décommandée à la dernière minute.* She was supposed to be coming, but she cried off at the last minute.

décongeler VERB
to thaw

déconner VERB (*rude*)
to talk rubbish ◇ *Non mais, sans déconner, c'est vrai?* No kidding, is that true?

déconseiller VERB
◆ **déconseiller à quelqu'un de faire quelque chose** to advise somebody not to do something ◇ *Je lui ai déconseillé d'y aller.* I advised him not to go.
◆ **C'est déconseillé.** It's not recommended.

décontracté ADJECTIVE
relaxed
◆ **s'habiller décontracté** to dress casually

se **décontracter** VERB
to relax ◇ *Il est allé faire du footing pour se décontracter.* He went jogging to relax.

le **décor** NOUN
décor

le **décorateur** NOUN
interior decorator

la **décoration** NOUN
decoration

la **décoratrice** NOUN
interior decorator

décorer VERB
to decorate

les **décors** MASC NOUN
1 *scenery* (*in play*)

PTO

2 *set* (*in film*)

décortiquer VERB
to shell
- **des crevettes décortiquées** peeled shrimps

découdre VERB
to unpick
- **se découdre** to come unstitched

découper VERB
1 *to cut out* ◇ *J'ai découpé cet article dans le journal.* I cut this article out of the paper.
2 *to carve* (*meat*)

décourageant ADJECTIVE
discouraging

décourager VERB
to discourage
- **se décourager** to get discouraged
◇ *Ne te décourage pas!* Don't give up!

décousu ADJECTIVE
unstitched ◇ *L'ourlet est décousu.* The hem's come unstitched.

le **découvert** NOUN
overdraft

la **découverte** NOUN
discovery

découvrir VERB
to discover

décrire VERB
to describe

décrocher VERB
1 *to take down* ◇ *Tu peux m'aider à décrocher les rideaux?* Can you help me take down the curtains?
2 *to pick up the phone* ◇ *Il a décroché et a composé le numéro.* He picked up the phone and dialled the number.
- **décrocher le téléphone** to take the phone off the hook

déçu VERB
disappointed

dédaigneux ADJECTIVE
(FEM SING **dédaigneuse**)
disdainful ◇ *d'un air dédaigneux* disdainfully

le **dédain** NOUN
disdain ◇ *avec dédain* with disdain

dedans ADVERB
inside ◇ *C'est une jolie boîte: qu'est-ce qu'il y a dedans?* That's a nice box: what's in it?
- **là-dedans (1)** in there ◇ *J'ai trouvé les clés là-dedans.* I found the keys in there.
- **là-dedans (2)** in that ◇ *Il y a du vrai là-dedans.* There's some truth in that.

dédicacé ADJECTIVE
- **un exemplaire dédicacé** a signed copy

dédier VERB
to dedicate

déduire VERB
to take off ◇ *Tu as déduit les vingt francs que je te devais?* Did you take off the twenty francs I owed you?
- **déduire que** to deduce that ◇ *J'en déduis qu'il m'a menti.* That means he must have been lying.

défaire VERB
to undo
- **se défaire** to come undone

la **défaite** NOUN
defeat

le **défaut** NOUN
fault

défavorable ADJECTIVE
unfavourable

défavorisé ADJECTIVE
underprivileged

défectueux ADJECTIVE
(FEM SING **défectueuse**)
faulty

défendu ADJECTIVE
forbidden ◇ *C'est défendu.* It's not allowed.

la **défense** NOUN
1 *defence* ◇ *prendre la défense de quelqu'un* to back somebody up
- **"défense de fumer"** "no smoking"
2 *tusk* (*of elephant*)

le **défi** NOUN
challenge
- **d'un air de défi** defiantly
- **sur un ton de défi** defiantly

défier VERB
1 *to challenge* ◇ *Je te défie de trouver un meilleur exemple.* I challenge you to find a better example.
2 *to dare* ◇ *Il m'a défié d'aller à l'école en pyjama.* He dared me to go to school in my pyjamas.

défigurer VERB
to disfigure

le **défilé** NOUN
1 *parade*
- **un défilé de mode** a fashion show
2 *march*

défiler VERB
to march

définir VERB
to define

définitif ADJECTIVE
(FEM SING **définitive**)
final
- **en définitive** in the end ◇ *En définitive, ils ont décidé de rester.* In the end, they decided to stay.

définitivement ADVERB

for good ◇ *Elle s'est définitivement installée en Écosse en 1980.* She settled in Scotland for good in 1980.

déformer VERB
to stretch ◇ *Ne tire pas sur ton pull, tu vas le déformer.* Don't pull at your sweater, you'll stretch it.
◆ **se déformer** to stretch ◇ *Ce tee-shirt s'est déformé au lavage.* This T-shirt has stretched in the wash.

défouler VERB
to unwind ◇ *Je fais du step pour me défouler.* I do step aerobics to unwind.

dégagé ADJECTIVE
◆ **d'un air dégagé** casually
◆ **sur un ton dégagé** casually

dégager VERB
1 *to free* ◇ *Ils ont mis une heure à dégager les victimes.* They took an hour to free the victims.
2 *to clear* ◇ *des gouttes qui dégagent le nez* drops to clear your nose
◆ **Ça se dégage.** It's clearing up. (*weather*)

dégarnir VERB
to go bald

dégâts MASC NOUN
damage

dégel NOUN
thaw

dégeler VERB
to thaw ◇ *faire dégeler un poulet congelé* to thaw out a frozen chicken

dégivrer VERB
1 *to defrost*
2 *to de-ice*

dégonfler VERB
to let down ◇ *Quelqu'un a dégonflé mes pneus.* Somebody let down my tyres.
◆ **se dégonfler** (*informal*) to chicken out

dégouliner VERB
to trickle

dégourdi ADJECTIVE
smart ◇ *Il n'est pas très dégourdi.* He's pretty clueless.

dégourdir VERB
◆ **se dégourdir les jambes** to stretch one's legs

dégoût NOUN
disgust ◇ *une expression de dégoût* a disgusted expression
◆ **avec dégoût** disgustedly

dégoûtant ADJECTIVE
disgusting

dégoûté ADJECTIVE
disgusted
◆ **être dégoûté de tout** to be sick of everything

dégoûter VERB
to disgust ◇ *Ce genre de comportement me dégoûte.* That kind of behaviour makes me sick.
◆ **dégoûter quelqu'un de quelque chose** to put somebody off something ◇ *Ça m'a dégoûté de la viande.* That put me off meat.

se **dégrader** VERB
to deteriorate

le **degré** NOUN
degree
◆ **de l'alcool à 90 degrés** surgical spirit

dégringoler VERB
1 *to rush down* ◇ *Il a dégringolé l'escalier.* He rushed down the stairs.
2 *to collapse* ◇ *Elle a fait dégringoler la pile de livres.* She knocked over the stack of books.

dégueulasse ADJECTIVE (*rude*)
disgusting

le **déguisement** NOUN
disguise

déguiser VERB
◆ **se déguiser en quelque chose** to dress up as something ◇ *Elle s'était déguisée en vampire.* She was dressed up as a vampire.

déguster VERB
1 *to taste* (*food, wine*)
2 *to enjoy*

dehors ADVERB
outside ◇ *Je t'attends dehors.* I'll wait for you outside.
◆ **jeter quelqu'un dehors** to throw somebody out
◆ **en dehors de** apart from ◇ *En dehors de lui, tout le monde était content.* Apart from him, everybody was happy.

déjà ADVERB
1 *already* ◇ *J'ai déjà fini.* I've already finished.
2 *before* ◇ *Tu es déjà venu en France?* Have you been to France before?

déjeuner VERB
see also déjeuner NOUN
to have lunch

le **déjeuner** NOUN
see also déjeuner VERB
lunch

le **délai** NOUN
1 *extension* ◇ *J'ai demandé un délai d'une semaine.* I've asked for a week's extension.
2 *time limit* ◇ *être dans les délais* to be within the time limit

délasser VERB
to relax ◇ *La lecture délasse.* Reading's relaxing.

PTO

- **se délasser** to relax ◇ *J'ai pris un bain pour me délasser.* I had a bath to relax.

délavé ADJECTIVE
faded ◇ *un jean délavé* a pair of faded jeans

le **délégué** NOUN
representative ◇ *les délégués de classe* the class representatives

In French schools, each class elects two representatives or délégués de classe, *one boy and one girl.*

la **déléguée** NOUN
representative

déléguer VERB
to delegate

délibéré ADJECTIVE
deliberate

délicat ADJECTIVE
1 *delicate* ◇ *avoir la peau délicate* to have delicate skin
2 *tricky* ◇ *une situation délicate* a tricky situation
3 *tactful* ◇ *Il est toujours très délicat.* He's always very tactful.
4 *thoughtful* ◇ *C'est une attention délicate de sa part.* That was a kind thought on his part.

délicatement ADVERB
1 *gently*
2 *tactfully*

le **délice** NOUN
delight ◇ *Vivre ici est un vrai délice.* Living here is a real delight. ◇ *Ce gâteau est un vrai délice.* This cake's a real treat.

délicieux ADJECTIVE
(FEM SING **délicieuse**)
delicious

la **délinquance** NOUN
crime ◇ *de nouvelles mesures pour combattre la délinquance juvénile* new measures to fight juvenile delinquency

le **délinquant** NOUN
criminal

la **délinquante** NOUN
criminal

délirer VERB
- **Mais tu délires!** (*informal*) You're crazy!

le **délit** NOUN
criminal offence

délivrer VERB
to set free (*prisoner*)

le **deltaplane** NOUN
hang-glider
- **faire du deltaplane** to go hang-gliding

demain ADVERB
tomorrow
- **À demain!** See you tomorrow!

la **demande** NOUN
request
- **une demande en mariage** an offer of marriage
- **"demandes d'emploi"** "situations wanted"

demandé ADJECTIVE
- **très demandé** very much in demand

demander VERB
1 *to ask for* ◇ *J'ai demandé la permission.* I've asked for permission. ◇ *Nous avons demandé notre chemin à un chauffeur de taxi.* We asked a taxi driver the way. ◇ *Je lui ai demandé de m'aider.* I asked him to help me.
2 *to require* ◇ *un travail qui demande beaucoup de concentration* a job that requires a lot of concentration
- **se demander** to wonder ◇ *Je me demande à quelle heure il va venir.* I wonder what time he'll come.

le **demandeur d'emploi** NOUN
job-seeker

la **démangeaison** NOUN
itching

démanger VERB
to itch ◇ *Ça me démange.* It itches.

le **démaquillant** NOUN
make-up remover

démaquiller VERB
- **se démaquiller** to remove one's make-up

la **démarche** NOUN
1 *walk* ◇ *Il a une drôle de démarche.* He's got a funny walk.
2 *step* ◇ *faire les démarches nécessaires pour obtenir quelque chose* to take the necessary steps to obtain something

démarrer VERB
to start (*car*)

démêler VERB
to untangle

le **déménagement** NOUN
move ◇ *C'était le jour de notre déménagement.* It was the day we moved house.
- **un camion de déménagement** a removal van

déménager VERB
to move house

le **déménageur** NOUN
removal man

dément ADJECTIVE
crazy

démentiel ADJECTIVE
(FEM SING **démentielle**)
insane ◇ *un projet démentiel* an insane scheme

se **démerder** VERB (*rude*)

to get by ◇ *Ne t'inquiète pas, il saura se démerder.* Don't worry, he'll get by.
- **Démerde-toi tout seul.** Sort things out for yourself.

demi ADJECTIVE, ADVERB
see also demi NOUN
half ◇ *Il a trois ans et demi.* He's three and a half.
- **Il est trois heures et demie.** It's half past three.
- **Il est midi et demi.** It's half past twelve.
- **à demi endormi** half-asleep

demi NOUN
see also demi ADJECTIVE
half pint of beer
- **Un demi, s'il vous plaît!** A beer please!

demi-baguette NOUN
half a baguette

demi-cercle NOUN
semicircle

demi-douzaine NOUN
half-dozen ◇ *une demi-douzaine d'œufs* half a dozen eggs

demie NOUN
half-hour ◇ *Le bus passe à la demie.* The bus comes by on the half-hour.

demi-écrémé ADJECTIVE
semi-skimmed

demi-finale NOUN
semifinal

demi-frère NOUN
half-brother

demi-heure NOUN
half an hour ◇ *dans une demi-heure* in half an hour ◇ *toutes les demi-heures* every half an hour

demi-journée NOUN
half-day ◇ *On peut louer un parasol à la demi-journée.* You can hire a sun umbrella for a half-day.

demi-litre NOUN
half litre ◇ *un demi-litre de lait* half a litre of milk

demi-livre NOUN
half-pound ◇ *une demi-livre de tomates* half a pound of tomatoes

demi-sel ADJECTIVE
- **du beurre demi-sel** slightly salted butter

demi-sœur NOUN
half-sister

démission NOUN
resignation
- **donner sa démission** to resign

démissionner VERB
to resign

demi-tarif NOUN
1 *half-price* ◇ *un billet à demi-tarif* a half-price season ticket
2 *half-fare* ◇ *voyager à demi-tarif* to travel half-fare

le **demi-tour** NOUN
- **faire demi-tour** to turn back ◇ *La nuit commence à tomber; il est temps de faire demi-tour.* It's getting dark; it's time we turned back.

la **démocratie** NOUN
democracy

démocratique ADJECTIVE
democratic

démodé ADJECTIVE
old-fashioned

la **demoiselle** NOUN
young lady
- **une demoiselle d'honneur** a bridesmaid

démolir VERB
to demolish

le **démon** NOUN
devil

démonter VERB
1 *to take down* (*tent*)
2 *to take apart* (*machine*)

démontrer VERB
to show

dénoncer VERB
to denounce
- **se dénoncer** to give oneself up ◇ *Il s'est dénoncé à la police.* He gave himself up to the police.

le **dénouement** NOUN
outcome

la **densité** NOUN
density

la **dent** NOUN
tooth ◇ *une dent de lait* a milk tooth ◇ *une dent de sagesse* a wisdom tooth

dentaire ADJECTIVE
dental

la **dentelle** NOUN
lace ◇ *un chemisier en dentelle* a lacy blouse

le **dentier** NOUN
denture

le **dentifrice** NOUN
toothpaste

le/la **dentiste** NOUN
dentist ◇ *Elle est dentiste.* She's a dentist.

le **déodorant** NOUN
deodorant

le **dépannage** NOUN
- **un service de dépannage** a breakdown service

dépanner VERB
1 *to fix* ◇ *Il a dépanné la voiture en cinq minutes.* He fixed the car in five minutes.

TO

2 *to help out* ◇ *Il m'a prêté cent francs pour me dépanner.* (*informal*) He lent me 100 francs to help me out.

la **dépanneuse** NOUN
breakdown lorry

le **départ** NOUN
departure ◇ *Le départ est à onze heures quinze.* The departure is at 11.15.
- **Je lui téléphonerai la veille de son départ.** I'll phone him the day before he leaves.

le **département** NOUN
1 *department* ◇ *le département d'anglais à l'université* the English department at the university
2 *administrative area*

France is divided into 96 départements, *administrative areas rather like counties.*

◇ *le département du Vaucluse* the Vaucluse region

dépasser VERB
1 *to overtake* ◇ *Il y a une voiture qui essaie de nous dépasser.* There's a car trying to overtake us.
2 *to pass* ◇ *Nous avons dépassé Dijon.* We've passed Dijon.
3 *to exceed* (*sum, limit*)

dépaysé ADJECTIVE
- **se sentir un peu dépaysé** to feel a bit lost

se **dépêcher** VERB
to hurry ◇ *Dépêche-toi!* Hurry up!

dépendre VERB
- **dépendre de** to depend on ◇ *Ça dépend du temps.* It depends on the weather.
- **dépendre de quelqu'un** to be dependent on somebody
- **Ça dépend.** It depends.

dépenser VERB
to spend (*money*)

dépensier ADJECTIVE
(FEM SING **dépensière**)
- **Il est dépensier.** He's a big spender.
- **Elle n'est pas dépensière.** She's not exactly extravagant.

dépilatoire ADJECTIVE
- **une crème dépilatoire** a hair-removing cream

le **dépit** NOUN
- **en dépit de** in spite of ◇ *Il y est allé en dépit de mes conseils.* He went in spite of my advice.

déplacé ADJECTIVE
uncalled-for ◇ *C'était une remarque déplacée.* That remark was uncalled-for.

le **déplacement** NOUN
trip ◇ *Ça vaut le déplacement.* It's worth the trip.

déplacer VERB
1 *to move* ◇ *Tu peux m'aider à déplacer la table?* Can you help me move the table?
2 *to put off* ◇ *déplacer un rendez-vous* to put off an appointment
- **se déplacer (1)** to travel around ◇ *Il se déplace beaucoup pour son travail.* He travels around a lot for his work.
- **se déplacer (2)** to get around ◇ *Il a du mal à se déplacer.* He has difficulty getting around.
- **se déplacer une vertèbre** to slip a disc

déplaire VERB
- **Cela me déplaît.** I dislike this.

déplaisant ADJECTIVE
unpleasant

le **dépliant** NOUN
leaflet

déplier VERB
to unfold

déposer VERB
1 *to leave* ◇ *J'ai déposé mon sac à la consigne.* I left my bag at the left luggage office.
2 *to put down* ◇ *Déposez le paquet sur la table.* Put the parcel down on the table.
- **déposer quelqu'un** to drop somebody off

dépourvu ADJECTIVE
- **prendre quelqu'un au dépourvu** to take somebody by surprise ◇ *Sa question m'a pris au dépourvu.* His question took me by surprise.

la **dépression** NOUN
depression
- **faire de la dépression** to be suffering from depression
- **faire une dépression** to have a breakdown

déprimant ADJECTIVE
depressing

déprimer VERB
to get depressed ◇ *Il déprime tout le temps.* He gets depressed all the time.
- **Ce genre de temps me déprime.** This kind of weather makes me depressed.

depuis PREPOSITION, ADVERB
1 *since* ◇ *Il habite Paris depuis 1983.* He's been living in Paris since 1983. ◇ *Je ne lui ai pas parlé depuis.* I haven't spoken to him since.
- **depuis que** since ◇ *Il a plu tous les jours depuis qu'elle est arrivée.* It's rained every day since she arrived.

2 *for* ◇ *Il habite Paris depuis cinq ans.*

He's been living in Paris for five years.

- **Depuis combien de temps?** How long? ◇ *Depuis combien de temps est-ce que vous le connaissez?* How long have you known him?
- **Depuis quand?** How long? ◇ *Depuis quand est-ce que vous le connaissez?* How long have you known him?

le **député** NOUN
Member of Parliament

la **députée** NOUN
Member of Parliament

déraciner VERB
to uproot

le **dérangement** NOUN
- **en dérangement** out of order ◇ *Le téléphone est en dérangement.* The phone's out of order.

déranger VERB
1 *to bother* ◇ *Excusez-moi de vous déranger.* I'm sorry to bother you.
- **Ne vous dérangez pas, je vais répondre au téléphone.** You stay there, I'll answer the phone.

2 *to disorganize* ◇ *Ne dérange pas mes livres, s'il te plaît.* Don't disorganize my books, please.

déraper VERB
to skid

la **dermatologue** NOUN
dermatologist ◇ *Elle est dermatologue.* She's a dermatologist.

dernier ADJECTIVE
(FEM SING **dernière**)
1 *last* ◇ *Il est arrivé dernier.* He arrived last. ◇ *la dernière fois* the last time
2 *latest* ◇ *le dernier film de Spielberg* Spielberg's latest film
- **en dernier** last ◇ *Ajoutez le lait en dernier.* Put the milk in last.

dernièrement ADVERB
recently

dérouler VERB
1 *to unroll*
2 *to unwind*
- **se dérouler** to take place ◇ *L'action se déroule dans les années vingt.* The action takes place in the 1920s.
- **Tout s'est déroulé comme prévu.** Everything went as planned.

derrière ADVERB, PREPOSITION
see also derrière NOUN
behind

le **derrière** NOUN
see also derrière ADVERB
1 *back* ◇ *la porte de derrière* the back door
2 *backside* ◇ *un coup de pied dans le derrière* a kick up the backside

des ARTICLE
des *is the contracted form of* **de** + **les**.
1 *some* ◇ *Tu veux des chips?* Would you like some crisps?
des *is sometimes not translated.*
◇ *J'ai des cousins en France.* I have cousins in France. ◇ *pendant des mois* for months
2 *any* ◇ *Tu as des frères?* Have you got any brothers? ◇ *la fin des vacances* the end of the holidays ◇ *la voiture des Durand* the Durands' car ◇ *Il arrive des États-Unis.* He's arriving from the United States.

dès PREPOSITION
as early as ◇ *dès le mois de novembre* from November
- **dès le début** right from the start
- **Il vous appellera dès son retour.** He'll call you as soon as he gets back.
- **dès que** as soon as ◇ *Il m'a reconnu dès qu'il m'a vu.* He recognized me as soon as he saw me.

désabusé ADJECTIVE
disillusioned

le **désaccord** NOUN
disagreement

désagréable ADJECTIVE
unpleasant

désaltérer VERB
- **L'eau gazeuse désaltère bien.** Sparkling water is very thirst-quenching.
- **se désaltérer** to quench one's thirst ◇ *Nous sommes allés dans un café pour nous désaltérer.* We went into a café to have a drink.

désapprobateur ADJECTIVE
(FEM SING **désapprobatrice**)
disapproving ◇ *un regard désapprobateur* a disapproving look

le **désastre** NOUN
disaster

le **désavantage** NOUN
disadvantage

désavantager VERB
- **désavantager quelqu'un** to put somebody at a disadvantage ◇ *Cette nouvelle loi va désavantager les femmes.* The new law will put women at a disadvantage.

descendre VERB
1 *to go down* ◇ *Je suis tombé en descendant l'escalier.* I fell as I was going down the stairs.
2 *to come down* ◇ *Attends en bas; je descends!* Wait downstairs; I'm coming down!

PTO

3 *to get down* ◇ *Vous pouvez descendre ma valise, s'il vous plaît?* Can you get my suitcase down, please?
4 *to get off* ◇ *Nous descendons à la prochaine station.* We're getting off at the next station.

la **descente** NOUN
way down ◇ *Je t'attendrai au bas de la descente.* I'll wait for you at the bottom of the hill.
◆ **une descente de police** a police raid

déséquilibré ADJECTIVE
unbalanced

déséquilibrer VERB
◆ **déséquilibrer quelqu'un** to throw somebody off balance ◇ *Le coup de poing l'a déséquilibré.* The punch threw him off balance.

désert ADJECTIVE
see also **désert** NOUN
deserted ◇ *Le dimanche, le centre commercial est désert.* On Sundays, the shopping centre is deserted.
◆ **une île déserte** a desert island

le **désert** NOUN
see also **désert** ADJECTIVE
desert

déserter VERB
to desert

désertique ADJECTIVE
desert ◇ *une région désertique* a desert region

désespéré ADJECTIVE
desperate

désespérer VERB
to despair ◇ *Il ne faut pas désespérer.* Don't despair.

le **désespoir** NOUN
despair

déshabiller VERB
to undress
◆ **se déshabiller** to get undressed

déshériter VERB
to disinherit
◆ **les déshérités** the underprivileged

déshydraté ADJECTIVE
dehydrated

désigner VERB
to choose ◇ *On l'a désignée pour remettre le prix.* She was chosen to present the prize.
◆ **désigner quelque chose du doigt** to point at something

le **désinfectant** NOUN
disinfectant

désinfecter VERB
to disinfect

désintéressé ADJECTIVE
1 *unselfish* ◇ *un acte désintéressé* an unselfish action
2 *impartial* ◇ *un conseil désintéressé* impartial advice

désintéresser VERB
◆ **se désintéresser de quelque chose** to lose interest in something

le **désir** NOUN
1 *wish* ◇ *Vos désirs sont des ordres.* Your wish is my command.
2 *will* ◇ *le désir de réussir* the will to succeed
3 *desire* ◇ *Ses yeux brillaient de désir.* Her eyes were shining with desire.

désirer VERB
to want ◇ *Vous désirez?* (*in shop*) What would you like?

désobéir VERB
◆ **désobéir à quelqu'un** to disobey somebody

désobéissant ADJECTIVE
disobedient

désobligeant ADJECTIVE
unpleasant ◇ *faire une remarque désobligeante* to make an unpleasant remark

le **désodorisant** NOUN
air freshener

désolé ADJECTIVE
sorry ◇ *Je suis vraiment désolé.* I'm very sorry.
◆ **Désolé!** Sorry!

désopilant ADJECTIVE
hilarious

désordonné ADJECTIVE
untidy

le **désordre** NOUN
untidiness
◆ **Quel désordre!** What a mess!
◆ **en désordre** untidy ◇ *Sa chambre est toujours en désordre.* His bedroom is always untidy.

désormais ADVERB
from now on ◇ *Désormais, je boirai de l'eau.* From now on I'll drink water.

desquelles PRONOUN
desquelles *is the contracted form of* **de + lesquelles**.
◇ *des négociations au cours desquelles les patrons ont fait des concessions* negotiations during which the employers made concessions

desquels PRONOUN
desquels *is the contracted form of* **de + lesquels**.
◇ *les lacs au bord desquels nous avons campé* the lakes on the banks of which we camped

dessécher VERB
to dry out ◇ *Le soleil dessèche la*

peau. The sun dries your skin out.

desserrer VERB
to loosen

dessert NOUN
pudding ◇ *Qu'est-ce que vous désirez comme dessert?* What would you like for pudding?

dessin NOUN
drawing ◇ *C'est un dessin de ma petite sœur.* It's a drawing my little sister did.
- **un dessin animé** a cartoon (*film*)
- **un dessin humoristique** a cartoon (*drawing*)

dessinateur NOUN
- **un dessinateur industriel** a draughtsman

dessiner VERB
to draw

dessous ADVERB
see also **dessous** NOUN
underneath
- **en dessous** underneath ◇ *Soulève le pot de fleurs, la clé est en dessous.* Lift the flowerpot, the key's underneath.
- **par-dessous** underneath ◇ *Le grillage ne sert à rien, les lapins passent par-dessous.* The fence is useless, the rabbits get in underneath.
- **là-dessous** under there ◇ *Il s'est caché là-dessous.* He hid under there.
- **ci-dessous** below ◇ *Complétez les phrases ci-dessous.* Complete the sentences below.
- **au-dessous de** below ◇ *vingt degrés au-dessous de zéro* 20 degrees below zero

dessous NOUN
see also **dessous** ADVERB
underneath
- **les voisins du dessous** the downstairs neighbours
- **les dessous** underwear ◇ *des dessous en soie* silk underwear

dessous-de-plat NOUN
(PL **les dessous-de-plat**)
tablemat

dessus ADVERB
see also **dessus** NOUN
on top ◇ *un gâteau avec des bougies dessus* a cake with candles on top
- **par-dessus** over ◇ *Nous avons sauté par-dessus la barrière.* We jumped over the gate.
- **au-dessus** above ◇ *la taille au-dessus* the size above ◇ *au-dessus du lit* above the bed
- **là-dessus (1)** on there ◇ *Tu peux écrire là-dessus.* You can write on there.
- **là-dessus (2)** with that ◇ *"Je démissionne!" Là-dessus, il est parti.* "I resign!" With that, he left.
- **ci-dessus** above ◇ *l'exemple ci-dessus* the example above

le **dessus** NOUN
see also **dessus** ADVERB
top
- **les voisins du dessus** the upstairs neighbours

le/la **destinataire** NOUN
addressee

la **destination** NOUN
destination
- **les passagers à destination de Paris** passengers travelling to Paris

le **détachant** NOUN
stain remover

détacher VERB
to undo

le **détail** NOUN
detail
- **en détail** in detail

le **détective** NOUN
detective ◇ *un détective privé* a private detective

déteindre VERB
to fade (*in wash*)

détendre VERB
to relax ◇ *La lecture, ça me détend.* I find reading relaxing.
- **se détendre** to relax ◇ *Il est allé prendre un bain pour se détendre.* He's gone to have a bath to relax.

la **détente** NOUN
relaxation

le **détenu** NOUN
prisoner

la **détenue** NOUN
prisoner

se **détériorer** VERB
to deteriorate

déterminé ADJECTIVE
1 *determined* ◇ *C'est un homme déterminé.* He's a determined man.
2 *specific* ◇ *un but déterminé* a specific aim

détestable ADJECTIVE
horrible

détester VERB
to hate

la **détonation** NOUN
bang ◇ *J'ai entendu une détonation.* I heard a bang.

le **détour** NOUN
detour
- **Ça vaut le détour.** It's worth the trip.

le **détournement** NOUN
- **un détournement d'avion** a hijacking

D

détrempé ADJECTIVE
waterlogged

les **détritus** MASC NOUN
litter

détruire VERB
to destroy

la **dette** NOUN
debt

le **deuil** NOUN
- **être en deuil** to be in mourning

deux NUMBER
two ◇ *Il était deux heures.* It was two o'clock. ◇ *Elle a deux ans.* She's two.
- **deux fois** twice
- **tous les deux** both ◇ *Nous y sommes allées toutes les deux.* We both went.
- **le deux février** the second of February

deuxième ADJECTIVE
second ◇ *au deuxième étage* on the second floor

deuxièmement ADVERB
secondly

devais, devait, devaient VERB *see* **devoir**

dévaliser VERB
to rob

devant ADVERB, PREPOSITION
see also devant NOUN
1 *in front* ◇ *Il marchait devant.* He was walking in front.
2 *in front of* ◇ *Il était assis devant moi.* He was sitting in front of me.
- **passer devant** to go past ◇ *Nous sommes passés devant chez toi.* We went past your house.

le **devant** NOUN
see also devant ADVERB
front ◇ *le devant de la maison* the front of the house
- **les pattes de devant** the front legs

le **développement** NOUN
development
- **les pays en voie de développement** developing countries

développer VERB
to develop ◇ *donner une pellicule à développer* to take a film to be developed
- **se développer** to develop

devenir VERB
to become

devez VERB *see* **devoir**

la **déviation** NOUN
diversion

deviez VERB *see* **devoir**

deviner VERB
to guess

la **devinette** NOUN
riddle ◇ *poser une devinette à quelqu'un* to ask somebody a riddle

devions VERB *see* **devoir**

dévisager VERB
- **dévisager quelqu'un** to stare at somebody

la **devise** NOUN
currency ◇ *les devises étrangères* foreign currency

dévisser VERB
to unscrew

dévoiler VERB
to unveil

devoir VERB
see also devoir NOUN

Present tense:	
je dois	*nous devons*
tu dois	*vous devez*
il/elle doit	*ils/elles doivent*
Past participle: *dû*	

1 *to have to* ◇ *Je dois partir.* I've got to go.
2 *must* ◇ *Tu dois être fatigué.* You must be tired.
3 *to be due to* ◇ *Le nouveau centre commercial doit ouvrir en mai.* The new shopping centre is due to open in May.
- **devoir quelque chose à quelqu'un** to owe somebody something ◇ *Combien est-ce que je vous dois?* How much do I owe you?

le **devoir** NOUN
see also devoir VERB
1 *exercise*
- **les devoirs** homework
- **un devoir sur table** a written test

2 *duty* ◇ *Aller voter fait partie des devoirs du citoyen.* Voting is part of one's duty as a citizen.

devons VERB *see* **devoir**

dévorer VERB
to devour

dévoué ADJECTIVE
devoted

devra, devrai, devras, devrez, devrons, devront VERB *see* **devoir**

le **diabète** NOUN
diabetes

diabétique ADJECTIVE
diabetic ◇ *Je suis diabétique.* I'm diabetic.

le **diable** NOUN
devil

le **diabolo** NOUN
fruit cordial and lemonade
- **un diabolo menthe** a mint cordial and lemonade

diagonal ADJECTIVE
(MASC PL **diagonaux**)
diagonal

diagonale NOUN
diagonal
- **en diagonale** diagonally

diagramme NOUN
diagram

dialecte NOUN
dialect

diamant NOUN
diamond

diamètre NOUN
diameter

diapo NOUN (*informal*)
slide
- **une pellicule diapo** a slide film

diapositive NOUN
slide ◇ *projeter des diapositives* to show some slides

diarrhée NOUN
diarrhoea ◇ *avoir la diarrhée* to have diarrhoea

dictateur NOUN
dictator

dictature NOUN
dictatorship

dictée NOUN
dictation

dicter VERB
to dictate

dictionnaire NOUN
dictionary

diététique ADJECTIVE
- **un magasin diététique** a health food shop

dieu NOUN
(PL les **dieux**)
god ◇ *Dieu* God ◇ *Mon Dieu!* Oh my God!

différent ADJECTIVE
1 *different* ◇ *pour des raisons différentes* for different reasons
2 *various* ◇ *pour différentes raisons* for various reasons
- **différent de** different to ◇ *Son point de vue est différent du mien.* His point of view is different to mine.

difficile ADJECTIVE
difficult ◇ *Son accent est difficile à comprendre.* His accent is difficult to understand.

difficilement ADVERB
- **faire quelque chose difficilement** to have trouble doing something ◇ *Ma grand-mère se déplace difficilement.* My grandmother has trouble getting around.
- **Je pouvais difficilement refuser.** It was difficult for me to refuse.

difficulté NOUN
difficulty ◇ *avec difficulté* with difficulty
- **être en difficulté** to be in difficulties

digérer VERB
to digest

digestif NOUN
after-dinner liqueur

digne ADJECTIVE
- **digne de** worthy of ◇ *digne de confiance* trustworthy

dignité NOUN
dignity

dilemme NOUN
dilemma ◇ *être devant un dilemme* to be faced with a dilemma

diluer VERB
to dilute

dimanche NOUN
1 *Sunday* ◇ *Aujourd'hui, nous sommes dimanche.* It's Sunday today.
2 *on Sunday* ◇ *Dimanche, nous allons déjeuner chez mes grands-parents.* On Sunday we're having lunch at my grandparents'.
- **le dimanche** on Sundays ◇ *Le dimanche, je fais la grasse matinée.* I have a lie-in on Sundays.
- **tous les dimanches** every Sunday
- **dimanche dernier** last Sunday
- **dimanche prochain** next Sunday

diminuer VERB
to decrease ◇ *Est-ce que tu peux diminuer le son?* Could you turn down the sound?

diminutif NOUN
pet name

diminution NOUN
1 *reduction*
2 *decrease*

dinde NOUN
turkey ◇ *la dinde de Noël* the Christmas turkey

dindon NOUN
turkey

le dindon *refers to a live turkey, whereas* **la dinde** *refers to the meat.*

dîner NOUN
see also dîner VERB
dinner (*evening meal*)

dîner VERB
see also dîner NOUN
to have dinner (*evening meal*)

dingue ADJECTIVE (*informal*)
crazy

diplomate ADJECTIVE
see also diplomate NOUN
diplomatic

diplomate NOUN
see also diplomate ADJECTIVE
diplomat

D

la **diplomatie** NOUN
diplomacy

le **diplôme** NOUN
qualification

diplômé ADJECTIVE
qualified

dire VERB
1 *to say* ◇ *Il a dit qu'il ne viendrait pas.* He said he wouldn't come.
- **on dit que...** they say that... ◇ *On dit que la nourriture est excellente là-bas.* They say that the food is excellent there.

2 *to tell*
- **dire quelque chose à quelqu'un** to tell somebody something ◇ *Elle m'a dit la vérité.* She told me the truth. ◇ *Il nous a dit de regarder cette émission.* He told us to watch this programme.
- **On dirait qu'il va pleuvoir.** It looks as if it's going to rain.

direct ADJECTIVE
direct
- **en direct** live ◇ *une émission en direct* a live broadcast

directement ADVERB
straight ◇ *Il est rentré directement chez lui.* He went straight home.

le **directeur** NOUN
1 *headteacher* ◇ *Il est directeur.* He's a headteacher.
2 *manager* ◇ *Il est directeur du personnel.* He's a personnel manager.

la **direction** NOUN
1 *management* ◇ *la direction et les ouvriers* the management and the workers
2 *direction* ◇ *"toutes directions"* "all directions"

la **directrice** NOUN
1 *headteacher* ◇ *Elle est directrice.* She's a headteacher.
2 *manager* ◇ *Elle est directrice commerciale.* She's a sales manager.

dirent VERB *see* **dire**

le **dirigeant** NOUN
leader

la **dirigeante** NOUN
leader

diriger VERB
to manage ◇ *Il dirige une petite entreprise.* He manages a small company.
- **se diriger vers** to head for ◇ *Il se dirigeait vers la gare.* He was heading for the station.

dis VERB *see* **dire**
- **Dis-moi la vérité!** Tell me the truth!
- **dis donc** hey ◇ *Il a drôlement changé, dis donc!* Hey, he's really changed! ◇ *Dis donc, tu te souviens de Sam?* Hey, do you remember Sam?

disaient, disais, disait VERB *see* **dire**

la **discothèque** NOUN
disco (*club*)

le **discours** NOUN
speech

discret ADJECTIVE
(FEM SING **discrète**)
discreet

la **discrimination** NOUN
discrimination ◇ *la discrimination raciale* racial discrimination ◇ *la discrimination sexuelle* sex discrimination

la **discussion** NOUN
discussion

discutable ADJECTIVE
debatable

discuter VERB
1 *to talk* ◇ *Nous avons discuté pendant des heures.* We talked for hours.
2 *to argue* ◇ *C'est ce que j'ai décidé, alors ne discutez pas!* That's what I've decided, so don't argue!

disent, disiez, disions VERB *see* **dire**

disons VERB *see* **dire**
let's say ◇ *C'est à, disons, une demi-heure à pied.* It's half an hour's walk, say.

disparaître VERB
to disappear
- **faire disparaître quelque chose (1)** to make something disappear ◇ *Il a fait disparaître le lapin dans son chapeau.* He made the rabbit disappear in his hat.
- **faire disparaître quelque chose (2)** to get rid of something ◇ *Ils ont fait disparaître tous les documents compromettants.* They got rid of all the incriminating documents.

la **disparition** NOUN
disappearance
- **une espèce en voie de disparition** an endangered species

disparu ADJECTIVE
- **être porté disparu** to be reported missing

le **dispensaire** NOUN
community clinic

dispensé ADJECTIVE
- **être dispensé de quelque chose** to be excused something ◇ *Elle est dispensée de gymnastique.* She's excused gym.

disperser VERB
to break up ◇ *La police a dispersé les manifestants.* The police broke up the

demonstrators.

- **se disperser** to break up ◇ *Une fois l'ambulance partie, la foule s'est dispersée.* Once the ambulance had left, the crowd broke up.

disponible ADJECTIVE
available

disposé ADJECTIVE
- **être disposé à faire quelque chose** to be willing to do something ◇ *Il était disposé à m'aider.* He was willing to help me.

disposer VERB
- **disposer de quelque chose** to have access to something ◇ *Je dispose d'un ordinateur.* I have access to a computer.

la **disposition** NOUN
- **prendre ses dispositions** to make arrangements ◇ *Est-ce que vous avez pris vos dispositions pour partir en France?* Have you made arrangements to go to France?
- **avoir quelque chose à sa disposition** to have something at one's disposal ◇ *J'ai une voiture à ma disposition pour la semaine.* I have a car at my disposal for the week.
- **Je suis à votre disposition.** I am at your service.
- **Je tiens ces livres à votre disposition.** The books are at your disposal.

la **dispute** NOUN
argument

se **disputer** VERB
to argue

le **disquaire** NOUN
record dealer

le **disque** NOUN
record
- **un disque compact** a compact disc
- **le disque dur** hard disk

la **disquette** NOUN
diskette

disséminé ADJECTIVE
scattered

disséquer VERB
to dissect

la **dissertation** NOUN
essay

dissimuler VERB
to conceal

se **dissiper** VERB
to clear ◇ *Le brouillard va se dissiper dans l'après-midi.* The fog will clear during the afternoon.

le **dissolvant** NOUN
nail polish remover

dissoudre VERB
to dissolve
- **se dissoudre** to dissolve

dissuader VERB
- **dissuader quelqu'un de faire quelque chose** to dissuade somebody from doing something ◇ *Elle m'a dissuadé d'aller voir ce film.* She dissuaded me from going to see the film.

la **distance** NOUN
distance

la **distillerie** NOUN
distillery

distingué ADJECTIVE
distinguished

distinguer VERB
to distinguish

la **distraction** NOUN
entertainment ◇ *Il lit beaucoup: c'est sa seule distraction.* He reads a lot: it's his only form of entertainment.

distraire VERB
- **Va voir un film, ça te distraira.** Go and see a film, it'll take your mind off things.

distrait ADJECTIVE
absent-minded

distribuer VERB
1 *to give out* ◇ *Distribue les livres, s'il te plaît.* Give out the books, please.
2 *to deal* (*cards*)

le **distributeur** NOUN
- **un distributeur automatique** a vending machine
- **un distributeur de billets** a cash dispenser

dit VERB *see* **dire**

dit ADJECTIVE
known as ◇ *Pierre, dit Pierrot* Pierre, known as Pierrot

dites VERB *see* **dire**
- **Dites-moi ce que vous pensez.** Tell me what you think.
- **dites donc** hey ◇ *Dites-donc, vous, là-bas!* Hey, you there!

divers ADJECTIVE
diverse
- **pour diverses raisons** for various reasons

se **divertir** VERB
to enjoy oneself

divin ADJECTIVE
divine

diviser VERB
to divide ◇ *Quatre divisé par deux égalent deux.* 4 divided by 2 equals 2.

le **divorcé** NOUN
divorcee

la **divorcée** NOUN
divorcee

divorcer VERB

PTO

to get divorced

dix NUMBER
ten ◇ *Elle a dix ans.* She's ten. ◇ *à dix heures* at ten o'clock
- **le dix février** the tenth of February

dix-huit NUMBER ◇ *Elle a dix-huit ans.* She's eighteen. ◇ *à dix-huit heures* at 6 p.m.

dixième ADJECTIVE
tenth ◇ *au dixième étage* on the tenth floor

dix-neuf NUMBER ◇ *Elle a dix-neuf ans.* She's nineteen. ◇ *à dix-neuf heures* at 7 p.m.

dix-sept NUMBER ◇ *Elle a dix-sept ans.* She's seventeen. ◇ *à dix-sept heures* at 5 p.m.

la **dizaine** NOUN
about ten ◇ *une dizaine de jours* about ten days

le **do** NOUN
1 *C* ◇ *en do majeur* in C major
2 *do* ◇ *do, ré, mi...* do, re, mi...

le **docteur** NOUN
doctor ◇ *Elle est docteur.* She's a doctor.

le **documentaire** NOUN
documentary

le/la **documentaliste** NOUN
librarian

documenter VERB
- **se documenter sur quelque chose** to gather information on something

dodu ADJECTIVE
plump

le **doigt** NOUN
finger
- **les doigts de pied** the toes

dois, doit, doivent VERB *see* **devoir**

le **domaine** NOUN
1 *estate* ◇ *Il possède un immense domaine en Normandie.* He owns a huge estate in Normandy.
2 *field* ◇ *La chimie n'est pas mon domaine.* Chemistry's not my field.

domestique ADJECTIVE
see also domestique NOUN
domestic
- **les animaux domestiques** pets

le/la **domestique** NOUN
see also domestique ADJECTIVE
servant

le **domicile** NOUN
place of residence
- **à domicile** at home ◇ *Il travaille à domicile.* He works at home.

domicilié ADJECTIVE
- **"domicilié à:..."** "address:..."

dominer VERB
to dominate
- **se dominer** to control oneself

les **dominos** MASC NOUN
dominoes ◇ *jouer aux dominos* to play dominoes

le **dommage** NOUN
damage ◇ *La tempête a causé d'importants dommages.* The storm caused a lot of damage.
- **C'est dommage.** It's a shame. ◇ *C'est dommage que tu ne puisses pas venir.* It's a shame you can't come.

dompter VERB
to tame

le **dompteur** NOUN
animal tamer

la **dompteuse** NOUN
animal tamer

le **don** NOUN
1 *donation*
2 *gift* ◇ *avoir un don pour quelque chose* to have a gift for something
- **Elle a le don de m'énerver.** She's got a knack of getting on my nerves.

donc CONJUNCTION
so

le **donjon** NOUN
keep (*of castle*)

les **données** FEM NOUN
data

donner VERB
1 *to give*
- **donner quelque chose à quelqu'un** to give somebody something ◇ *Elle m'a donné son adresse.* She gave me her address.
- **Ça m'a donné faim.** That made me feel hungry.

2 *to give away* ◇ *Tu as toujours ta veste en daim? – Non, je l'ai donnée.* Have you still got your suede jacket? – No, I gave it away.
- **donner sur quelque chose** to overlook something ◇ *une fenêtre qui donne sur la mer* a window overlooking the sea

dont PRONOUN
1 *of which* ◇ *deux livres, dont l'un est en anglais* two books, one of which is in English ◇ *le prix dont il est si fier* the prize he's so proud of
2 *of whom* ◇ *dix blessés, dont deux grièvement* ten people injured, two of them seriously ◇ *la fille dont je t'ai parlé* the girl I told you about

doré ADJECTIVE
golden ◇ *une étoile dorée* a golden star

dorénavant ADVERB
from now on ◇ *Dorénavant, tu feras*

attention. From now on, you'll be careful.

dorloter VERB
to pamper

dormir VERB
1 *to sleep* ◇ *Tu as bien dormi?* Did you sleep well?
2 *to be asleep* ◇ *Ne faites pas de bruit, il dort.* Don't make any noise, he's asleep.

le **dortoir** NOUN
dormitory

le **dos** NOUN
back ◇ *dos à dos* back to back
- **faire quelque chose dans le dos de quelqu'un** to do something behind somebody's back ◇ *Elle me critique dans mon dos.* She criticizes me behind my back.
- **de dos** from behind
- **nager le dos crawlé** to swim backstroke
- **"voir au dos"** "see over"

la **dose** NOUN
dose ◇ *Ne pas dépasser la dose prescrite.* Do not exceed the stated dose.

le **dossier** NOUN
1 *file* ◇ *une pile de dossiers* a stack of files
2 *report* ◇ *un bon dossier scolaire* a good school report
3 *feature* (*in magazine*)
4 *back* (*of chair*)

la **douane** NOUN
customs

le **douanier** NOUN
customs officer

le **double** NOUN
- **le double** twice as much ◇ *Il gagne le double.* He earns twice as much. ◇ *le double du prix normal* twice the normal price
- **en double** in duplicate ◇ *Garde cette photo, je l'ai en double.* Keep this photo, I've got a copy of it.
- **le double messieurs** the men's doubles (*tennis*)

doubler VERB
1 *to double* ◇ *Le prix a doublé en dix ans.* The price has doubled in 10 years.
2 *to overtake* ◇ *Il est dangereux de doubler sur cette route.* It's dangerous to overtake on this road.
- **un film doublé** a dubbed film

douce ADJECTIVE *see* **doux**

doucement ADVERB
1 *gently* ◇ *Il a frappé doucement à la porte.* He knocked gently at the door.
2 *slowly* ◇ *Roulez doucement!* Drive slowly! ◇ *Je ne comprends pas, parle plus doucement.* I don't understand, speak more slowly.

la **douceur** NOUN
1 *softness* ◇ *Cette crème maintient la douceur de votre peau.* This cream keeps your skin soft.
2 *gentleness* ◇ *parler avec douceur* to speak gently
- **L'avion a atterri en douceur.** The plane made a smooth landing.

la **douche** NOUN
shower
- **les douches** the shower room

se **doucher** VERB
to have a shower

doué ADJECTIVE
talented
- **être doué en quelque chose** to be good at something ◇ *Il est doué en maths.* He's good at maths.

douillet ADJECTIVE
(FEM SING **douillette**)
1 *cosy* ◇ *un anorak douillet* a cosy anorak
2 *soft* ◇ *Je ne supporte pas la douleur: je suis très douillette.* I can't stand pain: I'm a real softie.

la **douleur** NOUN
pain

douloureux ADJECTIVE
(FEM SING **douloureuse**)
painful

le **doute** NOUN
doubt
- **sans doute** probably

douter VERB
to doubt
- **douter de quelque chose** to doubt something ◇ *Je doute de sa sincérité.* I have my doubts about his sincerity.
- **se douter de quelque chose** to suspect something ◇ *Je ne me doutais de rien.* I didn't suspect anything.
- **Je m'en doutais.** I suspected as much.

douteux ADJECTIVE
(FEM SING **douteuse**)
1 *dubious* ◇ *une plaisanterie d'un goût douteux* a joke in dubious taste
2 *suspicious-looking* ◇ *un individu douteux* a suspicious-looking person

Douvres NOUN
Dover

doux ADJECTIVE
(FEM SING **douce**, MASC PL **doux**)
1 *soft* ◇ *un tissu doux* soft material ◇ *les drogues douces* soft drugs
2 *sweet* ◇ *du cidre doux* sweet cider
3 *mild* ◇ *Il fait doux aujourd'hui.* It's

PTO

mild today.
4 *gentle* ◇ *C'est quelqu'un de très doux.* He's a very gentle person.
◆ **en douce** on the quiet ◇ *Il m'a donné cinquante francs en douce.* He slipped me 50 francs on the quiet.

la **douzaine** NOUN
dozen ◇ *une douzaine d'œufs* a dozen eggs
◆ **une douzaine de personnes** about twelve people

douze NUMBER
twelve ◇ *Il a douze ans.* He's twelve.
◆ **le douze février** the twelfth of February

douzième ADJECTIVE
twelfth ◇ *au douzième étage* on the twelfth floor

la **dragée** NOUN
sugared almond

draguer VERB (*informal*)
◆ **draguer quelqu'un** to chat somebody up ◇ *Il est en train de la draguer.* He's chatting her up.
◆ **se faire draguer** to get chatted up ◇ *Elle aime se faire draguer.* She likes being chatted up.

le **dragueur** NOUN (*informal*)
flirt (*person*)

la **dragueuse** NOUN (*informal*)
flirt (*person*)

dramatique ADJECTIVE
tragic ◇ *une situation dramatique* a tragic situation
◆ **l'art dramatique** drama

le **drame** NOUN
drama (*incident*)
◆ **Ça n'est pas un drame si tu ne viens pas.** It's not the end of the world if you don't come.

le **drap** NOUN
sheet (*for bed*)

le **drapeau** NOUN
(PL les **drapeaux**)
flag ◇ *le drapeau français* the French flag

dressé ADJECTIVE
trained ◇ *un chien bien dressé* a well-trained dog

dresser VERB
1 *to draw up* ◇ *dresser une liste* to draw up a list
2 *to train* ◇ *dresser un chien* to train a dog
◆ **dresser l'oreille** to prick up one's ears ◇ *Quand elle a dit ça, il a dressé l'oreille.* When she said that, he pricked up his ears.

la **drogue** NOUN
drug ◇ *le problème de la drogue* the drugs problem ◇ *la lutte contre la drogue* the war against drugs
◆ **les drogues douces** soft drugs
◆ **les drogues dures** hard drugs

le **drogué** NOUN
drug addict

la **droguée** NOUN
drug addict

droguer VERB
◆ **droguer quelqu'un** to drug somebody
◆ **se droguer** to take drugs

la **droguerie** NOUN
hardware shop

droit ADJECTIVE, ADVERB
see also **droit** NOUN
1 *right* ◇ *le bras droit* the right arm ◇ *le côté droit* the right-hand side
2 *straight* ◇ *une ligne droite* a straight line ◇ *Tiens-toi droite!* Stand up straight!
◆ **tout droit** straight on

le **droit** NOUN
see also **droit** ADJECTIVE
1 *right* ◇ *les droits de l'homme* human rights
◆ **avoir le droit de faire quelque chose** to be allowed to do something ◇ *On n'a pas le droit de fumer à l'école.* We're not allowed to smoke at school.
2 *law* ◇ *faire son droit* to study law ◇ *un étudiant en droit* a law student

la **droite** NOUN
see also **droit** ADJECTIVE
right ◇ *sur votre droite* on your right
◆ **à droite (1)** on the right ◇ *la troisième rue à droite* the third street on the right
◆ **à droite (2)** to the right ◇ *à droite de la fenêtre* to the right of the window ◇ *Tournez à droite.* Turn right.
◆ **la voie de droite** the right-hand lane
◆ **la droite** the right (*in politics*) ◇ *Elle est très à droite.* She's very right-wing.

droitier ADJECTIVE
(FEM SING **droitière**)
right-handed ◇ *Elle est droitière.* She's right-handed.

drôle ADJECTIVE
funny ◇ *Ça n'est pas drôle.* It's not funny.
◆ **un drôle de temps** funny weather

drôlement ADVERB (*informal*)
really ◇ *C'est drôlement bon.* It's really good.

du ARTICLE
du *is the contracted form of* **de** + **le**.
1 *some* ◇ *Tu veux du fromage?* Would you like some cheese?
2 *any* ◇ *Tu as du chocolat?* Have you got any chocolate? ◇ *la porte du garage*

the door of the garage ◇ *la femme du directeur* the headmaster's wife

dû VERB *see* **devoir**

see also dû ADJECTIVE

◆ **Nous avons dû nous arrêter.** We had to stop.

dû ADJECTIVE

(FEM **due**, MASC PL **dus**)

see also dû VERB

◆ **dû à** due to ◇ *un retard dû au mauvais temps* a delay due to bad weather

duc NOUN

duke

duchesse NOUN

duchess

dupe ADJECTIVE

◆ **Elle me ment mais je ne suis pas dupe.** She lies to me but I'm not taken in by that.

duquel PRONOUN

(MASC PL **desquels**, FEM PL **desquelles**)

duquel *is the contracted form of* **de** + **lequel**.

◇ *l'homme duquel il parle* the man he is talking about

dur ADJECTIVE, ADVERB

hard ◇ *travailler dur* to work hard ◇ *être dur avec quelqu'un* to be hard on somebody

durant PREPOSITION

1 *during* ◇ *durant la nuit* during the night

2 *for* ◇ *durant des années* for years ◇ *des mois durant* for months

la **durée** NOUN

length ◇ *Quelle est la durée des études d'ingénieur?* How long does it take to train as an engineer?

◆ **pour une durée de quinze jours** for a period of two weeks

◆ **de courte durée** short ◇ *un séjour de courte durée* a short stay

◆ **de longue durée** long ◇ *une absence de longue durée* a long absence

durement ADVERB

harshly

durer VERB

to last

la **dureté** NOUN

harshness ◇ *traiter quelqu'un avec dureté* to treat somebody harshly

dynamique ADJECTIVE

dynamic

dyslexique ADJECTIVE

dyslexic

D

E

l'**eau** FEM NOUN
(PL les **eaux**)
water
- **l'eau minérale** mineral water
- **l'eau plate** still water
- **tomber à l'eau** to fall through ◇ *Nos projets sont tombés à l'eau.* Our plans have fallen through.

éblouir VERB
to dazzle

l'**éboueur** MASC NOUN
dustman

ébouillanter VERB
to scald

l'**écaille** FEM NOUN
scale (*of fish*)

s'**écailler** VERB
to flake

l'**écart** MASC NOUN
gap
- **à l'écart de** away from ◇ *Ils se sont assis à l'écart des autres.* They sat down away from the others.

écarté ADJECTIVE
remote
- **les bras écartés** arms outstretched
- **les jambes écartées** legs apart

écarter VERB
to open wide (*arms, legs*)
- **s'écarter** to move ◇ *Ils se sont écartés pour le laisser passer.* They moved to let him pass.

l'**échafaudage** MASC NOUN
scaffolding

l'**échalote** FEM NOUN
shallot

l'**échange** MASC NOUN
exchange ◇ *en échange de* in exchange for

échanger VERB
to swap ◇ *Je t'échange ce timbre contre celui-là.* I'll swap you this stamp for that one.

l'**échantillon** MASC NOUN
sample

échapper VERB
- **échapper à** to escape from ◇ *Le prisonnier a réussi à échapper à la police.* The prisoner managed to escape from the police.
- **s'échapper** to escape ◇ *Il s'est échappé de prison.* He escaped from prison.
- **l'échapper belle** to have a narrow escape ◇ *Nous l'avons échappé belle.* We had a narrow escape.

l'**écharde** FEM NOUN
splinter of wood

l'**écharpe** FEM NOUN
scarf

s'**échauffer** VERB
to warm up (*before exercise*)

l'**échec** MASC NOUN
failure

les **échecs** MASC NOUN
chess ◇ *jouer aux échecs* to play chess

l'**échelle** FEM NOUN
1 *ladder*
2 *scale* (*of map*)

échevelé ADJECTIVE
dishevelled

l'**écho** MASC NOUN
echo

échouer VERB
- **échouer à un examen** to fail an exam

éclabousser VERB
to splash

l'**éclair** MASC NOUN
flash of lightning
- **un éclair au chocolat** a chocolate éclair

l'**éclairage** MASC NOUN
lighting

l'**éclaircie** FEM NOUN
bright interval

éclairer VERB
- **Cette lampe éclaire bien.** This lamp gives a good light.

l'**éclat** MASC NOUN
1 *fragment* (*of glass*) ◇ *La vase a volé en éclats.* The vase smashed into pieces.
2 *brightness* (*of sun, colour*)
- **des éclats de rire** roars of laughter

éclatant ADJECTIVE
brilliant ◇ *des dents d'une blancheur éclatante* brilliant white teeth

éclater VERB
1 *to burst* (*tyre, balloon*)
- **éclater de rire** to burst out laughing
- **éclater en sanglots** to burst into tears

2 *to break out* ◇ *La Seconde Guerre mondiale a éclaté en 1939.* The Second World War broke out in 1939.

écœurant ADJECTIVE
sickly

écœurer VERB
- **Tous ces mensonges m'écœurent.** All these lies make me sick.

l'**école** FEM NOUN
school ◇ *aller à l'école* to go to school ◇ *une école publique* a state school

◇ *une école maternelle* a nursery school

The école maternelle *is a state school for 2-6 year-olds.*

l'**écolier** MASC NOUN
schoolboy

l'**écolière** FEM NOUN
schoolgirl

l'**écologie** FEM NOUN
ecology

écologique ADJECTIVE
ecological ◇ *une lessive écologique* an ecological washing powder

l'**économie** FEM NOUN
1 *economy* ◇ *l'économie de la France* the French economy
2 *economics* ◇ *un cours d'économie* an economics class

s'**économies** FEM NOUN
savings
- **faire des économies** to save up ◇ *Je fais des économies pour partir en vacances.* I'm saving up for my holidays.

économique ADJECTIVE
1 *economic* ◇ *une crise économique* an economic crisis
2 *economical* ◇ *Il est plus économique d'acheter une grande boîte de lessive.* It's more economical to buy a big box of washing powder. ◇ *Cette petite voiture est économique.* This little car is cheap to run.

économiser VERB
to save

l'**écorce** FEM NOUN
1 *bark* (*of tree*)
2 *peel* (*of orange, lemon*)

s'**écorcher** VERB
- **Je me suis écorché le genou.** I've grazed my knee.

écossais ADJECTIVE, NOUN
(FEM SING **écossaise**)
1 *Scottish* ◇ *Elle est écossaise.* She's Scottish.
- **un Écossais** a Scot (*man*)
- **une Écossaise** a Scot (*woman*)
- **les Écossais** the Scots

2 *tartan* ◇ *une jupe écossaise* a tartan skirt

l'**Écosse** FEM NOUN
Scotland
- **en Écosse (1)** in Scotland ◇ *Il a passé une semaine en Écosse.* He spent a week in Scotland.
- **en Écosse (2)** to Scotland ◇ *Nous allons en Écosse l'été prochain.* We're going to Scotland next summer.

s'**écouler** VERB
1 *to flow out* (*water*)
2 *to pass* ◇ *Le temps s'écoule trop vite.* Time passes too quickly.

écouter VERB
to listen to ◇ *J'aime écouter de la musique.* I like listening to music.
- **Écoute-moi!** Listen!

l'**écouteur** MASC NOUN
earpiece (*of phone*)

l'**écran** MASC NOUN
screen
- **le petit écran** television
- **l'écran total** sunblock

écraser VERB
1 *to crush* ◇ *Écrasez une gousse d'ail.* Crush a clove of garlic.
2 *to run over* ◇ *Regarde bien avant de traverser, sinon tu vas te faire écraser.* Look carefully before you cross or you'll get run over.
- **s'écraser** to crash ◇ *L'avion s'est écrasé dans le désert.* The plane crashed in the desert.

l'**écrevisse** FEM NOUN
crayfish

écrire VERB
to write ◇ *Nous nous écrivons régulièrement.* We write to each other regularly.
- **Ça s'écrit comment?** How do you spell that?

l'**écrit** MASC NOUN
written paper ◇ *L'écrit d'anglais a lieu la semaine prochaine.* The written paper in English is next week.
- **par écrit** in writing

l'**écriteau** MASC NOUN
(PL les **écriteaux**)
notice

l'**écriture** FEM NOUN
writing ◇ *J'ai du mal à lire son écriture.* I can't read his writing.

l'**écrivain** MASC NOUN
writer ◇ *Elle est écrivain.* She's a writer.

l'**écrou** MASC NOUN
nut (*metal*)

s'**écrouler** VERB
to collapse

écru ADJECTIVE
off-white

l'**écureuil** MASC NOUN
squirrel

l'**écurie** FEM NOUN
stable

EDF ABBREVIATION (= *Électricité de France*)
French electricity company

Édimbourg NOUN
Edinburgh

éditer VERB

PTO

to publish ◇ *On vient d'éditer un nouveau dictionnaire.* A new dictionary has just been published.

l'**éditeur** MASC NOUN
publisher

l'**édition** FEM NOUN
1 *edition* ◇ *une édition de poche* a paperback edition
2 *publishing* ◇ *Il travaille dans l'édition.* He works in publishing.

l'**édredon** MASC NOUN
eiderdown

l'**éducateur** MASC NOUN
teacher (*of people with special needs*)

éducatif ADJECTIVE
(FEM SING **éducative**)
educational ◇ *un jeu éducatif* an educational game

l'**éducation** FEM NOUN
1 *education* ◇ *l'éducation physique* physical education ◇ *Il n'a pas beaucoup d'éducation.* He's not very well educated.
2 *upbringing* ◇ *Il a reçu une éducation très stricte.* He had a very strict upbringing.

l'**éducatrice** FEM NOUN
teacher (*of people with special needs*)

éduquer VERB
to educate

effacer VERB
to rub out

effarant ADJECTIVE
amazing ◇ *Il a mangé une quantité effarante de pain.* He ate an amazing amount of bread.

effectivement ADVERB
indeed ◇ *Il est effectivement plus rapide de passer par là.* It is indeed quicker to go this way. ◇ *Oui, effectivement.* Yes, indeed.

effectuer VERB
1 *to make* ◇ *Ils ont effectué de nombreux changements.* They have made a lot of changes.
2 *to do* ◇ *On vient d'effectuer des travaux dans le bâtiment.* They have just done some work in the building.

effervescent ADJECTIVE
effervescent ◇ *un comprimé effervescent* an effervescent tablet

l'**effet** MASC NOUN
effect
- **faire de l'effet** to take effect ◇ *Ce médicament fait rapidement de l'effet.* This medicine takes effect quickly.
- **Ça m'a fait un drôle d'effet de le revoir.** It gave me a strange feeling to see him again.
- **en effet** yes indeed ◇ *Je ne me sens pas très bien.–En effet, tu as l'air pâle.* I don't feel very well.–Yes, you do look pale.

efficace ADJECTIVE
1 *efficient* ◇ *C'est une femme efficace.* She's an efficient woman.
2 *effective* ◇ *un remède efficace* an effective remedy

s'**effondrer** VERB
to collapse

s'**efforcer** VERB
- **s'efforcer de faire quelque chose** to try hard to do something ◇ *Il s'efforce d'être aimable avec la clientèle.* He tries hard to be polite to the customers.

l'**effort** MASC NOUN
effort ◇ *faire un effort* to make an effort

effrayant ADJECTIVE
frightening

effrayer VERB
to frighten

effronté ADJECTIVE
cheeky ◇ *Ce gamin est vraiment effronté.* This kid's really cheeky.

effroyable ADJECTIVE
horrifying

égal ADJECTIVE
(MASC PL **égaux**)
equal ◇ *une quantité égale de farine et de sucre* an equal quantity of flour and sugar
- **Ça m'est égal. (1)** I don't mind. ◇ *Tu préfères du riz ou des pâtes?–Ça m'est égal.* Would you rather have rice or pasta?–I don't mind.
- **Ça m'est égal. (2)** I don't care. ◇ *Fais ce que tu veux, ça m'est égal.* Do what you like, I don't care.

également ADVERB
also ◇ *On appelle également la France l'Hexagone à cause de sa forme.* France is also called the Hexagon because of its shape.

égaler VERB
to equal

l'**égalité** FEM NOUN
equality
- **être à égalité** to be level ◇ *Maintenant les deux joueurs sont à égalité.* The two players are now level.

l'**égard** MASC NOUN
- **à cet égard** in this respect

égarer VERB
to mislay ◇ *J'ai égaré mes clés.* I've mislaid my keys.
- **s'égarer** to get lost ◇ *Ils se sont égarés dans la forêt.* They got lost in

the forest.

l'église FEM NOUN
church ◇ *aller à l'église* to go to church

l'égoïsme MASC NOUN
selfishness

égoïste ADJECTIVE
selfish

l'égratignure FEM NOUN
scratch

l'Égypte FEM NOUN
Egypt

égyptien ADJECTIVE
(FEM SING **égyptienne**)
Egyptian

l'élan MASC NOUN
◆ **prendre de l'élan** to gather speed

s'élancer VERB
to hurl oneself

élargir VERB
to widen

l'élastique MASC NOUN
rubber band

l'électeur MASC NOUN
voter (*man*)

l'élection FEM NOUN
election ◇ *les élections présidentielles* the presidential election

l'électrice FEM NOUN
voter (*woman*)

l'électricien MASC NOUN
electrician

l'électricité FEM NOUN
electricity ◇ *une facture d'électricité* an electricity bill
◆ **allumer l'électricité** to turn on the light
◆ **éteindre l'électricité** to turn off the light

électrique ADJECTIVE
electric ◇ *le courant électrique* the electric current

l'électronique FEM NOUN
electronics

élégant ADJECTIVE
smart

élémentaire ADJECTIVE
elementary

l'éléphant MASC NOUN
elephant

l'élevage MASC NOUN
cattle rearing ◇ *faire de l'élevage* to rear cattle
◆ **un élevage de porcs** a pig farm
◆ **un élevage de poulets** a chicken farm
◆ **les truites d'élevage** farmed trout

élevé ADJECTIVE
high ◇ *Le prix est trop élevé.* The price is too high.
◆ **être bien élevé** to have good manners
◆ **être mal élevé** to have bad manners

l'élève MASC/FEM NOUN
pupil

élever VERB
1 *to bring up* ◇ *Il a été élevé par sa grand-mère.* He was brought up by his grandmother.
2 *to breed* ◇ *Son oncle élève des chevaux.* His uncle breeds horses.
◆ **élever la voix** to raise one's voice
◆ **s'élever à** to come to ◇ *À combien s'élèvent les dégâts?* How much does the damage come to?

l'éleveur MASC NOUN
breeder

éliminatoire ADJECTIVE
◆ **une note éliminatoire** a fail mark
◆ **une épreuve éliminatoire** a qualifying round (*sport*)

éliminer VERB
to eliminate

élire VERB
to elect

elle PRONOUN
1 *she* ◇ *Elle est institutrice.* She is a primary school teacher.
2 *her* ◇ *Vous pouvez avoir confiance en elle.* You can trust her.
3 *it* ◇ *Prends cette chaise: elle est plus confortable.* Take this chair: it's more comfortable.
elle *is also used for emphasis.*
◇ *Elle, elle est toujours en retard!* Oh, SHE's always late!
◆ **elle-même** herself ◇ *Elle l'a choisi elle-même.* She chose it herself.

elles PRONOUN
they ◇ *Où sont Anne et Rachel? – Elles sont allées au cinéma.* Where are Anne and Rachel? – They've gone to the cinema.
◆ **elles-mêmes** themselves

éloigné ADJECTIVE
distant

s'éloigner VERB
to go far away ◇ *Ne vous éloignez pas: le dîner est bientôt prêt!* Don't go far away: dinner will soon be ready!
◆ **Vous vous éloignez du sujet.** You are getting off the point.

l'Élysée MASC NOUN
Élysée Palace
The Élysée *is the residence of the French president.*

l'emballage MASC NOUN
◆ **le papier d'emballage** wrapping paper

emballer VERB
to wrap
◆ **s'emballer** (*informal*) to get excited

PTO

◇ *Il s'est emballé pour ce projet.* He got really excited about this plan.

l'**embarquement** MASC NOUN
boarding ◇ *L'embarquement des passagers n'a pas encore été annoncé.* Passenger boarding has not been announced yet.

l'**embarras** MASC NOUN
embarrassment ◇ *Votre question me met dans l'embarras.* It's difficult for me to answer your question.
- **Vous n'avez que l'embarras du choix.** The only problem is choosing.

embarrassant ADJECTIVE
embarrassing

embarrasser VERB
to embarrass ◇ *Cela m'embarrasse de vous demander encore un service.* I feel embarrassed to ask you to do something more for me.

embaucher VERB
to take on ◇ *L'entreprise vient d'embaucher cinquante ouvriers.* The firm has just taken on fifty workers.

les **embêtements** MASC NOUN
trouble

embêter VERB
to bother
- **s'embêter** to be bored ◇ *Qu'est-ce qu'on s'embête ici!* Isn't it boring here!

l'**embouteillage** MASC NOUN
traffic jam

embrasser VERB
to kiss ◇ *Ils se sont embrassés.* They kissed each other.

s'**embrouiller** VERB
to get confused ◇ *Il s'embrouille dans ses explications.* He gets confused when he explains things.

émerveiller VERB
to dazzle

l'**émeute** FEM NOUN
riot

émigrer VERB
to emigrate

l'**émission** FEM NOUN
programme ◇ *une émission de télévision* a TV programme

s'**emmêler** VERB
to get tangled ◇ *Ma laine s'est emmêlée.* My wool has got tangled.

emménager VERB
to move in ◇ *Nous venons d'emménager dans une nouvelle maison.* We've just moved into a new house.

emmener VERB
to take ◇ *Ils m'ont emmené au cinéma pour mon anniversaire.* They took me to the cinema for my birthday.

emmerder VERB (*rude*)
- **Ça m'emmerde!** It pisses me off!
- **Je t'emmerde!** Piss off!
- **s'emmerder** to be bored stiff

émotif ADJECTIVE
(FEM SING **émotive**)
emotional ◇ *Il est très émotif.* He's very emotional.

l'**émotion** FEM NOUN
emotion

émouvoir VERB
to move ◇ *Sa lettre l'a beaucoup émue.* She was deeply moved by his letter.

emparer VERB
- **s'emparer de** to grab ◇ *Il s'est emparé de ma valise.* He grabbed my case.

l'**empêchement** MASC NOUN
- **Nous avons eu un empêchement de dernière minute.** We were held up at the last minute.

empêcher VERB
to prevent ◇ *Le café le soir m'empêche de dormir.* Coffee at night keeps me awake.
- **Il n'a pas pu s'empêcher de rire.** He couldn't help laughing.

l'**empereur** MASC NOUN
emperor

s'**empiffrer** VERB (*informal*)
to stuff one's face ◇ *Arrête de t'empiffrer!* Stop stuffing your face!

empiler VERB
to pile up

empirer VERB
to worsen ◇ *La situation a encore empiré.* The situation got even worse.

l'**emplacement** MASC NOUN
site ◇ *Un panneau indique l'emplacement de la vieille abbaye.* A sign shows the site of the old abbey.

l'**emploi** MASC NOUN
1 *use* ◇ *prêt à l'emploi* ready for use
- **le mode d'emploi** directions for use

2 *job* ◇ *la création d'emplois* job creation
- **un emploi du temps** a timetable

l'**employé** MASC NOUN
employee
- **un employé de bureau** an office worker

l'**employée** FEM NOUN
employee
- **une employée de banque** a bank clerk

employer VERB
1 *to use* ◇ *Quelle méthode employez-vous?* What method do you use?

2 *to employ* ◇ *L'entreprise emploie*

dix ingénieurs. The firm employs ten engineers.

mployeur MASC NOUN
employer

mpoisonner VERB
to poison

mporter VERB
to take ◇ *N'emportez que le strict nécessaire.* Only take the bare minimum.
plats à emporter take-away meals
s'emporter to lose one's temper ◇ *Je m'emporte facilement et finis souvent par le regretter.* I'm quick to lose my temper and I'm often sorry afterwards.

mpreinte FEM NOUN
une empreinte digitale a fingerprint

mpresser VERB
s'empresser de faire quelque chose to be quick to do something ◇ *Ils se sont empressés de nous annoncer la nouvelle.* They were quick to tell us the news.

mprisonner VERB
to imprison

mprunt MASC NOUN
loan

mprunter VERB
to borrow
emprunter quelque chose à quelqu'un to borrow something from somebody ◇ *Est-ce que je peux t'emprunter dix francs?* Can I borrow ten francs from you?

mu ADJECTIVE
touched ◇ *J'ai été très ému par sa gentillesse.* I was very touched by her kindness.

n PREPOSITION, PRONOUN
1 *in* ◇ *Il habite en France.* He lives in France. ◇ *La mariée est en blanc.* The bride is in white. ◇ *Je le verrai en mai.* I'll see him in May.
2 *to* ◇ *Je vais en France cet été.* I'm going to France this summer.
3 *by* ◇ *C'est plus rapide en voiture.* It's quicker by car.
4 *made of* ◇ *C'est en verre.* It's made of glass. ◇ *un collier en argent* a silver necklace
5 *while* ◇ *Il s'est coupé le doigt en ouvrant une boîte de conserve.* He cut his finger while opening a tin.
Elle est sortie en courant. She ran out.

When **en** *is used with* **avoir** *and* **il y a**, *it is not translated in English.*

◇ *Est-ce que tu as un dictionnaire?–Oui, j'en ai un.* Have you got a dictionary?–Yes, I've got one.
◇ *Combien d'élèves y a-t-il dans ta classe?–Il y en a trente.* How many pupils are there in your class?–There are 30.

en *is also used with verbs and expressions normally followed by* **de** *to avoid repeating the same word.*

◇ *Si tu as un problème, tu peux m'en parler.* If you've got a problem, you can talk about it with me. ◇ *Est-ce que tu peux me rendre ce livre? J'en ai besoin.* Can you give me back that book? I need it. ◇ *Il a un beau jardin et il en est très fier.* He's got a beautiful garden and is very proud of it.
◆ **J'en ai assez.** I've had enough.

enceinte ADJECTIVE
pregnant ◇ *Elle est enceinte de six mois.* She's 6 months pregnant.

enchanté ADJECTIVE
delighted ◇ *Ma mère est enchantée de sa nouvelle voiture.* My mother's delighted with her new car.
◆ **Enchanté!** Pleased to meet you!

encombrant ADJECTIVE
bulky

encombrer VERB
to clutter

encore ADVERB
1 *still* ◇ *Il est encore au travail.* He's still at work. ◇ *Il reste encore deux morceaux de gâteau.* There are two bits of cake left.
2 *even* ◇ *C'est encore mieux.* That's even better.
3 *again* ◇ *Il m'a encore demandé de l'argent.* He asked me for money again.
◆ **encore une fois** once again
◆ **pas encore** not yet ◇ *Je n'ai pas encore fini.* I haven't finished yet.

encourager VERB
to encourage

l'encre FEM NOUN
ink

l'encyclopédie FEM NOUN
encyclopaedia

l'endive FEM NOUN
chicory

endommager VERB
to damage

endormi ADJECTIVE
asleep

endormir VERB
to deaden ◇ *Cette piqûre sert à endormir le nerf.* This injection is to deaden the nerve.
◆ **s'endormir** to go to sleep

l'endroit MASC NOUN
place ◇ *C'est un endroit très tranquille.* It's a very quiet place.

- **à l'endroit (1)** the right way out
- **à l'endroit (2)** the right way up

endurant ADJECTIVE
tough (*person*)

endurcir VERB
to toughen up ◇ *Ces exercices servent à endurcir les soldats.* These exercises are to toughen up the soldiers.
- **s'endurcir** to become hardened

endurer VERB
to endure

l'**énergie** FEM NOUN
1 *energy* ◇ *Je n'ai pas beaucoup d'énergie ce matin.* I haven't got much energy this morning.
2 *power* ◇ *l'énergie nucléaire* nuclear power
- **avec énergie** vigorously ◇ *Il a protesté avec énergie.* He protested vigorously.

énergique ADJECTIVE
energetic ◇ *C'est une femme très énergique.* She's a very energetic woman.
- **des mesures énergiques** strong measures

énerver VERB
- **Il m'énerve!** He gets on my nerves!
- **Ce bruit m'énerve.** This noise gets on my nerves.
- **s'énerver** to get worked up
- **Ne t'énerve pas!** Take it easy!

l'**enfance** FEM NOUN
childhood
- **Je le connais depuis l'enfance.** I've known him since I was a child.

l'**enfant** MASC/FEM NOUN
child

l'**enfer** MASC NOUN
hell

s'**enfermer** VERB
- **Il s'est enfermé dans sa chambre.** He shut himself up in his bedroom.

enfiler VERB
1 *to put on* ◇ *J'ai rapidement enfilé un pull avant de sortir.* I quickly put on a sweater before going out.
2 *to thread* ◇ *J'ai du mal à enfiler cette aiguille.* I am having difficulty threading this needle.

enfin ADVERB
at last ◇ *J'ai enfin réussi à le joindre.* I have at last managed to contact him.

enflé ADJECTIVE
swollen

enfler VERB
to swell

enfoncer VERB
- **Il marchait, les mains enfoncées dans les poches.** He was walking with his hands thrust into his pockets.
- **s'enfoncer** to sink ◇ *Les roues de la voiture s'enfonçaient dans la boue.* The wheels of the car were sinking into the mud.

s'**enfuir** VERB
to run off

l'**engagement** MASC NOUN
commitment

s'**engager** VERB
to commit oneself ◇ *Le Premier ministre s'est engagé à combattre le chômage.* The Prime Minister has committed himself to fighting unemployment.
- **Il s'est engagé dans l'armée à dix-huit ans.** He joined the army when he was 18.

les **engelures** FEM NOUN
chilblains

l'**engin** MASC NOUN
machine

s'**engourdir** VERB
to go numb ◇ *Mes doigts se sont engourdis avec le froid.* My fingers have gone numb with the cold.

engueuler VERB (*informal*)
- **engueuler quelqu'un** to tell somebody off ◇ *Tu vas te faire engueuler!* You're going to get a telling-off!

l'**énigme** FEM NOUN
riddle

s'**enivrer** VERB
to get drunk

enjamber VERB
to stride over ◇ *enjamber une barrière* to stride over a fence

l'**enlèvement** MASC NOUN
kidnapping

enlever VERB
1 *to take off* ◇ *Enlève donc ton manteau!* Take off your coat!
2 *to kidnap* ◇ *Un groupe terroriste a enlevé la femme de l'ambassadeur.* A terrorist group has kidnapped the ambassador's wife.

enneigé ADJECTIVE
snowed up ◇ *Les routes sont encore enneigées.* The roads are still snowed up.

l'**ennemi** MASC NOUN
enemy

l'**ennemie** FEM NOUN
enemy

l'**ennui** MASC NOUN
1 *boredom* ◇ *C'est à mourir d'ennui.* It's enough to bore you to death.
2 *problem* ◇ *avoir des ennuis* to

have problems

ennuyer VERB
to bother ◇ *J'espère que cela ne vous ennuie pas trop.* I hope it doesn't bother you too much.
- **s'ennuyer** to be bored

ennuyeux ADJECTIVE
(FEM SING **ennuyeuse**)
1 *boring*
2 *awkward* ◇ *Tu ne peux pas venir plus tôt? C'est bien ennuyeux.* You can't come any earlier? That's rather awkward.

énorme ADJECTIVE
huge

énormément ADVERB
- **Il a énormément grossi.** He's got terribly fat.
- **Il y a énormément de neige.** There's an enormous amount of snow.

enquête FEM NOUN
1 *investigation* ◇ *La police a ouvert une enquête.* The police have begun an investigation.
2 *survey* ◇ *une enquête parmi les étudiants a montré que...* a survey of students has shown that...

enquêter VERB
to investigate ◇ *La police enquête actuellement sur le crime.* The police are currently investigating the crime.

enrageant ADJECTIVE
infuriating

enrager VERB
to be furious ◇ *J'enrage de n'avoir pas pu profiter de cette occasion.* I'm furious I wasn't able to take advantage of this opportunity.

enregistrement MASC NOUN
recording
- **l'enregistrement des bagages** baggage check-in

enregistrer VERB
1 *to record* ◇ *Ils viennent d'enregistrer un nouvel album.* They've just recorded a new album.
2 *to check in* ◇ *Vous pouvez enregistrer plusieurs valises.* You can check in several cases.

enrhumer VERB
to catch a cold ◇ *Je suis enrhumé.* I've got a cold.

enrichir VERB
to get rich

enrouler VERB
to wind ◇ *Enroulez le fil autour de la bobine.* Wind the thread round the bobbin.

enseignant MASC NOUN
teacher

l'**enseignante** FEM NOUN
teacher

l'**enseignement** MASC NOUN
1 *education* ◇ *les réformes de l'enseignement* education reforms
2 *teaching* ◇ *l'enseignement des langues étrangères* the teaching of foreign languages

enseigner VERB
to teach ◇ *Mon père enseigne les maths dans un lycée.* My father teaches maths in a secondary school.

ensemble ADVERB
see also ensemble NOUN
together ◇ *tous ensemble* all together

l'**ensemble** NOUN
see also ensemble ADVERB
outfit ◇ *Elle portait un ensemble vert.* She was wearing a green outfit.
- **l'ensemble de** the whole of ◇ *La grève a été suivie par l'ensemble du personnel.* The whole workforce went on strike.
- **dans l'ensemble** on the whole

ensoleillé ADJECTIVE
sunny

ensuite ADVERB
then ◇ *Nous sommes allés au cinéma et ensuite au restaurant.* We went to the cinema and then to a restaurant.

entamer VERB
to start ◇ *Qui a entamé le gâteau?* Who's started the cake?

s'**entasser** VERB
to cram ◇ *Ils se sont tous entassés dans ma voiture.* They all crammed into my car.

entendre VERB
1 *to hear* ◇ *Je ne t'entends pas.* I can't hear you.
- **J'ai entendu dire qu'il est dangereux de nager ici.** I've heard that it's dangerous to swim here.
2 *to mean* ◇ *Qu'est-ce que tu entends par là?* What do you mean by that?
- **s'entendre** to get on ◇ *Il s'entend bien avec sa sœur.* He gets on well with his sister.

entendu ADJECTIVE
- **C'est entendu!** Agreed! ◇ *Je passerai te prendre à sept heures, c'est entendu.* That's agreed then, I'll pick you up at 7 o'clock.
- **bien entendu** of course ◇ *Il est bien entendu que je n'en parlerai à personne.* I won't tell anybody about it of course.

l'**enterrement** MASC NOUN
funeral (*burial*)

enterrer VERB
to bury

entêté ADJECTIVE
stubborn

s'**entêter** VERB
to persist ◇ *Il s'entête à refuser de voir le médecin.* He persists in refusing to go to the doctor.

l'**enthousiasme** MASC NOUN
enthusiasm

s'**enthousiasmer** VERB
to get enthusiastic ◇ *Il s'enthousiasme facilement.* He gets very enthusiastic about things.

entier ADJECTIVE
(FEM SING **entière**)
whole ◇ *Il a mangé une quiche entière.* He ate a whole quiche. ◇ *Je n'ai pas lu le livre en entier.* I haven't read the whole book.
◆ **le lait entier** full fat milk

entièrement ADVERB
completely

l'**entorse** FEM NOUN
sprain ◇ *Il s'est fait une entorse à la cheville.* He's sprained his ankle.

entourer VERB
to surround ◇ *Le jardin est entouré d'un mur de pierres.* The garden is surrounded by a stone wall.

l'**entracte** MASC NOUN
interval

l'**entraînement** MASC NOUN
training

entraîner VERB
1 *to lead* ◇ *Il se laisse facilement entraîner par les autres.* He's easily led.
2 *to train* ◇ *Il entraîne l'équipe de France depuis cinq ans.* He's been training the French team for five years.
3 *to involve* ◇ *Un mariage entraîne beaucoup de dépenses.* A wedding involves a lot of expense.
◆ **s'entraîner** to train ◇ *Il s'entraîne au foot tous les samedis matins.* He does football training every Saturday morning.

l'**entraîneur** MASC NOUN
trainer

entre PREPOSITION
between ◇ *Il est assis entre son père et son oncle.* He's sitting between his father and his uncle.
◆ **entre eux** among themselves
◆ **l'un d'entre eux** one of them

l'**entrecôte** FEM NOUN
rib steak

l'**entrée** FEM NOUN
1 *entrance*
2 *starter* (*of meal*) ◇ *Qu'est ce que vous prenez comme entrée?* What would you like for the starter?

entreprendre VERB
to start on ◇ *Elle a entrepris des démarches pour essayer d'adopter un enfant.* She's started on the procedures for adopting a child.

l'**entrepreneur** MASC NOUN
contractor

l'**entreprise** FEM NOUN
firm

entrer VERB
1 *to come in* ◇ *Entrez donc!* Come on in!
2 *to go in* ◇ *Ils sont tous entrés dans la maison.* They all went into the house
◆ **entrer à l'hôpital** to go into hospital

entre-temps ADVERB
meanwhile

l'**entretien** MASC NOUN
1 *maintenance* ◇ *un contrat d'entretien* a maintenance contract
2 *interview* ◇ *On m'a convoqué à un entretien pour un travail.* I've been called for a job interview.

l'**entrevue** FEM NOUN
interview ◇ *une entrevue avec le ministre* an interview with the minister

entrouvert ADJECTIVE
half-open ◇ *La porte était entrouverte.* The door was half open.

envahir VERB
to invade

l'**enveloppe** FEM NOUN
envelope

envelopper VERB
to wrap

envers PREPOSITION
see also envers NOUN
towards ◇ *Il est bien disposé envers elle.* He's well disposed towards her. ◇ *son attitude envers moi* his attitude to me

l'**envers** MASC NOUN
see also envers PREPOSITION
◆ **à l'envers** inside out ◇ *Je dois repasser ce chemisier à l'envers.* I have to iron this blouse inside out.

l'**envie** FEM NOUN
◆ **avoir envie de faire quelque chose** to feel like doing something ◇ *J'avais envie de pleurer.* I felt like crying. ◇ *J'ai envie d'aller aux toilettes.* I want to go to the toilet.
◆ **Cette glace me fait envie.** I fancy some of that ice cream.

envier VERB
to envy

nviron ADVERB
about ◇ *C'est à soixante kilomètres environ.* It's about 60 kilometres.

nvironnement MASC NOUN
environment

nvirons MASC NOUN
area ◇ *les environs de Nantes* the Nantes area ◇ *Il y a beaucoup de choses intéressantes à voir dans les environs.* There are a lot of interesting things to see in the area.
aux environs de dix-neuf heures around 7 p.m.

nvisager VERB
to consider ◇ *Est-ce que vous envisagez de travailler à l'étranger?* Are you considering working abroad?

nvoler VERB
1 *to fly away* ◇ *Le papillon s'est envolé.* The butterfly flew away.
2 *to blow away* ◇ *Toutes mes feuilles de cours se sont envolées.* All my lecture notes blew away.

nvoyer VERB
to send ◇ *Ma tante m'a envoyé une carte pour mon anniversaire.* My aunt sent me a card for my birthday.
envoyer quelqu'un chercher quelque chose to send somebody to get something ◇ *Sa mère l'a envoyé chercher du pain.* His mother sent him to get some bread.

pais ADJECTIVE
(FEM SING **épaisse**)
thick

paisseur FEM NOUN
thickness

patant ADJECTIVE (*informal*)
great ◇ *C'est un type épatant.* He's a great guy.

paule FEM NOUN
shoulder

pée FEM NOUN
sword

peler VERB
to spell ◇ *Est-ce que vous pouvez épeler votre nom s'il vous plaît?* Can you spell your name please?

pice FEM NOUN
spice

picé ADJECTIVE
spicy ◇ *Ce n'est pas assez épicé pour moi: je trouve ça trop fade.* It's not spicy enough for me: I think it's too bland.

picerie FEM NOUN
grocer's shop

picier MASC NOUN
grocer

picière FEM NOUN
grocer

l'**épidémie** FEM NOUN
epidemic

épiler VERB
◆ **s'épiler les jambes** to shave one's legs
◆ **s'épiler les sourcils** to pluck one's eyebrows

les **épinards** MASC NOUN
spinach

l'**épine** FEM NOUN
thorn

l'**épingle** FEM NOUN
pin
◆ **une épingle de sûreté** a safety pin

l'**épisode** MASC NOUN
episode

éplucher VERB
to peel

l'**éponge** FEM NOUN
sponge

l'**époque** FEM NOUN
time ◇ *à cette époque de l'année* at this time of year
◆ **à l'époque** at that time ◇ *À l'époque, beaucoup de gens n'avaient pas l'eau courante.* At that time a lot of people didn't have running water.

l'**épouse** FEM NOUN
wife

épouser VERB
to marry

épouvantable ADJECTIVE
awful

l'**épouvante** FEM NOUN
terror
◆ **un film d'épouvante** a horror film

épouvanter VERB
to terrify

l'**époux** MASC NOUN
husband
◆ **les nouveaux époux** the newly-weds

l'**épreuve** FEM NOUN
1 *test* ◇ *une épreuve orale* an oral test ◇ *une épreuve écrite* a written test
2 *event* (*sport*)

éprouver VERB
to feel ◇ *Qu'est-ce que vous avez éprouvé à ce moment-là?* What did you feel at that moment?

épuisé ADJECTIVE
exhausted

épuiser VERB
to wear out ◇ *Ce travail m'a complètement épuisé.* This job has completely worn me out.
◆ **s'épuiser** to wear oneself out ◇ *Il s'épuise à garder un jardin impeccable.* He wears himself out keeping his garden immaculate.

l'**Équateur** MASC NOUN
Ecuador

l'**équateur** MASC NOUN
equator

l'**équation** FEM NOUN
equation

l'**équerre** FEM NOUN
set square

l'**équilibre** MASC NOUN
balance ◇ *J'ai failli perdre l'équilibre.* I nearly lost my balance.

équilibré ADJECTIVE
well-balanced

l'**équipage** MASC NOUN
crew

l'**équipe** FEM NOUN
team

équipé ADJECTIVE
- **bien équipé** well-equipped

l'**équipement** MASC NOUN
equipment

les **équipements** MASC NOUN
facilities ◇ *les équipements sportifs* sports facilities

l'**équitation** FEM NOUN
riding ◇ *faire de l'équitation* to go riding

l'**équivalent** MASC NOUN
equivalent

l'**erreur** FEM NOUN
mistake
- **faire erreur** to be mistaken

es VERB *see* **être**
- **Tu es très gentille.** You're very kind.

l'**escabeau** MASC NOUN
(PL les **escabeaux**)
stepladder

l'**escalade** FEM NOUN
climbing ◇ *faire de l'escalade* to go climbing

escalader VERB
to climb

l'**escale** FEM NOUN
- **faire escale** to stop off

l'**escalier** MASC NOUN
stairs

l'**escargot** MASC NOUN
snail

l'**esclavage** MASC NOUN
slavery

l'**esclave** MASC/FEM NOUN
slave

l'**escrime** FEM NOUN
fencing

l'**escroc** MASC NOUN
crook

l'**espace** MASC NOUN
space

s'**espacer** VERB
to become less frequent ◇ *Ses visites se sont peu à peu espacées.* His visits became less and less frequent.

l'**espadrille** FEM NOUN
rope-soled sandal

l'**Espagne** FEM NOUN
Spain
- **en Espagne (1)** in Spain
- **en Espagne (2)** to Spain

espagnol ADJECTIVE, NOUN
Spanish ◇ *J'apprends l'espagnol.* I'm learning Spanish.
- **un Espagnol** a Spaniard (*man*)
- **une Espagnole** a Spaniard (*woman*)

l'**espèce** FEM NOUN
1 *sort* ◇ *Elle portait une espèce de cape en velours.* She was wearing a sort of velvet cloak.
2 *species* ◇ *une espèce en voie de disparition* an endangered species
- **Espèce d'idiot!** You idiot!

les **espèces** FEM NOUN
cash ◇ *payer en espèces* to pay cash

espérer VERB
to hope
- **J'espère bien.** I hope so. ◇ *Tu penses avoir réussi? – Oui, j'espère bien.* Do you think you've passed? – Yes, I hope so.

espiègle ADJECTIVE
mischievous

l'**espion** MASC NOUN
spy

l'**espionnage** MASC NOUN
spying
- **un roman d'espionnage** a spy novel

l'**espionne** FEM NOUN
spy

l'**espoir** MASC NOUN
hope

l'**esprit** MASC NOUN
mind ◇ *Ça ne m'est pas venu à l'esprit.* It didn't cross my mind.
- **avoir de l'esprit** to be witty ◇ *Il a beaucoup d'esprit.* He's very witty.

l'**esquimau** ®
(PL les **esquimaux**) MASC NOUN
ice lolly

l'**Esquimau** MASC NOUN
(PL les **Esquimaux**)
Eskimo

l'**Esquimaude** FEM NOUN
Eskimo

l'**essai** MASC NOUN
attempt ◇ *Ce n'est pas mal pour un coup d'essai.* It's not bad for a first attempt.
- **prendre quelqu'un à l'essai** to take somebody on for a trial period

essayer VERB

1 *to try* ◇ *Essaie de rentrer de bonne heure.* Try to come home early.
2 *to try on* ◇ *Essaie donc ce pull: il devrait bien t'aller.* Try this sweater on: it ought to look good on you.

ssence FEM NOUN
petrol

ssentiel ADJECTIVE
(FEM SING **essentielle**)
essential
Tu es là: c'est l'essentiel. You're here: that's the main thing.

ssouffler VERB
to get out of breath

ssuie-glace MASC NOUN
windscreen wiper

ssuyer VERB
to wipe
essuyer la vaisselle to dry the dishes
s'essuyer to dry oneself ◇ *Vous pouvez vous essuyer les mains avec cette serviette.* You can dry your hands on this towel.

st VERB *see* **être**
see also **est** ADJECTIVE, NOUN
Elle est merveilleuse. She's marvellous.

st ADJECTIVE
see also **est** VERB, NOUN
1 *east* ◇ *la côte est des États-Unis* the east coast of the United States
2 *eastern* ◇ *dans la partie est du pays* in the eastern part of the country

st MASC NOUN
see also **est** VERB, ADJECTIVE
east ◇ *Je vis dans l'est de la France.* I live in the East of France.
vers l'est eastwards
à l'est de Paris east of Paris
l'Europe de l'Est Eastern Europe
le vent d'est the east wind

st-ce que ADVERB
Est-ce que c'est cher? Is it expensive?
Quand est-ce qu'il part? When is he leaving?

sthéticienne FEM NOUN
beautician

stime FEM NOUN
J'ai beaucoup d'estime pour elle. I think a lot of her.

stimer VERB
estimer quelqu'un to have great respect for somebody ◇ *Mon père l'estime beaucoup.* My father has a lot of respect for him.
estimer que to consider that ◇ *J'estime que c'est de sa faute.* I consider that it's his fault.

stivant MASC NOUN
holiday-maker

l'**estivante** FEM NOUN
holiday-maker

l'**estomac** MASC NOUN
stomach

l'**Estonie** FEM NOUN
Estonia

l'**estrade** FEM NOUN
platform

et CONJUNCTION
and

établir VERB
to establish
◆ **s'établir à son compte** to set up in business

l'**établissement** MASC NOUN
establishment
◆ **un établissement scolaire** a school

l'**étage** MASC NOUN
floor ◇ *au premier étage* on the first floor
◆ **à l'étage** upstairs

l'**étagère** FEM NOUN
shelf

étaient VERB *see* **être**

l'**étain** MASC NOUN
tin

étais, était VERB *see* **être**
◆ **Il était très jeune.** He was very young.

l'**étalage** MASC NOUN
display

étaler VERB
to spread ◇ *Il a étalé la carte sur la table.* He spread the map on the table.

étanche ADJECTIVE
1 *watertight* ◇ *La toiture n'est pas étanche.* The roof isn't watertight.
2 *waterproof* (*watch*)

l'**étang** MASC NOUN
pond

étant VERB *see* **être**
◆ **Mes revenus étant limités...** My income being limited...

l'**étape** FEM NOUN
stage ◇ *une étape importante de la vie* an important stage in life
◆ **faire étape** to stop off

l'**État** MASC NOUN
state (*nation*) ◇ *un chef d'État* a head of state

l'**état** MASC NOUN
1 *state* (*country*)
2 *condition* ◇ *en mauvais état* in poor condition
◆ **remettre quelque chose en état** to repair something
◆ **le bureau d'état civil** the registry office

les **États-Unis** MASC NOUN
United States

E

PTO

- **aux États-Unis (1)** in the United States
- **aux États-Unis (2)** to the United States

été VERB *see* **être**

see also **été** NOUN

- **Il a été promu.** He's been promoted.

l'**été** MASC NOUN

see also **été** VERB

summer

- **en été** in the summer

éteindre VERB

1 *to switch off* ◇ *N'oubliez pas d'éteindre la lumière en sortant.* Don't forget to switch off the light when you leave.

2 *to put out* (*cigarette*)

étendre VERB

to spread ◇ *Elle a étendu une nappe propre sur la table.* She spread a clean cloth on the table.

- **étendre le linge** to hang out the washing
- **s'étendre** to lie down ◇ *Je vais m'étendre cinq minutes.* I'm going to lie down for five minutes.

l'**éternité** FEM NOUN

- **J'ai attendu une éternité chez le médecin.** I waited for ages at the doctor's.

éternuer VERB

to sneeze

êtes VERB *see* **être**

- **Vous êtes en retard.** You're late.

étiez VERB *see* **être**

étinceler VERB

to sparkle

étions VERB *see* **être**

l'**étiquette** FEM NOUN

label ◇ *L'étiquette du pot de confiture s'est décollée.* The label has come off the jam pot.

s'**étirer** VERB

to stretch ◇ *Elle s'est étirée paresseusement.* She stretched lazily.

l'**étoile** FEM NOUN

star

- **une étoile de mer** a starfish
- **une étoile filante** a shooting star
- **dormir à la belle étoile** to sleep under the stars

étonnant ADJECTIVE

amazing

étonner VERB

to surprise ◇ *Cela m'étonnerait que le colis soit déjà arrivé.* I'd be surprised if the parcel had arrived yet.

étouffer VERB

- **On étouffe ici: ouvre donc les fenêtres.** It's stifling in here: open the windows.
- **s'étouffer** to choke ◇ *Ne mange pas si vite: tu vas t'étouffer!* Don't eat so fast: you'll choke!

l'**étourderie** FEM NOUN

absent-mindedness

- **une erreur d'étourderie** a slip

étourdi ADJECTIVE

scatterbrained

l'**étourdissement** MASC NOUN

- **avoir des étourdissements** to feel dizzy

étrange ADJECTIVE

strange

étranger ADJECTIVE

(FEM SING **étrangère**)

see also **étranger** NOUN

foreign ◇ *un pays étranger* a foreign country

- **une personne étrangère** a stranger

l'**étranger** MASC NOUN

see also **étranger** ADJECTIVE

1 *foreigner*

2 *stranger*

- **à l'étranger** abroad

l'**étrangère** FEM NOUN

1 *foreigner*

2 *stranger*

étrangler VERB

to strangle

l'**être** MASC NOUN

see also **être** VERB

- **un être humain** a human being

être VERB

see also **être** NOUN

Present tense:	
je suis	*nous sommes*
tu es	*vous êtes*
il/elle est	*ils/elles sont*
Past participle: *été*	

1 *to be* ◇ *Je suis heureux.* I'm happy ◇ *Mon père est instituteur.* My father's a primary school teacher. ◇ *Il est dix heures.* It's 10 o'clock.

2 *to have* ◇ *Il n'est pas encore arrivé.* He hasn't arrived yet.

les **étrennes** FEM NOUN

- **Nous avons donné des étrennes à la gardienne.** We gave the caretaker a New Year gift.

étroit ADJECTIVE

narrow

- **être à l'étroit** to be cramped ◇ *Nous sommes un peu à l'étroit dans cet appartement.* We're a bit cramped in this flat.

l'**étude** FEM NOUN

study ◇ *une étude de cas* a case study

- **faire des études** to be studying ◇ *Il fait des études de droit.* He's studying law.

étudiant MASC NOUN
student

étudiante FEM NOUN
student

étudier VERB
to study

étui MASC NOUN
case ◇ *un étui à lunettes* a glasses case

eu VERB *see* **avoir**
- **J'ai eu une bonne note.** I got a good mark.

euh EXCLAMATION
er ◇ *Euh...je ne m'en souviens pas.* Er...I can't remember.

Europe FEM NOUN
Europe
- **en Europe (1)** in Europe
- **en Europe (2)** to Europe

européen ADJECTIVE
(FEM SING **européenne**)
European

eux PRONOUN
them ◇ *Je pense souvent à eux.* I often think of them.
eux *is also used for emphasis.*
◇ *Elle a accepté l'invitation, mais eux ont refusé.* She accepted the invitation, but THEY refused.

évacuer VERB
to evacuate

évader VERB
to escape

évangile MASC NOUN
gospel

évanouir VERB
to faint

évaporer VERB
to evaporate

évasif ADJECTIVE
(FEM SING **évasive**)
evasive

évasion FEM NOUN
escape ◇ *Ils ont préparé leur évasion pendant des mois.* They spent months planning their escape.

éveillé ADJECTIVE
1 *awake* ◇ *Il est resté éveillé toute la nuit.* He stayed awake all night.
2 *bright* ◇ *C'est un enfant très éveillé pour son âge.* He's very bright for his age.

éveiller VERB
to awaken

événement MASC NOUN
event

éventail MASC NOUN
fan (*hand-held*)
- **un large éventail de prix** a wide range of prices

l'**éventualité** FEM NOUN
- **dans l'éventualité d'un retard** in the event of a delay

éventuel ADJECTIVE
(FEM SING **éventuelle**)
possible ◇ *une solution éventuelle* a possible solution ◇ *les conséquences éventuelles* the possible consequences

éventuellement ADVERB
possibly ◇ *Nous pourrions éventuellement avoir besoin de vous.* We may need you. ◇ *les difficultés que vous pourriez éventuellement rencontrer* the difficulties that you may have

l'**évêque** MASC NOUN
bishop

évidemment ADVERB
1 *obviously* ◇ *Les tomates sont évidemment chères en cette saison.* Tomatoes are obviously dear at this time of year.
2 *of course* ◇ *Est-ce que je peux utiliser ton téléphone?–Évidemment, tu n'as pas besoin de demander.* Can I use your phone?–Of course, you don't need to ask.

l'**évidence** FEM NOUN
- **C'est une évidence.** It's quite obvious.
- **de toute évidence** obviously ◇ *De toute évidence, il ne veut pas nous voir.* Obviously he doesn't want to see us.
- **être en évidence** to be clearly visible ◇ *La lettre était en évidence sur la table.* The letter was clearly visible on the table.
- **mettre en évidence** to reveal

évident ADJECTIVE
obvious

l'**évier** MASC NOUN
sink

éviter VERB
to avoid

évolué ADJECTIVE
advanced

évoluer VERB
to progress ◇ *La chirurgie esthétique a beaucoup évolué.* Plastic surgery has progressed a great deal.
- **Il a beaucoup évolué.** He has come on a great deal.

l'**évolution** FEM NOUN
1 *development* ◇ *une évolution rapide* rapid development
2 *evolution* ◇ *la théorie de l'évolution* the theory of evolution

évoquer VERB
to mention ◇ *Il a évoqué divers problèmes dans son discours.* He mentioned various problems in his

PTO

speech.

exact ADJECTIVE
1 *right* ◇ *Avez-vous l'heure exacte?* Have you got the right time? ◇ *Votre voiture est garée dehors, n'est-ce pas?–C'est exact.* Your car's parked outside, isn't it?–That's right.
2 *exact* ◇ *Est-ce que vous pouvez m'indiquer le prix exact du billet?* Can you tell me the exact price of the ticket?

exactement ADVERB
exactly ◇ *C'est exactement ce que je cherchais.* That's exactly what I was looking for.

ex aequo ADJECTIVE
◆ **Ils sont arrivés ex aequo.** They finished neck and neck.

exagérer VERB
1 *to exaggerate* ◇ *Vous exagérez!* You're exaggerating!
2 *to go too far* ◇ *Ça fait trois fois que tu arrives en retard: tu exagères!* That's three times you've been late: you really go too far sometimes!

l'**examen** MASC NOUN
exam ◇ *Nous allons passer l'examen d'anglais vendredi matin.* We're doing our English exam on Friday morning.
◇ *un examen de français* a French exam
◆ **un examen médical** a medical

examiner VERB
to examine

exaspérant ADJECTIVE
infuriating

exaspérer VERB
to infuriate

l'**excédent** MASC NOUN
◆ **l' excédent de bagages** excess baggage

excéder VERB
to exceed ◇ *un contrat dont la durée n'excède pas deux ans* a contract for a period not exceeding two years
◆ **excéder quelqu'un** to drive somebody mad ◇ *Les cris des enfants l'excédaient.* The noise of the children was driving her mad.

excellent ADJECTIVE
excellent

excentrique ADJECTIVE
eccentric

excepté PREPOSITION
except ◇ *Toutes les chaussures excepté les sandales sont en solde.* All the shoes except sandals are reduced.

l'**exception** FEM NOUN
exception

exceptionnel ADJECTIVE
(FEM SING **exceptionnelle**)
exceptional

l'**excès** MASC NOUN
◆ **faire des excès** to overindulge ◇ *On fait souvent des excès aux environs de Noël.* People often overindulge around Christmas.
◆ **les excès de vitesse** speeding

excessif ADJECTIVE
(FEM SING **excessive**)
excessive

excitant ADJECTIVE
see also excitant NOUN
exciting

l'**excitant** MASC NOUN
see also excitant ADJECTIVE
stimulant ◇ *Le thé et le café sont des excitants.* Tea and coffee are stimulants.

l'**excitation** FEM NOUN
excitement

exciter VERB
to excite ◇ *Il était tout excité à l'idée de revoir ses cousins.* He was all excited about seeing his cousins again.
◆ **s'exciter** (*informal*) to get excited ◇ *Ne t'excite pas trop vite: ça ne va peut-être pas marcher!* Don't get excited too soon: it may not work!

l'**exclamation** FEM NOUN
exclamation

exclu ADJECTIVE
◆ **Il n'est pas exclu que...** It's not impossible that...

exclusif ADJECTIVE
(FEM SING **exclusive**)
exclusive

l'**excursion** FEM NOUN
1 *trip* ◇ *faire une excursion* to go on a trip
2 *walk* ◇ *une excursion dans la montagne* a walk in the hills

l'**excuse** FEM NOUN
1 *excuse* ◇ *Il trouve toujours une bonne excuse pour ne pas faire la vaisselle.* He always finds a good excuse for not doing the washing-up.
2 *apology* ◇ *présenter ses excuses* to offer one's apologies
◆ **un mot d'excuse** a note ◇ *Vous devez apporter un mot d'excuse signé par vos parents.* You have to bring a note signed by your parents.

excuser VERB
to excuse
◆ **Excusez-moi. (1)** Sorry!
◇ *Excusez-moi, je ne vous avais pas vu.* Sorry, I didn't see you.
◆ **Excusez-moi. (2)** Excuse me.
◇ *Excusez-moi, est-ce que vous avez l'heure?* Excuse me, have you got the

time?

- **s'excuser** to apologize ◇ *Il s'est excusé de son retard.* He apologized for being late.

exécuter VERB
1 *to execute* ◇ *Le prisonnier a été exécuté à l'aube.* The prisoner was executed at dawn.
2 *to perform* ◇ *Le pianiste va maintenant exécuter une valse de Chopin.* The pianist is now going to perform a waltz by Chopin.

exemplaire MASC NOUN
copy

exemple MASC NOUN
example ◇ *donner l'exemple* to set an example

- **par exemple** for example

exercer VERB
to practise

exercice MASC NOUN
exercise

exhiber VERB
to show off ◇ *Il aime bien exhiber ses décorations.* He likes showing off his medals.

- **s'exhiber** to expose oneself

exhibitionniste MASC NOUN
flasher

exigeant ADJECTIVE
hard to please ◇ *Elle est vraiment exigeante.* She's really hard to please.

exiger VERB
1 *to demand* ◇ *Le propriétaire exige d'être payé immédiatement.* The landlord is demanding to be paid immediately.
2 *to require* ◇ *Ce travail exige beaucoup de patience.* This job requires a lot of patience.

exil MASC NOUN
exile

exister VERB
to exist ◇ *Ça n'existe pas.* It doesn't exist. ◇ *Ce manteau existe également en rose.* This coat's also available in pink.

exotique ADJECTIVE
exotic ◇ *une plante exotique* an exotic plant ◇ *un yaourt aux fruits exotiques* a tropical fruit yoghurt

expédier VERB
to send ◇ *expédier un colis* to send a parcel

expéditeur MASC NOUN
sender

expédition FEM NOUN
expedition

- **l'expédition du courrier** the dispatch of the mail

l'expéditrice FEM NOUN
sender

l'expérience FEM NOUN
1 *experience* ◇ *Elle a plusieurs années d'expérience.* She's got several years' experience.
2 *experiment* ◇ *une expérience de chimie* a chemistry experiment

expérimenter VERB
to test ◇ *Ces produits de beauté n'ont pas été expérimentés sur des animaux.* These cosmetics have not been tested on animals.

l'expert MASC NOUN
expert

l'explication FEM NOUN
explanation

- **une explication de texte** a critical analysis (*of a text*)

expliquer VERB
to explain ◇ *Il m'a expliqué comment faire.* He explained to me how to do it.

- **ça s'explique** it's understandable

l'exploit MASC NOUN
achievement

l'exploitation FEM NOUN
exploitation ◇ *Cet organisme lutte contre l'exploitation des femmes.* This organization fights against the exploitation of women.

- **une exploitation agricole** a farm

exploiter VERB
to exploit ◇ *Il s'est fait exploiter par le patron du restaurant.* He was exploited by the owner of the restaurant.

explorer VERB
to explore

exploser VERB
to explode ◇ *La bombe a explosé en pleine rue.* The bomb exploded in the middle of the street.

l'explosif MASC NOUN
explosive

l'explosion FEM NOUN
explosion

l'exportateur MASC NOUN
exporter

l'exportation FEM NOUN
export

l'exportatrice FEM NOUN
exporter

exporter VERB
to export

l'exposé MASC NOUN
talk ◇ *On nous a demandé de faire un exposé sur l'environnement.* We were asked to give a talk on the environment.

exposer VERB

1 *to show* ◇ *Il expose ses peintures dans une galerie d'art.* He shows his paintings in a private art gallery.
2 *to expose* ◇ *N'exposez pas la pellicule à la lumière.* Do not expose the film to light.
3 *to set out* ◇ *Il nous a exposé les raisons de son départ.* He set out the reasons for his departure.
◆ **s'exposer au soleil** to stay out in the sun ◇ *Ne vous exposez pas trop longtemps au soleil.* Don't stay out too long in the sun.

l'**exposition** FEM NOUN
exhibition ◇ *une exposition de peinture* an exhibition of paintings

exprès ADVERB
1 *on purpose* ◇ *Je suis sûr qu'il l'a fait exprès.* I'm sure he did it on purpose.
2 *specially* ◇ *Goûtes-y: j'ai fait ce gâteau exprès pour toi.* Have a taste: I made this cake specially for you.

l'**express** MASC NOUN
1 *espresso* (*coffee*)
2 *fast train* ◇ *Il a décidé de prendre l'express de dix heures.* He decided to catch the fast train at 10 o'clock.

l'**expression** FEM NOUN
1 *expression*
2 *phrase*

exprimer VERB
to express
◆ **s'exprimer** to express oneself ◇ *Il s'exprime très bien pour un enfant de huit ans.* For a child of 8, he expresses himself very well.

exquis ADJECTIVE
exquisite

extérieur ADJECTIVE
see also extérieur NOUN
outside

l'**extérieur** MASC NOUN
see also extérieur ADJECTIVE
outside
◆ **à l'extérieur** outside ◇ *Les toilettes sont à l'extérieur.* The toilet is outside.

l'**externat** MASC NOUN
day school

l'**externe** MASC/FEM NOUN
day pupil

l'**extincteur** MASC NOUN
fire extinguisher

extra ADJECTIVE (MASC, FEM, PL)
excellent ◇ *Ce fromage est extra!* This cheese is excellent!

extraire VERB
to extract

l'**extrait** MASC NOUN
extract

extraordinaire ADJECTIVE
extraordinary

extravagant ADJECTIVE
extravagant

extrême ADJECTIVE
see also extrême NOUN
extreme ◇ *l'extrême droite et l'extrême gauche* the far right and the far left

l'**extrême** MASC NOUN
see also extrême ADJECTIVE
extreme

extrêmement ADVERB
extremely

l'**Extrême-Orient** MASC NOUN
the Far East

l'**extrémité** FEM NOUN
end ◇ *La gare est à l'autre extrémité de la ville.* The station is at the other end of the town.

F

F. ABBREVIATION
franc

fa NOUN
F

fabrication NOUN
manufacture

fabriquer VERB
to make ◇ *fabriqué en France* made in France
- **Qu'est-ce qu'il fabrique?** (*informal*) What's he up to?

fac NOUN (*informal*)
university

face NOUN
- **face à face** face to face
- **en face de** opposite ◇ *Le bus s'arrête en face de chez moi.* The bus stops opposite my house.
- **faire face à quelque chose** to face something
- **Pile ou face?–Face.** Heads or tails?–Heads.

fâché ADJECTIVE
angry
être fâché contre quelqu'un to be angry with somebody ◇ *Elle est fâchée contre moi.* She's angry with me.
être fâché avec quelqu'un to be on bad terms with somebody ◇ *Elle est fâchée avec sa sœur.* She's on bad terms with her sister.

fâcher VERB
se fâcher contre quelqu'un to lose one's temper with somebody
se fâcher avec quelqu'un to fall out with somebody ◇ *Il s'est fâché avec son frère.* He's fallen out with his brother.

facile ADJECTIVE
easy
facile à faire easy to do

facilement ADVERB
easily

façon NOUN
way ◇ *De quelle façon?* In what way?
de toute façon anyway

facteur NOUN
postman ◇ *Il est facteur.* He's a postman.

facture NOUN
bill ◇ *une facture de gaz* a gas bill

facultatif ADJECTIVE
(FEM SING **facultative**)
optional

fade ADJECTIVE
tasteless ◇ *La soupe est un peu fade.* The soup is a bit tasteless.

faible ADJECTIVE
weak ◇ *Je me sens encore faible.* I still feel a bit weak.
- **Il est faible en maths.** He's not very good at maths.

la **faiblesse** NOUN
weakness

la **faïence** NOUN
pottery

faillir VERB
- **J'ai failli tomber.** I nearly fell.

la **faim** NOUN
hunger
- **avoir faim** to be hungry

fainéant ADJECTIVE
lazy

faire VERB

Present tense:	
je fais	*nous faisons*
tu fais	*vous faites*
il/elle fait	*ils/elles font*

Past participle: *fait*

1 *to make* ◇ *Je vais faire un gâteau pour ce soir.* I'm going to make a cake for tonight. ◇ *Ils font trop de bruit.* They're making too much noise. ◇ *Je voudrais me faire de nouveaux amis.* I'd like to make new friends.
2 *to do* ◇ *Qu'est-ce que tu fais?* What are you doing? ◇ *Il fait de l'italien.* He's doing Italian. ◇ *Qui veut bien faire la vaisselle?* Who'll do the dishes?
3 *to play* ◇ *Il fait du piano.* He plays the piano.
4 *to be* ◇ *Qu'est-ce qu'il fait chaud!* Isn't it hot! ◇ *Espérons qu'il fera beau demain.* Let's hope it'll be nice weather tomorrow.
- **faire tomber** to knock over ◇ *Le chat a fait tomber le vase.* The cat knocked over the vase.
- **faire faire quelque chose** to get something done ◇ *Je dois faire réparer ma voiture.* I've got to get my car repaired.
- **Je vais me faire couper les cheveux.** I'm going to get my hair cut.
- **Ne t'en fais pas!** Don't worry!

fais, faisaient, faisais, faisait VERB
see **faire**

le **faisan** NOUN
pheasant

faisiez, faisions, faisons, fait VERB
see **faire**

le **fait** NOUN

PTO

fact ◇ *Le fait que...* The fact that...
- **au fait** by the way ◇ *Au fait, est-ce que tu as aimé le film d'hier?* By the way, did you enjoy the film yesterday?
- **en fait** actually ◇ *En fait je n'ai pas beaucoup de temps.* I haven't got much time actually.

faites VERB *see* **faire**

la **falaise** NOUN
cliff

falloir VERB *see* **faut, faudra, faudrait**

famé ADJECTIVE
- **un quartier mal famé** a rough area

fameux ADJECTIVE
(FEM SING **fameuse**)
- **Ce n'est pas fameux.** It's not great.

familial ADJECTIVE
(MASC PL **familiaux**)
family ◇ *une atmosphère familiale* a family atmosphere
- **les allocations familiales** child benefit

familier ADJECTIVE
(FEM SING **familière**)
familiar ◇ *C'est un nom qui m'est familier.* The name's familiar.

la **famille** NOUN
1 *family* ◇ *une famille nombreuse* a big family ◇ *Nous passons Noël en famille.* We have a family Christmas.
2 *relatives* ◇ *Il a de la famille à Paris.* He's got relatives in Paris.

la **famine** NOUN
famine

la **fanfare** NOUN
band

fantaisie ADJECTIVE
- **des bijoux fantaisie** costume jewellery

fantastique ADJECTIVE
fantastic

le **fantôme** NOUN
ghost

la **farce** NOUN
1 *stuffing* (*for chicken, turkey*)
2 *practical joke* ◇ *André aime faire des farces.* André likes to play practical jokes.

farci ADJECTIVE
stuffed ◇ *des tomates farcies* stuffed tomatoes

la **farine** NOUN
flour

fasciner VERB
to fascinate

fasse, fassent, fasses, fassiez, fassions VERB *see* **faire**
- **Pourvu qu'il fasse beau demain!** Let's hope it'll be fine tomorrow!

fatal ADJECTIVE
fatal
- **C'était fatal.** It was bound to happen.

la **fatalité** NOUN
fate

fatigant ADJECTIVE
tiring

la **fatigue** NOUN
tiredness

fatigué ADJECTIVE
tired

se **fatiguer** VERB
to get tired

fauché ADJECTIVE (*informal*)
hard up

faudra VERB
faudra *is the future tense of* **falloir**.
- **Il faudra qu'on soit plus rapide demain.** We'll have to be quicker tomorrow.

faudrait VERB
faudrait *is the conditional tense of* **falloir**.
- **Il faudrait qu'on fasse attention.** We ought to be careful.

se **faufiler** VERB
- **Il s'est faufilé à travers la foule.** He made his way through the crowd.

la **faune** NOUN
wildlife

fausse ADJECTIVE *see* **faux**

faut VERB
faut *is the present tense of* **falloir**.
- **Il faut faire attention.** You've got to be careful.
- **Nous n'avons pas le choix, il faut y aller.** We've no choice, we've got to go.
- **Il faut que je parte.** I've got to go.
- **Il faut du courage pour faire ce métier.** It takes courage to do that job.

la **faute** NOUN
1 *mistake* ◇ *faire une faute* to make a mistake
2 *fault* ◇ *Ce n'est pas de ma faute.* It's not my fault.
- **sans faute** without fail ◇ *Je t'appellerai sans faute.* I'll phone you without fail.

le **fauteuil** NOUN
armchair
- **un fauteuil roulant** a wheelchair

faux ADJECTIVE, ADVERB
(FEM SING **fausse**)
see also **faux** NOUN
untrue ◇ *C'est entièrement faux.* It's totally untrue.
- **faire un faux pas** to trip
- **Il chante faux.** He sings out of tune.

le **faux** NOUN
see also **faux** ADJECTIVE
fake ◇ *Ce tableau est un faux.* This painting is a fake.

la **faveur** NOUN

favour

avori ADJECTIVE
(FEM SING **favorite**)
favourite

avoriser VERB
to favour ◇ *Ce système d'examen favorise ceux qui ont de la mémoire.* This exam system favours people with good memories.

ax NOUN
fax

ée NOUN
fairy

eignant ADJECTIVE (*informal*)
lazy

élicitations FEM NOUN
congratulations

éliciter VERB
to congratulate

emelle NOUN
female (*animal*)

éminin ADJECTIVE
1 *female* ◇ *les personnages féminins du roman* the female characters in the novel
2 *feminine* ◇ *Elle est très féminine.* She's very feminine.
3 *women's* ◇ *Elle joue dans l'équipe féminine de France.* She plays in the French women's team.

éministe ADJECTIVE
feminist

emme NOUN
1 *woman*
2 *wife* ◇ *C'est la femme du directeur.* She's the headmaster's wife.
- **une femme au foyer** a housewife
- **une femme de ménage** a cleaning woman

endre VERB
to crack

enêtre NOUN
window

enouil NOUN
fennel

ente NOUN
slot

er NOUN
iron
- **un fer à cheval** a horseshoe
- **un fer à repasser** an iron

era, ferai, feras, ferez VERB *see* **faire**

érié ADJECTIVE
- **un jour férié** a public holiday

eriez, ferions VERB *see* **faire**

erme ADJECTIVE
see also **ferme** NOUN
firm ◇ *Elle s'est montrée très ferme à mon égard.* She was very firm with me.

la **ferme** NOUN
see also **ferme** ADJECTIVE
farm

fermé ADJECTIVE
1 *closed* ◇ *La pharmacie est fermée.* The chemist's is closed.
2 *off* ◇ *Est-ce que le gaz est fermé?* Is the gas off?

fermer VERB
1 *to close* ◇ *N'oublie pas de fermer la fenêtre.* Don't forget to close the window.
2 *to turn off* ◇ *As-tu bien fermé le robinet?* Have you turned the tap off?

la **fermeture** NOUN
- **les heures de fermeture** closing times
- **une fermeture éclair** ® a zip

le **fermier** NOUN
farmer

la **fermière** NOUN
1 *woman farmer*
2 *farmer's wife*

féroce ADJECTIVE
fierce ◇ *un animal féroce* a fierce animal

ferons, feront VERB *see* **faire**

les **fesses** FEM NOUN
buttocks

le **festival** NOUN
festival

la **fête** NOUN
1 *party* ◇ *Nous organisons une petite fête pour son anniversaire.* We're having a little party for his birthday.
- **faire la fête** to party

2 *name day* ◇ *C'est sa fête aujourd'hui.* It's his name day today.
- **une fête foraine** a funfair
- **la Fête Nationale** Bastille Day
- **les fêtes de fin d'année** the festive season

fêter VERB
to celebrate

le **feu** NOUN
(PL les **feux**)
1 *fire* ◇ *prendre feu* to catch fire ◇ *faire du feu* to make a fire
- **Au feu!** Fire!

2 *traffic light* ◇ *un feu rouge* a red light ◇ *Tournez à gauche aux feux.* Turn left at the lights.
- **Avez-vous du feu?** Have you got a light?

3 *heat* ◇ *...mijoter à feu doux* ...simmer over a gentle heat
- **un feu d'artifice** a firework display

le **feuillage** NOUN
leaves

F

la **feuille** NOUN
1 *leaf* ◇ *des feuilles mortes* fallen leaves
2 *sheet* ◇ *une feuille de papier* a sheet of paper
➔ **une feuille de maladie** a claim form for medical expenses

feuilleté ADJECTIVE
➔ **de la pâte feuilletée** flaky pastry

feuilleter VERB
to leaf through

le **feuilleton** NOUN
serial

le **feutre** NOUN
felt
➔ **un stylo-feutre** a felt-tip pen

la **fève** NOUN
broad bean

février MASC NOUN
February
➔ **en février** in February

fiable ADJECTIVE
reliable

les **fiançailles** FEM NOUN
engagement SING

fiancé ADJECTIVE
➔ **être fiancé à quelqu'un** to be engaged to somebody

se **fiancer** VERB
to get engaged

la **ficelle** NOUN
1 *string* ◇ *Passe-moi un bout de ficelle.* Give me a piece of string.
2 *thin baguette* (*bread*)

la **fiche** NOUN
form ◇ *Remplissez cette fiche s'il vous plaît.* Fill in this form please.

se **ficher** VERB (*informal*)
➔ **Je m'en fiche!** I don't care!
➔ **Fiche-moi la paix!** Leave me alone!
➔ **Quoi, tu n'as fait que ça? Tu te fiches de moi!** You've only done that much? You can't be serious!

fichu ADJECTIVE (*informal*)
➔ **Ce parapluie est fichu.** This umbrella's knackered.

fidèle ADJECTIVE
faithful

fier ADJECTIVE
(FEM SING **fière**)
proud

la **fierté** NOUN
pride

la **fièvre** NOUN
fever ◇ *J'ai de la fièvre.* I've got a temperature. ◇ *Il a trente-neuf de fièvre.* He's got a temperature of 39°C.

fiévreux ADJECTIVE
(FEM SING **fiévreuse**)
feverish

la **figue** NOUN
fig

la **figure** NOUN
1 *face* ◇ *Il a reçu le ballon en pleine figure.* The ball hit him smack in the face.
2 *figure* (*illustration*) ◇ *Voir figure 2.1, page 32.* See figure 2.1, page 32.

le **fil** NOUN
thread ◇ *le fil à coudre* sewing thread
➔ **le fil de fer** wire
➔ **un coup de fil** a phone call

la **file** NOUN
line (*of people, objects*)
➔ **une file d'attente** a queue ◇ *se mettre à la file* to join the queue
➔ **à la file** one after the other
➔ **en file indienne** in single file

filer VERB
to speed along ◇ *Les voitures filent sur l'autoroute.* The cars are speeding along the motorway.
➔ **File dans ta chambre!** Off to your room with you!

le **filet** NOUN
net

la **fille** NOUN
1 *girl* ◇ *C'est une école de filles.* It's a girls' school.
2 *daughter* ◇ *C'est leur fille aînée.* She's their oldest daughter.

la **fillette** NOUN
little girl

le **filleul** NOUN
godson

la **filleule** NOUN
goddaughter

le **film** NOUN
film
➔ **un film policier** a thriller
➔ **un film d'aventures** an adventure film
➔ **un film d'épouvante** a horror film

le **fils** NOUN
son

la **fin** NOUN
see also **fin** ADJECTIVE
end
➔ **sans fin** endless

fin ADJECTIVE
see also **fin** NOUN
fine
➔ **des fines herbes** mixed herbs

la **finale** NOUN
final ◇ *les quarts de finale* the quarter finals

finalement ADVERB
1 *at last* ◇ *Nous sommes finalement arrivés.* At last we arrived.

2 *after all* ◇ *Finalement, tu avais raison.* You were right after all.

fini ADJECTIVE
finished

finir VERB
to finish ◇ *Le cours finit à onze heures.* The lesson finishes at 11 o'clock. ◇ *Je viens de finir ce livre.* I've just finished this book.
➔ **Il a fini par se décider.** He made up his mind in the end.

finlandais ADJECTIVE, NOUN
Finnish ◇ *Ils parlent finlandais.* They speak Finnish.
➔ **un Finlandais** a Finn (*man*)
➔ **une Finlandaise** a Finn (*woman*)
➔ **les Finlandais** the Finnish

la **Finlande** NOUN
Finland

la **firme** NOUN
firm

fis VERB *see* **faire**

la **fissure** NOUN
crack

fit VERB *see* **faire**

fixe ADJECTIVE
1 *steady* ◇ *Il n'a pas d'emploi fixe.* He hasn't got a steady job.
2 *set* ◇ *Il mange toujours à heures fixes.* He always eats at set times.
➔ **un menu à prix fixe** a set menu

fixer VERB
1 *to fix* ◇ *Les volets sont fixés avec des crochets.* The shutters are fixed with hooks. ◇ *Nous avons fixé une heure pour nous retrouver.* We fixed a time to meet.
2 *to stare at* ◇ *Ne fixe pas les gens comme ça!* Don't stare at people like that!

le **flacon** NOUN
bottle ◇ *un flacon de parfum* a bottle of perfume

le **flageolet** NOUN
small haricot bean

flamand ADJECTIVE, NOUN
(FEM SING **flamande**)
1 *Flemish* ◇ *Il parle flamand chez lui.* He speaks Flemish at home.
2 *Fleming* (*Dutch-speaking Belgian*)
➔ **les Flamands** the Dutch-speaking Belgians

flambé ADJECTIVE
➔ **des bananes flambées** flambéed bananas

la **flamme** NOUN
flame
➔ **en flammes** on fire

le **flan** NOUN
baked custard

flâner VERB
to stroll

la **flaque** NOUN
puddle (*of water*)

le **flash** NOUN
(PL les **flashes**)
flash (*of camera*)
➔ **un flash d'information** a newsflash

flatter VERB
to flatter

la **flèche** NOUN
arrow

les **fléchettes** FEM NOUN
darts ◇ *jouer aux fléchettes* to play darts

la **fleur** NOUN
flower

fleuri ADJECTIVE
1 *full of flowers* ◇ *Son jardin était très fleuri.* Her garden was full of flowers.
2 *flowery* ◇ *un papier peint fleuri* flowery wallpaper

fleurir VERB
to flower ◇ *Cette plante fleurit en automne.* This plant flowers in autumn.

le/la **fleuriste** NOUN
florist

le **fleuve** NOUN
river

le **flic** (*informal*) NOUN
cop

le **flipper** NOUN
pinball machine

flirter VERB
to flirt

le **flocon** NOUN
flake

flotter VERB
to float

flou ADJECTIVE
blurred

le **fluor** NOUN
➔ **le dentifrice au fluor** fluoride toothpaste

la **flûte** NOUN
flute ◇ *Je joue de la flûte.* I play the flute.
➔ **Flûte!** (*informal*) Heck!

la **foi** NOUN
faith

le **foie** NOUN
liver
➔ **une crise de foie** a stomach upset

le **foin** NOUN
hay
➔ **un rhume des foins** hay fever

la **foire** NOUN
fair

F

la **fois** NOUN
time ◇ *la première fois* the first time ◇ *deux fois deux font quatre* 2 times 2 is 4
- **une fois** once
- **deux fois** twice ◇ *deux fois plus de gens* twice as many people
- **une fois que** once ◇ *Tu te sentiras mieux une fois que tu auras mangé.* You'll feel better once you've had something to eat.
- **à la fois** at once ◇ *Je ne peux pas faire deux choses à la fois.* I can't do two things at once.

la **folie** NOUN
madness ◇ *C'est de la folie pure!* It's absolute madness!
- **faire une folie** to be extravagant

folklorique ADJECTIVE
folk ◇ *de la musique folklorique* folk music

folle ADJECTIVE
(MASC SING **fou**)
mad

foncé ADJECTIVE
dark ◇ *bleu foncé* dark blue

foncer VERB (*informal*)
- **Je vais foncer à la boulangerie.** I'm just going to dash to the baker's.

la **fonction** NOUN
function
- **une voiture de fonction** a company car

le/la **fonctionnaire** NOUN
civil servant

fonctionner VERB
to work

le **fond** NOUN
1 *bottom* ◇ *Mon porte-monnaie est au fond de mon sac.* My purse is at the bottom of my bag.
2 *end* ◇ *Les toilettes sont au fond du couloir.* The toilets are at the end of the corridor.
- **dans le fond** all things considered ◇ *Dans le fond, ce n'est pas si grave.* All things considered, it's not that bad.

fonder VERB
to found

fondre VERB
to melt ◇ *La tablette de chocolat a fondu dans ma poche.* The bar of chocolate melted in my pocket.
- **fondre en larmes** to burst into tears

fondu ADJECTIVE
- **du beurre fondu** melted butter

font VERB *see* **faire**

la **fontaine** NOUN
fountain

le **foot** NOUN (*informal*)
football

le **football** NOUN
football ◇ *jouer au football* to play football

le **footballeur** NOUN
footballer

le **footing** NOUN
jogging ◇ *faire du footing* to go jogging

forain ADJECTIVE
see also forain NOUN
- **une fête foraine** a funfair

le **forain** NOUN
see also forain ADJECTIVE
fairground worker

la **force** NOUN
strength ◇ *Je n'ai pas beaucoup de force dans les bras.* I haven't got much strength in my arms.
- **à force de** by ◇ *Il a grossi à force de manger autant.* He got fat by eating so much.
- **de force** by force ◇ *Ils lui ont enlevé son pistolet de force.* They took the gun from him by force.

forcé ADJECTIVE
forced ◇ *un sourire forcé* a forced smile
- **C'est forcé.** (*informal*) It's inevitable.

forcément ADVERB
- **Ça devait forcément arriver.** That was bound to happen.
- **pas forcément** not necessarily

la **forêt** NOUN
forest

le **forfait** NOUN
all-in price
- **C'est compris dans le forfait.** It's included in the price.

la **formalité** NOUN
formality ◇ *Ce n'est qu'une simple formalité.* It's just a formality.

le **format** NOUN
size

la **formation** NOUN
training ◇ *la formation professionnelle* vocational training
- **Il a une formation d'ingénieur.** He is a trained engineer.

la **forme** NOUN
shape
- **être en forme** to be in good shape
- **Je ne suis pas en forme aujourd'hui.** I'm not feeling too good today.
- **Tu as l'air en forme.** You're looking well.

formellement ADVERB
strictly ◇ *Il est formellement interdit de fumer dans les couloirs.* It is strictly

forbidden to smoke in the corridors.

former VERB
to form

formidable ADJECTIVE
great

formulaire NOUN
form

fort ADJECTIVE, ADVERB
1 *strong* ◇ *Le café est trop fort.* The coffee's too strong.
2 *good* ◇ *Il est très fort en espagnol.* He's very good at Spanish.
3 *loud* ◇ *Est-ce vous pouvez parler plus fort?* Can you speak louder?
◆ **frapper fort** to hit hard

fortifiant NOUN
tonic (*medicine*)

fortune NOUN
fortune
◆ **de fortune** makeshift ◇ *Ils ont traversé la rivière sur un radeau de fortune.* They crossed the river on a makeshift raft.

fossé NOUN
ditch

fou ADJECTIVE
(FEM SING **folle**)
mad
◆ **Il y a un monde fou sur la plage!** (*informal*) There are loads of people on the beach!
◆ **attraper le fou rire** to get the giggles

foudre NOUN
lightning ◇ *L'arbre a été frappé par la foudre.* The tree was struck by lightning.

foudroyant ADJECTIVE
instant ◇ *un succès foudroyant* an instant hit

fouet NOUN
whisk

fougère NOUN
fern

fouiller VERB
to rummage

fouillis NOUN
mess ◇ *Il y a du fouillis dans sa chambre.* His bedroom is a mess.

foulard NOUN
scarf ◇ *un foulard en soie* a silk scarf

foule NOUN
crowd
◆ **une foule de** masses of ◇ *J'ai une foule de choses à faire ce week-end.* I've got masses of things to do this weekend.

four NOUN
oven ◇ *un four à micro-ondes* a microwave oven

fourchette NOUN
fork

fourmi NOUN
ant
◆ **avoir des fourmis dans les jambes** to have pins and needles

fourneau NOUN
(PL **les fourneaux**)
stove

fourni ADJECTIVE
thick (*beard, hair*)

fournir VERB
to supply

fournitures FEM NOUN
◆ **les fournitures scolaires** school stationery

fourré ADJECTIVE
filled ◇ *un gâteau fourré à la confiture d'abricot* a cake filled with apricot jam

fourrer (*informal*) VERB
to put ◇ *Où est-ce que tu as fourré mon passeport?* Where have you put my passport?

fourre-tout NOUN
(PL **les fourre-tout**)
holdall

fourrure NOUN
fur ◇ *un manteau de fourrure* a fur coat

foutre VERB (*rude*)
to do ◇ *Qu'est-ce qu'il fout?* What the hell is he doing?
◆ **Je n'en ai rien à foutre!** I don't give a damn!

foutu ADJECTIVE (*rude*)
1 *knackered* ◇ *Mon stylo est foutu.* My pen's knackered.
2 *bloody* ◇ *Qu'est-ce que j'ai fait de ce foutu stylo?* Where did I put that bloody pen?

foyer NOUN
home ◇ *dans la plupart des foyers français* in most French homes
◆ **un foyer de jeunes** a youth club

fracture NOUN
fracture

fragile ADJECTIVE
fragile ◇ *Attention, c'est fragile!* Be careful, it's fragile!

fragilité NOUN
fragility

fraîche ADJECTIVE *see* **frais**

fraîcheur NOUN
1 *cool* ◇ *la fraîcheur du soir* the cool of the evening
2 *freshness* ◇ *Je ne suis pas sûre de la fraîcheur du poisson.* I'm not sure about the freshness of the fish.

frais ADJECTIVE
(FEM SING **fraîche**)

PTO

see also frais NOUN

1 *fresh* ◇ *des œufs frais* fresh eggs ◇ *Cette salade n'est pas très fraîche.* This lettuce isn't very fresh.

2 *chilly* ◇ *Il fait un peu frais ce soir.* It's a bit chilly this evening.

3 *cool* ◇ *des boissons fraîches* cool drinks

- **"servir frais"** "serve chilled"
- **mettre au frais** to put in a cool place

les **frais** MASC NOUN

see also frais ADJECTIVE

expenses

la **fraise** NOUN

strawberry ◇ *une fraise des bois* a wild strawberry

la **framboise** NOUN

raspberry

franc ADJECTIVE

(FEM SING **franche**)

see also franc NOUN

frank

le **franc** NOUN

see also franc ADJECTIVE

franc

The franc *is the unit of currency in France, Belgium, Switzerland and many former French colonies; it is divided into 100* centimes.

français ADJECTIVE, NOUN

(FEM SING **française**)

French ◇ *Il parle français couramment.* He speaks French fluently.

- **un Français** a Frenchman
- **une Française** a Frenchwoman
- **les Français** the French

la **France** NOUN

France

- **en France (1)** in France ◇ *Je suis né en France.* I was born in France.
- **en France (2)** to France ◇ *Je pars en France pour Noël.* I'm going to France for Christmas.

franche ADJECTIVE *see* **franc**

franchement ADVERB

1 *frankly* ◇ *Il m'a parlé franchement.* He spoke to me frankly.

2 *really* ◇ *C'est franchement mauvais.* It's really bad.

franchir VERB

to get over

la **franchise** NOUN

frankness

francophone ADJECTIVE

French-speaking

la **frange** NOUN

fringe

la **frangipane** NOUN

almond cream

frapper VERB

to strike ◇ *Il l'a frappée au visage.* He struck her in the face. ◇ *Son air fatigué m'a frappé.* I was struck by how tired she looked.

fredonner VERB

to hum

le **freezer** NOUN

freezing compartment

le **frein** NOUN

brake

- **le frein à main** handbrake

freiner VERB

to brake

frêle ADJECTIVE

frail

le **frelon** NOUN

hornet

frémir VERB

shudder ◇ *Cette idée me fait frémir.* The idea makes me shudder.

fréquemment ADVERB

frequently

fréquent ADJECTIVE

frequent

fréquenté ADJECTIVE

busy ◇ *une rue très fréquentée* a very busy street

- **un bar mal fréquenté** a rough pub

fréquenter VERB

to see (*person*) ◇ *Je ne le fréquente pas beaucoup.* I don't see him often.

le **frère** NOUN

brother

le **friand** NOUN

- **un friand au fromage** a cheese puff

la **friandise** NOUN

sweet

le **fric** NOUN (*informal*)

cash

le **frigidaire ®** NOUN

refrigerator

le **frigo** NOUN (*informal*)

fridge

frileux ADJECTIVE

(FEM SING **frileuse**)

- **être frileux** to feel the cold ◇ *Je suis très frileuse.* I really feel the cold.

frimer VERB (*informal*)

to show off

les **fringues** FEM NOUN (*informal*)

clothes

fripé ADJECTIVE

crumpled

frire VERB

- **faire frire** to fry ◇ *Faites frire les boulettes dans de l'huile très chaude.* Fry the meatballs in very hot oil.

frisé ADJECTIVE

curly ◇ *Elle est très frisée.* She's got

very curly hair.

frisson NOUN
shiver

frissonner VERB
to shiver

frit ADJECTIVE
fried ◇ *du poisson frit* fried fish

frites FEM NOUN
chips

friture NOUN
1 *fried food* ◇ *On lui a conseillé d'éviter les fritures.* He's been advised to avoid fried food.
2 *fried fish* ◇ *Nous allons faire une friture ce soir.* We are going to have fried fish tonight.

froid ADJECTIVE
see also froid NOUN
cold ◇ *Ça me laisse froid.* It leaves me cold. ◇ *de la viande froide* cold meat

froid NOUN
see also froid ADJECTIVE
cold
- **Il fait froid.** It's cold.
- **avoir froid** to be cold ◇ *Est-ce que tu as froid?* Are you cold?

froisser VERB
1 *to crease* ◇ *Ce tissu se froisse très facilement.* This material creases very easily.
2 *to take offence* ◇ *Paul se froisse très facilement.* Paul's very quick to take offence.
- **se froisser un muscle** to strain a muscle

frôler VERB
1 *to brush against* ◇ *Le chat m'a frôlé au passage.* The cat brushed against me as it went past.
2 *to narrowly avoid* ◇ *Nous avons frôlé la catastrophe.* We narrowly avoided disaster.

le **fromage** NOUN
cheese
- **du fromage blanc** soft white cheese

le **froment** NOUN
wheat
- **une crêpe de froment** a pancake (*made with wheat flour*)

froncer VERB
- **froncer les sourcils** to frown

le **front** NOUN
forehead

la **frontière** NOUN
border

frotter VERB
to rub ◇ *se frotter les yeux* to rub one's eyes
- **frotter une allumette** to strike a match

le **fruit** NOUN
fruit
- **un fruit** a piece of fruit ◇ *Est-ce que vous voulez manger un fruit?* Would you like some fruit?
- **les fruits de mer** seafood

fruité ADJECTIVE
fruity

frustrer VERB
to frustrate

la **fugue** NOUN
- **faire une fugue** to run away

fuir VERB
1 *to flee* ◇ *fuir devant un danger* to flee from danger
2 *to drip* ◇ *Le robinet fuit.* The tap's dripping.

la **fuite** NOUN
1 *leak* ◇ *Il y a une fuite de gaz.* There is a gas leak.
2 *flight* (*escape*)
- **être en fuite** to be on the run

fumé ADJECTIVE
smoked ◇ *du saumon fumé* smoked salmon

la **fumée** NOUN
smoke

fumer VERB
to smoke

le **fumeur** NOUN
smoker

la **fumeuse** NOUN
smoker

fur
- **au fur et à mesure** ADVERB
as you go along ◇ *Je vérifie mon travail au fur et à mesure.* I check my work as I go along.
- **au fur et à mesure que** as ◇ *Je réponds à mon courrier au fur et à mesure que je le reçois.* I answer my mail as I receive it.

la **fureur** NOUN
fury
- **faire fureur** to be all the rage ◇ *Ce genre de sac fait fureur actuellement.* This sort of bag is all the rage at the moment.

furieux ADJECTIVE
(FEM SING **furieuse**)
furious

le **furoncle** NOUN
boil (*on skin*)

fus VERB *see* **être**

le **fuseau** NOUN
(PL les **fuseaux**)
ski pants

la **fusée** NOUN
rocket

F

le **fusil** NOUN
gun

fut VERB *see* **être**

futé ADJECTIVE
crafty

le **futur** NOUN
future

G

gâcher VERB
to waste ◇ *Je n'aime pas gâcher la nourriture.* I don't like to waste food.

gâchis NOUN
waste

gaffe NOUN
- **faire une gaffe** to do something stupid
- **Fais gaffe!** (*informal*) Watch out!
◇ *Fais gaffe: la peinture est encore humide!* Watch out: the paint's still wet!

gage NOUN
forfeit (*in a game*) ◇ *recevoir un gage* to pay a forfeit

gagnant NOUN
winner

gagnante NOUN
winner

gagner VERB
to win ◇ *Qui a gagné?* Who won?
- **gagner du temps** to gain time
- **Il gagne bien sa vie.** He makes a good living.

gai ADJECTIVE
cheerful ◇ *Elle est très gaie.* She's very cheerful.

gaieté NOUN
cheerfulness

galerie NOUN
gallery ◇ *une galerie de peinture* an art gallery
- **une galerie marchande** a shopping arcade

galet NOUN
pebble

galette NOUN
1 *round flat cake* ◇ *une galette de blé noir* a buckwheat pancake
2 *biscuit* ◇ *des galettes pur beurre* shortbread biscuits
- **la galette des Rois**

A galette des Rois *is a cake eaten on Twelfth Night containing a figurine. The person who finds it is the king (or queen) and gets a paper crown. They then choose someone else to be their queen (or king).*

Galles FEM NOUN
- **le pays de Galles** Wales
- **le prince de Galles** the Prince of Wales

gallois ADJECTIVE, NOUN
Welsh ◇ *un peintre gallois* a Welsh painter
- **un Gallois** a Welshman
- **une Galloise** a Welshwoman
- **les Gallois** the Welsh

le galop NOUN
gallop

galoper VERB
to gallop

le gamin NOUN (*informal*)
kid

la gamine NOUN (*informal*)
kid

la gamme NOUN
scale (*in music*) ◇ *Je dois faire des gammes tous les soirs.* I have to do my scales every night.
- **une gamme de produits** a range of products

gammée ADJECTIVE
- **la croix gammée** the swastika

le gant NOUN
glove ◇ *des gants en laine* woollen gloves
- **un gant de toilette** a face cloth

le garage NOUN
garage

le/la garagiste NOUN
1 *garage owner*
2 *mechanic*

la garantie NOUN
guarantee

garantir VERB
to guarantee

le garçon NOUN
1 *boy*
2 *waiter* (*in a café*)
- **un vieux garçon** a bachelor

le garde NOUN
see also la garde
1 *warder* (*in prison*)
2 *security man*
- **un garde du corps** a bodyguard

la garde NOUN
see also le garde
1 *guarding* ◇ *Il est chargé de la garde des prisonniers.* He's responsible for guarding the prisoners.
2 *guard* ◇ *la relève de la garde* the changing of the guard
- **être de garde** to be on duty ◇ *Mon père est de garde ce soir.* My father is on duty tonight. ◇ *La pharmacie de garde ce week-end est...* The duty chemist this weekend is...
- **mettre en garde** to warn ◇ *Elle m'a mis en garde contre les pickpockets.* She warned me about pickpockets.

garder VERB
1 *to keep* ◇ *Est-ce que tu as gardé toutes ses lettres?* Have you kept all his letters?

PTO

2 *to look after* ◇ *Je garde ma nièce samedi après-midi.* I'm looking after my niece on Saturday afternoon.
3 *to guard* ◇ *Ils ont pris un gros chien pour garder la maison.* They got a big dog to guard the house.
◆ **se garder** to keep ◇ *Ces crêpes se gardent bien.* These pancakes keep well.

la **garderie** NOUN
nursery

la **garde-robe** NOUN
wardrobe (*clothes*) ◇ *Elle a une garde-robe bien fournie.* She's got an extensive wardrobe.

le **gardien** NOUN
1 *caretaker*
2 *attendant* (*in a museum*)
◆ **un gardien de but** a goalkeeper
◆ **un gardien de la paix** a police officer

la **gardienne** NOUN
1 *caretaker*
2 *attendant* (*in a museum*)

la **gare** NOUN
see also gare EXCLAMATION
station ◇ *la gare routière* the bus station

gare EXCLAMATION
see also gare NOUN
◆ **Gare aux serpents!** Watch out for snakes!

garer VERB
to park
◆ **se garer** to park ◇ *Où t'es-tu garé?* Where are you parked?

garni ADJECTIVE
◆ **un plat garni** a dish served with accompaniments (*vegetables, chips, rice etc*)

le **gars** NOUN (*informal*)
guy

gaspiller VERB
to waste

le **gâteau** NOUN
(PL les **gâteaux**)
cake
◆ **les gâteaux secs** biscuits

gâter VERB
to spoil ◇ *Il aime gâter ses petits enfants.* He likes to spoil his grandchildren.
◆ **se gâter** to go bad ◇ *Le temps va se gâter.* The weather's going to break.

gauche ADJECTIVE
see also gauche NOUN
left ◇ *le bras gauche* the left arm ◇ *le côté gauche* the left-hand side

la **gauche** NOUN
see also gauche ADJECTIVE
left ◇ *sur votre gauche* on your left
◆ **à gauche (1)** on the left ◇ *la deuxième rue à gauche* the second street on the left
◆ **à gauche (2)** to the left ◇ *à gauche de l'armoire* to the left of the cupboard ◇ *Tournez à gauche.* Turn left.
◆ **la voie de gauche** the left-hand lane
◆ **la gauche** the left (*in politics*) ◇ *Il est de gauche.* He's left-wing.

gaucher ADJECTIVE
(FEM SING **gauchère**)
left-handed

la **gaufre** NOUN
waffle

la **gaufrette** NOUN
wafer

le **Gaulois** NOUN
Gaul ◇ *Astérix le Gaulois* Asterix the Gaul

gaulois ADJECTIVE
Gallic

le **gaz** NOUN
gas

gazeux ADJECTIVE
(FEM SING **gazeuse**)
◆ **une boisson gazeuse** a fizzy drink
◆ **de l'eau gazeuse** sparkling water

le **gazole** NOUN
diesel (*fuel*)

le **gazon** NOUN
lawn

le **géant** NOUN
giant

le **gel** NOUN
frost

la **gelée** NOUN
jelly

geler VERB
to freeze ◇ *Il a gelé cette nuit.* There was a frost last night.

la **gélule** NOUN
capsule (*containing medicine*)

les **Gémeaux** MASC NOUN
Gemini ◇ *Henry est Gémeaux.* Henry's Gemini.

gémir VERB
to moan

gênant ADJECTIVE
awkward ◇ *un silence gênant* an awkward silence

la **gencive** NOUN
gum (*in mouth*)

le **gendarme** NOUN
policeman

la **gendarmerie** NOUN
1 *police force*
2 *police station* ◇ *Vous devriez porter plainte à la gendarmerie.* You should go to the police station and report it.

le **gendre** NOUN

son-in-law

gêné ADJECTIVE
embarrassed

gêner VERB
1 *to bother* ◇ *Je ne voudrais pas vous gêner.* I don't want to bother you.
2 *to feel awkward* ◇ *Son regard la gênait.* The way he was looking at her made her feel awkward.

général ADJECTIVE
(MASC PL **généraux**)
see also général NOUN
general
◆ **en général** usually

le **général** NOUN
(PL les **généraux**)
see also général ADJECTIVE
general

généralement ADVERB
generally

la **généraliste** NOUN
family doctor

la **génération** NOUN
generation

généreux ADJECTIVE
(FEM SING **généreuse**)
generous

la **générosité** NOUN
generosity

le **genêt** NOUN
broom (*bush*)

la **génétique** NOUN
genetics

Genève NOUN
Geneva

génial ADJECTIVE (*informal*)
(MASC PL **géniaux**)
great ◇ *Le film d'hier soir était génial.* The film last night was great.

le **genou** NOUN
(PL les **genoux**)
knee ◇ *Elle est à genoux.* She's on her knees. ◇ *se mettre à genoux* to kneel down

le **genre** NOUN
kind ◇ *C'est un genre de gâteau à la crème.* It's a kind of cream cake.

les **gens** MASC NOUN
people

gentil ADJECTIVE
(FEM SING **gentille**)
1 *nice* ◇ *Nos voisins sont très gentils.* Our neighbours are very nice.
2 *kind* ◇ *C'était très gentil de votre part.* It was very kind of you.

la **gentillesse** NOUN
kindness ◇ *Je l'ai remerciée de sa gentillesse.* I thanked her for her kindness. ◇ *C'est un homme d'une grande gentillesse.* He is a very nice man.

gentiment ADVERB
1 *nicely* ◇ *Demande-le lui gentiment.* Ask him nicely.
2 *kindly* ◇ *Ils nous ont gentiment proposé de rester dîner.* They kindly invited us to stay for dinner.

la **géographie** NOUN
geography

la **géométrie** NOUN
geometry

gérer VERB
to manage

germain ADJECTIVE
◆ **un cousin germain** a first cousin

le **geste** NOUN
gesture ◇ *Il a voulu faire un geste.* He wanted to make a gesture.
◆ **Ne faites pas un geste!** Don't move!

la **gestion** NOUN
management

la **gifle** NOUN
slap across the face

gifler VERB
to slap across the face

gigantesque ADJECTIVE
gigantic

le **gigot** NOUN
leg of lamb

le **gilet** NOUN
1 *waistcoat* ◇ *un gilet en cuir* a leather waistcoat
2 *cardigan* ◇ *un gilet tricoté main* a hand-knitted cardigan
◆ **un gilet de sauvetage** a life jacket

le **gingembre** NOUN
ginger

la **girafe** NOUN
giraffe

le **gitan** NOUN
gipsy

la **gitane** NOUN
gipsy

le **gîte** NOUN
◆ **un gîte rural** a holiday house

la **glace** NOUN
1 *ice* ◇ *L'étang est recouvert de glace.* The pond is covered with ice.
2 *ice cream* ◇ *une glace à la fraise* a strawberry ice cream
3 *mirror* ◇ *Il se regarde souvent dans la glace.* He often looks at himself in the mirror.

glacé ADJECTIVE
1 *icy* ◇ *Il soufflait un vent glacé.* An icy wind was blowing.
2 *iced* ◇ *un thé glacé* an iced tea

glacial ADJECTIVE

PTO

(MASC PL **glaciaux**)
icy

le **glaçon** NOUN
ice cube

glissant ADJECTIVE
slippery

glisser VERB
1 *to slip* ◇ *Il a glissé sur une peau de banane.* He slipped on a banana skin.
2 *to be slippery* ◇ *Attention, ça glisse!* Watch out, it's slippery!

global ADJECTIVE
(MASC PL **globaux**)
total ◇ *la somme globale* the total amount

la **gloire** NOUN
glory

la **godasse** NOUN (*informal*)
shoe

le **goéland** NOUN
seagull

le **golf** NOUN
1 *golf* ◇ *Il joue au golf.* He plays golf.
2 *golf course* ◇ *un golf dix-huit trous* an 18-hole golf course

le **golfe** NOUN
gulf
◆ **le golfe de Gascogne** the Bay of Biscay

la **gomme** NOUN
rubber

gommer VERB
to rub out

gonfler VERB
1 *to blow up* ◇ *gonfler un ballon* to blow up a balloon
2 *to pump up* ◇ *Tu devrais gonfler ton pneu arrière.* You should pump up your back tyre.

la **gorge** NOUN
1 *throat* ◇ *J'ai mal à la gorge.* I've got a sore throat.
2 *gorge* ◇ *les gorges du Tarn* the Tarn gorges

la **gorgée** NOUN
sip ◇ *une gorgée d'eau* a sip of water

le **gorille** NOUN
gorilla

le/la **gosse** NOUN (*informal*)
kid

le **goudron** NOUN
tar

le **gouffre** NOUN
chasm
◆ **Cette voiture est un vrai gouffre!** This car eats up money!

la **gourde** NOUN
water bottle

gourmand ADJECTIVE
greedy

la **gourmandise** NOUN
greed

la **gousse** NOUN
◆ **une gousse d'ail** a clove of garlic

le **goût** NOUN
taste ◇ *Ça n'a pas de goût.* It's got no taste. ◇ *Elle a très bon goût.* She's got very good taste.

goûter VERB
see also goûter NOUN
1 *to taste* ◇ *Goûte donc ce fromage: tu verras comme il est bon!* Have a taste of this cheese: you'll see how nice it is!
2 *to have a snack* (*in the afternoon*) ◇ *Les enfants goûtent généralement vers quatre heures.* The children usually have a snack around 4 o'clock.

le **goûter** NOUN
see also goûter VERB
afternoon snack

la **goutte** NOUN
drop

le **gouvernement** NOUN
government

gouverner VERB
to govern

la **grâce** NOUN
◆ **grâce à** thanks to ◇ *Je suis arrivé à l'heure grâce à toi.* I arrived on time thanks to you.

gracieux ADJECTIVE
(FEM SING **gracieuse**)
graceful

les **gradins** MASC NOUN
terraces (*in stadium*)

graduel ADJECTIVE
(FEM SING **graduelle**)
gradual

le **grain** NOUN
grain ◇ *un grain de sable* a grain of sand
◆ **un grain de beauté** a beauty spot
◆ **un grain de café** a coffee bean
◆ **un grain de raisin** a grape

la **graine** NOUN
seed

la **graisse** NOUN
fat

la **grammaire** NOUN
grammar

le **gramme** NOUN
gramme

grand ADJECTIVE, ADVERB
1 *tall* ◇ *Il est grand pour son âge.* He's tall for his age.
2 *big* ◇ *une grande valise* a big suitcase ◇ *C'est sa grande sœur.* She's his big sister.
◆ **une grande personne** a grown-up

3 *long* ◇ *un grand voyage* a long journey
- **les grandes vacances** the summer holidays

4 *great* ◇ *C'est un grand ami à moi.* He's a great friend of mine.
- **un grand magasin** a department store
- **une grande surface** a hypermarket
- **les grandes écoles** top ranking colleges (*at university level*)
- **au grand air** out in the open air ◇ *Ça te fera beaucoup de bien d'être au grand air.* It'll be very good for you to be out in the open air.
- **grand ouvert** wide open

grand-chose NOUN
- **pas grand-chose** not much ◇ *Je n'ai pas acheté grand-chose au marché.* I didn't buy much at the market. ◇ *Voici un petit cadeau: ce n'est pas grand-chose.* Here's a little present: it's nothing much.

la **Grande-Bretagne** NOUN
Britain

la **grandeur** NOUN
size

grandir VERB
to grow ◇ *Il a beaucoup grandi.* He's grown a lot.

la **grand-mère** NOUN
(PL les **grands-mères**)
grandmother

grand-peine
- **à grand-peine** ADVERB
with great difficulty

le **grand-père** NOUN
(PL les **grands-pères**)
grandfather

les **grands-parents** MASC NOUN
grandparents

la **grange** NOUN
barn

la **grappe** NOUN
- **une grappe de raisin** a bunch of grapes

gras ADJECTIVE
(FEM SING **grasse**)
1 *fatty* (*food*) ◇ *Évitez les aliments gras.* Avoid fatty foods.
2 *greasy* ◇ *des cheveux gras* greasy hair
3 *oily* ◇ *une peau grasse* oily skin
- **faire la grasse matinée** to have a lie-in

gratis ADJECTIVE, ADVERB
free ◇ *J'ai eu ce stylo gratis.* I got this pen free.

le **gratte-ciel** NOUN
(PL les **gratte-ciel**)
skyscraper

gratter VERB
1 *to scratch* ◇ *Ne gratte pas tes piqûres de moustiques!* Don't scratch your mosquito bites!
2 *to be itchy* ◇ *C'est épouvantable comme ça gratte!* It's terribly itchy!

gratuit ADJECTIVE
free ◇ *entrée gratuite* entrance free

grave ADJECTIVE
1 *serious* ◇ *une maladie grave* a serious illness ◇ *Il avait l'air grave.* He was looking serious.
2 *deep* ◇ *Il a une voix grave.* He's got a deep voice.
- **Ce n'est pas grave.** It doesn't matter. ◇ *J'ai oublié ma clé. – Ce n'est pas grave, j'ai la mienne.* I've forgotten my key. – It doesn't matter, I've got mine.

gravement ADVERB
seriously ◇ *Il a été gravement blessé.* He was seriously injured.

grec ADJECTIVE, NOUN
(FEM SING **grecque**)
Greek
- **J'apprends le grec.** I'm learning Greek.
- **un Grec** a Greek (*man*)
- **une Grecque** a Greek (*woman*)
- **les Grecs** the Greeks

la **Grèce** NOUN
Greece
- **en Grèce (1)** in Greece
- **en Grèce (2)** to Greece

la **grêle** NOUN
hail

grêler VERB
- **Il grêle.** It's hailing.

grelotter VERB
to shiver

la **grenade** NOUN
1 *pomegranate*
2 *grenade*

le **grenier** NOUN
attic

la **grenouille** NOUN
frog

la **grève** NOUN
1 *strike*
- **en grève** on strike ◇ *Les ouvriers sont en grève depuis dix jours.* The workers have been on strike for ten days.
- **faire grève** to be on strike

2 *shore* ◇ *Nous nous sommes promenés le long de la grève.* We went for a walk along the shore.

le/la **gréviste** NOUN
striker

grièvement ADVERB
- **grièvement blessé** seriously injured

la **griffe** NOUN
1 *claw* ◇ *Le chat m'a donné un coup*

PTO

de griffe. The cat scratched me.
2 *label* ◇ *la griffe d'un grand couturier* the label of a top designer

griffer VERB
to scratch ◇ *Le chat m'a griffé.* The cat scratched me.

grignoter VERB
to nibble

la **grillade** NOUN
grilled food ◇ *une grillade d'agneau* grilled lamb

la **grille** NOUN
1 *wire fence* ◇ *L'usine est entourée d'une haute grille.* The factory is surrounded by a high wire fence.
2 *metal gate* ◇ *Le facteur a sonné à la grille du jardin.* The postman rang at the garden gate.

le **grille-pain** NOUN
(PL les **grille-pain**)
toaster

griller VERB
1 *to toast*
- **du pain grillé** toast
2 *to grill* ◇ *des saucisses grillées* grilled sausages

la **grimace** NOUN
- **faire des grimaces** to make faces

grimper VERB
to climb

grincer VERB
to creak

grincheux ADJECTIVE
(FEM SING **grincheuse**)
grumpy

la **grippe** NOUN
flu
- **avoir la grippe** to have flu ◇ *J'ai eu une mauvaise grippe l'hiver dernier.* I had a bad attack of flu last winter.

grippé ADJECTIVE
- **être grippé** to have flu

gris ADJECTIVE
grey

le **Groenland** NOUN
Greenland

grogner VERB
1 *to growl* ◇ *Le chien a grogné quand je me suis approché de lui.* The dog growled when I went near it.
2 *to complain* ◇ *Arrête donc de grogner!* Stop complaining!

gronder VERB
- **se faire gronder** to get a telling off ◇ *Tu vas te faire gronder par ton père!* You're going to get a telling off from your father!

gros ADJECTIVE
(FEM SING **grosse**)
1 *big* ◇ *une grosse pomme* a big apple
2 *fat* ◇ *Je suis trop grosse pour porter ça!* I'm too fat to wear that!

la **groseille** NOUN
- **la groseille rouge** redcurrant
- **la groseille à maquereau** gooseberry

la **grossesse** NOUN
pregnancy

grossier ADJECTIVE
(FEM SING **grossière**)
rude ◇ *Ne sois pas si grossier!* Don't be so rude!
- **une erreur grossière** a bad mistake

grossir VERB
to put on weight ◇ *Il a beaucoup grossi.* He's put on a lot of weight.

grosso modo ADVERB
roughly ◇ *Dis-moi grosso modo ce que tu en penses.* Give me a rough idea what you think of it.

la **grotte** NOUN
cave

le **groupe** NOUN
group ◇ *votre groupe sanguin* your blood group

grouper VERB
to group ◇ *On nous a groupés dans différentes classes selon notre niveau.* We were grouped in different classes according to our level.
- **se grouper** to gather ◇ *Nous nous sommes groupés autour du feu.* We gathered round the fire.

le **guépard** NOUN
cheetah

la **guêpe** NOUN
wasp

guérir VERB
to recover ◇ *Il est maintenant complètement guéri.* He's now completely recovered.

la **guérison** NOUN
recovery

la **guerre** NOUN
war ◇ *en guerre* at war

guetter VERB
to look out for ◇ *Elle guette l'arrivée du facteur tous les matins.* She looks out for the postman every morning.

la **gueule** NOUN
mouth (*rude when used for people*) ◇ *Le chat a ramené une souris dans sa gueule.* The cat brought in a mouse in its mouth.
- **Ta gueule!** (*rude*) Shut your face!
- **avoir la gueule de bois** (*informal*) to have a hangover

gueuler (*informal*) VERB
to bawl

guichet NOUN
counter (*in bank, booking office*)

guide NOUN
guide

guider VERB
to guide

guidon NOUN
handlebars

guillemets MASC NOUN
inverted commas ◇ *entre guillemets* in inverted commas

guirlande NOUN
tinsel ◇ *Nous avons décoré le sapin de Noël avec des guirlandes.* We decorated the Christmas tree with tinsel.
◆ **des guirlandes en papier** paper chains

la **guitare** NOUN
guitar ◇ *Sais-tu jouer de la guitare?* Can you play the guitar?

le **gymnase** NOUN
gym ◇ *Le lycée a un nouveau gymnase.* The school's got a new gym.

la **gymnastique** NOUN
gymnastics ◇ *faire de la gymnastique* to do one's exercises

H

habile ADJECTIVE
skilful ◇ *Il est très habile de ses mains.* He is very clever with his hands.

habillé ADJECTIVE
1 *dressed* ◇ *Il n'est pas encore habillé.* He's not dressed yet.
2 *smart* ◇ *Cette robe fait très habillé.* This dress looks very smart.

s'**habiller** VERB
1 *to get dressed* ◇ *Je me suis rapidement habillé.* I got dressed quickly.
2 *to dress up* ◇ *Est-ce qu'il faut s'habiller pour la réception?* Do you have to dress up to go to the party?

l'**habitant** MASC NOUN
inhabitant ◇ *Les habitants du quartier sont contre ce projet.* The local people are against this plan.

l'**habitante** FEM NOUN
inhabitant

habiter VERB
to live ◇ *Il habite à Montpellier.* He lives in Montpellier.

les **habits** MASC NOUN
clothes

l'**habitude** FEM NOUN
habit ◇ *une mauvaise habitude* a bad habit
- **avoir l'habitude de quelque chose** to be used to something ◇ *Elle a l'habitude des enfants.* She's used to children. ◇ *Je n'ai pas l'habitude de parler en public.* I'm not used to speaking in public.
- **d'habitude** usually
- **comme d'habitude** as usual

habituel ADJECTIVE
(FEM SING **habituelle**)
usual

s'**habituer** VERB
- **s'habituer à quelque chose** to get used to something ◇ *Il faudra que tu t'habitues à te lever tôt.* You'll have to get used to getting up early.

le **hachis** NOUN
mince
- **le hachis Parmentier** shepherd's pie

la **haie** NOUN
hedge

la **haine** NOUN
hatred

haïr VERB
to hate

l'**haleine** FEM NOUN
breath ◇ *avoir mauvaise haleine* to have bad breath ◇ *être hors d'haleine* to be out of breath

les **halles** FEM NOUN
covered market

la **halte** NOUN
stop ◇ *faire halte* to make a stop
- **Halte!** Stop!

l'**haltérophilie** FEM NOUN
weightlifting

l'**hameçon** MASC NOUN
fish hook

le **hamster** NOUN
hamster

la **hanche** NOUN
hip

le **handball** NOUN
handball ◇ *jouer au handball* to play handball

le **handicapé** NOUN
handicapped man

la **handicapée** NOUN
handicapped woman

le **hareng** NOUN
herring
- **un hareng saur** a kipper

le **haricot** NOUN
bean
- **les haricots verts** runner beans
- **les haricots blancs** haricot beans

l'**harmonica** MASC NOUN
mouth organ

la **harpe** NOUN
harp

le **hasard** NOUN
coincidence ◇ *C'était un pur hasard.* It was pure coincidence.
- **au hasard** at random ◇ *Choisis un numéro au hasard.* Choose a number at random.
- **par hasard** by chance ◇ *Je l'ai rencontrée tout à fait par hasard au supermarché.* I met her at the supermarket quite by chance.
- **à tout hasard (1)** just in case ◇ *Prends un parapluie à tout hasard.* Take an umbrella just in case.
- **à tout hasard (2)** on the off chance ◇ *Je ne sais pas s'il est chez lui, mais je vais l'appeler à tout hasard.* I don't know if he's at home, but I'll phone on the off chance.

la **hâte** NOUN
- **à la hâte** hurriedly ◇ *Elle s'est habillée à la hâte.* She got dressed hurriedly.
- **J'ai hâte de te voir.** I can't wait to see you.

la **hausse** NOUN

1 *increase* ◇ *la hausse des prix* price increase
2 *rise* ◇ *On annonce une légère hausse de température.* The forecast is for a slight rise in temperature.

hausser VERB
- **hausser les épaules** to shrug one's shoulders

haut ADJECTIVE, ADVERB
see also haut NOUN
1 *high* ◇ *une haute montagne* a high mountain
2 *aloud* ◇ *penser tout haut* to think aloud

haut NOUN
see also haut ADJECTIVE
top
- **un mur de trois mètres de haut** a wall 3 metres high
- **en haut (1)** upstairs ◇ *La salle de bain est en haut.* The bathroom is upstairs.
- **en haut (2)** at the top ◇ *Le nid est tout en haut de l'arbre.* The nest is right at the top of the tree.

la **hauteur** NOUN
height

le **haut-parleur** NOUN
loudspeaker

l'**hebdomadaire** MASC NOUN
weekly (*magazine*)

héberger VERB
to put up ◇ *Mon cousin a dit qu'il nous hébergerait.* My cousin said he would put us up.

hélas ADVERB
unfortunately ◇ *Hélas, il ne restait plus de billets.* Unfortunately there were no tickets left.

l'**hélicoptère** MASC NOUN
helicopter

l'**hémorragie** FEM NOUN
haemorrhage

l'**herbe** FEM NOUN
grass
- **les herbes de Provence** mixed herbs

le **hérisson** NOUN
hedgehog

hériter VERB
to inherit

l'**héritier** MASC NOUN
heir

l'**héritière** FEM NOUN
heiress

hermétique ADJECTIVE
airtight

l'**héroïne** FEM NOUN
1 *heroine* ◇ *l'héroïne du roman* the heroine of the novel
2 *heroin* (*drug*)

le **héros** NOUN
hero

l'**hésitation** FEM NOUN
hesitation

hésiter VERB
to hesitate ◇ *Il n'a pas hésité à nous aider.* He didn't hesitate to help us. ◇ *J'ai hésité entre le pull vert et le cardigan jaune.* I couldn't decide between the green pullover and the yellow cardigan. ◇ *Est-ce que tu viens ce soir?–J'hésite...* Are you coming this evening?–I'm not sure...
- **sans hésiter** without hesitating

l'**heure** FEM NOUN
1 *hour* ◇ *Le trajet dure six heures.* The journey lasts six hours.
2 *time* ◇ *Vous avez l'heure?* Have you got the time?
- **Quelle heure est-il?** What time is it?
- **À quelle heure?** What time? ◇ *À quelle heure arrivons-nous?* What time do we arrive?
- **deux heures du matin** 2 o'clock in the morning
- **être à l'heure** to be on time
- **une heure de français** a period of French

heureusement ADVERB
luckily ◇ *Heureusement qu'il n'a pas été blessé.* Luckily he wasn't hurt.

heureux ADJECTIVE
(FEM SING **heureuse**)
happy

heurter VERB
to hit

l'**hexagone** MASC NOUN
hexagon
- **l'Hexagone** France
France is often referred to as l'Hexagone *because of its six-sided shape.*

le **hibou** NOUN
(PL **les hiboux**)
owl

hier ADVERB
yesterday
- **avant-hier** the day before yesterday

la **hi-fi** NOUN
stereo
- **une chaîne hi-fi** a stereo system

hippique ADJECTIVE
- **un club hippique** a riding centre
- **un concours hippique** a horse show

l'**hippopotame** MASC NOUN
hippopotamus

l'**hirondelle** FEM NOUN
swallow (*bird*)

l'**histoire** FEM NOUN
1 *history* ◇ *un cours d'histoire* a

PTO

history lesson
2 *story* ◇ *Ce roman raconte l'histoire de deux enfants.* This novel tells the story of two children.
◆ **Ne fais pas d'histoires!** Don't make a fuss!

historique ADJECTIVE
historic ◇ *un monument historique* a historic monument

l'**hiver** MASC NOUN
winter
◆ **en hiver** in winter

la **HLM** NOUN (= *habitation à loyer modéré*)
council flat
◆ **des HLM** council housing

le **hockey** NOUN
hockey
◆ **le hockey sur glace** ice hockey

hollandais ADJECTIVE, NOUN
Dutch
◆ **J'apprends le hollandais.** I'm learning Dutch.
◆ **un Hollandais** a Dutch man
◆ **une Hollandaise** a Dutch woman
◆ **les Hollandais** the Dutch

la **Hollande** NOUN
Holland
◆ **en Hollande (1)** in Holland
◆ **en Hollande (2)** to Holland

le **homard** NOUN
lobster

homéopathique ADJECTIVE
homeopathic

l'**hommage** MASC NOUN
tribute

l'**homme** MASC NOUN
man
◆ **un homme d'affaires** a businessman

homosexuel ADJECTIVE
(FEM SING **homosexuelle**)
homosexual

la **Hongrie** NOUN
Hungary

hongrois ADJECTIVE
Hungarian

honnête ADJECTIVE
honest

l'**honnêteté** FEM NOUN
honesty

l'**honneur** MASC NOUN
honour

la **honte** NOUN
shame ◇ *avoir honte de quelque chose* to be ashamed of something

l'**hôpital** MASC NOUN
(PL les **hôpitaux**)
hospital

le **hoquet** NOUN
◆ **avoir le hoquet** to have hiccups

l'**horaire** MASC NOUN
timetable
◆ **les horaires de train** the train timetable

l'**horizon** MASC NOUN
horizon

horizontal ADJECTIVE
(MASC PL **horizontaux**)
horizontal

l'**horloge** FEM NOUN
clock

l'**horreur** FEM NOUN
horror ◇ *un film d'horreur* a horror film
◆ **avoir horreur de** to hate ◇ *J'ai horreur du chou.* I hate cabbage.

horrible ADJECTIVE
horrible

hors PREPOSITION
◆ **hors de** out of ◇ *Elle est hors de danger maintenant.* She's out of danger now.
◆ **hors taxes** duty-free

le **hors-d'œuvre** NOUN
(PL les **hors-d'œuvre**)
starter (*food*)

hospitalier ADJECTIVE
(FEM SING **hospitalière**)
hospitable ◇ *Ils sont très hospitaliers.* They're very hospitable.
◆ **les services hospitaliers** hospital services

l'**hospitalité** FEM NOUN
hospitality

hostile ADJECTIVE
hostile

l'**hôte** MASC/FEM NOUN
1 *host* ◇ *N'oubliez pas de remercier vos hôtes.* Don't forget to thank your hosts.
2 *guest* ◇ *Cette ferme accueille des hôtes payants.* This farm takes paying guests.

l'**hôtel** MASC NOUN
hotel
◆ **l'hôtel de ville** the town hall

l'**hôtesse** FEM NOUN
hostess
◆ **une hôtesse de l'air** a stewardess

le **houx** NOUN
holly

l'**huile** FEM NOUN
oil
◆ **l'huile solaire** suntan oil

huit NUMBER
eight ◇ *Il est huit heures du matin.* It's eight in the morning. ◇ *Il a huit ans.* He's eight.
◆ **le huit février** the eighth of February

huitaine NOUN
- **une huitaine de jours** about a week
  - *Nous serons de retour dans une huitaine de jours.* We'll be back in about a week.

huitième ADJECTIVE
eighth ◇ *au huitième étage* on the eighth floor

huître FEM NOUN
oyster

humain ADJECTIVE
see also humain NOUN
human

humain MASC NOUN
see also humain ADJECTIVE
human being

humeur FEM NOUN
mood ◇ *Il est de bonne humeur.* He's in a good mood. ◇ *Elle était de mauvaise humeur.* She was in a bad mood.

humide ADJECTIVE
damp ◇ *L'herbe est humide.* The grass is damp. ◇ *un climat humide* a damp climate

humilier VERB
to humiliate

humoristique ADJECTIVE
humorous
- **des dessins humoristiques** cartoons

l'**humour** MASC NOUN
humour ◇ *Il n'a pas beaucoup d'humour.* He hasn't got much sense of humour.

hurler VERB
to howl

la **hutte** NOUN
hut

hydratant ADJECTIVE
- **une crème hydratante** a moisturizing cream

hygiénique ADJECTIVE
hygienic
- **une serviette hygiénique** a sanitary towel
- **le papier hygiénique** toilet paper

l'**hymne** MASC NOUN
- **l'hymne national** the national anthem

l'**hypermarché** MASC NOUN
hypermarket

hypermétrope ADJECTIVE
long-sighted

hypocrite ADJECTIVE
hypocritical ◇ *Il est hypocrite.* He's a hypocrite.

l'**hypothèse** FEM NOUN
hypothesis

I

l'iceberg MASC NOUN
iceberg

ici ADVERB
here ◇ *Les assiettes sont ici.* The plates are here.
- **La mer monte parfois jusqu'ici.** The sea sometimes comes in as far as this.
- **Jusqu'ici nous n'avons eu aucun problème avec la voiture.** So far we haven't had any problems with the car.

idéal ADJECTIVE
(MASC PL **idéaux**)
ideal ◇ *C'est l'endroit idéal pour faire un pique-nique.* It's an ideal place to have a picnic.

l'idée FEM NOUN
idea ◇ *C'est une bonne idée.* It's a good idea.

identifier VERB
to identify ◇ *La police a identifié le meurtrier.* The police have identified the murderer.

identique ADJECTIVE
identical ◇ *Ils ont obtenu des résultats identiques.* They obtained identical results.

l'identité FEM NOUN
identity
- **une pièce d'identité** a form of identification ◇ *Avez-vous une pièce d'identité?* Have you got any form of identification?

idiot ADJECTIVE
see also **idiot** NOUN
1 *stupid* ◇ *une plaisanterie idiote* a stupid joke
2 *silly* ◇ *Ne sois pas idiot!* Don't be silly!

l'idiot MASC NOUN
see also **idiot** ADJECTIVE
idiot

l'idiote FEM NOUN
idiot

ignorant ADJECTIVE
ignorant

ignorer VERB
1 *not to know* ◇ *J'ignore son nom.* I don't know his name.
2 *to ignore* ◇ *Il m'a complètement ignoré.* He completely ignored me.

il PRONOUN
1 *he* ◇ *Il est parti ce matin de bonne heure.* He left early this morning.
2 *it* ◇ *Méfie-toi de ce chien: il mord.* Be careful of that dog: it bites. ◇ *Il pleut.* It's raining.

l'île FEM NOUN
island
- **les îles Anglo-Normandes** the Channel Islands
- **les îles Britanniques** the British Isles
- **les îles Féroé** the Faroe Islands

illégal ADJECTIVE
(MASC PL **illégaux**)
illegal

illimité ADJECTIVE
unlimited

illisible ADJECTIVE
illegible ◇ *une écriture illisible* illegible handwriting

illuminer VERB
to floodlight ◇ *Le château est illuminé tous les soirs pendant l'été.* The castle is floodlit every night in the summer.

l'illusion FEM NOUN
illusion ◇ *Tu te fais des illusions!* You're deluding yourself!

l'illustration FEM NOUN
illustration

illustré ADJECTIVE
see also **illustré** NOUN
illustrated

l'illustré MASC NOUN
see also **illustré** ADJECTIVE
comic

illustrer VERB
to illustrate ◇ *Vous pouvez illustrer votre rédaction avec des exemples.* You may illustrate your essay with examples.

ils PRONOUN
they ◇ *Ils nous ont appelés hier soir.* They phoned us last night.

l'image FEM NOUN
picture ◇ *Les films donnent une fausse image de l'Amérique.* Films give a false picture of America.

l'imagination FEM NOUN
imagination ◇ *Elle a beaucoup d'imagination.* She's got a vivid imagination.

imaginer VERB
to imagine

l'imbécile MASC/FEM NOUN
idiot

l'imitation FEM NOUN
imitation

imiter VERB
to imitate

l'immatriculation FEM NOUN
- **une plaque d'immatriculation** a numberplate

nmédiat MASC NOUN
dans l'immédiat for the moment ◇ *Je n'ai pas besoin de ce livre dans l'immédiat.* I don't need this book for the moment.
nmédiatement ADVERB
immediately
nmense ADJECTIVE
1 *huge* ◇ *une immense fortune* a huge fortune
2 *tremendous* ◇ *un immense soulagement* a tremendous relief
nmeuble MASC NOUN
block of flats
nmigration FEM NOUN
immigration
nmigré MASC NOUN
immigrant
nmigrée FEM NOUN
immigrant
nmobile ADJECTIVE
motionless
nmobilier ADJECTIVE
(FEM SING **immobilière**)
une agence immobilière an estate agent's
nmobiliser VERB
to immobilize
nmunisé ADJECTIVE
immunized
npact MASC NOUN
impact
npair ADJECTIVE
odd ◇ *un nombre impair* an odd number
npardonnable ADJECTIVE
unforgivable
npasse FEM NOUN
cul-de-sac
npatience FEM NOUN
impatience
npatient ADJECTIVE
impatient
npeccable ADJECTIVE
1 *immaculate* ◇ *Elle est toujours impeccable.* She's always immaculate.
2 *perfect* ◇ *Il a fait un travail impeccable.* He's done a perfect job.
◇ *C'est impeccable!* That's perfect!
npératif MASC NOUN
imperative
npératrice FEM NOUN
empress
nperméable MASC NOUN
raincoat
npertinent ADJECTIVE
cheeky ◇ *Ne sois pas impertinent!* Don't be cheeky!
npitoyable ADJECTIVE
merciless
impliquer VERB
to mean ◇ *Si tu vas à l'université, ça implique que tu vas devoir nous quitter.* If you go to university, it'll mean that you have to leave us.
◆ **être impliqué dans** to be involved in ◇ *Il est impliqué dans un scandale financier.* He's involved in a financial scandal.
impoli ADJECTIVE
rude
l'**importance** FEM NOUN
importance ◇ *C'est sans importance.* It doesn't matter.
important ADJECTIVE
1 *important* ◇ *un rôle important* an important role
2 *considerable* ◇ *une somme importante* a considerable sum
l'**importation** FEM NOUN
import ◇ *Les importations de pétrole ont baissé.* Oil imports have fallen.
importer VERB
see also n'importe
1 *to import* (*goods*)
2 *to matter* ◇ *Peu importe.* It doesn't matter.
imposant ADJECTIVE
imposing
imposer VERB
to impose
◆ **imposer quelque chose à quelqu'un** to make somebody do something
impossible ADJECTIVE
see also impossible NOUN
impossible
l'**impossible** MASC NOUN
see also impossible ADJECTIVE
◆ **Nous ferons l'impossible pour finir à temps.** We'll do our utmost to finish on time.
l'**impôt** MASC NOUN
tax
imprécis ADJECTIVE
imprecise
l'**impression** FEM NOUN
impression ◇ *Il a fait bonne impression à ma mère.* He made a good impression on my mother.
impressionnant ADJECTIVE
impressive
impressionner VERB
to impress
imprévisible ADJECTIVE
unpredictable
imprévu ADJECTIVE
unexpected
l'**imprimante** FEM NOUN

PTO

printer (*for computer*)

imprimé ADJECTIVE
printed ◇ *un tissu imprimé* a printed fabric ◇ *C'est imprimé en grandes lettres.* It's printed in large letters.

imprimer VERB
to print

impropre ADJECTIVE
◆ **impropre à la consommation** unfit for human consumption

improviser VERB
to improvise

improviste ADVERB
◆ **arriver à l'improviste** to arrive unexpectedly

l'**imprudence** FEM NOUN
carelessness
◆ **Ne fais pas d'imprudences!** Don't do anything silly!

imprudent ADJECTIVE
1 *unwise* ◇ *Il serait imprudent de prendre la voiture aujourd'hui.* It would be unwise to take the car today.
2 *careless* ◇ *un conducteur imprudent* a careless driver

impuissant ADJECTIVE
helpless ◇ *Elle se sentait complètement impuissante.* She felt completely helpless.

impulsif ADJECTIVE
(FEM SING **impulsive**)
impulsive

inabordable ADJECTIVE
prohibitive ◇ *des prix inabordables* prohibitive prices

inaccessible ADJECTIVE
inaccessible ◇ *Cette plage est inaccessible par la route.* This beach is inaccessible by road.

inachevé ADJECTIVE
unfinished

inadmissible ADJECTIVE
intolerable ◇ *Ce type de comportement est inadmissible!* This sort of behaviour is intolerable!

inanimé ADJECTIVE
unconscious ◇ *On l'a retrouvé inanimé sur la route.* He was found unconscious on the road.

inaperçu ADJECTIVE
◆ **passer inaperçu** to go unnoticed

inattendu ADJECTIVE
unexpected

l'**inattention** FEM NOUN
◆ **une faute d'inattention** a careless mistake

inaugurer VERB
to open (*an exhibition*)

incapable ADJECTIVE
incapable ◇ *être incapable de faire quelque chose* to be incapable of doing something

incassable ADJECTIVE
unbreakable

l'**incendie** MASC NOUN
fire ◇ *un incendie de forêt* a forest fire

incertain ADJECTIVE
1 *uncertain* ◇ *Son avenir est encore incertain.* His future is still uncertain.
2 *unsettled* ◇ *Le temps est incertain.* The weather is unsettled.

l'**incident** MASC NOUN
incident

inciter VERB
◆ **inciter quelqu'un à faire quelque chose** to encourage somebody to do something ◇ *J'ai incité mes parents à partir en voyage.* I encouraged my parents to go on a trip.

inclure VERB
to enclose ◇ *Veuillez inclure une enveloppe timbrée libellée à votre adresse.* Please enclose a stamped addressed envelope.
◆ **jusqu'au dix mars inclus** until 10th March inclusive

incohérent ADJECTIVE
incoherent

incollable ADJECTIVE
◆ **être incollable sur quelque chose** (*informal*) to know everything there is to know about something
◆ **le riz incollable** non-stick rice

incolore ADJECTIVE
colourless

incompétent ADJECTIVE
incompetent

incompris ADJECTIVE
misunderstood

l'**inconnu** MASC NOUN
stranger ◇ *Ne parle pas à des inconnus.* Don't speak to strangers.
◆ **l'inconnu** the unknown ◇ *la peur de l'inconnu* the fear of the unknown

l'**inconnue** FEM NOUN
stranger

inconsciemment ADVERB
unconsciously

inconscient ADJECTIVE
unconscious ◇ *Il est resté inconscient quelques minutes.* He was unconscious for several minutes.

incontestable ADJECTIVE
indisputable

incontournable ADJECTIVE
inevitable ◇ *l'incontournable petite robe noire* the inevitable little black dress

inconvénient MASC NOUN
disadvantage
◆ **si vous n'y voyez pas d'inconvénient** if you have no objection

incorrect ADJECTIVE
1 *incorrect* ◇ *une réponse incorrecte* an incorrect answer
2 *rude* ◇ *Il a été incorrect avec la voisine.* He was rude to the woman next door.

incroyable ADJECTIVE
incredible

inculper VERB
◆ **inculper de** to charge with ◇ *Il a été inculpé de meurtre.* He was charged with murder.

Inde FEM NOUN
India

indécis ADJECTIVE
1 *indecisive* ◇ *Il est constamment indécis.* He's always indecisive.
2 *undecided* ◇ *Je suis encore indécis.* I'm still undecided.

indéfiniment ADVERB
indefinitely

indélicat ADJECTIVE
tactless

indemne ADJECTIVE
unharmed ◇ *Il s'en est sorti indemne.* He escaped unharmed.

indemniser VERB
to compensate ◇ *Les victimes demandent maintenant à être indemnisées.* The victims are now demanding compensation.

indépendamment ADVERB
independently
◆ **indépendamment de** irrespective of ◇ *Les allocations familiales sont versées indépendamment des revenus.* Child benefit is given irrespective of income.

indépendance FEM NOUN
independence

indépendant ADJECTIVE
independent

index MASC NOUN
1 *index finger*
2 *index* (*in book*)

indicatif ADJECTIVE
(FEM SING **indicative**)
see also **indicatif** NOUN
◆ **à titre indicatif** for your information

indicatif MASC NOUN
see also **indicatif** ADJECTIVE
1 *dialling code*
2 *indicative* (*of verb*)
3 *theme tune* (*of TV programme*)

indications FEM NOUN
instructions ◇ *Il suffit de suivre les indications.* You just have to follow the instructions.

l'**indice** MASC NOUN
clue ◇ *La police cherche des indices.* The police are looking for clues.

indien ADJECTIVE, NOUN
(FEM SING **indienne**)
Indian
◆ **un Indien** an Indian (*man*)
◆ **une Indienne** an Indian (*woman*)

l'**indifférence** FEM NOUN
indifference

indifférent ADJECTIVE
indifferent

l'**indigène** MASC/FEM NOUN
native

indigeste ADJECTIVE
indigestible

l'**indigestion** FEM NOUN
indigestion

indigne ADJECTIVE
unworthy

indigner VERB
◆ **s'indigner de quelque chose** to get indignant about something

indiqué ADJECTIVE
advisable ◇ *Ce n'est pas très indiqué.* It's not really advisable.

indiquer VERB
to point out ◇ *Il m'a indiqué la mairie.* He pointed out the town hall.

indirect ADJECTIVE
indirect

indiscipliné ADJECTIVE
unruly

indiscret ADJECTIVE
(FEM SING **indiscrète**)
indiscreet

indispensable ADJECTIVE
indispensable

indisposé ADJECTIVE
indisposed
◆ **être indisposée** to be having one's period

l'**individu** MASC NOUN
individual

individuel ADJECTIVE
(FEM SING **individuelle**)
individual ◇ *servi en portions individuelles* served in individual portions
◆ **Vous aurez une chambre individuelle.** You'll have a room of your own.

indolore ADJECTIVE
painless

l'**Indonésie** FEM NOUN
Indonesia

indulgent ADJECTIVE
indulgent

PTO

- **Elle est trop indulgente avec son fils.** She's not firm enough with her son.

l'**industrie** FEM NOUN
industry

industriel ADJECTIVE
(FEM SING **industrielle**)
see also industriel NOUN
industrial

l'**industriel** MASC NOUN
see also industriel ADJECTIVE
industrialist

inédit ADJECTIVE
unpublished

inefficace ADJECTIVE
1 *ineffective* (*treatment*)
2 *inefficient* ◇ *un service de transports publics inefficace* an inefficient public transport system

inégal ADJECTIVE
(MASC PL **inégaux**)
1 *unequal* ◇ *un combat inégal* an unequal struggle
2 *uneven* ◇ *la qualité est inégale* the quality varies

inévitable ADJECTIVE
unavoidable

- **C'était inévitable!** That was bound to happen!

inexact ADJECTIVE
inaccurate

in extremis ADVERB

- **Il a réussi à attraper son train in extremis.** He just managed to catch his train.
- **Ils ont évité un accident in extremis.** They avoided an accident by the skin of their teeth.

l'**infarctus** MASC NOUN
coronary

infatigable ADJECTIVE
indefatigable ◇ *Il est infatigable.* He's indefatigable.

infect ADJECTIVE
revolting (*meal*)

s'**infecter** VERB
to go septic ◇ *La plaie s'est infectée.* The wound has gone septic.

l'**infection** FEM NOUN
infection

inférieur ADJECTIVE
lower ◇ *les membres inférieurs* the lower limbs ◇ *C'est moins cher, mais de qualité inférieure.* It's cheaper but of lower quality.

infernal ADJECTIVE
(MASC PL **infernaux**)
terrible ◇ *Ils faisaient un bruit infernal.* They were making a terrible noise.

l'**infini** MASC NOUN

- **à l'infini** indefinitely ◇ *On pourrait en parler à l'infini.* We could discuss this indefinitely.

l'**infinitif** MASC NOUN
infinitive

l'**infirme** MASC/FEM NOUN
disabled person

l'**infirmerie** FEM NOUN
medical room ◇ *Elle est à l'infirmerie.* She's in the medical room.

l'**infirmier** MASC NOUN
nurse

l'**infirmière** FEM NOUN
nurse

inflammable ADJECTIVE
inflammable

l'**influence** FEM NOUN
influence

influencer VERB
to influence

l'**informaticien** MASC NOUN
computer scientist

l'**informaticienne** FEM NOUN
computer scientist

les **informations** FEM NOUN
1 *news* (*on TV*) ◇ *les informations de vingt heures* the 8 o'clock news
2 *information* ◇ *Je voudrais quelques informations, s'il vous plaît.* I'd like some information, please.

- **une information** a piece of information

l'**informatique** FEM NOUN
computing

informer VERB
to inform

- **s'informer** to find out ◇ *Je ne connais pas les heures de fermeture, mais je vais m'informer.* I don't know when they close, but I'm going to find out.

infuser VERB
1 *to brew* (*tea*)
2 *to infuse* (*herbal tea*)

l'**infusion** FEM NOUN
herbal tea

l'**ingénieur** MASC NOUN
engineer

ingrat ADJECTIVE
ungrateful

l'**ingrédient** MASC NOUN
ingredient

inhabituel ADJECTIVE
(FEM SING **inhabituelle**)
unusual

inhumain ADJECTIVE
inhuman

initial ADJECTIVE
(MASC PL **initiaux**)
initial

l'**initiale** FEM NOUN

initial

initiation FEM NOUN
introduction ◇ *un stage d'initiation à la planche à voile* an introductory course in windsurfing

initiative FEM NOUN
initiative ◇ *avoir de l'initiative* to have initiative

injecter VERB
to inject

injection FEM NOUN
injection

injure FEM NOUN
1 *insult* ◇ *Il a pris ça comme une injure.* He took this as an insult.
2 *abuse* ◇ *lancer des injures à quelqu'un* to hurl abuse at somebody

injurieux ADJECTIVE
(FEM SING **injurieuse**)
abusive (*language*)

injuste ADJECTIVE
unfair

innocent ADJECTIVE
innocent

innombrable ADJECTIVE
innumerable

innover VERB
to break new ground

inoccupé ADJECTIVE
empty ◇ *un appartement inoccupé* an empty flat

inoffensif ADJECTIVE
(FEM SING **inoffensive**)
harmless

inondation FEM NOUN
flood

inoubliable ADJECTIVE
unforgettable

inoxydable ADJECTIVE
◆ **l'acier inoxydable** stainless steel

inquiet ADJECTIVE
(FEM SING **inquiète**)
worried

inquiétant ADJECTIVE
worrying

inquiéter VERB
to worry ◇ *Ne t'inquiète pas!* Don't worry!

inquiétude FEM NOUN
anxiety

insatisfait ADJECTIVE
dissatisfied

inscription FEM NOUN
registration (*for school, course*)

inscrire VERB
◆ **s'inscrire à (1)** to join ◇ *Je me suis inscrit au club de tennis.* I've joined the tennis club.
◆ **s'inscrire à (2)** to register ◇ *N'attends pas trop pour t'inscrire à la fac.* Don't leave it too long to register at the university.

l'**insecte** MASC NOUN
insect

insensible ADJECTIVE
insensitive ◇ *Il la trouve insensible.* He thinks she's insensitive.

l'**insigne** MASC NOUN
badge

insignifiant ADJECTIVE
insignificant

insister VERB
to insist
◆ **N'insiste pas!** Don't keep on!

l'**insolation** FEM NOUN
sunstroke

insolent ADJECTIVE
cheeky

insouciant ADJECTIVE
carefree

insoutenable ADJECTIVE
unbearable ◇ *une douleur insoutenable* an unbearable pain

inspecter VERB
to inspect

l'**inspecteur** MASC NOUN
inspector

l'**inspection** FEM NOUN
inspection

l'**inspectrice** FEM NOUN
inspector

inspirer VERB
to inspire
◆ **s'inspirer de** to take one's inspiration from ◇ *Le peintre s'est inspiré d'un poème.* The painter took his inspiration from a poem.

instable ADJECTIVE
1 *unsteady* (*piece of furniture*)
2 *unstable* (*person*)

les **installations** FEM NOUN
facilities ◇ *Cet appartement est pourvu de toutes les installations modernes.* This flat has all modern facilities.

installer VERB
1 *to put up* (*shelves*)
2 *to install* (*gas, telephone*)
◆ **s'installer** to settle in ◇ *Nous nous sommes installés dans notre nouvel appartement.* We've settled into our new flat.
◆ **Installez-vous, je vous en prie.** Have a seat please.

l'**instant** MASC NOUN
moment ◇ *dans un instant* in a moment ◇ *Le dîner sera prêt dans un instant.* Dinner will be ready in a moment. ◇ *pour l'instant* for the

PTO

moment

instantané ADJECTIVE
instant ◇ *du café instantané* instant coffee

l'**instinct** MASC NOUN
instinct

l'**institut** MASC NOUN
institute

l'**instituteur** MASC NOUN
primary school teacher

l'**institution** FEM NOUN
institution

l'**institutrice** FEM NOUN
primary school teacher

l'**instruction** FEM NOUN
1 *instruction* ◇ *J'ai suivi soigneusement ses instructions.* I followed his instructions carefully.
2 *education* ◇ *Il n'a pas beaucoup d'instruction.* He's not very well-educated.

s'**instruire** VERB
to educate oneself

instruit ADJECTIVE
educated

l'**instrument** MASC NOUN
instrument ◇ *un instrument de musique* a musical instrument

insuffisant ADJECTIVE
insufficient
◆ **"travail insuffisant"** (*on school report*) "must make more effort"

l'**insuline** FEM NOUN
insulin

l'**insulte** FEM NOUN
insult

insulter VERB
to insult

insupportable ADJECTIVE
unbearable

intact ADJECTIVE
intact

intégral ADJECTIVE
(MASC PL **intégraux**)
◆ **le texte intégral** unabridged version
◆ **un remboursement intégral** a full refund

l'**intégrisme** MASC NOUN
fundamentalism

l'**intelligence** FEM NOUN
intelligence

intelligent ADJECTIVE
intelligent

intense ADJECTIVE
intense

intensif ADJECTIVE
(FEM SING **intensive**)
intensive
◆ **un cours intensif** a crash course

l'**intention** FEM NOUN
intention
◆ **avoir l'intention de faire quelque chose** to intend to do something ◇ *J'ai l'intention de lui en parler.* I intend to speak to him about it.

l'**interdiction** FEM NOUN
◆ **"interdiction de stationner"** "no parking"
◆ **"interdiction de fumer"** "no smoking"

interdire VERB
to forbid ◇ *Ses parents lui ont interdit de sortir.* His parents have forbidden him to go out.

interdit ADJECTIVE
forbidden ◇ *Il est interdit de fumer dans les couloirs.* Smoking in the corridors is forbidden.

intéressant ADJECTIVE
interesting ◇ *un livre intéressant* an interesting book
◆ **On lui a fait une offre intéressante.** They made him an attractive offer.
◆ **On trouve des CD à des prix très intéressants dans ce magasin.** You can get very cheap CDs in this shop.

intéresser VERB
to interest
◆ **s'intéresser à** to be interested in ◇ *Est-ce que vous vous intéressez à la politique?* Are you interested in politics?

l'**intérêt** MASC NOUN
interest
◆ **avoir intérêt à faire quelque chose** to do well to do something ◇ *Tu as intérêt à te dépêcher si tu veux prendre le train de dix heures.* You'd better hurry up if you want to catch the 10 o'clock train.

l'**intérieur** MASC NOUN
inside ◇ *Il fait plus frais à l'intérieur de la maison.* It's cooler inside the house.

l'**interlocuteur** MASC NOUN
◆ **son interlocuteur** the man he's speaking to

l'**interlocutrice** FEM NOUN
◆ **son interlocutrice** the woman he's speaking to

l'**intermédiaire** MASC NOUN
intermediary
◆ **par l'intermédiaire de** through ◇ *Je l'ai rencontré par l'intermédiaire de sa sœur.* I met him through his sister.

l'**internat** MASC NOUN
boarding school

international ADJECTIVE
(MASC PL **internationaux**)
international

interne MASC/FEM NOUN
boarder

l'Internet MASC NOUN
Internet ◇ *sur Internet* on the Internet

l'interphone MASC NOUN
intercom

l'interprète MASC/FEM NOUN
interpreter

interpréter VERB
to interpret

interrogatif ADJECTIVE
(FEM SING **interrogative**)
interrogative

l'interrogation FEM NOUN
1 *question*
2 *test* ◇ *une interrogation écrite* a written test ◇ *une interrogation orale* an oral test

l'interrogatoire MASC NOUN
questioning
◆ **C'est un interrogatoire ou quoi?** Am I being cross-examined?

interroger VERB
to question

interrompre VERB
to interrupt

l'interrupteur MASC NOUN
switch

l'interruption FEM NOUN
interruption
◆ **sans interruption** without stopping ◇ *Il a parlé pendant deux heures sans interruption.* He spoke for two hours without stopping.

l'intervalle MASC NOUN
interval
◆ **dans l'intervalle** in the meantime

intervenir VERB
1 *to intervene*
2 *to take action* ◇ *La police est intervenue.* The police took action.

l'intervention FEM NOUN
intervention ◇ *une intervention militaire* a military intervention
◆ **une intervention chirurgicale** a surgical operation

l'interview FEM NOUN
interview (*on radio, TV*)

l'intestin MASC NOUN
intestine

intime ADJECTIVE
intimate
◆ **un journal intime** a diary

intimider VERB
to intimidate

l'intimité FEM NOUN
◆ **dans l'intimité** in private ◇ *Ce que vous faites dans l'intimité ne m'intéresse pas.* What you do in private doesn't interest me.
◆ **Le mariage a eu lieu dans l'intimité.** The wedding ceremony was private.

intitulé ADJECTIVE
entitled

intolérable ADJECTIVE
intolerable

l'intoxication FEM NOUN
◆ **une intoxication alimentaire** food poisoning

intransigeant ADJECTIVE
uncompromising

l'intrigue FEM NOUN
plot (*of book, film*)

l'introduction FEM NOUN
introduction

introduire VERB
to introduce

l'intuition FEM NOUN
intuition

inusable ADJECTIVE
hard-wearing

inutile ADJECTIVE
useless

l'invalide MASC/FEM NOUN
disabled person

l'invasion FEM NOUN
invasion

inventer VERB
1 *to invent*
2 *to make up* ◇ *inventer une excuse* to make up an excuse

l'inventeur MASC NOUN
inventor

l'invention FEM NOUN
invention

inverse ADJECTIVE
see also **inverse** NOUN
◆ **dans l'ordre inverse** in reverse order
◆ **en sens inverse** in the opposite direction

l'inverse MASC NOUN
see also **inverse** ADJECTIVE
reverse
◆ **Tu t'es trompé, c'est l'inverse.** You've got it wrong, it's the other way round.

l'investissement MASC NOUN
investment

invisible ADJECTIVE
invisible

l'invitation FEM NOUN
invitation

l'invité MASC NOUN
guest

l'invitée FEM NOUN
guest

inviter VERB
to invite

involontaire ADJECTIVE
unintentional ◇ *C'était tout à fait involontaire.* It was quite unintentional.

invraisemblable ADJECTIVE
unlikely ◇ *une histoire invraisemblable* an implausible story

ira, irai, iraient, irais VERB *see* **aller**
◆ **J'irai demain au supermarché.** I'll go to the supermarket tomorrow.

l'**Irak** MASC NOUN
Iraq

l'**Iran** MASC NOUN
Iran

iras, irez VERB *see* **aller**

irlandais ADJECTIVE, NOUN
(FEM SING **irlandaise**)
Irish
◆ **un Irlandais** an Irishman
◆ **une Irlandaise** an Irishwoman
◆ **les Irlandais** the Irish

l'**Irlande** FEM NOUN
Ireland
◆ **en Irlande (1)** in Ireland
◆ **en Irlande (2)** to Ireland
◆ **la République d'Irlande** the Irish Republic
◆ **l'Irlande du Nord** Northern Ireland

l'**ironie** FEM NOUN
irony

ironique ADJECTIVE
ironical

irons, iront VERB *see* **aller**
◆ **Nous irons à la plage cet après-midi.** We'll go to the beach this afternoon.

irrationnel ADJECTIVE
(FEM SING **irrationnelle**)
irrational

irréel ADJECTIVE
(FEM SING **irréelle**)
unreal

irrégulier ADJECTIVE
(FEM SING **irrégulière**)
irregular

irrésistible ADJECTIVE
irresistible

irritable ADJECTIVE
irritable

irriter VERB
to irritate

islamique ADJECTIVE
Islamic

l'**Islande** FEM NOUN
Iceland

isolé ADJECTIVE
isolated ◇ *une ferme isolée* an isolated farm

Israël MASC NOUN
Israel

israélien ADJECTIVE, NOUN
(FEM SING **israélienne**)
Israeli
◆ **un Israélien** an Israeli (*man*)
◆ **une Israélienne** an Israeli (*woman*)
◆ **les Israéliens** the Israelis

israélite ADJECTIVE
Jewish

l'**issue** FEM NOUN
◆ **une voie sans issue** a dead end
◆ **l'issue de secours** emergency exit

l'**Italie** FEM NOUN
Italy
◆ **en Italie (1)** in Italy
◆ **en Italie (2)** to Italy

italien ADJECTIVE, NOUN
(FEM SING **italienne**)
Italian ◇ *J'apprends l'italien.* I'm learning Italian.
◆ **un Italien** an Italian (*man*)
◆ **une Italienne** (*woman*)
◆ **les Italiens** the Italians

l'**itinéraire** MASC NOUN
route

l'**IUT** MASC NOUN (= *Institut universitaire de technologie*)
institute of technology (*at university level*)

ivre ADJECTIVE
drunk

l'**ivrogne** MASC/FEM NOUN
drunkard

J

' PRONOUN *see* **je**

alousie NOUN
jealousy

aloux ADJECTIVE
(FEM SING **jalouse**)
jealous

amais ADVERB
1 *never* ◇ *Est-ce que tu vas souvent au cinéma? – Non, jamais.* Do you go to the cinema often? – No, never. ◇ *Il ne boit jamais d'alcool.* He never drinks alcohol.
2 *ever*

Phrases with **jamais** *meaning* **ever** *are followed by a verb in the subjunctive.*

◇ *C'est la plus belle chose que j'aie jamais vue.* It's the most beautiful thing I've ever seen.

ambe NOUN
leg

ambon NOUN
ham
- **le jambon cru** Parma ham

ambonneau NOUN
(PL les **jambonneaux**)
knuckle of ham

anvier MASC NOUN
January
- **en janvier** in January

Japon NOUN
Japan
- **au Japon (1)** in Japan
- **au Japon (2)** to Japan

aponais ADJECTIVE, NOUN
Japanese ◇ *Elle parle japonais.* She speaks Japanese.
- **un Japonais** a Japanese (*man*)
- **une Japonaise** a Japanese (*woman*)
- **les Japonais** the Japanese

ardin NOUN
garden

ardinage NOUN
gardening

ardinier NOUN
gardener

ardinière NOUN
gardener

aune ADJECTIVE
see also **jaune** NOUN
yellow

aune NOUN
see also **jaune** ADJECTIVE
yellow
- **un jaune d'œuf** an egg yolk

aunir VERB
to turn yellow

la **jaunisse** NOUN
jaundice

Javel NOUN
- **l'eau de Javel** bleach

J.-C. ABBREVIATION (= *Jésus-Christ*)
- **44 avant J.-C.** 44 BC
- **115 après J.-C.** 115 AD

je PRONOUN

je *changes to* **j'** *before a vowel and most words beginning with "h".*

I ◇ *Je t'appellerai ce soir.* I'll phone you this evening. ◇ *J'arrive!* I'm coming! ◇ *J'hésite.* I'm not sure.

le **jean** NOUN
jeans

Jésus-Christ MASC NOUN
Jesus Christ

le **jet** NOUN
1 *jet* (*of water*)
2 *jet plane*

jetable ADJECTIVE
disposable

la **jetée** NOUN
jetty

jeter VERB
1 *to throw* ◇ *Il a jeté son manteau sur le lit.* He threw his coat onto the bed.
2 *to throw away* ◇ *Mes parents ne jettent jamais rien.* My parents never throw anything away.
- **jeter un coup d'œil** to have a look ◇ *Jette un coup d'œil pour voir s'il y a des erreurs.* Have a look to see if there are any mistakes.

le **jeton** NOUN
counter (*in board game*)

le **jeu** NOUN
(PL les **jeux**)
game ◇ *Je n'aime pas les jeux de société.* I don't like board games.
- **un jeu de cartes (1)** a pack of cards
- **un jeu de cartes (2)** a card game
- **un jeu de mots** a pun
- **les jeux vidéo** video games
- **en jeu** at stake ◇ *Des vies humaines sont en jeu.* Human lives are at stake.

le **jeudi** NOUN
1 *Thursday* ◇ *Aujourd'hui, nous sommes jeudi.* It's Thursday today.
2 *on Thursday* ◇ *Il arrivera jeudi matin.* He's arriving on Thursday morning.
- **le jeudi** on Thursdays ◇ *Le musée est fermé le jeudi.* The museum is closed on Thursdays.
- **tous les jeudis** every Thursday

PTO

- **jeudi dernier** last Thursday
- **jeudi prochain** next Thursday

jeun

- **à jeun** ADVERB
  on an empty stomach ◇ *à prendre à jeun* to be taken on an empty stomach ◇ *Il faut être à jeun pour la prise de sang.* You mustn't have eaten anything before giving a blood sample.

jeune ADJECTIVE
young ◇ *un jeune homme* a young man ◇ *une jeune femme* a young woman

- **une jeune fille** a girl

la **jeunesse** NOUN
youth

la **joie** NOUN
joy

joindre VERB
1 *to put together* ◇ *On va joindre les deux tables.* We're going to put the two tables together.
2 *to contact* ◇ *Vous arriverez peut-être à le joindre chez lui.* Maybe you'll be able to contact him at home.

joint ADJECTIVE

- **une pièce jointe** an enclosure (*in letter*)

joli ADJECTIVE
pretty

le **jonc** NOUN
rush

la **jonquille** NOUN
daffodil

la **joue** NOUN
cheek

jouer VERB
1 *to play* ◇ *Elle est allée jouer avec les petits voisins.* She's gone to play with the children next door.

- **jouer de** to play (*instrument*) ◇ *Il joue de la guitare et du piano.* He plays the guitar and the piano.
- **jouer à** to play (*sport, game*) ◇ *Elle joue au tennis.* She plays tennis. ◇ *jouer aux dames* to play draughts

2 *to act* ◇ *Je trouve qu'il joue très bien dans ce film.* I think he acts very well in this film.

- **On joue Hamlet au Théâtre de la Ville.** Hamlet is on at the Théâtre de la Ville.

le **jouet** NOUN
toy

le **joueur** NOUN
player

- **être mauvais joueur** to be a bad loser

la **joueuse** NOUN
player

le **jour** NOUN
day ◇ *J'ai passé trois jours chez mes cousins.* I stayed with my cousins for three days.

- **Il fait jour.** It's daylight.
- **mettre quelque chose à jour** to update something
- **un jour férié** a public holiday

le **journal** NOUN
(PL les **journaux**)
1 *newspaper*

- **le journal télévisé** the television news

2 *diary* ◇ *Elle tient un journal depuis l'âge de douze ans.* She has been keeping a diary since she was 12.

journalier ADJECTIVE
(FEM SING **journalière**)
daily

le **journalisme** NOUN
journalism

le/la **journaliste** NOUN
journalist ◇ *Elle est journaliste.* She's a journalist.

la **journée** NOUN
day

joyeux ADJECTIVE
(FEM SING **joyeuse**)
happy

- **Joyeux anniversaire!** Happy birthday!
- **Joyeux Noël!** Merry Christmas!

le **judo** NOUN
judo

le **juge** NOUN
judge

juger VERB
to judge

juif ADJECTIVE
(FEM SING **juive**)
Jewish ◇ *la cuisine juive* Jewish cooking

- **un juif** a Jew (*man*)
- **une juive** a Jew (*woman*)

juillet MASC NOUN
July

- **en juillet** in July

juin MASC NOUN
June

- **en juin** in June

le **jumeau** NOUN
(PL les **jumeaux**)
twin

jumeler VERB
to twin ◇ *Saint-Brieuc est jumelée avec Aberystwyth.* Saint-Brieuc is twinned with Aberystwyth.

la **jumelle** NOUN
twin

les **jumelles** FEM NOUN
binoculars

la **jument** NOUN
mare

jungle NOUN
jungle

jupe NOUN
skirt

jurer VERB
to swear ◇ *Je jure que c'est vrai!* I swear it's true!

juridique ADJECTIVE
legal

jury NOUN
jury

jus NOUN
juice
- **un jus de fruit** a fruit juice

jusqu'à PREPOSITION
1 *as far as* ◇ *Nous avons marché jusqu'au village.* We walked as far as the village.
2 *until* ◇ *Il fait généralement chaud jusqu'à la mi-août.* It's usually hot until mid-August.
- **jusqu'à ce que** until ◇ *Tu peux rester ici jusqu'à ce qu'il cesse de pleuvoir.* You can stay here until it stops raining.
- **jusqu'à présent** so far

juste ADJECTIVE, ADVERB
1 *fair* ◇ *Il est sévère, mais juste.* He's strict but fair.
2 *tight* ◇ *Cette veste est un peu juste.* This jacket is a bit tight.
- **juste assez** just enough
- **chanter juste** to sing in tune

justement ADVERB
just ◇ *C'est justement pour cela qu'il est parti!* That's just the reason why he left!

la **justesse** NOUN
- **de justesse** only just ◇ *Il a eu son permis de justesse.* He only just passed his driving test.

la **justice** NOUN
justice

justifier VERB
to justify

juteux ADJECTIVE
(FEM SING **juteuse**)
juicy

juvénile ADJECTIVE
youthful

K

kaki ADJECTIVE
khaki

le **kangourou** NOUN
kangaroo

le **karaté** NOUN
karate

la **kermesse** NOUN
fair

kidnapper VERB
to kidnap

le **kilo** NOUN
kilo

le **kilogramme** NOUN
kilogramme

le **kilomètre** NOUN
kilometre

le/la **kinésithérapeute** NOUN
physiotherapist

le **kiosque** NOUN
- **un kiosque à journaux** a news stand

le **klaxon** NOUN
horn (*of car*)

klaxonner VERB
to sound the horn

km ABBREVIATION (= *kilomètre*)
- **km/h** kph (= kilometres per hour)

K.-O. ADJECTIVE
knocked out
- **mettre quelqu'un K.-O.** to knock somebody out ◇ *Il l'a mis K.-O. au troisième round.* He knocked him out in the third round.
- **Je suis complètement K.-O.** (*informal*) I'm knackered.

le **K-way** NOUN
cagoule

L

l' ARTICLE, PRONOUN *see* **la, le**

la ARTICLE, PRONOUN

see also la NOUN

la *changes to* **l'** *before a vowel and most words beginning with "h".*

1 *the* ◇ *la maison* the house ◇ *l'actrice* the actress ◇ *l'herbe* the grass

2 *her* ◇ *Je la connais depuis longtemps.* I've known her for a long time. ◇ *C'est une femme intelligente: je l'admire beaucoup.* She's an intelligent woman: I admire her very much.

3 *it* ◇ *C'est une bonne émission: je la regarde toutes les semaines.* It's a good programme: I watch it every week.

4 *one's*

◆ **se mordre la langue** to bite one's tongue ◇ *Je me suis mordu la langue.* I've bitten my tongue.

◆ **dix francs la douzaine** 10 francs a dozen

la NOUN

see also la ARTICLE

1 *A* ◇ *en la bémol* in A flat

2 *la* ◇ *sol, la, si, do* so, la, ti, do

là ADVERB

1 *there* ◇ *Ton livre est là, sur la table.* Your book's there, on the table.

2 *here* ◇ *Elle n'est pas là.* She isn't here.

◆ **C'est là que... (1)** That's where... ◇ *C'est là que je suis né.* That's where I was born.

◆ **C'est là que... (2)** That's when... ◇ *C'est là que j'ai réalisé que je m'étais trompé.* That's when I realized that I had made a mistake.

là-bas ADVERB

over there

labo NOUN (*informal*)

lab

laboratoire NOUN

laboratory

labourer VERB

to plough

labyrinthe NOUN

maze

lac NOUN

lake

lacer VERB

to do up (*shoes*)

lacet NOUN

lace

◆ **des chaussures à lacets** lace-up shoes

lâche ADJECTIVE

see also lâche NOUN

1 *loose* ◇ *Le nœud est trop lâche.* The knot's too loose.

2 *cowardly*

◆ **Il est lâche.** He's a coward.

le **lâche** NOUN

see also lâche ADJECTIVE

coward

lâcher VERB

1 *to let go of* ◇ *Il n'a pas lâché ma main de tout le film.* He didn't let go of my hand until the end of the film.

2 *to drop* ◇ *Il a été tellement surpris qu'il a lâché son verre.* He was so surprised that he dropped his glass.

3 *to fail* ◇ *Les freins ont lâché.* The brakes failed.

la **lâcheté** NOUN

cowardice

lacrymogène ADJECTIVE

◆ **le gaz lacrymogène** tear gas

la **lacune** NOUN

gap

là-dedans ADVERB

in there ◇ *Qu'est-ce qu'il y a là-dedans?* What's in there?

là-dessous ADVERB

1 *under there* ◇ *Mon carnet d'adresses est quelque part là-dessous.* My address book is under there somewhere.

2 *behind it* ◇ *Il y a quelque chose de louche là-dessous.* There's something fishy behind it.

là-dessus ADVERB

on there

là-haut ADVERB

up there

laid ADJECTIVE

ugly

la **laideur** NOUN

ugliness

le **lainage** NOUN

woollen garment

la **laine** NOUN

wool ◇ *un pull en laine* a wool jumper

laïque ADJECTIVE

◆ **une école laïque** a state school

la **laisse** NOUN

lead ◇ *Tenez votre chien en laisse.* Keep your dog on a lead.

laisser VERB

1 *to leave* ◇ *J'ai laissé mon parapluie à la maison.* I've left my umbrella at home.

2 *to let* ◇ *Laisse-le parler.* Let him speak.

- **Elle se laisse aller.** She's letting herself go.

le **laisser-aller** NOUN
carelessness

le **lait** NOUN
milk
- **un café au lait** a white coffee

la **laitue** NOUN
lettuce

les **lambeaux** MASC NOUN
- **en lambeaux** tattered

la **lame** NOUN
blade ◇ *une lame de rasoir* a razor blade

la **lamelle** NOUN
thin strip

lamentable ADJECTIVE
appalling

se **lamenter** VERB
to moan

le **lampadaire** NOUN
standard lamp

la **lampe** NOUN
lamp
- **une lampe de poche** a torch

la **lance** NOUN
spear

le **lancement** NOUN
launch

lancer VERB
see also lancer NOUN
1 *to throw* ◇ *Lance-moi le ballon!* Throw me the ball!
2 *to launch* ◇ *Ils viennent de lancer un nouveau modèle.* They've just launched a new model.
- **se lancer** to embark on ◇ *Il s'est lancé là-dedans sans bien réfléchir.* He embarked on it without thinking properly.

le **lancer** NOUN
see also lancer VERB
- **le lancer de poids** putting the shot

lancinant ADJECTIVE
- **une douleur lancinante** a shooting pain

le **landau** NOUN
pram

la **lande** NOUN
moor

le **langage** NOUN
language

la **langouste** NOUN
crayfish

la **langue** NOUN
1 *tongue* ◇ *Un petit garçon m'a tiré la langue.* A little boy stuck out his tongue at me.
- **sa langue maternelle** his mother tongue

2 *language* ◇ *une langue vivante* a modern language

la **lanière** NOUN
strap

le **lapin** NOUN
rabbit

le **laps** NOUN
- **un laps de temps** a space of time

la **laque** NOUN
hair spray

laquelle PRONOUN
(PL **lesquelles**)
1 *which* ◇ *Laquelle de ces photos préfères-tu?* Which of these photos do you prefer? ◇ *À laquelle de tes sœurs ressembles-tu?* Which of your sisters do you look like?
2 *whom* ◇ *la personne à laquelle vous faites référence* the person to whom you are referring

laquelle *is often not translated in English.*
◇ *la personne à laquelle je pense* the person I'm thinking of

le **lard** NOUN
streaky bacon

les **lardons** MASC NOUN
chunks of bacon

large ADJECTIVE, ADVERB
see also large NOUN
wide
- **voir large** to allow a bit extra ◇ *Achète un autre pain: il vaut mieux voir large.* Buy another loaf of bread: it's better to have a bit extra.

le **large** NOUN
see also large ADJECTIVE
- **cinq mètres de large** 5 m wide
- **le large** the open sea
- **au large de** off the coast of ◇ *Le bateau est actuellement au large du Portugal.* The boat is off the coast of Portugal at the moment.

largement ADVERB
- **Vous avez largement le temps.** You have plenty of time.
- **C'est largement suffisant.** That's ample.

la **largeur** NOUN
width

la **larme** NOUN
tear ◇ *être en larmes* to be in tears

la **laryngite** NOUN
laryngitis

le **laser** NOUN
laser
- **une chaîne laser** a compact disc player
- **un disque laser** a compact disc

lasser VERB

- **se lasser de** to get tired of ◇ *Il s'est lassé de la tapisserie à fleurs du salon.* He's got tired of the flowery wallpaper in the sitting room.

atin NOUN
Latin

aurier NOUN
laurel tree ◇ *une feuille de laurier* a bay leaf

avable ADJECTIVE
washable

avabo NOUN
washbasin

avage NOUN
wash ◇ *Ce pull a rétréci au lavage.* This jumper has shrunk in the wash.

avande NOUN
lavender

ave-linge NOUN
(PL les **lave-linge**)
washing machine

aver VERB
to wash
- **se laver** to wash ◇ *se laver les mains* to wash one's hands

averie NOUN
- **une laverie automatique** a launderette

ave-vaisselle NOUN
(PL les **lave-vaisselle**)
dishwasher

e ARTICLE, PRONOUN

le *changes to* **l'** *before a vowel and most words beginning with "h".*

1 *the* ◇ *le livre* the book ◇ *l'arbre* the tree ◇ *l'hélicoptère* the helicopter
2 *him* ◇ *Daniel est un vieil ami: je le connais depuis plus de vingt ans.* Daniel is an old friend: I've known him for over 20 years.
3 *it* ◇ *Où est mon stylo? Je ne le trouve plus.* Where's my pen? I can't find it. ◇ *Où est le fromage?–Je l'ai mis au frigo.* Where's the cheese?–I've put it in the fridge.
4 *one's*
- **se laver le visage** to wash one's face ◇ *Évitez de vous laver le visage avec du savon.* Avoid washing your face with soap.
- **dix francs le kilo** 10 francs a kilo
- **Il est arrivé le douze mai.** He arrived on 12 May.

lécher VERB
to lick

lèche-vitrine NOUN
- **faire du lèche-vitrine** to go window-shopping

leçon NOUN
lesson

le **lecteur** NOUN
1 *reader*
2 *foreign language assistant* (*at a university*)
- **un lecteur de cassettes** a cassette player
- **un lecteur de CD** a CD player

la **lectrice** NOUN
1 *reader*
2 *foreign language assistant* (*at a university*)

la **lecture** NOUN
reading

légal ADJECTIVE
(MASC PL **légaux**)
legal

la **légende** NOUN
1 *legend*
2 *key* (*of map*)

léger ADJECTIVE
(FEM SING **légère**)
1 *light*
2 *slight* ◇ *un léger retard* a slight delay
- **à la légère** thoughtlessly ◇ *Il a agi à la légère.* He acted thoughtlessly.

légèrement ADVERB
1 *lightly* ◇ *Habille-toi légèrement: il va faire chaud.* Wear light clothes: it's going to be hot.
2 *slightly* ◇ *Il est légèrement plus grand que son frère.* He's slightly taller than his brother.

les **législatives** FEM NOUN
general election

le **légume** NOUN
vegetable

le **lendemain** NOUN
next day ◇ *le lendemain de son arrivée* the day after he arrived
- **le lendemain matin** the next morning

lent ADJECTIVE
slow

lentement ADVERB
slowly

la **lenteur** NOUN
slowness

la **lentille** NOUN
1 *contact lens* ◇ *Est-ce que tu portes des lentilles?* Do you wear contact lenses?
2 *lentil* ◇ *un rôti de porc aux lentilles* roast pork with lentils

le **léopard** NOUN
leopard

lequel PRONOUN
(FEM SING **laquelle**, MASC PL **lesquels**, FEM PL **lesquelles**)
1 *which* ◇ *Lequel de ces films as-tu*

PTO

préféré? Which of the films did you prefer?
2 *whom* ◇ *l'homme avec lequel elle a été vue pour la dernière fois* the man with whom she was last seen
lequel *is often not translated in English.*
◇ *le garçon avec lequel elle est sortie* the boy she went out with

les ARTICLE, PRONOUN
1 *the* ◇ *les arbres* the trees
2 *them* ◇ *Elle les a invités à dîner.* She invited them to dinner.
3 *one's*
◆ **se brosser les dents** to brush one's teeth ◇ *Elle s'est brossé les dents.* She brushed her teeth.
◆ **dix francs les cinq** 10 francs for 5

la **lesbienne** NOUN
lesbian

lesquels PRONOUN
(FEM **lesquelles**)
1 *which* ◇ *Lesquelles de ces photos as-tu choisies?* Which of the photos did you choose?
2 *whom* ◇ *les personnes avec lesquelles il est associé* the people with whom he is in partnership
lesquels *is often not translated in English.*
◇ *les gens chez lesquels nous avons dîné* the people we had dinner with

la **lessive** NOUN
1 *washing powder* ◇ *une marque de lessive* a brand of washing powder
2 *wash* ◇ *Est-ce que vous avez quelque chose à mettre à la lessive?* Have you got anything to go in the wash?
◆ **faire la lessive** to do the washing

leste ADJECTIVE
nimble

la **Lettonie** NOUN
Latvia

la **lettre** NOUN
letter ◇ *écrire une lettre* to write a lettre

les **lettres** FEM NOUN
arts ◇ *la faculté de lettres* the Faculty of Arts

leur ADJECTIVE, PRONOUN
1 *their* ◇ *leur ami* their friend
2 *them* ◇ *Je leur ai dit la vérité.* I told them the truth.
◆ **le leur** theirs ◇ *mon camion et le leur* my truck and theirs ◇ *Ma voiture est rouge, la leur est bleue.* My car's red, theirs is blue.

leurs ADJECTIVE, PRONOUN
their ◇ *leurs amis* their friends
◆ **les leurs** theirs ◇ *tes livres et les leurs* your books and theirs

levé ADJECTIVE
◆ **être levé** to be up ◇ *Est-ce qu'il est levé?* Is he up?

lever VERB
see also **lever** NOUN
to raise ◇ *Levez vos verres!* Raise your glasses! ◇ *Levez la main si vous connaissez la réponse.* Put your hand up if you know the answer.
◆ **lever les yeux** to look up
◆ **se lever (1)** to get up ◇ *Il se lève tous les jours à six heures.* He gets up at 6 o'clock every day. ◇ *Lève-toi!* Get up!
◆ **se lever (2)** to rise ◇ *Le soleil se lève actuellement à cinq heures.* At the moment the sun rises at 5 o'clock.

le **lever** NOUN
see also **lever** VERB
◆ **le lever du soleil** sunrise

le **levier** NOUN
lever

la **lèvre** NOUN
lip

le **lévrier** NOUN
greyhound

la **levure** NOUN
yeast
◆ **la levure chimique** baking powder

le **lexique** NOUN
word list

le **lézard** NOUN
lizard

la **liaison** NOUN
affair ◇ *Ils ont eu une liaison dans leur jeunesse.* They had an affair when they were younger.

la **libellule** NOUN
dragonfly

libérer VERB
to free ◇ *Les otages ont été libérés hier soir.* The hostages were freed last night.
◆ **se libérer** to find time ◇ *J'essaierai de me libérer cet après-midi.* I'll try to find time this afternoon.

la **liberté** NOUN
freedom
◆ **mettre en liberté** to release ◇ *Il a été mis en liberté au bout d'un an de prison.* He was released after a year in prison.

le/la **libraire** NOUN
bookseller

la **librairie** NOUN
bookshop

libre ADJECTIVE
1 *free* ◇ *Tu es libre de faire ce que tu veux.* You are free to do as you wish. ◇ *Est-ce que cette place est libre?* Is this seat free?

2 *clear* ◇ *La route est libre: vous pouvez traverser.* The road is clear: you can cross.

▸ **une école libre** a private school

ibre-service NOUN
(PL les **libres-services**)
self-service store

ibye NOUN
Libya

icence NOUN
1 *degree* ◇ *une licence de droit* a law degree
2 *licence* ◇ *une licence d'exportation* an export licence

icencié NOUN
graduate

icenciée NOUN
graduate

icencier VERB
to make redundant ◇ *Ils viennent de licencier sept employés.* They've just made 7 employees redundant.

iège NOUN
cork ◇ *des sets en liège* cork mats

▸ **un bouchon en liège** a cork (*for bottle*)

ien NOUN
connection ◇ *Il n'y aucun lien entre ces deux événements.* There's no connection between these two events.

▸ **un lien de parenté** a family tie

ier VERB

▸ **lier conversation avec quelqu'un** to get into conversation with somebody

▸ **se lier avec quelqu'un** to make friends with somebody ◇ *Je ne me lie pas facilement.* I don't make friends easily.

ierre NOUN
ivy

ieu NOUN
(PL les **lieux**)
place ◇ *votre lieu de travail* your place of work

▸ **avoir lieu** to take place ◇ *La cérémonie a eu lieu dans la salle des fêtes.* The ceremony took place in the village hall.

▸ **au lieu de** instead of ◇ *J'aimerais une pomme au lieu de la glace.* I'd like an apple instead of ice cream.

lièvre NOUN
hare

ligne NOUN
1 *line* (*phone, train*) ◇ *La ligne est mauvaise.* It's a bad line. ◇ *la ligne d'autobus numéro douze* the number 12 bus
2 *figure* ◇ *C'est mauvais pour la ligne.* It's bad for your figure.

ligoter VERB
to tie up

la **ligue** NOUN
league

le **lilas** NOUN
lilac

la **limace** NOUN
slug

la **lime** NOUN

▸ **une lime à ongles** a nail file

la **limitation** NOUN

▸ **la limitation de vitesse** the speed limit

la **limite** NOUN
1 *boundary* (*of property, football pitch*)
2 *limit* ◇ *Est-ce qu'il y a une limite d'âge?* Is there an age limit?

▸ **la date limite** the deadline

▸ **la date limite de vente** the sell-by-date

limiter VERB
to limit ◇ *Le nombre de billets est limité à deux par personne.* The number of tickets is limited to two per person.

la **limonade** NOUN
lemonade

le **lin** NOUN
linen ◇ *une veste en lin* a linen jacket

le **linge** NOUN
1 *linen* ◇ *le linge sale* dirty linen
2 *washing* ◇ *laver le linge* to do the washing

▸ **du linge de corps** underwear

la **lingerie** NOUN
underwear (*women's*)

le **lion** NOUN
lion

▸ **le Lion** Leo ◇ *Louise est Lion.* Louise is Leo.

la **lionne** NOUN
lioness

la **liqueur** NOUN
liqueur

liquide ADJECTIVE
see also liquide NOUN
liquid

le **liquide** NOUN
see also liquide ADJECTIVE
liquid

▸ **payer quelque chose en liquide** to pay cash for something

lire VERB
to read ◇ *Tu as lu "Madame Bovary"?* Have you read "Madame Bovary"?

lis, lisent, lisez VERB *see* **lire**

▸ **Je lis beaucoup.** I read a lot.

lisible ADJECTIVE
legible

lisse ADJECTIVE
smooth

la **liste** NOUN
list

L

PTO

- **faire la liste de** to make a list of ◇ *J'ai fait la liste de tout ce dont j'ai besoin.* I've made a list of all the things I need.

lit VERB *see* **lire**

le **lit** NOUN
bed ◇ *aller au lit* to go to bed
- **faire son lit** to make one's bed ◇ *Je n'ai pas eu le temps de faire mon lit ce matin.* I haven't had time to make my bed this morning.
- **un lit de camp** a campbed

la **literie** NOUN
bedding

la **litière** NOUN
1 *litter* (*for cat*)
2 *bedding* (*of caged pet*)

le **litre** NOUN
litre

littéraire ADJECTIVE
- **une œuvre littéraire** a work of literature

la **littérature** NOUN
literature

le **littoral** NOUN
(PL les **littoraux**)
coast

la **Lituanie** NOUN
Lithuania

la **livraison** NOUN
delivery
- **la livraison des bagages** baggage reclaim

le **livre** NOUN
see also la livre
book
- **un livre de poche** a paperback

la **livre** NOUN
see also le livre
pound
The French livre *is 500 grams.*
◇ *une livre de beurre* a pound of butter
- **la livre sterling** the pound sterling ◇ *Le guide coûte trois livres.* The guide book costs £3.

livrer VERB
to deliver

le **livret** NOUN
booklet
- **le livret scolaire** the school report book

le **livreur** NOUN
delivery man

local ADJECTIVE
(MASC PL **locaux**)
see also local NOUN
local

le **local** NOUN
(PL les **locaux**)
see also local ADJECTIVE
premises ◇ *Nous cherchons un local pour les répétitions.* We are looking for premises to rehearse in.

le/la **locataire** NOUN
1 *tenant*
2 *lodger* ◇ *Ils ont décidé de prendre un locataire.* They have decided to take a lodger.

la **location** NOUN
- **location de voitures** car rental
- **location de skis** ski hire

locaux ADJECTIVE, NOUN *see* **local**

la **locomotive** NOUN
locomotive

la **loge** NOUN
dressing room

le **logement** NOUN
1 *housing*
2 *accommodation*

loger VERB
to stay ◇ *Elle loge chez sa cousine quand elle revient dans la région.* She stays with her cousin when she comes back to the area.
- **trouver à se loger** to find somewhere to live ◇ *J'ai eu du mal à trouver à me loger.* I had difficulty finding somewhere to live.

le **logiciel** NOUN
software

logique ADJECTIVE
see also logique NOUN
logical

la **logique** NOUN
see also logique ADJECTIVE
logic

la **loi** NOUN
law

loin ADVERB
1 *far* ◇ *La gare n'est pas très loin d'ici.* The station is not very far from here.
2 *far off* ◇ *Noël n'est plus tellement loin.* Christmas isn't far off now.
3 *a long time ago* ◇ *Les vacances paraissent déjà tellement loin!* The holidays already seem such a long time ago!
- **au loin** in the distance ◇ *On aperçoit la mer au loin.* You can see the sea in the distance.
- **de loin (1)** from a long way away ◇ *On voit l'église de loin.* You can see the church from a long way away.
- **de loin (2)** by far ◇ *C'est de loin l'élève la plus brillante.* She is by far the brightest pupil.

lointain ADJECTIVE
see also lointain NOUN
distant ◇ *un pays lointain* a distant

country ◇ *C'est un parent lointain de ma mère.* He's a distant relation of my mother.

lointain NOUN

see also lointain ADJECTIVE

- **dans le lointain** in the distance

loir NOUN

dormouse

- **dormir comme un loir** to sleep like a log

loisirs MASC NOUN

1 *free time* ◇ *Qu'est-ce que vous faites pendant vos loisirs?* What do you do in your free time?

2 *hobby* ◇ *Le ski et l'équitation sont des loisirs coûteux.* Skiing and riding are expensive hobbies.

Londonien NOUN

Londoner

Londonienne NOUN

Londoner

Londres NOUN

London ◇ *le métro de Londres* the London underground

- **à Londres (1)** in London
- **à Londres (2)** to London

long ADJECTIVE

(FEM SING **longue**)

see also long NOUN

long

long NOUN

see also long ADJECTIVE

- **un bateau de trois mètres de long** a boat 3 m long
- **tout le long de** all along ◇ *Il y a des chemins de randonnée tout le long de la côte.* There are footpaths all along the coast.
- **marcher de long en large** to walk up and down

longtemps ADVERB

a long time ◇ *J'ai attendu longtemps chez le dentiste.* I waited a long time at the dentist's.

- **pendant longtemps** for a long time ◇ *On a cru pendant longtemps que la Terre était plate.* For a long time people thought the Earth was flat.
- **mettre longtemps à faire quelque chose** to take a long time to do something ◇ *Il a mis longtemps à répondre à ma lettre.* He took a long time to answer my letter.

longue ADJECTIVE *see* **long**

longue NOUN

- **à la longue** in the end ◇ *Elle a fini par agacer tout le monde à la longue.* In the end she got on everybody's nerves.

longuement ADVERB

at length ◇ *Elle m'a longuement parlé de ses projets d'avenir.* She talked to me at length about her plans for the future.

longueur NOUN

length

- **à longueur de journée** all day long ◇ *Elle mâche du chewing-gum à longueur de journée.* She chews gum all day long.

loques FEM NOUN

- **être en loques** to be torn to bits ◇ *Sa chemise était en loques.* His shirt was torn to bits.

lors de PREPOSITION

during ◇ *Je l'ai rencontré lors de mon stage en entreprise.* I met him during my work placement.

lorsque CONJUNCTION

when ◇ *J'allais composer ton numéro lorsque tu as appelé.* I was about to dial your number when you called.

lot NOUN

prize

- **le gros lot** the jackpot

loterie NOUN

1 *lottery* ◇ *la loterie nationale* the National Lottery

2 *raffle* ◇ *J'ai gagné cet ours en peluche dans une loterie.* I won this teddy in a raffle.

lotion NOUN

lotion ◇ *une bouteille de lotion solaire* a bottle of suntan lotion

- **une lotion après-rasage** an aftershave

lotissement NOUN

housing estate

loto NOUN

lottery

- **le loto sportif** the pools

loubard NOUN (*informal*)

lout

louche ADJECTIVE

see also louche NOUN

fishy ◇ *une histoire louche* a fishy story

louche NOUN

see also louche ADJECTIVE

ladle

loucher VERB

to squint

louer VERB

1 *to let* ◇ *Ils louent des chambres à des étudiants.* They let rooms to students.

- **"à louer"** "to let"

2 *to rent* ◇ *Je loue un petit appartement au centre-ville.* I rent a little flat in the centre of town.

3 *to hire* ◇ *Est-ce que vous louez des*

PTO

vélos? Do you hire bikes? ◇ *Nous allons louer une voiture pour le week-end.* We're going to hire a car for the weekend.

4 *to praise* ◇ *Les journaux ont loué le courage des pompiers.* The newspapers praised the courage of the firefighters.

le **loup** NOUN
wolf

la **loupe** NOUN
magnifying glass

louper VERB (*informal*)
to miss ◇ *Dépêche-toi, tu vas louper ton train!* Hurry up, you'll miss your train!

lourd ADJECTIVE
heavy ◇ *Mon sac est très lourd.* My bag's very heavy.

la **loutre** NOUN
otter

la **loyauté** NOUN
loyalty

le **loyer** NOUN
rent

lu VERB *see* **lire**

la **lucarne** NOUN
skylight

la **luge** NOUN
sledge

lugubre ADJECTIVE
gloomy

lui PRONOUN
1 *him* ◇ *Il a été très content du cadeau que je lui ai offert.* He was very pleased with the present I gave him. ◇ *C'est bien lui!* It's definitely him! ◇ *J'ai pensé à lui toute la journée.* I thought about him all day long.
2 *to him* ◇ *Mon père est d'accord: je lui ai parlé ce matin.* My father said yes: I spoke to him this morning.
3 *her* ◇ *Elle a été très contente du cadeau que je lui ai offert.* She was very pleased with the present I gave her.
4 *to her* ◇ *Ma mère est d'accord: je lui ai parlé ce matin.* My mother said yes: I spoke to her this morning.
5 *it* ◇ *Qu'est-ce que tu donnes à ton chat?–Je lui donne de la viande crue.* What do you give your cat?–I give it raw meat.

lui *is also used for emphasis.*

◇ *Lui, il est toujours en retard!* Oh him, he's always late!

◆ **lui-même** himself ◇ *Il a construit son bateau lui-même.* He built his boat himself.

la **lumière** NOUN
light

◆ **la lumière du jour** daylight

lumineux ADJECTIVE
(FEM SING **lumineuse**)

◆ **une enseigne lumineuse** a neon sign

lunatique ADJECTIVE
temperamental ◇ *Il est plutôt lunatique.* He's rather temperamental.

le **lundi** NOUN
1 *Monday* ◇ *Aujourd'hui, nous sommes lundi.* It's Monday today.
2 *on Monday* ◇ *Ils sont arrivés lundi.* They arrived on Monday.

◆ **le lundi** on Mondays ◇ *Le lundi, je vais à la piscine.* I go swimming on Mondays.

◆ **tous les lundis** every Monday

◆ **lundi dernier** last Monday

◆ **lundi prochain** next Monday

◆ **le lundi de Pâques** Easter Monday

la **lune** NOUN
moon

◆ **la lune de miel** honeymoon

les **lunettes** FEM NOUN
glasses

◆ **des lunettes de soleil** sunglasses

◆ **des lunettes de plongée** swimming goggles

la **lutte** NOUN
1 *fight* ◇ *la lutte contre le racisme* the fight against racism
2 *wrestling* ◇ *une épreuve de lutte* a wrestling bout

lutter VERB
to fight

le **luxe** NOUN
luxury

◆ **de luxe** luxury ◇ *un hôtel de luxe* a luxury hotel

luxueux ADJECTIVE
(FEM SING **luxueuse**)
luxurious

le **lycée** NOUN
secondary school

In France pupils go to a collège *between the ages of 11 and 15, and then to a* lycée *until the age of 18.*

le **lycéen** NOUN
secondary school pupil

la **lycéenne** NOUN
secondary school pupil

M

M. ABBREVIATION (= *Monsieur*)
Mr ◇ *M. Bernard* Mr Bernard

m' PRONOUN *see* **me**

ma ADJECTIVE
my ◇ *ma mère* my mother ◇ *ma montre* my watch

macaronis MASC NOUN
macaroni

Macédoine NOUN
Macedonia

macédoine NOUN
- **la macédoine de fruits** fruit salad
- **la macédoine de légumes** mixed vegetables

mâcher VERB
to chew

machin NOUN (*informal*)
thingy ◇ *Passe-moi le machin pour râper les carottes.* Pass me the thingy for grating carrots. ◇ *Qu'est-ce que c'est que ce vieux machin?* What's this old thing?

machine NOUN
machine
- **une machine à laver** a washing machine
- **une machine à écrire** a typewriter
- **une machine à coudre** a sewing machine
- **une machine à sous** a fruit machine

mâchoire NOUN
jaw

mâchonner VERB
to chew

maçon NOUN
bricklayer

Madame FEM NOUN
(PL **Mesdames**)
1 *Mrs* ◇ *Madame Legall* Mrs Legall
2 *lady* ◇ *Occupez-vous de Madame.* Could you look after this lady?
3 *Madam* ◇ *Madame,...* Dear Madam,... (*in letter*) ◇ *Madame! Vous avez oublié votre parapluie!* Excuse me! You've forgotten your umbrella!

Mademoiselle FEM NOUN
(PL **Mesdemoiselles**)
1 *Miss* ◇ *Mademoiselle Martin* Miss Martin
2 *Madam* ◇ *Mademoiselle,...* Dear Madam,... (*in letter*)

magasin NOUN
shop ◇ *Les magasins ouvrent à huit heures.* The shops open at 8 o'clock.

magazine NOUN
magazine

le **magicien** NOUN
magician

la **magicienne** NOUN
magician

la **magie** NOUN
magic ◇ *un tour de magie* a magic trick

magique ADJECTIVE
magic ◇ *une baguette magique* a magic wand

magistral ADJECTIVE
(MASC PL **magistraux**)
- **un cours magistral** a lecture (*at university*)

magnétique ADJECTIVE
magnetic

le **magnétophone** NOUN
tape recorder
- **un magnétophone à cassettes** a cassette recorder

le **magnétoscope** NOUN
video recorder

magnifique ADJECTIVE
superb

mai MASC NOUN
May
- **en mai** in May

maigre ADJECTIVE
1 *skinny* ◇ *Ma mère me trouve trop maigre.* My mother says I'm too skinny.
2 *lean* (*meat*)
3 *low-fat* (*cheese, yoghurt*)

maigrir VERB
to lose weight ◇ *Il fait un régime pour essayer de maigrir.* He's on a diet, to try to lose weight. ◇ *Elle a maigri de deux kilos en un mois.* She's lost two kilos in a month.

le **maillot de bain** NOUN
1 *swimsuit*
2 *swimming trunks*

la **main** NOUN
hand ◇ *Donne-moi la main!* Give me your hand!
- **serrer la main à quelqu'un** to shake hands with somebody
- **se serrer la main** to shake hands ◇ *Les deux présidents se sont serré la main.* The two presidents shook hands.
- **sous la main** to hand ◇ *Est-ce que tu as son adresse sous la main?* Have you got his address to hand?

maintenant ADVERB
1 *now* ◇ *Qu'est-ce que tu veux faire maintenant?* What do you want to do now? ◇ *C'est maintenant ou jamais.* It's

PTO

now or never.

2 *nowadays* ◇ *Maintenant la plupart des gens font leurs courses au supermarché.* Nowadays most people do their shopping at the supermarket.

maintenir VERB

to maintain ◇ *Il maintient qu'il n'était pas là le jour du crime.* He maintains he wasn't there on the day of the crime.

◆ **se maintenir** to hold ◇ *Espérons que le beau temps va se maintenir pour le week-end!* Let's hope the good weather will hold over the weekend!

le **maire** NOUN

mayor

la **mairie** NOUN

town hall

mais CONJUNCTION

but ◇ *C'est cher mais de très bonne qualité.* It's expensive, but very good quality.

le **maïs** NOUN

1 *maize*

2 *sweetcorn*

la **maison** NOUN

see also maison ADJECTIVE

house ◇ *Ils habitent dans la maison qui est au bout de la rue.* They live in the house at the end of the street.

◆ **à la maison (1)** at home ◇ *Je serai à la maison cet après-midi.* I'll be at home this afternoon.

◆ **à la maison (2)** home ◇ *Elle est rentrée à la maison.* She's gone home.

maison ADJECTIVE (MASC, FEM, PL)

see also maison NOUN

home-made ◇ *Je préfère les tartes maison à celles qui sont achetées.* I prefer home-made pies to bought ones.

le **maître** NOUN

1 *teacher* (*in primary school*)

2 *master* (*of dog*)

◆ **un maître d'hôtel** a head waiter (*in restaurant*)

◆ **un maître nageur** a lifeguard

la **maîtresse** NOUN

1 *teacher* (*in primary school*)

2 *mistress* ◇ *Il paraît qu'il a une maîtresse.* They say he's got a mistress.

la **maîtrise** NOUN

master's degree ◇ *Elle a une maîtrise d'anglais.* She's got a master's degree in English.

◆ **la maîtrise de soi** self-control

maîtriser VERB

◆ **se maîtriser** to control oneself ◇ *Il se met facilement en colère et a du mal à se maîtriser.* He loses his temper easily and finds it hard to control himself.

majestueux ADJECTIVE

(FEM SING **majestueuse**)

majestic

majeur ADJECTIVE

◆ **être majeur** to be 18 ◇ *Tu feras ce que tu voudras quand tu seras majeure.* You can do what you like once you're 18. ◇ *Elle sera majeure en août.* She comes of age in August.

◆ **la majeure partie** most ◇ *la majeure partie de mon salaire* most of my salary

la **majorité** NOUN

majority ◇ *dans la majorité des cas* in the majority of cases

◆ **la majorité et l'opposition** the government and the opposition

Majorque FEM NOUN

Majorca

la **majuscule** NOUN

capital letter ◇ *un M majuscule* a capital M

mal ADVERB, ADJECTIVE (MASC, FEM, PL)

see also mal NOUN

1 *badly* ◇ *Ce travail a été mal fait.* The work was badly done. ◇ *Il a mal compris.* He misunderstood.

2 *wrong* ◇ *C'est mal de mentir.* It's wrong to tell lies.

◆ **aller mal** to be ill ◇ *Son grand-père va très mal.* His grandfather is very ill.

◆ **pas mal** quite good ◇ *Je te trouve pas mal sur cette photo.* I think you look quite good in this photo.

le **mal** NOUN

(PL **les maux**)

see also mal ADVERB

1 *ache* ◇ *J'ai mal à la tête.* I've got a headache. ◇ *J'ai mal aux dents.* I've got toothache. ◇ *J'ai mal au dos.* My back hurts. ◇ *Est-ce que vous avez mal à la gorge?* Have you got a sore throat?

◆ **Ça fait mal.** It hurts.

◆ **Où est-ce que tu as mal?** Where does it hurt?

◆ **faire mal à quelqu'un** to hurt somebody ◇ *Attention, tu me fais mal!* Be careful, you're hurting me!

◆ **se faire mal** to hurt oneself ◇ *Je me suis fait mal au bras.* I hurt my arm.

◆ **se donner du mal pour faire quelque chose** to go to a lot of trouble to do something ◇ *Il s'est donné beaucoup de mal pour que cette soirée soit réussie.* He went to a lot of trouble to make the party a success.

◆ **avoir le mal de mer** to be seasick

◆ **avoir le mal du pays** to be homesick

2 *evil* ◇ *le bien et le mal* good and evil

◆ **dire du mal de quelqu'un** to speak ill of

somebody

malade ADJECTIVE

see also malade NOUN

ill

- **tomber malade** to fall ill

malade NOUN

see also malade ADJECTIVE

patient

maladie NOUN

illness

maladif ADJECTIVE

(FEM SING **maladive**)

sickly ◇ *C'est un enfant maladif.* He's a sickly child.

maladresse NOUN

clumsiness

maladroit ADJECTIVE

clumsy

malaise NOUN

- **avoir un malaise** to feel faint ◇ *Elle a eu un malaise après le déjeuner.* She felt faint after lunch.
- **Son arrivée a créé un malaise parmi les invités.** Her arrival made the guests feel uncomfortable.

malchance NOUN

bad luck

mâle ADJECTIVE

male

malédiction NOUN

curse

mal en point ADJECTIVE (MASC, FEM, PL)

- **Il avait l'air mal en point quand je l'ai vu hier soir.** He didn't look too good when I saw him last night.

malentendu NOUN

misunderstanding

malfaiteur NOUN

criminal

mal famé ADJECTIVE

(FEM **mal famée**, MASC PL **mal famés**)

- **un quartier mal famé** a seedy area

malgache ADJECTIVE

from Madagascar ◇ *Sa mère est malgache.* His mother's from Madagascar.

malgré PREPOSITION

in spite of ◇ *Il est toujours généreux malgré ses problèmes d'argent.* He's always generous in spite of his financial problems.

- **malgré tout** all the same ◇ *Il faisait mauvais mais nous sommes sortis malgré tout.* The weather was bad but we went out all the same.

malheur NOUN

tragedy ◇ *Elle a eu beaucoup de malheurs dans sa vie.* She's had a lot of tragedy in her life.

- **faire un malheur** (*informal*) to be a smash hit ◇ *Leur dernier album a fait un malheur.* Their latest album was a smash hit.

malheureusement ADVERB

unfortunately

malheureux ADJECTIVE

(FEM SING **malheureuse**)

miserable ◇ *Qu'est-ce que tu as? Tu as l'air malheureux.* What's wrong with you? You look miserable.

malhonnête ADJECTIVE

dishonest

la **malice** NOUN

mischief ◇ *Son regard était plein de malice.* His eyes were full of mischief.

malicieux ADJECTIVE

(FEM SING **malicieuse**)

mischievous

malin ADJECTIVE

(FEM SING **maligne**)

crafty

- **C'est malin!** (*informal*) That's clever! ◇ *Ah c'est malin! Nous voilà enfermés à cause de toi!* That's clever! You've got us locked in!

la **malle** NOUN

trunk

malodorant ADJECTIVE

foul-smelling

malpropre ADJECTIVE

dirty

malsain ADJECTIVE

unhealthy

Malte MASC NOUN

Malta

maltraiter VERB

to ill-treat ◇ *Il maltraite son chien.* He ill-treats his dog.

- **des enfants maltraités** battered children

malveillant ADJECTIVE

malicious ◇ *des rumeurs malveillantes* malicious rumours

la **maman** NOUN

mum

la **mamie** NOUN

granny

le **mammifère** NOUN

mammal

la **manche** NOUN

see also le manche

1 *sleeve* (*of clothes*)

2 *leg* (*of game*) ◇ *Ils ont remporté la première manche du match.* They won the first leg of the match.

- **la Manche** the Channel

le **manche** NOUN

see also la manche

PTO

handle (*of pan*)

la **mandarine** NOUN
mandarin orange

le **manège** NOUN
merry-go-round

la **manette** NOUN
lever

mangeable ADJECTIVE
edible ◇ *C'est à peine mangeable!* It's practically inedible!

manger VERB
to eat

la **mangue** NOUN
mango

maniaque ADJECTIVE
fussy

la **manie** NOUN
1 *obsession*
◆ **avoir la manie de** to be obsessive about ◇ *Il a la manie du rangement.* He's obsessive about tidying up.
2 *habit* ◇ *J'essaie de respecter ses petites manies.* I try to go along with her little ways.

manier VERB
to handle

la **manière**
see also les manières NOUN
way
◆ **de manière à** so as to ◇ *Nous sommes partis tôt de manière à éviter la circulation.* We left early so as to avoid the traffic.
◆ **de toute manière** in any case ◇ *Je n'aurais pas pu venir de toute manière.* I couldn't have come in any case.

maniéré ADJECTIVE
affected

les **manières**
see also la manière FEM NOUN
1 *manners* ◇ *apprendre les bonnes manières* to learn good manners
2 *fuss* ◇ *Ne fais pas de manières: mange ta soupe!* Don't make a fuss: eat your soup!

le **manifestant** NOUN
demonstrator

la **manifestante** NOUN
demonstrator

la **manifestation** NOUN
demonstration ◇ *une manifestation pour la paix* a peace demonstration

manifester VERB
to demonstrate

manipuler VERB
1 *to handle* ◇ *Ce vase doit être manipulé avec soin.* This vase must be handled with care.
2 *to manipulate* ◇ *Tous les partis essaient de manipuler l'opinion publique.* All the parties are trying to manipulate public opinion.

le **mannequin** NOUN
model ◇ *Elle est mannequin.* She's a model.

manœuvrer VERB
to manœuvre

le **manque** NOUN
◆ **le manque de** lack of ◇ *Le manque de sommeil peut provoquer toutes sortes de troubles.* Lack of sleep can cause all sorts of problems.
withdrawal ◇ *un drogué en état de manque* a drug addict suffering withdrawal symptoms

manqué ADJECTIVE
◆ **un garçon manqué** a tomboy

manquer VERB
to miss ◇ *Tu n'as rien manqué: le film n'était pas très bon.* You didn't miss anything: the film wasn't very good. ◇ *Il manque des pages à ce livre.* There are some pages missing from this book.
◆ **Mes parents me manquent.** I miss my parents.
◆ **Ma sœur me manque.** I miss my sister.
◆ **Il manque encore cent francs.** We are still 100 francs short.
◆ **manquer de** to lack ◇ *La quiche manque de sel.* The quiche hasn't got enough salt in it. ◇ *Je trouve qu'il a manqué de tact.* I don't think he was very tactful.
◆ **Il a manqué se tuer.** He nearly got killed.

le **manteau** NOUN
(PL les **manteaux**)
coat

manuel ADJECTIVE
(FEM SING **manuelle**)
see also manuel NOUN
manual

le **manuel** NOUN
see also manuel ADJECTIVE
1 *textbook*
2 *handbook*

le **maquereau** NOUN
(PL les **maquereaux**)
mackerel

la **maquette** NOUN
model ◇ *une maquette de bateau* a model boat

le **maquillage** NOUN
make-up

se **maquiller** VERB
to put on one's make-up ◇ *Je vais me maquiller en vitesse.* I'll just quickly put on my make-up.

marais NOUN
marsh
marbre NOUN
marble ◇ *une statue en marbre* a marble statue
marchand NOUN
1 *shopkeeper*
◆ **un marchand de journaux** a newsagent
2 *stallholder* (*in market*)
marchande NOUN
1 *shopkeeper*
◆ **une marchande de fruits et de légumes** a greengrocer
2 *stallholder* (*in market*)
marchander VERB
to haggle
marchandise NOUN
goods
marche NOUN
1 *step* ◇ *Fais attention à la marche!* Mind the step!
2 *walking* ◇ *La marche me fait du bien.* Walking does me good.
◆ **être en état de marche** to be in working order ◇ *Cette voiture est en parfait état de marche.* This car is in perfect running order.
◆ **Ne montez jamais dans un train en marche.** Never try to get into a moving train.
◆ **mettre en marche** to start ◇ *Comment est-ce qu'on met la machine à laver en marche?* How do you start the washing machine?
◆ **la marche arrière** reverse gear
◆ **faire marche arrière** to reverse
3 *march* ◇ *une marche militaire* a military march
marché NOUN
market
◆ **un marché aux puces** a flea market
marcher VERB
1 *to walk* ◇ *Elle marche cinq kilomètres par jour.* She walks 5 kilometres every day.
2 *to run* ◇ *Le métro marche normalement aujourd'hui.* The underground is running normally today.
3 *to work* ◇ *Est-ce que l'ascenseur marche?* Is the lift working?
4 *to go well* ◇ *Est-ce que les affaires marchent actuellement?* Is business going well at the moment?
◆ **Alors les études, ça marche?** (*informal*) How are you getting on at school?
◆ **faire marcher quelqu'un** to pull somebody's leg ◇ *Il essaie de te faire marcher.* He's pulling your leg.

le **marcheur** NOUN
walker
la **marcheuse** NOUN
walker
le **mardi** NOUN
1 *Tuesday* ◇ *Aujourd'hui, nous sommes mardi.* It's Tuesday today.
2 *on Tuesday* ◇ *Ils reviennent mardi.* They're coming back on Tuesday.
◆ **le mardi** on Tuesdays ◇ *Le mardi, je vais à la gym.* I go to the gym on Tuesdays.
◆ **tous les mardis** every Tuesday
◆ **mardi dernier** last Tuesday
◆ **mardi prochain** next Tuesday
◆ **Mardi gras** Shrove Tuesday
la **mare** NOUN
pond
le **marécage** NOUN
marsh
la **marée** NOUN
tide ◇ *la marée haute* high tide ◇ *la marée basse* low tide ◇ *la marée montante* the rising tide ◇ *la marée descendante* the ebb tide
la **margarine** NOUN
margarine
la **marge** NOUN
margin
le **mari** NOUN
husband ◇ *son mari* her husband
le **mariage** NOUN
1 *marriage*
2 *wedding* ◇ *un mariage civil* a registry office wedding ◇ *un mariage religieux* a church wedding
marié ADJECTIVE
see also marié NOUN
married
le **marié** NOUN
see also marié ADJECTIVE
bridegroom
◆ **les mariés** the bride and groom
la **mariée** NOUN
bride
se **marier** VERB
to marry ◇ *Elle s'est mariée avec un ami d'enfance.* She married a childhood friend.
marin ADJECTIVE
see also marin NOUN
sea ◇ *l'air marin* the sea air
◆ **un pull marin** a sailor's jersey
le **marin** NOUN
see also marin ADJECTIVE
sailor
marine ADJECTIVE (MASC, FEM, PL)
see also marine NOUN
◆ **bleu marine** navy-blue ◇ *un pull bleu*

PTO

marine a navy-blue sweater

la **marine** NOUN
see also marine ADJECTIVE
navy
- **la marine nationale** the French navy

la **marionnette** NOUN
puppet

la **marmelade** NOUN
stewed fruit
- **la marmelade de pommes** stewed apple
- **la marmelade d'oranges** marmalade

la **marmite** NOUN
cooking pot

marmonner VERB
to mumble

le **Maroc** NOUN
Morocco

marocain ADJECTIVE
Moroccan

la **maroquinerie** NOUN
leather goods shop

marquant ADJECTIVE
significant ◇ *un événement marquant* a significant event

la **marque** NOUN
1 *mark* ◇ *des marques de doigts* fingermarks
2 *make* ◇ *De quelle marque est ton jean?* What make are your jeans?
3 *brand* ◇ *une grande marque de cognac* a well-known brand of cognac
- **l'image de marque** the public image ◇ *Le ministre tient à son image de marque.* The minister cares about his public image.
- **une marque déposée** a registered trademark
- **A vos marques! prêts! partez!** Ready, steady, go!

marquer VERB
1 *to mark* ◇ *Peux-tu marquer sur la carte où se trouve le village?* Can you mark where the village is on the map?
2 *to score* ◇ *L'équipe adverse a marqué dix points.* The opposing team scored ten points.
3 *to celebrate* ◇ *On va sortir au restaurant pour marquer ton anniversaire.* We'll eat out to celebrate your birthday.

la **marraine** NOUN
godmother

marrant ADJECTIVE (*informal*)
funny

marre ADVERB (*informal*)
- **en avoir marre de quelque chose** to be fed up with something ◇ *J'en ai marre de faire la vaisselle.* I'm fed up with doing the dishes.

se **marrer** VERB (*informal*)
to have a good laugh ◇ *On s'est bien marrés.* We had a good laugh.

le **marron** NOUN
see also marron ADJECTIVE
chestnut ◇ *la crème de marrons* chestnut purée

marron ADJECTIVE (MASC, FEM, PL)
see also marron NOUN
brown ◇ *des chaussures marron* brown shoes

le **marronnier** NOUN
chestnut tree

mars MASC NOUN
March
- **en mars** in March

le **marteau** NOUN
(PL les **marteaux**)
hammer

martyriser VERB
to batter ◇ *des enfants martyrisés* battered children

masculin ADJECTIVE
1 *men's* ◇ *la mode masculine* men's fashion
2 *masculine* ◇ *"chat" est un nom masculin.* "chat" is a masculine noun. ◇ *Elle a une allure assez masculine.* She looks rather masculine.

le **masque** NOUN
mask

le **massacre** NOUN
massacre

massacrer VERB
to massacre

le **massage** NOUN
massage

la **masse** NOUN
- **une masse de** (*informal*) masses of ◇ *J'ai une masse de choses à faire.* I've got masses of things to do.
- **produire en masse** to mass-produce ◇ *Ces jouets sont produits en masse en Chine.* These toys are mass-produced in China.
- **venir en masse** to come en masse ◇ *Les gens sont venus en masse pour accueillir Nelson Mandela.* People came en masse to welcome Nelson Mandela.

masser VERB
to massage
- **se masser** to gather ◇ *Les manifestants se sont massés devant l'ambassade.* The demonstrators gathered in front of the embassy.

massif ADJECTIVE
(FEM SING **massive**)
1 *solid* (*gold, silver, wood*) ◇ *un bracelet en or massif* a solid gold bracelet
2 *massive* ◇ *une dose massive*

d'antibiotiques a massive dose of antibiotics

3 *mass* ◇ *des départs massifs* a mass exodus

mat ADJECTIVE

matt ◇ *blanc mat* matt white ◇ *Je voudrais mes photos en mat.* I would like my photos matt.

- **être mat** to be checkmate (*chess*)

le **match** NOUN

match ◇ *un match de football* a football match

- **le match aller** the first leg
- **le match retour** the second leg
- **faire match nul** to draw

le **matelas** NOUN

mattress

- **un matelas pneumatique** an air bed

matelassé ADJECTIVE

quilted ◇ *une veste matelassée* a quilted jacket

le **matelot** NOUN

sailor

les **matériaux** MASC NOUN

materials

le **matériel** NOUN

1 *equipment* ◇ *du matériel de laboratoire* laboratory equipment

2 *gear* ◇ *Il a pris tout son matériel de pêche avec lui.* He took all his fishing gear with him.

maternel ADJECTIVE

(FEM SING **maternelle**)

motherly ◇ *Elle est très maternelle.* She's very motherly.

- **ma grand-mère maternelle** my mother's mother
- **mon oncle maternel** my mother's brother

la **maternelle** NOUN

nursery school

The maternelle *is a state school for 2-6 year-olds.*

la **maternité** NOUN

- **le congé de maternité** maternity leave ◇ *Notre professeur de musique est en congé de maternité.* Our music teacher is on maternity leave.

les **mathématiques** FEM NOUN

mathematics

les **maths** FEM NOUN (*informal*)

maths

la **matière** NOUN

subject ◇ *Le latin est une matière facultative.* Latin is an optional subject.

- **sans matières grasses** fat-free
- **les matières premières** raw materials

le **matin** NOUN

morning ◇ *à trois heures du matin* at 3 o'clock in the morning ◇ *du matin au soir* from morning till night

- **Je suis du matin.** I'm at my best in the morning.
- **de bon matin** early in the morning

matinal ADJECTIVE

(MASC PL **matinaux**)

morning ◇ *Je fais ma gymnastique matinale avant de déjeuner.* I do my morning exercises before breakfast.

- **être matinal** to be up early ◇ *Tu es bien matinal aujourd'hui!* You're up early today!

la **matinée** NOUN

morning ◇ *Je t'appellerai demain dans la matinée.* I'll call you sometime tomorrow morning. ◇ *en début de matinée* early in the morning

le **matou** NOUN

tomcat

matrimonial ADJECTIVE

(MASC PL **matrimoniaux**)

- **une agence matrimoniale** a marriage bureau

maudire VERB

to curse

maudit ADJECTIVE (*informal*)

blasted ◇ *Où est passé ce maudit parapluie?* Where's that blasted umbrella got to?

maussade ADJECTIVE

sullen

mauvais ADJECTIVE, ADVERB

1 *bad* ◇ *une mauvaise note* a bad mark ◇ *Tu arrives au mauvais moment.* You've come at a bad time.

- **Il fait mauvais.** The weather's bad.
- **être mauvais en** to be bad at ◇ *Je suis mauvais en allemand.* I'm bad at German.

2 *poor* ◇ *J'ai trouvé que le film était mauvais.* I thought the film was poor. ◇ *Il est en mauvaise santé.* His health is poor.

- **Tu as mauvaise mine.** You don't look well.

3 *wrong* ◇ *Vous avez fait le mauvais numéro.* You've dialled the wrong number.

- **des mauvaises herbes** weeds
- **sentir mauvais** to smell

les **maux** MASC NOUN

- **des maux de ventre** stomachache
- **des maux de tête** headache

le **maximum** NOUN

maximum

- **au maximum (1)** as much as one can ◇ *Remplis le seau au maximum.* Fill the bucket as full as you can.

PTO

◆ **au maximum (2)** at the very most ◇ *Ça va vous coûter deux cents francs au maximum.* It'll cost you 200 francs at the very most.

la **mayonnaise** NOUN
mayonnaise

le **mazout** NOUN
fuel oil

me PRONOUN

me *changes to* **m'** *before a vowel and most words beginning with "h".*

1 *me* ◇ *Elle me téléphone tous les jours.* She phones me every day. ◇ *Il m'attend depuis une heure.* He's been waiting for me for an hour.

2 *to me* ◇ *Il me parle en allemand.* He talks to me in German. ◇ *Elle m'a expliqué la situation.* She explained the situation to me.

3 *myself* ◇ *Je vais me préparer quelque chose à manger.* I'm going to make myself something to eat.

With reflexive verbs, **me** *is often not translated.*

◇ *Je me lève à sept heures tous les matins.* I get up at 7 every morning.

le **mec** NOUN (*informal*)
guy

le **mécanicien** NOUN
mechanic

la **mécanicienne** NOUN
mechanic

la **mécanique** NOUN
1 *mechanics*
2 *mechanism* (*of watch, clock*)

le **mécanisme** NOUN
mechanism

méchamment ADVERB
nastily ◇ *Il lui a répondu méchamment.* He answered him nastily.

la **méchanceté** NOUN
nastiness

méchant ADJECTIVE
nasty ◇ *C'est un homme méchant.* He's a nasty man. ◇ *Ne sois pas méchant avec ton petit frère.* Don't be nasty to your little brother.

◆ **"Attention, chien méchant"** "Beware of the dog"

la **mèche** NOUN
lock (*of hair*)

mécontent ADJECTIVE

◆ **mécontent de** unhappy with ◇ *Elle est mécontente de sa coupe de cheveux.* She's unhappy with her haircut.

le **mécontentement** NOUN
displeasure ◇ *Il a exprimé son mécontentement.* He expressed his displeasure.

la **médaille** NOUN
medal

le **médecin** NOUN
doctor ◇ *aller chez le médecin* to go to the doctor

la **médecine** NOUN
medicine (*subject*) ◇ *Il fait médecine.* He's studying medicine.

les **médias** MASC NOUN
media

médical ADJECTIVE
(MASC PL **médicaux**)
medical ◇ *la recherche médicale* medical research

◆ **passer une visite médicale** to have a medical

le **médicament** NOUN
medicine (*drug*)

médiéval ADJECTIVE
(MASC PL **médiévaux**)
medieval

médiocre ADJECTIVE
poor ◇ *des notes médiocres* poor marks

méditer VERB
to meditate

la **Méditerranée** NOUN
Mediterranean

méditerranéen ADJECTIVE
(FEM SING **méditerranéenne**)
Mediterranean

la **méduse** NOUN
jellyfish

la **méfiance** NOUN
mistrust

méfiant ADJECTIVE
mistrustful

se **méfier** VERB

◆ **se méfier de quelqu'un** to distrust somebody ◇ *Si j'étais toi, je me méfierais de lui.* If I were you, I wouldn't trust him.

la **mégarde** NOUN

◆ **par mégarde** by mistake ◇ *J'ai emporté son livre par mégarde.* I took his book by mistake.

le **mégot** NOUN
cigarette end

meilleur ADJECTIVE, ADVERB, NOUN
better ◇ *Ce serait meilleur avec du fromage râpé.* It would be better with grated cheese. ◇ *Il paraît que le film est meilleur que le livre.* They say that the film is better than the book.

◆ **le meilleur** the best ◇ *C'est elle qui est la meilleure en sport.* She's the best at sport. ◇ *Je préfère garder le meilleur pour la fin.* I like to keep the best for last.

◆ **le meilleur des deux** the better of the two

◆ **meilleur marché** cheaper ◇ *La bière est meilleur marché en France.* Beer's cheaper in France.

mélancolique ADJECTIVE
melancholy

mélange NOUN
mixture

mélanger VERB
1 *to mix* ◇ *Mélangez le tout.* Mix everything together.
2 *to muddle up* ◇ *Tu mélanges tout!* You're muddling everything up!

mêlée NOUN
scrum

mêler VERB
◆ **se mêler** to mix ◇ *Il ne cherche pas à se mêler aux autres.* He doesn't try to mix with the others.
◆ **Mêle-toi de ce qui te regarde!** (*informal*) Mind your own business!

mélodie NOUN
melody

melon NOUN
melon

membre NOUN
1 *limb*
2 *member* ◇ *les pays membres de l'Union européenne* the member countries of the European Union

mémé NOUN (*informal*)
granny

même ADJECTIVE, ADVERB, PRONOUN
1 *same* ◇ *J'ai le même manteau.* I've got the same coat. ◇ *Tiens, c'est curieux j'ai le même!* That's strange, I've got the same one!
◆ **en même temps** at the same time
◆ **moi-même** myself ◇ *Je l'ai fait moi-même.* I did it myself.
2 *even* ◇ *Il n'a même pas pleuré.* He didn't even cry.

mémoire NOUN
memory

menace NOUN
threat

menacer VERB
to threaten

ménage NOUN
housework ◇ *faire le ménage* to do the housework
◆ **une femme de ménage** a cleaning woman

ménager ADJECTIVE
(FEM SING **ménagère**)
◆ **les travaux ménagers** housework

ménagère NOUN
housewife

mendiant NOUN
beggar

la **mendiante** NOUN
beggar

mendier VERB
to beg

mener VERB
to lead ◇ *Cette rue mène directement à la gare.* This street leads straight to the station.
◆ **Cela ne vous mènera à rien!** That will get you nowhere!

la **méningite** NOUN
meningitis

les **menottes** FEM NOUN
handcuffs

le **mensonge** NOUN
lie

la **mensualité** NOUN
monthly payment ◇ *en dix mensualités* in ten monthly payments

mensuel ADJECTIVE
(FEM SING **mensuelle**)
monthly

les **mensurations** FEM NOUN
measurements

la **mentalité** NOUN
mentality

le **menteur** NOUN
liar

la **menteuse** NOUN
liar

la **menthe** NOUN
mint

la **mention** NOUN
grade ◇ *Il a été reçu avec mention bien.* He got a grade B pass.

mentionner VERB
to mention

mentir VERB
to lie ◇ *Tu mens!* You're lying!

le **menton** NOUN
chin

menu ADJECTIVE, ADVERB
see also **menu** NOUN
1 *slim* ◇ *Elle est menue.* She's slim. ◇ *Elle est petite et menue.* She's petite.
2 *very fine* ◇ *Les oignons doivent être coupés menu.* The onions have to be cut up very fine.

le **menu** NOUN
see also **menu** ADJECTIVE
menu ◇ *le menu du jour* today's menu

la **menuiserie** NOUN
woodwork

le **menuisier** NOUN
joiner

le **mépris** NOUN
contempt ◇ *Il nous a traités avec mépris.* He treated us with contempt.

méprisant ADJECTIVE

M

PTO

contemptuous

mépriser VERB
to despise

la **mer** NOUN
1 *sea* ◇ *en mer* at sea
◆ **au bord de la mer** at the seaside
◆ **la mer du Nord** the North Sea
2 *tide* ◇ *La mer est basse.* The tide is out. ◇ *La mer sera haute à sept heures.* It'll be high tide at 7 o'clock.

la **mercerie** NOUN
1 *haberdashery*
2 *haberdasher's shop*

merci EXCLAMATION
thank you ◇ *Merci de m'avoir raccompagné.* Thank you for taking me home.
◆ **merci beaucoup** thank you very much

le **mercredi** NOUN
1 *Wednesday* ◇ *Aujourd'hui, nous sommes mercredi.* It's Wednesday today.
2 *on Wednesday* ◇ *Nous comptons partir mercredi.* We plan to leave on Wednesday.
◆ **le mercredi** on Wednesdays ◇ *Le musée est fermé le mercredi.* The museum is shut on Wednesdays.
◆ **tous les mercredis** every Wednesday
◆ **mercredi dernier** last Wednesday
◆ **mercredi prochain** next Wednesday

la **merde** NOUN (*rude*)
shit ◇ *Merde!* Shit!

la **mère** NOUN
mother

la **merguez** NOUN
spicy sausage

méridional ADJECTIVE
(MASC PL **méridionaux**)
southern ◇ *Il a un accent méridional.* He's got a southern accent.

la **meringue** NOUN
meringue

mériter VERB
to deserve

le **merlan** NOUN
whiting

le **merle** NOUN
blackbird

la **merveille** NOUN
◆ **Cet ordinateur est une vraie merveille!** This computer's really wonderful!
◆ **à merveille** wonderfully ◇ *Elle se porte à merveille depuis son opération.* She's been wonderfully well since the operation.

merveilleux ADJECTIVE
(FEM SING **merveilleuse**)
marvellous

mes ADJECTIVE
my ◇ *mes parents* my parents

Mesdames FEM NOUN
ladies ◇ *Bonjour, Mesdames.* Good morning, ladies.

Mesdemoiselles FEM NOUN
ladies ◇ *Bonjour, Mesdemoiselles.* Good morning, ladies.

mesquin ADJECTIVE
mean

le **message** NOUN
message

la **messe** NOUN
mass ◇ *aller à la messe* to go to mass ◇ *la messe de minuit* midnight mass

messieurs MASC NOUN
gentlemen ◇ *Que puis-je faire pour vous, Messieurs?* What can I do for you, gentlemen?
◆ **Messieurs,...** Dear Sirs,... (*in letter*)

la **mesure** NOUN
1 *measurement* ◇ *J'ai pris les mesures de la fenêtre.* I took the measurements of the window.
◆ **sur mesure** tailor-made ◇ *un costume sur mesure* a tailor-made suit
2 *measure* ◇ *L'établissement a pris des mesures pour lutter contre le vandalisme.* The school has taken measures to combat vandalism.
◆ **au fur et à mesure** as one goes along ◇ *Quand je cuisine, je préfère faire la vaisselle au fur et à mesure.* When I'm cooking, I prefer to wash up as I go along.
◆ **être en mesure de faire quelque chose** to be in a position to do something ◇ *Nous ne sommes pas en mesure de vous renseigner.* We are not in a position to give you any information.

mesurer VERB
to measure ◇ *Mesurez la longueur et la largeur.* Measure the length and the width.
◆ **Il mesure un mètre quatre-vingts.** He's 1 m 80 tall.

met VERB *see* **mettre**

le **métal** NOUN
(PL les **métaux**)
metal

métallique ADJECTIVE
metallic

la **météo** NOUN
weather forecast ◇ *Qu'est-ce que dit la météo pour cet après-midi?* What's the weather forecast for this afternoon?

la **méthode** NOUN
1 *method* ◇ *des méthodes d'enseignement modernes* modern

teaching methods
2 *tutor* ◇ *une méthode de guitare* a guitar tutor

métier NOUN
job ◇ *Quel métier est-ce que tu aimerais faire plus tard?* What job would you like to do when you're older?

mètre NOUN
metre
▸ **un mètre ruban** a tape measure

métro NOUN
underground ◇ *prendre le métro* to go by underground

mets VERB *see* **mettre**

metteur en scène NOUN
(PL les **metteurs en scène**)
1 *producer* (*of play*)
2 *director* (*of film*)

mettre VERB

Present tense:	
je mets	*nous mettons*
tu mets	*vous mettez*
il/elle met	*ils/elles mettent*
Past participle: *mis*	

1 *to put* ◇ *Où est-ce que tu as mis les clés?* Where have you put the keys?
2 *to put on* ◇ *Je mets mon manteau et j'arrive.* I'll put on my coat and then I'll be ready. ◇ *Il fait froid, je vais mettre le chauffage.* It's cold, I'm going to put the heating on.
3 *to wear* ◇ *Elle ne met pas souvent de jupe.* She doesn't often wear a skirt. ◇ *Je n'ai rien à me mettre!* I've got nothing to wear!
4 *to take* ◇ *Combien de temps as-tu mis pour aller à Lille?* How long did it take you to get to Lille? ◇ *Elle met des heures à se préparer.* She takes hours getting ready.
▸ **mettre en marche** to start ◇ *Comment met-on la machine à laver en marche?* How do you start the washing machine?
▸ **Vous pouvez vous mettre là.** You can sit there.
▸ **se mettre au lit** to get into bed
▸ **se mettre en maillot de bain** to put on one's swimsuit
▸ **se mettre à** to start ◇ *Il s'est mis à la peinture à cinquante ans.* He started painting when he was 50. ◇ *Il est temps de se mettre au travail.* It's time to start work. ◇ *Elle s'est mise à pleurer.* She started crying.

meuble NOUN
piece of furniture ◇ *Je me suis cogné contre un meuble.* I bumped into a piece of furniture. ◇ *Ce magasin vend de beaux meubles.* This shop sells nice furniture.

le **meublé** NOUN
1 *furnished flat*
2 *furnished room*

meubler VERB
to furnish

le **meurtre** NOUN
murder

le **meurtrier** NOUN
murderer

la **meurtrière** NOUN
murderess

Mexico NOUN
Mexico City

le **Mexique** NOUN
Mexico

le **mi** NOUN
1 *E* ◇ *mi bémol* E flat
2 *mi* ◇ *do, ré, mi...* do, re, mi...

mi- PREFIX
1 *half-* ◇ *mi-clos* half-shut
2 *mid-* ◇ *à la mi-janvier* in mid-January

miauler VERB
to mew

la **miche** NOUN
loaf

mi-chemin
▸ **à mi-chemin** ADVERB
halfway

le **micro** NOUN
microphone

le **microbe** NOUN
germ

le **micro-ondes** NOUN
microwave oven

le **micro-ordinateur** NOUN
microcomputer

le **microscope** NOUN
microscope

le **midi** NOUN
1 *midday* ◇ *à midi* at midday
▸ **midi et demi** half past twelve
2 *lunchtime* ◇ *On a bien mangé à midi.* We had a good meal at lunchtime.
▸ **le Midi** the South of France

la **mie** NOUN
breadcrumbs

le **miel** NOUN
honey

mien PRONOUN
▸ **le mien** mine ◇ *Ce vélo-là, c'est le mien.* That bike's mine.

mienne PRONOUN
▸ **la mienne** mine ◇ *Cette valise-là, c'est la mienne.* That case is mine.

miennes PRONOUN
▸ **les miennes** mine ◇ *Heureusement*

PTO

que tu as tes clés: j'ai oublié les miennes. It's lucky you've got your keys: I forgot mine.

miens PRONOUN

- **les miens** mine ◇ *Ces CD-là, ce sont les miens.* Those CDs are mine.

la **miette** NOUN

crumb (*of bread, cake*)

mieux ADVERB, ADJECTIVE, NOUN

better ◇ *Je la connais mieux que son frère.* I know her better than her brother. ◇ *Elle va mieux.* She's better. ◇ *Les cheveux courts lui vont mieux.* She looks better with short hair.

- **Il vaut mieux que tu appelles ta mère.** You'd better phone your mother.
- **le mieux** the best ◇ *C'est la région que je connais le mieux.* It's the region I know best.
- **faire de son mieux** to do one's best ◇ *Essaie de faire de ton mieux.* Try to do your best.

mignon ADJECTIVE

(FEM SING **mignonne**)

sweet ◇ *Qu'est-ce qu'il est mignon!* Isn't he sweet!

la **migraine** NOUN

migraine ◇ *J'ai la migraine.* I've got a migraine.

mijoter VERB

to simmer

le **milieu** NOUN

(PL les **milieux**)

1 *middle*

- **au milieu de** in the middle of ◇ *Place le vase au milieu de la table.* Put the vase in the middle of the table.
- **au beau milieu de** in the middle of ◇ *Quelqu'un a sonné à la porte au beau milieu de la nuit.* Somebody rang the bell in the middle of the night.

2 *background* ◇ *le milieu familial* the family background ◇ *Il vient d'un milieu modeste.* He comes from a modest background.

3 *environment* ◇ *le milieu marin* the marine environment

militaire ADJECTIVE

see also militaire NOUN

military ◇ *faire son service militaire* to do one's military service

le **militaire** NOUN

see also militaire ADJECTIVE

serviceman ◇ *Son père est militaire.* His father is in the services.

- **un militaire de carrière** a professional soldier

mille NUMBER

a thousand ◇ *mille francs* a thousand francs ◇ *deux mille personnes* two thousand people

le **millefeuille** NOUN

vanilla slice

le **milliard** NOUN

thousand million ◇ *cinq milliards de francs* five thousand million francs

le/la **milliardaire** NOUN

multimillionaire

le **millier** NOUN

thousand ◇ *des milliers de personnes* thousands of people

- **par milliers** by the thousand

le **milligramme** NOUN

milligramme

le **millimètre** NOUN

millimetre

le **million** NOUN

million ◇ *deux millions de personnes* two million people

le/la **millionnaire** NOUN

millionaire

le/la **mime** NOUN

mime artist

mimer VERB

to mimic

minable ADJECTIVE

1 *shabby* ◇ *un imperméable minable* a shabby raincoat

2 *pathetic* ◇ *Mon moniteur de ski était minable.* My skiing instructor was pathetic.

mince ADJECTIVE

1 *thin* ◇ *une mince tranche de jambon* a thin slice of ham

2 *slim* ◇ *Il est grand et mince.* He's tall and slim.

- **Mince alors!** (*informal*) Oh bother!

la **minceur** NOUN

1 *thinness* ◇ *la minceur des murs* the thinness of the walls

2 *slimness* ◇ *Elle enviait la minceur de sa sœur.* She envied her sister's slimness.

la **mine** NOUN

1 *expression*

2 *look* ◇ *Tu as bonne mine.* You look well. ◇ *Il a mauvaise mine.* He doesn't look well. ◇ *Elle avait une mine fatiguée.* She was looking tired.

3 *appearance* ◇ *Il ne faut pas juger les gens d'après leur mine.* You shouldn't judge people by their appearance.

4 *lead* (*of pencil*)

5 *mine* ◇ *une mine de charbon* a coal mine

- **faire mine de faire quelque chose** to pretend to do something ◇ *Elle a fait* *mine de le croire.* She pretended to believe him.

◆ **mine de rien** somehow or other ◇ *Elle a réussi mine de rien à le faire parler de lui.* Somehow or other she got him to talk about himself.

minéral ADJECTIVE
(MASC PL **minéraux**)
mineral ◇ *l'eau minérale* mineral water

minéralogique ADJECTIVE
◆ **une plaque minéralogique** a number plate

minet NOUN
pussycat

minette NOUN
pussycat (*female*)

mineur ADJECTIVE
see also **mineur** NOUN
minor

mineur NOUN
see also **mineur** ADJECTIVE
1 *boy under 18*
◆ **les mineurs** the under-18s
2 *miner* ◇ *Mon grand-père était mineur.* My grandfather was a miner.

mineure NOUN
girl under 18

minijupe NOUN
miniskirt

minimum NOUN
minimum ◇ *Il en fait le minimum.* He does the absolute minimum.
◆ **au minimum** at the very least

ministère NOUN
ministry ◇ *le ministère des Affaires étrangères* the Foreign Office

ministre NOUN
minister ◇ *le ministre des Affaires étrangères* the Foreign Secretary

Minitel ® NOUN
Minitel *is France Telecom's online data service. You can use it instead of a phone directory, and to make bookings for transport, exhibitions etc.*

minorité NOUN
minority

Minorque FEM NOUN
Minorca

minuit NOUN
midnight ◇ *à minuit et quart* at a quarter past midnight

minuscule ADJECTIVE
see also **minuscule** NOUN
tiny

minuscule NOUN
see also **minuscule** ADJECTIVE
small letter

minute NOUN
minute
◆ **à la minute** just this minute ◇ *Je viens de l'appeler à la minute.* I've just this minute called him.

minutieux ADJECTIVE
(FEM SING **minutieuse**)
meticulous
◆ **C'est un travail minutieux.** It's a fiddly job.

la **mirabelle** NOUN
small yellow plum

le **miracle** NOUN
miracle

le **miroir** NOUN
mirror

mis VERB *see* **mettre**

mis ADJECTIVE
◆ **bien mis** well turned out ◇ *Elle est toujours bien mise.* She's always well turned out.

miser VERB (*informal*)
to bank on ◇ *On ne peut pas miser là-dessus.* We can't bank on it.

misérable ADJECTIVE
shabby-looking ◇ *une femme d'aspect misérable* a shabby-looking woman

la **misère** NOUN
extreme poverty
◆ **un salaire de misère** starvation wages

le/la **missionnaire** NOUN
missionary

mit VERB *see* **mettre**

la **mi-temps** NOUN
1 *half* (*of match*) ◇ *la première mi-temps* the first half ◇ *la deuxième mi-temps* the second half
2 *half-time* ◇ *Je lui parlerai à la mi-temps.* I'll speak to him at half-time.
◆ **travailler à mi-temps** to work part-time

la **mitraillette** NOUN
submachine gun

mixte ADJECTIVE
◆ **une école mixte** a mixed school

Mlle ABBREVIATION (= *Mademoiselle*)
(PL **Mlles**)
Miss ◇ *Mlle Renoir* Miss Renoir

Mme ABBREVIATION (= *Madame*)
(PL **Mmes**)
Mrs ◇ *Mme Leroy* Mrs Leroy

le **mobile** NOUN
motive ◇ *Quel était le mobile du crime?* What was the motive for the crime?

le **mobilier** NOUN
furniture

moche ADJECTIVE (*informal*)
1 *awful* ◇ *Cette couleur est vraiment moche.* That colour's really awful. ◇ *Je me trouve moche!* I think I look awful!
2 *rotten* ◇ *Il a la grippe, c'est moche*

FTO

pour lui. He's got flu, that's rotten for him.

la **mode** NOUN

see also le mode

fashion ◇ *être à la mode* to be fashionable

le **mode** NOUN

see also la mode

- **le mode d'emploi** directions for use
- **le mode de vie** the way of life

le **modèle** NOUN

1 *model* ◇ *Le nouveau modèle sort en septembre.* The new model is coming out in September.

2 *style* (*of clothes*) ◇ *Est-ce que vous avez le même modèle en plus grand?* Have you got the same style in a bigger size?

modéré ADJECTIVE

moderate

moderne ADJECTIVE

modern

moderniser VERB

to modernize

modeste ADJECTIVE

modest ◇ *Ne sois pas si modeste!* Don't be so modest!

la **modestie** NOUN

modesty

moelleux ADJECTIVE

(FEM SING **moelleuse**)

soft ◇ *un coussin moelleux* a soft cushion

moi PRONOUN

me ◇ *Coucou, c'est moi!* Hello, it's me!

- **Moi, je pense que tu as tort.** I personally think you're wrong.
- **à moi** mine ◇ *Ce livre n'est pas à moi.* This book isn't mine. ◇ *un ami à moi* a friend of mine

moi-même PRONOUN

myself ◇ *J'ai tricoté ce pull moi-même.* I knitted this jumper myself.

moindre ADJECTIVE

- **le moindre** the slightest ◇ *Il ne fait pas le moindre effort.* He doesn't make the slightest effort. ◇ *Je n'en ai pas la moindre idée.* I haven't the slightest idea.

le **moine** NOUN

monk

le **moineau** NOUN

(PL les **moineaux**)

sparrow

moins ADVERB, PREPOSITION

1 *less* ◇ *Ça coûte moins de deux cents francs.* It costs less than 200 francs.

2 *fewer* ◇ *Il y a moins de gens aujourd'hui.* There are fewer people today.

- **Il est cinq heures moins dix.** It's 10 to 5.

3 *minus* ◇ *quatre moins trois* 4 minus 3 ◇ *Il a fait moins cinq la nuit dernière.* It was minus five last night.

- **le moins** the least ◇ *C'est le modèle le moins cher.* It's the least expensive model. ◇ *Ce sont les plages qui sont les moins polluées.* These are the least polluted beaches. ◇ *C'est l'album que j'aime le moins.* This is the album I like the least.
- **de moins en moins** less and less ◇ *Il vient nous voir de moins en moins.* He comes to see us less and less often.
- **Il a trois ans de moins que moi.** He's three years younger than me.
- **au moins** at least ◇ *Ne te plains pas: au moins il ne pleut pas!* Don't complain: at least it's not raining!
- **à moins que** unless

à moins que *is followed by a verb in the subjunctive.*

◇ *Je te retrouverai à dix heures à moins que le train n'ait du retard.* I'll meet you at 10 o'clock unless the train's late.

le **mois** NOUN

month

le **moisi** NOUN

- **Ça sent le moisi.** It smells musty.

moisir VERB

to go mouldy ◇ *Le pain a moisi.* The bread's gone mouldy.

la **moisson** NOUN

harvest

moite ADJECTIVE

sweaty ◇ *J'ai toujours les mains moites.* My hands are always sweaty.

la **moitié** NOUN

half ◇ *Il a mangé la moitié du gâteau à lui seul.* He ate half the cake all by himself.

- **la moitié du temps** half the time
- **à la moitié de** halfway through ◇ *Elle est partie à la moitié du film.* She left halfway through the film.
- **à moitié** half ◇ *Ton verre est encore à moitié plein.* Your glass is still half-full. ◇ *Ce sac était à moitié prix.* This bag was half-price.
- **partager moitié moitié** to go halves ◇ *On partage moitié moitié, d'accord?* We'll go halves, OK?

la **molaire** NOUN

back tooth

la **Moldavie** NOUN

Moldova

molle ADJECTIVE

lethargic ◇ *Je la trouve un peu molle.* I find her a bit lethargic.

le **mollet** NOUN
see also mollet ADJECTIVE
calf (*of leg*)

mollet ADJECTIVE
see also mollet NOUN
- **un œuf mollet** a soft-boiled egg

la **môme** (*informal*) NOUN
kid

le **moment** NOUN
moment
- **en ce moment** at the moment ◇ *Nous avons beaucoup de travail en ce moment.* We have a lot of work at the moment.
- **pour le moment** for the moment ◇ *Nous ne pensons pas déménager pour le moment.* We're not thinking of moving for the moment.
- **au moment où** just as ◇ *Il est arrivé au moment où j'allais partir.* He turned up just as I was leaving.
- **à tout moment (1)** at any moment ◇ *Elle peut arriver à tout moment.* She could arrive at any moment.
- **à tout moment (2)** constantly ◇ *Il nous dérange à tout moment pour des riens.* He's constantly bothering us about silly little things.
- **sur le moment** at the time ◇ *Sur le moment je n'ai rien dit.* At the time I didn't say anything.
- **par moments** at times ◇ *Elle se sent seule par moments.* She feels lonely at times.

momentané ADJECTIVE
momentary

la **momie** NOUN
mummy (*Egyptian*)

mon ADJECTIVE
(FEM SING **ma**, PL **mes**)
my ◇ *mon frère* my brother ◇ *mon ami* my friend

la **monarchie** NOUN
monarchy

le **monastère** NOUN
monastery

le **monde** NOUN
world ◇ *faire le tour du monde* to go round the world
- **Il y a du monde.** There are a lot of people.
- **beaucoup de monde** a lot of people ◇ *Il y avait beaucoup de monde au concert.* There were a lot of people at the concert.
- **peu de monde** not many people

mondial ADJECTIVE
(MASC PL **mondiaux**)
1 *world* ◇ *la population mondiale* the world population
2 *world-wide* ◇ *une crise mondiale* a world-wide crisis

le **moniteur** NOUN
1 *instructor* ◇ *un moniteur de voile* a sailing instructor
2 *supervisor*

la **monitrice** NOUN
1 *instructor* ◇ *une monitrice de ski* a ski instructor
2 *supervisor*

la **monnaie** NOUN
- **une pièce de monnaie** a coin
- **avoir de la monnaie** to have change ◇ *Est-ce que tu as de la monnaie?* Have you got any change? ◇ *Est-ce que vous avez la monnaie de cent francs?* Do you have change for 100 francs?
- **rendre la monnaie à quelqu'un** to give somebody their change

monotone ADJECTIVE
monotonous

Monsieur MASC NOUN
(PL **Messieurs**)
1 *Mr* ◇ *Monsieur Dupont* Mr Dupont
2 *man* ◇ *Il y a un monsieur qui veut te voir.* There's a man to see you.
3 *Sir* ◇ *Monsieur,...* Dear Sir,... (*in letter*) ◇ *Monsieur! Vous avez oublié votre parapluie!* Excuse me! You've forgotten your umbrella!

le **monstre** NOUN
see also monstre ADJECTIVE
monster

monstre ADJECTIVE
see also monstre NOUN
- **Nous avons un travail monstre.** We've got a terrific amount of work.

le **mont** NOUN
mount
- **le mont Everest** Mount Everest
- **le mont Blanc** Mont Blanc

la **montagne** NOUN
mountain ◇ *de hautes montagnes* high mountains ◇ *Nous passons tous les ans un mois à la montagne.* We spend a month in the mountains every year.
- **les montagnes russes** roller coaster

montagneux ADJECTIVE
(FEM SING **montagneuse**)
mountainous ◇ *une région montagneuse* a mountainous area

montant ADJECTIVE
1 *rising* ◇ *la marée montante* the rising tide
2 *high* ◇ *un pull à col montant* a high-necked jumper

monter VERB
1 *to go up* ◇ *Elle a du mal à monter les escaliers.* She has difficulty going upstairs. ◇ *Les prix ont encore monté.* Prices have gone up again.
2 *to assemble* ◇ *Est-ce que ces étagères sont difficiles à monter?* Are these shelves difficult to assemble?
- **monter dans** to get on ◇ *Il est temps de monter dans l'avion.* It's time to get on the plane.
- **monter sur** to stand on ◇ *Tu vas devoir monter sur une chaise pour changer l'ampoule.* You'll have to stand on a chair to change the light bulb.
- **monter à cheval** to ride

la **montre** NOUN
watch

montrer VERB
to show ◇ *Est-ce que vous pouvez me montrer la gare sur le plan?* Can you show me the station on the map?

la **monture** NOUN
frames (*of glasses*)

le **monument** NOUN
monument

se **moquer** VERB
- **se moquer de (1)** to make fun of ◇ *Ils se sont moqués de mes chaussures jaunes.* They made fun of my yellow shoes.
- **se moquer de (2)** (*informal*) not to care about ◇ *Il se moque complètement de la mode.* He couldn't care less about fashion.

la **moquette** NOUN
fitted carpet

moqueur ADJECTIVE
(FEM SING **moqueuse**)
mocking

le **moral** NOUN
- **Elle a le moral.** She's in good spirits.
- **J'ai le moral à zéro.** I'm feeling really down.

la **morale** NOUN
moral ◇ *La morale de cette histoire est...* The moral of the story is...
- **faire la morale à quelqu'un** to lecture somebody

le **morceau** NOUN
(PL les **morceaux**)
piece ◇ *un morceau de pain* a piece of bread

mordre VERB
to bite

mordu ADJECTIVE
- **Il est mordu de jazz.** (*informal*) He's crazy about jazz.

la **morgue** NOUN
mortuary

le **morse** NOUN
walrus

la **morsure** NOUN
bite

la **mort** NOUN
see also **mort** ADJECTIVE
death

mort ADJECTIVE
see also **mort** NOUN
dead ◇ *Nous avons trouvé un oiseau mort.* We found a dead bird.
◇ *Napoléon est mort en 1821.* Napoleon died in 1821.
- **Il était mort de peur.** He was scared to death.
- **Je suis morte de fatigue.** I'm dead tired.

mortel ADJECTIVE
(FEM SING **mortelle**)
1 *deadly* ◇ *un poison mortel* a deadly poison ◇ *Ces réunions de famille sont mortelles!* (*informal*) These family gatherings are deadly!
2 *fatal* ◇ *une chute mortelle* a fatal fall

la **morue** NOUN
cod

Moscou NOUN
Moscow

la **mosquée** NOUN
mosque

le **mot** NOUN
1 *word* ◇ *mot à mot* word for word
2 *line* ◇ *Je vais lui écrire un mot pour lui dire qu'on arrive.* I'll drop her a line to say we're coming.
- **des mots croisés** a crossword

le **motard** NOUN
1 *biker*
2 *motorcycle cop* (*informal*) ◇ *Il s'est fait arrêter par un motard pour excès de vitesse.* He was stopped for speeding by a motorcycle cop.

le **moteur** NOUN
engine
- **un bateau à moteur** a motor boat

le **motif** NOUN
pattern ◇ *des rideaux avec un motif d'oiseaux* curtains with a bird pattern
- **sans motif** for no reason ◇ *Il s'est fâché sans motif.* He got angry for no reason.

la **moto** NOUN
motorbike

le/la **motocycliste** NOUN
motorcyclist

mou ADJECTIVE
(FEM SING **molle**)

1 *soft* ◇ *Mon matelas est trop mou.* My mattress is too soft.
2 *lethargic* ◇ *Je le trouve un peu mou.* I find him a bit lethargic.

la **mouche** NOUN
fly

le **moucher** VERB
to blow one's nose

le **moucheron** NOUN
midge

le **mouchoir** NOUN
handkerchief
◆ **un mouchoir en papier** a tissue

moudre VERB
to grind

la **moue** NOUN
pout
◆ **faire la moue** to pout

la **mouette** NOUN
seagull

la **moufle** NOUN
mitt

mouillé ADJECTIVE
wet

mouiller VERB
to get wet ◇ *J'ai mouillé les manches de mon pull.* I got the sleeves of my jumper wet.
◆ **se mouiller** to get wet ◇ *Attention, tu vas te mouiller!* Careful, you'll get wet!

moulant ADJECTIVE
figure-hugging ◇ *une robe moulante* a figure-hugging dress

la **moule** NOUN
see also le moule
mussel

le **moule** NOUN
see also la moule
◆ **un moule à gâteaux** a cake tin

le **moulin** NOUN
mill

moulu VERB *see* **moudre**

mourir VERB
to die
◆ **mourir de faim** to starve ◇ *Des centaines de personnes sont mortes de faim.* Hundreds of people starved to death.
◆ **Je meurs de faim!** I'm starving!
◆ **mourir de froid** to die of exposure
◆ **Je meurs de froid!** I'm freezing!
◆ **mourir d'envie de faire quelque chose** to be dying to do something ◇ *Je meurs d'envie d'aller me baigner.* I'm dying to go for a swim.

la **mousse** NOUN
1 *moss* ◇ *un rocher recouvert de mousse* a rock covered with moss
2 *froth* (*on beer*)
3 *lather* (*of soap, shampoo*)
4 *mousse* ◇ *une mousse au chocolat* a chocolate mousse ◇ *une mousse de poisson* a fish mousse
◆ **la mousse à raser** shaving foam

mousseux ADJECTIVE
(FEM SING **mousseuse**)
◆ **un vin mousseux** a sparkling wine

la **moustache** NOUN
moustache
◆ **les moustaches** whiskers

le **moustique** NOUN
mosquito

la **moutarde** NOUN
mustard

le **mouton** NOUN
1 *sheep* ◇ *une peau de mouton* a sheepskin
2 *mutton* ◇ *un gigot de mouton* a leg of mutton

le **mouvement** NOUN
movement

mouvementé ADJECTIVE
eventful ◇ *des vacances mouvementées* eventful holidays

moyen ADJECTIVE
(FEM SING **moyenne**)
see also moyen NOUN
1 *average* ◇ *Je suis plutôt moyenne en langues.* I'm just average at languages.
2 *medium* ◇ *Elle est de taille moyenne.* She's of medium height.
◆ **le moyen âge** the Middle Ages

le **moyen** NOUN
see also moyen ADJECTIVE
way ◇ *Quel est le meilleur moyen de le convaincre?* What's the best way of convincing him?
◆ **Je n'en ai pas les moyens.** I can't afford it.
◆ **Ils n'ont pas les moyens de s'acheter une voiture.** They can't afford to buy a car.
◆ **un moyen de transport** a means of transport
◆ **par tous les moyens** by every possible means

la **moyenne** NOUN
◆ **avoir la moyenne** to get a pass mark ◇ *J'espère avoir la moyenne en maths.* I hope to get a pass mark in maths.
◆ **en moyenne** on average
◆ **la moyenne d'âge** the average age

le **Moyen-Orient** NOUN
Middle East

muet ADJECTIVE
(FEM SING **muette**)
dumb

PTO

◆ **un film muet** a silent film

le **muguet** NOUN
lily of the valley

multiple ADJECTIVE
numerous ◇ *en de multiples occasions* on numerous occasions

multiplier VERB
to multiply

municipal ADJECTIVE
(MASC PL **municipaux**)
◆ **la bibliothèque municipale** the public library

la **municipalité** NOUN
town council

les **munitions** FEM NOUN
ammunition

le **mur** NOUN
wall

mûr ADJECTIVE
1 *ripe* (*fruit*)
2 *mature* (*person*)

la **mûre** NOUN
bramble

mûrir VERB
1 *to ripen* ◇ *Les fraises ont mis du temps à mûrir.* The strawberries took a while to ripen.
2 *to make mature* ◇ *Cette expérience l'a beaucoup mûrie.* That experience has made her much more mature.

murmurer VERB
to whisper ◇ *Il m'a murmuré à l'oreille qu'il allait partir.* He whispered in my ear that he was going to go.

la **muscade** NOUN
nutmeg

le **muscat** NOUN
1 *muscat grape*
2 *muscatel* (*wine*) ◇ *un verre de muscat* a glass of muscatel

le **muscle** NOUN
muscle

musclé ADJECTIVE
muscular

le **museau** NOUN
(PL les **museaux**)
muzzle

le **musée** NOUN
museum

musical ADJECTIVE
(MASC PL **musicaux**)
musical
◆ **avoir l'oreille musicale** to be musical

le **music-hall** NOUN
variety ◇ *une chanteuse de music-hall* a variety singer

le **musicien** NOUN
musician

la **musicienne** NOUN
musician

la **musique** NOUN
music

musulman ADJECTIVE, NOUN
Muslim
◆ **un musulman** a Muslim (*man*)
◆ **une musulmane** a Muslim (*woman*)

la **mutation** NOUN
transfer ◇ *Il a demandé sa mutation à Paris.* He asked for a transfer to Paris.

myope ADJECTIVE
short-sighted

le **mystère** NOUN
mystery

mystérieux ADJECTIVE
(FEM SING **mystérieuse**)
mysterious

le **mythe** NOUN
myth

N

n' PRONOUN *see* **ne**

nage NOUN

- **traverser une rivière à la nage** to swim across a river

nageoire NOUN

fin

nager VERB

to swim

nageur NOUN

swimmer

nageuse NOUN

swimmer

naïf ADJECTIVE

(FEM SING **naïve**)

naïve

nain NOUN

dwarf

naissance NOUN

birth

- **votre date de naissance** your date of birth

naître VERB

to be born

- **Il est né en 1982.** He was born in 1982.

naïve ADJECTIVE *see* **naïf**

nana NOUN (*informal*)

girl

nappe NOUN

tablecloth

narine NOUN

nostril

natal ADJECTIVE

native ◇ *mon pays natal* my native country

natation NOUN

swimming ◇ *La natation est mon sport favori.* Swimming's my favourite sport.

national ADJECTIVE

(MASC PL **nationaux**)

national

- **la fête nationale espagnole** the national day of Spain

nationalité NOUN

nationality

natte NOUN

plait ◇ *Cécile avait des nattes.* Cécile had plaits.

nature NOUN

see also **nature** ADJECTIVE

nature

nature ADJECTIVE

see also **nature** NOUN

plain ◇ *un yaourt nature* a plain yoghurt

naturel ADJECTIVE

(FEM SING **naturelle**)

natural

naturellement ADVERB

of course ◇ *Vous viendrez à notre fête?–Naturellement!* Are you coming to our party?–Of course!

◇ *Naturellement, il est encore en retard.* Of course, he's late again.

le **naufrage** NOUN

shipwreck

nautique ADJECTIVE

water

- **les sports nautiques** water sports
- **le ski nautique** water-skiing

le **navet** NOUN

turnip

la **navette** NOUN

shuttle ◇ *la navette entre la gare et l'aéroport* the shuttle between the station and the airport

- **faire la navette** to commute ◇ *Je fais la navette entre Paris et Ivry.* I commute between Paris and Ivry.

la **navigation** NOUN

- **La navigation est interdite ici.** Boats are not allowed here.

naviguer VERB

to sail

le **navire** NOUN

ship

ne ADVERB

ne *is combined with words such as* **pas, personne, plus** *and* **jamais** *to form negative phrases.*

◇ *Je ne peux pas venir.* I can't come.

◇ *Ils ne vont jamais en boîte.* They never go to discos. ◇ *Je ne connais personne ici.* I don't know anyone here.

ne *changes to* **n'** *before a vowel and most words beginning with "h".*

◇ *Je n'ai pas d'argent.* I haven't got any money. ◇ *Il n'habite plus à Paris.* He doesn't live in Paris any more.

ne *is sometimes not translated.*

◇ *C'est plus loin que je ne le croyais.* It's further than I thought.

né VERB *see* **naître**

born ◇ *Elle est née en 1980.* She was born in 1980.

néanmoins ADVERB

nevertheless

nécessaire ADJECTIVE

necessary ◇ *Il est nécessaire de réserver.* It's necessary to book.

le **nectar** NOUN

- **le nectar d'abricot** apricot drink

néerlandais ADJECTIVE, NOUN

PTO

(FEM SING **néerlandaise**)
Dutch ◇ *Manon parle néerlandais.* Manon speaks Dutch.
- **un Néerlandais** a Dutchman
- **une Néerlandaise** a Dutchwoman
- **les Néerlandais** the Dutch

négatif ADJECTIVE
(FEM SING **négative**)
see also **négatif** NOUN
negative

le **négatif** NOUN
see also **négatif** ADJECTIVE
negative (*of photo*)

négligé ADJECTIVE
scruffy ◇ *une tenue négligée* scruffy clothes

la **neige** NOUN
snow
- **un bonhomme de neige** a snowman

neiger VERB
to snow

le **nénuphar** NOUN
water lily

le **néon** NOUN
neon ◇ *une lampe au néon* a neon light ◇ *La cuisine est éclairée au néon.* The kitchen has a neon light.

néo-zélandais ADJECTIVE, NOUN
(FEM SING **néo-zélandaise**)
New Zealand ◇ *Le champion néo-zélandais a gagné la course.* The New Zealand champion won the race.
- **un Néo-Zélandais** a New Zealander (*man*)
- **une Néo-Zélandaise** a New Zealander (*woman*)

le **nerf** NOUN
nerve
- **taper sur les nerfs de quelqu'un** to get on somebody's nerves ◇ *Il me tape sur les nerfs.* He's getting on my nerves.

nerveux ADJECTIVE
(FEM SING **nerveuse**)
nervous

la **nervosité** NOUN
nervousness

n'est-ce pas ADVERB
n'est-ce pas *is used to check that something is true.*
◇ *Nous sommes le douze aujourd'hui, n'est-ce pas?* It's the 12th today, isn't it? ◇ *Ils sont venus l'an dernier, n'est-ce pas?* They came last year, didn't they? ◇ *Elle aura dix-huit ans en octobre, n'est-ce pas?* She'll be 18 in October, won't she?

net ADJECTIVE, ADVERB
(FEM SING **nette**)
1 *clear* ◇ *L'image n'est pas nette.* The picture isn't very clear.
2 *net* ◇ *Poids net: 500 g.* Net weight: 500 g.
3 *flatly* ◇ *Il a refusé net de nous aider.* He flatly refused to help us.
- **s'arrêter net** to stop dead

nettement ADVERB
much ◇ *Ce magasin est nettement plus cher.* This shop is much more expensive.

le **nettoyage** NOUN
cleaning
- **le nettoyage à sec** dry cleaning

nettoyer VERB
to clean

neuf NUMBER
see also **neuf** ADJECTIVE
nine ◇ *Claire a neuf ans.* Claire's nine. ◇ *Il est neuf heures du matin.* It's nine in the morning.
- **le neuf février** the ninth of February

neuf ADJECTIVE
(FEM SING **neuve**)
see also **neuf** NUMBER
new ◇ *des chaussures neuves* new shoes

neutre ADJECTIVE
neutral

neuve ADJECTIVE *see* **neuf**

neuvième ADJECTIVE
ninth ◇ *au neuvième étage* on the ninth floor

le **neveu** NOUN
(PL les **neveux**)
nephew

le **nez** NOUN
nose
- **se trouver nez à nez avec quelqu'un** to come face to face with somebody

ni CONJUNCTION
- **ni...ni...** neither...nor... ◇ *Je n'aime ni les lentilles ni les épinards.* I like neither lentils nor spinach. ◇ *Elles ne sont venues ni l'une ni l'autre.* Neither of them came.

la **niche** NOUN
kennel

le **nid** NOUN
nest

la **nièce** NOUN
niece

nier VERB
to deny

n'importe ADVERB
- **n'importe qui** anybody ◇ *N'ouvre pas la porte à n'importe qui.* Don't open the door to just anybody.
- **n'importe quoi** anything ◇ *Je ferais n'importe quoi pour elle.* I'd do anything

for her.

- **Tu dis n'importe quoi.** You're talking rubbish.
- **n'importe où** anywhere ◇ *On trouve ces fleurs n'importe où.* You can find these flowers anywhere.
- **Ne laisse pas tes affaires n'importe où.** Don't leave your things lying everywhere.
- **n'importe quand** any time ◇ *Tu peux venir n'importe quand.* You can come any time.
- **n'importe comment** any old how ◇ *Ces livres sont rangés n'importe comment.* These books have been put away any old how.

le **niveau** NOUN
(PL les **niveaux**)
1 *level* ◇ *le niveau de l'eau* the water level
2 *standard* ◇ *Ces deux enfants n'ont pas le même niveau.* These two children aren't at the same level.
- **le niveau de vie** the standard of living

noble ADJECTIVE
noble

la **noblesse** NOUN
nobility

la **noce** NOUN
wedding
- **un repas de noce** a wedding reception

nocif ADJECTIVE
(FEM SING **nocive**)
harmful ◇ *une substance nocive* a harmful substance

nocturne ADJECTIVE
see also nocturne NOUN
1 *nocturnal* ◇ *un oiseau nocturne* a nocturnal bird
2 *by night* ◇ *Découvrez le Paris nocturne!* Discover Paris by night!

le **nocturne** NOUN
see also nocturne ADJECTIVE
late-night opening ◇ *Nocturne le vendredi jusqu'à vingt-trois heures.* Late-night opening until 11 p.m. on Fridays.

le **Noël** NOUN
Christmas ◇ *Qu'est-ce que tu as eu pour Noël?* What did you get for Christmas?
- **Joyeux Noël!** Merry Christmas!

le **nœud** NOUN
1 *knot* ◇ *Il a fait un nœud à la corde.* He tied a knot in the rope.
2 *bow* ◇ *Janet avait un nœud dans les cheveux.* Janet had a bow in her hair.
- **un nœud papillon** a bow tie

noir ADJECTIVE
see also noir NOUN
1 *black* ◇ *Elle porte une robe noire.* She's wearing a black dress. ◇ *Elle est noire.* She's black.
2 *dark* ◇ *Il fait noir dehors.* It's dark outside.

le **noir** NOUN
see also noir ADJECTIVE
dark ◇ *J'ai peur du noir.* I'm afraid of the dark.
- **le travail au noir** moonlighting

le **Noir** NOUN
black man
- **les Noirs** black people

la **Noire** NOUN
black woman

la **noisette** NOUN
hazelnut

la **noix** NOUN
(PL les **noix**)
walnut
- **une noix de coco** a coconut
- **les noix de cajou** cashew nuts
- **une noix de beurre** a knob of butter

le **nom** NOUN
1 *name* ◇ *votre nom* your name
- **mon nom de famille** my surname
- **son nom de jeune fille** her maiden name

2 *noun* (*in grammar*)

le **nombre** NOUN
number ◇ *Treize est un nombre impair.* Thirteen is an odd number. ◇ *un grand nombre d'amis* a large number of friends

nombreux ADJECTIVE
(FEM SING **nombreuse**)
1 *many* ◇ *Il a gagné de nombreux matchs.* He's won many matches.
2 *large* ◇ *une famille nombreuse* a large family
- **peu nombreux** few ◇ *Nous étions peu nombreux à la réunion.* There were few of us at the meeting.

le **nombril** NOUN
navel

nommer VERB
1 *to name* ◇ *Il n'a voulu nommer personne.* He didn't want to name anybody.
2 *to appoint* ◇ *Il a été nommé directeur.* He was appointed director.

non ADVERB
no ◇ *Tu as vu Jean-Pierre? – Non.* Have you seen Jean-Pierre? – No.
- **non seulement** not only ◇ *Il est non seulement intelligent, mais aussi très gentil.* Not only is he intelligent, he's also very nice.

PTO

- **moi non plus** Neither do I. ◇ *Je n'aime pas les hamburgers. – Moi non plus.* I don't like hamburgers. – Neither do I. ◇ *Il n'y est pas allé et moi non plus.* He didn't go and neither did I.

non alcoolisé ADJECTIVE
non-alcoholic ◇ *les boissons non alcoolisées* non-alcoholic drinks

le **non-fumeur** NOUN
non-smoker ◇ *Gavin est un non-fumeur.* Gavin's a non-smoker.
- **une voiture non-fumeurs** a no-smoking carriage

le **nord** NOUN
see also **nord** ADJECTIVE
north ◇ *Ils vivent dans le nord de l'île.* They live in the north of the island.
- **vers le nord** northwards
- **au nord de Paris** north of Paris
- **l'Afrique du Nord** North Africa
- **le vent du nord** the north wind

nord ADJECTIVE
see also **nord** NOUN
1 *north* ◇ *la face nord du Mont-Blanc* the north face of Mont-Blanc
- **le pôle Nord** the North Pole

2 *northern* ◇ *Nous avons visité la partie nord de l'île.* We visited the northern part of the island.

le **nord-est** NOUN
north-east ◇ *les régions du nord-est* north-eastern regions

le **nord-ouest** NOUN
north-west
- **l'Europe du nord-ouest** north-west Europe

normal ADJECTIVE
(MASC PL **normaux**)
1 *normal* ◇ *un bébé normal* a normal baby
2 *natural* ◇ *C'est tout à fait normal.* It's perfectly natural.
- **Vous trouvez que c'est normal?** Does that seem right to you?

normalement ADVERB
normally ◇ *Les aéroports fonctionnent tous normalement.* The airports are all working normally.
- **Normalement, elle doit arriver à huit heures.** She's supposed to arrive at 8 o'clock.
- **Tu es libre ce week-end? – Oui, normalement.** Are you free this weekend? – Yes, I should be.

normand ADJECTIVE
- **un village normand** a village in Normandy
- **la côte normande** the coast of Normandy

la **Normandie** NOUN
Normandy

la **Norvège** NOUN
Norway

norvégien ADJECTIVE, NOUN
(FEM SING **norvégienne**)
Norwegian
- **Elle parle norvégien.** She speaks Norwegian.
- **un Norvégien** a Norwegian (*man*)
- **une Norvégienne** a Norwegian (*woman*)

nos ADJECTIVE
our ◇ *Où sont nos affaires?* Where are our things?

le **notaire** NOUN
solicitor ◇ *Son père est notaire.* His father's a solicitor.

la **note** NOUN
1 *note* ◇ *J'ai pris des notes pendant la conférence.* I took notes at the lecture. ◇ *Il a joué quelques notes au piano.* He played a few notes on the piano.
2 *mark* ◇ *Vincent a de bonnes notes en maths.* Vincent's got good marks in maths.
3 *bill* ◇ *Il n'a pas payé sa note.* He didn't pay his bill.

noter VERB
to make a note of ◇ *Tu as noté leur adresse?* Did you make a note of their address?

les **notions** FEM NOUN
basics ◇ *Il faut avoir des notions d'anglais.* You have to have some basic English. ◇ *Elle a des notions de comptabilité.* She knows the basics of accounting.

notre ADJECTIVE
(PL **nos**)
our ◇ *Voici notre maison.* Here's our house.

nôtre PRONOUN
- **le nôtre** ours ◇ *À qui est ce chien? – C'est le nôtre.* Whose dog is it? – It's ours. ◇ *Leur voiture est rouge, la nôtre est bleue.* Their car is red, ours is blue.

nôtres PRONOUN
- **les nôtres** ours ◇ *Ces places-là sont les nôtres.* Those seats are ours.

nouer VERB
to tie

les **nouilles** FEM NOUN
noodles

nourrir VERB
to feed

la **nourriture** NOUN
food

nous PRONOUN

1 *we* ◇ *Nous avons deux enfants.* We have two children.
2 *us* ◇ *Viens avec nous.* Come with us.
◆ **nous-mêmes** ourselves

nouveau ADJECTIVE
(MASC SING ALSO **nouvel**, FEM SING **nouvelle**, MASC PL **nouveaux**)
see also nouveau NOUN
new ◇ *Il me faut un nouveau pantalon.* I need some new trousers. ◇ *Elle a une nouvelle voiture.* She's got a new car.
nouveau *changes to* **nouvel** *before a vowel and most words beginning with "h".*
◇ *Il y a un nouvel élève dans ma classe.* There's a new boy in my class.
◆ **le nouvel an** New Year

le **nouveau** NOUN
(PL les **nouveaux**)
see also nouveau ADJECTIVE
new pupil ◇ *Il y a plusieurs nouveaux dans la classe.* There are several new pupils in the class.
◆ **de nouveau** again ◇ *Il pleut de nouveau.* It's raining again.

la **nouveauté** NOUN
novelty

nouvel, nouvelle ADJECTIVE *see* **nouveau**

la **nouvelle** NOUN
1 *news* ◇ *Tu connais la nouvelle? Teresa a gagné au loto.* Have you heard the news? Teresa won the lottery. ◇ *C'est une bonne nouvelle.* That's good news.
2 *short story* ◇ *une nouvelle de Maupassant* a short story by Maupassant
◆ **les nouvelles** the news ◇ *J'ai écouté les nouvelles à la radio.* I listened to the news on the radio.
◆ **avoir des nouvelles de quelqu'un** to hear from somebody ◇ *Je n'ai pas eu de nouvelles de lui.* I haven't heard from him.

la **Nouvelle-Zélande** NOUN
New Zealand

novembre MASC NOUN
November
◆ **en novembre** in November

le **noyau** NOUN
(PL les **noyaux**)
stone (*of fruit*) ◇ *un noyau d'abricot* an apricot stone

le **noyer** NOUN
see also noyer VERB
walnut tree

se **noyer** VERB
see also noyer NOUN
to drown ◇ *Il s'est noyé dans la rivière.* He drowned in the river.

nu ADJECTIVE
1 *naked* ◇ *Ils se sont baignés nus.* They went for a swim naked. ◇ *tout nus* stark naked
2 *bare* ◇ *Elle avait les bras nus.* Her arms were bare. ◇ *Les murs étaient nus.* The walls were bare.

le **nuage** NOUN
cloud
◆ **un nuage de lait** a drop of milk

nuageux ADJECTIVE
(FEM SING **nuageuse**)
cloudy

nucléaire ADJECTIVE
nuclear ◇ *l'énergie nucléaire* nuclear power

le/la **nudiste** NOUN
nudist

la **nuit** NOUN
night ◇ *Ils ont fait du bruit toute la nuit.* They were noisy all night.
◆ **Il fait nuit.** It's dark.
◆ **cette nuit** tonight ◇ *Il va rentrer cette nuit.* He'll be back tonight.
◆ **Bonne nuit!** Good night!

nul ADJECTIVE
(FEM SING **nulle**)
rubbish
◆ **Ce film est nul.** (*informal*) This film's rubbish.
◆ **un match nul** a draw (*in sport*) ◇ *Ils ont fait match nul.* It was a draw.
◆ **nulle part** nowhere ◇ *Je ne le vois nulle part.* I can't see it anywhere.

le **numéro** NOUN
number ◇ *J'habite au numéro trois.* I live at number 3.
◆ **mon numéro de téléphone** my phone number

nu-pieds ADJECTIVE, ADVERB
barefoot ◇ *Il se promenait nu-pieds.* He was walking barefoot.

la **nuque** NOUN
nape of the neck

le **nylon** NOUN
nylon

N

O

obéir VERB
to obey
- **obéir à quelqu'un** to obey somebody ◇ *Elle refuse d'obéir à ses parents.* She refuses to obey her parents.

obéissant ADJECTIVE
obedient

l'**objet** MASC NOUN
object
- **les objets de valeur** valuables
- **les objets trouvés** the lost property office

obligatoire ADJECTIVE
compulsory

obliger VERB
- **obliger quelqu'un à faire quelque chose** to force somebody to do something
- **Je suis bien obligé d'accepter.** I can't really refuse.

obscur ADJECTIVE
dark

l'**obscurité** FEM NOUN
darkness ◇ *dans l'obscurité* in the dark

l'**obsédé** MASC NOUN
sex maniac
- **un obsédé sexuel** a sex maniac

obséder VERB
to obsess ◇ *Il est obsédé par le travail.* He's obsessed by work.

l'**observation** FEM NOUN
comment ◇ *J'ai une ou deux observations à faire.* I've got one or two comments to make.

observer VERB
1 *to watch* ◇ *Il observait les canards sur le lac.* He watched the ducks on the lake.
2 *to observe* ◇ *Ils observent le règlement.* They observe the rules.

l'**obstacle** MASC NOUN
1 *obstacle* ◇ *surmonter un obstacle* to overcome an obstacle
2 *fence* (*in show jumping*)
- **une course d'obstacles** an obstacle race

obtenir VERB
1 *to get* ◇ *Ils ont obtenu cinquante pour cent des voix.* They got 50% of the votes.
2 *to achieve* ◇ *Nous avons obtenu de bons résultats.* We achieved good results.

l'**occasion** FEM NOUN
1 *opportunity* ◇ *C'est une occasion à ne pas manquer.* It's an opportunity not to be missed.
2 *occasion* ◇ *à l'occasion de son anniversaire* on the occasion of his birthday ◇ *à plusieurs occasions* on several occasions
3 *bargain* ◇ *Cet ordinateur est une bonne occasion.* This computer's a real bargain.
- **d'occasion** second-hand ◇ *une voiture d'occasion* a second-hand car

l'**Occident** MASC NOUN
West
- **en Occident** in the West

occidental ADJECTIVE
(MASC PL **occidentaux**)
western
- **les pays occidentaux** the West

l'**occupation** FEM NOUN
occupation ◇ *la France sous l'Occupation* France during the Occupation

occupé ADJECTIVE
1 *busy* ◇ *Le directeur est très occupé.* The director's very busy.
2 *taken* ◇ *Est-ce que cette place est occupée?* Is this seat taken?
3 *engaged* ◇ *Les toilettes sont occupées.* The toilet's engaged. ◇ *La ligne est occupée.* The line's engaged.

occuper VERB
to occupy ◇ *Les enfants ne sont pas faciles à occuper quand il pleut.* Children aren't easy to keep occupied when it rains.
- **s'occuper de quelque chose (1)** to be in charge of something ◇ *Elle s'occupe d'un club de sport.* She's in charge of a sports club.
- **s'occuper de quelque chose (2)** to deal with something ◇ *Je vais m'occuper de ce dossier.* I'm going to deal with this file.
- **On s'occupe de vous?** (*in a shop*) Are you being attended to?

l'**océan** MASC NOUN
ocean ◇ *l'océan Indien* the Indian Ocean

octobre MASC NOUN
October
- **en octobre** in October

l'**odeur** FEM NOUN
smell ◇ *Il y a une drôle d'odeur ici.* There's a funny smell round here.

l'**œil** MASC NOUN
(PL **les yeux**)

eye ◇ *J'ai quelque chose dans l'œil.* I've got something in my eye.
- **à l'œil** (*informal*) for free ◇ *Il est entré à l'œil.* He got in for free.

l'**œillet** MASC NOUN
carnation

l'**œuf** MASC NOUN
egg
- **un œuf à la coque** a soft-boiled egg
- **un œuf dur** a hard-boiled egg
- **un œuf au plat** a fried egg
- **les œufs brouillés** scrambled eggs
- **un œuf de Pâques** an Easter egg

l'**œuvre** FEM NOUN
work ◇ *J'étudie une œuvre de Molière.* I'm studying one of Molière's works.
- **une œuvre d'art** a work of art

offert VERB *see* **offrir**

l'**office** MASC NOUN
- **un office du tourisme** a tourist office

officiel ADJECTIVE
(FEM SING **officielle**)
official

l'**officier** MASC NOUN
officer ◇ *Il est officier de marine.* He's a naval officer.

l'**offre** FEM NOUN
offer ◇ *une offre spéciale* a special offer
- **"offres d'emploi"** "situations vacant"

offrir VERB
- **offrir quelque chose (1)** to offer something ◇ *On lui a offert un poste de secrétaire.* They offered her a secretarial post. ◇ *Elle lui a offert à boire.* She offered him a drink.
- **offrir quelque chose (2)** to give something ◇ *Il lui a offert des roses.* He gave her roses.
- **s'offrir quelque chose** to treat oneself to something ◇ *Je me suis offert une nouvelle paire de chaussures.* I treated myself to a new pair of shoes.

l'**oie** FEM NOUN
goose

l'**oignon** MASC NOUN
onion

l'**oiseau** MASC NOUN
(PL **les oiseaux**)
bird

l'**olive** FEM NOUN
olive ◇ *l'huile d'olive* olive oil

olympique ADJECTIVE
- **les Jeux Olympiques** the Olympic Games

l'**ombre** FEM NOUN
1 *shade* ◇ *Je vais me mettre à l'ombre.* I'm going to sit in the shade.
2 *shadow*
- **l'ombre à paupières** eye shadow

l'**omelette** FEM NOUN
omelette

on PRONOUN
1 *we* ◇ *On va à la plage demain.* We're going to the beach tomorrow. ◇ *On a pensé que ça te ferait plaisir.* We thought you'd be pleased.
2 *someone* ◇ *On m'a volé mon porte-monnaie.* Someone has stolen my purse.
- **On m'a dit d'attendre.** I was told to wait.
- **On vous demande au téléphone.** There's a phone call for you.

3 *you* ◇ *On peut visiter le château en été.* You can visit the castle in the summer. ◇ *D'ici on peut voir la côte française.* From here you can see the French coast.

l'**oncle** MASC NOUN
uncle

l'**onde** FEM NOUN
wave (*on radio*) ◇ *sur les grandes ondes* on long wave

l'**ongle** MASC NOUN
nail
- **se couper les ongles** to cut one's nails ◇ *Elle s'est coupé les ongles.* She cut her nails.

ont VERB *see* **avoir**
- **Ils ont beaucoup d'argent.** They've got lots of money.
- **Elles ont passé de bonnes vacances.** They had a good holiday.

l'**ONU** FEM NOUN (= *Organisation des Nations unies*)
UN (= United Nations)

onze NUMBER
eleven ◇ *Elle a onze ans.* She's eleven. ◇ *à onze heures* at eleven o'clock
- **le onze février** the eleventh of February

onzième ADJECTIVE
eleventh ◇ *au onzième étage* on the eleventh floor

l'**opéra** MASC NOUN
opera

l'**opération** FEM NOUN
operation

opérer VERB
to operate on ◇ *Elle a été opérée de l'appendicite.* She was operated on for appendicitis.
- **se faire opérer** to have an operation ◇ *Elle s'est fait opérer.* She's had an operation.

l'**opinion** FEM NOUN

PTO

opinion

opposé ADJECTIVE

see also opposé NOUN

opposite ◇ *Elle est partie dans la direction opposée.* She went off in the opposite direction.

- **être opposé à quelque chose** to be opposed to something

l'**opposé** MASC NOUN

see also opposé ADJECTIVE

the opposite

opposer VERB

- **opposer quelqu'un à quelqu'un** to pit somebody against somebody ◇ *Ce match oppose les Français aux Allemands.* This match pits the French against the Germans.
- **s'opposer** to conflict ◇ *Ces deux points de vue s'opposent.* These two points of view conflict.
- **s'opposer à quelque chose** to oppose something ◇ *Son père s'oppose à son mariage.* Her father's against her marriage.

l'**opposition** FEM NOUN

opposition

- **par opposition à** as opposed to ◇ *la littérature contemporaine par opposition à la littérature classique* modern literature, as opposed to classics
- **faire opposition à un chèque** to stop a cheque

l'**opticien** MASC NOUN

optician ◇ *Il est opticien.* He's an optician.

l'**opticienne** FEM NOUN

optician ◇ *Elle est opticienne.* She's an optician.

optimiste ADJECTIVE

optimistic

l'**option** FEM NOUN

option

- **une matière à option** an optional subject

l'**or** MASC NOUN

see also or CONJUNCTION

gold ◇ *un bracelet en or* a gold bracelet

or CONJUNCTION

see also or NOUN

and yet ◇ *Il était sûr de gagner, or il a perdu.* He was sure he would win, and yet he lost.

l'**orage** MASC NOUN

thunderstorm

orageux ADJECTIVE

(FEM SING **orageuse**)

stormy

oral ADJECTIVE

(MASC PL **oraux**)

see also oral NOUN

- **une épreuve orale** an oral exam
- **à prendre par voie orale** to be taken orally

l'**oral** MASC NOUN

(PL les **oraux**)

see also oral ADJECTIVE

oral (*exam*) ◇ *un oral de français* a French oral

l'**orange** FEM NOUN

see also orange ADJECTIVE

orange (*fruit*)

orange ADJECTIVE (MASC, FEM, PL)

see also orange NOUN

orange (*in colour*) ◇ *des fleurs orange* orange flowers

l'**orchestre** MASC NOUN

1 *orchestra* ◇ *un orchestre symphonique* a symphony orchestra

2 *band* ◇ *un orchestre de jazz* a jazz band

ordinaire ADJECTIVE

see also ordinaire NOUN

1 *ordinary* ◇ *des gens ordinaires* ordinary people

2 *standard* ◇ *un format ordinaire* a standard size

l'**ordinaire** MASC NOUN

see also ordinaire ADJECTIVE

two-star (petrol)

- **sortir de l'ordinaire** to be out of the ordinary

l'**ordinateur** MASC NOUN

computer

l'**ordonnance** FEM NOUN

prescription

ordonné ADJECTIVE

tidy

ordonner VERB

- **ordonner à quelqu'un de faire quelque chose** to order somebody to do something ◇ *Il m'a ordonné de sortir.* He ordered me to leave.

l'**ordre** MASC NOUN

order ◇ *par ordre alphabétique* in alphabetical order

- **mettre en ordre** to tidy up
- **jusqu'à nouvel ordre** until further notice

les **ordures** FEM NOUN

rubbish

- **jeter quelque chose aux ordures** to throw something in the bin

l'**oreille** FEM NOUN

ear

l'**oreiller** MASC NOUN

pillow

les **oreillons** MASC NOUN

mumps

rgane MASC NOUN
organ (*in body*)

rganisateur MASC NOUN
organizer

rganisation FEM NOUN
organization

rganisatrice FEM NOUN
organizer

rganiser VERB
to organize
s'organiser to get organized ◇ *Il ne sait pas s'organiser.* He can't get himself organized.

rganisme MASC NOUN
body (*organization*)

rgue MASC NOUN
organ ◇ *Carl joue de l'orgue.* Carl plays the organ.

rgueilleux ADJECTIVE
(FEM SING **orgueilleuse**)
proud

Orient MASC NOUN
East
en Orient in the East

riental ADJECTIVE
(MASC PL **orientaux**)
1 *oriental* ◇ *un palais oriental* an oriental palace
2 *eastern* ◇ *la frontière orientale de la Pologne* Poland's eastern border

rientation FEM NOUN
orientation
avoir le sens de l'orientation to have a good sense of direction
l'orientation professionnelle careers advice

riginaire ADJECTIVE
Elle est originaire de Paris. She's from Paris.

riginal ADJECTIVE
(MASC PL **originaux**)
see also original NOUN
original ◇ *un film en version originale* a film in the original language

riginal MASC NOUN
(PL les **originaux**)
see also original ADJECTIVE
original ◇ *L'original est au Louvre.* The original is in the Louvre.
un vieil original an old eccentric

rigine FEM NOUN
origin
à l'origine originally

rphelin MASC NOUN
orphan

rpheline FEM NOUN
orphan

rteil MASC NOUN
toe

l'**orthographe** FEM NOUN
spelling

l'**os** MASC NOUN
bone

oser VERB
to dare
◆ **oser faire quelque chose** to dare to do something

l'**otage** MASC NOUN
hostage

ôter VERB
1 *to take off* ◇ *Elle a ôté son manteau.* She took off her coat.
2 *to take away*

ou CONJUNCTION
or
◆ **ou...ou...** either...or...
◆ **ou bien** or else ◇ *On pourrait aller au cinéma ou bien rentrer directement.* We could go to the cinema or else go straight home.

où PRONOUN, ADVERB
1 *where* ◇ *Où est Nick?* Where's Nick? ◇ *Où allez-vous?* Where are you going? ◇ *Je sais où il est.* I know where he is. ◇ *C'est la maison où je suis né.* That's the house where I was born. ◇ *la ville d'où je viens* the town I come from
2 *that* ◇ *Le jour où il est parti, tout le monde a pleuré.* The day that he left, everyone cried.
◆ **Par où allons-nous passer?** Which way are we going to go?

l'**ouate** FEM NOUN
cotton wool

oublier VERB
1 *to forget* ◇ *N'oublie pas de fermer la porte.* Don't forget to shut the door.
2 *to leave* ◇ *J'ai oublié mon sac chez Sabine.* I left my bag at Sabine's.

l'**ouest** MASC NOUN
see also ouest ADJECTIVE
west ◇ *Elle vit dans l'ouest de l'Angleterre.* She lives in the West of England.
◆ **à l'ouest de Paris** west of Paris
◆ **vers l'ouest** westwards
◆ **l'Europe de l'Ouest** Western Europe
◆ **le vent d'ouest** the west wind

ouest ADJECTIVE (MASC, FEM, PL)
see also ouest NOUN
1 *west* ◇ *la côte ouest de l'Écosse* the west coast of Scotland
2 *western* ◇ *la partie ouest du pays* the western part of the country

ouf EXCLAMATION
phew!

oui ADVERB

PTO

yes

l'**ouragan** MASC NOUN
hurricane

l'**ourlet** MASC NOUN
seam

l'**ours** MASC NOUN
bear
◆ **un ours en peluche** a teddy bear

l'**outil** MASC NOUN
tool

ouvert VERB *see* **ouvrir**

ouvert ADJECTIVE
1 *open* ◇ *Le magasin est ouvert.* The shop's open.
2 *on* ◇ *Il a laissé le robinet ouvert.* He left the tap on.
◆ **avoir l'esprit ouvert** to be open-minded

l'**ouverture** FEM NOUN
opening ◇ *les heures d'ouverture* opening hours

l'**ouvre-boîte** MASC NOUN
tin opener

l'**ouvre-bouteille** MASC NOUN
bottle-opener

l'**ouvrier** NOUN
worker ◇ *Son père est ouvrier dans une usine.* His father's a factory worke

l'**ouvrière** NOUN
worker

ouvrir VERB
to open ◇ *Ouvrez!* Open up! ◇ *Elle a ouvert la porte.* She opened the door.
◆ **s'ouvrir** to open ◇ *La porte s'est ouverte.* The door opened.

l'**ovni** MASC NOUN (= *objet volant non identifié*)
UFO

l'**oxygène** MASC NOUN
oxygen

P

acifique NOUN
Pacific ◇ *l'océan Pacifique* the Pacific Ocean
agaille NOUN
mess SING ◇ *Quelle pagaille!* What a mess!
age NOUN
page ◇ *Tournez la page.* Turn the page.
aie NOUN
wages
aiement NOUN
payment
aillasson NOUN
doormat
aille NOUN
straw
ain NOUN
1 *bread* ◇ *un morceau de pain* a piece of bread ◇ *une tranche de pain* a slice of bread
2 *loaf* ◇ *J'ai acheté un pain.* I bought a loaf of bread.
le pain complet wholemeal bread
le pain d'épice gingerbread
le pain de mie sandwich loaf
le pain grillé toast
air ADJECTIVE
even ◇ *un nombre pair* an even number
une jeune fille au pair an au pair
aire NOUN
pair ◇ *une paire de chaussures* a pair of shoes
aisible ADJECTIVE
peaceful ◇ *un village paisible* a peaceful village
aix NOUN
peace
faire la paix (1) to make peace ◇ *Les deux pays ont fait la paix.* The two countries have made peace with each other.
faire la paix (2) to make it up ◇ *Laure a fait la paix avec son frère.* Laure made it up with her brother.
avoir la paix to have peace and quiet ◇ *J'aimerais bien avoir la paix.* I'd like to have a bit of peace and quiet.
Fiche-lui la paix! (*informal*) Leave him alone!
alais NOUN
1 *palace* ◇ *le palais de Buckingham* Buckingham Palace
2 *palate* (*in mouth*)
âle ADJECTIVE
pale ◇ *bleu pâle* pale blue
la **Palestine** NOUN
Palestine
la **pâleur** NOUN
paleness
le **palier** NOUN
landing ◇ *Il m'attendait sur le palier.* He was waiting for me on the landing.
pâlir VERB
to go pale
la **palme** NOUN
flipper (*for swimming*)
palmé ADJECTIVE
webbed ◇ *Les canards ont les pieds palmés.* Ducks have webbed feet.
le **palmier** NOUN
palm tree
palpitant ADJECTIVE
thrilling ◇ *un roman palpitant* a thrilling novel
le **pamplemousse** NOUN
grapefruit
le **panaché** NOUN
shandy
la **pancarte** NOUN
sign ◇ *Il y a une pancarte dans la vitrine.* There's a sign in the window.
pané ADJECTIVE
fried in breadcrumbs ◇ *du poisson pané* fish in breadcrumbs
le **panier** NOUN
basket
la **panique** NOUN
panic
paniquer VERB
to panic
la **panne** NOUN
breakdown
- **être en panne** to have broken down ◇ *L'ascenseur est en panne.* The lift's not working.
- **tomber en panne** to break down ◇ *Nous sommes tombés en panne sur l'autoroute.* We broke down on the motorway. ◇ *Nous sommes tombés en panne d'essence.* We've run out of petrol.
- **une panne de courant** a power cut

le **panneau** NOUN
(PL les **panneaux**)
sign ◇ *Ce panneau dit que la maison est à vendre.* This sign says that the house is for sale.
- **panneau d'affichage (1)** advertising hoarding
- **panneau d'affichage (2)** arrivals and

TO

departures board (*in station*)

le **panorama** NOUN
panorama

le **pansement** NOUN
1 *dressing* (*bandage*)
2 *sticking plaster*

le **pantalon** NOUN
trousers PL ◇ *Son pantalon est trop court.* His trousers are too short.
- **un pantalon de ski** a pair of ski pants

la **panthère** NOUN
panther

la **pantoufle** NOUN
slipper

le **paon** NOUN
peacock

le **papa** NOUN
dad

le **pape** NOUN
pope

la **papeterie** NOUN
stationer's

le **papi** NOUN (*informal*)
granddad

le **papier** NOUN
paper ◇ *une feuille de papier* a sheet of paper
- **Vos papiers, s'il vous plaît.** Your identity papers, please.
- **les papiers d'identité** identity papers
- **le papier à lettres** writing paper
- **le papier hygiénique** toilet paper
- **le papier peint** wallpaper

le **papillon** NOUN
butterfly

le **paquebot** NOUN
liner

la **pâquerette** NOUN
daisy

Pâques MASC NOUN
Easter ◇ *Je viendrai te voir à Pâques.* I'll come and see you at Easter.
- **les œufs de Pâques** Easter eggs

In France, Easter eggs are said to be brought by the Easter bells or cloches de Pâques *which fly from Rome and drop them in people's gardens.*

le **paquet** NOUN
1 *packet* ◇ *Je voudrais un paquet de cigarettes.* I'd like a packet of cigarettes.
2 *parcel* ◇ *Sa mère lui a envoyé un paquet.* His mother sent him a parcel.

le **paquet-cadeau** NOUN
(PL les **paquets-cadeaux**)
gift-wrapped parcel ◇ *La vendeuse m'a fait un paquet-cadeau.* The shop assistant gift-wrapped it for me.

par PREPOSITION
1 *by* ◇ *Le Tour de France a été remporté par un Écossais.* The Tour de France was won by a Scotsman.
- **deux par deux** two by two ◇ *Les élèves sont entrés deux par deux.* The pupils went in two by two.

2 *with* ◇ *Son nom commence par un H.* His name begins with H.
3 *out of* ◇ *Elle regardait par la fenêtre.* She was looking out of the window. ◇ *par habitude* out of habit
4 *via* ◇ *Nous sommes passés par Lyon pour aller à Grenoble.* We went via Lyons to Grenoble.
5 *through* ◇ *Il faut passer par la douane avant de prendre l'avion.* You have to go through customs before boarding the plane.
6 *per* ◇ *Prenez trois cachets par jour.* Take three tablets per day. ◇ *Le voyage coûte deux mille francs par personne.* The trip costs two thousand francs per person.
- **par ici (1)** this way ◇ *Il faut passer par ici pour y arriver.* You have to go this way to get there.
- **par ici (2)** round here ◇ *Il y a beaucoup de touristes par ici.* There are lots of tourists round here.
- **par-ci, par-là** here and there

le **parachute** NOUN
parachute

le/la **parachutiste** NOUN
parachutist

le **paradis** NOUN
heaven

les **parages** MASC NOUN
- **dans les parages** in the area ◇ *Il n'y pas d'hôtel dans les parages.* There are no hotels in the area.

le **paragraphe** NOUN
paragraph

paraître VERB
1 *to seem* ◇ *Ça paraît incroyable.* It seems unbelievable.
2 *to look* ◇ *Elle paraît plus jeune que son frère.* She looks younger than her brother.
- **il paraît que** it seems that ◇ *Il paraît que c'est la faute de la direction.* It seems that it's the management's fault.

le **parallèle** NOUN
see also la parallèle
parallel ◇ *Il a fait un parallèle entre ces deux événements.* He drew a parallel between the two events.

la **parallèle** NOUN
see also le parallèle
parallel line

paralysé ADJECTIVE

paralysed

parapluie NOUN
umbrella

parasol NOUN
parasol

parc NOUN
1 *park* ◇ *Le dimanche, Chantal va se promener au parc.* On Sundays Chantal goes for a walk in the park.
◆ **un parc d'attractions** an amusement park
2 *grounds* ◇ *Le château est situé au milieu d'un grand parc.* The castle is surrounded by extensive grounds.

parce que CONJUNCTION
because ◇ *Il n'est pas venu parce qu'il n'avait pas de voiture.* He didn't come because he didn't have a car.

parcmètre NOUN
parking meter

parcourir VERB
1 *to cover* ◇ *Gavin a parcouru cinquante kilomètres à vélo.* Gavin covered 50 kilometres on his bike.
2 *to glance through* ◇ *J'ai parcouru le journal d'aujourd'hui.* I glanced through today's newspaper.

parcours NOUN
journey

par-dessous ADVERB
underneath ◇ *Il portait un pull et une chemise par-dessous.* He was wearing a jumper with a shirt underneath.

pardessus NOUN
overcoat

par-dessus ADVERB, PREPOSITION
1 *on top* ◇ *Elle porte un chemisier et un pull rouge par-dessus.* She's wearing a blouse with a red jumper on top.
2 *over* ◇ *Elle a sauté par-dessus le mur.* She jumped over the wall.
◆ **en avoir par-dessus la tête** to have had enough ◇ *J'en ai par-dessus la tête de tous ces problèmes.* I've had enough of all these problems.

pardon NOUN
see also pardon EXCLAMATION
forgiveness

pardon EXCLAMATION
see also pardon NOUN
1 *sorry!* ◇ *Oh, pardon! J'espère que je ne vous ai pas fait mal.* Oh, sorry! I hope I didn't hurt you.
◆ **demander pardon à quelqu'un** to apologize to somebody ◇ *Il leur a demandé pardon.* He apologized to them.
◆ **Je vous demande pardon.** I'm sorry.
2 *excuse me!* ◇ *Pardon, madame! Pouvez-vous me dire où se trouve la poste?* Excuse me! Could you tell me where the post office is?
3 *pardon?* ◇ *Pardon? Je n'ai pas compris ce que vous avez dit.* Pardon? I didn't understand what you said.

pardonner VERB
to forgive ◇ *Nous lui avons pardonné de nous avoir menti.* We forgave him for lying to us.

le **pare-brise** NOUN
(PL les **pare-brise**)
windscreen

le **pare-chocs** NOUN
bumper

pareil ADJECTIVE
(FEM SING **pareille**)
1 *the same* ◇ *Ces deux maisons ne sont pas pareilles.* These two houses aren't the same.
2 *like that* ◇ *J'aime bien sa voiture. J'en voudrais une pareille.* I like his car. I'd like one like that.
3 *such* ◇ *Je refuse d'écouter des bêtises pareilles.* I won't listen to such nonsense.
◆ **sans pareil** unequalled ◇ *Il a joué cette symphonie avec un talent sans pareil.* He played this symphony with unequalled talent.

la **parenthèse** NOUN
bracket ◇ *entre parenthèses* in brackets

les **parents** MASC NOUN
parents

la **paresse** NOUN
laziness

paresseux ADJECTIVE
(FEM SING **paresseuse**)
lazy

parfait ADJECTIVE
perfect

parfaitement ADVERB
perfectly ◇ *Il parle parfaitement l'arabe.* He speaks perfect Arabic.

parfois ADVERB
sometimes

le **parfum** NOUN
1 *perfume*
2 *flavour* ◇ *Je voudrais une glace. – Quel parfum veux-tu?* I'd like an ice cream. – What flavour would you like?

parfumé ADJECTIVE
1 *fragrant* ◇ *une rose très parfumée* a very fragrant rose
2 *flavoured* ◇ *des biscuits parfumés au café* coffee-flavoured biscuits

la **parfumerie** NOUN

PTO

perfume shop

le **pari** NOUN
bet

parier VERB
to bet

Paris NOUN
Paris

- **à Paris (1)** in Paris
- **à Paris (2)** to Paris

parisien ADJECTIVE, NOUN
(FEM SING **parisienne**)
1 *Parisian* ◇ *un célèbre couturier parisien* a famous Parisian designer
2 *Paris* ◇ *le métro parisien* the Paris metro

- **un Parisien** a Parisian (*man*)
- **une Parisienne** a Parisian (*woman*)

le **parking** NOUN
car park

le **parlement** NOUN
parliament

parler VERB
1 *to speak* ◇ *Vous parlez français?* Do you speak French?
2 *to talk* ◇ *Nous étions en train de parler quand le directeur est entré.* We were talking when the headmaster came in.

- **parler de quelque chose à quelqu'un** to tell somebody about something ◇ *Il m'a parlé de sa nouvelle voiture.* He told me about his new car.

parmi PREPOSITION
among ◇ *Ils étaient parmi les meilleurs de la classe.* They were among the best pupils in the class.

la **paroi** NOUN
wall

la **paroisse** NOUN
parish

la **parole** NOUN
1 *speech* ◇ *l'usage de la parole* the power of speech
2 *word* ◇ *Il m'a donné sa parole.* He gave me his word. ◇ *Elle a tenu parole.* She kept her word.

- **les paroles** lyrics ◇ *J'aime les paroles de cette chanson.* I like the lyrics of this song.

le **parquet** NOUN
floor (*wooden*)

le **parrain** NOUN
godfather

parrainer VERB
to sponsor ◇ *Cette entreprise parraine notre équipe de rugby.* This firm is sponsoring our rugby team.

pars VERB *see* **partir**

la **part** NOUN
1 *share* ◇ *Vous n'avez pas eu votre part.* You haven't had your share.
2 *piece* ◇ *une part de gâteau* a piece of cake

- **prendre part à quelque chose** to take part in something ◇ *Il va prendre part à la réunion.* He's going to take part in the meeting.
- **de la part de (1)** on behalf of ◇ *Je dois vous remercier de la part de mon frère.* I must thank you on behalf of my brother.
- **de la part de (2)** from ◇ *C'est un cadeau pour toi, de la part de Françoise.* It's a present for you, from Françoise.
- **à part** except ◇ *Ils sont tous venus, à part Christian.* They all came, except Christian.

partager VERB
1 *to share* ◇ *Ils partagent un appartement.* They share a flat.
2 *to divide* ◇ *Janet a partagé le gâteau en quatre.* Janet divided the cake into four.

le/la **partenaire** NOUN
partner

le **parti** NOUN
party ◇ *le Parti socialiste* the Socialist Party

le **participant** NOUN
participant

la **participante** NOUN
participant

la **participation** NOUN
participation

le **participe** NOUN
participle

- **le participe passé** the past participle
- **le participe présent** the present participle

participer VERB

- **participer à quelque chose (1)** to take part in something ◇ *André va participer à la course.* André is going to take part in the race.
- **participer à quelque chose (2)** to contribute to something ◇ *Je voudrais participer aux frais.* I would like to contribute to the cost.

la **particularité** NOUN
characteristic

particulier ADJECTIVE
(FEM SING **particulière**)
1 *private* ◇ *une maison particulière* a private house
2 *distinctive* ◇ *Ce vin a un arôme particulier.* This wine has a distinctive flavour.
3 *particular* ◇ *Dans ce cas particulier,*

je ne peux rien faire. In this particular case, I can't do anything.

- **en particulier (1)** particularly ◇ *J'aime les fruits, en particulier les fraises.* I like fruit, particularly strawberries.
- **en particulier (2)** in private ◇ *Est-ce que je peux vous parler en particulier?* Can I speak to you in private?

particulièrement ADVERB

particularly

partie NOUN

1 *part* ◇ *Une partie du groupe partira en Italie.* Part of the group will go to Italy.

2 *game* ◇ *Nous avons fait une partie de tennis.* We played a game of tennis. ◇ *une partie de cartes* a game of cards

- **en partie** partly ◇ *Cela explique en partie le problème.* That partly explains the problem.
- **en grande partie** largely ◇ *Son histoire est en grande partie vraie.* His story is largely true.
- **faire partie de** to be part of ◇ *Ce tableau fait partie d'une très belle collection.* This picture is part of a very beautiful collection.

partiel ADJECTIVE

(FEM SING **partielle**)

partial

partir VERB

to go ◇ *Je lui ai téléphoné mais il était déjà parti.* I phoned him but he'd already gone.

- **partir en vacances** to go on holiday
- **partir de** to leave ◇ *Il est parti de Nice à sept heures.* He left Nice at 7.
- **à partir de** from ◇ *Je serai chez moi à partir de huit heures.* I'll be at home from eight o'clock onwards.

partition NOUN

score (*in music*) ◇ *une partition de piano* a piano score

partout ADVERB

everywhere

paru VERB *see* **paraître**

parution NOUN

publication ◇ *Ce roman a eu beaucoup de succès dès sa parution.* This novel was very successful from the moment it came out.

parvenir VERB

- **parvenir à faire quelque chose** to manage to do something ◇ *Elle est finalement parvenue à ouvrir la porte.* She finally managed to open the door.
- **faire parvenir quelque chose à quelqu'un** to send something to somebody ◇ *Je vous ferai parvenir le colis avant lundi.* I'll send you the parcel before Monday.

pas ADVERB

see also pas NOUN

- **ne...pas** not ◇ *Il ne pleut pas.* It's not raining. ◇ *Elle n'est pas venue.* She didn't come. ◇ *Ils n'ont pas de voiture.* They haven't got a car.
- **Vous viendrez à notre soirée, n'est-ce pas?** You're coming to our party, aren't you?
- **C'est Harry qui a gagné, n'est-ce pas?** Harry won, didn't he?
- **pas moi** not me ◇ *Elle veut aller au cinéma, pas moi.* She wants to go to the cinema, but I don't.
- **pas du tout** not at all ◇ *Je n'aime pas du tout ça.* I don't like that at all.
- **pas mal** not bad ◇ *Ce n'est pas mal pour un début.* That's not bad for a first attempt. ◇ *Comment allez-vous?–Pas mal.* How are you?–Not bad.
- **pas mal de** quite a lot of ◇ *Il y avait pas mal de monde au concert.* There were quite a lot of people at the concert.

le **pas** NOUN

see also pas ADVERB

1 *pace* ◇ *Il marchait d'un pas rapide.* He walked at a fast pace.

2 *step* ◇ *Faites trois pas en avant.* Take three steps forward.

3 *footstep* ◇ *J'entends des pas dans l'escalier.* I can hear footsteps on the stairs.

- **au pas** at walking pace ◇ *Le cheval est parti au pas.* The horse set off at walking pace.
- **faire les cent pas** to pace up and down ◇ *Il faisait les cent pas dans le corridor.* He was pacing up and down the corridor.

le **passage** NOUN

passage ◇ *J'ai traduit un passage de ce livre.* I translated a passage from this book.

- **Il a été éclaboussé au passage de la voiture.** He was soaked by a passing car.
- **de passage** passing through ◇ *Nous sommes de passage à Toulouse.* We're just passing through Toulouse.
- **un passage clouté** a pedestrian crossing
- **un passage souterrain** a subway

passager ADJECTIVE

(FEM SING **passagère**)

see also passager NOUN

temporary

le **passager** NOUN

PTO

see also passager ADJECTIVE
passenger
- **un passager clandestin** a stowaway

la **passagère** NOUN
passenger

le **passant** NOUN
passer-by

la **passante** NOUN
passer-by

passé ADJECTIVE
see also passé NOUN
1 *last* ◇ *Je l'ai vu la semaine passée.* I saw him last week.
2 *past* ◇ *Il est minuit passé.* It's past midnight.

le **passé** NOUN
see also passé ADJECTIVE
1 *past* ◇ *dans le passé* in the past
2 *past tense* ◇ *Mettez ce verbe au passé.* Put this verb into the past tense.
- **le passé composé** the perfect tense
- **le passé simple** the past historic

le **passeport** NOUN
passport

passer VERB
1 *to cross* ◇ *Nous avons passé la frontière belge.* We crossed the Belgian border.
2 *to go through* ◇ *Il faut passer la douane en sortant.* You have to go through customs on the way out.
3 *to take* ◇ *Gordon a passé ses examens la semaine dernière.* Gordon took his exams last week.
4 *to spend* ◇ *Elle a passé la journée à ne rien faire.* She spent the day doing nothing. ◇ *Ils passent toujours leurs vacances au Danemark.* They always spend their holidays in Denmark.
5 *to pass* ◇ *Passe-moi le sel, s'il te plaît.* Pass me the salt, please.
6 *to show* ◇ *On passe "Le Kid" au cinéma cette semaine.* They're showing "The Kid" at the cinema this week.
7 *to call in* ◇ *Je passerai chez vous ce soir.* I'll call in this evening.
- **Ne quittez pas, je vous passe Madame Chevalier.** Hold on please, I'm putting you through to Mrs Chevalier.
- **passer par** to go through ◇ *Ils sont passés par Paris pour aller à Tours.* They went through Paris to get to Tours.
- **en passant** in passing ◇ *Je lui ai dit en passant que j'allais me marier.* I told him in passing that I was getting married.
- **laisser passer** to let through ◇ *Il m'a laissé passer.* He let me through.
- **se passer (1)** to take place ◇ *Cette histoire se passe au moyen âge.* This story takes place in the Middle Ages.
- **se passer (2)** to go ◇ *Comment se sont passés tes examens?* How did your exams go?
- **se passer (3)** to happen ◇ *Que s'est-il passé? Un accident?* What happened? Was there an accident?
- **Qu'est-ce qui se passe? Pourquoi est-ce qu'elle pleure?** What's the matter? Why is she crying?
- **se passer de** to do without ◇ *Je me passerai de café ce matin.* I'll do without coffee this morning.

la **passerelle** NOUN
1 *footbridge* (*over river*)
2 *gangway* (*onto plane, boat*)

le **passe-temps** NOUN
pastime

passif ADJECTIVE
(FEM SING **passive**)
see also passif NOUN
passive

le **passif** NOUN
see also passif ADJECTIVE
passive ◇ *Mettez ce verbe au passif.* Put this verb into the passive.

la **passion** NOUN
passion

passionnant ADJECTIVE
fascinating

passionné ADJECTIVE
keen ◇ *Donald est un lecteur passionné.* Donald is a keen reader.
- **Il est passionné de voile.** He's a sailing fanatic.

passionner VERB
- **Son travail le passionne.** He's passionate about his work.
- **se passionner pour quelque chose** to have a passion for something ◇ *Harry se passionne pour les perroquets.* Harry has a passion for parrots.

la **passoire** NOUN
sieve

la **pastèque** NOUN
watermelon

le **pasteur** NOUN
minister (*priest*)

la **patate** NOUN (*informal*)
potato
- **une patate douce** a sweet potato

la **pâte** NOUN
1 *pastry*
2 *dough*
3 *cake mixture*
- **la pâte à crêpes** pancake batter
- **la pâte à modeler** Plasticine ®
- **la pâte d'amandes** marzipan

âté NOUN
pâté ◇ *Nous avons mangé du pâté en entrée.* We had pâté as a starter.
un pâté de maisons a block (*of houses*)
aternel ADJECTIVE
(FEM SING **paternelle**)
ma grand-mère paternelle my father's mother
mon oncle paternel my father's brother
âtes FEM NOUN
pasta
atience NOUN
patience
atient ADJECTIVE
see also patient NOUN
patient
atient NOUN
see also patient ADJECTIVE
patient
atiente NOUN
patient
atienter VERB
to wait ◇ *Veuillez patienter un instant, s'il vous plaît.* Please wait a moment.
atin NOUN
1 *skate* ◇ *Nic a enfilé ses patins.* Nic put her skates on.
2 *skating* ◇ *Ils font du patin tous les mercredis.* They go skating every Wednesday.
• **les patins à glace** ice skates
• **les patins à roulettes** roller skates
atinage NOUN
skating
• **le patinage artistique** figure skating
atiner VERB
to skate
atineur NOUN
skater
atineuse NOUN
skater
atinoire NOUN
ice rink
âtisserie NOUN
cake shop
• **faire de la pâtisserie** to bake ◇ *J'adore faire de la pâtisserie.* I love baking.
• **les pâtisseries** cakes
âtissier NOUN
confectioner
âtissière NOUN
confectioner
atrie NOUN
homeland
atron NOUN
1 *boss*
2 *pattern* (*for dressmaking*)

la **patronne** NOUN
boss
• **Elle est patronne de café.** She runs a café.
patronner VERB
to sponsor ◇ *Le festival est patronné par des entreprises locales.* The festival is sponsored by local businesses.
la **patrouille** NOUN
patrol
la **patte** NOUN
1 *paw* (*of dog, cat*)
2 *leg* (*of bird, animal*)
paumer VERB (*informal*)
to lose ◇ *J'ai paumé mes clefs.* I've lost my keys.
la **paupière** NOUN
eyelid
la **pause** NOUN
1 *break* ◇ *Ils font une pause.* They're having a break.
2 *pause* ◇ *Il y a eu une pause dans la conversation.* There was a pause in the conversation.
pauvre ADJECTIVE
poor ◇ *Sa famille est pauvre.* His family is poor. ◇ *Pauvre Jean-Pierre! Il n'a pas eu de chance!* Poor Jean-Pierre! He was unlucky!
la **pauvreté** NOUN
poverty
pavé ADJECTIVE
cobbled ◇ *Les rues étaient pavées.* The streets were cobbled.
le **pavillon** NOUN
house ◇ *Ils habitent un pavillon de banlieue.* They've got a house in the suburbs.
payant ADJECTIVE
paying ◇ *Ce sont des hôtes payants.* They're paying guests.
• **C'est payant.** You have to pay. ◇ *L'entrée de la boîte est payante.* You have to pay to get into the nightclub.
la **paye** NOUN
wages
payer VERB
1 *to pay for* ◇ *Combien as-tu payé ta voiture?* How much did you pay for your car?
• **J'ai payé ce T-shirt vingt francs.** I paid 20 francs for this T-shirt.
2 *to pay* ◇ *Elle a été payée aujourd'hui.* She got paid today. ◇ *Son métier paye bien.* His job pays good money.
• **faire payer quelque chose à quelqu'un** to charge somebody for something ◇ *Il me l'a fait payer dix francs.* He

PTO

charged me 10 francs for it.

- **payer quelque chose à quelqu'un** to buy somebody something ◇ *Allez, je vous paye un verre.* Come on, I'll buy you a drink.

le **pays** NOUN
country
- **du pays** local ◇ *le vin du pays* the local wine

le **paysage** NOUN
landscape

le **paysan** NOUN
farmer

la **paysanne** NOUN
farmer

les **Pays-Bas** MASC NOUN
Netherlands
- **aux Pays-Bas (1)** in the Netherlands
- **aux Pays-Bas (2)** to the Netherlands

le **Pays de Galles** NOUN
Wales
- **au Pays de Galles (1)** in Wales ◇ *Daphne habite au Pays de Galles.* Daphne lives in Wales.
- **au Pays de Galles (2)** to Wales ◇ *Elle part au Pays de Galles la semaine prochaine.* She is going to Wales next week.

le **PC** NOUN
see also PC ABBREVIATION
PC (= personal computer) ◇ *Il a tapé le rapport sur son PC.* He typed the report on his PC.

PC ABBREVIATION (= *Parti communiste*)
see also PC NOUN
Communist Party

le **PDG** ABBREVIATION (= *président-directeur général*)
MD (= managing director)

le **péage** NOUN
1 *toll* ◇ *Nous avons payé cinquante francs de péage.* We paid a toll of 50 francs.
2 *tollbooth* ◇ *Sabine s'est arrêtée au péage de l'autoroute.* Sabine stopped at the motorway tollbooth.
French motorways charge a toll.

la **peau** NOUN
(PL les **peaux**)
skin ◇ *Elle a la peau douce.* She's got soft skin.

le/la **Peau-Rouge** NOUN
(PL les **Peaux-Rouges**)
Red Indian

la **pêche** NOUN
1 *peach*
2 *fishing*
- **aller à la pêche** to go fishing
- **la pêche à la ligne** angling

le **péché** NOUN
sin

pêcher VERB
1 *to fish for* ◇ *Ils sont partis pêcher la truite.* They've gone fishing for trout.
2 *to catch* ◇ *Jacques a pêché deux saumons.* Jacques caught two salmon.

le **pêcheur** NOUN
fisherman ◇ *Son père est pêcheur.* His father's a fisherman.
- **un pêcheur à la ligne** an angler

pédagogique ADJECTIVE
educational

la **pédale** NOUN
pedal

pédestre ADJECTIVE
- **une randonnée pédestre** a ramble

le **peigne** NOUN
comb

peigner VERB
to comb ◇ *Elle peigne sa poupée.* She's combing her doll's hair.
- **se peigner** to comb one's hair ◇ *Il faut que je me peigne.* I must comb my hair.

le **peignoir** NOUN
dressing gown
- **un peignoir de bain** a bathrobe

peindre VERB
to paint

la **peine** NOUN
trouble
- **avoir de la peine à faire quelque chose** to have trouble doing something ◇ *J'ai eu beaucoup de peine à la convaincre.* I had a lot of trouble convincing her.
- **se donner de la peine** to make a real effort ◇ *Il s'est donné beaucoup de peine pour obtenir ces renseignements.* He made a real effort to get this information.
- **prendre la peine de faire quelque chose** to go to the trouble of doing something ◇ *Il a pris la peine de me rapporter ma valise.* He went to the trouble of returning my case to me.
- **faire de la peine à quelqu'un** to upset somebody ◇ *Ça me fait de la peine de la voir pleurer.* It upsets me to see her crying.
- **ce n'est pas la peine** there's no point ◇ *Ce n'est pas la peine de téléphoner.* There's no point in phoning.
- **à peine (1)** hardly ◇ *J'ai à peine eu le temps de me changer.* I hardly had time to get changed.
- **à peine (2)** only just ◇ *Elle vient à peine de se lever.* She's only just got

up.

eintre NOUN
painter

einture NOUN
1 *painting* ◇ *On expose des peintures de Gautier au musée.* There's an exhibition of Gautier's paintings at the museum.
2 *paint* ◇ *J'ai acheté de la peinture verte.* I bought some green paint.
"peinture fraîche" "wet paint"

êle-mêle ADVERB
higgledy-piggledy

elle NOUN
1 *shovel*
2 *spade*

ellicule NOUN
film ◇ *une pellicule couleur* a colour film

ellicules FEM NOUN
dandruff SING

elote NOUN
ball ◇ *une pelote de laine* a ball of wool

elouse NOUN
lawn

eluche NOUN
un animal en peluche a soft toy

encher VERB
to tilt ◇ *Ce tableau penche vers la droite.* The picture's tilting to the right.
se pencher (1) to lean over ◇ *Françoise s'est penchée sur son cahier.* Françoise leant over her exercise book.
se pencher (2) to bend down ◇ *Il s'est penché pour ramasser sa casquette.* He bent down to pick his cap up.
se pencher (3) to lean out ◇ *Annick s'est penchée par la fenêtre.* Annick leant out of the window.

endant PREPOSITION
during ◇ *Ça s'est passé pendant l'été.* It happened during the summer.
pendant que while ◇ *Christian a téléphoné pendant que Chantal prenait son bain.* Christian phoned while Chantal was having a bath.

endentif NOUN
pendant

enderie NOUN
wardrobe (*for hanging clothes*)

endre VERB
to hang ◇ *Il a pendu sa veste dans l'armoire.* He hung his jacket in the wardrobe.
pendre quelqu'un to hang somebody ◇ *L'assassin a été pendu.* The murderer was hanged.

endule NOUN
clock

pénétrer VERB
1 *to enter* ◇ *Ils ont pénétré dans la maison en passant par le jardin.* They entered the house through the garden.
2 *to penetrate* ◇ *L'armée a pénétré sur le territoire ennemi.* The army penetrated enemy territory.

pénible ADJECTIVE
hard ◇ *Travailler sur un chantier est pénible.* Working on a building site is hard.
◆ **Il est vraiment pénible.** He's a real nuisance.

péniblement ADVERB
with difficulty

la **péniche** NOUN
barge

le **pénis** NOUN
penis

la **pénombre** NOUN
half-light

la **pensée** NOUN
thought ◇ *Il était perdu dans ses pensées.* He was lost in thought.

penser VERB
to think ◇ *Je pense que Yann a eu raison de partir.* I think Yann was right to leave.
◆ **penser à quelque chose** to think about something ◇ *Je pense à mes vacances.* I'm thinking about my holidays. ◇ *C'est une bonne occasion, pensez-y.* It's a good opportunity, think about it.
◆ **faire penser quelqu'un à quelque chose** to remind someone of something ◇ *Cette photo me fait penser à la Grèce.* This photo reminds me of Greece.
◆ **faire penser quelqu'un à faire quelque chose** to remind someone to do something ◇ *Fais-moi penser à téléphoner à Claire.* Remind me to phone Claire.
◆ **penser faire quelque chose** to be planning to do something ◇ *Ils pensent partir en Espagne en juillet.* They're planning to go to Spain in July.

la **pension** NOUN
1 *boarding school* ◇ *Leur fille est en pension.* Their daughter is at boarding school.
2 *pension* ◇ *Ma grand-mère reçoit sa pension tous les mois.* My grandma gets her pension every month.
3 *boarding house*
◆ **la pension complète** full board

le/la **pensionnaire** NOUN

P

PTO

boarder

le **pensionnat** NOUN
boarding school

la **pente** NOUN
slope ◇ *une pente raide* a steep slop
- **en pente** sloping ◇ *Le toit de cette maison est en pente.* This house has a sloping roof.

la **Pentecôte** NOUN
Whitsun

le **pépin** NOUN
1 *pip* ◇ *Cette orange est pleine de pépins.* This orange is full of pips.
2 *problem* ◇ *avoir un pépin* (*informal*) to have a slight problem

perçant ADJECTIVE
1 *sharp* ◇ *Il a une vue perçante.* He has very sharp eyes.
2 *piercing* ◇ *un cri perçant* a piercing cry

percer VERB
to pierce ◇ *Christèle s'est fait percer les oreilles.* Christèle has had her ears pierced.

le **perdant** NOUN
loser

la **perdante** NOUN
loser

perdre VERB
to lose ◇ *Cécile a perdu ses clés.* Cécile's lost her keys.
- **J'ai perdu mon chemin.** I've lost my way.
- **perdre du temps** to waste time ◇ *J'ai perdu beaucoup de temps ce matin.* I've wasted a lot of time this morning. ◇ *Nous avons perdu notre temps à cette réunion.* That meeting was a waste of time.
- **se perdre** to get lost ◇ *Je me suis perdu en route.* I got lost on the way here.

perdu VERB *see* **perdre**

le **père** NOUN
father
- **le père Noël** Father Christmas

perfectionné ADJECTIVE
sophisticated

perfectionner VERB
to improve ◇ *Elle a besoin de perfectionner son anglais.* She needs to improve her English.

périmé ADJECTIVE
out-of-date ◇ *Mon passeport est périmé.* My passport's out of date.
- **Ces yaourts sont périmés.** These yoghurts are past their use-by date.

la **période** NOUN
period

périodique ADJECTIVE
periodic

périphérique ADJECTIVE
see also périphérique NOUN
outlying ◇ *un quartier périphérique* a outlying district

le **périphérique** NOUN
see also périphérique ADJECTIVE
ring road

la **perle** NOUN
pearl

la **permanence** NOUN
- **assurer une permanence** to operate a basic service ◇ *Ma banque assure une permanence le samedi matin.* My bank operates a basic service on Saturday mornings.
- **être de permanence** to be on duty ◇ *Sophie ne peut pas venir, elle est de permanence ce soir.* Sophie can't come she's on duty tonight.
- **en permanence** permanently ◇ *Elle se plaint en permanence.* She's always complaining.

permanent ADJECTIVE
1 *permanent* ◇ *Il a un poste permanent.* He has a permanent job.
2 *continuous* ◇ *J'en ai assez de tes critiques permanentes.* I've had enough of your constant criticism.

la **permanente** NOUN
perm

permettre VERB
to allow
- **permettre à quelqu'un de faire quelque chose** to allow somebody to do something ◇ *Sa mère lui permet de sortir le soir.* His mother allows him to go out at night.

le **permis** NOUN
permit ◇ *Il vous faut un permis pour camper ici.* You need a permit to camp here.
- **le permis de conduire** driving licence
- **un permis de séjour** a residence permit
- **un permis de travail** a work permit

la **permission** NOUN
permission ◇ *Qui t'a donné la permission d'entrer?* Who gave you permission to come in?
- **avoir la permission de faire quelque chose** to have permission to do something ◇ *J'ai la permission d'utiliser sa chaîne hi-fi.* I've got his permission to use his hi-fi.
- **être en permission** to be on leave (*from the army*)

le **Pérou** NOUN
Peru

perpétuel ADJECTIVE
(FEM SING **perpétuelle**)
perpetual

perroquet NOUN
parrot

perruche NOUN
budgie

perruque NOUN
wig

persil NOUN
parsley

personnage NOUN
1 *figure* ◇ *les grands personnages de l'histoire de France* the important figures in French history
2 *character* ◇ *le personnage principal du film* the main character in the film

personnalité NOUN
1 *personality* ◇ *Ray a une personnalité forte.* Ray has a strong personality.
2 *prominent figure* ◇ *Il y avait beaucoup de personnalités politiques à ce dîner.* There were lots of prominent political figures at the dinner.

personne NOUN
see also **personne** PRONOUN
person ◇ *Il y avait une trentaine de personnes dans la pièce.* There were about 30 people in the room. ◇ *une personne âgée* an elderly person
- **en personne** in person

personne PRONOUN
see also **personne** NOUN
1 *nobody* ◇ *Il n'y a personne à la maison.* There's nobody at home. ◇ *Personne n'est venu le chercher.* Nobody came to fetch him.
2 *anybody* ◇ *Elle ne veut voir personne.* She doesn't want to see anybody.

personnel ADJECTIVE
(FEM SING **personnelle**)
see also **personnel** NOUN
personal

personnel NOUN
see also **personnel** ADJECTIVE
staff ◇ *Il nous faut plus de personnel.* We need more staff.
- **le service du personnel** the personnel department

personnellement ADVERB
personally ◇ *Personnellement, je ne suis pas d'accord.* Personally, I don't agree.

perspective NOUN
prospect ◇ *Les perspectives sont encourageantes.* The prospects are encouraging.
- **perspectives d'avenir** prospects ◇ *Il y a des perspectives d'avenir dans ce métier.* This job has good prospects.
- **en perspective (1)** in prospect ◇ *Il y a des changements en perspective.* Changes are in prospect.
- **en perspective (2)** in perspective ◇ *Il a dessiné la maison en perspective.* He drew the house in perspective.

persuader VERB
to persuade
- **persuader quelqu'un de faire quelque chose** to persuade somebody to do something ◇ *Elle m'a persuadé de l'accompagner au cinéma.* She persuaded me to go to the cinema with her.

la **perte** NOUN
1 *loss* ◇ *des pertes d'emploi* job losses
2 *waste* ◇ *Cette réunion a été une perte de temps.* The meeting was a waste of time.

perturber VERB
to disrupt ◇ *Un camion en panne perturbait la circulation.* A lorry had broken down and was disrupting the traffic.

le **pèse-personne** NOUN
bathroom scales PL

peser VERB
to weigh ◇ *Elle pèse cent kilos.* She weighs 100 kilos.

pessimiste ADJECTIVE
pessimistic

le **pétale** NOUN
petal

la **pétanque** NOUN
pétanque *is a type of bowls played in France, especially in the south.*

le **pétard** NOUN
firecracker

péter VERB (*rude*)
to fart

petit ADJECTIVE
1 *small* ◇ *Sonia habite une petite ville.* Sonia lives in a small town.
2 *little* ◇ *Phyllis a une jolie petite maison.* Phyllis has a nice little house.
- **petit à petit** bit by bit
- **un petit ami** a boyfriend
- **une petite amie** a girlfriend
- **le petit déjeuner** breakfast
- **un petit pain** a bread roll
- **les petites annonces** the small ads
- **des petits pois** garden peas
- **les petits** young (*of animal*) ◇ *la lionne et ses petits* the lioness and her young

la **petite-fille** NOUN
(PL **les petites-filles**)

PTO

granddaughter

le **petit-fils** NOUN
(PL les **petits-fils**)
grandson

les **petits-enfants** MASC NOUN
grandchildren

le **pétrole** NOUN
oil ◇ *une lampe à pétrole* an oil lamp

peu ADVERB, NOUN
not much ◇ *J'ai peu mangé à midi.* I didn't eat much for lunch. ◇ *Il voyage peu.* He doesn't travel much.
- **un peu** a bit ◇ *Elle est un peu timide.* She's a bit shy. ◇ *un peu de gâteau* a bit of cake
- **un petit peu** a little bit ◇ *un petit peu de crème* a little bit of cream
- **peu de (1)** not many ◇ *Il y a peu de bons films au cinéma.* There aren't very many good films on at the cinema. ◇ *Elle a peu d'amis.* She hasn't got many friends.
- **peu de (2)** not much ◇ *Il a peu d'espoir de réussir.* He doesn't have much hope of succeeding. ◇ *Il lui reste peu d'argent.* He hasn't got much money left.
- **à peu près (1)** more or less ◇ *J'ai à peu près fini.* I've more or less finished.
- **à peu près (2)** about ◇ *Le voyage prend à peu près deux heures.* The journey takes about two hours.
- **peu à peu** little by little
- **peu avant** shortly before
- **peu après** shortly afterwards
- **de peu** only just ◇ *Chantal a manqué son train de peu.* Chantal only just missed her train.

le **peuple** NOUN
people ◇ *le peuple français* the French people

la **peur** NOUN
fear
- **avoir peur de** to be afraid of ◇ *Il a peur du noir.* He's afraid of the dark.
- **avoir peur de faire quelque chose** to be frightened of doing something ◇ *Elle a peur d'y aller toute seule.* She's frightened of going on her own.
- **faire peur à quelqu'un** to frighten somebody ◇ *Cet homme-là me fait peur.* That man frightens me.

peureux ADJECTIVE
(FEM SING **peureuse**)
fearful

peut VERB *see* **pouvoir**
- **Il ne peut pas venir.** He can't come.

peut-être ADVERB
perhaps ◇ *Je l'ai peut-être oublié à la maison.* Perhaps I've left it at home.
- **peut-être que** perhaps ◇ *Peut-être qu'elles n'ont pas pu téléphoner.* Perhaps they weren't able to phone.

peuvent, peux VERB *see* **pouvoir**
- **Je ne peux pas le faire.** I can't do it.

p. ex. ABBREVIATION (= *par exemple*)
e.g.

le **phare** NOUN
1 *lighthouse* ◇ *On voit le phare depuis le pont du bateau.* You can see the lighthouse from the ship's deck.
2 *headlight* ◇ *Il a laissé les phares de sa voiture allumés.* He left his headlights on.

la **pharmacie** NOUN
chemist's

Chemist's shops in France are identified by a special green cross outside the shop.

le **pharmacien** NOUN
pharmacist

la **pharmacienne** NOUN
pharmacist

le **phénomène** NOUN
phenomenon

la **philosophie** NOUN
philosophy

le **phoque** NOUN
seal (*animal*)

la **photo** NOUN
photograph ◇ *Elle a fait développer ses photos.* She's had her photographs developed.
- **en photo** in photographs ◇ *Je n'ai vu Venise qu'en photo.* I've only seen Venice in photographs.
- **prendre quelqu'un en photo** to take a photo of somebody ◇ *Claire nous a pris en photo.* Claire took a photo of us.
- **une photo d'identité** a passport photograph

la **photocopie** NOUN
photocopy

photocopier VERB
to photocopy

la **photocopieuse** NOUN
photocopier

le/la **photographe** NOUN
photographer

la **photographie** NOUN
1 *photography*
2 *photograph*

photographier VERB
to photograph

la **phrase** NOUN
sentence

physique ADJECTIVE
see also physique NOUN
physical

physique NOUN

see also la physique *and* physique ADJECTIVE

- **Il a un physique agréable.** He's quite good-looking.

physique NOUN

see also le physique *and* physique ADJECTIVE

physics ◇ *Il est professeur de physique.* He's a physics teacher.

pianiste NOUN

pianist ◇ *Elle est pianiste.* She's a pianist.

piano NOUN

piano

pic NOUN

peak ◇ *les pics enneigés des Pyrénées* the snowy peaks of the Pyrenees

- **à pic (1)** vertically ◇ *La falaise tombe à pic dans la mer.* The cliff drops vertically into the sea.
- **à pic (1)** just at the right time ◇ *Tu es arrivé à pic.* You arrived just at the right time.

pièce NOUN

1 *room* ◇ *Mon lit est au centre de la pièce.* My bed is in the middle of the room.

- **un cinq-pièces** a five-roomed flat

2 *play* ◇ *On joue une pièce d'Anouilh au théâtre.* There's a play by Anouilh on at the theatre.

3 *part* ◇ *Il faut changer une pièce du moteur.* There's an engine part which needs changing.

4 *coin* ◇ *des pièces d'un franc* some one-franc coins

- **cinquante francs pièce** 50 francs each ◇ *J'ai acheté ces T-shirts dix francs pièce.* I bought these T-shirts for ten francs each.
- **un maillot une pièce** a one-piece swimsuit
- **un maillot deux-pièces** a bikini
- **Avez-vous une pièce d'identité?** Have you got any identification?

le **pied** NOUN

foot ◇ *J'ai mal aux pieds.* My feet are hurting.

- **à pied** on foot
- **avoir pied** to be able to touch the bottom ◇ *Justine n'aime pas nager là où elle n'a pas pied.* Justine doesn't like swimming where she can't touch the bottom.

le **pied-noir** NOUN

(PL les **pieds-noirs**)

A pied-noir *is a French person born in Algeria; most of them moved to France during the Algerian war in the 1950s.*

◇ *Sa grand-mère est pied-noir.* His grandmother was born in Algeria.

le **piège** NOUN

trap

- **prendre quelqu'un au piège** to trap somebody

piéger VERB

to trap

- **un colis piégé** a parcel bomb
- **une voiture piégée** a car bomb

la **pierre** NOUN

stone

- **une pierre précieuse** a precious stone

le **piéton** NOUN

pedestrian

la **piétonne** NOUN

pedestrian

piétonnier ADJECTIVE

(FEM SING **piétonnière**)

- **une rue piétonnière** a pedestrianized street
- **un quartier piétonnier** a pedestrianized area

la **pieuvre** NOUN

octopus

le **pigeon** NOUN

pigeon

piger VERB (*informal*)

to understand

la **pile** NOUN

see also pile ADVERB

1 *pile* ◇ *Il y a une pile de disques sur la table.* There's a pile of records on the table.

2 *battery* ◇ *Les piles de mon magnétophone sont usées.* The batteries in my tape recorder have run out.

pile ADVERB

see also pile NOUN

- **à deux heures pile** at two on the dot
- **jouer à pile ou face** to toss up
- **Pile ou face?** Heads or tails?

le **pilote** NOUN

pilot

- **un pilote de course** a racing driver
- **un pilote de ligne** an airline pilot

piloter VERB

to fly (*a plane*)

la **pilule** NOUN

pill

- **prendre la pilule** to be on the pill

le **piment** NOUN

chilli

le **pin** NOUN

pine

le **pinard** NOUN (*informal*)

wine

la **pince** NOUN

1 *pliers* PL (*tool*)

2 *pincer* (*of crab*)

PTO

- **une pince à épiler** tweezers
- **une pince à linge** a clothes peg

le **pinceau** NOUN
(PL les **pinceaux**)
paintbrush

la **pincée** NOUN
- **une pincée de sel** a pinch of salt

pincer VERB
to pinch ◇ *Elle m'a pincé le bras.* She pinched my arm.

le **pingouin** NOUN
penguin

le **ping-pong** NOUN
table tennis ◇ *jouer au ping-pong* to play table tennis

la **pintade** NOUN
guinea fowl

le **pion** NOUN
1 *pawn* (*in chess*)
2 *piece* (*in draughts*)
3 *supervisor* (*man*)

In French secondary schools, the teachers are not responsible for supervising the pupils outside class. This job is done by people called pions *or* surveillants.

la **pionne** NOUN
supervisor (*woman*)

la **pipe** NOUN
pipe ◇ *Mon grand-père fume la pipe.* My granddad smokes a pipe.

piquant ADJECTIVE
1 *prickly*
2 *spicy*

le **pique** NOUN
see also la pique
spades PL ◇ *l'as de pique* the ace of spades

la **pique** NOUN
see also le pique
cutting remark ◇ *envoyer des piques à quelqu'un* to make cutting remarks to somebody

le **pique-nique** NOUN
picnic

piquer VERB
1 *to bite* ◇ *Nous avons été piqués par les moustiques.* We were bitten by mosquitoes.
2 *to burn* ◇ *Cette sauce me pique la langue.* This sauce is burning my tongue.
3 *to steal* ◇ *On m'a piqué mon porte-monnaie.* (*informal*) I've had my purse stolen.
- **se piquer** to prick oneself ◇ *Il s'est piqué avec une aiguille.* He pricked himself with a needle.

le **piquet** NOUN
1 *post* ◇ *Le chien est attaché à un piquet.* The dog is tied to a post.
2 *peg* ◇ *Il nous manque un des piquets de la tente.* One of our tent pegs is missing.

la **piqûre** NOUN
1 *injection* ◇ *Le médecin lui a fait une piqûre.* The doctor gave him an injection.
2 *bite* ◇ *une piqûre de moustique* a mosquito bite
3 *sting* ◇ *une piqûre d'abeille* a bee sting

le **pirate** NOUN
pirate

pire ADJECTIVE, NOUN
worse ◇ *C'est encore pire qu'avant.* It's even worse than before.
- **le pire** the worst ◇ *C'est la pire journée que j'aie jamais passée.* That's the worst day I've ever had. ◇ *Ce gamin est le pire de la bande.* That boy is the worst in the group.
- **le pire de** the worst of ◇ *Le pire de tout, c'est qu'on s'ennuie tout le temps.* The worst of it is that we're always bored.

la **piscine** NOUN
swimming pool

la **pistache** NOUN
pistachio ◇ *une glace à la pistache* a pistachio ice cream

la **piste** NOUN
1 *lead* ◇ *La police est sur une piste.* The police are following a lead.
2 *runway* ◇ *L'avion s'est posé sur la piste.* The plane landed on the runway.
3 *ski run* ◇ *Le skieur a descendu la piste.* The skier came down the ski run.
- **une piste artificielle** a dry ski slope
- **la piste de danse** the dance floor
- **une piste cyclable** a cycle track

le **pistolet** NOUN
pistol

pistonner VERB
- **Il a été pistonné pour avoir ce travail.** They pulled some strings to get him this job.

la **pitié** NOUN
pity
- **Il me fait pitié.** I feel sorry for him.
- **avoir pitié de quelqu'un** to feel sorry for somebody

pittoresque ADJECTIVE
picturesque

le **placard** NOUN
cupboard

la **place** NOUN
1 *place* ◇ *Vincent a eu la troisième place au concours.* Vincent got third

place in the competition.
2 *square* ◇ *la place du village* the village square
3 *space* ◇ *Il ne reste plus de place pour se garer.* There's no more space to park. ◇ *Ça prend de la place.* It takes up a lot of room.
4 *seat* ◇ *Toutes les places ont été vendues.* All the seats have been sold. ◇ *Il y a vingt places assises.* There are 20 seats. ◇ *remettre quelque chose en place* to put something back in its place
sur place on the spot
à la place instead ◇ *Il ne reste plus de tarte; désirez-vous quelque chose d'autre à la place?* There's no pie left; would you like something else instead?
à la place de instead of
placer VERB
1 *to seat* ◇ *Nous étions placés à côté du directeur.* We were seated next to the manager.
2 *to invest* ◇ *Il a placé ses économies en Bourse.* He invested his money on the Stock Exchange.
plafond NOUN
ceiling
plage NOUN
beach
plaie NOUN
wound
plaindre VERB
plaindre quelqu'un to feel sorry for somebody ◇ *Je te plains.* I feel sorry for you.
se plaindre to complain ◇ *Il n'arrête pas de se plaindre.* He never stops complaining.
se plaindre à quelqu'un to complain to somebody ◇ *Ils se sont plaints au directeur.* They complained to the manager.
se plaindre de quelque chose to complain about something ◇ *Elle s'est plainte du bruit.* She complained about the noise.
plaine NOUN
plain (*level area*)
plainte NOUN
complaint
porter plainte to lodge a complaint
plaire VERB
Ce cadeau me plaît beaucoup. I like this present a lot.
Ce film plaît beaucoup aux jeunes. The film is very popular with young people.
Elle lui plaît. He fancies her.
s'il te plaît please
◆ **s'il vous plaît** please
plaisanter VERB
to joke
la **plaisanterie** NOUN
joke
le **plaisir** NOUN
pleasure
◆ **faire plaisir à quelqu'un** to please somebody ◇ *J'y suis allé pour lui faire plaisir.* I went there to please him. ◇ *Ce cadeau me fait très plaisir.* I'm very pleased with this present.
plaît VERB *see* **plaire**
le **plan** NOUN
plan
◆ **au premier plan** in the foreground
la **planche** NOUN
plank
◆ **une planche à repasser** an ironing board
◆ **une planche à roulettes** a skateboard
le **plancher** NOUN
floor
planer VERB
1 *to glide* ◇ *L'avion planait dans le ciel.* The plane was gliding in the sky.
2 *to have one's head in the clouds* ◇ *Ce garçon plane complètement.* (*informal*) He's not with us at all.
la **planète** NOUN
planet
la **plante** NOUN
plant
planter VERB
1 *to plant* ◇ *Daphné a planté des tomates.* Daphne planted some tomatoes.
2 *to hammer in* ◇ *Jean-Pierre a planté un clou dans le mur.* Jean-Pierre hammered a nail into the wall.
3 *to pitch* ◇ *André a planté sa tente au bord du lac.* André pitched his tent next to the lake.
◆ **Ne reste pas planté là!** Don't just stand there!
◆ **se planter** (*informal*) to fail ◇ *Je me suis planté en maths.* I failed maths.
la **plaque** NOUN
(metal) plate
◆ **une plaque de verglas** a patch of ice
◆ **une plaque de chocolat** a bar of chocolate
◆ **une plaque d'immatriculation** a number plate (*of car*)
plaqué ADJECTIVE
◆ **plaqué or** gold-plated
◆ **plaqué argent** silver-plated
plaquer VERB (*informal*)
1 *to ditch* ◇ *Elle a plaqué son copain.*

PTO

She ditched her boyfriend.
2 *to pack in* ◇ *Il a plaqué son boulot.* He packed in his job.

la **plaquette** NOUN
- **une plaquette de chocolat** a bar of chocolate
- **une plaquette de beurre** a pack of butter

le **plastique** NOUN
plastic

plat ADJECTIVE
see also plat NOUN
flat
- **être à plat ventre** to be lying face down
- **l'eau plate** still water

le **plat** NOUN
see also plat ADJECTIVE
1 *dish* ◇ *un plat en inox* a stainless steel dish
2 *course* ◇ *le plat principal* the main course
- **un plat cuisiné** a pre-cooked meal
- **le plat de résistance** the main course
- **le plat du jour** the dish of the day

le **platane** NOUN
plane tree

le **plateau** NOUN
(PL les **plateaux**)
1 *tray*
- **un plateau de fromages** a selection of cheeses

2 *plateau*

le **platine** NOUN
see also la platine
platinum

la **platine** NOUN
see also le platine
turntable (*of record player*)
- **une platine laser** a CD player

le **plâtre** NOUN
plaster ◇ *une statue en plâtre* a statue made of plaster ◇ *avoir un bras dans le plâtre* to have an arm in plaster

plein ADJECTIVE
see also plein NOUN
full
- **à plein temps** full-time ◇ *Elle travaille à plein temps.* She works full-time.
- **en plein air** in the open air
- **en pleine nuit** in the middle of the night
- **en plein jour** in broad daylight

le **plein** NOUN
see also plein ADJECTIVE
- **faire le plein** to fill up (*petrol tank*) ◇ *Faites le plein, s'il vous plaît.* Fill it up, please.

pleurer VERB
to cry

pleut VERB *see* **pleuvoir**

pleuvoir VERB
to rain ◇ *Il pleut.* It's raining.

le **pli** NOUN
1 *fold*
2 *pleat* ◇ *Elle a repassé les plis de sa jupe.* She ironed the pleats of her skirt.
3 *crease* ◇ *Il y a un pli sur la manche de ta chemise.* There's a crease in the sleeve of your shirt.

pliant ADJECTIVE
folding ◇ *un lit pliant* a folding bed

plier VERB
1 *to fold* ◇ *Elle a plié sa serviette.* She folded her towel.
2 *to bend* ◇ *Elle a plié le bras.* She bent her arm.

le **plomb** NOUN
1 *lead* ◇ *Ces jouets sont en plomb.* These toys are made of lead.
2 *fuse* ◇ *Les plombs ont sauté.* The fuses have blown.
- **l'essence sans plomb** unleaded petrol

le **plombier** NOUN
plumber
- **Il est plombier.** He's a plumber.

la **plongée** NOUN
diving ◇ *faire de la plongée* to go diving

le **plongeoir** NOUN
diving board

le **plongeon** NOUN
dive

plonger VERB
to dive ◇ *Jean a plongé dans la piscine.* Jean dived into the swimming pool.
- **J'ai plongé ma main dans l'eau.** I plunged my hand into the water.

plu VERB *see* **plaire, pleuvoir**

la **pluie** NOUN
rain ◇ *sous la pluie* in the rain

la **plume** NOUN
feather ◇ *une plume d'oiseau* a bird's feather
- **un stylo à plume** a fountain pen

plupart
- **la plupart** PRONOUN
most (of them) ◇ *La plupart ont moins de quinze ans.* Most of them are under 15.
- **la plupart des** most ◇ *La plupart des gens ont vu ce film.* Most people have seen this film.
- **la plupart du temps** most of the time

le **pluriel** NOUN
plural

plus ADVERB, PREPOSITION
- **ne...plus (1)** not...any more ◇ *Je ne*

veux plus le voir. I don't want to see him any more.
ne...plus (2) no longer ◇ *Il ne travaille plus ici.* He's no longer working here.
Je n'ai plus de pain. I've got no bread left.
plus...que more...than ◇ *Il est plus intelligent que son frère.* He's more intelligent than his brother. ◇ *Il travaille plus que moi.* He works more than me. ◇ *Elle est plus grande que moi.* She's bigger than me.
C'est le plus grand de la famille. He's the tallest in his family.
plus...plus... the more...the more... ◇ *Plus il gagne d'argent, plus il en veut.* The more money he earns, the more he wants.
plus de (1) more ◇ *Il nous faut plus de pain.* We need more bread.
plus de (2) more than ◇ *Il y avait plus de dix personnes.* There were more than 10 people.
de plus more ◇ *Il nous faut un joueur de plus.* We need one more player. ◇ *Le voyage a pris trois heures de plus que prévu.* The journey took 3 hours more than planned.
en plus more ◇ *J'ai apporté quelques gâteaux en plus.* I brought a few more cakes.
de plus en plus more and more ◇ *Il y a de plus en plus de touristes par ici.* There are more and more tourists round here. ◇ *Il fait de plus en plus chaud.* It's getting hotter and hotter.
plus ou moins more or less
Quatre plus deux égalent six. 4 plus 2 is 6.

usieurs PRONOUN
several ◇ *Elle a acheté plusieurs chemises.* She bought several shirts. ◇ *Il y en a plusieurs.* There are several of them.

us-que-parfait NOUN
pluperfect

utôt ADVERB
1 *quite* ◇ *Elle est plutôt jolie.* She's quite pretty.
2 *rather* ◇ *L'eau est plutôt froide.* The water's rather cold.
3 *instead* ◇ *Demande-leur plutôt de venir avec toi.* Ask them to come with you instead.
plutôt que rather than ◇ *Invite Marie plutôt que Nathalie.* Invite Marie rather than Nathalie.

uvieux ADJECTIVE
(FEM SING **pluvieuse**)
rainy

le **pneu** NOUN
tyre

la **pneumonie** NOUN
pneumonia

la **poche** NOUN
pocket
◆ **l'argent de poche** pocket money
◆ **un livre de poche** a paperback

la **poêle** NOUN
frying pan
◆ **une poêle à frire** a frying pan

le **poème** NOUN
poem

la **poésie** NOUN
1 *poetry*
2 *poem*

le **poète** NOUN
poet

le **poids** NOUN
weight ◇ *vendre quelque chose au poids* to sell something by weight
◆ **prendre du poids** to put on weight ◇ *Il a pris du poids.* He's put on weight.
◆ **perdre du poids** to lose weight ◇ *Elle a perdu du poids.* She's lost weight.
◆ **un poids lourd** a lorry

la **poignée** NOUN
1 *handful* ◇ *une poignée de sel* a handful of salt
2 *handle* ◇ *la poignée de la porte* the door handle
◆ **une poignée de main** a handshake

le **poignet** NOUN
1 *wrist* ◇ *Je me suis fait mal au poignet.* I've hurt my wrist.
2 *cuff* (*of shirt*)

le **poil** NOUN
1 *hair* ◇ *Il y a des poils de chat partout sur la moquette.* There are cat hairs all over the carpet.
2 *fur* ◇ *Ton chien a un beau poil.* Your dog's got lovely fur.

poilu ADJECTIVE
hairy

poinçonner VERB
to punch ◇ *Le contrôleur a poinçonné les billets.* The conductor punched the tickets.

le **poing** NOUN
fist
◆ **un coup de poing** a punch

le **point** NOUN
1 *point* ◇ *Je ne suis pas d'accord sur ce point.* I don't agree with this point. ◇ *Son point faible, c'est qu'elle est trop gentille.* Her weak point is she's too nice.
◆ **point de vue** point of view

PTO

2 *full stop*

- **être sur le point de faire quelque chose** to be just about to do something ◇ *J'étais sur le point de te téléphoner.* I was just about to phone you.
- **mettre au point** to finalize
- **Ce n'est pas encore au point.** It's not finalized yet.
- **à point** medium ◇ *Comment voulez-vous votre steak?–À point.* How would you like your steak?–Medium.
- **un point d'exclamation** an exclamation mark
- **un point d'interrogation** a question mark

la **pointe** NOUN
point ◇ *la pointe d'un couteau* the point of a knife
- **être à la pointe du progrès** to be in the forefront of progress
- **sur la pointe des pieds** on tiptoe
- **les heures de pointe** peak hours

le **pointillé** NOUN
dotted line

pointu ADJECTIVE
pointed ◇ *un chapeau pointu* a pointed hat

la **pointure** NOUN
size (*of shoes*) ◇ *Quelle est votre pointure?* What size shoes do you take?

le **point-virgule** NOUN
semicolon

la **poire** NOUN
pear

le **poireau** NOUN
(PL les **poireaux**)
leek ◇ *la soupe aux poireaux* leek soup

le **pois** NOUN
pea
- **les petits pois** peas
- **les pois chiches** chickpeas
- **à pois** spotted ◇ *une robe à pois* a spotted dress

le **poison** NOUN
poison

le **poisson** NOUN
fish ◇ *Je n'aime pas le poisson.* I don't like fish. ◇ *André a pêché deux poissons.* André caught two fish.
- **les Poissons** Pisces ◇ *Monique est Poissons.* Monique is Pisces.
- **Poisson d'avril!** April fool!

Pinning a paper fish to somebody's back is a traditional April fool joke in France.

- **un poisson rouge** a goldfish

la **poissonnerie** NOUN
fish shop

le **poissonnier** NOUN
fishmonger

la **poitrine** NOUN
1 *chest* ◇ *J'ai mal à la poitrine.* My chest hurts.
2 *bust* ◇ *Quel est votre tour de poitrine?* What's your bust size?

le **poivre** NOUN
pepper (*spice*)

le **poivron** NOUN
pepper (*vegetable*)

le **pôle** NOUN
pole
- **le pôle Nord** the North Pole
- **le pôle Sud** the South Pole

poli ADJECTIVE
polite

la **police** NOUN
police ◇ *La police recherche le voleur.* The police are looking for the thief.
- **police secours** emergency services ◇ *Ils ont appelé police secours.* They phoned the emergency services.
- **une police d'assurance** an insurance policy

policier ADJECTIVE
(FEM SING **policière**)
see also **policier** NOUN
- **un roman policier** a detective novel

le **policier** NOUN
see also **policier** ADJECTIVE
policeman ◇ *Il est policier.* He's a policeman.

la **politesse** NOUN
politeness

la **politique** NOUN
politics ◇ *La politique ne l'intéresse pas du tout.* He's not at all interested in politics.
- **un homme politique** a politician

la **pollution** NOUN
pollution

le **polo** NOUN
polo shirt

la **Pologne** NOUN
Poland

polonais ADJECTIVE, NOUN
(FEM SING **polonaise**)
Polish ◇ *Elle parle polonais.* She speaks Polish.
- **un Polonais** a Pole (*man*)
- **une Polonaise** a Pole (*woman*)
- **les Polonais** the Polish

la **Polynésie** NOUN
Polynesia

la **pommade** NOUN
ointment

la **pomme** NOUN
apple
- **les pommes de terre** potatoes

les pommes frites chips

pompe NOUN
pump
une pompe à essence a petrol pump
les pompes funèbres undertakers

pompier NOUN
fireman

pondre VERB
to lay (*eggs*)

poney NOUN
pony

pont NOUN
1 *bridge*
2 *deck* (*of ship*)
faire le pont to take a long weekend ◇ *Nous faisons le pont pour la Pentecôte.* We're taking a long weekend for Whitsun.

populaire ADJECTIVE
1 *popular* ◇ *Ce chanteur est très populaire en France.* This singer's very popular in France.
2 *working-class* ◇ *un quartier populaire de la ville* a working-class area of town

population NOUN
population

porc NOUN
1 *pig* ◇ *Ils élèvent des porcs.* They breed pigs.
2 *pork* ◇ *du rôti de porc* roast pork

porcelaine NOUN
china ◇ *une tasse en porcelaine* a china cup

port NOUN
1 *harbour*
2 *port*

portail NOUN
gate

portatif ADJECTIVE
(FEM SING **portative**)
portable

porte NOUN
1 *door* ◇ *Ferme la porte, s'il te plaît.* Close the door, please.
◆ **la porte d'entrée** the front door
2 *gate* ◇ *Vol 432 à destination de Paris: porte numéro trois.* Flight 432 to Paris: gate 3.
◆ **mettre quelqu'un à la porte** to sack somebody

porte-bagages NOUN
luggage rack

porte-clés NOUN
key ring

portée NOUN
◆ **à portée de la main** within arm's reach
◆ **hors de portée** out of reach

portefeuille NOUN
wallet

le **portemanteau** NOUN
(PL les **portemanteaux**)
1 *coat hanger*
2 *coat rack*

le **porte-monnaie** NOUN
(PL les **porte-monnaie**)
purse

porter VERB
1 *to carry* ◇ *Il portait une valise.* He was carrying a suitcase.
2 *to wear* ◇ *Elle porte une jolie robe bleue.* She's wearing a lovely blue dress.
◆ **se porter bien** to be well
◆ **se porter mal** to be unwell

la **portière** NOUN
door (*of car*)

la **portion** NOUN
portion

le **porto** NOUN
port (*wine*)

le **portrait** NOUN
portrait

portugais ADJECTIVE, NOUN
(FEM SING **portugaise**)
Portuguese ◇ *Il parle portugais.* He speaks Portuguese.
◆ **un Portugais** a Portuguese (*man*)
◆ **une Portugaise** a Portuguese (*woman*)
◆ **les Portugais** the Portuguese

le **Portugal** NOUN
Portugal
◆ **au Portugal (1)** in Portugal
◆ **au Portugal (2)** to Portugal

poser VERB
1 *to put down* ◇ *J'ai posé la cafetière sur la table.* I put the coffee pot down on the table.
2 *to pose* ◇ *Cela pose un problème.* That poses a problem.
◆ **poser une question à quelqu'un** to ask somebody a question
◆ **se poser** to land ◇ *L'avion s'est posé à huit heures.* The plane landed at 8 o'clock.

positif ADJECTIVE
(FEM SING **positive**)
positive

la **position** NOUN
position

posséder VERB
to own ◇ *Ils possèdent une jolie maison.* They own a lovely house.

la **possibilité** NOUN
possibility

possible ADJECTIVE
possible ◇ *Alain leur a dit que ce n'était pas possible.* Alain told them it wasn't possible.

PTO

- **le plus de gens possible** as many people as possible
- **le plus tôt possible** as early as possible
- **le moins d'argent possible** as little money as possible
- **Il travaille le moins possible.** He works as little as possible.
- **dès que possible** as soon as possible
- **faire son possible** to do all one can ◇ *Je ferai tout mon possible.* I'll do all I can.

la **poste** NOUN

see also le poste

1 *post* ◇ *Je vais l'envoyer par la poste.* I'm going to send it by post.

2 *post office* ◇ *Je vais à la poste pour acheter des timbres.* I'm going to the post office to buy some stamps.

- **mettre une lettre à la poste** to post a letter

le **poste** NOUN

see also la poste

1 *post* ◇ *Jean-Pierre a trouvé un poste de professeur.* Jean-Pierre has found a teaching post.

2 *extension* (*phone*) ◇ *Pouvez-vous me passer le poste de M. Salzedo?* Can you put me through to Mr Salzedo's extension?

3 *set* ◇ *un poste de radio* a radio set

- **un poste de police** a police station

poster VERB

see also poster NOUN

to post ◇ *Je vais poster ce colis.* I'm going to post this parcel.

le **poster** NOUN

see also poster VERB

poster ◇ *un poster de la Grèce* a poster of Greece

postérieur ADJECTIVE

1 *later* ◇ *Ce document est postérieur à mille trois cent quatorze.* This document is from later than 1314.

2 *back* ◇ *la partie postérieure de ma jambe* the back of my leg

le **pot** NOUN

jar ◇ *J'ai fait trois pots de confiture.* I've made three jars of jam.

- **prendre un pot** (*informal*) to have a drink ◇ *On va prendre un pot ce soir.* We're going for a drink tonight.
- **un pot de fleurs** a plant pot

potable ADJECTIVE

- **eau potable** drinking water
- **"eau non potable"** "not drinking water"

le **potage** NOUN

soup

le **potager** NOUN

vegetable garden

le **pot-au-feu** NOUN

(PL les **pot-au-feu**)

beef stew

le **pote** NOUN (*informal*)

mate ◇ *Je sors avec mes potes ce soi*

I'm going out with my mates tonight.

le **poteau** NOUN

(PL les **poteaux**)

post ◇ *Il s'est appuyé contre un poteau*

He leant against a post.

- **un poteau indicateur** a signpost

potentiel ADJECTIVE

(FEM SING **potentielle**)

potential

la **poterie** NOUN

1 *pottery* ◇ *Elle fait de la poterie à l'école.* She does pottery at school.

2 *piece of pottery* ◇ *J'ai acheté deux poteries.* I bought two pieces of pottery.

le **potier** NOUN

potter

le **pou** NOUN

(PL les **poux**)

louse

la **poubelle** NOUN

dustbin

le **pouce** NOUN

1 *thumb* ◇ *Je me suis coincé le pouc dans la porte.* I trapped my thumb in the door.

2 *inch* ◇ *Un pouce fait à peu près deux virgule cinq centimètres.* 1 inch equals roughly 2.5 centimetres.

- **manger sur le pouce** to have a quick snack

la **poudre** NOUN

1 *powder*

2 *face powder*

- **la poudre à laver** washing powder
- **le lait en poudre** powdered milk
- **le café en poudre** instant coffee

le **poulain** NOUN

foal

la **poule** NOUN

hen

le **poulet** NOUN

1 *chicken* ◇ *J'adore le poulet.* I love chicken.

2 *cop* ◇ *Il s'est fait attraper par les poulets.* (*informal*) He got caught by the cops.

le **pouls** NOUN

pulse ◇ *Il m'a pris le pouls.* He took my pulse.

le **poumon** NOUN

lung

la **poupée** NOUN

doll

pour PREPOSITION
for ◇ *C'est un cadeau pour toi.* It's a present for you. ◇ *Qu'est-ce que tu veux pour ton petit déjeuner?* What would you like for breakfast?
pour faire quelque chose to do something ◇ *Je lui ai téléphoné pour l'inviter.* I phoned him to invite him.
pour que so that
pour que *is followed by a verb in the subjunctive.*
◇ *Je lui ai prêté mon pull pour qu'elle n'ait pas froid.* I lent her my jumper so that she wouldn't be cold.
pour cent per cent

pourboire NOUN
tip ◇ *Il a donné un pourboire au garçon.* He gave the waiter a tip.

pourcentage NOUN
percentage

pourquoi ADVERB, CONJUNCTION
why ◇ *Pourquoi est-ce qu'il ne vient pas avec nous?* Why isn't he coming with us? ◇ *Elle ne m'a pas dit pourquoi.* She didn't tell me why.

pourra, pourrai, pourras, pourrez VERB *see* **pouvoir**

pourri ADJECTIVE
rotten

pourrir VERB
to go bad ◇ *Ces poires ont pourri.* These pears have gone bad.

pourrons, pourront VERB *see* **pouvoir**

poursuite NOUN
chase
se lancer à la poursuite de quelqu'un to chase after somebody

poursuivre VERB
to carry on with ◇ *Ils ont poursuivi leur travail.* They carried on with their work.
se poursuivre to go on ◇ *Le concert s'est poursuivi très tard.* The concert went on very late.

pourtant ADVERB
yet ◇ *Il a raté son examen. Pourtant, il n'est pas bête.* He failed his exam, yet he's not stupid.
C'est pourtant facile! But it's easy!

pourvu ADJECTIVE
pourvu que... let's hope that...
pourvu que *is followed by a verb in the subjunctive.*
◇ *Pourvu qu'il ne pleuve pas!* Let's hope it doesn't rain!

pousser VERB
1 *to push* ◇ *Ils ont dû pousser la voiture.* They had to push the car.
2 *to grow* ◇ *Mes cheveux poussent vite.* My hair grows quickly.
pousser un cri to give a cry
se pousser to move over
◇ *Pousse-toi, je ne vois rien.* Move over, I can't see a thing.

la **poussette** NOUN
pushchair

la **poussière** NOUN
1 *dust* ◇ *La table est couverte de poussière.* The table's covered in dust.
2 *speck of dust* ◇ *J'ai une poussière dans l'œil.* I've got a speck of dust in my eye.

poussiéreux ADJECTIVE
(FEM SING **poussiéreuse**)
dusty

le **poussin** NOUN
chick

le **pouvoir** NOUN
see also pouvoir VERB
power ◇ *Le Premier ministre a beaucoup de pouvoir.* The prime minister has a lot of power.

pouvoir VERB
see also pouvoir NOUN

Present tense:	
je peux	*nous pouvons*
tu peux	*vous pouvez*
il/elle peut	*ils/elles peuvent*
Past participle: *pu*	

can ◇ *Je peux lui téléphoner si tu veux.* I can phone her if you want. ◇ *Puis-je venir vous voir samedi?* May I come and see you on Saturday? ◇ *Je ne pourrai pas venir samedi.* I can't come on Saturday. ◇ *J'ai fait tout ce que j'ai pu.* I did all I could.
Je n'en peux plus. I'm exhausted.
Il se peut que... It's possible that...
il se peut que *is followed by a verb in the subjunctive.*
◇ *Il se peut qu'elle ait déménagé.* It's possible that she's moved house. ◇ *Il se peut que j'y aille.* I might go.

la **prairie** NOUN
meadow

la **pratique** NOUN
see also pratique ADJECTIVE
practice ◇ *Je manque de pratique.* I'm out of practice.

pratique ADJECTIVE
see also pratique NOUN
practical ◇ *Ce sac est très pratique.* This bag's very practical.

pratiquement ADVERB
virtually ◇ *J'ai pratiquement fini.* I've virtually finished.

P

pratiquer VERB
to practise ◇ *Je dois pratiquer mon espagnol.* I need to practise my Spanish.
◆ **Pratiquez-vous un sport?** Do you do any sport?

le **pré** NOUN
meadow

la **précaution** NOUN
precaution ◇ *prendre ses précautions* to take precautions
◆ **par précaution** as a precaution ◇ *Il a pris une assurance par précaution.* He took out insurance as a precaution.
◆ **"à manipuler avec précaution"** "handle with care"

précédemment ADVERB
previously

précédent ADJECTIVE
previous

précieux ADJECTIVE
(FEM SING **précieuse**)
precious
◆ **une pierre précieuse** a precious stone
◆ **de précieux conseils** invaluable advice

le **précipice** NOUN
ravine ◇ *Leur voiture est tombée dans un précipice.* Their car fell into a ravine.

précipitamment ADVERB
hurriedly ◇ *Chantal est partie précipitamment.* Chantal left hurriedly.

la **précipitation** NOUN
haste ◇ *Il a agi avec précipitation.* He acted hastily.

se **précipiter** VERB
to rush

précis ADJECTIVE
precise

précisément ADVERB
precisely

préciser VERB
1 *to be more specific about*
◇ *Pouvez-vous préciser ce que vous voulez dire?* Can you be more specific about what you want to say?
2 *to specify* ◇ *Pouvez-vous préciser les raisons de ce changement?* Can you specify the reasons for this change?

la **précision** NOUN
1 *precision*
2 *detail* ◇ *Je vais vous donner quelques précisions.* I'm going to give you some details.

la **préfecture** NOUN
A préfecture *is the headquarters of a* département, *one of the 96 administrative areas of France.*
◆ **la préfecture de police** the police headquarters

préférable ADJECTIVE
preferable

préféré ADJECTIVE
favourite

la **préférence** NOUN
preference ◇ *Je n'ai pas de préférence.* I've no preference.
◆ **de préférence** preferably

préférer VERB
to prefer ◇ *Je préfère la cuisine de Teresa.* I prefer Teresa's cooking. ◇ *Je préfère manger à la cantine.* I prefer to eat in the canteen.
◆ **Je préférerais du thé.** I'd rather have tea.
◆ **préférer quelqu'un à quelqu'un** to prefer somebody to somebody ◇ *Je le préfère à son frère.* I prefer him to his brother.

préhistorique ADJECTIVE
prehistoric

le **préjugé** NOUN
prejudice ◇ *avoir des préjugés contre quelqu'un* to be prejudiced against somebody

premier ADJECTIVE
(FEM SING **première**)
see also première NOUN
first ◇ *au premier étage* on the first floor ◇ *C'est notre premier jour de vacances.* It's the first day of our holiday. ◇ *C'est la première fois que je viens ici.* It's the first time I've been here. ◇ *le premier mai* the first of May ◇ *Il est arrivé premier.* He came first.
◆ **le Premier ministre** the Prime Minister

la **première** NOUN
see also premier ADJECTIVE
1 *first class* ◇ *Nous avons voyagé en première.* We travelled first class.
2 *first gear* ◇ *Passe en première pour prendre ce virage.* Change into first to go round this bend.
3 *lower sixth form*
In French secondary schools, years are counted from the sixième *(youngest) to* première *and* terminale *(oldest).*
◇ *Ma sœur est en première.* My sister's in the lower sixth.

premièrement ADVERB
firstly

prendre VERB
to take ◇ *Prends tes affaires et viens avec moi.* Take your things and come with me.
◆ **prendre quelque chose à quelqu'un** to take something from somebody ◇ *Il m'a pris mon stylo!* He's taken my pen!
◆ **passer prendre** to pick up ◇ *Je dois passer prendre Richard.* I have to pick

up Richard.
prendre à gauche to turn left ◇ *Prenez à gauche en arrivant au rond-point.* Turn left at the roundabout.
Il se prend pour Napoléon. He thinks he's Napoleon.
s'en prendre à quelqu'un to lay into somebody (*verbally*) ◇ *Il s'en est pris à moi.* He laid into me.
s'y prendre to set about it ◇ *Tu t'y prends mal!* You're setting about it the wrong way!

rénom NOUN
first name ◇ *Quel est votre prénom?* What's your first name?

réparation NOUN
preparation

réparer VERB
1 *to prepare* ◇ *Elle prépare le dîner.* She's preparing dinner.
2 *to make* ◇ *Je vais préparer le café.* I'm going to make the coffee.
3 *to prepare for* ◇ *Laure prépare son examen d'économie.* Laure's preparing for her economics exam.
se préparer to get ready ◇ *Ils se préparent à partir.* They're getting ready to go.

réposition NOUN
preposition

rès ADVERB
tout près nearby ◇ *J'habite tout près.* I live nearby.
près de (1) near (to) ◇ *Est-ce que c'est près d'ici?* Is it near here?
près de (2) next to ◇ *Assieds-toi près de moi.* Sit down next to me.
près de (3) nearly ◇ *Il y avait près de cinq cents spectateurs.* There were nearly 500 spectators.
de près closely ◇ *Il a regardé la photo de près.* He looked closely at the photo.
à peu de chose près more or less

résence NOUN
1 *presence* ◇ *Sa présence est rassurante.* His presence is reassuring.
2 *attendance* ◇ *La présence aux cours est obligatoire.* Attendance at lessons is compulsory.

résent ADJECTIVE
see also présent NOUN
present

résent NOUN
see also présent ADJECTIVE
present tense
à présent now

résentation NOUN
presentation
faire les présentations to do the introductions

présenter VERB
to present ◇ *Il présentait le spectacle.* He presented the show.
présenter quelqu'un à quelqu'un to introduce somebody to somebody ◇ *Il m'a présenté à sa sœur.* He introduced me to his sister.
Marc, je te présente Anaïs. Marc, this is Anaïs.
se présenter (1) to introduce oneself ◇ *Elle s'est présentée à ses collègues.* She introduced herself to her colleagues.
se présenter (2) to arise ◇ *Si l'occasion se présente, nous irons en Écosse.* If the chance arises, we'll go to Scotland.
se présenter (3) to stand ◇ *Monsieur Legros se présente encore aux élections.* Mr Legros is standing for election again.

le **préservatif** NOUN
condom

préserver VERB
to protect
préserver de to protect from ◇ *Nous avons ramassé les chaises du jardin pour les préserver de l'humidité.* We brought the garden chairs in to protect them from the damp.

le **président** NOUN
1 *president* ◇ *le président des États-Unis* the president of the United States
2 *chairman* ◇ *le président du conseil d'administration* the chairman of the board of directors
le président directeur général the chairman and managing director

présider VERB
1 *to chair* ◇ *Duncan a présidé la réunion.* Duncan chaired the meeting.
2 *to be the guest of honour* ◇ *Il présidait à table.* He was the guest of honour at the table.

presque ADVERB
nearly ◇ *Il est presque six heures.* It's nearly 6 o'clock. ◇ *Nous sommes presque arrivés.* We're nearly there.
presque rien hardly anything ◇ *Elle n'a presque rien mangé.* She's hardly eaten anything.
presque pas hardly at all ◇ *Il ne dort presque pas.* He hardly sleeps at all.
presque pas de hardly any ◇ *Il n'y a presque pas de place.* There's hardly any space.

la **presqu'île** NOUN
peninsula

la **presse** NOUN
press ◇ *les représentants de la presse* representatives of the press

pressé ADJECTIVE
1 *in a hurry* ◇ *Je ne peux pas rester, je suis pressé.* I can't stay, I'm in a hurry.
2 *urgent* ◇ *Ce n'est pas très pressé.* It's not very urgent.
- **une orange pressée** a fresh orange juice

presser VERB
1 *to squeeze* ◇ *Tu peux me presser un citron?* Can you squeeze me a lemon?
2 *to be urgent* ◇ *Est-ce que ça presse?* Is it urgent?
- **se presser** to hurry up ◇ *Allez, presse-toi, on va être en retard!* Come on, hurry up, we're going to be late!
- **Rien ne presse.** There's no hurry.

le **pressing** NOUN
dry-cleaner's

la **pression** NOUN
1 *pressure*
- **faire pression sur quelqu'un** to put pressure on somebody

2 *draught beer* (*informal*)

prêt ADJECTIVE
see also prêt NOUN
ready ◇ *Le déjeuner est prêt.* Lunch is ready. ◇ *Tu es prête?* Are you ready?

le **prêt** NOUN
see also prêt ADJECTIVE
loan

le **prêt-à-porter** NOUN
ready-to-wear clothes

prétendre VERB
- **prétendre que** to claim that ◇ *Il prétend qu'il ne la connaît pas.* He claims he doesn't know her.

prétendu ADJECTIVE
so-called ◇ *un prétendu expert* a so-called expert

prétentieux ADJECTIVE
(FEM SING **prétentieuse**)
pretentious

prêter VERB
- **prêter quelque chose à quelqu'un** to lend something to someone ◇ *Il m'a prêté sa voiture.* He lent me his car.
- **prêter attention à quelque chose** to pay attention to something

le **prétexte** NOUN
excuse ◇ *Il avait un prétexte pour ne pas venir.* He had an excuse for not coming.
- **sous aucun prétexte** on no account ◇ *Ne le dérangez sous aucun prétexte.* On no account must you disturb him.

prétexter VERB
to give as an excuse ◇ *Elle a prétexté une réunion.* She gave a meeting as her excuse. ◇ *Il a prétexté qu'il avait un rendez-vous.* He gave the excuse that he had an appointment.

le **prêtre** NOUN
priest

la **preuve** NOUN
1 *evidence* ◇ *Il y a des preuves contre lui.* There's evidence against him.
2 *proof* ◇ *Vous n'avez aucune preuve.* You haven't got any proof.
- **faire preuve de courage** to show courage
- **faire ses preuves** to prove oneself ◇ *Pour être embauché ici, il faut faire ses preuves.* To be employed here, you need to prove yourself.

prévenir VERB
- **prévenir quelqu'un** to warn somebody ◇ *Je te préviens, il est de mauvaise humeur.* I'm warning you, he's in a bad mood.

la **prévention** NOUN
prevention
- **des mesures de prévention** preventative measures
- **la prévention routière** road safety

la **prévision** NOUN
- **les prévisions météorologiques** the weather forecast
- **en prévision de quelque chose** in anticipation of something

prévoir VERB
1 *to plan* ◇ *Nous prévoyons un pique-nique pour dimanche.* We're planning to have a picnic on Sunday.
- **Le départ est prévu pour dix heures.** The departure's scheduled for 10 o'clock.

2 *to allow* ◇ *J'ai prévu assez à manger pour quatre.* I allowed enough food for four.
3 *to foresee* ◇ *J'avais prévu qu'il serait en retard.* I'd foreseen that he'd be late.
- **Je prévois qu'il me faudra une heure de plus.** I reckon on it taking me another hour.

prier VERB
to pray to ◇ *Les Grecs priaient Dionysos.* The Greeks prayed to Dionysos.
- **prier quelqu'un de faire quelque chose** to ask somebody to do something ◇ *Elle l'a prié de sortir.* She asked him to leave.

- **je vous en prie (1)** please do ◇ *Je peux m'asseoir?–Je vous en prie.* May I sit down?–Please do.
- **je vous en prie (2)** please ◇ *Je vous en prie, ne me laissez pas seule.* Please, don't leave me alone.
- **je vous en prie (3)** don't mention it ◇ *Merci pour votre aide.–Je vous en prie.* Thanks for your help.–Don't mention it.

prière NOUN
prayer ◇ *faire ses prières* to say one's prayers
- **"prière de ne pas fumer"** "no smoking please"

primaire NOUN
primary education ◇ *Ses enfants sont encore en primaire.* His children are still in primary education.
- **l'école primaire** primary school

prime NOUN
1 *bonus* ◇ *Il a eu une prime en récompense de son travail.* He received a bonus for his work.
2 *free gift* ◇ *J'ai eu ce stylo en prime avec l'agenda.* I got this pen as a free gift with the diary.
3 *premium* ◇ *une prime d'assurance* an insurance premium

primevère NOUN
primrose

prince NOUN
prince ◇ *le prince Charles* Prince Charles

princesse NOUN
princess ◇ *la princesse Diana* Princess Diana

principal ADJECTIVE
(MASC PL **principaux**)
see also principal NOUN
main ◇ *le rôle principal* the main role

principal NOUN
(PL les **principaux**)
see also principal ADJECTIVE
1 *headmaster* ◇ *le principal du collège* the headmaster of the school
2 *main thing* ◇ *Personne n'a été blessé; c'est le principal.* Nobody was injured; that's the main thing.

principe NOUN
principle
- **pour le principe** on principle
- **en principe (1)** as a rule ◇ *Il déjeune en principe à midi et demi.* As a rule he has lunch at 12.30.
- **en principe (2)** in theory ◇ *En principe Anne doit arriver lundi.* In theory, Anne should arrive on Monday.

printemps NOUN
spring
- **au printemps** in spring

la **priorité** NOUN
1 *priority* ◇ *C'est à faire en priorité.* It needs to be done as a priority.
2 *right of way* ◇ *Tu n'as pas la priorité.* You haven't got right of way.

pris VERB *see* **prendre**

pris ADJECTIVE
1 *taken* ◇ *Est-ce que cette place est prise?* Is this seat taken?
2 *busy* ◇ *Je serai très pris la semaine prochaine.* I'll be very busy next week.
- **avoir le nez pris** to have a stuffy nose
- **être pris de panique** to be panic-stricken

la **prise** NOUN
1 *plug*
2 *socket*
- **une prise de courant** a power point
- **une prise multiple** an adaptor
- **une prise de sang** a blood test

la **prison** NOUN
prison ◇ *aller en prison* to go to prison ◇ *être en prison* to be in prison

prisonnier ADJECTIVE
see also prisonnier NOUN
captive

le **prisonnier** NOUN
see also prisonnier ADJECTIVE
prisoner

la **prisonnière** NOUN
prisoner

prit VERB *see* **prendre**

privé ADJECTIVE
private ◇ *la propriété privée* private property ◇ *ma vie privée* my private life
- **en privé** in private

priver VERB
- **priver quelqu'un de quelque chose** to deprive somebody of something ◇ *Le prisonnier a été privé de nourriture.* The prisoner was deprived of food.
- **Tu seras privé de dessert!** You won't get any pudding!

le **prix** NOUN
1 *price* ◇ *Je n'arrive pas à lire le prix de ce livre.* I can't see the price of this book.
2 *prize* ◇ *Cécile a eu le prix de la meilleure actrice.* Cécile got the prize for best actress.
- **hors de prix** exorbitantly priced ◇ *Les repas sont hors de prix ici!* The price of meals here is exorbitant!
- **à aucun prix** not at any price ◇ *Je n'irai là-bas à aucun prix.* I'm not going there, not at any price.
- **à tout prix** at all costs ◇ *Je veux à tout*

prix voir ce film. I want to see this film at all costs.

probable ADJECTIVE
likely ◇ *Il est probable qu'elle viendra.* It's likely she'll come.
- **C'est peu probable.** That's unlikely.

probablement ADVERB
probably

le **problème** NOUN
problem

le **procédé** NOUN
process

le **procès** NOUN
trial ◇ *Le procès du meurtrier commence mardi.* The murder trial starts on Tuesday.
- **Il est en procès avec son employeur.** He's involved in a lawsuit with his employer.

prochain ADJECTIVE
next ◇ *Nous descendons au prochain arrêt.* We're getting off at the next stop.
- **la prochaine fois** next time
- **la semaine prochaine** next week
- **À la prochaine!** See you!

prochainement ADVERB
soon

proche ADJECTIVE
1 *near* ◇ *Les magasins les plus proches étaient à trois kilomètres.* The nearest shops were 3 kilometres away. ◇ *dans un proche avenir* in the near future
2 *close* ◇ *un ami proche* a close friend
- **proche de** near to ◇ *La cathédrale est proche du château.* The cathedral is near the castle.
- **le Proche-Orient** the Middle East

les **proches** MASC NOUN
close relatives

proclamer VERB
to proclaim

procurer VERB
- **procurer quelque chose à quelqu'un** to get something for somebody ◇ *C'est lui qui m'a procuré ce travail.* He got me this job.
- **se procurer quelque chose** to get something ◇ *Je me suis procuré leur dernier catalogue.* I got their latest catalogue.

le **producteur** NOUN
producer

la **production** NOUN
production

la **productrice** NOUN
producer

produire VERB
to produce
- **se produire** to take place ◇ *Ces changements se sont produits l'an dernier.* The changes took place last year.

le **produit** NOUN
product ◇ *les produits de beauté* beauty products

le **prof** NOUN (*informal*)
teacher ◇ *Elle est prof de maths.* She' a maths teacher.

le **professeur** NOUN
1 *teacher* ◇ *Philippe est professeur d'histoire.* Philippe's a history teacher.
2 *professor* ◇ *le professeur Dupont* Professor Dupont
- **un professeur de faculté** a university lecturer

la **profession** NOUN
profession ◇ *Quelle est votre profession?* What's your profession?
- **"sans profession"** "unemployed"

professionnel ADJECTIVE
(FEM SING **professionnelle**)
professional

le **profil** NOUN
1 *profile* (*of person*) ◇ *de profil* in profile
2 *contours* (*of object*)

le **profit** NOUN
profit ◇ *La société a fait des profits importants.* The company made significant profits.
- **tirer profit de quelque chose** to profit from something
- **au profit de** in aid of ◇ *un spectacle au profit de l'UNICEF* a show in aid of UNICEF

profiter VERB
- **profiter de quelque chose** to take advantage of something ◇ *Profitez du beau temps pour aller faire du vélo.* Take advantage of the good weather and go cycling.
- **Profitez-en bien!** Make the most of it!

profond ADJECTIVE
deep

la **profondeur** NOUN
depth

le **programme** NOUN
1 *programme* ◇ *le programme du festival* the festival programme
2 *syllabus* ◇ *le programme de maths* the maths syllabus
3 *program* ◇ *un programme informatique* a computer program

programmer VERB
1 *to show* ◇ *Ce film est programmé dimanche soir.* The film is scheduled for Sunday evening.

2 *to program* ◇ *Mon ordinateur n'est pas programmé pour ça.* My computer isn't programmed to do that.

progrès NOUN
progress ◇ *faire des progrès* to make progress

progresser VERB
to progress

progressif ADJECTIVE
(FEM SING **progressive**)
progressive

projecteur NOUN
1 *projector* ◇ *Le projecteur de diapositives est en panne.* The slide projector is broken.
2 *spotlight* ◇ *Elle était sous les projecteurs.* She was under the spotlight.

projet NOUN
1 *plan* ◇ *des projets de vacances* holiday plans
2 *draft* ◇ *le projet de construction d'un musée* the draft for the construction of a museum
- **un projet de loi** a bill (*in parliament*)

projeter VERB
1 *to plan* ◇ *Ils projettent d'acheter une maison.* They're planning to buy a house.
2 *to cast* ◇ *une ombre projetée sur le mur* a shadow cast onto the wall
- **Elle a été projetée hors de la voiture.** She was thrown out of the car.

prolonger VERB
1 *to prolong* ◇ *Je vais prolonger mes vacances en Espagne.* I'm going to prolong my holidays in Spain.
2 *to extend* ◇ *Je vais prolonger mon abonnement.* I'm going to extend my subscription.
- **se prolonger** to go on ◇ *La réunion s'est prolongée tard.* The meeting went on late.

promenade NOUN
walk ◇ *Il y a de belles promenades par ici.* There are some nice walks round here.
- **faire une promenade** to go for a walk
- **faire une promenade en voiture** to go for a drive
- **faire une promenade à vélo** to go for a bike ride

promener VERB
to take for a walk ◇ *Cordelia promène son chien tous les jours.* Cordelia takes her dog for a walk every day.
- **se promener** to go for a walk ◇ *Chantal est partie se promener.* Chantal has gone for a walk.

la **promesse** NOUN
promise ◇ *faire une promesse* to make a promise ◇ *tenir sa promesse* to keep one's promise

promettre VERB
to promise ◇ *On m'a promis une augmentation.* They promised me a pay rise. ◇ *Elle m'a promis de me téléphoner.* She promised to phone me.

la **promotion** NOUN
promotion ◇ *Il espère avoir bientôt une promotion.* He's hoping to get promotion soon.
- **être en promotion** to be on special offer ◇ *Les côtes de porc sont en promotion.* Pork chops are on special offer.

le **pronom** NOUN
pronoun

prononcer VERB
1 *to pronounce* ◇ *Le russe est difficile à prononcer.* Russian is difficult to pronounce.
2 *to deliver* ◇ *prononcer un discours* to deliver a speech
- **se prononcer** to be pronounced ◇ *Le "e" final ne se prononce pas.* The final "e" isn't pronounced.

la **prononciation** NOUN
pronunciation

la **propagande** NOUN
propaganda

se **propager** VERB
to spread ◇ *Le feu s'est propagé rapidement.* The fire spread quickly.

la **proportion** NOUN
proportion

le **propos** NOUN
- **à propos** by the way ◇ *À propos, quand est-ce que tu viens?* By the way, when are you coming?
- **à propos de quelque chose** about something ◇ *C'est à propos de la soirée de vendredi.* It's about the party on Friday.

proposer VERB
- **proposer quelque chose à quelqu'un (1)** to suggest something to somebody ◇ *Nous lui avons proposé une promenade en bateau.* We suggested going on a boat ride to him.
- **proposer quelque chose à quelqu'un (2)** to offer somebody something ◇ *Ils m'ont proposé des chocolats.* They offered me some chocolates.

la **proposition** NOUN
offer ◇ *J'accepte ta proposition avec plaisir.* I'll be pleased to accept your offer.

propre ADJECTIVE
see also propre NOUN
1 *clean* ◇ *Ce mouchoir n'est pas propre.* This handkerchief isn't clean.
2 *own* ◇ *Gordon l'a fabriqué de ses propres mains.* Gordon made it with his own hands.
◆ **propre à** characteristic of ◇ *C'est une coutume propre au Berry.* It's a custom you find in the Berry region.

le **propre** NOUN
see also propre ADJECTIVE
◆ **recopier quelque chose au propre** to make a fair copy of something

proprement ADVERB
properly ◇ *Mange proprement!* Eat properly!
◆ **le village proprement dit** the village itself
◆ **à proprement parler** strictly speaking

la **propreté** NOUN
cleanliness

le **propriétaire** NOUN
see also la propriétaire
1 *owner*
2 *landlord*

la **propriétaire** NOUN
see also le propriétaire
1 *owner*
2 *landlady*

la **propriété** NOUN
property ◇ *la propriété privée* private property

le **prospectus** NOUN
leaflet

prospère ADJECTIVE
prosperous

la **prostituée** NOUN
prostitute

protecteur ADJECTIVE
(FEM SING **protectrice**)
1 *protective* ◇ *un vernis protecteur* a protective varnish
2 *patronizing* ◇ *un ton protecteur* a patronizing tone

la **protection** NOUN
protection

protéger VERB
to protect

la **protéine** NOUN
protein

protestant ADJECTIVE
(FEM SING **protestante**)
Protestant ◇ *une église protestante* a Protestant church
◆ **Il est protestant.** He's a Protestant.

la **protestation** NOUN
protest

protester VERB
to protest ◇ *Ils protestent contre leurs conditions de travail.* They're protesting about their working conditions.

prouver VERB
to prove

la **provenance** NOUN
origin
◆ **un avion en provenance de Berlin** a plane arriving from Berlin

provenir VERB
◆ **provenir de (1)** to come from ◇ *Ces tomates proviennent d'Espagne.* These tomatoes come from Spain.
◆ **provenir de (2)** to be the result of ◇ *Cela provient d'un manque d'organisation.* This is the result of a lack of organization.

le **proverbe** NOUN
proverb

la **province** NOUN
province
◆ **en province** in the provinces ◇ *Ils habitent en province.* They live in the provinces.

le **proviseur** NOUN
headteacher (*of state secondary school*)
◇ *Elle est proviseur.* She's a headteacher.

la **provision** NOUN
supply ◇ *une provision de pommes de terre* a supply of potatoes

les **provisions** FEM NOUN
food ◇ *Nous n'avons plus beaucoup de provisions.* We haven't got much food left.

provisoire ADJECTIVE
temporary ◇ *un emploi provisoire* a temporary job

provoquer VERB
1 *to provoke* ◇ *Il l'a provoquée en la traitant d'imbécile.* He provoked her by calling her stupid.
2 *to cause* ◇ *Cet accident a provoqué la mort de quarante personnes.* The accident caused the death of 40 people.

la **proximité** NOUN
proximity
◆ **à proximité** nearby ◇ *Sabine habite à proximité.* Sabine lives nearby.

prudemment ADVERB
1 *carefully* ◇ *Conduisez prudemment.* Drive carefully.
2 *wisely* ◇ *Prudemment, il a fait des économies.* Wisely, he saved some money.

la **prudence** NOUN
caution
◆ **avec prudence** carefully ◇ *Ils ont conduit avec prudence.* They drove

carefully.

prudent ADJECTIVE
1 *careful* ◇ *Soyez prudents!* Be careful!
2 *wise* ◇ *Laisse ton passeport à la maison, c'est plus prudent.* It would be wiser to leave your passport at home.

prune NOUN
plum

pruneau NOUN
(PL les **pruneaux**)
prune

psychiatre NOUN
psychiatrist

psychologie NOUN
psychology

psychologique ADJECTIVE
psychological

psychologue NOUN
psychologist

PTT FEM NOUN (= *Postes et Télécommunications*)
Post Office

pu VERB *see* **pouvoir**
◆ **Je n'ai pas pu venir.** I couldn't come.

pub NOUN (*informal*)
1 *advertising* ◇ *Il y a trop de pub à la télé.* There's too much advertising on TV.
2 *adverts* ◇ *Le film a été coupé par la pub.* The film was interrupted by adverts.

public ADJECTIVE
(FEM SING **publique**)
see also public NOUN
public ◇ *un jardin public* a public park
◆ **une école publique** a state school

public NOUN
see also public ADJECTIVE
1 *public* ◇ *Ce parc est ouvert au public.* The park's open to the public.
2 *audience* ◇ *Le public a applaudi le chanteur.* The audience applauded the singer.
◆ **en public** in public ◇ *Je déteste parler en public.* I hate speaking in public.

publicitaire ADJECTIVE
◆ **une agence publicitaire** an advertising agency
◆ **un film publicitaire** a publicity film

publicité NOUN
1 *advertising* ◇ *Muriel travaille dans la publicité.* Muriel works in advertising.
2 *advert* ◇ *Il y a trop de publicités dans ce journal.* There are too many adverts in this newspaper.

publier VERB
to publish ◇ *Bob vient de publier son nouveau roman.* Bob has just published his new novel.

publique ADJECTIVE *see* **public**

la **puce** NOUN
1 *flea* ◇ *Ce chien a des puces.* This dog has fleas.
2 *chip* ◇ *une puce électronique* a microchip
◆ **une carte à puce** a smart card

les **puces** FEM NOUN
flea market

puer VERB
to stink ◇ *Ça pue le tabac ici!* It stinks of tobacco round here!

puéril ADJECTIVE
childish

puis VERB
see also puis ADVERB *see* **pouvoir**
◆ **Puis-je venir vous voir samedi?** May I come and see you on Saturday?

puis ADVERB
see also puis VERB
then ◇ *Faites dorer le poulet, puis ajoutez le vin blanc.* Fry the chicken till golden, then add white wine.

puisque CONJUNCTION
since ◇ *Puisque c'est si cher, nous irons manger ailleurs.* Since it's so expensive, we'll eat elsewhere.

la **puissance** NOUN
power

puissant ADJECTIVE
powerful

le **puits** NOUN
well ◇ *Il a un puits dans son jardin.* He's got a well in his garden.

le **pull** NOUN
jumper

le **pull-over** NOUN
jumper

le **pulvérisateur** NOUN
spray ◇ *un pulvérisateur de parfum* a perfume spray

pulvériser VERB
1 *to pulverize* ◇ *L'explosion a pulvérisé le bâtiment.* The explosion pulverized the building.
2 *to spray* ◇ *Il a pulvérisé de l'insecticide sur ses plantes.* He sprayed insecticide on his plants.

la **punaise** NOUN
drawing pin

punir VERB
to punish ◇ *Il a été puni pour avoir menti.* He was punished for lying.

la **punition** NOUN
punishment

le **pupitre** NOUN
desk (*for pupil*)

pur ADJECTIVE

PTO

1 *pure* ◇ *L'eau de cette source est très pure.* The water from this spring is very pure.

2 *neat* (*undiluted*) ◇ *du whisky pur* neat whisky ◇ *de l'eau de Javel pure* concentrated bleach

◆ **c'est de la folie pure** it's sheer madness

la **purée** NOUN
mashed potatoes

◆ **la purée de marrons** chestnut purée

la **putain** NOUN (*rude*)
whore

le **puzzle** NOUN
jigsaw puzzle

le **p.-v.** NOUN (= *procès-verbal*)
parking ticket

le **pyjama** NOUN
pyjamas PL

la **pyramide** NOUN
pyramid

les **Pyrénées** FEM NOUN
Pyrenees

◆ **dans les Pyrénées** in the Pyrenees

Q

le **QI** NOUN (= *quotient intellectuel*)
IQ

le **quai** NOUN
1 *quay* ◇ *être à quai* to be alongside the quay
2 *platform* ◇ *Le train partira du quai numéro quatre.* The train will leave from platform 4.

qualifier VERB
- **se qualifier** to qualify ◇ *Bob s'est qualifié pour la demi-finale.* Bob has qualified for the semifinal.

la **qualité** NOUN
quality ◇ *Ces outils sont de très bonne qualité.* These are very good quality tools.

quand CONJUNCTION, ADVERB
when ◇ *Quand est-ce que tu pars en vacances?* When are you going on holiday? ◇ *Quand je serai riche, j'achèterai une belle maison.* When I'm rich, I'll buy a nice house.
- **quand même** all the same ◇ *Je ne voulais pas de dessert, mais j'en ai mangé quand même.* I didn't want any dessert, but I had some all the same.

quant à PREPOSITION
regarding ◇ *Quant au problème de chauffage...* Regarding the problem with the heating... ◇ *Quant à moi, je n'arriverai qu'à dix heures.* As for me, I won't be arriving till 10 o'clock.

la **quantité** NOUN
amount
- **des quantités de** a great deal of ◇ *Ils ont invité des quantités de gens.* They invited a lot of people.

la **quarantaine** NOUN
about forty ◇ *une quarantaine de personnes* about forty people
- **Elle a la quarantaine.** She's in her forties.

quarante NUMBER
forty ◇ *Elle a quarante ans.* She's forty.
- **quarante et un** forty-one
- **quarante-deux** forty-two

le **quart** NOUN
quarter
- **le quart de** a quarter of ◇ *Elle a mangé le quart du gâteau.* She ate a quarter of the cake.
- **trois quarts** three quarters
- **un quart d'heure** a quarter of an hour
- **deux heures et quart** a quarter past two
- **dix heures moins le quart** a quarter to ten
- **Un quart d'eau minérale, s'il vous plaît.** A small bottle of mineral water, please.

le **quartier** NOUN
1 *area* (*of town*) ◇ *un quartier tranquille* a quiet area
- **un cinéma de quartier** a local cinema
2 *piece* ◇ *un quartier d'orange* a piece of orange

le **quartz** NOUN
- **une montre à quartz** a quartz watch

quasi ADVERB
nearly ◇ *La quasi-totalité des récoltes a été détruite.* Nearly all of the crop was destroyed.

quasiment ADVERB
nearly ◇ *Le film est quasiment fini.* The film's nearly finished.
- **quasiment jamais** hardly ever ◇ *Ils ne vont quasiment jamais en boîte.* They hardly ever go clubbing.

quatorze NUMBER
fourteen ◇ *Mon frère a quatorze ans.* My brother's fourteen. ◇ *à quatorze heures* at 2 p.m.
- **le quatorze février** the fourteenth of February

quatre NUMBER
four ◇ *Il est quatre heures du matin.* It's four in the morning. ◇ *Il a quatre ans.* He's four.
- **le quatre février** the fourth of February
- **faire les quatre cents coups** to be a bit wild ◇ *Todd a fait les quatre cents coups dans sa jeunesse.* Todd was a bit wild in his youth.

quatre-vingts NUMBER
eighty

quatre-vingts *is spelt with an* **-s** *when it is followed by a noun, but not when it is followed by another number.*

◇ *quatre-vingts francs* eighty francs
◇ *Elle a quatre-vingt-deux ans.* She's eighty-two.
- **quatre-vingt-dix** ninety
- **quatre-vingt-onze** ninety-one
- **quatre-vingt-quinze** ninety-five
- **quatre-vingt-dix-huit** ninety-eight

quatrième ADJECTIVE
fourth ◇ *au quatrième étage* on the fourth floor

la **quatrième** NOUN
third year

In French secondary schools, years are counted from the sixième *(youngest) to* première *and* terminale *(oldest).*

◇ *Mon frère est en quatrième.* My

PTO

brother's in third year.

que CONJUNCTION, PRONOUN, ADVERB

1 *that* ◇ *Il sait que tu es là.* He knows that you're here. ◇ *la dame que j'ai rencontrée hier* the lady that I met yesterday ◇ *Le gâteau qu'elle a fait est délicieux.* The cake she's made is delicious.

- **Je veux que tu viennes.** I want you to come.

2 *what* ◇ *Que fais-tu?* What are you doing? ◇ *Que vas-tu lui dire?* What are you going to tell him?

- **Qu'est-ce que...?** What...? ◇ *Qu'est-ce que tu fais?* What are you doing? ◇ *Qu'est-ce que c'est?* What's that?
- **plus...que** more...than ◇ *C'est plus difficile que je ne le pensais.* It's more difficult than I thought. ◇ *Il est plus grand que moi.* He's bigger than me.
- **aussi...que** as...as ◇ *Elle est aussi jolie que sa sœur.* She's as pretty as her sister. ◇ *Le train est aussi cher que l'avion.* The train is as expensive as the plane.
- **ne...que** only ◇ *Il ne boit que de l'eau.* He only drinks water. ◇ *Je ne l'ai vu qu'une fois.* I've only seen him once.
- **Qu'il est bête!** He's so silly!

quel ADJECTIVE

(FEM SING **quelle**)

1 *who* ◇ *Quel est ton chanteur préféré?* Who's your favourite singer?

2 *what* ◇ *Quelle est ta couleur préférée?* What's your favourite colour? ◇ *Quelle heure est-il?* What time is it? ◇ *Quelle bonne surprise!* What a surprise!

3 *which* ◇ *Quel groupe préfères-tu?* Which band do you like best?

- **quel que soit (1)** whoever ◇ *quel que soit le coupable* whoever is guilty
- **quel que soit (2)** whatever ◇ *quel que soit votre avis* whatever your opinion

quelle ADJECTIVE *see* **quel**

quelque ADJECTIVE, ADVERB

1 *some* ◇ *Il a quelques amis à Paris.* He has some friends in Paris. ◇ *J'ai acheté quelques disques.* I bought some records.

2 *a few* ◇ *Il reste quelques bouteilles.* There are a few bottles left.

3 *few* ◇ *Ils ont fini les quelques bouteilles qui restaient.* They finished the few bottles that were left.

- **quelque chose (1)** something ◇ *J'ai quelque chose pour toi.* I've got something for you. ◇ *Je voudrais quelque chose de moins cher.* I'd like something cheaper.
- **quelque chose (2)** anything ◇ *Avez-vous quelque chose à déclarer?* Have you got anything to declare? ◇ *Tu as pensé à quelque chose d'autre?* Did you think of anything else?
- **quelque part (1)** somewhere ◇ *J'ai oublié mon sac quelque part.* I've left my bag somewhere.
- **quelque part (2)** anywhere ◇ *Vous allez quelque part ce week-end?* Are you going anywhere this weekend?

quelquefois ADVERB

sometimes

quelques-uns PRONOUN

(FEM **quelques-unes**)

some ◇ *As-tu vu ses films? J'en ai vu quelques-uns.* Have you seen his films? I've seen some of them.

quelqu'un PRONOUN

1 *somebody* ◇ *Quelqu'un t'a appelé.* Somebody phoned you. ◇ *Il y a quelqu'un à la porte.* There's somebody at the door.

2 *anybody* ◇ *Est-ce que quelqu'un a vu mon parapluie?* Has anybody seen my umbrella? ◇ *Il y a quelqu'un?* Is there anybody there?

la **querelle** NOUN

quarrel

qu'est-ce que *see* **que**

qu'est-ce qui *see* **qui**

la **question** NOUN

1 *question* ◇ *Je t'ai posé une question.* I asked you a question.

2 *matter* ◇ *Ils se sont disputés pour des questions d'argent.* They argued over money matters.

- **Il n'en est pas question.** There's no question of it. ◇ *Il n'est pas question que je paye.* There's no question of me paying.
- **De quoi est-il question?** What's it about?
- **Il est question de l'organisation du concert.** It's about the organization of the concert.
- **hors de question** out of the question ◇ *Il est hors de question que nous restions ici.* It's out of the question that we stay here.

le **questionnaire** NOUN

questionnaire

questionner VERB

to question

la **queue** NOUN

1 *tail* ◇ *Le chien a agité la queue.* The dog wagged its tail.

- **faire la queue** to queue
- **une queue de cheval** a ponytail

2 *rear* ◇ *en queue du train* at the rear of the train

3 *bottom* ◇ *en queue de liste* at the bottom of the list

4 *stalk* (*of fruit, leaf*) ◇ *la queue d'une cerise* a cherry stalk

qui PRONOUN

1 *who* ◇ *Qui a téléphoné?* Who phoned? ◇ *Le peintre qui a peint ce tableau est un génie.* The artist who painted this picture is a genius.

2 *whom* ◇ *C'est la personne à qui j'ai parlé hier.* It's the person whom I spoke to yesterday.

3 *that* ◇ *Donne-moi la veste qui est sur la chaise.* Give me the jacket that's on the chair.

- **Qui est-ce qui...?** Who...? ◇ *Qui est-ce qui t'emmène au spectacle?* Who's taking you to the show?
- **Qui est-ce que...?** Who...? ◇ *Qui est-ce que tu as vu à cette soirée?* Who did you see at the party?
- **Qu'est-ce qui...?** What...? ◇ *Qu'est-ce qui est sur la table?* What's on the table? ◇ *Qu'est-ce qui te prend?* What's the matter with you?
- **À qui est ce sac?** Whose bag is this?
- **À qui parlais-tu?** Who were you talking to?

quille NOUN

- **un jeu de quilles** skittles

quincaillerie NOUN

ironmonger's (shop)

quinzaine NOUN

about fifteen ◇ *Il y avait une quinzaine de personnes.* There were about fifteen people there.

- **une quinzaine de jours** a fortnight

quinze NUMBER

fifteen ◇ *Anaïs a quinze ans.* Anaïs is fifteen. ◇ *à quinze heures* at 3 p.m.

- **le quinze février** the fifteenth of February
- **dans quinze jours** in a fortnight's time

quitter VERB

to leave ◇ *J'ai quitté la maison à huit heures.* I left the house at 8 o'clock.

- **se quitter** to part ◇ *Les deux amis se sont quittés devant le café.* The two friends parted in front of the café.
- **Ne quittez pas.** (*on telephone*) Hold the line. ◇ *Ne quittez pas, je vous passe Monsieur Divan.* Hold the line, I'll put you through to Monsieur Divan.

quoi PRONOUN

what? ◇ *À quoi penses-tu?* What are you thinking about? ◇ *C'est quoi, ce truc?* What's this thing?

- **Quoi de neuf?** What's new?
- **As-tu de quoi écrire?** Have you got anything to write with?
- **Je n'ai pas de quoi acheter une voiture.** I can't afford to buy a car.
- **Quoi qu'il arrive.** Whatever happens.
- **Il n'y a pas de quoi.** Don't mention it.
- **Il n'y a pas de quoi s'énerver.** There's no reason for getting worked up.
- **En quoi puis-je vous aider?** How may I help you?

quoique CONJUNCTION

even though ◇ *Il va l'acheter quoique ce soit cher.* He's going to buy it even though it's expensive.

quotidien ADJECTIVE

(FEM SING **quotidienne**)

see also quotidien NOUN

daily ◇ *Il est parti faire sa promenade quotidienne.* He's gone for his daily walk.

le **quotidien** NOUN

see also quotidien ADJECTIVE

daily paper ◇ *Le Monde est un quotidien.* Le Monde is a daily paper.

R

le **rab** NOUN (*informal*)
seconds (*of meal*) ◇ *Il y a du rab?* Are there any seconds?

le **rabais** NOUN
reduction (*in price*)
◆ **au rabais** at a discount

raccompagner VERB
to take home ◇ *Tu peux me raccompagner?* Can you take me home?

le **raccourci** NOUN
shortcut

raccrocher VERB
to hang up (*telephone*)

la **race** NOUN
1 *race* ◇ *la race humaine* the human race
2 *breed* ◇ *De quelle race est ton chat?* What breed is your cat?
◆ **de race** pedigree ◇ *un chien de race* a pedigree dog

racheter VERB
1 *to buy another* ◇ *J'ai racheté un portefeuille.* I've bought another wallet. ◇ *racheter du lait* to buy more milk
2 *to buy* ◇ *Il m'a racheté ma moto.* He bought my bike from me.

la **racine** NOUN
root

raciste ADJECTIVE
racist

raconter VERB
◆ **raconter quelque chose à quelqu'un** to tell somebody about something ◇ *Raconte-moi ce qui s'est passé.* Tell me what happened. ◇ *Raconte-moi une histoire.* Tell me a story.
◆ **Qu'est-ce que tu racontes?** What are you talking about?

le **radar** NOUN
radar

le **radiateur** NOUN
radiator
◆ **un radiateur électrique** an electric heater

radin ADJECTIVE (*informal*)
stingy

la **radio** NOUN
1 *radio* ◇ *à la radio* on the radio
2 *X-ray*
◆ **passer une radio** to have an X-ray ◇ *Elle a passé une radio des poumons.* She had a chest X-ray.

le **radio-réveil** NOUN
(PL les **radios-réveils**)
clock radio

le **radis** NOUN
radish

raffoler VERB
◆ **raffoler de** to be crazy about ◇ *Elle raffole de la tarte aux pommes.* She really loves apple tart.

rafraîchir VERB
to cool down
◆ **se rafraîchir (1)** to get cooler ◇ *Le temps se rafraîchit.* The weather's getting cooler.
◆ **se rafraîchir (2)** to freshen up ◇ *Il a pris une douche pour se rafraîchir.* He had a shower to freshen up.

rafraîchissant ADJECTIVE
refreshing

la **rage** NOUN
rabies
◆ **une rage de dents** raging toothache

le **ragoût** NOUN
stew

raide ADJECTIVE
1 *steep* ◇ *Cette pente est raide.* This is a steep slope.
2 *straight* ◇ *Laure a les cheveux raides.* Laure has straight hair.
3 *stiff* ◇ *Son bras est encore raide.* His arm's still stiff.
4 *flat broke* ◇ *Je suis raide ce mois-ci.* (*informal*) I'm flat broke this month.

la **raie** NOUN
1 *skate* (*fish*)
2 *parting* (*in hair*)

le **rail** NOUN
rail ◇ *par rail* by rail

le **raisin** NOUN
grapes ◇ *le raisin blanc* green grapes
◆ **des raisins secs** raisins

la **raison** NOUN
reason ◇ *sans raison* for no reason ◇ *Raison de plus pour y aller.* All the more reason for going.
◆ **Ce n'est pas une raison.** That's no excuse.
◆ **avoir raison** to be right ◇ *Tu as raison.* You're right.
◆ **en raison de** because of ◇ *en raison d'une grève* because of a strike

raisonnable ADJECTIVE
sensible ◇ *Elle est très raisonnable pour son âge.* She's very sensible for her age.

le **raisonnement** NOUN
reasoning ◇ *J'ai du mal à suivre son raisonnement.* I have difficulty

following his reasoning.

rajouter VERB
to add

ralentir VERB
to slow down

râler VERB (*informal*)
to moan

le **ramassage** NOUN
- **le ramassage scolaire** the school bus service

ramasser VERB
1 *to pick up* ◇ *Il a ramassé son crayon.* He picked up his pencil.
2 *to take in* ◇ *Il a ramassé les copies.* He took in the exam papers.

la **rame** NOUN
1 *oar* (*of boat*)
2 *train* (*on the underground*)

le **rameau** NOUN
(PL les **rameaux**)
branch
- **le dimanche des Rameaux** Palm Sunday

ramener VERB
1 *to bring back* ◇ *Je t'ai ramené un souvenir de Grèce.* I've brought you back a present from Greece.
2 *to take home* ◇ *Tu me ramènes?* Will you take me home?

ramer VERB
to row ◇ *C'est Jean-Pierre qui ramait.* Jean-Pierre was rowing.

la **rampe** NOUN
banister

la **rancune** NOUN
- **garder rancune à quelqu'un** to bear somebody a grudge
- **Sans rancune!** No hard feelings!

rancunier ADJECTIVE
(FEM SING **rancunière**)
vindictive

la **randonnée** NOUN
- **une randonnée à vélo** a bike ride
- **une randonnée pédestre** a ramble

le **rang** NOUN
row (*line*) ◇ *au premier rang* in the front row ◇ *se mettre en rangs* to get into rows

la **rangée** NOUN
row (*line*) ◇ *une rangée de chaises* a row of chairs

ranger VERB
1 *to put away* ◇ *J'ai rangé tes affaires.* I've put your things away.
2 *to tidy up* ◇ *Va ranger ta chambre.* Go and tidy up your room.

le **rap** NOUN
rap ◇ *Robert est chanteur de rap.* Robert's a rap singer.

râper VERB
to grate ◇ *le fromage râpé* grated cheese

rapide ADJECTIVE
1 *fast* ◇ *Cette voiture est très rapide.* This is a very fast car.
2 *quick* ◇ *J'ai jeté un coup d'œil rapide sur ton travail.* I had a quick glance at your work.

rapidement ADVERB
quickly

le **rappel** NOUN
1 *booster* (*vaccination*)
2 *curtain call*

rappeler VERB
to call back ◇ *Je te rappelle dans cinq minutes.* I'll call you back in 5 minutes.
- **rappeler quelque chose à quelqu'un** to remind somebody of something ◇ *Cette odeur me rappelle mon enfance.* This smell reminds me of my childhood.
- **rappeler à quelqu'un de faire quelque chose** to remind somebody to do something ◇ *Rappelle-moi d'acheter des billets.* Remind me to get tickets.
- **se rappeler** to remember ◇ *Il s'est rappelé qu'il avait une course à faire.* He remembered he had some shopping to do.

le **rapport** NOUN
see also les rapports
1 *report* ◇ *Il a écrit un rapport.* He wrote a report.
2 *connection* ◇ *Je ne vois pas le rapport.* I can't see the connection.
- **par rapport à** in comparison with

rapporter VERB
to bring back ◇ *Je leur ai rapporté un cadeau.* I brought them back a present.

le **rapporteur** NOUN
telltale

la **rapporteuse** NOUN
telltale

les **rapports** MASC NOUN
see also le rapport
relations ◇ *Leurs rapports avec leurs voisins se sont améliorés.* Their relations with their neighbours have improved.
- **les rapports sexuels** sexual intercourse

rapprocher VERB
1 *to bring together* ◇ *Cet accident a rapproché les deux frères.* The accident brought the two brothers together.
2 *to bring closer* ◇ *Il a rapproché le fauteuil de la télé.* He brought the armchair closer to the TV.
- **se rapprocher** to come closer

PTO

◇ *Rapproche-toi, tu verras mieux.* Come closer, you'll see better.

la **raquette** NOUN
1 *racket* (*tennis*)
2 *bat* (*table tennis*)

rare ADJECTIVE
rare ◇ *une plante rare* a rare plant

rarement ADVERB
rarely

ras ADJECTIVE, ADVERB
short ◇ *un chien à poil ras* a short-haired dog
◆ **à ras bords** to the brim ◇ *Il a rempli son verre à ras bords.* He filled his glass to the brim.
◆ **en avoir ras le bol de quelque chose** (*informal*) to be fed up with something
◆ **un pull ras du cou** a crew-neck jumper

raser VERB
to shave off ◇ *Ray a rasé sa barbe.* Ray has shaved off his beard.
◆ **se raser** to shave

le **rasoir** NOUN
see also rasoir ADJECTIVE
razor

rasoir ADJECTIVE (MASC, FEM, PL) (*informal*)
see also rasoir NOUN
dead boring

rassembler VERB
to assemble ◇ *Il a rassemblé les enfants dans la cour.* He assembled the children in the playground.
◆ **se rassembler** to gather together ◇ *Les passagers se sont rassemblés près du car.* The passengers gathered near the coach.

rassurer VERB
to reassure
◆ **Je suis rassuré.** I don't need to worry any more.
◆ **se rassurer** to be reassured ◇ *Rassure-toi!* Don't worry!

le **rat** NOUN
rat

raté ADJECTIVE
unsuccessful ◇ *Le gâteau est raté.* The cake's a failure.

le **râteau** NOUN
(PL les **râteaux**)
rake

rater VERB
1 *to miss* ◇ *Chantal a raté son train.* Chantal missed her train.
2 *to fail* ◇ *J'ai raté mon examen de maths.* I failed my maths exam. ◇ *Elle a raté sa quiche.* Her quiche didn't turn out right.

RATP ABBREVIATION
Paris transport authority

rattacher VERB
to tie up again ◇ *rattacher ses lacets* to tie up one's laces

rattraper VERB
1 *to recapture* ◇ *La police a rattrapé le voleur.* The police recaptured the thief.
2 *to catch up with* ◇ *Je vais rattraper Cécile.* I'll catch up with Cécile.
3 *to make up for* ◇ *Il faut rattraper le temps perdu.* We must make up for lost time.
◆ **se rattraper** to make up for it ◇ *Je n'ai pas le temps de sortir mais je me rattraperai après les examens.* I haven't got time to go out, but I'll make up for it after the exams.

la **rature** NOUN
correction ◇ *un texte sans ratures* a text with no corrections

ravi ADJECTIVE
◆ **être ravi** to be delighted ◇ *Ils étaient ravis de nous voir.* They were delighted to see us. ◇ *Je suis ravi que vous puissiez venir.* I'm delighted that you can come.

rayé ADJECTIVE
striped ◇ *une chemise rayée* a striped shirt

rayer VERB
1 *to scratch* ◇ *Il a rayé la peinture de sa voiture.* He scratched the paintwork of his car.
2 *to cross off* ◇ *Son nom a été rayé de la liste.* His name has been crossed off the list.

le **rayon** NOUN
1 *ray* ◇ *un rayon de soleil* a ray of sunshine
2 *radius* ◇ *le rayon d'un cercle* the radius of a circle
3 *shelf* ◇ *les rayons d'une bibliothèque* the shelves of a bookcase
4 *department* ◇ *le rayon hi-fi vidéo* the hi-fi and video department
◆ **les rayons X** X-rays

la **rayure** NOUN
stripe

le **ré** NOUN
1 *D* ◇ *en ré majeur* in D major
2 *re* ◇ *do, ré, mi...* do, re, mi...

la **réaction** NOUN
reaction

réagir VERB
to react

le **réalisateur** NOUN
director (*of film*) ◇ *Il est réalisateur.* He's a film director.

la **réalisatrice** NOUN

director (*of film*) ◇ *Elle est réalisatrice.* She's a film director.

réaliser VERB
1 *to carry out* ◇ *Ils ont réalisé leur projet.* They carried out their plan.
2 *to fulfil* ◇ *Il a réalisé son rêve.* He has fulfilled his dream.
3 *to realize* ◇ *Tu réalises ce que tu dis?* Do you realize what you're saying?
4 *to make* ◇ *réaliser un film* to make a film
◆ **se réaliser** to come true ◇ *Mon rêve s'est réalisé.* My dream has come true.

réaliste ADJECTIVE
realistic

la **réalité** NOUN
reality
◆ **en réalité** in fact

rebondir VERB
to bounce

le **rebord** NOUN
edge ◇ *le rebord du lavabo* the edge of the washbasin
◆ **le rebord de la fenêtre** the window ledge

recaler VERB (*informal*)
◆ **J'ai été recalé en maths.** I failed maths.

récemment ADVERB
recently

récent ADJECTIVE
recent

la **réception** NOUN
reception desk

/la **réceptionniste** NOUN
receptionist ◇ *Elle est réceptionniste.* She's a receptionist.

la **recette** NOUN
recipe

recevoir VERB
1 *to receive* ◇ *J'ai reçu une lettre.* I received a letter.
2 *to see* ◇ *Il a reçu trois clients ce matin.* He has seen three clients this morning.
3 *to have round* ◇ *Je reçois des amis à dîner.* I'm having friends for dinner.
◆ **être reçu à un examen** to pass an exam

le **rechange** NOUN
◆ **de rechange** spare (*battery, bulb*) ◇ *des vêtements de rechange* a change of clothes

la **recharge** NOUN
refill

le **réchaud** NOUN
stove

réchauffer VERB
1 *to reheat* ◇ *Je vais réchauffer les légumes.* I'll reheat the vegetables.
2 *to warm up* ◇ *Un bon café va te réchauffer.* A nice cup of coffee will warm you up.
◆ **se réchauffer** to warm oneself ◇ *Je vais me réchauffer près du feu.* I'll go and warm myself by the fire.

la **recherche** NOUN
research ◇ *Je voudrais faire de la recherche.* I'd like to do research.
◆ **être à la recherche de quelque chose** to be looking for something ◇ *Je suis à la recherche d'un emploi.* I'm looking for a job.
◆ **les recherches** search ◇ *La police a interrompu les recherches.* The police called off the search.

rechercher VERB
to look for ◇ *La police recherche l'assassin.* The police are looking for the killer.

la **rechute** NOUN
relapse

le **récipient** NOUN
container

le **récit** NOUN
story

réciter VERB
to recite

la **réclamation** NOUN
complaint ◇ *J'ai une réclamation à faire.* I want to make a complaint.
◆ **les réclamations** the complaints department

la **réclame** NOUN
advert ◇ *une réclame de lessive* an advert for washing powder
◆ **en réclame** on special offer ◇ *Le saumon était en réclame au supermarché.* Salmon was on special offer at the supermarket.

réclamer VERB
1 *to demand* ◇ *Nous réclamons la semaine de trente heures.* We demand a 30-hour week.
2 *to complain* ◇ *Elles sont toujours en train de réclamer.* They're always complaining about something.

reçois VERB *see* **recevoir**

la **récolte** NOUN
harvest

récolter VERB
1 *to harvest* ◇ *Ils ont récolté le blé.* They harvested the wheat.
2 *to collect* ◇ *Ils ont récolté deux mille francs.* They collected 2000 francs.
3 *to get* ◇ *Il a récolté une amende.* (*informal*) He got a fine.

le **recommandé** NOUN
◆ **en recommandé** by registered mail

PTO

◇ *Je voudrais envoyer ce paquet en recommandé.* I'd like to send this parcel registered.

recommander VERB
to recommend ◇ *Je vous recommande ce restaurant.* I recommend this restaurant.

recommencer VERB
1 *to start again* ◇ *Il a recommencé à pleuvoir.* It's started raining again.
2 *to do again* ◇ *S'il n'est pas puni, il va recommencer.* If he's not punished he'll do it again.

la **récompense** NOUN
reward

récompenser VERB
to reward ◇ *Il m'a récompensée de mes efforts.* He rewarded me for my efforts.

réconcilier VERB
◆ **se réconcilier avec quelqu'un** to be make it up with somebody ◇ *Il s'est réconcilié avec sa sœur.* He has made it up with his sister.

reconnaissant ADJECTIVE
grateful

reconnaître VERB
1 *to recognize* ◇ *Je ne l'ai pas reconnu.* I didn't recognize him.
2 *to admit* ◇ *Je reconnais que j'ai eu tort.* I admit I was wrong.

reconstruire VERB
to rebuild

le **record** NOUN
record ◇ *battre un record* to break a record

recouvrir VERB
to cover ◇ *La neige recouvre le sol.* The ground is covered in snow.

la **récréation** NOUN
break ◇ *Les élèves sont en récréation.* The pupils are having their break.
◆ **la cour de récréation** the playground (*of school*)

le **rectangle** NOUN
rectangle

rectangulaire ADJECTIVE
rectangular

rectifier VERB
to correct

le **reçu** NOUN
see also reçu VERB
receipt

reçu VERB *see* **recevoir**
see also reçu NOUN
◆ **J'ai reçu un colis ce matin.** I received a parcel this morning.
◆ **être reçu à un examen** to pass an exam

reculer VERB
1 *to step back* ◇ *Il a reculé pour la laisser entrer.* He stepped back to let her in.
2 *to reverse* ◇ *J'ai reculé pour laisser passer le camion.* I reversed to let the lorry past.
3 *to postpone* ◇ *Ils ont reculé la date du spectacle.* They postponed the show.

reculons
◆ **à reculons** ADVERB
backwards ◇ *Elle est entrée à reculons.* She came in backwards.

récupérer VERB
1 *to get back* ◇ *Je vais récupérer ma voiture au garage.* I'm going to get my car back from the garage.
2 *to make up* ◇ *J'ai des heures à récupérer.* I've got time to make up.
3 *to recover* ◇ *J'ai besoin de récupérer.* I need to recover.

recycler VERB
to recycle
◆ **se recycler** to retrain ◇ *Il a décidé de se recycler en informatique.* He decided to retrain as a computer programmer.

la **rédaction** NOUN
essay

redemander VERB
1 *to ask again for* ◇ *Je vais lui redemander son adresse.* I'll ask him for his address again.
2 *to ask for more* ◇ *Je vais redemander des carottes.* I'm going to ask for more carrots.

redescendre VERB
to go back down ◇ *Il est redescendu au premier étage.* He went back down to the first floor. ◇ *Elle a redescendu l'escalier.* She went back down the stairs.

rédiger VERB
to write (*an essay*)

redoubler VERB
to repeat a year ◇ *Il a raté son examen et doit redoubler.* He's failed his exam and will have to repeat the year.

la **réduction** NOUN
1 *reduction* ◇ *une réduction du nombre des touristes* a reduction in the number of tourists
2 *discount* ◇ *une réduction de cent francs* a 100 franc discount

réduire VERB
to cut ◇ *Ils ont réduit leurs prix.* They've cut their prices. ◇ *Il a réduit de moitié ses dépenses.* He has cut his spending by half.

réel ADJECTIVE

(FEM SING **réelle**)
real

réellement ADVERB
really

refaire VERB
1 *to do again* ◇ *Je dois refaire ce rapport.* I've got to do this report again.
2 *to take up again* ◇ *Je voudrais refaire de la gym.* I'd like to take up gymnastics again.

le **réfectoire** NOUN
refectory

la **référence** NOUN
reference
- **faire référence à quelque chose** to refer to something
- **Ce n'est pas une référence!** That's no recommendation!

réfléchi ADJECTIVE
reflexive (*verb*)
- **C'est tout réfléchi.** My mind's made up.

réfléchir VERB
to think ◇ *Il est en train de réfléchir.* He's thinking.
- **réfléchir à quelque chose** to think about something ◇ *Je vais réfléchir à ta proposition.* I'll think about your suggestion.

le **reflet** NOUN
reflection ◇ *les reflets du soleil sur la mer* the reflection of the sun on the sea

refléter VERB
to reflect

le **réflexe** NOUN
reflex ◇ *avoir de bons réflexes* to have good reflexes

la **réflexion** NOUN
1 *thought* ◇ *Elle est en pleine réflexion.* She's deep in thought.
2 *remark* ◇ *faire des réflexions désagréables* to make nasty remarks
- **réflexion faite** on reflection

le **refrain** NOUN
chorus (*of song*)

le **réfrigérateur** NOUN
refrigerator

refroidir VERB
to cool ◇ *Laissez le gâteau refroidir.* Leave the cake to cool.
- **se refroidir** to get colder ◇ *Le temps se refroidit.* It's getting colder.

se **réfugier** VERB
to take shelter ◇ *Je me suis réfugié sous un arbre.* I took shelter under a tree.

le **refus** NOUN
refusal
- **Ce n'est pas de refus.** I wouldn't say no. ◇ *Voulez-vous une bière? – Ce n'est pas de refus.* Would you like a beer? – I wouldn't say no.

refuser VERB
to refuse ◇ *Il a refusé de payer sa part.* He refused to pay his share. ◇ *On lui a refusé une augmentation.* He was refused a pay rise.
- **Je refuse qu'on me parle ainsi!** I won't let anybody talk to me like that!

se **régaler** VERB
- **Merci beaucoup: je me suis régalé!** Thank you very much: it was absolutely delicious!

le **regard** NOUN
look ◇ *Il lui a jeté un regard interrogateur.* He gave him an enquiring look. ◇ *On voyait à son regard qu'elle était contrariée.* You could tell from the look in her eyes that she was upset.
- **Tous les regards se sont tournés vers lui.** All eyes turned towards him.

regarder VERB
1 *to look at* ◇ *Il regardait ses photos de vacances.* He was looking at his holiday photos. ◇ *Regarde! J'ai presque fini.* Look! I've nearly finished.
2 *to watch* ◇ *Je regarde la télévision.* I'm watching television. ◇ *Regarde où tu mets les pieds!* Watch where you put your feet!
3 *to concern* ◇ *Ça ne nous regarde pas.* It doesn't concern us.
- **ne pas regarder à la dépense** to spare no expense

le **régime** NOUN
1 *régime* (*of a country*)
2 *diet* ◇ *un régime sans sel* a salt-free diet ◇ *se mettre au régime* to go on a diet ◇ *suivre un régime* to be on a diet
- **un régime de bananes** a bunch of bananas

la **région** NOUN
region

régional ADJECTIVE
(MASC PL **régionaux**)
regional

le **registre** NOUN
register

la **règle** NOUN
1 *ruler* ◇ *Il a souligné son nom avec une règle.* He underlined his name with a ruler.
2 *rule* ◇ *C'est la règle.* That's the rule. ◇ *en règle générale* as a general rule
- **être en règle** to be in order ◇ *Mes papiers sont en règle.* My papers are in

R

PTO

order.
- **les règles** period (*menstruation*)

le **règlement** NOUN
rules ◇ *Le règlement est affiché à l'entrée.* The rules are up on the wall by the entrance.

régler VERB
1 *to adjust* ◇ *Il faut que je règle mon rétroviseur.* I'll have to adjust my rear-view mirror.
2 *to tune* ◇ *J'ai réglé ma radio sur 476 FM.* I tuned my radio to 476 FM.
3 *to set* ◇ *J'ai réglé le thermostat à vingt degrés.* I've set the thermostat to 20 degrees.
4 *to solve* ◇ *Le problème est réglé.* The problem's solved.
5 *to settle* ◇ *Elle a réglé sa facture.* She's settled her bill. ◇ *J'ai réglé Jean-Pierre pour l'essence.* I've settled up with Jean-Pierre for the petrol.

la **réglisse** NOUN
liquorice

le **règne** NOUN
reign ◇ *sous le règne de Henri IV* in the reign of Henry IV

régner VERB
to reign

le **regret** NOUN
regret
- **à regret** reluctantly

regretter VERB
1 *to regret* ◇ *Elle regrette ce qu'elle a dit.* She regrets saying what she did.
- **Je regrette.** I'm sorry. ◇ *Je regrette, je ne peux pas vous aider.* I'm sorry, I can't help you.

2 *to miss* ◇ *Je regrette mon ancien travail.* I miss my old job.

regrouper VERB
to group together ◇ *Nous avons regroupé les enfants suivant leur âge.* We grouped the children together according to age.
- **se regrouper** to gather together ◇ *Les agriculteurs se sont regroupés pour constituer un syndicat.* The farmers joined together to form a union.

régulier ADJECTIVE
(FEM SING **régulière**)
1 *regular* ◇ *des livraisons régulières* regular deliveries ◇ *des bus réguliers* a regular bus service
2 *steady* ◇ *à un rythme régulier* at a steady rate
3 *scheduled* ◇ *des vols réguliers pour Marseille* scheduled flights to Marseilles

régulièrement ADVERB
regularly

le **rein** NOUN
kidney
- **les reins** back (*of body*) ◇ *J'ai mal aux reins.* My back hurts.

la **reine** NOUN
queen

rejoindre VERB
to go back to ◇ *J'ai rejoint mes amis.* I went back to my friends.
- **Je te rejoins au café.** I'll see you at the café.
- **se rejoindre** to meet up ◇ *Elles se sont rejointes une heure après.* They met up an hour later.

relâcher VERB
to release (*prisoner, animal*)
- **se relâcher** to get slack ◇ *Il se relâche dans son travail.* His work is getting careless.

le **relais** NOUN
relay race ◇ *le relais quatre fois cent mètres* the 4 x 100 metre relay
- **prendre le relais** to take over

la **relation** NOUN
relationship
- **les relations franco-britanniques** Anglo-French relations

se **relaxer** VERB
to relax

se **relayer** VERB
- **se relayer pour faire quelque chose** to take it in turns to do something

le **relevé** NOUN
- **un relevé de compte** a bank statement

relever VERB
1 *to collect* ◇ *Je relève les copies dans cinq minutes.* I'll collect the papers in five minutes.
2 *to react to* ◇ *Je n'ai pas relevé sa réflexion.* I didn't react to his remark.
- **relever la tête** to look up
- **se relever** to get up ◇ *Il est tombé mais s'est relevé aussitôt.* He fell, but got up immediately.

la **religieuse** NOUN
1 *nun* ◇ *Marie est religieuse.* Marie is a nun.
2 *choux cream bun* ◇ *des religieuses au chocolat* choux buns with chocolate cream and icing

religieux ADJECTIVE
(FEM **religieuse**)
religious

la **religion** NOUN
religion

relire VERB
1 *to read over* ◇ *Il a relu sa copie avant de la rendre.* He read his exam paper over before handing it in.

2 *to read again* ◇ *Je voudrais relire ce roman.* I'd like to read this novel again.

remarquable ADJECTIVE
remarkable

la **remarque** NOUN
1 *remark* ◇ *Il a fait une remarque désagréable.* He made a nasty remark.
2 *comment* ◇ *Avez-vous des remarques à faire?* Have you any comments to make?

remarquer VERB
to notice ◇ *J'ai remarqué qu'elle avait l'air triste.* I noticed she was looking sad.
- **faire remarquer quelque chose à quelqu'un** to point something out to somebody ◇ *Je lui ai fait remarquer que c'était un peu cher.* I pointed out to him that it was rather expensive.
- **Remarquez, il n'est pas si bête que ça.** Mind you, he's not as stupid as all that.
- **se remarquer** to be noticeable ◇ *David ne s'est pas rasé ce matin. Ça se remarque.* It's obvious David didn't shave this morning.
- **se faire remarquer** to call attention to oneself

le **remboursement** NOUN
refund

rembourser VERB
to pay back ◇ *Il m'a remboursé l'argent qu'il me devait.* He paid me back the money he owed me.
- **"satisfait ou remboursé"** "satisfaction or your money back"

remercier VERB
to thank ◇ *Je te remercie pour ton cadeau.* Thank you for your present.
- **remercier quelqu'un d'avoir fait quelque chose** to thank somebody for doing something ◇ *Je vous remercie de m'avoir invité.* Thank you for inviting me.

remettre VERB
1 *to put back on* ◇ *Elle a remis son pull.* She put her sweater back on.
2 *to put back* ◇ *Il a remis sa veste dans l'armoire.* He put his jacket back in the wardrobe.
3 *to put off* ◇ *J'ai dû remettre mon rendez-vous.* I've had to put my appointment off.
- **se remettre** to recover (*from illness*) ◇ *Mélusine s'est bien remise de son opération.* Mélusine has fully recovered from her operation.

le **remonte-pente** NOUN
ski-lift

remonter VERB
1 *to go back up* ◇ *Il est remonté au premier étage.* He has gone back up to the first floor.
2 *to go up* ◇ *Ils ont remonté la pente.* They went up the hill.
3 *to buck up* ◇ *Cette nouvelle m'a un peu remontée.* The news bucked me up a bit.
- **remonter le moral à quelqu'un** to cheer somebody up

le **remords** NOUN
- **avoir des remords** to feel remorse

la **remorque** NOUN
trailer (*of car*)

le **remplaçant** NOUN
supply teacher

la **remplaçante** NOUN
supply teacher

remplacer VERB
to replace ◇ *Il faut remplacer cette ampoule.* We need to replace this bulb. ◇ *Il remplace le prof de maths.* He's replacing the maths teacher.
- **remplacer par** to replace with

rempli ADJECTIVE
busy ◇ *une journée bien remplie* a very busy day
- **rempli de** full of ◇ *La salle était remplie de monde.* The room was full of people.

remplir VERB
1 *to fill up* ◇ *Elle a rempli son verre de vin.* She filled her glass with wine.
2 *to fill in* ◇ *Tu as rempli ton formulaire?* Have you filled in your form?
- **se remplir** to fill up ◇ *La salle s'est remplie de monde.* The room filled up with people.

remuer VERB
1 *to move* ◇ *Elle a remué le bras.* She moved her arm.
2 *to stir* ◇ *Remuez la sauce pendant deux minutes.* Stir the sauce for two minutes.
- **se remuer** (*informal*) to go to a lot of trouble ◇ *Ils se sont beaucoup remués pour organiser cette soirée.* They went to a lot of trouble organizing this party.

le **renard** NOUN
fox

la **rencontre** NOUN
- **faire la rencontre de quelqu'un** to meet somebody ◇ *J'ai fait la rencontre de personnes intéressantes ce soir.* I met some interesting people this evening.
- **aller à la rencontre de quelqu'un** to go and meet somebody ◇ *Je viendrai à ta*

PTO

rencontre. I'll come and meet you.

rencontrer VERB
to meet
- **se rencontrer** to meet ◇ *Ils se sont rencontrés il y a deux ans.* They met two years ago.

le **rendez-vous** NOUN
1 *appointment* ◇ *J'ai rendez-vous chez le coiffeur.* I've got an appointment at the hairdresser's. ◇ *prendre rendez-vous avec quelqu'un* to make an appointment with somebody
2 *date* ◇ *Tu sors ce soir?–Oui, j'ai un rendez-vous.* Are you going out tonight?–Yes, I've got a date.
- **donner rendez-vous à quelqu'un** to arrange to meet somebody

rendre VERB
1 *to give back* ◇ *J'ai rendu ses disques à Christine.* I've given Christine her records back.
2 *to take back* ◇ *J'ai rendu mes livres à la bibliothèque.* I've taken my books back to the library.
- **rendre quelqu'un célèbre** to make somebody famous
- **se rendre** to give oneself up ◇ *Le meurtrier s'est rendu à la police.* The murderer gave himself up to the police.
- **se rendre compte de quelque chose** to realize something

le **renfermé** NOUN
- **sentir le renfermé** to smell stuffy

renifler VERB
to sniff

le **renne** NOUN
reindeer

renommé ADJECTIVE
renowned ◇ *La Bretagne est renommée pour ses plages.* Brittany is renowned for its beaches.

renoncer VERB
- **renoncer à** to give up ◇ *Ils ont renoncé à leur projet.* They've given up their plan.
- **renoncer à faire quelque chose** to give up the idea of doing something

renouveler VERB
to renew (*passport, contract*)
- **se renouveler** to happen again ◇ *J'espère que ça ne se renouvellera pas.* I hope that won't happen again.

le **renseignement** NOUN
piece of information ◇ *Il me manque un renseignement.* There's one piece of information I still need.
- **les renseignements (1)** information ◇ *Il m'a donné des renseignements.* He gave me some information.
- **les renseignements (2)** information desk
- **les renseignements (3)** directory inquiries

renseigner VERB
- **renseigner quelqu'un sur quelque chose** to give somebody information about something
- **Est-ce que je peux vous renseigner?** Can I help you?
- **se renseigner** to find out ◇ *Je vais me renseigner pour voir s'il n'y a pas un vol direct.* I'm going to find out if there's a direct flight.

rentable ADJECTIVE
profitable

la **rentrée** NOUN
- **la rentrée (des classes)** the start of the new school year

rentrer VERB
1 *to come in* ◇ *Rentre, tu vas prendre froid.* Come in, you'll catch cold.
2 *to go in* ◇ *Elle est rentrée dans le magasin.* She went into the shop.
3 *to get home* ◇ *Je suis rentré à sept heures hier soir.* I got home at 7 o'clock last night.
4 *to put away* ◇ *Tu as rentré la voiture?* Have you put the car away?
- **rentrer dans** to crash into ◇ *Sa voiture est rentrée dans un arbre.* He crashed into a tree.
- **rentrer dans l'ordre** to get back to normal

la **renverse** NOUN
- **tomber à la renverse** to fall backwards

renverser VERB
1 *to knock over* ◇ *J'ai renversé mon verre.* I knocked my glass over.
2 *to knock down* ◇ *Elle a été renversée par une voiture.* She was knocked down by a car.
3 *to spill* ◇ *Il a renversé de l'eau partout.* He has spilt water everywhere.
- **se renverser** to fall over (*glass, vase*)

renvoyer VERB
1 *to send back* ◇ *Je t'ai renvoyé ton courrier.* I've sent your mail back to you.
2 *to dismiss* ◇ *On a renvoyé deux employés.* Two employees have been dismissed.

la **réparation** NOUN
repair

réparer VERB
to repair

repartir VERB
to set off again ◇ *Il s'est arrêté pour déjeuner avant de repartir.* He stopped

for lunch before setting off again.
◇ *Maree était là tout à l'heure, mais elle est repartie.* Maree was here a moment ago, but she's gone again.
- **repartir à zéro** to start again from scratch

le **repas** NOUN
meal
- **le repas de midi** lunch
- **le repas du soir** dinner

repasser VERB
1 *to come back* ◇ *Je repasserai demain.* I'll come back tomorrow.
2 *to go back* ◇ *Je dois repasser au magasin.* I've got to go back to the shop.
3 *to iron* ◇ *J'ai repassé ma chemise.* I've ironed my shirt.
4 *to resit* ◇ *Elle doit repasser son examen de maths.* She's got to resit her maths exam.

repérer VERB
to spot ◇ *J'ai repéré deux fautes.* I spotted two mistakes.
- **se repérer** to find one's way around ◇ *J'ai du mal à me repérer de nuit.* I have difficulty finding my way around when it's dark.

répéter VERB
1 *to repeat* ◇ *Elle répète toujours la même chose.* She keeps repeating the same thing.
2 *to rehearse* ◇ *Les acteurs répètent une scène.* The actors are rehearsing a scene.
- **se répéter** to happen again ◇ *J'espère que cela ne se répétera pas!* I hope this won't happen again!

la **répétition** NOUN
1 *repetition* ◇ *Il y a beaucoup de répétitions dans ce texte.* There's a lot of repetition in this text.
- **des grèves à répétition** repeated strikes

2 *rehearsal* ◇ *Ils ont une répétition cet après-midi.* They've got a rehearsal this afternoon.
- **la répétition générale** the dress rehearsal

le **répondeur** NOUN
answering machine

répondre VERB
to answer ◇ *répondre à quelqu'un* to answer somebody

la **réponse** NOUN
answer ◇ *C'est la bonne réponse.* That's the right answer.

le **reportage** NOUN
1 *report* ◇ *J'ai vu ce reportage aux informations.* I saw that report on the news.
2 *story* ◇ *J'ai lu ce reportage dans "La Gazette".* I read that story in "La Gazette".

le **reporter** NOUN
reporter ◇ *Christian est reporter.* Christian is a reporter.

le **repos** NOUN
rest

reposer VERB
to put back down ◇ *Elle a reposé son verre sur la table.* She put her glass back down on the table.
- **se reposer** to have a rest ◇ *Tu pourras te reposer demain.* You'll be able to have a rest tomorrow.
- **se reposer sur quelqu'un** to rely on somebody

repousser VERB
1 *to grow again* ◇ *Ses cheveux ont repoussé.* Her hair has grown again.
2 *to postpone* ◇ *Le voyage est repoussé.* The trip's been postponed.

reprendre VERB
1 *to take back* ◇ *Il a repris son livre.* He's taken his book back.
2 *to go back to* ◇ *Elle a repris le travail.* She went back to work.
3 *to start again* ◇ *La réunion reprendra à deux heures.* The meeting will start again at 2 o'clock.
- **reprendre du pain** to take more bread
- **reprendre la route** to set off again
- **reprendre son souffle** to get one's breath back

le **représentant** NOUN
rep ◇ *Il est représentant chez Harper Collins.* He's a rep for Harper Collins.

la **représentante** NOUN
rep ◇ *Elle est représentante.* She'a a sales rep.

la **représentation** NOUN
performance ◇ *la dernière représentation d'une pièce* the final performance of a play

représenter VERB
to show ◇ *Le tableau représente un enfant et un chat.* The picture shows a child with a cat.
- **se représenter** to arise again ◇ *Cette occasion ne se représentera pas.* This opportunity won't arise again.

le **reproche** NOUN
- **faire des reproches à quelqu'un** to reproach somebody

reprocher VERB
- **reprocher quelque chose à quelqu'un** to reproach somebody for something ◇ *Il m'a reproché mon retard.* He

R

PTO

reproached me for being late.
- **Qu'est-ce que tu lui reproches?** What have you got against him?

la **reproduction** NOUN
reproduction

reproduire VERB
to reproduce
- **se reproduire** to happen again ◇ *Je te promets que ça ne se reproduira pas!* I promise it won't happen again!

républicain ADJECTIVE
republican

la **république** NOUN
republic ◇ *la République française* the French Republic

répugnant ADJECTIVE
repulsive

la **réputation** NOUN
reputation

le **requin** NOUN
shark

le **RER** NOUN
Greater Paris high-speed train service

le **réseau** NOUN
(PL les **réseaux**)
network

la **réservation** NOUN
reservation

la **réserve** NOUN
stock ◇ *avoir quelque chose en réserve* to have a stock of something
- **mettre quelque chose en réserve** to put something aside

réserver VERB
1 *to reserve* ◇ *Cette table est réservée.* This table is reserved.
2 *to book* ◇ *Nous avons réservé une chambre.* We've booked a room.
3 *to save* ◇ *Je t'ai réservé une part de gâteau.* I've saved you a piece of cake.

le **réservoir** NOUN
petrol tank

la **résidence** NOUN
block of flats
- **une résidence secondaire** a second home

résistant ADJECTIVE
1 *hard-wearing* ◇ *Ce tissu est résistant.* This fabric is hard-wearing.
2 *robust* ◇ *Il est très résistant.* He's very robust.

résister VERB
to resist

résolu ADJECTIVE
- **Le problème est résolu.** The problem's solved.

résoudre VERB
to solve

le **respect** NOUN
respect

respecter VERB
to respect

la **respiration** NOUN
breathing

respirer VERB
to breathe

la **responsabilité** NOUN
responsibility

responsable ADJECTIVE
see also responsable NOUN
responsible ◇ *être responsable de quelque chose* to be responsible for something

le/la **responsable** NOUN
see also responsable ADJECTIVE
1 *person in charge* ◇ *Je voudrais parler au responsable.* I'd like to speak to the person in charge.
2 *person responsible* ◇ *Il faut punir les responsables.* Those responsible must be punished.

ressembler VERB
- **ressembler à (1)** to look like ◇ *Elle ne ressemble pas à sa sœur.* She doesn't look like her sister.
- **ressembler à (2)** to be like ◇ *Ça ressemble à un conte de fées.* It's like a fairy tale.
- **se ressembler (1)** to look alike ◇ *Les deux frères ne se ressemblent pas.* The two brothers don't look alike.
- **se rassembler (2)** to be alike ◇ *Ces deux pays ne se ressemblent pas.* These two countries aren't alike.

le **ressort** NOUN
spring (*metal*) ◇ *Le ressort est cassé.* The spring is broken.

ressortir VERB
to go out again

le **restaurant** NOUN
restaurant

le **reste** NOUN
rest
- **un reste de poulet** some left-over chicken
- **les restes** the left-overs

rester VERB
1 *to stay* ◇ *Je reste à la maison ce week-end.* I'm staying at home this weekend.
2 *to be left* ◇ *Il reste du pain.* There's some bread left. ◇ *Il me reste assez de temps.* I still have enough time.
- **Il ne me reste plus qu'à...** I've just got to... ◇ *Il ne me reste plus qu'à ranger mes affaires.* I've just got to put my things away.

- **Restons-en là.** Let's leave it at that.

le **résultat** NOUN
result ◇ *le résultat des examens* the exam results

le **résumé** NOUN
summary

résumer VERB
to summarize

le **retard** NOUN
delay ◇ *un retard de livraison* a delay in delivery
- **avoir du retard** to be late
- **être en retard de deux heures** to be two hours late
- **prendre du retard** to be delayed

retarder VERB
1 *to be slow* ◇ *Ma montre retarde.* My watch is slow.
2 *to put back* ◇ *Je dois retarder la pendule d'une heure.* I've got to put the clock back an hour.
- **être retardé** to be delayed ◇ *J'ai été retardé par un coup de téléphone.* I was held up by a phone call.

retenir VERB
1 *to remember* ◇ *Tu as retenu leur adresse?* Do you remember their address?
2 *to book* ◇ *J'ai retenu une chambre à l'hôtel.* I've booked a room at the hotel.
- **retenir son souffle** to hold one's breath

retenu ADJECTIVE
1 *reserved* ◇ *Cette place est retenue.* This seat is reserved.
2 *held up* ◇ *J'ai été retenu par un coup de téléphone.* I was held up by a phone call.

la **retenue** NOUN
detention ◇ *Gerry est en retenue.* Gerry's in detention.

retirer VERB
1 *to withdraw* ◇ *Elle a retiré de l'argent.* She withdrew some money.
2 *to take off* ◇ *Il a retiré son pull.* He took off his sweater.

le **retour** NOUN
return
- **être de retour** to be back ◇ *Je serai de retour la semaine prochaine.* I'll be back next week.

retourner VERB
1 *to go back* ◇ *Est-ce que tu es retourné à Londres?* Have you been back to London?
2 *to turn over* ◇ *Elle a retourné la crêpe.* She turned the pancake over. ◇ *Il a retourné la poubelle.* He turned the bin upside down.
- **se retourner (1)** to turn round ◇ *Janet s'est retournée.* Janet turned round.
- **se retourner (2)** to turn over ◇ *La voiture s'est retournée.* The car turned over.

la **retraite** NOUN
- **être à la retraite** to be retired
- **prendre sa retraite** to retire

retraité ADJECTIVE
see also retraité NOUN
retired ◇ *Mon oncle est maintenant retraité.* My uncle's now retired.

le **retraité** NOUN
see also retraité ADJECTIVE
pensioner

la **retraitée** NOUN
pensioner

rétrécir VERB
to shrink ◇ *Son pull a rétréci au lavage.* Her sweater shrank in the wash.
- **se rétrécir** to get narrower ◇ *La rue se rétrécit.* The street gets narrower.

retrouver VERB
1 *to find* ◇ *J'ai retrouvé mon portefeuille.* I've found my wallet.
2 *to meet up with* ◇ *Je te retrouve au café à trois heures.* I'll meet you at the café at 3 o'clock.
- **se retrouver (1)** to meet up ◇ *Ils se sont retrouvés devant le cinéma.* They met up in front of the cinema.
- **se retrouver (2)** to find one's way around ◇ *Je n'arrive pas à me retrouver.* I can't find my way around.

le **rétroviseur** NOUN
rear-view mirror

la **réunion** NOUN
meeting

se **réunir** VERB
to meet ◇ *Ils se sont réunis à cinq heures.* They met at 5 o'clock.

réussi ADJECTIVE
successful ◇ *une soirée très réussie* a very successful party
- **être réussi** to be a success ◇ *Le repas était très réussi.* The meal was delicious.

réussir VERB
to be successful ◇ *Tous ses enfants ont très bien réussi.* All her children are very successful.
- **réussir à faire quelque chose** to succeed in doing something
- **réussir à un examen** to pass an exam

la **réussite** NOUN
success

la **revanche** NOUN
return match
- **prendre sa revanche** to get one's own

back ◇ *Il a pris sa revanche en refusant de lui prêter son vélo.* He got his own back by refusing to lend him his bike.
- **en revanche** on the other hand ◇ *C'est cher mais en revanche c'est de la bonne qualité.* It is dear but on the other hand it's good quality.

le **rêve** NOUN
dream
- **de rêve** fantastic ◇ *des vacances de rêve* fantastic holidays

le **réveil** NOUN
alarm clock

le **réveille-matin** NOUN
(PL les **réveille-matin**)
alarm clock

réveiller VERB
to wake up ◇ *réveiller quelqu'un* to wake somebody up
- **se réveiller** to wake up

le **réveillon** NOUN
- **le réveillon du premier de l'an** New Year's Eve celebrations
- **le réveillon de Noël** Christmas Eve celebrations

réveillonner VERB
1 *to celebrate New Year's Eve*
2 *to celebrate Christmas Eve*

revenir VERB
to come back ◇ *Reviens vite!* Come back soon! ◇ *Son nom m'est revenu cinq minutes après.* His name came back to me five minutes later.
- **Ça revient au même.** It comes to the same thing.
- **Ça revient cher.** It costs a lot.
- **Je n'en reviens pas!** I can't get over it!
- **revenir sur ses pas** to retrace one's steps

le **revenu** NOUN
income

rêver VERB
to dream
- **rêver de quelque chose** to dream of something ◇ *J'ai rêvé de mes vacances cette nuit.* I dreamt about my holidays last night.

le **réverbère** NOUN
street lamp

le **revers** NOUN
1 *backhand* ◇ *Becker a un excellent revers.* Becker has an excellent backhand.
2 *lapel* (*of jacket*)
- **le revers de la médaille** the other side of the coin

revient VERB *see* **revenir**

réviser VERB
1 *to revise* ◇ *Je dois réviser mon anglais.* I've got to revise my English.
2 *to service* ◇ *Je dois faire réviser ma voiture.* I must get my car serviced.

la **révision** NOUN
revision

revoir VERB
1 *to see again* ◇ *J'ai revu Sophie hier soir.* I saw Sophie again last night.
2 *to revise* ◇ *Il est en train de revoir sa géographie.* He's revising his geography.
- **au revoir** goodbye

la **révolution** NOUN
revolution ◇ *la Révolution française* the French Revolution

le **revolver** NOUN
revolver

la **revue** NOUN
magazine

le **rez-de-chaussée** NOUN
ground floor ◇ *au rez-de-chaussée* on the ground floor

le **Rhin** NOUN
Rhine

le **rhinocéros** NOUN
rhinoceros

le **Rhône** NOUN
Rhone

la **rhubarbe** NOUN
rhubarb

le **rhum** NOUN
rum

le **rhume** NOUN
cold ◇ *J'ai attrapé un rhume.* I've caught a cold.
- **un rhume de cerveau** a head cold
- **le rhume des foins** hay fever

ri VERB *see* **rire**
- **Nous avons bien ri.** We had a good laugh.

riche ADJECTIVE
1 *well-off* ◇ *Sa famille est très riche.* His family's very well-off.
2 *rich* ◇ *riche en vitamines* rich in vitamins

le **rideau** NOUN
(PL les **rideaux**)
curtain ◇ *tirer les rideaux* to draw the curtains

ridicule ADJECTIVE
ridiculous ◇ *Je trouve ça complètement ridicule.* I think that's absolutely ridiculous.

rien PRONOUN
see also **rien** NOUN
1 *nothing* ◇ *Qu'est-ce que tu as acheté? – Rien.* What have you bought? – Nothing. ◇ *Ça n'a rien à voir.* It has nothing to do with it.
- **rien d'intéressant** nothing interesting

rien d'autre nothing else
rien du tout nothing at all
2 *anything* ◇ *Il n'a rien dit.* He didn't say anything.
rien que (1) just ◇ *rien que pour lui faire plaisir* just to please him ◇ *Rien que la voiture coûte un million.* The car alone costs a million.
rien que (2) nothing but ◇ *rien que la vérité* nothing but the truth
De rien! Not at all! ◇ *Merci beaucoup! – De rien!* Thank you very much! – Not at all!
en NOUN
see also **rien** PRONOUN
pour un rien at the slightest thing ◇ *Il se met en colère pour un rien.* He loses his temper over the slightest thing.
en un rien de temps in no time at all
goler VERB (*informal*)
1 *to laugh* ◇ *Elle a rigolé en le voyant tomber.* She laughed when she saw him fall.
2 *to have fun* ◇ *On a bien rigolé hier soir.* We had good fun last night.
3 *to be joking* ◇ *Ne te fâche pas, je rigolais.* Don't get upset, I was only joking.
pour rigoler for a laugh
golo ADJECTIVE (*informal*)
(FEM SING **rigolote**)
funny
ncer VERB
to rinse
re VERB
see also **rire** NOUN
to laugh ◇ *Ce film m'a vraiment fait rire.* That film really made me laugh. ◇ *Nous avons bien ri.* We had a good laugh.
pour rire for a laugh
re NOUN
see also **rire** VERB
laughter ◇ *Il a un rire communicatif.* He has an infectious laugh.
sque NOUN
1 *risk* ◇ *prendre des risques* to take risks ◇ *à tes risques et périls* at your own risk
2 *danger* ◇ *Il n'y a pas de risque qu'il le sache.* There's no danger of him finding out.
squé ADJECTIVE
risky
squer VERB
to risk
Ça ne risque rien. It's quite safe.
Il risque de se tuer. He could get himself killed.
◆ **C'est ce qui risque de se passer.** That's what might well happen.

le **rivage** NOUN
shore
la **rivière** NOUN
river
le **riz** NOUN
rice
le **RMI** NOUN
Income Support ◇ *Il touche le RMI.* He's on Income Support.
RN ABBREVIATION (= *route nationale*)
A road
la **robe** NOUN
dress
◆ **une robe de soirée** an evening dress
◆ **une robe de mariée** a wedding dress
◆ **une robe de chambre** a dressing gown
le **robinet** NOUN
tap
le **robot** NOUN
robot
la **roche** NOUN
rock (*stone*)
le **rocher** NOUN
rock
le **rock** NOUN
rock (*music*) ◇ *un chanteur de rock* a rock singer
les **rognons** MASC NOUN
kidneys (*in cooking*)
le **roi** NOUN
king
◆ **le jour des Rois** Twelfth Night
le **rôle** NOUN
role
romain ADJECTIVE
Roman ◇ *des ruines romaines* Roman remains
le **roman** NOUN
novel
◆ **un roman policier** a detective story
◆ **un roman d'espionnage** a spy story
le **romancier** NOUN
novelist
rompre VERB
1 *to split up* ◇ *Paul et Justine ont rompu.* Paul and Justine have split up.
2 *to break off* ◇ *Ils ont rompu leurs fiançailles.* They've broken off their engagement.
les **ronces** FEM NOUN
brambles
ronchonner VERB (*informal*)
to grouse
rond ADJECTIVE
see also **rond** NOUN
1 *round* ◇ *La Terre est ronde.* The earth is round.

R

- **ouvrir des yeux ronds** to stare in amazement

2 *chubby* ◇ *Il a les joues rondes.* He has chubby cheeks.

3 *drunk* ◇ *Il est complètement rond.* (*informal*) He's completely drunk.

le **rond** NOUN

see also rond ADJECTIVE

circle ◇ *Elle a dessiné un rond sur le sable.* She drew a circle in the sand.

- **en rond** in a circle ◇ *Ils se sont assis en rond.* They sat down in a circle.
- **tourner en rond** to go round in circles
- **Je n'ai plus un rond.** (*informal*) I haven't a penny left.

la **rondelle** NOUN

slice ◇ *une rondelle de citron* a slice of lemon

le **rond-point** NOUN

(PL les **ronds-points**)

roundabout ◇ *La voiture s'est arrêtée au rond-point.* The car stopped at the roundabout.

ronfler VERB

to snore

le **rosbif** NOUN

roast beef

la **rose** NOUN

see also rose ADJECTIVE

rose

rose ADJECTIVE

see also rose NOUN

pink

le **rosé** NOUN

rosé (wine) ◇ *Je prendrai un verre de rosé.* I'll have a glass of rosé.

le **rosier** NOUN

rosebush

le **rôti** NOUN

roast meat

- **un rôti de bœuf** a joint of beef

rôtir VERB

to roast ◇ *faire rôtir quelque chose* to roast something

la **roue** NOUN

wheel ◇ *une roue de secours* a spare wheel

rouge ADJECTIVE

see also rouge NOUN

red

le **rouge** NOUN

see also rouge ADJECTIVE

1 *red* ◇ *Le rouge est ma couleur préférée.* Red is my favourite colour.

2 *red wine* ◇ *un verre de rouge* a glass of red wine

- **passer au rouge (1)** to change to red ◇ *Le feu est passé au rouge.* The light changed to red.
- **passer au rouge (2)** to go through a red light ◇ *Jean-Pierre est passé au rouge.* Jean-Pierre went through a red light.
- **un rouge à lèvres** a lipstick

la **rougeole** NOUN

measles

rougir VERB

1 *to blush* ◇ *Il a rougi en me voyant.* He blushed when he saw me.

2 *to flush* ◇ *Il a rougi de colère.* He flushed with anger.

la **rouille** NOUN

rust

rouillé ADJECTIVE

rusty

rouiller VERB

to go rusty

roulant ADJECTIVE

- **un fauteuil roulant** a wheelchair
- **une table roulante** a trolley

le **rouleau** NOUN

(PL les **rouleaux**)

roll ◇ *un rouleau de papier peint* a roll of wallpaper

- **un rouleau à pâtisserie** a rolling pin

rouler VERB

1 *to go* ◇ *Le train roulait à 250 km/h.* The train was going at 250 km an hour

2 *to drive* ◇ *Il a roulé sans s'arrêter.* He drove without stopping.

3 *to roll* ◇ *Gilles a roulé une cigarette.* Gilles rolled a cigarette.

4 *to roll up* ◇ *Il a roulé le tapis.* He rolled the carpet up.

5 *to con* ◇ *Ils se sont fait rouler.* (*informal*) They were conned.

- **Alors, ça roule?** (*informal*) How's it going?

la **Roumanie** NOUN

Romania

le **rouquin** NOUN (*informal*)

redhead

la **rouquine** NOUN (*informal*)

redhead

rousse ADJECTIVE *see* **roux**

la **rousse** NOUN

redhead

la **route** NOUN

1 *road* ◇ *au bord de la route* at the roadside

- **une route nationale** an A road

2 *way* ◇ *Je ne connais pas la route.* I don't know the way.

- **Il y a trois heures de route.** It's a 3-hour journey.
- **en route** on the way ◇ *Ils se sont arrêtés en route pour pique-niquer.* They stopped on the way for a picnic.

mettre en route to start up ◇ *Il a mis le moteur en route.* He started the engine up.

se mettre en route to set off ◇ *Il s'est mis en route à cinq heures.* He set off at 5 o'clock.

outier NOUN

1 *lorry driver* ◇ *Son père est routier.* His father's a lorry driver.

2 *transport café* ◇ *Nous avons mangé dans un routier.* We ate in a transport café.

outine NOUN

routine

oux ADJECTIVE

(FEM SING **rousse**)

see also **roux** NOUN

1 *red* ◇ *Harry a les cheveux roux.* Harry has red hair.

2 *red-haired* ◇ *Isobel est rousse.* Isobel's red-haired.

oux NOUN

see also **roux** ADJECTIVE

redhead

oyal ADJECTIVE

(MASC PL **royaux**)

royal

oyaume NOUN

kingdom

le Royaume-Uni the United Kingdom

uban NOUN

ribbon

le ruban adhésif adhesive tape

ubéole NOUN

German measles

uche NOUN

hive

udement ADVERB (*informal*)

terribly ◇ *C'était rudement bon.* It was terribly good.

la **rue** NOUN

street

la **ruelle** NOUN

alley

le **rugby** NOUN

rugby ◇ *Yann joue au rugby.* Yann plays rugby.

la **ruine** NOUN

ruin ◇ *les ruines de la cathédrale* the ruins of the cathedral

ruiner VERB

to ruin

le **ruisseau** NOUN

(PL les **ruisseaux**)

stream

la **rumeur** NOUN

rumour

la **rupture** NOUN

break-up

la **ruse** NOUN

trickery ◇ *une ruse* a trick

rusé ADJECTIVE

cunning

russe ADJECTIVE, NOUN

Russian ◇ *Il parle russe.* He speaks Russian.

◆ **un Russe** a Russian (*man*)

◆ **une Russe** a Russian (*woman*)

◆ **les Russes** the Russians

la **Russie** NOUN

Russia

le **rythme** NOUN

1 *rhythm* ◇ *J'aime le rythme de cette musique.* I like the beat of this music.

2 *pace* ◇ *Il marche à un bon rythme.* He walks at a good pace.

S

s' PRONOUN *see* **se**

sa ADJECTIVE
1 *his* ◇ *Paul est allé voir sa grand-mère.* Paul's gone to see his grandmother.
2 *her* ◇ *Elle a embrassé sa mère.* She kissed her mother.

le **sable** NOUN
sand
➔ **des sables mouvants** quicksand

le **sablé** NOUN
shortbread biscuit

le **sabot** NOUN
1 *clog*
2 *hoof* (*of horse*)

le **sac** NOUN
bag
➔ **un sac de voyage** a travel bag
➔ **un sac de couchage** a sleeping bag
➔ **un sac à main** a handbag
➔ **un sac à dos** a rucksack

le **sachet** NOUN
sachet (*of sugar, coffee*)
➔ **du potage en sachet** packet soup
➔ **un sachet de thé** a tea bag

la **sacoche** NOUN
bag
➔ **une sacoche de bicyclette** a saddlebag

sacré ADJECTIVE
sacred

sage ADJECTIVE
1 *good* (*well-behaved*) ◇ *Sois sage.* Be good.
2 *wise* (*sensible*) ◇ *Il serait plus sage d'attendre.* It would be wiser to wait.

la **sagesse** NOUN
wisdom ◇ *Il a eu la sagesse de ne pas y aller.* He wisely didn't go.
➔ **une dent de sagesse** a wisdom tooth

le **Sagittaire** NOUN
Sagittarius ◇ *Michèle est Sagittaire.* Michèle is Sagittarius.

saignant ADJECTIVE
rare (*meat*)

saigner VERB
to bleed
➔ **saigner du nez** to have a nosebleed

sain ADJECTIVE
healthy
➔ **sain et sauf** safe and sound

saint ADJECTIVE
see also saint NOUN
holy ◇ *la semaine sainte* Holy Week ◇ *le Saint-Esprit* the Holy Spirit
➔ **la Sainte Vierge** the Blessed Virgin
➔ **le vendredi saint** Good Friday

le **saint** NOUN
see also saint ADJECTIVE
saint

la **sainte** NOUN
saint

sais VERB *see* **savoir**
➔ **Je ne sais pas.** I don't know.

saisir VERB
to take hold of
➔ **saisir l'occasion de faire quelque chose** to seize the opportunity to do something

la **saison** NOUN
season ◇ *Ce n'est pas la saison des fraises.* Strawberries are out of season. ◇ *un temps de saison* seasonable weather
➔ **la saison des vendanges** harvest time

sait VERB *see* **savoir**
➔ **Il sait que...** He knows that...

la **salade** NOUN
1 *lettuce*
2 *salad* ◇ *une salade composée* a mixed salad ◇ *une salade de fruits* a fruit salad

le **saladier** NOUN
salad bowl

le **salaire** NOUN
salary

le **salarié** NOUN
salaried employee

la **salariée** NOUN
salaried employee

le **salaud** NOUN (*rude*)
bastard

sale ADJECTIVE
dirty

salé ADJECTIVE
1 *salty* ◇ *La soupe est trop salée.* The soup's too salty.
2 *salted* ◇ *du beurre salé* salted butter
3 *savoury* ◇ *des biscuits salés* savoury biscuits

saler VERB
to put salt in ◇ *J'ai oublié de saler la soupe.* I forgot to put salt in the soup.

la **saleté** NOUN
dirt ◇ *J'ai horreur de la saleté.* I hate dirt. ◇ *Il y a une saleté sur ta chemise.* There's some dirt on your shirt.
➔ **faire des saletés** to make a mess

salir VERB
➔ **salir quelque chose** to get something dirty
➔ **se salir** to get oneself dirty ◇ *Mets un tablier, sinon tu vas te salir.* Put on an

apron or you'll get yourself dirty.

alle NOUN
1 *room*
2 *audience* ◇ *Toute la salle l'a applaudi.* The whole audience applauded him.
3 *ward* (*in hospital*) ◇ *Il est à la salle douze.* He's in Ward 12.
- **la salle à manger** the dining room
- **la salle de séjour** the living room
- **la salle de bains** the bathroom
- **la salle d'attente** the waiting room
- **une salle de classe** a classroom
- **une salle de concert** a concert hall
- **la salle d'embarquement** the departure lounge

salon NOUN
lounge
- **un salon de thé** a tearoom
- **un salon de coiffure** a hair salon
- **un salon de beauté** a beauty salon

salope NOUN (*rude*)
bitch

salopette NOUN
1 *dungarees*
2 *overalls*

saluer VERB
- **saluer quelqu'un (1)** to say hello to somebody ◇ *Je l'ai croisé dans la rue et il m'a salué.* I met him in the street and he said hello.
- **saluer quelqu'un (2)** to say goodbye to somebody ◇ *Il nous a salués et il est parti.* He said goodbye and left.

salut EXCLAMATION (*informal*)
Hi!

samedi NOUN
1 *Saturday* ◇ *Aujourd'hui, nous sommes samedi.* It's Saturday today.
2 *on Saturday* ◇ *Nous sommes allés au cinéma samedi.* We went to the cinema on Saturday.
- **le samedi** on Saturdays ◇ *Le magasin ferme à dix-huit heures le samedi.* The shop closes at 6 p.m. on Saturdays.
- **tous les samedis** every Saturday
- **samedi dernier** last Saturday
- **samedi prochain** next Saturday

SAMU NOUN
ambulance service

sandale NOUN
sandal

sang NOUN
blood
- **en sang** covered in blood

sang-froid NOUN
- **garder son sang-froid** to keep calm
- **perdre son sang-froid** to lose one's cool
- **faire quelque chose de sang-froid** to do something in cold blood

le **sanglier** NOUN
wild boar

le **sanglot** NOUN
- **éclater en sanglots** to burst into tears

la **Sanisette** ® NOUN
Superloo ®

sans PREPOSITION
without ◇ *Elle est venue sans son frère.* She came without her brother.
- **un pull sans manches** a sleeveless sweater

le/la **sans-abri** NOUN
(PL les **sans-abri**)
homeless person ◇ *les sans-abri* the homeless

sans-gêne ADJECTIVE
inconsiderate

la **santé** NOUN
health ◇ *en bonne santé* in good health
- **Santé!** Cheers!

saoudien ADJECTIVE, NOUN
(FEM SING **saoudienne**)
Saudi Arabian
- **un Saoudien** a Saudi Arabian (*man*)
- **une Saoudienne** a Saudi Arabian (*woman*)

le **sapeur-pompier** NOUN
(PL les **sapeurs-pompiers**)
fireman
- **les sapeurs-pompiers** the fire brigade

le **sapin** NOUN
fir tree
- **un sapin de Noël** a Christmas tree

la **Sardaigne** NOUN
Sardinia

satisfaire VERB
to satisfy

satisfaisant ADJECTIVE
satisfactory

satisfait ADJECTIVE
satisfied ◇ *être satisfait de quelque chose* to be satisfied with something

la **sauce** NOUN
1 *sauce*
2 *gravy*

la **saucisse** NOUN
sausage

le **saucisson** NOUN
salami

sauf PREPOSITION
except ◇ *Tout le monde est venu sauf lui.* Everyone came except him.
- **sauf si** unless ◇ *Nous irons pique-niquer, sauf s'il fait mauvais.* We'll go for a picnic, unless the weather's bad.
- **sauf que** except that ◇ *Tout s'est bien passé, sauf que nous sommes arrivés en*

PTO

retard. Everything went OK, except that we arrived late.

le **saumon** NOUN
salmon

saur ADJECTIVE
- **un hareng saur** a kipper

le **saut** NOUN
jump
- **le saut en longueur** the long jump
- **le saut en hauteur** the high jump
- **le saut à la perche** the pole vault
- **le saut à l'élastique** bungee jumping
- **un saut périlleux** a somersault

sauter VERB
to jump ◇ *Nous avons sauté par-dessus la barrière.* We jumped over the gate.
- **sauter à la corde** to skip (*with a rope*)
- **faire sauter quelque chose** to blow something up ◇ *On a fait sauter le commissariat de police la nuit dernière.* The police station was blown up last night.

la **sauterelle** NOUN
grasshopper

sauvage ADJECTIVE
1 *wild* ◇ *les animaux sauvages* wild animals ◇ *faire du camping sauvage* to camp in the wild
- **une région sauvage** an unspoiled area

2 *shy* ◇ *Il est un peu sauvage.* He's a bit shy.

sauver VERB
to save
- **se sauver (1)** to run away ◇ *Il s'est sauvé à toutes jambes.* He ran away as fast as he could.
- **se sauver (2)** (*informal*) to be off ◇ *Allez, je me sauve!* Right, I'm off.

le **sauvetage** NOUN
rescue

le **sauveur** NOUN
saviour

savais, savait VERB *see* **savoir**
- **Je ne savais pas qu'il devait venir.** I didn't know he was going to come.

le **savant** NOUN
scientist

savent VERB *see* **savoir**
- **Ils ne savent pas ce qu'ils veulent.** They don't know what they want.

la **saveur** NOUN
flavour

savez VERB *see* **savoir**
- **Est-ce que vous savez où elle habite?** Do you know where she lives?

savoir VERB
to know ◇ *Je ne sais pas où il est allé.* I don't know where he's gone. ◇ *Nous ne savons pas s'il est bien arrivé.* We don't know if he's arrived safely. ◇ *Tu savais que Canberra était la capitale de l'Australie?* Did you know that Canberra was the capital of Australia? ◇ *Il ne sait pas ce qu'il va faire ce week-end.* He doesn't know what he's going to do this weekend.
- **Tu sais nager?** Can you swim?

le **savon** NOUN
soap

la **savonnette** NOUN
bar of soap

savons VERB *see* **savoir**

savoureux ADJECTIVE
(FEM SING **savoureuse**)
tasty

le **saxo** NOUN (*informal*)
see also la saxo
1 *sax*
2 *sax player*

la **saxo** NOUN (*informal*)
see also le saxo
sax player

le **scandale** NOUN
scandal
- **faire scandale** to cause a scandal ◇ *Ce film a fait scandale.* The film caused a scandal.

scandaleux ADJECTIVE
(FEM SING **scandaleuse**)
outrageous

le/la **Scandinave** NOUN
Scandinavian

scandinave ADJECTIVE
Scandinavian

la **Scandinavie** NOUN
Scandinavia

le **scarabée** NOUN
beetle

la **scène** NOUN
scene ◇ *une scène d'amour* a love scene ◇ *la scène du crime* the scene of the crime ◇ *Il m'a fait une scène.* He made a scene.
- **une scène de ménage** a domestic row

sceptique ADJECTIVE
sceptical

le **schéma** NOUN
diagram

schématique ADJECTIVE
- **l'explication schématique d'une théorie** the broad outline of a theory
- **Cette interprétation est un peu trop schématique.** This interpretation is a bit oversimplified.

la **scie** NOUN
saw
- **une scie à métaux** a hacksaw

science NOUN
science
les sciences physiques physics
les sciences naturelles biology
sciences po (*informal*) politics ◇ *Mon frère fait sciences po à Paris.* My brother is studying politics in Paris.

scientifique ADJECTIVE
see also scientifique NOUN
scientific

scientifique NOUN
see also scientifique ADJECTIVE
1 *scientist*
2 *science student*

scier VERB
to saw

scolaire ADJECTIVE
school ◇ *l'année scolaire* the school year ◇ *les vacances scolaires* the school holidays ◇ *mon livret scolaire* my school report

Scorpion NOUN
Scorpio ◇ *Catherine est Scorpion.* Catherine is Scorpio.

Scotch ® NOUN
adhesive tape

scrupule NOUN
scruple

sculpter VERB
to sculpt

sculpteur NOUN
sculptor

sculpture NOUN
sculpture

SDF NOUN (= *sans domicile fixe*)
homeless person
◆ **les SDF** the homeless

se PRONOUN
se *forms part of reflexive constructions.*
1 *himself* ◇ *Il se regarde dans la glace.* He's looking at himself in the mirror.
2 *herself* ◇ *Elle se regarde dans la glace.* She's looking at herself in the mirror.
3 *itself* ◇ *Le chien s'est fait mal.* The dog hurt itself.
4 *oneself* ◇ *se regarder dans une glace* to look at oneself in a mirror
5 *themselves* ◇ *Ils se sont regardés dans la glace.* They looked at themselves in the mirror.
se *changes to* **s'** *before a vowel and most words beginning with "h".*
◇ *Elle s'admire dans sa nouvelle robe.* She's admiring herself in her new dress.
6 *each other* ◇ *Ils s'aiment.* They love each other.

séance NOUN
1 *session* ◇ *une séance de rééducation* a physiotherapy session
2 *showing* (*at the cinema*) ◇ *La prochaine séance est à dix-neuf heures.* The next showing is at 7 p.m.

le **seau** NOUN
(PL les **seaux**)
bucket

sec ADJECTIVE
(FEM SING **sèche**)
1 *dry* ◇ *Mon jean n'est pas encore sec.* My jeans aren't dry yet.
2 *dried* ◇ *des figues sèches* dried figs

le **sèche-cheveux** NOUN
(PL les **sèche-cheveux**)
hair dryer

le **sèche-linge** NOUN
(PL les **sèche-linge**)
tumble dryer

sécher VERB
1 *to dry*
2 *to be stumped* ◇ *J'ai complètement séché à l'interro de maths.* (*informal*) I was completely stumped in the maths test.
◆ **se sécher** to dry oneself ◇ *Sèche-toi avec cette serviette.* Dry yourself with this towel.

la **sécheresse** NOUN
drought ◇ *une terrible sécheresse* a terrible drought

second ADJECTIVE
see also second NOUN
second ◇ *Il est arrivé second.* He came second.

le **second** NOUN
see also second ADJECTIVE
second floor ◇ *Elle habite au second.* She lives on the second floor.

secondaire ADJECTIVE
secondary ◇ *l'enseignement secondaire* secondary education
◆ **des effets secondaires** side effects

la **seconde** NOUN
1 *second* ◇ *Attends une seconde!* Wait a second!
2 *fifth year*
In French secondary schools, years are counted from the sixième *(youngest) to* première *and* terminale *(oldest).*
◇ *Ma sœur est en seconde.* My sister's in fifth year.
3 *second class* ◇ *voyager en seconde* to travel second-class

secouer VERB
to shake ◇ *secouer la tête* to shake one's head

secourir VERB
to rescue

S

le **secourisme** NOUN
first aid ◇ *J'ai un brevet de secourisme.* I've got a first aid qualification.

le **secours** NOUN
help ◇ *Il est allé chercher du secours.* He went to get help. ◇ *Au secours!* Help!
- **les premiers secours** first aid
- **une sortie de secours** an emergency exit
- **la roue de secours** the spare wheel

le **secret** NOUN
see also secret ADJECTIVE
secret

secret ADJECTIVE
(FEM SING **secrète**)
see also secret NOUN
secret

le **secrétaire** NOUN
see also la secrétaire
1 *secretary*
2 *writing desk*

la **secrétaire** NOUN
see also le secrétaire
secretary

le **secrétariat** NOUN
secretary's office

le **secteur** NOUN
sector ◇ *le secteur public* the public sector ◇ *le secteur privé* the private sector

la **sécu** NOUN (*informal*)
Social Security

la **sécurité** NOUN
1 *safety*
- **être en sécurité** to be safe ◇ *On ne se sent pas en sécurité dans ce quartier.* You don't feel safe in this neighbourhood.
- **la sécurité routière** road safety
- **une ceinture de sécurité** a seatbelt

2 *security* ◇ *par mesure de sécurité* as a security measure
- **la sécurité sociale** Social Security
- **la sécurité de l'emploi** job security

séduisant ADJECTIVE
attractive

le **seigle** NOUN
rye ◇ *un pain de seigle* a loaf of rye bread

le **seigneur** NOUN
lord
- **le Seigneur** the Lord

le **sein** NOUN
breast
- **au sein de** within ◇ *Chaque pays est autonome au sein de l'Europe.* Each country is independent within Europe.

seize NUMBER
sixteen ◇ *Elle a seize ans.* She's sixteen. ◇ *à seize heures* at 4 p.m.
- **le seize février** the sixteenth of February

seizième ADJECTIVE
sixteenth

le **séjour** NOUN
stay ◇ *J'ai fait un séjour d'une semaine en Italie.* I stayed in Italy for a week.

le **sel** NOUN
salt

sélectionner VERB
to select

le **self** NOUN (*informal*)
self-service restaurant

le **self-service** NOUN
self-service restaurant

la **selle** NOUN
saddle

selon PREPOSITION
according to ◇ *selon lui* according to him ◇ *selon mon humeur* according to what mood I'm in ◇ *Ils sont répartis selon leur âge.* They're divided up according to age.

la **semaine** NOUN
week
- **en semaine** on weekdays

semblable ADJECTIVE
similar

le **semblant** NOUN
- **faire semblant de faire quelque chose** to pretend to do something ◇ *Il fait semblant de dormir.* He's pretending to be asleep.

sembler VERB
to seem ◇ *Le temps semble s'améliorer.* The weather seems to be improving. ◇ *Il me semble inutile de s'en inquiéter.* It seems pointless to me to worry about it.

la **semelle** NOUN
1 *sole*
2 *insole*

la **semoule** NOUN
semolina

le **sens** NOUN
1 *sense* ◇ *avoir le sens de l'humour* to have a sense of humour ◇ *Je n'ai pas le sens de l'orientation.* I've got no sense of direction. ◇ *Ça n'a pas de sens.* It doesn't make sense.
- **le bon sens** common sense

2 *direction* ◇ *Tu tournes la poignée dans le mauvais sens.* You're turning the handle in the wrong direction.
- **sens dessus dessous** upside down
- **un sens interdit** a one-way street

◇ *J'ai failli prendre un sens interdit.* I nearly went the wrong way down a one-way street.

un sens unique a one-way street

ensé ADJECTIVE
sensible

ensible ADJECTIVE
1 *sensitive* ◇ *Elle est très sensible.* She's very sensitive. ◇ *Ce film est déconseillé aux personnes sensibles.* This film contains scenes which some viewers may find disturbing.
2 *visible* ◇ *une amélioration sensible* a visible improvement

ensiblement ADVERB
1 *visibly* ◇ *Elle a sensiblement progressé.* She's made visible progress.
2 *approximately* ◇ *Nous sommes sensiblement de la même taille.* We're approximately the same height.

entence NOUN
sentence (*judgement*)

entier NOUN
path

entiment NOUN
feeling

entimental ADJECTIVE
(MASC PL **sentimentaux**)
sentimental

entir VERB
1 *to smell* ◇ *Ça sent bon.* That smells good. ◇ *Ça sent mauvais.* It smells bad.
2 *to smell of* ◇ *Ça sent les frites ici.* It smells of chips in here.
3 *to taste* ◇ *Est-ce que tu sens l'ail dans le rôti?* Can you taste the garlic in the roast?
4 *to feel* ◇ *Ça t'a fait mal?–Non, je n'ai rien senti.* Did it hurt?–No, I didn't feel a thing. ◇ *Je ne me sens pas bien.* I don't feel well.

◆ **Il ne peut pas la sentir.** (*informal*) He can't stand her.

éparé ADJECTIVE
separated ◇ *Mes parents sont séparés.* My parents are separated.

éparément ADVERB
separately

éparer VERB
to separate ◇ *Séparez le blanc du jaune.* Separate the yolk from the white.

◆ **se séparer** to separate ◇ *Mes parents se sont séparés l'année dernière.* My parents separated last year.

ept NUMBER
seven ◇ *Il est arrivé à sept heures.* He arrived at seven o'clock. ◇ *Elle a sept ans.* She's seven.

◆ **le sept février** the seventh of February

septembre MASC NOUN
September

◆ **en septembre** in September

le **septennat** NOUN
le septennat *is the seven-year term of office of the French President.*

septième ADJECTIVE
seventh ◇ *au septième étage* on the seventh floor

sera, serai, seras, serez VERB *see* **être**

◆ **Je serai de retour à dix heures.** I'll be back at 10 o'clock.

la **série** NOUN
series

sérieusement ADVERB
seriously

sérieux ADJECTIVE
(FEM SING **sérieuse**)
see also sérieux NOUN
1 *serious* ◇ *Il plaisantait?–Non, il était sérieux.* Was he joking?–No, he was serious.
2 *responsible* ◇ *C'est un employé très sérieux.* He's a very responsible employee.

le **sérieux** NOUN
see also sérieux ADJECTIVE

◆ **garder son sérieux** to keep a straight face ◇ *J'ai eu du mal à garder mon sérieux.* I had trouble keeping a straight face.

◆ **prendre quelque chose au sérieux** to take something seriously

◆ **prendre quelqu'un au sérieux** to take somebody seriously

◆ **Il manque un peu de sérieux.** He's not very responsible.

la **seringue** NOUN
syringe

séronégatif ADJECTIVE
(FEM SING **séronégative**)
HIV-negative

serons, seront VERB *see* **être**

séropositif ADJECTIVE
(FEM SING **séropositive**)
HIV-positive

le **serpent** NOUN
snake

la **serre** NOUN
greenhouse

◆ **l'effet de serre** the greenhouse effect

serré ADJECTIVE
1 *tight* ◇ *Mon pantalon est trop serré.* My trousers are too tight.
2 *close-fought* ◇ *Ça a été un match serré.* It was a close-fought game.

serrer VERB

PTO

- **Ce pantalon me serre trop.** These trousers are too tight for me.
- **serrer la main à quelqu'un** to shake hands with somebody
- **se serrer** to squeeze up ◇ *Serrez-vous un peu pour que je puisse m'asseoir.* Squeeze up a bit so I can sit down.
- **serrer quelqu'un dans ses bras** to hug somebody

la **serrure** NOUN
lock

sers, sert VERB *see* **servir**

le **serveur** NOUN
waiter

la **serveuse** NOUN
waitress

serviable ADJECTIVE
helpful

le **service** NOUN
1 *service* (*in restaurant*) ◇ *Le service est compris.* Service is included.
- **être de service** to be on duty
- **hors service** out of order
- **faire le service** to serve (*at table*) ◇ *Tu peux faire le service s'il te plaît?* Could you serve please?

2 *favour* ◇ *rendre service à quelqu'un* to do somebody a favour ◇ *Est-ce que je peux te demander un service?* Can I ask you a favour?
3 *serve* (*sport*) ◇ *Il a un bon service.* He's got a good serve.
- **le service militaire** military service
- **les services sociaux** the social services
- **les services secrets** the secret service

la **serviette** NOUN
1 *towel* ◇ *une serviette de bain* a bath towel
- **une serviette hygiénique** a sanitary towel

2 *serviette* (*napkin*)
3 *briefcase*

servir VERB
to serve ◇ *On vous sert?* Are you being served?
- **À toi de servir.** (*tennis*) It's your serve.
- **se servir** to help oneself ◇ *Servez-vous.* Help yourself.
- **se servir de** to use ◇ *Tu te sers souvent de ton vélo?* Do you use your bike a lot?
- **servir à quelqu'un** to be of use to somebody ◇ *Ça m'a beaucoup servi.* It was very useful.
- **À quoi ça sert?** What's it for?
- **Ça ne sert à rien.** It's no use. ◇ *Ça ne sert à rien d'insister.* It's no use insisting.

ses ADJECTIVE
1 *his* ◇ *Il est parti voir ses grands-parents.* He's gone to see his grandparents.
2 *her* ◇ *Delphine a oublié ses baskets* Delphine's forgotten her trainers.
3 *its* ◇ *la ville et ses alentours* the town and its surroundings

seul ADJECTIVE, ADVERB
1 *alone* ◇ *vivre seul* to live alone
2 *by oneself* ◇ *Elle est venue seule.* She came by herself.
- **faire quelque chose tout seul** to do something by oneself ◇ *Elle a fait ça toute seule?* Did she do it by herself?
- **se sentir seul** to feel lonely
- **un seul livre** one book only ◇ *Vous avez droit à un seul livre.* You're entitled to one book only.
- **Il reste une seule nectarine.** There's only one nectarine left.
- **le seul livre que...** the only book that... ◇ *C'est le seul Agatha Christie que je n'aie pas lu.* That's the only Agatha Christie I haven't read.
- **le seul** the only one ◇ *C'est la seule que je ne connaisse pas.* She's the only one I don't know.

seulement ADVERB
only
- **non seulement...mais** not only...but ◇ *Non seulement il a plu, mais en plus il a fait froid.* Not only did it rain, but it was cold as well.

sévère ADJECTIVE
strict ◇ *Mon prof de maths est très sévère.* My maths teacher is very strict.

sexuel ADJECTIVE
(FEM SING **sexuelle**)
sexual ◇ *la discrimination sexuelle* sexual discrimination ◇ *l'éducation sexuelle* sex education

le **shampooing** NOUN
shampoo
- **se faire un shampooing** to wash one's hair

le **short** NOUN
shorts ◇ *Il était en short.* He was wearing shorts.

le **si** NOUN
see also **si** CONJUNCTION
1 *B* ◇ *en si bémol* in B flat
2 *ti* ◇ *la, si, do* la, ti, do

si CONJUNCTION, ADVERB
see also **si** NOUN
1 *if* ◇ *si tu veux* if you like ◇ *Je me demande si elle va venir.* I wonder if she'll come. ◇ *si seulement* if only
2 *so* ◇ *Elle est si gentille.* She's so kind. ◇ *Tout s'est passé si vite.*

Everything happened so fast.
3 *yes* ◇ *Tu n'es pas allé à l'école habillé comme ça?–Si.* You didn't go to school dressed like that?–Yes I did.

Sicile NOUN
Sicily

sida NOUN
AIDS ◇ *Il a le sida.* He's got AIDS.

siècle NOUN
century ◇ *le vingtième siècle* the twentieth century

siège NOUN
1 *seat* (*in vehicle*)
2 *head office*

sien PRONOUN
- **le sien (1)** his ◇ *C'est le vélo de Paul?–Oui, c'est le sien.* Is this Paul's bike?–Yes, it's his.
- **le sien (2)** hers ◇ *C'est le vélo d'Isabelle?–Oui, c'est le sien.* Is this Isabelle's bike?–Yes, it's hers.

sienne PRONOUN
- **la sienne (1)** his ◇ *C'est la montre de Paul?–Oui, c'est la sienne.* Is this Paul's watch?–Yes, it's his.
- **la sienne (2)** hers ◇ *C'est la montre d'Isabelle?–Oui, c'est la sienne.* Is this Isabelle's watch?–Yes, it's hers.

siennes PRONOUN
- **les siennes (1)** his ◇ *Ce sont les cassettes de Christian?–Oui, ce sont les siennes.* Are these Christian's cassettes?–Yes, they're his.
- **les siennes (2)** hers ◇ *Ce sont les lunettes de Daphne?–Oui, ce sont les siennes.* Are these Daphne's glasses?–Yes, they're hers.

siens PRONOUN
- **les siens (1)** his ◇ *Ce sont les sandwichs de Pierre?–Oui, ce sont les siens.* Are these Pierre's sandwiches?–Yes, they're his.
- **les siens (2)** hers ◇ *Ce sont les sandwichs de Justine?–Oui, ce sont les siens.* Are these Justine's sandwiches?–Yes, they're hers.

sieste NOUN
nap ◇ *faire la sieste* to have a nap

siffler VERB
to whistle

sifflet NOUN
whistle

sigle NOUN
acronym

signal NOUN
(PL les **signaux**)
signal

signe NOUN
sign
- **faire un signe de la main** to wave
- **faire signe à quelqu'un d'entrer** to beckon to somebody to come in

signer VERB
to sign

la **signification** NOUN
meaning

signifier VERB
to mean ◇ *Que signifie ce mot?* What does this word mean?

le **silence** NOUN
silence
- **Silence!** Be quiet!

silencieux ADJECTIVE
(FEM SING **silencieuse**)
1 *silent* ◇ *Elle est restée silencieuse.* She remained silent.
2 *quiet* ◇ *C'est très silencieux ici.* It's very quiet here.

la **silhouette** NOUN
figure ◇ *J'ai vu une silhouette dans le brouillard.* I saw a figure in the mist.

similaire ADJECTIVE
similar

le **simple** NOUN
singles (*tennis*) ◇ *le simple messieurs* the men's singles ◇ *le simple dames* the ladies' singles

simuler VERB
to simulate

simultané ADJECTIVE
simultaneous

sincère ADJECTIVE
sincere

la **sincérité** NOUN
sincerity

le **singe** NOUN
monkey

le **singulier** NOUN
singular ◇ *au féminin singulier* in the feminine singular

sinistre ADJECTIVE
sinister

sinon CONJUNCTION
otherwise ◇ *Dépêche-toi, sinon je pars sans toi.* Hurry up, otherwise I'll leave without you.

la **sinusite** NOUN
sinusitis ◇ *avoir de la sinusite* to have sinusitis

la **sirène** NOUN
mermaid
- **la sirène d'alarme** the fire alarm

le **sirop** NOUN
syrup
- **le sirop contre la toux** cough mixture

le **site** NOUN
setting ◇ *un site très sauvage* a totally unspoiled setting

PTO

- **un site pittoresque** a beauty spot
- **un site touristique** a tourist attraction
- **un site archéologique** an archaeological site

sitôt ADVERB
- **sitôt dit, sitôt fait** no sooner said than done
- **pas de sitôt** not for a long time ◇ *On ne le reverra pas de sitôt.* We won't see him again for a long time.

la **situation** NOUN
1 *situation*
- **la situation de famille** marital status

2 *job* ◇ *Il a une belle situation.* He's got a good job.

se **situer** VERB
to be situated ◇ *Versailles se situe à l'ouest de Paris.* Versailles is situated to the west of Paris.
- **bien situé** well situated

six NUMBER
six ◇ *Il est rentré à six heures.* He got back at six o'clock. ◇ *Il a six ans.* He's six.
- **le six février** the sixth of February

sixième ADJECTIVE
see also sixième NOUN
sixth ◇ *au sixième étage* on the sixth floor

la **sixième** NOUN
see also sixième ADJECTIVE
first year
In French secondary schools, years are counted from the sixième *(youngest) to* première *and* terminale *(oldest).*
◇ *Mon frère est en sixième.* My brother's in first year.

le **ski** NOUN
1 *ski* ◇ *J'ai loué des skis.* I hired skis.
2 *skiing* ◇ *J'adore le ski.* I love skiing. ◇ *faire du ski* to go skiing
- **le ski de fond** cross-country skiing
- **le ski nautique** water-skiing
- **le ski de piste** downhill skiing
- **le ski de randonnée** cross-country skiing

skier VERB
to ski

le **skieur** NOUN
skier

la **skieuse** NOUN
skier

le **slip** NOUN
pants
- **un slip de bain** swimming trunks

la **Slovaquie** NOUN
Slovakia

la **Slovénie** NOUN
Slovenia

le **SMIC** NOUN
guaranteed minimum wage ◇ *Il touche le SMIC.* He's on the legal minimum wage.

le **smoking** NOUN
dinner suit

la **SNCF** NOUN (= *Société nationale des chemins de fer français*)
French railways

snob ADJECTIVE
(FEM SING **snob**)
snobbish

sobre ADJECTIVE
1 *sober*
2 *plain* ◇ *C'est une veste très sobre.* It's a very plain jacket.

social ADJECTIVE
(MASC PL **sociaux**)
social

le/la **socialiste** NOUN
socialist

la **société** NOUN
1 *society*
2 *company* ◇ *une société d'ingénierie* an engineering company

la **sociologie** NOUN
sociology

la **socquette** NOUN
ankle sock

la **sœur** NOUN
sister
- **une bonne sœur** (*informal*) a nun

soi PRONOUN
oneself ◇ *avoir confiance en soi* to have confidence in oneself
- **rester chez soi** to stay at home
- **Ça va de soi.** It goes without saying.

soi-disant ADVERB, ADJECTIVE
supposedly ◇ *Il était soi-disant parti à Paris.* He had supposedly left for Paris.
- **un soi-disant poète** a so-called poet

la **soie** NOUN
silk

la **soif** NOUN
thirst
- **avoir soif** to be thirsty

soigner VERB
to look after (*ill person, animal*)
◇ *Soigne-toi bien ce week-end!* Take good care of yourself this weekend!

soigneux ADJECTIVE
(FEM SING **soigneuse**)
careful ◇ *Tu devrais être plus soigneux avec tes livres.* You should be more careful with your books.

soi-même PRONOUN
oneself ◇ *Il vaut mieux le faire soi-même.* It's better to do it oneself.

le **soin** NOUN

care
- **prendre soin de quelque chose** to take care of something ◇ *Prends bien soin de ce livre.* Take good care of this book.

soins MASC NOUN
treatment
les premiers soins first aid
- **"aux bons soins de Madame Martin"** (*on letter*) "c/o Mrs Martin"

soir NOUN
evening ◇ *ce soir* this evening
- **demain soir** tomorrow night
hier soir last night

soirée NOUN
evening ◇ *en tenue de soirée* in evening dress

sois VERB *see* **être**
- **Sois tranquille!** Be quiet!

soit CONJUNCTION
- **soit..., soit...** either...or... ◇ *soit lundi, soit mardi* either Monday or Tuesday

soixantaine NOUN
about sixty ◇ *une soixantaine de personnes* about sixty people
- **Elle a la soixantaine.** She's in her sixties.

soixante NUMBER
sixty ◇ *Il a soixante ans.* He's sixty.
◇ *soixante et un* sixty-one
◇ *soixante-deux* sixty-two
- **soixante et onze** seventy-one
- **soixante-quinze** seventy-five

soixante-dix NUMBER
seventy ◇ *Il a soixante-dix ans.* He's seventy.

soja NOUN
soya
- **des germes de soja** beansprouts

sol NOUN
1 *floor* ◇ *un sol carrelé* a tiled floor
- **à même le sol** on the floor
2 *soil* ◇ *sur le sol français* on French soil
3 *G* ◇ *sol dièse* G sharp
4 *so* ◇ *do, ré, mi, fa, sol...* do, re, mi, fa, so...

solaire ADJECTIVE
solar ◇ *le système solaire* the solar system
- **la crème solaire** sun cream

soldat NOUN
soldier

solde NOUN
- **être en solde** to be reduced ◇ *Les chemisiers sont en solde.* The blouses are reduced.
- **les soldes** the sales ◇ *faire les soldes* to go round the sales ◇ *les soldes de janvier* the January sales

soldé ADJECTIVE
- **être soldé** to be reduced ◇ *un article soldé à dix francs* an item reduced to 10 francs

la **sole** NOUN
sole (*fish*)

le **soleil** NOUN
sun ◇ *au soleil* in the sun
- **Il y a du soleil.** It's sunny.

le **solfège** NOUN
musical theory ◇ *Il joue du violon sans connaître le solfège.* He plays the violin but he can't read music.

solidaire ADJECTIVE
- **être solidaire de quelqu'un** to back somebody up

solide ADJECTIVE
1 *strong* (*person*)
2 *solid* (*object*)

solitaire ADJECTIVE
see also solitaire NOUN
solitary

le/la **solitaire** NOUN
see also solitaire ADJECTIVE
loner

la **solitude** NOUN
loneliness

la **solution** NOUN
solution
- **une solution de facilité** an easy way out

sombre ADJECTIVE
dark

la **somme** NOUN
see also le somme
sum

le **somme** NOUN
see also la somme
nap ◇ *faire un somme* to take a nap

le **sommeil** NOUN
sleep
- **avoir sommeil** to be sleepy

sommes VERB *see* **être**
- **Nous sommes en vacances.** We're on holiday.

le **sommet** NOUN
summit

le **somnifère** NOUN
sleeping pill

somptueux ADJECTIVE
(FEM SING **somptueuse**)
sumptuous

son ADJECTIVE
(FEM SING **sa**, PL **ses**)
see also son NOUN
1 *his* ◇ *son père* his father ◇ *Il a perdu son portefeuille.* He's lost his wallet.
2 *her* ◇ *son père* her father ◇ *Elle a*

PTO

perdu son sac. She's lost her bag.

le **son** NOUN

see also **son** ADJECTIVE

1 *sound* ◇ *Le son n'est pas très bon.* The sound's not very good. ◇ *baisser le son* to turn the sound down

2 *bran*

◆ **le pain de son** brown bread

le **sondage** NOUN

survey

◆ **un sondage d'opinion** an opinion poll

sonner VERB

to ring ◇ *On a sonné.* Somebody rang the doorbell. ◇ *Le téléphone a sonné.* The phone rang.

la **sonnerie** NOUN

bell (*electric*) ◇ *La sonnerie du téléphone l'a réveillé.* He was woken by the phone ringing.

la **sonnette** NOUN

bell ◇ *la sonnette d'alarme* the alarm bell

la **sono** NOUN (*informal*)

sound system

sont VERB *see* **être**

◆ **Ils sont en vacances.** They're on holiday.

sophistiqué ADJECTIVE

sophisticated

le **sort** NOUN

1 *spell* ◇ *jeter un sort à quelqu'un* to cast a spell on somebody

◆ **un mauvais sort** a curse

2 *fate* ◇ *abandonner quelqu'un à son triste sort* to leave somebody to their fate

◆ **tirer au sort** to draw lots

la **sorte** NOUN

sort ◇ *C'est une sorte de gâteau.* It's a sort of cake. ◇ *toutes sortes de choses* all sorts of things

la **sortie** NOUN

way out ◇ *Où est la sortie?* Where's the way out?

◆ **la sortie de secours** the emergency exit

◆ **Attends-moi à la sortie de l'école.** Meet me after school.

sortir VERB

1 *to go out* ◇ *Il est sorti sans rien dire.* He went out without saying a word. ◇ *Il est sorti acheter un journal.* He's gone out to buy a newspaper. ◇ *J'aime sortir.* I like going out.

2 *to come out* ◇ *Elle sort de l'hôpital demain.* She's coming out of hospital tomorrow. ◇ *Je l'ai rencontré en sortant de la pharmacie.* I met him coming out of the chemist's. ◇ *Ce modèle vient juste de sortir.* This model has just come out.

3 *to take out* ◇ *Elle a sorti son porte-monnaie de son sac.* She took her purse out of her handbag. ◇ *Je vais sortir la voiture du garage.* I'll get the car out of the garage.

◆ **sortir avec quelqu'un** to be going out with somebody ◇ *Tu sors avec lui?* Are you going out with him?

◆ **s'en sortir** to manage ◇ *Ne t'en fais pas, tu t'en sortiras.* Don't worry, you'll manage OK.

la **sottise** NOUN

◆ **Ne fais pas de sottises.** Don't do anything silly.

◆ **Ne dis pas de sottises.** Don't talk nonsense.

le **sou** NOUN

◆ **une machine à sous** a fruit machine

◆ **Je n'ai pas un sou sur moi.** I haven't got a penny on me.

◆ **être près de ses sous** (*informal*) to be tight-fisted

le **souci** NOUN

worry

◆ **se faire du souci** to worry

soucieux ADJECTIVE

(FEM SING **soucieuse**)

worried ◇ *Tu as l'air soucieux.* You look worried.

la **soucoupe** NOUN

saucer

◆ **une soucoupe volante** a flying saucer

soudain ADJECTIVE, ADVERB

1 *sudden* ◇ *une douleur soudaine* a sudden pain

2 *suddenly* ◇ *Soudain, il s'est fâché.* Suddenly, he got angry.

le **souffle** NOUN

breath

◆ **à bout de souffle** out of breath

le **soufflé** NOUN

soufflé ◇ *un soufflé au fromage* a cheese soufflé

souffler VERB

1 *to blow* ◇ *Le vent soufflait fort.* The wind was blowing hard.

2 *to blow out* ◇ *Souffle les bougies!* Blow out the candles!

la **souffrance** NOUN

suffering

souffrir VERB

to be in pain ◇ *Il souffre beaucoup.* He's in a lot of pain.

◆ **Il ne peux pas la souffrir.** (*informal*) He can't stand her.

le **souhait** NOUN

wish ◇ *faire un souhait* to make a wish ◇ *Tous nos souhaits de réussite.*

All our best wishes for your success.
◇ *les souhaits de bonne année* New Year's wishes
Atchoum! – À tes souhaits!
Atchoo! – Bless you!

souhaiter VERB
to wish ◇ *Il souhaite aller à l'université.* He wishes to go to university. ◇ *Nous vous souhaitons une bonne année.* We wish you a happy New Year.

soûl ADJECTIVE (*informal*)
drunk

soulager VERB
to relieve

soulever VERB
1 *to lift* ◇ *Je n'arrive pas à soulever cette valise.* I can't lift this suitcase.
2 *to raise* ◇ *Il faudra soulever la question lors de la réunion.* We'll have to raise the matter at the meeting.

soulier NOUN
shoe

souligner VERB
to underline

soupçon NOUN
suspicion
◆ **un soupçon de** a dash of ◇ *Ajoutez un soupçon de rhum.* Add a dash of rum.

soupçonner VERB
to suspect

soupe NOUN
soup

soupir NOUN
sigh

soupirer VERB
to sigh

souple ADJECTIVE
1 *supple* (*person*)
2 *flexible* (*system*)

source NOUN
spring ◇ *l'eau de source* spring water

sourcil NOUN
eyebrow

sourd ADJECTIVE
deaf

souriant ADJECTIVE
cheerful

sourire NOUN
see also sourire VERB
smile

sourire VERB
see also sourire NOUN
to smile ◇ *sourire à quelqu'un* to smile at somebody

souris NOUN
mouse

sournois ADJECTIVE
sly

sous PREPOSITION
under
◆ **sous terre** underground
◆ **sous la pluie** in the rain

sous-entendu ADJECTIVE
see also sous-entendu NOUN
implied

le **sous-entendu** NOUN
see also sous-entendu ADJECTIVE
insinuation

sous-marin ADJECTIVE
see also sous-marin NOUN
underwater

le **sous-marin** NOUN
see also sous-marin ADJECTIVE
submarine

le **sous-sol** NOUN
basement

le **sous-titre** NOUN
subtitle

sous-titré ADJECTIVE
with subtitles

la **soustraction** NOUN
subtraction

les **sous-vêtements** MASC NOUN
underwear SING

soutenir VERB
to support ◇ *Il m'a toujours soutenu contre elle.* He's always supported me against her.
◆ **soutenir que** to maintain that ◇ *Elle soutenait que c'était impossible.* She maintained that it was impossible.
◆ **soutenir l'allure** to keep up ◇ *Il marchait trop vite et je n'arrivais pas à soutenir l'allure.* He was walking too fast and I couldn't keep up.

souterrain ADJECTIVE
see also souterrain NOUN
underground

le **souterrain** NOUN
see also souterrain ADJECTIVE
underground passage

le **soutien** NOUN
support

le **soutien-gorge** NOUN
(PL les **soutiens-gorge**)
bra

le **souvenir** NOUN
see also se souvenir VERB
1 *memory* ◇ *garder un bon souvenir de quelque chose* to have happy memories of something
2 *souvenir* ◇ *un souvenir de Lourdes* a souvenir of Lourdes
◆ **Garde ce livre en souvenir de moi.** Keep the book: it'll remind you of me.

se **souvenir** VERB
see also souvenir NOUN
◆ **se souvenir de quelque chose** to

S

PTO

remember something ◇ *Je ne me souviens pas de son adresse.* I can't remember his address.

◆ **se souvenir que** to remember that ◇ *Je me souviens qu'il neigeait ce jour-là.* I remember it was snowing that day.

souvent ADVERB
often

soyez, soyons VERB *see* **être**

◆ **Soyons clairs!** Let's be clear about this!

spacieux ADJECTIVE
(FEM SING **spacieuse**)
spacious

les **spaghettis** MASC NOUN
spaghetti

le **sparadrap** NOUN
sticking plaster

le **speaker** NOUN
announcer

la **speakerine** NOUN
announcer

spécial ADJECTIVE
(MASC PL **spéciaux**)
1 *special* ◇ *Qu'est-ce que tu fais ce week-end? – Rien de spécial.* What are you doing this weekend? – Nothing special.
◆ **les effets spéciaux** special effects
2 *peculiar* ◇ *Elle a des goûts un peu spéciaux.* She has rather peculiar tastes.

spécialement ADVERB
1 *specially* ◇ *Il est venu spécialement pour te parler.* He came specially to speak to you.
2 *particularly* ◇ *Ce n'est pas spécialement difficile.* It's not particularly difficult.

se **spécialiser** VERB
◆ **se spécialiser dans quelque chose** to specialize in something ◇ *Je me suis spécialisé en histoire contemporaine.* I specialized in modern history.

le/la **spécialiste** NOUN
specialist

la **spécialité** NOUN
speciality

spécifier VERB
to specify

le **spectacle** NOUN
show

spectaculaire ADJECTIVE
spectacular

le **spectateur** NOUN
1 *member of the audience*
2 *spectator*

la **spectatrice** NOUN
1 *member of the audience*
2 *spectator*

la **spéléologie** NOUN
potholing

spirituel ADJECTIVE
1 *spiritual*
2 *witty*

splendide ADJECTIVE
magnificent

spontané ADJECTIVE
spontaneous

le **sport** NOUN
see also sport ADJECTIVE
sport ◇ *faire du sport* to do sport
◆ **les sports d'hiver** winter sports

sport ADJECTIVE (MASC, FEM, PL)
see also sport NOUN
casual ◇ *une veste sport* a casual jacket

sportif ADJECTIVE
(FEM SING **sportive**)
see also sportif NOUN
1 *sporty* ◇ *Elle est très sportive.* She's very sporty.
2 *sports* ◇ *un club sportif* a sports club

le **sportif** NOUN
see also sportif ADJECTIVE
sportsman

la **sportive** NOUN
sportswoman

le **spot** NOUN
spotlight
◆ **un spot publicitaire** a commercial break

le **square** NOUN
public gardens

le **squelette** NOUN
skeleton

stable ADJECTIVE
stable
◆ **un emploi stable** a steady job

le **stade** NOUN
stadium

le **stage** NOUN
training course

le/la **stagiaire** NOUN
see also stagiaire ADJECTIVE
trainee

stagiaire ADJECTIVE
see also stagiaire NOUN
trainee ◇ *un professeur stagiaire* a trainee teacher

le **stand** NOUN
1 *stand* (*at exhibition*)
2 *stall* (*at fair*)

le/la **standardiste** NOUN
operator

la **station** NOUN
◆ **une station de métro** an underground station
◆ **une station de taxis** a taxi rank

◆ **une station de ski** a ski resort
stationnement NOUN
parking
◆ **"stationnement interdit"** "no parking"
stationner VERB
to park
station-service NOUN
(PL les **stations-service**)
service station
statistique NOUN
statistic
steak NOUN
steak
◆ **un steak frites** steak and chips
◆ **un steak haché** a hamburger
sténo NOUN
shorthand ◇ *un cours de sténo* a shorthand course
sténodactylo NOUN
shorthand typist
stérile ADJECTIVE
sterile
stimulant ADJECTIVE
stimulating
stimuler VERB
to stimulate
stop NOUN
stop sign
◆ **faire du stop** to hitchhike
stopper VERB
to stop
store NOUN
1 *blind* (*on window*)
2 *awning*
strapontin NOUN
foldaway seat
stratégie NOUN
strategy
stratégique ADJECTIVE
strategic
stressant ADJECTIVE
stressful
strict ADJECTIVE
1 *strict* (*person*) ◇ *Ma prof de français est très stricte.* My French teacher's very strict.
2 *severe* (*clothes*) ◇ *une tenue très stricte* a very severe outfit
◆ **le strict minimum** the bare minimum
strophe NOUN
stanza
studieux ADJECTIVE
(FEM SING **studieuse**)
studious
studio NOUN
1 *studio flat*
2 *studio* ◇ *un studio de télévision* a television studio
stupéfait ADJECTIVE
astonished
les **stupéfiants** MASC NOUN
narcotics
stupéfier VERB
to astonish ◇ *Sa réponse m'a stupéfié.* I was astonished by his answer.
la **stupidité** NOUN
stupidity
le/la **styliste** NOUN
designer
le **stylo** NOUN
pen
◆ **un stylo plume** a fountain pen
◆ **un stylo bille** a ballpoint pen
◆ **un stylo-feutre** a felt-tip pen
su VERB *see* **savoir**
◆ **Si j'avais su...** If I'd known...
subir VERB
to suffer (*defeat*)
◆ **subir une opération** to have an operation
subit ADJECTIVE
sudden
subitement ADVERB
suddenly
subjectif ADJECTIVE
(FEM SING **subjective**)
subjective
le **subjonctif** NOUN
subjunctive
substituer VERB
to substitute ◇ *substituer un mot à un autre* to substitute one word for another
subtil ADJECTIVE
subtle
la **subvention** NOUN
subsidy
subventionner VERB
to subsidize
le **succès** NOUN
success ◇ *avoir du succès* to be successful
le **successeur** NOUN
successor
la **succursale** NOUN
branch (*of company*)
sucer VERB
to suck
la **sucette** NOUN
lollipop
le **sucre** NOUN
sugar
◆ **un sucre** a sugar-lump ◇ *Je prends deux sucres dans mon café.* I take two lumps of sugar in my coffee.
◆ **du sucre en morceaux** lump sugar
◆ **un sucre d'orge** a barley sugar
◆ **du sucre en poudre** caster sugar

PTO

- **du sucre glace** icing sugar

sucré ADJECTIVE
1 *sweet* ◇ *Ce gâteau est un peu trop sucré.* This cake is a bit too sweet.
2 *sweetened* ◇ *du lait concentré sucré* sweetened condensed milk

les **sucreries** FEM NOUN
sweet things

le **sucrier** NOUN
sugar bowl

le **sud** NOUN
see also **sud** ADJECTIVE
south ◇ *Ils vivent dans le sud de la France.* They live in the South of France.
- **vers le sud** southwards
- **au sud de Paris** south of Paris
- **l'Amérique du Sud** South America
- **le vent du sud** the south wind

sud ADJECTIVE
see also **sud** NOUN
1 *south* ◇ *la côte sud de l'Espagne* the south coast of Spain
- **le pôle sud** the South Pole

2 *southern* ◇ *Nous avons visité la partie sud du pays.* We visited the southern part of the country.

sud-africain ADJECTIVE
South African

sud-américain ADJECTIVE
South American

le **sud-est** NOUN
south-east ◇ *au sud-est* in the south-east

le **sud-ouest** NOUN
south-west ◇ *au sud-ouest* in the south-west

la **Suède** NOUN
Sweden

suédois ADJECTIVE, NOUN
(FEM SING **suédoise**)
Swedish ◇ *Ils parlent suédois.* They speak Swedish.
- **un Suédois** a Swede (*man*)
- **une Suédoise** a Swede (*woman*)
- **les Suédois** the Swedes

suer VERB
to sweat

la **sueur** NOUN
sweat
- **en sueur** sweating

suffire VERB
to be enough ◇ *Tiens, voilà dix francs. Ça te suffit?* Here's 10 francs. Is that enough for you?
- **Ça suffit!** That's enough!

suffisamment ADVERB
enough ◇ *Ça n'est pas suffisamment grand.* It's not big enough. ◇ *Il n'y a pas suffisamment de chaises.* There aren't enough chairs.

suffisant ADJECTIVE
1 *sufficient* ◇ *Ça n'est pas une raison suffisante.* That's not sufficient reason.
2 *smug* ◇ *Il est un peu trop suffisant.* He's rather smug.

suffoquer VERB
to suffocate

suggérer VERB
to suggest

se **suicider** VERB
to commit suicide

suis VERB *see* **être**, *see* **suivre**
- **Je suis écossais.** I'm Scottish.
- **Suis-moi.** Follow me.

suisse ADJECTIVE, NOUN
see also la Suisse
Swiss ◇ *le franc suisse* the Swiss franc
- **un Suisse** a Swiss man
- **une Suisse** a Swiss woman
- **les Suisses** the Swiss

la **Suisse** NOUN
see also **suisse** ADJECTIVE
Switzerland ◇ *la Suisse allemande* German-speaking Switzerland ◇ *la Suisse romande* French-speaking Switzerland

la **suite** NOUN
1 *rest* ◇ *Je vous raconterai la suite de l'histoire demain.* I'll tell you the rest of the story tomorrow.
2 *sequel* (*to book, film*)
- **tout de suite** straightaway ◇ *J'y vais tout de suite.* I'll go straightaway.
- **de suite** in succession ◇ *Il a commis la même erreur trois fois de suite.* He made the same mistake three times in succession.
- **par la suite** subsequently ◇ *Il s'est avéré par la suite qu'il était coupable.* He subsequently turned out to be guilty.

suivant ADJECTIVE
following ◇ *le jour suivant* the following day ◇ *l'exercice suivant* the following exercise
- **Au suivant!** Next!

suivre VERB
1 *to follow* ◇ *Il m'a suivie jusque chez moi.* He followed me home. ◇ *Vous me suivez ou est-ce que je parle trop vite?* Are you following me or am I speaking too fast?
2 *to do* ◇ *Je suis un cours d'anglais à la fac.* I'm doing an English course at college.
3 *to keep up* ◇ *Il n'arrive pas à suivre en maths.* He can't keep up in maths. ◇ *J'aime suivre l'actualité.* I like to keep

up with the news.
- **"à suivre"** "to be continued"
- **suivre un régime** to be on a diet

sujet ADJECTIVE
(FEM SING **sujette**)
see also sujet NOUN
- **être sujet à** to be prone to ◇ *Il est sujet au vertige.* He suffers from vertigo.

sujet NOUN
see also sujet ADJECTIVE
subject
- **au sujet de** about ◇ *C'est à quel sujet? – C'est au sujet de l'annonce parue dans "Le Monde" d'aujourd'hui.* What's it about? – It's about the advertisement in today's "Le Monde".
- **un sujet de conversation** a topic of conversation
- **un sujet d'examen** an examination question
- **un sujet de plaisanterie** something to joke about

super NOUN
4-star petrol

superficiel ADJECTIVE
(FEM SING **superficielle**)
superficial

superflu ADJECTIVE
superfluous

supérieur ADJECTIVE
see also supérieur NOUN
1 *upper* ◇ *la lèvre supérieure* the upper lip
2 *superior* ◇ *qualité supérieure* superior quality ◇ *Il a toujours l'air tellement supérieur!* He always looks so superior!
- **supérieur à** greater than ◇ *Choisissez un nombre supérieur à cent.* Choose a number greater than 100.

le **supérieur** NOUN
see also supérieur ADJECTIVE
superior ◇ *mon supérieur hiérarchique* my immediate superior

le **superlatif** NOUN
superlative

le **supermarché** NOUN
supermarket

superposé ADJECTIVE
- **des lits superposés** bunk beds

superstitieux ADJECTIVE
(FEM SING **superstitieuse**)
superstitious

le **suppléant** NOUN
supply teacher

la **suppléante** NOUN
supply teacher

le **supplément** NOUN
- **payer un supplément** to pay an additional charge
- **Le vin est en supplément.** Wine is extra.
- **un supplément de travail** extra work

supplémentaire ADJECTIVE
additional ◇ *Voici quelques exercices supplémentaires.* Here are some additional exercises.
- **faire des heures supplémentaires** to do overtime

le **supplice** NOUN
torture ◇ *C'était un supplice.* It was torture.

supplier VERB
- **supplier quelqu'un de faire quelque chose** to beg somebody to do something ◇ *Je t'en supplie!* I'm begging you!

supportable ADJECTIVE
bearable

supporter VERB
to stand (*tolerate*) ◇ *Je ne supporte pas l'hypocrisie.* I can't stand hypocrisy. ◇ *Elle ne supporte pas qu'on la critique.* She can't stand being criticized. ◇ *Je ne peux pas la supporter.* I can't stand her. ◇ *Je supporte mal la chaleur.* I can't stand hot weather.

supposer VERB
to suppose

supprimer VERB
1 *to cut* ◇ *Deux mille emplois ont été supprimés dans le secteur public.* Two thousand jobs have been cut in the public sector.
2 *to cancel* ◇ *Le train de Londres a été supprimé.* The train to London has been cancelled.
3 *to get rid of* ◇ *Ils ont supprimé les témoins gênants.* They got rid of the awkward witnesses.

sur PREPOSITION
1 *on* ◇ *Pose-le sur la table.* Put it down on the table. ◇ *Vous verrez l'hôpital sur votre droite.* You'll see the hospital on your right. ◇ *une conférence sur Balzac* a lecture on Balzac
2 *in* ◇ *une personne sur dix* 1 person in 10
3 *out of* ◇ *J'ai eu quatorze sur vingt en maths.* I got 14 out of 20 in maths.
4 *by* ◇ *quatre mètres sur deux* 4 metres by 2

sûr ADJECTIVE
1 *sure* ◇ *Tu es sûr?* Are you sure?
- **sûr et certain** absolutely certain
2 *reliable* ◇ *C'est quelqu'un de très sûr.* He's a very reliable person.

3 *safe* ◇ *Ce quartier n'est pas très sûr la nuit.* This neighbourhood isn't very safe at night.

- **sûr de soi** self-confident ◇ *Elle est très sûre d'elle.* She's very self-confident.

sûrement ADVERB
certainly ◇ *Sûrement pas!* Certainly not! ◇ *Il est sûrement déjà parti.* He's sure to have already left.

la **sûreté** NOUN
- **mettre quelque chose en sûreté** to put something in a safe place

le **surf** NOUN
surfing

la **surface** NOUN
surface
- **les grandes surfaces** the supermarkets

surgelé ADJECTIVE
frozen ◇ *des frites surgelées* frozen chips

les **surgelés** MASC NOUN
frozen food

surhumain ADJECTIVE
superhuman

sur-le-champ ADVERB
immediately

le **surlendemain** NOUN
- **le surlendemain de son arrivée** two days after he arrived
- **le surlendemain dans la matinée** two days later, in the morning

se **surmener** VERB
to work too hard ◇ *Ne te surmène pas trop pendant le week-end.* Don't work too hard over the weekend.

surmonter VERB
to overcome ◇ *Il nous reste de nombreux obstacles à surmonter.* We still have many obstacles to overcome.

surnaturel ADJECTIVE
(FEM SING **surnaturelle**)
supernatural

le **surnom** NOUN
nickname

surnommer NOUN
to nickname ◇ *On l'a surnommé "Kiki".* We nicknamed him "Kiki".

surpeuplé ADJECTIVE
overpopulated

surprenant ADJECTIVE
surprising

surprendre VERB
to surprise ◇ *Ça me surprendrait beaucoup qu'il arrive à l'heure.* I'd be very surprised if he arrived on time.
- **surprendre quelqu'un en train de faire quelque chose** to catch somebody doing something ◇ *Je l'ai surpris en train de fouiller dans mon placard.* I caught him rummaging in my cupboard.

surpris ADJECTIVE
surprised ◇ *Il était surpris de me voir.* He was surprised to see me.

la **surprise** NOUN
surprise ◇ *faire une surprise à quelqu'un* to give somebody a surprise

sursauter VERB
to jump ◇ *J'ai sursauté en entendant mon nom.* I jumped when I heard my name.

surtout ADVERB
1 *especially* ◇ *Il est assez timide, surtout avec les filles.* He's rather shy, especially with girls.
2 *above all* ◇ *Ce canapé est joli et surtout, il n'est pas salissant.* This sofa is pretty, and even more important, it doesn't show the dirt. ◇ *Surtout, ne répète pas ce que je t'ai dit!* Whatever you do, don't repeat what I told you!

le **surveillant** NOUN
supervisor (*man*)

In French secondary schools, the teachers are not responsible for supervising the pupils outside class. This job is done by people called surveillants *or* pions.

la **surveillante** NOUN
supervisor (*woman*)

surveiller VERB
1 *to keep an eye on* ◇ *Tu peux surveiller mes bagages?* Can you keep an eye on my luggage?
2 *to keep a watch on* ◇ *La police a surveillé la maison pendant une semaine.* The police kept the house under surveillance for a week.
3 *to supervise* ◇ *Nous sommes toujours surveillés pendant la récréation.* We're always supervised during break.
- **surveiller un examen** to invigilate an exam
- **surveiller sa ligne** to watch one's figure

le **survêtement** NOUN
tracksuit ◇ *un haut de survêtement* a tracksuit top ◇ *un pantalon de survêtement* tracksuit bottoms

la **survie** NOUN
survival

le **survivant** NOUN
survivor

la **survivante** NOUN
survivor

survivre VERB
to survive ◇ *survivre à un accident* to survive an accident

survoler VERB
to fly over

susceptible ADJECTIVE
touchy

suspect ADJECTIVE
suspicious ◇ *dans des circonstances suspectes* under suspicious circumstances

suspecter VERB
to suspect

le **suspense** NOUN
suspense
◆ **un film à suspense** a thriller

la **suture** NOUN
◆ **un point de suture** a stitch

svelte ADJECTIVE
slender

SVP ABBREVIATION (= *s'il vous plaît*)
please

la **syllabe** NOUN
syllable

symbolique ADJECTIVE
symbolic

symboliser VERB
to symbolize

symétrique ADJECTIVE
symmetrical

sympa ADJECTIVE (*informal*)
nice ◇ *Elle est très sympa.* She's a really nice person.

la **sympathie** NOUN
◆ **J'ai beaucoup de sympathie pour lui.** I like him a lot.

sympathique ADJECTIVE
nice ◇ *Ce sont des gens très sympathiques.* They're very nice people.

sympathiser VERB
to get on well ◇ *Nous avons immédiatement sympathisé avec nos voisins.* We got on well with our neighbours straight away.

le **symptôme** NOUN
symptom

le **syndicat** NOUN
trade union
◆ **le syndicat d'initiative** the tourist information office

synonyme ADJECTIVE
see also synonyme NOUN
synonymous ◇ *être synonyme de* to be synonymous with

le **synonyme** NOUN
see also synonyme ADJECTIVE
synonym

synthétique ADJECTIVE
synthetic

la **Syrie** NOUN
Syria

syrien ADJECTIVE
(FEM SING **syrienne**)
Syrian

systématique ADJECTIVE
systematic

le **système** NOUN
system

T

t' PRONOUN *see* **te**

ta ADJECTIVE
your ◇ *J'ai vu ta sœur hier.* I saw your sister yesterday.

le **tabac** NOUN
1 *tobacco* ◇ *le tabac blond* light tobacco ◇ *le tabac brun* dark tobacco
2 *smoking* ◇ *Le tabac est mauvais pour la santé.* Smoking is bad for you.

la **table** NOUN
table
- **mettre la table** to lay the table
- **se mettre à table** to sit down to eat
- **À table!** Dinner's ready!
- **une table de nuit** a bedside table
- **"table des matières"** "contents"

le **tableau** NOUN
(PL les **tableaux**)
painting ◇ *un tableau de Monet* a painting by Monet
- **le tableau d'affichage** the notice board
- **le tableau noir** the blackboard

la **tablette** NOUN
- **une tablette de chocolat** a bar of chocolate

le **tablier** NOUN
apron

le **tabouret** NOUN
stool

la **tache** NOUN
mark (*stain*)
- **des taches de rousseur** freckles

la **tâche** NOUN
task

tacher VERB
to leave a stain

le **tact** NOUN
tact ◇ *avoir du tact* to be tactful

la **tactique** NOUN
tactics
- **changer de tactique** to try something different

la **taie** NOUN
- **une taie d'oreiller** a pillowcase

la **taille** NOUN
1 *waist* ◇ *Elle a la taille fine.* She has a slim waist.
2 *height* ◇ *un homme de taille moyenne* a man of average height
3 *size* ◇ *Avez-vous ma taille?* Have you got my size?

le **taille-crayon** NOUN
pencil sharpener

le **tailleur** NOUN
1 *tailor*
2 *suit* (*lady's*)
- **Il est assis en tailleur.** He's sitting cross-legged.

se **taire** VERB
to stop talking
- **Taisez-vous!** Be quiet!

le **talon** NOUN
heel

le **tambour** NOUN
drum

la **Tamise** NOUN
Thames

le **tampon** NOUN
pad ◇ *un tampon à récurer* a scouring pad
- **un tampon hygiénique** a tampon

tamponneuse ADJECTIVE
- **les autos tamponneuses** dodgems

tandis que CONJUNCTION
while ◇ *Il a toujours de bonnes notes, tandis que les miennes sont mauvaises.* He always gets good marks, while mine are poor.

tant ADVERB
so much ◇ *Je l'aime tant!* I love him so much!
- **tant de (1)** so much ◇ *tant de nourriture* so much food
- **tant de (2)** so many ◇ *tant de livres* so many books
- **tant que (1)** until ◇ *Tu ne sortiras pas tant que tu n'auras pas fini tes devoirs.* You're not going out until you've finished your homework.
- **tant que (2)** while ◇ *Profites-en tant que tu peux.* Make the most of it while you can.
- **tant mieux** so much the better
- **tant pis** never mind

la **tante** NOUN
aunt

tantôt ADVERB
sometimes ◇ *Nous venons tantôt à pied, tantôt en bus.* Sometimes we walk, sometimes we come by bus.

le **tapage** NOUN
1 *racket* ◇ *Ils ont fait du tapage toute la nuit.* They made a racket all night long.
2 *fuss* ◇ *On a fait beaucoup de tapage autour de cette affaire.* There was a lot of fuss about that business.

taper VERB
to beat down ◇ *Le soleil tape.* The sun's really beating down.
- **taper quelqu'un** to hit somebody ◇ *Maman, il m'a tapé!* Mum, he hit me!

- **taper sur quelque chose** to bang on something
- **taper des pieds** to stamp one's feet
- **taper des mains** to clap one's hands
- **taper à la machine** to type ◇ *Tu sais taper à la machine?* Can you type? ◇ *Je vais taper cette lettre.* I'm going to type this letter.

le **tapis** NOUN
carpet

tapisser VERB
to paper

la **tapisserie** NOUN
1 *wallpaper* ◇ *Tu aimes la tapisserie de ma chambre?* Do you like the wallpaper in my bedroom?
2 *tapestry*

taquiner VERB
to tease

tard ADVERB
late
- **plus tard** later on
- **au plus tard** at the latest

tardif ADJECTIVE
(FEM SING **tardive**)
late ◇ *un petit déjeuner tardif* a late breakfast

le **tarif** NOUN
- **le tarif des consommations** the price list (*in café*)
- **une communication à tarif réduit** an off-peak phone call
- **un billet de train à tarif réduit** a concessionary train ticket
- **un billet de train à plein tarif** a full-price train ticket
- **Est-ce que vous faites un tarif de groupe?** Is there a reduction for groups?

la **tarte** NOUN
tart

la **tartine** NOUN
slice of bread ◇ *une tartine de confiture* a slice of bread and jam

tartiner VERB
to spread
- **le fromage à tartiner** cheese spread

le **tas** NOUN
heap ◇ *un tas de charbon* a heap of coal
- **un tas de** (*informal*) loads of ◇ *J'ai lu un tas de livres pendant les vacances.* I read loads of books in the holidays.

la **tasse** NOUN
cup

le **taureau** NOUN
(PL les **taureaux**)
bull
- **le Taureau** Taurus ◇ *Ils sont tous les deux Taureau.* They're both Taurus.

le **taux** NOUN
rate ◇ *le taux de change* the exchange rate

la **taxe** NOUN
tax
- **la boutique hors taxes** the duty-free shop

le **taxi** NOUN
taxi

tchèque ADJECTIVE
Czech
- **la République tchèque** the Czech Republic

te PRONOUN
te *changes to* **t'** *before a vowel and most words beginning with "h".*
1 *you* ◇ *Je te vois.* I can see you. ◇ *Il t'a vu?* Did he see you?
2 *to you* ◇ *Est-ce qu'il te parle en français?* Does he talk to you in French? ◇ *Elle t'a parlé?* Did she speak to you?
3 *yourself* ◇ *Tu vas te rendre malade.* You'll make yourself sick.
With reflexive verbs, **te** *is often not translated.*
◇ *Comment tu t'appelles?* What's your name?

le **technicien** NOUN
technician

la **technicienne** NOUN
technician

technique ADJECTIVE
see also technique NOUN
technical

la **technique** NOUN
see also technique ADJECTIVE
technique

la **technologie** NOUN
technology

le **teint** NOUN
complexion ◇ *Elle a le teint clair.* She's got a fair complexion.

la **teinte** NOUN
shade (*colour*)

le **teinturier** NOUN
dry cleaner's ◇ *Je vais porter ce manteau chez le teinturier.* I'm going to take this coat to the dry cleaner's.

tel ADJECTIVE
(FEM SING **telle**)
- **Il a un tel enthousiasme!** He's got such enthusiasm!
- **rien de tel** nothing like ◇ *Il n'y a rien de tel qu'une bonne nuit de sommeil.* There's nothing like a good night's sleep.
- **J'ai tout laissé tel quel.** I left everything as it was.

PTO

- **tel que** such as

la **télé** NOUN
telly ◇ *à la télé* on telly

la **télécarte** NOUN
phonecard

la **télécommande** NOUN
remote control

la **télécopie** NOUN
fax

le **télégramme** NOUN
telegram

le **téléphérique** NOUN
cable car

le **téléphone** NOUN
telephone ◇ *Elle est au téléphone.* She's on the phone.

téléphoner VERB
to phone ◇ *Je vais téléphoner à Claire.* I'll phone Claire. ◇ *Je peux téléphoner?* Can I make a phone call?

le **télésiège** NOUN
chairlift

le **téléski** NOUN
ski-tow

le **téléspectateur** NOUN
viewer (*TV*)

la **téléspectatrice** NOUN
viewer (*TV*)

le **téléviseur** NOUN
television set

la **télévision** NOUN
television ◇ *à la télévision* on television

telle ADJECTIVE
- **Je n'ai jamais eu une telle peur.** I've never had such a fright.
- **telle que** such as

tellement ADVERB
1 *so* ◇ *Andrew est tellement gentil.* Andrew's so nice. ◇ *Il travaille tellement.* He works so hard.
2 *so much* ◇ *Il a tellement mangé que...* He ate so much that...
3 *so many* ◇ *Il y avait tellement de monde.* There were so many people.

telles ADJECTIVE
such ◇ *Je n'ai jamais entendu de telles âneries!* I've never heard such nonsense!

tels ADJECTIVE
such ◇ *Nous n'avons pas de tels orages chez nous.* We don't have such storms back home.

le **témoignage** NOUN
testimony

témoigner VERB
to testify

le **témoin** NOUN
witness

la **température** NOUN
temperature ◇ *avoir de la température* to have a temperature

la **tempête** NOUN
storm

temporaire ADJECTIVE
temporary

le **temps** NOUN
1 *weather* ◇ *Quel temps fait-il?* What's the weather like?
2 *time* ◇ *Je n'ai pas le temps.* I haven't got time. ◇ *Prends ton temps.* Take your time. ◇ *Il est temps de partir.* It's time to go.
- **juste à temps** just in time
- **de temps en temps** from time to time
- **en même temps** at the same time
- **à temps** in time ◇ *Il est arrivé à temps pour le match.* He arrived in time for the match.
- **à plein temps** full time ◇ *Elle travaille à plein temps.* She works full time.
- **à temps partiel** part time ◇ *le travail à temps partiel* part-time work
- **dans le temps** at one time ◇ *Dans le temps, on pouvait circuler en vélo sans danger.* At one time, it was safe to go around by bike.

3 *tense* (*of verb*)

tenais, tenait VERB *see* **tenir**

la **tendance** NOUN
- **avoir tendance à faire quelque chose** to tend to do something ◇ *Il a tendance à exagérer.* He tends to exaggerate.

tendre ADJECTIVE
see also tendre VERB
tender

tendre VERB
see also tendre ADJECTIVE
to stretch out ◇ *Ils ont tendu une corde entre deux arbres.* They stretched out a rope between two trees.
- **tendre quelque chose à quelqu'un** to hold something out to somebody ◇ *Il lui a tendu les clés.* He held out the keys to her.
- **tendre la main** to hold out one's hand
- **tendre le bras** to reach out
- **tendre un piège à quelqu'un** to set a trap for someone

tendrement ADVERB
tenderly

la **tendresse** NOUN
tenderness

tendu ADJECTIVE
tense ◇ *Il était très tendu aujourd'hui.* He was very tense today.

tenir VERB

to hold ◇ *Tu peux tenir la lampe, s'il te plaît?* Can you hold the torch, please? ◇ *Il tenait un enfant par la main.* He was holding a child by the hand.

- **Tenez votre chien en laisse.** Keep your dog on the lead.
- **tenir à quelqu'un** to be attached to somebody ◇ *Il tient beaucoup à elle.* He's very attached to her.
- **tenir à faire quelque chose** to be determined to do something ◇ *Elle tient à y aller.* She's determined to go.
- **tenir de quelqu'un** to take after somebody ◇ *Il tient de son père.* He takes after his father.
- **Tiens, voilà un stylo.** Here's a pen.
- **Tiens, c'est Alain là-bas!** Look, that's Alain over there!
- **Tiens?** Really?
- **se tenir (1)** to stand ◇ *Il se tenait près de la porte.* He was standing by the door.
- **se tenir (2)** to be held ◇ *La foire va se tenir place du marché.* The fair will be held in the market place.
- **se tenir droit (1)** to stand up straight ◇ *Tiens-toi droit pour que je puisse te mesurer.* Stand up straight so I can measure you.
- **se tenir droit (2)** to sit up straight ◇ *Arrête de manger le nez dans ton assiette, tiens-toi droit.* Don't slouch while you're eating, sit up straight.
- **Tiens-toi bien!** Behave yourself!

le **tennis** NOUN
[1] *tennis* ◇ *Elle joue au tennis.* She plays tennis.
[2] *tennis court* ◇ *Il est au tennis.* He's at the tennis court.
- **les tennis** trainers

tentant ADJECTIVE
tempting

la **tentation** NOUN
temptation

la **tentative** NOUN
attempt

la **tente** NOUN
tent

tenter VERB
to tempt ◇ *J'ai été tenté de tout abandonner.* I was tempted to give up. ◇ *Ça ne me tente vraiment pas d'aller à la piscine.* I don't really fancy going to the swimming pool.
- **tenter de faire quelque chose** to try to do something ◇ *Il a tenté plusieurs fois de s'évader.* He tried several times to escape.

tenu VERB *see* **tenir**

la **tenue** NOUN
clothes
- **en tenue de soirée** in evening dress

le **terme** NOUN
- **à court terme** short-term
- **à long terme** long-term

la **terminale** NOUN
final year

> *In French secondary schools, years are counted from the* sixième *(youngest) to* première *and* terminale *(oldest).*

terminer VERB
to finish
- **se terminer** to end ◇ *Les vacances se terminent demain.* The holidays end tomorrow.

le **terminus** NOUN
terminus

le **terrain** NOUN
land ◇ *Il veut acheter un terrain en Normandie.* He wants to buy some land in Normandy.
- **un terrain de camping** a campsite
- **un terrain de football** a football pitch
- **un terrain de golf** a golf course
- **un terrain de jeu** a playground
- **un terrain de sport** a sports ground
- **un terrain vague** a piece of waste ground

la **terrasse** NOUN
terrace
- **Si on s'asseyait en terrasse?** Shall we sit outside? *(at café)*

la **terre** NOUN
earth
- **la Terre** the Earth
- **Elle s'est assise par terre.** She sat on the floor.
- **Il est tombé par terre.** He fell down.
- **la terre cuite** terracotta ◇ *un pot en terre cuite* a terracotta pot
- **la terre glaise** clay

terrible ADJECTIVE
terrible ◇ *Quelque chose de terrible est arrivé.* Something terrible has happened.
- **pas terrible** *(informal)* nothing special ◇ *Ce film n'est pas terrible.* The film's nothing special.

la **terrine** NOUN
pâté

le **territoire** NOUN
territory

le/la **terroriste** NOUN
terrorist

tes ADJECTIVE
your ◇ *J'aime bien tes baskets.* I like your trainers.

le **test** NOUN

PTO

test

le **testament** NOUN
will ◇ *Il est mort sans testament.* He died without leaving a will.

tester VERB
to test

le **tétanos** NOUN
tetanus

le **têtard** NOUN
tadpole

la **tête** NOUN
head ◇ *de la tête aux pieds* from head to foot
- **se laver la tête** to wash one's hair
- **la tête la première** headfirst
- **tenir tête à quelqu'un** to stand up to somebody
- **faire la tête** to sulk
- **en avoir par-dessus la tête** to be fed up

têtu ADJECTIVE
stubborn

le **texte** NOUN
text

le **TGV** NOUN (= *train à grande vitesse*)
high-speed train

le **thé** NOUN
tea ◇ *Je vous offre un thé?* Would you like a cup of tea?

le **théâtre** NOUN
theatre
- **faire du théâtre** to act ◇ *Est-ce que tu as déjà fait du théâtre?* Have you ever acted?

la **théière** NOUN
teapot

le **thème** NOUN
1 *subject* ◇ *Quel est le thème de l'émission?* What's the programme about?
2 *prose* (*translation into the foreign language*)

la **théorie** NOUN
theory

le **thermomètre** NOUN
thermometer

le **thon** NOUN
tuna

le **tibia** NOUN
1 *shinbone* ◇ *une fracture du tibia* a broken shinbone
2 *shin* ◇ *Il m'a donné un coup de pied dans le tibia.* He kicked me in the shin.

le **tic** NOUN
nervous twitch

le **ticket** NOUN
ticket ◇ *un ticket de métro* an underground ticket
- **le ticket de caisse** the till receipt

tiède ADJECTIVE
1 *warm* (*water, air*)
2 *lukewarm* (*food, drink*)

tien PRONOUN
- **le tien** yours ◇ *J'ai oublié mon stylo. Tu peux me prêter le tien?* I've forgotten my pen. Can you lend me yours?

tienne PRONOUN
- **la tienne** yours ◇ *Ce n'est pas ma raquette, c'est la tienne.* It's not my racket, it's yours.
- **À la tienne!** Cheers!

tiennes PRONOUN
- **les tiennes** yours ◇ *J'ai pris mes baskets, mais j'ai oublié les tiennes.* I've brought my trainers, but I've forgotten yours.

tiens PRONOUN
- **les tiens** yours ◇ *Je ne trouve pas mes feutres. Je peux utiliser les tiens?* I can't find my felt pens. Can I use yours?

tiens, tient VERB *see* **tenir**

le **tiers** NOUN
third ◇ *Un tiers de la classe était pour.* A third of the class were in favour.
- **le tiers monde** the Third World

la **tige** NOUN
stem

le **tigre** NOUN
tiger

le **tilleul** NOUN
lime tea

le **timbre** NOUN
stamp

timide ADJECTIVE
shy

timidement ADVERB
shyly

la **timidité** NOUN
shyness

le **tir** NOUN
shooting
- **le tir à l'arc** archery

le **tirage** NOUN
- **par tirage au sort** by drawing lots ◇ *Les prix seront attribués par tirage au sort.* The prizes will be awarded by drawing lots.

le **tire-bouchon** NOUN
corkscrew

la **tirelire** NOUN
money box

tirer VERB
1 *to pull* ◇ *Elle a tiré un mouchoir de son sac.* She pulled a handkerchief out of her bag. ◇ *Il m'a tiré les cheveux.* He pulled my hair. ◇ *"Tirer"* "Pull"
2 *to draw* ◇ *tirer les rideaux* to draw

the curtains ◇ *tirer un trait* to draw a line ◇ *tirer des conclusions* to draw conclusions
- **tirer au sort** to draw lots

3 *to fire* ◇ *Il a tiré plusieurs coups de feu.* He fired several shots. ◇ *Il a tiré sur les policiers.* He fired at the police.

le **tiret** NOUN
dash (*hyphen*)

le **tiroir** NOUN
drawer

la **tisane** NOUN
herbal tea

tisser VERB
to weave

le **tissu** NOUN
material
- **un sac en tissu** a cloth bag

le **titre** NOUN
title
- **les gros titres** the headlines
- **un titre de transport** a travel ticket

tituber VERB
to stagger

le **toast** NOUN
1 *piece of toast*
2 *toast* ◇ *porter un toast à quelqu'un* to drink a toast to somebody

le **toboggan** NOUN
slide

toi PRONOUN
you ◇ *Ça va?–Oui, et toi?* How are you?–Fine, and you? ◇ *J'ai faim, pas toi?* I'm hungry, aren't you?
- **Assieds-toi.** Sit down.
- **C'est à toi de jouer.** It's your turn to play.
- **Est-ce que ce stylo est à toi?** Is this pen yours?

la **toile** NOUN
- **un pantalon de toile** cotton trousers
- **un sac de toile** a canvas bag
- **une toile cirée** an oilcloth
- **une toile d'araignée** a cobweb

la **toilette** NOUN
1 *wash* ◇ *faire sa toilette* to have a wash
2 *outfit* ◇ *une toilette élégante* an elegant outfit

les **toilettes** FEM NOUN
toilet

toi-même PRONOUN
yourself ◇ *Tu as fait ça toi-même?* Did you do it yourself?

le **toit** NOUN
roof
- **un toit ouvrant** a sunroof

tolérant ADJECTIVE
tolerant

tolérer VERB
to tolerate

la **tomate** NOUN
tomato

la **tombe** NOUN
grave

le **tombeau** NOUN
(PL les **tombeaux**)
tomb

la **tombée** NOUN
- **à la tombée de la nuit** at nightfall

tomber VERB
to fall ◇ *Attention, tu vas tomber!* Be careful, you'll fall!
- **laisser tomber (1)** to drop ◇ *Elle a laissé tomber son stylo.* She dropped her pen.
- **laisser tomber (2)** to give up ◇ *Il a laissé tomber le piano.* He gave up the piano.
- **laisser tomber (3)** to let down ◇ *Il ne laisse jamais tomber ses amis.* He never lets his friends down.
- **tomber sur quelqu'un** to bump into someone ◇ *Je suis tombé sur lui en sortant de chez Pierre.* I bumped into him coming out of Pierre's place.
- **Ça tombe bien.** That's lucky.
- **Il tombe de sommeil.** He's asleep on his feet.

ton ADJECTIVE
(FEM SING **ta**, PL **tes**)
see also ton NOUN
your ◇ *C'est ton stylo?* Is this your pen?

le **ton** NOUN
see also ton ADJECTIVE
1 *tone of voice* ◇ *Ne me parle pas sur ce ton.* Don't speak to me in that tone of voice.
2 *colour* ◇ *J'adore les tons pastel.* I love pastel colours.

la **tonalité** NOUN
dialling tone

la **tondeuse** NOUN
lawnmower

tondre VERB
to mow

tonique ADJECTIVE
fortifying

la **tonne** NOUN
tonne

le **tonneau** NOUN
(PL les **tonneaux**)
barrel

le **tonnerre** NOUN
thunder

le **tonus** NOUN
- **avoir du tonus** to be energetic

T

le **torchon** NOUN
tea towel

tordre VERB
- **se tordre la cheville** to twist one's ankle

tordu ADJECTIVE
1 *bent* ◇ *Ce clou est un peu tordu.* This nail's a bit bent.
2 *crazy* ◇ *une histoire complètement tordue* a crazy story

le **torrent** NOUN
mountain stream

le **torse** NOUN
chest ◇ *Il était torse nu.* He was bare-chested.

le **tort** NOUN
- **avoir tort** to be wrong
- **donner tort à quelqu'un** to lay the blame on somebody

le **torticolis** NOUN
stiff neck ◇ *J'ai le torticolis.* I've got a stiff neck.

la **tortue** NOUN
tortoise

la **torture** NOUN
torture

torturer VERB
to torture

tôt ADVERB
early
- **au plus tôt** at the earliest
- **tôt ou tard** sooner or later

total ADJECTIVE
(MASC PL **totaux**)
see also total NOUN
total

le **total** NOUN
(PL les **totaux**)
see also total ADJECTIVE
total ◇ *faire le total* to work out the total
- **au total** in total

totalement ADVERB
totally

la **totalité** NOUN
- **la totalité des profs** all the teachers
- **la totalité du personnel** the entire staff

touchant ADJECTIVE
touching

toucher VERB
1 *to touch* ◇ *Ne touche pas à mes livres!* Don't touch my books!
- **Nos deux jardins se touchent.** Our gardens are next to each other.

2 *to feel* ◇ *Ce pull a l'air doux. Je peux toucher?* That sweater looks soft. Can I feel it?
3 *to hit* ◇ *La balle l'a touché en pleine poitrine.* The bullet hit him right in the chest.
4 *to affect* ◇ *Ces nouvelles réformes ne nous touchent pas.* The new reforms don't affect us.
5 *to receive* ◇ *Il a touché une grosse somme d'argent.* He received a large sum of money.

toujours ADVERB
1 *always* ◇ *Il est toujours très gentil.* He's always very nice.
- **pour toujours** forever

2 *still* ◇ *Quand nous sommes revenus, il était toujours là.* When we got back he was still there.

le **toupet** NOUN (*informal*)
- **avoir du toupet** to have a nerve

la **tour** NOUN
see also le tour
1 *tower* ◇ *la Tour Eiffel* the Eiffel Tower
2 *tower block* ◇ *Il y a beaucoup de tours dans ce quartier.* There are a lot of tower blocks in this area.

le **tour** NOUN
see also la tour
turn ◇ *C'est ton tour de jouer.* It's your turn to play.
- **faire un tour** to go for a walk ◇ *Allons faire un tour dans le parc.* Let's go for a walk in the park.
- **faire un tour en voiture** to go for a drive
- **faire un tour à vélo** to go for a ride ◇ *Tu veux aller faire un tour à vélo?* Do you want to go for a bike ride?
- **faire le tour du monde** to travel round the world

le **tourbillon** NOUN
whirlpool

le/la **touriste** NOUN
tourist

se **tourmenter** VERB
to fret ◇ *Ne te tourmente pas, ça s'arrangera.* Don't fret about it, it'll be all right.

le **tournant** NOUN
1 *bend* ◇ *Il y a beaucoup de tournants dangereux sur cette route.* There are a lot of dangerous bends on this road.
2 *turning point* ◇ *Ça a été un tournant dans sa vie.* It was a turning point in his life.

la **tournée** NOUN
1 *round* ◇ *Le facteur commence sa tournée à sept heures du matin.* The postman starts his round at 7 o'clock in the morning. ◇ *Allez, qu'est-ce que vous voulez boire? C'est ma tournée.* Right, what are you drinking? It's my round.

2 *tour* ◇ *Il est en tournée aux États-Unis.* He's on tour in the United States.

tourner VERB
1 *to turn* ◇ *Tournez à droite au prochain feu.* Turn right at the lights. ◇ *Tourne-toi un peu plus vers moi, et souris!* Turn towards me a bit more, and smile!
2 *to go sour* ◇ *Le lait a tourné.* The milk's gone sour.
◆ **mal tourner** to go wrong ◇ *Ça a mal tourné.* It all went wrong.
◆ **tourner le dos à quelqu'un** to have one's back to somebody

e**tournesol** NOUN
sunflower

e**tournevis** NOUN
screwdriver

e**tournoi** NOUN
tournament

la**tourte** NOUN
pie ◇ *une tourte aux poireaux* a leek pie

tous ADJECTIVE, PRONOUN *see* **tout**

la**Toussaint** NOUN
All Saints' Day

tousser VERB
to cough

tout ADJECTIVE, ADVERB, PRONOUN
(MASC PL **tous**, FEM PL **toutes**)
1 *all* ◇ *tout le lait* all the milk ◇ *toute la nuit* all night ◇ *tous les livres* all the books ◇ *toutes les filles* all the girls ◇ *tout le temps* all the time ◇ *C'est tout.* That's all. ◇ *Je les connais tous.* I know them all. ◇ *Nous y sommes toutes allées.* We all went. ◇ *Ça fait combien en tout?* How much is that all together?
◆ **Il est tout seul.** He's all alone.
◆ **pas du tout** not at all
2 *every* ◇ *tous les jours* every day ◇ *tous les deux jours* every two days
◆ **tout le monde** everybody
◆ **tous les deux** both ◇ *Nous y sommes allés tous les deux.* We both went.
◆ **tous les trois** all three ◇ *Je les ai invités tous les trois.* I invited all three of them.
3 *everything* ◇ *Il a tout organisé.* He organized everything.
4 *very* ◇ *Elle habite tout près.* She lives very close.
◆ **tout en haut** right at the top
◆ **tout droit** straight ahead
◆ **tout d'abord** first of all
◆ **tout à coup** suddenly
◆ **tout à fait** absolutely
◆ **tout à l'heure (1)** just now ◇ *Je l'ai vu tout à l'heure.* I saw him just now.
◆ **tout à l'heure (2)** in a moment ◇ *Je finirai ça tout à l'heure.* I'll finish it in a moment.
◆ **À tout à l'heure!** See you later!
◆ **tout de suite** straight away

toutefois ADVERB
however

toutes ADJECTIVE, PRONOUN *see* **tout**

la**toux** NOUN
cough

le/la**toxicomane** NOUN
drug addict

le**trac** NOUN
◆ **avoir le trac** to be feeling nervous

la**trace** NOUN
1 *trace* ◇ *Le voleur n'a pas laissé de traces.* The thief left no traces.
2 *mark* ◇ *des traces de doigts* finger marks
◆ **des traces de pas** footprints

tracer VERB
to draw ◇ *tracer un trait* to draw a line

le**tracteur** NOUN
tractor

la**tradition** NOUN
tradition

traditionnel ADJECTIVE
(FEM SING **traditionnelle**)
traditional

le**traducteur** NOUN
translator

la**traduction** NOUN
translation

la**traductrice** NOUN
translator

traduire VERB
to translate

le**trafic** NOUN
traffic
◆ **le trafic de drogue** drug trafficking

le**trafiquant** NOUN
◆ **un trafiquant de drogue** a drug trafficker

tragique ADJECTIVE
tragic

trahir VERB
to betray

la**trahison** NOUN
betrayal

le**train** NOUN
train
◆ **un train électrique** a train set
◆ **Il est en train de manger.** He's eating.

le**traîneau** NOUN
(PL les **traîneaux**)
sledge

traîner VERB
1 *to wander around* ◇ *J'ai vu des*

T

PTO

jeunes qui traînaient en ville. I saw some young people wandering around town.
2 *to hang about* ◇ *Dépêche-toi, ne traîne pas!* Hurry up, don't hang about!
3 *to drag on* ◇ *La réunion a traîné jusqu'à midi.* The meeting dragged on till 12 o'clock.
- **traîner des pieds** to drag one's feet

le **train-train** NOUN
humdrum routine

traire VERB
to milk

le **trait** NOUN
1 *line* ◇ *Tracez un trait.* Draw a line.
2 *feature* ◇ *Elle a les traits fins.* She has delicate features.
- **boire quelque chose d'un trait** to drink something down in one gulp
- **un trait d'union** a hyphen

le **traitement** NOUN
treatment
- **le traitement de texte** word processing

traiter VERB
to treat ◇ *Elle le traite comme un chien.* She treats him like a dog.
- **Il m'a traité d'imbécile.** He called me an idiot.
- **traiter de** to be about ◇ *Cet article traite des sans-abri.* This article is about the homeless.

le **traiteur** NOUN
caterer

le **trajet** NOUN
1 *journey* ◇ *Il n'a pas arrêté de parler pendant tout le trajet.* He talked for the whole journey. ◇ *J'ai une heure de trajet pour aller au travail.* My journey to work takes an hour.
2 *route* ◇ *C'est le trajet le plus court.* It's the shortest route.

le **tramway** NOUN
tram

tranchant ADJECTIVE
sharp (*knife*)

la **tranche** NOUN
slice

tranquille ADJECTIVE
quiet ◇ *Cette rue est très tranquille.* This is a very quiet street.
- **Sois tranquille, il ne va rien lui arriver.** Don't worry, nothing will happen to him.
- **Tiens-toi tranquille!** Be quiet!
- **Laisse-moi tranquille.** Leave me alone.
- **Laisse ça tranquille.** Leave it alone.

la **tranquillité** NOUN
peace and quiet

transférer VERB
to transfer

transformer VERB
1 *to transform* ◇ *Son séjour en France l'a transformé.* His stay in France has transformed him.
2 *to convert* ◇ *Ils ont transformé la grange en garage.* They've converted the barn into a garage.
- **se transformer en** to turn into ◇ *La chenille se transforme en papillon.* The caterpillar turns into a butterfly.

la **transfusion** NOUN
- **une transfusion sanguine** a blood transfusion

transiger VERB
to compromise

transmettre VERB
- **transmettre quelque chose à quelqu'un** to pass something on to somebody

transpercer VERB
to go through ◇ *La pluie a transpercé mes vêtements.* The rain went through my clothes.

la **transpiration** NOUN
perspiration

transpirer VERB
to perspire

le **transport** NOUN
transport
- **les transports en commun** public transport

transporter VERB
1 *to carry* ◇ *Le train transportait des marchandises.* The train was carrying freight.
2 *to move* ◇ *Je ne sais pas comment je vais transporter mes affaires.* I don't know how I'm going to move my stuff.

traumatiser VERB
to traumatize

le **travail** NOUN
(PL les **travaux**)
1 *work* ◇ *J'ai beaucoup de travail.* I've got a lot of work.
2 *job* ◇ *Il a un travail intéressant.* He's got an interesting job.
- **le travail au noir** moonlighting

travailler VERB
to work

travailleur ADJECTIVE
(FEM SING **travailleuse**)
see also travailleur NOUN
hard-working

le **travailleur** NOUN
see also travailleur ADJECTIVE
worker

la **travailleuse** NOUN
worker

les **travaillistes** MASC NOUN

the Labour Party

s**travaux** MASC NOUN
1 *work* ◇ *des travaux de construction* building work
2 *roadworks* ◇ *Il y a beaucoup de bruit à cause des travaux dans la rue.* There's a lot of noise from the roadworks.
- **être en travaux** to be undergoing alterations
- **les travaux dirigés** supervised practical work
- **les travaux manuels** handicrafts
- **les travaux ménagers** housework

e**travers** NOUN
- **en travers de** across ◇ *Il y avait un arbre en travers de la route.* There was a tree lying across the road.
- **de travers** crooked ◇ *Son chapeau était de travers.* His hat was crooked.
- **comprendre de travers** to misunderstand ◇ *Elle comprend toujours tout de travers.* She always gets the wrong idea.
- **J'ai avalé de travers.** Something went down the wrong way.
- **à travers** through ◇ *Cette vitre est tellement sale qu'on ne voit rien à travers.* This window is so dirty you can't see anything through it.

a**traversée** NOUN
crossing

traverser VERB
1 *to cross* ◇ *Traversez la rue.* Cross the street.
2 *to go through* ◇ *Nous avons traversé la France pour aller en Espagne.* We went through France on the way to Spain. ◇ *La pluie a traversé mon manteau.* The rain went through my coat.

le**traversin** NOUN
bolster

trébucher VERB
to trip up

le**trèfle** NOUN
1 *clover*
2 *clubs* (*at cards*) ◇ *le roi de trèfle* the king of clubs

treize NUMBER
thirteen ◇ *Il a treize ans.* He's thirteen. ◇ *à treize heures* at 1 p.m.
- **le treize février** the thirteenth of February

treizième ADJECTIVE
thirteenth

le**tréma** NOUN
diaeresis

le**tremblement de terre** NOUN
earthquake

trembler VERB
to shake ◇ *trembler de peur* to shake with fear
- **trembler de froid** to shiver

trempé ADJECTIVE
soaking wet

tremper VERB
to soak
- **tremper sa main dans l'eau** to dip one's hand in the water

le**tremplin** NOUN
springboard

la**trentaine** NOUN
about thirty ◇ *une trentaine de personnes* about thirty people
- **Il a la trentaine.** He's in his thirties.

trente NUMBER
thirty ◇ *Elle a trente ans.* She's thirty.
- **le trente janvier** the thirtieth of January
- **trente et un** thirty-one
- **trente-deux** thirty-two

trentième ADJECTIVE
thirtieth

très ADVERB
very

le**trésor** NOUN
treasure

la**tresse** NOUN
plait

la**tribu** NOUN
tribe

le**tribunal** NOUN
(PL les **tribunaux**)
court

tricher VERB
to cheat

tricolore ADJECTIVE
three-coloured
- **le drapeau tricolore** the French tricolour

le drapeau tricolore *is the French flag which is blue, white and red.*

le**tricot** NOUN
1 *knitting* ◇ *On fait du tricot à l'école.* We do knitting at school.
2 *sweater* ◇ *Mets un tricot, il fait froid.* Put a sweater on, it's cold.

tricoter VERB
to knit

trier VERB
to sort out ◇ *Je vais trier mes papiers avant de partir en vacances.* I'm going to sort out my papers before I go on holiday.

le**trimestre** NOUN
term

trinquer VERB
to clink glasses

le **triomphe** NOUN
triumph
triompher VERB
to triumph
les **tripes** FEM NOUN
tripe
le **triple** NOUN
- **Ça m'a coûté le triple.** It cost me three times as much.
- **Il gagne le triple de mon salaire.** He earns three times my salary.

tripler VERB
to treble
les **triplés** MASC NOUN
triplets
triste ADJECTIVE
sad
la **tristesse** NOUN
sadness
le **trognon** NOUN
core ◇ *un trognon de pomme* an apple core
trois NUMBER
three ◇ *à trois heures du matin* at three in the morning ◇ *Elle a trois ans.* She's three. ◇ *trois fois* three times
- **le trois février** the third of February

troisième ADJECTIVE
see also troisième NOUN
third ◇ *au troisième étage* on the third floor
la **troisième** NOUN
see also troisième ADJECTIVE
fourth year
In French secondary schools, years are counted from the sixième *(youngest) to* première *and* terminale *(oldest).*
◇ *Mon frère est en troisième.* My brother's in fourth year.
les **trois-quarts** MASC NOUN
three-quarters ◇ *les trois-quarts de la classe* three-quarters of the class
le **trombone** NOUN
1 *trombone* ◇ *Il joue du trombone.* He plays the trombone.
2 *paper clip*
la **trompe** NOUN
trunk ◇ *la trompe d'un éléphant* an elephant's trunk
tromper VERB
to deceive
- **se tromper** to make a mistake ◇ *Tout le monde peut se tromper.* Anyone can make a mistake.
- **se tromper de jour** to get the wrong day
- **Vous vous êtes trompé de numéro.** You've got the wrong number.

la **trompette** NOUN
trumpet ◇ *Il joue de la trompette.* He plays the trumpet.
- **Il a le nez en trompette.** He's got a turned-up nose.

le **tronc** NOUN
trunk ◇ *un tronc d'arbre* a tree trunk
trop ADVERB
1 *too* ◇ *Il conduit trop vite.* He drives too fast.
2 *too much* ◇ *J'ai trop mangé.* I've eaten too much.
- **trop de (1)** too much ◇ *J'ai acheté trop de pain.* I bought too much bread. ◇ *trois francs de trop* 3 francs too much
- **trop de (2)** too many ◇ *J'ai apporté trop de vêtements.* I've brought too many clothes.
- **trois personnes de trop** 3 people too many

le **tropique** NOUN
tropic
le **trottoir** NOUN
pavement
le **trou** NOUN
hole
- **J'ai eu un trou de mémoire.** My mind went blank.

trouble ADJECTIVE, ADVERB
cloudy ◇ *L'eau est trouble.* The water's cloudy.
- **Sans mes lunettes je vois trouble.** Without my glasses I can't see properly.

les **troubles** MASC NOUN
- **une période de troubles politiques** a period of political instability

trouer VERB
to make a hole in ◇ *Il a troué la moquette avec sa cigarette.* He made a hole in the carpet with his cigarette.
la **trouille** NOUN
- **avoir la trouille** (*informal*) to be scared to death

la **troupe** NOUN
troop
- **une troupe de théâtre** a theatre company

le **troupeau** NOUN
(PL les **troupeaux**)
- **un troupeau de moutons** a flock of sheep
- **un troupeau de vaches** a herd of cows

la **trousse** NOUN
pencil case
- **une trousse de toilette** a toilet bag

trouver VERB
1 *to find* ◇ *Je ne trouve pas mes lunettes.* I can't find my glasses.
2 *to think* ◇ *Je trouve que c'est bête.* I think it's stupid.

se trouver to be ◇ *Où se trouve la poste?* Where is the post office? ◇ *Marseille se trouve dans le sud de la France.* Marseilles is in the South of France.

se trouver mal to pass out

c NOUN (*informal*)

1 *thing* ◇ *un truc en plastique* a thing made of plastic ◇ *J'ai plein de trucs à faire ce week-end.* I've got loads of things to do this weekend.

2 *trick* ◇ *Je vais te montrer un truc qui réussit à tous les coups.* I'll show you a trick that never fails.

ite NOUN

trout

VP ABBREVIATION (= *tournez s'il vous plaît*)

PTO (= please turn over)

PRONOUN

you ◇ *Est-ce que tu as un animal familier?* Have you got a pet?

ba NOUN

1 *tuba* ◇ *Je joue du tuba.* I play the tuba.

2 *snorkel*

be NOUN

1 *tube* ◇ *un tube de dentifrice* a tube of toothpaste

un tube de rouge à lèvres a lipstick

2 *hit* ◇ *Ça va être le tube de l'été.* It's going to be this summer's hit.

er VERB

to kill

se tuer to get killed ◇ *Il s'est tué dans un accident de voiture.* He got killed in a car accident.

e-tête

à tue-tête ADVERB

at the top of one's voice ◇ *crier à tue-tête* to shout at the top of one's voice ◇ *Il chantait à tue-tête.* He was singing at the top of his voice.

ile NOUN

tile ◇ *un toit en tuiles* a tiled roof

nique NOUN

tunic

nisie NOUN

Tunisia

tunisien ADJECTIVE

(FEM SING **tunisienne**)

Tunisian

le **tunnel** NOUN

tunnel

◆ **le tunnel sous la Manche** the Channel Tunnel

turbulent ADJECTIVE

boisterous

turc ADJECTIVE, NOUN

(FEM SING **turque**)

Turkish ◇ *Il parle turc.* He speaks Turkish.

◆ **un Turc** a Turk (*man*)

◆ **une Turque** a Turk (*woman*)

la **Turquie** NOUN

Turkey

tutoyer VERB

◆ **tutoyer quelqu'un** to address somebody as "tu"

> **tutoyer quelqu'un** *means to use* **tu** *when speaking to someone, rather than* **vous**. *Use* **tu** *only when talking to one person and when that person is someone of your own age or whom you know well; use* **vous** *to everyone else. If in doubt use* **vous**.

◆ **On se tutoie?** Shall we use "tu" to each other?

le **tuyau** NOUN

(PL **les tuyaux**)

1 *pipe*

◆ **un tuyau d'arrosage** a hosepipe

2 *tip* ◇ *Il m'a donné un bon tuyau.* (*informal*) He gave me a handy tip.

la **TVA** NOUN (= *taxe sur la valeur ajoutée*)

VAT

le **tympan** NOUN

eardrum

le **type** NOUN (*informal*)

guy ◇ *C'est un type formidable.* He's a great guy.

typique ADJECTIVE

typical

le **tyran** NOUN

tyrant ◇ *C'est un vrai tyran.* He's a real tyrant.

le/la **tzigane** NOUN

gipsy

U

un ARTICLE, PRONOUN, ADJECTIVE
1 *a* ◇ *un garçon* a boy
an ◇ *un œuf* an egg
2 *one* ◇ *l'un des meilleurs* one of the best ◇ *un citron et deux oranges* one lemon and two oranges ◇ *Combien de timbres?–Un.* How many stamps?–One. ◇ *Elle a un an.* She's one year old.
- **l'un..., l'autre...** one..., the other... ◇ *L'un est grand, l'autre est petit.* One is tall, the other is short.
- **les uns..., les autres...** some..., others... ◇ *Les uns marchaient, les autres couraient.* Some were walking, others were running.
- **l'un ou l'autre** either of them ◇ *Prends l'un ou l'autre, ça m'est égal.* Take either of them, I don't mind.
- **un par un** one by one ◇ *Ils entraient un par un.* They went in one by one.

unanime ADJECTIVE
unanimous

l'**unanimité** FEM NOUN
- **à l'unanimité** unanimously

une ARTICLE, PRONOUN, ADJECTIVE
1 *a* ◇ *une fille* a girl
an ◇ *une pomme* an apple
2 *one* ◇ *une pomme et deux bananes* one apple and two bananas ◇ *Combien de cartes postales?–Une.* How many postcards?–One. ◇ *à une heure du matin* at one in the morning ◇ *l'une des meilleures* one of the best
- **l'une..., l'autre...** one..., the other... ◇ *L'une est grande, l'autre est petite.* One is tall, the other is short.
- **les unes..., les autres...** some..., others... ◇ *Les unes marchaient, les autres couraient.* Some were walking, others were running.
- **l'une ou l'autre** either of them ◇ *Prends l'une ou l'autre, ça m'est égal.* Take either of them, I don't mind.
- **une par une** one by one ◇ *Elles entraient une par une.* They went in one by one.

uni ADJECTIVE
1 *plain* ◇ *un tissu uni* a plain fabric
2 *close-knit* ◇ *une famille unie* a close-knit family

l'**uniforme** MASC NOUN
uniform

l'**union** FEM NOUN
union
- **l'ex-Union soviétique** the former Soviet Union

unique ADJECTIVE
unique ◇ *Tout individu a des empreintes uniques.* Everyone's fingerprints are unique. ◇ *C'est une occasion unique.* It's a unique opportunity.
- **Il est fils unique.** He's an only child.
- **Elle est fille unique.** She's an only child.

uniquement ADVERB
only

l'**unité** FEM NOUN
1 *unity* ◇ *l'unité européenne* European unity
2 *unit* ◇ *une unité de mesure* a unit of measurement

l'**univers** MASC NOUN
universe

universitaire ADJECTIVE
university ◇ *un diplôme universitaire* university degree
- **faire des études universitaires** to study at university

l'**université** FEM NOUN
university ◇ *aller à l'université* to go to university

l'**urgence** FEM NOUN
- **C'est une urgence.** It's urgent.
- **Il n'y a pas urgence.** It's not urgent.
- **le service des urgences** the accident and emergency department
- **Il a été transporté d'urgence à l'hôpital** He was rushed to hospital.
- **Téléphonez d'urgence.** Phone as soon as possible.

urgent ADJECTIVE
urgent

l'**urine** FEM NOUN
urine

les **USA** MASC NOUN
USA
- **aux USA (1)** in the USA
- **aux USA (2)** to the USA

l'**usage** MASC NOUN
use ◇ *à usage interne* for internal use ◇ *à usage externe* for external use only
- **hors d'usage** out of action ◇ *Cet appareil est hors d'usage.* That machine's out of action.

usagé ADJECTIVE
1 *old* ◇ *un manteau usagé* an old coat
2 *used* ◇ *une seringue usagée* a used syringe

l'**usager** MASC NOUN
user ◇ *les usagers de la route* road

users

usé ADJECTIVE
worn ◇ *Mon jean est un peu usé.* My jeans are a bit worn.

user VERB
to wear out ◇ *Mes baskets se sont usées en quinze jours.* My trainers wore out in two weeks.

usine FEM NOUN
factory ◇ *une usine de sardines* a sardine factory

ustensile MASC NOUN
un ustensile de cuisine a kitchen utensil

usuel ADJECTIVE
(FEM SING **usuelle**)
everyday ◇ *la langue usuelle* everyday language

utile ADJECTIVE
useful

l'**utilisation** FEM NOUN
use ◇ *L'utilisation des calculatrices est interdite.* It is forbidden to use calculators.

utiliser VERB
to use

l'**utilité** FEM NOUN
use ◇ *Ce gadget n'est pas d'une grande utilité.* This gadget isn't much use.

V

va VERB *see* **aller**

les **vacances** FEM NOUN
holidays ◇ *aller en vacances* to go on holiday ◇ *être en vacances* to be on holiday
➔ **les grandes vacances** the summer holidays

le **vacancier** NOUN
holiday-maker

la **vacancière** NOUN
holiday-maker

le **vacarme** NOUN
racket ◇ *Qu'est-ce que c'est que ce vacarme?* What's all this racket?

le **vaccin** NOUN
vaccination

la **vaccination** NOUN
vaccination ◇ *La vaccination est obligatoire.* Vaccination is compulsory.

vacciner VERB
to vaccinate ◇ *se faire vacciner contre la rubéole* to be vaccinated against German measles

la **vache** NOUN
see also vache ADJECTIVE
cow

vache ADJECTIVE (*informal*)
see also vache NOUN
mean ◇ *C'est vraiment vache, ce qu'il a dit.* What he said was really mean. ◇ *Il est vache.* He's a mean sod.

vachement ADVERB (*informal*)
really ◇ *Viens te baigner, l'eau est vachement chaude.* Come in the water, it's really warm.

le **vagabond** NOUN
tramp

le **vagin** NOUN
vagina

la **vague** NOUN
see also vague ADJECTIVE
wave (*in sea*)

vague ADJECTIVE
see also vague NOUN
vague ◇ *J'ai un vague souvenir de lui.* I vaguely remember him.

vain ADJECTIVE
➔ **en vain** in vain

vaincre VERB
1 *to defeat* ◇ *L'armée a été vaincue.* The army was defeated.
2 *to overcome* ◇ *Il a réussi à vaincre sa timidité.* He managed to overcome his shyness.

le **vainqueur** NOUN
winner

vais VERB *see* **aller**
➔ **Je vais écrire à mes cousins.** I'm going to write to my cousins.

le **vaisseau** NOUN
(PL les **vaisseaux**)
➔ **un vaisseau spatial** a spaceship
➔ **un vaisseau sanguin** a blood vessel

la **vaisselle** NOUN
1 *washing-up* ◇ *Je vais faire la vaisselle.* I'll do the washing-up.
2 *dishes* ◇ *Tu peux ranger la vaisselle s'il te plaît?* Can you put the dishes away please?

valable ADJECTIVE
valid ◇ *Ce billet d'avion est valable un an.* This plane ticket is valid for one year.

le **valet** NOUN
jack (*in card games*) ◇ *le valet de carreau* the jack of diamonds

la **valeur** NOUN
value ◇ *sans valeur* of no value
➔ **des objets de valeur** valuables ◇ *Ne laissez pas d'objets de valeur dans votre chambre.* Don't leave any valuables in your room.

valider VERB
to stamp ◇ *Vous devez faire valider votre billet avant votre départ.* You must get your ticket stamped before you leave.

la **valise** NOUN
suitcase

la **vallée** NOUN
valley

valoir VERB
to be worth ◇ *Ça vaut combien?* How much is it worth? ◇ *Cette voiture vaut très cher.* This car's worth a lot of money.
➔ **Ça vaut mieux.** That would be better. ◇ *Il vaut mieux ne rien dire.* It would be better to say nothing.
➔ **valoir la peine** to be worth it ◇ *Ça vaudrait la peine d'essayer.* It would be worth a try.

le **vampire** NOUN
vampire

le **vandalisme** NOUN
vandalism

la **vanille** NOUN
vanilla ◇ *une glace à la vanille* a vanilla ice cream

la **vanité** NOUN
vanity

vaniteux ADJECTIVE

(FEM SING **vaniteuse**)
conceited

anter VERB
to boast

apeur NOUN
steam ◇ *des légumes cuits à la vapeur* steamed vegetables

arappe NOUN
rock climbing ◇ *faire de la varappe* to go rock climbing

ariable ADJECTIVE
changeable (*weather*)

aricelle NOUN
chickenpox ◇ *Elle a la varicelle.* She's got chickenpox.

arié ADJECTIVE
varied ◇ *Son travail est très varié.* His job is very varied.

arier VERB
to vary
- **Le menu varie tous les jours.** The menu changes every day.

ariété NOUN
variety ◇ *Il n'y a pas beaucoup de variété.* There isn't much variety.
- **une émission de variétés** a television variety show

as VERB *see* **aller**

ase NOUN
see also la vase
vase

ase NOUN
see also le vase
mud

aste ADJECTIVE
vast

audrait, vaut VERB *see* **valoir**

autour NOUN
vulture

eau NOUN
(PL les **veaux**)
1 *calf* (*animal*)
2 *veal* (*meat*)

écu VERB *see* **vivre**
- **Il a vécu à Paris pendant dix ans.** He lived in Paris for ten years.

edette NOUN
1 *star* ◇ *une vedette de cinéma* a film star
2 *motor boat*
- **une vedette de police** a police launch

égétal ADJECTIVE
(MASC PL **végétaux**)
vegetable ◇ *l'huile végétale* vegetable oil

égétarien ADJECTIVE
(FEM SING **végétarienne**)
vegetarian ◇ *Je suis végétarien.* I'm a vegetarian.

la **végétation** NOUN
vegetation

le **véhicule** NOUN
vehicle

la **veille** NOUN
the day before ◇ *la veille de son départ* the day before he left ◇ *la veille au soir* the previous evening
- **la veille de Noël** Christmas Eve
- **la veille du jour de l'An** New Year's Eve

veinard ADJECTIVE (*informal*)
- **Qu'est-ce qu'il est veinard!** He's such a lucky devil!

la **veine** NOUN
vein
- **avoir de la veine** (*informal*) to be lucky

le/la **véliplanchiste** NOUN
windsurfer

le **vélo** NOUN
bike ◇ *faire du vélo* to go cycling
- **un vélo tout-terrain** a mountain bike

le **vélomoteur** NOUN
moped

le **velours** NOUN
velvet ◇ *une robe en velours* a velvet dress
- **le velours côtelé** corduroy ◇ *un pantalon en velours côtelé* corduroy trousers

les **vendanges** FEM NOUN
grape harvest ◇ *On fait les vendanges en septembre.* The grape harvest is in September.

le **vendeur** NOUN
shop assistant

la **vendeuse** NOUN
shop assistant

vendre VERB
to sell
- **vendre quelque chose à quelqu'un** to sell somebody something ◇ *Il m'a vendu son vélo.* He sold me his bike.
- **"à vendre"** "for sale"

le **vendredi** NOUN
1 *Friday* ◇ *Aujourd'hui, nous sommes vendredi.* It's Friday today.
2 *on Friday* ◇ *Il est venu vendredi.* He came on Friday.
- **le vendredi** on Fridays ◇ *Je joue au foot le vendredi.* I play football on Fridays.
- **tous les vendredis** every Friday
- **vendredi dernier** last Friday
- **vendredi prochain** next Friday
- **le Vendredi saint** Good Friday

vénéneux ADJECTIVE
(FEM SING **vénéneuse**)
poisonous (*plant*) ◇ *un champignon vénéneux* a poisonous mushroom

V

la **vengeance** NOUN
revenge

se **venger** VERB
to get revenge

venimeux ADJECTIVE
(FEM SING **venimeuse**)
poisonous (*animal*) ◇ *un serpent venimeux* a poisonous snake

le **venin** NOUN
poison

venir VERB
to come ◇ *Il viendra demain.* He'll come tomorrow. ◇ *Il est venu nous voir.* He came to see us.
◆ **venir de** to have just ◇ *Je viens de le voir.* I've just seen him. ◇ *Je viens de lui téléphoner.* I've just phoned him.
◆ **faire venir quelqu'un** to call somebody out ◇ *faire venir le médecin* to call the doctor out

le **vent** NOUN
wind ◇ *Il y a du vent.* It's windy.

la **vente** NOUN
sale ◇ *une vente de charité* a jumble sale
◆ **une vente aux enchères** an auction

le **ventilateur** NOUN
fan (*for cooling*)

le **ventre** NOUN
stomach ◇ *avoir mal au ventre* to have stomachache

venu VERB *see* **venir**

le **ver** NOUN
worm
◆ **un ver de terre** an earthworm

le **verbe** NOUN
verb

le **verdict** NOUN
verdict

le **verger** NOUN
orchard

verglacé ADJECTIVE
icy ◇ *La route était verglacée.* The road was icy.

le **verglas** NOUN
black ice

véridique ADJECTIVE
truthful

la **vérification** NOUN
check ◇ *une vérification d'identité* an identity check

vérifier VERB
to check

véritable ADJECTIVE
real ◇ *C'était un véritable cauchemar.* It was a real nightmare.
◆ **en cuir véritable** made of real leather

la **vérité** NOUN
truth ◇ *dire la vérité* to tell the truth

verni ADJECTIVE
varnished
◆ **des chaussures vernies** patent leather shoes

vernir VERB
to varnish

le **vernis** NOUN
varnish ◇ *le vernis à ongles* nail varnish

verra, verrai, verras VERB *see* **voir**
◆ **on verra...** we'll see...

le **verre** NOUN
1 *glass* ◇ *une table en verre* a glass table ◇ *un verre d'eau* a glass of water
◆ **boire un verre** to have a drink
2 *lens* (*of spectacles*) ◇ *des verres de contact* contact lenses

verrez, verrons, verront VERB *see* **voir**

le **verrou** NOUN
bolt (*on door*)

verrouiller VERB
to bolt ◇ *N'oublie pas de verrouiller la porte du garage.* Don't forget to bolt the garage door.

la **verrue** NOUN
wart

le **vers** NOUN
see also **vers** PREPOSITION
line (*of poetry*) ◇ *au troisième vers* in the third line

vers PREPOSITION
see also **vers** NOUN
1 *towards* ◇ *Il allait vers la gare.* He was going towards the station.
2 *at about* ◇ *Il est rentré chez lui vers cinq heures.* He went home at about 5 o'clock.

verse
◆ **à verse** ADVERB ◇ *Il pleut à verse.* It's pouring with rain.

le **Verseau** NOUN
Aquarius ◇ *Georges est Verseau.* Georges is Aquarius.

le **versement** NOUN
instalment ◇ *en cinq versements* in 5 instalments

verser VERB
to pour ◇ *Est-ce que tu peux me verser un verre d'eau?* Could you pour me a glass of water?

la **version** NOUN
1 *version*
2 *translation* (*from the foreign language*)
◆ **un film en version originale** a film in the original language

le **verso** NOUN
back (*of sheet of paper*)
◆ **voir au verso** see overleaf

ert ADJECTIVE
green

ertèbre NOUN
vertebra

ertical ADJECTIVE
(MASC PL **verticaux**)
vertical

ertige NOUN
vertigo ◇ *avoir le vertige* to have vertigo

erveine NOUN
verbena tea

essie NOUN
bladder

este NOUN
jacket

estiaire NOUN
1 *cloakroom* (*in theatre, museum*)
2 *changing room* (*at sports ground*)

estibule NOUN
hall

êtement NOUN
garment
les vêtements clothes

étérinaire NOUN
vet ◇ *Elle est vétérinaire.* She's a vet.

euf NOUN
widower ◇ *Il est veuf.* He's a widower.

euille, veuillez, veuillons, veulent, veut VERB *see* **vouloir**
Veuillez fermer la porte en sortant. Please shut the door when you go out.

euve NOUN
widow ◇ *Elle est veuve.* She's a widow.

eux VERB *see* **vouloir**

exer VERB
vexer quelqu'un to hurt somebody's feelings
se vexer to be offended

iande NOUN
meat
la viande hachée mince

ibrer VERB
to vibrate

ice NOUN
vice

icieux ADJECTIVE
(FEM SING **vicieuse**)
lecherous ◇ *Il est un peu vicieux.* He's a bit of a lecher.

ictime NOUN
victim

ictoire NOUN
victory

ide ADJECTIVE
see also **vide** NOUN
empty

le **vide** NOUN
see also **vide** ADJECTIVE
vacuum ◇ *emballé sous vide* vacuum-packed
◆ **avoir peur du vide** to be afraid of heights

la **vidéo** NOUN
see also **vidéo** ADJECTIVE
video

vidéo ADJECTIVE (MASC, FEM, PL)
see also **vidéo** NOUN
video ◇ *une cassette vidéo* a video cassette ◇ *un jeu vidéo* a video game ◇ *une caméra vidéo* a video camera

le **vidéoclip** NOUN
music video

le **vidéoclub** NOUN
video shop

vider VERB
to empty

la **vie** NOUN
life
◆ **être en vie** to be alive

vieil ADJECTIVE
vieil *is used with a masculine singular noun in place of* **vieux** *when the noun begins with a vowel sound.*
old ◇ *un vieil arbre* an old tree ◇ *un vieil homme* an old man

le **vieillard** NOUN
old man

vieille ADJECTIVE
(MASC SING **vieux**)
see also **vieille** NOUN
old ◇ *une vieille dame* an old lady
◆ **une vieille fille** an old maid

la **vieille** NOUN
see also **vieille** ADJECTIVE
old woman
◆ **Eh bien, ma vieille...** (*informal*) Well, my dear...

la **vieillesse** NOUN
old age

vieillir VERB
to age ◇ *Il a beaucoup vieilli depuis la dernière fois que je l'ai vu.* He's aged a lot since I last saw him.

viendrai, vienne, viens VERB *see* **venir**
◆ **Je viendrai dès que possible.** I'll come as soon as possible.
◆ **Je voudrais que tu viennes.** I'd like you to come.
◆ **Viens ici!** Come here!

la **Vierge** NOUN
see also **vierge** ADJECTIVE
Virgo ◇ *Pascal est Vierge.* Pascal is Virgo.
◆ **la Vierge** the Virgin Mary

vierge ADJECTIVE
see also Vierge NOUN
1 *virgin* ◇ *Il est vierge.* He's a virgin.
2 *blank* ◇ *une cassette vierge* a blank cassette

le **Viêt-Nam** NOUN
Vietnam

vietnamien ADJECTIVE, NOUN
(FEM SING **vietnamienne**)
Vietnamese
◆ **un Vietnamien** a Vietnamese (*man*)
◆ **une Vietnamienne** a Vietnamese (*woman*)
◆ **les Vietnamiens** the Vietnamese

vieux ADJECTIVE
(FEM SING **vieille**)
see also vieux NOUN
old ◇ *Il fait plus vieux que son âge.* He looks older than he is.
◆ **un vieux garçon** a bachelor

le **vieux** NOUN
see also vieux ADJECTIVE
old man ◇ *Eh bien, mon vieux...* (*informal*) Well, my old mate...
◆ **les vieux** old people

vieux jeu ADJECTIVE (MASC, FEM, PL)
old-fashioned ◇ *Il est un peu vieux jeu.* He's a bit old-fashioned.

vif ADJECTIVE
(FEM SING **vive**)
1 *sharp* (*mentally*) ◇ *Il est très vif.* He's very sharp.
◆ **avoir l'esprit vif** to be quick-witted
2 *crisp* ◇ *L'air est plus vif à la campagne qu'en ville.* The air is crisper in the country than in the town.
3 *bright* (*colour*) ◇ *un bleu vif* a bright blue

la **vigne** NOUN
vine
◆ **des champs de vigne** vineyards

le **vigneron** NOUN
wine grower

la **vignette** NOUN
tax disc

le **vignoble** NOUN
vineyard

vilain ADJECTIVE
1 *naughty* ◇ *C'est très vilain de dire des mensonges.* It's very naughty to tell lies.
2 *ugly* ◇ *Il n'est pas vilain.* He's not bad-looking.

la **villa** NOUN
villa ◇ *une villa en multipropriété* a time-share villa

le **village** NOUN
village

le **villageois** NOUN
villager

la **villageoise** NOUN
villager

la **ville** NOUN
town ◇ *Je vais en ville.* I'm going int town.
◆ **une grande ville** a city

le **vin** NOUN
wine ◇ *le vin de pays* the local wine ◇ *le vin ordinaire* the table wine

le **vinaigre** NOUN
vinegar

la **vinaigrette** NOUN
French dressing

vingt NUMBER
twenty ◇ *Elle a vingt ans.* She's twenty. ◇ *à vingt heures* at 8 p.m.
◆ **le vingt février** the twentieth of February
◆ **vingt et un** twenty-one
◆ **vingt-deux** twenty-two

la **vingtaine** NOUN
about twenty ◇ *une vingtaine de personnes* about twenty people
◆ **Il a une vingtaine d'années.** He's abou twenty.

vingtième ADJECTIVE
twentieth

le **viol** NOUN
rape

violemment ADVERB
violently

la **violence** NOUN
violence

violent ADJECTIVE
violent

violer VERB
to rape

violet ADJECTIVE
(FEM SING **violette**)
purple

la **violette** NOUN
violet (*flower*)

le **violon** NOUN
violin ◇ *Je joue du violon.* I play the violin.

le **violoncelle** NOUN
cello ◇ *Elle joue du violoncelle.* She plays the cello.

le/la **violoniste** NOUN
violinist

la **vipère** NOUN
viper

le **virage** NOUN
bend ◇ *une route pleine de virages dangereux* a road full of dangerous bends

la **virgule** NOUN
1 *comma*

2 *decimal point* ◇ *trois virgule cinq* three point five

irus NOUN
virus

is VERB *see* **vivre**
see also **vis** NOUN
• **Je vis en Écosse.** I live in Scotland.

is NOUN
see also **vis** VERB
screw

isa NOUN
visa

isage NOUN
face ◇ *Elle a le visage rond.* She's got a round face.

is-à-vis de PREPOSITION
with regard to ◇ *Ce n'est pas très juste vis-à-vis de lui.* It's not very fair to him.

iser VERB
to aim at ◇ *Il faut viser la cible.* You have to aim at the target.

isibilité NOUN
visibility

isible ADJECTIVE
visible

isière NOUN
peak (*of cap*)

isite NOUN
visit
• **rendre visite à quelqu'un** to visit somebody ◇ *Je vais rendre visite à mon grand-père.* I'm going to visit my grandfather.
• **avoir de la visite** to have visitors ◇ *Nous avons de la visite aujourd'hui.* We've got visitors today.
• **une visite médicale** a medical examination

isiter VERB
to visit

isiteur NOUN
visitor

isiteuse NOUN
visitor

ison NOUN
mink (*fur*) ◇ *un manteau en vison* a mink coat

it VERB *see* **vivre**
• **Il vit chez ses parents.** He lives with his parents.

ital ADJECTIVE
(MASC PL **vitaux**)
vital ◇ *C'est une question vitale.* It's of vital importance.

itamine NOUN
vitamin

ite ADVERB
1 *quick* ◇ *Vite, ils arrivent!* Quick, they're coming! ◇ *Je peux aller dire au revoir à Claire?–Oui, mais fais vite!* Can I go and say goodbye to Claire?–Yes, but be quick! ◇ *Prenons la voiture, ça ira plus vite.* Let's take the car, it'll be quicker.
• **Le temps passe vite.** Time flies.
2 *fast* ◇ *Il roule trop vite.* He drives too fast.
3 *soon* ◇ *Il va vite oublier.* He'll soon forget.
• **Il a vite compris.** He understood immediately.

la **vitesse** NOUN
1 *speed* ◇ *à toute vitesse* at top speed ◇ *Nous sommes rentrés à toute vitesse.* We rushed back home.
2 *gear* ◇ *en première vitesse* in first gear

le **vitrail** NOUN
(PL les **vitraux**)
stained-glass window

la **vitre** NOUN
window ◇ *Il a cassé une vitre.* He broke a window.

la **vitrine** NOUN
shop window

vivant ADJECTIVE
1 *living* ◇ *les êtres vivants* living creatures ◇ *les expériences sur les animaux vivants* experiments on live animals
2 *lively* ◇ *Elle est très vivante.* She's very lively.

vive ADJECTIVE
(MASC SING **vif**)
see also **vive** EXCLAMATION
1 *sharp* (*mentally*) ◇ *Elle est très vive.* She's very sharp.
2 *bright* (*colour*)
• **à vive allure** at a brisk pace
• **de vive voix** in person ◇ *Je te le dirai de vive voix.* I'll tell you about it when I see you.

vive EXCLAMATION
see also **vive** ADJECTIVE
• **Vive le roi!** Long live the king!

vivement EXCLAMATION
• **Vivement les vacances!** Roll on the holidays!

vivre VERB
to live ◇ *J'aimerais vivre à l'étranger.* I'd like to live abroad. ◇ *Et ton grand-père? Il vit encore?* What about your grandfather? Is he still alive?

vlan EXCLAMATION
wham!

la **VO** NOUN
• **un film en VO** a film in the original

V

PTO

language

le **vocabulaire** NOUN
vocabulary

la **vocation** NOUN
vocation

le **vœu** NOUN
(PL les **vœux**)
wish ◇ *faire un vœu* to make a wish ◇ *Meilleurs vœux de bonne année!* Best wishes for the New Year!

la **vogue** NOUN
fashion ◇ *C'est très en vogue en ce moment.* It's very fashionable at the moment.

voici PREPOSITION
1 *this is* ◇ *Voici mon frère et voilà ma sœur.* This is my brother and that's my sister.
2 *here is* ◇ *Tu as perdu ton stylo? Tiens, en voici un autre.* Have you lost your pen? Here's another one.
◆ **Le voici!** Here he is! ◇ *Tu veux tes clés? Tiens, les voici!* You want your keys? Here you are!

la **voie** NOUN
lane ◇ *une route à trois voies* a 3-lane road
◆ **par voie buccale** orally ◇ *à prendre par voie buccale* to be taken orally
◆ **la voie ferrée** the railway track

voilà PREPOSITION
1 *there is* ◇ *Tiens! Voilà Paul.* Look! There's Paul. ◇ *Tu as perdu ton stylo? Tiens, en voilà un autre.* Have you lost your pen? There's another one.
◆ **Les voilà!** There they are!
2 *that is* ◇ *Voilà ma sœur.* That's my sister.

le **voile** NOUN
see also la voile
veil ◇ *un voile de mariée* a wedding veil

la **voile** NOUN
see also le voile
1 *sail*
2 *sailing* ◇ *faire de la voile* to go sailing
◆ **un bateau à voiles** a sailing boat

le **voilier** NOUN
sailing boat

voir VERB

Present tense:	
je vois	*nous voyons*
tu vois	*vous voyez*
il/elle voit	*ils/elles voient*
Past participle: *vu*	

to see ◇ *Venez me voir quand vous serez à Paris.* Come and see me when you're in Paris. ◇ *Je ne vois pas pourquoi il a fait ça.* I can't see why he did that.
◆ **faire voir quelque chose à quelqu'un** to show somebody something ◇ *Il m'a fait voir sa collection de timbres.* He showed me his stamp collection.
◆ **se voir** to be obvious ◇ *Est-ce que cette tache se voit?* Does that stain show? ◇ *Ça fait des années qu'elle n'a pas joué au tennis – Oui, ça se voit!* She hasn't played tennis for years – Yes, you can tell!
◆ **avoir quelque chose à voir avec** to have something to do with ◇ *Ça n'a rien à voir avec lui, c'est entre toi et moi.* It's nothing to do with him, it's between you and me.
◆ **Je ne peux vraiment pas la voir.** (*informal*) I really can't stand her.

le **voisin** NOUN
neighbour

le **voisinage** NOUN
◆ **dans le voisinage** in the vicinity

la **voisine** NOUN
neighbour

la **voiture** NOUN
car ◇ *une voiture de sport* a sports car

la **voix** NOUN
(PL les **voix**)
1 *voice* ◇ *à voix basse* in a low voice
◆ **à haute voix** aloud
2 *vote* ◇ *Il a obtenu cinquante pour cent des voix.* He got 50% of the votes.

le **vol** NOUN
1 *flight*
◆ **à vol d'oiseau** as the crow flies
◆ **le vol à voile** gliding
2 *theft* ◇ *un vol à main armée* an armed robbery

la **volaille** NOUN
poultry

le **volant** NOUN
1 *steering wheel* ◇ *Est-ce que tu veux que je prenne le volant?* Do you want me to take the wheel?
2 *shuttlecock*

le **volcan** NOUN
volcano

la **volée** NOUN
volley (*in tennis*)
◆ **rattraper une balle à la volée** to catch a ball in mid-air

voler VERB
1 *to fly* ◇ *J'aimerais savoir voler.* I'd like to be able to fly.
2 *to steal* ◇ *On a volé mon appareil photo.* My camera's been stolen.
◆ **voler quelque chose à quelqu'un** to steal something from somebody ◇ *Ça*

n'est pas son stylo, il me l'a volé. That's not his pen, he stole it from me.

- **voler quelqu'un** to rob somebody

volet NOUN
shutter

voleur NOUN
thief

voleuse NOUN
thief

volley NOUN
volleyball ◇ *jouer au volley* to play volleyball

volontaire NOUN
volunteer

volonté NOUN
willpower ◇ *Il a beaucoup de volonté.* He's got a lot of willpower.

- **la bonne volonté** goodwill
- **la mauvaise volonté** lack of goodwill

volontiers ADVERB
1 *gladly* ◇ *Je l'aiderais volontiers s'il me le demandais.* I'd gladly help him if he asked me.
2 *please* ◇ *Voulez-vous boire quelque chose?–Volontiers!* Would you like something to drink?–Yes, please!

volume NOUN
volume ◇ *un dictionnaire en deux volumes* a two-volume dictionary

volumineux ADJECTIVE
(FEM SING **volumineuse**)
bulky

vomir VERB
to vomit ◇ *Il a vomi toute la nuit.* He was vomiting all night.

vont VERB *see* **aller**

vos ADJECTIVE
your ◇ *Rangez vos jouets, les enfants!* Children, put your toys away! ◇ *Merci pour vos fleurs, M. Durand.* Thanks for your flowers, Mr Durand.

vote NOUN
vote

voter VERB
to vote

votre ADJECTIVE
(PL **vos**)
your ◇ *C'est votre manteau?* Is this your coat?

vôtre PRONOUN
- **le vôtre** yours ◇ *J'aime bien notre prof de maths, mais le vôtre est plus patient.* I like our maths teacher, but yours is more patient. ◇ *À qui est cette écharpe? C'est la vôtre?* Whose is this scarf? Is it yours?
- **À la vôtre!** Cheers!

vôtres PRONOUN
- **les vôtres** yours ◇ *J'ai oublié mes lunettes de soleil. Vous avez apporté les vôtres?* I've forgotten my sunglasses. Have you brought yours?

voudra, voudrai, voudrais, voudras, voudrez, voudrons, voudront VERB *see* **vouloir**
- **Je voudrais...** I'd like... ◇ *Je voudrais deux litres de lait, s'il vous plaît.* I'd like two litres of milk, please.

vouloir VERB

Present tense:	
je veux	*nous voulons*
tu veux	*vous voulez*
il/elle veut	*ils/elles veulent*
Past participle: *voulu*	

to want ◇ *Elle veut un vélo pour Noël.* She wants a bike for Christmas. ◇ *Je ne veux pas de dessert.* I don't want any pudding. ◇ *Il ne veut pas venir.* He doesn't want to come. ◇ *On va au cinéma?–Si tu veux.* Shall we go to the cinema?–If you like.

- **Je veux bien.** I'll be happy to. ◇ *Je veux bien le faire à ta place si ça t'arrange.* I don't mind doing it for you if you prefer.
- **Voulez-vous une tasse de thé?–Je veux bien.** Would you like a cup of tea?–Yes please.
- **sans le vouloir** without meaning to ◇ *Je l'ai vexé sans le vouloir.* I upset him without meaning to.
- **en vouloir à quelqu'un** to be angry at somebody ◇ *Il m'en veut de ne pas l'avoir invité à mon anniversaire.* He's angry at me for not inviting him to my birthday party.
- **vouloir dire** to mean ◇ *Qu'est-ce que ça veut dire?* What does that mean?

voulu VERB *see* **vouloir**

vous PRONOUN
1 *you* ◇ *Vous aimez la pizza?* Do you like pizza?
2 *to you* ◇ *Je vous écrirai bientôt.* I'll write to you soon.
3 *yourself* ◇ *Vous vous êtes fait mal?* Have you hurt yourself?
- **vous-même** yourself ◇ *Vous l'avez fait vous-même?* Did you do it yourself?

vouvoyer VERB
- **vouvoyer quelqu'un** to address somebody as "vous"

vouvoyer quelqu'un *means to use* **vous** *when speaking to someone, rather than* **tu**. *Use* **tu** *only when talking to one person and when that person is someone of your own age or whom you know well; use* **vous** *to everyone else. If in doubt use* **vous**.

- **Est-ce que je dois vouvoyer ta sœur?**

Should I use "vous" to your sister?

le **voyage** NOUN
journey ◇ *Avez-vous fait bon voyage?* Did you have a good journey?
➔ **Bon voyage!** Have a good trip!

voyager VERB
to travel

le **voyageur** NOUN
passenger

la **voyageuse** NOUN
passenger

voyaient, voyais, voyait VERB *see* **voir**

la **voyelle** NOUN
vowel

voyez, voyiez, voyions VERB *see* **voir**

voyons VERB *see* **voir**
1 *let's see* ◇ *Voyons ce qu'on peut faire.* Let's see what we can do.
2 *come on* ◇ *Voyons, sois raisonnable!* Come on, be reasonable!

le **voyou** NOUN
hooligan

vrac
➔ **en vrac** ADVERB
loose ◇ *du thé en vrac* loose tea

vrai ADJECTIVE
true ◇ *une histoire vraie* a true story
◇ *C'est vrai?* Is that true?
➔ **à vrai dire** to tell the truth

vraiment ADVERB
really

vraisemblable ADJECTIVE
likely ◇ *C'est peu vraisemblable.* That's not very likely. ◇ *Il va falloir trouver une excuse vraisemblable.* We'll have to find a convincing excuse.

le **VTT** NOUN (= *vélo tout-terrain*)
mountain bike

vu VERB *see* **voir**
➔ **être bien vu** to be popular (*person*) ◇ *Est-ce qu'il est bien vu à l'école?* Is he popular at school?
➔ **être mal vu** to be disapproved of ◇ *C'est mal vu de fumer ici.* They don't like people smoking here.

la **vue** NOUN
1 *eyesight* ◇ *J'ai une mauvaise vue.* I've got bad eyesight.
2 *view* ◇ *Il y a une belle vue d'ici.* There's a lovely view from here.
➔ **à vue d'œil** visibly ◇ *Elle grandit à vue d'œil.* Every time you see her, she's got taller.

vulgaire ADJECTIVE
vulgar ◇ *Ne dit pas ça, c'est très vulgaire.* Don't say that, it's very vulgar

W

agon NOUN
railway carriage

agon-lit NOUN
(PL les **wagons-lits**)
sleeper (*on train*)

agon-restaurant NOUN
(PL les **wagons-restaurants**)
restaurant car

alkman ® NOUN
Walkman ®

allon ADJECTIVE, NOUN
(FEM SING **wallonne**)
Walloon (*French-speaking Belgian*)

◆ **les Wallons** the French-speaking Belgians

la **Wallonie** NOUN
French-speaking Belgium

les **W.-C.** MASC NOUN
toilet

le **week-end** NOUN
weekend

le **western** NOUN
western (*film*)

le **whisky** NOUN
(PL les **whiskies**)
whisky

X

ylophone NOUN
xylophone ◇ *Elle joue du xylophone.* She plays the xylophone.

Y

PRONOUN
there ◇ *Nous y sommes allés l'été dernier.* We went there last summer. ◇ *Regarde dans le tiroir: je pense que les clés y sont.* Look in the drawer: I think the keys are in there.

y *replaces phrases with* **à** *in constructions like the ones below.*

▸ **Je pensais à l'examen. – Mais arrête d'y penser!** I was thinking about the exam. – Well, stop thinking about it!

▸ **Je ne m'attendais pas à ça. – Eh bien moi, je m'y attendais.** I wasn't expecting that. – Well, I was expecting it.

aourt NOUN
yoghurt ◇ *un yaourt nature* a plain yoghurt ◇ *un yaourt aux fruits* a fruit yoghurt

les **yeux** MASC NOUN
(SING **œil**)
eyes ◇ *Elle a les yeux bleus.* She's got blue eyes.

le **yoga** NOUN
yoga

le **yoghourt** NOUN
yoghurt

la **Yougoslavie** NOUN
Yugoslavia

◆ **l'ex-Yougoslavie** the former Yugoslavia

youpi EXCLAMATION
Yippee!

le **yoyo** NOUN
yo-yo

Z

zapper VERB
to channel hop

le **zèbre** NOUN
zebra

le **zéro** NOUN
zero
- **Ils ont gagné trois à zéro.** They won three-nil.

zézayer VERB
to lisp ◇ *Il zézaie.* He's got a lisp.

le **zigzag** NOUN
- **faire des zigzags** to zigzag

la **zone** NOUN
zone
- **une zone industrielle** an industrial estate

le **zoo** NOUN
zoo

zut EXCLAMATION
Oh heck!

PUZZLES AND WORDGAMES

Introduction

he puzzles and wordgames on the following pages have been designed to give ou practice in using your dictionary. Make sure you read the "How to use the ictionary" section at the front of this book before you start. Don't worry, there are nswers at the end of the wordgames in case you get really stuck!

WORDGAME 1

CHOOSING THE RIGHT TRANSLATION

Complete the crossword below by looking up the English words in the list and finding the correct French translations. There is a slight catch, however! All the English words have more than one French translation, but only one will fit correct into each part of the crossword.

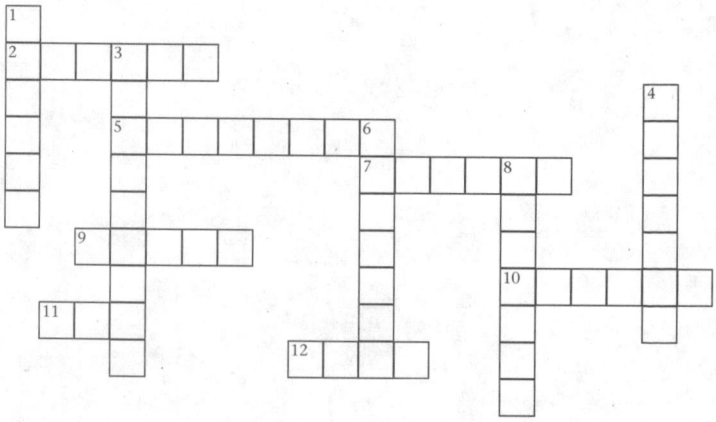

1. CLASS
2. THROW
3. KNOW
4. FIND
5. NUT
6. TAKE
7. CALF
8. PLACE
9. DINNER
10. STAY
11. HARD
12. LATE

WORDGAME 2

NOUNS, ADJECTIVES, ADVERBS & VERBS

In each sentence below a word has been shaded. Put a tick in the appropriate box to show whether it's a **noun**, **adjective**, **adverb** or **verb** each time. Look in the section "How to use the dictionary" at the front of the book to remind you what nouns, adjectives, adverbs and verbs are. Remember, there may be more than one entry for each word.

SENTENCE	Noun	Adj	Adv	Verb
1. La ferme de mes parents est en Alsace.				
2. Il n'est pas franc.				
3. Le magasin ferme dans deux minutes.				
4. Le dîner est à 20 heures.				
5. Tu veux goûter ma mousse au chocolat?				
6. Je n'aime pas la bière.				
7. C'est un faux passeport.				
8. J'entends des pas dans l'escalier.				
9. Ce film nous a fait rire.				
10. Cette voiture est mal garée.				

WORDGAME 3

NOUNS

This list contains the feminine form of some French nouns. Use your dictionary to find the **masculine** form. Remember, the masculine form usually appears in a separate entry.

MASCULINE	FEMININE
	danseuse
	boulangère
	Américaine
	animatrice
	avocate
	Parisienne
	libraire
	téléspectatrice
	pionne
	veuve

Use your dictionary to find the **plural** of the following nouns. Remember, the plural form appears in brackets and in bold on the line below the singular form.

SINGULAR	PLURAL
chou	
canal	
bateau	
sapeur-pompier	
neveu	
travail	
vœu	
voix	
œil	
croque-monsieur	

WORDGAME 4

ADJECTIVES

Use the French-English side of your dictionary to find the **feminine singular** form of these adjectives. Remember, the feminine singular form appears in brackets and in bold on the line below the masculine form.

MASCULINE	FEMININE
1. naturel	
2. beau	
3. heureux	
4. américain	
5. gros	
6. blanc	
7. faux	
8. sec	
9. favori	
10. frais	
11. bon	
12. fou	
13. public	
14. naïf	

WORDGAME 5

VERB TENSES

Use the verb tables on pages 284 to 297 to help you fill in the blanks in the table below.

INFINITIVE	PRESENT	IMPERFECT	FUTURE
faire		je	
se laver	il		
voir			nous
finir			elle
avoir		il	
aller	vous		
être	elles		
vouloir		ils	
devoir	tu		
mettre			je
dire		il	
pouvoir			nous

WORDGAME 6

«MOTS CODÉS»

In the boxes below, the letters of eight French words have been replaced by numbers. A number represents the same letter each time.

Try to crack the code and find the eight words. If you need help, use your dictionary.

Here is a clue: all the words you are looking for have something to do with CLOTHES.

1. P[1] [2] [3] [4] [2] [5] [6] [3]

2. [7] [8] P[1] E[9]

3. [10] [11] [3] [11] [7] [8] P[1] [9]

4. [10] [2] [3] [4] [9] [2] [8]

5. P[1] [8] [5] [5]

6. [12] [13] [2] P[1] [9] [2] [8]

7. [12] [13] [2] [8] [14] [14] [9] [4] [4] [9]

8. [12] [13] [2] [8] [14] [14] [8] [15] [9]

WORDGAME 7

«MOTS CUISINÉS»

Here is a list of French words for things you will find in the kitchen. Unfortunately, they have all been jumbled up. Try to work out what each word is and put the word in the boxes on the right. You will see there are five shaded boxes below. The five letters in the shaded boxes make up *another* French word for an object you can find in the kitchen.

1. féac — **Tu prends du sucre dans ton _____ ?**

2. rever — **Encore un _____ de vin?**

3. lesvisale — **je déteste faire la _____.**

4. rascosele — **Elle a fait cuire les pâtes dans une grande _____.**

5. grifo — **Le fromage est dans le _____.**

The word you are looking for is:

ANSWERS

WORDGAME 1

1. classe
2. lancer
3. connaître
4. trouver
5. noisette
6. emmener
7. mollet
8. endroit
9. dîner
10. rester
11. dur
12. tard

WORDGAME 2

1. noun
2. adjective
3. verb
4. noun
5. verb
6. adverb
7. adjective
8. noun
9. verb
10. adverb

WORDGAME 3

Masculine forms

1. danseur
2. boulanger
3. Américain
4. animateur
5. avocat
6. Parisien
7. libraire
8. téléspectateur
9. pion
10. veuf

WORDGAME 3

Plural forms

1. choux
2. canaux
3. bateaux
4. sapeurs-pompiers
5. neveux
6. travaux
7. voeux
8. voix
9. yeux
10. croque-monsieur

WORDGAME 4

1. naturelle
2. belle
3. heureuse
4. américaine
5. grosse
6. blanche
7. fausse
8. sèche
9. favorite
10. fraîche
11. bonne
12. folle
13. publique
14. naïve

WORDGAME 5

1. je faisais
2. il se lave
3. nous verrons
4. elle finira
5. il avait
6. vous allez
7. elles sont
8. ils voulaient
9. tu dois
10. je mettrai
11. il disait
12. nous pourrons

WORDGAME 6

1. pantalon
2. jupe
3. minijupe
4. manteau
5. pull
6. chapeau
7. chaussette
8. chaussure

WORDGAME 7

1. café
2. verre
3. vaisselle
4. casserole
5. frigo

Missing word – évier

FRENCH VERB TABLES

CONTENTS

Introduction 282

Verb Tables:

AIMER (regular "–er" verb) 284
FINIR (regular "–ir" verb) 285
ATTENDRE (regular "–re" verb) 286
SE LAVER (reflexive verb) 287
AVOIR 288
ÊTRE 289
ALLER 290
DEVOIR 291
DIRE 292
FAIRE 293
METTRE 294
POUVOIR 295
VOIR 296
VOULOIR 297

French irregular verb forms 298

FRENCH VERB TABLES

This section contains fourteen important French verbs that you need to learn. All French verbs fall into two main categories – **regular** and **irregular** – and it is important to learn which verbs fall into which category.

The tables are arranged in the following order:

1. Regular verbs – **aimer**, **finir**, **attendre** and **se laver**
2. Very important irregular verbs – **avoir** and **être**
3. Other common irregular verbs – **aller**, **devoir**, **dire**, **faire**, **mettre**, **pouvoir**, **voir** and **vouloir**

At the top of each table you will find the infinitive, the imperative and the past participle. The lower section of the table shows you how to form six tenses of the verb:

PRESENT	e.g. je fais = I **do** *or* **I am doing**
*PRESENT SUBJUNCTIVE**	e.g. je fasse = I **do**
IMPERFECT	e.g. je faisais = I **was doing** *or* **I did**
PERFECT	e.g. j'ai fait = I **did** *or* **I have done**
FUTURE	e.g. je ferai = I **will do**
CONDITIONAL	e.g. je ferais = I **would do**

***The French side of your dictionary will tell you which words must be followed by the subjunctive.**

1. REGULAR VERBS

There are three groups of regular verbs:

1. "-ER" verbs = verbs that end in **-er** like **aimer** on p284 and **se laver** on p287
2. "-IR" verbs = verbs that end in **-ir** like **finir** on p285
3. "-RE" verbs = verbs that end in **-re** like **attendre** on p286

They are called regular verbs because they follow one of three set patterns. When you have learnt these patterns, you will be able to form *any* regular verb.

HOW TO FORM A REGULAR VERB

i. a) To form the present, imperfect or present subjunctive tense, take the infinitive minus the last two letters. This is called the **stem** e.g. *aimer* → **aim-**, *finir* → **fin-**, and *attendre* → **attend-**

b) To form the future or conditional tense, the stem is the whole infinitive for "-ER" and "-IR" verbs and the infinitive minus its final "e" for "-RE" verbs e.g. *aimer* → **aimer**, *finir* → **finir** and *attendre* → **attendr-**

ii. Next add the appropriate **ending**. You need to ask yourself three questions:

a) **What sort of** verb am I using (-ER, -IR, -RE)?
b) **Who** is doing the verb? (je, tu, il *etc*)?
c) **When** are they doing it (in the present, the past or the future)?

Look at the verb tables for **aimer**, **finir** and **attendre**. The verb endings are in red and underlined. These endings can be tagged onto the stem of *any* regular verb.

2. AVOIR AND ÊTRE

Avoir (to have) and **être** (to be) are very important verbs which **must** be learnt. You use them when you want to say "**I have**" *etc* or "**I am**" *etc*. The present tense of **avoir** or **être** is also used to form the **perfect tense**. In most cases, **avoir** is used to form the perfect, but verbs of movement like **aller** (to go) and **venir** (to come) use **être** – e.g. the French for both "he's gone" and "he went" is **il *est* allé**, not **il *a* allé**. You will have to learn which verbs use être.

HOW TO FORM THE PERFECT TENSE

a) Take the infinitive of a French verb e.g. **donner**
b) Does it use **avoir** or **être** to form the perfect tense? e.g. **donner** uses **avoir**
c) Take the present tense form of **avoir** or **être** that goes with the person who **did** the action e.g. **he** gave – the French for "he" is **il**, so to form the perfect tense of **donner** we use **il a**
d) Add the **past participle** – this is shown near the top of each verb table. If you want to form the past participle of *any* regular verb, simply take the infinitive of the verb, knock off the last two letters and add the following endings:

"-ER" verbs add **é** – e.g. aimer → aim**é**
"-IR" verbs add **i** – e.g. finir → fin**i**
"-RE" verbs add **u** – e.g. attendre → attend**u**

In our example, **donner** is a regular "-ER" verb, so the past participle is donn + é → **donné**
e) The French for "he gave" is "**il a donné**"

3. IRREGULAR VERBS

Many French verbs are irregular and this means you have to learn them individually. There are tables of the most important irregular verbs such as **avoir** (to have), **être** (to be) and **faire** (to do) in this section. When you are translating from French and meet an unfamiliar verb form, you may be able to guess from the context that it comes from one of these verbs, and you can use the verb table to check. The most common irregular verb parts are listed on the French side of the dictionary, so you could also look there.

HOW TO USE THE VERB TABLES

You will find some useful example phrases at the top of each verb table, but if you can't find what you need to say or write in French there, use the verb table itself to help you. Imagine that you want to find the French for "he wants". Here's how to do it:

a) Look up **want** on the English-French side of the dictionary to find the French translation
b) French translation = **vouloir**
c) Turn to the verb tables section of your dictionary and find **vouloir**
d) When does he want it? He wants it **now**, so look for the heading ***PRESENT***
e) Who wants it? **He** does. The French for "he" is **il** so look for **il** under the ***PRESENT*** heading
f) The French for "he wants" is "**il veut**"

aimer

to like *or* to love

IMPERATIVE

aime
aimons
aimez

EXAMPLE PHRASES

*Tu **aimes** le chocolat?* Do you like chocolate?
*Je t'**aime**.* I love you.
*J'**aimerais** aller en Grèce.* I'd like to go to Greece.

PAST PARTICIPLE

aimé

PRESENT

j' aime
tu aimes
il aime
nous aimons
vous aimez
ils aiment

PRESENT SUBJUNCTIVE

j' aime
tu aimes
il aime
nous aimions
vous aimiez
ils aiment

PERFECT

j' ai aimé
tu as aimé
il a aimé
nous avons aimé
vous avez aimé
ils ont aimé

IMPERFECT

j' aimais
tu aimais
il aimait
nous aimions
vous aimiez
ils aimaient

FUTURE

j' aimerai
tu aimeras
il aimera
nous aimerons
vous aimerez
ils aimeront

CONDITIONAL

j' aimerais
tu aimerais
il aimerait
nous aimerions
vous aimeriez
ils aimeraient

finir

to finish

EXAMPLE PHRASES

***Finis** ta soupe!* Finish your soup!
*J'**ai fini!*** I've finished!
*Je **finirai** mes devoirs demain.* I'll finish my homework tomorrow.

IMPERATIVE

fin is
fin issons
fin issez

PAST PARTICIPLE

fin i

PRESENT

je fin is
tu fin is
il fin it
nous fin issons
vous fin issez
ils fin issent

PERFECT

j' ai fin i
tu as fin i
il a fin i
nous avons fin i
vous avez fin i
ils ont fin i

FUTURE

j' finir ai
tu finir as
il finir a
nous finir ons
vous finir ez
ils finir ont

PRESENT SUBJUNCTIVE

je fin isse
tu fin isses
il fin isse
nous fin issions
vous fin issiez
ils fin issent

IMPERFECT

je fin issais
tu fin issais
il fin issait
nous fin issions
vous fin issiez
ils fin issaient

CONDITIONAL

je finir ais
tu finir ais
il finir ait
nous finir ions
vous finir iez
ils finir aient

attendre

to wait

IMPERATIVE

attends
attendons
attendez

EXAMPLE PHRASES

***Attends**–moi!* Wait for me!
*Tu **attends** depuis longtemps?* Have you been waiting long?
*Je l'**ai attendu** à la poste.* I waited for him at the post office.

PAST PARTICIPLE

attendu

PRESENT

j' attends
tu attends
il attend
nous attendons
vous attendez
ils attendent

PRESENT SUBJUNCTIVE

j' attende
tu attendes
il attende
nous attendions
vous attendiez
ils attendent

PERFECT

j' ai attendu
tu as attendu
il a attendu
nous avons attendu
vous avez attendu
ils ont attendu

IMPERFECT

j' attendais
tu attendais
il attendait
nous attendions
vous attendiez
ils attendaient

FUTURE

j' attendrai
tu attendras
il attendra
nous attendrons
vous attendrez
ils attendront

CONDITIONAL

j' attendrais
tu attendrais
il attendrait
nous attendrions
vous attendriez
ils attendraient

se laver

to wash (oneself)

EXAMPLE PHRASES

*Je **me lave** chaque matin.* I have a wash every morning.
*Il **s'est lavé** les mains.* He washed his hands.
*Elle va **se laver** les cheveux.* She's going to wash her hair.

IMPERATIVE

lav e-toi
lav ons-nous
lav ez-vous

PAST PARTICIPLE

lav é

PRESENT

je me lav e
tu te lav es
il se lav e
nous nous lav ons
vous vous lav ez
ils se lav ent

PERFECT

je me suis lav é
tu t'es lav é
il s'est lav es
nous nous sommes lav és
vous vous êtes lav és
ils se sont lav és

FUTURE

je me laver ai
tu te laver as
il se laver a
nous nous laver ons
vous vous laver ez
ils se laver ont

PRESENT SUBJUNCTIVE

je me lav e
tu te lav es
il se lav e
nous nous lav ions
vous vous lav iez
ils se lav ent

IMPERFECT

je me lav ais
tu te lav ais
il se lav ait
nous nous lav ions
vous vous lav iez
ils se lav aient

CONDITIONAL

je me laver ais
tu te laver ais
il se laver ait
nous nous laver ions
vous vous laver iez
ils se laver aient

avoir

to have

IMPERATIVE

aie
ayons
ayez

EXAMPLE PHRASES

*Il **a** les yeux bleus.* He's got blue eyes.
*Quel âge **as**-tu?* How old are you?
*Il **a eu** un accident.* He's had an accident.
*j'**avais** faim.* I was hungry.

PAST PARTICIPLE

eu

PRESENT

j'ai
tu as
il a
nous avons
vous avez
ils ont

PERFECT

j' ai eu
tu as eu
il a eu
nous avons eu
vous avez eu
ils ont eu

FUTURE

j'aurai
tu auras
il aura
nous aurons
vous aurez
ils auront

PRESENT SUBJUNCTIVE

j'aie
tu aies
il ait
nous ayons
vous ayez
ils aient

IMPERFECT

j' avais
tu avais
il avait
nous avions
vous aviez
ils avaient

CONDITIONAL

j'aurais
tu aurais
il aurait
nous aurions
vous auriez
ils auraient

être

to be

EXAMPLE PHRASES

*Mon père **est** professeur.* My father's a teacher.
*Quelle heure **est**-il? Il **est** 10 heures.* What time is it? – It's 10 o'clock
*Ils ne **sont** pas encore arrivés.* They haven't arrived yet.

IMPERATIVE

sois
soyons
soyez

PAST PARTICIPLE

été

PRESENT

je suis
tu es
il est
nous sommes
vous êtes
ils sont

PRESENT SUBJUNCTIVE

je sois
tu sois
il soit
nous soyons
vous soyez
ils soient

PERFECT

j' ai été
tu as été
il a étés
nous avons été
vous avez été
ils ont été

IMPERFECT

j' étais
tu étais
il était
nous étions
vous étiez
ils étaient

FUTURE

je serai
tu seras
il sera
nous serons
vous serez
ils seront

CONDITIONAL

je serais
tu serais
il serait
nous serions
vous seriez
ils seraient

aller

to go

IMPERATIVE

va
allons
allez

EXAMPLE PHRASES

*Vous **allez** au cinéma?* Are you going to the cinema?
*Je **suis allé** à Londres.* I went to London.
*Est-ce que tu **es** déjà **allé** en Allemagne?* Have you ever been to Germany?

PAST PARTICIPLE

allé

PRESENT

je vais
tu vas
il va
nous allons
vous allez
ils vont

PRESENT SUBJUNCTIVE

j' aille
tu ailles
il aille
nous allions
vous alliez
ils aillent

PERFECT

je suis allé
tu es allé
il est allé
nous sommes allés
vous êtes allé(s)
ils sont allés

IMPERFECT

j' allais
tu allais
il allait
nous allions
vous alliez
ils allaient

FUTURE

j' irai
tu iras
il ira
nous irons
vous irez
ils iront

CONDITIONAL

j' irais
tu irais
il irait
nous irions
vous iriez
ils iraient

devoir

to have to

EXAMPLE PHRASES

e ***dois*** *aller faire les courses ce matin.*
have to do the shopping this morning.
l ***a dû*** *faire ses devoirs hier soir.* He had
o do his homework last night.
l ***devait*** *prendre le train pour aller*
ravailler. He had to go to work by train.

IMPERATIVE

dois
dev ons
dev ez

PAST PARTICIPLE

dû

PRESENT

je dois
tu dois
il doit
nous dev ons
vous dev ez
ils doivent

PERFECT

j' ai dû
tu as dû
il a dû
nous avons dû
vous avez dû
ils ont dû

FUTURE

je dev rai
tu dev ras
il dev ra
nous dev rons
vous dev rez
ils dev ront

PRESENT SUBJUNCTIVE

je doive
tu doives
il doive
nous dev ions
vous dev iez
ils doivent

IMPERFECT

je dev ais
tu dev ais
il dev ait
nous dev ions
vous dev iez
ils dev aient

CONDITIONAL

je dev rais
tu dev rais
il dev rait
nous dev rions
vous dev riez
ils dev raient

dire

to say

IMPERATIVE

dis
disons
dites

EXAMPLE PHRASES

Qu'est-ce qu'elle ***dit?*** What is she saying?
"Bonjour!" ***a****-t-il* ***dit****.* "Hello!" he said.
*Il m'****a dit*** *que le film était nul.* He told me that the film was rubbish.

PAST PARTICIPLE

dit

PRESENT

je dis
tu dis
il dit
nous disons
vous dites
ils disent

PERFECT

j' ai dit
tu as dit
il a dit
nous avons dit
vous avez dit
ils ont dit

FUTURE

je dir<u>ai</u>
tu dir<u>as</u>
il dir<u>a</u>
nous dir<u>ons</u>
vous dir<u>ez</u>
ils dir<u>ont</u>

PRESENT SUBJUNCTIVE

je dise
tu dises
il dise
nous disions
vous disiez
ils disent

IMPERFECT

je disais
tu disais
il disait
nous disions
vous disiez
ils disaient

CONDITIONAL

je dir<u>ais</u>
tu dir<u>ais</u>
il dir<u>ait</u>
nous dir<u>ions</u>
vous dir<u>iez</u>
ils dir<u>aient</u>

faire

to do *or* to make

EXAMPLE PHRASES

Qu'est-ce que tu ***fais****?* What are you doing?
Qu'est-ce qu'il ***a fait****?* What has he done *or* What did he do?
*J'****ai fait*** *un gâteau.* I've made a cake *or* I made a cake.

IMPERATIVE

fais
faisons
faites

PAST PARTICIPLE

fait

PRESENT

je fais
tu fais
il fait
nous faisons
vous faites
ils font

PERFECT

j' ai fait
tu as fait
il a fait
nous avons fait
vous avez fait
ils ont fait

FUTURE

je ferai
tu feras
il fera
nous ferons
vous ferez
ils feront

PRESENT SUBJUNCTIVE

je fasse
tu fasses
il fasse
nous fassions
vous fassiez
ils fassent

IMPERFECT

je faisais
tu faisais
il faisait
nous faisions
vous faisiez
ils faisaient

CONDITIONAL

je ferais
tu ferais
il ferait
nous ferions
vous feriez
ils feraient

mettre

to put

IMPERATIVE

mets
mettons
mettez

EXAMPLE PHRASES

***Mets** ton manteau!* Put your coat on!
*Où est-ce que tu **as mis** les clés?* Where have you put the keys?
*J'**ai mis** le livre sur la table.* I put the book on the table.

PAST PARTICIPLE

mis

PRESENT

je mets
tu mets
il met
nous mettons
vous mettez
ils mettent

PERFECT

j' ai mis
tu as mis
il a mis
nous avons mis
vous avez mis
ils ont mis

FUTURE

je mettrai
tu mettras
il mettra
nous mettrons
vous mettrez
ils mettront

PRESENT SUBJUNCTIVE

je mette
tu mettes
il mette
nous mettions
vous mettiez
ils mettent

IMPERFECT

je mettais
tu mettais
il mettait
nous mettions
vous mettiez
ils mettaient

CONDITIONAL

je mettrais
tu mettrais
il mettrait
nous mettrions
vous mettriez
ils mettraient

pouvoir

to be able

EXAMPLE PHRASES

*Je **peux** t'aider, si tu veux?* I can help you if you like?
*J'ai fait tout ce que j'**ai pu**.* I did all I could.
*Je ne **pourrai** pas venir samedi.* I won't be able to come on Saturday.

IMPERATIVE

the imperative of **pouvoir** is not used

PAST PARTICIPLE

pu

PRESENT

je peux
tu peux
il peut
nous pouvons
vous pouvez
ils peuvent

PERFECT

j' ai pu
tu as pu
il a pu
nous avons pu
vous avez pu
ils ont pu

FUTURE

je pourrai
tu pourras
il pourra
nous pourrons
vous pourrez
ils pourront

PRESENT SUBJUNCTIVE

je puisse
tu puisses
il puisse
nous puissions
vous puissiez
ils puissent

IMPERFECT

je pouvais
tu pouvais
il pouvait
nous pouvions
vous pouviez
ils pouvaient

CONDITIONAL

je pourrais
tu pourrais
il pourrait
nous pourrions
vous pourriez
ils pourraient

voir

to see

IMPERATIVE

vois
voyons
voyez

EXAMPLE PHRASES

*Venez me **voir** quand vous serez à Paris.*
Come and see me when you're in Paris.
*Je ne **vois** rien sans mes lunettes.*
I can't see anything without my glasses.
*Est-ce que tu l'**as vu**?* Did you see him? *or* Have you seen him?

PAST PARTICIPLE

vu

PRESENT

je vois
tu vois
il voit
nous voyons
vous voyez
ils voient

PRESENT SUBJUNCTIVE

je voie
tu voies
il voie
nous voyions
vous voyiez
ils voient

PERFECT

j' ai vu
tu as vu
il a vu
nous avons vu
vous avez vu
ils ont vu

IMPERFECT

je voyais
tu voyais
il voyait
nous voyions
vous voyiez
ils voyaient

FUTURE

je verrai
tu verras
il verra
nous verrons
vous verrez
ils verront

CONDITIONAL

je verrais
tu verrais
il verrait
nous verrions
vous verriez
ils verraient

vouloir

to want

EXAMPLE PHRASES

*Elle **veut** un vélo pour Noël.* She wants a bike for Christmas.
*Ils **voulaient** aller au cinéma.* They wanted to go to the cinema.
*Tu **voudrais** une tasse de thé?* Would you like a cup of tea?

IMPERATIVE

veuille
veuillons
veuillez

PAST PARTICIPLE

voul u

PRESENT

je veux
tu veux
il veut
nous voul ons
vous voul ez
ils veulent

PERFECT

j' ai voul u
tu as voul u
il a voul u
nous avons voul u
vous avez voul u
ils ont voul u

FUTURE

je voudrai
tu voudras
il voudra
nous voudrons
vous voudrez
ils voudront

PRESENT SUBJUNCTIVE

je veuille
tu veuilles
il veuille
nous voul ions
vous voul iez
ils veuillent

IMPERFECT

je voul ais
tu voul ais
il voul ait
nous voul ions
vous voul iez
ils voul aient

CONDITIONAL

je voudrais
tu voudrais
il voudrait
nous voudrions
vous voudriez
ils voudraient

FRENCH IRREGULAR VERB FORMS

The following list is a summary of the main forms of other irregular verbs that you are likely to come across. The **infinitive** appears in red and is followed by a series of numbers from 1 to 5. These tell you which **tenses** are listed:

1 = present
2 = past participle
3 = Imperfect
4 = future
5 = present subjunctive

For the present tense, all **je** and **nous** forms are shown. The **il**, **vous** and **ils** forms are also included wherever the part of the verb that goes with them follows an unusual pattern. For the imperfect, future and present subjunctive tenses, only the **je** form is given.

acheter **1** j'achète, nous achetons, ils achètent **2** acheté **3** j'achetais **4** j'achèterai **5** j'achète

appeler **1** j'appelle, il appelle, nous appelons **2** appelé **3** j'appelais **4** j'appellerai **5** j'appelle

apprendre **1** j'apprends, nous apprenons, vous apprenez, ils apprennent **2** appris **3** j'apprenais **4** j'apprendrai **5** j'apprenne

s'asseoir **1** je m'assieds, nous nous asseyons, vous vous asseyez, ils s'asseyent **2** assis **3** je m'asseyais **4** je m'assiérai **5** je m'asseye

battre **1** je bats, il bat, nous battons **2** battu **3** je battais **5** je batte

boire **1** je bois, nous buvons, ils boivent **2** bu **3** je buvais **4** je boirai **5** je boive

bouillir **1** je bous, nous bouillons **2** bouilli **3** je bouillais **5** je bouille

conclure **1** je conclus, nous concluons **2** conclu **3** je concluais **5** je conclue

conduire **1** je conduis, nous conduisons **2** conduit **3** je conduisais **5** je conduise

connaître **1** je connais, il connaît, nous connaissons **2** connu **3** je connaissais **4** je connaîtrai **5** je connaisse

coudre **1** je couds, nous cousons, vous cousez, ils cousent **2** cousu **3** je cousais **4** je coudrai **5** je couse

courir **1** je cours, nous courons **2** couru **3** je courais **4** je courrai **5** je coure

couvrir **1** je couvre, nous couvrons **2** couvert **3** je couvrais **4** je couvrirai **5** je couvre

craindre **1** je crains, nous craignons **2** craint **3** je craignais **5** je craigne

créer **1** je crée, nous créons **2** créé **3** je créais **4** je créerai **5** je crée

croire **1** je crois, nous croyons, ils croient **2** cru **3** je croyais **4** je croirai **5** je croie

croître **1** je croîs, nous croissons **2** crû, crue, crus, crues **3** je croissais **5** je croisse

cueillir **1** je cueille, nous cueillons **2** cueilli **3** je cueillais **4** je cueillerai **5** je cueille

cuire **1** je cuis, nous cuisons, ils cuisent **2** cuit **3** je cuisais **4** je cuirai **5** je cuise

dormir **1** je dors, nous dormons **2** dormi **3** je dormais **4** je dormirai **5** je dorme

écrire **1** j'écris, nous écrivons **2** écrit **3** j'écrivais **4** j'écrirai **5** j'écrive

falloir **1** il faut **2** fallu **3** il fallait **4** il faudra **5** il faille

fuir **1** je fuis, nous fuyons, ils fuient **2** fui **3** je fuyais **5** je fuie

haïr **1** je hais, nous haïssons, ils haïssent **2** haï **3** je haïssais **4** je haïrai **5** je haïsse

jeter **1** je jette, nous jetons, ils jettent **2** jeté **3** je jetais **4** je jetterai **5** je jette

joindre **1** je joins, nous joignons **2** joint **3** je joignais **5** je joigne

lever **1** je lève, nous levons, ils lèvent **2** levé **3** je levais **4** je lèverai **5** je lève

lire **1** je lis, nous lisons **2** lu **3** je lisais **4** je lirai **5** je lise

manger **1** je mange, nous mangeons **2** mangé **3** je mangeais **4** je mangerai **5** je mange

mentir **1** je mens, nous mentons **2** menti **3** je mentais **5** je mente

mourir **1** je meurs, nous mourons, ils meurent **2** mort **3** je mourais **4** je mourrai **5** je meure

naître **1** je nais, il naît, nous naissons **2** né **3** je naissais **4** je naîtrai **5** je naisse

offrir **1** j'offre, nous offrons **2** offert **3** j'offrais **5** j'offre

paraître **1** je parais, il paraît, nous paraissons **2** paru **3** je paraissais **4** je paraîtrai **5** je paraisse

partir **1** je pars, nous partons **2** parti **3** je partais **4** je partirai **5** je parte

plaire **1** je plais, il plaît, nous plaisons **2** plu **3** je plaisais **4** je plairai **5** je plaise

pleuvoir **1** il pleut **2** plu **3** il pleuvait **4** il pleuvra **5** il pleuve

prendre **1** je prends, nous prenons, ils prennent **2** pris **3** je prenais **4** je prendrai **5** je prenne

recevoir **1** je reçois, il reçoit, ils reçoivent **2** reçu **3** je recevais **4** je recevrai **5** je reçoive

rire **1** je ris, nous rions **2** ri **3** je riais **4** je rirai **5** je rie

savoir **1** je sais, nous savons, ils savent **2** su **3** je savais **4** je saurai **5** je sache

servir **1** je sers, nous servons **2** servi **3** je servais **5** je serve

sortir **1** je sors, nous sortons **2** sorti **3** je sortais **5** je sorte

souffrir **1** je souffre, nous souffrons **2** souffert **3** je souffrais **5** je souffre

suffire **1** je suffis, nous suffisons **2** suffi **3** je suffisais **5** je suffise

suivre **1** je suis, nous suivons **2** suivi **3** je suivais **4** je suivrai **5** je suive

se taire **1** je me tais, nous nous taisons **2** tu **3** je me taisais **4** je me tairai **5** je me taise

tenir **1** je tiens, nous tenons, ils tiennent **2** tenu **3** je tenais **4** je tiendrai **5** je tienne

vaincre **1** je vaincs, il vainc, nous vainquons **2** vaincu **3** je vainquais **5** je vainque

valoir **1** je vaux, il vaut, nous valons **2** valu **3** je valais **4** je vaudrai **5** je vaille

venir **1** je viens, nous venons, ils viennent **2** venu **3** je venais **4** je viendrai **5** je vienne

vivre **1** je vis, nous vivons **2** vécu **3** je vivais **4** je vivrai **5** je vive

If you would like to see fuller tables for these verbs, look in **Collins Pocket French Verb Tables.**

LES NOMBRES

1	un (une)
2	deux
3	trois
4	quatre
5	cinq
6	six
7	sept
8	huit
9	neuf
10	dix
11	onze
12	douze
13	treize
14	quatorze
15	quinze
16	seize
17	dix-sept
18	dix-huit
19	dix-neuf
20	vingt
21	vingt et un (une)
22	vingt-deux
30	trente
40	quarante
50	cinquante
60	soixante
70	soixante-dix
71	soixante et onze
72	soixante-douze
80	quatre-vingts
81	quatre-vingt-un (-une)
90	quatre-vingt-dix
91	quatre-vingt-onze
100	cent
101	cent un (une)
300	trois cents
301	trois cent un (une)
1000	mille
2000	deux mille
1,000,000	un million

1st	premier (**1**er), première (**1**re)
2nd	deuxième (**2**e *or* **2**ème)
3rd	troisième (**3**e *or* **3**ème)
4th	quatrième (**4**e *or* **4**ème)
5th	cinquième (**5**e *or* **5**ème)
6th	sixième (**6**e *or* **6**ème)
7th	septième (**7**e *or* **7**ème)
8th	huitième (**8**e *or* **8**ème)
9th	neuvième (**9**e *or* **9**ème)
10th	dixième (**10**e *or* **10**ème)
11th	onzième (**11**e *or* **11**ème)
12th	douzième (**12**e *or* **12**ème)
13th	treizième (**13**e *or* **13**ème)
14th	quatorzième (**14**e *or* **14**ème)
15th	quinzième (**15**e *or* **15**ème)
16th	seizième (**16**e *or* **16**ème)
17th	dix-septième (**17**e *or* **17**ème)
18th	dix-huitième (**18**e *or* **18**ème)
19th	dix-neuvième (**19**e *or* **19**ème)
20th	vingtième (**20**e *or* **20**ème)
21st	vingt et unième (**21**e *or* **21**ème)
22nd	vingt-deuxième (**22**e *or* **22**ème)
30th	trentième (**30**e *or* **30**ème)
100th	centième (**100**e *or* **100**ème)
101st	cent unième (**101**e *or* **101**ème)
1000th	millième (**1000**e *or* **1000**ème)

Fractions etc

$\frac{1}{2}$	un demi
$\frac{1}{3}$	un tiers
$\frac{2}{3}$	deux tiers
$\frac{1}{4}$	un quart
$\frac{1}{5}$	un cinquième
0.5	zéro virgule cinq (0,5)
3.4	trois virgule quatre (3,4)
10%	dix pour cent
100%	cent pour cent

EXEMPLES

il habite au dix
à la page dix-neuf
au chapitre sept
il habite au cinquième (étage)
il est arrivè troisième
échelle au vingt-cinq millième

EXAMPLES

he lives at number ten
on page nineteen
in chapter seven
he lives on the fifth floor
he came in third
scale one to twenty-five thousand

L'HEURE

uelle heure est-il? What time is it?
est... It's...

une heure

une heure dix

une heure et quart

une heure et demie

deux heures moins vingt

deux heures moins le quart

À quelle heure? At what time?

à minuit

à midi

à une heure (de l'après-midi)

à huit heures (du soir)

In France times are often given in the twenty-four hour clock.

à 11.15 *or*
onze heures quinze

à 20.45 *or*
vingt heures quarante-cinq

LA DATE

LES JOURS DE LA SEMAINE

lundi
mardi
mercredi
jeudi
vendredi
samedi
dimanche

Quand?
lundi
le lundi
tous les lundis
mardi dernier
vendredi prochain
samedi en huit
samedi en quinze

DAYS OF THE WEEK

Monday
Tuesday
Wednesday
Thursday
Friday
Saturday
Sunday

When?
on Monday
on Mondays
every Monday
last Tuesday
next Friday
a week on Saturday
two weeks on Saturday

LES MOIS

janvier
février
mars
avril
mai
juin
juillet
août
septembre
octobre
novembre
décembre

Quand?

en février
le 1er décembre
le premier décembre
en 1998
en mille neuf cent quatre-vingt-dix-huit

Quel jour sommes-nous? What day is it?

FEB 26 MON lundi 26 février *or*
lundi vingt-six février

VOCABULAIRE

Quand?

aujourd'hui
ce matin
cet après-midi
ce soir

Souvent?

tous les jours
tous les deux jours
une fois par semaine
deux fois par semaine
une fois par mois

Ça s'est passé quand?

le matin
le soir
hier
hier soir
avant-hier
il y a une semaine
il y a quinze jours
l'an dernier *or* l'année dernière

Ça va se passer quand?

demain
demain matin
après-demain
dans deux jours
dans une semaine
dans quinze jours
le mois prochain
l'an prochain or l'année prochaine

MONTHS OF THE YEAR

January
February
March
April
May
June
July
August
September
October
November
December

When?

in February
on December 1st
on December first
in 1998
in nineteen ninety-eight

Nous sommes le... It's...

OCT 1 SUN dimanche 1er octobre *or*
dimanche premier octobre

USEFUL VOCABULARY

When?

today
this morning
this afternoon
this evening

How often?

every day
every other day
once a week
twice a week
once a month

When *did* it happen?

in the morning
in the evening
yesterday
yesterday evening
the day before yesterday
a week ago
two weeks ago
last year

When *is it going* to happen?

tomorrow
tomorrow morning
the day after tomorrow
in two days
in a week
in two weeks
next month
next year

A

a ARTICLE

Use **un** *for masculine nouns,* **une** *for feminine nouns.*

un MASC ◇ *a book* un livre ◇ *a year ago* il y a un an

une FEM ◇ *an apple* une pomme

You do not translate **a** *when you want to describe somebody's job in French.*

◇ *He's a butcher.* Il est boucher. ◇ *She's a doctor.* Elle est médecin.

- **once a week** une fois par semaine
- **10 km an hour** dix kilomètres à l'heure
- **30 pence a kilo** trente pence le kilo
- **a hundred pounds** cent livres

abandon VERB

abandonner

abbey NOUN

l' *abbaye* FEM

abbreviation NOUN

l' *abréviation* FEM

ability NOUN

- **to have the ability to do something** être capable de faire quelque chose

able ADJECTIVE

- **to be able to do something** être capable de faire quelque chose

abolish VERB

abolir

abortion NOUN

l' *avortement* MASC

- **She had an abortion.** Elle s'est fait avorter.

about PREPOSITION, ADVERB

1 *à propos de* (*concerning*) ◇ *I'm phoning you about tomorrow's meeting.* Je vous appelle à propos de la réunion de demain.

2 *environ* (*approximately*) ◇ *It takes about 10 hours.* Ça prend dix heures environ.

- **about a hundred pounds** une centaine de livres
- **at about 11 o'clock** vers onze heures

3 *dans* (*around*) ◇ *to walk about the town* se promener dans la ville

4 *sur* ◇ *a book about London* un livre sur Londres

- **to be about to do something** être sur le point de faire quelque chose ◇ *I was about to go out.* J'étais sur le point de sortir.
- **to talk about something** parler de quelque chose
- **What's it about?** De quoi s'agit-il?
- **How about going to the cinema?** Et si nous allions au cinéma?

above PREPOSITION, ADVERB

1 *au-dessus de* (*higher than*) ◇ *He put his hands above his head.* Il a mis ses mains au-dessus de sa tête.

- **the flat above** l'appartement du dessus
- **mentioned above** mentionné ci-dessus
- **above all** par-dessus tout

2 *plus de* (*more than*) ◇ *above 40 degrees* plus de quarante degrés

abroad ADVERB

à l'étranger ◇ *to go abroad* partir à l'étranger

abrupt ADJECTIVE

brusque ◇ *He was a bit abrupt with me.* Il s'est montré un peu brusque avec moi.

abruptly ADVERB

brusquement ◇ *He got up abruptly.* Il s'est levé brusquement.

absence NOUN

l' *absence* FEM

absent ADJECTIVE

absent

absent-minded ADJECTIVE

distrait ◇ *She's a bit absent-minded.* Elle est un peu distraite.

absolutely ADVERB

1 *tout à fait* (*completely*) ◇ *Chantal's absolutely right.* Chantal a tout à fait raison.

2 *absolument* ◇ *Do you think it's a good idea?–Absolutely!* Tu trouves que c'est une bonne idée?–Absolument!

absurd ADJECTIVE

absurde ◇ *That's absurd!* C'est absurde!

academic ADJECTIVE

universitaire ◇ *the academic year* l'année universitaire FEM

academy NOUN

le *collège* ◇ *a military academy* un collège militaire

to **accelerate** VERB

accélérer

accelerator NOUN

l' *accélérateur* MASC

accent NOUN

l' *accent* MASC ◇ *He's got a French accent.* Il a l'accent français.

to **accept** VERB

accepter

acceptable ADJECTIVE

acceptable

access NOUN

1 l' *accès* MASC ◇ *He has access to confidential information.* Il a accès à des renseignements confidentiels.

PTO

2 le *droit de visite* ◇ *Her ex-husband has access to the children.* Son ex-mari a le droit de visite.

accessible ADJECTIVE
accessible

accessory NOUN
l' *accessoire* MASC ◇ *fashion accessories* les accessoires de mode

accident NOUN
l' *accident* MASC ◇ *to have an accident* avoir un accident

- **by accident (1)** (*by mistake*) accidentellement ◇ *The burglar killed him by accident.* Le cambrioleur l'a tué accidentellement.
- **by accident (2)** (*by chance*) par hasard ◇ *She met him by accident.* Elle l'a rencontré par hasard.

accidental ADJECTIVE
accidentel MASC
accidentelle FEM

to **accommodate** VERB
recevoir ◇ *The hotel can accommodate 50 people.* L'hôtel peut recevoir cinquante personnes.

accommodation NOUN
le *logement*

to **accompany** VERB
accompagner

accord NOUN
- **of his own accord** de son plein gré ◇ *He left of his own accord.* Il est parti de son plein gré.

according to PREPOSITION
selon ◇ *According to him, everyone had gone.* Selon lui, tout le monde était parti.

account NOUN
1 le *compte* ◇ *a bank account* un compte en banque
- **to do the accounts** tenir la comptabilité

2 (*report*)
le *compte rendu*
(les *comptes rendus* PL)
◇ *He gave a detailed account of what happened.* Il a donné un compte rendu détaillé des événements.
- **to take something into account** tenir compte de quelque chose
- **on account of** à cause de ◇ *We couldn't go out on account of the bad weather.* Nous n'avons pas pu sortir à cause du mauvais temps.

accountancy NOUN
la *comptabilité*

accountant NOUN
le/la *comptable* ◇ *She's an accountant.* Elle est comptable.

accuracy NOUN
l' *exactitude* FEM

accurate ADJECTIVE
précis ◇ *accurate information* les renseignements précis MASC

accurately ADVERB
avec précision

to **accuse** VERB
- **to accuse somebody of something** accuser quelqu'un de quelque chose ◇ *The police are accusing her of murder.* La police l'accuse de meurtre.

ace NOUN
l' *as* MASC ◇ *the ace of hearts* l'as de cœur

ache NOUN
see also ache VERB
la *douleur*

to **ache** VERB
see also ache NOUN
- **My leg's aching.** J'ai mal à la jambe.

to **achieve** VERB
1 *atteindre* (*an aim*)
2 *remporter* (*victory*)

achievement NOUN
l' *exploit* MASC ◇ *That was quite an achievement.* C'était un véritable exploit.

acid NOUN
l' *acide* MASC

acid rain NOUN
les *pluies acides* FEM PL

acne NOUN
l' *acné* FEM

acrobat NOUN
l' *acrobate* MASC/FEM ◇ *He's an acrobat.* Il est acrobate.

across PREPOSITION, ADVERB
de l'autre côté de ◇ *the shop across the road* la boutique de l'autre côté de la rue
- **to walk across the road** traverser la rue
- **to run across the road** traverser la rue en courant
- **across from** (*opposite*) en face de ◇ *He sat down across from her.* Il s'est assis en face d'elle.

to **act** VERB
see also act NOUN
1 *jouer* (*in play, film*) ◇ *He acts really well.* Il joue vraiment bien. ◇ *She's acting the part of Juliet.* Elle joue le rôle de Juliette.
2 *agir* (*take action*) ◇ *The police acted quickly.* La police a agi rapidement.
- **She acts as his interpreter.** Elle lui sert d'interprète.

act NOUN
see also act VERB
l' *acte* MASC (*in play*) ◇ *in the first act* au

premier acte

action NOUN
l' *action* FEM ◇ *The film was full of action.* Il y avait beaucoup d'action dans le film.
◆ **to take firm action against** prendre des mesures énergiques contre

active ADJECTIVE
actif MASC
active FEM
◇ *He's a very active person.* Il est très actif.
◆ **an active volcano** un volcan en activité

activity NOUN
l' *activité* FEM ◇ *outdoor activities* les activités de plein air

actor NOUN
l' *acteur* MASC ◇ *Brad Pitt is a well-known actor.* Brad Pitt est un acteur connu.

actress NOUN
l' *actrice* FEM ◇ *Julia Roberts is a well-known actress.* Julia Roberts est une actrice connue.

actually ADVERB
1 *vraiment* (*really*) ◇ *Did it actually happen?* Est-ce que c'est vraiment arrivé?
2 *en fait* (*in fact*) ◇ *Actually, I don't know him at all.* En fait, je ne le connais pas du tout.

ad NOUN
1 l' *annonce* FEM (*in paper*)
2 la *pub* (*on TV, radio*)

AD ABBREVIATION
ap. J.-C. (= après Jésus-Christ) ◇ *in 800 AD* en huit cents après Jésus-Christ

adapt VERB
adapter ◇ *His novel was adapted for television.* Son roman a été adapté pour la télévision.
◆ **to adapt to something** (*get used to*) s'adapter à quelque chose ◇ *He adapted to his new school very quickly.* Il s'est adapté très vite à sa nouvelle école.

adaptor NOUN
l' *adaptateur* MASC

add VERB
ajouter ◇ *Add two eggs to the mixture.* Ajoutez deux œufs au mélange.
◆ **to add up** additionner ◇ *Add the figures up.* Additionnez les chiffres.

addict NOUN
(*drug addict*)
le *drogué*
la *droguée*
◆ **Jean-Pierre's a football addict.** Jean-Pierre est un mordu de football.

addicted ADJECTIVE
◆ **to be addicted to** (*drug*) s'adonner à ◇ *She's addicted to heroin.* Elle s'adonne à l'héroïne.
◆ **She's addicted to soap operas.** C'est une mordue des soaps.

addition NOUN
◆ **in addition** en plus ◇ *He's broken his leg and, in addition, he's caught a cold.* Il s'est cassé la jambe et en plus, il a attrapé un rhume.
◆ **in addition to** en plus de ◇ *In addition to the price of the cassette, there's a charge for postage.* En plus du prix de la cassette, il y a des frais de port.

address NOUN
l' *adresse* FEM ◇ *What's your address?* Quelle est votre adresse?

adjective NOUN
l' *adjectif* MASC

to **adjust** VERB
régler ◇ *You can adjust the height of the chair.* Tu peux régler la hauteur de la chaise.
◆ **to adjust to something** (*get used to*) s'adapter à quelque chose ◇ *He adjusted to his new school very quickly.* Il s'est adapté très vite à sa nouvelle école.

adjustable ADJECTIVE
réglable

administration NOUN
l' *administration* FEM

admiral NOUN
l' *amiral* MASC

to **admire** VERB
admirer

admission NOUN
l' *entrée* FEM ◇ *"admission free"* "entrée gratuite"

to **admit** VERB
1 *admettre* (*agree*) ◇ *I must admit that...* Je dois admettre que...
2 *reconnaître* (*confess*) ◇ *He admitted that he'd done it.* Il a reconnu qu'il l'avait fait.

adolescence NOUN
l' *adolescence* FEM

adolescent NOUN
l' *adolescent* MASC
l' *adolescente* FEM

to **adopt** VERB
adopter ◇ *Phil was adopted.* Phil a été adopté.

adopted ADJECTIVE
adoptif MASC
adoptive FEM
◇ *an adopted son* un fils adoptif

adoption NOUN
l' *adoption* FEM

to **adore** VERB

adorer

Adriatic Sea NOUN
la *mer Adriatique*

adult NOUN
l' *adulte* MASC/FEM

- **adult education** l'enseignement pour adultes MASC

to **advance** VERB
see also advance NOUN
1 *avancer* (*move forward*) ◇ *The troops are advancing.* Les troupes avancent.
2 *progresser* (*progress*) ◇ *Technology has advanced a lot.* La technologie a beaucoup progressé.

advance NOUN
see also advance VERB

- **in advance** à l'avance ◇ *They bought the tickets in advance.* Ils ont acheté les billets à l'avance.

advance booking NOUN

- **Advance booking is essential.** Il est indispensable de réserver.

advanced ADJECTIVE
avancé

advantage NOUN
l' *avantage* MASC ◇ *Going to university has many advantages.* Aller à l'université présente de nombreux avantages.

- **to take advantage of something** profiter de quelque chose ◇ *He took advantage of the good weather to go for a walk.* Il a profité du beau temps pour faire une promenade.
- **to take advantage of somebody** exploiter quelqu'un ◇ *The company was taking advantage of its employees.* La société exploitait ses employés.

adventure NOUN
l' *aventure* FEM

adverb NOUN
l' *adverbe* MASC

advert, advertisement NOUN
1 la *publicité* (*on TV*)
2 l' *annonce* FEM (*in newspaper*)

advertising NOUN
la *publicité*

advice NOUN
les *conseils* MASC PL ◇ *to give somebody advice* donner des conseils à quelqu'un

- **a piece of advice** un conseil ◇ *He gave me a good piece of advice.* Il m'a donné un bon conseil.

to **advise** VERB
conseiller ◇ *He advised me to wait.* Il m'a conseillé d'attendre. ◇ *He advised me not to go there.* Il m'a conseillé de ne pas y aller.

aerial NOUN
l' *antenne* FEM

aerobics PL NOUN
l' *aérobic* FEM ◇ *I'm going to aerobics tonight.* Je vais au cours d'aérobic ce soir.

aeroplane NOUN
l' *avion* MASC

aerosol NOUN
la *bombe*

affair NOUN
1 l' *aventure* FEM (*romantic*) ◇ *to have an affair with somebody* avoir une aventure avec quelqu'un
2 l' *affaire* FEM (*event*)

to **affect** VERB
affecter

affectionate ADJECTIVE
affectueux MASC
affectueuse FEM

to **afford** VERB
avoir les moyens d'acheter ◇ *I can't afford a new pair of jeans.* Je n'ai pas les moyens d'acheter un nouveau jean.

- **We can't afford to go on holiday.** Nous n'avons pas les moyens de partir en vacances.

afraid ADJECTIVE

- **to be afraid of something** avoir peur de quelque chose ◇ *I'm afraid of spiders.* J'ai peur des araignées.
- **I'm afraid I can't come.** Je crains de ne pouvoir venir.
- **I'm afraid so.** Hélas oui.
- **I'm afraid not.** Hélas non.

Africa NOUN
l' *Afrique* FEM

- **in Africa** en Afrique

African ADJECTIVE
see also African NOUN
africain MASC
africaine FEM

African NOUN
see also African ADJECTIVE
l' *Africain* MASC
l' *Africaine* FEM

after PREPOSITION, ADVERB, CONJUNCTION
après ◇ *after dinner* après le dîner ◇ *He ran after me.* Il a couru après moi. ◇ *soon after* peu après

- **after I'd had a rest** après m'être reposé
- **after having asked** après avoir demandé
- **after all** après tout

afternoon NOUN
l' *après-midi* MASC/FEM ◇ *3 o'clock in the afternoon* trois heures de l'après-midi ◇ *this afternoon* cet après-midi ◇ *on Saturday afternoon* samedi après-midi

afters NOUN
le *dessert*

after-shave NOUN

l' *after-shave* MASC

afterwards ADVERB
après ◇ *She left not long afterwards.* Elle est partie peu de temps après.

again ADVERB
1 *de nouveau* (*once more*) ◇ *They're friends again.* Ils sont de nouveau amis.
2 *encore une fois* (*one more time*) ◇ *Can you tell me again?* Tu peux me le dire encore une fois?
- **not...again** ne...plus ◇ *I won't go there again.* Je n'y retournerai plus.
- **Do it again!** Refais-le!
- **again and again** à plusieurs reprises

against PREPOSITION
contre ◇ *He leant against the wall.* Il s'est appuyé contre le mur. ◇ *I'm against nuclear testing.* Je suis contre les essais nucléaires.

age NOUN
l' *âge* MASC ◇ *at the age of 16* à l'âge de seize ans ◇ *an age limit* une limite d'âge
- **I haven't been to the cinema for ages.** Ça fait une éternité que je ne suis pas allé au cinéma.

aged ADJECTIVE
- **aged 10** âgé de dix ans

agenda NOUN
l' *ordre du jour* MASC

agent NOUN
l' *agent* MASC ◇ *an estate agent* un agent immobilier ◇ *a travel agent* un agent de voyage

aggressive ADJECTIVE
agressif MASC
agressive FEM

ago ADVERB
- **two days ago** il y a deux jours
- **two years ago** il y a deux ans
- **not long ago** il n'y a pas longtemps
- **How long ago did it happen?** Il y a combien de temps que c'est arrivé?

agony NOUN
- **to be in agony** souffrir le martyre ◇ *He was in agony.* Il souffrait le martyre.

agree VERB
- **to agree with** être d'accord avec ◇ *I agree with Carol.* Je suis d'accord avec Carol.
- **to agree to do something** accepter de faire quelque chose ◇ *He agreed to go and pick her up.* Il a accepté d'aller la chercher.
- **to agree that...** admettre que... ◇ *I agree that it's difficult.* J'admets que c'est difficile.
- **Garlic doesn't agree with me.** Je ne supporte pas l'ail.

agreed ADJECTIVE
convenu ◇ *at the agreed time* au moment convenu

agreement NOUN
l' *accord* MASC
- **to be in agreement** être d'accord ◇ *Everybody was in agreement with Ray.* Tout le monde était d'accord avec Ray.

agricultural ADJECTIVE
agricole

agriculture NOUN
l' *agriculture* FEM

ahead ADVERB
devant ◇ *She looked straight ahead.* Elle regardait droit devant elle.
- **ahead of time** en avance
- **to plan ahead** organiser à l'avance
- **The French are 5 points ahead.** Les Français ont cinq points d'avance.
- **Go ahead!** Allez-y!

aid NOUN
- **in aid of charity** au profit d'associations caritatives

AIDS NOUN
le *sida*

to **aim** VERB
see also aim NOUN
- **to aim at** braquer sur ◇ *He aimed a gun at me.* Il a braqué un revolver sur moi.
- **The film is aimed at children.** Le film est destiné aux enfants.
- **to aim to do something** avoir l'intention de faire quelque chose ◇ *Janice aimed to leave at 5 o'clock.* Janice avait l'intention de partir à cinq heures.

aim NOUN
see also aim VERB
l' *objectif* ◇ *The aim of the festival is to raise money.* L'objectif du festival est de collecter des fonds.

air NOUN
l' *air* MASC ◇ *to get some fresh air* prendre l'air
- **by air** en avion ◇ *I prefer to travel by air.* Je préfère voyager en avion.

air-conditioned ADJECTIVE
climatisé

air conditioning NOUN
la *climatisation*

Air Force NOUN
l' *armée de l'air* FEM

air hostess NOUN
l' *hôtesse de l'air* ◇ *She's an air hostess.* Elle est hôtesse de l'air.

airline NOUN
la *compagnie aérienne*

airmail NOUN
- **by airmail** par avion

airport NOUN
l' *aéroport* MASC

aisle NOUN
l' *allée centrale* FEM

alarm NOUN
l' *alarme* FEM (*warning*)
- **a fire alarm** un avertisseur d'incendie

alarm clock NOUN
le *réveil*

album NOUN
l' *album* MASC

alcohol NOUN
l' *alcool* MASC

alcoholic NOUN
see also alcoholic ADJECTIVE
l' *alcoolique* MASC/FEM ◇ *He's an alcoholic.* C'est un alcoolique.

alcoholic ADJECTIVE
see also alcoholic NOUN
alcoolisé ◇ *alcoholic drinks* des boissons alcoolisées

alert ADJECTIVE
1 (*bright*)
vif MASC
vive FEM
◇ *He's a very alert baby.* C'est un bébé très vif.
2 (*paying attention*)
vigilant ◇ *We must stay alert.* Nous devons rester vigilants.

A levels PL NOUN
le *baccalauréat* SING

The baccalauréat *(or* bac *for short) is taken at the age of 17 or 18. Students have to sit one of a variety of set subject combinations, rather than being able to choose any combination of subjects they want. If you pass you have the right to a place at university.*

Algeria NOUN
l' *Algérie* FEM
- **in Algeria** en Algérie

alike ADVERB
- **to look alike** se ressembler ◇ *The two sisters look alike.* Les deux sœurs se ressemblent.

alive ADJECTIVE
vivant

all ADJECTIVE, PRONOUN, ADVERB
tout
(*tous* MASC PL)
◇ *all the time* tout le temps ◇ *I ate all of it.* J'ai tout mangé. ◇ *all day* toute la journée ◇ *all the books* tous les livres ◇ *all the apples* toutes les pommes
- **All of us went.** Nous y sommes tous allés.
- **after all** après tout ◇ *After all, nobody can make us go.* Après tout, personne ne peut nous obliger à y aller.
- **all alone** tout seul ◇ *She's all alone.* Elle est toute seule.
- **not at all** pas du tout ◇ *I'm not tired at all.* Je ne suis pas du tout fatigué.
- **The score is 5 all.** Le score est de cinq partout.

allergic ADJECTIVE
allergique
- **to be allergic to something** être allergique à quelque chose ◇ *I'm allergic to cats' hair.* Je suis allergique aux poils de chat.

alley NOUN
la *ruelle*

to **allow** VERB
- **to be allowed to do something** être autorisé à faire quelque chose ◇ *He's not allowed to go out at night.* Il n'est pas autorisé à sortir le soir.
- **to allow somebody to do something** permettre à quelqu'un de faire quelque chose ◇ *His mum allowed him to go out.* Sa mère lui a permis de sortir.

all right ADVERB
1 *bien* (*okay*) ◇ *Everything turned out all right.* Tout s'est bien terminé.
- **Are you all right?** Ça va?
2 *pas mal* (*not bad*) ◇ *The film was all right.* Le film n'était pas mal.
3 *d'accord* (*when agreeing*) ◇ *We'll talk about it later.* – *All right.* On en reparlera plus tard. – D'accord.
- **Is that all right with you?** Tu es d'accord?

almond NOUN
l' *amande* FEM

almost ADVERB
presque ◇ *I've almost finished.* J'ai presque fini.

alone ADJECTIVE, ADVERB
seul ◇ *She lives alone.* Elle habite seule.
- **to leave somebody alone** laisser quelqu'un tranquille ◇ *Leave her alone!* Laisse-la tranquille!
- **to leave something alone** ne pas toucher à quelque chose ◇ *Leave my things alone!* Ne touche pas à mes affaires!

along PREPOSITION, ADVERB
le long de ◇ *Chris was walking along the beach.* Chris se promenait le long de la plage.
- **all along** depuis le début ◇ *He was lying to me all along.* Il m'a menti depuis le début.

aloud ADVERB
à haute voix ◇ *He read the poem aloud.* Il a lu le poème à haute voix.

alphabet NOUN
l' *alphabet* MASC

Alps PL NOUN
les *Alpes* FEM PL

already ADVERB
déjà ◇ *Liz had already gone.* Liz était déjà partie.

also ADVERB
aussi

altar NOUN
l' *autel* MASC

alter VERB
changer

alternate ADJECTIVE
◆ **on alternate days** tous les deux jours

alternative NOUN
see also alternative ADJECTIVE
le *choix* ◇ *You have no alternative.* Tu n'a pas le choix.
◆ **Fruit is a healthy alternative to chocolate.** Les fruits sont plus sains que le chocolat.
◆ **There are several alternatives.** Il y a plusieurs possibilités.

alternative ADJECTIVE
see also alternative NOUN
autre ◇ *They made alternative plans.* Ils ont pris d'autres dispositions.
◆ **an alternative solution** une solution de rechange
◆ **alternative medicine** la médecine douce

alternatively ADVERB
◆ **Alternatively, we could just stay at home.** On pourrait aussi rester à la maison.

although CONJUNCTION
bien que
bien que *has to be followed by a verb in the subjunctive.*
◇ *Although she was tired, she stayed up late.* Bien qu'elle soit fatiguée, elle s'est couchée tard.

altogether ADVERB
1 *en tout* (*in total*) ◇ *You owe me £20 altogether.* Tu me dois vingt livres en tout.
2 *tout à fait* (*completely*) ◇ *I'm not altogether happy with your work.* Je ne suis pas tout à fait satisfait de votre travail.

aluminium NOUN
l' *aluminium* MASC

always ADVERB
toujours ◇ *He's always moaning.* Il est toujours en train de ronchonner.

am VERB *see* **be**

a.m. ABBREVIATION
du matin ◇ *at 4 a.m.* à quatre heures du matin

amateur NOUN
l' *amateur* MASC

to **amaze** VERB
◆ **to be amazed** être stupéfait ◇ *I was amazed that I managed to do it.* J'étais stupéfait d'avoir réussi.

amazing ADJECTIVE
1 (*surprising*)
stupéfiant ◇ *That's amazing news!* C'est une nouvelle stupéfiante!
2 (*excellent*)
exceptionnel MASC
exceptionnelle FEM
◇ *Vivian's an amazing cook.* Vivian est une cuisinière exceptionnelle.

ambassador NOUN
l' *ambassadeur* MASC
l' *ambassadrice* FEM

amber ADJECTIVE
◆ **an amber light** un feu orange

ambition NOUN
l' *ambition* FEM

ambitious ADJECTIVE
ambitieux MASC
ambitieuse FEM
◇ *She's very ambitious.* Elle est très ambitieuse.

ambulance NOUN
l' *ambulance* FEM

amenities PL NOUN
les *aménagements* MASC
◆ **The hotel has very good amenities.** L'hôtel est très bien aménagé.

America NOUN
l' *Amérique* FEM
◆ **in America** en Amérique
◆ **to America** en Amérique

American ADJECTIVE
see also American NOUN
américain ◇ *He's American.* Il est américain. ◇ *She's American.* Elle est américaine.

American NOUN
see also American ADJECTIVE
l' *Américain* MASC
l' *Américaine* FEM
◆ **the Americans** les Américains

amount NOUN
1 la *somme* ◇ *a large amount of money* une grosse somme d'argent
2 la *quantité*
◆ **a huge amount of rice** une énorme quantité de riz

amp NOUN
1 l' *ampère* MASC (*of electricity*)
2 l' *ampli* MASC (*for hi-fi*)

amplifier NOUN
l' *amplificateur* MASC (*for hi-fi*)

to **amuse** VERB

amuser ◇ *He was most amused by the story.* L'histoire l'a beaucoup amusé.

amusement arcade NOUN
la *salle de jeux électroniques*

an ARTICLE *see* **a**

to **analyse** VERB
analyser

analysis NOUN
l' *analyse* FEM

ancestor NOUN
l' *ancêtre* MASC/FEM

anchor NOUN
l' *ancre* FEM

ancient ADJECTIVE
1 (*civilization*)
antique ◇ *ancient Greece* la Grèce antique
2 (*custom, building*)
ancien MASC
ancienne FEM
◇ *an ancient monument* un monument ancien

and CONJUNCTION
et ◇ *you and me* toi et moi ◇ *2 and 2 are 4* deux et deux font quatre
◆ **Please try and come!** Essaie de venir!
◆ **He talked and talked.** Il n'a pas arrêté de parler.
◆ **better and better** de mieux en mieux

angel NOUN
l' *ange* MASC

anger NOUN
la *colère*

angle NOUN
l' *angle* MASC

angler NOUN
le *pêcheur à la ligne*
la *pêcheuse à la ligne*

angling NOUN
la *pêche à la ligne*

angry ADJECTIVE
en colère ◇ *Dad looks very angry.* Papa a l'air très en colère.
◆ **to be angry with somebody** être furieux contre quelqu'un ◇ *Mum's really angry with you.* Maman est vraiment furieuse contre toi.
◆ **to get angry** se fâcher

animal NOUN
l' *animal* MASC
(les *animaux* PL)

ankle NOUN
la *cheville*

anniversary NOUN
l' *anniversaire* MASC ◇ *a wedding anniversary* un anniversaire de mariage

to **announce** VERB
annoncer

announcement NOUN
l' *annonce* FEM

to **annoy** VERB
agacer ◇ *He's really annoying me.* Il m'agace vraiment.
◆ **to get annoyed** se fâcher ◇ *Don't get so annoyed!* Ne vous fâchez pas!

annoying ADJECTIVE
agaçant ◇ *It's really annoying.* C'est vraiment agaçant.

annual ADJECTIVE
annuel MASC
annuelle FEM
◇ *an annual meeting* une réunion annuelle

anorak NOUN
l' *anorak* MASC

another ADJECTIVE
un autre
une autre
◇ *Would you like another piece of cake?* Tu veux un autre morceau de gâteau?
◇ *Have you got another skirt?* Tu as une autre jupe?

to **answer** VERB
see also answer NOUN
répondre à ◇ *Can you answer my question?* Peux-tu répondre à ma question? ◇ *to answer the phone* répondre au téléphone
◆ **to answer the door** aller ouvrir ◇ *Can you answer the door please?* Tu peux aller ouvrir s'il te plaît?

answer NOUN
see also answer VERB
1 la *réponse* (*to question*)
2 la *solution* (*to problem*)

answering machine NOUN
le *répondeur*

ant NOUN
la *fourmi*

Antarctic NOUN
l' *Antarctique* FEM

anthem NOUN
◆ **the national anthem** l'hymne national MASC

antibiotic NOUN
l' *antibiotique* MASC

antique NOUN
le *meuble ancien* (*furniture*)

antique shop NOUN
le *magasin d'antiquités*

antiseptic NOUN
l' *antiseptique* MASC

any ADJECTIVE, PRONOUN, ADVERB
Use **du**, **de la** *or* **des** *to translate* **any** *according to the gender of the French noun that follows it.* **du** *and* **de la** *become* **de l'** *when they're followed by a noun starting with a vowel.*

1 *du* ◇ *Would you like any bread?* Voulez-vous du pain?
de la ◇ *Would you like any beer?* Voulez-vous de la bière?
de l' ◇ *Have you got any mineral water?* Avez-vous de l'eau minérale?
des ◇ *Have you got any Blur CDs?* Avez-vous des CD de Blur?

If you want to say you haven't got any of something, use **de** *whatever the gender of the following noun is.* **de** *becomes* **d'** *when it comes before a noun starting with a vowel.*

2 *de* ◇ *I haven't got any books.* Je n'ai pas de livres.
d' ◇ *I haven't got any money.* Je n'ai pas d'argent.

Use **en** *where there is no noun after* any.

3 *en* ◇ *Sorry, I haven't got any.* Désolé, je n'en ai pas.

◆ **any more (1)** (*additional*) encore de ◇ *Would you like any more coffee?* Est-ce que tu veux encore du café?

◆ **any more (2)** (*no longer*) ne...plus ◇ *I don't love him any more.* Je ne l'aime plus.

anybody PRONOUN
1 *quelqu'un* (*in question*) ◇ *Has anybody got a pen?* Est-ce que quelqu'un a un stylo?
2 *n'importe qui* (*no matter who*) ◇ *Anybody can learn to swim.* N'importe qui peut apprendre à nager.

Use **ne...personne** *in a negative sentence.* **ne** *comes before the verb,* **personne** *after it.*

3 *ne...personne* ◇ *I can't see anybody.* Je ne vois personne.

anyhow ADVERB
de toute façon ◇ *He doesn't want to go out and anyhow he's not allowed.* Il ne veut pas sortir et de toute façon il n'y est pas autorisé.

anyone PRONOUN
1 *quelqu'un* (*in question*) ◇ *Has anyone got a pen?* Est-ce que quelqu'un a un stylo?
2 *n'importe qui* (*no matter who*) ◇ *Anyone can learn to swim.* N'importe qui peut apprendre à nager.

Use **ne...personne** *in a negative sentence.* **ne** *comes before the verb,* **personne** *after it.*

3 *ne...personne* ◇ *I can't see anyone.* Je ne vois personne.

anything PRONOUN
1 *quelque chose* (*in question*) ◇ *Would you like anything to eat?* Tu veux manger quelque chose?
2 *n'importe quoi* (*no matter what*) ◇ *Anything could happen.* Il pourrait arriver n'importe quoi.

Use **ne...rien** *in a negative sentence.* **ne** *comes before the verb,* **rien** *after it.*

3 *ne...rien* ◇ *I can't hear anything.* Je n'entends rien.

anyway ADVERB
de toute façon ◇ *He doesn't want to go out and anyway he's not allowed.* Il ne veut pas sortir et de toute façon il n'y est pas autorisé.

anywhere ADVERB
1 *quelque part* (*in question*) ◇ *Have you seen my coat anywhere?* Est-ce que tu as vu mon manteau quelque part?
2 *n'importe où* ◇ *You can buy stamps almost anywhere.* On peut acheter des timbres presque n'importe où.

Use **ne...nulle part** *in a negative sentence.* **ne** *comes before the verb,* **nulle part** *after it.*

3 *ne...nulle part* ◇ *I can't find it anywhere.* Je ne le trouve nulle part.

apart ADVERB
◆ **The two towns are 10 kilometres apart.** Les deux villes sont à dix kilomètres l'une de l'autre.
◆ **apart from** à part ◇ *Apart from that, everything's fine.* À part ça, tout va bien.

apartment NOUN
l' *appartement* MASC

to **apologize** VERB
s'excuser ◇ *He apologized for being late.* Il s'est excusé de son retard.
◆ **I apologize!** Je vous prie de m'excuser.

apology NOUN
les *excuses* FEM PL

apostrophe NOUN
l' *apostrophe* FEM

apparatus NOUN
1 le *matériel* (*in lab*)
2 les *agrès* MASC PL (*in gym*)

apparent ADJECTIVE
apparent

apparently ADVERB
apparemment

to **appeal** VERB
see also appeal NOUN
lancer un appel ◇ *They appealed for help.* Ils ont lancé un appel au secours.
◆ **Greece doesn't appeal to me.** Ça ne me tente pas d'aller en Grèce.
◆ **Does that appeal to you?** Ça te tente?

appeal NOUN
see also appeal VERB
l' *appel* MASC ◇ *They have launched an appeal.* Ils ont lancé un appel.

to **appear** VERB
1 *apparaître* (*come into view*) ◇ *The bus appeared around the corner.* Le bus est apparu au coin de la rue.
◆ **to appear on TV** passer à la télé

PTO

2 *paraître* (*seem*) ◇ *She appeared to be asleep.* Elle paraissait dormir.

appearance NOUN
l' *apparence* FEM (*looks*) ◇ *She takes great care over her appearance.* Elle prend grand soin de son apparence.

appendicitis NOUN
l' *appendicite* FEM

appetite NOUN
l' *appétit* MASC

to **applaud** VERB
applaudir

applause NOUN
les *applaudissements* MASC PL

apple NOUN
la *pomme*
◆ **an apple tree** un pommier

application NOUN
◆ **a job application** une candidature

application form NOUN
1 le *dossier de candidature* (*for job*)
2 le *dossier d'inscription* (*for university*)

to **apply** VERB
◆ **to apply for a job** poser sa candidature à un poste
◆ **to apply to** (*be relevant*) s'appliquer à ◇ *This rule doesn't apply to us.* Ce règlement ne s'applique pas à nous.

appointment NOUN
le *rendez-vous* ◇ *I've got a dental appointment.* J'ai rendez-vous chez le dentiste.

to **appreciate** VERB
être reconnaissant de ◇ *I really appreciate your help.* Je vous suis extrêmement reconnaissant de votre aide.

apprentice NOUN
l' *apprenti* MASC
l' *apprentie* FEM

to **approach** VERB
1 *s'approcher de* (*get nearer to*) ◇ *He approached the house.* Il s'est approché de la maison.
2 *aborder* (*tackle*) ◇ *to approach a problem* aborder un problème

appropriate ADJECTIVE
approprié ◇ *That dress isn't very appropriate for an interview.* Cette robe n'est pas très appropriée pour un entretien.

to **approve** VERB
◆ **to approve of** approuver ◇ *I don't approve of his choice.* Je n'approuve pas son choix.
◆ **They didn't approve of his girlfriend.** Sa copine ne leur a pas plu.

approximate ADJECTIVE
approximatif MASC
approximative FEM

apricot NOUN
l' *abricot* MASC

April NOUN
avril MASC
◆ **in April** en avril
◆ **April Fool's Day** le premier avril

apron NOUN
le *tablier*

Aquarius NOUN
le *Verseau* ◇ *I'm Aquarius.* Je suis Verseau.

Arab ADJECTIVE
see also Arab NOUN
arabe ◇ *the Arab countries* les pays arabes

Arab NOUN
see also Arab ADJECTIVE
l' *Arabe* MASC / FEM

arch NOUN
l' *arc* MASC

archaeologist NOUN
l' *archéologue* MASC / FEM ◇ *He's an archaeologist.* Il est archéologue.

archaeology NOUN
l' *archéologie* FEM

archbishop NOUN
l' *archevêque* MASC

architect NOUN
l' *architecte* MASC / FEM ◇ *She's an architect.* Elle est architecte.

architecture NOUN
l' *architecture* FEM

Arctic NOUN
l' *Arctique* MASC

are VERB *see* **be**

area NOUN
1 la *région* ◇ *She lives in the Paris area.* Elle habite dans la région parisienne.
2 le *quartier* ◇ *My favourite area of Paris is Montmartre.* Montmartre est le quartier de Paris que je préfère.
3 la *superficie* ◇ *The field has an area of 1500m².* Le champ a une superficie de mille cinq cent mètres carrés.

Argentina NOUN
l' *Argentine* FEM
◆ **in Argentina** en Argentine

Argentinian ADJECTIVE
argentin

to **argue** VERB
se disputer ◇ *They never stop arguing.* Ils n'arrêtent pas de se disputer.

argument NOUN
◆ **to have an argument** se disputer ◇ *They had an argument.* Ils se sont disputés.

Aries NOUN

le *Bélier* ◇ *I'm Aries.* Je suis Bélier.

arm NOUN
le *bras*

armchair NOUN
le *fauteuil*

armour NOUN
l' *armure* FEM

army NOUN
l' *armée* FEM

around PREPOSITION, ADVERB
1 *autour de* ◇ *She wore a scarf around her neck.* Elle portait une écharpe autour du cou.
2 *environ* (*approximately*) ◇ *It costs around £100.* Cela coûte environ cent livres.
3 *vers* (*date, time*) ◇ *Let's meet at around 8 p.m.* Retrouvons-nous vers vingt heures.
- **around here (1)** (*nearby*) près d'ici ◇ *Is there a chemist's around here?* Est-ce qu'il y a une pharmacie près d'ici?
- **around here (2)** (*in this area*) dans les parages ◇ *He lives around here.* Il habite dans les parages.

arrange VERB
- **to arrange to do something** prévoir de faire quelque chose ◇ *They arranged to go out together on Friday.* Ils ont prévu de sortir ensemble vendredi.
- **to arrange a meeting** convenir d'un rendez-vous ◇ *Can we arrange a meeting?* Pouvons-nous convenir d'un rendez-vous?
- **to arrange a party** organiser une fête

arrangement NOUN
l' *arrangement* MASC (*plan*)
- **They made arrangements to go out on Friday night.** Ils ont organisé une sortie vendredi soir.

arrest VERB
see also arrest NOUN
arrêter ◇ *The police have arrested 5 people.* La police a arrêté cinq personnes.

arrest NOUN
see also arrest VERB
l' *arrestation* FEM ◇ *You're under arrest!* Vous êtes en état d'arrestation!

arrival NOUN
l' *arrivée* FEM

arrive VERB
arriver ◇ *I arrived at 5 o'clock.* Je suis arrivé à cinq heures.

arrow NOUN
la *flèche*

art NOUN
l' *art* MASC

artery NOUN
l' *artère* FEM

art gallery NOUN
le *musée*

article NOUN
l' *article* MASC ◇ *a newspaper article* un article de journal

artificial ADJECTIVE
artificiel MASC
artificielle FEM

artist NOUN
l' *artiste* MASC/FEM ◇ *She's an artist.* C'est une artiste.

artistic ADJECTIVE
artistique

as CONJUNCTION, ADVERB
1 *au moment où* (*while*) ◇ *He came in as I was leaving.* Il est arrivé au moment où je partais.
2 *puisque* (*since*) ◇ *As it's Sunday, you can have a lie-in.* Tu peux faire la grasse matinée, puisque c'est dimanche.
- **as...as** aussi...que ◇ *Pierre's as tall as Michel.* Pierre est aussi grand que Michel.
- **twice as...as** deux fois plus...que ◇ *Her coat cost twice as much as mine.* Son manteau a coûté deux fois plus cher que le mien.
- **as much...as** autant...que ◇ *I haven't got as much money as you.* Je n'ai pas autant d'argent que toi.
- **as soon as possible** dès que possible ◇ *I'll do it as soon as possible.* Je le ferai dès que possible.
- **as from tomorrow** à partir de demain ◇ *As from tomorrow, the shop will stay open until 10 p.m.* À partir de demain, le magasin restera ouvert jusqu'à vingt-deux heures.
- **as though** comme si ◇ *She acted as though she hadn't seen me.* Elle a fait comme si elle ne m'avait pas vu.
- **as if** comme si
- **He works as a waiter in the holidays.** Il travaille comme serveur pendant les vacances.

asap ABBREVIATION (= *as soon as possible*)
dès que possible

ashamed ADJECTIVE
- **to be ashamed** avoir honte ◇ *You should be ashamed of yourself!* Tu devrais avoir honte!

ashtray NOUN
le *cendrier*

Asia NOUN
l' *Asie* FEM
- **in Asia** en Asie

Asian ADJECTIVE
see also Asian NOUN
asiatique ◇ *He's Asian.* C'est un

TO

Asiatique. ◇ *She's Asian.* C'est une Asiatique.

Asian NOUN

see also Asian ADJECTIVE

l' *Asiatique* MASC/FEM

to **ask** VERB

1 *demander* (*inquire, request*) ◇ *"Have you finished?" she asked.* "Tu as fini?" a-t-elle demandé.

- **to ask somebody something** demander quelque chose à quelqu'un ◇ *He asked her how old she was.* Il lui a demandé quel âge elle avait.
- **to ask for something** demander quelque chose ◇ *He asked for a cup of tea.* Il a demandé une tasse de thé.
- **to ask somebody to do something** demander à quelqu'un de faire quelque chose ◇ *She asked him to do the shopping.* Elle lui a demandé de faire les courses.
- **to ask about something** se renseigner sur quelque chose ◇ *I asked about train times to Leeds.* Je me suis renseigné sur les horaires des trains pour Leeds.
- **to ask somebody a question** poser une question à quelqu'un

2 *inviter* ◇ *Have you asked Matthew to the party?* Est-ce que tu as invité Matthew à la fête?

- **He asked her out.** (*on a date*) Il lui a demandé de sortir avec lui.

asleep ADJECTIVE

- **to be asleep** dormir ◇ *He's asleep.* Il dort.
- **to fall asleep** s'endormir ◇ *I fell asleep in front of the TV.* Je me suis endormi devant la télé.

asparagus NOUN

les *asperges* FEM PL

aspect NOUN

l' *aspect* MASC

aspirin NOUN

l' *aspirine* FEM

assignment NOUN

le *devoir* (*in school*)

assistance NOUN

l' *aide* FEM

assistant NOUN

1 (*in shop*)

le *vendeur*

la *vendeuse*

2 (*helper*)

l' *assistant* MASC

l' *assistante* FEM

association NOUN

l' *association* FEM

assortment NOUN

l' *assortiment* MASC

to **assume** VERB

supposer ◇ *I assume she won't be coming.* Je suppose qu'elle ne viendra pas.

to **assure** VERB

assurer ◇ *He assured me he was coming.* Il m'a assuré qu'il viendrait.

asthma NOUN

l' *asthme* MASC ◇ *I've got asthma.* J'ai de l'asthme.

astrology NOUN

l' *astrologie* FEM

astronaut NOUN

l' *astronaute* MASC/FEM

astronomy NOUN

l' *astronomie* FEM

at PREPOSITION

à+le *becomes* **au, à+les** *becomes* **aux.**

à ◇ *at 4 o'clock* à quatre heures ◇ *at Christmas* à Noël ◇ *at 50 km/h* à cinquante km/h ◇ *at home* à la maison ◇ *two at a time* deux à la fois ◇ *at school* à l'école

au ◇ *at the office* au bureau

aux ◇ *at the races* aux courses

- **at night** la nuit
- **What are you doing at the weekend?** Qu'est-ce que tu fais ce week-end?

ate VERB *see* **eat**

Athens NOUN

Athènes

- **in Athens** à Athènes

athlete NOUN

l' *athlète* MASC/FEM

athletic ADJECTIVE

athlétique

athletics NOUN

l' *athlétisme* MASC ◇ *I like watching the athletics on TV.* J'aime bien regarder les épreuves d'athlétisme à la télé.

Atlantic NOUN

l' *océan Atlantique* MASC

atlas NOUN

l' *atlas* MASC

atmosphere NOUN

l' *atmosphère* FEM

atom NOUN

l' *atome* MASC

atomic ADJECTIVE

atomique ◇ *an atomic bomb* une bombe atomique

to **attach** VERB

fixer ◇ *They attached a rope to the car.* Ils ont fixé une corde à la voiture.

- **Please find attached...** Veuillez trouver ci-joint...

attached ADJECTIVE

- **to be attached to** être attaché à ◇ *He's very attached to his family.* Il est très attaché à sa famille.

attack VERB
see also attack NOUN
attaquer ◇ *The dog attacked her.* Le chien l'a attaquée.

attack NOUN
see also attack VERB
l' *attaque* FEM

attempt NOUN
see also attempt VERB
la *tentative* ◇ *She gave up after several attempts.* Elle y a renoncé après plusieurs tentatives.

attempt VERB
see also attempt NOUN
◆ **to attempt to do something** essayer de faire quelque chose ◇ *I attempted to write a song.* J'ai essayé d'écrire une chanson.

attend VERB
assister à ◇ *to attend a meeting* assister à une réunion

attention NOUN
l' *attention* FEM
◆ **to pay attention to** faire attention à ◇ *He didn't pay attention to what I was saying.* Il ne faisait pas attention à ce que je disais.

attic NOUN
le *grenier*

attitude NOUN
l' *attitude* FEM (*way of thinking*) ◇ *I really don't like your attitude!* Je n'aime pas du tout ton attitude!

attract VERB
attirer ◇ *The Lake District attracts lots of tourists.* La région des lacs attire de nombreux touristes.

attraction NOUN
l' *attraction* FEM ◇ *a tourist attraction* une attraction touristique

attractive ADJECTIVE
séduisant ◇ *She's very attractive.* Elle est très séduisante.

aubergine NOUN
l' *aubergine* FEM

auction NOUN
la *vente aux enchères*

audience NOUN
les *spectateurs* MASC PL (*in theatre*)

audition NOUN
l' *audition* FEM

August NOUN
août MASC
◆ **in August** en août

aunt, aunty NOUN
la *tante* ◇ *my aunt* ma tante

au pair NOUN
la *jeune fille au pair* ◇ *She's an au pair.* Elle est jeune fille au pair.

Australia NOUN
l' *Australie* FEM
◆ **in Australia** en Australie
◆ **to Australia** en Australie

Australian ADJECTIVE
see also Australian NOUN
australien MASC
australienne FEM
◇ *He's Australian.* Il est australien.

Australian NOUN
see also Australian ADJECTIVE
l' *Australien* MASC
l' *Australienne* FEM
◆ **the Australians** les Australiens

Austria NOUN
l' *Autriche* FEM
◆ **in Austria** en Autriche

Austrian ADJECTIVE
see also Austrian NOUN
autrichien MASC
autrichienne FEM
◇ *She's Austrian.* Elle est autrichienne.

Austrian NOUN
see also Austrian ADJECTIVE
l' *Autrichien* MASC
l' *Autrichienne* FEM
◆ **the Austrians** les Autrichiens

author NOUN
l' *auteur* MASC ◇ *She's a famous author.* C'est un auteur connu.

autobiography NOUN
l' *autobiographie* FEM

autograph NOUN
l' *autographe* MASC

automatic ADJECTIVE
automatique ◇ *an automatic door* une porte automatique

automatically ADVERB
automatiquement

autumn NOUN
l' *automne* MASC
◆ **in autumn** en automne

availability NOUN
la *disponibilité*

available ADJECTIVE
disponible ◇ *Free brochures are available on request.* Des brochures gratuites sont disponibles sur demande. ◇ *Is Mr Cooke available today?* Est-ce que Monsieur Cooke est disponible aujourd'hui?

avalanche NOUN
l' *avalanche* FEM

avenue NOUN
l' *avenue* FEM

average NOUN
see also average ADJECTIVE
la *moyenne* ◇ *on average* en

PTO

moyenne

average ADJECTIVE
see also average NOUN
moyen MASC
moyenne FEM
◇ *the average price* le prix moyen

avocado NOUN
l' *avocat* MASC

to **avoid** VERB
éviter ◇ *He avoids her when she's in a bad mood.* Il l'évite lorsqu'elle est de mauvaise humeur.
◆ **to avoid doing something** éviter de faire quelque chose ◇ *Avoid going out on your own at night.* Évite de sortir seul le soir.

awake ADJECTIVE
◆ **to be awake** être réveillé ◇ *Is she awake?* Elle est réveillée?
◆ **He was still awake.** Il ne dormait pas encore.

award NOUN
le *prix* ◇ *He's won an award.* Il a remporté un prix. ◇ *the award for the best actor* le prix du meilleur acteur

away ADJECTIVE, ADVERB
absent (*not here*) ◇ *André's away today.* André est absent aujourd'hui.
◆ **He's away for a week.** Il est parti pour une semaine.
◆ **The town's 2 kilometres away.** La ville est à deux kilomètres d'ici.
◆ **The coast is 2 hours away by car.** La côte est à deux heures de route.
◆ **Go away!** Va-t'en!
◆ **to put something away** ranger quelque chose ◇ *He put his toys away in the cupboard.* Il a rangé ses jouets dans le placard.

away match NOUN
le *match à l'extérieur*
(les *matchs à l'extérieur* PL)

awful ADJECTIVE
affreux MASC
affreuse FEM
◇ *That's awful!* C'est affreux!
◆ **an awful lot of...** énormément de...

awkward ADJECTIVE
1 *délicat* (*difficult to deal with*) ◇ *an awkward situation* une situation délicate
2 *gênant* (*embarrassing*) ◇ *an awkward question* une question gênante
◆ **It's a bit awkward for me to come and see you.** Ce n'est pas très pratique pour moi de venir vous voir.

axe NOUN
la *hache*

B

baby NOUN
le *bébé*

babysit VERB
faire du baby-sitting

babysitter NOUN
le/la *baby-sitter*

babysitting NOUN
le *baby-sitting*

bachelor NOUN
le *célibataire* ◇ *He's a bachelor.* Il est célibataire.

back NOUN
see also back ADJECTIVE, VERB
1 le *dos* (*of person, horse, book*)
2 l' *arrière* MASC (*of car, house*) ◇ *in the back* à l'arrière
3 le *verso* (*of page*) ◇ *on the back* au verso
4 le *fond* (*of room, garden*) ◇ *at the back* au fond

back ADJECTIVE, ADVERB
see also back NOUN, VERB
arrière MASC, FEM, PL ◇ *the back seat* le siège arrière ◇ *the back wheel of my bike* la roue arrière de mon vélo
- **the back door** la porte de derrière
- **to get back** rentrer ◇ *What time did you get back?* À quelle heure est-ce que tu es rentré?
- **We went there by bus and walked back.** Nous y sommes allés en bus et nous sommes rentrés à pied.
- **He's not back yet.** Il n'est pas encore rentré.
- **to call somebody back** rappeler quelqu'un ◇ *I'll call back later.* Je rappellerai plus tard.

back VERB
see also back NOUN, ADJECTIVE
soutenir (*support*) ◇ *I'm backing Tony Blair.* Je soutiens Tony Blair.
- **to back a horse** parier sur un cheval
- **to back out** se désister ◇ *They promised to help and then backed out.* Ils avaient promis de nous aider et ils se sont désistés.
- **to back somebody up** soutenir quelqu'un

backache NOUN
le *mal au dos* ◇ *to have backache* avoir mal au dos

backbone NOUN
la *colonne vertébrale*

backfire VERB
échouer (*go wrong*)

background NOUN
1 l' *arrière-plan* MASC (*of picture*) ◇ *a house in the background* une maison à l'arrière-plan
- **background noise** les bruits de fond MASC PL

2 le *milieu* (les *milieux* PL)
◇ *his family background* son milieu familial

backhand NOUN
le *revers*

backing NOUN
le *soutien* (*support*)

backpack NOUN
le *sac à dos*

back pain NOUN
le *mal au dos* ◇ *to have back pain* avoir mal au dos

backside NOUN
le *derrière*

backup NOUN
le *soutien* (*support*)
- **a backup file** une sauvegarde

backwards ADVERB
en arrière ◇ *to take a step backwards* faire un pas en arrière
- **to fall backwards** tomber à la renverse

back yard NOUN
la *cour*

bacon NOUN
1 le *lard* (*French type*)
2 le *bacon* (*British type*) ◇ *bacon and eggs* des œufs au bacon

bad ADJECTIVE
1 *mauvais* ◇ *a bad film* un mauvais film ◇ *the bad weather* le mauvais temps ◇ *to be in a bad mood* être de mauvaise humeur
- **to be bad at something** être mauvais en quelque chose ◇ *I'm really bad at maths.* Je suis vraiment mauvais en maths.

2 *grave* (*serious*) ◇ *a bad accident* un accident grave
3 *vilain* (*naughty*) ◇ *You bad boy!* Vilain!
- **to go bad** (*food*) se gâter
- **I feel bad about it.** Ça m'ennuie.
- **not bad** pas mal ◇ *That's not bad at all.* Ce n'est pas mal du tout.

badge NOUN
le *badge*

badly ADVERB
mal ◇ *badly paid* mal payé
- **badly wounded** grièvement blessé
- **He badly needs a rest.** Il a sérieusement

PTO

besoin de se reposer.

badminton NOUN
le *badminton* ◇ *to play badminton* jouer au badminton

bad-tempered ADJECTIVE
◆ **to be bad-tempered (1)** (*by nature*) avoir mauvais caractère ◇ *He's a really bad-tempered person.* Il a vraiment mauvais caractère.
◆ **to be bad-tempered (2)** (*temporarily*) être de mauvaise humeur ◇ *He was really bad-tempered yesterday.* Il était vraiment de mauvaise humeur hier.

bag NOUN
le *sac*
◆ **an old bag** (*person*) une vieille peau

baggage NOUN
les *bagages* MASC PL

baggage reclaim NOUN
la *livraison des bagages*

bagpipes PL NOUN
la *cornemuse* SING ◇ *Ed plays the bagpipes.* Ed joue de la cornemuse.

to **bake** VERB
◆ **to bake a cake** faire un gâteau

baker NOUN
le *boulanger*
la *boulangère*
◇ *He's a baker.* Il est boulanger.

bakery NOUN
la *boulangerie*

baking ADJECTIVE
◆ **It's baking in here!** Il fait une chaleur torride ici!

balance NOUN
l' *équilibre* MASC ◇ *to lose one's balance* perdre l'équilibre

balanced ADJECTIVE
équilibré

balcony NOUN
le *balcon*

bald ADJECTIVE
chauve

ball NOUN
1 la *balle* (*tennis, golf, cricket*)
2 le *ballon* (*football, rugby*)

ballet NOUN
le *ballet* ◇ *We went to a ballet.* Nous sommes allés voir un ballet.
◆ **ballet lessons** les cours de danse

ballet dancer NOUN
le *danseur classique*
la *danseuse classique*

ballet shoes PL NOUN
les *chaussons de danse* MASC PL

balloon NOUN
le *ballon* (*for parties*)
◆ **a hot-air balloon** une montgolfière

ballpoint pen NOUN
le *stylo à bille*

ban NOUN
see also ban VERB
l' *interdiction* FEM

to **ban** VERB
see also ban NOUN
interdire

banana NOUN
la *banane* ◇ *a banana skin* une peau de banane

band NOUN
1 le *groupe* (*rock band*)
2 la *fanfare* (*brass band*)

bandage NOUN
see also bandage VERB
le *bandage*

to **bandage** VERB
see also bandage NOUN
mettre un bandage à ◇ *The nurse bandaged his arm.* L'infirmière lui a mis un bandage au bras.

bandit NOUN
le *bandit*

bang NOUN
see also bang VERB
1 la *détonation* ◇ *I heard a loud bang.* J'ai entendu une forte détonation.
2 le *coup* ◇ *a bang on the head* un coup sur la tête
◆ **Bang!** Pan!

to **bang** VERB
see also bang NOUN
se cogner (*part of body*) ◇ *I banged my head.* Je me suis cogné la tête.
◆ **to bang the door** claquer la porte
◆ **to bang on the door** cogner à la porte

bank NOUN
1 la *banque* (*financial*)
2 le *bord* (*of river, lake*)

bank account NOUN
le *compte en banque*

banker NOUN
le *banquier*

bank holiday NOUN
le *jour férié*

banknote NOUN
le *billet de banque*

banned ADJECTIVE
interdit

bar NOUN
1 le *bar* (*pub*)
2 le *comptoir* (*counter*)
◆ **a bar of chocolate** une tablette de chocolat
◆ **a bar of soap** une savonnette

barbaric ADJECTIVE
barbare

barbecue NOUN
le *barbecue*

arber NOUN
le *coiffeur pour hommes*

are ADJECTIVE
nu

arefoot ADJECTIVE, ADVERB
nu-pieds MASC, FEM, PL ◇ *The children go around barefoot.* Les enfants se promènent nu-pieds.
to be barefoot avoir les pieds nus
◇ *She was barefoot.* Elle avait les pieds nus.

argain NOUN
l' *affaire* FEM ◇ *It was a bargain!* C'était une affaire!

arge NOUN
la *péniche*

ark VERB
aboyer

armaid NOUN
la *barmaid* ◇ *She's a barmaid.* Elle est barmaid.

arman NOUN
le *barman* ◇ *He's a barman.* Il est barman.

arn NOUN
la *grange*

arrel NOUN
le *tonneau*
(les *tonneaux* PL)

arrier NOUN
la *barrière*

ase NOUN
la *base*

aseball NOUN
le *base-ball*
◆ **a baseball cap** une casquette de base-ball

ased ADJECTIVE
◆ **based on** fondé sur

asement NOUN
le *sous-sol*

ash VERB
see also bash NOUN
◆ **to bash something** taper sur quelque chose

ash NOUN
see also bash VERB
◆ **I'll have a bash.** Je vais essayer.

asic ADJECTIVE
1 *de base* ◇ *It's a basic model.* C'est un modèle de base.
2 *rudimentaire* ◇ *The accommodation is pretty basic.* Le logement est plutôt rudimentaire.

asically ADVERB
tout simplement ◇ *Basically, I just don't like him.* Tout simplement, je ne l'aime pas.

asics PL NOUN
les *rudiments* MASC PL

asin NOUN
le *lavabo* (*washbasin*)

asis NOUN
◆ **on a daily basis** quotidiennement
◆ **on a regular basis** régulièrement

asketball NOUN
le *basket*

ass NOUN
1 la *basse* (*guitar, singer*) ◇ *He plays the bass.* Il joue de la basse. ◇ *He's a bass.* Il est basse.
◆ **a bass guitar** une guitare basse
◆ **a double bass** une contrebasse
2 les *graves* MASC PL (*on hi-fi*)

ass drum NOUN
la *grosse caisse*

assoon NOUN
le *basson* ◇ *I play the bassoon.* Je joue du basson.

astard NOUN
le *salaud* (*rude*) ◇ *You bastard!* Salaud!

at NOUN
1 (*for cricket, rounders*)
la *batte*
2 (*for table tennis*)
la *raquette*
3 (*animal*)
la *chauve-souris*
(les *chauves-souris* PL)

ath NOUN
1 le *bain* ◇ *to have a bath* prendre un bain
◆ **a hot bath** un bain chaud
2 la *baignoire* (*bathtub*) ◇ *There's a spider in the bath.* Il y a une araignée dans la baignoire.

to **athe** VERB
se baigner

athroom NOUN
la *salle de bains*

aths PL NOUN
la *piscine* SING

ath towel NOUN
la *serviette de bain*

atter NOUN
la *pâte à frire*

attery NOUN
1 la *pile* (*for torch, toy*)
2 la *batterie* (*of car*)

attle NOUN
la *bataille* ◇ *the Battle of Hastings* la bataille de Hastings
◆ **It was a battle, but we managed in the end.** Il a fallu se battre, mais on a fini par y arriver.

attleship NOUN
le *cuirassé*

ay NOUN

PTO

la *baie*

BC ABBREVIATION (= *before Christ*)
av. J.-C. (= avant Jésus-Christ) ◇ *in 200 BC* en deux cents avant Jésus-Christ

to **be** VERB
être ◇ *I'm tired.* Je suis fatigué. ◇ *You're late.* Tu es en retard. ◇ *She's English.* Elle est anglaise. ◇ *Edinburgh is in Scotland.* Édimbourg est en Écosse. ◇ *It's 4 o'clock.* Il est quatre heures. ◇ *We are all happy.* Nous sommes tous heureux. ◇ *They are in Paris at the moment.* Ils sont à Paris en ce moment. ◇ *I've been ill.* J'ai été malade.
- **It's the 28th of October today.** Nous sommes le vingt-huit octobre.
- **Have you been to Greece before?** Est-ce que tu es déjà allé en Grèce?
- **I've never been to Paris.** Je ne suis jamais allé à Paris.
- **to be killed** être tué

When you are saying what somebody's occupation is, you leave out the "a" in French.
◇ *She's a doctor.* Elle est médecin. ◇ *He's a student.* Il est étudiant.

With certain adjectives, such as "cold", "hot", "hungry" and "thirsty", use **avoir** *instead of* **être**.
- **I'm cold.** J'ai froid.
- **I'm hungry.** J'ai faim.

When saying how old somebody is, use **avoir** *not* **être**.
- **I'm fourteen.** J'ai quatorze ans.
- **How old are you?** Quel âge as-tu?

When referring to the weather, use **faire**.
- **It's cold.** Il fait froid.
- **It's too hot.** Il fait trop chaud.
- **It's a nice day.** Il fait beau.

beach NOUN
la *plage*

bead NOUN
la *perle*

beam NOUN
le *rayon*

beans NOUN
1 les *haricots* MASC PL
2 les *haricots blancs à la sauce tomate* MASC PL (*baked beans*) ◇ *I had beans on toast.* J'ai mangé des haricots blancs à la sauce tomate sur du pain grillé.
- **broad beans** les fèves FEM
- **green beans** les haricots verts MASC
- **kidney beans** les haricots rouges MASC

bear NOUN
see also **bear** VERB
l' *ours* MASC

to **bear** VERB
see also **bear** NOUN
- **I can't bear it!** C'est insupportable!
- **to bear up** tenir le coup
- **Bear up!** Tiens bon!

beard NOUN
la *barbe*
- **He's got a beard.** Il est barbu.
- **a man with a beard** un barbu

bearded ADJECTIVE
barbu

beat NOUN
see also **beat** VERB
le *rythme*

to **beat** VERB
see also **beat** NOUN
battre ◇ *We beat them 3-0.* On les a battus trois à zéro.
- **Beat it!** Fiche le camp! (*informal*)
- **to beat somebody up** tabasser quelqu'un (*informal*)

beautiful ADJECTIVE
beau MASC
belle FEM
(*beaux* MASC PL)

beautifully ADVERB
admirablement

beauty NOUN
la *beauté*

beauty spot NOUN
le *site pittoresque*

became VERB *see* **become**

because CONJUNCTION
parce que ◇ *I did it because...* Je l'ai fait parce que...
- **because of** à cause de ◇ *because of the weather* à cause du temps

to **become** VERB
devenir ◇ *He became a famous writer.* Il est devenu un grand écrivain.

bed NOUN
le *lit* ◇ *in bed* au lit
- **to go to bed** aller se coucher
- **to go to bed with somebody** coucher avec quelqu'un

bed and breakfast NOUN
la *chambre d'hôte* ◇ *We stayed in a bed and breakfast.* Nous avons logé dans une chambre d'hôte.
- **How much is it for bed and breakfast?** C'est combien pour la chambre et le petit déjeuner?

bedclothes PL NOUN
les *draps et les couvertures* MASC PL

bedding NOUN
la *literie*

bedroom NOUN
la *chambre*

bedspread NOUN
le *dessus-de-lit*
(les *dessus-de-lit* PL)

bedtime NOUN

- **Ten o'clock is my usual bedtime.** Je me couche généralement à dix heures.
- **Bedtime!** Au lit!

bee NOUN
l' *abeille* FEM

beef NOUN
le *bœuf*
- **roast beef** le rosbif

beefburger NOUN
le *hamburger*

been VERB *see* **be**

beer NOUN
la *bière*

beetle NOUN
le *scarabée*

beetroot NOUN
la *betterave rouge*

before PREPOSITION, CONJUNCTION, ADVERB
1 *avant* ◇ *before Tuesday* avant mardi
2 *avant de* ◇ *before going* avant de partir ◇ *Before opening the packet, read the instructions.* Avant d'ouvrir le paquet, lisez le mode d'emploi. ◇ *I'll phone before I leave.* J'appellerai avant de partir.
3 *déjà* (*already*) ◇ *I've seen this film before.* J'ai déjà vu ce film. ◇ *Have you been to Scotland before?* Vous êtes déjà venu en Écosse?
- **the day before** la veille
- **the week before** la semaine précédente

beforehand ADVERB
à l'avance

beg VERB
1 *mendier* (*for money*)
2 *supplier* ◇ *He begged me to stop.* Il m'a supplié d'arrêter.

began VERB *see* **begin**

beggar NOUN
le *mendiant*
la *mendiante*

begin VERB
commencer
- **to begin doing something** commencer à faire quelque chose

beginner NOUN
le *débutant*
la *débutante*
◇ *I'm just a beginner.* Je ne suis qu'un débutant.

beginning NOUN
le *début* ◇ *in the beginning* au début

behalf NOUN
- **on behalf of somebody** pour quelqu'un

behave VERB
se comporter ◇ *He behaved like an idiot.* Il s'est comporté comme un idiot. ◇ *She behaved very badly.* Elle s'est très mal comportée.
- **to behave oneself** être sage ◇ *Did the children behave themselves?* Est-ce que les enfants ont été sages?
- **Behave!** Sois sage!

behaviour NOUN
le *comportement*

behind PREPOSITION, ADVERB
see also behind NOUN
derrière ◇ *behind the television* derrière la télévision
- **to be behind** (*late*) avoir du retard ◇ *I'm behind with my revision.* J'ai du retard dans mes révisions.

behind NOUN
see also behind PREPOSITION, ADVERB
le *derrière*

beige ADJECTIVE
beige

Belgian ADJECTIVE
see also Belgian NOUN
belge ◇ *Belgian chocolate* le chocolat belge ◇ *She's Belgian.* Elle est belge.

Belgian NOUN
see also Belgian ADJECTIVE
le/la *Belge*
- **the Belgians** les Belges

Belgium NOUN
la *Belgique*
- **in Belgium** en Belgique

to **believe** VERB
croire ◇ *I don't believe you.* Je ne te crois pas.
- **to believe in something** croire à quelque chose ◇ *Do you believe in ghosts?* Tu crois aux fantômes?
- **to believe in God** croire en Dieu

bell NOUN
1 la *sonnette* (*doorbell*)
- **to ring the bell** sonner à la porte
2 la *cloche* (*in church*)
3 la *sonnerie* (*in school*)
4 la *clochette* ◇ *Our cat has a bell on its neck.* Notre chat a une clochette sur son collier.

belly NOUN
le *ventre*

to **belong** VERB
- **to belong to somebody** être à quelqu'un ◇ *Who does it belong to?* C'est à qui? ◇ *That belongs to me.* C'est à moi.
- **Do you belong to any clubs?** Est-ce que tu es membre d'un club?
- **Where does this belong?** Où est-ce que ça va?

belongings PL NOUN
les *affaires* FEM PL

below PREPOSITION, ADVERB
1 *au-dessous de* ◇ *below the castle*

au-dessous du château
2 *en dessous* ◇ *on the floor below* à l'étage en dessous
◆ **10 degrees below freezing** moins dix

belt NOUN
la *ceinture*

bench NOUN
1 le *banc* (*seat*)
2 l' *établi* MASC (*for woodwork*)

bend NOUN
see also bend VERB
1 le *virage* (*in road*)
2 le *coude* (*in river*)

to **bend** VERB
see also bend NOUN
1 *courber* (*back*)
2 *plier* (*leg, arm*) ◇ *I can't bend my arm.* Je n'arrive pas à plier le bras.
◆ **"do not bend"** "ne pas plier"
3 *tordre* (*object*) ◇ *You've bent it.* Tu l'as tordu.
4 *se tordre* ◇ *It bends easily.* Ça se tord facilement.
◆ **to bend down** se baisser
◆ **to bend over** se pencher

beneath PREPOSITION
sous

benefit NOUN
see also benefit VERB
l' *avantage* MASC (*advantage*)
◆ **unemployment benefit** les allocations de chômage

to **benefit** VERB
see also benefit NOUN
◆ **He'll benefit from the change.** Le changement lui fera du bien.

bent VERB *see* **bend**

bent ADJECTIVE
tordu ◇ *a bent fork* une fourchette tordue

beret NOUN
le *béret*

berserk ADJECTIVE
◆ **to go berserk** devenir fou furieux ◇ *She went berserk.* Elle est devenue folle furieuse.

berth NOUN
la *couchette*

beside PREPOSITION
à côté de ◇ *beside the television* à côté de la télévision
◆ **He was beside himself.** Il était hors de lui.
◆ **That's beside the point.** Cela n'a rien à voir.

besides ADVERB
en plus ◇ *Besides, it's too expensive.* En plus, c'est trop cher.

best ADJECTIVE, ADVERB
1 *meilleur* ◇ *He's the best player in the team.* Il est le meilleur joueur de l'équipe. ◇ *Janet's the best at maths.* Janet est la meilleure en maths.
2 *le mieux* ◇ *Emma sings best.* C'est Emma qui chante le mieux. ◇ *That's the best I can do.* Je ne peux pas faire mieux.
◆ **to do one's best** faire de son mieux ◇ *It's not perfect, but I did my best.* Ça n'est pas parfait, mais j'ai fait de mon mieux.
◆ **to make the best of it** s'en contenter ◇ *We'll have to make the best of it.* Il va falloir nous en contenter.

best man NOUN
le *garçon d'honneur*

bet NOUN
see also bet VERB
le *pari* ◇ *to make a bet* faire un pari

to **bet** VERB
see also bet NOUN
parier ◇ *I bet you he won't come.* Je te parie qu'il ne viendra pas. ◇ *I bet he forgot.* Je parie qu'il a oublié.

to **betray** VERB
trahir

better ADJECTIVE, ADVERB
1 *meilleur* ◇ *This one's better than that one.* Celui-ci est meilleur que celui-là. ◇ *a better way to do it* une meilleure façon de le faire
2 *mieux* ◇ *That's better!* C'est mieux comme ça.
◆ **better still** encore mieux ◇ *Go and see her tomorrow, or better still, go today.* Va la voir demain, ou encore mieux, vas-y aujourd'hui.
◆ **to get better (1)** (*improve*) s'améliorer ◇ *I hope the weather gets better soon.* J'espère que le temps va s'améliorer bientôt. ◇ *My French is getting better.* Mon français s'améliore.
◆ **to get better (2)** (*from illness*) se remettre ◇ *I hope you get better soon.* J'espère que tu vas vite te remettre.
◆ **to feel better** se sentir mieux ◇ *Are you feeling better now?* Tu te sens mieux maintenant?
◆ **You'd better do it straight away.** Vous feriez mieux de le faire immédiatement.
◆ **I'd better go home.** Je ferais mieux de rentrer.

betting shop NOUN
le *bureau de paris*

between PREPOSITION
entre ◇ *Stroud is between Oxford and Bristol.* Stroud est entre Oxford et Bristol. ◇ *between 15 and 20 minutes* entre quinze et vingt minutes

beyond PREPOSITION
au-delà de ◇ *There was a lake beyond the mountain.* Il y avait un lac au-delà de la montagne.
◆ **beyond belief** incroyable
◆ **beyond repair** irréparable

biased ADJECTIVE
partial

Bible NOUN
la *Bible*

bicycle NOUN
le *vélo*

bifocals PL NOUN
les *verres à double foyer* MASC PL

big ADJECTIVE
1 *grand* ◇ *a big house* une grande maison ◇ *my big brother* mon grand frère ◇ *her big sister* sa grande sœur
◆ **He's a big guy.** C'est un grand gaillard.
2 (*car, animal, book, parcel*)
gros MASC
grosse FEM
◇ *a big car* une grosse voiture

bigheaded ADJECTIVE
◆ **to be bigheaded** avoir la grosse tête

bike NOUN
le *vélo* ◇ *by bike* en vélo

bikini NOUN
le *bikini*

bilingual ADJECTIVE
bilingue

bill NOUN
1 l' *addition* FEM (*in restaurant*) ◇ *Can we have the bill, please?* L'addition, s'il vous plaît.
2 la *facture* (*for gas, electricity, telephone*)

billiards NOUN
le *billard* ◇ *to play billiards* jouer au billard

billion NOUN
le *milliard*

bin NOUN
la *poubelle*

binoculars PL NOUN
les *jumelles* FEM PL
◆ **a pair of binoculars** des jumelles

biochemistry NOUN
la *biochimie*

biography NOUN
la *biographie*

biology NOUN
la *biologie*

bird NOUN
l' *oiseau* MASC
(les *oiseaux* PL)

birdwatching NOUN
◆ **My hobby's birdwatching.** Mon passe-temps favori est d'observer les oiseaux.

Biro ® NOUN
le *bic* ®

birth NOUN
la *naissance* ◇ *date of birth* la date de naissance

birth certificate NOUN
l' *acte de naissance* MASC

birth control NOUN
la *contraception*

birthday NOUN
l' *anniversaire* MASC ◇ *When's your birthday?* Quelle est la date de ton anniversaire?
◆ **a birthday cake** un gâteau d'anniversaire
◆ **I'm going to have a birthday party.** Je vais faire une fête pour mon anniversaire.

biscuit NOUN
le *gâteau sec*

bishop NOUN
l' *évêque* MASC

bit VERB *see* **bite**

bit NOUN
le *morceau*
(les *morceaux* PL)
◇ *Would you like another bit?* Est-ce que tu en veux un autre morceau?
◆ **a bit of (1)** (*piece of*) un morceau de ◇ *a bit of cake* un morceau de gâteau
◆ **a bit of (2)** (*a little*) un peu de ◇ *a bit of music* un peu de musique
◆ **It's a bit of a nuisance.** C'est ennuyeux.
◆ **a bit** un peu ◇ *He's a bit mad.* Il est un peu fou. ◇ *a bit too hot* un peu trop chaud ◇ *Wait a bit!* Attends un peu! ◇ *Do you play football?–A bit.* Tu joues au football?–Un peu.
◆ **to fall to bits** se désintégrer
◆ **to take something to bits** démonter quelque chose
◆ **bit by bit** petit à petit

bitch NOUN
1 la *garce* (*person*)
2 la *chienne* (*female dog*)

to **bite** VERB
see also bite NOUN
1 *mordre* (*person, dog*)
2 *piquer* (*insect*) ◇ *I got bitten by mosquitoes.* Je me suis fait piquer par des moustiques.
◆ **to bite one's nails** se ronger les ongles

bite NOUN
see also bite VERB
1 la *piqûre* (*insect bite*)
2 la *morsure* (*animal bite*)
◆ **to have a bite to eat** manger un morceau

bitter ADJECTIVE

PTO

see also bitter NOUN
1 *amer* MASC
amère FEM
2 (*weather, wind*)
glacial
(*glaciaux* MASC PL)
◇ *It's bitter today.* Il fait glacial aujourd'hui.

bitter NOUN
see also bitter ADJECTIVE
la *bière brune*

black ADJECTIVE
noir ◇ *a black jacket* une veste noire
◇ *She's black.* Elle est noire.

blackberry NOUN
la *mûre*

blackbird NOUN
le *merle*

blackboard NOUN
le *tableau noir*

black coffee NOUN
le *café*

blackcurrant NOUN
le *cassis*

blackmail NOUN
see also blackmail VERB
le *chantage* ◇ *That's blackmail!* C'est du chantage!

to **blackmail** VERB
see also blackmail NOUN
◆ **to blackmail somebody** faire chanter quelqu'un ◇ *He blackmailed her.* Il l'a fait chanter.

blackout NOUN
la *panne d'électricité* (*power cut*)
◆ **to have a blackout** (*faint*) s'évanouir

black pudding NOUN
le *boudin*

blade NOUN
la *lame*

to **blame** VERB
◆ **Don't blame me!** Ça n'est pas ma faute!
◆ **I blame the police.** À mon avis, c'est la faute de la police.
◆ **He blamed it on my sister.** Il a dit que c'était la faute de ma sœur.

blank ADJECTIVE
see also blank NOUN
1 (*paper*)
blanc MASC
blanche FEM
2 (*cassette, video, page*)
vierge
◆ **My mind went blank.** J'ai eu un trou.

blank NOUN
see also blank ADJECTIVE
le *blanc* ◇ *Fill in the blanks.* Remplissez les blancs.

blank cheque NOUN
le *chèque en blanc*

blanket NOUN
la *couverture*

blast NOUN
◆ **a bomb blast** une explosion

blatant ADJECTIVE
flagrant

blaze NOUN
l' *incendie* MASC

blazer NOUN
le *blazer*

bleach NOUN
l' *eau de Javel* FEM

bleached ADJECTIVE
décoloré ◇ *bleached hair* les cheveux décolorés

to **bleed** VERB
saigner ◇ *My nose is bleeding.* Je saigne du nez.

bleeper NOUN
le *bip*

blender NOUN
le *mixer*

to **bless** VERB
bénir (*religiously*)
◆ **Bless you!** (*after sneezing*) À tes souhaits!

blew VERB *see* **blow**

blind ADJECTIVE
see also blind NOUN
aveugle

blind NOUN
see also blind ADJECTIVE
le *store* (*for window*)

blindfold NOUN
see also blindfold VERB
le *bandeau*
(les *bandeaux* PL)

to **blindfold** VERB
see also blindfold NOUN
◆ **to blindfold somebody** bander les yeux à quelqu'un

to **blink** VERB
cligner des yeux

bliss NOUN
◆ **It was bliss!** C'était merveilleux!

blister NOUN
l' *ampoule* FEM

blizzard NOUN
la *tempête de neige*

blob NOUN
la *goutte* ◇ *a blob of glue* une goutte de colle

block NOUN
see also block VERB
l' *immeuble* MASC ◇ *He lives in our block.* Il habite dans notre immeuble.
◆ **a block of flats** un immeuble

to **block** VERB
see also block NOUN

bloquer

blockage NOUN
l' *obstruction* FEM

bloke NOUN
le *mec* (*informal*)

blonde ADJECTIVE
blond ◇ *She's got blonde hair.* Elle a les cheveux blonds.

blood NOUN
le *sang*

blood pressure NOUN
- **to have high blood pressure** faire de la tension

blood sports NOUN
les *sports sanguinaires* MASC PL

blood test NOUN
la *prise de sang*

bloody ADJECTIVE
- **bloody difficult** sacrément difficile
- **that bloody television** cette putain de télévision
- **Bloody hell!** Merde!

blouse NOUN
le *chemisier*

blow NOUN
see also blow VERB
le *coup*

blow VERB
see also blow NOUN
souffler (*wind, person*)
- **to blow one's nose** se moucher
- **to blow a whistle** siffler
- **to blow out a candle** éteindre une bougie
- **to blow up (1)** faire sauter ◇ *The terrorists blew up a police station.* Les terroristes ont fait sauter un commissariat de police.
- **to blow up (2)** gonfler ◇ *to blow up a balloon* gonfler un ballon
- **The house blew up.** La maison a sauté.

blow-dry NOUN
le *brushing*
- **A cut and blow-dry, please.** Une coupe brushing, s'il vous plaît.

blue ADJECTIVE
bleu ◇ *a blue dress* une robe bleue
- **a blue film** un film pornographique
- **It came out of the blue.** C'était complètement inattendu.

blues PL NOUN
le *blues* SING

bluff VERB
see also bluff NOUN
bluffer

bluff NOUN
see also bluff VERB
le *bluff* ◇ *It's just a bluff.* C'est du bluff.

blunder NOUN
la *gaffe*

blunt ADJECTIVE
1 *brusque* (*person*)
2 *émoussé* (*knife*)

to **blush** VERB
rougir

board NOUN
1 (*wooden*)
la *planche*
2 (*blackboard*)
le *tableau*
(les *tableaux* PL)
◇ *on the board* au tableau
3 (*noticeboard*)
le *panneau*
(les *panneaux* PL)
4 (*for board games*)
le *jeu*
(les *jeux* PL)
5 (*for chess*)
l' *échiquier* MASC
- **on board** à bord
- **"full board"** "pension complète"

boarder NOUN
l' *interne* MASC/FEM

board game NOUN
le *jeu de société*
(les *jeux de société* PL)

boarding card NOUN
la *carte d'embarquement*

boarding school NOUN
le *pensionnat*
- **I go to boarding school.** Je suis interne.

to **boast** VERB
se vanter ◇ *Stop boasting!* Arrête de te vanter!
- **to boast about something** se vanter de quelque chose

boat NOUN
le *bateau*
(les *bateaux* PL)

body NOUN
le *corps*

bodybuilding NOUN
le *culturisme*

bodyguard NOUN
le *garde du corps*

bog NOUN
la *tourbière* (*marsh*)

boil NOUN
see also boil VERB
le *furoncle*

to **boil** VERB
see also boil NOUN
1 *faire bouillir* ◇ *to boil some water* faire bouillir de l'eau
- **to boil an egg** faire cuire un œuf
2 *bouillir* ◇ *The water's boiling.* L'eau bout. ◇ *The water's boiled.* L'eau a

bouilli.
- **to boil over** déborder

boiled ADJECTIVE
à l'eau ◇ *boiled potatoes* des pommes de terre à l'eau
- **a boiled egg** un œuf à la coque

boiling ADJECTIVE
- **It's boiling in here!** Il fait une chaleur torride ici!
- **boiling hot** torride ◇ *a boiling hot day* une journée torride

bolt NOUN
1 le *verrou* (*on door*)
2 le *boulon* (*with nut*)

bomb NOUN
see also bomb VERB
la *bombe*

to **bomb** VERB
see also bomb NOUN
bombarder

bomber NOUN
le *bombardier*

bombing NOUN
l' *attentat à la bombe* MASC

bond NOUN
le *lien*

bone NOUN
1 l' *os* MASC (*of human, animal*)
2 l' *arête* FEM (*of fish*)

bone dry ADJECTIVE
complètement sec MASC
complètement sèche FEM

bonfire NOUN
le *feu*
(les *feux* PL)

bonnet NOUN
le *capot* (*of car*)

book NOUN
see also book VERB
le *livre*

to **book** VERB
see also book NOUN
réserver ◇ *We haven't booked.* Nous n'avons pas réservé.

bookcase NOUN
la *bibliothèque*

booklet NOUN
la *brochure*

bookshelf NOUN
l' *étagère à livres* FEM

bookshop NOUN
la *librairie*

boot NOUN
1 le *coffre* (*of car*)
2 la *botte* (*fashion boot*)
3 la *chaussure de marche* (*for hiking*)
- **football boots** des chaussures de foot

booze NOUN
l' *alcool* MASC

border NOUN
la *frontière*

bored ADJECTIVE
- **to be bored** s'ennuyer ◇ *I was bored.* Je m'ennuyais.
- **to get bored** s'ennuyer

boredom NOUN
l' *ennui* MASC

boring ADJECTIVE
ennuyeux MASC
ennuyeuse FEM

born ADJECTIVE
- **to be born** naître ◇ *I was born in 1982.* Je suis né en mille neuf cent quatre-vingt-deux.

to **borrow** VERB
emprunter ◇ *Can I borrow your pen?* Je peux emprunter ton stylo?
- **to borrow something from somebody** emprunter quelque chose à quelqu'un ◇ *I borrowed some money from a friend.* J'ai emprunté de l'argent à un ami.

Bosnia NOUN
la *Bosnie*

Bosnian ADJECTIVE
bosniaque

boss NOUN
le *patron*
la *patronne*

to **boss around** VERB
- **to boss somebody around** donner des ordres à quelqu'un

bossy ADJECTIVE
autoritaire

both ADJECTIVE, PRONOUN
tous les deux MASC PL
(*toutes les deux* FEM PL)
◇ *We both went.* Nous y sommes allés tous les deux. ◇ *Emma and Jane both went.* Emma et Jane y sont allées toutes les deux. ◇ *Both of your answers are wrong.* Vos réponses sont toutes les deux mauvaises. ◇ *Both of them have left.* Ils sont partis tous les deux. ◇ *Both of us went.* Nous y sommes allés tous les deux. ◇ *Both Maggie and John are against it.* Maggie et John sont tous les deux contre.
- **He speaks both German and Italian.** Il parle allemand et italien.

to **bother** VERB
1 *tracasser* (*worry*) ◇ *What's bothering you?* Qu'est-ce qui te tracasse?
2 *déranger* (*disturb*) ◇ *I'm sorry to bother you.* Je suis désolé de vous déranger.
- **no bother** aucun problème
- **Don't bother!** Ça n'est pas la peine!
- **to bother to do something** prendre la

peine de faire quelque chose ◇ *He didn't bother to tell me about it.* Il n'a pas pris la peine de m'en parler.

bottle NOUN
la *bouteille*

bottle bank NOUN
le *conteneur à verre*

bottle-opener NOUN
l' *ouvre-bouteille* MASC

bottom NOUN
see also bottom ADJECTIVE
1 le *fond* (*of container, bag, sea*)
2 le *derrière* (*buttocks*)
3 le *bas* (*of page, list*)

bottom ADJECTIVE
see also bottom NOUN
inférieur ◇ *the bottom shelf* l'étagère inférieure
◆ **the bottom sheet** le drap de dessous

bought VERB *see* **buy**

bounce VERB
rebondir

bouncer NOUN
le *videur*

bound ADJECTIVE
◆ **He's bound to fail.** Il va sûrement échouer.

boundary NOUN
la *frontière*

bow NOUN
see also bow VERB
1 le *nœud* (*knot*) ◇ *to tie a bow* faire un nœud
2 l' *arc* MASC ◇ *a bow and arrows* un arc et des flèches

bow VERB
see also bow NOUN
faire une révérence

bowels PL NOUN
les *intestins* MASC PL

bowl NOUN
see also bowl VERB
le *bol* (*for soup, cereal*)

bowl VERB
see also bowl NOUN
lancer la balle (*in cricket*)

bowler NOUN
le *lanceur* (*in cricket*)

bowling NOUN
le *bowling*
◆ **to go bowling** jouer au bowling
◆ **a bowling alley** un bowling

bowls NOUN
les *boules* FEM PL ◇ *to play bowls* jouer aux boules

bow tie NOUN
le *nœud papillon*

box NOUN
la *boîte* ◇ *a box of matches* une boîte d'allumettes
◆ **a cardboard box** un carton

boxer NOUN
le *boxeur*

boxer shorts PL NOUN
le *caleçon* SING

boxing NOUN
la *boxe*

Boxing Day NOUN
le *lendemain de Noël* ◇ *on Boxing Day* le lendemain de Noël

boy NOUN
le *garçon*

boyfriend NOUN
le *copain* ◇ *Have you got a boyfriend?* Est-ce que tu as un copain?

bra NOUN
le *soutien-gorge*
(les *soutiens-gorge* PL)

brace NOUN
l' *appareil* MASC (*on teeth*) ◇ *She wears a brace.* Elle a un appareil.

bracelet NOUN
le *bracelet*

brackets PL NOUN
◆ **in brackets** entre parenthèses

brain NOUN
le *cerveau*
(les *cerveaux* PL)

brainy ADJECTIVE
intelligent

brake NOUN
see also brake VERB
le *frein*

to **brake** VERB
see also brake NOUN
freiner

branch NOUN
1 la *branche* (*of tree*)
2 l' *agence* FEM (*of bank*)

brand-new ADJECTIVE
tout neuf MASC
toute neuve FEM

brandy NOUN
le *cognac*

brass NOUN
le *cuivre*
◆ **the brass section** les cuivres

brass band NOUN
la *fanfare*

brat NOUN
◆ **He's a spoiled brat.** C'est un enfant gâté.

brave ADJECTIVE
courageux MASC
courageuse FEM

Brazil NOUN
le *Brésil*
◆ **in Brazil** au Brésil

B

bread NOUN
le *pain* ◇ *brown bread* le pain complet ◇ *white bread* le pain blanc
- **bread and butter** les tartines de pain beurrées FEM

break NOUN
see also break VERB
1 la *pause* (*rest*) ◇ *to take a break* faire une pause
2 la *récréation* (*at school*) ◇ *during morning break* pendant la récréation du matin
- **the Christmas break** les vacances de Noël
- **Give me a break!** Laisse-moi tranquille!

to **break** VERB
see also break NOUN
1 *casser* ◇ *Careful, you'll break something!* Attention, tu vas casser quelque chose!
2 *se casser* (*get broken*) ◇ *Careful, it'll break!* Attention, ça va se casser!
- **to break one's leg** se casser la jambe ◇ *I broke my leg.* Je me suis cassé la jambe.
- **He broke his arm.** Il s'est cassé le bras.
- **to break a promise** rompre une promesse
- **to break a record** battre un record
- **to break the law** violer la loi

to **break down** VERB
tomber en panne ◇ *The car broke down.* La voiture est tombée en panne.

breakdown NOUN
1 la *panne* (*in vehicle*) ◇ *to have a breakdown* tomber en panne
2 la *dépression* (*mental*) ◇ *to have a breakdown* faire une dépression

breakdown van NOUN
la *dépanneuse*

breakfast NOUN
le *petit déjeuner* ◇ *What would you like for breakfast?* Qu'est-ce vous voulez pour le petit déjeuner?

to **break in** VERB
entrer par effraction

break-in NOUN
le *cambriolage*

to **break open** VERB
forcer (*door, cupboard*)

to **break out** VERB
1 *se déclarer* (*fire*)
2 *éclater* (*war*)
3 *s'évader* (*prisoner*)
- **to break out in a rash** être couvert de boutons

to **break up** VERB
1 *se disperser* (*crowd*)
2 *se terminer* (*meeting, party*)
3 *se séparer* (*couple*)
- **to break up a fight** mettre fin à une bagarre
- **We break up next Wednesday.** Nos vacances commencent mercredi.

breast NOUN
le *sein* (*of woman*)
- **chicken breast** le blanc de poulet

to **breast-feed** VERB
allaiter

breaststroke NOUN
la *brasse*

breath NOUN
l' *haleine* FEM ◇ *to have bad breath* avoir mauvaise haleine
- **to be out of breath** être essoufflé
- **to get one's breath back** reprendre son souffle

to **breathe** VERB
respirer

to **breed** VERB
see also breed NOUN
se reproduire (*reproduce*)
- **to breed dogs** faire de l'élevage de chiens

breed NOUN
see also breed VERB
la *race*

breeze NOUN
la *brise*

brewery NOUN
la *brasserie*

brick NOUN
la *brique*
- **a brick wall** un mur en brique

bricklayer NOUN
le *maçon*

bride NOUN
la *mariée*

bridegroom NOUN
le *marié*

bridesmaid NOUN
la *demoiselle d'honneur*

bridge NOUN
1 le *pont* ◇ *a suspension bridge* un pont suspendu
2 le *bridge* ◇ *to play bridge* jouer au bridge

brief ADJECTIVE
bref MASC
brève FEM

briefcase NOUN
la *serviette*

briefly ADVERB
brièvement

briefs PL NOUN
le *slip* SING
- **a pair of briefs** un slip

bright ADJECTIVE

1 (*colour, light*)
vif MASC
vive FEM
◇ *a bright colour* une couleur vive
◆ **bright blue** bleu vif ◇ *a bright blue car* une voiture bleu vif
2 *intelligent* ◇ *He's not very bright.* Il n'est pas très intelligent.

brilliant ADJECTIVE
1 (*wonderful*)
génial
(*géniaux* MASC PL)
◇ *Brilliant!* Génial!
2 (*clever*)
brillant ◇ *a brilliant scientist* un savant brillant

bring VERB
1 *apporter* ◇ *Bring warm clothes.* Apportez des vêtements chauds. ◇ *Could you bring me my trainers?* Tu peux m'apporter mes baskets?
2 *amener* (*person*) ◇ *Can I bring a friend?* Est-ce que je peux amener un ami?
◆ **to bring back** rapporter
◆ **to bring up** élever ◇ *She brought up 5 children on her own.* Elle a élevé cinq enfants toute seule.

Britain NOUN
la *Grande-Bretagne*
◆ **in Britain** en Grande-Bretagne
◆ **to Britain** en Grande-Bretagne
◆ **I'm from Britain.** Je suis britannique.
◆ **Great Britain** la Grande-Bretagne

British ADJECTIVE
britannique
◆ **the British** les Britanniques MASC PL
◆ **the British Isles** les îles Britanniques FEM PL

Brittany NOUN
la *Bretagne*
◆ **in Brittany** en Bretagne
◆ **to Brittany** en Bretagne
◆ **She's from Brittany.** Elle est bretonne.

broad ADJECTIVE
large (*wide*)
◆ **in broad daylight** en plein jour

broadcast NOUN
see also broadcast VERB
l' *émission* FEM

broadcast VERB
see also broadcast NOUN
diffuser ◇ *The interview was broadcast all over the world.* L'interview a été diffusé dans le monde entier.
◆ **to broadcast live** retransmettre en direct

broad-minded ADJECTIVE
large d'esprit

broccoli NOUN
les *brocolis* MASC PL

brochure NOUN
la *brochure*

broke VERB *see* **break**

broke ADJECTIVE
◆ **to be broke** (*without money*) être fauché

broken ADJECTIVE
cassé ◇ *It's broken.* C'est cassé. ◇ *a broken leg* une jambe cassée ◇ *He's got a broken arm.* Il a le bras cassé.

bronchitis NOUN
la *bronchite*

bronze NOUN
le *bronze* ◇ *the bronze medal* la médaille de bronze

brooch NOUN
la *broche*

broom NOUN
le *balai*

brother NOUN
le *frère* ◇ *my brother* mon frère ◇ *my big brother* mon grand frère

brother-in-law NOUN
le *beau-frère*
(les *beaux-frères* PL)

brought VERB *see* **bring**

brown ADJECTIVE
1 *marron* MASC, FEM, PL (*clothes*)
2 (*hair*)
brun
3 (*tanned*)
bronzé
◆ **brown bread** le pain complet

bruise NOUN
le *bleu*

brush NOUN
see also brush VERB
1 la *brosse*
2 (*paintbrush*)
le *pinceau*
(les *pinceaux* PL)

to **brush** VERB
see also brush NOUN
brosser
◆ **to brush one's hair** se brosser les cheveux ◇ *I brushed my hair.* Je me suis brossé les cheveux.
◆ **to brush one's teeth** se brosser les dents ◇ *I brush my teeth every night.* Je me brosse les dents tous les soirs.

Brussels NOUN
Bruxelles
◆ **in Brussels** à Bruxelles
◆ **to Brussels** à Bruxelles

Brussels sprouts PL NOUN
les *choux de Bruxelles* MASC PL

brutal ADJECTIVE
brutal

PTO

(*brutaux* MASC PL)

bubble NOUN
la *bulle*

bubble bath NOUN
le *bain moussant*

bubble gum NOUN
le *chewing-gum*

bucket NOUN
le *seau*
(les *seaux* PL)

buckle NOUN
la *boucle* (*on belt, watch, shoe*)

Buddhism NOUN
le *bouddhisme*

Buddhist ADJECTIVE
bouddhiste

budget NOUN
le *budget*

budgie NOUN
la *perruche*

buffet NOUN
le *buffet*

buffet car NOUN
la *voiture-bar*

bug NOUN
1 l' *insecte* MASC (*insect*)
2 le *microbe* (*infection*) ◇ *There's a bug going round.* Il y a un microbe qui traîne.
◆ **a stomach bug** une gastroentérite
3 le *bug* (*in computer*)

bugged ADJECTIVE
sur écoute ◇ *The room was bugged.* La pièce était sur écoute.

to **build** VERB
construire ◇ *They're going to build houses here.* On va construire des maisons ici.
◆ **to build up** (*increase*) s'accumuler

builder NOUN
1 l' *entrepreneur* MASC (*owner of firm*)
2 le *maçon* (*worker*)

building NOUN
le *bâtiment*

built VERB *see* **build**

bulb NOUN
l' *ampoule* FEM (*electric*)

bull NOUN
le *taureau*
(les *taureaux* PL)

bullet NOUN
la *balle*

bullfighting NOUN
la *tauromachie*

bully NOUN
see also bully VERB
la *brute* ◇ *He's a big bully.* C'est une brute.

to **bully** VERB
see also bully NOUN
tyranniser

bum NOUN
le *derrière* (*bottom*)

bump NOUN
see also bump VERB
1 la *bosse* (*lump*)
2 l' *accrochage* MASC (*minor accident*) ◇ *We had a bump.* Nous avons eu un accrochage.

to **bump** VERB
see also bump NOUN
◆ **to bump into something** rentrer dans quelque chose ◇ *We bumped into his car.* Nous sommes rentrés dans sa voiture.
◆ **to bump into somebody (1)** (*literally*) rentrer dans quelqu'un ◇ *He stopped suddenly and I bumped into him.* Il s'est arrêté subitement et je lui suis rentré dedans.
◆ **to bump into somebody (2)** (*meet by chance*) rencontrer par hasard
◆ **I bumped into Jane in the supermarket.** J'ai rencontré Jane par hasard au supermarché.

bumper NOUN
le *pare-chocs*
(les *pare-chocs* PL)

bumpy ADJECTIVE
cahoteux MASC
cahoteuse FEM

bun NOUN
le *petit pain au lait*

bunch NOUN
◆ **a bunch of flowers** un bouquet de fleurs
◆ **a bunch of grapes** une grappe de raisin
◆ **a bunch of keys** un trousseau de clés

bunches PL NOUN
les *couettes* FEM ◇ *She has her hair in bunches.* Elle a des couettes.

bungalow NOUN
le *bungalow*

bunk NOUN
la *couchette*

burglar NOUN
le *cambrioleur*
la *cambrioleuse*

burglary NOUN
le *cambriolage*

burn NOUN
see also burn VERB
la *brûlure*

to **burn** VERB
see also burn NOUN
1 *brûler* (*rubbish, documents*)
2 *faire brûler* (*food*) ◇ *I burned the cake.* J'ai fait brûler le gâteau.
◆ **to burn oneself** se brûler ◇ *I burned myself on the oven door.* Je me suis brûlé

sur la porte du four.
- **I've burned my hand.** Je me suis brûlé la main.
- **to burn down** brûler ◇ *The factory burned down.* L'usine a brûlé.

burst VERB
éclater ◇ *The balloon burst.* Le ballon a éclaté.
- **to burst a balloon** faire éclater un ballon
- **to burst out laughing** éclater de rire
- **to burst into flames** prendre feu
- **to burst into tears** fondre en larmes

bury VERB
enterrer

bus NOUN
l' *autobus* MASC ◇ *the bus driver* le conducteur d'autobus ◇ *a bus stop* un arrêt d'autobus
- **the school bus** le car scolaire
- **a bus pass** une carte d'abonnement pour le bus
- **a bus station** une gare routière
- **a bus ticket** un ticket de bus

bush NOUN
le *buisson*

business NOUN
1 l' *entreprise* FEM (*firm*) ◇ *He's got his own business.* Il a sa propre entreprise.
2 les *affaires* FEM PL (*commerce*) ◇ *He's away on business.* Il est en voyage d'affaires.
- **a business trip** un voyage d'affaires
- **It's none of my business.** Ça ne me regarde pas.

businessman NOUN
l' *homme d'affaires* MASC

businesswoman NOUN
la *femme d'affaires*

busker NOUN
le *musicien de rue*
la *musicienne de rue*

bust NOUN
la *poitrine* (*chest*)

busy ADJECTIVE
1 *occupé* (*person, phone line*)
2 *chargé* (*day, schedule*)
3 *très fréquenté* (*shop, street*)

but CONJUNCTION
mais ◇ *I'd like to come, but I'm busy.* J'aimerais venir mais je suis occupé.

butcher NOUN
le *boucher* ◇ *He's a butcher.* Il est boucher.

butcher's NOUN
la *boucherie*

butter NOUN
le *beurre*

butterfly NOUN
le *papillon*

buttocks PL NOUN
les *fesses* FEM PL

button NOUN
le *bouton*

to **buy** VERB
see also buy NOUN
acheter ◇ *He bought me an ice cream.* Il m'a acheté une glace. ◇ *I bought him an ice cream.* Je lui ai acheté une glace.
- **to buy something from somebody** acheter quelque chose à quelqu'un ◇ *I bought a watch from him.* Je lui ai acheté une montre.

buy NOUN
see also buy VERB
- **It was a good buy.** C'était une bonne affaire.

by PREPOSITION
1 *par* ◇ *The thieves were caught by the police.* Les voleurs ont été arrêtés par la police.
2 *de* ◇ *a painting by Picasso* un tableau de Picasso ◇ *a book by Balzac* un livre de Balzac
3 *en* ◇ *by car* en voiture ◇ *by train* en train ◇ *by bus* en autobus
4 *à côté de* (*close to*) ◇ *Where's the bank?–It's by the post office.* Où est la banque?–Elle est à côté de la poste.
5 *avant* (*not later than*) ◇ *We have to be there by 4 o'clock.* Nous devons y être avant quatre heures.
- **by the time...** quand... ◇ *By the time I got there it was too late.* Quand je suis arrivé il était déjà trop tard. ◇ *It'll be ready by the time you get back.* Ça sera prêt quand vous reviendrez.
- **That's fine by me.** Ça me va.
- **all by himself** tout seul
- **all by herself** toute seule
- **I did it all by myself.** Je l'ai fait tout seul.
- **by the way** au fait

bypass NOUN
la *route de contournement*

C

cab NOUN
le *taxi*

cabbage NOUN
le *chou*
(les *choux* PL)

cabin NOUN
la *cabine* (*on ship*)

cabinet NOUN
- **a bathroom cabinet** une armoire de salle de bain
- **a drinks cabinet** un bar

cable NOUN
le *câble*

cable car NOUN
le *téléphérique*

cable television NOUN
la *télévision par câble*

cactus NOUN
le *cactus*

cadet NOUN
- **a police cadet** un élève policier
- **a cadet officer** un élève officier

café NOUN
le *café*

Cafés in France sell both alcoholic and non-alcoholic drinks.

cage NOUN
la *cage*

cagoule NOUN
le *K-way* ®

cake NOUN
le *gâteau*
(les *gâteaux* PL)

to **calculate** VERB
calculer

calculation NOUN
le *calcul*

calculator NOUN
la *machine à calculer*

calendar NOUN
le *calendrier*

calf NOUN
1 (*of cow*)
le *veau*
(les *veaux* PL)
2 (*of leg*)
le *mollet*

call NOUN
see also call VERB
l' *appel* MASC (*by phone*) ◇ *Thanks for your call.* Merci de votre appel.
- **a phone call** un coup de téléphone
- **to be on call** (*doctor*) être de permanence ◇ *He's on call this evening.* Il est de permanence ce soir.

to **call** VERB
see also call NOUN
appeler ◇ *I'll tell him you called.* Je lui dirai que vous avez appelé. ◇ *This is the number to call.* C'est le numéro à appeler. ◇ *We called the police.* Nous avons appelé la police. ◇ *Everyone calls him Jimmy.* Tout le monde l'appelle Jimmy.
- **to be called** s'appeler ◇ *He's called Fluffy.* Il s'appelle Fluffy. ◇ *What's she called?* Elle s'appelle comment?
- **to call somebody names** insulter quelqu'un
- **He called me an idiot.** Il m'a traité d'idiot.
- **to call back** (*phone again*) rappeler ◇ *I'll call back at 6 o'clock.* Je rappellerai à six heures.
- **to call for** passer prendre ◇ *I'll call for you at 2.30.* Je passerai te prendre à deux heures et demie.
- **to call off** annuler ◇ *The match was called off.* Le match a été annulé.

call box NOUN
la *cabine téléphonique*

calm ADJECTIVE
calme

to **calm down** VERB
se calmer ◇ *Calm down!* Calme-toi!

Calor gas ® NOUN
le *butane*

calorie NOUN
la *calorie*

calves PL NOUN *see* **calf**

Cambodia NOUN
le *Cambodge*
- **in Cambodia** au Cambodge

camcorder NOUN
le *caméscope*

came VERB *see* **come**

camel NOUN
le *chameau*
(les *chameaux* PL)

camera NOUN
1 (*for photos*)
l' *appareil photo* MASC
(les *appareils photo* PL)
2 (*for filming, TV*)
la *caméra*

cameraman NOUN
le *caméraman*

to **camp** VERB
see also camp NOUN
camper

camp NOUN
see also camp VERB

le *camp*
- **a camp bed** un lit de camp

campaign NOUN
la *campagne*

camper NOUN
1 (*person*)
le *campeur*
la *campeuse*
2 (*van*)
le *camping-car*

camping NOUN
le *camping*
- **to go camping** faire du camping ◇ *We went camping in Cornwall.* Nous avons fait du camping en Cornouailles.

camping gas ® NOUN
le *butane*

campsite NOUN
le *terrain de camping*

campus NOUN
le *campus*

can NOUN
see also can VERB
1 la *boîte* (*tin*) ◇ *a can of sweetcorn* une boîte de maïs ◇ *a can of beer* une boîte de bière
2 le *bidon* (*jerry can*) ◇ *a can of petrol* un bidon d'essence

can VERB
see also can NOUN
1 *pouvoir* (*be able to, be allowed to*) ◇ *I can't come.* Je ne peux pas venir. ◇ *Can I help you?* Est-ce que je peux vous aider? ◇ *Can I use your phone?* Est-ce que je peux me servir de votre téléphone? ◇ *You could hire a bike.* Tu pourrais louer un vélo. ◇ *I couldn't sleep because of the noise.* Je ne pouvais pas dormir à cause du bruit.
can *is sometimes not translated.*
◇ *I can't hear you.* Je ne t'entends pas. ◇ *I can't remember.* Je ne m'en souviens pas. ◇ *Can you speak French?* Parlez-vous français?
2 *savoir* (*have learnt how to*) ◇ *I can swim.* Je sais nager. ◇ *He can't drive.* Il ne sait pas conduire.
- **That can't be true!** Ce n'est pas possible!
- **You could be right.** Vous avez peut-être raison.

Canada NOUN
le *Canada*
- **in Canada** au Canada
- **to Canada** au Canada

Canadian ADJECTIVE
see also Canadian NOUN
canadien MASC
canadienne FEM

Canadian NOUN
see also Canadian ADJECTIVE
le *Canadien*
la *Canadienne*

canal NOUN
le *canal*
(les *canaux* PL)

canary NOUN
le *canari*

to **cancel** VERB
annuler ◇ *The match was cancelled.* Le match a été annulé.

cancellation NOUN
l' *annulation* FEM

cancer NOUN
1 le *cancer* ◇ *He's got cancer.* Il a le cancer.
2 le *Cancer* ◇ *I'm Cancer.* Je suis Cancer.

candidate NOUN
le *candidat*
la *candidate*

candle NOUN
la *bougie*

candyfloss NOUN
la *barbe à papa*

cannabis NOUN
le *cannabis*

canned ADJECTIVE
en conserve (*food*)

cannot VERB *see* **can**

canoe NOUN
le *canoë*

canoeing NOUN
- **to go canoeing** faire du canoë ◇ *We went canoeing.* Nous avons fait du canoë.

can-opener NOUN
l' *ouvre-boîte* MASC

can't VERB *see* **can**

canteen NOUN
la *cantine*

to **canter** VERB
aller au petit galop

canvas NOUN
la *toile*

cap NOUN
1 la *casquette* (*hat*)
2 le *bouchon* (*of bottle, tube*)

capable ADJECTIVE
capable

capacity NOUN
la *capacité*

capital NOUN
1 la *capitale* ◇ *Cardiff is the capital of Wales.* Cardiff est la capitale du pays de Galles.
2 la *majuscule* (*letter*) ◇ *Write your address in capitals.* Écris ton adresse en majuscules.

C

capitalism NOUN
le *capitalisme*

capital punishment NOUN
la *peine capitale*

Capricorn NOUN
le *Capricorne* ◇ *I'm Capricorn.* Je suis Capricorne.

to **capsize** VERB
chavirer

captain NOUN
le *capitaine* ◇ *She's captain of the hockey team.* Elle est capitaine de l'équipe de hockey.

to **capture** VERB
capturer

car NOUN
la *voiture*
- **to go by car** aller en voiture ◇ *We went by car.* Nous y sommes allés en voiture.
- **a car crash** un accident de voiture

caramel NOUN
le *caramel*

caravan NOUN
la *caravane* ◇ *a caravan site* un camping pour caravanes

card NOUN
la *carte*
- **a card game** un jeu de cartes

cardboard NOUN
le *carton*

cardigan NOUN
le *cardigan*

cardphone NOUN
le *téléphone à carte*

care NOUN
see also care VERB
le *soin* ◇ *with care* avec soin
- **to take care of** s'occuper de ◇ *I take care of the children on Saturdays.* Le samedi, je m'occupe des enfants.
- **Take care! (1)** (*Be careful!*) Fais attention!
- **Take care! (2)** (*Look after yourself!*) Prends bien soin de toi!

to **care** VERB
see also care NOUN
- **to care about** se soucier de ◇ *They don't care about their image.* Ils se soucient peu de leur image.
- **I don't care!** Ça m'est égal! ◇ *She doesn't care.* Ça lui est égal.
- **to care for somebody** (*patients, old people*) s'occuper de quelqu'un

career NOUN
la *carrière*

careful ADJECTIVE
- **Be careful!** Fais attention!

carefully ADVERB
1 *soigneusement* ◇ *She carefully avoided talking about it.* Elle évitait soigneusement d'en parler.
2 *prudemment* (*safely*) ◇ *Drive carefully!* Conduisez prudemment!
- **Think carefully!** Réfléchis bien!

careless ADJECTIVE
1 (*work*)
peu soigné
- **a careless mistake** une faute d'inattention

2 (*person*)
peu soigneux MASC
peu soigneuse FEM
◇ *She's very careless.* Elle est bien peu soigneuse.
3 *imprudent* ◇ *a careless driver* un conducteur imprudent

caretaker NOUN
le *gardien*
la *gardienne*

car-ferry NOUN
le *ferry*

cargo NOUN
la *cargaison*

car hire NOUN
la *location de voitures*

Caribbean ADJECTIVE
see also Caribbean NOUN
antillais ◇ *Caribbean food* la cuisine antillaise

Caribbean NOUN
see also Caribbean ADJECTIVE
1 les *Caraïbes* FEM PL (*islands*) ◇ *We're going to the Caribbean.* Nous allons aux Caraïbes.
- **He's from the Caribbean.** Il est antillais.

2 la *mer des Caraïbes* (*sea*)

carnation NOUN
l' *œillet* MASC

carnival NOUN
le *carnaval*

carol NOUN
- **a Christmas carol** un chant de Noël

car park NOUN
le *parking*

carpenter NOUN
le *charpentier* ◇ *He's a carpenter.* Il est charpentier.

carpentry NOUN
la *menuiserie*

carpet NOUN
1 le *tapis* ◇ *a Persian carpet* un tapis persan
2 la *moquette* (*fitted*)

car phone NOUN
le *téléphone de voiture*

carriage NOUN
la *voiture*

carrier bag NOUN

le *sac en plastique*

carrot NOUN
la *carotte*

carry VERB
1 *porter* ◇ *I'll carry your bag.* Je vais porter ton sac.
2 *transporter* ◇ *a plane carrying 100 passengers* un avion transportant cent passagers
◆ **to carry on** continuer ◇ *Carry on!* Continue! ◇ *She carried on talking.* Elle a continué à parler.
◆ **to carry out** (*orders*) exécuter

carrycot NOUN
le *porte-bébé*

cart NOUN
la *charrette*

carton NOUN
la *brique* (*of milk, juice*)

cartoon NOUN
1 le *dessin animé* (*film*)
2 le *dessin humoristique* (*in newspaper*)
◆ **a strip cartoon** une bande dessinée

cartridge NOUN
la *cartouche*

carve VERB
découper (*meat*)

case NOUN
1 la *valise* ◇ *I've packed my case.* J'ai fait ma valise.
2 le *cas*
(les *cas* PL)
◇ *in some cases* dans certains cas
◆ **in that case** dans ce cas ◇ *I don't want it.–In that case, I'll take it.* Je n'en veux pas.–Dans ce cas, je le prends.
◆ **in case** au cas où ◇ *in case it rains* au cas où il pleuvrait
◆ **just in case** à tout hasard ◇ *Take some money, just in case.* Prends de l'argent à tout hasard.

cash NOUN
l' *argent* MASC ◇ *I'm a bit short of cash.* Je suis un peu à court d'argent.
◆ **in cash** en liquide ◇ *£2000 in cash* deux mille livres en liquide
◆ **to pay cash** payer comptant
◆ **a cash card** une carte de retrait
◆ **the cash desk** la caisse
◆ **a cash dispenser** un distributeur automatique de billets
◆ **a cash register** une caisse

cashew NOUN
la *noix de cajou*

cashier NOUN
le *caissier*
la *caissière*

cashmere NOUN
le *cachemire* ◇ *a cashmere sweater* un pull en cachemire

casino NOUN
le *casino*

casserole NOUN
le *ragoût* ◇ *I'm going to make a casserole.* Je vais faire un ragoût.
◆ **a casserole dish** une cocotte

cassette NOUN
la *cassette*
◆ **a cassette player** un lecteur de cassettes
◆ **a cassette recorder** un magnétophone

cast NOUN
les *acteurs* MASC PL ◇ *After the play, we met the cast.* Après la représentation, nous avons rencontré les acteurs.

castle NOUN
le *château*
(les *châteaux* PL)

casual ADJECTIVE
1 *décontracté* ◇ *I prefer casual clothes.* Je préfère les vêtements décontractés.
2 *désinvolte* ◇ *a casual attitude* une attitude désinvolte
3 *en passant* ◇ *It was just a casual remark.* C'était juste une remarque en passant.

casually ADVERB
◆ **to dress casually** s'habiller de façon décontractée

casualty NOUN
les *urgences* FEM PL (*in hospital*)

cat NOUN
(*female*)
le *chat*
la *chatte*
◇ *Have you got a cat?* Est-ce que tu as un chat?

catalogue NOUN
le *catalogue*

catalytic converter NOUN
le *catalyseur*

catarrh NOUN
le *rhume chronique*

catastrophe NOUN
la *catastrophe*

to **catch** VERB
1 *attraper* ◇ *to catch a thief* attraper un voleur ◇ *My cat catches birds.* Mon chat attrape des oiseaux.
◆ **to catch somebody doing something** attraper quelqu'un en train de faire quelque chose ◇ *If they catch you smoking...* S'ils t'attrapent en train de fumer...
◆ **to catch a cold** attraper un rhume
2 *prendre* (*bus, train*) ◇ *We caught the last bus.* Nous avons pris le dernier bus.
3 *saisir* (*hear*) ◇ *I didn't catch his name.*

Je n'ai pas saisi son nom.

- **to catch up** rattraper son retard ◇ *I've got to catch up: I was away last week.* Je dois rattraper mon retard: j'étais absent la semaine dernière.

catching ADJECTIVE
contagieux MASC
contagieuse FEM
◇ *It's not catching.* Ce n'est pas contagieux.

catering NOUN
la *restauration*

cathedral NOUN
la *cathédrale*

Catholic ADJECTIVE
see also Catholic NOUN
catholique

Catholic NOUN
see also Catholic ADJECTIVE
le/la *catholique* ◇ *I'm a Catholic.* Je suis catholique.

cattle PL NOUN
le *bétail* SING

caught VERB *see* **catch**

cauliflower NOUN
le *chou-fleur*
(les *choux-fleurs* PL)

cause NOUN
see also cause VERB
la *cause*

to **cause** VERB
see also cause NOUN
provoquer ◇ *to cause an accident* provoquer un accident

cautious ADJECTIVE
prudent

cave NOUN
la *grotte*

CD NOUN
le *CD*
(les *CD* PL)

CD player NOUN
la *platine laser*

CD-ROM NOUN
le *CD-ROM*
(les *CD-ROM* PL)

ceiling NOUN
le *plafond*

to **celebrate** VERB
fêter (*birthday*)

celebrity NOUN
la *célébrité*

celery NOUN
le *céleri*

cell NOUN
la *cellule*

cellar NOUN
la *cave* ◇ *a wine cellar* une cave à vins

cello NOUN
le *violoncelle* ◇ *I play the cello.* Je joue du violoncelle.

cement NOUN
le *ciment*

cemetery NOUN
le *cimetière*

cent NOUN
le *cent* ◇ *twenty cents* vingt cents

centenary NOUN
le *centenaire*

centigrade ADJECTIVE
centigrade ◇ *20 degrees centigrade* vingt degrés centigrade

centimetre NOUN
le *centimètre*

central ADJECTIVE
central
(*centraux* MASC PL)

central heating NOUN
le *chauffage central*

centre NOUN
le *centre* ◇ *a sports centre* un centre sportif

century NOUN
le *siècle* ◇ *the 20th century* le vingtième siècle ◇ *the 21st century* le vingt et unième siècle

cereal NOUN
les *céréales* FEM PL ◇ *I have cereal for breakfast.* Je prends des céréales au petit déjeuner.

ceremony NOUN
la *cérémonie*

certain ADJECTIVE
certain ◇ *a certain person* une certaine personne ◇ *I'm absolutely certain it was him.* Je suis absolument certain que c'était lui.

- **I don't know for certain.** Je n'en suis pas certain.
- **to make certain** s'assurer ◇ *I made certain the door was locked.* Je me suis assuré que la porte était fermée à clé.

certainly ADVERB
vraiment ◇ *I certainly expected something better.* Je m'attendais vraiment à quelque chose de mieux.

- **Certainly not!** Certainement pas!
- **So it was a surprise? – It certainly was!** C'était donc une surprise? – Ça oui alors!

certificate NOUN
le *certificat*

chain NOUN
la *chaîne*

chair NOUN
1 la *chaise* ◇ *a table and 4 chairs* une table et quatre chaises
2 le *fauteuil* (*armchair*)

chairlift NOUN

le *télésiège*

chairman NOUN
le *président*

chalet NOUN
le *chalet*

chalk NOUN
la *craie*

challenge NOUN
see also challenge VERB
le *défi*

challenge VERB
see also challenge NOUN
- **She challenged me to a race.** Elle m'a proposé de faire la course avec elle.

challenging ADJECTIVE
stimulant ◇ *a challenging job* un travail stimulant

champagne NOUN
le *champagne*

champion NOUN
le *champion*
la *championne*

championship NOUN
le *championnat*

chance NOUN
1 la *chance* ◇ *Do you think I've got any chance?* Tu crois que j'ai une chance? ◇ *Their chances of winning are very good.* Ils ont de fortes chances de gagner.
- **No chance!** Pas question!

2 l' *occasion* FEM ◇ *I'd like to have a chance to travel.* J'aimerais avoir l'occasion de voyager.
- **I'll write when I get the chance.** J'écrirai quand j'aurai un moment.
- **by chance** par hasard ◇ *We met by chance.* Nous nous sommes rencontrés par hasard.
- **to take a chance** prendre un risque ◇ *I'm taking no chances!* Je ne veux prendre aucun risque!

Chancellor of the Exchequer NOUN
le *chancelier de l'Échiquier*

change VERB
see also change NOUN
1 *changer* ◇ *The town has changed a lot.* La ville a beaucoup changé. ◇ *I'd like to change £50.* Je voudrais changer cinquante livres.

Use **changer de** *when you change one thing for another.*

2 *changer de* ◇ *You have to change trains in Paris.* Il faut changer de train à Paris. ◇ *I'm going to change my shoes.* Je vais changer de chaussures. ◇ *He wants to change his job.* Il veut changer d'emploi.
- **to change one's mind** changer d'avis ◇ *I've changed my mind.* J'ai changé d'avis.
- **to change gear** changer de vitesse

3 *se changer* ◇ *She's changing to go out.* Elle est en train de se changer pour sortir.
- **to get changed** se changer ◇ *I'm going to get changed.* Je vais me changer.

4 *échanger* (*swap*) ◇ *Can I change this sweater? It's too small.* Est-ce que je peux échanger ce pull? Il est trop petit.

change NOUN
see also change VERB
1 le *changement* ◇ *There's been a change of plan.* Il y a eu un changement de programme.
2 la *monnaie* (*money*) ◇ *I haven't got any change.* Je n'ai pas de monnaie.
- **a change of clothes** des vêtements de rechange
- **for a change** pour changer ◇ *Let's play tennis for a change.* Si on jouait au tennis pour changer?

changeable ADJECTIVE
variable

changing room NOUN
1 le *salon d'essayage* (*in shop*)
2 le *vestiaire* (*for sport*)

channel NOUN
la *chaîne* (*TV*) ◇ *There's football on the other channel.* Il y a du football sur l'autre chaîne.
- **the Channel** la Manche
- **the Channel Islands** les îles Anglo-Normandes FEM PL
- **the Channel Tunnel** le tunnel sous la Manche

chaos NOUN
le *chaos*

chap NOUN
le *type* ◇ *He's a nice chap.* C'est un type sympa.

chapel NOUN
la *chapelle* (*part of church*)

chapter NOUN
le *chapitre*

character NOUN
1 le *caractère* ◇ *Give me some idea of his character.* Décris-moi un peu son caractère.
- **She's quite a character.** C'est un drôle de numéro.

2 le *personnage* (*in play, film*) ◇ *The character played by Depardieu...* Le personnage joué par Depardieu...

characteristic NOUN
la *caractéristique*

charcoal NOUN
le *charbon de bois*

charge NOUN

see also charge VERB
les *frais* MASC PL ◇ *Is there a charge for delivery?* Est-ce qu'il y a des frais de livraison?
- **an extra charge** un supplément
- **free of charge** gratuit
- **to reverse the charges** appeler en P.C.V. ◇ *I'd like to reverse the charges.* Je voudrais appeler en P.C.V.
- **to be on a charge** être inculpé ◇ *He's on a charge of murder.* Il est inculpé de meurtre.
- **to be in charge** être responsable ◇ *Mrs Munday was in charge of the group.* Madame Munday était responsable du groupe.

to **charge** VERB
see also charge NOUN
1 *prendre* (*money*) ◇ *How much did he charge you?* Combien est-ce qu'il vous a pris? ◇ *They charge £10 an hour.* Ils prennent dix livres de l'heure.
2 *inculper* (*with crime*) ◇ *The police have charged him with murder.* La police l'a inculpé de meurtre.

charity NOUN
l' *association caritative* FEM ◇ *He gave the money to charity.* Il a donné l'argent à une association caritative.

charm NOUN
le *charme* ◇ *He's got a lot of charm.* Il a beaucoup de charme.

charming ADJECTIVE
charmant

chart NOUN
le *tableau*
(les *tableaux* PL)
◇ *The chart shows the rise of unemployment.* Le tableau indique la progression du chômage.
- **the charts** le hit-parade ◇ *This album is number one in the charts.* Cet album est numéro un au hit-parade.

charter flight NOUN
le *charter*

to **chase** VERB
see also chase NOUN
pourchasser

chase NOUN
see also chase VERB
la *poursuite* ◇ *a car chase* une poursuite en voiture

chat NOUN
- **to have a chat** bavarder

chat show NOUN
le *talk-show*

cheap ADJECTIVE
bon marché MASC, FEM, PL ◇ *a cheap T-shirt* un T-shirt bon marché

cheaper ADJECTIVE
moins cher MASC
moins chère FEM
◇ *It's cheaper by bus.* C'est moins cher en bus.

to **cheat** VERB
see also cheat NOUN
tricher ◇ *You're cheating!* Tu triches!

cheat NOUN
see also cheat VERB
le *tricheur*
la *tricheuse*

check NOUN
see also check VERB
le *contrôle* ◇ *a security check* un contrôle de sécurité

to **check** VERB
see also check NOUN
vérifier ◇ *I'll check the time of the train.* Je vais vérifier l'heure du train. ◇ *Could you check the oil, please?* Pourriez-vous vérifier le niveau d'huile, s'il vous plaît?
- **to check in (1)** (*at airport*) se présenter à l'enregistrement ◇ *What time do I have to check in?* À quelle heure est-ce que je dois me présenter à l'enregistrement?
- **to check in (2)** (*in hotel*) se présenter à la réception
- **to check out** (*from hotel*) régler sa note

check-in NOUN
l' *enregistrement* MASC

checkout NOUN
la *caisse*

check-up NOUN
l' *examen de routine* MASC

cheek NOUN
1 la *joue* ◇ *He kissed her on the cheek.* Il l'a embrassée sur la joue.
2 le *culot* ◇ *What a cheek!* Quel culot!

cheeky ADJECTIVE
effronté ◇ *Don't be cheeky!* Ne sois pas effronté!
- **a cheeky smile** un sourire malicieux

cheer NOUN
see also cheer VERB
les *hourras* MASC PL
- **to give a cheer** pousser des hourras
- **Cheers! (1)** (*good health*) À la vôtre!
- **Cheers! (2)** (*thanks*) Merci!

to **cheer** VERB
see also cheer NOUN
applaudir
- **to cheer somebody up** remonter le moral à quelqu'un ◇ *I was trying to cheer him up.* J'essayais de lui remonter le moral.
- **Cheer up!** Ne te laisse pas abattre!

cheerful ADJECTIVE
gai

cheerio EXCLAMATION
salut!

cheese NOUN
le *fromage*

chef NOUN
le *chef*

chemical NOUN
le *produit chimique*

chemist NOUN
1 (*dispenser*)
le *pharmacien*
la *pharmacienne*
2 (*shop*)
la *pharmacie* ◇ *You get it from the chemist.* C'est vendu en pharmacie.

Chemist's shops in France are identified by a special green cross outside the shop.

3 (*scientist*)
le/la *chimiste*

chemistry NOUN
la *chimie* ◇ *the chemistry lab* le laboratoire de chimie

cheque NOUN
le *chèque* ◇ *to write a cheque* faire un chèque ◇ *to pay by cheque* payer par chèque

chequebook NOUN
le *carnet de chèques*

cherry NOUN
la *cerise*

chess NOUN
les *échecs* MASC PL ◇ *to play chess* jouer aux échecs

chessboard NOUN
l' *échiquier* MASC

chest NOUN
la *poitrine* (*of person*) ◇ *his chest measurement* son tour de poitrine
◆ **a chest of drawers** une commode

chestnut NOUN
le *marron* ◇ *We have turkey with chestnuts.* Nous mangeons de la dinde aux marrons.

chewing gum NOUN
le *chewing-gum*

chicken NOUN
le *poulet*

chickenpox NOUN
la *varicelle*

child NOUN
l' *enfant* MASC/FEM ◇ *all the children* tous les enfants

childish ADJECTIVE
puéril

child minder NOUN
la *nourrice*

children PL NOUN *see* **child**

Chile NOUN
le *Chili*
◆ **in Chile** au Chili

to **chill** VERB
mettre au frais ◇ *Put the wine in the fridge to chill.* Mets le vin au frais dans le réfrigérateur.

chilli NOUN
le *piment*

chimney NOUN
la *cheminée*

chin NOUN
le *menton*

china NOUN
la *porcelaine* ◇ *a china plate* une assiette en porcelaine

China NOUN
la *Chine*
◆ **in China** en Chine

Chinese ADJECTIVE
see also Chinese NOUN
chinois ◇ *a Chinese restaurant* un restaurant chinois
◆ **a Chinese man** un Chinois
◆ **a Chinese woman** une Chinoise

Chinese NOUN
see also Chinese ADJECTIVE
le *chinois* (*language*)
◆ **the Chinese** (*people*) les Chinois

chip NOUN
1 la *frite* (*food*) ◇ *We bought some chips.* Nous avons acheté des frites.
2 la *puce* (*in computer*)

chiropodist NOUN
le/la *pédicure* ◇ *He's a chiropodist.* Il est pédicure.

chives PL NOUN
la *ciboulette* SING

chocolate NOUN
le *chocolat* ◇ *a chocolate cake* un gâteau au chocolat
◆ **hot chocolate** le chocolat chaud

choice NOUN
le *choix* ◇ *I had no choice.* Je n'avais pas le choix.

choir NOUN
la *chorale* ◇ *I sing in the school choir.* Je chante dans la chorale de l'école.

to **choose** VERB
choisir ◇ *It's difficult to choose.* C'est difficile de choisir.

to **chop** VERB
see also chop NOUN
émincer ◇ *Chop the onions.* Émincez les oignons.

chop NOUN
see also chop VERB
la *côte* ◇ *a pork chop* une côte de porc

chopsticks PL NOUN
les *baguettes* FEM PL

chose, chosen VERB *see* **choose**

C

Christ NOUN
le *Christ* ◇ *the birth of Christ* la naissance du Christ

christening NOUN
le *baptême*

Christian NOUN
see also Christian ADJECTIVE
le *chrétien*
la *chrétienne*

Christian ADJECTIVE
see also Christian NOUN
chrétien MASC
chrétienne FEM

Christian name NOUN
le *prénom*

Christmas NOUN
Noël MASC ◇ *Happy Christmas!* Joyeux Noël!

- **Christmas Day** le jour de Noël
- **Christmas Eve** la veille de Noël
- **a Christmas tree** un arbre de Noël
- **a Christmas card** une carte de Noël

*The French more often send greetings cards (*une carte de vœux*) in January rather than at Christmas, with best wishes for the New Year.*

- **Christmas dinner** le repas de Noël

*Most French people have their Christmas meal (*réveillon de Noël*) on the evening of Christmas Eve, though some have a* repas de Noël *on Christmas Day.*

- **Christmas pudding**

*The French usually have a Yule log (*une bûche de Noël*) for pudding at the Christmas meal. You could explain what Christmas pudding is using the example given.*

◇ *Christmas pudding is made with dried fruit and spices, and steamed.* Le "Christmas pudding" est un gâteau avec des raisins secs, parfumé avec des épices et cuit à la vapeur.

chunk NOUN
le *gros morceau*
(les *gros morceaux* PL)
◇ *Cut the meat into chunks.* Coupez la viande en gros morceaux.

church NOUN
l' *église* FEM ◇ *I don't go to church every Sunday.* Je ne vais pas à l'église tous les dimanches.

- **the Church of England** l'Église anglicane

cider NOUN
le *cidre*

cigar NOUN
le *cigare*

cigarette NOUN
la *cigarette*

cinema NOUN
le *cinéma* ◇ *I'm going to the cinema this evening.* Je vais au cinéma ce soir.

circle NOUN
le *cercle*

circular ADJECTIVE
circulaire

circulation NOUN
1 la *circulation* (*of blood*)
2 le *tirage* (*of newspaper*)

circumflex NOUN
l' *accent circonflexe* MASC

circumstances PL NOUN
les *circonstances* FEM PL

circus NOUN
le *cirque*

citizen NOUN
le *citoyen*
la *citoyenne*
◇ *a French citizen* un citoyen français

city NOUN
la *ville*

- **the city centre** le centre-ville ◇ *It's in the city centre.* C'est au centre-ville.

city technology college NOUN
le *collège technique*

civilization NOUN
la *civilisation*

civil servant NOUN
le/la *fonctionnaire* ◇ *She's a civil servant.* Elle est fonctionnaire.

civil war NOUN
la *guerre civile*

to **claim** VERB
see also claim NOUN
1 *prétendre* ◇ *He claims to have found the money.* Il prétend avoir trouvé l'argent.
2 *percevoir* (*receive*) ◇ *She's claiming unemployment benefit.* Elle perçoit des allocations chômage.

- **She can't claim unemployment benefit.** Elle n'a pas droit aux allocations chômage.
- **to claim on one's insurance** se faire rembourser par son assurance ◇ *We claimed on our insurance.* Nous nous sommes fait rembourser par notre assurance.

claim NOUN
see also claim VERB
la *demande d'indemnité* (*on insurance policy*) ◇ *to make a claim* faire une demande d'indemnité

to **clap** VERB
applaudir (*applaud*)

- **to clap one's hands** frapper dans ses mains ◇ *I've trained my dog to sit when I clap my hands.* J'ai dressé mon chien à s'asseoir quand je frappe dans mes mains.

clarinet NOUN
la *clarinette* ◇ *I play the clarinet.* Je joue de la clarinette.

clash VERB
1 *jurer* (*colours*) ◇ *These two colours clash.* Ces deux couleurs jurent.
2 *tomber en même temps* (*events*) ◇ *The concert clashes with Ann's party.* Le concert tombe en même temps que la soirée d'Ann.

clasp NOUN
le *fermoir* (*of necklace*)

class NOUN
1 la *classe* (*group*) ◇ *We're in the same class.* Nous sommes dans la même classe.
2 le *cours* (*lesson*) ◇ *I go to dancing classes.* Je vais à des cours de danse.

classic ADJECTIVE
see also classic NOUN
classique ◇ *a classic example* un cas classique

classic NOUN
see also classic ADJECTIVE
le *classique* (*book, film*)

classical ADJECTIVE
classique ◇ *I like classical music.* J'aime la musique classique.

classroom NOUN
la *classe*

claw NOUN
1 la *griffe* (*of cat, dog*)
2 la *serre* (*of bird*)
3 la *pince* (*of crab, lobster*)

clean ADJECTIVE
see also clean VERB
propre ◇ *a clean shirt* une chemise propre

clean VERB
see also clean ADJECTIVE
nettoyer

cleaner NOUN
la *femme de ménage* ◇ *She's a cleaner.* Elle est femme de ménage.

cleaner's NOUN
la *teinturerie*

clear ADJECTIVE
see also clear VERB
1 *clair* ◇ *a clear explanation* une explication claire ◇ *It's clear you don't believe me.* Il est clair que tu ne me crois pas.
2 *libre* (*road, way*) ◇ *The road's clear now.* La route est libre maintenant.

clear VERB
see also clear ADJECTIVE
1 *dégager* ◇ *The police are clearing the road after the accident.* La police dégage la route après l'accident.
2 *se dissiper* (*fog, mist*) ◇ *The mist soon cleared.* La brume s'est vite dissipée.
◆ **to be cleared of a crime** être reconnu non coupable d'un crime ◇ *She was cleared of murder.* Elle a été reconnue non coupable du meurtre.
◆ **to clear the table** débarrasser la table ◇ *I'll clear the table.* Je vais débarrasser la table.
◆ **to clear up** ranger ◇ *Who's going to clear all this up?* Qui va ranger tout ça?
◆ **I think it's going to clear up.** (*weather*) Je pense que le temps va se lever.

clearly ADVERB
1 *clairement* ◇ *She explained it very clearly.* Elle l'a expliqué très clairement.
2 *nettement* ◇ *The French coast was clearly visible.* On distinguait nettement la côte française.
3 *distinctement* ◇ *to speak clearly* parler distinctement

clementine NOUN
la *clémentine*

clever ADJECTIVE
1 *intelligent* ◇ *She's very clever.* Elle est très intelligente.
2 (*ingenious*)
astucieux MASC
astucieuse FEM
◇ *a clever system* un système astucieux
◆ **What a clever idea!** Quelle bonne idée!

client NOUN
le *client*
la *cliente*

cliff NOUN
la *falaise*

climate NOUN
le *climat*

to **climb** VERB
1 *escalader* ◇ *We're going to climb Snowdon.* Nous allons escalader le Snowdon.
2 *monter* (*stairs*)

climber NOUN
le *grimpeur*
la *grimpeuse*

climbing NOUN
l' *escalade* FEM
◆ **to go climbing** faire de l'escalade ◇ *We're going climbing in Scotland.* Nous allons faire de l'escalade en Écosse.

clinic NOUN
le *centre médical*
(les *centres médicaux* PL)

cloakroom NOUN
1 le *vestiaire* (*for coats*)
2 les *toilettes* FEM PL (*toilet*)

clock NOUN

PTO

1 l' *horloge* FEM ◇ *the church clock* l'horloge de l'église
2 la *pendule* (*smaller*)
- **an alarm clock** un réveil
- **a clock-radio** un radio-réveil

clog NOUN
le *sabot*

close ADJECTIVE, ADVERB
see also close VERB
1 *près* (*near*) ◇ *The shops are very close.* Les magasins sont tout près.
- **close to** près de ◇ *The youth hostel is close to the station.* L'auberge de jeunesse est près de la gare.
- **Come closer.** Rapproche-toi.

2 *proche* (*in relationship*) ◇ *We're just inviting close relations.* Nous n'invitons que les parents proches. ◇ *She's a close friend of mine.* C'est une proche amie. ◇ *I'm very close to my sister.* Je suis très proche de ma sœur.
3 *très serré* (*contest*) ◇ *It's going to be very close.* Ça va être très serré.
4 *lourd* (*weather*) ◇ *It's close this afternoon.* Il fait lourd cet après-midi.

to **close** VERB
see also close ADJECTIVE
1 *fermer* ◇ *What time does the pool close?* La piscine ferme à quelle heure? ◇ *The shops close at 5.30.* Les magasins ferment à cinq heures et demie. ◇ *Please close the door.* Fermez la porte, s'il vous plaît.
2 *se fermer* ◇ *The doors close automatically.* Les portes se ferment automatiquement.

closed ADJECTIVE
fermé ◇ *The bank's closed.* La banque est fermée.

closely ADVERB
de près (*look, examine*)

cloth NOUN
le *tissu* (*material*)
- **a cloth** un chiffon ◇ *Wipe it with a damp cloth.* Nettoyez-le avec un chiffon humide.

clothes PL NOUN
les *vêtements* MASC PL ◇ *new clothes* des vêtements neufs
- **a clothes line** un fil à linge
- **a clothes peg** une pince à linge

cloud NOUN
le *nuage*

cloudy ADJECTIVE
nuageux MASC
nuageuse FEM

clove NOUN
- **a clove of garlic** une gousse d'ail

clown NOUN
le *clown*

club NOUN
le *club* ◇ *a golf club* (*society and for playing golf*) un club de golf
- **the youth club** la maison des jeunes
- **clubs** (*in cards*) le trèfle ◇ *the ace of clubs* l'as de trèfle

to **club together** VERB
se cotiser ◇ *We clubbed together to buy her a present.* Nous nous sommes cotisés pour lui acheter un cadeau.

clue NOUN
l' *indice* MASC ◇ *an important clue* un indice important
- **I haven't a clue.** Je n'en ai pas la moindre idée.

clumsy ADJECTIVE
maladroit

coach NOUN
1 le *car* MASC ◇ *We went there by coach.* Nous y sommes allés en car.
- **the coach station** la gare routière
- **a coach trip** une excursion en car

2 l' *entraîneur* MASC (*trainer*) ◇ *the French coach* l'entraîneur de l'équipe de France

coal NOUN
le *charbon*
- **a coal mine** une mine de charbon
- **a coal miner** un mineur

coast NOUN
la *côte* ◇ *It's on the west coast of Scotland.* C'est sur la côte ouest de l'Écosse.

coat NOUN
le *manteau*
(les *manteaux* PL)
◇ *a warm coat* un manteau chaud
- **a coat of paint** une couche de peinture

coat hanger NOUN
le *cintre*

cocaine NOUN
la *cocaïne*

cockerel NOUN
le *coq*

cockney NOUN
le *cockney* ◇ *I'm a cockney.* Je suis cockney.

cocoa NOUN
le *cacao* ◇ *a cup of cocoa* une tasse de cacao

coconut NOUN
la *noix de coco*

cod NOUN
le *cabillaud*

code NOUN
le *code*

coffee NOUN
le *café*

◆ **A cup of coffee, please.** Un café, s'il vous plaît.

coffeepot NOUN
la *cafetière*

coffee table NOUN
la *table basse*

coffin NOUN
le *cercueil*

coin NOUN
la *pièce de monnaie*

◆ **a 5 franc coin** une pièce de cinq francs

coincidence NOUN
la *coïncidence*

coinphone NOUN
le *téléphone à pièces*

Coke ® NOUN
le *coca* ◇ *a can of Coke ®* une boîte de coca

colander NOUN
la *passoire*

cold ADJECTIVE
see also cold NOUN
froid ◇ *The water's cold.* L'eau est froide.

◆ **It's cold today.** Il fait froid aujourd'hui.

◆ **to be cold** (*person*) avoir froid ◇ *I'm cold.* J'ai froid. ◇ *Are you cold?* Est-ce que tu as froid?

cold NOUN
see also cold ADJECTIVE
1 le *froid* ◇ *I can't stand the cold.* Je ne supporte pas le froid.
2 le *rhume* ◇ *to catch a cold* attraper un rhume

◆ **to have a cold** avoir un rhume ◇ *I've got a bad cold.* J'ai un gros rhume.

◆ **a cold sore** un bouton de fièvre

coleslaw NOUN
la *salade de chou cru à la mayonnaise*

collapse VERB
s'effondrer ◇ *He collapsed.* Il s'est effondré.

collar NOUN
1 le *col* (*of coat, shirt*)
2 le *collier* (*for animal*)

collarbone NOUN
la *clavicule* ◇ *I broke my collarbone.* Je me suis cassé la clavicule.

colleague NOUN
le/la *collègue*

collect VERB
1 *ramasser* ◇ *The teacher collected the exercise books.* Le professeur a ramassé les cahiers. ◇ *They collect the rubbish twice a week.* Ils ramassent les ordures deux fois par semaine.
2 *faire collection de* ◇ *I collect stamps.* Je fais collection de timbres.
3 *aller chercher* ◇ *Their mother collects them from school.* Leur mère va les chercher à l'école.
4 *faire une collecte* ◇ *They're collecting for charity.* Ils font une collecte pour une association caritative.

collection NOUN
1 la *collection* ◇ *my CD collection* ma collection de CD
2 la *collecte* ◇ *a collection for charity* une collecte pour une association caritative

collector NOUN
le *collectionneur*
la *collectionneuse*

college NOUN
le *collège* ◇ *a technical college* un collège d'enseignement technique

to **collide** VERB
entrer en collision

collie NOUN
le *colley*

colliery NOUN
la *houillère*

collision NOUN
la *collision*

colonel NOUN
le *colonel*

colour NOUN
la *couleur* ◇ *What colour is it?* C'est de quelle couleur?

◆ **a colour film** (*for camera*) une pellicule en couleur

colourful ADJECTIVE
coloré

colouring NOUN
le *colorant* (*for food*)

comb NOUN
see also comb VERB
le *peigne*

to **comb** VERB
see also comb NOUN

◆ **to comb one's hair** se peigner ◇ *You haven't combed your hair.* Tu ne t'es pas peigné.

combination NOUN
la *combinaison*

to **combine** VERB
1 *allier* ◇ *The film combines humour with suspense.* Le film allie l'humour au suspense.
2 *concilier* ◇ *It's difficult to combine a career with a family.* Il est difficile de concilier carrière et vie de famille.

to **come** VERB
1 *venir* ◇ *Can I come too?* Est-ce que je peux venir aussi? ◇ *Some friends came to see us.* Quelques amis sont venus nous voir. ◇ *I'll come with you.* Je viens avec toi.

PTO

2 *arriver* (*arrive*) ◇ *I'm coming!* J'arrive! ◇ *They came late.* Ils sont arrivés en retard. ◇ *The letter came this morning.* La lettre est arrivée ce matin.

- **to come back** revenir ◇ *Come back!* Reviens!
- **to come down (1)** (*person, lift*) descendre
- **to come down (2)** (*prices*) baisser
- **to come from** venir de ◇ *Where do you come from?* Tu viens d'où?
- **to come in** entrer ◇ *Come in!* Entrez!
- **Come on!** Allez!
- **to come out** sortir ◇ *when we came out of the cinema* quand nous sommes sortis du cinéma ◇ *It's just come out on video.* Ça vient de sortir en vidéo.
- **None of my photos came out.** Mes photos n'ont rien donné.
- **to come round** reprendre connaissance (*after faint, operation*)
- **to come up** monter ◇ *Come up here!* Monte!
- **to come up to somebody (1)** s'approcher de quelqu'un ◇ *She came up to me and kissed me.* Elle s'est approchée de moi et m'a embrassé.
- **to come up to somebody (2)** (*to speak to them*) aborder quelqu'un ◇ *A man came up to me and said...* Un homme m'a abordé et m'a dit...

comedian NOUN
le *comique*

comedy NOUN
la *comédie*

comfortable ADJECTIVE
1 *confortable* (*bed, chair*)
2 *à l'aise* (*person*) ◇ *I'm very comfortable, thanks.* Je suis parfaitement à l'aise, merci.

comic NOUN
l' *illustré* MASC (*magazine*)

comic strip NOUN
la *bande dessinée*

coming ADJECTIVE
prochain ◇ *in the coming months* au cours des prochains mois

comma NOUN
la *virgule*

command NOUN
l' *ordre* MASC

comment NOUN
see also comment VERB
le *commentaire* ◇ *He made no comment.* Il n'a fait aucun commentaire.
- **No comment!** Je n'ai rien à dire!

to **comment** VERB
see also comment NOUN
- **to comment on something** faire des commentaires sur quelque chose

commentary NOUN
le *reportage en direct* (*on TV, radio*)

commentator NOUN
le *commentateur sportif*
la *commentatrice sportive*

commercial NOUN
le *spot publicitaire*

commission NOUN
la *commission* ◇ *Salesmen work on commission.* Les représentants travaillent à la commission.

to **commit** VERB
- **to commit a crime** commettre un crime
- **to commit oneself** s'engager ◇ *I don't want to commit myself.* Je ne veux pas m'engager.
- **to commit suicide** se suicider ◇ *He committed suicide.* Il s'est suicidé.

committee NOUN
le *comité*

common ADJECTIVE
see also common NOUN
courant ◇ *"Smith" is a very common surname.* "Smith" est un nom de famille très courant.
- **in common** en commun ◇ *We've got a lot in common.* Nous avons beaucoup de choses en commun.

common NOUN
see also common ADJECTIVE
le *terrain communal* ◇ *We went for a walk on the common.* Nous sommes allés nous promener sur le terrain communal.

common sense NOUN
le *bon sens* ◇ *Use your common sense!* Sers-toi de ton bon sens!

to **communicate** VERB
communiquer

communication NOUN
la *communication*

communion NOUN
la *communion* ◇ *my First Communion* ma première communion

communism NOUN
le *communisme*

communist NOUN
see also communist ADJECTIVE
le/la *communiste*

communist ADJECTIVE
see also communist NOUN
communiste
- **the Communist Party** le Parti communiste

community NOUN
la *communauté*

to **commute** VERB
faire la navette ◇ *She commutes between Liss and London.* Elle fait la navette entre Liss et Londres.

compact disc NOUN
le *disque compact*
◆ **a compact disc player** une platine laser

companion NOUN
le *compagnon*
la *compagne*

company NOUN
1 la *société* ◇ *He works for a big company.* Il travaille pour une grosse société.
2 la *compagnie* ◇ *an insurance company* une compagnie d'assurance ◇ *a theatre company* une compagnie théâtrale
◆ **to keep somebody company** tenir compagnie à quelqu'un ◇ *I'll keep you company.* Je vais te tenir compagnie.

comparatively ADVERB
relativement

compare VERB
comparer ◇ *People always compare him with his brother.* On le compare toujours à son frère.
◆ **compared with** en comparaison de ◇ *Oxford is small compared with London.* Oxford est une petite ville en comparaison de Londres.

comparison NOUN
la *comparaison*

compartment NOUN
le *compartiment*

compass NOUN
la *boussole*

compensation NOUN
l' *indemnité* FEM ◇ *They got £2000 compensation.* Ils ont reçu une indemnité de deux mille livres.

compere NOUN
l' *animateur* MASC
l' *animatrice* FEM

compete VERB
participer ◇ *I'm competing in the marathon.* Je participe au marathon.
◆ **to compete for something** se disputer quelque chose ◇ *There are 50 students competing for 6 places.* Ils sont cinquante étudiants à se disputer six places.

competent ADJECTIVE
compétent

competition NOUN
le *concours* ◇ *a singing competition* un concours de chant

competitor NOUN
le *concurrent*
la *concurrente*

complain VERB
se plaindre ◇ *I'm going to complain to the manager.* Je vais me plaindre au directeur. ◇ *We complained about the noise.* Nous nous sommes plaints du bruit.

complaint NOUN
la *plainte* ◇ *There were lots of complaints about the food.* Il y a eu beaucoup de plaintes à propos de la nourriture.

complete ADJECTIVE
complet MASC
complète FEM

completely ADVERB
complètement

complexion NOUN
le *teint*

complicated ADJECTIVE
compliqué

compliment NOUN
see also compliment VERB
le *compliment*

to **compliment** VERB
see also compliment NOUN
complimenter ◇ *They complimented me on my French.* Ils m'ont complimenté sur mon français.

composer NOUN
le *compositeur*
la *compositrice*

comprehensive school NOUN
1 le *collège*
2 le *lycée*
In France pupils go to a collège *between the ages of 11 and 15, and then to a* lycée *until the age of 18.*

compromise NOUN
le *compromis* ◇ *We reached a compromise.* Nous sommes parvenus à un compromis.

compulsory ADJECTIVE
obligatoire

computer NOUN
l' *ordinateur* MASC

computer game NOUN
le *jeu électronique*
(les *jeux électroniques* PL)

computer programmer NOUN
le *programmeur*
la *programmeuse*
◇ *She's a computer programmer.* Elle est programmeuse.

computing NOUN
l' *informatique* FEM

to **concentrate** VERB
se concentrer ◇ *I couldn't concentrate.* Je n'arrivais pas à me concentrer.

concentration NOUN
la *concentration*

concerned ADJECTIVE
◆ **to be concerned** s'inquiéter ◇ *His*

PTO

mother is concerned about him. Sa mère s'inquiète à son sujet.

- **as far as I'm concerned** en ce qui me concerne

concert NOUN
le *concert*

concrete NOUN
le *béton*

condition NOUN
1 la *condition* ◇ *I'll do it, on one condition...* Je veux bien le faire, à une condition...
2 l' *état* MASC ◇ *in good condition* en bon état

conditional NOUN
le *conditionnel*

conditioner NOUN
le *baume démêlant* (*for hair*)

condom NOUN
le *préservatif*

to **conduct** VERB
diriger (*orchestra*)

conductor NOUN
le *chef d'orchestre*

cone NOUN
le *cornet* ◇ *an ice-cream cone* un cornet de glace

conference NOUN
la *conférence*

to **confess** VERB
avouer ◇ *He finally confessed.* Il a fini par avouer. ◇ *He confessed to the murder.* Il a avoué avoir commis le meurtre.

confession NOUN
la *confession*

confidence NOUN
1 la *confiance* ◇ *I've got confidence in you.* J'ai confiance en toi.
2 l' *assurance* FEM ◇ *She lacks confidence.* Elle manque d'assurance.

confident ADJECTIVE
sûr ◇ *I'm confident everything will be okay.* Je suis sûr que tout ira bien.

- **She's seems quite confident.** Elle a l'air sûre d'elle.

confidential ADJECTIVE
confidentiel MASC
confidentielle FEM

to **confirm** VERB
confirmer (*booking*)

confirmation NOUN
la *confirmation*

conflict NOUN
le *conflit*

to **confuse** VERB

- **to confuse somebody** embrouiller les idées de quelqu'un ◇ *Don't confuse me!* Ne m'embrouille pas les idées!

confused ADJECTIVE
désorienté

confusing ADJECTIVE

- **The traffic signs are confusing.** Les panneaux de signalisation ne sont pas clairs.

confusion NOUN
la *confusion*

to **congratulate** VERB
féliciter ◇ *My friends congratulated me on passing the test.* Mes amis m'ont félicité d'avoir réussi à l'examen.

congratulations PL NOUN
les *félicitations* FEM PL ◇ *Congratulations on your new job!* Félicitations pour votre nouveau poste!

conjurer NOUN
le *prestidigitateur*

connection NOUN
1 le *rapport* ◇ *There's no connection between the two events.* Il n'y a aucun rapport entre les deux événements.
2 le *contact* (*electrical*) ◇ *There's a loose connection.* Il y a un mauvais contact.
3 la *correspondance* (*of trains, planes*) ◇ *We missed our connection.* Nous avons raté la correspondance.

to **conquer** VERB
conquérir

conscience NOUN
la *conscience*

conscious ADJECTIVE
conscient

consciousness NOUN
la *connaissance*

- **to lose consciousness** perdre connaissance ◇ *I lost consciousness.* J'ai perdu connaissance.

consequently ADVERB
par conséquent

conservation NOUN
la *protection*

conservative ADJECTIVE
see also conservative NOUN
conservateur MASC
conservatrice FEM

- **the Conservative Party** le Parti conservateur

Conservative NOUN
see also conservative ADJECTIVE
le *conservateur*
la *conservatrice*

- **to vote Conservative** voter conservateur
- **the Conservatives** les conservateurs

conservatory NOUN
le *jardin d'hiver*

to **consider** VERB
1 *considérer* ◇ *He considers it a waste*

of time. Il considère que c'est une perte de temps.
2 *envisager* ◇ *We considered cancelling our holiday.* Nous avons envisagé d'annuler nos vacances.
◆ **I'm considering the idea.** J'y songe.

considerate ADJECTIVE
délicat

considering PREPOSITION
1 *étant donné* ◇ *Considering we were there for a month...* Étant donné que nous étions là pour un mois...
2 *tout compte fait* ◇ *I got a good mark, considering.* J'ai eu une bonne note, tout compte fait.

consist VERB
◆ **to consist of** être composé de ◇ *The band consists of three guitarists and a drummer.* Le groupe est composé de trois guitaristes et un batteur.

consonant NOUN
la *consonne*

constant ADJECTIVE
constant

constantly ADVERB
constamment

constipated ADJECTIVE
constipé

construct VERB
construire

construction NOUN
la *construction*

consult VERB
consulter

contact NOUN
see also contact VERB
le *contact* ◇ *I'm in contact with her.* Je suis en contact avec elle.

contact VERB
see also contact NOUN
joindre ◇ *Where can we contact you?* Où pouvons-nous vous joindre?

contact lenses PL NOUN
les *verres de contact* MASC PL

contain VERB
contenir

container NOUN
le *récipient*

contest NOUN
le *concours*

contestant NOUN
le *concurrent*
la *concurrente*

context NOUN
le *contexte*

continent NOUN
le *continent* ◇ *How many continents are there?* Combien y a-t-il de continents?
◆ **the Continent** l'Europe FEM ◇ *I've never been to the Continent.* Je ne suis jamais allé en Europe.

continental breakfast NOUN
le *petit déjeuner à la française*

to **continue** VERB
1 *continuer* ◇ *She continued talking to her friend.* Elle a continué à parler à son amie.
2 *reprendre* (*after interruption*) ◇ *We continued working after lunch.* Nous avons repris le travail après le déjeuner.

continuous ADJECTIVE
continu
◆ **continuous assessment** le contrôle continu

contraceptive NOUN
le *contraceptif*

contract NOUN
le *contrat*

to **contradict** VERB
contredire

contrary NOUN
le *contraire*
◆ **on the contrary** au contraire

contrast NOUN
le *contraste*

to **contribute** VERB
1 *contribuer* (*to success, achievement*) ◇ *The treaty will contribute to world peace.* Le traité va contribuer à la paix dans le monde.
2 *participer* (*share in*) ◇ *He didn't contribute to the discussion.* Il n'a pas participé à la discussion.
3 *donner* (*give*) ◇ *She contributed £10.* Elle a donné dix livres.

contribution NOUN
la *contribution*

control NOUN
see also control VERB
le *contrôle*
◆ **to lose control** (*of vehicle*) perdre le contrôle ◇ *He lost control of the car.* Il a perdu le contrôle de son véhicule.
◆ **the controls** les commandes FEM (*of machine*)
◆ **to be in control** être maître de la situation
◆ **to keep control** (*of people*) se faire obéir ◇ *He can't keep control of the class.* Il n'arrive pas à se faire obéir de sa classe.
◆ **out of control** (*child, class*) déchaîné

to **control** VERB
see also control NOUN
1 *diriger* (*country, organization*)
2 *se faire obéir de* ◇ *He can't control the class.* Il n'arrive pas à se faire obéir de sa classe.

PTO

3 *maîtriser* ◇ *I couldn't control the horse.* Je ne suis pas arrivé à maîtriser le cheval.

➔ **to control oneself** se contrôler

controversial ADJECTIVE
controversé ◇ *a controversial book* un livre controversé

convenient ADJECTIVE
bien situé (*place*) ◇ *The hotel's convenient for the airport.* L'hôtel est bien situé par rapport à l'aéroport.

➔ **It's not a convenient time for me.** C'est une heure qui ne m'arrange pas.

➔ **Would Monday be convenient for you?** Est-ce que lundi vous conviendrait?

conventional ADJECTIVE
conventionnel MASC
conventionnelle FEM

convent school NOUN
l' *institution religieuse* FEM

conversation NOUN
la *conversation* ◇ *a French conversation class* un cours de conversation française

to **convert** VERB
transformer ◇ *We've converted the loft into a spare room.* Nous avons transformé le grenier en chambre d'amis.

to **convict** VERB
reconnaître coupable ◇ *He was convicted of the murder.* Il a été reconnu coupable du meurtre.

to **convince** VERB
persuader ◇ *I'm not convinced.* Je n'en suis pas persuadé.

to **cook** VERB
see also cook NOUN
1 *faire la cuisine* ◇ *I can't cook.* Je ne sais pas faire la cuisine.
2 *préparer* ◇ *She's cooking lunch.* Elle est en train de préparer le déjeuner.
3 *faire cuire* ◇ *Cook the pasta for 10 minutes.* Faites cuire les pâtes pendant dix minutes.

➔ **to be cooked** être cuit ◇ *When the potatoes are cooked...* Lorsque les pommes de terre sont cuites...

cook NOUN
see also cook VERB
le *cuisinier*
la *cuisinière*
◇ *Matthew's an excellent cook.* Matthew est un excellent cuisinier.

cookbook NOUN
le *livre de cuisine*

cooker NOUN
la *cuisinière* ◇ *a gas cooker* une cuisinière à gaz

cookery NOUN
la *cuisine*

cooking NOUN
la *cuisine* ◇ *I like cooking.* J'aime bien faire la cuisine.

cool ADJECTIVE
frais MASC
fraîche FEM
◇ *a cool place* un endroit frais

➔ **to stay cool** (*keep calm*) garder son calme ◇ *He stayed cool.* Il a gardé son calme.

cooperation NOUN
la *coopération*

cop NOUN
le *flic* (*informal*)

to **cope** VERB
se débrouiller ◇ *It was hard, but we coped.* C'était dur, mais nous nous sommes débrouillés.

➔ **to cope with** faire face à ◇ *She's got a lot of problems to cope with.* Elle doit faire face à de nombreux problèmes.

copper NOUN
1 le *cuivre* ◇ *a copper bracelet* un bracelet en cuivre
2 le *flic* (*informal: policeman*)

copy NOUN
see also copy VERB
1 la *copie* (*of letter, document*)
2 l' *exemplaire* MASC (*of book*)

to **copy** VERB
see also copy NOUN
copier ◇ *The teacher accused him of copying.* Le professeur l'a accusé d'avoir copié.

cork NOUN
1 le *bouchon* (*of bottle*)
2 le *liège* (*material*) ◇ *a cork table mat* un set de table en liège

corkscrew NOUN
le *tire-bouchon*

corn NOUN
1 le *blé* (*wheat*)
2 le *maïs* (*sweetcorn*)

➔ **corn on the cob** l'épi de maïs MASC

corner NOUN
1 le *coin* ◇ *in a corner of the room* dans un coin de la pièce

➔ **the shop on the corner** la boutique au coin de la rue

➔ **He lives just round the corner.** Il habite tout près d'ici.

2 le *corner* (*in football*)

cornet NOUN
1 le *cornet à pistons* ◇ *He plays the cornet.* Il joue du cornet à pistons.
2 le *cornet* (*ice cream*)

cornflakes PL NOUN
les *corn-flakes* MASC PL

Cornwall NOUN
la *Cornouailles*
in Cornwall en Cornouailles
corporal NOUN
le *caporal*
corporal punishment NOUN
le *châtiment corporel*
corpse NOUN
le *cadavre*
correct ADJECTIVE
see also correct VERB
exact ◇ *That's correct.* C'est exact.
the correct choice le bon choix
the correct answer la bonne réponse
correct VERB
see also correct ADJECTIVE
corriger
correction NOUN
la *correction*
corridor NOUN
le *couloir*
corruption NOUN
la *corruption*
Corsica NOUN
la *Corse*
in Corsica en Corse
cosmetics PL NOUN
les *produits de beauté* MASC PL
cost VERB
see also cost NOUN
coûter ◇ *The meal costs a hundred francs.* Le repas coûte cent francs. ◇ *How much does it cost?* Combien est-ce que ça coûte? ◇ *It costs too much.* Ça coûte trop cher.
cost NOUN
see also cost VERB
le *coût*
◆ **the cost of living** le coût de la vie
◆ **at all costs** à tout prix
costume NOUN
le *costume*
cosy ADJECTIVE
douillet MASC
douillette FEM
cot NOUN
le *lit d'enfant*
cottage NOUN
le *cottage*
◆ **a thatched cottage** une chaumière
cotton NOUN
le *coton* ◇ *a cotton shirt* une chemise en coton
◆ **cotton wool** le coton hydrophile
couch NOUN
le *canapé*
couchette NOUN
la *couchette*
cough VERB
see also cough NOUN
tousser
cough NOUN
see also cough VERB
la *toux* ◇ *a bad cough* une mauvaise toux
◆ **I've got a cough.** Je tousse.
could VERB *see* **can**
council NOUN
le *conseil*
The nearest French equivalent of a local council would be a conseil municipal, *which administers a* commune.
◆ **He's on the council.** Il fait partie du conseil municipal.
◆ **a council estate** une cité HLM
◆ **a council house** une HLM
HLM *stands for* habitation à loyer modéré *which means "low-rent home".*
councillor NOUN
◆ **She's a local councillor.** Elle fait partie du conseil municipal.
to **count** VERB
compter
◆ **to count on** compter sur ◇ *You can count on me.* Tu peux compter sur moi.
counter NOUN
1 le *comptoir* (*in shop*)
2 le *guichet* (*in post office, bank*)
3 le *jeton* (*in game*)
country NOUN
1 le *pays* ◇ *the border between the two countries* la frontière entre les deux pays
2 la *campagne* ◇ *I live in the country.* J'habite à la campagne.
◆ **country dancing** la danse folklorique
countryside NOUN
la *campagne*
county NOUN
le *comté*
The nearest French equivalent of a county would be a département.
◆ **the county council**
The nearest French equivalent of a county council would be a conseil général, *which administers a* département.
couple NOUN
le *couple* ◇ *the couple who live next door* le couple qui habite à côté
◆ **a couple** deux ◇ *a couple of hours* deux heures
◆ **Could you wait a couple of minutes?** Pourriez-vous attendre quelques minutes?
courage NOUN
le *courage*
courier NOUN
1 (*for tourists*)
l' *accompagnateur* MASC

PTO

l' *accompagnatrice* FEM
[2] (*delivery service*)
le *coursier* ◇ *They sent it by courier.* Ils l'ont envoyé par coursier.

course NOUN
[1] le *cours* ◇ *a French course* un cours de français ◇ *to go on a course* suivre un cours
[2] le *plat* ◇ *the main course* le plat principal
◆ **the first course** l'entrée FEM
[3] le *terrain* ◇ *a golf course* un terrain de golf
◆ **of course** bien sûr ◇ *Do you love me?–Of course I do!* Tu m'aimes?–Bien sûr que oui!

court NOUN
[1] (*of law*)
le *tribunal*
(les *tribunaux* PL)
◇ *He was in court last week.* Il est passé devant le tribunal la semaine dernière.
[2] (*tennis*)
le *court* ◇ *There are tennis and squash courts.* Il y a des courts de tennis et de squash.

courtyard NOUN
la *cour*

cousin NOUN
le *cousin*
la *cousine*

cover NOUN
see also cover VERB
[1] la *couverture* (*of book*)
[2] la *housse* (*of duvet*)

to **cover** VERB
see also cover NOUN
[1] *couvrir* ◇ *My face was covered with mosquito bites.* J'avais le visage couvert de piqûres de moustique.
[2] *prendre en charge* ◇ *Our insurance didn't cover it.* Notre assurance ne l'a pas pris en charge.
◆ **to cover up a scandal** étouffer un scandale

cow NOUN
la *vache*

coward NOUN
le *lâche* ◇ *She's a coward.* Elle est lâche.

cowardly ADJECTIVE
lâche

cowboy NOUN
le *cow-boy*

crab NOUN
le *crabe*

crack NOUN
see also crack VERB
[1] la *fissure* (*in wall*)
[2] la *fêlure* (*in cup, window*)
[3] le *crack* (*drug*)
◆ **I'll have a crack at it.** Je vais tenter le coup.

to **crack** VERB
see also crack NOUN
casser (*nut, egg*)
◆ **to crack a joke** sortir une blague

cracked ADJECTIVE
fêlé (*cup, window*)

cracker NOUN
[1] le *cracker* (*biscuit*)
[2] le *diablotin* (*Christmas cracker*)

cradle NOUN
le *berceau*
(les *berceaux* PL)

craft NOUN
les *travaux manuels* MASC PL ◇ *We do craft at school.* Nous avons des cours de travaux manuels à l'école.
◆ **a craft centre** un centre artisanal

craftsman NOUN
l' *artisan* MASC

to **cram** VERB
[1] *entasser* ◇ *We crammed our stuff into the boot.* Nous avons entassé nos affaires dans le coffre.
[2] *bachoter* (*for exams*)

to **crash** VERB
see also crash NOUN
avoir un accident ◇ *He's crashed his car.* Il a eu un accident de voiture.
◆ **The plane crashed.** L'avion s'est écrasé.

crash NOUN
see also crash VERB
[1] la *collision* (*of car*)
[2] l' *accident* MASC (*of plane*)
◆ **a crash helmet** un casque
◆ **a crash course** un cours intensif

to **crawl** VERB
see also crawl NOUN
marcher à quatre pattes (*baby*)

crawl NOUN
see also crawl VERB
le *crawl* ◇ *to do the crawl* nager le crawl

crazy ADJECTIVE
fou MASC
folle FEM

cream ADJECTIVE
see also cream NOUN
crème MASC, FEM, PL (*colour*)

cream NOUN
see also cream ADJECTIVE
la *crème* ◇ *strawberries and cream* les fraises à la crème
◆ **a cream cake** un gâteau à la crème
◆ **cream cheese** le fromage à la crème
◆ **sun cream** la crème solaire

rease NOUN
le *pli*
reased ADJECTIVE
froissé
reate VERB
créer
reation NOUN
la *création*
reative ADJECTIVE
créatif MASC
créative FEM
reature NOUN
la *créature*
rèche NOUN
la *crèche*
redit NOUN
le *crédit* ◇ *on credit* à crédit
redit card NOUN
la *carte de crédit*
ress NOUN
le *cresson*
rew NOUN
1 l' *équipage* MASC (*of ship, plane*)
2 l' *équipe* FEM ◇ *a film crew* une équipe de tournage
rew cut NOUN
les *cheveux en brosse* MASC PL
ricket NOUN
1 le *cricket* ◇ *I play cricket.* Je joue au cricket.
• **a cricket bat** une batte de cricket
2 le *grillon* (*insect*)
rime NOUN
1 le *délit* ◇ *Murder is a crime.* Le meurtre est un délit.
2 la *criminalité* (*lawlessness*)
• **Crime is rising.** La criminalité augmente.
riminal NOUN
see also criminal ADJECTIVE
le *criminel*
la *criminelle*
riminal ADJECTIVE
see also criminal NOUN
criminel MASC
criminelle FEM
◇ *It's criminal!* C'est criminel!
• **It's a criminal offence.** C'est un crime puni par la loi.
• **to have a criminal record** avoir un casier judiciaire
risis NOUN
la *crise*
risp ADJECTIVE
croquant (*food*)
risps PL NOUN
les *chips* FEM PL ◇ *a bag of crisps* un paquet de chips
riterion NOUN
le *critère*
critic NOUN
le *critique*
critical ADJECTIVE
critique
• **a critical remark** une critique
criticism NOUN
la *critique*
to **criticize** VERB
critiquer
Croatia NOUN
la *Croatie*
• **in Croatia** en Croatie
to **crochet** VERB
crocheter
crocodile NOUN
le *crocodile*
crook NOUN
l' *escroc* MASC (*criminal*)
crop NOUN
la *récolte* ◇ *a good crop of apples* une bonne récolte de pommes
cross NOUN
see also cross ADJECTIVE, VERB
la *croix*
cross ADJECTIVE
see also cross NOUN, VERB
fâché ◇ *to be cross about something* être fâché à propos de quelque chose
to **cross** VERB
see also cross ADJECTIVE, NOUN
traverser (*street, bridge*)
• **to cross out** barrer
• **to cross over** traverser
cross-country NOUN
le *cross* (*race*)
• **cross-country skiing** le ski de fond
crossing NOUN
1 la *traversée* (*by boat*) ◇ *the crossing from Dover to Calais* la traversée de Douvres à Calais
2 le *passage clouté* (*for pedestrians*)
crossroads NOUN
le *carrefour*
crossword NOUN
les *mots croisés* MASC PL ◇ *I like doing crosswords.* J'aime faire les mots croisés.
crow NOUN
le *corbeau*
(les *corbeaux* PL)
crowd NOUN
la *foule*
• **the crowd** (*at sports match*) les spectateurs
crowded ADJECTIVE
bondé
crown NOUN
la *couronne*
crucifix NOUN
le *crucifix*

C

crude ADJECTIVE
(*vulgar*)
grossier MASC
grossière FEM

cruel ADJECTIVE
cruel MASC
cruelle FEM

cruise NOUN
la *croisière* ◇ *to go on a cruise* faire une croisière

crumb NOUN
la *miette*

to **crush** VERB
écraser

crutch NOUN
la *béquille*

to **cry** VERB
pleurer ◇ *The baby's crying.* Le bébé pleure.

crystal NOUN
le *cristal*
(les *cristaux* PL)

CTC NOUN (= *city technology college*)
le *collège technique*

cub NOUN
1 (*animal*)
le *petit*
2 (*scout*)
le *louveteau*
(les *louveteaux* PL)

cube NOUN
le *cube*

cubic ADJECTIVE
◆ **a cubic metre** un mètre cube

cucumber NOUN
le *concombre*

cue NOUN
la *queue de billard* (*for snooker, pool*)

culottes PL NOUN
la *jupe-culotte* SING

culture NOUN
la *culture*

cunning ADJECTIVE
1 (*person*)
rusé
2 (*plan, idea*)
astucieux MASC
astucieuse FEM

cup NOUN
1 la *tasse* ◇ *a china cup* une tasse en porcelaine
◆ **a cup of coffee** un café
2 la *coupe* (*trophy*)

cupboard NOUN
le *placard*

to **cure** VERB
see also cure NOUN
guérir

cure NOUN
see also cure VERB
le *remède*

curious ADJECTIVE
curieux MASC
curieuse FEM

curly ADJECTIVE
1 *bouclé* (*loosely curled*)
2 *frisé* (*tightly curled*)

currant NOUN
le *raisin de Corinthe* (*dried fruit*)

currency NOUN
la *devise* ◇ *foreign currency* les devises étrangères

current NOUN
see also current ADJECTIVE
le *courant* ◇ *The current is very strong.* Le courant est très fort.

current ADJECTIVE
see also current NOUN
actuel MASC
actuelle FEM
◇ *the current situation* la situation actuelle

current affairs PL NOUN
l' *actualité* FEM

curriculum NOUN
le *programme*

curriculum vitae NOUN
le *curriculum vitae*

curry NOUN
le *curry*

curse NOUN
la *malédiction* (*spell*)

curtain NOUN
le *rideau*
(les *rideaux* PL)
◆ **to draw the curtains** tirer les rideaux

cushion NOUN
le *coussin*

custard NOUN
la *crème anglaise* (*for pouring*)

custody NOUN
la *garde* (*of child*)

custom NOUN
la *coutume* MASC ◇ *It's an old custom.* C'est une ancienne coutume.

customer NOUN
le *client*
la *cliente*

customs PL NOUN
la *douane* SING

customs officer NOUN
le *douanier*
la *douanière*

cut NOUN
see also cut VERB
1 la *coupure* ◇ *He's got a cut on his forehead.* Il a une coupure au front.
2 la *coupe* ◇ *a cut and blow-dry* une

coupe brushing
3 la *réduction* (*in price, spending*)

cut VERB
see also cut NOUN
1 *couper* ◇ *I'll cut some bread.* Je vais couper du pain.
- **to cut oneself** se couper ◇ *I cut my foot on a piece of glass.* Je me suis coupé au pied avec un morceau de verre.

2 *réduire* (*price, spending*)
- **to cut down** abattre (*tree*)
- **to cut off** couper ◇ *The electricity was cut off.* L'électricité a été coupée.
- **to cut up** hacher (*vegetables, meat*)

cutlery NOUN
les *couverts* MASC PL

CV NOUN
le *C.V.*

cycle VERB
see also cycle NOUN
faire de la bicyclette ◇ *I like cycling.* J'aime faire de la bicyclette.
- **I cycle to school.** Je vais à l'école à bicyclette.

cycle NOUN
see also cycle VERB
la *bicyclette*
- **a cycle ride** une promenade à bicyclette

cycling NOUN
le *cyclisme*

cyclist NOUN
le/la *cycliste*

cylinder NOUN
le *cylindre*

Cyprus NOUN
Chypre
- **in Cyprus** à Chypre
- **We went to Cyprus.** Nous sommes allés à Chypre.

Czech ADJECTIVE
see also Czech NOUN
tchèque
- **the Czech Republic** la République tchèque

Czech NOUN
see also Czech ADJECTIVE
1 le/la *Tchèque* (*person*)
2 le *tchèque* (*language*)

C

D

dad NOUN
1 le *père* ◇ *my dad* mon père ◇ *his dad* son père
2 le *papa*
Use **papa** *only when you are talking to your father or using it as his name; otherwise use* **père**.
➔ **Dad!** Papa! ◇ *I'll ask Dad.* Je vais demander à papa.

daffodil NOUN
la *jonquille*

daft ADJECTIVE
idiot

daily ADJECTIVE, ADVERB
1 *quotidien* MASC
quotidienne FEM
◇ *It's part of my daily routine.* Ça fait partie de mes occupations quotidiennes.
2 *tous les jours* ◇ *The pool is open daily from 9 a.m. to 6 p.m.* La piscine est ouverte tous les jours de neuf heures à dix-huit heures.

dairy NOUN
la *crémerie* (*shop*)

dairy products PL NOUN
les *produits laitiers* MASC PL

daisy NOUN
la *pâquerette*

dam NOUN
le *barrage*

damage NOUN
see also damage VERB
les *dégâts* MASC PL ◇ *The storm did a lot of damage.* La tempête a fait beaucoup de dégâts.

to **damage** VERB
see also damage NOUN
endommager

damn NOUN
see also damn ADJECTIVE
➔ **I don't give a damn!** Je m'en fiche! (*informal*)
➔ **Damn!** Zut! (*informal*)

damn ADJECTIVE, ADVERB
see also damn NOUN
➔ **It's a damn nuisance!** Quelle barbe!

damp ADJECTIVE
humide

dance NOUN
see also dance VERB
1 la *danse* ◇ *The last dance was a waltz.* La dernière danse était une valse.
2 le *bal* ◇ *Are you going to the dance tonight?* Tu vas au bal ce soir?

to **dance** VERB
see also dance NOUN
danser
➔ **to go dancing** aller danser ◇ *Let's go dancing!* Si on allait danser?

dancer NOUN
le *danseur*
la *danseuse*

dandruff NOUN
les *pellicules* FEM PL

Dane NOUN
1 le *Danois*
2 la *Danoise*

danger NOUN
le *danger*
➔ **in danger** en danger ◇ *His life is in danger.* Sa vie est en danger.
➔ **to be in danger of** risquer de ◇ *We were in danger of missing the plane.* Nous risquions de rater l'avion.

dangerous ADJECTIVE
dangereux MASC
dangereuse FEM

Danish ADJECTIVE
see also Danish NOUN
danois

Danish NOUN
see also Danish ADJECTIVE
le *danois* (*language*)

to **dare** VERB
oser
➔ **to dare to do something** oser faire quelque chose ◇ *I didn't dare to tell my parents.* Je n'ai pas osé le dire à mes parents.
➔ **I dare say it'll be okay.** Je suppose que ça va aller.

daring ADJECTIVE
audacieux MASC
audacieuse FEM

dark ADJECTIVE
see also dark NOUN
1 *sombre* (*room*) ◇ *It's dark.* (*inside*) Il fait sombre.
➔ **It's dark outside.** Il fait nuit dehors.
➔ **It's getting dark.** La nuit tombe.
2 *foncé* (*colour*) ◇ *She's got dark hair.* Elle a les cheveux foncés. ◇ *a dark green sweater* un pull vert foncé

dark NOUN
see also dark ADJECTIVE
le *noir* ◇ *I'm afraid of the dark.* J'ai peur du noir.
➔ **after dark** après la tombée de la nuit

darkness NOUN
l' *obscurité* FEM ◇ *The room was in darkness.* La chambre était dans l'obscurité.

darling NOUN

le *chéri*
la *chérie*
◇ *Thank you, darling!* Merci, chéri!

dart NOUN
la *fléchette* ◇ *to play darts* jouer aux fléchettes

data PL NOUN
les *données* FEM PL

database NOUN
la *base de données* (*on computer*)

date NOUN
1 la *date* ◇ *my date of birth* ma date de naissance
- **What's the date today?** Quel jour sommes-nous?
- **to have a date with somebody** sortir avec quelqu'un ◇ *She's got a date with Ian tonight.* Elle sort avec Ian ce soir.
- **out of date (1)** (*passport*) périmé
- **out of date (2)** (*technology*) dépassé
- **out of date (3)** (*clothes*) démodé

2 la *datte* (*fruit*)

daughter NOUN
la *fille*

daughter-in-law NOUN
la *belle-fille*
(les *belles-filles* PL)

dawn NOUN
l' *aube* FEM ◇ *at dawn* à l'aube

day NOUN
Use **jour** *to refer to the whole 24-hour period.* **journée** *only refers to the time when you are awake.*
1 le *jour* ◇ *We stayed in Nice for three days.* Nous sommes restés trois jours à Nice.
- **every day** tous les jours

2 la *journée* ◇ *during the day* dans la journée ◇ *I stayed at home all day.* Je suis resté à la maison toute la journée.
- **the day before** la veille ◇ *the day before my birthday* la veille de mon anniversaire
- **the day after** le lendemain
- **the day after tomorrow** après-demain ◇ *We're leaving the day after tomorrow.* Nous partons après-demain.
- **the day before yesterday** avant-hier ◇ *He arrived the day before yesterday.* Il est arrivé avant-hier.

dead ADJECTIVE, ADVERB
1 *mort* ◇ *He was already dead when the doctor came.* Il était déjà mort quand le docteur est arrivé.
- **He was shot dead.** Il a été abattu.

2 *absolument* (*totally*) ◇ *You're dead right!* Tu as absolument raison!
- **dead on time** à l'heure pile ◇ *The train arrived dead on time.* Le train est arrivé à l'heure pile.

dead end NOUN
l' *impasse* FEM

deadline NOUN
la *date limite* ◇ *The deadline for entries is May 2nd.* La date limite d'inscription est le deux mai.

deaf ADJECTIVE
sourd

deafening ADJECTIVE
assourdissant

deal NOUN
see also deal VERB
le *marché*
- **It's a deal!** Marché conclu!
- **a great deal** beaucoup ◇ *a great deal of money* beaucoup d'argent

to **deal** VERB
see also deal NOUN
donner (*cards*) ◇ *It's your turn to deal.* C'est à toi de donner.
- **to deal with something** s'occuper de quelque chose ◇ *He promised to deal with it immediately.* Il a promis de s'en occuper immédiatement.

dear ADJECTIVE
1 *cher* MASC
chère FEM
◇ *Dear Mrs Duval* Chère Madame Duval
- **Dear Sir/Madam** (*in a circular*) Madame, Monsieur

2 (*expensive*)
coûteux MASC
coûteuse FEM

death NOUN
la *mort* ◇ *after his death* après sa mort
- **I was bored to death.** Je me suis ennuyé à mourir.

debate NOUN
see also debate VERB
le *débat*

to **debate** VERB
see also debate NOUN
débattre

debt NOUN
la *dette* ◇ *He's got a lot of debts.* Il a beaucoup de dettes.
- **to be in debt** avoir des dettes

decade NOUN
la *décennie*

decaffeinated ADJECTIVE
décaféiné

to **deceive** VERB
tromper

December NOUN
décembre MASC
- **in December** en décembre

decent ADJECTIVE
convenable ◇ *a decent education* une

PTO

éducation convenable

to **decide** VERB
1 *décider* ◇ *I decided to write to her.* J'ai décidé de lui écrire. ◇ *I decided not to go.* J'ai décidé de ne pas y aller.
2 *se décider* ◇ *I can't decide.* Je n'arrive pas à me décider. ◇ *Haven't you decided yet?* Tu ne t'es pas encore décidé?

decimal ADJECTIVE
décimal ◇ *the decimal system* le système décimal

decision NOUN
la *décision*
◆ **to make a decision** prendre une décision

decisive ADJECTIVE
décidé (*person*)

deck NOUN
1 (*of ship*)
le *pont*
◆ **on deck** sur le pont
2 (*of cards*)
le *jeu*
(les *jeux* PL)

deckchair NOUN
la *chaise longue*

to **declare** VERB
déclarer

to **decorate** VERB
1 *décorer* ◇ *I decorated the cake with glacé cherries.* J'ai décoré le gâteau avec des cerises confites.
2 *peindre* (*paint*)
3 *tapisser* (*wallpaper*)

decrease NOUN
see also decrease VERB
la *diminution* ◇ *a decrease in the number of unemployed people* une diminution du nombre de chômeurs

to **decrease** VERB
see also decrease NOUN
diminuer

dedicated ADJECTIVE
dévoué ◇ *a very dedicated teacher* un professeur très dévoué

to **deduct** VERB
déduire

deep ADJECTIVE
1 (*water, hole, cut*)
profond ◇ *Is it deep?* Est-ce que c'est profond?
◆ **How deep is the lake?** Quelle est la profondeur du lac?
◆ **a hole 4 metres deep** un trou de quatre mètres de profondeur
2 (*layer*)
épais MASC
épaisse FEM
◇ *a deep layer of snow* une épaisse couche de neige ◇ *The snow was really deep.* Il y avait une épaisse couche de neige.
◆ **He's got a deep voice.** Il a la voix grave.
◆ **to take a deep breath** respirer à fond

deeply ADVERB
profondément (*depressed*)

deer NOUN
1 le *cerf* (*red deer*)
2 le *daim* (*fallow deer*)
3 le *chevreuil* (*roe deer*)

defeat NOUN
see also defeat VERB
la *défaite*

to **defeat** VERB
see also defeat NOUN
battre

defect NOUN
le *défaut*

defence NOUN
la *défense*

to **defend** VERB
défendre

defender NOUN
le *défenseur*

to **define** VERB
définir

definite ADJECTIVE
1 *précis* ◇ *I haven't got any definite plans.* Je n'ai pas de projets précis.
2 *net* MASC
nette FEM
◇ *It's a definite improvement.* Cela constitue une nette amélioration.
3 *sûr* ◇ *Perhaps we'll go to Spain, but it's not definite.* Nous irons peut-être en Espagne, mais ce n'est pas sûr.
◆ **He was definite about it.** Il a été catégorique.

definitely ADVERB
vraiment ◇ *He's definitely the best player.* C'est vraiment lui le meilleur joueur.
◆ **He's the best player.–Definitely!** C'est le meilleur joueur.–C'est sûr!
◆ **I definitely think he'll come.** Je suis sûr qu'il va venir.

definition NOUN
la *définition*

degree NOUN
1 le *degré* ◇ *a temperature of 30 degrees* une température de trente degrés
2 la *licence* ◇ *a degree in English* une licence d'anglais

to **delay** VERB
see also delay NOUN
1 *retarder* ◇ *We decided to delay our*

departure. Nous avons décidé de retarder notre départ.
2 *tarder* ◇ *Don't delay!* Ne tarde pas!
◆ **to be delayed** être retardé ◇ *Our flight was delayed.* Notre vol a été retardé.

delay NOUN
see also delay VERB
le *délai* ◇ *without delay* sans délai

delete VERB
effacer (*on computer, tape*)

deliberate ADJECTIVE
délibéré

deliberately ADVERB
exprès ◇ *She did it deliberately.* Elle l'a fait exprès.

delicate ADJECTIVE
délicat

delicatessen NOUN
l' *épicerie fine* FEM

delicious ADJECTIVE
délicieux MASC
délicieuse FEM

delighted ADJECTIVE
ravi ◇ *He'll be delighted to see you.* Il sera ravi de vous voir.

delightful ADJECTIVE
(*meal, evening*)
délicieux MASC
délicieuse FEM

deliver VERB
1 *livrer* ◇ *I deliver newspapers.* Je livre les journaux.
2 *distribuer* (*mail*)

delivery NOUN
la *livraison*

demand VERB
see also demand NOUN
exiger

demand NOUN
see also demand VERB
la *demande* (*for product*)

demanding ADJECTIVE
astreignant ◇ *It's a very demanding job.* C'est un travail très astreignant.

demo NOUN
la *manif* (*protest*)

democracy NOUN
la *démocratie*

democratic ADJECTIVE
démocratique

demolish VERB
démolir

demonstrate VERB
1 *faire une démonstration de* (*show*)
◇ *She demonstrated the technique.* Elle a fait une démonstration de la technique.
2 *manifester* (*protest*)
◆ **to demonstrate against something** manifester contre quelque chose

demonstration NOUN
1 la *démonstration* (*of method, technique*)
2 la *manifestation* (*protest*)

demonstrator NOUN (*protester*)
le *manifestant*
la *manifestante*

denim NOUN
le *jean* ◇ *a denim jacket* une veste en jean

denims PL NOUN
le *jean* SING (*jeans*)

Denmark NOUN
le *Danemark*
◆ **in Denmark** au Danemark
◆ **to Denmark** au Danemark

dense ADJECTIVE
1 (*crowd, fog*)
dense
2 (*smoke*)
épais MASC
épaisse FEM
◆ **He's so dense!** Il est vraiment bouché!

dent NOUN
see also dent VERB
la *bosse*

to **dent** VERB
see also dent NOUN
cabosser

dental ADJECTIVE
dentaire
◆ **dental floss** le fil dentaire

dentist NOUN
le/la *dentiste* ◇ *Catherine is a dentist.* Catherine est dentiste.

to **deny** VERB
nier ◇ *She denied everything.* Elle a tout nié.

deodorant NOUN
le *déodorant*

to **depart** VERB
partir

department NOUN
1 le *rayon* (*in shop*) ◇ *the shoe department* le rayon chaussures
2 le *département* (*university, school*)
◇ *the English department* le département d'anglais

department store NOUN
le *grand magasin*

departure NOUN
le *départ*

to **depend** VERB
◆ **to depend on** dépendre de ◇ *The price depends on the quality.* Le prix dépend de la qualité.
◆ **depending on the weather** selon le temps
◆ **It depends.** Ça dépend.

to **deport** VERB

expulser

deposit NOUN
1 les *arrhes* FEM PL (*part payment*) ◇ *You have to pay a deposit when you book.* Il faut verser des arrhes lors de la réservation.
2 la *caution* (*when hiring something*) ◇ *You get the deposit back when you return the bike.* On vous remboursera la caution quand vous ramènerez le vélo.
3 la *consigne* (*on bottle*)

depressed ADJECTIVE
déprimé ◇ *I'm feeling depressed.* Je suis déprimé.

depressing ADJECTIVE
déprimant

depth NOUN
la *profondeur*

deputy head NOUN
le *directeur adjoint*
la *directrice adjointe*

to **descend** VERB
descendre

to **describe** VERB
décrire

description NOUN
la *description*

desert NOUN
le *désert*

desert island NOUN
l' *île déserte* FEM

to **deserve** VERB
mériter

design NOUN
see also design VERB
1 la *conception* ◇ *It's a completely new design.* C'est une conception entièrement nouvelle.
2 le *motif* ◇ *a geometric design* un motif géométrique
◆ **fashion design** le stylisme

to **design** VERB
see also design NOUN
dessiner (*clothes, furniture*)

designer NOUN
le/la *styliste* (*of clothes*)
◆ **designer clothes** les vêtements griffés

desire NOUN
see also desire VERB
le *désir*

to **desire** VERB
see also desire NOUN
désirer

desk NOUN
1 (*in office*)
le *bureau*
(les *bureaux* PL)
2 (*for pupil*)
le *pupitre*
3 (*in hotel*)
la *réception*
4 (*at airport*)
le *comptoir*

despair NOUN
le *désespoir*
◆ **I was in despair.** J'étais désespéré.

desperate ADJECTIVE
désespéré ◇ *a desperate situation* une situation désespérée
◆ **to get desperate** désespérer ◇ *I was getting desperate.* Je commençais à désespérer.

to **despise** VERB
mépriser

despite PREPOSITION
malgré

dessert NOUN
le *dessert* ◇ *for dessert* comme dessert

destination NOUN
la *destination*

to **destroy** VERB
détruire

destruction NOUN
la *destruction*

detached house NOUN
le *pavillon*

detail NOUN
le *détail* ◇ *in detail* en détail

detailed ADJECTIVE
détaillé

detective NOUN
l' *inspecteur de police*
◆ **a private detective** un détective privé
◆ **a detective story** un roman policier

detention NOUN
◆ **to get a detention** être consigné

detergent NOUN
le *détergent*

determined ADJECTIVE
déterminé
◆ **to be determined to do something** être déterminé à faire quelque chose
◇ *She's determined to succeed.* Elle est déterminée à réussir

detour NOUN
le *détour*

devaluation NOUN
la *dévaluation*

devastated ADJECTIVE
anéanti ◇ *I was devastated.* J'étais anéanti.

devastating ADJECTIVE
1 (*upsetting*)
accablant
2 (*flood, storm*)
dévastateur MASC
dévastatrice FEM

to **develop** VERB

1 *développer* ◇ *to get a film developed* faire développer un film
2 *se développer* ◇ *Girls develop faster than boys.* Les filles se développent plus vite que les garçons.
◆ **to develop into** se transformer en ◇ *The argument developed into a fight.* La dispute s'est transformée en bagarre.
◆ **a developing country** un pays en voie de développement

development NOUN
le *développement* ◇ *the latest developments* les derniers développements

devil NOUN
le *diable* ◇ *Poor devil!* Pauvre diable!

devise VERB
concevoir

devoted ADJECTIVE
dévoué ◇ *He's completely devoted to her.* Il lui est très dévoué.

diabetes NOUN
le *diabète*

diabetic NOUN
le/la *diabétique* ◇ *I'm a diabetic.* Je suis diabétique.

diagonal ADJECTIVE
diagonal
(*diagonaux* MASC PL)

diagram NOUN
le *diagramme*

dial VERB
composer (*number*)

dialling tone NOUN
la *tonalité*

dialogue NOUN
le *dialogue*

diamond NOUN
le *diamant* ◇ *a diamond ring* une bague en diamant
◆ **diamonds** (*at cards*) le carreau SING

diarrhoea NOUN
la *diarrhée* ◇ *I've got diarrhoea.* J'ai la diarrhée.

diary NOUN
1 l' *agenda* MASC ◇ *I've got her phone number in my diary.* J'ai son numéro de téléphone dans mon agenda.
2 le *journal*
(les *journaux* PL)
◇ *I keep a diary.* Je tiens un journal.

dice NOUN
le *dé*

dictation NOUN
la *dictée*

dictionary NOUN
le *dictionnaire*

did VERB *see* **do**

die VERB
mourir ◇ *He died last year.* Il est mort l'année dernière.
◆ **to be dying to do something** mourir d'envie de faire quelque chose ◇ *I'm dying to see you.* Je meurs d'envie de te voir.

diesel NOUN
1 le *gazole* (*fuel*) ◇ *30 litres of diesel, please.* Trente litres de gazole, s'il vous plaît.
2 la *voiture diesel* (*car*) ◇ *Our car's a diesel.* Nous avons une voiture diesel.

diet NOUN
1 l' *alimentation* FEM ◇ *a healthy diet* une alimentation saine
2 le *régime* (*for slimming*) ◇ *I'm on a diet.* Je suis au régime.

difference NOUN
la *différence* ◇ *There's not much difference in age between us.* Il n'y a pas une grande différence d'âge entre nous.
◆ **It makes no difference.** Ça revient au même.

different ADJECTIVE
différent ◇ *We are very different.* Nous sommes très différents. ◇ *Paris is different from London.* Paris est différent de Londres.

difficult ADJECTIVE
difficile ◇ *It's difficult to choose.* C'est difficile de choisir.

difficulty NOUN
la *difficulté* ◇ *without difficulty* sans difficulté
◆ **to have difficulty doing something** avoir du mal à faire quelque chose

to **dig** VERB
1 *creuser* (*hole*)
2 *bêcher* (*garden*)
◆ **to dig something up** déterrer quelque chose

digestion NOUN
la *digestion*

digital watch NOUN
la *montre à affichage numérique*

dim ADJECTIVE
1 *faible* (*light*)
2 *limité* (*stupid*)

dimension NOUN
la *dimension*

to **diminish** VERB
diminuer

din NOUN
le *vacarme*

dinghy NOUN
◆ **a rubber dinghy** un canot pneumatique
◆ **a sailing dinghy** un dériveur

dining car NOUN
le *wagon-restaurant*

(les *wagons-restaurants* PL)

dining room NOUN
la *salle à manger*

dinner NOUN
1 le *déjeuner* (*at midday*)
2 le *dîner* (*in the evening*)

dinner party NOUN
le *dîner*

dinner time NOUN
1 l' *heure du déjeuner* FEM (*midday*)
2 l' *heure du dîner* FEM (*in the evening*)

dinosaur NOUN
le *dinosaure*

diploma NOUN
le *diplôme* ◇ *a diploma in social work* un diplôme d'assistante sociale

diplomat NOUN
le/la *diplomate*

diplomatic ADJECTIVE
diplomatique

direct ADJECTIVE, ADVERB
see also direct VERB
direct ◇ *the most direct route* le chemin le plus direct ◇ *You can't fly to Marseilles direct from Manchester.* Il n'y a pas de vols directs de Manchester à Marseille.

to **direct** VERB
see also direct ADJECTIVE
1 *réaliser* (*film, programme*)
2 *mettre en scène* (*play, show*)

direction NOUN
la *direction* ◇ *We're going in the wrong direction.* Nous allons dans la mauvaise direction.
◆ **to ask somebody for directions** demander son chemin à quelqu'un

director NOUN
1 (*of company*)
le *directeur*
la *directrice*
2 (*of play*)
le *metteur en scène*
(les *metteurs en scène* PL)
3 (*of film, programme*)
le *réalisateur*
la *réalisatrice*

directory NOUN
l' *annuaire* MASC

dirt NOUN
la *saleté*

dirty ADJECTIVE
sale
◆ **to get dirty** se salir
◆ **to get something dirty** salir quelque chose

disabled ADJECTIVE
handicapé
◆ **the disabled** les handicapés

disadvantage NOUN
le *désavantage*

to **disagree** VERB
◆ **We always disagree.** Nous ne sommes jamais d'accord.
◆ **I disagree!** Je ne suis pas d'accord!
◆ **He disagrees with me.** Il n'est pas d'accord avec moi.

disagreement NOUN
le *désaccord*

to **disappear** VERB
disparaître

disappearance NOUN
la *disparition*

disappointed ADJECTIVE
déçu

disappointing ADJECTIVE
décevant

disappointment NOUN
la *déception*

disaster NOUN
le *désastre*

disastrous ADJECTIVE
désastreux MASC
désastreuse FEM

discipline NOUN
la *discipline*

disc jockey NOUN
le *disc-jockey*

disco NOUN
la *soirée disco* ◇ *There's a disco at the school tonight.* Il y a une soirée disco à l'école ce soir.

to **disconnect** VERB
1 *débrancher* (*electrical equipment*)
2 *couper* (*telephone, water supply*)

discount NOUN
la *réduction* ◇ *a discount for students* une réduction pour les étudiants

to **discourage** VERB
décourager
◆ **to get discouraged** se décourager
◇ *Don't get discouraged!* Ne te décourage pas!

to **discover** VERB
découvrir

discrimination NOUN
la *discrimination* ◇ *racial discrimination* la discrimination raciale

to **discuss** VERB
1 *discuter de* ◇ *I'll discuss it with my parents.* Je vais en discuter avec mes parents.
2 *discuter sur* (*topic*) ◇ *We discussed the problem of pollution.* Nous avons discuté du problème de la pollution.

discussion NOUN
la *discussion*

disease NOUN

la *maladie*

disgraceful ADJECTIVE
scandaleux MASC
scandaleuse FEM

disguise VERB
déguiser ◇ *He was disguised as a policeman.* Il était déguisé en policier.

disgusted ADJECTIVE
dégoûté ◇ *I was absolutely disgusted.* J'étais complètement dégoûté.

disgusting ADJECTIVE
1 *dégoûtant* (*food, smell*) ◇ *It looks disgusting.* Ça a l'air dégoûtant.
2 *honteux* (*disgraceful*) ◇ *That's disgusting!* C'est honteux!

dish NOUN
le *plat* ◇ *a china dish* un plat en porcelaine ◇ *a vegetarian dish* un plat végétarien
- **to do the dishes** faire la vaisselle ◇ *He never does the dishes.* Il ne fait jamais la vaisselle.

dishonest ADJECTIVE
malhonnête

dishwasher NOUN
le *lave-vaisselle*
(les *lave-vaisselle* PL)

disinfectant NOUN
le *désinfectant*

disk NOUN
le *disque*
- **a floppy disk** une disquette
- **the hard disk** le disque dur

dislike VERB
see also dislike NOUN
ne pas aimer ◇ *I really dislike cabbage.* Je n'aime vraiment pas le chou.

dislike NOUN
see also dislike VERB
- **my likes and dislikes** ce que j'aime et ce que je n'aime pas

dismiss VERB
renvoyer (*employee*)

disobedient ADJECTIVE
désobéissant

display NOUN
see also display VERB
l' *étalage* MASC ◇ *There was a lovely display of fruit in the window.* Il y avait un superbe étalage de fruits en vitrine.
- **to be on display** être exposé ◇ *Her best paintings were on display.* Ses meilleurs tableaux étaient exposés.
- **a firework display** un feu d'artifice

display VERB
see also display NOUN
1 *montrer* ◇ *She proudly displayed her medal.* Elle a montré sa médaille avec fierté.
2 *exposer* (*in shop window*)

disposable ADJECTIVE
jetable

to **disqualify** VERB
disqualifier
- **to be disqualified** être disqualifié ◇ *He was disqualified.* Il a été disqualifié.

to **disrupt** VERB
perturber ◇ *Protesters disrupted the meeting.* Des manifestants ont perturbé la réunion. ◇ *Train services are being disrupted by the strike.* Les horaires de train sont perturbés par la grève.

dissatisfied ADJECTIVE
- **We were dissatisfied with the service.** Nous n'étions pas satisfaits du service.

to **dissolve** VERB
dissoudre

distance NOUN
la *distance* ◇ *a distance of 40 kilometres* une distance de quarante kilomètres
- **It's within walking distance.** On peut y aller à pied.
- **in the distance** au loin

distant ADJECTIVE
lointain ◇ *in the distant future* dans un avenir lointain

distillery NOUN
la *distillerie* ◇ *a whisky distillery* une distillerie de whisky

distinction NOUN
1 la *distinction* ◇ *to make a distinction between...* faire la distinction entre...
2 la *mention très bien* ◇ *I got a distinction in my piano exam.* J'ai eu la mention très bien à mon examen de piano.

distinctive ADJECTIVE
distinctif MASC
distinctive FEM

to **distract** VERB
distraire

to **distribute** VERB
distribuer

district NOUN
1 le *quartier* (*of town*)
2 la *région* (*of country*)

to **disturb** VERB
déranger ◇ *I'm sorry to disturb you.* Je suis désolé de vous déranger.

ditch NOUN
see also ditch VERB
le *fossé*

to **ditch** VERB
see also ditch NOUN
plaquer (*informal*) ◇ *She's just ditched her boyfriend.* Elle vient de plaquer son copain.

dive NOUN
see also dive VERB
le *plongeon*

to **dive** VERB
see also dive NOUN
plonger

diver NOUN
le *plongeur*
la *plongeuse*

diversion NOUN
la *déviation* (*for traffic*)

to **divide** VERB
1 *diviser* ◇ *Divide the pastry in half.* Divisez la pâte en deux. ◇ *12 divided by 3 is 4.* Douze divisé par trois également quatre.
2 *se diviser* ◇ *We divided into two groups.* Nous nous sommes divisés en deux groupes.

diving NOUN
la *plongée*
◆ **a diving board** un plongeoir

division NOUN
la *division*

divorce NOUN
le *divorce*

divorced ADJECTIVE
divorcé ◇ *My parents are divorced.* Mes parents sont divorcés.

DIY NOUN
le *bricolage* ◇ *to do DIY* faire du bricolage ◇ *a DIY shop* un magasin de bricolage

dizzy ADJECTIVE
◆ **to feel dizzy** avoir la tête qui tourne ◇ *I feel dizzy.* J'ai la tête qui tourne.

DJ NOUN
le *disc-jockey*

to **do** VERB
1 *faire* ◇ *What are you doing this evening?* Qu'est-ce que tu fais ce soir? ◇ *I do a lot of cycling.* Je fais beaucoup de vélo. ◇ *I haven't done my homework.* Je n'ai pas fait mes devoirs. ◇ *She did it by herself.* Elle l'a fait toute seule. ◇ *I'll do my best.* Je ferai de mon mieux.
◆ **to do well** marcher bien ◇ *The firm is doing well.* L'entreprise marche bien. ◇ *She's doing well at school.* Ses études marchent bien.
2 *aller* (*be enough*) ◇ *It's not very good, but it'll do.* Ce n'est pas très bon, mais ça ira.
◆ **That'll do, thanks.** Ça ira, merci.

In English do *is used to make questions. In French questions are made either with* **est-ce que** *or by reversing the order of verb and subject.*

◇ *Do you like French food?* Est-ce que vous aimez la cuisine française? ◇ *Where does he live?* Où est-ce qu'il habite? ◇ *Do you speak English?* Parlez-vous anglais? ◇ *What do you do in your free time?* Qu'est-ce que vous faites pendant vos loisirs? ◇ *Where did you go for your holidays?* Où es-tu allé pendant tes vacances?

Use **ne...pas** *in negative sentences for* don't.

◇ *I don't understand.* Je ne comprends pas. ◇ *Why didn't you come?* Pourquoi n'êtes-vous pas venus?

do *is not translated when it is used in place of another verb.*

◇ *I hate maths.–So do I.* Je déteste les maths.–Moi aussi. ◇ *I didn't like the film.–Neither did I.* Je n'ai pas aimé le film.–Moi non plus. ◇ *Do you like horses?–No I don't.* Est-ce que tu aimes les chevaux?–Non.

Use **n'est-ce pas** *to check information.*

◇ *You go swimming on Fridays, don't you?* Tu fais de la natation le vendredi, n'est-ce pas? ◇ *The bus stops at the youth hostel, doesn't it?* Le bus s'arrête à l'auberge de jeunesse, n'est-ce pas?
◆ **How do you do?** Enchanté!
◆ **to do up (1)** (*shoes*) lacer ◇ *Do up your shoes!* Lace tes chaussures!
◆ **to do up (2)** (*renovate*) retaper ◇ *They're doing up an old cottage.* Ils retapent une vieille maison.
◆ **to do up (3)** (*shirt, cardigan*) boutonner
◆ **Do up your zip!** (*on trousers*) Ferme ta braguette!
◆ **to do without** se passer de ◇ *I couldn't do without my computer.* Je ne pourrais pas me passer de mon ordinateur.

dock NOUN
le *dock* (*for ships*)

doctor NOUN
le *médecin* ◇ *She's a doctor.* Elle est médecin. ◇ *I'd like to be a doctor.* Je voudrais être médecin.

document NOUN
le *document*

documentary NOUN
le *documentaire*

to **dodge** VERB
échapper à (*attacker*)

dodgems PL NOUN
les *autos tamponneuses* FEM PL ◇ *to go on the dodgems* aller faire un tour d'autos tamponneuses

does VERB *see* **do**

doesn't = **does not**

dog NOUN
(*female*)
le *chien*
la *chienne*

◇ *Have you got a dog?* Est-ce que tu as un chien?

do-it-yourself NOUN
le *bricolage*

dole NOUN
les *allocations chômage* FEM PL
- **to be on the dole** toucher le chômage
  ◇ *A lot of people are on the dole.* Beaucoup de gens touchent le chômage.
- **to go on the dole** s'inscrire au chômage

doll NOUN
la *poupée*

dollar NOUN
le *dollar*

dolphin NOUN
le *dauphin*

domestic ADJECTIVE
- **a domestic flight** un vol intérieur

dominoes PL NOUN
- **to have a game of dominoes** faire une partie de dominos

donate VERB
donner

done VERB *see* **do**

donkey NOUN
l' *âne* MASC

don't = **do not**

door NOUN
1 la *porte* ◇ *the first door on the right* la première porte à droite
2 la *portière* (*of car, train*)

doorbell NOUN
la *sonnette*
- **to ring the doorbell** sonner
- **Suddenly the doorbell rang.** Soudain, on a sonné.

doorman NOUN
le *portier*

doorstep NOUN
le *pas de la porte*

dormitory NOUN
le *dortoir*

dose NOUN
la *dose*

dosh NOUN
le *fric* (*informal: money*)

dot NOUN
le *point* (*on letter "i", in e-mail address*)
- **on the dot** à l'heure pile ◇ *He arrived at 9 o'clock on the dot.* Il est arrivé à neuf heures pile.

double VERB
see also double ADJECTIVE
doubler ◇ *The number of attacks has doubled.* Le nombre d'agressions a doublé.

double ADJECTIVE, ADVERB
see also double VERB
double ◇ *a double helping* une double portion
- **to cost double** coûter le double
  ◇ *First-class tickets cost double.* Les billets de première classe coûtent le double.
- **a double bed** un grand lit
- **a double room** une chambre pour deux personnes
- **a double-decker bus** un autobus à impériale

double bass NOUN
la *contrebasse* ◇ *I play the double bass.* Je joue de la contrebasse.

double glazing NOUN
le *double vitrage*

doubles PL NOUN
le *double* SING (*in tennis*) ◇ *to play mixed doubles* jouer en double mixte

doubt NOUN
see also doubt VERB
le *doute* ◇ *I have my doubts.* J'ai des doutes.

to **doubt** VERB
see also doubt NOUN
douter de
- **I doubt it.** J'en doute.
- **to doubt that** douter que
  douter que *has to be followed by a verb in the subjunctive.*
  ◇ *I doubt he'll agree.* Je doute qu'il soit d'accord.

doubtful ADJECTIVE
- **to be doubtful about doing something** hésiter à faire quelque chose ◇ *I'm doubtful about going by myself.* J'hésite à y aller tout seul.
- **It's doubtful.** Ce n'est pas sûr.
- **You sound doubtful.** Tu n'as pas l'air sûr.

dough NOUN
la *pâte*

doughnut NOUN
le *beignet* ◇ *a jam doughnut* un beignet à la confiture

Dover NOUN
Douvres ◇ *We went from Dover to Boulogne.* Nous sommes allés de Douvres à Boulogne.
- **in Dover** à Douvres

down ADVERB, ADJECTIVE, PREPOSITION
1 *en bas* (*below*) ◇ *His office is down on the first floor.* Son bureau est en bas, au premier étage. ◇ *It's down there.* C'est là-bas.
2 *à terre* (*to the ground*) ◇ *He threw down his racket.* Il a jeté sa raquette à terre.
- **They live just down the road.** Ils habitent tout à côté.

PTO

- **to come down** descendre ◇ *Come down here!* Descends!
- **to go down** descendre ◇ *The rabbit went down the hole.* Le lapin est descendu dans le terrier.
- **to sit down** s'asseoir ◇ *Sit down!* Asseyez-vous!
- **to feel down** avoir le cafard ◇ *I'm feeling a bit down.* J'ai un peu le cafard.
- **The computer's down.** L'ordinateur est en panne.

downpour NOUN
la *pluie torrentielle* ◇ *a sudden downpour* une pluie soudaine et torrentielle

downstairs ADVERB, ADJECTIVE
1 *au rez-de-chaussée* ◇ *The bathroom's downstairs.* La salle de bain est au rez-de-chaussée.
2 *du rez-de-chaussée* ◇ *the downstairs bathroom* la salle de bain du rez-de-chaussée
- **the people downstairs** les voisins du dessous

to **doze** VERB
sommeiller
- **to doze off** s'assoupir

dozen NOUN
la *douzaine* ◇ *two dozen* deux douzaines ◇ *a dozen eggs* une douzaine d'œufs
- **I've told you that dozens of times.** Je t'ai dit ça des centaines de fois.

drab ADJECTIVE
terne (*clothes*)

to **drag** VERB
see also drag NOUN
traîner (*thing, person*)

drag NOUN
see also drag VERB
- **It's a real drag!** C'est la barbe! (*informal*)
- **in drag** travesti ◇ *He was in drag.* Il était travesti.

dragon NOUN
le *dragon*

drain NOUN
see also drain VERB
l' *égout* MASC ◇ *The drains are blocked.* Les égouts sont bouchés.

to **drain** VERB
see also drain NOUN
égoutter (*vegetables, pasta*)

draining board NOUN
l' *égouttoir* MASC

drainpipe NOUN
le *tuyau d'écoulement*

drama NOUN
l' *art dramatique* MASC ◇ *Drama is my favourite subject.* L'art dramatique est ma matière préférée.
- **drama school** l'école d'art dramatique ◇ *I'd like to go to drama school.* J'aimerais entrer dans une école d'art dramatique.
- **Greek drama** le théâtre grec

dramatic ADJECTIVE
spectaculaire ◇ *It was really dramatic!* C'était vraiment spectaculaire! ◇ *a dramatic improvement* une amélioration spectaculaire
- **dramatic news** une nouvelle extraordinaire

drank VERB *see* **drink**

drastic ADJECTIVE
(*change*)
radical
(*radicaux* MASC PL)
- **to take drastic action** prendre des mesures énergiques

draught NOUN
le *courant d'air*

draughts NOUN
les *dames* FEM PL ◇ *to play draughts* jouer aux dames

to **draw** VERB
see also draw NOUN
1 *dessiner* ◇ *He's good at drawing.* Il dessine bien.
- **to draw a picture** faire un dessin
- **to draw a picture of somebody** faire le portrait de quelqu'un
- **to draw a line** tirer un trait

2 *faire match nul* (*sport*) ◇ *We drew 2-2.* Nous avons fait match nul deux à deux.
- **to draw the curtains** tirer les rideaux
- **to draw lots** tirer au sort

draw NOUN
see also draw VERB
1 le *match nul* (*sport*) ◇ *The game ended in a draw.* La partie s'est soldée par un match nul.
2 le *tirage au sort* (*in lottery*) ◇ *The draw takes place on Saturday.* Le tirage au sort a lieu samedi.

drawback NOUN
l' *inconvénient* MASC

drawer NOUN
le *tiroir*

drawing NOUN
le *dessin*

drawing pin NOUN
la *punaise*

drawn VERB *see* **draw**

dreadful ADJECTIVE
1 *terrible* ◇ *a dreadful mistake* une terrible erreur
2 *affreux* MASC
affreuse FEM

◇ *The weather was dreadful.* Il a fait un temps affreux.

- **I feel dreadful.** Je ne me sens vraiment pas bien.
- **You look dreadful.** (*ill*) Tu as une mine affreuse.

dream VERB
see also dream NOUN
rêver ◇ *I dreamed I was in Belgium.* J'ai rêvé que j'étais en Belgique.

dream NOUN
see also dream VERB
le *rêve* ◇ *It was just a dream.* Ce n'était qu'un rêve.

- **a bad dream** un cauchemar

drench VERB
- **to get drenched** se faire tremper ◇ *We got drenched.* Nous nous sommes fait tremper.

dress NOUN
see also dress VERB
la *robe*

dress VERB
see also dress NOUN
s'habiller ◇ *I got up, dressed, and went downstairs.* Je me suis levé, je me suis habillé et je suis descendu.

- **to dress somebody** habiller quelqu'un ◇ *She dressed the children.* Elle a habillé les enfants.
- **to get dressed** s'habiller ◇ *I got dressed quickly.* Je me suis habillé rapidement.
- **to dress up** se déguiser ◇ *I dressed up as a ghost.* Je me suis déguisé en fantôme.

dressed ADJECTIVE
habillé ◇ *I'm not dressed yet.* Je ne suis pas encore habillé. ◇ *How was she dressed?* Comment est-ce qu'elle était habillée?

- **She was dressed in a green sweater and jeans.** Elle portait un pull vert et un jean.

dresser NOUN
le *vaisselier* (*furniture*)

dressing gown NOUN
la *robe de chambre*

dressing table NOUN
la *coiffeuse*

drew VERB *see* **draw**

drier NOUN
le *séchoir*

drift NOUN
see also drift VERB
- **a snow drift** une congère

drift VERB
see also drift NOUN
1 *aller à la dérive* (*boat*)
2 *s'amonceler* (*snow*)

drill NOUN
see also drill VERB
la *perceuse*

to **drill** VERB
see also drill NOUN
percer

to **drink** VERB
see also drink NOUN
boire ◇ *What would you like to drink?* Qu'est-ce que voulez boire? ◇ *She drank three cups of tea.* Elle a bu trois tasses de thé. ◇ *He'd been drinking.* Il avait bu.

- **I don't drink.** Je ne bois pas d'alcool.

drink NOUN
see also drink VERB
1 la *boisson* ◇ *a cold drink* une boisson fraîche ◇ *a hot drink* une boisson chaude
2 le *verre* (*alcoholic*) ◇ *They've gone out for a drink.* Ils sont allés prendre un verre.

- **to have a drink** prendre un verre

drive NOUN
see also drive VERB
1 le *tour en voiture*

- **to go for a drive** aller faire un tour en voiture ◇ *We went for a drive in the country.* Nous sommes allés faire un tour à la campagne.
- **We've got a long drive tomorrow.** Nous avons une longue route à faire demain.

2 l' *allée* FEM (*of house*) ◇ *He parked his car in the drive.* Il a garé sa voiture dans l'allée.

to **drive** VERB
see also drive NOUN
1 *conduire* (*a car*) ◇ *She's learning to drive.* Elle apprend à conduire. ◇ *Can you drive?* Tu sais conduire?
2 *aller en voiture* (*go by car*) ◇ *Did you go by train?–No, we drove.* Vous êtes partis en train?–Non, nous y sommes allés en voiture.
3 *emmener en voiture* ◇ *My mother drives me to school.* Ma mère m'emmène à l'école en voiture.

- **to drive somebody home** raccompagner quelqu'un ◇ *He offered to drive me home.* Il m'a proposé de me raccompagner.
- **to drive somebody mad** rendre quelqu'un fou ◇ *He drives her mad.* Il la rend folle.

driver NOUN
1 le *conducteur*
la *conductrice*
◇ *She's an excellent driver.* C'est une excellente conductrice.

PTO

2 le *chauffeur* (*of taxi, bus*) ◇ *He's a bus driver.* Il est chauffeur d'autobus.

driving instructor NOUN
le *moniteur d'auto-école* ◇ *He's a driving instructor.* Il est moniteur d'auto-école.

driving lesson NOUN
la *leçon de conduite*

driving licence NOUN
le *permis de conduire*

driving test NOUN
- **to take one's driving test** passer son permis de conduire ◇ *He's taking his driving test tomorrow.* Il passe son permis de conduire demain.
- **She's just passed her driving test.** Elle vient d'avoir son permis.

drop NOUN
see also drop VERB
la *goutte* ◇ *a drop of water* une goutte d'eau

to **drop** VERB
see also drop NOUN
1 *laisser tomber* ◇ *I dropped the glass and it broke.* J'ai laissé tomber le verre et il s'est cassé. ◇ *I'm going to drop chemistry.* Je vais laisser tomber la chimie.
2 *déposer* ◇ *Could you drop me at the station?* Pouvez-vous me déposer à la gare?

drought NOUN
la *sécheresse*

drove VERB *see* **drive**

to **drown** VERB
se noyer ◇ *A boy drowned here yesterday.* Un jeune garçon s'est noyé ici hier.

drug NOUN
1 le *médicament* (*medicine*) ◇ *They need food and drugs.* Ils ont besoin de nourriture et de médicaments.
2 la *drogue* (*illegal*) ◇ *hard drugs* les drogues dures ◇ *soft drugs* les drogues douces
- **to take drugs** se droguer
- **a drug addict** un drogué ◇ *She's a drug addict.* C'est une droguée.
- **a drug pusher** un dealer
- **a drug smuggler** un trafiquant de drogue
- **the drugs squad** la brigade antidrogue

drum NOUN
le *tambour* ◇ *an African drum* un tambour africain
- **a drum kit** une batterie
- **drums** la batterie SING ◇ *I play drums.* Je joue de la batterie.

drummer NOUN
(*in rock group*)
le *batteur*
la *batteuse*

drunk ADJECTIVE
see also drunk NOUN
ivre ◇ *He was drunk.* Il était ivre.

drunk NOUN
see also drunk ADJECTIVE
l' *ivrogne* MASC/FEM ◇ *The streets were full of drunks.* Les rues étaient pleines d'ivrognes.

dry ADJECTIVE
see also dry VERB
1 *sec* MASC
sèche FEM
◇ *The paint isn't dry yet.* La peinture n'est pas encore sèche.
2 *sans pluie* (*weather*) ◇ *a long dry period* une longue période sans pluie

to **dry** VERB
see also dry ADJECTIVE
1 *sécher* ◇ *The washing will dry quickly in the sun.* Le linge va sécher vite au soleil. ◇ *some dried flowers* des fleurs séchées
- **to dry one's hair** se sécher les cheveux ◇ *I haven't dried my hair yet.* Je ne me suis pas encore séché les cheveux.

2 *faire sécher* (*clothes*) ◇ *There's nowhere to dry clothes here.* Il n'y a pas d'endroit où faire sécher les vêtements ici.
- **to dry the dishes** essuyer la vaisselle

dry-cleaner's NOUN
la *teinturerie*

dryer NOUN
le *séchoir* (*for clothes*)
- **a tumble dryer** un séchoir à linge
- **a hair dryer** un sèche-cheveux

dubbed ADJECTIVE
doublé ◇ *The film was dubbed into French.* Le film était doublé en français.

dubious ADJECTIVE
réticent ◇ *My parents were a bit dubious about it.* Mes parents étaient un peu réticents à ce sujet.

duck NOUN
le *canard*

due ADJECTIVE, ADVERB
- **to be due to do something** devoir faire quelque chose ◇ *He's due to arrive tomorrow.* Il doit arriver demain.
- **The plane's due in half an hour.** L'avion doit arriver dans une demi-heure.
- **When's the baby due?** Le bébé est prévu pour quand?
- **due to** à cause de ◇ *The trip was cancelled due to bad weather.* Le voyage

a été annulé à cause du mauvais temps.

dug VERB *see* **dig**

dull ADJECTIVE
1 *ennuyeux* MASC
ennuyeuse FEM
◇ *He's nice, but a bit dull.* Il est sympathique, mais un peu ennuyeux.
2 *maussade* (*weather, day*)

dumb ADJECTIVE
1 *muet* MASC
muette FEM
◆ **She's deaf and dumb.** Elle est sourde-muette.
2 *bête* (*stupid*) ◇ *That was a really dumb thing I did!* C'était vraiment bête de ma part!

dummy NOUN
la *tétine* (*for baby*)

dump NOUN
see also dump VERB
◆ **It's a real dump!** C'est un endroit minable!
◆ **a rubbish dump** une décharge

dump VERB
see also dump NOUN
1 *déposer* (*waste*) ◇ *"no dumping"* "défense de déposer des ordures"
2 *plaquer* (*informal*) ◇ *He's just dumped his girlfriend.* Il vient de plaquer sa copine.

dungarees PL NOUN
la *salopette* SING

dungeon NOUN
le *cachot*

duration NOUN
la *durée*

during PREPOSITION
pendant ◇ *during the day* pendant la journée

dusk NOUN
le *crépuscule* ◇ *at dusk* au crépuscule

dust NOUN
see also dust VERB
la *poussière*

dust VERB
see also dust NOUN
épousseter ◇ *I dusted the shelves.* J'ai épousseté les étagères.
◆ **I hate dusting!** Je déteste faire les poussières!

dustbin NOUN
la *poubelle*

dustman NOUN
l' *éboueur* MASC ◇ *He's a dustman.* Il est éboueur.

dusty ADJECTIVE
poussiéreux MASC
poussiéreuse FEM

Dutch ADJECTIVE
see also Dutch NOUN
hollandais ◇ *She's Dutch.* Elle est hollandaise.

Dutch NOUN
see also Dutch ADJECTIVE
le *hollandais* (*language*)
◆ **the Dutch** les Hollandais

Dutchman NOUN
le *Hollandais*

Dutchwoman NOUN
la *Hollandaise*

duty NOUN
le *devoir* ◇ *It was his duty to tell the police.* C'était son devoir de prévenir la police.
◆ **to be on duty (1)** (*policeman*) être de service
◆ **to be on duty (2)** (*doctor, nurse*) être de garde

duty-free ADJECTIVE
hors taxes FEM+PL
◆ **the duty-free shop** la boutique hors taxes

duvet NOUN
la *couette*

dwarf NOUN
le *nain*
la *naine*

dynamic ADJECTIVE
dynamique

dyslexia NOUN
la *dyslexie*

E

each ADJECTIVE, PRONOUN
1 *chaque* ◇ *each day* chaque jour ◇ *Each house in our street has its own garden.* Chaque maison dans notre rue a son propre jardin.
2 *chacun* MASC
chacune FEM
◇ *The girls each have their own bedroom.* Les filles ont chacune leur chambre. ◇ *They have 10 points each.* Ils ont dix points chacun. ◇ *The plates cost £5 each.* Les assiettes coûtent cinq livres chacune. ◇ *He gave each of us £10.* Il nous a donné dix livres à chacun.
Use a reflexive verb to translate each other.
- **They hate each other.** Ils se détestent.
- **We wrote to each other.** Nous nous sommes écrit.
- **They don't know each other.** Ils ne se connaissent pas.

ear NOUN
l' *oreille* FEM

earache NOUN
- **to have earache** avoir mal aux oreilles

earlier ADVERB
1 *tout à l'heure* ◇ *I saw him earlier.* Je l'ai vu tout à l'heure.
2 *plus tôt* (*in the morning*) ◇ *I ought to get up earlier.* Je devrais me lever plus tôt.

early ADVERB, ADJECTIVE
1 *tôt* (*early in the day*) ◇ *I have to get up early.* Je dois me lever tôt.
- **to have an early night** se coucher tôt

2 *en avance* (*ahead of time*) ◇ *I came early to get a good seat.* Je suis venu en avance pour avoir une bonne place.

to **earn** VERB
gagner ◇ *She earns £5 an hour.* Elle gagne cinq livres de l'heure.

earnings PL NOUN
le *salaire* SING

earring NOUN
la *boucle d'oreille*

earth NOUN
la *terre*

earthquake NOUN
le *tremblement de terre*

easily ADVERB
facilement

east ADJECTIVE, ADVERB
see also east NOUN
1 *est* MASC, FEM, PL ◇ *the east coast* la côte est
- **an east wind** un vent d'est
- **east of** à l'est de ◇ *It's east of London.* C'est à l'est de Londres.

2 *vers l'est* ◇ *We were travelling east.* Nous allions vers l'est.

east NOUN
see also east ADJECTIVE
l' *est* MASC ◇ *in the east* dans l'est

Easter NOUN
Pâques FEM ◇ *at Easter* à Pâques ◇ *We went to my grandparents' for Easter.* Nous sommes allés chez mes grands-parents à Pâques.

Easter egg NOUN
l' *œuf de Pâques* MASC

eastern ADJECTIVE
- **the eastern part of the island** la partie est de l'île
- **Eastern Europe** l'Europe de l'Est

easy ADJECTIVE
facile

easy chair NOUN
le *fauteuil*

easy-going ADJECTIVE
facile à vivre
(*faciles à vivre* PL)
◇ *She's very easy-going.* Elle est très facile à vivre.

to **eat** VERB
manger
- **Would you like something to eat?** Est-ce que tu veux manger quelque chose?

EC NOUN (= *European Community*)
la *CE* (= Communauté européenne)

eccentric ADJECTIVE
excentrique

echo NOUN
l' *écho* MASC

ecology NOUN
l' *écologie* FEM

economic ADJECTIVE
rentable (*profitable*)

economics NOUN
l' *économie* FEM ◇ *He's studying economics.* Il fait des études d'économie.

to **economize** VERB
faire des économies ◇ *to economize on something* faire des économies sur quelque chose

economy NOUN
l' *économie* FEM

ecstasy NOUN
l' *ecstasy* FEM (*drug*)
- **to be in ecstasy** s'extasier

ecu NOUN (= *European Currency Unit*)
l' *écu* MASC

eczema NOUN
l' *eczéma* MASC

edge NOUN
le *bord*

edgy ADJECTIVE
tendu

Edinburgh NOUN
Édimbourg

editor NOUN
(*of newspaper*)
le *rédacteur en chef*
la *rédactrice en chef*

educated ADJECTIVE
cultivé

education NOUN
1 l' *éducation* FEM ◇ *There should be more investment in education.* On devrait investir plus dans l'éducation.
2 l' *enseignement* MASC (*teaching*) ◇ *She works in education.* Elle travaille dans l'enseignement.

educational ADJECTIVE
(*experience, toy*)
éducatif MASC
éducative FEM
◇ *It was very educational.* C'était très éducatif.

effect NOUN
l' *effet* MASC ◇ *special effects* les effets spéciaux

effective ADJECTIVE
efficace

efficient ADJECTIVE
efficace

effort NOUN
l' *effort* MASC

e.g. ABBREVIATION
p. ex. (= par exemple)

egg NOUN
l' *œuf* MASC ◇ *a hard-boiled egg* un œuf dur ◇ *a soft-boiled egg* un œuf à la coque ◇ *a fried egg* un œuf sur le plat
◆ **scrambled eggs** les œufs brouillés

egg cup NOUN
le *coquetier*

Egypt NOUN
l' *Égypte* FEM
◆ **in Egypt** en Égypte

Eiffel Tower NOUN
la *tour Eiffel*

eight NUMBER
huit ◇ *She's eight.* Elle a huit ans.

eighteen NUMBER
dix-huit ◇ *She's eighteen.* Elle a dix-huit ans.

eighth ADJECTIVE
huitième ◇ *the eighth floor* le huitième étage
◆ **the eighth of August** le huit août

eighty NUMBER
quatre-vingts

Eire NOUN
la *République d'Irlande*
◆ **in Eire** en République d'Irlande

either ADVERB, CONJUNCTION, PRONOUN
non plus ◇ *I don't like milk, and I don't like eggs either.* Je n'aime pas le lait, et je n'aime pas les œufs non plus. ◇ *I've never been to Spain. – I haven't either.* Je ne suis jamais allé en Espagne. – Moi non plus.
◆ **either...or...** soit...soit... ◇ *You can have either ice cream or yoghurt.* Tu peux prendre soit une glace soit un yaourt.
◆ **either of them** l'un ou l'autre ◇ *Take either of them.* Prends l'un ou l'autre.
◆ **I don't like either of them.** Je n'aime ni l'un ni l'autre.

elastic NOUN
l' *élastique* MASC

elastic band NOUN
l' *élastique* MASC

elbow NOUN
le *coude*

elder ADJECTIVE
aîné ◇ *my elder sister* ma sœur aînée

elderly ADJECTIVE
âgé
◆ **the elderly** les personnes âgées

eldest ADJECTIVE
aîné ◇ *my eldest sister* ma sœur aînée ◇ *He's the eldest.* C'est l'aîné.

to **elect** VERB
élire

election NOUN
l' *élection* FEM

electric ADJECTIVE
électrique ◇ *an electric fire* un radiateur électrique ◇ *an electric guitar* une guitare électrique
◆ **an electric blanket** une couverture chauffante

electrical ADJECTIVE
électrique
◆ **an electrical engineer** un ingénieur électricien

electrician NOUN
l' *électricien* MASC ◇ *He's an electrician.* Il est électricien.

electricity NOUN
l' *électricité* FEM

electronic ADJECTIVE
électronique

electronics NOUN
l' *électronique* FEM ◇ *My hobby is electronics.* Ma passion, c'est l'électronique.

elegant ADJECTIVE

PTO

élégant

elephant NOUN
l' *éléphant* MASC

eleven NUMBER
onze ◇ *She's 11.* Elle a onze ans.

eleventh ADJECTIVE
onzième ◇ *the 11th floor* le onzième étage ◇ *the 11th of August* le onze août

else ADVERB
d'autre ◇ *somebody else* quelqu'un d'autre ◇ *nobody else* personne d'autre ◇ *nothing else* rien d'autre
- **something else** autre chose
- **anything else** autre chose ◇ *Would you like anything else?* Désirez-vous autre chose?
- **I don't want anything else.** Je ne veux rien d'autre.
- **somewhere else** ailleurs
- **anywhere else** autre part

e-mail NOUN
le *courrier électronique*

embankment NOUN
le *talus*

embarrassed ADJECTIVE
gêné ◇ *I was really embarrassed.* J'étais vraiment gêné.

embarrassing ADJECTIVE
gênant ◇ *It was so embarrassing.* C'était tellement gênant.

embassy NOUN
l' *ambassade* FEM ◇ *the British Embassy* l'ambassade de Grande-Bretagne ◇ *the French Embassy* l'ambassade de France

to **embroider** VERB
broder

embroidery NOUN
la *broderie* ◇ *I do embroidery.* Je fais de la broderie.

emergency NOUN
l' *urgence* FEM ◇ *This is an emergency!* C'est une urgence!
- **in an emergency** en cas d'urgence
- **an emergency exit** une sortie de secours
- **an emergency landing** un atterrissage forcé
- **the emergency services** les services d'urgence

to **emigrate** VERB
émigrer

emotion NOUN
l' *émotion* FEM

emotional ADJECTIVE
(*person*)
émotif MASC
émotive FEM

emperor NOUN
l' *empereur* MASC

to **emphasize** VERB
- **to emphasize something** insister sur quelque chose
- **to emphasize that...** souligner que...

empire NOUN
l' *empire* MASC

to **employ** VERB
employer ◇ *The factory employs 600 people.* L'usine emploie six cents personnes.

employee NOUN
l' *employé* MASC
l' *employée* FEM

employer NOUN
l' *employeur* MASC

employment NOUN
l' *emploi* MASC

empty ADJECTIVE
see also empty VERB
vide

to **empty** VERB
see also empty ADJECTIVE
vider
- **to empty something out** vider quelque chose

to **encourage** VERB
encourager
- **to encourage somebody to do something** encourager quelqu'un à faire quelque chose

encouragement NOUN
l' *encouragement* MASC

encyclopedia NOUN
l' *encyclopédie* FEM

end NOUN
see also end VERB
1 la *fin* ◇ *the end of the film* la fin du film ◇ *the end of the holidays* la fin des vacances
- **in the end** en fin de compte ◇ *In the end I decided to stay at home.* En fin de compte j'ai décidé de rester à la maison.
- **It turned out all right in the end.** Ça s'est bien terminé.

2 le *bout* ◇ *at the end of the street* au bout de la rue ◇ *at the other end of the table* à l'autre bout de la table
- **for hours on end** des heures entières

to **end** VERB
see also end NOUN
finir ◇ *What time does the film end?* À quelle heure est-ce que le film finit?
- **to end up doing something** finir par faire quelque chose ◇ *I ended up walking home.* J'ai fini par rentrer chez moi à pied.

ending NOUN
la *fin* ◇ *It was an exciting film, especially the ending.* C'était un film passionnant,

surtout la fin.

endless ADJECTIVE
interminable ◇ *The journey seemed endless.* Le voyage a paru interminable.

enemy NOUN
l' *ennemi* MASC
l' *ennemie* FEM

energetic ADJECTIVE
énergique (*person*)

energy NOUN
l' *énergie* FEM

engaged ADJECTIVE
1 *occupé* (*busy, in use*) ◇ *I phoned, but it was engaged.* J'ai téléphoné, mais c'était occupé.
2 *fiancé* (*to be married*) ◇ *She's engaged to Brian.* Elle est fiancée à Brian.
- **to get engaged** se fiancer

engagement NOUN
les *fiançailles* FEM PL ◇ *an engagement ring* une bague de fiançailles

engine NOUN
le *moteur*

engineer NOUN
l' *ingénieur* MASC ◇ *He's an engineer.* Il est ingénieur.

engineering NOUN
l' *ingénierie* FEM

England NOUN
l' *Angleterre* FEM
- **in England** en Angleterre
- **to England** en Angleterre
- **I'm from England.** Je suis anglais.

English ADJECTIVE
see also English NOUN
anglais ◇ *I'm English.* Je suis anglais.
- **English people** les Anglais

English NOUN
see also English ADJECTIVE
l' *anglais* MASC (*language*) ◇ *Do you speak English?* Est-ce que vous parlez anglais?
- **the English** les Anglais

Englishman NOUN
l' *Anglais* MASC

Englishwoman NOUN
l' *Anglaise* FEM

enjoy VERB
aimer ◇ *Did you enjoy the film?* Est-ce que vous avez aimé le film?
- **to enjoy oneself** s'amuser ◇ *I really enjoyed myself.* Je me suis vraiment bien amusé. ◇ *Did you enjoy yourselves at the party?* Est-ce que vous vous êtes bien amusés à la fête?

enjoyable ADJECTIVE
agréable

enlargement NOUN
l' *agrandissement* MASC (*of photo*)

enormous ADJECTIVE
énorme

enough PRONOUN, ADJECTIVE
assez de ◇ *enough time* assez de temps ◇ *I didn't have enough money.* Je n'avais pas assez d'argent. ◇ *Have you got enough?* Tu en as assez? ◇ *I've had enough!* J'en ai assez!
- **big enough** suffisamment grand
- **warm enough** suffisamment chaud
- **That's enough.** Ça suffit.

to **enquire** VERB
- **to enquire about something** se renseigner sur quelque chose ◇ *I am going to enquire about train times.* Je vais me renseigner sur les horaires de trains.

to **enter** VERB
entrer
- **to enter a room** entrer dans une pièce
- **to enter a competition** s'inscrire à une compétition

to **entertain** VERB
recevoir (*guests*)

entertainer NOUN
l' *artiste de variétés* MASC/FEM

entertaining ADJECTIVE
amusant

enthusiasm NOUN
l' *enthousiasme* MASC

enthusiast NOUN
- **a railway enthusiast** un passionné des trains
- **She's a DIY enthusiast.** C'est une passionnée de bricolage.

enthusiastic ADJECTIVE
enthousiaste

entire ADJECTIVE
entier MASC
entière FEM
◇ *the entire world* le monde entier

entirely ADVERB
entièrement

entrance NOUN
l' *entrée* FEM
- **an entrance exam** un concours d'entrée
- **entrance fee** le prix d'entrée

entry NOUN
l' *entrée* FEM
- **"no entry" (1)** (*on door*) "défense d'entrer"
- **"no entry" (2)** (*on road sign*) "sens interdit"
- **an entry form** une feuille d'inscription

entry phone NOUN
l' *interphone* MASC

envelope NOUN
l' *enveloppe* FEM

envious ADJECTIVE
envieux MASC
envieuse FEM

E

environment NOUN
l' *environnement* MASC

environmental ADJECTIVE
écologique

environment-friendly ADJECTIVE
écologique

envy NOUN
see also envy VERB
l' *envie* FEM

to **envy** VERB
see also envy NOUN
envier ◇ *I don't envy you!* Je ne t'envie pas!

epileptic NOUN
l' *épileptique* MASC/FEM

episode NOUN
l' *épisode* MASC (*of TV programme, story*)

equal ADJECTIVE
égal
(*égaux* MASC PL)

equality NOUN
l' *égalité* FEM

to **equalize** VERB
égaliser (*in sport*)

equator NOUN
l' *équateur* MASC

equipment NOUN
l' *équipement* MASC ◇ *fishing equipment* l'équipement de pêche ◇ *skiing equipment* l'équipement de ski

equipped ADJECTIVE
◆ **equipped with** équipé de
◆ **to be well equipped** être bien équipé

equivalent NOUN
l' *équivalent* MASC
◆ **equivalent to** équivalent à

error NOUN
l' *erreur* FEM

escalator NOUN
l' *escalier roulant* MASC

escape NOUN
see also escape VERB
l' *évasion* FEM (*from prison*)

to **escape** VERB
see also escape NOUN
s'échapper ◇ *A lion has escaped.* Un lion s'est échappé.
◆ **to escape from prison** s'évader de prison

escort NOUN
l' *escorte* FEM ◇ *a police escort* une escorte de police

Eskimo NOUN
l' *Esquimau* MASC
l' *Esquimaude* FEM
◆ **the Eskimos** les Esquimaux

especially ADVERB
surtout ◇ *It's very hot there, especially in the summer.* Il fait très chaud là-bas, surtout en été.

essay NOUN
la *dissertation* ◇ *a history essay* une dissertation d'histoire

essential ADJECTIVE
essentiel MASC
essentielle FEM
◇ *It's essential to bring warm clothes.* Il est essentiel d'apporter des vêtements chauds.

estate NOUN
la *cité* (*housing estate*) ◇ *I live on an estate.* J'habite dans une cité.

estate agent NOUN
l' *agent immobilier* MASC

estate car NOUN
le *break*

etc ABBREVIATION (= *et cetera*)
etc.

Ethiopia NOUN
l' *Éthiopie* FEM
◆ **in Ethiopia** en Éthiopie

ethnic ADJECTIVE
1 *ethnique* (*racial*) ◇ *an ethnic minority* une minorité ethnique
2 *folklorique* (*clothes, music*)

EU NOUN (= *European Union*)
l' *Union européenne*

Eurocheque NOUN
l' *eurochèque* MASC

Europe NOUN
l' *Europe* FEM
◆ **in Europe** en Europe
◆ **to Europe** en Europe

European ADJECTIVE
see also European NOUN
européen MASC
européenne FEM

European NOUN
see also European ADJECTIVE
(*person*)
l' *Européen* MASC
l' *Européenne* FEM

to **evacuate** VERB
évacuer

eve NOUN
◆ **Christmas Eve** la veille de Noël
◆ **New Year's Eve** la Saint-Sylvestre

even ADVERB
see also even ADJECTIVE
même ◇ *I like all animals, even snakes.* J'aime tous les animaux, même les serpents.
◆ **even if** même si ◇ *I'd never do that, even if you asked me.* Je ne ferais jamais ça, même si tu me le demandais.
◆ **not even** même pas ◇ *He never stops working, not even at the weekend.* Il n'arrête jamais de travailler, même pas

le week-end.

- **even though** bien que

bien que *has to be followed by a verb in the subjunctive.*

◇ *He's never got any money, even though his parents are quite rich.* Il n'a jamais d'argent, bien que ses parents soient assez riches.

- **even more** encore plus ◇ *I liked Boulogne even more than Paris.* J'ai encore plus aimé Boulogne que Paris.

even ADJECTIVE

see also even ADVERB

régulier MASC

régulière FEM

◇ *an even layer of snow* une couche régulière de neige

- **an even number** un nombre pair
- **to get even with somebody** prendre sa revanche sur quelqu'un ◇ *He wanted to get even with her.* Il voulait prendre sa revanche sur elle.

evening NOUN

le *soir* ◇ *in the evening* le soir

◇ *yesterday evening* hier soir

◇ *tomorrow evening* demain soir

- **all evening** toute la soirée
- **Good evening!** Bonsoir!

evening class NOUN

le *cours du soir*

(les *cours du soir* PL)

event NOUN

l' *événement* MASC

- **a sporting event** une épreuve sportive

eventful ADJECTIVE

mouvementé

eventually ADVERB

finalement

ever ADVERB

- **Have you ever been to Germany?** Est-ce que tu es déjà allé en Allemagne?
- **Have you ever seen her?** Vous l'avez déjà vue?
- **I haven't ever done that.** Je ne l'ai jamais fait.
- **the best I've ever seen** le meilleur que j'aie jamais vu
- **for the first time ever** pour la première fois
- **ever since** depuis que ◇ *ever since I met him* depuis que je l'ai rencontré
- **ever since then** depuis ce moment-là

every ADJECTIVE

chaque ◇ *every pupil* chaque élève

- **every time** chaque fois ◇ *Every time I see him he's depressed.* Chaque fois que je le vois il est déprimé.
- **every day** tous les jours
- **every week** toutes les semaines
- **every now and then** de temps en temps

everybody PRONOUN

tout le monde ◇ *Everybody had a good time.* Tout le monde s'est bien amusé. ◇ *Everybody makes mistakes.* Tout le monde peut se tromper.

everyone PRONOUN

tout le monde ◇ *Everyone opened their presents.* Tout le monde a ouvert ses cadeaux. ◇ *Everyone should have a hobby.* Tout le monde devrait avoir un passe-temps.

everything PRONOUN

tout ◇ *You've thought of everything!* Tu as pensé à tout!

- **Have you remembered everything?** Est-ce que tu n'as rien oublié?
- **Money isn't everything.** L'argent ne fait pas le bonheur.

everywhere ADVERB

partout ◇ *I looked everywhere, but I couldn't find it.* J'ai regardé partout, mais je n'ai pas pu le trouver. ◇ *There were policemen everywhere.* Il y avait des policiers partout.

evil ADJECTIVE

mauvais

ex- PREFIX

ex- ◇ *his ex-wife* son ex-femme

exact ADJECTIVE

exact

exactly ADVERB

exactement ◇ *exactly the same* exactement le même ◇ *Not exactly.* Pas exactement.

- **It's exactly 10 o'clock.** Il est dix heures précises.

to **exaggerate** VERB

exagérer

exaggeration NOUN

l' *exagération* FEM

exam NOUN

l' *examen* MASC ◇ *a French exam* un examen de français ◇ *the exam results* les résultats des examens MASC

examination NOUN

l' *examen* MASC

to **examine** VERB

examiner ◇ *He examined her passport.* Il a examiné son passeport. ◇ *The doctor examined him.* Le docteur l'a examiné.

examiner NOUN

l' *examinateur* MASC

l' *examinatrice* FEM

example NOUN

l' *exemple* MASC

- **for example** par exemple

excellent ADJECTIVE

excellent ◇ *Her results were excellent.*

PTO

Elle a eu d'excellents résultats.
- **It was excellent fun.** C'était vraiment super.

except PREPOSITION
sauf ◇ *everyone except me* tout le monde sauf moi
- **except for** sauf
- **except that** sauf que ◇ *The weather was great, except that it was a bit cold.* Il a fait un temps superbe, sauf qu'il a fait un peu froid.

exception NOUN
l' *exception* FEM
- **to make an exception** faire une exception

exceptional ADJECTIVE
exceptionnel MASC
exceptionnelle FEM

excess baggage NOUN
l' *excédent de bagages* MASC

to **exchange** VERB
échanger ◇ *I exchanged the book for a video.* J'ai échangé le livre contre une vidéo.

exchange rate NOUN
le *taux de change*

excited ADJECTIVE
excité

exciting ADJECTIVE
passionnant

excuse NOUN
see also excuse VERB
l' *excuse* FEM

to **excuse** VERB
see also excuse NOUN
- **Excuse me!** Pardon!

to **execute** VERB
exécuter

execution NOUN
l' *exécution* FEM

executive NOUN
le *cadre* (*in business*) ◇ *He's an executive.* Il est cadre.

exercise NOUN
l' *exercice* MASC
- **an exercise bike** un vélo d'appartement
- **an exercise book** un cahier

exhausted ADJECTIVE
épuisé

exhaust fumes PL NOUN
les *gaz d'échappement* MASC PL

exhaust pipe NOUN
le *tuyau d'échappement*

exhibition NOUN
l' *exposition* FEM

ex-husband NOUN
l' *ex-mari* MASC

to **exist** VERB
exister

exit NOUN
la *sortie*

exotic ADJECTIVE
exotique

to **expect** VERB
1 *attendre* ◇ *I'm expecting him for dinner.* Je l'attends pour dîner. ◇ *She's expecting a baby.* Elle attend un enfant.
2 *s'attendre à* ◇ *I was expecting the worst.* Je m'attendais au pire.
3 *supposer* ◇ *I expect it's a mistake.* Je suppose qu'il s'agit d'une erreur.

expedition NOUN
l' *expédition* FEM

to **expel** VERB
- **to get expelled** (*from school*) se faire renvoyer

expenses PL NOUN
les *frais* MASC PL

expensive ADJECTIVE
cher MASC
chère FEM

experience NOUN
l' *expérience* FEM

experienced ADJECTIVE
expérimenté

experiment NOUN
l' *expérience* FEM

expert NOUN
le *spécialiste*
la *spécialiste*
◇ *He's a computer expert.* C'est un spécialiste en informatique.
- **He's an expert cook.** Il cuisine très bien.

to **expire** VERB
expirer

to **explain** VERB
expliquer

explanation NOUN
l' *explication* FEM

to **explode** VERB
exploser

to **exploit** VERB
exploiter

exploitation NOUN
l' *exploitation* FEM

to **explore** VERB
explorer (*place*)

explorer NOUN
l' *explorateur* MASC
l' *exploratrice* FEM

explosion NOUN
l' *explosion* FEM

explosive ADJECTIVE
see also explosive NOUN
explosif MASC
explosive FEM

explosive NOUN

see also explosive ADJECTIVE
l' *explosif* MASC

express VERB
exprimer
- **to express oneself** s'exprimer ◇ *It's not easy to express oneself in a foreign language.* Ce n'est pas facile de s'exprimer dans une langue étrangère.

expression NOUN
l' *expression* FEM ◇ *It's an English expression.* C'est une expression anglaise.

extension NOUN
1 l' *annexe* FEM (*of building*)
2 le *poste* (*telephone*)
In France phone numbers are broken into groups of two digits where possible.
- **Extension 3137, please.** Poste trente et un trente-sept, s'il vous plaît.

extent NOUN
- **to some extent** dans une certaine mesure

exterior ADJECTIVE
extérieur

extinct ADJECTIVE
- **to become extinct** disparaître
- **to be extinct** avoir disparu ◇ *The species is almost extinct.* Cette espèce a presque disparu.

extinguisher NOUN
l' *extincteur* MASC (*fire extinguisher*)

extortionate ADJECTIVE
exorbitant

extra ADJECTIVE, ADVERB
supplémentaire ◇ *an extra blanket* une couverture supplémentaire
- **to pay extra** payer un supplément
- **Breakfast is extra.** Il y a un supplément pour le petit déjeuner.
- **It costs extra.** Il y a un supplément.

extraordinary ADJECTIVE
extraordinaire

extravagant ADJECTIVE
(*person*)
dépensier MASC
dépensière FEM

extreme ADJECTIVE
extrême

extremely ADVERB
extrêmement

extremist NOUN
l' *extrémiste* MASC/FEM

eye NOUN
l' *œil* MASC
(les *yeux* PL)
◇ *I've got green eyes.* J'ai les yeux verts.
- **to keep an eye on something** surveiller quelque chose

eyebrow NOUN
le *sourcil*

eyelash NOUN
le *cil*

eyelid NOUN
la *paupière*

eyeliner NOUN
l' *eye-liner* MASC

eye shadow NOUN
l' *ombre à paupières* FEM

eyesight NOUN
la *vue*

E

F

fabric NOUN
le *tissu*

fabulous ADJECTIVE
formidable ◇ *The show was fabulous.* Le spectacle était formidable.

face NOUN
see also face VERB
1 le *visage* (*of person*)
2 le *cadran* (*of clock*)
3 la *paroi* (*of cliff*)
◆ **on the face of it** à première vue
◆ **in the face of these difficulties** face à ces difficultés
◆ **face to face** face à face
◆ **a face cloth** un gant de toilette

to **face** VERB
see also face NOUN
faire face à (*place, problem*)
◆ **to face up to something** faire face à quelque chose ◇ *You must face up to your responsibilities.* Vous devez faire face à vos responsabilités.

facilities PL NOUN
l' *équipement* MASC SING ◇ *This school has excellent facilities.* Cette école dispose d'un excellent équipement.
◆ **toilet facilities** les toilettes FEM
◆ **cooking facilities** la cuisine équipée SING

fact NOUN
le *fait*
◆ **in fact** en fait

factory NOUN
l' *usine* FEM

to **fade** VERB
1 *passer* (*colour*) ◇ *The colour has faded in the sun.* La couleur a passé au soleil
◆ **My jeans have faded.** Mon jean est délavé.
2 *baisser* ◇ *The light was fading fast.* La lumière baissait rapidement.
3 *diminuer* ◇ *The noise gradually faded.* Le bruit a diminué peu à peu.

to **fail** VERB
see also fail NOUN
1 *rater* ◇ *I failed the history exam.* J'ai raté l'examen d'histoire.
2 *échouer* ◇ *In our class, no one failed.* Dans notre classe, personne n'a échoué.
3 *lâcher* ◇ *My brakes failed.* Mes freins ont lâché.
◆ **to fail to do something** ne pas faire quelque chose ◇ *She failed to return her library books.* Elle n'a pas rendu ses livres à la bibliothèque.

fail NOUN
see also fail VERB
◆ **without fail** sans faute

failure NOUN
1 l' *échec* MASC ◇ *feelings of failure* un sentiment d'échec SING
2 le *raté*
la *ratée*
◇ *He's a failure.* C'est un raté.
3 la *défaillance* ◇ *a mechanical failure* une défaillance mécanique

faint ADJECTIVE
see also faint VERB
faible ◇ *His voice was very faint.* Sa voix était très faible.
◆ **to feel faint** se trouver mal

to **faint** VERB
see also faint ADJECTIVE
s'évanouir ◇ *All of a sudden she fainted.* Tout à coup elle s'est évanouie.

fair ADJECTIVE
see also fair NOUN
1 *juste* ◇ *That's not fair.* Ce n'est pas juste.
2 (*hair*)
blond ◇ *He's got fair hair.* Il a les cheveux blonds.
3 (*skin*)
clair ◇ *people with fair skin* les gens qui ont la peau claire
4 (*weather*)
beau MASC
belle FEM
◇ *The weather was fair.* Il faisait beau.
5 (*good enough*)
assez bon MASC
assez bonne FEM
◇ *I have a fair chance of winning.* J'ai d'assez bonnes chances de gagner.
6 (*sizeable*)
considérable ◇ *That's a fair distance.* Ça représente une distance considérable.

fair NOUN
see also fair ADJECTIVE
la *foire* ◇ *They went to the fair.* Ils sont allés à la foire.
◆ **a trade fair** une foire commerciale

fairly ADVERB
1 *équitablement* ◇ *The cake was divided fairly.* Le gâteau a été partagé équitablement.
2 *assez* (*quite*) ◇ *That's fairly good.* C'est assez bien.

fairness NOUN
la *justice*

fairy NOUN

la *fée*

airy tale NOUN
le *conte de fées*
(les *contes de fées* PL)

aith NOUN
1 la *foi* ◇ *the Catholic faith* la foi catholique
2 la *confiance* ◇ *People have lost faith in the government.* Les gens ont perdu confiance dans le gouvernement.

aithful ADJECTIVE
fidèle

aithfully ADVERB
◆ **Yours faithfully...** (*in letter*) Veuillez agréer mes salutations distinguées...

ake NOUN
see also fake ADJECTIVE
le *faux* ◇ *The painting was a fake.* Le tableau était un faux.

ake ADJECTIVE
see also fake NOUN
faux MASC
fausse FEM
◇ *She wore fake fur.* Elle portait une fausse fourrure.

all NOUN
see also fall VERB
la *chute* ◇ *a fall of snow* une chute de neige ◇ *She had a nasty fall.* Elle a fait une mauvaise chute.
◆ **the Niagara Falls** les chutes du Niagara

all VERB
see also fall NOUN
1 *tomber* ◇ *He tripped and fell.* Il a trébuché et il est tombé.
2 *baisser* ◇ *Prices are falling.* Les prix baissent.
◆ **to fall down (1)** (*person*) tomber ◇ *She's fallen down.* Elle est tombée.
◆ **to fall down (2)** (*building*) s'écrouler ◇ *The house is slowly falling down.* La maison est en train de s'écrouler.
◆ **to fall for (1)** se laisser prendre à ◇ *They fell for it.* Ils s'y sont laissé prendre.
◆ **to fall for (2)** tomber amoureux de ◇ *She's falling for him.* Elle est en train de tomber amoureuse de lui.
◆ **to fall off** tomber de ◇ *The book fell off the shelf.* Le livre est tombé de l'étagère.
◆ **to fall through** tomber à l'eau ◇ *Our plans have fallen through.* Nos projets sont tombés à l'eau.

alse ADJECTIVE
faux MASC
fausse FEM
◆ **a false alarm** une fausse alerte
◆ **false teeth** les fausses dents

ame NOUN
la *renommée*

familiar ADJECTIVE
familier MASC
familière FEM
◇ *a familiar face* un visage familier
◆ **to be familiar with something** bien connaître quelque chose ◇ *I'm familiar with his work.* Je connais bien ses œuvres.

family NOUN
la *famille*
◆ **the Cooke family** la famille Cooke

famine NOUN
la *famine*

famous ADJECTIVE
célèbre

fan NOUN
1 l' *éventail* MASC (*hand-held*)
2 le *ventilateur* (*electric*)
3 le/la *fan* (*of person, band*) ◇ *I'm a fan of Take That.* Je suis une fan de Take That.
4 le/la *supporter* (*of sport*) ◇ *football fans* les supporters de football

fanatic NOUN
le/la *fanatique*

to **fancy** VERB
◆ **to fancy something** avoir envie de quelque chose ◇ *I fancy an ice cream.* J'ai envie d'une glace.
◆ **to fancy doing something** avoir envie de faire quelque chose
◆ **He fancies her.** Elle lui plaît.

fancy dress NOUN
le *déguisement* ◇ *He was wearing fancy dress.* Il portait un déguisement.
◆ **a fancy-dress ball** un bal costumé

fantastic ADJECTIVE
fantastique

far ADJECTIVE, ADVERB
loin ◇ *Is it far?* Est-ce que c'est loin?
◆ **far from** loin de ◇ *It's not far from London.* Ce n'est pas loin de Londres. ◇ *It's far from easy.* C'est loin d'être facile.
◆ **How far is it?** C'est à quelle distance?
◆ **How far is it to Geneva?** Combien y a-t-il jusqu'à Genève?
◆ **How far have you got?** (*with a task*) Où en êtes-vous?
◆ **at the far end** à l'autre bout ◇ *at the far end of the room* à l'autre bout de la pièce
◆ **far better** beaucoup mieux
◆ **as far as I know** pour autant que je sache

fare NOUN
1 le *prix du billet* (*on trains, buses*)
2 le *prix de la course* (*in taxi*)
◆ **half fare** le demi-tarif
◆ **full fare** le plein tarif

F

Far East NOUN
l' *Extrême-Orient* MASC
◆ **in the Far East** en Extrême-Orient

farm NOUN
la *ferme*

farmer NOUN
l' *agriculteur* MASC
l' *agricultrice* FEM
◇ *He's a farmer.* Il est agriculteur.

farmhouse NOUN
la *ferme*

farming NOUN
l' *agriculture* FEM
◆ **dairy farming** l'industrie laitière

fascinating ADJECTIVE
fascinant

fashion NOUN
la *mode*
◆ **in fashion** à la mode

fashionable ADJECTIVE
à la mode ◇ *Jane wears very fashionable clothes.* Jane porte des vêtements très à la mode. ◇ *a fashionable restaurant* un restaurant à la mode

fast ADJECTIVE, ADVERB
1 *vite* ◇ *He can run fast.* Il sait courir vite.
2 *rapide* ◇ *a fast car* une voiture rapide
◆ **That clock's fast.** Cette pendule avance.
◆ **He's fast asleep.** Il est profondément endormi.

fat ADJECTIVE
see also fat NOUN
gros MASC
grosse FEM

fat NOUN
see also fat ADJECTIVE
1 le *gras* (*on meat, in food*) ◇ *It's very high in fat.* C'est très gras.
2 la *matière grasse* (*for cooking*)

fatal ADJECTIVE
1 (*causing death*)
mortel MASC
mortelle FEM
◇ *a fatal accident* un accident mortel
2 (*disastrous*)
fatal ◇ *He made a fatal mistake.* Il a fait une erreur fatale..

father NOUN
le *père* ◇ *my father* mon père

father-in-law NOUN
le *beau-père*
(les *beaux-pères* PL)

fault NOUN
1 la *faute* (*mistake*) ◇ *It's my fault.* C'est de ma faute.
2 le *défaut* (*defect*) ◇ *There's a fault in this material.* Ce tissu a un défaut.
◆ **a mechanical fault** une défaillance mécanique

faulty ADJECTIVE
défectueux MASC
défectueuse FEM
◇ *This machine is faulty.* Cette machine est défectueuse.

favour NOUN
le *service*
◆ **to do somebody a favour** rendre service à quelqu'un ◇ *Could you do me a favour?* Tu peux me rendre service?
◆ **to be in favour of something** être pour quelque chose ◇ *I'm in favour of nuclear disarmament.* Je suis pour le désarmement nucléaire.

favourite ADJECTIVE
see also favourite NOUN
favori MASC
favorite FEM
◇ *Blue's my favourite colour.* Le bleu est ma couleur favorite.

favourite NOUN
see also favourite ADJECTIVE
1 le *favori*
2 la *favorite* ◇ *Liverpool are favourites to win the Cup.* L'équipe de Liverpool est favorite pour la coupe.

fear NOUN
see also fear VERB
la *peur*

to **fear** VERB
see also fear NOUN
craindre ◇ *You have nothing to fear.* Vous n'avez rien à craindre.

feather NOUN
la *plume*

feature NOUN
la *caractéristique* (*of person, object*) ◇ *an important feature* une caractéristique essentielle

February NOUN
février MASC
◆ **in February** en février

fed VERB *see* **feed**

fed up ADJECTIVE
◆ **to be fed up with something** en avoir marre de quelque chose ◇ *I'm fed up of waiting for him.* J'en ai marre de l'attendre.

to **feed** VERB
donner à manger à ◇ *Have you fed the cat?* Est-ce que tu as donné à manger au chat?
◆ **He worked hard to feed his family.** Il travaillait dur pour nourrir sa famille.

to **feel** VERB
1 *se sentir* ◇ *I don't feel well.* Je ne me

sens pas bien. ◇ *I feel a bit lonely.* Je me sens un peu seul.
2 *sentir* ◇ *I didn't feel much pain.* Je n'ai presque rien senti.
3 *toucher* ◇ *The doctor felt his forehead.* Le docteur lui a touché le front.
◆ **I was feeling hungry.** J'avais faim.
◆ **I was feeling cold, so I went inside.** J'avais froid, donc je suis rentré.
◆ **I feel like...** (*want*) J'ai envie de... ◇ *Do you feel like an ice cream?* Tu as envie d'une glace?

eeling NOUN
1 la *sensation* (*physical*) ◇ *a burning feeling* une sensation de brûlure
2 le *sentiment* (*emotional*) ◇ *a feeling of satisfaction* un sentiment de satisfaction

eet PL NOUN *see* **foot**

ell VERB *see* **fall**

elt VERB *see* **feel**

elt-tip pen NOUN
le *stylo-feutre*

emale ADJECTIVE
see also female NOUN
1 *femelle* ◇ *a female animal* un animal femelle
2 *féminin* ◇ *the female sex* le sexe féminin

emale NOUN
see also female ADJECTIVE
la *femelle* (*animal*)

eminine ADJECTIVE
féminin

eminist NOUN
le/la *féministe*

ence NOUN
la *barrière*

ern NOUN
la *fougère*

erocious ADJECTIVE
féroce

erry NOUN
le *ferry*

ertile ADJECTIVE
fertile

ertilizer NOUN
l' *engrais* MASC

estival NOUN
le *festival* ◇ *a jazz festival* un festival de jazz

etch VERB
1 *aller chercher* ◇ *Fetch the bucket.* Va chercher le seau.
2 *se vendre* (*sell for*) ◇ *His painting fetched £5000.* Son tableau s'est vendu cinq mille livres.

ever NOUN
la *fièvre* (*temperature*)

few ADJECTIVE, PRONOUN
peu de (*not many*) ◇ *few books* peu de livres
◆ **a few (1)** quelques ◇ *a few hours* quelques heures
◆ **a few (2)** quelques-uns ◇ *How many apples do you want?–A few.* Tu veux combien de pommes?–Quelques-unes.
◆ **quite a few people** pas mal de monde

fewer ADJECTIVE
moins de ◇ *There are fewer people than there were yesterday.* Il y a moins de monde qu'hier. ◇ *There are fewer pupils in this class.* Il y a moins d'élèves dans cette classe.

fiancé NOUN
le *fiancé* ◇ *He's my fiancé.* C'est mon fiancé.

fiancée NOUN
la *fiancée* ◇ *She's my fiancée.* C'est ma fiancée.

fiction NOUN
les *romans* MASC PL (*novels*)

field NOUN
1 le *champ* (*in countryside*) ◇ *a field of wheat* un champ de blé
2 le *terrain* (*for sport*) ◇ *a football field* un terrain de football
3 le *domaine* (*subject*) ◇ *He's an expert in his field.* C'est un expert dans son domaine.

fierce ADJECTIVE
1 *féroce* ◇ *The dog looked very fierce.* Le chien avait l'air très féroce.
2 *violent* ◇ *The wind was very fierce.* Le vent était très violent. ◇ *a fierce attack* une attaque violente

fifteen NUMBER
quinze ◇ *I'm fifteen.* J'ai quinze ans.

fifth ADJECTIVE
cinquième ◇ *the fifth floor* le cinquième étage
◆ **the fifth of August** le cinq août

fifty NUMBER
cinquante ◇ *He's fifty.* Il a cinquante ans.

fifty-fifty ADJECTIVE, ADVERB
moitié-moitié ◇ *They split the prize money fifty-fifty.* Ils ont partagé l'argent du prix moitié-moitié.
◆ **a fifty-fifty chance** une chance sur deux

fight NOUN
see also fight VERB
1 la *bagarre* ◇ *There was a fight in the pub.* Il y a eu une bagarre au pub.
2 la *lutte* ◇ *the fight against cancer* la lutte contre le cancer

to **fight** VERB
see also fight NOUN

F

1 *se battre* ◇ *They were fighting.* Ils se battaient.
2 *lutter contre* ◇ *The doctors tried to fight the disease.* Les médecins ont essayé de lutter contre la maladie. ◇ *He fought against the urge to smoke.* Il a lutté contre son envie de fumer.

fighting NOUN
les *bagarres* FEM PL ◇ *Fighting broke out outside the pub.* Des bagarres ont éclaté devant le pub.

figure NOUN
1 le *chiffre* (*number*) ◇ *Can you give me the exact figures?* Pouvez-vous me donner les chiffres exacts?
2 la *silhouette* (*outline of person*) ◇ *Hélène saw the figure of a man on the bridge.* Hélène a vu la silhouette d'un homme sur le pont.
- **She's got a good figure.** Elle est bien faite.
- **I have to watch my figure.** Je dois faire attention à ma ligne.

3 le *personnage* (*personality*) ◇ *She's an important political figure.* C'est un personnage politique important.

to figure out VERB
1 *calculer* ◇ *I'll try to figure out how much it'll cost.* Je vais essayer de calculer combien ça va coûter.
2 *voir* ◇ *I couldn't figure out what it meant.* Je n'arrivais pas à voir ce que ça voulait dire.
3 *cerner* ◇ *I can't figure him out at all.* Je n'arrive pas du tout à le cerner.

file NOUN
see also file VERB
1 le *dossier* (*document*) ◇ *Have we got a file on the suspect?* Est-ce que nous avons un dossier sur le suspect?
2 la *chemise* (*folder*) ◇ *She keeps all her letters in a cardboard file.* Elle garde toutes ses lettres dans une chemise en carton.
3 le *classeur* (*ring binder*)
4 le *fichier* (*on computer*)
5 la *lime* (*for nails, metal*)

to file VERB
see also file NOUN
1 *classer* (*papers*)
2 *limer* (*nails, metal*) ◇ *to file one's nails* se limer les ongles

to fill VERB
remplir ◇ *She filled the glass with water.* Elle a rempli le verre d'eau.
- **to fill in (1)** remplir ◇ *Can you fill this form in please?* Est-ce que vous pouvez remplir ce formulaire s'il vous plaît?
- **to fill in (2)** boucher ◇ *He filled the hole in with soil.* Il a bouché le trou avec de la terre.
- **to fill up** remplir ◇ *He filled the cup up to the brim.* Il a rempli la tasse à ras bords.
- **Fill it up, please.** (*at petrol station*) Le plein, s'il vous plaît.

film NOUN
1 le *film* (*movie*)
2 la *pellicule* (*for camera*)

film star NOUN
la *vedette de cinéma* ◇ *He's a film star.* C'est une vedette de cinéma.

filthy ADJECTIVE
dégoûtant

final ADJECTIVE
see also final NOUN
1 (*last*)
dernier MASC
dernière FEM
◇ *our final farewells* nos derniers adieux
2 (*definite*)
définitif MASC
définitive FEM
◇ *a final decision* une décision définitive
- **I'm not going and that's final.** Je n'y vais pas, un point c'est tout.

final NOUN
see also final ADJECTIVE
la *finale* ◇ *Boris Becker is in the final.* Boris Becker va disputer la finale.

finally ADVERB
1 *enfin* (*lastly*) ◇ *Finally, I would like to say...* Enfin, je voudrais dire...
2 *finalement* (*eventually*) ◇ *They finally decided to leave on Saturday instead of Friday.* Ils ont finalement décidé de partir samedi au lieu de vendredi.

to find VERB
1 *trouver* ◇ *I can't find the exit.* Je ne trouve pas la sortie.
2 *retrouver* (*something lost*) ◇ *Did you find your pen?* Est-ce que tu as retrouvé ton crayon?
- **to find something out** découvrir quelque chose ◇ *I'm determined to find out the truth.* Je suis décidé à découvrir la vérité.
- **to find out about (1)** (*make enquiries*) se renseigner sur ◇ *Try to find out about the cost of a hotel.* Essaye de te renseigner sur le prix d'un hôtel.
- **to find out about (2)** (*by chance*) apprendre ◇ *I found out about their affair.* J'ai appris leur liaison.

fine ADJECTIVE, ADVERB
see also fine NOUN
1 *excellent* (*very good*) ◇ *He's a fine musician.* C'est un excellent musicien.

to be fine aller bien ◇ *How are you?–I'm fine.* Comment ça va?–Ça va bien.
I feel fine. Je me sens bien.
The weather is fine today. Il fait beau aujourd'hui.
2 *fin* (*not coarse*) ◇ *She's got very fine hair.* Elle a les cheveux très fins.

ne NOUN
see also fine ADJECTIVE
1 l' *amende* FEM ◇ *She got a £50 fine.* Elle a eu une amende de cinquante livres.
2 la *contravention* (*for traffic offence*) ◇ *I got a fine for driving through a red light.* J'ai eu une contravention pour avoir grillé un feu rouge.

nger NOUN
le *doigt*
my little finger mon petit doigt

ngernail NOUN
l' *ongle* MASC

nish NOUN
see also finish VERB
l' *arrivée* FEM (*of race*) ◇ *We saw the finish of the London Marathon.* Nous avons vu l'arrivée du marathon de Londres.

nish VERB
see also finish NOUN
1 *finir* ◇ *I've finished!* J'ai fini!
to finish doing something finir de faire quelque chose
2 *terminer* ◇ *I've finished the book.* J'ai terminé ce livre. ◇ *The film has finished.* Le film est terminé.

inland NOUN
la *Finlande*
in Finland en Finlande
to Finland en Finlande

inn NOUN
le *Finlandais*
la *Finlandaise*

innish ADJECTIVE
see also Finnish NOUN
finlandais

innish NOUN
see also Finnish ADJECTIVE
le *finnois* (*language*)

re NOUN
see also fire VERB
1 le *feu*
(les *feux* PL)
◇ *He made a fire to warm himself up.* Il a fait du feu pour se réchauffer.
to be on fire être en feu
2 l' *incendie* MASC (*accidental*) ◇ *The house was destroyed by fire.* La maison a été détruite par un incendie.
3 le *radiateur* (*heater*) ◇ *Turn the fire on.* Allume le radiateur.
the fire brigade les pompiers MASC PL
a fire alarm un avertisseur d'incendie
a fire engine une voiture de pompiers
a fire escape un escalier de secours
a fire extinguisher un extincteur
a fire station une caserne de pompiers

to fire VERB
see also fire NOUN
tirer (*shoot*) ◇ *She fired twice.* Elle a tiré deux fois.
to fire at somebody tirer sur quelqu'un ◇ *The terrorist fired at the crowd.* Le terroriste a tiré sur la foule.
to fire a gun tirer un coup de feu
to fire somebody mettre quelqu'un à la porte ◇ *He was fired from his job.* Il a été mis à la porte.

fireman NOUN
le *pompier* ◇ *He's a fireman.* Il est pompier.

fireplace NOUN
la *cheminée*

fireworks PL NOUN
le *feu d'artifice* SING ◇ *Are you going to see the fireworks?* Est-ce que tu vas voir le feu d'artifice?

firm ADJECTIVE
see also firm NOUN
ferme ◇ *to be firm with somebody* se montrer ferme avec quelqu'un

firm NOUN
see also firm ADJECTIVE
l' *entreprise* FEM ◇ *He works for a large firm in London.* Il travaille pour une grande entreprise à Londres.

first ADJECTIVE, ADVERB
see also first NOUN
1 *premier* MASC
première FEM
◇ *the first of September* le premier septembre ◇ *the first time* la première fois
to come first (*in exam, race*) arriver premier ◇ *Rachel came first.* Rachel est arrivée première.
2 *d'abord* ◇ *I want to get a job, but first I have to pass my exams.* Je veux trouver du travail, mais d'abord je dois réussir à mes examens.
first of all tout d'abord

first NOUN
see also first ADJECTIVE
le *premier*
la *première*
◇ *She was the first to arrive.* Elle est arrivée la première.
at first au début

F

first aid NOUN
les *premiers secours* MASC PL
- **a first aid kit** une trousse de secours

first-class ADJECTIVE
1 *de première classe* ◇ *She has booked a first-class ticket.* Elle a réservé un billet de première classe.
2 *excellent* ◇ *a first-class meal* un excellent repas
- **a first-class stamp**

In France there is no first-class or second-class postage. However letters cost more to send than postcards, so you have to remember to say what you are sending when buying stamps.

firstly ADVERB
premièrement ◇ *Firstly, let's see what the book is about.* Premièrement, voyons de quoi parle ce livre.

fish NOUN
see also fish VERB
le *poisson* ◇ *I caught three fish.* J'ai pêché trois poissons. ◇ *I don't like fish.* Je n'aime pas le poisson.

to **fish** VERB
see also fish NOUN
pêcher
- **to go fishing** aller à la pêche ◇ *We went fishing in the River Dee.* Nous sommes allés à la pêche sur la Dee.

fisherman NOUN
le *pêcheur* ◇ *He's a fisherman.* Il est pêcheur.

fishing NOUN
la *pêche* ◇ *My hobby is fishing.* La pêche est mon passe-temps favori.

fishing boat NOUN
le *bateau de pêche*

fishing rod NOUN
la *canne à pêche*

fishing tackle NOUN
le *matériel de pêche*

fist NOUN
le *poing*

to **fit** VERB
see also fit ADJECTIVE, NOUN
1 *être la bonne taille* (*be the right size*) ◇ *Does it fit?* Est-ce que c'est la bonne taille?

In French you usually specify whether something is too big, small, tight etc.

- **These trousers don't fit me. (1)** (*too big*) Ce pantalon est trop grand pour moi.
- **These trousers don't fit me. (2)** (*too small*) Ce pantalon est trop petit pour moi.

2 *installer* (*fix up*) ◇ *He fitted an alarm in his car.* Il a installé une alarme dans sa voiture.
3 *adapter* (*attach*) ◇ *She fitted a plug to the hair dryer.* Elle a adapté une prise au sèche-cheveux.
- **to fit in (1)** (*match up*) correspondre ◇ *That story doesn't fit in with what he told us.* Cette histoire ne correspond pas à ce qu'il nous a dit.
- **to fit in (2)** (*person*) s'adapter ◇ *She fitted in well at her new school.* Elle s'est bien adaptée à sa nouvelle école.

fit ADJECTIVE
see also fit VERB, NOUN
en forme (*in condition*) ◇ *He felt relaxed and fit after his holiday.* Il se sentait détendu et en forme après ses vacances.

fit NOUN
see also fit ADJECTIVE, VERB
- **to have a fit (1)** (*epileptic*) avoir une crise d'épilepsie
- **to have a fit (2)** (*be angry*) piquer une crise de nerfs ◇ *My Mum will have a fit when she sees the carpet!* Ma mère va piquer une crise de nerfs quand elle va voir la moquette!

fitted carpet NOUN
la *moquette*

fitted kitchen NOUN
la *cuisine aménagée*

fitting room NOUN
la *cabine d'essayage*

five NUMBER
cinq ◇ *He's five.* Il a cinq ans.

to **fix** VERB
1 *réparer* (*mend*) ◇ *Can you fix my bike?* Est-ce que tu peux réparer mon vélo?
2 *fixer* (*decide*) ◇ *Let's fix a date for the party.* Fixons une date pour la soirée. ◇ *They fixed a price for the car.* Ils ont fixé un prix pour la voiture.
3 *préparer* ◇ *Janice fixed some food for us.* Janice nous a préparé à manger.

fixed ADJECTIVE
fixe ◇ *at a fixed time* à une heure fixe ◇ *at a fixed price* à un prix fixe ◇ *a fixed-price menu* un menu à prix fixe
- **My parents have very fixed ideas.** Mes parents ont des idées très arrêtées.

fizzy ADJECTIVE
gazeux MASC
gazeuse FEM
◇ *I don't like fizzy drinks.* Je n'aime pas les boissons gazeuses.

flabby ADJECTIVE
flasque

flag NOUN
le *drapeau*
(les *drapeaux* PL)

flame NOUN
la *flamme*

amingo NOUN
le *flamant rose*

an NOUN
1 la *tarte* (*sweet*) ◇ *a raspberry flan* une tarte aux framboises
2 la *quiche* (*savoury*) ◇ *a cheese and onion flan* une quiche au fromage et aux oignons

annel NOUN
le *gant de toilette* (*for face*)

ap VERB
battre de ◇ *The bird flapped its wings.* L'oiseau battait des ailes.

ash NOUN
see also flash VERB
le *flash*
(les *flashes* PL)
◇ *Has your camera got a flash?* Est-ce que ton appareil photo a un flash?
a flash of lightning un éclair
◆ **in a flash** en un clin d'œil

ash VERB
see also flash NOUN
1 *clignoter* ◇ *The police car's blue light was flashing.* Le gyrophare de la voiture de police clignotait.
2 *projeter* ◇ *They flashed a torch in his face.* Ils lui ont projeté la lumière d'une torche en plein visage.
She flashed her headlights. Elle a fait un appel de phares.

at ADJECTIVE
see also flat NOUN
1 *plat* ◇ *a flat roof* un toit plat ◇ *flat shoes* des chaussures plates
2 *crevé* (*tyre*) ◇ *I've got a flat tyre.* J'ai un pneu crevé.

at NOUN
see also flat ADJECTIVE
l' *appartement* MASC ◇ *She lives in a flat.* Elle habite un appartement.

atter VERB
flatter

avour NOUN
1 le *goût* (*taste*) ◇ *This cheese has a very strong flavour.* Ce fromage a un goût très fort.
2 le *parfum* (*variety*) ◇ *Which flavour of ice cream would you like?* Quel parfum de glace est-ce que tu veux?

lavouring NOUN
le *parfum*

lew VERB *see* **fly**

lexible ADJECTIVE
flexible ◇ *flexible working hours* les horaires flexibles

lick VERB
appuyer sur ◇ *She flicked the switch to turn the light on.* Elle a appuyé sur le bouton pour allumer la lumière.
◆ **to flick through a book** feuilleter un livre

to **flicker** VERB
trembloter ◇ *The light flickered.* La lumière a trembloté.

flight NOUN
le *vol* ◇ *What time is the flight to Paris?* À quelle heure est le vol pour Paris?
◆ **a flight of stairs** un escalier

to **fling** VERB
jeter ◇ *He flung the dictionary onto the floor.* Il a jeté le dictionnaire par terre.

to **float** VERB
flotter ◇ *A leaf was floating on the water.* Une feuille flottait sur l'eau.

flock NOUN
◆ **a flock of sheep** un troupeau de moutons
◆ **a flock of birds** un vol d'oiseaux

flood NOUN
see also flood VERB
1 l' *inondation* FEM ◇ *The rain has caused many floods.* La pluie a provoqué de nombreuses inondations.
2 le *flot* ◇ *He received a flood of letters.* Il a reçu un flot de lettres.

to **flood** VERB
see also flood NOUN
inonder ◇ *The river has flooded the village.* La rivière a inondé le village.

flooding NOUN
les *inondations* FEM PL

floor NOUN
1 le *sol* ◇ *a tiled floor* un sol carrelé
◆ **on the floor** par terre
2 l' *étage* MASC (*storey*) ◇ *the first floor* le premier étage
◆ **the ground floor** le rez-de-chaussée
◆ **on the third floor** au troisième étage

floppy disk NOUN
la *disquette*

florist NOUN
le/la *fleuriste*

flour NOUN
la *farine*

to **flow** VERB
1 *couler* (*river*)
2 *s'écouler* (*flow out*) ◇ *Water was flowing from the pipe.* De l'eau s'écoulait du tuyau.

flower NOUN
see also flower VERB
la *fleur*

to **flower** VERB
see also flower NOUN
fleurir

flown VERB *see* **fly**

flu NOUN

F

PTO

la *grippe* ◇ *She's got flu.* Elle a la grippe.

fluent ADJECTIVE
- **He speaks fluent French.** Il parle couramment le français.

flung VERB *see* **fling**

flush NOUN
see also flush VERB
la *chasse d'eau* (*of toilet*)

to **flush** VERB
see also flush NOUN
- **to flush the toilet** tirer la chasse

flute NOUN
la *flûte* ◇ *I play the flute.* Je joue de la flûte.

fly NOUN
see also fly VERB
la *mouche* (*insect*)

to **fly** VERB
see also fly NOUN
1 *voler* ◇ *The plane flies at a speed of 400 km per hour.* L'avion vole à quatre cents kilomètres à l'heure.
2 *aller en avion* (*passenger*) ◇ *He flew from Paris to New York.* Il est allé de Paris à New York en avion.
- **to fly away** s'envoler ◇ *The bird flew away.* L'oiseau s'est envolé.

foal NOUN
le *poulain*

focus NOUN
see also focus VERB
- **to be out of focus** être flou ◇ *The house is out of focus in this photo.* La maison est floue sur cette photo.

to **focus** VERB
see also focus NOUN
mettre au point ◇ *Try to focus the binoculars.* Essaye de mettre les jumelles au point.
- **to focus on something (1)** (*with camera, telescope*) régler la mise au point sur quelque chose ◇ *The cameraman focused on the bird.* Le caméraman a réglé la mise au point sur l'oiseau.
- **to focus on something (2)** (*concentrate*) se concentrer sur quelque chose ◇ *Let's focus on the plot of the play.* Concentrons-nous sur l'intrigue de la pièce.

fog NOUN
le *brouillard*

foggy ADJECTIVE
- **It's foggy.** Il y a du brouillard.
- **a foggy day** un jour de brouillard

foil NOUN (*kitchen foil*)
le *papier d'aluminium* ◇ *She wrapped the meat in foil.* Elle a enveloppé la viande dans du papier d'aluminium.

fold NOUN
see also fold VERB
le *pli*

to **fold** VERB
see also fold NOUN
plier ◇ *He folded the newspaper in half.* Il a plié le journal en deux.
- **to fold something up** plier quelque chose
- **to fold one's arms** croiser ses bras ◇ *She folded her arms.* Elle a croisé les bras.

folder NOUN
1 la *chemise* ◇ *She kept all her letters in a folder.* Elle gardait toutes ses lettres dans une chemise.
2 le *classeur* (*ring binder*)

folding ADJECTIVE
- **a folding chair** une chaise pliante
- **a folding bed** un lit pliant

to **follow** VERB
suivre ◇ *She followed him.* Elle l'a suivi. ◇ *You go first and I'll follow.* Va devant, je te suis.

following ADJECTIVE
suivant ◇ *the following day* le jour suivant

fond ADJECTIVE
- **to be fond of somebody** aimer beaucoup quelqu'un ◇ *I'm very fond of her.* Je l'aime beaucoup.

food NOUN
la *nourriture*
- **We need to buy some food.** Nous devons acheter à manger.
- **cat food** la nourriture pour chat
- **dog food** la nourriture pour chien

fool NOUN
l' *idiot* MASC
l' *idiote* FEM

foot NOUN
1 le *pied* (*of person*) ◇ *My feet are aching.* J'ai mal aux pieds.
2 la *patte* (*of animal*) ◇ *The dog's foot was injured.* Le chien était blessé à la patte.
- **on foot** à pied
3 le *pied* (*12 inches*)
In France measurements are in metres and centimetres rather than feet and inches. A foot is about 30 centimetres.
- **Dave is 6 foot tall.** Dave mesure un mètre quatre-vingt.
- **That mountain is 5000 feet high.** Cette montagne fait mille six cents mètres de haut.

football NOUN
1 le *football* (*game*) ◇ *I like playing football.* J'aime jouer au football.

2 le *ballon* (*ball*) ◇ *Paul threw the football over the fence.* Paul a envoyé le ballon par dessus la clôture.

football player NOUN
le *joueur de football*
la *joueuse de football*
◇ *He's a famous football player.* C'est un joueur de football célèbre.

footpath NOUN
le *sentier* ◇ *Jane followed the footpath through the forest.* Jane a suivi le sentier à travers la forêt.

footprint NOUN
la *trace de pas* ◇ *He saw some footprints in the sand.* Il a vu des traces de pas sur le sable.

footstep NOUN
le *pas* ◇ *I can hear footsteps on the stairs.* J'entends des pas dans l'escalier.

for PREPOSITION
There are several ways of translating for. *Scan the examples to find one that is similar to what you want to say.*
1 *pour* ◇ *a present for me* un cadeau pour moi ◇ *the train for London* le train pour Londres ◇ *He works for the government.* Il travaille pour le gouvernement. ◇ *I'll do it for you.* Je vais le faire pour toi. ◇ *Can you do it for tomorrow?* Est-ce que vous pouvez le faire pour demain? ◇ *Are you for or against the idea?* Êtes-vous pour ou contre cette idée? ◇ *Oxford is famous for its university.* Oxford est célèbre pour son université.
When referring to periods of time, use **pendant** *for the future and completed actions in the past, and* **depuis** *(with the French verb in the present tense) for something that started in the past and is still going on.*
2 *pendant* ◇ *He worked in France for two years.* Il a travaillé en France pendant deux ans. ◇ *She will be away for a month.* Elle sera absente pendant un mois. ◇ *There are road works for three kilometres.* Il y a des travaux pendant trois kilomètres.
3 *depuis* ◇ *He's been learning French for two years.* Il apprend le français depuis deux ans. ◇ *She's been away for a month.* Elle est absente depuis un mois.
When talking about amounts of money, you do not translate for.
◇ *I sold it for £5.* Je l'ai vendu cinq livres. ◇ *He paid fifty pence for his ticket.* Il a payé son billet cinquante pence.
◆ **What's the French for "lion"?** Comment dit-on "lion" en français?
◆ **It's time for lunch.** C'est l'heure du déjeuner.
◆ **What for?** Pour quoi faire? ◇ *Give me some money! – What for?* Donne-moi de l'argent! – Pour quoi faire?
◆ **What's it for?** Ça sert à quoi?
◆ **for sale** à vendre ◇ *The factory's for sale.* L'usine est en vente.

to **forbid** VERB
défendre
◆ **to forbid somebody to do something** défendre à quelqu'un de faire quelque chose ◇ *I forbid you to go out tonight!* Je te défends de sortir ce soir.

forbidden ADJECTIVE
défendu ◇ *Smoking is strictly forbidden.* Il est strictement défendu de fumer.

force NOUN
see also force VERB
la *force* ◇ *the force of the explosion* la force de l'explosion
◆ **in force** en vigueur ◇ *No-smoking rules are now in force.* Un règlement qui interdit de fumer est maintenant en vigueur.

to **force** VERB
see also force NOUN
forcer ◇ *They forced him to open the safe.* Ils l'ont obligé à ouvrir le coffre-fort.

forecast NOUN
◆ **the weather forecast** la météo

foreground NOUN
le *premier plan* ◇ *in the foreground* au premier plan

forehead NOUN
le *front*

foreign ADJECTIVE
étranger MASC
étrangère FEM

foreigner NOUN
l' *étranger* MASC
l' *étrangère* FEM

to **foresee** VERB
prévoir ◇ *He had foreseen the problem.* Il avait prévu ce problème.

forest NOUN
la *forêt*

forever ADVERB
1 *pour toujours* ◇ *He's gone forever.* Il est parti pour toujours.
2 *toujours* (*always*) ◇ *She's forever complaining.* Elle est toujours en train de se plaindre.

forgave VERB *see* **forgive**

to **forge** VERB
contrefaire ◇ *She tried to forge his signature.* Elle a essayé de contrefaire sa signature.

forged ADJECTIVE

PTO

faux MASC
fausse FEM
◇ *forged banknotes* des faux billets

to **forget** VERB
oublier ◇ *I've forgotten his name.* J'ai oublié son nom. ◇ *I'm sorry, I completely forgot!* Je suis désolé, j'ai complètement oublié!

to **forgive** VERB
- **to forgive somebody** pardonner à quelqu'un ◇ *I forgive you.* Je te pardonne.
- **to forgive somebody for doing something** pardonner à quelqu'un d'avoir fait quelque chose ◇ *She forgave him for forgetting her birthday.* Elle lui a pardonné d'avoir oublié son anniversaire.

fork NOUN
1 la *fourchette* (*for eating*)
2 la *fourche* (*for gardening*)
3 la *bifurcation* (*in road*)

form NOUN
1 le *formulaire* (*paper*) ◇ *to fill in a form* remplir un formulaire
2 la *forme* (*type*) ◇ *I'm against hunting in any form.* Je suis contre la chasse sous toutes ses formes.
- **in top form** en pleine forme
- **She's in the fourth form.** Elle est en troisième.

formal ADJECTIVE
1 (*occasion*)
officiel MASC
officielle FEM
◇ *a formal dinner* un dîner officiel
2 (*person*)
guindé
3 (*language*)
soutenu ◇ *In English, "residence" is a formal term.* En anglais, "residence" est un terme soutenu.
- **formal clothes** une tenue habillée
- **He's got no formal education.** Il n'a pas fait beaucoup d'études.

former ADJECTIVE
ancien MASC
ancienne FEM
◇ *a former pupil* un ancien élève ◇ *the former Prime Minister* l'ancien Premier ministre

fort NOUN
le *fort*

forth ADVERB
- **to go back and forth** aller et venir
- **and so forth** et ainsi de suite

fortnight NOUN
- **a fortnight** quinze jours ◇ *I'm going on holiday for a fortnight.* Je pars en vacances pendant quinze jours.

fortunate ADJECTIVE
- **to be fortunate** avoir de la chance ◇ *He was extremely fortunate to survive.* Il a eu énormément de chance de survivre.
- **It's fortunate that I remembered the map.** C'est une chance que j'aie pris la carte.

fortunately ADVERB
heureusement ◇ *Fortunately, it didn't rain.* Heureusement, il n'a pas plu.

fortune NOUN
la *fortune* ◇ *Kate earns a fortune!* Kate gagne une fortune!
- **to tell somebody's fortune** dire la bonne aventure à quelqu'un

forty NUMBER
quarante ◇ *He's forty.* Il a quarante ans.

forward ADVERB
see also forward VERB
- **to move forward** avancer

to **forward** VERB
see also forward ADVERB
faire suivre ◇ *He forwarded all Janette's letters.* Il a fait suivre toutes les lettres de Janette.

foster child NOUN
l' *enfant adoptif* MASC
l' *enfant adoptive* FEM

fought VERB *see* **fight**

foul ADJECTIVE
see also foul NOUN
infect ◇ *The weather was foul.* Le temps était infect. ◇ *What a foul smell!* Quelle odeur infecte!

foul NOUN
see also foul ADJECTIVE
la *faute* ◇ *Ferguson committed a foul.* Ferguson a fait une faute.

found VERB *see* **find**

to **found** VERB
fonder ◇ *Baden Powell founded the Scout Movement.* Baden Powell a fondé le mouvement scout.

foundations PL NOUN
les *fondations* FEM PL

fountain NOUN
la *fontaine*

fountain pen NOUN
le *stylo à encre*

four NUMBER
quatre ◇ *She's four.* Elle a quatre ans.

fourteen NUMBER
quatorze ◇ *I'm fourteen.* J'ai quatorze ans.

fourth ADJECTIVE
quatrième ◇ *the fourth floor* le

quatrième étage
- **the fourth of July** le quatre juillet

fox NOUN
le *renard*

fragile ADJECTIVE
fragile

frame NOUN
le *cadre* (*for picture*)

France NOUN
la *France*
- **in France** en France
- **to France** en France
- **He's from France.** Il est français.

frantic ADJECTIVE
- **I was going frantic.** J'étais dans tous mes états.
- **to be frantic with worry** être folle d'inquiétude

fraud NOUN
1 la *fraude* (*crime*) ◇ *He was jailed for fraud.* On l'a mis en prison pour fraude.
2 l' *imposteur* MASC (*person*) ◇ *He's not a real doctor, he's a fraud.* Ce n'est pas un vrai médecin, c'est un imposteur.

free ADJECTIVE
see also **free** VERB
1 *gratuit* (*free of charge*) ◇ *a free brochure* une brochure gratuite
2 *libre* (*not busy, not taken*) ◇ *Is this seat free?* Est-ce que cette place est libre? ◇ *Are you free after school?* Tu es libre après l'école?

free VERB
see also **free** ADJECTIVE
libérer

freedom NOUN
la *liberté*

freeze VERB
1 *geler* ◇ *The water had frozen.* L'eau avait gelé.
2 *congeler* (*food*) ◇ *She froze the rest of the raspberries.* Elle a congelé le reste des framboises.

freezer NOUN
le *congélateur*

freezing ADJECTIVE
- **It's freezing!** Il fait un froid de canard! (*informal*)
- **I'm freezing!** Je suis gelé! (*informal*)
- **3 degrees below freezing** moins trois

freight NOUN
la *cargaison* (*goods*)
- **a freight train** un train de marchandises

French ADJECTIVE
see also **French** NOUN
français ◇ *He's French.* Il est français. ◇ *She's French.* Elle est française.

French NOUN
see also **French** ADJECTIVE
le *français* (*language*) ◇ *Do you speak French?* Est-ce que tu parles français?
- **the French** (*people*) les Français

French beans PL NOUN
les *haricots verts*

French fries PL NOUN
les *frites* FEM PL

French horn NOUN
le *cor (d'harmonie)* ◇ *I play the French horn.* Je joue du cor.

French kiss NOUN
le *baiser profond*

French loaf NOUN
la *baguette*

Frenchman NOUN
le *Français*

Frenchwoman NOUN
la *Française*

frequent ADJECTIVE
fréquent ◇ *frequent showers* des averses fréquentes
- **There are frequent buses to the town centre.** Il y a beaucoup de bus pour le centre ville.

fresh ADJECTIVE
frais MASC
fraîche FEM
- **I need some fresh air.** J'ai besoin de prendre l'air.

to **freshen up** VERB
faire un brin de toilette ◇ *I'd like to go and freshen up.* Je voudrais faire un brin de toilette.

to **fret** VERB
se tracasser ◇ *Philip was fretting about his exams.* Philip se tracassait au sujet de ses examens.

Friday NOUN
le *vendredi* ◇ *on Friday* vendredi ◇ *on Fridays* le vendredi ◇ *every Friday* tous les vendredis ◇ *last Friday* vendredi dernier ◇ *next Friday* vendredi prochain

fridge NOUN
le *frigo*

fried ADJECTIVE
frit ◇ *fried vegetables* des légumes frits
- **a fried egg** un œuf sur le plat

friend NOUN
l' *ami* MASC
l' *amie* FEM

friendly ADJECTIVE
1 *gentil* MASC
gentille FEM
◇ *She's really friendly.* Elle est vraiment gentille.
2 *accueillant* ◇ *Liverpool is a very friendly city.* Liverpool est une ville très accueillante.

friendship NOUN

PTO

l' *amitié* FEM

fright NOUN
la *peur* ◇ *I got a terrible fright!* Ça m'a fait une peur terrible!

to **frighten** VERB
faire peur à ◇ *Horror films frighten him.* Les films d'horreur lui font peur.

frightened ADJECTIVE
- **to be frightened** avoir peur ◇ *I'm frightened!* J'ai peur!
- **to be frightened of something** avoir peur de quelque chose ◇ *Anna's frightened of spiders.* Anna a peur des araignées.

frightening ADJECTIVE
effrayant

fringe NOUN
la *frange* (*of hair*) ◇ *She's got a fringe.* Elle a une frange.

Frisbee ® NOUN
le *Frisbee* ® ◇ *to play Frisbee* jouer au Frisbee

fro ADVERB
- **to go to and fro** aller et venir

frog NOUN
la *grenouille*
- **frogs' legs** les cuisses de grenouille

from PREPOSITION
de ◇ *Where do you come from?* D'où venez-vous? ◇ *I come from Perth.* Je viens de Perth. ◇ *a letter from my sister* une lettre de ma sœur ◇ *The hotel is one kilometre from the beach.* L'hôtel est à un kilomètre de la plage.
- **from...to...** de...à... ◇ *He flew from London to Paris.* Il a pris l'avion de Londres à Paris. ◇ *from 1 o'clock to 2* d'une heure à deux heures ◇ *The price was reduced from £10 to £5.* Ils ont réduit le prix de dix livres à cinq.
- **from...onwards** à partir de... ◇ *We'll be at home from 7 o'clock onwards.* Nous serons chez nous à partir de sept heures.

front NOUN
see also front ADJECTIVE
le *devant* ◇ *the front of the house* le devant de la maison
- **in front** devant ◇ *a house with a car in front* une maison avec une voiture devant ◇ *the car in front* la voiture de devant
- **in front of** devant ◇ *in front of the house* devant la maison ◇ *the car in front of us* la voiture devant nous
- **in the front** (*of car*) à l'avant ◇ *I was sitting in the front.* J'étais assis à l'avant.
- **at the front of the train** à l'avant du train

front ADJECTIVE
see also front NOUN
1 *de devant* ◇ *the front row* la rangée de devant
2 *avant* ◇ *the front seats of the car* les sièges avant de la voiture
- **the front door** la porte d'entrée

frontier NOUN
la *frontière*

frost NOUN
le *gel*

frosty ADJECTIVE
- **It's frosty today.** Il gèle aujourd'hui.

to **frown** VERB
froncer les sourcils ◇ *He frowned.* Il a froncé les sourcils.

froze VERB *see* **freeze**

frozen ADJECTIVE
see also freeze
surgelé (*food*) ◇ *frozen chips* des frites surgelées

fruit NOUN
le *fruit*
- **fruit juice** le jus de fruits
- **a fruit salad** une salade de fruits

fruit machine NOUN
la *machine à sous*

frustrated ADJECTIVE
frustré

to **fry** VERB
faire frire ◇ *Fry the onions for 5 minutes.* Faites frire les oignons pendant cinq minutes.

frying pan NOUN
la *poêle*

fuel NOUN
le *carburant* (*for car, aeroplane*) ◇ *to run out of fuel* avoir une panne de carburant

to **fulfil** VERB
réaliser ◇ *Robert fulfilled his dream to visit China.* Robert a réalisé son rêve de visiter la Chine.

full ADJECTIVE, ADVERB
1 *plein* ◇ *The tank's full.* Le réservoir est plein.
2 *complet* MASC
complète FEM
◇ *He asked for full information on the job.* Il a demandé des renseignements complets sur le poste.
- **your full name** vos nom et prénoms ◇ *My full name is Ian John Marr.* Je m'appelle Ian John Marr.
- **I'm full.** (*after meal*) J'ai bien mangé.
- **at full speed** à toute vitesse ◇ *He drove at full speed.* Il conduisait à toute vitesse
- **There was a full moon.** C'était la pleine lune.

full stop NOUN
le *point*

ıll-time ADJECTIVE, ADVERB
à plein temps ◇ *She's got a full-time job.* Elle a un travail à plein temps. ◇ *She works full-time.* Elle travaille à plein temps.

ılly ADVERB
complètement ◇ *He hasn't fully recovered from his illness.* Il n'est pas complètement remis de sa maladie.

ımes PL NOUN
les *fumées* FEM PL ◇ *The factory gave out dangerous fumes.* L'usine rejetait des fumées dangereuses.
exhaust fumes les gaz d'échappement

ın ADJECTIVE
see also fun NOUN
marrant ◇ *She's a fun person.* Elle est marrante.

ın NOUN
see also fun ADJECTIVE
to have fun s'amuser ◇ *We had great fun playing in the snow.* Nous nous sommes bien amusés à jouer dans la neige.
for fun pour rire ◇ *He entered the competition just for fun.* Il a participé à la compétition juste pour rire.
to make fun of somebody se moquer de quelqu'un ◇ *They made fun of him.* Ils se sont moqués de lui.
It's fun! C'est chouette!
Have fun! Amuse-toi bien!

ınds PL NOUN
les *fonds* MASC ◇ *to raise funds* collecter des fonds

ıneral NOUN
l' *enterrement* MASC

ınfair NOUN
la *fête foraine*

ınny ADJECTIVE
1 *drôle* (*amusing*) ◇ *It was really funny.* C'était vraiment drôle.
2 *bizarre* (*strange*) ◇ *There's something funny about him.* Il est un peu bizarre.

ır NOUN
1 la *fourrure* ◇ *a fur coat* un manteau de fourrure
2 le *poil* ◇ *the dog's fur* le poil du chien

furious ADJECTIVE
furieux MASC
furieuse FEM
◇ *Dad was furious with me.* Papa était furieux contre moi.

furniture NOUN
les *meubles* MASC PL ◇ *a piece of furniture* un meuble

further ADVERB, ADJECTIVE
plus loin ◇ *London is further from Manchester than Leeds is.* Londres est plus loin de Manchester que Leeds.
➔ **How much further is it?** C'est encore loin?

further education NOUN
l' *enseignement postscolaire* MASC

fuse NOUN
le *fusible* ◇ *The fuse has blown.* Le fusible a sauté.

fuss NOUN
l' *agitation* FEM ◇ *What's all the fuss about?* Qu'est-ce que c'est que toute cette agitation?
➔ **to make a fuss** faire des histoires ◇ *He's always making a fuss about nothing.* Il fait toujours des histoires pour rien.

fussy ADJECTIVE
difficile ◇ *She is very fussy about her food.* Elle est très difficile sur la nourriture.

future NOUN
1 l' *avenir* MASC ◇ *What are your plans for the future?* Quels sont vos projets pour l'avenir?
➔ **in future** à l'avenir ◇ *Be more careful in future.* Sois plus prudent à l'avenir.
2 le *futur* (*in grammar*) ◇ *Put this sentence into the future.* Mettez cette phrase au futur.

F

G

to **gain** VERB
- **to gain weight** prendre du poids
- **to gain speed** prendre de la vitesse

gallery NOUN
le *musée* ◇ *an art gallery* un musée d'art

to **gamble** VERB
jouer ◇ *He gambled £100 at the casino.* Il a joué cent livres au casino.

gambler NOUN
le *joueur*

gambling NOUN
le *jeu* ◇ *He likes gambling.* Il aime le jeu.

game NOUN
1 le *jeu*
(les *jeux* PL)
◇ *The children were playing a game.* Les enfants jouaient à un jeu.
2 le *match* (*sport*) ◇ *a game of football* un match de football
- **a game of cards** une partie de cartes

gang NOUN
la *bande*

gangster NOUN
le *gangster*

gap NOUN
1 le *trou* ◇ *There's a gap in the hedge.* Il y a un trou dans la haie.
2 l' *intervalle* MASC ◇ *a gap of four years* un intervalle de quatre ans

garage NOUN
le *garage*

garden NOUN
le *jardin*

gardener NOUN
le *jardinier* ◇ *He's a gardener.* Il est jardinier.

gardening NOUN
le *jardinage* ◇ *Margaret loves gardening.* Margaret aime le jardinage.

gardens PL NOUN
le *jardin public* SING

garlic NOUN
l' *ail* MASC

garment NOUN
le *vêtement*

gas NOUN
le *gaz*
- **a gas cooker** une cuisinière à gaz
- **a gas cylinder** une bouteille de gaz
- **a gas fire** un radiateur à gaz
- **a gas leak** une fuite de gaz

gate NOUN
1 le *portail* (*of garden*)
2 la *barrière* (*of field*)
3 la *porte* (*at airport*)

gateau NOUN
le *gâteau à la crème*

to **gather** VERB
se rassembler (*assemble*) ◇ *People gathered in front of Buckingham Palace.* Les gens se sont rassemblés devant Buckingham Palace.
- **to gather speed** prendre de la vitesse ◇ *The train gathered speed.* Le train a pris de la vitesse.

gave VERB *see* **give**

gay ADJECTIVE
homosexuel MASC
homosexuelle FEM

to **gaze** VERB
- **to gaze at something** fixer quelque chose du regard ◇ *He gazed at her.* Il l'a fixée du regard.

gear NOUN
1 la *vitesse* (*in car*) ◇ *in first gear* en première vitesse ◇ *to change gear* changer de vitesse
2 le *matériel* ◇ *camping gear* le matériel de camping
- **your sports gear** (*clothes*) tes affaires de sport

gear lever NOUN
le *levier de vitesse*

geese PL NOUN *see* **goose**

gel NOUN
le *gel*
- **hair gel** le gel pour les cheveux

gem NOUN
la *pierre précieuse*

Gemini NOUN
les *Gémeaux* MASC PL ◇ *I'm Gemini.* Je suis Gémeaux.

general NOUN
see also general ADJECTIVE
le *général*
(les *généraux* PL)

general ADJECTIVE
see also general NOUN
général
(*généraux* MASC PL)
- **in general** en général

general election NOUN
les *élections législatives* FEM PL

general knowledge NOUN
les *connaissances générales* FEM PL

generally ADVERB
généralement ◇ *I generally go shopping on Saturday.* Généralement, je fais mes courses le samedi.

generation NOUN

la *génération* ◇ *the younger generation* la nouvelle génération

generator NOUN
le *générateur*

generous ADJECTIVE
généreux MASC
généreuse FEM
◇ *That's very generous of you.* C'est très généreux de votre part.

Geneva NOUN
Genève
- **in Geneva** à Genève
- **to Geneva** à Genève
- **Lake Geneva** le lac Léman

genius NOUN
le *génie* ◇ *She's a genius!* C'est un génie!

gentle ADJECTIVE
doux MASC
douce FEM

gentleman NOUN
le *monsieur*
(les *messieurs* PL)
◇ *Good morning, gentlemen.* Bonjour messieurs.

gently ADVERB
doucement

gents NOUN
les *toilettes pour hommes* FEM PL
◇ *Can you tell me where the gents is, please?* Pouvez-vous me dire où sont les toilettes, s'il vous plaît?
- **"gents"** (*on sign*) "messieurs"

genuine ADJECTIVE
1 *véritable* (*real*) ◇ *These are genuine diamonds.* Ce sont de véritables diamants.
2 *sincère* (*sincere*) ◇ *She's a very genuine person.* C'est quelqu'un de très sincère.

geography NOUN
la *géographie*

germ NOUN
le *microbe*

German ADJECTIVE
see also German NOUN
allemand

German NOUN
see also German ADJECTIVE
1 (*person*)
l' *Allemand* MASC
l' *Allemande* FEM
2 (*language*)
l' *allemand* ◇ *Do you speak German?* Parlez-vous allemand?

Germany NOUN
l' *Allemagne* FEM
- **in Germany** en Allemagne
- **to Germany** en Allemagne

to get VERB
There are several ways of translating get. *Scan the examples to find one that is similar to what you want to say.*
1 *avoir* (*have, receive*) ◇ *I got lots of presents.* J'ai eu beaucoup de cadeaux. ◇ *He got first prize.* Il a eu le premier prix. ◇ *Jackie got good exam results.* Jackie a eu de bons résultats aux examens. ◇ *How many have you got?* Combien en avez-vous?
2 *aller chercher* (*fetch*) ◇ *Quick, get help!* Allez vite chercher de l'aide!
3 *attraper* (*catch*) ◇ *They've got the thief.* Ils ont attrapé le voleur.
4 *prendre* (*train, bus*) ◇ *I'm getting the bus into town.* Je prends le bus pour aller en ville.
5 *comprendre* (*understand*) ◇ *I don't get the joke.* Je ne comprends pas cette blague.
6 *aller* (*go*) ◇ *How do you get to the castle?* Comment est-ce qu'on va au château?
7 *arriver* (*arrive*) ◇ *He should get here soon.* Il devrait arriver bientôt.
8 *devenir* (*become*) ◇ *to get old* devenir vieux
- **to get something done** faire faire quelque chose ◇ *to get one's hair cut* se faire couper les cheveux
- **to get something for somebody** trouver quelque chose pour quelqu'un ◇ *The librarian got the book for me.* Le bibliothécaire m'a trouvé le livre.
- **to have got to do something** devoir faire quelque chose ◇ *I've got to tell him.* Je dois le lui dire.
- **to get back (1)** rentrer ◇ *What time did you get back?* Tu es rentré à quelle heure?
- **to get back (2)** récupérer ◇ *He got his money back.* Il a récupéré son argent.
- **to get in** rentrer ◇ *What time did you get in last night?* Tu es rentré à quelle heure hier soir?
- **to get into** monter dans ◇ *Sharon got into the car.* Sharon est montée dans la voiture.
- **to get off** descendre de (*vehicle, bike*) ◇ *Isobel got off the train.* Isobel est descendue du train.
- **to get on (1)** (*vehicle*) monter dans ◇ *Phyllis got on the bus.* Phyllis est montée dans le bus.
- **to get on (2)** (*bike*) enfourcher ◇ *Carol got on her bike.* Carol a enfourché son vélo.
- **to get on with somebody** s'entendre

PTO

avec quelqu'un ◇ *He doesn't get on with his parents.* Il ne s'entend pas avec ses parents. ◇ *We got on really well.* Nous nous sommes très bien entendus.

- **to get out** sortir ◇ *Hélène got out of the car.* Hélène est sortie de la voiture. ◇ *Get out!* Sortez!
- **to get something out** sortir quelque chose ◇ *She got the map out.* Elle a sorti la carte.
- **to get up** se lever ◇ *What time do you get up?* Tu te lèves à quelle heure?

ghetto blaster NOUN
le *radiocassette portable*

ghost NOUN
le *fantôme*

giant ADJECTIVE
see also giant NOUN
énorme ◇ *They ate a giant meal.* Ils ont mangé un énorme repas.

giant NOUN
see also giant ADJECTIVE
le *géant*
la *géante*

gift NOUN
1 (*present*)
le *cadeau*
(les *cadeaux* PL)
2 (*talent*)
le *don*

- **to have a gift for something** être doué pour quelque chose ◇ *Dave has a gift for painting.* Dave est doué pour la peinture.

gifted ADJECTIVE
doué ◇ *Janice is a gifted dancer.* Janice est douée pour la danse.

gift shop NOUN
la *boutique de cadeaux*

gigantic ADJECTIVE
gigantesque

gin NOUN
le *gin*

ginger NOUN
see also ginger ADJECTIVE
le *gingembre* ◇ *Add a teaspoon of ginger.* Ajoutez une cuillère à café de gingembre.

ginger ADJECTIVE
see also ginger NOUN
roux MASC
rousse FEM
◇ *Chris has ginger hair.* Chris a les cheveux roux.

giraffe NOUN
la *girafe*

girl NOUN
1 la *fille* ◇ *They've got a girl and two boys.* Ils ont une fille et deux garçons.
2 la *petite fille* (*young*) ◇ *a five-year-old girl* une petite fille de cinq ans
3 la *jeune fille* (*older*) ◇ *a sixteen-year-old girl* une jeune fille de seize ans ◇ *an English girl* une jeune Anglaise

girlfriend NOUN
1 la *copine* (*lover*) ◇ *Damon's girlfriend is called Justine.* La copine de Damon s'appelle Justine.
2 l' *amie* FEM (*friend*) ◇ *She often went out with her girlfriends.* Elle sortait souvent avec ses amies.

to **give** VERB
donner

- **to give something to somebody** donner quelque chose à quelqu'un ◇ *He gave me £10.* Il m'a donné dix livres.
- **to give something back to somebody** rendre quelque chose à quelqu'un ◇ *I gave the book back to him.* Je lui ai rendu le livre.
- **to give something out** distribuer quelque chose ◇ *The teacher gave out the books.* Le professeur a distribué les livres.
- **to give in** céder ◇ *His Mum gave in and let him go out.* Sa mère a cédé et l'a laissé sortir.
- **to give up** laisser tomber ◇ *I couldn't do it, so I gave up.* Je n'arrivais pas à le faire, alors j'ai laissé tomber.
- **to give up doing something** arrêter de faire quelque chose ◇ *He gave up smoking.* Il a arrêté de fumer.
- **to give oneself up** se rendre ◇ *The thief gave himself up.* Le voleur s'est rendu.
- **to give way** céder la priorité (*in traffic*)

glad ADJECTIVE
content ◇ *She's glad she's done it.* Elle est contente de l'avoir fait.

to **glance** VERB
see also glance NOUN

- **to glance at something** jeter un coup d'œil à quelque chose ◇ *Peter glanced at his watch.* Peter a jeté un coup d'œil à sa montre.

glance NOUN
see also glance VERB
le *coup d'œil* ◇ *at first glance* au premier coup d'œil

to **glare** VERB

- **to glare at somebody** lancer un regard furieux à quelqu'un ◇ *He glared at me.* Il m'a lancé un regard furieux.

glaring ADJECTIVE

- **a glaring mistake** une erreur qui saute

aux yeux

glass NOUN
le *verre* ◇ *a glass of milk* un verre de lait

glasses PL NOUN
les *lunettes* FEM ◇ *Jean-Pierre wears glasses.* Jean-Pierre porte des lunettes.

glider NOUN
le *planeur*

gliding NOUN
le *vol à voile* ◇ *My hobby is gliding.* Je fais du vol à voile.

global ADJECTIVE
mondial
(*mondiaux* MASC PL)
◆ **on a global scale** à l'échelle mondiale

global warming NOUN
le *réchauffement de la planète*

globe NOUN
le *globe*

glove NOUN
le *gant*

glove compartment NOUN
la *boîte à gants*

glue NOUN
la *colle*

go NOUN
see also **go** VERB
◆ **to have a go at doing something** essayer de faire quelque chose ◇ *He had a go at making a cake.* Il a essayé de faire un gâteau.
◆ **Whose go is it?** À qui le tour?

go VERB
see also **go** NOUN
1 *aller* ◇ *I'm going to the cinema tonight.* Je vais au cinéma ce soir.
2 *partir* (*leave*) ◇ *Where's Pierre?–He's gone.* Où est Pierre?–Il est parti.
3 *s'en aller* (*go away*) ◇ *I'm going now.* Je m'en vais.
4 *marcher* (*vehicle*) ◇ *My car won't go.* Ma voiture ne marche pas.
◆ **to go home** rentrer à la maison ◇ *I go home at about 4 o'clock.* Je rentre à la maison vers quatre heures.
◆ **to go for a walk** aller se promener ◇ *Shall we go for a walk?* Si on allait se promener?
◆ **How did it go?** Comment est-ce que ça s'est passé?
◆ **I'm going to do it tomorrow.** Je vais le faire demain.
◆ **It's going to be difficult.** Ça va être difficile.

go after VERB
suivre ◇ *Quick, go after them!* Vite, suivez-les!

to **go away** VERB
s'en aller ◇ *Go away!* Allez-vous-en!

to **go back** VERB
Use **rentrer** *only when you are entering a building, usually your home; otherwise use* **retourner**.
1 *retourner* ◇ *We went back to the same place.* Nous sommes retournés au même endroit.
2 *rentrer* ◇ *Is he still here?–No, he's gone back home.* Est-ce qu'il est encore là?–Non, il est rentré chez lui.

to **go by** VERB
passer ◇ *Two policemen went by.* Deux policiers sont passés.

to **go down** VERB
1 *descendre* (*person*) ◇ *to go down the stairs* descendre l'escalier
2 *baisser* (*decrease*) ◇ *The price of computers has gone down.* Le prix des ordinateurs a baissé.
3 *se dégonfler* (*deflate*) ◇ *My airbed kept going down.* Mon matelas pneumatique se dégonflait constamment.
◆ **My brother's gone down with flu.** Mon frère a attrapé la grippe.

to **go for** VERB
attaquer (*attack*) ◇ *Suddenly the dog went for me.* Soudain, le chien m'a attaqué.
◆ **Go for it!** (*go on!*) Vas-y, fonce!

to **go in** VERB
entrer ◇ *He knocked on the door and went in.* Il a frappé à la porte et il est entré.

to **go off** VERB
1 *exploser* (*bomb*) ◇ *The bomb went off.* La bombe a explosé.
2 *se déclencher* (*alarm, gun*) ◇ *The fire alarm went off.* L'avertisseur d'incendie s'est déclenché.
3 *sonner* (*alarm clock*) ◇ *My alarm clock goes off at seven every morning.* Mon réveil sonne à sept heures tous les matins.
4 *tourner* (*food*) ◇ *The milk's gone off.* Le lait a tourné.
5 *partir* (*go away*) ◇ *He went off in a huff.* Il est parti de mauvaise humeur.

to **go on** VERB
1 *se passer* (*happen*) ◇ *What's going on?* Qu'est-ce qui se passe?
2 *continuer* (*carry on*) ◇ *The concert went on until 11 o'clock at night.* Le concert a continué jusqu'à onze heures du soir.
◆ **to go on doing something** continuer à faire quelque chose ◇ *He went on*

PTO

reading. Il a continué à lire.

- **to go on at somebody** être sur le dos de quelqu'un ◇ *My parents always go on at me.* Mes parents sont toujours sur mon dos.
- **Go on!** Allez! ◇ *Go on, tell me what the problem is!* Allez, dis-moi quel est le problème!

to **go out** VERB

1 *sortir* (*person*) ◇ *Are you going out tonight?* Tu sors ce soir?

- **to go out with somebody** sortir avec quelqu'un ◇ *Are you going out with him?* Est-ce que tu sors avec lui?

2 *s'éteindre* (*light, fire, candle*) ◇ *Suddenly the lights went out.* Soudain, les lumières se sont éteintes.

to **go past** VERB

- **to go past something** passer devant quelque chose ◇ *He went past the shop.* Il est passé devant la boutique.

to **go round** VERB

- **to go round a corner** prendre un tournant
- **to go round to somebody's house** aller chez quelqu'un
- **to go round a museum** visiter un musée
- **to go round the shops** faire les boutiques
- **There's a bug going round.** Il y a un microbe qui circule.

to **go through** VERB

traverser ◇ *We went through Paris to get to Rennes.* Nous avons traversé Paris pour aller à Rennes.

to **go up** VERB

1 *monter* (*person*) ◇ *to go up the stairs* monter l'escalier

2 *augmenter* (*increase*) ◇ *The price has gone up.* Le prix a augmenté.

- **to go up in flames** s'embraser ◇ *The whole factory went up in flames.* L'usine toute entière s'est embrasée.

to **go with** VERB

aller avec ◇ *Does this blouse go with that skirt?* Est-ce que ce chemisier va avec cette jupe?

goal NOUN

le *but* ◇ *to score a goal* marquer un but ◇ *His goal is to become the world champion.* Son but est de devenir champion du monde.

goalkeeper NOUN

le *gardien de but*

goat NOUN

la *chèvre*

- **goat's cheese** le fromage de chèvre

god NOUN

le *dieu*

(les *dieux* PL)

◇ *I believe in God.* Je crois en Dieu.

gold NOUN

l'*or* MASC ◇ *They found some gold.* Ils ont trouvé de l'or. ◇ *a gold necklace* un collier en or

goldfish NOUN

le *poisson rouge* ◇ *I've got five goldfish.* J'ai cinq poissons rouges.

golf NOUN

le *golf* ◇ *My dad plays golf.* Mon père joue au golf.

- **a golf club** un club de golf

golf course NOUN

le *terrain de golf*

gone VERB *see* **go**

good ADJECTIVE

1 *bon* MASC

bonne FEM

◇ *It's a very good film.* C'est un très bon film. ◇ *Vegetables are good for you.* Les légumes sont bons pour la santé.

- **to be good at something** être bon en quelque chose ◇ *Jane's very good at maths.* Jane est très bonne en maths.

2 (*kind*)

gentil MASC

gentille FEM

◇ *They were very good to me.* Ils ont été très gentils avec moi. ◇ *That's very good of you.* C'est très gentil de votre part.

3 (*not naughty*)

sage ◇ *Be good!* Sois sage!

- **for good** pour de bon ◇ *One day he left for good.* Un jour il est parti pour de bon.
- **Good morning!** Bonjour!
- **Good afternoon!** Bonjour!
- **Good evening!** Bonsoir!
- **Good night!** Bonne nuit!
- **It's no good complaining.** Cela ne sert à rien de se plaindre.

goodbye EXCLAMATION

au revoir!

Good Friday NOUN

le *Vendredi saint*

good-looking ADJECTIVE

beau MASC

belle FEM

(*beaux* MASC PL)

◇ *He's very good-looking.* Il est très beau.

goods PL NOUN

les *marchandises* FEM (*in shop*)

- **a goods train** un train de marchandises

goose NOUN

l'*oie* FEM

gorgeous ADJECTIVE

1 *superbe* ◇ *She's gorgeous!* Elle est superbe!

2 *splendide* ◇ *The weather was gorgeous.* Il a fait un temps splendide.

gorilla NOUN
le *gorille*

gossip NOUN
see also gossip VERB
1 les *cancans* MASC PL (*rumours*) ◇ *Tell me the gossip!* Raconte-moi les cancans!
2 la *commère* (*woman*) ◇ *She's such a gossip!* C'est une vraie commère!
3 le *bavard* (*man*) ◇ *What a gossip!* Quel bavard!

gossip VERB
see also gossip NOUN
1 *bavarder* (*chat*) ◇ *They were always gossiping.* Elles étaient tout le temps en train de bavarder.
2 *faire des commérages* (*about somebody*) ◇ *They gossiped about her.* Elles faisaient des commérages à son sujet.

got VERB *see* **get**

government NOUN
le *gouvernement*

grab VERB
saisir

graceful ADJECTIVE
élégant

grade NOUN
la *note* (*at school*) ◇ *He got good grades in his exams.* Il a eu de bonnes notes à ses examens.

gradual ADJECTIVE
progressif MASC
progressive FEM

gradually ADVERB
peu à peu ◇ *We gradually got used to it.* Nous nous y sommes habitués peu à peu.

graduate NOUN
le *diplômé*
la *diplômée*

graffiti PL NOUN
les *graffiti* MASC

grain NOUN
le *grain*

gram NOUN
le *gramme*

grammar NOUN
la *grammaire*

grammar school NOUN
1 le *collège*
2 le *lycée*

In France pupils go to a collège *between the ages of 11 and 15, and then to a* lycée *until the age of 18. French schools are mostly non-selective.*

grammatical ADJECTIVE
grammatical
(*grammaticaux* MASC PL)

gramme NOUN
le *gramme* ◇ *500 grammes of cheese* cinq cents grammes de fromage

grand ADJECTIVE
somptueux MASC
somptueuse FEM
◇ *Samantha lives in a very grand house.* Samantha habite une maison somptueuse.

grandchildren PL NOUN
les *petits-enfants* MASC PL

granddad NOUN
le *papi* ◇ *my granddad* mon papi

granddaughter NOUN
la *petite-fille*
(les *petites-filles* PL)

grandfather NOUN
le *grand-père*
(les *grands-pères* PL)
◇ *my grandfather* mon grand-père

grandma NOUN
la *mamie* ◇ *my grandma* ma mamie

grandmother NOUN
la *grand-mère*
(les *grands-mères* PL)
◇ *my grandmother* ma grand-mère

grandpa NOUN
le *papi* ◇ *my grandpa* mon papi

grandparents PL NOUN
les *grands-parents* MASC PL ◇ *my grandparents* mes grands-parents

grandson NOUN
le *petit-fils*
(les *petits-fils* PL)

granny NOUN
la *mamie* ◇ *my granny* ma mamie

grape NOUN
le *raisin*

grapefruit NOUN
le *pamplemousse*

graph NOUN
le *graphique*

to **grasp** VERB
saisir

grass NOUN
l' *herbe* FEM ◇ *The grass is long.* L'herbe est haute.
◆ **to cut the grass** tondre le gazon

grasshopper NOUN
la *sauterelle*

to **grate** VERB
râper ◇ *to grate some cheese* râper du fromage

grateful ADJECTIVE
reconnaissant

grave NOUN
la *tombe*

gravel NOUN
le *gravier*

G

graveyard NOUN
le *cimetière*

gravy NOUN
la *sauce au jus de viande*

grease NOUN
le *lubrifiant*

greasy ADJECTIVE
gras MASC
grasse FEM
◇ *He has greasy hair.* Il a les cheveux gras. ◇ *The food was very greasy.* La nourriture était très grasse.

great ADJECTIVE
1 *génial*
(*géniaux* MASC PL)
◇ *That's great!* C'est génial!
2 *grand* ◇ *a great mansion* un grand manoir

Great Britain NOUN
la *Grande-Bretagne*
➔ **in Great Britain** en Grande-Bretagne
➔ **to Great Britain** en Grande-Bretagne
➔ **I'm from Great Britain.** Je suis britannique.

great-grandfather NOUN
l' *arrière-grand-père* MASC
(les *arrière-grands-pères* PL)

great-grandmother NOUN
l' *arrière-grand-mère* FEM
(les *arrière-grands-mères* PL)

Greece NOUN
la *Grèce*
➔ **in Greece** en Grèce
➔ **to Greece** en Grèce

greedy ADJECTIVE
1 *gourmand* (*for food*) ◇ *I want some more cake.* – *Don't be so greedy!* Je veux encore du gâteau. – Ne sois pas si gourmand!
2 *avide* (*for money*)

Greek ADJECTIVE
see also Greek NOUN
grec MASC
grecque FEM
◇ *Dionysis is Greek.* Dionysis est grec.
◇ *She's Greek.* Elle est grecque.

Greek NOUN
see also Greek ADJECTIVE
1 (*person*)
le *Grec*
la *Grecque*
2 (*language*)
le *grec*

green ADJECTIVE
see also green NOUN
1 *vert* ◇ *a green car* une voiture verte ◇ *a green salad* une salade verte
2 *écologiste* (*movement, candidate*) ◇ *the Green Party* le parti écologiste

green NOUN
see also green ADJECTIVE
le *vert* ◇ *a dark green* un vert foncé
➔ **greens** (*vegetables*) les légumes verts
➔ **the Greens** (*party*) les Verts MASC

greengrocer's NOUN
le *marchand de fruits et légumes*

greenhouse NOUN
la *serre*
➔ **the greenhouse effect** l'effet de serre MASC

Greenland NOUN
le *Groenland*

to **greet** VERB
accueillir ◇ *He greeted me with a kiss.* Il m'a accueillie en me donnant un baiser.

greeting NOUN
➔ **Greetings from Bangor!** Bonjour de Bangor!

greetings card NOUN
la *carte de vœux*

grew VERB *see* **grow**

grey ADJECTIVE
gris ◇ *She's got grey hair.* Elle a les cheveux gris.
➔ **He's going grey.** Il grisonne.

grey-haired ADJECTIVE
grisonnant

grid NOUN
1 (*in road*)
la *grille*
2 (*of electricity*)
le *réseau*
(les *réseaux* PL)

grief NOUN
le *chagrin*

grill NOUN
see also grill VERB
le *gril* (*of cooker*)
➔ **a mixed grill** les grillades FEM PL

to **grill** VERB
see also grill NOUN
➔ **to grill something** faire griller quelque chose

grim ADJECTIVE
sinistre

to **grin** VERB
see also grin NOUN
sourire ◇ *Dave grinned at me.* Dave m'a souri.

grin NOUN
see also grin VERB
le *large sourire*

to **grind** VERB
moudre (*coffee, pepper*)

to **grip** VERB
saisir

gripping ADJECTIVE

palpitant (*exciting*)

it NOUN
le *gravillon*

oan VERB
see also groan NOUN
gémir ◇ *He groaned with pain.* Il a gémi sous l'effet de la douleur.

oan NOUN
see also groan VERB
le *gémissement* (*of pain*)

ocer NOUN
l' *épicier* MASC ◇ *He's a grocer.* Il est épicier.

oceries PL NOUN
les *provisions* FEM

ocer's (shop) NOUN
l' *épicerie* FEM

oom NOUN
le *marié* (*bridegroom*) ◇ *the groom and his best man* le marié et son témoin

ope VERB
to grope for something chercher quelque chose à tâtons ◇ *He groped for the light switch.* Il a cherché à tâtons l'interrupteur.

oss ADJECTIVE
dégoûtant (*revolting*) ◇ *It was really gross!* C'était vraiment dégoûtant!

ossly ADVERB
largement ◇ *We're grossly underpaid.* Nous sommes largement sous-payés.

ound NOUN
see also ground VERB
1 le *sol* (*earth*) ◇ *The ground's wet.* Le sol est mouillé.
2 le *terrain* (*for sport*) ◇ *a football ground* un terrain de football
3 la *raison* (*reason*) ◇ *We've got grounds for complaint.* Nous avons des raisons de nous plaindre.
on the ground par terre ◇ *We sat on the ground.* Nous nous sommes assis par terre.

round VERB *see* **grind**
see also ground NOUN
ground coffee le café moulu

roup NOUN
le *groupe*

row VERB
1 *pousser* (*plant*) ◇ *Grass grows quickly.* L'herbe pousse vite.
2 *grandir* (*person, animal*) ◇ *Haven't you grown!* Comme tu as grandi!
3 *augmenter* (*increase*) ◇ *The number of unemployed people has grown.* Le nombre de chômeurs a augmenté.
4 *faire pousser* (*cultivate*) ◇ *My Dad grows potatoes.* Mon père fait pousser des pommes de terre.
- **to grow a beard** se laisser pousser la barbe
- **to grow up** grandir ◇ *Oh, grow up!* Ne fais pas l'enfant!
- **He's grown out of his jacket.** Sa veste est devenue trop petite pour lui.

to **growl** VERB
grogner

grown VERB *see* **grow**

growth NOUN
la *croissance* ◇ *economic growth* la croissance économique

grub NOUN
la *bouffe* (*informal*)

grudge NOUN
la *rancune*
- **to bear a grudge against somebody** garder rancune à quelqu'un

gruesome ADJECTIVE
horrible

guarantee NOUN
see also guarantee VERB
la *garantie*
- **a five-year guarantee** une garantie de cinq ans

to **guarantee** VERB
see also guarantee NOUN
garantir ◇ *I can't guarantee he'll come.* Je ne peux pas garantir qu'il viendra.

to **guard** VERB
see also guard NOUN
garder ◇ *They guarded the palace.* Ils gardaient le palais.
- **to guard against something** protéger contre quelque chose

guard NOUN
see also guard VERB
le *chef de train* (*of train*)
- **a security guard** un vigile
- **a guard dog** un chien de garde

to **guess** VERB
see also guess NOUN
deviner ◇ *Can you guess what it is?* Devine ce que c'est!
- **to guess wrong** se tromper ◇ *Janice guessed wrong.* Janice s'est trompée.

guess NOUN
see also guess VERB
la *supposition* ◇ *It's just a guess.* C'est une simple supposition.
- **Have a guess!** Devine!

guest NOUN
1 l' *invité* MASC
l' *invitée* FEM
◇ *We have guests staying with us.* Nous avons des invités.
2 (*of hotel*)
le *client*
la *cliente*

G

guide NOUN
1 le *guide* (*book, person*) ◇ *We bought a guide to Paris.* Nous avons acheté un guide sur Paris. ◇ *The guide showed us round the castle.* Le guide nous a fait visiter le château.
2 l' *éclaireuse* FEM (*girl guide*)
◆ **the Guides** les Éclaireuses

guidebook NOUN
le *guide*

guide dog NOUN
le *chien d'aveugle*

guilty ADJECTIVE
coupable ◇ *to feel guilty* se sentir coupable ◇ *She was found guilty.* Elle a été reconnue coupable.

guinea pig NOUN
le *cobaye*

guitar NOUN
la *guitare* ◇ *I play the guitar.* Je joue de la guitare.

gum NOUN
le *chewing-gum* (*sweet*)
◆ **gums** (*in mouth*) les gencives FEM

gun NOUN
1 le *revolver* (*small*)
2 le *fusil* (*rifle*)

gust NOUN
◆ **a gust of wind** une rafale de vent

guy NOUN
le *type* ◇ *Who's that guy?* C'est qui ce type? ◇ *He's a nice guy.* C'est un type sympa.

gym NOUN
la *gym* ◇ *I go to the gym every day.* Je vais tous les jours à la gym.
◆ **gym classes** les cours de gym

gymnast NOUN
le/la *gymnaste* ◇ *She's a gymnast.* Elle est gymnaste.

gymnastics NOUN
la *gymnastique* ◇ *to do gymnastics* faire de la gymnastique

H

abit NOUN
l' *habitude* ◇ *a bad habit* une mauvaise habitude

ad VERB *see* **have**

adn't = **had not**

ail NOUN
see also **hail** VERB
la *grêle*

ail VERB
see also **hail** NOUN
grêler ◇ *It's hailing.* Il grêle.

air NOUN
1 les *cheveux* MASC PL ◇ *She's got long hair.* Elle a les cheveux longs. ◇ *He's got black hair.* Il a les cheveux noirs. ◇ *He's losing his hair.* Il perd ses cheveux.
to brush one's hair se brosser les cheveux ◇ *I brush my hair every morning.* Je me brosse les cheveux tous les matins.
to wash one's hair se laver les cheveux ◇ *I need to wash my hair.* Il faut que je me lave les cheveux.
to have one's hair cut se faire couper les cheveux ◇ *I've just had my hair cut.* Je viens de me faire couper les cheveux.
a hair (1) (*from head*) un cheveu
a hair (2) (*from body*) un poil
2 le *pelage* (*fur of animal*)

airbrush NOUN
la *brosse à cheveux*

aircut NOUN
la *coupe*
to have a haircut se faire couper les cheveux ◇ *I've just had a haircut.* Je viens de me faire couper les cheveux.

airdresser NOUN
le *coiffeur*
la *coiffeuse*
◇ *He's a hairdresser.* Il est coiffeur.

airdresser's NOUN
le *coiffeur* ◇ *at the hairdresser's* chez le coiffeur

air dryer NOUN
le *sèche-cheveux*
(les *sèche-cheveux* PL)

air gel NOUN
le *gel pour les cheveux*

airgrip NOUN
la *pince à cheveux*

air spray NOUN
la *laque*

airstyle NOUN
la *coiffure*

airy ADJECTIVE
poilu ◇ *He's got hairy legs.* Il a les jambes poilues.

half NOUN
see also **half** ADJECTIVE
1 la *moitié* ◇ *half of the cake* la moitié du gâteau
2 le *billet demi-tarif* (*ticket*) ◇ *A half to York, please.* Un billet demi-tarif pour York, s'il vous plaît.
◆ **two and a half** deux et demi
◆ **half an hour** une demi-heure
◆ **half past ten** dix heures et demie
◆ **half a kilo** cinq cents grammes
◆ **to cut something in half** couper quelque chose en deux

half ADJECTIVE, ADVERB
see also **half** NOUN
1 *demi* ◇ *a half chicken* un demi-poulet
2 *à moitié* ◇ *He was half asleep.* Il était à moitié endormi.

half-hour NOUN
la *demi-heure*

half-price ADJECTIVE, ADVERB
◆ **at half-price** à moitié prix

half-time NOUN
la *mi-temps*

halfway ADVERB
1 *à mi-chemin* ◇ *halfway between Oxford and London* à mi-chemin entre Oxford et Londres
2 *à la moitié* ◇ *halfway through the chapter* à la moitié du chapitre

hall NOUN
1 l' *entrée* FEM (*in house*)
2 la *salle* ◇ *the village hall* la salle des fêtes

Hallowe'en NOUN
la *veille de la Toussaint*

hallway NOUN
le *vestibule*

halt NOUN
◆ **to come to a halt** s'arrêter

ham NOUN
le *jambon*
◆ **a ham sandwich** un sandwich au jambon

hamburger NOUN
le *hamburger*

hammer NOUN
le *marteau*
(les *marteaux* PL)

hamster NOUN
le *hamster*

hand NOUN
see also **hand** VERB
1 la *main* (*of person*)

PTO

- **to give somebody a hand** donner un coup de main à quelqu'un ◇ *Can you give me a hand?* Tu peux me donner un coup de main?
- **on the one hand..., on the other hand...** d'une part..., d'autre part...

2 l' *aiguille* FEM (*of clock*)

to **hand** VERB

see also hand NOUN

passer ◇ *He handed me the book.* Il m'a passé le livre.

- **to hand something in** rendre quelque chose ◇ *Martin handed his exam paper in.* Martin a rendu sa copie d'examen.
- **to hand something out** distribuer quelque chose ◇ *The teacher handed out the books.* Le professeur a distribué les livres.
- **to hand something over** remettre quelque chose ◇ *She handed the keys over to me.* Elle m'a remis les clés.

handbag NOUN
le *sac à main*
(les *sacs à main* PL)

handbook NOUN
le *manuel*

handcuffs PL NOUN
les *menottes* FEM

handkerchief NOUN
le *mouchoir*

handle NOUN

see also handle VERB

1 la *poignée* (*of door*)
2 l' *anse* FEM (*of cup*)
3 le *manche* (*of knife*)
4 la *queue* (*of saucepan*)

to **handle** VERB

see also handle NOUN

- **He handled it well.** Il s'en est bien tiré.
- **Kath handled the travel arrangements.** Kath s'est occupée de l'organisation du voyage.
- **She's good at handling children.** Elle sait s'y prendre bien avec les enfants.

handlebars PL NOUN
le *guidon* SING

handmade ADJECTIVE
fait à la main

handsome ADJECTIVE
beau MASC
belle FEM
◇ *He's very handsome.* Il est très beau.

handwriting NOUN
l' *écriture* FEM

handy ADJECTIVE

1 *pratique* ◇ *This knife's very handy.* Ce couteau est très pratique.
2 *sous la main* ◇ *Have you got a pen handy?* Est-ce que tu as un stylo sous la main?

to **hang** VERB

1 *accrocher* ◇ *Mike hung the painting on the wall.* Mike a accroché le tableau au mur.
2 *pendre* ◇ *They hanged the criminal.* Ils ont pendu le criminel.

- **to hang around** traîner ◇ *On Saturdays we hang around in the park.* Le samedi nous traînons dans le parc.
- **to hang on** patienter ◇ *Hang on a minute please.* Patientez une minute s'il vous plaît.
- **to hang up (1)** (*clothes*) accrocher ◇ *Hang your jacket up on the hook.* Accrochez votre veste au portemanteau.
- **to hang up (2)** (*phone*) raccrocher ◇ *I tried to phone him but he hung up on me.* J'ai essayé de l'appeler, mais il m'a raccroché au nez.

hang-gliding NOUN
le *deltaplane*

- **to go hang-gliding** faire du deltaplane

hangover NOUN
la *gueule de bois* ◇ *to have a hangover* avoir la gueule de bois

to **happen** VERB

se passer ◇ *What's happened?* Qu'est-ce qui s'est passé?

- **as it happens** justement ◇ *As it happens, I don't want to go.* Justement, je ne veux pas y aller.

happily ADVERB

1 *joyeusement* ◇ *"Don't worry!" he said happily.* "Ne te fais pas de souci!" dit-il joyeusement.
2 *heureusement* (*fortunately*) ◇ *Happily, everything went well.* Heureusement, tout s'est bien passé.

happiness NOUN
le *bonheur*

happy ADJECTIVE
heureux MASC
heureuse FEM
◇ *Janet looks happy.* Janet a l'air heureuse.

- **I'm very happy with your work.** Je suis très satisfait de ton travail.
- **Happy birthday!** Bon anniversaire!

harbour NOUN
le *port*

hard ADJECTIVE, ADVERB

1 *dur* ◇ *This cheese is very hard.* Ce fromage est très dur. ◇ *He's worked very hard.* Il a travaillé très dur.
2 *difficile* ◇ *This question's too hard for me.* Cette question est trop difficile pour moi.

hard disk NOUN

le *disque dur* (*of computer*)

hardly ADVERB
- **I've hardly got any money.** Je n'ai presque pas d'argent.
- **I hardly know you.** Je te connais à peine.
- **hardly ever** presque jamais

hard up ADJECTIVE
fauché

hare NOUN
le *lièvre*

harm VERB
- **to harm somebody** faire du mal à quelqu'un ◇ *I didn't mean to harm you.* Je ne voulais pas te faire de mal.
- **to harm something** nuire à quelque chose ◇ *Chemicals harm the environment.* Les produits chimiques nuisent à l'environnement.

harmful ADJECTIVE
nuisible ◇ *harmful chemicals* des produits chimiques nuisibles

harmless ADJECTIVE
inoffensif MASC
inoffensive FEM
◇ *Most spiders are harmless.* La plupart des araignées sont inoffensives.

has VERB *see* **have**

hasn't = **has not**

hat NOUN
le *chapeau*
(les *chapeaux* PL)

hate VERB
détester ◇ *I hate maths.* Je déteste les maths.

hatred NOUN
la *haine*

have VERB
1 *avoir* ◇ *Have you got a sister?* Tu as une sœur? ◇ *He's got blue eyes.* Il a les yeux bleus. ◇ *I've got a cold.* J'ai un rhume. ◇ *He's done it, hasn't he?* Il l'a fait, non? ◇ *Have you got any money?–No, I haven't!* Est-ce que tu as de l'argent?–Non, je n'en ai pas!

The perfect tense of some verbs is formed with **être**.

2 *être* ◇ *They have arrived.* Ils sont arrivés. ◇ *Has he gone?* Est-ce qu'il est parti?

3 *prendre* ◇ *He had his breakfast.* Il a pris son petit déjeuner. ◇ *to have a shower* prendre une douche
- **to have got to do something** devoir faire quelque chose ◇ *She's got to do it.* Elle doit le faire.
- **to have a party** faire une fête
- **to have one's hair cut** se faire couper les cheveux

haven't = **have not**

hay NOUN
le *foin*

hay fever NOUN
le *rhume des foins* ◇ *Do you get hay fever?* Est-ce que vous êtes sujet au rhume des foins?

hazelnut NOUN
la *noisette*

he PRONOUN
il ◇ *He loves dogs.* Il aime les chiens.

head NOUN
see also **head** VERB
1 (*of person*)
la *tête* ◇ *The wine went to my head.* Le vin m'est monté à la tête.
2 (*of private or primary school*)
le *directeur*
la *directrice*
3 (*of state secondary school*)
le *proviseur*
4 (*leader*)
le *chef* ◇ *a head of state* un chef d'État
- **to have a head for figures** être doué pour les chiffres
- **Heads or tails?–Heads.** Pile ou face?–Face.

to **head** VERB
see also **head** NOUN
- **to head for something** se diriger vers quelque chose ◇ *They headed for the church.* Ils se sont dirigés vers l'église.

headache NOUN
- **I've got a headache.** J'ai mal à la tête.

headlight NOUN
le *phare*

headline NOUN
le *titre*

headmaster NOUN
1 le *directeur* (*of private or primary school*)
2 le *proviseur* (*of state secondary school*)

headmistress NOUN
1 la *directrice* (*of private or primary school*)
2 le *proviseur* (*of state secondary school*)

headphones PL NOUN
les *écouteurs* MASC

headteacher NOUN
1 (*of private or primary school*)
le *directeur*
la *directrice*
2 (*of state secondary school*)
le *proviseur* ◇ *She's a headteacher.* Elle est proviseur.

health NOUN
la *santé*

healthy ADJECTIVE
1 *en bonne santé* (*person*) ◇ *Lesley's a healthy person.* Lesley est en bonne santé.
2 *sain* (*climate, food*) ◇ *a healthy diet*

PTO

une alimentation saine

heap NOUN
le *tas* ◇ *a rubbish heap* un tas d'ordures

to **hear** VERB
1 *entendre* ◇ *He heard the dog bark.* Il a entendu le chien aboyer. ◇ *She can't hear very well.* Elle entend mal. ◇ *I heard that she was ill.* J'ai entendu dire qu'elle était malade.
◆ **to hear about something** entendre parler de quelque chose
2 *apprendre* (*news*) ◇ *Did you hear the good news?* Est-ce que tu as appris la bonne nouvelle?
◆ **to hear from somebody** avoir des nouvelles de quelqu'un ◇ *I haven't heard from him recently.* Je n'ai pas eu de ses nouvelles récemment.

heart NOUN
le *cœur*
◆ **to learn something by heart** apprendre quelque chose par cœur
◆ **the ace of hearts** l'as de cœur

heart attack NOUN
la *crise cardiaque*

heartbroken ADJECTIVE
◆ **to be heartbroken** avoir le cœur brisé

heat NOUN
see also **heat** VERB
la *chaleur*

to **heat** VERB
see also **heat** NOUN
faire chauffer ◇ *Heat gently for 5 minutes.* Faire chauffer à feu doux pendant cinq minutes.
◆ **to heat up (1)** (*cooked food*) faire réchauffer ◇ *He heated the soup up.* Il a fait réchauffer la soupe.
◆ **to heat up (2)** (*water, oven*) chauffer ◇ *The water is heating up.* L'eau chauffe.

heater NOUN
le *radiateur* ◇ *an electric heater* un radiateur électrique

heating NOUN
le *chauffage*

heaven NOUN
le *paradis*

heavily ADVERB
lourdement ◇ *The car was heavily loaded.* La voiture était lourdement chargée.
◆ **He drinks heavily.** C'est un gros buveur.

heavy ADJECTIVE
1 *lourd* ◇ *This bag's very heavy.* Ce sac est très lourd.
◆ **heavy rain** une grosse averse
2 *chargé* (*busy*) ◇ *I've got a very heavy week ahead.* Je vais avoir une semaine très chargée.
◆ **to be a heavy drinker** être un gros buveur

he'd = **he would, he had**

hedge NOUN
la *haie*

hedgehog NOUN
le *hérisson*

heel NOUN
le *talon*

height NOUN
1 la *taille* (*of person*)
2 la *hauteur* (*of object*)
3 l' *altitude* FEM (*of mountain*)

heir NOUN
l' *héritier* MASC

heiress NOUN
l' *héritière* FEM

held VERB *see* **hold**

helicopter NOUN
l' *hélicoptère* MASC

hell NOUN
l' *enfer* MASC
◆ **Hell!** Merde! (*rude*)

he'll = **he will, he shall**

hello EXCLAMATION
bonjour!

helmet NOUN
le *casque*

to **help** VERB
see also **help** NOUN
aider ◇ *Can you help me?* Est-ce que vous pouvez m'aider?
◆ **Help!** Au secours!
◆ **Help yourself!** Servez-vous!
◆ **He can't help it.** Il n'y peut rien.

help NOUN
see also **help** VERB
l' *aide* FEM ◇ *Do you need any help?* Vous avez besoin d'aide?

helpful ADJECTIVE
serviable ◇ *He was very helpful.* Il a été très serviable.

hen NOUN
la *poule*

her ADJECTIVE
see also **her** PRONOUN
son MASC ◇ *her father* son père
sa FEM ◇ *her mother* sa mère
ses PL ◇ *her parents* ses parents
sa *becomes* **son** *before a vowel sound.*
◆ **her friend (1)** (*male*) son ami
◆ **her friend (2)** (*female*) son amie
Do not use **son/sa/ses** *with parts of the body.* ◇ *She's going to wash her hair.* Elle va se laver les cheveux. ◇ *She's cleaning her teeth.* Elle se brosse les dents. ◇ *She's hurt her foot.* Elle s'est fait mal au pied.

her PRONOUN
see also **her** ADJECTIVE
la *becomes* **l'** *before a vowel sound.*
1 *la* ◇ *I can see her.* Je la vois. ◇ *Look at her!* Regarde-la!
l' ◇ *I saw her.* Je l'ai vue.
Use **lui** *when* her *means* to her.
2 *lui* ◇ *I gave her a book.* Je lui ai donné un livre. ◇ *I told her the truth.* Je lui ai dit la vérité.
Use **elle** *after prepositions.*
3 *elle* ◇ *I'm going with her.* Je vais avec elle. ◇ *He sat next to her.* Il s'est assis à côté d'elle.
elle *is also used in comparisons.*
◇ *I'm older than her.* Je suis plus âgé qu'elle.

herb NOUN
l' *herbe*

here ADVERB
ici ◇ *I live here.* J'habite ici.
◆ **here is...** voici... ◇ *Here's Helen.* Voici Helen. ◇ *Here he is!* Le voici!
◆ **here are...** voici... ◇ *Here are the books.* Voici les livres.

hero NOUN
le *héros* ◇ *He's a real hero!* C'est un véritable héros!

heroin NOUN
l' *héroïne* ◇ *Heroin is a hard drug.* L'héroïne est une drogue dure.
◆ **a heroin addict** un héroïnomane ◇ *She's a heroin addict.* C'est une héroïnomane.

heroine NOUN
l' *héroïne* ◇ *the heroine of the novel* l'héroïne du roman

hers PRONOUN
le sien + MASC NOUN ◇ *Is this her coat?–No, hers is black.* C'est son manteau?–Non, le sien est noir.
la sienne + FEM NOUN ◇ *Is this her car?–No, hers is white.* C'est sa voiture?–Non, la sienne est blanche.
les siens + MASC PL NOUN ◇ *my parents and hers* mes parents et les siens
les siennes + FEM PL NOUN ◇ *my reasons and hers* mes raisons et les siennes
◆ **Is this hers?** C'est à elle? ◇ *This book is hers.* Ce livre est à elle. ◇ *Whose is this?–It's hers.* C'est à qui?–À elle.

herself PRONOUN
1 *se* ◇ *She's hurt herself.* Elle s'est blessée.
2 *elle* (*after preposition*) ◇ *She talked mainly about herself.* Elle a surtout parlé d'elle.
3 *elle-même* ◇ *She did it herself.* Elle l'a fait elle-même.
◆ **by herself** toute seule ◇ *She doesn't like travelling by herself.* Elle n'aime pas voyager toute seule.

he's = **he is, he has**

to **hesitate** VERB
hésiter

heterosexual ADJECTIVE
hétérosexuel MASC
hétérosexuelle FEM

hi EXCLAMATION
salut!

to **hide** VERB
se cacher ◇ *He hid behind a bush.* Il s'est caché derrière un buisson.
◆ **to hide something** cacher quelque chose ◇ *Paula hid the present.* Paula a caché le cadeau.

hide-and-seek NOUN
◆ **to play hide-and-seek** jouer à cache-cache

hideous ADJECTIVE
hideux MASC
hideuse FEM

hi-fi NOUN
la *chaîne hi-fi*
(les *chaînes hi-fi* PL)

high ADJECTIVE, ADVERB
1 *haut* ◇ *It's too high.* C'est trop haut.
◆ **How high is the wall?** Quelle est la hauteur du mur?
◆ **The wall's 2 metres high.** Le mur fait deux mètres de haut.
2 *élevé* ◇ *a high price* un prix élevé ◇ *a high temperature* une température élevée
◆ **at high speed** à grande vitesse
◆ **It's very high in fat.** C'est très gras.
◆ **She's got a very high voice.** Elle a la voix très aiguë.
◆ **to be high** (*on drugs*) être défoncé (*informal*)
◆ **to get high** se défoncer (*informal*) ◇ *to get high on crack* se défoncer au crack

high-heeled ADJECTIVE
à hauts talons
◆ **high-heeled shoes** des chaussures à hauts talons

high jump NOUN
le *saut en hauteur* (*sport*)

highlight NOUN
le *clou* ◇ *the highlight of the evening* le clou de la soirée

high-rise NOUN
la *tour* ◇ *I live in a high-rise.* J'habite dans une tour.

high school NOUN
le *lycée*

to **hijack** VERB
détourner

H

hijacker NOUN
le *pirate de l'air*

hike NOUN
la *randonnée*

hiking NOUN
◆ **to go hiking** faire une randonnée

hilarious ADJECTIVE
hilarant ◇ *It was hilarious!* C'était hilarant!

hill NOUN
la *colline* ◇ *She walked up the hill.* Elle a gravi la colline.

hill-walking NOUN
la *randonnée de basse montagne*
◇ *to go hill-walking* faire de la randonnée de basse montagne

him PRONOUN
le *becomes* **l'** *before a vowel sound.*
1 *le* ◇ *I can see him.* Je le vois. ◇ *Look at him!* Regarde-le!
l' ◇ *I saw him.* Je l'ai vu.
Use **lui** *when* him *means* to him, *and after prepositions.*
2 *lui* ◇ *I gave him a book.* Je lui ai donné un livre. ◇ *I told him the truth.* Je lui ai dit la vérité. ◇ *I'm going with him.* Je vais avec lui. ◇ *She sat next to him.* Elle s'est assise à côté de lui.
lui *is also used in comparisons.*
◇ *I'm older than him.* Je suis plus âgé que lui.

himself PRONOUN
1 *se* ◇ *He's hurt himself.* Il s'est blessé.
2 *lui* ◇ *He talked mainly about himself.* Il a surtout parlé de lui.
3 *lui-même* ◇ *He did it himself.* Il l'a fait lui-même.
◆ **by himself** tout seul ◇ *He was travelling by himself.* Il voyageait tout seul.

Hindu ADJECTIVE
hindou ◇ *a Hindu temple* un temple hindou

hip NOUN
la *hanche*

hippie NOUN
le *hippie*
la *hippie*

hippo NOUN
l' *hippopotame* MASC

to **hire** VERB
see also hire NOUN
1 *louer* ◇ *to hire a car* louer une voiture
2 *engager* (*person*) ◇ *They hired a cleaner.* Ils ont engagé une femme de ménage.

hire NOUN
see also hire VERB
la *location*
◆ **car hire** location de voitures
◆ **for hire** à louer

hire car NOUN
la *voiture de location*

his ADJECTIVE
see also his PRONOUN
son MASC ◇ *his father* son père
sa FEM ◇ *his mother* sa mère
ses PL ◇ *his parents* ses parents
sa *becomes* **son** *before a vowel sound.*
◆ **his friend (1)** (*male*) son ami
◆ **his friend (2)** (*female*) son amie
Do not use **son/sa/ses** *with parts of the body.*
◇ *He's going to wash his hair.* Il va se laver les cheveux. ◇ *He's cleaning his teeth.* Il se brosse les dents. ◇ *He's hurt his foot.* Il s'est fait mal au pied.

his PRONOUN
see also his ADJECTIVE
le sien + MASC NOUN ◇ *Is this his coat?–No, his is black.* C'est son manteau?–Non, le sien est noir.
la sienne + FEM NOUN ◇ *Is this his car?–No, his is white.* C'est sa voiture?–Non, la sienne est blanche.
les siens + MASC PL NOUN ◇ *my parents and his* mes parents et les siens
les siennes + FEM PL NOUN ◇ *my reasons and his* mes raisons et les siennes
◆ **Is this his?** C'est à lui? ◇ *This book is his.* Ce livre est à lui. ◇ *Whose is this?–It's his.* C'est à qui?–À lui.

history NOUN
l' *histoire* FEM

to **hit** VERB
see also hit NOUN
1 *frapper* ◇ *Andrew hit him.* Andrew l'a frappé.
2 *renverser* ◇ *He was hit by a car.* Il a été renversé par une voiture.
3 *toucher* ◇ *The arrow hit the target.* La flèche a touché la cible.
◆ **to hit it off with somebody** bien s'entendre avec quelqu'un ◇ *She hit it off with his parents.* Elle s'est bien entendue avec ses parents.

hit NOUN
see also hit VERB
1 le *tube* (*song*) ◇ *Blur's latest hit* le dernier tube de Blur
2 le *succès* (*success*) ◇ *The film was a massive hit.* Le film a eu un immense succès.

hitch NOUN
le *contretemps* ◇ *There's been a slight hitch.* Il y a eu un léger contretemps.

to **hitchhike** VERB
faire de l'auto-stop

hitchhiker NOUN
l' *auto-stoppeur* MASC
l' *auto-stoppeuse* FEM

hitchhiking NOUN
l' *auto-stop* MASC ◇ *Hitchhiking can be dangerous.* Il peut être dangereux de faire de l'auto-stop.

hit man NOUN
le *tueur à gages*

HIV-negative ADJECTIVE
séronégatif MASC
séronégative FEM

HIV-positive ADJECTIVE
séropositif MASC
séropositive FEM

hobby NOUN
le *passe-temps favori* ◇ *What are your hobbies?* Quels sont tes passe-temps favoris?

hockey NOUN
le *hockey* ◇ *I play hockey.* Je joue au hockey.

hold VERB
1 *tenir* (*hold on to*) ◇ *She held the baby.* Elle tenait le bébé.
2 *contenir* (*contain*) ◇ *This bottle holds one litre.* Cette bouteille contient un litre.
- **to hold a meeting** avoir une réunion
- **Hold the line!** (*on telephone*) Ne quittez pas!
- **Hold it!** (*wait*) Attends!
- **to get hold of something** (*obtain*) trouver quelque chose ◇ *I couldn't get hold of it.* Je n'ai pas réussi à en trouver.

hold on VERB
1 *tenir bon* (*keep hold*) ◇ *The cliff was slippery but he managed to hold on.* La falaise était glissante, mais il est parvenu à tenir bon.
- **to hold on to something** se cramponner à quelque chose ◇ *He held on to the chair.* Il se cramponnait à la chaise.
2 *attendre* (*wait*) ◇ *Hold on, I'm coming!* Attends, je viens!
- **Hold on!** (*on telephone*) Ne quittez pas!

hold up VERB
- **to hold up one's hand** lever la main ◇ *Pierre held up his hand.* Pierre a levé la main.
- **to hold somebody up** (*delay*) retenir quelqu'un ◇ *I was held up at the office.* J'ai été retenu au bureau.
- **to hold up a bank** (*rob*) braquer une banque (*informal*)

hold-up NOUN
1 le *hold-up* (*at bank*)
2 le *retard* (*delay*)
3 le *bouchon* (*traffic jam*)

hole NOUN
le *trou*

holiday NOUN
1 les *vacances* FEM PL ◇ *Did you have a good holiday?* Tu as passé de bonnes vacances? ◇ *our holidays in France* nos vacances en France
- **on holiday** en vacances ◇ *to go on holiday* partir en vacances ◇ *We are on holiday.* Nous sommes en vacances.
- **the school holidays** les vacances scolaires
2 le *jour férié* (*public holiday*) ◇ *Next Wednesday is a holiday.* Mercredi prochain est un jour férié.
3 le *jour de congé* (*day off*) ◇ *He took a day's holiday.* Il a pris un jour de congé.
- **a holiday camp** un camp de vacances

Holland NOUN
la *Hollande*
- **in Holland** en Hollande
- **to Holland** en Hollande

hollow ADJECTIVE
creux MASC
creuse FEM

holy ADJECTIVE
saint

home NOUN
see also home ADVERB
la *maison*
- **at home** à la maison
- **Make yourself at home.** Faites comme chez vous.

home ADVERB
see also home NOUN
à la maison ◇ *I'll be home at 5 o'clock.* Je serai à la maison à cinq heures.
- **to get home** rentrer ◇ *What time did he get home?* Il est rentré à quelle heure?

home address NOUN
l' *adresse* FEM ◇ *What's your home address?* Quelle est votre adresse?

homeland NOUN
la *patrie*

homeless ADJECTIVE
sans abri MASC, FEM, PL
- **the homeless** les sans-abri

home match NOUN
le *match à domicile*

homesick ADJECTIVE
- **to be homesick** avoir le mal du pays

homework NOUN
les *devoirs* MASC PL ◇ *Have you done your homework?* Est-ce que tu as fait tes devoirs? ◇ *my geography homework* mes devoirs de géographie

homosexual ADJECTIVE
see also homosexual NOUN

PTO

homosexuel MASC
homosexuelle FEM

homosexual NOUN
see also homosexual ADJECTIVE
l' *homosexuel*

honest ADJECTIVE
1 (*trustworthy*)
honnête ◇ *She's a very honest person.* Elle est très honnête.
2 (*sincere*)
franc MASC
franche FEM
◇ *He was very honest with her.* Il a été très franc avec elle.

honestly ADVERB
franchement ◇ *I honestly don't know.* Franchement, je n'en sais rien.

honesty NOUN
l' *honnêteté* FEM

honey NOUN
le *miel*

honeymoon NOUN
la *lune de miel*

honour NOUN
l' *honneur* MASC

hood NOUN
la *capuche* ◇ *a coat with a hood* un manteau à capuche

hook NOUN
le *crochet* ◇ *He hung the painting on the hook.* Il a suspendu le tableau au crochet.
◆ **to take the phone off the hook** décrocher le téléphone
◆ **a fish-hook** un hameçon

hooligan NOUN
le *voyou*
(les *voyoux* PL)

hooray EXCLAMATION
hourra!

Hoover ® NOUN
l' *aspirateur* MASC

to **hoover** VERB
passer l'aspirateur ◇ *to hoover the lounge* passer l'aspirateur dans le salon

to **hope** VERB
see also hope NOUN
espérer ◇ *I hope he comes.* J'espère qu'il va venir. ◇ *I'm hoping for good results.* J'espère avoir de bons résultats.
◆ **I hope so.** Je l'espère.
◆ **I hope not.** J'espère que non.

hope NOUN
see also hope VERB
l' *espoir* MASC
◆ **to give up hope** perdre espoir ◇ *Don't give up hope!* Ne perds pas espoir!

hopeful ADJECTIVE
1 *plein d'espoir* ◇ *I'm hopeful.* Je suis plein d'espoir.
◆ **He's hopeful of winning.** Il a bon espoir de gagner.
2 (*situation*)
prometteur MASC
prometteuse FEM
◇ *The prospects look hopeful.* Les perspectives semblent prometteuses.

hopefully ADVERB
avec un peu de chance ◇ *Hopefully he'll make it in time.* Avec un peu de chance, il arrivera à temps.

hopeless ADJECTIVE
nul MASC
nulle FEM
◇ *I'm hopeless at maths.* Je suis nul en maths.

horizon NOUN
l' *horizon*

horizontal ADJECTIVE
horizontal
(*horizontaux* MASC PL)

horn NOUN
1 le *klaxon* ◇ *He sounded his horn.* Il a klaxonné.
2 le *cor* ◇ *I play the horn.* Je joue du cor.

horoscope NOUN
l' *horoscope* MASC

horrible ADJECTIVE
horrible ◇ *What a horrible dress!* Quelle robe horrible!

horror NOUN
l' *horreur* FEM

horror film NOUN
le *film d'horreur*

horse NOUN
le *cheval*
(les *chevaux* PL)

horse-racing NOUN
les *courses de chevaux* FEM PL

horseshoe NOUN
le *fer à cheval*

hose NOUN
le *tuyau*
(les *tuyaux* PL)
◇ *a garden hose* un tuyau d'arrosage

hosepipe NOUN
le *tuyau d'arrosage*

hospital NOUN
l' *hôpital* MASC
(les *hôpitaux* PL)
◇ *Take me to the hospital!* Emmenez-moi à l'hôpital! ◇ *in hospital* à l'hôpital

hospitality NOUN
l' *hospitalité* FEM

hostage NOUN
l' *otage* MASC
◆ **to take somebody hostage** prendre

quelqu'un en otage

hostile ADJECTIVE
hostile

hot ADJECTIVE
1 *chaud* (*warm*) ◇ *a hot bath* un bain chaud ◇ *a hot country* un pays chaud

When you are talking about a person being hot, you use **avoir chaud**.

◇ *I'm hot.* J'ai chaud. ◇ *I'm too hot.* J'ai trop chaud.

When you mean that the weather is hot, you use **faire chaud**.

◇ *It's hot.* Il fait chaud. ◇ *It's very hot today.* Il fait très chaud aujourd'hui.

2 *épicé* (*spicy*) ◇ *a very hot curry* un curry très épicé

hot dog NOUN
le *hot-dog*

hotel NOUN
l' *hôtel* ◇ *We stayed in a hotel.* Nous avons logé à l'hôtel.

hour NOUN
l' *heure* FEM ◇ *She always takes hours to get ready.* Elle passe toujours des heures à se préparer.
- **a quarter of an hour** un quart d'heure
- **half an hour** une demi-heure
- **two and a half hours** deux heures et demie

hourly ADJECTIVE, ADVERB
toutes les heures ◇ *There are hourly buses.* Il y a des bus toutes les heures.
- **to be paid hourly** être payé à l'heure

house NOUN
la *maison*
- **at his house** chez lui
- **We stayed at their house.** Nous avons séjourné chez eux.

housewife NOUN
la *femme au foyer* ◇ *She's a housewife.* Elle est femme au foyer.

housework NOUN
le *ménage*
- **to do the housework** faire le ménage

hovercraft NOUN
l' *aéroglisseur* MASC

how ADVERB
comment ◇ *How are you?* Comment allez-vous?
- **How many?** Combien?
- **How many...?** Combien de...? ◇ *How many pupils are there in the class?* Combien d'élèves y a-t-il dans la classe?
- **How much?** Combien?
- **How much...?** Combien de...? ◇ *How much sugar do you want?* Combien de sucres voulez-vous?
- **How old are you?** Quel âge as-tu?
- **How far is it to Edinburgh?** Combien y a-t-il de kilomètres d'ici à Édimbourg?
- **How long have you been here?** Depuis combien de temps êtes-vous là?

however CONJUNCTION
pourtant ◇ *This, however, isn't true.* Pourtant, ce n'est pas vrai.

to **howl** VERB
hurler

to **hug** VERB
see also **hug** NOUN
serrer dans ses bras ◇ *He hugged her.* Il l'a serrée dans ses bras.

hug NOUN
see also **hug** VERB
- **to give somebody a hug** serrer quelqu'un dans ses bras ◇ *She gave them a hug.* Elle les a serrés dans ses bras.

huge ADJECTIVE
immense

to **hum** VERB
fredonner

human ADJECTIVE
humain ◇ *the human body* le corps humain

human being NOUN
l' *être humain* MASC

humour NOUN
l' *humour* MASC
- **to have a sense of humour** avoir le sens de l'humour

hundred NUMBER
- **a hundred** cent ◇ *a hundred francs* cent francs
- **five hundred** cinq cents
- **five hundred and one** cinq cent un
- **hundreds of people** des centaines de personnes

hung VERB *see* **hang**

Hungary NOUN
la *Hongrie*
- **in Hungary** en Hongrie
- **to Hungary** en Hongrie

hunger NOUN
la *faim*

hungry ADJECTIVE
- **to be hungry** avoir faim ◇ *I'm hungry.* J'ai faim.

to **hunt** VERB
1 *chasser* (*animal*) ◇ *People used to hunt wild boar.* On chassait le sanglier autrefois.
- **to go hunting** aller à la chasse

2 *pourchasser* (*criminal*) ◇ *The police are hunting the killer.* La police pourchasse le criminel.
- **to hunt for something** (*search*) chercher quelque chose partout ◇ *I hunted everywhere for that book.* J'ai cherché ce

PTO

livre partout.

hunting NOUN
la *chasse* ◇ *I'm against hunting.* Je suis contre la chasse.
- **fox-hunting** la chasse au renard

hurricane NOUN
l' *ouragan* MASC

to **hurry** VERB
see also hurry NOUN
se dépêcher ◇ *Sharon hurried back home.* Sharon s'est dépêchée de rentrer chez elle.
- **Hurry up!** Dépêche-toi!

hurry NOUN
see also hurry VERB
- **to be in a hurry** être pressé
- **to do something in a hurry** faire quelque chose en vitesse
- **There's no hurry.** Rien ne presse.

to **hurt** VERB
see also hurt ADJECTIVE
- **to hurt somebody (1)** (*physically*) faire mal à quelqu'un ◇ *You're hurting me!* Tu me fais mal!
- **to hurt somebody (2)** (*emotionally*) blesser quelqu'un ◇ *His remarks really hurt me.* Ses remarques m'ont vraiment blessé.
- **to hurt oneself** se faire mal ◇ *I fell over and hurt myself.* Je me suis fait mal en tombant.
- **That hurts.** Ça fait mal. ◇ *It hurts to have a tooth out.* Ça fait mal de se faire arracher une dent.
- **My leg hurts.** J'ai mal à la jambe.

hurt ADJECTIVE
see also hurt VERB
blessé ◇ *Is he badly hurt?* Est-ce qu'il est grièvement blessé? ◇ *He was hurt in the leg.* Il a été blessé à la jambe. ◇ *I was hurt by what he said.* J'ai été blessé par ce qu'il a dit.
- **Luckily, nobody got hurt.** Heureusement, il n'y a pas eu de blessés.

husband NOUN
le *mari*

hut NOUN
la *hutte*

hymn NOUN
le *cantique*

hypermarket NOUN
l' *hypermarché* MASC

hyphen NOUN
le *trait d'union*

I PRONOUN
1 *je* ◇ *I speak French.* Je parle français.
je *changes to* **j'** *before a vowel and most words beginning with "h".*
◇ *I love cats.* J'aime les chats.
2 *moi* ◇ *Ann and I* Ann et moi

ice NOUN
1 la *glace* ◇ *There was ice on the lake.* Il y avait de la glace sur le lac.
2 le *verglas* (*on road*)

iceberg NOUN
l' *iceberg* MASC

ice cream NOUN
la *glace* ◇ *vanilla ice cream* la glace à la vanille

ice cube NOUN
le *glaçon*

ice hockey NOUN
le *hockey sur glace*

Iceland NOUN
l' *Islande* FEM
◆ **in Iceland** en Islande
◆ **to Iceland** en Islande

ice lolly NOUN
la *glace à l'eau*

ice rink NOUN
la *patinoire*

ice-skating NOUN
le *patinage sur glace*
◆ **to go ice-skating** faire du patin à glace

icing NOUN
le *glaçage* (*on cake*)
◆ **icing sugar** le sucre glace

icy ADJECTIVE
glacial
(*glaciaux* MASC PL)
◇ *There was an icy wind.* Il y avait un vent glacial.
◆ **The roads are icy.** Il y a du verglas sur les routes.

I'd = **I had, I would**

idea NOUN
l' *idée* FEM ◇ *Good idea!* Bonne idée!

ideal ADJECTIVE
idéal
(*idéaux* MASC PL)

identical ADJECTIVE
identique

identification NOUN
l' *identification* FEM

identify VERB
identifier

identity card NOUN
la *carte d'identité*

idiot NOUN
l' *idiot* MASC
l' *idiote* FEM

idiotic ADJECTIVE
stupide

i.e. ABBREVIATION
c.-à-d. (= c'est-à-dire)

if CONJUNCTION
si ◇ *You can have it if you like.* Tu peux le prendre si tu veux.
si *changes to* **s'** *before* **il** *and* **ils**.
◇ *Do you know if he's there?* Savez-vous s'il est là?
◆ **if only** si seulement ◇ *If only I had more money!* Si seulement j'avais plus d'argent!
◆ **if not** sinon ◇ *Are you coming? If not, I'll go with Mark.* Est-ce que tu viens? Sinon, j'irai avec Mark.

ignorant ADJECTIVE
ignorant

to **ignore** VERB
◆ **to ignore something** ne tenir aucun compte de quelque chose ◇ *She ignored my advice.* Elle n'a tenu aucun compte de mes conseils.
◆ **to ignore somebody** ignorer quelqu'un ◇ *She saw me, but she ignored me.* Elle m'a vu, mais elle m'a ignoré.
◆ **Just ignore him!** Ne fais pas attention à lui!

ill ADJECTIVE
malade (*sick*)
◆ **to be taken ill** tomber malade ◇ *She was taken ill while on holiday.* Elle est tombée malade pendant qu'elle était en vacances.

I'll = **I will**

illegal ADJECTIVE
illégal
(*illégaux* MASC PL)

illegible ADJECTIVE
illisible

illness NOUN
la *maladie*

to **ill-treat** VERB
maltraiter

illusion NOUN
l' *illusion* FEM

illustration NOUN
l' *illustration* FEM

image NOUN
l' *image* FEM ◇ *The company has changed its image.* La société a changé d'image.

imagination NOUN
l' *imagination* FEM

to **imagine** VERB

imaginer ◇ *You can imagine how I felt!* Tu peux imaginer ce que j'ai ressenti! ◇ *Is he angry?–I imagine so.* Est-ce qu'il est en colère?–J'imagine que oui.

to **imitate** VERB
imiter

imitation NOUN
l' *imitation* FEM

immediate ADJECTIVE
immédiat

immediately ADVERB
immédiatement ◇ *I'll do it immediately.* Je vais le faire immédiatement.

immigrant NOUN
l' *immigré* MASC
l' *immigrée* FEM

immigration NOUN
l' *immigration* FEM

immoral ADJECTIVE
immoral
(*immoraux* MASC PL)

impartial ADJECTIVE
impartial
(*impartiaux* MASC PL)

impatience NOUN
l' *impatience* FEM

impatient ADJECTIVE
impatient
◆ **to get impatient** s'impatienter ◇ *People are getting impatient.* Les gens commencent à s'impatienter.

impatiently ADVERB
avec impatience ◇ *We waited impatiently.* Nous avons attendu avec impatience.

impersonal ADJECTIVE
impersonnel MASC
impersonnelle FEM

importance NOUN
l' *importance* FEM

important ADJECTIVE
important

impossible ADJECTIVE
impossible

to **impress** VERB
impressionner ◇ *She's trying to impress you.* Elle essaie de t'impressionner.

impressed ADJECTIVE
impressionné ◇ *I'm very impressed!* Je suis très impressionné!

impression NOUN
l' *impression* FEM ◇ *I was under the impression that...* J'avais l'impression que...

impressive ADJECTIVE
impressionnant

to **improve** VERB
1 *améliorer* (*make better*) ◇ *They have improved the service.* Ils ont amélioré le service.
2 *s'améliorer* (*get better*) ◇ *The weather is improving.* Le temps s'améliore. ◇ *My French has improved.* Mon français s'est amélioré.

improvement NOUN
1 l' *amélioration* FEM (*of condition*) ◇ *It's a great improvement.* C'est une nette amélioration.
2 le *progrès* (*of learner*) ◇ *There's been an improvement in his French.* Il a fait des progrès en français.

in PREPOSITION, ADVERB

There are several ways of translating in. *Scan the examples to find one that is similar to what you want to say. For other expressions with* in, *see the verbs* go, come, get, give *etc.*

1 *dans* ◇ *in the house* dans la maison ◇ *in my bag* dans mon sac ◇ *in the sixties* dans les années soixante ◇ *I'll see you in three weeks.* Je te verrai dans trois semaines.
2 *à* ◇ *in the country* à la campagne ◇ *in school* à l'école ◇ *in hospital* à l'hôpital ◇ *in London* à Londres ◇ *in spring* au printemps ◇ *in the sun* au soleil ◇ *in the shade* à l'ombre ◇ *in a loud voice* à voix haute ◇ *the boy in the blue shirt* le garçon à la chemise bleue ◇ *It was written in pencil.* C'était écrit au crayon.
3 *en* ◇ *in French* en français ◇ *in summer* en été ◇ *in May* en mai ◇ *in 1996* en dix-neuf cent quatre-vingt seize ◇ *I did it in 3 hours.* Je l'ai fait en trois heures. ◇ *in town* en ville ◇ *in prison* en prison ◇ *in tears* en larmes ◇ *in good condition* en bon état

When in *refers to a country which is feminine, use* **en**; *when the country is masculine, use* **au**; *when the country is plural, use* **aux**.

◇ *in France* en France ◇ *in Portugal* au Portugal ◇ *in the United States* aux États-Unis
4 *de* ◇ *the best pupil in the class* le meilleur élève de la classe ◇ *the best team in the world* la meilleure équipe du monde ◇ *the tallest person in the family* le plus grand de la famille ◇ *at 4 o'clock in the afternoon* à quatre heures de l'après-midi ◇ *at 6 in the morning* à six heures du matin
◆ **in the afternoon** l'après-midi
◆ **You look good in that dress.** Tu es jolie avec cette robe.
◆ **in time** à temps ◇ *We arrived in time for dinner.* Nous sommes arrivés à temps pour le dîner.

- **in here** ici ◇ *It's hot in here.* Il fait chaud ici.
- **in the rain** sous la pluie
- **one person in ten** une personne sur dix
- **to be in** (*at home, work*) être là ◇ *He wasn't in.* Il n'était pas là.
- **to ask somebody in** inviter quelqu'un à entrer

inaccurate ADJECTIVE
inexact

incentive NOUN
- **There is no incentive to work.** Il n'y a rien qui incite à travailler.

inch NOUN
le *pouce*

In France measurements are in metres and centimetres rather than feet and inches. An inch is about 2.5 centimetres.

- **6 inches** quinze centimètres

incident NOUN
l' *incident* MASC

inclined ADJECTIVE
- **to be inclined to do something** avoir tendance à faire quelque chose ◇ *He's inclined to arrive late.* Il a tendance à arriver en retard.

include VERB
comprendre ◇ *Service is not included.* Le service n'est pas compris.

including PREPOSITION
compris ◇ *It will be 200 francs, including tax.* Ça coûtera deux cents francs, toutes taxes comprises.

inclusive ADJECTIVE
compris ◇ *The inclusive price is 200 francs.* Ça coûte deux cents francs tout compris.
- **inclusive of tax** taxes comprises

income NOUN
le *revenu*

income tax NOUN
l' *impôt sur le revenu* MASC

incompetent ADJECTIVE
incompétent

incomplete ADJECTIVE
incomplet MASC
incomplète FEM

inconvenience NOUN
- **I don't want to cause any inconvenience.** Je ne veux pas vous déranger.

inconvenient ADJECTIVE
- **That's very inconvenient for me.** Ça ne m'arrange pas du tout.

incorrect ADJECTIVE
incorrect

increase NOUN
see also increase VERB
l' *augmentation* FEM ◇ *an increase in road accidents* une augmentation des accidents de la route

to **increase** VERB
see also increase NOUN
augmenter

incredible ADJECTIVE
incroyable

indecisive ADJECTIVE
indécis (*person*)

indeed ADVERB
vraiment ◇ *It's very hard indeed.* C'est vraiment très difficile.
- **Know what I mean?–Indeed I do.** Tu vois ce que je veux dire?–Oui, tout à fait.
- **Thank you very much indeed!** Merci beaucoup!

independence NOUN
l' *indépendance* FEM

independent ADJECTIVE
indépendant
- **an independent school** une école privée

index NOUN
l' *index* MASC (*in book*)

India NOUN
l' *Inde* FEM
- **in India** en Inde
- **to India** en Inde

Indian ADJECTIVE
see also Indian NOUN
indien MASC
indienne FEM

Indian NOUN
see also Indian ADJECTIVE
(*person*)
l' *Indien* MASC
l' *Indienne* FEM
- **an American Indian** un Indien d'Amérique

to **indicate** VERB
indiquer

indigestion NOUN
l' *indigestion* FEM
- **I've got indigestion.** J'ai une indigestion.

indoor ADJECTIVE
- **an indoor swimming pool** une piscine couverte

indoors ADVERB
à l'intérieur ◇ *They're indoors.* Ils sont à l'intérieur.
- **to go indoors** rentrer ◇ *We'd better go indoors.* Nous ferions mieux de rentrer.

industrial ADJECTIVE
industriel MASC
industrielle FEM

industrial estate NOUN
la *zone industrielle*

industry NOUN

PTO

l' *industrie* FEM ◇ *the tourist industry* l'industrie du tourisme ◇ *the oil industry* l'industrie pétrolière ◇ *I'd like to work in industry.* J'aimerais travailler dans l'industrie.

inefficient ADJECTIVE
inefficace

inevitable ADJECTIVE
inévitable

inexpensive ADJECTIVE
bon marché MASC, FEM, PL ◇ *an inexpensive hotel* un hôtel bon marché ◇ *inexpensive holidays* des vacances bon marché

inexperienced ADJECTIVE
inexpérimenté

infant school NOUN
CP (cours préparatoire) is the equivalent of first-year infants, and CE1 (cours élémentaire première année) the equivalent of second-year infants.
◇ *He's just started at infant school.* Il vient d'entrer au cours préparatoire.

infection NOUN
l' *infection* FEM ◇ *an ear infection* une infection de l'oreille
➔ **a throat infection** une angine

infectious ADJECTIVE
contagieux MASC
contagieuse FEM
◇ *It's not infectious.* Ce n'est pas contagieux.

infinitive NOUN
l' *infinitif* MASC

infirmary NOUN
l' *hôpital* MASC
(les *hôpitaux* PL)

inflatable ADJECTIVE
gonflable (*mattress, dinghy*)

inflation NOUN
l' *inflation* FEM

influence NOUN
see also influence VERB
l' *influence* FEM ◇ *He's a bad influence on her.* Il a mauvaise influence sur elle.

to **influence** VERB
see also influence NOUN
influencer

influenza NOUN
la *grippe*

to **inform** VERB
informer
➔ **to inform somebody of something** informer quelqu'un de quelque chose
◇ *Nobody informed me of the new plan.* Personne ne m'a informé de ce nouveau projet.

informal ADJECTIVE
1 (*person, party*)
décontracté ◇ *"informal dress"* "tenue décontractée"
2 (*colloquial*)
familier MASC
familière FEM
◇ *informal language* le langage familier
➔ **an informal visit** une visite non officielle

information NOUN
les *renseignements* MASC PL ◇ *important information* les renseignements importants
➔ **a piece of information** un renseignement
➔ **Could you give me some information about trains to Paris?** Pourriez-vous me renseigner sur les trains pour Paris?

information office NOUN
le *bureau des renseignements*

infuriating ADJECTIVE
exaspérant

ingredient NOUN
l' *ingrédient* MASC

inhabitant NOUN
l' *habitant* MASC
l' *habitante* FEM

to **inherit** VERB
hériter de ◇ *She inherited her father's house.* Elle a hérité de la maison de son père.

initials PL NOUN
les *initiales* FEM PL ◇ *Her initials are CDT.* Ses initiales sont CDT.

initiative NOUN
l' *initiative* FEM

to **inject** VERB
injecter (*drug*)

injection NOUN
la *piqûre*

to **injure** VERB
blesser

injured ADJECTIVE
blessé

injury NOUN
la *blessure*

injury time NOUN
les *arrêts de jeu* MASC PL

injustice NOUN
l' *injustice* FEM

ink NOUN
l' *encre* FEM

in-laws PL NOUN
les *beaux-parents* MASC PL

inn NOUN
l' *auberge* FEM

inner ADJECTIVE
intérieur
➔ **the inner city** les quartiers déshérités du centre ville

nner tube NOUN
la *chambre à air*

nnocent ADJECTIVE
innocent

nquest NOUN
l' *enquête* FEM

nquiries office NOUN
le *bureau des renseignements*

nquisitive ADJECTIVE
curieux MASC
curieuse FEM

nsane ADJECTIVE
fou MASC
folle FEM

nscription NOUN
l' *inscription* FEM

nsect NOUN
l' *insecte* MASC

nsect repellent NOUN
l' *insectifuge* MASC

nside NOUN
see also inside ADVERB
l' *intérieur* MASC

nside ADVERB, PREPOSITION
see also inside NOUN
à l'intérieur ◇ *They're inside.* Ils sont à l'intérieur. ◇ *inside the house* à l'intérieur de la maison
◆ **to go inside** rentrer
◆ **Come inside!** Rentrez!

nsincere ADJECTIVE
peu sincère

nsist VERB
insister ◇ *I didn't want to, but he insisted.* Je ne voulais pas, mais il a insisté.
◆ **to insist on doing something** insister pour faire quelque chose ◇ *She insisted on paying.* Elle a insisté pour payer.
◆ **He insisted he was innocent.** Il affirmait qu'il était innocent.

nspector NOUN
l' *inspecteur* MASC (*police*) ◇ *Inspector Jill Brown* l'inspecteur Jill Brown
◆ **ticket inspector** (*on buses*) le contrôleur

nstance NOUN
◆ **for instance** par exemple

nstant ADJECTIVE
immédiat ◇ *It was an instant success.* Ça a été un succès immédiat.
◆ **instant coffee** le café instantané

nstantly ADVERB
tout de suite

nstead ADVERB
◆ **instead of (1)** (*followed by noun*) à la place de ◇ *He went instead of Peter.* Il y est allé à la place de Peter.
◆ **instead of (2)** (*followed by verb*) au lieu de ◇ *We played tennis instead of going swimming.* Nous avons joué au tennis au lieu d'aller nager.
◆ **The pool was closed, so we played tennis instead.** La piscine était fermée, alors nous avons joué au tennis.

instinct NOUN
l' *instinct* MASC

institution NOUN
l' *institution* FEM

to **instruct** VERB
◆ **to instruct somebody to do something** donner l'ordre à quelqu'un de faire quelque chose ◇ *She instructed us to wait outside.* Elle nous a donné l'ordre d'attendre dehors.

instructions PL NOUN
1 les *instructions* FEM PL ◇ *Follow the instructions carefully.* Suivez soigneusement les instructions.
2 le *mode d'emploi* SING (*booklet*) ◇ *Where are the instructions?* Où est le mode d'emploi?

instructor NOUN
le *moniteur*
la *monitrice*
◇ *a skiing instructor* un moniteur de ski
◇ *a driving instructor* un moniteur d'auto-école

instrument NOUN
l' *instrument* MASC ◇ *Do you play an instrument?* Est-ce que tu joues d'un instrument?

insufficient ADJECTIVE
insuffisant

insulin NOUN
l' *insuline* FEM

insult NOUN
see also insult VERB
l' *insulte* FEM

to **insult** VERB
see also insult NOUN
insulter

insurance NOUN
l' *assurance* FEM ◇ *his car insurance* son assurance automobile
◆ **an insurance policy** une police d'assurance

intelligent ADJECTIVE
intelligent

to **intend** VERB
◆ **to intend to do something** avoir l'intention de faire quelque chose ◇ *I intend to do French at university.* J'ai l'intention d'étudier le français à l'université.

intense ADJECTIVE
intense

intensive ADJECTIVE
intensif MASC

PTO

intensive FEM

intention NOUN
l' *intention* FEM

intercom NOUN
l' *interphone* MASC

interest NOUN
see also interest VERB
l' *intérêt* MASC ◇ *to show an interest in something* manifester de l'intérêt pour quelque chose
- **What interests do you have?** Quels sont tes centres d'intérêt?
- **My main interest is music.** Ce qui m'intéresse le plus c'est la musique.

to **interest** VERB
see also interest NOUN
intéresser ◇ *It doesn't interest me.* Ça ne m'intéresse pas.
- **to be interested in something** s'intéresser à quelque chose ◇ *I'm not interested in politics.* Je ne m'intéresse pas à la politique.

interesting ADJECTIVE
intéressant

interior NOUN
l' *intérieur* MASC

interior designer NOUN
le/la *designer*

intermediate ADJECTIVE
(*course, level*)
moyen MASC
moyenne FEM

internal ADJECTIVE
interne

international ADJECTIVE
international
(*internationaux* MASC PL)

Internet NOUN
l' *Internet* MASC ◇ *on the Internet* sur Internet

to **interpret** VERB
servir d'interprète ◇ *Steve couldn't speak French, so his friend interpreted.* Comme Steve ne savait pas le français, son ami a servi d'interprète.

interpreter NOUN
l' *interprète* MASC/FEM

to **interrupt** VERB
interrompre

interruption NOUN
l' *interruption* FEM

interval NOUN
l' *entracte* MASC (*in play, concert*)

interview NOUN
see also interview VERB
1 l' *interview* FEM (*on TV, radio*)
2 l' *entretien* MASC (*for job*)

to **interview** VERB
see also interview NOUN
interviewer (*on TV, radio*) ◇ *I was interviewed on the radio.* J'ai été interviewé à la radio.

interviewer NOUN
l' *interviewer* MASC (*on TV, radio*)

intimate ADJECTIVE
intime

into PREPOSITION
1 *dans* ◇ *He got into the car.* Il est monté dans la voiture.
2 *en* ◇ *I'm going into town.* Je vais en ville. ◇ *Translate it into French.* Traduisez ça en français. ◇ *Divide into two groups.* Répartissez-vous en deux groupes.

to **introduce** VERB
présenter ◇ *He introduced me to his parents.* Il m'a présenté à ses parents.

introduction NOUN
l' *introduction* FEM (*in book*)

intruder NOUN
l' *intrus* MASC
l' *intruse* FEM

intuition NOUN
l' *intuition* FEM

to **invade** VERB
envahir

invalid NOUN
le/la *malade*

to **invent** VERB
inventer

invention NOUN
l' *invention* FEM

inventor NOUN
l' *inventeur* MASC
l' *inventrice* FEM

investigation NOUN
l' *enquête* FEM (*police*)

invigilator NOUN
le *surveillant*
la *surveillante*

invisible ADJECTIVE
invisible

invitation NOUN
l' *invitation* FEM

to **invite** VERB
inviter ◇ *He's not invited.* Il n'est pas invité.
- **to invite somebody to a party** inviter quelqu'un à une fête

to **involve** VERB
nécessiter ◇ *His job involves a lot of travelling.* Son travail nécessite de nombreux déplacements.
- **to be involved in something** (*crime, drugs*) être impliqué dans quelque chose
- **to be involved with somebody** (*in relationship*) avoir une relation avec quelqu'un

Q NOUN (= *intelligence quotient*)
le *Q.I.* (= quotient intellectuel)

an NOUN
l' *Iran* MASC
in Iran en Iran

aq NOUN
l' *Iraq* MASC
in Iraq en Iraq

eland NOUN
l' *Irlande* FEM
in Ireland en Irlande
to Ireland en Irlande
I'm from Ireland. Je suis irlandais.

ish ADJECTIVE
see also Irish NOUN
irlandais ◇ *Irish music* la musique irlandaise

ish NOUN
see also Irish ADJECTIVE
l' *irlandais* (*language*)
the Irish (*people*) les Irlandais

ishman NOUN
l' *Irlandais* MASC

ishwoman NOUN
l' *Irlandaise* FEM

on NOUN
see also iron VERB
1 le *fer* (*metal*)
2 le *fer à repasser* (*for clothes*)

on VERB
see also iron NOUN
repasser

ronic ADJECTIVE
ironique

roning NOUN
le *repassage* ◇ *to do the ironing* faire le repassage

roning board NOUN
la *planche à repasser*

ronmonger's (shop) NOUN
la *quincaillerie*

rrelevant ADJECTIVE
hors de propos ◇ *That's irrelevant.* C'est hors de propos.

rresponsible ADJECTIVE (*person*)
irresponsable ◇ *That was irresponsible of him.* C'était irresponsable de sa part.

rritating ADJECTIVE
irritant

s VERB *see* **be**

slam NOUN
l' *Islam* MASC

slamic ADJECTIVE
islamique ◇ *Islamic law* la loi islamique
Islamic fundamentalists les intégristes musulmans

sland NOUN
l' *île* FEM

isle NOUN
the Isle of Man l'île de Man
the Isle of Wight l'île de Wight

isolated ADJECTIVE
isolé

Israel NOUN
Israël MASC
in Israel en Israël

Israeli ADJECTIVE
see also Israeli NOUN
israélien MASC
israélienne FEM

Israeli NOUN
see also Israeli ADJECTIVE
l' *Israélien* MASC
l' *Israélienne* FEM

issue NOUN
see also issue VERB
1 la *question* (*matter*) ◇ *a controversial issue* une question controversée
2 le *numéro* (*of magazine*)

to **issue** VERB
see also issue NOUN
distribuer (*equipment, supplies*)

it PRONOUN
Remember to check if it *stands for a masculine or feminine noun.*
1 *il* ◇ *Where's my book? – It's on the table.* Où est mon livre? – Il est sur la table.
elle ◇ *When does the pool close? – It closes at 8.* La piscine ferme à quelle heure? – Elle ferme à vingt heures.
Use **le** *or* **la** *when* it *is the object of the sentence.* **le** *and* **la** *change to* **l'** *before a vowel and most words beginning with "h".*
2 *le* ◇ *There's a croissant left. Do you want it?* Il reste un croissant. Tu le veux?
l' ◇ *It's a good film. Did you see it?* C'est un bon film. L'as-tu vu?
la ◇ *I don't want this apple. Take it.* Je ne veux pas de cette pomme. Prends-la.
l' ◇ *He's got a new car. – Yes, I saw it.* Il a une nouvelle voiture. – Oui, je l'ai vue.
It's raining. Il pleut.
It's 6 o'clock. Il est six heures.
It's Friday tomorrow. Demain c'est vendredi.
Who is it? – It's me. Qui est-ce? – C'est moi.
It's expensive. C'est cher.

Italian ADJECTIVE
see also Italian NOUN
italien MASC
italienne FEM

Italian NOUN
see also Italian ADJECTIVE
1 (*person*)
l' *Italien* MASC

PTO

l' *Italienne* FEM
2 (*language*)
l' *italien* MASC

Italy NOUN
l' *Italie* FEM
◆ **in Italy** en Italie
◆ **to Italy** en Italie

to **itch** VERB
◆ **It itches.** Ça me démange.
◆ **My head's itching.** J'ai des démangeaisons à la tête.

it'd = **it had, it would**

item NOUN
l' *article* MASC (*object*)

itinerary NOUN
l' *itinéraire* MASC

it'll = **it will**

its ADJECTIVE
Remember to check if **its** *refers to a masculine, feminine or plural noun.*
son MASC ◇ *What's its name?* Quel est son nom?
sa FEM ◇ *Every thing in its place.* Chaque chose à sa place.
ses PL ◇ *The dog is losing its hair.* Le chien perd ses poils.

it's = **it is, it has**

itself PRONOUN
se
se *changes to* **s'** *before a vowel and most words beginning with "h".*
◇ *The heating switches itself off.* Le chauffage s'arrête automatiquement.

I've = **I have**

J

jab NOUN
la *piqûre* (*injection*)

jack NOUN
1 le *cric* (*for car*)
2 le *valet* (*playing card*)

jacket NOUN
la *veste*
• **jacket potatoes** les pommes de terre en robe des champs

jackpot NOUN
le *gros lot*
• **to win the jackpot** gagner le gros lot

jail NOUN
see also **jail** VERB
la *prison*
• **to go to jail** aller en prison

jail VERB
see also **jail** NOUN
emprisonner

jam NOUN
la *confiture* ◇ *strawberry jam* la confiture de fraises
• **a traffic jam** un embouteillage

jam jar NOUN
le *pot à confiture*

jammed ADJECTIVE
coincé ◇ *The window's jammed.* La fenêtre est coincée.

jam-packed ADJECTIVE
bondé ◇ *The room was jam-packed.* La salle était bondée.

janitor NOUN
le *concierge* ◇ *He's a janitor.* Il est concierge.

January NOUN
janvier MASC
• **in January** en janvier

Japan NOUN
le *Japon*
• **in Japan** au Japon
• **from Japan** du Japon

Japanese ADJECTIVE
see also **Japanese** NOUN
japonais

Japanese NOUN
see also **Japanese** ADJECTIVE
1 (*person*)
le *Japonais*
la *Japonaise*
• **the Japanese** les Japonais
2 (*language*)
le *japonais*

jar NOUN
le *bocal*
(les *bocaux* PL)
◇ *an empty jar* un bocal vide
• **a jar of honey** un pot de miel

jaundice NOUN
la *jaunisse*

javelin NOUN
le *javelot*

jaw NOUN
la *mâchoire*

jazz NOUN
le *jazz*

jealous ADJECTIVE
jaloux MASC
jalouse FEM

jeans PL NOUN
le *jean* SING

Jehovah's Witness NOUN
le *témoin de Jéhovah* ◇ *She's a Jehovah's Witness.* Elle est témoin de Jéhovah.

jelly NOUN
la *gelée*

jellyfish NOUN
la *méduse*

jersey NOUN (*pullover*)
le *pull-over*

Jesus NOUN
Jésus MASC

jet NOUN
le *jet* (*plane*)

jetlag NOUN
• **to be suffering from jetlag** être sous le coup du décalage horaire

jetty NOUN
la *jetée*

Jew NOUN
le *Juif*
la *Juive*

jewel NOUN
le *bijou*
(les *bijoux* PL)

jeweller NOUN
le *bijoutier*
la *bijoutière*
◇ *He's a jeweller.* Il est bijoutier.

jeweller's shop NOUN
la *bijouterie*

jewellery NOUN
les *bijoux* MASC PL

Jewish ADJECTIVE
juif MASC
juive FEM

jigsaw NOUN
le *puzzle*

job NOUN
1 l' *emploi* MASC ◇ *He's lost his job.* Il a perdu son emploi.
• **I've got a Saturday job.** Je travaille le

PTO

samedi.
2 (*chore, task*)
le *travail*
(les *travaux* PL)
◇ *That was a difficult job.* C'était un travail difficile.

job centre NOUN
l' *agence pour l'emploi* FEM

jobless ADJECTIVE
sans emploi

jockey NOUN
le *jockey*

to **jog** VERB
faire du jogging

jogging NOUN
le *jogging*
➔ **to go jogging** faire du jogging

to **join** VERB
1 *s'inscrire à* (*become member of*) ◇ *I'm going to join the ski club.* Je vais m'inscrire au club de ski.
2 *se joindre à* ◇ *Do you mind if I join you?* Puis-je me joindre à vous?

joiner NOUN
le *menuisier* ◇ *He's a joiner.* Il est menuisier.

joint NOUN
1 l' *articulation* FEM (*in body*)
2 le *rôti* (*of meat*)
3 le *joint* (*drugs*)

joke NOUN
see also joke VERB
la *plaisanterie*
➔ **to tell a joke** raconter une plaisanterie

to **joke** VERB
see also joke NOUN
plaisanter ◇ *I'm only joking.* Je plaisante.

jolly ADJECTIVE
jovial
(*joviaux* MASC PL)

Jordan NOUN
la *Jordanie* (*country*)
➔ **in Jordan** en Jordanie

to **jot down** VERB
noter

jotter NOUN
(*pad*)
le *bloc-notes*
(les *blocs-notes* PL)

journalism NOUN
le *journalisme*

journalist NOUN
le/la *journaliste* ◇ *She's a journalist.* Elle est journaliste.

journey NOUN
1 le *voyage* ◇ *I don't like long journeys.* Je n'aime pas les longs voyages.
➔ **to go on a journey** faire un voyage
2 le *trajet* (*to school, work*) ◇ *The journey to school takes about half an hour.* Il y a une demi-heure de trajet pour aller à l'école.
➔ **a bus journey** un trajet en autobus

joy NOUN
la *joie*

joystick NOUN
le *manette de jeu* (*for computer game*)

judge NOUN
see also judge VERB
le *juge* ◇ *She's a judge.* Elle est juge.

to **judge** VERB
see also judge NOUN
juger

judo NOUN
le *judo* ◇ *My hobby is judo.* Je fais du judo.

jug NOUN
le *pot*

juice NOUN
le *jus* ◇ *orange juice* le jus d'orange

July NOUN
juillet MASC
➔ **in July** en juillet

to **jump** VERB
sauter
➔ **to jump over something** sauter par-dessus quelque chose
➔ **to jump out of the window** sauter par la fenêtre
➔ **to jump off the roof** sauter du toit

jumper NOUN
le *pull-over* (*pullover*)

junction NOUN
le *carrefour* (*of roads*)

June NOUN
juin MASC
➔ **in June** en juin

jungle NOUN
la *jungle*

junior NOUN
➔ **the juniors** (*in school*) les élèves des petites classes

junior school NOUN
l' *école primaire* FEM

junk NOUN
le *bric-à-brac* NO PL (*old things*) ◇ *The attic's full of junk.* Le grenier est rempli de bric-à-brac.
➔ **to eat junk food** manger n'importe comment
➔ **a junk shop** un magasin de brocante

jury NOUN
le *jury*

just ADVERB
juste ◇ *just after Christmas* juste après Noël ◇ *We had just enough money.* Nous avions juste assez d'argent. ◇ *just*

in time juste à temps
- **just here** ici
- **I'm rather busy just now.** Je suis assez occupé en ce moment.
- **I did it just now.** Je viens de le faire.
- **He's just arrived.** Il vient d'arriver.
- **I'm just coming!** J'arrive!
- **It's just a suggestion.** Ce n'est qu'une suggestion.

justice NOUN
la *justice*

to **justify** VERB
justifier

K

kangaroo NOUN
le *kangourou*

karate NOUN
le *karaté*

keen ADJECTIVE
enthousiaste ◇ *He doesn't seem very keen.* Il n'a pas l'air très enthousiaste.
- **She's a keen student.** C'est une étudiante assidue.
- **to be keen on something** aimer quelque chose ◇ *I'm keen on maths.* J'aime les maths. ◇ *I'm not very keen on maths.* Je n'aime pas trop les maths.
- **to be keen on somebody** (*fancy them*) être très attiré par quelqu'un ◇ *He's keen on her.* Il est très attiré par elle.
- **to be keen on doing something** avoir très envie de faire quelque chose ◇ *I'm not very keen on going.* Je n'ai pas très envie d'y aller.

to **keep** VERB
1 *garder* (*retain*) ◇ *You can keep it.* Tu peux le garder.
2 *rester* (*remain*) ◇ *Keep still!* Reste tranquille!
- **Keep quiet!** Tais-toi!
- **I keep forgetting my keys.** J'oublie tout le temps mes clés.
- **to keep on doing something (1)** (*continue*) continuer à faire quelque chose ◇ *He kept on reading.* Il a continué à lire.
- **to keep on doing something (2)** (*repeatedly*) ne pas arrêter de faire quelque chose ◇ *The car keeps on breaking down.* La voiture n'arrête pas de tomber en panne.
- **"keep out"** "défense d'entrer"

keep-fit NOUN
la *gymnastique d'entretien*
- **I go to keep-fit classes.** Je vais à des cours de gymnastique.

kennel NOUN
la *niche*

kettle NOUN
la *bouilloire*

key NOUN
la *clé*

keyboard NOUN
le *clavier* ◇ *...with Mike Moran on keyboards* ...avec Mike Moran aux claviers

keyring NOUN
le *porte-clés*

kick NOUN
see also kick VERB
le *coup de pied*

to **kick** VERB
see also kick NOUN
- **to kick somebody** donner un coup de pied à quelqu'un ◇ *He kicked me.* Il m'a donné un coup de pied. ◇ *He kicked the ball hard.* Il a donné un bon coup de pied dans le ballon.
- **to kick off** (*in football*) donner le coup d'envoi

kick-off NOUN
le *coup d'envoi* ◇ *The kick-off is at 10 o'clock.* Le coup d'envoi sera donné à dix heures.

kid NOUN
see also kid VERB
le/la *gosse* (*child*)

to **kid** VERB
see also kid NOUN
plaisanter ◇ *I'm just kidding.* Je plaisante.

to **kidnap** VERB
kidnapper

kidney NOUN
1 le *rein* (*human*) ◇ *He's got kidney trouble.* Il a des problèmes de reins.
2 le *rognon* (*to eat*) ◇ *I don't like kidneys.* Je n'aime pas les rognons.

to **kill** VERB
tuer ◇ *He was killed in a car accident.* Il a été tué dans un accident de voiture.
- **Luckily, nobody was killed.** Il n'y a heureusement pas eu de victimes.
- **Six people were killed in the accident.** L'accident a fait six morts.
- **to kill oneself** se suicider ◇ *He killed himself.* Il s'est suicidé.

killer NOUN
1 (*murderer*)
le *meurtrier*
la *meurtrière*
◇ *The police are searching for the killer.* La police recherche le meurtrier.
2 (*hit man*)
le *tueur*
la *tueuse*
◇ *a hired killer* un tueur à gages
- **Meningitis can be a killer.** La méningite peut être mortelle.

kilo NOUN
le *kilo* ◇ *10 francs a kilo* dix francs le kilo

kilometre NOUN
le *kilomètre*

kilt NOUN
le *kilt*

kind ADJECTIVE
see also kind NOUN
gentil MASC
gentille FEM
- **to be kind to somebody** être gentil avec quelqu'un
- **Thank you for being so kind.** Merci pour votre gentillesse.

kind NOUN
see also kind ADJECTIVE
la *sorte* ◇ *It's a kind of sausage.* C'est une sorte de saucisse.

kindergarten NOUN
l' *école maternelle* FEM

kindness NOUN
la *gentillesse*

king NOUN
le *roi*

kingdom NOUN
le *royaume*

kiosk NOUN
la *cabine téléphonique* (*phone box*)

kipper NOUN
le *hareng fumé*

kiss NOUN
see also kiss VERB
le *baiser* ◇ *a passionate kiss* un baiser passionné

kiss VERB
see also kiss NOUN
1 *embrasser* ◇ *He kissed her passionately.* Il l'a embrassée passionnément.
2 *s'embrasser* ◇ *They kissed.* Ils se sont embrassés.

kit NOUN
1 les *affaires* FEM PL (*clothes for sport*) ◇ *I've forgotten my gym kit.* J'ai oublié mes affaires de gym.
2 la *trousse* ◇ *a tool kit* une trousse à outils ◇ *a first aid kit* une trousse de secours ◇ *a puncture repair kit* une trousse de réparations
- **a drum kit** une batterie
- **a sewing kit** un nécessaire à couture

kitchen NOUN
la *cuisine* ◇ *a fitted kitchen* une cuisine aménagée
- **the kitchen units** les éléments de cuisine
- **a kitchen knife** un couteau de cuisine

kite NOUN
le *cerf-volant*
(les *cerfs-volants* PL)

kitten NOUN
le *chaton*

knee NOUN
le *genou*
(les *genoux* PL)
- **He was on his knees.** Il était à genoux.

to **kneel (down)** VERB
s'agenouiller

knew VERB *see* **know**

knickers PL NOUN
la *culotte* SING
- **a pair of knickers** une culotte

knife NOUN
le *couteau*
(les *couteaux* PL)
- **a kitchen knife** un couteau de cuisine
- **a sheath knife** un couteau à gaine
- **a penknife** un canif

to **knit** VERB
tricoter

knitting NOUN
le *tricot* ◇ *I like knitting.* J'aime faire du tricot.

knives PL NOUN *see* **knife**

to **knock** VERB
see also knock NOUN
frapper ◇ *Someone's knocking at the door.* Quelqu'un frappe à la porte.
- **to knock somebody down** renverser quelqu'un ◇ *She was knocked down by a car.* Elle a été renversée par une voiture.
- **to knock somebody out (1)** (*defeat*) éliminer ◇ *They were knocked out early in the tournament.* Ils ont été éliminés au début du tournoi.
- **to knock somebody out (2)** (*stun*) assommer ◇ *They knocked out the watchman.* Ils ont assommé le gardien.

knock NOUN
see also knock VERB
le *coup*

knot NOUN
le *nœud*
- **to tie a knot in something** faire un nœud à quelque chose

to **know** VERB
Use **savoir** *for knowing facts,* **connaître** *for knowing people and places.*
1 *savoir* ◇ *It's a long way.* – *Yes, I know.* C'est loin. – Oui, je sais. ◇ *I don't know.* Je ne sais pas. ◇ *I don't know what to do.* Je ne sais pas quoi faire. ◇ *I don't know how to do it.* Je ne sais pas comment faire.
2 *connaître* ◇ *I know her.* Je la connais. ◇ *I know Paris well.* Je connais bien Paris.
- **I don't know any German.** Je ne parle pas du tout allemand.
- **to know that...** savoir que... ◇ *I know that you like chocolate.* Je sais que tu aimes le chocolat. ◇ *I didn't know that your Dad was a policeman.* Je ne savais pas que ton père était policier.

PTO

- **to know about something (1)** (*be aware of*) être au courant de quelque chose ◇ *Do you know about the meeting this afternoon?* Tu es au courant de la réunion de cet après-midi?
- **to know about something (2)** (*be knowledgeable about*) s'y connaître en quelque chose ◇ *He knows a lot about cars.* Il s'y connaît en voitures. ◇ *I don't know much about computers.* Je ne m'y connais pas bien en informatique.
- **to get to know somebody** apprendre à connaître quelqu'un
- **How should I know?** (*I don't know!*) Comment veux-tu que je le sache?
- **You never know!** On ne sait jamais!

know-all NOUN
le/la *je-sais-tout* ◇ *He's such a know-all!* C'est Monsieur je-sais-tout!

know-how NOUN
le *savoir-faire*

knowledge NOUN
la *connaissance*

knowledgeable ADJECTIVE
- **to be knowledgeable about something** s'y connaître en quelque chose ◇ *She's very knowledgeable about computers.* Elle s'y connaît bien en informatique.

Koran NOUN
le *Coran*

Korea NOUN
la *Corée*
- **in Korea** en Corée

kosher ADJECTIVE
kascher MASC, FEM, PL

L

lab NOUN (= *laboratory*)
le *labo*
◆ **a lab technician** un laborantin
label NOUN
l' *étiquette* FEM
laboratory NOUN
le *laboratoire*
Labour NOUN
les *travaillistes* MASC PL ◇ *My parents vote Labour.* Mes parents votent pour les travaillistes.
◆ **the Labour Party** le parti travailliste
labourer NOUN
le *manœuvre*
◆ **a farm labourer** un ouvrier agricole
lace NOUN
1 le *lacet* (*of shoe*)
2 la *dentelle* ◇ *a lace collar* un col en dentelle
lacquer NOUN
la *laque*
lad NOUN
le *gars*
ladder NOUN
l' *échelle* FEM
lady NOUN
la *dame*
◆ **a young lady** une jeune fille
◆ **Ladies and gentlemen...** Mesdames, Messieurs...
◆ **the ladies'** les toilettes pour dames FEM
ladybird NOUN
la *coccinelle*
lag behind VERB
rester en arrière
lager NOUN
la *bière blonde*
laid VERB *see* **lay**
laid-back ADJECTIVE
relaxe
lain VERB *see* **lie**
lake NOUN
le *lac*
◆ **Lake Geneva** le lac Léman
lamb NOUN
l' *agneau* MASC
(les *agneaux* PL)
◆ **a lamb chop** une côtelette d'agneau
lame ADJECTIVE
boiteux ◇ *My pony is lame.* Mon poney boîte.
lamp NOUN
la *lampe*
lamppost NOUN
le *réverbère*
land NOUN
see also **land** VERB
la *terre*
◆ **a piece of land** un terrain
to **land** VERB
see also **land** NOUN
atterrir (*plane, passenger*)
landing NOUN
1 l' *atterrissage* MASC (*of plane*)
2 le *palier* (*of staircase*)
landlady NOUN
la *propriétaire*
landlord NOUN
le *propriétaire*
landowner NOUN
le *propriétaire terrien*
landscape NOUN
le *paysage*
lane NOUN
1 le *chemin* (*in country*)
2 la *voie* (*on motorway*)
language NOUN
la *langue* ◇ *French isn't a difficult language.* Le français n'est pas une langue difficile.
◆ **to use bad language** dire des grossièretés
language laboratory NOUN
le *laboratoire de langues*
lap NOUN
le *tour de piste* (*sport*) ◇ *I ran ten laps.* J'ai fait dix tours de piste en courant.
◆ **on my lap** sur mes genoux
laptop NOUN (*computer*)
le *portable*
larder NOUN
le *garde-manger*
(les *garde-manger* PL)
large ADJECTIVE
1 *grand* ◇ *a large house* une grande maison
2 (*person, animal*)
gros MASC
grosse FEM
◇ *a large dog* un gros chien
laser NOUN
le *laser*
lass NOUN
la *jeune fille*
last ADJECTIVE, ADVERB
see also **last** VERB
1 *dernier* MASC
dernière FEM
◇ *last Friday* vendredi dernier ◇ *last week* la semaine dernière ◇ *last summer* l'été dernier
2 *en dernier* ◇ *He arrived last.* Il est

PTO

arrivé en dernier.

3 *pour la dernière fois* ◇ *I've lost my bag.–When did you see it last?* J'ai perdu mon sac.–Quand est-ce que tu l'as vu pour la dernière fois? ◇ *When I last saw him, he was wearing a blue shirt.* La dernière fois que je l'ai vu, il portait une chemise bleue.

- **the last time** la dernière fois ◇ *the last time I saw her* la dernière fois que je l'ai vue ◇ *That's the last time I take your advice!* C'est la dernière fois que je suis tes conseils!
- **last night (1)** (*evening*) hier soir ◇ *I got home at midnight last night.* Je suis rentré à minuit hier soir.
- **last night (2)** (*sleeping hours*) la nuit dernière ◇ *I couldn't sleep last night.* J'ai eu du mal à dormir la nuit dernière.
- **at last** enfin

to **last** VERB

see also last ADJECTIVE

durer ◇ *The concert lasts two hours.* Le concert dure deux heures.

late ADJECTIVE, ADVERB

1 *en retard* ◇ *Hurry up or you'll be late!* Dépêche-toi, sinon tu vas être en retard! ◇ *I'm often late for school.* J'arrive souvent en retard à l'école.

- **to arrive late** arriver en retard ◇ *She arrived late.* Elle est arrivée en retard.

2 *tard* ◇ *I went to bed late.* Je me suis couché tard.

- **in the late afternoon** en fin d'après-midi
- **in late May** fin mai

lately ADVERB

ces derniers temps ◇ *I haven't seen him lately.* Je ne l'ai pas vu ces derniers temps.

later ADVERB

plus tard ◇ *I'll do it later.* Je ferai ça plus tard.

- **See you later!** À tout à l'heure!

latest ADJECTIVE

dernier MASC
dernière FEM

◇ *their latest album* leur dernier album

- **at the latest** au plus tard ◇ *by 10 o'clock at the latest* à dix heures au plus tard

Latin NOUN

le *latin* ◇ *I do Latin.* Je fais du latin.

Latin America NOUN

l' *Amérique latine* FEM

- **in Latin America** en Amérique latine

Latin American ADJECTIVE

latino-américain

laugh NOUN

see also laugh VERB

le *rire*

- **It was a good laugh.** (*it was fun*) On s'est bien amusés.

to **laugh** VERB

see also laugh NOUN

rire

- **to laugh at something** se moquer de quelque chose ◇ *They laughed at her.* Ils se sont moqués d'elle.

Launderette ® NOUN

la *laverie*

laundry NOUN

le *linge* (*clothes*)

lavatory NOUN

les *toilettes* FEM PL

lavender NOUN

la *lavande*

law NOUN

1 la *loi* ◇ *The laws are very strict.* Les lois sont très sévères.

- **It's against the law.** C'est illégal.

2 le *droit* (*subject*) ◇ *My sister's studying law.* Ma sœur fait des études de droit.

lawn NOUN

la *pelouse*

lawnmower NOUN

la *tondeuse à gazon*

lawyer NOUN

l' *avocat* MASC
l' *avocate* FEM

◇ *My mother's a lawyer.* Ma mère est avocate.

to **lay** VERB

lay *is also a form of* lie VERB.

mettre ◇ *She laid the baby in her cot.* Elle a mis le bébé dans son lit.

- **to lay the table** mettre la table
- **to lay something on (1)** (*provide*) organiser quelque chose ◇ *They laid on extra buses.* Ils ont organisé un service de bus supplémentaire.
- **to lay something on (2)** (*prepare*) préparer quelque chose ◇ *They laid on a special meal.* Ils ont préparé un repas soigné.

lay-by NOUN

l' *aire de stationnement* FEM

lazy ADJECTIVE

paresseux MASC
paresseuse FEM

lead NOUN

This word has two pronunciations. Make sure you choose the right translation.

see also lead VERB

1 le *fil* (*cable*)

2 la *laisse* (*for dog*)

- **to be in the lead** être en tête ◇ *Our team is in the lead.* Notre équipe est en

tête.
3 le *plomb* (*metal*)

lead VERB
see also lead NOUN
mener ◇ *the street that leads to the station* la rue qui mène à la gare
- **to lead the way** montrer le chemin
- **to lead somebody away** emmener quelqu'un ◇ *The police led the man away.* La police a emmené l'homme.

leaded petrol NOUN
l' *essence au plomb* FEM

leader NOUN
1 (*of expedition, gang*)
le *chef*
2 (*of political party*)
le *dirigeant*
la *dirigeante*

lead-free ADJECTIVE
- **lead-free petrol** de l'essence sans plomb

lead singer NOUN
le *chanteur principal*
la *chanteuse principale*

leaf NOUN
la *feuille*

leaflet NOUN
la *brochure*

league NOUN
le *championnat* ◇ *They are at the top of the league.* Ils sont en tête du championnat.
- **the Premier League** la première division

leak NOUN
see also leak VERB
la *fuite* ◇ *a gas leak* une fuite de gaz

leak VERB
see also leak NOUN
fuir (*pipe, water, gas*)

lean VERB
se pencher ◇ *Don't lean over too far.* Ne te penche pas trop. ◇ *She leant out of the window.* Elle s'est penchée par la fenêtre.
- **to lean forward** se pencher en avant
- **to lean on something** s'appuyer contre quelque chose ◇ *He leant on the wall.* Il s'est appuyé contre le mur.
- **to be leaning against something** être appuyé contre quelque chose ◇ *The ladder was leaning against the wall.* L'échelle était appuyée contre le mur.
- **to lean something against a wall** appuyer quelque chose contre un mur ◇ *He leant his bike against the wall.* Il a appuyé son vélo contre le mur.

leap year NOUN
l' *année bissextile* FEM

learn VERB
apprendre ◇ *I'm learning to ski.* J'apprends à skier.

learner NOUN
- **She's a quick learner.** Elle apprend vite.
- **French learners** (*people learning French*) ceux qui apprennent le français

learner driver NOUN
le *conducteur débutant*
la *conductrice débutante*

least ADVERB, ADJECTIVE, PRONOUN
- **the least (1)** (*followed by noun*) le moins de ◇ *It takes the least time.* C'est ce qui prend le moins de temps.
- **the least (2)** (*after a verb*) le moins ◇ *Maths is the subject I like the least.* Les maths sont la matière que j'aime le moins.

When least *is followed by adjective, the translation depends on whether the noun referred to is masculine, feminine or plural.*

- **the least... (1)** le moins... ◇ *the least expensive hotel* l'hôtel le moins cher
- **the least... (2)** la moins... ◇ *the least expensive seat* la place la moins chère
- **the least... (3)** les moins... ◇ *the least expensive hotels* les hôtels les moins chers ◇ *the least expensive seats* les places les moins chères
- **It's the least I can do.** C'est le moins que je puisse faire.
- **at least (1)** au moins ◇ *It'll cost at least £200.* Ça va coûter au moins deux cents livres.
- **at least (2)** du moins ◇ *...but at least nobody was hurt.* ...mais du moins personne n'a été blessé. ◇ *It's totally unfair–at least, that's my opinion.* C'est vraiment injuste–du moins c'est ce que je pense.

leather NOUN
le *cuir* ◇ *a black leather jacket* un blouson en cuir noir

to leave VERB
see also leave NOUN
1 *laisser* (*deliberately*) ◇ *Don't leave your camera in the car.* Ne laisse pas ton appareil-photo dans la voiture.
2 *oublier* (*by mistake*) ◇ *I've left my book at home.* J'ai oublié mon livre à la maison. ◇ *Make sure you haven't left anything behind.* Vérifiez bien que vous n'avez rien oublié.
3 *partir* (*go*) ◇ *The bus leaves at 8.* Le car part à huit heures. ◇ *She's just left.* Elle vient de partir.
4 *quitter* (*go away from*) ◇ *We leave London at six o'clock.* Nous quittons Londres à six heures. ◇ *My sister left home last year.* Ma sœur a quitté la

PTO

maison l'an dernier.

- **to leave somebody alone** laisser quelqu'un tranquille ◇ *Leave me alone!* Laisse-moi tranquille!

leave NOUN

see also leave VERB

1 le *congé* (*from job*)

2 la *permission* (*from army*) ◇ *My brother is on leave for a week.* Mon frère est en permission pendant une semaine.

leaves PL NOUN *see* **leaf**

Lebanon NOUN

le *Liban*

- **in Lebanon** au Liban

lecture NOUN

see also lecture VERB

1 (*public*)

la *conférence*

2 (*at university*)

le *cours magistral*

(les *cours magistraux* PL)

to **lecture** VERB

see also lecture NOUN

1 *enseigner* ◇ *She lectures at the technical college.* Elle enseigne au collège technique.

2 *faire la morale* ◇ *He's always lecturing us.* Il n'arrête pas de nous faire la morale.

lecturer NOUN

le *professeur d'université* ◇ *She's a lecturer.* Elle est professeur d'université.

led VERB *see* **lead**

leek NOUN

le *poireau*

(les *poireaux* PL)

left VERB *see* **leave**

left ADJECTIVE, ADVERB

see also left NOUN

1 *gauche* (*not right*) ◇ *my left hand* ma main gauche ◇ *on the left side of the road* sur le côté gauche de la route

2 *à gauche* ◇ *Turn left at the traffic lights.* Tournez à gauche aux prochains feux.

- **I haven't got any money left.** Il ne me reste plus d'argent.

left NOUN

see also left ADJECTIVE

la *gauche*

- **on the left** à gauche ◇ *Remember to drive on the left.* N'oubliez pas de conduire à gauche.

left-hand ADJECTIVE

- **the left-hand side** la gauche ◇ *It's on the left-hand side.* C'est à gauche.

left-handed ADJECTIVE

gaucher MASC

gauchère FEM

left-luggage office NOUN

la *consigne*

leg NOUN

la *jambe* ◇ *She's broken her leg.* Elle s'est cassé la jambe.

- **a chicken leg** une cuisse de poulet
- **a leg of lamb** un gigot d'agneau

legal ADJECTIVE

légal

(*légaux* MASC PL)

leggings NOUN

le *caleçon* SING

leisure NOUN

les *loisirs* MASC PL ◇ *What do you do in your leisure time?* Qu'est-ce que tu fais pendant tes loisirs?

leisure centre NOUN

le *centre de loisirs*

lemon NOUN

le *citron*

lemonade NOUN

la *limonade*

to **lend** VERB

prêter ◇ *I can lend you some money.* Je peux te prêter de l'argent.

length NOUN

la *longueur*

- **It's about a metre in length.** Ça fait environ un mètre de long.

lens NOUN

1 la *lentille* (*contact lens*)

2 le *verre* (*of spectacles*)

3 l' *objectif* MASC (*of camera*)

Lent NOUN

le *carême*

lent VERB *see* **lend**

lentil NOUN

la *lentille*

Leo NOUN

le *Lion* ◇ *I'm Leo.* Je suis Lion.

leotard NOUN

le *justaucorps*

lesbian NOUN

la *lesbienne*

less PRONOUN, ADVERB, ADJECTIVE

1 *moins* ◇ *He's less intelligent than her.* Il est moins intelligent qu'elle. ◇ *A bit less, please.* Un peu moins, s'il vous plaît.

2 *moins de* ◇ *I've got less time for hobbies now.* J'ai moins de temps pour les loisirs maintenant.

- **less than (1)** (*with amounts*) moins de ◇ *It's less than a kilometre from here.* C'est à moins d'un kilomètre d'ici. ◇ *It costs less than 100 francs.* Ça coûte moins de cent francs. ◇ *less than half* moins de la moitié
- **less than (2)** (*in comparisons*) moins que

◇ *He spent less than me.* Il a dépensé moins que moi. ◇ *I've got less than you.* J'en ai moins que toi. ◇ *It cost less than we thought.* Ça a coûté moins cher que nous ne le pensions.

lesson NOUN
1 la *leçon* ◇ *a French lesson* une leçon de français
◇ *"Lesson Sixteen"* (*in textbook*) "Leçon seize"
2 le *cours* (*class*) ◇ *The lessons last forty minutes each.* Chaque cours dure quarante minutes.

let VERB
1 *laisser* (*allow*)
◆ **to let somebody do something** laisser quelqu'un faire quelque chose ◇ *Let me have a look.* Laisse-moi voir. ◇ *My parents won't let me stay out that late.* Mes parents ne me laissent pas sortir aussi tard.
◆ **to let somebody know** faire savoir à quelqu'un ◇ *I'll let you know as soon as possible.* Je vous le ferai savoir dès que possible.
◆ **to let somebody go** lâcher quelqu'un ◇ *Let me go!* Lâche-moi!
◆ **to let in** laisser entrer ◇ *They wouldn't let me in because I was under 18.* Ils ne m'ont pas laissé entrer parce que j'avais moins de dix-huit ans.

To make suggestions using let's, *you can ask questions beginning with* **si on**.

◇ *Let's go to the cinema!* Si on allait au cinéma?
◆ **Let's go!** Allons-y!
2 *louer* (*hire out*)
◆ **"to let"** "à louer"

letter NOUN
la *lettre*

letterbox NOUN
la *boîte à lettres*

lettuce NOUN
la *salade*

leukaemia NOUN
la *leucémie*

level ADJECTIVE
see also level NOUN
plan
◇ *A snooker table must be perfectly level.* Un billard doit être parfaitement plan.

level NOUN
see also level ADJECTIVE
le *niveau*
(les *niveaux* PL)
◇ *The level of the river is rising.* Le niveau de la rivière monte.
◆ **"A" levels** le baccalauréat

The French baccalauréat *(or* bac *for short) is taken at the age of 17 or 18. Students have to sit one of a variety of set subject combinations, rather than being able to choose any combination of subjects they want. If you pass you have the right to a place at university.*

level crossing NOUN
le *passage à niveau*

lever NOUN
le *levier*

liable ADJECTIVE
◆ **He's liable to lose his temper.** Il se met facilement en colère.

liar NOUN
le *menteur*
la *menteuse*

liberal ADJECTIVE
(*opinions*)
libéral
(*libéraux* MASC PL)
◆ **the Liberal Democrats** le parti libéral-démocrate

liberation NOUN
la *libération*

Libra NOUN
la *Balance* ◇ *I'm Libra.* Je suis Balance.

librarian NOUN
le/la *bibliothécaire* ◇ *She's a librarian.* Elle est bibliothécaire.

library NOUN
la *bibliothèque*

Libya NOUN
la *Libye*
◆ **in Libya** en Libye

licence NOUN
le *permis*
◆ **a driving licence** un permis de conduire

to **lick** VERB
lécher

lid NOUN
le *couvercle*

to **lie** VERB
see also lie NOUN
mentir (*not tell the truth*) ◇ *I know she's lying.* Je sais qu'elle ment.
◆ **to lie down** s'allonger
◆ **to be lying down** être allongé
◆ **He was lying on the sofa.** Il était allongé sur le canapé. ◇ *When I'm on holiday I lie on the beach all day.* Quand je suis en vacances, je reste allongé sur la plage toute la journée.

lie NOUN
see also lie VERB
le *mensonge*
◆ **to tell a lie** mentir
◆ **That's a lie!** Ce n'est pas vrai!

lie-in NOUN
◆ **to have a lie-in** faire la grasse matinée

◇ *I have a lie-in on Sundays.* Je fais la grasse matinée le dimanche.

lieutenant NOUN
le *lieutenant*

life NOUN
la *vie*

lifebelt NOUN
la *bouée de sauvetage*

lifeboat NOUN
le *canot de sauvetage*

lifeguard NOUN
le *maître nageur*

life jacket NOUN
le *gilet de sauvetage*

life-saving NOUN
le *sauvetage* ◇ *I've done a course in life-saving.* J'ai pris des cours de sauvetage.

lifestyle NOUN
le *style de vie*

to **lift** VERB
see also lift NOUN
soulever ◇ *It's too heavy, I can't lift it.* C'est trop lourd, je ne peux pas le soulever.

lift NOUN
see also lift VERB
l' *ascenseur* MASC ◇ *The lift isn't working.* L'ascenseur est en panne.
- **He gave me a lift to the cinema.** Il m'a emmené au cinéma en voiture.
- **Would you like a lift?** Est-ce que je peux vous déposer quelque part?

light ADJECTIVE
see also light NOUN, VERB
1 (*not heavy*)
léger MASC
légère FEM
◇ *a light jacket* une veste légère ◇ *a light meal* un repas léger
2 (*colour*)
clair ◇ *a light blue sweater* un pull bleu clair

light NOUN
see also light ADJECTIVE, VERB
1 la *lumière* ◇ *to switch on the light* allumer la lumière ◇ *to switch off the light* éteindre la lumière
2 la *lampe* ◇ *There's a light by my bed.* Il y a une lampe près de mon lit.
- **the traffic lights** les feux MASC
- **Have you got a light?** (*for cigarette*) Avez-vous du feu?

to **light** VERB
see also light ADJECTIVE, NOUN
allumer (*candle, cigarette, fire*)

light bulb NOUN
l' *ampoule* FEM

lighter NOUN
le *briquet* (*for cigarettes*)

lighthouse NOUN
le *phare*

lightning NOUN
les *éclairs* MASC PL
- **a flash of lightning** un éclair

to **like** VERB
see also like PREPOSITION
1 *aimer* ◇ *I don't like mustard.* Je n'aime pas la moutarde. ◇ *I like riding.* J'aime monter à cheval.
Note that **aimer** *also means to love, so make sure you use* **aimer bien** *for just liking somebody.*
2 *aimer bien* ◇ *I like Paul, but I don't want to go out with him.* J'aime bien Paul, mais je ne veux pas sortir avec lui.
- **I'd like...** Je voudrais... ◇ *I'd like an orange juice, please.* Je voudrais un jus d'orange, s'il vous plaît. ◇ *Would you like some coffee?* Voulez-vous du café?
- **I'd like to...** J'aimerais... ◇ *I'd like to go to Russia one day.* J'aimerais aller en Russie un jour. ◇ *I'd like to wash my hands.* J'aimerais me laver les mains.
- **Would you like to go for a walk?** Tu veux aller faire une promenade?
- **...if you like** ...si tu veux

like PREPOSITION
see also like VERB
comme ◇ *It's fine like that.* C'est bien comme ça. ◇ *Do it like this.* Fais-le comme ça. ◇ *a city like Paris* une ville comme Paris ◇ *It's a bit like salmon.* C'est un peu comme du saumon.
- **What's the weather like?** Quel temps fait-il?
- **to look like somebody** ressembler à quelqu'un ◇ *You look like my brother.* Tu ressembles à mon frère.

likely ADJECTIVE
probable ◇ *That's not very likely.* C'est peu probable.
- **She's likely to come.** Elle viendra probablement.
- **She's not likely to come.** Elle ne viendra probablement pas.

lily of the valley NOUN
le *muguet*

lime NOUN
le *citron vert* (*fruit*)

limit NOUN
la *limite* ◇ *The speed limit is 70 mph.* La vitesse est limitée à cent dix kilomètres à l'heure.

limousine NOUN
la *limousine*

to **limp** VERB
boiter

line NOUN

1 la *ligne* ◇ *a straight line* une ligne droite
2 le *trait* (*to divide, cancel*) ◇ *Draw a line under each answer.* Tirez un trait après chaque réponse.
3 la *voie* (*railway track*)
- **Hold the line, please.** Ne quittez pas.
- **It's a very bad line.** La ligne est très mauvaise.

linen NOUN
le *lin* ◇ *a linen jacket* une veste en lin

liner NOUN
le *paquebot* (*ship*)

linguist NOUN
- **to be a good linguist** être doué pour les langues ◇ *She's a good linguist.* Elle est douée pour les langues.

link NOUN
see also link VERB
le *rapport* ◇ *the link between smoking and cancer* le rapport entre le tabagisme et le cancer

link VERB
see also link NOUN
relier

lino NOUN
le *linoléum*

lion NOUN
le *lion*

lioness NOUN
la *lionne*

lip NOUN
la *lèvre*

lip-read VERB
lire sur les lèvres

lip salve NOUN
la *pommade pour les lèvres*

lipstick NOUN
le *rouge à lèvres*

liqueur NOUN
la *liqueur*

liquid NOUN
le *liquide*

liquidizer NOUN
le *mixer*

list NOUN
see also list VERB
la *liste*

list VERB
see also list NOUN
faire une liste de ◇ *List your hobbies!* Fais une liste de tes hobbies!

listen VERB
écouter ◇ *Listen to this!* Écoutez ceci! ◇ *Listen to me!* Écoutez-moi!

listener NOUN
l' *auditeur* MASC
l' *auditrice* FEM

lit VERB *see* **light**

literally ADVERB
vraiment (*completely*) ◇ *It was literally impossible to find a seat.* Il était vraiment impossible de trouver une place.
- **to translate literally** faire une traduction littérale

literature NOUN
la *littérature* ◇ *I'm studying English Literature.* J'étudie la littérature anglaise.

litre NOUN
le *litre*

litter NOUN
les *ordures* FEM PL

litter bin NOUN
la *poubelle*

little ADJECTIVE
petit ◇ *a little girl* une petite fille
- **a little** un peu ◇ *How much would you like?–Just a little.* Combien en voulez-vous?–Juste un peu.
- **very little** très peu ◇ *We've got very little time.* Nous avons très peu de temps.
- **little by little** petit à petit

live ADJECTIVE
see also live VERB
1 *vivant* (*animal*)
2 *en direct* (*broadcast*)
- **There's live music on Fridays.** Il y a des musiciens qui jouent le vendredi.

to **live** VERB
see also live ADJECTIVE
1 *vivre* ◇ *I live with my grandmother.* Je vis avec ma grand-mère. ◇ *They're not married, they're living together.* Il ne sont pas mariés, ils vivent ensemble.
- **to live on something** vivre de quelque chose ◇ *He lives on benefit.* Il vit de ses indemnités.

2 *habiter* (*reside*) ◇ *Where do you live?* Où est-ce que tu habites? ◇ *I live in Edinburgh.* J'habite à Édimbourg.

liver NOUN
le *foie*

lives PL NOUN
les *vies* FEM

living NOUN
- **to make a living** gagner sa vie
- **What does she do for a living?** Qu'est-ce qu'elle fait dans la vie?

living room NOUN
la *salle de séjour*

lizard NOUN
le *lézard*

load NOUN
see also load VERB
- **loads of** un tas de ◇ *loads of people* un tas de gens ◇ *loads of money* un tas d'argent

PTO

- **You're talking a load of rubbish!** Tu ne dis que des bêtises!

to **load** VERB
see also load NOUN
charger ◇ *a trolley loaded with luggage* un chariot chargé de bagages

loaf NOUN
le *pain*
- **a loaf of bread** un pain

loan NOUN
see also loan VERB
le *prêt*

to **loan** VERB
see also loan NOUN
prêter

to **loathe** VERB
détester ◇ *I loathe her.* Je la déteste.

loaves PL NOUN *see* **loaf**

lobster NOUN
le *homard*

local ADJECTIVE
local
(*locaux* MASC PL)
◇ *the local paper* le journal local
- **a local call** une communication urbaine

loch NOUN
le *loch*

lock NOUN
see also lock VERB
la *serrure* ◇ *The lock is broken.* La serrure est cassée.

to **lock** VERB
see also lock NOUN
fermer à clé ◇ *Make sure you lock your door.* N'oubliez pas de fermer votre porte à clé.

locker NOUN
le *casier*
- **the locker room** le vestiaire
- **the left-luggage lockers** la consigne automatique

locket NOUN
le *médaillon*

lodger NOUN
le/la *locataire*

loft NOUN
le *grenier*

log NOUN
la *bûche* (*of wood*)

logical ADJECTIVE
logique

lollipop NOUN
la *sucette*

lolly NOUN
la *glace à l'eau* (*ice lolly*)

London NOUN
Londres
- **in London** à Londres
- **to London** à Londres
- **I'm from London.** Je suis de Londres.

Londoner NOUN
le *Londonien*
la *Londonienne*

loneliness NOUN
la *solitude*

lonely ADJECTIVE
seul
- **to feel lonely** se sentir seul ◇ *She feels a bit lonely.* Elle se sent un peu seule.

long ADJECTIVE, ADVERB
see also long VERB
long MASC
longue FEM
◇ *She's got long hair.* Elle a les cheveux longs. ◇ *The room is 6 metres long.* La pièce fait six mètres de long.
- **How long?** (*time*) Combien de temps? ◇ *How long did you stay there?* Combien de temps êtes-vous resté là-bas? ◇ *How long have you been here?* Depuis combien de temps êtes-vous ici? ◇ *How long is the flight?* Combien de temps dure le vol?
- **I've been waiting a long time.** J'attends depuis longtemps.
- **It takes a long time.** Ça prend du temps.
- **as long as** si ◇ *I'll come as long as it's not too expensive.* Je viendrai si ce n'est pas trop cher.

to **long** VERB
see also long ADJECTIVE
- **to long to do something** attendre avec impatience de faire quelque chose
- **I'm longing to see my boyfriend again.** J'attends avec impatience de revoir mon copain.

long-distance ADJECTIVE
- **a long-distance call** une communication interurbaine

longer ADVERB
see also long ADJECTIVE
- **They're no longer going out together.** Ils ne sortent plus ensemble.
- **I can't stand it any longer.** Je ne peux plus le supporter.

long jump NOUN
le *saut en longueur*

loo NOUN
les *toilettes* FEM PL ◇ *Where's the loo?* Où sont les toilettes?

look NOUN
see also look VERB
- **to have a look** regarder ◇ *Have a look at this!* Regardez ceci!
- **I don't like the look of it.** Ça ne me dit rien.

to **look** VERB

see also **look** NOUN

1 *regarder* ◇ *Look!* Regardez!

- **to look at something** regarder quelque chose ◇ *Look at the picture.* Regardez cette image.

2 *avoir l'air* (*seem*) ◇ *She looks surprised.* Elle a l'air surprise. ◇ *That cake looks nice.* Ce gâteau a l'air bon. ◇ *It looks fine.* Ça a l'air bien.

- **to look like somebody** ressembler à quelqu'un ◇ *He looks like his brother.* Il ressemble à son frère.
- **What does she look like?** Comment est-elle physiquement?
- **Look out!** Attention!
- **to look after** s'occuper de ◇ *I look after my little sister.* Je m'occupe de ma petite sœur.
- **to look for** chercher ◇ *I'm looking for my passport.* Je cherche mon passeport.
- **to look forward to something** attendre quelque chose avec impatience ◇ *I'm looking forward to the holidays.* J'attends les vacances avec impatience.
- **Looking forward to hearing from you...** J'espère avoir bientôt de tes nouvelles...
- **to look round (1)** (*look behind*) se retourner ◇ *I shouted and he looked round.* J'ai crié et il s'est retourné.
- **to look round (2)** (*have a look*) jeter un coup d'œil ◇ *I'm just looking round.* Je jette simplement un coup d'œil.
- **to look round a museum** visiter un musée
- **I like looking round the shops.** J'aime faire les boutiques.
- **to look up** (*word, name*) chercher ◇ *If you don't know a word, look it up in the dictionary.* Si vous ne connaissez pas un mot, cherchez-le dans le dictionnaire.

loose ADJECTIVE

ample (*clothes*)

- **loose change** la petite monnaie

lord NOUN

le *seigneur* (*feudal*)

- **the House of Lords** la Chambre des lords
- **Good Lord!** Mon Dieu!

lorry NOUN

le *camion*

lorry driver NOUN

le *routier* ◇ *He's a lorry driver.* Il est routier.

lose VERB

perdre ◇ *I've lost my purse.* J'ai perdu mon porte-monnaie.

- **to get lost** se perdre ◇ *I was afraid of getting lost.* J'avais peur de me perdre.

loss NOUN

la *perte*

lost VERB *see* **lose**

lost ADJECTIVE

perdu

lot NOUN

- **a lot** beaucoup
- **a lot of** beaucoup de ◇ *We saw a lot of interesting things.* Nous avons vu beaucoup de choses intéressantes.
- **lots of** un tas de ◇ *She's got lots of money.* Elle a un tas d'argent. ◇ *He's got lots of friends.* Il a un tas d'amis.
- **What did you do at the weekend? – Not a lot.** Qu'as-tu fait ce week-end? – Pas grand-chose.
- **Do you like football? – Not a lot.** Tu aimes le football? – Pas tellement.
- **That's the lot.** C'est tout.

lottery NOUN

la *loterie*

- **to win the lottery** gagner à la loterie

loud ADJECTIVE

fort ◇ *The television is too loud.* La télévision est trop forte.

loudly ADVERB

fort

loudspeaker NOUN

le *haut-parleur*

lounge NOUN

le *salon*

lousy ADJECTIVE

infect ◇ *The food in the canteen is lousy.* La nourriture de la cantine est infecte.

- **I feel lousy.** Je suis mal fichu. (*informal*)

love NOUN

see also **love** VERB

l' *amour* MASC

- **to be in love** être amoureux ◇ *She's in love with Paul.* Elle est amoureuse de Paul.
- **to make love** faire l'amour
- **Give Delphine my love.** Embrasse Delphine pour moi.
- **Love, Rosemary.** Amitiés, Rosemary.

to **love** VERB

see also **love** NOUN

1 *aimer* (*be in love with*) ◇ *I love you.* Je t'aime.

2 *aimer beaucoup* (*like a lot*) ◇ *Everybody loves her.* Tout le monde l'aime beaucoup. ◇ *I'd love to come.* J'aimerais beaucoup venir.

3 *adorer* (*things*) ◇ *I love chocolate.* J'adore le chocolat. ◇ *I love skiing.* J'adore le ski.

lovely ADJECTIVE

charmant ◇ *What a lovely surprise!* Quelle charmante surprise! ◇ *She's a lovely person.* Elle est charmante.

- **It's a lovely day.** Il fait très beau aujourd'hui.
- **Is your meal OK? – Yes, it's lovely.** Est-ce que c'est bon? – Oui, c'est délicieux.
- **They've got a lovely house.** Ils ont une très belle maison.
- **Have a lovely time!** Amusez-vous bien!

low ADJECTIVE, ADVERB
(*price, level*)
bas MASC
basse FEM
◇ *That plane is flying very low.* Cet avion vole très bas.
- **the low season** la basse saison ◇ *in the low season* en basse saison

lower sixth NOUN
la *première* ◇ *He's in the lower sixth.* Il est en première.

low-fat ADJECTIVE
allégé ◇ *a low-fat yoghurt* un yaourt allégé

loyalty NOUN
la *fidélité*

L-plates PL NOUN
les *plaques de conducteur débutant* FEM PL

luck NOUN
la *chance* ◇ *She hasn't had much luck.* Elle n'a pas eu beaucoup de chance.
- **Good luck!** Bonne chance!
- **Bad luck!** Pas de chance!

luckily ADVERB
heureusement

lucky ADJECTIVE
- **to be lucky (1)** (*be fortunate*) avoir de la chance ◇ *He's lucky, he's got a job.* Il a de la chance, il a un emploi. ◇ *He wasn't hurt. – That was lucky!* Il n'a pas été blessé. – C'est une chance!
- **to be lucky (2)** (*bring luck*) porter bonheur ◇ *Black cats are lucky in Britain.* Les chats noirs portent bonheur en Grande-Bretagne.
- **a lucky horseshoe** un fer à cheval porte-bonheur

luggage NOUN
les *bagages* MASC PL

lump NOUN
1 le *morceau*
(les *morceaux* PL)
◇ *a lump of butter* un morceau de beurre
2 la *bosse* (*swelling*) ◇ *He's got a lump on his forehead.* Il a une bosse sur le front.

lunatic NOUN
le *fou*
la *folle*
◇ *He's an absolute lunatic.* Il est complètement fou.

lunch NOUN
le *déjeuner*
- **to have lunch** déjeuner ◇ *We have lunch at 12.30.* Nous déjeunons à midi et demie.

luncheon voucher NOUN
le *ticket-restaurant*

lung NOUN
le *poumon*
- **lung cancer** le cancer du poumon

luscious ADJECTIVE
délicieux MASC
délicieuse FEM

lush ADJECTIVE
luxuriant

lust NOUN
le *désir*

Luxembourg NOUN
1 le *Luxembourg* (*country*)
- **in Luxembourg** au Luxembourg
- **to Luxembourg** au Luxembourg

2 *Luxembourg* (*city*)
- **in Luxembourg** à Luxembourg

luxurious ADJECTIVE
luxueux MASC
luxueuse FEM

luxury NOUN
le *luxe* ◇ *It was luxury!* C'était un vrai luxe!
- **a luxury hotel** un hôtel de luxe

lying VERB *see* **lie**

lyrics PL NOUN
les *paroles* FEM PL (*of song*)

M

nac NOUN
l' *imper* MASC

nacaroni NOUN
les *macaronis* MASC PL

nachine NOUN
la *machine*

nachinery NOUN
les *machines* FEM PL

nackerel NOUN
le *maquereau*
(les *maquereaux* PL)

nad ADJECTIVE
1 (*insane*)
fou MASC
folle FEM
◇ *You're mad!* Tu es fou!
2 (*angry*)
furieux MASC
furieuse FEM
◇ *She'll be mad when she finds out.* Elle sera furieuse quand elle va s'en apercevoir.
◆ **to be mad about (1)** (*sport, activity*) être enragé de ◇ *He's mad about football.* Il est enragé de foot.
◆ **to be mad about (2)** (*person, animal*) adorer ◇ *She's mad about horses.* Elle adore les chevaux.

nadam NOUN
madame FEM ◇ *Would you like to order, Madam?* Désirez-vous commander, Madame?

nade VERB *see* **make**

nadly ADVERB
◆ **They're madly in love.** Ils sont éperdument amoureux.

nadman NOUN
le *fou*

nagazine NOUN
le *magazine*

naggot NOUN
l' *asticot* MASC

nagic ADJECTIVE
see also **magic** NOUN
1 *magique* (*magical*) ◇ *a magic wand* une baguette magique
2 *super* (*brilliant*)
◆ **It was magic!** C'était super!

magic NOUN
see also **magic** ADJECTIVE
la *magie*
◆ **a magic trick** un tour de magie
◆ **My hobby is magic.** Je fais des tours de magie.

magician NOUN
le *prestidigitateur* (*conjurer*)

magnificent ADJECTIVE
1 *magnifique* (*beautiful*) ◇ *a magnificent view* une vue magnifique
2 *superbe* (*outstanding*) ◇ *It was a magnificent effort.* Ils ont fait un superbe effort.

maid NOUN
la *domestique* (*servant*)
◆ **an old maid** (*spinster*) une vieille fille

maiden name NOUN
le *nom de jeune fille*

mail NOUN
le *courrier* ◇ *Here's your mail.* Voici ton courrier.
◆ **e-mail** (*electronic mail*) le courrier électronique
◆ **by mail** par la poste

main ADJECTIVE
principal
(*principaux* MASC PL)
◇ *the main problem* le principal problème
◆ **the main thing is to...** l'essentiel est de...

mainly ADVERB
principalement

main road NOUN
la *grande route* ◇ *I don't like cycling on main roads.* Je n'aime pas faire du vélo sur les grandes routes.

to **maintain** VERB
entretenir (*machine, building*)

maintenance NOUN
l' *entretien* MASC (*of machine, building*)

maize NOUN
le *maïs*

major ADJECTIVE
majeur ◇ *a major problem* un problème majeur
◆ **in C major** en do majeur

Majorca NOUN
Majorque FEM ◇ *We went to Majorca in August.* Nous sommes allés à Majorque en août.

majority NOUN
la *majorité*

make NOUN
see also **make** VERB
la *marque* ◇ *What make is that car?* De quelle marque est cette voiture?

to **make** VERB
see also **make** NOUN
1 *faire* ◇ *I'm going to make a cake.* Je vais faire un gâteau. ◇ *He made it himself.* Il l'a fait lui-même. ◇ *I make my bed every morning.* Je fais mon lit tous les matins. ◇ *2 and 2 make 4.* Deux et deux font quatre.

2 *fabriquer* (*manufacture*) ◇ *made in France* fabriqué en France
3 *gagner* (*earn*) ◇ *He makes a lot of money.* Il gagne beaucoup d'argent.
- **to make somebody do something** obliger quelqu'un à faire quelque chose ◇ *My mother makes me do my homework.* Ma mère m'oblige à faire mes devoirs.
- **to make lunch** préparer le repas ◇ *She's making lunch.* Elle prépare le repas.
- **to make a phone call** donner un coup de téléphone ◇ *I'd like to make a phone call.* J'aimerais donner un coup de téléphone.
- **to make fun of somebody** se moquer de quelqu'un ◇ *They made fun of him.* Ils se sont moqués de lui.
- **What time do you make it?** Quelle heure avez-vous?

to **make up** VERB
1 *inventer* (*invent*) ◇ *He made up the whole story.* Il a inventé cette histoire de toutes pièces.
2 *se réconcilier* (*after argument*) ◇ *They had a quarrel, but soon made up.* Ils se sont disputés, mais se sont vite réconciliés.
- **to make oneself up** se maquiller ◇ *She spends hours making herself up.* Elle passe des heures à se maquiller.

make-up NOUN
le *maquillage*

Malaysia NOUN
la *Malaisie*
- **in Malaysia** en Malaisie

male ADJECTIVE
1 *mâle* (*animals, plants*) ◇ *a male kitten* un chaton mâle
2 *masculin* (*person, on official forms*) ◇ *Sex: male.* Sexe : masculin.
- **Most football players are male.** La plupart des joueurs de football sont des hommes.
- **a male chauvinist** un macho
- **a male nurse** un infirmier

Malta NOUN
Malte
- **in Malta** à Malte
- **to Malta** à Malte

mammoth NOUN
see also mammoth ADJECTIVE
le *mammouth*

mammoth ADJECTIVE
see also mammoth NOUN
monstre ◇ *a mammoth task* un travail monstre

man NOUN
l' *homme* MASC ◇ *an old man* un vieil homme

to **manage** VERB
1 *gérer* (*be in charge of*) ◇ *She manages a big store.* Elle dirige un grand magasin. ◇ *He manages our football team.* Il dirige notre équipe de foot.
2 *se débrouiller* (*get by*) ◇ *We haven't got much money, but we manage.* Nous n'avons pas beaucoup d'argent, mais nous nous débrouillons. ◇ *It's okay, I can manage.* Ça va, je me débrouille.
- **Can you manage okay?** Tu y arrives?
- **to manage to do something** réussir à faire quelque chose ◇ *Luckily I managed to pass the exam.* J'ai heureusement réussi à avoir mon examen.
- **I can't manage all that.** (*food*) C'est trop pour moi.

manageable ADJECTIVE
faisable (*task*)

management NOUN
1 la *gestion* (*organization*) ◇ *He's responsible for the management of the company.* Il est responsable de la gestion de la société.
2 la *direction* (*people in charge*) ◇ *"under new management"* "changement de direction"

manager NOUN
1 (*of company*)
le *directeur*
la *directrice*
2 (*of shop, restaurant*)
le *gérant*
la *gérante*
3 (*of team, performer*)
le *manager*

manageress NOUN
la *gérante*

mandarin NOUN
la *mandarine* (*fruit*)

mango NOUN
la *mangue*

mania NOUN
la *manie*

maniac NOUN
le *fou*
la *folle*
◇ *He drives like a maniac.* Il conduit comme un fou.
- **a religious maniac** un fanatique religieux

man-made ADJECTIVE
synthétique (*fibre*)

manner NOUN
la *façon*
- **She behaves in an odd manner.** Elle se comporte de façon étrange.

- **He has a confident manner.** Il a de l'assurance.

manners PL NOUN
les *manières* FEM PL ◇ *good manners* les bonnes manières ◇ *Her manners are appalling.* Elle a de très mauvaises manières.
- **It's bad manners to speak with your mouth full.** Ce n'est pas poli de parler la bouche pleine.

manpower NOUN
la *main-d'œuvre*

mansion NOUN
le *manoir*

mantelpiece NOUN
la *cheminée*

manual NOUN
le *manuel*

manufacture VERB
fabriquer

manufacturer NOUN
le *fabricant*

manure NOUN
le *fumier*

manuscript NOUN
le *manuscrit*

many ADJECTIVE, PRONOUN
beaucoup de ◇ *The film has many special effects.* Le film a beaucoup d'effets spéciaux. ◇ *He hasn't got many friends.* Il n'a pas beaucoup d'amis. ◇ *Were there many people at the concert?* Est-ce qu'il y avait beaucoup de gens au concert?
- **very many** beaucoup de ◇ *I haven't got very many CDs.* Je n'ai pas beaucoup de CD.
- **Not many.** Pas beaucoup.
- **How many?** Combien? ◇ *How many do you want?* Combien en veux-tu?
- **how many...?** combien de...? ◇ *How many francs do you get for £1?* Combien de francs a-t-on pour une livre?
- **too many** trop ◇ *That's too many.* C'est trop.
- **too many...** trop de... ◇ *She makes too many mistakes.* Elle fait trop d'erreurs.
- **so many** autant ◇ *I didn't know there would be so many.* Je ne pensais pas qu'il y en aurait autant.
- **so many...** autant de... ◇ *I've never seen so many policemen.* Je n'ai jamais vu autant de policiers.

map NOUN
1 la *carte* (*of country, area*)
2 le *plan* (*of town*)

marathon NOUN
le *marathon* ◇ *the London marathon* le marathon de Londres

marble NOUN
le *marbre* ◇ *a marble statue* une statue en marbre
- **to play marbles** jouer aux billes

March NOUN
mars MASC
- **in March** en mars

march NOUN
see also **march** VERB
la *manifestation* (*demonstration*)

to **march** VERB
see also **march** NOUN
1 *marcher au pas* (*soldiers*)
2 *défiler* (*protesters*)

mare NOUN
la *jument*

margarine NOUN
la *margarine*

margin NOUN
la *marge* ◇ *Write notes in the margin.* Écrivez vos notes dans la marge.

marijuana NOUN
la *marijuana*

marital status NOUN
la *situation de famille*

mark NOUN
see also **mark** VERB
1 la *note* (*in school*) ◇ *I get good marks for French.* J'ai de bonnes notes en français.
2 la *tache* (*stain*) ◇ *You've got a mark on your skirt.* Tu as une tache sur ta jupe.
3 le *mark* (*German currency*)

to **mark** VERB
see also **mark** NOUN
corriger ◇ *The teacher hasn't marked my homework yet.* Le professeur n'a pas encore corrigé mon devoir.

market NOUN
le *marché*

marketing NOUN
le *marketing*

marmalade NOUN
la *confiture d'oranges*

maroon ADJECTIVE
bordeaux MASC, FEM, PL (*colour*)

marriage NOUN
le *mariage*

married ADJECTIVE
marié ◇ *They are not married.* Ils ne sont pas mariés. ◇ *They have been married for 15 years.* Ils sont mariés depuis quinze ans. ◇ *a married couple* un couple marié

to **marry** VERB
épouser ◇ *He wants to marry her.* Il veut l'épouser.
- **to get married** se marier ◇ *My sister's getting married in June.* Ma sœur se

M

PTO

marie en juin.

marvellous ADJECTIVE
1 *excellent* ◇ *She's a marvellous cook.* C'est une excellente cuisinière.
2 *superbe* ◇ *The weather was marvellous.* Il a fait un temps superbe.

marzipan NOUN
la *pâte d'amandes*

mascara NOUN
le *mascara*

masculine ADJECTIVE
masculin

mashed potatoes PL NOUN
la *purée* ◇ *sausages and mashed potatoes* des saucisses avec de la purée

mask NOUN
le *masque*

mass NOUN
1 la *multitude* ◇ *a mass of books and papers* une multitude de livres et de papiers
2 la *messe* (*in church*) ◇ *We go to mass on Sunday.* Nous allons à la messe le dimanche.
◆ **the mass media** les médias

massage NOUN
le *massage*

massive ADJECTIVE
énorme

to **master** VERB
maîtriser

masterpiece NOUN
le *chef-d'œuvre*
(les *chefs-d'œuvre* PL)

mat NOUN
le *paillasson* (*doormat*)
◆ **a table mat** un set de table
◆ **a beach mat** un tapis de plage

match NOUN
see also match VERB
1 l' *allumette* FEM ◇ *a box of matches* une boîte d'allumettes
2 (*sport*)
le *match*
(les *matchs* PL)
◇ *a football match* un match de foot

to **match** VERB
see also match NOUN
être assorti à ◇ *The jacket matches the trousers.* La veste est assortie au pantalon.
◆ **These colours don't match.** Ces couleurs ne vont pas ensemble.

matching ADJECTIVE
assorti ◇ *My bedroom has matching wallpaper and curtains.* Ma chambre a du papier peint et des rideaux assortis.

mate NOUN
le *pote* (*informal*) ◇ *On Friday night I go out with my mates.* Vendredi soir, je sors avec mes potes.

material NOUN
1 le *tissu* (*cloth*)
2 la *documentation* (*information, data*) ◇ *I'm collecting material for my project.* Je rassemble une documentation pour mon dossier.
◆ **raw materials** les matières premières FEM

mathematics NOUN
les *mathématiques* FEM PL

maths NOUN
les *maths* FEM PL

matron NOUN
l' *infirmière-chef* FEM (*in hospital*)

matter NOUN
see also matter VERB
la *question* ◇ *It's a matter of life and death.* C'est une question de vie ou de mort.
◆ **What's the matter?** Qu'est-ce qui ne va pas?
◆ **as a matter of fact** en fait

to **matter** VERB
see also matter NOUN
◆ **it doesn't matter (1)** (*I don't mind*) ça ne fait rien ◇ *I can't give you the money today.–It doesn't matter.* Je ne peux pas te donner l'argent aujourd'hui.–Ça ne fait rien.
◆ **it doesn't matter (2)** (*it makes no difference*) ça n'a pas d'importance ◇ *Shall I phone today or tomorrow?–Whenever, it doesn't matter.* Est-ce que j'appelle aujourd'hui ou demain?–Quand tu veux, ça n'a pas d'importance.
◆ **It matters a lot to me.** C'est très important pour moi.

mattress NOUN
le *matelas*

mature ADJECTIVE
mûr ◇ *She's quite mature for her age.* Elle est très mûre pour son âge.

maximum NOUN
see also maximum ADJECTIVE
le *maximum*

maximum ADJECTIVE
see also maximum NOUN
maximum MASC, FEM, PL ◇ *The maximum speed is 100 km/h.* La vitesse maximum autorisée est de cent kilomètres à l'heure.
◆ **the maximum amount** le maximum

May NOUN
mai MASC
◆ **in May** en mai
◆ **May Day** le Premier Mai

may VERB
◆ **He may come.** Il va peut-être venir.

◇ *It may rain.* Il va peut-être pleuvoir.
◆ **Are you going to the party?–I don't know, I may.** Est-ce que tu vas à la soirée?–Je ne sais pas, peut-être.
◆ **May I smoke?** Est-ce que je peux fumer?

maybe ADVERB
peut-être ◇ *maybe not* peut-être pas ◇ *a bit boring, maybe* peut-être un peu ennuyeux ◇ *Maybe she's at home.* Elle est peut-être chez elle. ◇ *Maybe he'll change his mind.* Il va peut-être changer d'avis.

mayonnaise NOUN
la *mayonnaise*

mayor NOUN
le *maire*

me PRONOUN
me *becomes* **m'** *before a vowel sound.*
1 *me* ◇ *Could you lend me your pen?* Est-ce que tu peux me prêter ton stylo? *m'* ◇ *Can you tell me the way to the station?* Est-ce que vous pouvez m'indiquer le chemin de la gare? ◇ *Can you help me?* Est-ce que tu peux m'aider? ◇ *He heard me.* Il m'a entendu.
moi *is used in exclamations.*
2 *moi* ◇ *Me too!* Moi aussi! ◇ *Excuse me!* Excusez-moi! ◇ *Look at me!* Regarde-moi! ◇ *Wait for me!* Attends-moi! ◇ *Come with me!* Suivez-moi!
moi *is also used after prepositions and in comparisons.*
◇ *You're after me.* Tu es après moi. ◇ *Is it for me?* C'est pour moi? ◇ *She's older than me.* Elle est plus âgée que moi.

meal NOUN
le *repas*

mealtime NOUN
◆ **at mealtimes** aux heures des repas

mean VERB
see also mean ADJECTIVE *and* means NOUN
vouloir dire ◇ *What does "complet" mean?* Qu'est-ce que "complet" veut dire? ◇ *I don't know what it means.* Je ne sais pas ce que ça veut dire. ◇ *What do you mean?* Qu'est que vous voulez dire? ◇ *That's not what I meant.* Ce n'est pas ce que je voulais dire.
◆ **Which one do you mean?** Duquel veux-tu parler?
◆ **Do you really mean it?** Tu es sérieux?
◆ **to mean to do something** avoir l'intention de faire quelque chose ◇ *I didn't mean to offend you.* Je n'avais pas l'intention de vous blesser.

mean ADJECTIVE
see also mean VERB *and* means NOUN
1 *radin* (*with money*) ◇ *He's too mean to buy Christmas presents.* Il est trop radin pour acheter des cadeaux de Noël.
2 *méchant* (*unkind*) ◇ *You're being mean to me.* Tu es méchant avec moi.
◆ **That's a really mean thing to say!** Ce n'est vraiment pas gentil de dire ça!

meaning NOUN
le *sens*

means NOUN
see also mean VERB *and* ADJECTIVE
le *moyen* ◇ *He'll do it by any possible means.* Il le fera par tous les moyens. ◇ *a means of transport* un moyen de transport
◆ **by means of** au moyen de ◇ *He got in by means of a stolen key.* Il est entré au moyen d'une clé volée.
◆ **by all means** bien sûr ◇ *Can I come?–By all means!* Est-ce que je peux venir?–Bien sûr!

meant VERB *see* **mean**

measles NOUN
la *rougeole*

to **measure** VERB
1 *mesurer* ◇ *I measured the page.* J'ai mesuré la page.
2 *faire* ◇ *The room measures 3 metres by 4.* La pièce fait trois mètres sur quatre.

measurements PL NOUN
1 les *dimensions* FEM (*of object*) ◇ *What are the measurements of the room?* Quelles sont les dimensions de la pièce?
2 les *mensurations* FEM (*of body*) ◇ *What are your measurements?* Quelles sont tes mensurations?
◆ **my waist measurement** mon tour de taille
◆ **What's your neck measurement?** Quel est votre tour de cou?

meat NOUN
la *viande* ◇ *I don't eat meat.* Je ne mange pas de viande.

Mecca NOUN
[La] Mecque

mechanic NOUN
le *mécanicien* ◇ *He's a mechanic.* Il est mécanicien.

mechanical ADJECTIVE
mécanique MASC, FEM

medal NOUN
la *médaille*
◆ **the gold medal** la médaille d'or

media PL NOUN
les *médias* MASC

medical ADJECTIVE
see also medical NOUN
médical
(*médicaux* MASC PL)

◇ *medical treatment* les soins médicaux
◆ **medical insurance** l'assurance maladie
◆ **to have medical problems** avoir des problèmes de santé
◆ **She's a medical student.** Elle est étudiante en médecine.

medical NOUN
see also medical ADJECTIVE
◆ **to have a medical** passer une visite médicale

medicine NOUN
1 la *médecine* (*subject*) ◇ *I want to study medicine.* Je veux faire médecine.
◆ **alternative medicine** la médecine douce
2 le *médicament* (*medication*) ◇ *I need some medicine.* J'ai besoin d'un médicament.

Mediterranean ADJECTIVE
méditerranéen MASC
méditerranéenne FEM
◆ **the Mediterranean** la Méditerranée

medium ADJECTIVE
moyen MASC
moyenne FEM
◇ *a man of medium height* un homme de taille moyenne

medium-sized ADJECTIVE
de taille moyenne ◇ *a medium-sized town* une ville de taille moyenne

to **meet** VERB
1 *rencontrer* (*by chance*) ◇ *I met Paul when I was walking the dog.* J'ai rencontré Paul alors que je promenais mon chien. ◇ *Have you met him before?* Est-ce que tu l'as déjà rencontré?
2 *se rencontrer* ◇ *We met by chance in the shopping centre.* Nous nous sommes rencontrés par hasard dans le centre commercial.
3 *retrouver* (*by arrangement*) ◇ *I'm going to meet my friends.* Je vais retrouver mes amis.
4 *se retrouver* ◇ *Let's meet in front of the tourist office.* Retrouvons-nous devant l'office de tourisme.
◆ **I like meeting new people.** J'aime faire de nouvelles connaissances.
5 *aller chercher* (*pick up*) ◇ *I'll meet you at the station.* J'irai te chercher à la gare.

meeting NOUN
1 la *réunion* (*for work*) ◇ *a business meeting* une réunion d'affaires
2 la *rencontre* (*socially*) ◇ *their first meeting* leur première rencontre

mega ADJECTIVE
◆ **He's mega rich.** Il est hyper-riche. (*informal*)

melody NOUN
la *mélodie*

melon NOUN
le *melon*

to **melt** VERB
fondre ◇ *The snow is melting.* La neige est en train de fondre.

member NOUN
le *membre*
◆ **a Member of Parliament** un député

membership card NOUN
la *carte de membre*

memorial NOUN
le *monument* ◇ *a war memorial* un monument aux morts

to **memorize** VERB
apprendre par cœur

memory NOUN
1 la *mémoire* ◇ *I haven't got a good memory.* Je n'ai pas une bonne mémoire
2 le *souvenir* (*recollection*) ◇ *to bring back memories* rappeler des souvenirs

men PL NOUN *see* **man**
les *hommes* MASC

to **mend** VERB
réparer

meningitis NOUN
la *méningite*

mental ADJECTIVE
1 *mental*
(*mentaux* MASC PL)
◇ *a mental illness* une maladie mentale
2 (*mad*)
fou MASC
folle FEM
◇ *You're mental!* Tu es fou!
◆ **a mental hospital** un hôpital psychiatrique

to **mention** VERB
mentionner
◆ **Thank you! – Don't mention it!** Merci! – Il n'y a pas de quoi!

menu NOUN
le *menu* ◇ *Could I have the menu please?* Est-ce que je pourrais avoir le menu s'il vous plaît?

merchant NOUN
le *marchand* ◇ *a wine merchant* un marchand de vin

mercy NOUN
la *pitié*

meringue NOUN
la *meringue*

merry ADJECTIVE
◆ **Merry Christmas!** Joyeux Noël!

merry-go-round NOUN
le *manège*

mess NOUN
le *fouillis* ◇ *My bedroom's usually in a mess.* Il y a généralement du fouillis

dans ma chambre.

mess about VERB
- **to mess about with something** (*interfere with*) tripoter quelque chose ◇ *Stop messing about with my computer!* Arrête de tripoter mon ordinateur!
- **Don't mess about with my things!** Ne touche pas à mes affaires!

mess up VERB
- **to mess something up** mettre la pagaille dans quelque chose ◇ *My little brother has messed up my cassettes.* Mon petit frère a mis la pagaille dans mes cassettes.

message NOUN
le *message*

messenger NOUN
le *messager*

messy ADJECTIVE
1 *salissant* (*dirty*) ◇ *a messy job* un travail salissant
2 *en désordre* (*untidy*) ◇ *Your desk is really messy.* Ton bureau est vraiment en désordre.
3 *désordonnée* (*person*) ◇ *She's so messy!* Elle est tellement désordonnée!
- **My writing is terribly messy.** J'ai une écriture de cochon.

met VERB *see* **meet**

metal NOUN
le *métal*
(les *métaux* PL)

meter NOUN
1 le *compteur* (*for gas, electricity, taxi*)
2 le *parcmètre* (*parking meter*)

method NOUN
la *méthode*

Methodist NOUN
le/la *méthodiste* ◇ *I'm a Methodist.* Je suis méthodiste.

metre NOUN
le *mètre*

metric ADJECTIVE
métrique

Mexico NOUN
le *Mexique*
- **in Mexico** au Mexique
- **to Mexico** au Mexique

miaow VERB
miauler

mice PL NOUN *see* **mouse**

microchip NOUN
la *puce*

microphone NOUN
le *microphone*

microscope NOUN
le *microscope*

microwave oven NOUN
le *four à micro-ondes*

mid ADJECTIVE
- **in mid May** à la mi-mai

midday NOUN
le *midi*
- **at midday** à midi

middle NOUN
le *milieu* ◇ *in the middle of the road* au milieu de la route ◇ *in the middle of the night* au milieu de la nuit ◇ *the middle seat* la place du milieu

middle-aged ADJECTIVE
d'un certain âge ◇ *a middle-aged man* un homme d'un certain âge
- **to be middle-aged** avoir la cinquantaine
- **She's middle-aged.** Elle a la cinquantaine.

middle-class ADJECTIVE
de la classe moyenne ◇ *a middle-class family* une famille de la classe moyenne

Middle East NOUN
le *Moyen-Orient*
- **in the Middle East** au Moyen-Orient

middle name NOUN
le *deuxième nom*

midge NOUN
le *moucheron*

midnight NOUN
minuit MASC
- **at midnight** à minuit

might VERB
Use **peut-être** *to express possibility.*
◇ *He might come later.* Il va peut-être venir plus tard. ◇ *We might go to Spain next year.* Nous irons peut-être en Espagne l'an prochain. ◇ *She might not have understood.* Elle n'a peut-être pas compris.

migraine NOUN
la *migraine* ◇ *I've got a migraine.* J'ai la migraine.

mike NOUN
le *micro*

mild ADJECTIVE
doux MASC
douce FEM
◇ *The winters are quite mild.* Les hivers sont assez doux.

mile NOUN
le *mille*
In France distances are expressed in kilometres. A mile is about 1.6 kilometres.
◇ *It's 5 miles from here.* C'est à huit kilomètres d'ici.
- **We walked miles!** Nous avons fait des kilomètres à pied!

military ADJECTIVE
militaire MASC, FEM

milk NOUN

PTO

see also milk VERB

le *lait* ◇ *tea with milk* du thé au lait

to **milk** VERB

see also milk NOUN

traire

milk chocolate NOUN

le *chocolat au lait*

milkman NOUN

In France milk is not delivered to people's homes.

◇ *He's a milkman.* Il livre le lait à domicile.

milk shake NOUN

le *milk-shake*

mill NOUN

le *moulin* (*for grain*)

millimetre NOUN

le *millimètre*

million NOUN

le *million*

millionaire NOUN

le *millionnaire*

to **mimic** VERB

imiter

mince NOUN

la *viande hachée*

to **mind** VERB

see also mind NOUN

1 *garder* ◇ *Could you mind the baby this afternoon?* Est-ce que tu pourrais garder le bébé cet après-midi?

2 *surveiller* (*keep an eye on*) ◇ *Could you mind my bags for a few minutes?* Est-ce que vous pourriez surveiller mes bagages pendant quelques minutes?

◆ **Do you mind if I open the window?** Est-ce que je pourrais ouvrir la fenêtre?

◆ **I don't mind.** Ça ne me dérange pas. ◇ *I don't mind the noise.* Le bruit ne me dérange pas.

◆ **Never mind!** Ça ne fait rien!

◆ **Mind that bike!** Attention au vélo!

◆ **Mind the step!** Attention à la marche!

mind NOUN

see also mind VERB

◆ **to make up one's mind** se décider ◇ *I haven't made up my mind yet.* Je ne me suis pas encore décidé.

◆ **to change one's mind** changer d'avis ◇ *He's changed his mind.* Il a changé d'avis.

◆ **Are you out of your mind?** Tu as perdu la tête?

mine PRONOUN

see also mine NOUN

le mien + MASC NOUN ◇ *Is this your coat?–No, mine's black.* C'est ton manteau?–Non, le mien est noir.

la mienne + FEM NOUN ◇ *Is this your car?–No, mine's green.* C'est ta voiture?–Non, la mienne est verte.

les miens + MASC PL NOUN ◇ *her parents and mine* ses parents et les miens

les miennes + FEM PL NOUN ◇ *Your hands are dirty, mine are clean.* Tes mains sont sales, les miennes sont propres.

◆ **It's mine.** C'est à moi. ◇ *This book is mine.* Ce livre est à moi. ◇ *Whose is this?–It's mine.* C'est à qui?–À moi.

mine NOUN

see also mine PRONOUN

la *mine* ◇ *a coal mine* une mine de charbon ◇ *a land mine* une mine terrestre

miner NOUN

le *mineur*

mineral water NOUN

l' *eau minérale* FEM

miniature ADJECTIVE

see also miniature NOUN

miniature ◇ *a miniature version* une version miniature

miniature NOUN

see also miniature ADJECTIVE

la *miniature*

minibus NOUN

le *minibus*

minimum NOUN

see also minimum ADJECTIVE

le *minimum*

minimum ADJECTIVE

see also minimum NOUN

minimum MASC, FEM, PL ◇ *There's no minimum wage in Britain.* Il n'y a pas de salaire minimum en Grande-Bretagne. ◇ *The minimum age for driving is 17.* L'âge minimum pour conduire est dix-sept ans.

◆ **the minimum amount** le minimum

miniskirt NOUN

la *mini-jupe*

minister NOUN

1 le *ministre* (*in government*)

2 le *pasteur* (*of church*)

minor ADJECTIVE

mineur ◇ *a minor problem* un problème mineur

◆ **in D minor** en ré mineur

◆ **a minor operation** une opération bénigne

minority NOUN

la *minorité*

mint NOUN

1 la *menthe* (*plant*) ◇ *mint sauce* la sauce à la menthe

2 le *bonbon à la menthe* (*sweet*)

minus PREPOSITION

moins ◇ *16 minus 3 is 13.* Seize moins trois égale treize. ◇ *It's minus two degrees outside.* Il fait moins deux dehors. ◇ *I got a B minus.* J'ai eu un B moins.

minute NOUN
see also minute ADJECTIVE
la *minute* ◇ *Wait a minute!* Attends une minute!

minute ADJECTIVE
see also minute NOUN
minuscule ◇ *Her flat is minute.* Son appartement est minuscule.

miracle NOUN
le *miracle*

mirror NOUN
1 la *glace* (*on wall*)
2 le *rétroviseur* (*in car*)

misbehave VERB
se conduire mal

mischief NOUN
les *bêtises* FEM PL ◇ *My little sister's always up to mischief.* Ma petite sœur fait constamment des bêtises.

mischievous ADJECTIVE
coquin

miser NOUN
l' *avare* MASC / FEM

miserable ADJECTIVE
1 (*person*)
malheureux MASC
malheureuse FEM
◇ *You're looking miserable.* Tu as l'air malheureux.
2 (*weather*)
épouvantable ◇ *The weather was miserable.* Il faisait un temps épouvantable.
◆ **to feel miserable** ne pas avoir le moral ◇ *I'm feeling miserable.* Je n'ai pas le moral.

misfortune NOUN
le *malheur*

mishap NOUN
la *mésaventure*

misjudge VERB
mal juger (*person*) ◇ *I've misjudged her.* Je l'ai mal jugée.
◆ **He misjudged the bend.** Il a mal pris le virage.

mislay VERB
égarer ◇ *I've mislaid my passport.* J'ai égaré mon passeport.

misleading ADJECTIVE
trompeur MASC
trompeuse FEM

Miss NOUN
1 *Mademoiselle*
(*Mesdemoiselles* PL)
2 (*in address*)
Mlle
(*Mlles* PL)

to **miss** VERB
1 *rater* ◇ *Hurry or you'll miss the bus.* Dépêche-toi ou tu vas rater le bus. ◇ *He missed the target.* Il a raté la cible.
2 *manquer* ◇ *to miss an opportunity* manquer une occasion
◆ **I miss you.** Tu me manques. ◇ *I'm missing my family.* Ma famille me manque. ◇ *I miss him.* Il me manque. ◇ *I miss them.* Ils me manquent.

missing ADJECTIVE
manquant ◇ *the missing part* la pièce manquante
◆ **to be missing** avoir disparu ◇ *My rucksack is missing.* Mon sac à dos a disparu. ◇ *Two members of the group are missing.* Deux membres du groupe ont disparu.

missionary NOUN
le/la *missionnaire*

mist NOUN
la *brume*

mistake NOUN
see also mistake VERB
1 la *faute* (*slip*) ◇ *a spelling mistake* une faute d'orthographe
◆ **to make a mistake (1)** (*in writing, speaking*) faire une faute
◆ **to make a mistake (2)** (*get mixed up*) se tromper ◇ *I'm sorry, I made a mistake.* Je suis désolé, je me suis trompé.
2 l' *erreur* FEM (*misjudgement*) ◇ *It was a mistake to buy those yellow shoes.* J'ai fait une erreur en achetant ces chaussures jaunes.
◆ **by mistake** par erreur ◇ *I took his bag by mistake.* J'ai pris son sac par erreur.

to **mistake** VERB
see also mistake NOUN
◆ **He mistook me for my sister.** Il m'a prise pour ma sœur.

mistaken ADJECTIVE
◆ **to be mistaken** se tromper ◇ *If you think I'm going to get up at 6 o'clock, you're mistaken.* Si tu penses que je vais me lever à six heures, tu te trompes.

mistletoe NOUN
le *gui*

mistook VERB *see* **mistake**

mistress NOUN
1 le *professeur* (*teacher*) ◇ *our French mistress* notre professeur de français
2 la *maîtresse* (*lover*) ◇ *He's got a mistress.* Il a une maîtresse.

to **mistrust** VERB
se méfier de

misty ADJECTIVE
brumeux MASC

PTO

brumeuse FEM
◇ *a misty morning* un matin brumeux

to **misunderstand** VERB
mal comprendre ◇ *Sorry, I misunderstood you.* Je suis désolé, je t'avais mal compris.

misunderstanding NOUN
le *malentendu*

mix NOUN
see also mix VERB
le *mélange* ◇ *It's a mix of science fiction and comedy.* C'est un mélange de science-fiction et de comédie.
◆ **a cake mix** une préparation pour gâteau

to **mix** VERB
see also mix NOUN
1 *mélanger* ◇ *Mix the flour with the sugar.* Mélangez la farine au sucre.
2 *combiner* ◇ *He's mixing business with pleasure.* Il combine les affaires et le plaisir.
◆ **to mix with somebody** (*associate*) fréquenter quelqu'un
◆ **He doesn't mix much.** Il se tient à l'écart.
◆ **to mix up** (*people*) confondre ◇ *He always mixes me up with my sister.* Il me confond toujours avec ma sœur.
◆ **The travel agent mixed up the bookings.** L'agence de voyage s'est embrouillée dans les réservations.
◆ **I'm getting mixed up.** Je ne m'y retrouve plus.

mixed ADJECTIVE
◆ **a mixed salad** une salade composée
◆ **a mixed school** une école mixte
◆ **a mixed grill** un assortiment de grillades

mixture NOUN
le *mélange* ◇ *a mixture of spices* un mélange d'épices
◆ **cough mixture** le sirop pour la toux

mix-up NOUN
la *confusion*

to **moan** VERB
râler ◇ *She's always moaning.* Elle est toujours en train de râler.

mobile home NOUN
le *mobile home*

mobile phone NOUN
le *téléphone portatif*

to **mock** VERB
see also mock ADJECTIVE
ridiculiser

mock ADJECTIVE
see also mock VERB
◆ **a mock exam** un examen blanc

model NOUN
see also model ADJECTIVE
1 le *modèle* (*type*) ◇ *His car is the latest model.* Sa voiture est le tout dernier modèle.
2 la *maquette* (*mock-up*) ◇ *a model of the castle* une maquette du château
3 le *mannequin* (*fashion*) ◇ *She's a famous model.* C'est un mannequin célèbre.

model ADJECTIVE
see also model NOUN
◆ **a model plane** un modèle réduit d'avion
◆ **a model railway** un modèle réduit de voie ferrée
◆ **He's a model pupil.** C'est un élève modèle.

modem NOUN
le *modem*

moderate ADJECTIVE
modéré ◇ *His views are quite moderate.* Ses opinions sont assez modérées.
◆ **a moderate amount of** un peu de
◆ **a moderate price** un prix raisonnable

modern ADJECTIVE
moderne

to **modernize** VERB
moderniser

modest ADJECTIVE
modeste

to **modify** VERB
modifier

moisture NOUN
l' *humidité* FEM

moisturizer NOUN
1 la *crème hydratante* (*cream*)
2 le *lait hydratant* (*lotion*)

mole NOUN
1 la *taupe* (*animal*)
2 le *grain de beauté* (*on skin*)

moment NOUN
l' *instant* MASC ◇ *Could you wait a moment?* Pouvez-vous attendre un instant? ◇ *in a moment* dans un instant ◇ *Just a moment!* Un instant!
◆ **at the moment** en ce moment
◆ **any moment now** d'un moment à l'autre ◇ *They'll be arriving any moment now.* Ils vont arriver d'un moment à l'autre.

Monaco NOUN
Monaco
◆ **in Monaco** à Monaco

monarch NOUN
le *monarque*

monarchy NOUN
la *monarchie*

monastery NOUN
le *monastère*

Monday NOUN
le *lundi* ◇ *on Monday* lundi ◇ *on*

Mondays le lundi ◇ *every Monday* tous les lundis ◇ *last Monday* lundi dernier ◇ *next Monday* lundi prochain

money NOUN
l' *argent* MASC ◇ *I need to change some money.* J'ai besoin de changer de l'argent.
◆ **to make money** gagner de l'argent

mongrel NOUN
le *bâtard* ◇ *My dog's a mongrel.* Mon chien est un bâtard.

monitor NOUN
le *moniteur* (*of computer*)

monk NOUN
le *moine*

monkey NOUN
le *singe*

monotonous ADJECTIVE
monotone

monster NOUN
le *monstre*

month NOUN
le *mois* ◇ *this month* ce mois-ci ◇ *next month* le mois prochain ◇ *last month* le mois dernier ◇ *every month* tous les mois ◇ *at the end of the month* à la fin du mois

monthly ADJECTIVE
mensuel MASC
mensuelle FEM

monument NOUN
le *monument*

mood NOUN
l' *humeur* FEM
◆ **to be in a bad mood** être de mauvaise humeur
◆ **to be in a good mood** être de bonne humeur

moody ADJECTIVE
1 *lunatique* (*temperamental*)
2 *maussade* (*in a bad mood*)

moon NOUN
la *lune* ◇ *There's a full moon tonight.* Il y a pleine lune ce soir.
◆ **to be over the moon** (*happy*) être aux anges

moor NOUN
see also **moor** VERB
la *lande*

moor VERB
see also **moor** NOUN
amarrer (*boat*)

mop NOUN
le *balai laveur* (*for floor*)

moped NOUN
le *cyclomoteur*

moral ADJECTIVE
see also **moral** NOUN
moral
(*moraux* MASC PL)

moral NOUN
see also **moral** ADJECTIVE
la *morale* ◇ *the moral of the story* la morale de l'histoire
◆ **morals** la moralité

morale NOUN
le *moral* ◇ *Their morale is very low.* Leur moral est très bas.

more ADJECTIVE, PRONOUN, ADVERB
When comparing one amount with another, you usually use **plus**.
1 *plus* ◇ *Beer is more expensive in Britain.* La bière est plus chère en Grande-Bretagne. ◇ *Could you speak more slowly?* Est-ce que vous pourriez parler plus lentement? ◇ *a bit more* un peu plus ◇ *There isn't any more.* Il n'y en a plus.
◆ **more...than** plus...que ◇ *He's more intelligent than me.* Il est plus intelligent que moi. ◇ *She practises more than I do.* Elle s'entraîne plus que moi. ◇ *More girls than boys do French.* Il y a plus de filles que de garçons qui font du français.
2 *plus de* (*followed by noun*) ◇ *There are more girls in the class.* Il y a plus de filles dans la classe. ◇ *I get more homework than you do.* J'ai plus de devoirs que toi. ◇ *I spent more than 500 francs.* J'ai dépensé plus de cinq cents francs.
When referring to an additional amount, more than there is already, you usually use **encore**.
3 *encore* ◇ *Is there any more?* Est-ce qu'il y en a encore? ◇ *Would you like some more?* Vous en voulez encore? ◇ *It'll take a few more days.* Ça prendra encore quelques jours.
4 *encore de* (*followed by noun*) ◇ *Could I have some more chips?* Est-ce que je pourrais avoir encore des frites? ◇ *Do you want some more tea?* Voulez-vous encore du thé?
◆ **more or less** plus ou moins
◆ **more than ever** plus que jamais

morning NOUN
le *matin* ◇ *this morning* ce matin ◇ *tomorrow morning* demain matin ◇ *every morning* tous les matins
◆ **in the morning** le matin ◇ *at 7 o'clock in the morning* à sept heures du matin
◆ **a morning paper** un journal du matin

Morocco NOUN
le *Maroc*
◆ **in Morocco** au Maroc

Moscow NOUN
Moscou
◆ **in Moscow** à Moscou

Moslem NOUN

M

PTO

le *musulman*
la *musulmane*
◇ *He's a Moslem.* Il est musulman.

mosque NOUN
la *mosquée*

mosquito NOUN
le *moustique*
◆ **a mosquito bite** une piqûre de moustique

most ADVERB, ADJECTIVE, PRONOUN

Use **la plupart de** *when* most (of) *is followed by a plural noun and* **la majeure partie (de)** *when* most (of) *is followed by a singular noun.*

1 *la plupart de* ◇ *most of my friends* la plupart de mes amis ◇ *most people* la plupart des gens ◇ *Most cats are affectionate.* La plupart des chats sont affectueux.
◆ **most of them** la plupart d'entre eux
◆ **most of the time** la plupart du temps
2 *la majeure partie de* ◇ *most of the work* la majeure partie du travail ◇ *most of the class* la majeure partie de la classe ◇ *most of the night* la majeure partie de la nuit
◆ **the most** le plus ◇ *He's the one who talks the most.* C'est lui qui parle le plus.

When most *is followed by adjective, the translation depends on whether the noun referred to is masculine, feminine or plural.*

◆ **the most... (1)** le plus... ◇ *the most expensive restaurant* le restaurant le plus cher
◆ **the most... (2)** la plus... ◇ *the most expensive seat* la place la plus chère
◆ **the most... (3)** les plus... ◇ *the most expensive restaurants* les restaurants les plus chers ◇ *the most expensive seats* les places les plus chères
◆ **to make the most of something** profiter au maximum de quelque chose
◆ **at the most** au maximum ◇ *Two hours at the most.* Deux heures au maximum.

mostly ADVERB
◆ **The teachers are mostly quite nice.** La plupart des professeurs sont assez gentils.

motel NOUN
le *motel*

mother NOUN
la *mère* ◇ *my mother* ma mère
◆ **mother tongue** la langue maternelle

mother-in-law NOUN
la *belle-mère*
(les *belles-mères* PL)

Mother's Day NOUN
la *fête des Mères*

Mother's Day is usually on the last Sunday of May in France.

motionless ADJECTIVE
immobile

motivated ADJECTIVE
motivé ◇ *He is highly motivated.* Il est très motivé.

motivation NOUN
la *motivation*

motive NOUN
le *mobile* ◇ *the motive for the killing* le mobile du crime

motor NOUN
le *moteur* ◇ *The boat has a motor.* Le bateau a un moteur.

motorbike NOUN
la *moto*

motorboat NOUN
le *bateau à moteur*

motorcycle NOUN
le *vélomoteur*

motorcyclist NOUN
le *motard*

motorist NOUN
l' *automobiliste* MASC/FEM

motor mechanic NOUN
le *mécanicien garagiste*

motor racing NOUN
la *course automobile*

motorway NOUN
l' *autoroute* FEM ◇ *on the motorway* sur l'autoroute

mouldy ADJECTIVE
moisi

mountain NOUN
la *montagne*
◆ **a mountain bike** un VTT (= vélo tout-terrain)

mountaineer NOUN
l' *alpiniste* MASC/FEM

mountaineering NOUN
l' *alpinisme* MASC ◇ *I go mountaineering.* Je fais de l'alpinisme.

mountainous ADJECTIVE
montagneux MASC
montagneuse FEM

mouse NOUN
la *souris* (*also for computer*) ◇ *white mice* des souris blanches

mousse NOUN
1 la *mousse* (*food*) ◇ *chocolate mousse* la mousse au chocolat
2 la *mousse coiffante* (*for hair*)

moustache NOUN
la *moustache* ◇ *He's got a moustache.* Il a une moustache.
◆ **a man with a moustache** un moustachu

mouth NOUN
la *bouche*

mouthful NOUN
la *bouchée*

outh organ NOUN
l' *harmonica* MASC ◇ *I play the mouth organ.* Je joue de l'harmonica.

ove NOUN
see also move VERB
1 le *tour* ◇ *It's your move.* C'est ton tour.
2 le *déménagement* ◇ *Our move from Oxford to Luton...* Notre déménagement d'Oxford à Luton...
to get a move on se remuer ◇ *Get a move on!* Remue-toi!

ove VERB
see also move NOUN
1 *bouger* ◇ *Don't move!* Ne bouge pas! ◇ *Could you move your stuff please?* Est-ce que tu peux bouger tes affaires s'il te plaît?
2 *avancer* ◇ *The car was moving very slowly.* La voiture avançait très lentement.
3 *émouvoir* ◇ *I was very moved by the film.* J'ai été très émue par ce film.
- **to move house** déménager ◇ *We're moving in July.* Nous allons déménager en juillet.
- **to move forward** avancer
- **to move in** emménager ◇ *They're moving in next week.* Ils emménagent la semaine prochaine.
to move over se pousser ◇ *Could you move over a bit?* Est-ce que vous pouvez vous pousser un peu?

ovement NOUN
le *mouvement*

ovie NOUN
le *film*
- **the movies** le cinéma ◇ *Let's go to the movies!* Si on allait au cinéma?

oving ADJECTIVE
1 *en marche* (*not stationary*) ◇ *a moving bus* un bus en marche
2 *touchant* (*touching*) ◇ *a moving story* une histoire touchante

ow VERB
tondre
- **to mow the lawn** tondre le gazon

ower NOUN
la *tondeuse à gazon*

P NOUN
le *député* ◇ *She's an MP.* Elle est député.

Mr NOUN
1 *Monsieur*
(*Messieurs* PL)
2 (*in address*)
M.
(*MM.* PL)

Mrs NOUN
1 *Madame*
(*Mesdames* PL)
2 (*in address*)
Mme
(*Mmes* PL)

Ms NOUN
1 *Madame*
(*Mesdames* PL)
2 (*in address*)
Mme
(*Mmes* PL)

There isn't a direct equivalent of Ms *in French. If you are writing to somebody and don't know whether she is married, use* Madame.

much ADJECTIVE, ADVERB, PRONOUN
1 *beaucoup* (*with verb*) ◇ *Do you go out much?* Tu sors beaucoup? ◇ *I don't like sport much.* Je n'aime pas beaucoup le sport. ◇ *I feel much better now.* Je me sens beaucoup mieux maintenant.
2 *beaucoup de* (*followed by noun*) ◇ *I haven't got much money.* Je n'ai pas beaucoup d'argent. ◇ *I don't want much rice.* Je ne veux pas beaucoup de riz.
- **very much (1)** (*with verb*) beaucoup ◇ *I enjoyed the film very much.* J'ai beaucoup apprécié le film. ◇ *Thank you very much.* Merci beaucoup.
- **very much (2)** (*followed by noun*) beaucoup de ◇ *I haven't got very much money.* Je n'ai pas beaucoup d'argent.
- **not much (1)** pas beaucoup ◇ *Have you got a lot of luggage?–No, not much.* As-tu beaucoup de bagages?–Non, pas beaucoup.
- **not much (2)** pas grand-chose ◇ *What's on TV?–Not much.* Qu'est-ce qu'il y a à la télé?–Pas grand-chose. ◇ *What did you think of it?–Not much.* Qu'est-ce que tu en as pensé?–Pas grand-chose.
- **How much?** Combien? ◇ *How much do you want?* Tu en veux combien? ◇ *How much time have you got?* Tu as combien de temps? ◇ *How much is it?* (*cost*) Combien est-ce que ça coûte?
- **too much** trop ◇ *That's too much!* C'est trop! ◇ *It costs too much.* Ça coûte trop cher. ◇ *They give us too much homework.* Ils nous donnent trop de devoirs.
- **so much** autant ◇ *I didn't think it would cost so much.* Je ne pensais pas que ça coûterait autant. ◇ *I've never seen so much traffic.* Je n'ai jamais vu autant de circulation.

mud NOUN
la *boue*

muddle NOUN

PTO

le *désordre* ◇ *The photos are in a muddle.* Les photos sont en désordre.

to **muddle up** VERB
confondre (*people*) ◇ *He muddles me up with my sister.* Il me confond avec ma sœur.
◆ **to get muddled up** s'embrouiller ◇ *I'm getting muddled up.* Je m'embrouille.

muddy ADJECTIVE
boueux MASC
boueuse FEM

muesli NOUN
le *muesli*

mug NOUN
see also mug VERB
la *grande tasse* ◇ *Do you want a cup or a mug?* Est-ce que vous voulez une tasse normale ou une grande tasse?
◆ **a beer mug** une chope à bière

to **mug** VERB
see also mug NOUN
agresser ◇ *He was mugged in the city centre.* Il s'est fait agresser au centre ville.

mugger NOUN
l' *agresseur* MASC

mugging NOUN
l' *agression* FEM

muggy ADJECTIVE
lourd ◇ *It's muggy today.* Il fait lourd aujourd'hui.

multiplication NOUN
la *multiplication*

to **multiply** VERB
multiplier ◇ *to multiply 6 by 3* multiplier six par trois

multi-storey car park NOUN
le *parking à plusieurs étages*

mum NOUN
You use **maman** *only when you are talking to your mother or using it as her name; otherwise use* **mère**.
1 la *mère* ◇ *my mum* ma mère ◇ *her mum* sa mère
2 la *maman* ◇ *Mum!* Maman! ◇ *I'll ask Mum.* Je vais demander à maman.

mummy NOUN
1 la *maman* (*mum*) ◇ *Mummy says I can go.* Maman dit que je peux y aller.
2 la *momie* (*Egyptian*)

mumps NOUN
les *oreillons* MASC PL

murder NOUN
see also murder VERB
le *meurtre* MASC

to **murder** VERB
see also murder NOUN
assassiner ◇ *He was murdered.* Il a été assassiné.

murderer NOUN
l' *assassin* MASC

muscle NOUN
le *muscle*

muscular ADJECTIVE
musclé

museum NOUN
le *musée*

mushroom NOUN
le *champignon* ◇ *mushroom omelette* l'omelette aux champignons

music NOUN
la *musique*

musical ADJECTIVE
see also musical NOUN
doué pour la musique ◇ *I'm not musical.* Je ne suis pas doué pour la musique.
◆ **a musical instrument** un instrument de musique

musical NOUN
see also musical ADJECTIVE
la *comédie musicale*

music centre NOUN
la *chaîne stéréo*

musician NOUN
le *musicien*
la *musicienne*

Muslim NOUN
le *musulman*
la *musulmane*
◇ *He's a Muslim.* Il est musulman.

mussel NOUN
la *moule*

must VERB
When must *means that you assume or suppose something, use* **devoir**; *when it means it's necessary to do something, eg* I must buy some presents, *use* **il faut que...**, *which comes from the verb* **falloir** *and is followed by a verb in the subjunctive.*
1 *devoir* (*I suppose*) ◇ *You must be tired.* Tu dois être fatigué. ◇ *They must have plenty of money.* Ils doivent avoir beaucoup d'argent. ◇ *There must be some problem.* Il doit y avoir un problème.
2 *il faut que* ◇ *I must buy some presents.* Il faut que j'achète des cadeaux. ◇ *I really must go now.* Il faut que j'y aille.
◆ **You mustn't forget to send her a card.** N'oublie surtout pas de lui envoyer une carte.
◆ **You must come and see us.** (*invitation*) Venez donc nous voir.

mustard NOUN
la *moutarde*

to **mutter** VERB

marmonner

my ADJECTIVE
mon MASC ◇ *my father* mon père
ma FEM ◇ *my aunt* ma tante
mes PL ◇ *my parents* mes parents
ma *becomes* **mon** *before a vowel sound.*
my friend (1) (*male*) mon ami
my friend (2) (*female*) mon amie
Do not use **mon/ma/mes** *with parts of the body.*
◇ *I want to wash my hair.* Je voudrais me laver les cheveux. ◇ *I'm going to clean my teeth.* Je vais me brosser les dents. ◇ *I've hurt my foot.* Je me suis fait mal au pied.

myself PRONOUN
1 *me* ◇ *I've hurt myself.* Je me suis fait mal. ◇ *I really enjoyed myself.* Je me suis vraiment bien amusé. ◇ *...when I look at myself in the mirror.* ...quand je me regarde dans la glace.
2 *moi* ◇ *I don't like talking about myself.* Je n'aime pas parler de moi.
3 *moi-même* ◇ *I made it myself.* Je l'ai fait moi-même.
◆ **by myself** tout seul ◇ *I don't like travelling by myself.* Je n'aime pas voyager tout seul.

mysterious ADJECTIVE
mystérieux MASC
mystérieuse FEM

mystery NOUN
le *mystère*
◆ **a murder mystery** (*novel*) un roman policier

myth NOUN
1 le *mythe* (*legend*) ◇ *a Greek myth* un mythe grec
2 l' *idée reçue* FEM (*untrue idea*)
◇ *That's a myth.* C'est une idée reçue.

mythology NOUN
la *mythologie*

N

naff ADJECTIVE
nul MASC
nulle FEM

to **nag** VERB
harceler (*scold*) ◇ *She's always nagging me.* Elle me harcèle constamment.

nail NOUN
1 l' *ongle* MASC (*on finger, toe*) ◇ *Don't bite your nails!* Ne te ronge pas les ongles!
2 le *clou* (*made of metal*)

nailbrush NOUN
la *brosse à ongles*

nailfile NOUN
la *lime à ongles*

nail scissors PL NOUN
les *ciseaux à ongles* MASC

nail varnish NOUN
le *vernis à ongles*
◆ **nail varnish remover** le dissolvant

naked ADJECTIVE
nu

name NOUN
le *nom*
◆ **What's your name?** Comment vous appelez-vous?

nanny NOUN
la *garde d'enfants* ◇ *She's a nanny.* C'est une garde d'enfants.

nap NOUN
le *petit somme*
◆ **to have a nap** faire un petit somme

napkin NOUN
la *serviette*

nappy NOUN
la *couche*

narrow ADJECTIVE
étroit

narrow-minded ADJECTIVE
borné

nasty ADJECTIVE
1 *mauvais* (*bad*) ◇ *a nasty cold* un mauvais rhume ◇ *a nasty smell* une mauvaise odeur
2 *méchant* (*unfriendly*) ◇ *He gave me a nasty look.* Il m'a regardé d'un air méchant.

nation NOUN
la *nation*

national ADJECTIVE
national
(*nationaux* MASC PL)
◇ *He's the national champion.* C'est le champion national.
◆ **the national elections** les élections législatives

national anthem NOUN
l' *hymne national* MASC

National Health Service NOUN
la *Sécurité sociale*
In France you have to pay for medical treatment when you receive it, and then claim it back from the Sécurité sociale.

nationalism NOUN
le *nationalisme* ◇ *Scottish nationalism* le nationalisme écossais

nationalist NOUN
le/la *nationaliste*

nationality NOUN
la *nationalité*

national park NOUN
le *parc national*
(les *parcs nationaux* PL)

native ADJECTIVE
natal ◇ *my native country* mon pays natal
◆ **native language** la langue maternelle ◇ *English is not their native language.* L'anglais n'est pas leur langue maternelle.

natural ADJECTIVE
naturel MASC
naturelle FEM

naturalist NOUN
le *naturaliste*

naturally ADVERB
naturellement ◇ *Naturally, we were very disappointed.* Nous avons naturellement été très déçus.

nature NOUN
la *nature*

naughty ADJECTIVE
vilain ◇ *Naughty girl!* Vilaine! ◇ *Don't be naughty!* Ne fais pas le vilain!

navy NOUN
la *marine* ◇ *He's in the navy.* Il est dans la marine.

navy-blue ADJECTIVE
bleu marine MASC, FEM, PL ◇ *a navy-blue skirt* une jupe bleu marine

Nazi NOUN
le *Nazi*
la *Nazie*
◇ *the Nazis* les Nazis

near ADJECTIVE
see also near PREPOSITION
proche ◇ *It's fairly near.* C'est assez proche.
◆ **It's near enough to walk.** On peut facilement y aller à pied.
◆ **the nearest** le plus proche ◇ *Where's the nearest service station?* Où est la station-service la plus proche? ◇ *The*

nearest shops were three kilometres away. Les magasins les plus proches étaient à trois kilomètres.

near PREPOSITION, ADVERB

see also near ADJECTIVE

près de ◇ *I live near Liverpool.* J'habite près de Liverpool. ◇ *near my house* près de chez moi

◆ **near here** près d'ici ◇ *Is there a bank near here?* Est-ce qu'il y a une banque près d'ici?

◆ **near to** près de ◇ *It's very near to the school.* C'est tout près de l'école.

nearby ADVERB

see also nearby ADJECTIVE

à proximité ◇ *There's a supermarket nearby.* Il y a un supermarché à proximité.

nearby ADJECTIVE

see also nearby ADVERB

1 *proche* (*close*) ◇ *a nearby garage* un garage proche

2 *voisin* (*neighbouring*) ◇ *We went to the nearby village of Torrance.* Nous sommes allés à Torrance, le village voisin.

nearly ADVERB

presque ◇ *Dinner's nearly ready.* Le dîner est presque prêt. ◇ *I'm nearly 15.* J'ai presque quinze ans.

◆ **I nearly missed the train.** J'ai failli rater le train.

neat ADJECTIVE

soigné ◇ *She has very neat writing.* Elle a une écriture très soignée.

◆ **a neat whisky** un whisky sec

neatly ADVERB

soigneusement ◇ *neatly folded* soigneusement plié

◆ **neatly dressed** impeccable

necessarily ADVERB

◆ **not necessarily** pas forcément

necessary ADJECTIVE

nécessaire

necessity NOUN

la *chose nécessaire* ◇ *A car is a necessity, not a luxury.* Une voiture est une chose nécessaire et non pas un luxe.

neck NOUN

1 le *cou* (*of body*)

◆ **a stiff neck** un torticolis

2 l' *encolure* FEM (*of garment*) ◇ *a V-neck sweater* un pull avec une encolure en V

necklace NOUN

le *collier*

need VERB

see also need NOUN

avoir besoin de ◇ *I need a bigger size.* J'ai besoin d'une plus grande taille.

◆ **to need to do something** avoir besoin de faire quelque chose ◇ *I need to change some money.* J'ai besoin de changer de l'argent.

need NOUN

see also need VERB

◆ **There's no need to book.** Il n'est pas nécessaire de réserver.

needle NOUN

l' *aiguille* FEM

needlework NOUN

la *couture* ◇ *We have needlework lessons at school.* Nous avons des cours de couture à l'école.

negative NOUN

see also negative ADJECTIVE

le *négatif* (*photo*)

negative ADJECTIVE

see also negative NOUN

négatif MASC

négative FEM

◇ *He's got a very negative attitude.* Il a une attitude très négative.

neglected ADJECTIVE

mal tenu (*untidy*) ◇ *The garden is neglected.* Le jardin est mal tenu.

negligee NOUN

le *déshabillé*

neighbour NOUN

le *voisin*

la *voisine*

◇ *the neighbours' garden* le jardin des voisins

neighbourhood NOUN

le *quartier*

neither PRONOUN, CONJUNCTION, ADVERB

aucun des deux

aucune des deux

◇ *Carrots or peas? – Neither, thanks.* Des carottes ou des petits pois? – Aucun des deux merci. ◇ *Neither of them is coming.* Aucun des deux ne vient.

◆ **neither...nor...** ni...ni... ◇ *Neither Sarah nor Tamsin is coming to the party.* Ni Sarah ni Tamsin ne vient à la soirée.

◆ **Neither do I.** Moi non plus. ◇ *I don't like him. – Neither do I!* Je ne l'aime pas. – Moi non plus!

◆ **Neither have I.** Moi non plus. ◇ *I've never been to Spain. – Neither have I.* Je ne suis jamais allé en Espagne. – Moi non plus.

neon NOUN

le *néon*

◆ **a neon light** une lampe au néon

nephew NOUN

le *neveu*

(les *neveux* PL)

◇ *my nephew* mon neveu

N

nerve NOUN
1 le *nerf* ◇ *She sometimes gets on my nerves.* Elle me tape quelquefois sur les nerfs.
2 le *toupet* (*cheek*) ◇ *He's got a nerve!* Il a du toupet!

nerve-racking ADJECTIVE
angoissant

nervous ADJECTIVE
tendu (*tense*) ◇ *I bite my nails when I'm nervous.* Je me ronge les ongles quand je suis tendu.
◆ **to be nervous about something** appréhender de faire quelque chose ◇ *I'm a bit nervous about flying to Paris by myself.* J'appréhende un peu d'aller toute seule en avion à Paris.

nest NOUN
le *nid*

net NOUN
le *filet* ◇ *a fishing net* un filet de pêche

Netherlands PL NOUN
les *Pays-Bas* MASC
◆ **in the Netherlands** aux Pays-Bas

network NOUN
le *réseau*
(les *réseaux* PL)

neurotic ADJECTIVE
névrosé

never ADVERB
1 *jamais* ◇ *Have you ever been to Germany?–No, never.* Est-ce que tu es déjà allé en Allemagne?–Non, jamais. ◇ *When are you going to phone him?–Never!* Quand est-ce que tu vas l'appeler?–Jamais!
Add **ne** *if the sentence contains a verb.*
2 *ne...jamais* ◇ *I never write letters.* Je n'écris jamais. ◇ *I have never been camping.* Je n'ai jamais fait de camping. ◇ *Never leave valuables in your car.* Ne laissez jamais d'objets de valeur dans votre voiture.
◆ **Never again!** Plus jamais!
◆ **Never mind.** Ça ne fait rien.

new ADJECTIVE
1 *nouveau* MASC
nouvelle FEM
(*nouveaux* MASC PL)
◇ *her new boyfriend* son nouveau copain ◇ *I need a new dress.* J'ai besoin d'une nouvelle robe.
2 (*brand new*)
neuf MASC
neuve FEM
◇ *They've got a new car.* Ils ont une voiture neuve.

newcomer NOUN
le *nouveau venu*
(les *nouveaux venus* MASC PL)
la *nouvelle venue*

news NOUN
1 les *nouvelles* FEM PL ◇ *good news* de bonnes nouvelles ◇ *I've had some bad news.* J'ai reçu de mauvaises nouvelles. ◇ *It was nice to have your news.* J'ai été content d'avoir de tes nouvelles.
2 la *nouvelle* (*single piece of news*) ◇ *That's wonderful news!* Quelle bonne nouvelle!
3 le *journal télévisé* (*on TV*) ◇ *I watch the news every evening.* Je regarde le journal télévisé tous les soirs.
4 les *informations* FEM PL (*on radio*) ◇ *I listen to the news every morning.* J'écoute les informations tous les matins.

newsagent NOUN
le *marchand de journaux*

newspaper NOUN
le *journal*
(les *journaux* PL)
◇ *I deliver newspapers.* Je distribue des journaux.

newsreader NOUN
le *présentateur*
la *présentatrice*

New Year NOUN
le *Nouvel An* ◇ *to celebrate New Year* fêter le Nouvel An
◆ **Happy New Year!** Bonne Année!
◆ **New Year's Day** le premier de l'An
◆ **New Year's Eve** la veille du premier de l'An ◇ *a New Year's Eve party* un réveillon du premier de l'An

New Zealand NOUN
la *Nouvelle-Zélande*
◆ **in New Zealand** en Nouvelle-Zélande

New Zealander NOUN
le *Néo-Zélandais*
la *Néo-Zélandaise*

next ADJECTIVE, ADVERB, PREPOSITION
1 *prochain* (*in time*) ◇ *next Saturday* samedi prochain ◇ *next year* l'année prochaine ◇ *next summer* l'été prochain
2 *suivant* (*in sequence*) ◇ *the next train* le train suivant ◇ *Next please!* Au suivant!
3 *ensuite* (*afterwards*) ◇ *What shall I do next?* Qu'est-ce que je fais ensuite? ◇ *What happened next?* Qu'est-ce qui s'est passé ensuite?
◆ **next to** à côté de ◇ *next to the bank* à côté de la banque
◆ **the next day** le lendemain ◇ *The next day we visited Versailles.* Le lendemain nous avons visité Versailles.
◆ **the next time** la prochaine fois ◇ *the next time you see her* la prochaine fois

que tu la verras

- **next door** à côté ◇ *They live next door.* Ils habitent à côté. ◇ *the people next door* les gens d'à côté
- **the next room** la pièce d'à côté

NHS NOUN
la *Sécurité sociale*

In France you have to pay for medical treatment when you receive it, and then claim it back from the Sécurité sociale.

nice ADJECTIVE
1 (*kind*)
gentil MASC
gentille FEM
◇ *Your parents are very nice.* Tes parents sont très gentils. ◇ *It was nice of you to remember my birthday.* C'était gentil de ta part de te souvenir de mon anniversaire.
- **to be nice to somebody** être gentil avec quelqu'un

2 (*pretty*)
joli ◇ *That's a nice dress!* Qu'est-ce qu'elle est jolie, cette robe! ◇ *Aix is a nice town.* Aix est une jolie ville.
3 (*food*)
bon MASC
bonne FEM
◇ *It's very nice.* C'est très bon. ◇ *a nice cup of coffee* une bonne tasse de café
- **Have a nice time!** Amuse-toi bien!
- **nice weather** le beau temps
- **It's a nice day.** Il fait beau.

nickname NOUN
le *surnom*

niece NOUN
la *nièce* ◇ *my niece* ma nièce

Nigeria NOUN
le *Nigéria*
- **in Nigeria** au Nigéria

night NOUN
1 la *nuit* ◇ *I want a single room for two nights.* Je veux une chambre à un lit pour deux nuits.
- **at night** la nuit
- **Goodnight!** Bonne nuit!
- **a night club** une boîte de nuit

2 le *soir* (*evening*) ◇ *last night* hier soir

nightie NOUN
la *chemise de nuit*

nightlife NOUN
- **There's plenty of nightlife.** Il y a plein de choses à faire le soir.

nightmare NOUN
le *cauchemar* ◇ *It was a real nightmare!* Ça a été un vrai cauchemar!
- **to have a nightmare** faire un cauchemar

nil NOUN
le *zéro* ◇ *We won one-nil.* Nous avons gagné un à zéro.

nine NUMBER
neuf MASC
neuve FEM
◇ *She's nine.* Elle a neuf ans.

nineteen NUMBER
dix-neuf ◇ *She's nineteen.* Elle a dix-neuf ans.

ninety NUMBER
quatre-vingt-dix

ninth ADJECTIVE
neuvième ◇ *the ninth floor* le neuvième étage
- **the ninth of August** le neuf août

no ADVERB, ADJECTIVE
1 *non* ◇ *Are you coming?–No.* Est-ce que vous venez?–Non. ◇ *Would you like some more?–No thank you.* Vous en voulez encore?–Non merci.
2 *pas de* (*not any*) ◇ *There's no hot water.* Il n'y a pas d'eau chaude. ◇ *There are no trains on Sundays.* Il n'y a pas de trains le dimanche. ◇ *No problem.* Pas de problème.
- **I've got no idea.** Je n'en ai aucune idée.
- **No way!** Pas question!
- **"no smoking"** "défense de fumer"

nobody PRONOUN
1 *personne* ◇ *Who's going with you?–Nobody.* Qui t'accompagne?–Personne.

Add **ne** *if the sentence contains a verb.*

2 *ne...personne* ◇ *There was nobody in the office.* Il n'y avait personne au bureau.
- **Nobody likes him.** Personne ne l'aime.

noise NOUN
le *bruit* ◇ *Please make less noise.* Faites moins de bruit s'il vous plaît.

noisy ADJECTIVE
bruyant

none PRONOUN
1 *aucun* MASC
aucune FEM
◇ *How many sisters have you got?–None.* Tu as combien de sœurs?–Aucune. ◇ *What sports do you do?–None.* Qu'est-ce que tu fais comme sport?–Je n'en fais aucun.

Add **ne** *if the sentence contains a verb.*

2 *aucun...ne* ◇ *None of my friends wanted to come.* Aucun de mes amis n'a voulu venir.
- **There's none left.** Il n'y en a plus.
- **There are none left.** Il n'y en a plus.

nonsense NOUN
les *bêtises* FEM PL ◇ *She talks a lot of nonsense.* Elle dit beaucoup de bêtises. ◇ *Nonsense!* Ne dis pas de bêtises!

non-smoker NOUN
le *non-fumeur* ◇ *He's a non-smoker.* Il est non-fumeur.

non-smoking ADJECTIVE
non-fumeur ◇ *a non-smoking carriage* une voiture non-fumeurs

non-stop ADJECTIVE, ADVERB
1 *direct* ◇ *a non-stop flight* un vol direct ◇ *We flew non-stop.* Nous avons pris un vol direct.
2 *sans arrêt* ◇ *He talks non-stop.* Il parle sans arrêt.

noodles PL NOUN
les *nouilles* FEM PL

noon NOUN
midi ◇ *at noon* à midi

no one PRONOUN
1 *personne* ◇ *Who's going with you?–No one.* Qui t'accompagne?–Personne.
Add **ne** *if the sentence contains a verb.*
2 *ne...personne* ◇ *There was no one in the office.* Il n'y avait personne au bureau.
- **No one likes him.** Personne ne l'aime.

nor CONJUNCTION
- **neither...nor** ni...ni ◇ *neither the cinema nor the swimming pool* ni le cinéma, ni la piscine
- **Nor do I.** Moi non plus. ◇ *I didn't like the film.–Nor did I.* Je n'ai pas aimé le film.–Moi non plus.
- **Nor have I.** Moi non plus. ◇ *I haven't seen him.–Nor have I.* Je ne l'ai pas vu.–Moi non plus.

normal ADJECTIVE
1 (*usual*)
habituel MASC
habituelle FEM
◇ *at the normal time* à l'heure habituelle
2 (*standard*)
normal
(*normaux* MASC PL)
◇ *a normal car* une voiture normale

normally ADVERB
1 *généralement* (*usually*) ◇ *I normally arrive at nine o'clock.* J'arrive généralement à neuf heures.
2 *normalement* (*as normal*) ◇ *In spite of the strike, the airports are working normally.* Malgré la grève, les aéroports fonctionnent normalement.

Normandy NOUN
la *Normandie*
- **in Normandy** en Normandie
- **to Normandy** en Normandie

north ADJECTIVE, ADVERB
see also north NOUN
1 *nord* MASC, FEM, PL ◇ *the north coast* la côte nord
- **a north wind** un vent du nord
2 *vers le nord* ◇ *We were travelling north.* Nous allions vers le nord.
- **north of** au nord de ◇ *It's north of London.* C'est au nord de Londres.

north NOUN
see also north ADJECTIVE
le *nord* ◇ *in the north* dans le nord

North America NOUN
l' *Amérique du Nord* FEM

northeast NOUN
le *nord-est* ◇ *in the northeast* au nord-est

northern ADJECTIVE
- **the northern part of the island** la partie nord de l'île
- **Northern Europe** l'Europe du Nord

Northern Ireland NOUN
l' *Irlande du Nord* FEM
- **in Northern Ireland** en Irlande du Nord
- **to Northern Ireland** en Irlande du Nord
- **I'm from Northern Ireland.** Je viens d'Irlande du Nord.

North Pole NOUN
le *pôle Nord*

North Sea NOUN
la *mer du Nord*

northwest NOUN
le *nord-ouest* ◇ *in the northwest* au nord-ouest

Norway NOUN
la *Norvège*
- **in Norway** en Norvège

Norwegian ADJECTIVE
see also Norwegian NOUN
norvégien MASC
norvégienne FEM

Norwegian NOUN
see also Norwegian ADJECTIVE
1 (*person*)
le *Norvégien*
la *Norvégienne*
2 (*language*)
le *norvégien*

nose NOUN
le *nez*
(les *nez* PL)

nosebleed NOUN
- **to have a nosebleed** saigner du nez ◇ *I often get nosebleeds.* Je saigne souvent du nez.

nosey ADJECTIVE
- **to be nosey** se mêler de tout ◇ *She's very nosey.* Elle se mêle de tout.

not ADVERB
1 *pas* ◇ *Are you coming or not?* Est-ce que tu viens ou pas?
- **not really** pas vraiment

- **not at all** pas du tout
- **not yet** pas encore ◇ *Have you finished?–Not yet.* As-tu fini?–Pas encore.

Add **ne** *before a verb.*

2 *ne...pas* ◇ *I'm not sure.* Je ne suis pas sûr. ◇ *It's not raining.* Il ne pleut pas. ◇ *You shouldn't do that.* Tu ne devrais pas faire ça. ◇ *They haven't arrived yet.* Ils ne sont pas encore arrivés.

3 *non* ◇ *I hope not.* J'espère que non. ◇ *Can you lend me £10?–I'm afraid not.* Est-ce que tu peux me prêter dix livres?–Non, désolé.

note NOUN

1 la *note* ◇ *to take notes* prendre des notes

2 le *mot* (*letter*) ◇ *I'll write her a note.* Je vais lui écrire un mot.

3 le *billet* (*banknote*) ◇ *a £5 note* un billet de cinq livres

note down VERB

noter

notebook NOUN

le *carnet*

notepad NOUN

le *bloc-notes*

(les *blocs-notes* PL)

notepaper NOUN

le *papier à lettres*

nothing NOUN

1 *rien* ◇ *What's wrong?–Nothing.* Qu'est-ce qui ne va pas?–Rien. ◇ *nothing special* rien de particulier

Add **ne** *if the sentence contains a verb.*

2 *ne...rien* ◇ *He does nothing.* Il ne fait rien. ◇ *He ate nothing for breakfast.* Il n'a rien mangé au petit-déjeuner.

- **Nothing is open on Sundays.** Rien n'est ouvert le dimanche.

notice NOUN

see also notice VERB

(*sign*)

le *panneau*

(les *panneaux* PL)

- **to put up a notice** mettre un panneau
- **a warning notice** un avertissement
- **Don't take any notice of him!** Ne fais pas attention à lui!

notice VERB

see also notice NOUN

remarquer

notice board NOUN

le *panneau d'affichage*

(les *panneaux d'affichage* PL)

nought NOUN

le *zéro*

noun NOUN

le *nom*

novel NOUN

le *roman*

novelist NOUN

le *romancier*

la *romancière*

November NOUN

novembre MASC

- **in November** en novembre

now ADVERB, CONJUNCTION

maintenant ◇ *What are you doing now?* Qu'est-ce que tu fais maintenant?

- **just now** en ce moment ◇ *I'm rather busy just now.* Je suis très occupé en ce moment.
- **I did it just now.** Je viens de le faire.
- **He should be there by now.** Il doit être arrivé à l'heure qu'il est.
- **It should be ready by now.** Ça devrait être déjà prêt.
- **now and then** de temps en temps

nowhere ADVERB

nulle part ◇ *nowhere else* nulle part ailleurs

nuclear ADJECTIVE

nucléaire ◇ *nuclear power* l'énergie nucléaire ◇ *a nuclear power station* une centrale nucléaire

nude ADJECTIVE

see also nude NOUN

nu

- **to sunbathe nude** faire du bronzage intégral

nude NOUN

see also nude ADJECTIVE

- **in the nude** nu

nudist NOUN

le/la *nudiste*

nuisance NOUN

- **It's a nuisance.** C'est très embêtant.
- **Sorry to be a nuisance.** Désolé de vous déranger.

number NOUN

1 le *nombre* (*total amount*) ◇ *a large number of people* un grand nombre de gens

2 le *numéro* (*of house, telephone, bank account*) ◇ *They live at number 5.* Ils habitent au numéro cinq. ◇ *What's your phone number?* Quel est votre numéro de téléphone? ◇ *You've got the wrong number.* Vous vous êtes trompé de numéro.

3 le *chiffre* (*figure, digit*) ◇ *I can't read the second number.* Je n'arrive pas à lire le deuxième chiffre.

number plate NOUN

la *plaque d'immatriculation*

nun NOUN

la *religieuse* ◇ *She's a nun.* Elle est

PTO

religieuse.

nurse NOUN
l' *infirmier* MASC
l' *infirmière* FEM
◇ *She's a nurse.* Elle est infirmière.

nursery NOUN
1 la *crèche* (*for children*)
2 la *pépinière* (*for plants*)

nursery school NOUN
l' *école maternelle* FEM

The école maternelle *is a state school for 2-6 year-olds.*

nursery slope NOUN
la *piste pour débutants*

nut NOUN
1 (*peanut*)
la *cacahuète*
2 (*hazelnut*)
la *noisette*
3 (*walnut*)
la *noix*
(les *noix* PL)
4 (*made of metal*)
l' *écrou* MASC

nutmeg NOUN
la *noix de muscade*

nutritious ADJECTIVE
nourrissant

nutter NOUN
◆ **He's a nutter.** Il est complètement cinglé. (*informal*)

nylon NOUN
le *nylon*

O

oak NOUN
le *chêne* ◇ *an oak table* une table en chêne

oar NOUN
l' *aviron* MASC

oats NOUN
l' *avoine* FEM

obedient ADJECTIVE
obéissant

obey VERB
◆ **to obey the rules** respecter le règlement

object NOUN
l' *objet* MASC ◇ *a familiar object* un objet familier

objection NOUN
l' *objection* FEM

objective NOUN
l' *objectif* MASC

oblong ADJECTIVE
rectangulaire

oboe NOUN
le *hautbois* ◇ *I play the oboe.* Je joue du hautbois.

obscene ADJECTIVE
obscène

observant ADJECTIVE
observateur MASC
observatrice FEM

observe VERB
observer

obsolete ADJECTIVE
dépassé

obstacle NOUN
l' *obstacle* MASC

obstinate ADJECTIVE
obstiné

obstruct VERB
bloquer ◇ *A lorry was obstructing the traffic.* Un camion bloquait la circulation.

obtain VERB
obtenir

obvious ADJECTIVE
évident

obviously ADVERB
1 *évidemment* (*of course*) ◇ *Do you want to pass the exam?–Obviously!* Tu veux être reçu à l'examen?–Évidemment!
◆ **Obviously not!** Bien sûr que non!
2 *manifestement* (*visibly*) ◇ *She was obviously exhausted.* Elle était manifestement épuisée.

occasion NOUN
l' *occasion* FEM ◇ *a special occasion* une occasion spéciale
◆ **on several occasions** à plusieurs reprises

occasionally ADVERB
de temps en temps

occupation NOUN
la *profession*

to **occupy** VERB
occuper ◇ *That seat is occupied.* Cette place est occupée.

to **occur** VERB
avoir lieu (*happen*) ◇ *The accident occurred yesterday.* L'accident a eu lieu hier.
◆ **It suddenly occurred to me that...** Il m'est soudain venu à l'esprit que...

ocean NOUN
l' *océan* MASC

o'clock ADVERB
◆ **at four o'clock** à quatre heures
◆ **It's five o'clock.** Il est cinq heures.

October NOUN
octobre MASC
◆ **in October** en octobre

octopus NOUN
la *pieuvre*

odd ADJECTIVE
1 *bizarre* ◇ *That's odd!* C'est bizarre!
2 *impair* ◇ *an odd number* un chiffre impair

of PREPOSITION
1 *de* ◇ *some photos of my holiday* des photos de mes vacances ◇ *a boy of ten* un garçon de dix ans

de *changes to* **d'** *before a vowel and most words beginning with "h".*

d' ◇ *a kilo of oranges* un kilo d'oranges

de + **le** *changes to* **du**, *and* **de** + **les** *changes to* **des**.

du ◇ *the end of the film* la fin du film
des ◇ *the end of the holidays* la fin des vacances
2 *en* (*with quantity, amount*) ◇ *He's got four sisters. I've met two of them.* Il a quatre sœurs. J'en ai rencontré deux. ◇ *Can I have half of that?* Je peux en avoir la moitié?
◆ **three of us** trois d'entre nous
◆ **a friend of mine** un de mes amis
◆ **the 14th of September** le quatorze septembre
◆ **That's very kind of you.** C'est très gentil de votre part.
◆ **It's made of wood.** C'est en bois.

off ADVERB, PREPOSITION, ADJECTIVE

For other expressions with **off**, *see the verbs* **get**, **take**, **turn** *etc.*

PTO

1 *éteint* (*heater, light, TV*) ◇ *All the lights are off.* Toutes les lumières sont éteintes.
2 *fermé* (*tap, gas*) ◇ *Are you sure the tap is off?* Tu es sûr que le robinet est fermé?
3 *annulé* (*cancelled*) ◇ *The match is off.* Le match est annulé.
- **to be off sick** être malade
- **a day off** un jour de congé ◇ *to take a day off work* prendre un jour de congé
- **She's off school today.** Elle n'est pas à l'école aujourd'hui.
- **I must be off now.** Je dois m'en aller maintenant.
- **I'm off.** Je m'en vais.

offence NOUN
le *délit* (*crime*)

offensive ADJECTIVE
choquant

offer NOUN
see also offer VERB
la *proposition* ◇ *a good offer* une proposition intéressante
- **"on special offer"** "en promotion"

to **offer** VERB
see also offer NOUN
proposer ◇ *He offered to help me.* Il m'a proposé de m'aider. ◇ *I offered to go with them.* Je leur ai proposé de les accompagner.

office NOUN
le *bureau*
(les *bureaux* PL)
◇ *She works in an office.* Elle travaille dans un bureau.

officer NOUN
l' *officier* MASC

official ADJECTIVE
officiel MASC
officielle FEM

off-licence NOUN
le *marchand de vins et spiritueux*

offside ADJECTIVE
hors jeu (*in football*)

often ADVERB
souvent ◇ *It often rains.* Il pleut souvent. ◇ *How often do you go to the gym?* Tu vas souvent à la gym? ◇ *I'd like to go skiing more often.* J'aimerais aller skier plus souvent.

oil NOUN
see also oil VERB
1 l' *huile* FEM (*for lubrication, cooking*)
- **an oil painting** une peinture à l'huile
2 le *pétrole* (*crude oil*) ◇ *North Sea oil* le pétrole de la mer du Nord

to **oil** VERB
see also oil NOUN
graisser

oil rig NOUN
la *plateforme pétrolière* ◇ *He works on an oil rig.* Il travaille sur une plateforme pétrolière.

oil slick NOUN
la *marée noire*

oil well NOUN
le *puits de pétrole*
(les *puits de pétrole* PL)

ointment NOUN
la *pommade* MASC

okay EXCLAMATION, ADJECTIVE
d'accord (*agreed*) ◇ *Could you call back later?–Okay!* Tu peux rappeler plus tard?–D'accord! ◇ *I'll meet you at six o'clock, okay?* Je te retrouve à six heures, d'accord? ◇ *Is that okay?* C'est d'accord?
- **I'll do it tomorrow, if that's okay with you.** Je le ferai demain, si tu es d'accord.
- **Are you okay?** Ça va?
- **How was your holiday?–It was okay.** C'était comment tes vacances?–Pas mal.
- **What's your teacher like?–He's okay.** Il est comment ton prof?–Il est sympa. (*informal*)

old ADJECTIVE
1 *vieux* MASC
vieille FEM
◇ *an old dog* un vieux chien ◇ *an old house* une vieille maison

vieux *changes to* **vieil** *before a vowel and most words beginning with "h".*

vieil ◇ *an old man* un vieil homme

When talking about people it is more polite to use **âgé** *instead of* **vieux**.

âgé ◇ *old people* les personnes âgées
2 (*former*)
ancien MASC
ancienne FEM
◇ *my old English teacher* mon ancien professeur d'anglais
- **How old are you?** Quel âge as-tu?
- **He's ten years old.** Il a dix ans.
- **my older brother** mon frère aîné ◇ *my older sister* ma sœur aînée
- **She's two years older than me.** Elle a deux ans de plus que moi.
- **I'm the oldest in the family.** Je suis l'aîné de la famille.

old age pensioner NOUN
le *retraité*
la *retraitée*
◇ *She's an old age pensioner.* Elle est retraitée.

old-fashioned ADJECTIVE
1 *démodé* ◇ *She wears old-fashioned clothes.* Elle porte des vêtements démodés.
2 *vieux jeu* MASC, FEM, PL (*person*) ◇ *My*

parents are rather old-fashioned. Mes parents sont plutôt vieux jeu.

olive NOUN
l' *olive* FEM

olive oil NOUN
l' *huile d'olive* FEM

Olympic ADJECTIVE
olympique
- **the Olympics** les Jeux olympiques MASC

omelette NOUN
l' *omelette* FEM

on PREPOSITION, ADVERB
see also on ADJECTIVE
There are several ways of translating on. *Scan the examples to find one that is similar to what you want to say. For other expressions with* on, *see the verbs* go, put, turn *etc.*
1 *sur* ◇ *on the table* sur la table ◇ *on an island* sur une île
2 *à* ◇ *on the left* à gauche ◇ *on the 2nd floor* au deuxième étage ◇ *I go to school on my bike.* Je vais à l'école à vélo.
- **on TV** à la télé ◇ *What's on TV?* Qu'est-ce qu'il y a à la télé?
- **on the radio** à la radio ◇ *I heard it on the radio.* Je l'ai entendu à la radio.
- **on the bus (1)** (*by bus*) en bus ◇ *I go into town on the bus.* Je vais en ville en bus.
- **on the bus (2)** (*inside*) dans le bus ◇ *There were no empty seats on the bus.* Il n'y avait pas de places libres dans le bus.
- **on holiday** en vacances ◇ *They're on holiday.* Ils sont en vacances.
- **on strike** en grève

With days and dates on *is not translated.*
◇ *on Friday* vendredi ◇ *on Fridays* le vendredi ◇ *on Christmas Day* le jour de Noël ◇ *on June 20th* le vingt juin ◇ *on my birthday* le jour de mon anniversaire

on ADJECTIVE
see also on PREPOSITION
1 *allumé* (*heater, light, TV*) ◇ *I think I left the light on.* Je crois que j'ai laissé la lumière allumée.
2 *ouvert* (*tap, gas*) ◇ *Leave the tap on.* Laisse le robinet ouvert.
3 *en marche* (*machine*) ◇ *Is the dishwasher on?* Est-ce que le lave-vaisselle est en marche?
- **What's on at the cinema?** Qu'est-ce qui passe au cinéma?

once ADVERB
une fois ◇ *once a week* une fois par semaine ◇ *once more* encore une fois ◇ *I've been to France once before.* J'ai déjà été une fois en France.
- **Once upon a time...** Il était une fois...
- **at once** tout de suite
- **once in a while** de temps en temps

one NUMBER, PRONOUN
Use **un** *for masculine nouns and* **une** *for feminine nouns.*
1 *un* ◇ *one day* un jour ◇ *Do you need a stamp?–No thanks, I've got one.* Est-ce que tu as besoin d'un timbre?–Non merci, j'en ai un.
une ◇ *one minute* une minute ◇ *I've got one brother and one sister.* J'ai un frère et une sœur.
2 *on* (*impersonal*) ◇ *One never knows.* On ne sait jamais.
- **this one (1)** celui-ci (*masculine*) ◇ *Which foot is hurting?–This one.* Quel pied te fait mal?–Celui-ci.
- **this one (2)** celle-ci (*feminine*) ◇ *Which is the best photo?–This one.* Quelle est la meilleure photo?–Celle-ci.
- **that one (1)** celui-là (*masculine*) ◇ *Which bag is yours?–That one.* Lequel est ton sac?–Celui-là.
- **that one (2)** celle-là (*feminine*) ◇ *Which seat do you want?–That one.* Quelle place voulez-vous?–Celle-là.

oneself PRONOUN
1 *se* ◇ *to hurt oneself* se faire mal
2 *soi-même* ◇ *It's quicker to do it oneself.* C'est plus rapide de le faire soi-même.

one-way ADJECTIVE
- **a one-way street** une impasse

onion NOUN
l' *oignon* MASC ◇ *onion soup* la soupe à l'oignon

only ADVERB, ADJECTIVE, CONJUNCTION
1 *seul* ◇ *Monday is the only day I'm free.* Le lundi est le seul jour où je suis libre. ◇ *French is the only subject I like.* Le français est la seule matière que j'aime.
2 *seulement* ◇ *How much was it?–Only 10 francs.* Combien c'était?–Seulement dix francs.
3 *ne...que* ◇ *We only want to stay for one night.* Nous ne voulons rester qu'une nuit. ◇ *These cassettes are only 30 francs.* Ces cassettes ne coûtent que trente francs.
4 *mais* ◇ *I'd like the same sweater, only in black.* Je voudrais le même pull, mais en noir.
- **an only child** un enfant unique

onwards ADVERB
à partir de ◇ *from July onwards* à partir de juillet

open ADJECTIVE
see also open VERB

PTO

ouvert ◇ *The baker's is open on Sunday morning.* La boulangerie est ouverte le dimanche matin.

◆ **in the open air** en plein air

to **open** VERB

see also open ADJECTIVE

1 *ouvrir* ◇ *Can I open the window?* Est-ce que je peux ouvrir la fenêtre? ◇ *What time do the shops open?* Les magasins ouvrent à quelle heure?

2 *s'ouvrir* ◇ *The door opens automatically.* La porte s'ouvre automatiquement. ◇ *The door opened and in came the teacher.* La porte s'est ouverte et le professeur est entré.

opening hours PL NOUN

les *heures d'ouverture* FEM

opera NOUN

l' *opéra* MASC

operation NOUN

l' *opération* FEM ◇ *a major operation* une grave opération

◆ **to have an operation** se faire opérer ◇ *I have never had an operation.* Je ne me suis jamais fait opérer.

operator NOUN

le/la *standardiste* (*on telephone*)

opinion NOUN

l' *avis* MASC ◇ *in my opinion* à mon avis ◇ *He asked me my opinion.* Il m'a demandé mon avis.

◆ **What's your opinion?** Qu'est-ce vous en pensez?

opinion poll NOUN

le *sondage*

opponent NOUN

l' *adversaire* MASC/FEM

opportunity NOUN

l' *occasion* FEM

◆ **to have the opportunity to do something** avoir l'occasion de faire quelque chose ◇ *I've never had the opportunity to go to France.* Je n'ai jamais eu l'occasion d'aller en France.

opposing ADJECTIVE

opposé (*team*)

opposite ADJECTIVE, ADVERB, PREPOSITION

1 *opposé* ◇ *It's in the opposite direction.* C'est dans la direction opposée.

2 *en face* ◇ *They live opposite.* Ils habitent en face.

3 *en face de* ◇ *the girl sitting opposite me* la fille assise en face de moi

◆ **the opposite sex** l'autre sexe

opposition NOUN

l' *opposition* FEM

optician NOUN

l' *opticien* MASC

l' *opticienne* FEM

◇ *She's an optician.* Elle est opticienne.

optimist NOUN

l' *optimiste* MASC/FEM

optimistic ADJECTIVE

optimiste

option NOUN

1 le *choix* (*choice*) ◇ *I've got no option.* Je n'ai pas le choix.

2 la *matière à option* (*optional subject*) ◇ *I'm doing geology as my option.* La géologie est ma matière à option.

optional ADJECTIVE

facultatif MASC

facultative FEM

or CONJUNCTION

1 *ou* ◇ *Would you like tea or coffee?* Est-ce que tu veux du thé ou du café?

Use **ni...ni** *in negative sentences.*

◇ *I don't eat meat or fish.* Je ne mange ni viande, ni poisson.

2 *sinon* (*otherwise*) ◇ *Hurry up or you'll miss the bus.* Dépêche-toi, sinon tu vas rater le bus.

◆ **Give me the money, or else!** Donne-moi l'argent, sinon tu vas le regretter!

oral ADJECTIVE

see also oral NOUN

oral

(*oraux* MASC PL)

◆ **an oral exam** un oral

oral NOUN

see also oral ADJECTIVE

l' *oral* MASC

(les *oraux* PL)

◇ *I've got my French oral soon.* Je vais bientôt passer mon oral de français.

orange NOUN

see also orange ADJECTIVE

l' *orange* FEM

◆ **an orange juice** un jus d'orange

orange ADJECTIVE

see also orange NOUN

orange MASC, FEM, PL

orchard NOUN

le *verger*

orchestra NOUN

l' *orchestre* MASC ◇ *I play in the school orchestra.* Je joue dans l'orchestre de l'école.

order NOUN

see also order VERB

1 l' *ordre* MASC (*sequence*) ◇ *in alphabetical order* dans l'ordre alphabétique

2 la *commande* (*instruction*) ◇ *The waiter took our order.* Le garçon a pris notre commande.

- **in order to** pour ◇ *He does it in order to earn money.* Il le fait pour gagner de l'argent.
- **"out of order"** "en panne"

order VERB

see also order NOUN

commander ◇ *We ordered steak and chips.* Nous avons commandé un steak frites. ◇ *Are you ready to order?* Vous êtes prêt à commander?

ordinary ADJECTIVE

1 *ordinaire* ◇ *an ordinary day* une journée ordinaire

2 *comme les autres* (*people*) ◇ *an ordinary family* une famille comme les autres ◇ *He's just an ordinary guy.* C'est un type comme les autres.

organ NOUN

l' *orgue* MASC (*instrument*) ◇ *I play the organ.* Je joue de l'orgue.

organic ADJECTIVE

biologique (*vegetables, fruit*)

organization NOUN

l' *organisation* FEM

organize VERB

organiser

original ADJECTIVE

original

(*originaux* MASC PL)

◇ *It's a very original idea.* C'est une idée très originale.

- **Our original plan was to go camping.** A l'origine nous avions l'intention de faire du camping.

originally ADVERB

à l'origine

Orkneys PL NOUN

les *Orcades* FEM PL

- **in the Orkneys** dans les Orcades

ornament NOUN

le *bibelot*

orphan NOUN

l' *orphelin* MASC

l' *orpheline* FEM

ostrich NOUN

l' *autruche* FEM

other ADJECTIVE, PRONOUN

autre ◇ *Have you got these jeans in other colours?* Est-ce que vous avez ce jean dans d'autres couleurs? ◇ *on the other side of the street* de l'autre côté de la rue ◇ *the other day* l'autre jour

- **the other one** l'autre ◇ *This one?–No, the other one.* Celui-ci?–Non, l'autre.
- **the others** les autres ◇ *The others are going but I'm not.* Les autres y vont mais pas moi.

otherwise ADVERB, CONJUNCTION

1 *sinon* (*if not*) ◇ *Note down the number, otherwise you'll forget it.* Note le numéro, sinon tu vas l'oublier. ◇ *Put some sunscreen on, you'll get burned otherwise.* Mets une crème solaire, sinon tu vas attraper des coups de soleil.

2 *à part ça* (*in other ways*) ◇ *I'm tired, but otherwise I'm fine.* Je suis fatigué, mais à part ça, ça va.

ought VERB

To translate ought to *use the conditional tense of* **devoir**.

◇ *I ought to phone my parents.* Je devrais appeler mes parents. ◇ *You ought not to do that.* Tu ne devrais pas faire ça. ◇ *He ought to win.* Il devrait gagner.

our ADJECTIVE

notre ◇ *Our house is quite big.* Notre maison est plutôt grande.

nos PL ◇ *Our neighbours are very nice.* Nos voisins sont très gentils.

ours PRONOUN

le nôtre + MASC NOUN ◇ *Your garden is very big, ours is much smaller.* Votre jardin est très grand, le nôtre est beaucoup plus petit.

la nôtre + FEM NOUN ◇ *Your school is very different from ours.* Votre école est très différente de la nôtre.

les nôtres + PL NOUN ◇ *Our teachers are strict.–Ours are too.* Nos professeurs sont sévères.–Les nôtres aussi.

- **Is this ours?** C'est à nous? ◇ *This car is ours.* Cette voiture est à nous. ◇ *Whose is this?–It's ours.* C'est à qui?–À nous.

ourselves PRONOUN

1 *nous* ◇ *We really enjoyed ourselves.* Nous nous sommes vraiment bien amusés.

2 *nous-mêmes* ◇ *We built our garage ourselves.* Nous avons construit notre garage nous-mêmes.

out ADVERB

There are several ways of translating out. *Scan the examples to find one that is similar to what you want to say. For other expressions with* out, *see the verbs* go, put, turn *etc.*

1 *dehors* (*outside*) ◇ *It's cold out.* Il fait froid dehors.

2 *éteint* (*light, fire*) ◇ *All the lights are out.* Toutes les lumières sont éteintes.

- **She's out.** Elle est sortie.
- **She's out shopping.** Elle est sortie faire des courses.
- **She's out for the afternoon.** Elle ne sera pas là de tout l'après-midi.
- **out there** dehors ◇ *It's cold out there.* Il fait froid dehors.
- **to go out** sortir ◇ *I'm going out tonight.*

Je sors ce soir.

- **to go out with somebody** sortir avec quelqu'un ◇ *I've been going out with him for two months.* Je sors avec lui depuis deux mois.
- **out of (1)** dans ◇ *to drink out of a glass* boire dans un verre
- **out of (2)** sur ◇ *in 9 cases out of 10* dans neuf cas sur dix
- **out of (3)** en dehors de ◇ *He lives out of town.* Il habite en dehors de la ville.
- **3 km out of town** à trois kilomètres de la ville
- **out of curiosity** par curiosité
- **out of work** sans emploi
- **That is out of the question.** C'est hors de question.
- **You're out!** (*in game*) Tu es éliminé!
- **"way out"** "sortie"

outdoor ADJECTIVE
en plein air ◇ *an outdoor swimming pool* une piscine en plein air
- **outdoor activities** les activités de plein air

outdoors ADVERB
au grand air

outing NOUN
la *sortie* ◇ *to go on an outing* faire une sortie

outline NOUN
1 les *grandes lignes* FEM (*summary*) ◇ *This is an outline of the plan.* Voici les grandes lignes du projet.
2 les *contours* MASC PL (*shape*) ◇ *We could see the outline of the mountain in the mist.* Nous distinguions les contours de la montagne dans la brume.

outrageous ADJECTIVE
1 (*behaviour*)
scandaleux MASC
scandaleuse FEM
2 (*price*)
exorbitant

outset NOUN
le *début* ◇ *at the outset* dès le début

outside NOUN
see also outside ADJECTIVE
l' *extérieur* MASC

outside ADJECTIVE, ADVERB, PREPOSITION
see also outside NOUN
1 *extérieur* ◇ *the outside walls* les murs extérieurs
2 *dehors* ◇ *It's very cold outside.* Il fait très froid dehors.
3 *en dehors de* ◇ *outside the school* en dehors de l'école ◇ *outside school hours* en dehors des heures de cours

outsize ADJECTIVE
énorme

outskirts PL NOUN
la *banlieue* ◇ *on the outskirts of the town* dans les banlieues de la ville

outstanding ADJECTIVE
remarquable

oval ADJECTIVE
ovale

oven NOUN
le *four*

over PREPOSITION, ADVERB, ADJECTIVE
When there is movement over something, use **par-dessus**; *when something is located above something, use* **au-dessus de**.
1 *par-dessus* ◇ *The ball went over the wall.* Le ballon est passé par-dessus le mur.
2 *au-dessus de* ◇ *There's a mirror over the washbasin.* Il y a une glace au-dessus du lavabo.
3 *plus de* (*more than*) ◇ *It's over twenty kilos.* Ça pèse plus de vingt kilos. ◇ *The temperature was over thirty degrees.* Il faisait une température de plus de trente degrés.
4 *pendant* (*during*) ◇ *over the holidays* pendant les vacances ◇ *over Christmas* pendant les fêtes de Noël
5 *terminé* (*finished*) ◇ *I'll be happy when the exams are over.* Je serai content quand les examens seront terminés.
- **over here** ici
- **over there** là-bas
- **all over Scotland** dans toute l'Écosse
- **The baker's is over the road.** La boulangerie est de l'autre côté de la rue.
- **I spilled coffee over my shirt.** J'ai renversé du café sur ma chemise.

overall ADVERB
dans l'ensemble (*generally*) ◇ *My results were quite good overall.* Mes résultats étaient assez bons dans l'ensemble.

overalls PL NOUN
les *bleus de travail* MASC PL

to **overcharge** VERB
- **He overcharged me.** Il m'a fait payer trop cher.
- **They overcharged us for the meal.** Ils nous ont fait payer de trop pour le repas.

overdone ADJECTIVE
trop cuit (*food*)

overdose NOUN
l' *overdose* FEM (*of drugs*) ◇ *to take an overdose* prendre une overdose

to **overestimate** VERB
surestimer

overhead projector NOUN
le *rétroprojecteur*

overlook VERB
1 *donner sur* (*have view of*) ◇ *The hotel overlooked the beach.* L'hôtel donnait sur la plage.
2 *négliger* (*forget about*) ◇ *He had overlooked one important problem.* Il avait négligé un problème important.

overseas ADVERB
à l'étranger ◇ *I'd like to work overseas.* J'aimerais travailler à l'étranger.

oversight NOUN
l' *oubli* MASC

oversleep VERB
se réveiller en retard ◇ *I overslept this morning.* Je me suis réveillé en retard ce matin.

overtake VERB
dépasser

overtime NOUN
les *heures supplémentaires* FEM PL ◇ *to work overtime* faire des heures supplémentaires

overweight ADJECTIVE
trop gros MASC
trop grosse FEM

owe VERB
devoir
◆ **to owe somebody something** devoir quelque chose à quelqu'un ◇ *I owe you 50 francs.* Je te dois cinquante francs.

owing to PREPOSITION
en raison de ◇ *owing to bad weather* en raison du mauvais temps

owl NOUN
le *hibou*
(les *hiboux* PL)

to **own** VERB
see also **own** ADJECTIVE
posséder

own ADJECTIVE
see also **own** VERB
propre ◇ *I've got my own bathroom.* J'ai ma propre salle de bain.
◆ **I'd like a room of my own.** J'aimerais avoir une chambre à moi.
◆ **on his own** tout seul ◇ *on her own* toute seule ◇ *on our own* tout seuls

owner NOUN
le/la *propriétaire*

oxygen NOUN
l' *oxygène* MASC

oyster NOUN
l' *huître* FEM

ozone layer NOUN
la *couche d'ozone*

P

PA NOUN
la *secrétaire de direction* (*personal assistant*) ◇ *She's a PA.* Elle est secrétaire de direction.
- **the PA system** (*public address*) les haut-parleurs

pace NOUN
l' *allure* FEM (*speed*) ◇ *He was walking at a brisk pace.* Il marchait à vive allure.

Pacific NOUN
le *Pacifique*

to **pack** VERB
see also pack NOUN
faire ses bagages ◇ *I'll help you pack.* Je vais t'aider à faire tes bagages.
- **I've already packed my case.** J'ai déjà fait ma valise.
- **Pack it in!** (*stop it*) Laisse tomber!

pack NOUN
see also pack VERB
1 le *paquet* (*packet*) ◇ *a pack of cigarettes* un paquet de cigarettes
2 le *pack* (*of yoghurts, cans*) ◇ *a six-pack* un pack de six
- **a pack of cards** un jeu de cartes

package NOUN
le *paquet*
- **a package holiday** un voyage organisé

packed ADJECTIVE
bondé ◇ *The cinema was packed.* Le cinéma était bondé.

packed lunch NOUN
le *repas froid* ◇ *I take a packed lunch to school.* J'apporte un repas froid à l'école.

packet NOUN
le *paquet* ◇ *a packet of cigarettes* un paquet de cigarettes

pad NOUN
(*notepad*)
le *bloc-notes*
(les *blocs-notes* PL)

to **paddle** VERB
see also paddle NOUN
1 *pagayer* (*canoe*)
2 *faire trempette* (*in water*)

paddle NOUN
see also paddle VERB
la *pagaie* (*for canoe*)
- **to go for a paddle** faire trempette

padlock NOUN
le *cadenas*

page NOUN
la *page* (*of book*)

paid VERB *see* **pay**

paid ADJECTIVE
1 *rémunéré* (*work*)
2 *payé* ◇ *3 weeks' paid holiday* trois semaines de congés payés

pail NOUN
le *seau*
(les *seaux* PL)

pain NOUN
la *douleur* ◇ *A terrible pain.* une douleur insupportable
- **I've got a pain in my stomach.** J'ai mal à l'estomac.
- **to be in pain** souffrir ◇ *She's in a lot of pain.* Elle souffre beaucoup.
- **He's a real pain.** Il est vraiment pénible.

painful ADJECTIVE
douloureux MASC
douloureuse FEM
◇ *to suffer from painful periods* souffrir de règles douloureuses
- **Is it painful?** Ça te fait mal?

painkiller NOUN
l' *analgésique* MASC

paint NOUN
see also paint VERB
la *peinture*

to **paint** VERB
see also paint NOUN
peindre ◇ *to paint something green* peindre quelque chose en vert

paintbrush NOUN
le *pinceau*
(les *pinceaux* PL)

painter NOUN
le *peintre*

painting NOUN
1 la *peinture* ◇ *My hobby is painting.* Je fais de la peinture.
2 (*picture*)
le *tableau*
(les *tableaux* PL)
◇ *a painting by Picasso* un tableau de Picasso

pair NOUN
la *paire* ◇ *a pair of shoes* une paire de chaussures ◇ *a pair of scissors* une paire de ciseaux
- **a pair of trousers** un pantalon
- **a pair of jeans** un jean
- **a pair of pants (1)** (*briefs*) un slip
- **a pair of pants (2)** (*boxer shorts*) un caleçon
- **in pairs** deux par deux ◇ *We work in pairs.* Nous travaillons deux par deux.

Pakistan NOUN
le *Pakistan*
- **in Pakistan** au Pakistan

◆ **to Pakistan** au Pakistan
◆ **He's from Pakistan.** Il est pakistanais.

Pakistani NOUN
see also Pakistani ADJECTIVE
le *Pakistanais*
la *Pakistanaise*

Pakistani ADJECTIVE
see also Pakistani NOUN
pakistanais MASC
pakistanaise FEM

pal NOUN
le *copain*
la *copine*

palace NOUN
le *palais*

pale ADJECTIVE
pâle ◇ *a pale blue shirt* une chemise bleu pâle

Palestine NOUN
la *Palestine*
◆ **in Palestine** en Palestine

Palestinian ADJECTIVE
see also Palestinian NOUN
palestinien MASC
palestinienne FEM

Palestinian NOUN
see also Palestinian ADJECTIVE
le *Palestinien*
la *Palestinienne*

palm NOUN
la *paume* (*of hand*)
◆ **a palm tree** un palmier

pamphlet NOUN
la *brochure*

pan NOUN
1 la *casserole* (*saucepan*)
2 la *poêle* (*frying pan*)

pancake NOUN
la *crêpe*

panic NOUN
see also panic VERB
la *panique*

panic VERB
see also panic NOUN
s'affoler ◇ *Don't panic!* Pas de panique!

panther NOUN
la *panthère*

panties PL NOUN
le *slip* SING

pantomime NOUN
le *spectacle de Noël pour enfants*

pants PL NOUN
1 le *slip* SING (*briefs*) ◇ *a pair of pants* un slip
2 le *caleçon* SING (*boxer shorts*) ◇ *a pair of pants* un caleçon

paper NOUN
1 le *papier* ◇ *a piece of paper* un morceau de papier ◇ *a paper towel* une serviette en papier
2 (*newspaper*)
le *journal*
(les *journaux* PL)
◇ *I saw an advert in the paper.* J'ai vu une annonce dans le journal.
◆ **an exam paper** une épreuve écrite

paperback NOUN
le *livre de poche*

paper clip NOUN
le *trombone*

parachute NOUN
le *parachute*

parade NOUN
le *défilé*

paradise NOUN
le *paradis*

paraffin NOUN
le *pétrole* ◇ *a paraffin lamp* une lampe à pétrole

paragraph NOUN
le *paragraphe*

parallel ADJECTIVE
parallèle

paralysed ADJECTIVE
paralysé

parcel NOUN
le *colis*

pardon NOUN
◆ **Pardon?** Pardon?

parent NOUN
1 le *père* (*father*)
2 la *mère* (*mother*)
◆ **my parents** mes parents MASC

Paris NOUN
Paris FEM
◆ **in Paris** à Paris
◆ **to Paris** à Paris
◆ **She's from Paris.** Elle est parisienne.

Parisian ADJECTIVE
see also Parisian NOUN
parisien MASC
parisienne FEM

Parisian NOUN
see also Parisian ADJECTIVE
le *Parisien*
la *Parisienne*

park NOUN
see also park VERB
le *parc*
◆ **a national park** un parc national
◆ **a theme park** un parc à thème
◆ **a car park** un parking

to **park** VERB
see also park NOUN
1 *garer* ◇ *Where can I park my car?* Où est-ce que je peux garer ma voiture?
2 *se garer* ◇ *We couldn't find anywhere*

PTO

to park. Nous avons eu du mal à nous garer.

parking NOUN
le *stationnement* ◇ *"no parking"* "stationnement interdit"

parking meter NOUN
le *parcmètre*

parking ticket NOUN
le *p.-v.* (*informal*)

parliament NOUN
le *parlement*

parrot NOUN
le *perroquet*

parsley NOUN
le *persil*

part NOUN
1 la *partie* (*section*) ◇ *The first part of the film was boring.* La première partie du film était ennuyeuse.
2 la *pièce* (*component*) ◇ *spare parts* les pièces de rechange
3 le *rôle* (*in play, film*)
➔ **to take part in something** participer à quelque chose ◇ *A lot of people took part in the demonstration.* Beaucoup de gens ont participé à la manifestation.

particular ADJECTIVE
particulier MASC
particulière FEM
◇ *Are you looking for anything particular?* Est-ce que vous voulez quelque chose de particulier?
➔ **nothing in particular** rien de particulier

particularly ADVERB
particulièrement

parting NOUN
la *raie* (*in hair*)

partly ADVERB
en partie

partner NOUN
1 (*in game*)
le/la *partenaire*
2 (*in business*)
l' *associé* MASC
l' *associée* FEM
3 (*in dance*)
le *cavalier*
la *cavalière*
4 (*boyfriend*)
le *compagnon*
la *compagne* (*girlfriend*)

part-time ADJECTIVE, ADVERB
à temps partiel ◇ *a part-time job* un travail à temps partiel ◇ *She works part-time.* Elle travaille à temps partiel.

party NOUN
1 la *fête* ◇ *a birthday party* une fête d'anniversaire ◇ *a Christmas party* une fête de Noël ◇ *a New Year party* une fête du Nouvel An
2 la *soirée* (*more formal*) ◇ *I'm going to a party on Saturday.* Je vais à une soirée samedi.
3 le *parti* (*political*) ◇ *the Conservative Party* le Parti conservateur
4 le *groupe* (*group*) ◇ *a party of tourists* un groupe de touristes

pass NOUN
see also pass VERB
1 le *col* (*in mountains*) ◇ *The pass was blocked with snow.* Le col était enneigé.
2 la *passe* (*in football*)
➔ **to get a pass** (*in exam*) être reçu ◇ *She got a pass in her piano exam.* Elle a été reçue à son examen de piano. ◇ *I got six passes.* J'ai été reçu dans six matières.
➔ **a bus pass** une carte de bus

to **pass** VERB
see also pass NOUN
1 *passer* ◇ *Could you pass me the salt, please?* Est-ce que vous pourriez me passer le sel, s'il vous plaît? ◇ *The time has passed quickly.* Le temps a passé rapidement.
2 *passer devant* ◇ *I pass his house on my way to school.* Je passe devant chez lui en allant à l'école.
3 *être reçu* (*exam*) ◇ *Did you pass?* Tu as été reçu?
➔ **to pass an exam** être reçu à un examen ◇ *I hope I'll pass the exam.* J'espère que je serai reçu à l'examen.

to **pass out** VERB
s'évanouir (*faint*)

passage NOUN
1 le *passage* (*piece of writing*) ◇ *Read the passage carefully.* Lisez attentivement le passage.
2 le *couloir* (*corridor*)

passenger NOUN
le *passager*
la *passagère*

passion NOUN
la *passion*

passive ADJECTIVE
passif MASC
passive FEM
➔ **passive smoking** le tabagisme passif

Passover NOUN
la *Pâque juive* ◇ *at Passover* à la Pâque juive

passport NOUN
le *passeport* ◇ *passport control* le contrôle des passeports

password NOUN
le *mot de passe*

past ADVERB, PREPOSITION
see also past NOUN

après (*beyond*) ◇ *It's on the right, just past the station.* C'est sur la droite, juste après la gare.

- **to go past (1)** passer ◇ *The bus went past without stopping.* Le bus est passé sans s'arrêter.
- **to go past (2)** passer devant ◇ *The bus goes past our house.* Le bus passe devant notre maison.
- **It's half past ten.** Il est dix heures et demie.
- **It's quarter past nine.** Il est neuf heures et quart.
- **It's ten past eight.** Il est huit heures dix.
- **It's past midnight.** Il est minuit passé.

past NOUN
see also past ADVERB
le *passé* ◇ *She lives in the past.* Elle vit dans le passé.
- **in the past** (*previously*) autrefois ◇ *This was common in the past.* C'était courant autrefois.

pasta NOUN
les *pâtes* FEM PL ◇ *Pasta is easy to cook.* Les pâtes sont faciles à préparer.

paste NOUN
la *colle* (*glue*)

pasteurized ADJECTIVE
pasteurisé

pastime NOUN
le *passe-temps*
(les *passe-temps* PL)
◇ *Her favourite pastime is knitting.* Son passe-temps favori est le tricot.

pastry NOUN
la *pâte*
- **pastries** les pâtisseries FEM

patch NOUN
1 la *pièce* ◇ *a patch of material* une pièce de tissu
2 la *rustine* (*for flat tyre*)
- **He's got a bald patch.** Il a le crâne dégarni.

patched ADJECTIVE
rapiécé ◇ *a pair of patched jeans* un jean rapiécé

pâté NOUN
le *pâté*

path NOUN
1 le *chemin* (*footpath*)
2 l' *allée* FEM (*in garden, park*)

pathetic ADJECTIVE
lamentable ◇ *Our team was pathetic.* Notre équipe a été lamentable.

patience NOUN
1 la *patience* ◇ *He hasn't got much patience.* Il n'a pas beaucoup de patience.
2 la *réussite* (*card game*) ◇ *to play patience* faire une réussite

patient NOUN
see also patient ADJECTIVE
le *patient*
la *patiente*

patient ADJECTIVE
see also patient NOUN
patient

patio NOUN
le *patio*

patriotic ADJECTIVE
patriote

patrol NOUN
la *patrouille*

patrol car NOUN
la *voiture de police*

pattern NOUN
le *motif* ◇ *a geometric pattern* un motif géométrique
- **a sewing pattern** un patron

pause NOUN
la *pause*

pavement NOUN
le *trottoir*

pavilion NOUN
le *pavillon*

paw NOUN
la *patte*

pay NOUN
see also pay VERB
le *salaire*

to **pay** VERB
see also pay NOUN
1 *payer* ◇ *They pay me more on Sundays.* Je suis payé davantage le dimanche.
2 *régler* ◇ *to pay by cheque* régler par chèque ◇ *to pay by credit card* régler par carte de crédit
- **to pay for something** payer quelque chose ◇ *I paid for my ticket.* J'ai payé mon billet. ◇ *I paid 50 francs for it.* Je l'ai payé cinquante francs.
- **to pay extra for something** payer un supplément pour quelque chose ◇ *You have to pay extra for parking.* Il faut payer un supplément pour le parking.
- **to pay attention** faire attention ◇ *Don't pay any attention to him!* Ne fais pas attention à lui!
- **to pay somebody a visit** rendre visite à quelqu'un ◇ *Paul paid us a visit last night.* Paul nous a rendu visite hier soir.
- **to pay somebody back** rembourser quelqu'un ◇ *I'll pay you back tomorrow.* Je te rembourserai demain.

payment NOUN
le *paiement*

payphone NOUN

PTO

le *téléphone public*

PC NOUN (= *personal computer*)
le *PC* ◇ *She typed the report on her PC.* Elle a tapé le rapport sur son PC.

pea NOUN
le *petit pois*

peace NOUN
1 la *paix* (*after war*)
2 le *calme* (*quietness*)

peaceful ADJECTIVE
1 *paisible* (*calm*) ◇ *a peaceful afternoon* un après-midi paisible
2 *pacifique* (*not violent*) ◇ *a peaceful protest* une manifestation pacifique

peach NOUN
la *pêche*

peacock NOUN
le *paon*

peak NOUN
la *cime* (*of mountain*)
◆ **the peak rate** le plein tarif ◇ *You pay the peak rate for calls at this time of day.* On paie le plein tarif quand on appelle à cette heure-ci.
◆ **in peak season** en haute saison

peanut NOUN
la *cacahuète* ◇ *a packet of peanuts* un paquet de cacahuètes

peanut butter NOUN
le *beurre de cacahuètes* ◇ *a peanut-butter sandwich* un sandwich au beurre de cacahuètes

pear NOUN
la *poire*

pearl NOUN
la *perle*

pebble NOUN
le *galet* ◇ *a pebble beach* une plage de galets

peculiar ADJECTIVE
bizarre ◇ *He's a peculiar person.* Il est bizarre. ◇ *It tastes peculiar.* Ça a un goût bizarre.

pedal NOUN
la *pédale*

pedestrian NOUN
le *piéton*

pedestrian crossing NOUN
le *passage pour piétons*

pedestrianized ADJECTIVE
◆ **a pedestrianized street** une rue piétonne

pedigree ADJECTIVE
de race (*animal*) ◇ *a pedigree dog* un chien de race ◇ *A pedigree labrador.* Un labrador de pure race.

pee NOUN
◆ **to have a pee** faire pipi

peel NOUN
see also peel VERB
l' *écorce* FEM (*of orange*)

to **peel** VERB
see also peel NOUN
1 *éplucher* ◇ *Shall I peel the potatoes?* J'épluche les pommes de terre?
2 *peler* ◇ *My nose is peeling.* Mon nez pèle.

peg NOUN
1 (*for coats*)
le *portemanteau*
(les *portemanteaux* PL)
2 (*clothes peg*)
la *pince à linge*
3 (*tent peg*)
le *piquet*

Pekinese NOUN
le *pékinois*

pellet NOUN
le *plomb* (*for gun*)

pelvis NOUN
le *bassin*

pen NOUN
le *stylo*

to **penalize** VERB
pénaliser

penalty NOUN
1 la *peine* (*punishment*)
◆ **the death penalty** la peine de mort
2 le *penalty* (*in football*)
3 la *pénalité* (*in rugby*)
◆ **a penalty shoot-out** les tirs au but

pence PL NOUN
les *pence* MASC PL

pencil NOUN
le *crayon*
◆ **in pencil** au crayon

pencil case NOUN
la *trousse*

pencil sharpener NOUN
le *taille-crayon*

pendant NOUN
le *pendentif*

penfriend NOUN
le *correspondant*
la *correspondante*

penguin NOUN
le *pingouin*

penicillin NOUN
la *pénicilline*

penis NOUN
le *pénis*

penknife NOUN
le *canif*

penny NOUN
le *penny*
(les *pence* PL)

pension NOUN
la *retraite*

pensioner NOUN
le *retraité*
la *retraitée*

pentathlon NOUN
le *pentathlon*

people PL NOUN
1 les *gens* MASC ◇ *The people were nice.* Les gens étaient sympathiques. ◇ *a lot of people* beaucoup de gens
2 les *personnes* FEM (*individuals*) ◇ *six people* six personnes ◇ *several people* plusieurs personnes
- **How many people are there in your family?** Vous êtes combien dans votre famille?
- **French people** les Français
- **black people** les Noirs
- **People say that...** On dit que...

pepper NOUN
1 le *poivre* (*spice*) ◇ *Pass the pepper, please.* Passez-moi le poivre, s'il vous plaît.
2 le *poivron* (*vegetable*) ◇ *a green pepper* un poivron vert

peppermill NOUN
le *moulin à poivre*

peppermint NOUN
la *pastille de menthe* (*sweet*)
- **peppermint chewing gum** le chewing-gum à la menthe

per PREPOSITION
par ◇ *per day* par jour ◇ *per week* par semaine
- **30 miles per hour** trente miles à l'heure

per cent ADVERB
pour cent ◇ *fifty per cent* cinquante pour cent

percolator NOUN
la *cafetière électrique*

percussion NOUN
la *percussion* ◇ *I play percussion.* Je joue des percussions.

perfect ADJECTIVE
parfait ◇ *Chantal speaks perfect English.* Chantal parle un anglais parfait.

perfectly ADVERB
parfaitement

perform VERB
jouer (*act, play*)

performance NOUN
1 le *spectacle* (*show*) ◇ *The performance lasts two hours.* Le spectacle dure deux heures.
2 l' *interprétation* FEM (*acting*) ◇ *his performance as Hamlet* son interprétation d'Hamlet
3 la *performance* (*results*) ◇ *the team's poor performance* la médiocre performance de l'équipe

perfume NOUN
le *parfum*

perhaps ADVERB
peut-être ◇ *a bit boring, perhaps* peut-être un peu ennuyeux ◇ *Perhaps he's ill.* Il est peut-être malade.
- **perhaps not** peut-être pas

period NOUN
1 la *période* ◇ *for a limited period* pour une période limitée
2 l' *époque* FEM (*in history*) ◇ *the Victorian period* l'époque victorienne
3 les *règles* FEM (*menstruation*) ◇ *I'm having my period.* J'ai mes règles.
4 le *cours* (*lesson time*) ◇ *Each period lasts forty minutes.* Chaque cours dure quarante minutes.

perm NOUN
la *permanente* ◇ *She's got a perm.* Elle a une permanente.
- **to have a perm** se faire faire une permanente

permanent ADJECTIVE
permanent

permission NOUN
la *permission* ◇ *Could I have permission to leave early?* Pourrais-je avoir la permission de partir plus tôt?

permit NOUN
le *permis* ◇ *a fishing permit* un permis de pêche

to **persecute** VERB
persécuter

Persian ADJECTIVE
- **a Persian cat** un chat persan

persistent ADJECTIVE
tenace (*person*)

person NOUN
la *personne* ◇ *She's a very nice person.* C'est une personne très sympathique.
- **in person** en personne

personal ADJECTIVE
personnel MASC
personnelle FEM

personality NOUN
la *personnalité*

personally ADVERB
personnellement ◇ *I don't know him personally.* Je ne le connais pas personnellement. ◇ *Personally I don't agree.* Personnellement, je ne suis pas d'accord.

personal stereo NOUN
le *walkman* ®

personnel NOUN
le *personnel*

perspiration NOUN
la *transpiration*

to **persuade** VERB
persuader
- **to persuade somebody to do something** persuader quelqu'un de faire quelque chose ◇ *She persuaded me to go with her.* Elle m'a persuadé de l'accompagner.

pessimist NOUN
le/la *pessimiste* ◇ *I'm a pessimist.* Je suis pessimiste.

pessimistic ADJECTIVE
pessimiste

pest NOUN
le/la *casse-pieds* (*person*) ◇ *He's a real pest!* C'est un vrai casse-pieds!

to **pester** VERB
importuner

pet NOUN
l' *animal familier* MASC ◇ *Have you got a pet?* Est-ce que tu as un animal familier?
- **She's the teacher's pet.** C'est la chouchoute de la maîtresse.

petition NOUN
la *pétition*

petrified ADJECTIVE
pétrifié

petrol NOUN
l' *essence* FEM
- **unleaded petrol** l'essence sans plomb
- **leaded petrol** l'essence au plomb
- **4-star petrol, please.** Du super, s'il vous plaît.

petrol station NOUN
la *station-service*
(les *stations-service* PL)

petrol tank NOUN
le *réservoir d'essence*

phantom NOUN
le *fantôme*

pharmacy NOUN
la *pharmacie*
Pharmacies in France are identified by a special green cross outside the shop.

pheasant NOUN
le *faisan*

philosophy NOUN
la *philosophie*

phobia NOUN
la *phobie*

phone NOUN
see also phone VERB
le *téléphone* ◇ *Where's the phone?* Où est le téléphone? ◇ *Is there a phone here?* Est-ce qu'il y a un téléphone ici?
- **by phone** par téléphone
- **to be on the phone** être au téléphone ◇ *She's on the phone at the moment.* Elle est au téléphone en ce moment.
- **Can I use the phone, please?** Est-ce que je peux téléphoner, s'il vous plaît?

to **phone** VERB
see also phone NOUN
appeler ◇ *I'll phone the station.* Je vais appeler la gare.

phone bill NOUN
la *facture de téléphone*

phone book NOUN
l' *annuaire* MASC

phone box NOUN
la *cabine téléphonique*

phone call NOUN
l' *appel* MASC ◇ *There's a phone call for you.* Il y a un appel pour vous.
- **to make a phone call** téléphoner ◇ *Can I make a phone call?* Est-ce que peux téléphoner?

phonecard NOUN
la *carte de téléphone*

phone number NOUN
le *numéro de téléphone*

photo NOUN
la *photo*
- **to take a photo** prendre une photo
- **to take a photo of somebody** prendre quelqu'un en photo

photocopier NOUN
la *photocopieuse*

photocopy NOUN
see also photocopy VERB
la *photocopie*

to **photocopy** VERB
see also photocopy NOUN
photocopier

photograph NOUN
see also photograph VERB
la *photo*
- **to take a photograph** prendre une photo
- **to take a photograph of somebody** prendre quelqu'un en photo

to **photograph** VERB
see also photograph NOUN
photographier

photographer NOUN
le/la *photographe* ◇ *She's a photographer.* Elle est photographe.

photography NOUN
la *photo* ◇ *My hobby is photography.* Je fais de la photo.

phrase NOUN
l' *expression* FEM

phrase book NOUN
le *guide de conversation*

physical ADJECTIVE
physique

physicist NOUN
le *physicien*
la *physicienne*

◇ *He's a physicist.* Il est physicien.

physics NOUN
la *physique* ◇ *She teaches physics.* Elle enseigne la physique.

physiotherapist NOUN
le/la *kinésithérapeute*

physiotherapy NOUN
la *kinésithérapie*

pianist NOUN
le/la *pianiste*

piano NOUN
le *piano* ◇ *I play the piano.* Je joue du piano. ◇ *I have piano lessons.* Je prends des leçons de piano.

pick NOUN
see also pick VERB
• **Take your pick!** Faites votre choix!

pick VERB
see also pick NOUN
1 *choisir* (*choose*) ◇ *I picked the biggest piece.* J'ai choisi le plus gros morceau.
2 *sélectionner* (*for team*) ◇ *I've been picked for the team.* J'ai été sélectionné pour faire partie de l'équipe.
3 *cueillir* (*fruit, flowers*)
• **to pick on somebody** harceler quelqu'un ◇ *She's always picking on me.* Elle me harcèle constamment.
• **to pick out** choisir ◇ *I like them all–it's difficult to pick one out.* Ils me plaisent tous–c'est difficile d'en choisir un.
• **to pick up (1)** (*collect*) venir chercher ◇ *We'll come to the airport to pick you up.* Nous irons vous chercher à l'aéroport.
• **to pick up (2)** (*from floor*) ramasser ◇ *Could you help me pick up the toys?* Tu peux m'aider à ramasser les jouets?
• **to pick up (3)** (*learn*) apprendre ◇ *I picked up some Spanish during my holiday.* J'ai appris quelque mots d'espagnol pendant mes vacances.

pickpocket NOUN
le *pickpocket*

picnic NOUN
le *pique-nique*
• **to have a picnic** pique-niquer ◇ *We had a picnic on the beach.* Nous avons pique-niqué sur la plage.

picture NOUN
1 l' *illustration* FEM ◇ *Children's books have lots of pictures.* Il y a beaucoup d'illustrations dans les livres pour enfants.
2 la *photo* ◇ *My picture was in the paper.* Ma photo était dans le journal.
3 (*painting*)
le *tableau*
(les *tableaux* PL)
◇ *a famous picture* un tableau célèbre
• **to paint a picture of something** peindre quelque chose
4 (*drawing*)
le *dessin*
• **to draw a picture of something** dessiner quelque chose
• **the pictures** (*cinema*) le cinéma ◇ *Shall we go to the pictures?* On va au cinéma?

picturesque ADJECTIVE
pittoresque

pie NOUN
la *tourte* ◇ *an apple pie* une tourte aux pommes

piece NOUN
le *morceau*
(les *morceaux* PL)
◇ *A small piece, please.* Un petit morceau, s'il vous plaît.
• **a piece of furniture** un meuble
• **a piece of advice** un conseil

pier NOUN
la *jetée*

pierced ADJECTIVE
percé ◇ *I've got pierced ears.* J'ai les oreilles percées.

pig NOUN
le *cochon*

pigeon NOUN
le *pigeon*

piggy bank NOUN
la *tirelire*

pigtail NOUN
la *natte*

pile NOUN
1 le *tas* (*untidy heap*)
2 la *pile* (*tidy stack*)

pill NOUN
la *pilule*
• **to be on the pill** prendre la pilule

pillar NOUN
le *pilier*

pillar box NOUN
la *boîte aux lettres*

pillow NOUN
l' *oreiller* MASC

pilot NOUN
le *pilote* ◇ *He's a pilot.* Il est pilote.

pimple NOUN
le *bouton*

pin NOUN
l' *épingle* FEM
• **I've got pins and needles.** J'ai des fourmis dans les jambes.

PIN NOUN (= *personal identification number*)
le *code confidentiel*

pinafore NOUN
le *tablier*

pinball NOUN
le *flipper* ◇ *to play pinball* jouer au

P

PTO

flipper
- **a pinball machine** un flipper

to **pinch** VERB
1 *pincer* ◇ *He pinched me!* Il m'a pincé!
2 *piquer* (*informal: steal*) ◇ *Who's pinched my pen?* Qui est-ce qui m'a piqué mon stylo?

pine NOUN
le *pin* ◇ *a pine table* une table en pin

pineapple NOUN
l' *ananas* MASC

pink ADJECTIVE
rose

pint NOUN
la *pinte*
In France measurements are in litres and centilitres. A pint is about 0.6 litres.
- **to have a pint** boire une bière ◇ *He's gone out for a pint.* Il est parti boire une bière.

pipe NOUN
1 la *conduite* (*for water, gas*) ◇ *The pipes froze.* Les conduites d'eau ont gelé.
2 la *pipe* (*for smoking*) ◇ *He smokes a pipe.* Il fume la pipe.
- **the pipes** (*bagpipes*) la cornemuse ◇ *He plays the pipes.* Il joue de la cornemuse.

pirate NOUN
le *pirate*

pirated ADJECTIVE
pirate ◇ *a pirated video* une vidéo pirate

Pisces NOUN
les *Poissons* MASC ◇ *I'm Pisces.* Je suis Poissons.

pissed ADJECTIVE
bourré (*informal*)

pistol NOUN
le *pistolet*

pitch NOUN
see also pitch VERB
le *terrain* ◇ *a football pitch* un terrain de football

to **pitch** VERB
see also pitch NOUN
dresser (*tent*) ◇ *We pitched our tent near the beach.* Nous avons dressé notre tente près de la plage.

pity NOUN
see also pity VERB
la *pitié*
- **What a pity!** Quel dommage!

to **pity** VERB
see also pity NOUN
plaindre

pizza NOUN
la *pizza*

place NOUN
see also place VERB
1 l' *endroit* MASC (*location*) ◇ *It's a quiet place.* C'est un endroit tranquille.
◇ *There are a lot of interesting places to visit.* Il y a beaucoup d'endroits intéressants à visiter.
2 la *place* (*space*) ◇ *a parking place* une place de parking ◇ *a university place* une place à l'université
- **to change places** changer de place ◇ *Tamsin, change places with Delphine!* Tamsin, change de place avec Delphine!
- **to take place** avoir lieu
- **at your place** chez toi ◇ *Shall we meet at your place?* On se retrouve chez toi?
- **to my place** chez moi ◇ *Do you want to come round to my place?* Tu veux venir chez moi?

to **place** VERB
see also place NOUN
1 *poser* ◇ *He placed his hand on hers.* Il a posé la main sur la sienne.
2 *classer* (*in competition, contest*)

plaid ADJECTIVE
écossais ◇ *a plaid shirt* une chemise écossaise

plain NOUN
see also plain ADJECTIVE
la *plaine*

plain ADJECTIVE, ADVERB
see also plain NOUN
1 *uni* (*not patterned*) ◇ *a plain carpet* un tapis uni
2 *simple* (*not fancy*) ◇ *a plain white blouse* un simple chemisier blanc

plain chocolate NOUN
le *chocolat à croquer*

plait NOUN
la *natte* ◇ *She wears her hair in a plait.* Elle a une natte.

plan NOUN
see also plan VERB
1 le *projet* ◇ *What are your plans for the holidays?* Quels sont tes projets pour les vacances? ◇ *to make plans* faire des projets
- **Everything went according to plan.** Tout s'est passé comme prévu.
2 le *plan* (*map*) ◇ *a plan of the campsite* un plan du terrain de camping
- **my essay plan** le plan de ma dissertation

to **plan** VERB
see also plan NOUN
1 *préparer* (*make plans for*) ◇ *We're planning a trip to France.* Nous préparons un voyage en France.
2 *planifier* (*make schedule for*) ◇ *Plan your revision carefully.* Planifiez vos

révisions avec soin.
to plan to do something avoir l'intention de faire quelque chose ◇ *I'm planning to get a job in the holidays.* J'ai l'intention de trouver un job pour les vacances.

plane NOUN
l' *avion* MASC ◇ *by plane* en avion

planet NOUN
la *planète*

planning NOUN
la *préparation* ◇ *The trip needs careful planning.* Le voyage nécessite une préparation méticuleuse.
family planning le planning familial

plant NOUN
see also plant VERB
1 la *plante* ◇ *to water the plants* arroser les plantes
2 l' *usine* FEM (*factory*)

plant VERB
see also plant NOUN
planter

plaster NOUN
1 le *pansement adhésif* (*sticking plaster*) ◇ *Have you got a plaster, by any chance?* Vous n'auriez pas un pansement adhésif, par hasard?
2 le *plâtre* (*for fracture*) ◇ *Her leg's in plaster.* Elle a la jambe dans le plâtre.

plastic NOUN
see also plastic ADJECTIVE
le *plastique* ◇ *It's made of plastic.* C'est en plastique.

plastic ADJECTIVE
see also plastic NOUN
en plastique ◇ *a plastic bag* un sac en plastique ◇ *a plastic mac* un imperméable en plastique

plate NOUN
l' *assiette* FEM (*for food*)

platform NOUN
1 le *quai* (*at station*) ◇ *on platform 7* sur le quai numéro sept
2 l' *estrade* FEM (*for performers*)

play NOUN
see also play VERB
la *pièce* ◇ *a play by Shakespeare* une pièce de Shakespeare
• **to put on a play** monter une pièce

play VERB
see also play NOUN
1 *jouer* ◇ *He's playing with his friends.* Il joue avec ses amis. ◇ *What sort of music do they play?* Quel genre de musique jouent-ils?
2 *jouer contre* (*against person, team*) ◇ *France will play Scotland next month.* La France jouera contre l'Écosse le mois prochain.
3 *jouer à* (*sport, game*) ◇ *I play hockey.* Je joue au hockey. ◇ *Can you play pool?* Tu sais jouer au billard américain?
4 *jouer de* (*instrument*) ◇ *I play the guitar.* Je joue de la guitare.
5 *écouter* (*record, cassette, music*) ◇ *She's always playing that record.* Elle écoute tout le temps ce disque.

player NOUN
1 (*of sport*)
le *joueur*
la *joueuse*
◇ *a football player* un joueur de football
2 (*of instrument*)
le *musicien*
la *musicienne*
• **a piano player** un pianiste
• **a saxophone player** un saxophoniste

playful ADJECTIVE
espiègle

playground NOUN
1 la *cour de récréation* (*at school*)
2 l' *aire de jeux* FEM (*in park*)

playgroup NOUN
la *garderie*

playing field NOUN
le *terrain de sport*

playtime NOUN
la *récréation*

playwright NOUN
le *dramaturge*

pleasant ADJECTIVE
agréable

please EXCLAMATION
1 *s'il vous plaît* (*polite form*) ◇ *Two coffees, please.* Deux cafés, s'il vous plaît.
2 *s'il te plaît* (*familiar form*) ◇ *Please write back soon.* Réponds vite, s'il te plaît.

pleased ADJECTIVE
content ◇ *My mother's not going to be very pleased.* Ma mère ne va pas être contente du tout. ◇ *It's beautiful: she'll be pleased with it.* C'est beau: elle va être contente.
• **Pleased to meet you!** Enchanté!

pleasure NOUN
le *plaisir* ◇ *I read for pleasure.* Je lis pour le plaisir.

plenty NOUN
largement assez ◇ *I've got plenty.* J'en ai largement assez. ◇ *That's plenty, thanks.* Ça suffit largement, merci.
• **plenty of (1)** (*a lot*) beaucoup de ◇ *I've got plenty to do.* J'ai beaucoup de choses à faire.
• **plenty of (2)** (*enough*) largement assez de

◇ *I've got plenty of money.* J'ai largement assez d'argent. ◇ *We've got plenty of time.* Nous avons largement le temps.

plot NOUN

see also plot VERB

1 l' *intrigue* FEM (*of story, play*)

2 la *conspiration* (*against somebody*) ◇ *a plot against the president* une conspiration contre le président

3 le *carré* (*of land*) ◇ *a vegetable plot* un carré de légumes

to **plot** VERB

see also plot NOUN

comploter ◇ *They were plotting to kill him.* Ils complotaient de le tuer.

plough NOUN

see also plough VERB

la *charrue*

to **plough** VERB

see also plough NOUN

labourer

plug NOUN

1 la *prise de courant* (*electrical*) ◇ *The plug is faulty.* La prise est défectueuse.

2 le *bouchon* (*for sink*)

to **plug in** VERB

brancher ◇ *Is it plugged in?* Est-ce que c'est branché?

plum NOUN

la *prune* ◇ *plum jam* la confiture de prunes

plumber NOUN

le *plombier* ◇ *He's a plumber.* Il est plombier.

plump ADJECTIVE

dodu

to **plunge** VERB

plonger

plural NOUN

le *pluriel*

plus PREPOSITION, ADJECTIVE

plus ◇ *4 plus 3 equals 7.* Quatre plus trois égalent sept. ◇ *three children plus a dog* trois enfants plus un chien

- **I got a B plus.** J'ai eu un Bien.

p.m. ABBREVIATION

- **at 8 p.m.** à huit heures du soir

In France times are often given using the 24-hour clock.

- **at 2 p.m.** à quatorze heures

pneumonia NOUN

la *pneumonie*

poached ADJECTIVE

poché ◇ *a poached egg* un œuf poché

pocket NOUN

la *poche*

- **pocket money** l'argent de poche MASC ◇ *£8 a week pocket money* huit livres d'argent de poche par semaine

pocket calculator NOUN

la *calculette*

poem NOUN

le *poème*

poet NOUN

le *poète*

poetry NOUN

la *poésie*

point NOUN

see also point VERB

1 le *point* (*spot, score*) ◇ *a point on the horizon* un point à l'horizon ◇ *They scored 5 points.* Ils ont marqué cinq points.

2 la *remarque* (*comment*) ◇ *He made some interesting points.* Il a fait quelque remarques intéressantes.

3 la *pointe* (*tip*) ◇ *a pencil with a sharp point* un crayon à la pointe aiguisée

4 le *moment* (*in time*) ◇ *At that point, we decided to leave.* À ce moment-là, nous avons décidé de partir.

- **a point of view** un point de vue
- **to get the point** comprendre ◇ *Sorry, I don't get the point.* Désolé, je ne comprends pas.
- **That's a good point!** C'est vrai!
- **There's no point.** Cela ne sert à rien. ◇ *There's no point in waiting.* Cela ne sert à rien d'attendre.
- **What's the point?** À quoi bon? ◇ *What's the point of leaving so early?* À quoi bon partir si tôt?
- **Punctuality isn't my strong point.** La ponctualité n'est pas mon fort.
- **two point five (2.5)** deux virgule cinq (2,5)

to **point** VERB

see also point NOUN

montrer du doigt ◇ *Don't point!* Ne montre pas du doigt!

- **to point at somebody** montrer quelqu'un du doigt ◇ *She pointed at Anne.* Elle a montré Anne du doigt.
- **to point a gun at somebody** braquer un revolver sur quelqu'un
- **to point something out (1)** (*show*) montrer quelque chose ◇ *The guide pointed out Notre-Dame to us.* Le guide nous a montré Notre-Dame.
- **to point something out (2)** (*mention*) signaler quelque chose ◇ *I should point out that...* Je dois vous signaler que...

pointless ADJECTIVE

inutile ◇ *It's pointless to argue.* Il est inutile de discuter.

poison NOUN

see also poison VERB

le *poison*

poison VERB
see also poison NOUN
empoisonner

poisonous ADJECTIVE
1 (*snake*)
venimeux MASC
venimeuse FEM
2 (*plant, mushroom*)
vénéneux MASC
vénéneuse FEM
3 (*gas*)
toxique

poker NOUN
le *poker* ◇ *I play poker.* Je joue au poker.

Poland NOUN
la *Pologne*
- **in Poland** en Pologne
- **to Poland** en Pologne

polar bear NOUN
l' *ours blanc* MASC

Pole NOUN
(*Polish person*)
le *Polonais*
la *Polonaise*

pole NOUN
le *poteau*
(les *poteaux* PL)
◇ *a telegraph pole* un poteau télégraphique
- **a tent pole** un montant de tente
- **a ski pole** un bâton de ski
- **the North Pole** le pôle Nord
- **the South Pole** le pôle Sud

pole vault NOUN
le *saut à la perche*

police PL NOUN
la *police* ◇ *We called the police.* Nous avons appelé la police.
- **a police car** une voiture de police
- **a police station** un commissariat de police

policeman NOUN
le *policier* ◇ *He's a policeman.* Il est policier.

policewoman NOUN
la *femme policier* ◇ *She's a policewoman.* Elle est femme policier.

polio NOUN
la *polio*

Polish ADJECTIVE
see also Polish NOUN
polonais

Polish NOUN
see also Polish ADJECTIVE
le *polonais* (*language*)

polish NOUN
see also polish VERB
1 le *cirage* (*for shoes*)
2 la *cire* (*for furniture*)

to **polish** VERB
see also polish NOUN
1 *cirer* (*shoes, furniture*)
2 *faire briller* (*glass*)

polite ADJECTIVE
poli

politely ADVERB
poliment

politeness NOUN
la *politesse*

political ADJECTIVE
politique

politician NOUN
le *politicien*
la *politicienne*

politics PL NOUN
la *politique* SING ◇ *I'm not interested in politics.* La politique ne m'intéresse pas.

pollen NOUN
le *pollen*

to **pollute** VERB
polluer

polluted ADJECTIVE
pollué

pollution NOUN
la *pollution*

polo-necked sweater NOUN
le *pull à col roulé*

polo shirt NOUN
le *polo*

polythene bag NOUN
le *sac en plastique*

pond NOUN
1 l' *étang* MASC (*big*)
2 la *mare* (*smaller*)
3 le *bassin* ◇ *We've got a pond in our garden.* Nous avons un bassin dans notre jardin.

pony NOUN
le *poney*

ponytail NOUN
la *queue de cheval* ◇ *He's got a ponytail.* Il a une queue de cheval.

pony trekking NOUN
- **to go pony trekking** faire une randonnée à dos de poney

poodle NOUN
le *caniche*

pool NOUN
1 la *flaque* (*puddle*)
2 l' *étang* MASC (*pond*)
3 la *piscine* (*for swimming*)
4 le *billard américain* (*game*) ◇ *Shall we have a game of pool?* Si on jouait au billard américain?
- **the pools** (*football*) le loto sportif ◇ *to do the pools* jouer au loto sportif

poor ADJECTIVE

P

PTO

1 *pauvre* ◇ *a poor family* une famille pauvre ◇ *Poor David, he's very unlucky!* Le pauvre David, il n'a vraiment pas de chance!

➔ **the poor** les pauvres MASC

2 *médiocre* (*bad*) ◇ *a poor mark* une note médiocre

poorly ADJECTIVE

souffrant ◇ *She's poorly.* Elle est souffrante.

pop ADJECTIVE

pop ◇ *pop music* la musique pop ◇ *a pop star* une pop star ◇ *a pop group* un groupe pop ◇ *a pop song* une chanson pop

popcorn NOUN

le *pop-corn*

pope NOUN

le *pape*

poppy NOUN

le *coquelicot*

popular ADJECTIVE

populaire ◇ *She's a very popular girl.* C'est une fille très populaire. ◇ *This is a very popular style.* C'est un style très populaire.

population NOUN

la *population*

porch NOUN

le *porche*

pork NOUN

le *porc* ◇ *a pork chop* une côtelette de porc ◇ *I don't eat pork.* Je ne mange pas de porc.

porn NOUN

see also porn ADJECTIVE

le *porno*

porn ADJECTIVE

see also porn NOUN

porno MASC, FEM, PL ◇ *a porn film* un film porno ◇ *a porn mag* un magazine porno

pornographic ADJECTIVE

pornographique ◇ *a pornographic magazine* un magazine pornographique

pornography NOUN

la *pornographie*

porridge NOUN

le *porridge*

port NOUN

1 le *port* (*harbour*)

2 le *porto* (*wine*) ◇ *a glass of port* un verre de porto

porter NOUN

1 le *portier* (*in hotel*)

2 le *porteur* (*at station*)

portion NOUN

la *portion* ◇ *a large portion of chips* une grosse portion de frites

portrait NOUN

le *portrait*

Portugal NOUN

le *Portugal*

➔ **in Portugal** au Portugal

➔ **We went to Portugal.** Nous sommes allés au Portugal.

Portuguese ADJECTIVE

see also Portuguese NOUN

portugais

Portuguese NOUN

see also Portuguese ADJECTIVE

1 (*person*)

le *Portugais*

la *Portugaise*

2 (*language*)

le *portugais*

posh ADJECTIVE

chic MASC, FEM, PL ◇ *a posh hotel* un hôtel chic

position NOUN

la *position* ◇ *an uncomfortable position* une position inconfortable

positive ADJECTIVE

1 (*good*)

positif MASC

positive FEM

◇ *a positive attitude* une attitude positive

2 (*sure*)

certain ◇ *I'm positive.* J'en suis certain.

to **possess** VERB

posséder

possession NOUN

➔ **Have you got all your possessions?** Est-ce tu as toutes tes affaires?

possibility NOUN

➔ **It's a possibility.** C'est possible.

possible ADJECTIVE

possible ◇ *as soon as possible* aussitôt que possible

possibly ADVERB

peut-être (*perhaps*) ◇ *Are you coming to the party?–Possibly.* Est-ce que tu viens à la soirée?–Peut-être.

➔ **...if you possibly can.** ...si cela vous est possible.

➔ **I can't possibly come.** Je ne peux vraiment pas venir.

post NOUN

see also post VERB

1 (*letters*)

le *courrier* ◇ *Is there any post for me?* Est-ce qu'il y a du courrier pour moi?

2 (*pole*)

le *poteau*

(les *poteaux* PL)

◇ *The ball hit the post.* Le ballon a heurté le poteau.

to **post** VERB

see also post NOUN
poster ◇ *I've got some cards to post.* J'ai quelques cartes à poster.

postage NOUN
l' *affranchissement* MASC

postbox NOUN
la *boîte aux lettres*

postcard NOUN
la *carte postale*

postcode NOUN
le *code postal*

poster NOUN
1 le *poster* ◇ *I've got posters on my bedroom walls.* J'ai des posters sur les murs de ma chambre.
2 l' *affiche* FEM (*advertising*) ◇ *There are posters all over town.* Il y a des affiches dans toute la ville.

postman NOUN
le *facteur* ◇ *He's a postman.* Il est facteur.

postmark NOUN
le *cachet de la poste*

post office NOUN
la *poste* ◇ *Where's the post office, please?* Où est la poste, s'il vous plaît? ◇ *She works for the post office.* Elle travaille à la poste.

postpone VERB
remettre à plus tard ◇ *The match has been postponed.* Le match a été remis à plus tard.

postwoman NOUN
la *factrice* ◇ *She's a postwoman.* Elle est factrice.

pot NOUN
1 le *pot* ◇ *a pot of jam* un pot de confiture
2 la *théière* (*teapot*)
3 la *cafetière* (*coffeepot*)
4 l' *herbe* FEM (*marijuana*) ◇ *to smoke pot* fumer de l'herbe
the pots and pans les casseroles

potato NOUN
la *pomme de terre* ◇ *potato salad* la salade de pommes de terre
mashed potatoes la purée
a baked potato une pomme de terre en robe des champs

potential NOUN
see also potential ADJECTIVE
He has great potential. Il a de l'avenir.

potential ADJECTIVE
see also potential NOUN
possible ◇ *a potential problem* un problème possible

pothole NOUN
le *nid de poule* (*in road*)

pot plant NOUN
la *plante en pot*

pottery NOUN
la *poterie*

pound NOUN
see also pound VERB
la *livre* (*weight, money*) ◇ *a pound of carrots* une livre de carottes ◇ *How many francs do you get for a pound?* Combien de francs a-t-on pour une livre? ◇ *a pound coin* une pièce d'une livre

to **pound** VERB
see also pound NOUN
battre ◇ *My heart was pounding.* J'avais le cœur qui battait.

to **pour** VERB
1 *verser* (*liquid*) ◇ *She poured some water into the pan.* Elle a versé de l'eau dans la casserole.
- **She poured him a drink.** Elle lui a servi à boire.
- **Shall I pour you a cup of tea?** Je vous sers une tasse de thé?

2 *pleuvoir à verse* (*rain*) ◇ *It's pouring.* Il pleut à verse.
- **in the pouring rain** sous une pluie torrentielle

poverty NOUN
la *pauvreté*

powder NOUN
la *poudre*

power NOUN
1 le *courant* (*electricity*) ◇ *The power's off.* Le courant est coupé.
- **a power cut** une coupure de courant
- **a power point** une prise de courant
- **a power station** une centrale électrique

2 l' *énergie* FEM (*energy*) ◇ *nuclear power* l'énergie nucléaire ◇ *solar power* l'énergie solaire
3 le *pouvoir* (*authority*) ◇ *to be in power* être au pouvoir

powerful ADJECTIVE
puissant

practical ADJECTIVE
pratique ◇ *a practical suggestion* un conseil pratique
- **She's very practical.** Elle a l'esprit pratique.

practically ADVERB
pratiquement ◇ *It's practically impossible.* C'est pratiquement impossible.

practice NOUN
l' *entraînement* MASC (*for sport*) ◇ *football practice* l'entraînement de foot
- **I've got to do my piano practice.** Je dois travailler mon piano.
- **It's normal practice in our school.** C'est

P

PTO

ce qui se fait dans notre école.

- **in practice** en pratique
- **a medical practice** un cabinet médical

to **practise** VERB

1 *s'exercer* (*music, hobby*) ◇ *I ought to practise more.* Je devrais m'exercer davantage.

2 *travailler* (*instrument*) ◇ *I practise the flute every evening.* Je travaille ma flûte tous les soirs.

3 *pratiquer* (*language*) ◇ *I practised my French when we were on holiday.* J'ai pratiqué mon français pendant les vacances.

4 *s'entraîner* (*sport*) ◇ *The team practises on Thursdays.* L'équipe s'entraîne le jeudi. ◇ *I don't practise enough.* Je ne m'entraîne pas assez.

practising ADJECTIVE
pratiquant ◇ *She's a practising Catholic.* Elle est catholique pratiquante.

pram NOUN
le *landau*

prawn NOUN
la *crevette*

prawn cocktail NOUN
le *cocktail de crevettes*

to **pray** VERB
prier ◇ *to pray for something* prier pour quelque chose

prayer NOUN
la *prière*

precaution NOUN
la *précaution*

- **to take precautions** prendre ses précautions

preceding ADJECTIVE
précédent

precinct NOUN

- **a shopping precinct** un centre commercial
- **a pedestrian precinct** une zone piétonnière

precious ADJECTIVE
précieux MASC
précieuse FEM

precise ADJECTIVE
précis ◇ *at that precise moment* à cet instant précis

precisely ADVERB
précisément ◇ *Precisely!* Précisément!

- **at 10 a.m. precisely** à dix heures précises

to **predict** VERB
prédire

predictable ADJECTIVE
prévisible

prefect NOUN
French schools do not have prefects. You could explain what a prefect is using the example given

- **My sister's a prefect.** Ma sœur est en dernière année et est chargée de maintenir la discipline.

to **prefer** VERB
préférer ◇ *Which would you prefer?* Lequel préfères-tu? ◇ *I prefer French to chemistry.* Je préfère le français à la chimie.

preference NOUN
la *préférence*

pregnant ADJECTIVE
enceinte ◇ *She's six months pregnant.* Elle est enceinte de six mois.

prehistoric ADJECTIVE
préhistorique

prejudice NOUN

1 le *préjugé* ◇ *That's just a prejudice.* C'est un préjugé.

2 les *préjugés* MASC PL ◇ *There's a lot of racial prejudice.* Il y a beaucoup de préjugés raciaux.

prejudiced ADJECTIVE

- **to be prejudiced against somebody** avoir des préjugés contre quelqu'un

premature ADJECTIVE
prématuré

- **a premature baby** un prématuré

Premier League NOUN
la *première division* ◇ *in the Premier League* en première division

premises PL NOUN
les *locaux* MASC ◇ *They're moving to new premises.* Ils vont occuper de nouveaux locaux.

premonition NOUN
la *prémonition*

preoccupied ADJECTIVE
préoccupé

prep NOUN
les *devoirs* MASC PL (*homework*) ◇ *history prep* les devoirs d'histoire

preparation NOUN
la *préparation*

to **prepare** VERB
préparer ◇ *She has to prepare lessons in the evening.* Elle doit préparer ses cours le soir.

- **to prepare for something** se préparer pour quelque chose ◇ *We're preparing for our skiing holiday.* Nous nous préparons pour nos vacances à la neige.

prepared ADJECTIVE

- **to be prepared to do something** être prêt à faire quelque chose ◇ *I'm prepared to help you.* Je suis prêt à t'aider.

prep school NOUN

l' *école primaire privée* FEM

resbyterian NOUN
see also Presbyterian ADJECTIVE
le *presbytérien*
la *presbytérienne*

resbyterian ADJECTIVE
see also Presbyterian NOUN
presbytérien MASC
presbytérienne FEM

rescribe VERB
prescrire

rescription NOUN
l' *ordonnance* FEM ◇ *You can't get it without a prescription.* On ne peut pas se le procurer sans ordonnance.

resence NOUN
la *présence*
presence of mind présence d'esprit

resent ADJECTIVE
see also present NOUN, VERB
1 (*in attendance*)
présent ◇ *He wasn't present at the meeting.* Il n'était pas présent à la réunion.
2 (*current*)
actuel MASC
actuelle FEM
◇ *the present situation* la situation actuelle
the present tense le présent

resent NOUN
see also present ADJECTIVE, VERB
1 (*gift*)
le *cadeau*
(les *cadeaux* PL)
◇ *I'm going to buy presents.* Je vais acheter des cadeaux.
to give somebody a present offrir un cadeau à quelqu'un
2 (*time*)
le *présent* ◇ *up to the present* jusqu'à présent
• **for the present** pour l'instant
• **at present** en ce moment

resent VERB
see also present ADJECTIVE, NOUN
• **to present somebody with something** (*prize, medal*) remettre quelque chose à quelqu'un

resenter NOUN
(*on TV*)
le *présentateur*
la *présentatrice*

resently ADVERB
1 *bientôt* (*soon*) ◇ *You'll feel better presently.* Tu vas bientôt te sentir mieux.
2 *actuellement* (*at present*) ◇ *They're presently on tour.* Ils sont actuellement en tournée.

president NOUN
le *président*
la *présidente*

press NOUN
see also press VERB
la *presse*
• **a press conference** une conférence de presse

to **press** VERB
see also press NOUN
1 *appuyer* ◇ *Don't press too hard!* N'appuie pas trop fort!
2 *appuyer sur* ◇ *He pressed the accelerator.* Il a appuyé sur l'accélérateur.

pressed ADJECTIVE
• **We are pressed for time.** Le temps nous manque.

press-up NOUN
• **to do press-ups** faire des pompes ◇ *I do twenty press-ups every morning.* Je fais vingt pompes tous les matins.

pressure NOUN
see also pressure VERB
la *pression* ◇ *He's under a lot of pressure at work.* Il est sous pression au travail.
• **a pressure group** un groupe de pression

to **pressure** VERB
see also pressure NOUN
faire pression sur ◇ *My parents are pressuring me.* Mes parents font pression sur moi.

prestige NOUN
le *prestige*

prestigious ADJECTIVE
prestigieux MASC
prestigieuse FEM

presumably ADVERB
vraisemblablement

to **presume** VERB
supposer ◇ *I presume so.* Je suppose que oui.

to **pretend** VERB
• **to pretend to do something** faire semblant de faire quelque chose ◇ *He pretended to be asleep.* Il faisait semblant de dormir.

pretty ADJECTIVE, ADVERB
1 *joli* ◇ *She's very pretty.* Elle est très jolie.
2 *plutôt* (*rather*) ◇ *That film was pretty bad.* Ce film était plutôt mauvais.
• **The weather was pretty awful.** Il faisait un temps minable.
• **It's pretty much the same.** C'est pratiquement la même chose.

to **prevent** VERB

PTO

empêcher

◆ **to prevent somebody from doing something** empêcher quelqu'un de faire quelque chose ◇ *They try to prevent us from smoking.* Ils essaient de nous empêcher de fumer.

previous ADJECTIVE
précédent

previously ADVERB
auparavant

prey NOUN
la *proie* ◇ *a bird of prey* un oiseau de proie

price NOUN
le *prix*

price list NOUN
la *liste des prix*

to **prick** VERB
piquer ◇ *I've pricked my finger.* Je me suis piqué le doigt.

pride NOUN
la *fierté*

priest NOUN
le *prêtre* ◇ *He's a priest.* Il est prêtre.

primarily ADVERB
principalement

primary ADJECTIVE
principal
(*principaux* MASC PL)

primary school NOUN
l' *école primaire* FEM ◇ *She's still at primary school.* Elle est encore à l'école primaire.

prime minister NOUN
le *Premier ministre*

primitive ADJECTIVE
primitif MASC
primitive FEM

prince NOUN
le *prince* ◇ *the Prince of Wales* le prince de Galles

princess NOUN
la *princesse* ◇ *Princess Anne* la princesse Anne

principal ADJECTIVE
see also principal NOUN
principal
(*principaux* MASC PL)

principal NOUN
see also principal ADJECTIVE
le *principal* (*of college*)

principle NOUN
le *principe*
(les *principaux* PL)

◆ **on principle** par principe

print NOUN
1 le *tirage* (*photo*) ◇ *colour prints* des tirages en couleur
2 les *caractères* MASC (*letters*) ◇ *in small print* en petits caractères
3 l' *empreinte digitale* FEM (*fingerprint*)
4 la *gravure* FEM (*picture*) ◇ *a framed print* une gravure encadrée

printer NOUN
l' *imprimante* FEM (*machine*)

print-out NOUN
la *copie papier*

priority NOUN
la *priorité*

prison NOUN
la *prison*

◆ **in prison** en prison

prisoner NOUN
le *prisonnier*
la *prisonnière*

privacy NOUN
l' *intimité* FEM

private ADJECTIVE
privé ◇ *a private school* une école privée

◆ **private property** la propriété privée
◆ **"private"** (*on envelope*) "personnel"
◆ **a private bathroom** une salle de bain individuelle
◆ **I have private lessons.** Je prends des cours particuliers.

to **privatize** VERB
privatiser

privilege NOUN
le *privilège*

prize NOUN
le *prix* ◇ *to win a prize* gagner un prix

prize-giving NOUN
la *distribution des prix*

prizewinner NOUN
le *gagnant*
la *gagnante*

pro NOUN

◆ **the pros and cons** le pour et le contre ◇ *We weighed up the pros and cons.* Nous avons pesé le pour et le contre.

probability NOUN
la *probabilité*

probable ADJECTIVE
probable

probably ADVERB
probablement ◇ *probably not* probablement pas

problem NOUN
le *problème* ◇ *No problem!* Pas de problème!

proceeds PL NOUN
la *recette* SING

process NOUN
le *processus* ◇ *the peace process* le processus de paix

◆ **to be in the process of doing something** être en train de faire quelque chose ◇ *We're in the process of painting the kitchen.* Nous sommes en train de peindre la cuisine.

procession NOUN
la *procession* (*religious*)

produce VERB
1 *produire* (*manufacture*)
2 *monter* (*play, show*)

producer NOUN
(*of play, show*)
le *metteur en scène*
(les *metteurs en scène* PL)

product NOUN
le *produit*

production NOUN
1 la *production* ◇ *They're increasing production of luxury models.* Ils augmentent la production des modèles de luxe.
2 la *mise en scène* (*play, show*) ◇ *a production of "Hamlet"* une mise en scène de "Hamlet"

profession NOUN
la *profession*

professional NOUN
see also professional ADJECTIVE
le *professionnel*
la *professionnelle*

professional ADJECTIVE
see also professional NOUN
(*player*)
professionnel MASC
professionnelle FEM
◇ *a professional musician* un musicien professionnel
a very professional piece of work un vrai travail de professionnel

professionally ADVERB
She sings professionally. C'est une chanteuse professionnelle.

professor NOUN
le *professeur d'université*
He's the French professor. Il est titulaire de la chaire de français.

profit NOUN
le *bénéfice*

profitable ADJECTIVE
rentable

program NOUN
see also program VERB
le *programme* ◇ *a computer program* un programme informatique

program VERB
see also program NOUN
programmer (*computer*)

programme NOUN
1 l' *émission* FEM (*on TV, radio*)
2 le *programme* (*of events*)

programmer NOUN
le *programmeur*
la *programmeuse*
◇ *She's a programmer.* Elle est programmeuse.

programming NOUN
la *programmation*

progress NOUN
le *progrès* ◇ *You're making progress!* Vous faites des progrès!

to **prohibit** VERB
interdire ◇ *Smoking is prohibited.* Il est interdit de fumer.

project NOUN
1 le *projet* (*plan*) ◇ *a development project* un projet de développement
2 le *dossier* (*research*) ◇ *I'm doing a project on education in France.* Je prépare un dossier sur l'éducation en France.

projector NOUN
le *projecteur*

promenade NOUN
le *front de mer*

promise NOUN
see also promise VERB
la *promesse* ◇ *He made me a promise.* Il m'a fait une promesse.
◆ **That's a promise!** C'est promis!

to **promise** VERB
see also promise NOUN
promettre ◇ *She promised to write.* Elle a promis d'écrire. ◇ *I'll write, I promise!* J'écrirai, c'est promis!

promising ADJECTIVE
◆ **a promising player** un joueur qui a de l'avenir

to **promote** VERB
◆ **to be promoted** être promu ◇ *She was promoted after six months.* Elle a été promue au bout de six mois.

promotion NOUN
la *promotion*

prompt ADJECTIVE, ADVERB
rapide ◇ *a prompt reply* une réponse rapide
◆ **at eight o'clock prompt** à huit heures précises

promptly ADVERB
◆ **We left promptly at seven.** Nous sommes partis à sept heures précises.

pronoun NOUN
le *pronom*

to **pronounce** VERB
prononcer ◇ *How do you pronounce that word?* Comment est-ce qu'on prononce ce mot?

pronunciation NOUN
la *prononciation*

proof NOUN
la *preuve*

proper ADJECTIVE
1 *vrai* (*genuine*) ◇ *proper French bread* du vrai pain français ◇ *We didn't have a proper lunch, just sandwiches.* Nous n'avons pas pris de vrai repas, juste des sandwichs.
◆ **It's difficult to get a proper job.** Il est difficile de trouver un travail correct.
2 *adéquat* ◇ *You have to have the proper equipment.* Il faut avoir l'équipement adéquat. ◇ *We need proper training.* Il nous faut une formation adéquate.
◆ **If you had come at the proper time...** Si tu étais venu à l'heure dite...

properly ADVERB
1 *comme il faut* (*correctly*) ◇ *You're not doing it properly.* Tu ne t'y prends pas comme il faut.
2 *convenablement* (*appropriately*) ◇ *Dress properly for your interview.* Habille-toi convenablement pour ton entretien.

property NOUN
la *propriété*
◆ **"private property"** "propriété privée"
◆ **stolen property** les objets volés

proportional ADJECTIVE
proportionnel MASC
proportionnelle FEM
◇ *proportional representation* la représentation proportionnelle

proposal NOUN
la *proposition* (*suggestion*)

to **propose** VERB
proposer ◇ *I propose a new plan.* Je propose un changement de programme.
◆ **to propose to do something** avoir l'intention de faire quelque chose ◇ *What do you propose to do?* Qu'est-ce que tu as l'intention de faire?
◆ **to propose to somebody** (*for marriage*) demander quelqu'un en mariage ◇ *He proposed to her at the restaurant.* Il l'a demandée en mariage au restaurant.

prospect NOUN
la *perspective* ◇ *It'll improve my career prospects.* Ça va améliorer mes perspectives d'avenir.

prospectus NOUN
le *prospectus*

prostitute NOUN
la *prostituée*
◆ **a male prostitute** un prostitué

to **protect** VERB
protéger

protection NOUN
la *protection*

protein NOUN
la *protéine*

protest NOUN
see also protest VERB
la *protestation* ◇ *He ignored their protests.* Il a ignoré leurs protestations.
◆ **a protest march** une manifestation

to **protest** VERB
see also protest NOUN
protester

Protestant NOUN
see also Protestant ADJECTIVE
le *protestant*
la *protestante*
◇ *I'm a Protestant.* Je suis protestant.

Protestant ADJECTIVE
see also Protestant NOUN
protestant ◇ *a Protestant church* une église protestante

protester NOUN
le *manifestant*
la *manifestante*

proud ADJECTIVE
fier MASC
fière FEM
◇ *Her parents are proud of her.* Ses parents sont fiers d'elle.

to **prove** VERB
prouver ◇ *The police couldn't prove it.* La police n'a pas pu le prouver.

proverb NOUN
le *proverbe*

to **provide** VERB
fournir
◆ **to provide somebody with something** fournir quelque chose à quelqu'un ◇ *They provided us with maps.* Ils nous ont fourni des cartes.

provided CONJUNCTION
à condition que
à condition que *has to be followed by the subjunctive.*
◇ *He'll play in the next match provided he's fit.* Il jouera dans le prochain match, à condition qu'il soit en forme.

provisional ADJECTIVE
provisoire

prowler NOUN
le *rôdeur*
la *rôdeuse*

prune NOUN
le *pruneau*
(les *pruneaux* PL)

pseudonym NOUN
le *pseudonyme*

psychiatrist NOUN
le/la *psychiatre* ◇ *She's a psychiatrist.* Elle est psychiatre.

psychoanalyst NOUN
le/la *psychanalyste*

psychological ADJECTIVE
psychologique
psychologist NOUN
le/la *psychologue* ◇ *He's a psychologist.* Il est psychologue.
psychology NOUN
la *psychologie*
PTO ABBREVIATION (= *please turn over*)
T.S.V.P. (= tournez, s'il vous plaît)
pub NOUN
le *pub*
public NOUN
see also public ADJECTIVE
le *public* ◇ *open to the public* ouvert au public
◆ **in public** en public
public ADJECTIVE
see also public NOUN
public MASC
publique FEM
◆ **a public holiday** un jour férié
◆ **public opinion** l'opinion publique FEM
◆ **the public address system** les haut-parleurs
publicity NOUN
la *publicité*
public school NOUN
l' *école privée* FEM
public transport NOUN
les *transports en commun* MASC PL
to **publish** VERB
publier
publisher NOUN
l' *éditeur* MASC
pudding NOUN
le *dessert* ◇ *What's for pudding?* Qu'est-ce qu'il y a comme dessert?
◆ **rice pudding** le riz au lait
◆ **black pudding** le boudin noir
puddle NOUN
la *flaque*
puff pastry NOUN
la *pâte feuilletée*
to **pull** VERB
tirer ◇ *Pull!* Tirez!
◆ **He pulled the trigger.** Il a appuyé sur la gâchette.
◆ **to pull a muscle** se froisser un muscle ◇ *I pulled a muscle when I was training.* Je me suis froissé un muscle à l'entraînement.
◆ **You're pulling my leg!** Tu me fais marcher!
◆ **to pull down** démolir
◆ **to pull out (1)** arracher (*tooth, weed*)
◆ **to pull out (2)** déboîter (*car*) ◇ *The car pulled out to overtake.* La voiture a déboîté pour doubler.
◆ **to pull out (3)** se retirer (*withdraw*) ◇ *She pulled out of the tournament.* Elle s'est retirée du tournoi.
◆ **to pull through** s'en sortir ◇ *They think he'll pull through.* Ils pensent qu'il va s'en sortir.
pullover NOUN
le *pull-over*
pulse NOUN
le *pouls* ◇ *The nurse felt his pulse.* L'infirmière a pris son pouls.
pulses PL NOUN
les *légumes secs* MASC
pump NOUN
see also pump VERB
1 la *pompe* ◇ *a bicycle pump* une pompe à vélo ◇ *a petrol pump* une pompe à essence
2 la *chaussure de sport* (*shoe*)
to **pump** VERB
see also pump NOUN
pomper
◆ **to pump up** gonfler (*tyre*)
pumpkin NOUN
le *potiron*
punch NOUN
see also punch VERB
1 le *coup de poing* (*blow*) ◇ *He gave me a punch.* Il m'a donné un coup de poing.
2 le *punch* (*drink*)
to **punch** VERB
see also punch NOUN
1 *donner un coup de poing à* (*hit*) ◇ *He punched me!* Il m'a donné un coup de poing!
2 *composter* (*in ticket machine*) ◇ *Punch your ticket before you get on the train.* Compostez votre billet avant de monter dans le train.
3 *poinçonner* (*by hand*) ◇ *He forgot to punch my ticket.* Il a oublié de poinçonner mon billet.
punch-up NOUN
la *bagarre* (*informal*)
punctual ADJECTIVE
ponctuel MASC
ponctuelle FEM
punctuation NOUN
la *ponctuation*
puncture NOUN
la *crevaison* ◇ *I had to mend a puncture.* J'ai dû réparer une crevaison.
◆ **to have a puncture** crever ◇ *I had a puncture on the motorway.* J'ai crevé sur l'autoroute.
to **punish** VERB
punir
◆ **to punish somebody for something** punir quelqu'un de quelque chose

- **to punish somebody for doing something** punir quelqu'un d'avoir fait quelque chose

punishment NOUN
la *punition*

punk NOUN
le/la *punk* (*person*)
- **a punk rock band** un groupe de punk rock

pupil NOUN
l' *élève* MASC / FEM

puppet NOUN
la *marionnette*

puppy NOUN
le *chiot*

to **purchase** VERB
acheter

pure ADJECTIVE
pur ◇ *pure orange juice* du pur jus d'orange ◇ *He's doing pure maths.* Il fait des maths pures.

purple ADJECTIVE
violet MASC
violette FEM

purpose NOUN
le *but* ◇ *What is the purpose of these changes?* Quel est le but de ces changements? ◇ *his purpose in life* son but dans la vie
- **on purpose** exprès ◇ *He did it on purpose.* Il l'a fait exprès.

to **purr** VERB
ronronner

purse NOUN
le *porte-monnaie*
(les *porte-monnaie* PL)

to **pursue** VERB
poursuivre

pursuit NOUN
l' *activité* FEM ◇ *outdoor pursuits* les activités de plein air

push NOUN
see also push VERB
- **to give somebody a push** pousser quelqu'un ◇ *He gave me a push.* Il m'a poussé.

to **push** VERB
see also push NOUN
1 *pousser* ◇ *Don't push!* Arrêtez de pousser!
2 *appuyer sur* (*button*)
- **to push somebody to do something** pousser quelqu'un à faire quelque chose ◇ *My parents are pushing me to go to university.* Mes parents me poussent à entrer à l'université.
- **to push drugs** revendre de la drogue
- **Push off!** Dégage!

pushchair NOUN
la *poussette*

pusher NOUN
(*of drugs*)
le *revendeur*
la *revendeuse*

to **put** VERB
1 *mettre* (*place*) ◇ *Where shall I put my things?* Où est-ce que je peux mettre mes affaires? ◇ *She's putting the baby to bed.* Elle met le bébé au lit.
2 *écrire* (*write*) ◇ *Don't forget to put your name on the paper.* N'oubliez pas d'écrire votre nom sur la feuille.

to **put away** VERB
ranger ◇ *Can you put away the dishes, please?* Tu peux ranger la vaisselle, s'il te plaît?

to **put back** VERB
remettre en place (*replace*) ◇ *Put it back when you've finished with it.* Remets-le en place une fois que tu auras fini.

to **put down** VERB
1 *poser* ◇ *I'll put these bags down for a minute.* Je vais poser ces sacs une minute.
2 *noter* (*in writing*) ◇ *I've put down a few ideas.* J'ai noté quelques idées.
- **to have an animal put down** faire piquer un animal ◇ *We had to have our old dog put down.* Nous avons dû faire piquer notre vieux chien.

to **put off** VERB
1 *éteindre* (*switch off*) ◇ *Shall I put the light off?* Est-ce que j'éteins la lumière?
2 *remettre à plus tard* (*postpone*) ◇ *I keep putting it off.* Je n'arrête pas de remettre ça à plus tard.
3 *déranger* (*distract*) ◇ *Stop putting me off!* Arrête de me déranger!
4 *décourager* (*discourage*) ◇ *He's not easily put off.* Il ne se laisse pas facilement décourager.

to **put on** VERB
1 *mettre* (*clothes, lipstick, record*) ◇ *I'll put my coat on.* Je vais mettre mon manteau.
2 *allumer* (*light, heater, telly*) ◇ *Shall I put the heater on?* J'allume le chauffage?
3 *monter* (*play, show*) ◇ *We're putting on "Bugsy Malone".* Nous sommes en train de monter "Bugsy Malone".
4 *mettre à cuire* ◇ *I'll put the potatoes on.* Je vais mettre les pommes de terre à cuire.
- **to put on weight** grossir ◇ *He's put on a lot of weight.* Il a beaucoup grossi.

to **put out** VERB
éteindre (*light, cigarette, fire*) ◇ *It took them five hours to put out the fire.* Ils ont

mis cinq heures à éteindre l'incendie.

put through VERB

passer ◇ *Can you put me through to the manager?* Est-ce que vous pouvez me passer le directeur?

◆ **I'm putting you through.** Je vous passe la communication.

put up VERB

1 *mettre* (*pin up*) ◇ *The poster's great. I'll put it up on my wall.* Le poster est super. Je vais le mettre au mur.

2 *monter* (*tent*) ◇ *We put up our tent in a field.* Nous avons monté la tente dans un champ.

3 *augmenter* (*price*) ◇ *They've put up the price.* Ils ont augmenté le prix.

4 *héberger* (*accommodate*) ◇ *My friend will put me up for the night.* Mon ami va m'héberger pour la nuit.

◆ **to put one's hand up** lever la main ◇ *If you have any questions, put up your hand.* Si vous avez une question, levez la main.

◆ **to put up with something** supporter quelque chose ◇ *I'm not going to put up with it any longer.* Je ne vais pas supporter ça plus longtemps.

puzzle NOUN

le *puzzle* (*jigsaw*)

puzzled ADJECTIVE

perplexe ◇ *You look puzzled!* Tu as l'air perplexe!

puzzling ADJECTIVE

déconcertant

pyjamas PL NOUN

le *pyjama* SING ◇ *my pyjamas* mon pyjama

◆ **a pair of pyjamas** un pyjama

◆ **a pyjama top** un haut de pyjama

pyramid NOUN

la *pyramide*

Pyrenees PL NOUN

les *Pyrénées* FEM

◆ **in the Pyrenees** dans les Pyrénées

◆ **We went to the Pyrenees.** Nous sommes allés dans les Pyrénées.

Q

quaint ADJECTIVE
pittoresque (*house, village*)

qualification NOUN
le *diplôme* ◇ *to leave school without any qualifications* quitter l'école sans aucun diplôme
◆ **vocational qualifications** des qualifications professionnelles

qualified ADJECTIVE
1 *qualifié* (*trained*) ◇ *a qualified driving instructor* un moniteur d'auto-école qualifié
2 *diplômé* (*nurse, teacher*) ◇ *a qualified nurse* une infirmière diplômée

to **qualify** VERB
1 *obtenir son diplôme* (*for job*) ◇ *She qualified as a teacher last year.* Elle a obtenu son diplôme de professeur l'année dernière.
2 *se qualifier* (*in competition*) ◇ *Our team didn't qualify.* Notre équipe ne s'est pas qualifiée.

quality NOUN
la *qualité* ◇ *a good quality of life* une bonne qualité de vie ◇ *good-quality ingredients* des ingrédients de bonne qualité ◇ *She's got lots of good qualities.* Elle a beaucoup de qualités.

quantity NOUN
la *quantité*

quarantine NOUN
la *quarantaine* ◇ *in quarantine* en quarantaine

quarrel NOUN
see also quarrel VERB
la *dispute*

to **quarrel** VERB
see also quarrel NOUN
se disputer

quarry NOUN
la *carrière* (*for stone*)

quarter NOUN
le *quart*
◆ **three quarters** trois quarts
◆ **a quarter of an hour** un quart d'heure ◇ *three quarters of an hour* trois quarts d'heure
◆ **a quarter past ten** dix heures et quart
◆ **a quarter to eleven** onze heures moins le quart

quarter final NOUN
le *quart de finale*

quartet NOUN
le *quatuor* ◇ *a string quartet* un quatuor à cordes

quay NOUN
le *quai*

queasy ADJECTIVE
◆ **to feel queasy** avoir mal au cœur ◇ *I'm feeling queasy.* J'ai mal au cœur.

queen NOUN
1 la *reine* ◇ *Queen Elizabeth* la reine Élisabeth
2 la *dame* (*playing card*) ◇ *the queen of hearts* la dame de cœur
◆ **the Queen Mother** la reine mère

query NOUN
la *question*

question NOUN
see also question VERB
la *question* ◇ *Can I ask a question?* Est-ce que je peux poser une question? ◇ *That's a difficult question.* C'est une question difficile.
◆ **It's out of the question.** C'est hors de question.

to **question** VERB
see also question NOUN
interroger ◇ *He was questioned by the police.* Il a été interrogé par la police.

question mark NOUN
le *point d'interrogation*

questionnaire NOUN
le *questionnaire*

queue NOUN
see also queue VERB
la *queue*

to **queue** VERB
see also queue NOUN
faire la queue
◆ **to queue for something** faire la queue pour avoir quelque chose ◇ *We had to queue for tickets.* Nous avons dû faire la queue pour avoir les billets.

quick ADJECTIVE, ADVERB
rapide ◇ *a quick lunch* un déjeuner rapide ◇ *It's quicker by train.* C'est plus rapide en train.
◆ **Be quick!** Dépêche-toi!
◆ **She's a quick learner.** Elle apprend vite.
◆ **Quick, phone the police!** Téléphonez vite à la police!

quickly ADVERB
vite ◇ *It was all over very quickly.* Ça s'est passé très vite.

quiet ADJECTIVE
1 (*not talkative or noisy*)
silencieux MASC
silencieuse FEM
◇ *You're very quiet today.* Tu es bien silencieux aujourd'hui. ◇ *The engine's very quiet.* Le moteur est très silencieux.

2 (*peaceful*) *tranquille* ◇ *a quiet little town* une petite ville tranquille ◇ *a quiet weekend* un week-end tranquille

- **Be quiet!** Tais-toi!
- **Quiet!** Silence!

quietly ADVERB

1 *doucement* (*speak*) ◇ *"She's dead," he said quietly.* "Elle est morte" dit-il doucement.

2 *silencieusement* (*move*) ◇ *He quietly opened the door.* Il a ouvert la porte sans faire de bruit.

quilt NOUN

la *couette* (*duvet*)

quite ADVERB

1 *assez* (*rather*) ◇ *It's quite warm today.* Il fait assez bon aujourd'hui. ◇ *I quite liked the film, but...* J'ai trouvé le film assez bon, mais...

2 *tout à fait* (*entirely*) ◇ *I'm not quite sure.* Je n'en suis pas tout à fait sûr. ◇ *It's not quite the same.* Ce n'est pas tout à fait la même chose.

- **quite good** pas mal
- **I've been there quite a lot.** J'y suis allé pas mal de fois.
- **quite a lot of money** pas mal d'argent
- **It costs quite a lot to go abroad.** Ça coûte assez cher d'aller à l'étranger.
- **It's quite a long way.** C'est assez loin.
- **It was quite a shock.** Ça a été un sacré choc.
- **There were quite a few people there.** Il y avait pas mal de gens.

quiz NOUN

le *jeu-concours*

quota NOUN

le *quota*

quotation NOUN

la *citation* ◇ *a quotation from Shakespeare* une citation de Shakespeare

quote NOUN

la *citation* ◇ *a Shakespeare quote* une citation de Shakespeare

- **quotes** (*quotation marks*) les guillemets MASC ◇ *in quotes* entre guillemets

R

rabbi NOUN
le *rabbin*
rabbit NOUN
le *lapin*
◆ **a rabbit hutch** un clapier
rabies NOUN
la *rage*
◆ **a dog with rabies** un chien enragé
race NOUN
see also race VERB
1 la *course* (*sport*) ◇ *a cycle race* une course cycliste
2 la *race* (*species*) ◇ *the human race* la race humaine
◆ **race relations** les relations interraciales FEM
to **race** VERB
see also race NOUN
1 *courir* ◇ *We raced to catch the bus.* Nous avons couru pour attraper le bus.
2 *faire la course* (*have a race*)
◆ **I'll race you!** On fait la course!
racecourse NOUN
le *champ de courses*
racehorse NOUN
le *cheval de course*
(les *chevaux de course* PL)
racer NOUN
le *vélo de course* (*bike*)
racetrack NOUN
la *piste*
racial ADJECTIVE
racial
(*raciaux* MASC PL)
◇ *racial discrimination* la discrimination raciale
racing car NOUN
la *voiture de course*
racing driver NOUN
le *pilote de course*
racism NOUN
le *racisme*
racist ADJECTIVE
see also racist NOUN
raciste
racist NOUN
see also racist ADJECTIVE
le/la *raciste*
rack NOUN (*for luggage*)
le *porte-bagages*
(les *porte-bagages* PL)
racket NOUN
1 la *raquette* (*for sport*) ◇ *my tennis racket* ma raquette de tennis
2 le *boucan* (*noise*) ◇ *They're making a terrible racket.* Ils font un boucan de tous les diables. (*informal*)
racquet NOUN
la *raquette*
radar NOUN
le *radar*
radiation NOUN
la *radiation*
radiator NOUN
le *radiateur*
radio NOUN
la *radio*
◆ **on the radio** à la radio
◆ **a radio station** une station de radio
radioactive ADJECTIVE
radioactif MASC
radioactive FEM
radio cassette NOUN
le *radiocassette*
radio-controlled ADJECTIVE
téléguidé (*model plane, car*)
radish NOUN
le *radis*
RAF NOUN (= *Royal Air Force*)
la *R.A.F.* ◇ *He's in the RAF.* Il est dans la R.A.F.
raffle NOUN
la *tombola* ◇ *a raffle ticket* un billet de tombola
raft NOUN
le *radeau*
(les *radeaux* PL)
rag NOUN
le *chiffon* ◇ *a piece of rag* un chiffon
◆ **dressed in rags** en haillons
rage NOUN
la *rage* ◇ *mad with rage* fou de rage
◆ **to be in a rage** être furieux ◇ *She was in a rage.* Elle était furieuse.
◆ **It's all the rage.** Ça fait fureur.
raid NOUN
see also raid VERB
1 (*burglary*)
le *hold-up*
(les *hold-up* PL)
◇ *There was a bank raid near my house.* Il y a eu un hold-up dans une banque près de chez moi.
2 la *descente* ◇ *a police raid* une descente de police
to **raid** VERB
see also raid NOUN
faire une descente dans (*police*) ◇ *The police raided a club in Soho.* La police a fait une descente dans un club de Soho.
rail NOUN
1 la *rampe* (*on stairs*)

2 la *balustrade* (*on bridge, balcony*) ◇ *Don't lean over the rail!* Ne vous penchez pas sur la balustrade!
3 le *rail* (*on railway line*)
◆ **by rail** en train

railway NOUN
le *chemin de fer* ◇ *the privatization of the railways* la privatisation des chemins de fer
◆ **a railway line** une ligne de chemin de fer
◆ **a railway station** une gare

rain NOUN
see also rain VERB
la *pluie* ◇ *in the rain* sous la pluie

to **rain** VERB
see also rain NOUN
pleuvoir ◇ *It rains a lot here.* Il pleut beaucoup par ici.
◆ **It's raining.** Il pleut.

rainbow NOUN
l' *arc-en-ciel* MASC
(les *arcs-en-ciel* PL)

raincoat NOUN
l' *imperméable* MASC

rainforest NOUN
la *forêt tropicale humide*

rainy ADJECTIVE
pluvieux MASC
pluvieuse FEM

to **raise** VERB
1 *lever* (*lift*) ◇ *He raised his hand.* Il a levé la main.
2 *améliorer* (*improve*) ◇ *They want to raise standards in schools.* Ils veulent améliorer le niveau dans les écoles.
◆ **to raise money** collecter des fonds ◇ *The school is raising money for a new gym.* L'école collecte des fonds pour un nouveau gymnase.

raisin NOUN
le *raisin sec*

rake NOUN
le *râteau*
(les *râteaux* PL)

rally NOUN
1 le *rassemblement* (*of people*)
2 le *rallye* (*sport*) ◇ *a rally driver* un pilote de rallye
3 l' *échange* MASC (*in tennis*)

ramble NOUN
la *randonnée* ◇ *to go for a ramble* faire une randonnée

rambler NOUN
le *randonneur*
la *randonneuse*

ramp NOUN
la *rampe d'accès* (*for wheelchairs*)

ran VERB *see* **run**

ranch NOUN
le *ranch*

random ADJECTIVE
◆ **a random selection** une sélection effectuée au hasard
◆ **at random** au hasard ◇ *We picked the number at random.* Nous avons choisi le numéro au hasard.

rang VERB *see* **ring**

range NOUN
see also range VERB
le *choix* ◇ *There's a wide range of colours.* Il y a un grand choix de coloris.
◆ **a range of subjects** diverses matières ◇ *We study a range of subjects.* Nous étudions diverses matières.
◆ **a mountain range** une chaîne de montagnes

to **range** VERB
see also range NOUN
◆ **to range from...to** se situer entre...et ◇ *Temperatures in summer range from 20 to 35 degrees.* Les températures estivales se situent entre vingt et trente-cinq degrés.
◆ **Tickets range from £2 to £20.** Les billets coûtent entre deux et vingt livres.

rank NOUN
◆ **a taxi rank** une station de taxis

ransom NOUN
la *rançon*

rap NOUN
le *rap* (*music*)

rape NOUN
see also rape VERB
le *viol*

to **rape** VERB
see also rape NOUN
violer

rapids PL NOUN
les *rapides* MASC PL

rapist NOUN
le *violeur*

rare ADJECTIVE
1 *rare* (*unusual*) ◇ *a rare plant* une plante rare
2 *saignant* (*steak*)

rash NOUN
l' *éruption de boutons* FEM ◇ *I've got a rash on my chest.* J'ai une éruption de boutons sur la poitrine.

rasher NOUN
la *tranche* ◇ *an egg and two rashers of bacon* un œuf et deux tranches de bacon

raspberry NOUN
la *framboise* ◇ *raspberry jam* la confiture de framboises

rat NOUN
le *rat*

rate NOUN
1 le *tarif* (*price*) ◇ *There are reduced rates for students.* Il y a des tarifs réduits pour les étudiants.
2 le *taux* (*level*) ◇ *the divorce rate* le taux de divorce ◇ *a high rate of interest* un taux d'intérêt élevé

rather ADVERB
plutôt ◇ *I was rather disappointed.* J'étais plutôt déçu. ◇ *£20! That's rather a lot!* Vingt livres! C'est plutôt cher!
- **rather a lot of** pas mal de ◇ *I've got rather a lot of homework to do.* J'ai pas mal de devoirs à faire.
- **rather than** plutôt que ◇ *We decided to camp, rather than stay at a hotel.* Nous avons décidé de camper plutôt que d'aller à l'hôtel.
- **I'd rather...** J'aimerais mieux... ◇ *I'd rather stay in tonight.* J'aimerais mieux rester à la maison ce soir. ◇ *Would you like a sweet?–I'd rather have an apple.* Tu veux un bonbon?–J'aimerais mieux une pomme.

rattle NOUN
le *hochet* (*for baby*)

rattlesnake NOUN
le *serpent à sonnette*

to **rave** VERB
see also rave NOUN
s'extasier ◇ *They raved about the film.* Ils se sont extasiés sur le film.

rave NOUN
see also rave VERB
la *rave* (*party*)
- **rave music** le rave

raven NOUN
le *corbeau*
(les *corbeaux* PL)

ravenous ADJECTIVE
- **to be ravenous** avoir une faim de loup ◇ *I'm ravenous!* J'ai une faim de loup!

raving ADJECTIVE
- **raving mad** fou à lier ◇ *She's raving mad!* Elle est folle à lier.

raw ADJECTIVE
cru (*food*)
- **raw materials** les matières premières FEM

razor NOUN
le *rasoir* ◇ *some disposable razors* des rasoirs jetables
- **a razor blade** une lame de rasoir

RE NOUN
l' *éducation religieuse* FEM

reach NOUN
see also reach VERB
- **out of reach** hors de portée ◇ *The light switch was out of reach.* L'interrupteur était hors de portée.
- **within easy reach of** à proximité de ◇ *The hotel is within easy reach of the town centre.* L'hôtel se trouve à proximité du centre-ville.

to **reach** VERB
see also reach NOUN
1 *arriver à* ◇ *We reached the hotel at 7 p.m.* Nous sommes arrivés à l'hôtel à sept heures du soir.
- **We hope to reach the final.** Nous espérons aller en finale.

2 *parvenir à* (*decision*) ◇ *Eventually they reached a decision.* Ils sont finalement parvenus à une décision.
- **He reached for his gun.** Il a tendu la main pour prendre son revolver.

to **react** VERB
réagir

reaction NOUN
la *réaction*

reactor NOUN
le *réacteur* ◇ *a nuclear reactor* un réacteur nucléaire

to **read** VERB
lire ◇ *I don't read much.* Je ne lis pas beaucoup. ◇ *Have you read "Animal Farm"?* Est-ce que tu as lu "La ferme des animaux"? ◇ *Read the text out loud.* Lis le texte à haute voix.

reader NOUN
(*person*)
le *lecteur*
la *lectrice*

reading NOUN
la *lecture* ◇ *Reading is one of my hobbies.* La lecture est l'une de mes activités favorites.

ready ADJECTIVE
prêt ◇ *She's nearly ready.* Elle est presque prête. ◇ *He's always ready to help.* Il est toujours prêt à rendre service.
- **a ready meal** un plat cuisiné
- **to get ready** se préparer ◇ *She's getting ready to go out.* Elle est en train de se préparer pour sortir.
- **to get something ready** préparer quelque chose ◇ *He's getting the dinner ready.* Il est en train de préparer le dîner.

real ADJECTIVE
1 *vrai* ◇ *He wasn't a real policeman.* Ce n'était pas un vrai policier. ◇ *Her real name is Cordelia.* Son vrai nom est Cordelia.
2 *véritable* ◇ *It's real leather.* C'est du cuir véritable. ◇ *It was a real nightmare.* C'était un véritable cauchemar.
- **in real life** dans la réalité

realistic ADJECTIVE
réaliste
reality NOUN
la *réalité*
realize VERB
◆ **to realize that...** se rendre compte que... ◇ *We realized that something was wrong.* Nous nous sommes rendu compte que quelque chose n'allait pas.
really ADVERB
vraiment ◇ *She's really nice.* Elle est vraiment sympathique. ◇ *Do you want to go?–Not really.* Tu veux y aller?–Pas vraiment.
◆ **I'm learning German.–Really?** J'apprends l'allemand.–Ah bon?
◆ **Do you really think so?** Tu es sûr?
rear ADJECTIVE
see also rear NOUN
arrière MASC, FEM, PL ◇ *a rear wheel* une roue arrière
rear NOUN
see also rear ADJECTIVE
l' *arrière* MASC ◇ *at the rear of the train* à l'arrière du train
reason NOUN
la *raison* ◇ *There's no reason to think that...* Il n'y a aucune raison de penser que...
◆ **for security reasons** pour des raisons de sécurité
◆ **That was the main reason I went.** C'est surtout pour ça que j'y suis allé.
reasonable ADJECTIVE
1 *raisonnable* (*sensible*) ◇ *Be reasonable!* Sois raisonnable!
2 *correct* (*not bad*) ◇ *He wrote a reasonable essay.* Sa dissertation était correcte.
reassure VERB
rassurer
reassuring ADJECTIVE
rassurant
rebellious ADJECTIVE
rebelle
receipt NOUN
le *reçu*
receive VERB
recevoir
receiver NOUN
le *combiné* (*of phone*)
◆ **to pick up the receiver** décrocher
recent ADJECTIVE
récent
recently ADVERB
ces derniers temps ◇ *I've been doing a lot of training recently.* Je me suis beaucoup entraîné ces derniers temps.
reception NOUN
la *réception* ◇ *Please leave your key at reception.* Merci de laisser votre clé à la réception. ◇ *The reception will be at a big hotel.* La réception aura lieu dans un grand hôtel.
receptionist NOUN
le/la *réceptionniste*
recession NOUN
la *récession*
recipe NOUN
la *recette*
to **reckon** VERB
penser ◇ *What do you reckon?* Qu'est-ce que tu en penses?
reclining ADJECTIVE
◆ **a reclining seat** un siège inclinable
recognizable ADJECTIVE
reconnaissable
to **recognize** VERB
reconnaître ◇ *You'll recognize me by my red hair.* Vous me reconnaîtrez à mes cheveux roux.
to **recommend** VERB
conseiller ◇ *What do you recommend?* Qu'est-ce que vous me conseillez?
to **reconsider** VERB
reconsidérer
record NOUN
see also record VERB
1 le *disque* (*recording*) ◇ *my favourite record* mon disque préféré
2 le *record* (*sport*) ◇ *the world record* le record du monde
◆ **in record time** en un temps record ◇ *She finished the job in record time.* Elle a terminé le travail en un temps record.
◆ **a criminal record** un casier judiciaire ◇ *He's got a criminal record.* Il a un casier judiciaire.
◆ **records** (*of police, hospital*) les archives FEM ◇ *I'll check in the records.* Je vais vérifier dans les archives.
◆ **There is no record of your booking.** Il n'y a aucune trace de votre réservation.
to **record** VERB
see also record NOUN
enregistrer (*on film, tape*) ◇ *They've just recorded their new album.* Ils viennent d'enregistrer leur nouveau disque.
recorded delivery NOUN
◆ **to send something recorded delivery** envoyer quelque chose en recommandé
recorder NOUN
la *flûte à bec* (*instrument*) ◇ *She plays the recorder.* Elle joue de la flûte à bec.
◆ **a cassette recorder** un magnétophone à cassettes
◆ **a video recorder** un magnétoscope
recording NOUN

R

l' *enregistrement* MASC

record player NOUN

le *tourne-disque*

to **recover** VERB

se remettre ◇ *He's recovering from a knee injury.* Il se remet d'une blessure au genou.

recovery NOUN

le *rétablissement*

◆ **Best wishes for a speedy recovery!** Meilleurs vœux de prompt rétablissement!

rectangle NOUN

le *rectangle*

rectangular ADJECTIVE

rectangulaire

to **recycle** VERB

recycler

recycling NOUN

le *recyclage*

red ADJECTIVE

1 *rouge* ◇ *a red rose* une rose rouge ◇ *red meat* la viande rouge

◆ **a red light** (*traffic light*) un feu rouge ◇ *to go through a red light* brûler un feu rouge

2 (*hair*)

roux MASC

rousse FEM

◇ *Tamsin's got red hair.* Tamsin a les cheveux roux.

Red Cross NOUN

la *Croix-Rouge*

redcurrant NOUN

la *groseille*

to **redecorate** VERB

1 *retapisser* (*with wallpaper*)

2 *refaire les peintures* (*with paint*)

red-haired ADJECTIVE

roux MASC

rousse FEM

red-handed ADJECTIVE

◆ **to catch somebody red-handed** prendre quelqu'un la main dans le sac ◇ *He was caught red-handed.* Il a été pris la main dans le sac.

redhead NOUN

le *roux*

la *rousse*

to **redo** VERB

refaire

to **reduce** VERB

réduire ◇ *at a reduced price* à prix réduit

◆ **"reduce speed now"** "ralentir"

reduction NOUN

la *réduction* ◇ *a 5% reduction* une réduction de cinq pour cent

◆ **"huge reductions!"** "prix sacrifiés!"

redundancy NOUN

le *licenciement* ◇ *There were fifty redundancies.* Il y a eu cinquante licenciements.

◆ **his redundancy payment** ses indemnités de licenciement

redundant ADJECTIVE

◆ **to be made redundant** être licencié ◇ *He was made redundant yesterday.* Il a été licencié hier.

reed NOUN

(*plant*)

le *roseau*

(les *roseaux* PL)

reel NOUN

la *bobine* (*of thread*)

to **refer** VERB

◆ **to refer to** faire allusion à ◇ *What are you referring to?* À quoi faites-vous allusion?

referee NOUN

l' *arbitre* MASC

reference NOUN

1 l' *allusion* FEM ◇ *He made no reference to the murder.* Il n'a fait aucune allusion au meurtre.

2 les *références* FEM (*for job application*) ◇ *Would you please give me a reference?* Pouvez-vous me fournir des références?

◆ **a reference book** un ouvrage de référence

to **refill** VERB

remplir à nouveau ◇ *He refilled my glass.* Il a rempli mon verre à nouveau.

refinery NOUN

la *raffinerie*

to **reflect** VERB

refléter (*light, image*)

reflection NOUN

le *reflet* (*in mirror*)

reflex NOUN

le *réflexe*

reflexive ADJECTIVE

réfléchi ◇ *a reflexive verb* un verbe réfléchi

refresher course NOUN

le *cours de recyclage*

refreshing ADJECTIVE

rafraîchissant

refreshments PL NOUN

les *rafraîchissements* MASC PL

refrigerator NOUN

le *réfrigérateur*

to **refuel** VERB

se ravitailler en carburant ◇ *The plane stops in Boston to refuel.* L'avion s'arrête à Boston pour se ravitailler en carburant.

refuge NOUN

le *refuge*

refugee NOUN
le *réfugié*
la *réfugiée*

refund NOUN
see also refund VERB
le *remboursement*

refund VERB
see also refund NOUN
rembourser

refusal NOUN
le *refus*

refuse VERB
see also refuse NOUN
refuser

refuse NOUN
see also refuse VERB
les *ordures* FEM PL
◆ **refuse collection** le ramassage des ordures

regain VERB
◆ **to regain consciousness** reprendre connaissance

regard NOUN
see also regard VERB
◆ **Give my regards to Alice.** Transmettez mon bon souvenir à Alice.
◆ **Louis sends his regards.** Vous avez le bonjour de Louis.
◆ **"with kind regards"** "bien cordialement"

regard VERB
see also regard NOUN
◆ **to regard something as** considérer quelque chose comme
◆ **as regards...** concernant...

regarding PREPOSITION
relatif à MASC
relative à FEM
◇ *the laws regarding the export of animals* les lois relatives à l'exportation des animaux
◆ **Regarding John,...** Quant à John,...

regiment NOUN
le *régiment*

region NOUN
la *région*

regional ADJECTIVE
régional
(*régionaux* PL)

register NOUN
see also register VERB
le *registre d'absences* (*in school*)

register VERB
see also register NOUN
s'inscrire (*at school, college*)

registered ADJECTIVE
◆ **a registered letter** une lettre recommandée

registration NOUN
1 l' *appel* MASC (*roll call*)
2 le *numéro d'immatriculation* (*of car*)

regret NOUN
see also regret VERB
le *regret*
◆ **I've got no regrets.** Je ne regrette rien.

to **regret** VERB
see also regret NOUN
regretter ◇ *Give me the money or you'll regret it!* Donne-moi l'argent, sinon tu vas le regretter!
◆ **to regret doing something** regretter d'avoir fait quelque chose ◇ *I regret saying that.* Je regrette d'avoir dit ça.

regular ADJECTIVE
1 *régulier* MASC
régulière FEM
◇ *at regular intervals* à intervalles réguliers ◇ *a regular verb* un verbe régulier
◆ **to take regular exercise** faire régulièrement de l'exercice
2 (*average*)
normal
(*normaux* PL)
◇ *a regular portion of fries* une portion de frites normale

regularly ADVERB
régulièrement

regulation NOUN
le *règlement*

rehearsal NOUN
la *répétition*

to **rehearse** VERB
répéter

rein NOUN
la *rêne* ◇ *the reins* les rênes

reindeer NOUN
le *renne*

to **reject** VERB
rejeter (*idea, suggestion*) ◇ *We rejected that idea straight away.* Nous avons immédiatement rejeté cette idée.
◆ **I applied but they rejected me.** J'ai posé ma candidature mais ils l'ont rejetée.

relapse NOUN
la *rechute* ◇ *to have a relapse* faire une rechute

related ADJECTIVE
apparenté (*people*) ◇ *We're related.* Nous sommes apparentés.
◆ **The two events were not related.** Il n'y avait aucun rapport entre les deux événements.

relation NOUN
1 (*person*)
le *parent*
la *parente*

R

PTO

◇ *He's a distant relation.* C'est un parent éloigné. ◇ *my close relations* mes parents proches

Remember that in French, **mes parents** *usually only refers to your mother and father.*

◆ **my relations** ma famille

◆ **I've got relations in London.** J'ai de la famille à Londres.

2 (*connection*)

le *rapport* ◇ *It has no relation to reality.* Cela n'a aucun rapport avec la réalité.

◆ **in relation to** par rapport à

relationship NOUN

les *relations* FEM PL ◇ *We have a good relationship.* Nous avons de bonnes relations.

◆ **I'm not in a relationship at the moment.** Je ne sors avec personne en ce moment.

relative NOUN

le *parent*

la *parente*

◇ *my close relatives* mes proches parents

◆ **all her relatives** toute sa famille

relatively ADVERB

relativement

to **relax** VERB

se détendre ◇ *I relax listening to music.* Je me détends en écoutant de la musique.

◆ **Relax! Everything's fine.** Ne t'en fais pas! Tout va bien.

relaxation NOUN

la *détente* ◇ *I don't have much time for relaxation.* Je n'ai pas beaucoup de moments de détente.

relaxed ADJECTIVE

détendu

relaxing ADJECTIVE

reposant

◆ **I find cooking relaxing.** Cela me détend de faire la cuisine.

relay NOUN

◆ **a relay race** une course de relais

to **release** VERB

see also release NOUN

1 *libérer* (*prisoner*)

2 *divulguer* (*report, news*)

3 *sortir* (*record, video*)

release NOUN

see also release VERB

la *libération* (*from prison*) ◇ *the release of Nelson Mandela* la libération de Nelson Mandela

◆ **the band's latest release** le dernier disque du groupe

relegated ADJECTIVE

déclassé (*sport*)

relevant ADJECTIVE

approprié (*documents*)

◆ **That's not relevant.** Ça n'a aucun rapport.

◆ **to be relevant to something** être en rapport avec quelque chose

◇ *Education should be relevant to real life.* L'enseignement devrait être en rapport avec la réalité.

reliable ADJECTIVE

fiable ◇ *a reliable car* une voiture fiable ◇ *He's not very reliable.* Il n'est pas très fiable.

relief NOUN

le *soulagement* ◇ *That's a relief!* Quel soulagement!

to **relieve** VERB

soulager ◇ *This injection will relieve the pain.* Cette piqûre va soulager la douleur.

relieved ADJECTIVE

soulagé ◇ *I was relieved to hear...* J'ai été soulagé d'apprendre...

religion NOUN

la *religion* ◇ *What religion are you?* Quelle est votre religion?

religious ADJECTIVE

1 *religieux* MASC

religieuse FEM

◇ *my religious beliefs* mes croyances religieuses

2 *croyant* ◇ *I'm not religious.* Je ne suis pas croyant.

reluctant ADJECTIVE

◆ **to be reluctant to do something** être peu disposé à faire quelque chose

◇ *They were reluctant to help us.* Ils étaient peu disposés à nous aider.

reluctantly ADVERB

à contrecœur ◇ *She reluctantly accepted.* Elle a accepté à contrecœur.

to **rely on** VERB

compter sur ◇ *I'm relying on you.* Je compte sur toi.

to **remain** VERB

rester

◆ **to remain silent** garder le silence

remaining ADJECTIVE

le reste de ◇ *the remaining ingredients* le reste des ingrédients

remains PL NOUN

les *restes* MASC PL ◇ *the remains of the picnic* les restes du pique-nique

◇ *human remains* des restes humains

◆ **Roman remains** les vestiges romains

remake NOUN

le *remake* (*of film*)

remark NOUN

la *remarque*

remarkable ADJECTIVE

remarquable

remarkably ADVERB
remarquablement

remarry VERB
se remarier ◇ *She remarried three years ago.* Elle s'est remariée il y a trois ans.

remedy NOUN
le *remède* ◇ *a good remedy for a sore throat* un bon remède contre le mal de gorge

remember VERB
se souvenir de ◇ *I can't remember his name.* Je ne me souviens pas de son nom. ◇ *I don't remember.* Je ne m'en souviens pas.

In French you often say "don't forget" instead of remember.

◇ *Remember your passport!* N'oublie pas ton passeport! ◇ *Remember to write your name on the form.* N'oubliez pas d'écrire votre nom sur le formulaire.

Remembrance Day NOUN
le *jour de l'Armistice* MASC ◇ *on Remembrance Day* le jour de l'Armistice

remind VERB
rappeler ◇ *It reminds me of Scotland.* Cela me rappelle l'Écosse. ◇ *I'll remind you tomorrow.* Je te le rappellerai demain. ◇ *Remind me to speak to Daniel.* Rappelle-moi de parler à Daniel.

remorse NOUN
le *remords* ◇ *He showed no remorse.* Il a manifesté aucun remords.

remote ADJECTIVE
isolé ◇ *a remote village* un village isolé

remote control NOUN
la *télécommande*

removable ADJECTIVE
amovible

removal NOUN
le *déménagement* (*from house*)
◆ **a removal van** un camion de déménagement

remove VERB
1 *enlever* ◇ *Please remove your bag from my seat.* Est-ce que vous pouvez enlever votre sac de mon siège?
2 *faire partir* (*stain*) ◇ *Did you remove the stain?* Est-ce que tu as fait partir la tache?

rendezvous NOUN
le *rendez-vous*
(les *rendez-vous* PL)

renew VERB
renouveler (*passport, licence*)

renewable ADJECTIVE
renouvelable (*energy, resource*)

renovate VERB
rénover ◇ *The building's been renovated.* Le bâtiment a été rénové.

renowned ADJECTIVE
renommé

rent NOUN
see also rent VERB
le *loyer*

to **rent** VERB
see also rent NOUN
louer ◇ *We rented a car.* Nous avons loué une voiture.

rental NOUN
la *location* ◇ *Car rental is included in the price.* Le prix comprend la location d'une voiture.

to **reorganize** VERB
réorganiser

rep NOUN (= *representative*)
le *représentant*
la *représentante*

to **repair** VERB
see also repair NOUN
réparer
◆ **to get something repaired** faire réparer quelque chose ◇ *I got the washing machine repaired.* J'ai fait réparer la machine à laver.

repair NOUN
see also repair VERB
la *réparation*

to **repay** VERB
rembourser (*money*)

repayment NOUN
le *remboursement*

to **repeat** VERB
see also repeat NOUN
répéter

repeat NOUN
see also repeat VERB
la *reprise* ◇ *There are too many repeats on TV.* Il y a trop de reprises à la télé.

repeatedly ADVERB
à plusieurs reprises

repellent NOUN
◆ **insect repellent** l'insectifuge MASC

repetitive ADJECTIVE
(*movement, work*)
répétitif MASC
répétitive FEM

to **replace** VERB
remplacer

replay NOUN
see also replay VERB
◆ **There will be a replay on Friday.** Le match sera rejoué vendredi.

to **replay** VERB
see also replay NOUN
rejouer (*match*)

replica NOUN
la *réplique*

reply NOUN
see also reply VERB
la *réponse*

to **reply** VERB
see also reply NOUN
répondre

report NOUN
see also report VERB
1 (*of event*)
le *compte rendu*
(les *comptes rendus* PL)
2 (*news report*)
le *reportage* ◇ *a report in the paper* un reportage dans le journal
3 (*at school*)
le *bulletin scolaire* ◇ *I got a good report this term.* J'ai un bon bulletin scolaire ce trimestre.

to **report** VERB
see also report NOUN
1 *signaler* ◇ *I reported the theft to the police.* J'ai signalé le vol au commissariat.
2 *se présenter* ◇ *Report to reception when you arrive.* Présentez-vous à la réception à votre arrivée.

reporter NOUN
le *reporter* ◇ *I'd like to be a reporter.* J'aimerais être reporter.

to **represent** VERB
représenter

representative ADJECTIVE
représentatif MASC
représentative FEM

reproduction NOUN
la *reproduction*

republic NOUN
la *république*

repulsive ADJECTIVE
repoussant

reputation NOUN
la *réputation*

request NOUN
see also request VERB
la *demande*

to **request** VERB
see also request NOUN
demander

requirement NOUN
la *condition requise*
➔ **What are the requirements for the job?** Quelles sont les conditions requises pour le poste?
➔ **entry requirements** (*for university*) les critères d'entrée

to **rescue** VERB
see also rescue NOUN
sauver

rescue NOUN
see also rescue VERB
1 le *sauvetage* ◇ *a rescue operation* une opération de sauvetage
➔ **a mountain rescue team** une équipe de sauvetage en montagne
2 le *secours* ◇ *the rescue services* les services de secours
➔ **to come to somebody's rescue** venir au secours de quelqu'un ◇ *He came to my rescue.* Il est venu à mon secours.

research NOUN
1 la *recherche* (*experimental*) ◇ *He's doing research.* Il fait de la recherche.
2 les *recherches* FEM PL (*theoretical*) ◇ *She's doing some research in the library.* Elle fait des recherches à la bibliothèque.

resemblance NOUN
la *ressemblance*

reservation NOUN
la *réservation* (*booking*) ◇ *I've got a reservation for two nights.* J'ai une réservation pour deux nuits. ◇ *I'd like to make a reservation for this evening.* J'aimerais faire une réservation pour ce soir.

reserve NOUN
see also reserve VERB
1 (*place*)
la *réserve* ◇ *a nature reserve* une réserve naturelle
2 (*person*)
le *remplaçant*
la *remplaçante*
◇ *I was reserve in the game last Saturday.* J'étais remplaçant dans le match de samedi dernier.

to **reserve** VERB
see also reserve NOUN
réserver ◇ *I'd like to reserve a table for tomorrow evening.* J'aimerais réserver une table pour demain soir.

reserved ADJECTIVE
réservé ◇ *a reserved seat* une place réservée ◇ *He's quite reserved.* Il est assez réservé.

resident NOUN
le *résident*
la *résidente*

residential ADJECTIVE
résidentiel MASC
résidentielle FEM
◇ *a residential area* un quartier résidentiel

to **resign** VERB
donner sa démission

resistance NOUN
➔ **He was in the resistance.** Il faisait de la résistance.

◆ **the French Resistance** la Résistance

resit VERB
repasser ◇ *I'm resitting the exam in December.* Je vais repasser l'examen en décembre.

resolution NOUN
la *résolution*
◆ **Have you made any new year's resolutions?** Tu as pris de bonnes résolutions pour l'année nouvelle?

resort NOUN
la *station balnéaire* (*at seaside*) ◇ *It's a resort on the Costa del Sol.* C'est une station balnéaire sur la Costa del Sol.
◆ **a ski resort** une station de ski
◆ **as a last resort** en dernier recours

resource NOUN
la *ressource*

respect NOUN
see also respect VERB
le *respect*

respect VERB
see also respect NOUN
respecter

respectable ADJECTIVE
1 *respectable*
2 *correct* (*standard, marks*)

respectively ADVERB
respectivement

responsibility NOUN
la *responsabilité*

responsible ADJECTIVE
1 (*in charge*)
responsable
◆ **to be responsible for something** être responsable de quelque chose ◇ *He's responsible for booking the tickets.* Il est responsable de la réservation des billets.
◆ **It's a responsible job.** C'est un poste à responsabilités.
2 (*mature*)
sérieux MASC
sérieuse FEM
◇ *You should be more responsible.* Tu devrais être un peu plus sérieux.

rest NOUN
see also rest VERB
1 le *repos* (*relaxation*) ◇ *five minutes' rest* cinq minutes de repos
◆ **to have a rest** se reposer ◇ *We stopped to have a rest.* Nous nous sommes arrêtés pour nous reposer.
2 le *reste* (*remainder*) ◇ *I'll do the rest.* Je ferai le reste. ◇ *the rest of the money* le reste de l'argent
◆ **the rest of them** les autres ◇ *The rest of them went swimming.* Les autres sont allés nager.

rest VERB
see also rest NOUN
1 *se reposer* (*relax*) ◇ *She's resting in her room.* Elle se repose dans sa chambre.
2 *ménager* (*not overstrain*) ◇ *He has to rest his knee.* Il doit ménager son genou.
3 *appuyer* (*lean*) ◇ *I rested my bike against the window.* J'ai appuyé mon vélo contre la fenêtre.

restaurant NOUN
le *restaurant* ◇ *We don't often go to restaurants.* Nous n'allons pas souvent au restaurant.
◆ **a restaurant car** un wagon-restaurant

restful ADJECTIVE
reposant

restoration NOUN
la *restauration*

to **restore** VERB
restaurer (*building, picture*)

to **restrict** VERB
limiter

result NOUN
le *résultat* ◇ *my exam results* mes résultats d'examen ◇ *What was the result?–One-nil.* Quel a été le résultat?–Un à zéro.

to **retire** VERB
prendre sa retraite ◇ *He retired last year.* Il a pris sa retraite l'an dernier.

retired ADJECTIVE
retraité ◇ *She's retired.* Elle est retraitée.
◆ **a retired teacher** un professeur à la retraite

retirement NOUN
la *retraite*

to **retrace** VERB
◆ **to retrace one's steps** revenir sur ses pas ◇ *I retraced my steps.* Je suis revenu sur mes pas.

return NOUN
see also return VERB
1 le *retour* ◇ *after our return* à notre retour
◆ **the return journey** le voyage de retour
◆ **a return match** un match retour
2 l' *aller retour* MASC (*ticket*) ◇ *A return to Avignon, please.* Un aller retour pour Avignon, s'il vous plaît.
◆ **in return** en échange ◇ *...and I help her in return* ...et je l'aide en échange
◆ **in return for** en échange de
◆ **Many happy returns!** Bon anniversaire!

to **return** VERB
see also return NOUN
1 *revenir* (*come back*) ◇ *I've just returned from holiday.* Je viens de revenir de vacances.
◆ **to return home** rentrer à la maison

PTO

2 *retourner* (*go back*) ◇ *He returned to France the following year.* Il est retourné en France l'année suivante.

3 *rendre* (*give back*) ◇ *She borrows my things and doesn't return them.* Elle m'emprunte mes affaires et ne me les rend pas.

reunion NOUN
la *réunion*

to **reuse** VERB
réutiliser

to **reveal** VERB
révéler

revenge NOUN
la *vengeance* ◇ *in revenge* par vengeance
◆ **to take revenge** se venger ◇ *They planned to take revenge on him.* Ils voulaient se venger de lui.

to **reverse** VERB
see also reverse ADJECTIVE
faire marche arrière (*car*) ◇ *He reversed without looking.* Il a fait marche arrière sans regarder.
◆ **to reverse the charges** (*telephone*) appeler en PCV
In France, reversing the charges is only possible for international calls.
◇ *I'd like to make a reverse charge call to Britain.* Je voudrais appeler la Grande-Bretagne en PCV.

reverse ADJECTIVE
see also reverse VERB
inverse ◇ *in reverse order* dans l'ordre inverse
◆ **in reverse gear** en marche arrière

to **revise** VERB
réviser ◇ *I haven't started revising yet.* Je n'ai pas encore commencé à réviser.
◆ **I've revised my opinion.** J'ai changé d'opinion.

revision NOUN
les *révisions* FEM PL ◇ *Have you done a lot of revision?* Est-ce que tu as fait beaucoup de révisions?

to **revive** VERB
ranimer ◇ *The nurses tried to revive him.* Les infirmières ont essayé de le ranimer.

revolting ADJECTIVE
dégoûtant

revolution NOUN
la *révolution*
◆ **the French Revolution** la Révolution française

revolutionary ADJECTIVE
révolutionnaire

revolver NOUN
le *revolver*

reward NOUN
la *récompense*

rewarding ADJECTIVE
gratifiant ◇ *a rewarding job* un travail gratifiant

to **rewind** VERB
rembobiner ◇ *to rewind a cassette* rembobiner une cassette

rheumatism NOUN
le *rhumatisme*

Rhine NOUN
le *Rhin*

Rhone NOUN
le *Rhône*

rhubarb NOUN
la *rhubarbe* ◇ *a rhubarb tart* une tarte à la rhubarbe

rhythm NOUN
le *rythme*

rib NOUN
la *côte*

ribbon NOUN
le *ruban*

rice NOUN
le *riz*
◆ **rice pudding** le riz au lait

rich ADJECTIVE
riche
◆ **the rich** les riches MASC

to **rid** VERB
◆ **to get rid of** se débarrasser de ◇ *I want to get rid of some old clothes.* Je veux me débarrasser de vieux vêtements.

ride NOUN
see also ride VERB
◆ **to go for a ride (1)** (*on horse*) monter à cheval
◆ **to go for a ride (2)** (*on bike*) faire un tour en vélo ◇ *We went for a bike ride.* Nous sommes allés faire un tour en vélo.
◆ **It's a short bus ride to the town centre.** Ce n'est pas loin du centre-ville en bus.

to **ride** VERB
see also ride NOUN
monter à cheval (*on horse*) ◇ *I'm learning to ride.* J'apprends à monter à cheval.
◆ **to ride a bike** faire du vélo ◇ *Can you ride a bike?* Tu sais faire du vélo?

rider NOUN
1 (*on horse*)
le *cavalier*
la *cavalière*
◇ *She's a good rider.* C'est une bonne cavalière.
2 (*on bike*)
le/la *cycliste*

ridiculous ADJECTIVE
ridicule ◇ *Don't be ridiculous!* Ne sois

pas ridicule!

iding NOUN
l' *équitation* FEM
to go riding faire de l'équitation
a riding school une école d'équitation

ifle NOUN
le *fusil* ◇ *a hunting rifle* un fusil de chasse

ig NOUN
an oil rig une plate-forme pétrolière

ight ADJECTIVE, ADVERB
see also right NOUN
There are several ways of translating right. *Scan the examples to find one that is similar to what you want to say.*
1 (*factually correct, suitable*)
bon MASC
bonne FEM
◇ *the right answer* la bonne réponse ◇ *It isn't the right size.* Ce n'est pas la bonne taille. ◇ *We're on the right train.* Nous sommes dans le bon train.
Is this the right road for Arles? Est-ce que c'est bien la route pour aller à Arles?
2 (*correctly*)
correctement ◇ *Am I pronouncing it right?* Est-ce que je prononce ça correctement?
to be right (1) (*person*) avoir raison ◇ *You were right!* Tu avais raison!
to be right (2) (*statement, opinion*) être vrai ◇ *That's right!* C'est vrai!
3 (*accurate*)
juste ◇ *Do you have the right time?* Est-ce que vous avez l'heure juste?
4 (*morally correct*)
bien ◇ *It's not right to behave like that.* Ce n'est pas bien d'agir comme ça.
I think you did the right thing. Je pense que tu as bien fait.
5 (*not left*)
droit ◇ *my right hand* ma main droite
6 (*turn, look*)
à droite ◇ *Turn right at the traffic lights.* Tournez à droite aux prochains feux.
• **Right! Let's get started.** Bon! On commence.
• **right away** tout de suite ◇ *I'll do it right away.* Je vais le faire tout de suite.

right NOUN
see also right ADJECTIVE
1 le *droit*
• **You've got no right to do that.** Vous n'avez pas le droit de faire ça.
2 la *droite* (*not left*)
• **on the right** à droite ◇ *Remember to drive on the right.* N'oubliez pas de conduire à droite.
• **right of way** la priorité ◇ *It was our right of way.* Nous avions la priorité.

right-hand ADJECTIVE
• **the right-hand side** la droite ◇ *It's on the right-hand side.* C'est à droite.

right-handed ADJECTIVE
droitier MASC
droitière FEM

rim NOUN
la *monture* ◇ *glasses with wire rims* des lunettes avec une monture métallique

ring NOUN
see also ring VERB
1 l' *anneau* MASC
(les *anneaux* PL)
◇ *a gold ring* un anneau en or
2 la *bague* (*with stones*) ◇ *a diamond ring* une bague de diamants
• **a wedding ring** une alliance
3 le *cercle* (*circle*) ◇ *to stand in a ring* se mettre en cercle
4 le *coup de sonnette* (*of bell*) ◇ *I was woken by a ring at the door.* J'ai été réveillé par un coup de sonnette.
• **to give somebody a ring** appeler quelqu'un ◇ *I'll give you a ring this evening.* Je t'appellerai ce soir.

to **ring** VERB
see also ring NOUN
1 *téléphoner* ◇ *Your mother rang this morning.* Ta mère a téléphoné ce matin.
• **to ring somebody** appeler quelqu'un ◇ *I'll ring you tomorrow morning.* Je t'appellerai demain matin.
• **to ring somebody up** donner un coup de fil à quelqu'un
2 *sonner* ◇ *The phone's ringing.* Le téléphone sonne.
• **to ring the bell** (*doorbell*) sonner à la porte ◇ *I rang the bell three times.* J'ai sonné trois fois à la porte.
• **to ring back** rappeler ◇ *I'll ring back later.* Je rappellerai plus tard.

ring binder NOUN
le *classeur*

ring road NOUN
1 la *rocade* (*ordinary road*)
2 le *périphérique* (*motorway*)

rink NOUN
1 la *patinoire* (*for ice-skating*)
2 la *piste* (*for roller-skating*)

to **rinse** VERB
rincer

riot NOUN
see also riot VERB
l' *émeute* FEM

to **riot** VERB
see also riot NOUN
faire une émeute

to **rip** VERB
1 *déchirer* ◇ *I've ripped my jeans.* J'ai déchiré mon jean.
2 *se déchirer* ◇ *My skirt's ripped.* Ma jupe s'est déchirée.

ripe ADJECTIVE
mûr

rip-off NOUN
◆ **It's a rip-off!** C'est de l'arnaque! (*informal*)

rise NOUN
see also rise VERB
1 la *hausse* (*in prices, temperature*) ◇ *a sudden rise in temperature* une hausse subite de température
2 l' *augmentation* FEM (*pay rise*)

to **rise** VERB
see also rise NOUN
1 *augmenter* (*increase*) ◇ *Prices are rising.* Les prix augmentent.
2 *se lever* ◇ *The sun rises early in June.* Le soleil se lève tôt en juin.

riser NOUN
◆ **to be an early riser** être matinal

risk NOUN
see also risk VERB
le *risque*
◆ **to take risks** prendre des risques
◆ **It's at your own risk.** C'est à vos risques et périls.

to **risk** VERB
see also risk NOUN
risquer ◇ *You risk getting a fine.* Vous risquez de recevoir une amende.
◆ **I wouldn't risk it if I were you.** À votre place, je ne prendrais pas ce risque.

risky ADJECTIVE
risqué

rival NOUN
see also rival ADJECTIVE
le *rival*
(les *rivaux* PL)
la *rivale*

rival ADJECTIVE
see also rival NOUN
1 *rival* ◇ *a rival gang* une bande rivale
2 *concurrent* ◇ *a rival company* une société concurrente

rivalry NOUN
la *rivalité* (*between towns, schools*)

river NOUN
1 la *rivière* ◇ *The river runs alongside the canal.* La rivière longe le canal.
2 le *fleuve* (*major*) ◇ *the rivers of France* les fleuves de France
◆ **the river Seine** la Seine

Riviera NOUN
◆ **the French Riviera** la Côte d'Azur
◆ **the Italian Riviera** la Riviera italienne

road NOUN
1 la *route* ◇ *There's a lot of traffic on the roads.* Il y a beaucoup de circulation sur les routes.
2 la *rue* (*street*) ◇ *They live across the road.* Ils habitent de l'autre côté de la rue.

road map NOUN
la *carte routière*

road sign NOUN
le *panneau de signalisation*
(les *panneaux de signalisation* PL)

roadworks PL NOUN
les *travaux* MASC PL

roast ADJECTIVE
rôti ◇ *roast chicken* le poulet rôti ◇ *roast potatoes* les pommes de terre rôties
◆ **roast pork** le rôti de porc
◆ **roast beef** le rôti de bœuf

to **rob** VERB
◆ **to rob somebody** voler quelqu'un ◇ *I've been robbed.* On m'a volé.
◆ **to rob somebody of something** voler quelque chose à quelqu'un ◇ *He was robbed of his wallet.* On lui a volé son portefeuille.
◆ **to rob a bank** dévaliser une banque

robber NOUN
le *voleur*
◆ **a bank-robber** un cambrioleur de banques

robbery NOUN
le *vol*
◆ **a bank robbery** un hold-up
◆ **armed robbery** le vol à main armée

robot NOUN
le *robot*

rock NOUN
1 la *roche* (*substance*) ◇ *They tunnelled through the rock.* Ils ont creusé un tunnel dans la roche.
2 le *rocher* (*boulder*) ◇ *I sat on a rock.* Je me suis assis sur un rocher.
3 la *pierre* (*stone*) ◇ *The crowd started to throw rocks.* La foule s'est mise à lancer des pierres.
4 le *rock* (*music*) ◇ *a rock concert* un concert de rock ◇ *He's a rock star.* C'est une rock star.
5 le *sucre d'orge* (*sweet*) ◇ *a stick of rock* un bâton de sucre d'orge
◆ **rock and roll** le rock'n'roll

rockery NOUN
la *rocaille*

rocket NOUN
la *fusée* (*firework, spacecraft*)

rocking chair NOUN
le *rocking-chair*

rocking horse NOUN
le *cheval à bascule*

rod NOUN
la *canne à pêche* (*for fishing*)

rode VERB *see* **ride**

role NOUN
le *rôle*

role play NOUN
le *jeu de rôle*
(les *jeux de rôles* PL)
◇ *to do a role play* faire un jeu de rôle

roll NOUN
see also roll VERB
1 le *rouleau*
(les *rouleaux* PL)
◇ *a roll of tape* un rouleau de ruban adhésif ◇ *a toilet roll* un rouleau de papier hygiénique
2 le *petit pain* (*bread*)

roll VERB
see also roll NOUN
rouler
◆ **to roll out the pastry** abaisser la pâte

roll call NOUN
l' *appel* MASC

roller NOUN
le *rouleau*
(les *rouleaux* PL)

rollercoaster NOUN
les *montagnes russes* FEM PL

roller skates PL NOUN
les *patins à roulettes* MASC

roller-skating NOUN
le *patin à roulettes*
◆ **to go roller-skating** faire du patin à roulettes

rolling pin NOUN
le *rouleau à pâtisserie*

Roman ADJECTIVE, NOUN
romain (*ancient*) ◇ *a Roman villa* une villa romaine ◇ *the Roman empire* l'empire romain
◆ **the Romans** les Romains

Roman Catholic NOUN
le/la *catholique* ◇ *He's a Roman Catholic.* Il est catholique.

romance NOUN
1 les *romans d'amour* MASC PL (*novels*)
◇ *I read a lot of romance.* Je lis beaucoup de romans d'amour.
2 le *charme* (*glamour*) ◇ *the romance of Paris* le charme de Paris
◆ **a holiday romance** une idylle de vacances

Romania NOUN
la *Roumanie*
◆ **in Romania** en Roumanie

Romanian ADJECTIVE
roumain

romantic ADJECTIVE
romantique

roof NOUN
le *toit*

roof rack NOUN
la *galerie*

room NOUN
1 la *pièce* ◇ *the biggest room in the house* la plus grande pièce de la maison
2 la *chambre* (*bedroom*) ◇ *She's in her room.* Elle est dans sa chambre.
◆ **a single room** une chambre pour une personne
◆ **a double room** une chambre pour deux personnes
3 la *salle* (*in school*) ◇ *the music room* la salle de musique
4 la *place* (*space*) ◇ *There's no room for that box.* Il n'y a pas de place pour cette boîte.

roommate NOUN
le/la *camarade de chambre*

root NOUN
la *racine*

rope NOUN
la *corde*

rose VERB *see* **rise**

rose NOUN
la *rose* (*flower*)

to **rot** NOUN VERB
pourrir

rotten ADJECTIVE
pourri (*decayed*) ◇ *a rotten apple* une pomme pourrie
◆ **rotten weather** un temps pourri
◆ **That's a rotten thing to do.** Ce n'est vraiment pas gentil.
◆ **to feel rotten** être mal fichu (*informal*)

rough ADJECTIVE
1 (*surface*)
rêche ◇ *My hands are rough.* J'ai les mains rêches.
2 (*game*)
violent ◇ *Rugby's a rough sport.* Le rugby est un sport violent.
3 (*place*)
difficile ◇ *It's a rough area.* C'est un quartier difficile.
4 (*water*)
houleux MASC
houleuse FEM
◇ *The sea was rough.* La mer était houleuse.
5 *approximatif* MASC
approximative FEM
◆ **I've got a rough idea.** J'en ai une idée approximative.
◆ **to feel rough** ne pas être dans son assiette ◇ *I feel rough.* Je ne suis pas

R

PTO

dans mon assiette.

roughly ADVERB

à peu près ◇ *It weighs roughly 20 kilos.* Ça pèse à peu près vingt kilos.

round ADJECTIVE, ADVERB, PREPOSITION

see also round NOUN

1 *rond* ◇ *a round table* une table ronde

2 *autour de* (*around*) ◇ *We were sitting round the table.* Nous étions assis autour de la table. ◇ *She wore a scarf round her neck.* Elle portait une écharpe autour du cou.

- **It's just round the corner.** (*very near*) C'est tout près.
- **to go round to somebody's house** aller chez quelqu'un ◇ *I went round to my friend's house.* Je suis allé chez mon ami.
- **to have a look round** faire un tour ◇ *We're going to have a look round.* Nous allons faire un tour.
- **to go round a museum** visiter un musée
- **round here** près d'ici ◇ *Is there a chemist's round here?* Est-ce qu'il y a une pharmacie près d'ici?
- **He lives round here.** Il habite dans les parages.
- **all round** partout ◇ *There were vineyards all round.* Il y avait des vignobles partout.
- **all year round** toute l'année
- **round about** (*roughly*) environ ◇ *It costs round about £100.* Cela coûte environ cent livres. ◇ *round about 8 o'clock* à huit heures environ

round NOUN

see also round ADJECTIVE

1 la *manche* (*of tournament*)

2 le *round* (*of boxing match*)

- **a round of golf** une partie de golf
- **a round of drinks** une tournée ◇ *He bought a round of drinks.* Il a offert une tournée.

roundabout NOUN

1 (*at junction*) le *rond-point* (les *ronds-points* PL)

2 (*at funfair*) le *manège*

route NOUN

1 l' *itinéraire* MASC ◇ *We're planning our route.* Nous établissons notre itinéraire.

2 le *parcours* (*of bus*)

routine NOUN

- **my daily routine** mes occupations quotidiennes

row NOUN

see also row VERB

1 la *rangée* ◇ *a row of houses* une rangée de maisons

2 le *rang* (*of seats*) ◇ *Our seats are in the front row.* Nos places se trouvent au premier rang.

- **five times in a row** cinq fois d'affilée

3 le *vacarme* (*noise*) ◇ *What's that terrible row?* Qu'est-ce que c'est que ce vacarme?

4 la *dispute* (*quarrel*)

- **to have a row** se disputer ◇ *They've had a row.* Ils se sont disputés.

to **row** VERB

see also row NOUN

1 *ramer* ◇ *We took turns to row.* Nous avons ramé à tour de rôle.

2 *faire de l'aviron* (*as sport*)

rowing NOUN

l' *aviron* MASC (*sport*) ◇ *My hobby is rowing.* Je fais de l'aviron.

- **a rowing boat** un bateau à rames

royal ADJECTIVE

royal (*royaux* MASC PL)

- **the royal family** la famille royale

to **rub** VERB

1 *frotter* (*stain*)

2 *se frotter* (*part of body*) ◇ *Don't rub your eyes!* Ne te frotte pas les yeux!

- **to rub something out** effacer quelque chose

rubber NOUN

1 le *caoutchouc* ◇ *rubber soles* des semelles en caoutchouc

2 la *gomme* (*eraser*) ◇ *Can I borrow your rubber?* Je peux emprunter ta gomme?

- **a rubber band** un élastique

rubbish NOUN

see also rubbish ADJECTIVE

1 les *ordures* FEM PL (*refuse*) ◇ *When do they collect the rubbish?* Quand est-ce qu'ils ramassent les ordures?

2 la *camelote* (*junk*) ◇ *They sell a lot of rubbish at the market.* Ils vendent beaucoup de camelote au marché.

3 les *bêtises* FEM PL (*nonsense*) ◇ *Don't talk rubbish!* Ne dis pas de bêtises!

- **That's a load of rubbish!** C'est vraiment n'importe quoi! (*informal*)
- **a rubbish bin** une poubelle
- **a rubbish dump** une décharge

rubbish ADJECTIVE

see also rubbish NOUN

nul MASC

nulle FEM

◇ *They're a rubbish team!* Cette équipe est nulle!

rucksack NOUN

le *sac à dos*

rude ADJECTIVE

1 (*impolite*)
impoli ◇ *It's rude to interrupt.* C'est impoli de couper la parole aux gens.

2 (*offensive*)
grossier MASC
grossière FEM
◇ *a rude joke* une plaisanterie grossière
◇ *He was very rude to me.* Il a été très grossier avec moi.

◆ **a rude word** un gros mot

rug NOUN

1 le *tapis* ◇ *a Persian rug* un tapis persan

2 la *couverture* (*blanket*) ◇ *a tartan rug* une couverture écossaise

rugby NOUN

le *rugby* ◇ *I play rugby.* Je joue au rugby.

ruin NOUN

see also ruin VERB

la *ruine* ◇ *the ruins of the castle* les ruines du château

◆ **in ruins** en ruine

ruin VERB

see also ruin NOUN

1 *abîmer* ◇ *You'll ruin your shoes.* Tu vas abîmer tes chaussures.

2 *gâcher* ◇ *It ruined our holiday.* Ça a gâché nos vacances.

3 *ruiner* (*financially*)

rule NOUN

1 la *règle* ◇ *the rules of grammar* les règles de grammaire

◆ **as a rule** en règle générale

2 le *règlement* (*regulation*) ◇ *It's against the rules.* C'est contre le règlement.

ruler NOUN

la *règle* ◇ *Can I borrow your ruler?* Je peux emprunter ta règle?

rum NOUN

le *rhum*

rumour NOUN

la *rumeur* ◇ *It's just a rumour.* Ce n'est qu'une rumeur.

run NOUN

see also run VERB

le *point* (*in cricket*) ◇ *to score a run* marquer un point

◆ **to go for a run** courir ◇ *I go for a run every morning.* Je cours tous les matins.

◆ **I did a ten-kilometre run.** J'ai couru dix kilomètres.

◆ **on the run** en fuite ◇ *The criminals are still on the run.* Les criminels sont toujours en fuite.

◆ **in the long run** à long terme

to **run** VERB

see also run NOUN

1 *courir* ◇ *I ran five kilometres.* J'ai couru cinq kilomètres.

◆ **to run a marathon** participer à un marathon

2 *diriger* (*manage*) ◇ *He runs a large company.* Il dirige une grosse société.

3 *organiser* (*organize*) ◇ *They run music courses in the holidays.* Ils organisent des cours de musique pendant les vacances.

4 *couler* (*water*) ◇ *Don't leave the tap running.* Ne laisse pas couler le robinet.

◆ **to run a bath** faire couler un bain

5 *conduire* (*by car*) ◇ *I can run you to the station.* Je peux te conduire à la gare.

◆ **to run away** s'enfuir ◇ *They ran away before the police came.* Ils se sont enfuis avant l'arrivée de la police.

◆ **Time is running out.** Il ne reste plus beaucoup de temps.

◆ **to run out of something** se trouver à court de quelque chose ◇ *We ran out of money.* Nous nous sommes trouvés à court d'argent.

◆ **to run somebody over** écraser quelqu'un

◆ **to get run over** se faire écraser ◇ *Be careful, or you'll get run over!* Fais attention, sinon tu vas te faire écraser!

rung VERB *see* **ring**

runner NOUN

le *coureur*
la *coureuse*

runner beans PL NOUN

les *haricots verts* MASC PL

runner-up NOUN

le *second*
la *seconde*

running NOUN

la *course* ◇ *Running is my favourite sport.* La course est mon sport préféré.

runway NOUN

la *piste*

rural ADJECTIVE

rural
(*ruraux* MASC PL)

rush NOUN

see also rush VERB

la *hâte*

◆ **In a rush.** à la hâte

to **rush** VERB

see also rush NOUN

1 *se précipiter* (*run*) ◇ *Everyone rushed outside.* Tout le monde s'est précipité dehors.

2 *se dépêcher* (*hurry*) ◇ *There's no need to rush.* Ce n'est pas la peine de se

PTO

dépêcher.

rush hour NOUN
les *heures de pointe* FEM PL ◇ *in the rush hour* aux heures de pointe

rusk NOUN
la *biscotte*

Russia NOUN
la *Russie*
◆ **in Russia** en Russie
◆ **to Russia** en Russie

Russian ADJECTIVE
see also Russian NOUN
russe

Russian NOUN
see also Russian ADJECTIVE
1 le/la *Russe* (*person*)
2 le *russe* (*language*)

rust NOUN
la *rouille*

rusty ADJECTIVE
rouillé ◇ *a rusty bike* un vélo rouillé ◇ *My French is very rusty.* Mon français est très rouillé.

ruthless ADJECTIVE
sans pitié

rye NOUN
le *seigle*
◆ **rye bread** le pain de seigle

S

Sabbath NOUN
1 le *dimanche* (*Christian*)
2 le *sabbat* (*Jewish*)
sack NOUN
see also sack VERB
le *sac*
• **to get the sack** être mis à la porte
sack VERB
see also sack NOUN
• **to sack somebody** mettre quelqu'un à la porte ◇ *He was sacked.* On l'a mis à la porte.
sacred ADJECTIVE
sacré
sacrifice NOUN
le *sacrifice*
sad ADJECTIVE
triste
saddle NOUN
la *selle*
saddlebag NOUN
la *sacoche*
sadly ADVERB
1 *tristement* ◇ *"She's gone," he said sadly.* "Elle est partie," a-t-il dit tristement.
2 *malheureusement* (*unfortunately*) ◇ *Sadly, it was too late.* Malheureusement, il était trop tard.
safe NOUN
see also safe ADJECTIVE
le *coffre-fort*
(les *coffres-forts* PL)
◇ *She put the money in the safe.* Elle a mis l'argent dans le coffre-fort.
safe ADJECTIVE
see also safe NOUN
1 *sans danger* ◇ *Don't worry, it's perfectly safe.* Ne vous inquiétez pas, c'est absolument sans danger.
• **Is it safe?** Ça n'est pas dangereux?
2 *sûr* (*machine, ladder*) ◇ *This car isn't safe.* Cette voiture n'est pas sûre.
3 *hors de danger* (*out of danger*) ◇ *You're safe now.* Vous êtes hors de danger maintenant.
• **to feel safe** se sentir en sécurité
• **safe sex** le sexe sans risques
safety NOUN
la *sécurité*
• **a safety belt** une ceinture de sécurité
• **a safety pin** une épingle de nourrice
Sagittarius NOUN
le/la *Sagittaire* ◇ *I'm Sagittarius.* Je suis Sagittaire.
Sahara NOUN
• **the Sahara Desert** le Sahara
said VERB *see* **say**
sail NOUN
see also sail VERB
la *voile*
to **sail** VERB
see also sail NOUN
1 *naviguer* (*travel*)
2 *prendre la mer* (*set off*) ◇ *The boat sails at eight o'clock.* Le bateau prend la mer à huit heures.
sailing NOUN
la *voile* ◇ *His hobby is sailing.* Son passe-temps, c'est la voile.
• **to go sailing** faire de la voile
• **a sailing boat** un voilier
• **a sailing ship** un grand voilier
sailor NOUN
le *marin* ◇ *He's a sailor.* Il est marin.
saint NOUN
le *saint*
la *sainte*
sake NOUN
• **for the sake of** dans l'intérêt de
salad NOUN
la *salade*
• **salad cream** la mayonnaise
• **salad dressing** la vinaigrette
salami NOUN
le *salami*
salary NOUN
le *salaire*
sale NOUN
les *soldes* MASC PL (*reductions*) ◇ *There's a sale on at Harrods.* Ce sont les soldes chez Harrods.
• **on sale** en vente
• **The factory's for sale.** L'usine est en vente.
• **"for sale"** "à vendre"
sales assistant NOUN
le *vendeur*
la *vendeuse*
◇ *She's a sales assistant.* Elle est vendeuse.
salesman NOUN
1 le *représentant* (*sales rep*) ◇ *He's a salesman.* Il est représentant.
• **a double-glazing salesman** un représentant en doubles vitrages
2 le *vendeur* (*sales assistant*)
sales rep NOUN
le *représentant*
la *représentante*
saleswoman NOUN
1 la *représentante* (*sales rep*) ◇ *She's a*

PTO

saleswoman. Elle est représentante.
2 la *vendeuse* (*sales assistant*)

salmon NOUN
le *saumon*

salon NOUN
le *salon* ◇ *a hair salon* un salon de coiffure ◇ *a beauty salon* un salon de beauté

saloon car NOUN
la *berline*

salt NOUN
le *sel*

salty ADJECTIVE
salé

to **salute** VERB
saluer

Salvation Army NOUN
l' *armée du Salut* FEM

same ADJECTIVE
même ◇ *the same model* le même modèle ◇ *at the same time* en même temps
◆ **They're exactly the same.** Ils sont exactement pareils.
◆ **It's not the same.** Ça n'est pas pareil.

sand NOUN
le *sable*

sandal NOUN
la *sandale* ◇ *a pair of sandals* une paire de sandales

sand castle NOUN
le *château de sable*
(les *châteaux de sable* PL)

sandwich NOUN
le *sandwich* ◇ *a cheese sandwich* un sandwich au fromage

sandwich course NOUN
le *cours avec stage pratique*

sang VERB *see* **sing**

sanitary towel NOUN
la *serviette hygiénique*

sank VERB *see* **sink**

Santa Claus NOUN
le *père Noël*

sarcastic ADJECTIVE
sarcastique

sat VERB *see* **sit**

satchel NOUN
le *cartable*

satellite NOUN
le *satellite*
◆ **a satellite dish** une antenne parabolique
◆ **satellite television** la télévision par satellite

satisfactory ADJECTIVE
satisfaisant

satisfied ADJECTIVE
satisfait

Saturday NOUN
le *samedi* ◇ *on Saturday* samedi ◇ *on Saturdays* le samedi ◇ *every Saturday* tous les samedis ◇ *last Saturday* samedi dernier ◇ *next Saturday* samedi prochain
◆ **I've got a Saturday job.** Je travaille le samedi.

sauce NOUN
la *sauce*

saucepan NOUN
la *casserole*

saucer NOUN
la *soucoupe*

Saudi Arabia NOUN
l' *Arabie Saoudite* FEM
◆ **in Saudi Arabia** en Arabie Saoudite

sauna NOUN
le *sauna*

sausage NOUN
1 la *saucisse*
2 le *saucisson* (*salami*)
◆ **a sausage roll** un friand à la saucisse

to **save** VERB
1 *mettre de côté* (*save up money*) ◇ *I've saved £50 already.* J'ai déjà mis cinquante livres de côté.
2 *économiser* (*spend less*) ◇ *I saved £20 by waiting for the sales.* J'ai économisé vingt livres en attendant les soldes.
◆ **to save time** gagner du temps ◇ *We took a taxi to save time.* Nous avons pris un taxi pour gagner du temps. ◇ *It saved us time.* Ça nous a fait gagner du temps.
3 *sauver* (*rescue*) ◇ *Luckily, all the passengers were saved.* Heureusement, tous les passagers ont été sauvés.
4 *sauvegarder* (*on computer*) ◇ *I saved the file onto a diskette.* J'ai sauvegardé le fichier sur disquette.
◆ **to save up** mettre de l'argent de côté ◇ *I'm saving up for a new bike.* Je mets de l'argent à côté pour un nouveau vélo.

savings PL NOUN
les *économies* FEM PL ◇ *She spent all her savings on a computer.* Elle a dépensé toutes ses économies en achetant un ordinateur.

savoury ADJECTIVE
salé ◇ *Is it sweet or savoury?* C'est sucré ou salé?

saw VERB *see* **see**

saw NOUN
la *scie*

sax NOUN
le *saxo* (*informal*) ◇ *I play the sax.* Je joue du saxo.

saxophone NOUN

le *saxophone* ◇ *I play the saxophone.* Je joue du saxophone.

say VERB

dire ◇ *What did he say?* Qu'est-ce qu'il a dit? ◇ *Did you hear what she said?* Tu as entendu ce qu'elle a dit?

Could you say that again? Pourriez-vous répéter s'il vous plaît?

That goes without saying. Cela va sans dire.

saying NOUN

le *dicton* ◇ *It's just a saying.* C'est juste un dicton.

scale NOUN

1 l' *échelle* FEM (*of map*) ◇ *a large-scale map* une carte à grande échelle

2 l' *ampleur* FEM (*size, extent*) ◇ *a disaster on a massive scale* un désastre d'une ampleur incroyable

3 la *gamme* (*in music*)

scales PL NOUN

la *balance* SING (*in kitchen, shop*)

bathroom scales le pèse-personne SING

scampi PL NOUN

les *scampi* MASC PL

scandal NOUN

1 le *scandale* (*outrage*) ◇ *It caused a scandal.* Ça a fait scandale.

2 les *ragots* MASC PL (*gossip*) ◇ *It's just scandal.* Ce ne sont que des ragots.

Scandinavia NOUN

la *Scandinavie*

in Scandinavia en Scandinavie

Scandinavian ADJECTIVE

scandinave

scar NOUN

la *cicatrice*

scare NOUN

see also scare VERB

la *panique*

a bomb scare une alerte à la bombe

scare VERB

see also scare NOUN

to scare somebody faire peur à quelqu'un ◇ *He scares me.* Il me fait peur.

scarecrow NOUN

l' *épouvantail* MASC

scared ADJECTIVE

to be scared avoir peur ◇ *I was scared stiff.* J'avais terriblement peur.

to be scared of avoir peur de ◇ *Are you scared of him?* Est-ce que tu as peur de lui?

scarf NOUN

1 l' *écharpe* FEM (*long*)

2 le *foulard* (*square*)

scary ADJECTIVE

effrayant ◇ *It was really scary.* C'était vraiment effrayant.

scene NOUN

1 les *lieux* MASC PL (*place*) ◇ *The police were soon on the scene.* La police est vite arrivée sur les lieux. ◇ *the scene of the crime* les lieux du crime

2 le *spectacle* (*event, sight*) ◇ *It was an amazing scene.* C'était un spectacle étonnant.

→ **to make a scene** faire une scène

scenery NOUN

le *paysage* (*landscape*)

scent NOUN

le *parfum* (*perfume*)

schedule NOUN

le *programme* ◇ *a busy schedule* un programme chargé

→ **on schedule** comme prévu

→ **to be behind schedule** avoir du retard

scheduled flight NOUN

le *vol régulier*

scheme NOUN

1 le *truc* (*idea*) ◇ *a crazy scheme he dreamed up* un truc farfelu qu'il a inventé

2 le *projet* (*project*) ◇ *a council road-widening scheme* un projet municipal d'élargissement des routes

scholarship NOUN

la *bourse*

school NOUN

l' *école* FEM

→ **to go to school** aller à l'école

schoolbook NOUN

le *livre scolaire*

schoolboy NOUN

l' *écolier* MASC

schoolchildren NOUN

les *écoliers* MASC PL

schoolgirl NOUN

l' *écolière* FEM

science NOUN

la *science*

science fiction NOUN

la *science-fiction*

scientific ADJECTIVE

scientifique

scientist NOUN

(*doing research*)

le *chercheur*

la *chercheuse*

◇ *She's a scientist.* Elle est chercheuse.

→ **He trained as a scientist.** Il a une formation scientifique.

scissors PL NOUN

les *ciseaux* MASC PL ◇ *a pair of scissors* une paire de ciseaux

to **scoff** VERB

bouffer (*eat*) ◇ *My brother scoffed all*

PTO

the sandwiches. Mon frère a bouffé tous les sandwichs.

scooter NOUN
1 le *scooter*
2 la *trottinette* (*child's toy*)

score NOUN
see also score VERB
le *score* ◇ *The score was three nil.* Le score était trois à zéro.

to **score** VERB
see also score NOUN
1 *marquer* (*goal, point*) ◇ *to score a goal* marquer un but
◆ **to score 6 out of 10** obtenir un score de six sur dix
2 *compter les points* (*keep score*) ◇ *Who's going to score?* Qui va compter les points?

Scorpio NOUN
le *Scorpion* ◇ *I'm Scorpio.* Je suis Scorpion.

Scot NOUN
l' *Écossais* MASC
l' *Écossaise* FEM

Scotland NOUN
l' *Écosse* FEM
◆ **in Scotland** en Écosse
◆ **to Scotland** en Écosse
◆ **I'm from Scotland.** Je suis écossais.

Scots ADJECTIVE
écossais ◇ *a Scots accent* un accent écossais

Scotsman NOUN
l' *Écossais* MASC

Scotswoman NOUN
l' *Écossaise* FEM

Scottish ADJECTIVE
écossais ◇ *a Scottish accent* un accent écossais

scout NOUN
le *scout* ◇ *I'm in the Scouts.* Je suis scout.

scrambled eggs PL NOUN
les *œufs brouillés* MASC PL

scrap NOUN
see also scrap VERB
1 le *bout* ◇ *a scrap of paper* un bout de papier
2 la *bagarre* (*fight*)
◆ **scrap iron** la ferraille

to **scrap** VERB
see also scrap NOUN
abandonner (*plan, idea*) ◇ *In the end the plan was scrapped.* Finalement le projet a été abandonné.

scrapbook NOUN
l' *album* MASC

to **scratch** VERB
see also scratch NOUN
se gratter ◇ *Stop scratching!* Arrête de te gratter!

scratch NOUN
see also scratch VERB
l' *égratignure* FEM (*on skin*)
◆ **to start from scratch** partir de zéro

scream NOUN
see also scream VERB
le *hurlement*

to **scream** VERB
see also scream NOUN
hurler

screen NOUN
l' *écran* MASC

screwdriver NOUN
le *tournevis*

to **scribble** VERB
griffonner

to **scrub** VERB
récurer ◇ *to scrub a pan* récurer une casserole

sculpture NOUN
la *sculpture*

sea NOUN
la *mer*

seafood NOUN
les *fruits de mer* MASC PL ◇ *I don't like seafood.* Je n'aime pas les fruits de mer.

seagull NOUN
la *mouette*

seal NOUN
see also seal VERB
1 le *phoque* (*animal*)
2 le *cachet* (*on letter*)

to **seal** VERB
see also seal NOUN
1 *sceller* (*document*)
2 *coller* (*letter*)

seaman NOUN
le *marin*

to **search** VERB
see also search NOUN
fouiller ◇ *They searched the woods for her.* Ils ont fouillé les bois pour la trouver.
◆ **to search for something** chercher quelque chose ◇ *He searched for evidence.* Il cherchait des preuves.

search NOUN
see also search VERB
la *fouille*

search party NOUN
l' *expédition de secours* FEM

seashore NOUN
le *bord de la mer* ◇ *on the seashore* au bord de la mer

seasick ADJECTIVE
◆ **to be seasick** avoir le mal de mer

seaside NOUN

le *bord de la mer* ◇ *at the seaside* au bord de la mer

season NOUN
la *saison* ◇ *What's your favourite season?* Quelle est ta saison préférée?
out of season hors saison ◇ *It's cheaper to go there out of season.* C'est moins cher d'y aller hors saison.
during the holiday season en période de vacances
a season ticket une carte d'abonnement

seat NOUN
le *siège*

seat belt NOUN
la *ceinture de sécurité*

sea water NOUN
l' *eau de mer* FEM

seaweed NOUN
les *algues* FEM PL

second ADJECTIVE
see also second NOUN
deuxième ◇ *on the second page* à la deuxième page
to come second (*in race*) arriver deuxième
to travel second class voyager en seconde
the second of March le deux mars

second NOUN
see also second ADJECTIVE
la *seconde* ◇ *It'll only take a second.* Ça va prendre juste une seconde.

secondary school NOUN
1 le *collège*
2 le *lycée*
In France pupils go to a collège *between the ages of 11 and 15, and then to a* lycée *until the age of 18.*

second-class ADJECTIVE, ADVERB
1 *de seconde classe* (*ticket, compartment*)
to travel second-class voyager en seconde
2 *à tarif réduit* (*stamp, letter*) ◇ *to send something second-class* envoyer quelque chose à tarif réduit

secondhand ADJECTIVE
d'occasion ◇ *a secondhand car* une voiture d'occasion

secondly ADVERB
deuxièmement
firstly...secondly... d'abord...ensuite... ◇ *Firstly, it's too expensive. Secondly, it wouldn't work anyway.* D'abord, c'est trop cher. Ensuite, ça ne marcherait quand même pas.

secret ADJECTIVE
see also secret NOUN
secret MASC
secrète FEM
◇ *a secret mission* une mission secrète

secret NOUN
see also secret ADJECTIVE
le *secret* ◇ *It's a secret.* C'est un secret. ◇ *Can you keep a secret?* Tu sais garder un secret?
in secret en secret

secretary NOUN
le/la *secrétaire* ◇ *She's a secretary.* Elle est secrétaire.

secretly NOUN
secrètement

section NOUN
la *section*

security guard NOUN
le *vigile* ◇ *She's a security guard.* Elle est vigile.

to **see** VERB
voir ◇ *I can't see.* Je n'y vois rien. ◇ *I saw him yesterday.* Je l'ai vu hier. ◇ *Have you seen him?* Est-ce que tu l'as vu?
See you! Salut!
See you soon! À bientôt!
to see to something s'occuper de quelque chose ◇ *The window's stuck again. Can you see to it please?* La fenêtre est encore coincée. Tu peux t'en occuper s'il te plaît?

seed NOUN
la *graine* ◇ *sunflower seeds* des graines de tournesol

to **seem** VERB
avoir l'air ◇ *She seems tired.* Elle a l'air fatiguée. ◇ *The shop seemed to be closed.* Le magasin avait l'air d'être fermé.
That seems like a good idea. Ce n'est pas une mauvaise idée.
It seems that... Il paraît que... ◇ *It seems she's getting married.* Il paraît qu'elle va se marier.
There seems to be a problem. Il semble y avoir un problème.

seen VERB *see* **see**

seesaw NOUN
le *tapecul*

see-through ADJECTIVE
transparent

to **select** VERB
sélectionner

selection NOUN
la *sélection*

self-assured ADJECTIVE
sûr de soi ◇ *He's very self-assured.* Il est très sûr de lui.

self-catering ADJECTIVE
a self-catering apartment un

S

PTO

appartement de vacances

self-centred ADJECTIVE
égocentrique

self-confidence NOUN
la *confiance en soi* ◇ *He hasn't got much self-confidence.* Il n'a pas très confiance en lui.

self-conscious ADJECTIVE
- **to be self-conscious (1)** (*embarrassed*) être mal à l'aise ◇ *She was really self-conscious at first.* Elle était vraiment mal à l'aise au début.
- **to be self-conscious (2)** (*shy*) manquer d'assurance ◇ *He's always been rather self-conscious.* Il a toujours manqué un peu d'assurance.

self-contained ADJECTIVE
- **a self-contained flat** un appartement indépendant

self-control NOUN
le *sang-froid*

self-defence NOUN
l' *autodéfense* FEM ◇ *self-defence classes* les cours d'autodéfense
- **She killed him in self-defence.** Elle l'a tué en légitime défense.

self-discipline NOUN
l' *autodiscipline* FEM

self-employed ADJECTIVE
- **to be self-employed** travailler à son compte ◇ *He's self-employed.* Il travaille à son compte.
- **the self-employed** les travailleurs indépendants

selfish ADJECTIVE
égoïste ◇ *Don't be so selfish.* Ne sois pas si égoïste.

self-respect NOUN
l' *amour-propre* MASC

self-service ADJECTIVE
- **It's self-service.** (*café, shop*) C'est un self-service.
- **a self-service restaurant** un restaurant self-service

to **sell** VERB
vendre ◇ *He sold it to me.* Il me l'a vendu.
- **to sell off** liquider
- **The tickets are all sold out.** Il ne reste plus de billets.
- **The tickets sold out in three hours.** Tous les billets ont été vendus en trois heures.

sell-by date NOUN
la *date limite de vente*

selling price NOUN
le *prix de vente*

Sellotape ® NOUN
le *scotch* ®

semi NOUN
la *maison jumelée* ◇ *We live in a semi* Nous habitons dans une maison jumelée.

semicircle NOUN
le *demi-cercle*

semicolon NOUN
le *point-virgule*

semi-detached house NOUN
la *maison jumelée* ◇ *We live in a semi-detached house.* Nous habitons dans une maison jumelée.

semi-final NOUN
la *demi-finale*

semi-skimmed milk NOUN
le *lait demi-écrémé*

to **send** VERB
envoyer ◇ *She sent me a birthday card.* Elle m'a envoyé une carte d'anniversaire
- **to send back** renvoyer
- **to send off (1)** (*goods, letter*) envoyer
- **to send off (2)** (*in sports match*) renvoyer du terrain ◇ *He was sent off.* On l'a renvoyé du terrain.
- **to send off for something (1)** (*free*) se faire envoyer quelque chose ◇ *I've sent off for a brochure.* Je me suis fait envoyer une brochure.
- **to send off for something (2)** (*paid for*) commander quelque chose par correspondance ◇ *She sent off for a book.* Elle a commandé un livre par correspondance.
- **to send out** envoyer

sender NOUN
l' *expéditeur* MASC
l' *expéditrice* FEM

senior ADJECTIVE
haut placé
- **senior management** les cadres supérieurs
- **senior school** le lycée
- **senior pupils** les grandes classes

senior citizen NOUN
la *personne du troisième âge* (les *personnes du troisième âge* PL)

sensational ADJECTIVE
sensationnel MASC
sensationnelle FEM

sense NOUN
1 le *bon sens* (*wisdom*) ◇ *Use your common sense!* Un peu de bon sens, voyons!
- **It makes sense.** C'est logique.
- **It doesn't make sense.** Ça n'a pas de sens.

2 le *sens* (*faculty*) ◇ *the five senses* les cinq sens
- **the sense of touch** le toucher

the sense of smell l'odorat MASC
the sixth sense le sixième sens
sense of humour le sens de l'humour
◇ *He's got no sense of humour.* Il n'a aucun sens de l'humour.

senseless ADJECTIVE
insensé

sensible ADJECTIVE
raisonnable ◇ *Be sensible!* Sois raisonnable!
It would be sensible to check first. Il serait sage de vérifier d'abord.

sensitive ADJECTIVE
sensible ◇ *She's very sensitive.* Elle est très sensible.

sensuous ADJECTIVE
sensuel MASC
sensuelle FEM

sent VERB *see* **send**

sentence NOUN
see also sentence VERB
1 la *phrase* ◇ *What does this sentence mean?* Que veut dire cette phrase?
2 la *condamnation* (*judgment*)
3 la *peine* (*punishment*) ◇ *the death sentence* la peine de mort
He got a life sentence. Il a été condamné à la réclusion à perpétuité.

sentence VERB
see also sentence NOUN
to sentence somebody to life imprisonment condamner quelqu'un à la réclusion à perpétuité
to sentence somebody to death condamner quelqu'un à mort

sentimental ADJECTIVE
sentimental
(*sentimentaux* MASC PL)

separate ADJECTIVE
see also separate VERB
séparé ◇ *I wrote it on a separate sheet.* Je l'ai écrit sur une feuille séparée.
The children have separate rooms. Les enfants ont chacun leur chambre.
on separate occasions à différentes reprises

separate VERB
see also separate ADJECTIVE
1 *séparer*
2 *se séparer* (*married couple*)

separately ADVERB
séparément

separation NOUN
la *séparation*

September NOUN
septembre MASC
in September en septembre

sequel NOUN
la *suite* (*book, film*)

sequence NOUN
1 l' *ordre* MASC
◆ **in sequence** par ordre
◆ **a sequence of events** une succession d'événements
2 la *séquence* (*in film*)

sergeant NOUN
1 le *sergent* (*army*)
2 le *brigadier* (*police*)

serial NOUN
le *feuilleton*

series NOUN
1 la *série* ◇ *a TV series* une série télévisée
2 la *suite* (*of numbers*)

serious ADJECTIVE
1 *sérieux* MASC
sérieuse FEM
◇ *You look very serious.* Tu as l'air sérieux.
◆ **Are you serious?** Sérieusement?
2 *grave* (*illness, mistake*)

seriously ADVERB
sérieusement ◇ *No, but seriously...* Non, mais sérieusement...
◆ **to take somebody seriously** prendre quelqu'un au sérieux
◆ **seriously injured** gravement blessé
◆ **Seriously?** Vraiment?

sermon NOUN
le *sermon*

servant NOUN
le/la *domestique*

to **serve** VERB
see also serve NOUN
1 *servir* ◇ *Dinner is served.* Le dîner est servi. ◇ *It's Agassi's turn to serve.* C'est à Agassi de servir.
2 *purger* (*prison sentence*)
◆ **to serve time** être en prison
◆ **It serves you right.** C'est bien fait pour toi.

serve NOUN
see also serve VERB
le *service* (*tennis*)
◆ **It's your serve.** C'est à toi de servir.

to **service** VERB
see also service NOUN
réviser (*car, washing machine*)

service NOUN
see also service VERB
1 le *service* ◇ *Service is included.* Le service est compris.
2 la *révision* (*of car*)
3 l' *office* MASC (*church service*)
◆ **the Fire Service** les sapeurs-pompiers
◆ **the armed services** les forces armées

service area NOUN
l' *aire de service* FEM

service charge NOUN
le *service* ◇ *There's no service charge.* Le service est compris.
serviceman NOUN
le *militaire* ◇ *He's a serviceman.* Il est militaire.
service station NOUN
la *station-service*
(les *stations-service* PL)
serviette NOUN
la *serviette*
session NOUN
la *séance*
set NOUN
see also **set** VERB
1 le *jeu*
(les *jeux* PL)
◇ *a set of keys* un jeu de clés ◇ *a chess set* un jeu d'échecs
◆ **a train set** un train électrique
2 le *set* (*in tennis*)
to **set** VERB
see also **set** NOUN
1 *mettre à sonner* (*alarm clock*) ◇ *I set the alarm for 7 o'clock.* J'ai mis le réveil à sept heures.
2 *établir* (*record*) ◇ *The world record was set last year.* Le record du monde a été établi l'année dernière.
3 *se coucher* (*sun*) ◇ *The sun was setting.* Le soleil se couchait.
◆ **The film is set in Morocco.** L'action du film se déroule au Maroc.
◆ **to set off** partir ◇ *We set off for London at 9 o'clock.* Nous sommes partis pour Londres à neuf heures.
◆ **to set out** partir ◇ *We set out for London at 9 o'clock.* Nous sommes partis pour Londres à neuf heures.
◆ **to set sail** prendre la mer
◆ **to set the table** mettre le couvert
settee NOUN
le *canapé*
to **settle** VERB
1 *résoudre* (*problem*)
2 *régler* (*argument, account*)
◆ **to settle down** (*calm down*) se calmer
◆ **Settle down!** Du calme!
◆ **to settle in** s'installer
◆ **to settle on something** opter pour quelque chose
seven NUMBER
sept ◇ *She's seven.* Elle a sept ans.
seventeen NUMBER
dix-sept ◇ *He's seventeen.* Il a dix-sept ans.
seventh ADJECTIVE
septième ◇ *the seventh floor* le septième étage
◆ **the seventh of August** le sept août
seventy NUMBER
soixante-dix
several ADJECTIVE, PRONOUN
plusieurs ◇ *several schools* plusieurs écoles
◆ **several of them** plusieurs ◇ *I've seen several of them.* J'en ai vu plusieurs.
to **sew** VERB
coudre
◆ **to sew up** (*tear*) recoudre
sewing NOUN
la *couture* ◇ *I like sewing.* J'aime faire de la couture.
◆ **a sewing machine** une machine à coudre
sewn VERB *see* **sew**
sex NOUN
le *sexe*
◆ **to have sex with somebody** coucher avec quelqu'un
◆ **sex education** l'éducation sexuelle FEM
sexism NOUN
le *sexisme*
sexist ADJECTIVE
sexiste
sexual ADJECTIVE
sexuel MASC
sexuelle FEM
◇ *sexual discrimination* la discrimination sexuelle ◇ *sexual harassment* le harcèlement sexuel
sexuality NOUN
la *sexualité*
sexy ADJECTIVE
sexy MASC, FEM, PL
shabby ADJECTIVE
miteux MASC
miteuse FEM
shade NOUN
1 l' *ombre* FEM
◆ **in the shade** à l'ombre ◇ *It was 35 degrees in the shade.* Il faisait trente-cinq à l'ombre.
2 la *nuance* (*colour*) ◇ *a shade of blue* une nuance de bleu
shadow NOUN
l' *ombre* FEM
to **shake** VERB
1 *secouer* ◇ *She shook the rug.* Elle a secoué le tapis.
2 *trembler* (*tremble*) ◇ *He was shaking with cold.* Il tremblait de froid.
◆ **to shake one's head** (*in refusal*) faire non de la tête
◆ **to shake hands with somebody** serrer la main à quelqu'un ◇ *They shook hands.* Ils se sont serré la main.
shaken ADJECTIVE

secoué ◇ *I was feeling a bit shaken.* J'étais un peu secoué.

haky ADJECTIVE
tremblant (*hand, voice*)

hall VERB
Shall I shut the window? Vous voulez que je ferme la fenêtre?
Shall we ask him to come with us? Si on lui demandait de venir avec nous?

hallow ADJECTIVE
peu profond (*water, pool*)

hambles NOUN
la *pagaille* ◇ *It's a complete shambles.* C'est la pagaille complète.

hame NOUN
la *honte* ◇ *The shame of it!* Quelle honte!
What a shame! Quel dommage!
It's a shame that... c'est dommage que...
c'est dommage que *has to be followed by a verb in the subjunctive.*
◇ *It's a shame he isn't here.* C'est dommage qu'il ne soit pas ici.

hampoo NOUN
le *shampooing* ◇ *a bottle of shampoo* une bouteille de shampooing

handy NOUN
le *panaché*

han't = **shall not**

hape NOUN
la *forme*

hare NOUN
see also share VERB
1 l' *action* FEM (*in company*) ◇ *They've got shares in British Gas.* Ils ont des actions de British Gas.
2 *la part* ◇ *Everybody pays their share.* Tout le monde paie sa part.

hare VERB
see also share NOUN
partager ◇ *to share a room with somebody* partager une chambre avec quelqu'un
to share out distribuer ◇ *They shared the sweets out among the children.* Ils ont distribué les bonbons aux enfants.

hark NOUN
le *requin*

harp ADJECTIVE
1 *tranchant* (*razor, knife*)
2 *pointu* (*spike, point*)
3 *intelligent* (*clever*) ◇ *She's very sharp.* Elle est très intelligente.
at two o'clock sharp à deux heures pile

have VERB
se raser (*have a shave*)
to shave one's legs se raser les jambes

haver NOUN
an electric shaver un rasoir électrique

shaving cream NOUN
la *crème à raser*

shaving foam NOUN
la *mousse à raser*

she PRONOUN
elle ◇ *She's very nice.* Elle est très gentille.

shed NOUN
la *remise*

she'd = **she had, she would**

sheep NOUN
le *mouton*

sheepdog NOUN
le *chien de berger*
(les *chiens de berger* PL)

sheer ADJECTIVE
pur ◇ *It's sheer greed.* C'est de l'avidité pure.

sheet NOUN
le *drap* (*on bed*)
◆ **a sheet of paper** une feuille de papier

shelf NOUN
1 l' *étagère* FEM (*in house*)
2 le *rayon* (*in shop*)

shell NOUN
1 le *coquillage* (*on beach*)
2 la *coquille* (*of egg, nut*)
3 l' *obus* MASC (*explosive*)

she'll = **she will**

shellfish NOUN
les *fruits de mer* MASC PL

shell suit NOUN
le *survêtement*

shelter NOUN
◆ **to take shelter** se mettre à l'abri
◆ **a bus shelter** un arrêt d'autobus

shelves PL NOUN *see* **shelf**

shepherd NOUN
le *berger*

sheriff NOUN
le *shérif*

sherry NOUN
le *xérès*

she's = **she is, she has**

Shetland Islands NOUN
les *îles Shetland* FEM PL

shield NOUN
le *bouclier*

shift NOUN
see also shift VERB
le *service* ◇ *His shift starts at 8 o'clock.* Il prend son service à huit heures. ◇ *the night shift* le service de nuit
◆ **to do shift work** faire les trois-huit

to **shift** VERB
see also shift NOUN
déplacer (*move*) ◇ *I couldn't shift the wardrobe on my own.* Je n'ai pas pu déplacer l'armoire tout seul.

PTO

- **Shift yourself!** Pousse-toi de là! (*informal*)

shifty ADJECTIVE
1 *louche* (*person*) ◇ *He looked shifty.* Il avait l'air louche.
2 *fuyant* (*eyes*)

shin NOUN
le *tibia*

to **shine** VERB
briller ◇ *The sun was shining.* Le soleil brillait.

shiny ADJECTIVE
brillant

ship NOUN
1 le *bateau* (les *bateaux* PL)
2 le *navire* (*warship*)

shipbuilding NOUN
la *construction navale*

shipwreck NOUN
le *naufrage*

shipwrecked ADJECTIVE
- **to be shipwrecked** faire naufrage

shipyard NOUN
le *chantier naval*

shirt NOUN
1 la *chemise* (*man's*)
2 le *chemisier* (*woman's*)

shit EXCLAMATION
Merde! (*rude*)

to **shiver** VERB
frissonner

shock NOUN
le *choc*
- **to get a shock (1)** (*surprise*) avoir un choc
- **to get a shock (2)** (*electric*) recevoir une décharge
- **an electric shock** une décharge

shocked ADJECTIVE
choqué ◇ *He'll be shocked if you say that.* Tu vas le choquer si tu dis ça.

shocking ADJECTIVE
choquant ◇ *It's shocking!* C'est choquant!
- **a shocking waste** un gaspillage épouvantable

shoe NOUN
la *chaussure*

shoelace NOUN
le *lacet*

shoe polish NOUN
le *cirage*

shoe shop NOUN
le *magasin de chaussures*

shone VERB *see* **shine**

shook VERB *see* **shake**

to **shoot** VERB
1 *abattre* (*kill*) ◇ *He was shot by a sniper.* Il a été abattu par un franc-tireur.
2 *fusiller* (*execute*) ◇ *He was shot at dawn.* Il a été fusillé à l'aube.
3 *tirer* (*gun*) ◇ *Don't shoot!* Ne tirez pas!
- **to shoot at somebody** tirer sur quelqu'un
- **He shot himself with a revolver.** (*dead*) Il s'est suicidé d'un coup de revolver.
- **He was shot in the leg.** (*wounded*) Il a reçu une balle dans la jambe.
- **to shoot an arrow** envoyer une flèche
4 *tourner* (*film*) ◇ *The film was shot in Prague.* Le film a été tourné à Prague.
5 *shooter* (*in football*)

shooting NOUN
1 les *coups de feu* MASC PL ◇ *They heard shooting.* Ils ont entendu des coups de feu.
- **a shooting** une fusillade
2 la *chasse* (*hunting*) ◇ *to go shooting* aller à la chasse

shop NOUN
le *magasin* ◇ *a sports shop* un magasin de sports

shop assistant NOUN
le *vendeur*
la *vendeuse*
◇ *She's a shop assistant.* Elle est vendeuse.

shopkeeper NOUN
le *commerçant*
la *commerçante*
◇ *He's a shopkeeper.* Il est commerçant

shoplifting NOUN
le *vol à l'étalage*

shopping NOUN
les *courses* FEM PL (*purchases*) ◇ *Can you get the shopping from the car?* Tu peux aller chercher les courses dans la voiture
- **I love shopping.** J'adore faire du shopping.
- **to go shopping (1)** (*for food*) faire des courses
- **to go shopping (2)** (*for pleasure*) faire du shopping
- **a shopping bag** un sac à provisions
- **a shopping centre** un centre commercial

shop window NOUN
la *vitrine*

shore NOUN
le *rivage*
- **on shore** à terre

short ADJECTIVE
1 *court* ◇ *a short skirt* une jupe courte ◇ *short hair* les cheveux courts
- **too short** trop court ◇ *It was a great holiday, but too short.* C'étaient des vacances super, mais trop courtes.

2 *petit* (*person, period of time*) ◇ *She's quite short.* Elle est assez petite. ◇ *a short break* une petite pause ◇ *a short walk* une petite promenade

- **to be short of something** être à court de quelque chose ◇ *I'm short of money.* Je suis à court d'argent.
- **at short notice** au dernier moment
- **In short, the answer's no.** Bref, la réponse est non.

shortage NOUN
la *pénurie* ◇ *a water shortage* une pénurie d'eau

short cut NOUN
le *raccourci* ◇ *I took a short cut.* J'ai pris un raccourci.

shorthand NOUN
la *sténo*

shortly ADVERB
bientôt

shorts PL NOUN
le *short* SING

- **a pair of shorts** un short

short-sighted ADJECTIVE
myope

short story NOUN
la *nouvelle*

shot VERB *see* **shoot**

shot NOUN
1 (*gunshot*)
le *coup de feu*
(les *coups de feu* PL)
2 (*photo*)
la *photo* ◇ *a shot of Edinburgh Castle* une photo du château d'Édimbourg
3 (*vaccination*)
le *vaccin*

shotgun NOUN
le *fusil de chasse*
(les *fusils de chasse* PL)

should VERB
When should *means "ought to", use* **devoir**.
devoir ◇ *You should take more exercise.* Vous devriez faire plus d'exercice. ◇ *He should be there by now.* Il devrait être arrivé maintenant. ◇ *That shouldn't be too hard.* Ça ne devrait pas être trop difficile.

- **should have** avoir dû ◇ *I should have told you before.* J'aurais dû te le dire avant.

When should *means "would", use the conditional tense.*

- **I should go if I were you.** Si j'étais vous, j'irais.
- **I should be so lucky!** Ça serait trop beau!

shoulder NOUN
l' *épaule* FEM

- **a shoulder bag** un sac à bandoulière

shouldn't = **should not**

to **shout** VERB
see also shout NOUN
crier ◇ *Don't shout!* Ne criez pas! ◇ *"Go away!" he shouted.* "Allez-vous-en!" a-t-il crié.

shout NOUN
see also shout VERB
le *cri*

shovel NOUN
la *pelle*

show NOUN
see also show VERB
1 le *spectacle* (*performance*)
2 l' *émission* FEM (*programme*)
3 le *salon* (*exhibition*)

to **show** VERB
see also show NOUN
1 *montrer*

- **to show somebody something** montrer quelque chose à quelqu'un ◇ *Have I shown you my new trainers?* Je t'ai montré mes nouvelles baskets?

2 *faire preuve de* ◇ *She showed great courage.* Elle a fait preuve de beaucoup de courage.

- **It shows.** Ça se voit. ◇ *I've never been riding before.–It shows.* Je n'ai jamais fait de cheval.–Ça se voit.
- **to show off** frimer (*informal*)
- **to show up** (*turn up*) se pointer ◇ *He showed up late as usual.* Il s'est pointé en retard comme d'habitude.

shower NOUN
1 la *douche*

- **to have a shower** prendre une douche

2 l' *averse* FEM (*of rain*)

showerproof ADJECTIVE
imperméabilisé

showing NOUN
la *projection* (*of film*)

shown VERB *see* **show**

show-off NOUN
le *frimeur*
la *frimeuse*

shrank VERB *see* **shrink**

to **shriek** VERB
hurler

shrimps PL NOUN
les *crevettes* FEM PL

to **shrink** VERB
rétrécir (*clothes, fabric*)

Shrove Tuesday NOUN
le *mardi gras*

to **shrug** VERB

- **to shrug one's shoulders** hausser les épaules

shrunk VERB *see* **shrink**

S

to **shudder** VERB
frissonner

to **shuffle** VERB
- **to shuffle the cards** battre les cartes

to **shut** VERB
fermer ◇ *What time do you shut?* À quelle heure est-ce que vous fermez? ◇ *What time do the shops shut?* À quelle heure est-ce que les magasins ferment?
- **to shut down** fermer ◇ *The cinema shut down last year.* Le cinéma a fermé l'année dernière.
- **to shut up (1)** (*close*) fermer
- **to shut up (2)** (*be quiet*) se taire ◇ *Shut up!* Tais-toi!

shutters NOUN
les *volets* MASC PL

shuttle NOUN
la *navette*

shuttlecock NOUN
le *volant* (*badminton*)

shy ADJECTIVE
timide

Sicily NOUN
la *Sicile*
- **in Sicily** en Sicile
- **to Sicily** en Sicile

sick ADJECTIVE
1 *malade* (*ill*) ◇ *He was sick for four days.* Il a été malade pendant quatre jours.
2 *de mauvais goût* (*joke, humour*) ◇ *That's really sick!* C'est vraiment de mauvais goût!
- **to be sick** (*vomit*) vomir ◇ *I feel sick.* J'ai envie de vomir.
- **to be sick of something** en avoir assez de quelque chose ◇ *I'm sick of your jokes.* J'en ai assez de tes plaisanteries.

sickening ADJECTIVE
écœurant

sick leave NOUN
le *congé de maladie*

sickness NOUN
la *maladie*

sick note NOUN
1 le *mot d'absence* (*from parents*)
2 le *certificat médical* (*from doctor*)

sick pay NOUN
l' *indemnité de maladie* FEM

side NOUN
1 le *côté* (*of object, building, car*) ◇ *He was driving on the wrong side of the road.* Il roulait du mauvais côté de la route.
2 le *bord* (*of pool, river, road*) ◇ *by the side of the lake* au bord du lac
3 le *flanc* (*of hill*)
4 l' *équipe* FEM (*team*)
- **He's on my side. (1)** (*on my team*) Il est dans mon équipe.
- **He's on my side. (2)** (*supporting me*) Il est de mon côté.
- **side by side** côte à côte
- **the side entrance** l'entrée latérale
- **to take sides** prendre parti ◇ *She always takes his side.* Elle prend toujours son parti.

sideboard NOUN
le *buffet*

side-effect NOUN
l' *effet secondaire* MASC

side street NOUN
la *petite rue transversale*

sideways ADVERB
1 *de côté* (*look, be facing*)
2 *de travers* (*move*)
- **sideways on** de profil

sieve NOUN
la *passoire*

sigh NOUN
see also sigh VERB
le *soupir*

to **sigh** VERB
see also sigh NOUN
soupirer

sight NOUN
1 la *vue* ◇ *to have poor sight* avoir une mauvaise vue
- **to know somebody by sight** connaître quelqu'un de vue

2 le *spectacle* ◇ *It was an amazing sight.* C'était un spectacle étonnant.
- **in sight** visible
- **out of sight** hors de vue
- **the sights** (*tourist spots*) les attractions touristiques
- **to see the sights of London** visiter Londres

sightseeing NOUN
le *tourisme*
- **to go sightseeing** faire du tourisme

sign NOUN
see also sign VERB
1 (*notice*)
le *panneau*
(les *panneaux* PL)
◇ *There was a big sign saying "private".* Il y avait un grand panneau indiquant "privé".
- **a road sign** un panneau

2 (*gesture, indication*)
le *signe* ◇ *There's no sign of improvement.* Il n'y a aucun signe d'amélioration.
- **What sign are you?** (*star sign*) Tu es de quel signe?

to **sign** VERB
see also sign NOUN

signer

- **to sign on (1)** (*as unemployed*) s'inscrire au chômage
- **to sign on (2)** (*for course*) s'inscrire

signal NOUN
see also signal VERB
le *signal*
(les *signaux* PL)

signal VERB
see also signal NOUN
- **to signal to somebody** faire un signe à quelqu'un

signalman NOUN
l' *aiguilleur* MASC

signature NOUN
la *signature*

significance NOUN
l' *importance* FEM

significant ADJECTIVE
important

sign language NOUN
le *langage par signes*

signpost NOUN
le *poteau indicateur*

silence NOUN
le *silence*

silent ADJECTIVE
silencieux MASC
silencieuse FEM

silicon chip NOUN
la *puce électronique*

silk NOUN
see also silk ADJECTIVE
la *soie*

silk ADJECTIVE
see also silk NOUN
en soie ◇ *a silk scarf* un foulard en soie

silky ADJECTIVE
soyeux MASC
soyeuse FEM

silly ADJECTIVE
bête

silver NOUN
l' *argent* MASC ◇ *a silver medal* une médaille d'argent

similar ADJECTIVE
semblable
- **similar to** semblable à

simple ADJECTIVE
1 *simple* ◇ *It's very simple.* C'est très simple.
2 (*simple-minded*)
simplet MASC
simplette FEM
◇ *He's a bit simple.* Il est un peu simplet.

simply ADVERB
simplement ◇ *It's simply not possible.* Ça n'est tout simplement pas possible.

simultaneous ADJECTIVE
simultané

sin NOUN
see also sin VERB
le *péché*

to **sin** VERB
see also sin NOUN
pécher

since PREPOSITION, ADVERB, CONJUNCTION
1 *depuis* ◇ *since Christmas* depuis Noël ◇ *since then* depuis ce moment-là ◇ *I haven't seen him since.* Je ne l'ai pas vu depuis.
- **ever since** depuis ce moment-là

2 *depuis que* ◇ *I haven't seen her since she left.* Je ne l'ai pas vue depuis qu'elle est partie.
3 *puisque* (*because*) ◇ *Since you're tired, let's stay at home.* Puisque tu es fatigué, restons à la maison.

sincere ADJECTIVE
sincère

sincerely ADVERB
- **Yours sincerely... (1)** (*in business letter*) Veuillez agréer l'expression de mes sentiments les meilleurs...
- **Yours sincerely... (2)** (*in personal letter*) Cordialement...

to **sing** VERB
chanter ◇ *He sang out of tune.* Il chantait faux. ◇ *Have you ever sung this tune before?* Vous avez déjà chanté cet air-là?

singer NOUN
le *chanteur*
la *chanteuse*

singing NOUN
le *chant*

single ADJECTIVE
see also single NOUN
célibataire (*unmarried*)
- **a single room** une chambre pour une personne
- **not a single thing** rien du tout

single NOUN
see also single ADJECTIVE
1 l' *aller simple* MASC (*ticket*) ◇ *A single to Toulouse, please.* Un aller simple pour Toulouse, s'il vous plaît.
2 le *45 tours* (*record*)
- **a CD single** un CD single

single parent NOUN
- **She's a single parent.** Elle élève ses enfants toute seule.
- **a single parent family** une famille monoparentale

singles PL NOUN
le *simple* SING (*in tennis*) ◇ *the women's singles* le simple dames

singular NOUN
le *singulier* ◇ *in the singular* au singulier

sinister ADJECTIVE
sinistre

sink NOUN
see also sink VERB
l' *évier* MASC

to **sink** VERB
see also sink NOUN
couler

sir NOUN
monsieur MASC
◆ **Yes sir.** Oui, Monsieur.

siren NOUN
la *sirène*

sister NOUN
1 la *sœur* ◇ *my little sister* ma petite sœur
2 l' *infirmière en chef* FEM (*nurse*)

sister-in-law NOUN
la *belle-sœur*
(les *belles-sœurs* PL)

to **sit** VERB
s'asseoir
◆ **to sit on something** s'asseoir sur quelque chose ◇ *She sat on the chair.* Elle s'est assise sur la chaise.
◆ **to sit down** s'asseoir
◆ **to be sitting** être assis
◆ **to sit an exam** passer un examen

sitcom NOUN
la *comédie de situation*
(les *comédies de situation* PL)

site NOUN
1 le *site* ◇ *an archaeological site* un site archéologique
◆ **the site of the accident** le lieu de l'accident
2 le *camping* (*campsite*)
◆ **a building site** un chantier

sitting room NOUN
le *salon*

situated ADJECTIVE
◆ **to be situated** être situé ◇ *The village is situated on the side of a hill.* Le village est situé sur le flanc d'une colline.

situation NOUN
la *situation*

six NUMBER
six ◇ *He's six.* Il a six ans.

sixteen NUMBER
seize ◇ *He's sixteen.* Il a seize ans.

sixth ADJECTIVE
sixième ◇ *the sixth floor* le sixième étage
◆ **the sixth of August** le six août

sixty NUMBER
soixante

size NOUN
France uses the European system to show clothing and shoe sizes.
1 la *taille* (*of object, clothing*) ◇ *What size do you take?* Quelle taille est-ce que vous faites?
◆ **I'm a size ten.** Je fais du trente-huit.
2 la *pointure* (*of shoes*)
◆ **I take size six.** Je fais du trente-neuf.

to **skate** VERB
1 *faire du patin à glace* (*ice-skate*)
2 *faire du patin à roulettes* (*roller-skate*)

skateboard NOUN
le *skateboard*

skateboarding NOUN
le *skateboard* ◇ *to go skateboarding* faire du skateboard

skates NOUN
les *patins* MASC PL

skating NOUN
le *patin à glace* ◇ *to go skating* faire du patin à glace
◆ **a skating rink** une patinoire

skeleton NOUN
le *squelette*

sketch NOUN
see also sketch VERB
le *croquis* (*drawing*)

to **sketch** VERB
see also sketch NOUN
◆ **to sketch something** faire un croquis de quelque chose

to **ski** VERB
see also ski NOUN
skier ◇ *Can you ski?* Tu sais skier?

ski NOUN
see also ski VERB
le *ski*
◆ **ski boots** les chaussures de ski FEM
◆ **a ski lift** un remonte-pente
◆ **ski pants** le fuseau SING
◆ **a ski pole** un bâton de ski
◆ **a ski slope** une piste de ski
◆ **a ski suit** une combinaison de ski

to **skid** VERB
déraper

skiing NOUN
le *ski* ◇ *to go skiing* faire du ski
◆ **to go on a skiing holiday** aller aux sports d'hiver

skilful ADJECTIVE
adroit

skilled ADJECTIVE
◆ **a skilled worker** un ouvrier spécialisé

skimmed milk NOUN
le *lait écrémé*

skimpy ADJECTIVE
1 *minuscule* (*clothes*)
2 *maigre* (*meal*)

skin NOUN
la *peau*
(les *peaux* PL)
- **skin cancer** le cancer de la peau

skinhead NOUN
le/la *skinhead*

skinny ADJECTIVE
maigre

skin-tight ADJECTIVE
collant

skip NOUN
see also skip VERB
la *benne* (*container*)

to **skip** VERB
see also skip NOUN
sauter ◇ *to skip a meal* sauter un repas
- **to skip a lesson** sécher un cours

skirt NOUN
la *jupe*

skittles NOUN
les *quilles* FEM PL ◇ *to play skittles* jouer aux quilles

to **skive** VERB
tirer au flanc (*be lazy*)
- **to skive off** sécher (*informal*) ◇ *to skive off school* sécher les cours

skull NOUN
le *crâne*

sky NOUN
le *ciel*

skyscraper NOUN
le *gratte-ciel*
(les *gratte-ciel* PL)

slack ADJECTIVE
1 *lâche* (*rope*)
2 *négligent* (*person*)

to **slag off** VERB
- **to slag somebody off** dire du mal de quelqu'un

to **slam** VERB
claquer ◇ *The door slammed.* La porte a claqué. ◇ *She slammed the door.* Elle a claqué la porte.

slang NOUN
l' *argot* MASC

slap NOUN
see also slap VERB
la *claque*

to **slap** VERB
see also slap NOUN
- **to slap somebody** donner une claque à quelqu'un

slate NOUN
l' *ardoise* FEM

sledge NOUN
la *luge*

sledging NOUN
- **to go sledging** faire de la luge

sleep NOUN
see also sleep VERB
le *sommeil*
- **I need some sleep.** J'ai besoin de dormir.
- **to go to sleep** s'endormir

to **sleep** VERB
see also sleep NOUN
dormir ◇ *I couldn't sleep last night.* J'ai mal dormi la nuit dernière.
- **to sleep with somebody** coucher avec quelqu'un
- **to sleep together** coucher ensemble

sleeping bag NOUN
le *sac de couchage*
(les *sacs de couchage* PL)

sleeping car NOUN
le *wagon-lit*
(les *wagons-lits* PL)

sleeping pill NOUN
le *somnifère*

sleepy ADJECTIVE
- **to feel sleepy** avoir sommeil ◇ *I was feeling sleepy.* J'avais sommeil.
- **a sleepy little village** un petit village tranquille

sleet NOUN
see also sleet VERB
la *neige fondue*

to **sleet** VERB
see also sleet NOUN
- **It's sleeting.** Il tombe de la neige fondue.

sleeve NOUN
1 la *manche* ◇ *long sleeves* les manches longues ◇ *short sleeves* les manches courtes
2 la *pochette* (*record sleeve*)

sleigh NOUN
le *traîneau*
(les *traîneaux* PL)

slept VERB *see* **sleep**

slice NOUN
see also slice VERB
la *tranche*

to **slice** VERB
see also slice NOUN
couper en tranches

slick NOUN
- **an oil slick** une marée noire

slide NOUN
see also slide VERB
1 le *toboggan* (*in playground*)
2 la *diapositive* (*photo*)
3 la *barrette* (*hair slide*)

to **slide** VERB
see also slide NOUN
glisser

slight ADJECTIVE
léger MASC

S

PTO

légère FEM
◇ *a slight problem* un léger problème
◇ *a slight improvement* une légère amélioration

slightly ADVERB
légèrement

slim ADJECTIVE
see also slim VERB
mince

to **slim** VERB
see also slim ADJECTIVE
faire un régime (*be on a diet*) ◇ *I'm slimming.* Je fais un régime.

sling NOUN
l' *écharpe* FEM ◇ *She had her arm in a sling.* Elle avait le bras en écharpe.

slip NOUN
see also slip VERB
1 l' *erreur* FEM (*mistake*)
2 le *jupon* (*underskirt*)
3 la *combinaison* (*full-length underskirt*)
◆ **a slip of paper** un bout de papier
◆ **a slip of the tongue** un lapsus

to **slip** VERB
see also slip NOUN
glisser ◇ *He slipped on the ice.* Il a glissé sur le verglas.
◆ **to slip up** faire une erreur (*make a mistake*)

slipper NOUN
le *chausson*
◆ **a pair of slippers** des chaussons

slippery ADJECTIVE
glissant

slip-up NOUN
l' *erreur* FEM

slope NOUN
la *pente*

sloppy ADJECTIVE
1 *bâclé* (*work*)
2 *négligé* (*person, appearance*)

slot NOUN
la *fente*

slot machine NOUN
1 la *machine à sous* (*for gambling*)
2 le *distributeur automatique* (*vending machine*)

slow ADJECTIVE, ADVERB
1 *lent* ◇ *He's a bit slow.* Il est un peu lent.
2 *lentement* ◇ *to go slow* (*person, car*) aller lentement ◇ *Drive slower!* Conduisez plus lentement!
◆ **My watch is slow.** Ma montre retarde.

to **slow down** VERB
ralentir

slowly ADVERB
lentement

slug NOUN
la *limace*

slush NOUN
la *neige fondue*

sly ADJECTIVE
rusé (*person*)
◆ **a sly smile** un sourire sournois

smack NOUN
see also smack VERB
la *tape*

to **smack** VERB
see also smack NOUN
◆ **to smack somebody** donner une tape à quelqu'un

small ADJECTIVE
petit
◆ **small change** la petite monnaie

smart ADJECTIVE
1 *chic* MASC, FEM, PL (*elegant*)
2 (*clever*) *intelligent*
◆ **a smart idea** une idée astucieuse

smash NOUN
see also smash VERB
l' *accident* MASC

to **smash** VERB
see also smash NOUN
1 *casser* (*break*) ◇ *I've smashed my watch.* J'ai cassé ma montre.
2 *se briser* (*get broken*) ◇ *The glass smashed into tiny pieces.* Le verre s'est brisé en mille morceaux.

smashing ADJECTIVE
formidable ◇ *I think he's smashing.* Je le trouve formidable.

smell NOUN
see also smell VERB
l' *odeur* FEM
◆ **the sense of smell** l'odorat MASC

to **smell** VERB
see also smell NOUN
1 *sentir mauvais* ◇ *That old dog really smells!* Qu'est-ce qu'il sent mauvais, ce vieux chien!
◆ **to smell of something** sentir quelque chose ◇ *It smells of petrol.* Ça sent l'essence.
2 *sentir* (*detect*) ◇ *I can't smell anything.* Je ne sens rien.

smelly ADJECTIVE
qui sent mauvais ◇ *He's got smelly feet.* Il a les pieds qui sentent mauvais.

smile NOUN
see also smile VERB
le *sourire*

to **smile** VERB
see also smile NOUN
sourire

smoke NOUN
see also smoke VERB

la *fumée*

smoke VERB
see also smoke NOUN
fumer ◇ *I don't smoke.* Je ne fume pas. ◇ *He smokes cigars.* Il fume le cigare.

smoker NOUN
le *fumeur*
la *fumeuse*

smoking NOUN
- **to give up smoking** arrêter de fumer
- **Smoking is bad for you.** Le tabac, est mauvais pour la santé.
- **"no smoking"** "défense de fumer"

smooth ADJECTIVE
1 (*surface*)
lisse
2 (*person*)
mielleux MASC
mielleuse FEM

smudge NOUN
la *bavure*

smug ADJECTIVE
suffisant

smuggle VERB
passer en contrebande

smuggler NOUN
le *contrebandier*
la *contrebandière*

smuggling NOUN
la *contrebande*

smutty ADJECTIVE
cochon MASC
cochonne FEM
◇ *a smutty story* une histoire cochonne

snack NOUN
l' *en-cas* MASC
(les *en-cas* PL)
- **to have a snack** prendre un en-cas

snack bar NOUN
le *snack-bar*

snail NOUN
l' *escargot* MASC

snake NOUN
le *serpent*

snap VERB
casser net (*break*) ◇ *The branch snapped.* La branche a cassé net.
- **to snap one's fingers** faire claquer ses doigts

snapshot NOUN
la *photo*

snarl VERB
gronder (*animal*)

snatch VERB
- **to snatch something from somebody** arracher quelque chose à quelqu'un ◇ *He snatched the keys from my hand.* Il m'a arraché les clés des mains.
- **My bag was snatched.** On m'a arraché mon sac.

to **sneak** VERB
- **to sneak in** entrer furtivement
- **to sneak out** sortir furtivement
- **to sneak up on somebody** s'approcher de quelqu'un sans faire de bruit

to **sneeze** VERB
éternuer

to **sniff** VERB
1 *renifler* ◇ *Stop sniffing!* Arrête de renifler!
2 *flairer* ◇ *The dog sniffed my hand.* Le chien m'a flairé la main.
- **to sniff glue** sniffer de la colle

snob NOUN
le/la *snob*

snooker NOUN
le *billard* ◇ *to play snooker* jouer au billard

snooze NOUN
le *petit somme* ◇ *to have a snooze* faire un petit somme

to **snore** VERB
ronfler

snow NOUN
see also snow VERB
la *neige*

to **snow** VERB
see also snow NOUN
neiger ◇ *It's snowing.* Il neige.

snowball NOUN
la *boule de neige*
(les *boules de neige* PL)

snowflake NOUN
le *flocon de neige*
(les *flocons de neige* PL)

snowman NOUN
le *bonhomme de neige*
(les *bonshommes de neige* PL)
◇ *to build a snowman* faire un bonhomme de neige

so CONJUNCTION, ADVERB
1 *alors* ◇ *The shop was closed, so I went home.* Le magasin était fermé, alors je suis rentré chez moi. ◇ *So, have you always lived in London?* Alors, vous avez toujours vécu à Londres?
- **So what?** Et alors?

2 *donc* (*so that*) ◇ *It rained, so I got wet.* Il pleuvait, donc j'ai été mouillé.
3 *tellement* (*very*) ◇ *It was so heavy!* C'était tellement lourd! ◇ *He was talking so fast I couldn't understand.* Il parlait tellement vite que je ne comprenais pas.
- **It's not so heavy!** Ça n'est pas si lourd que ça!
- **How's your father?–Not so good.** Comment va ton père?–Pas très bien.
- **so much** (*a lot*) tellement ◇ *I love you*

PTO

so much. Je t'aime tellement.

- **so much..., so many...** tellement de... ◇ *I've got so much work.* J'ai tellement de travail. ◇ *I've got so many things to do today.* J'ai tellement de choses à faire aujourd'hui.

4 *aussi* (*in comparisons*) ◇ *He's like his sister but not so clever.* Il est comme sa sœur mais pas aussi intelligent.

- **so do I** moi aussi ◇ *I love horses.–So do I.* J'aime les chevaux.–Moi aussi.
- **so have we** nous aussi ◇ *I've been to France twice.–So have we.* Je suis allé en France deux fois.–Nous aussi.
- **I think so.** Je crois.
- **I hope so.** J'espère bien.
- **That's not so.** Ça n'est pas le cas.
- **so far** jusqu'à présent ◇ *It's been easy so far.* Ça a été facile jusqu'à présent.
- **so far so good** jusqu'ici ça va
- **ten or so people** environ dix personnes
- **at five o'clock or so** à environ cinq heures

to **soak** VERB
tremper

soaked ADJECTIVE
trempé ◇ *By the time we got back we were soaked.* Nous sommes rentrés trempés.

soaking ADJECTIVE
trempé ◇ *By the time we got back we were soaking.* Nous sommes rentrés trempés.

- **soaking wet** trempé ◇ *Your shoes are soaking wet.* Tes chaussures sont trempées.

soap NOUN
le *savon*

soap opera NOUN
le *feuilleton à l'eau de rose*
(les *feuilletons à l'eau de rose* PL)

soap powder NOUN
la *lessive*

to **sob** VERB
sangloter ◇ *She was sobbing.* Elle sanglotait.

sober ADJECTIVE
sobre

to **sober up** VERB
dessoûler

soccer NOUN
le *football* ◇ *to play soccer* jouer au football

- **a soccer player** un joueur de football

social ADJECTIVE
social
(*sociaux* MASC PL)
◇ *a social class* une classe sociale

- **I have a good social life.** Je vois beaucoup de monde.

socialism NOUN
le *socialisme*

socialist ADJECTIVE
see also socialist NOUN
socialiste

socialist NOUN
see also socialist ADJECTIVE
le/la *socialiste*

social security NOUN
1 l' *aide sociale* FEM (*money*)

- **to be on social security** recevoir de l'aide sociale

2 la *sécurité sociale* (*organization*)

social worker NOUN
1 (*woman*)
l' *assistante sociale* FEM ◇ *She's a social worker.* Elle est assistante sociale.
2 (*man*)
le *travailleur social*
(les *travailleurs sociaux* PL)
◇ *He's a social worker.* Il est travailleur social.

society NOUN
1 la *société* ◇ *We live in a multi-cultural society.* Nous vivons dans une société multiculturelle.
2 le *club* ◇ *a drama society* un club de théâtre

sociology NOUN
la *sociologie*

sock NOUN
la *chaussette*

socket NOUN
la *prise de courant*
(les *prises de courant* PL)

soda NOUN
le *soda* (*soda water*)

sofa NOUN
le *canapé*

soft ADJECTIVE
1 (*fabric, texture*)
doux MASC
douce FEM
2 (*pillow, bed*)
mou MASC
molle FEM

- **soft cheeses** les fromages à pâte molle

3 (*hair*)
fin

- **to be soft on somebody** (*be kind to*) être indulgent avec quelqu'un
- **a soft drink** une boisson non alcoolisée
- **soft drugs** les drogues douces FEM
- **a soft option** une solution de facilité

software NOUN
le *logiciel*

soggy ADJECTIVE
1 (*soaked*)

trempé ◇ *a soggy tissue* un mouchoir trempé
2 (*not crisp*)
mou MASC
molle FEM
◇ *soggy chips* des frites molles

soil NOUN
la *terre*

solar power NOUN
l' *énergie solaire* FEM

sold VERB *see* **sell**

soldier NOUN
le *soldat* ◇ *He's a soldier.* Il est soldat.

solicitor NOUN
1 (*for lawsuits*)
l' *avocat* MASC
l' *avocate* FEM
◇ *He's a solicitor.* Il est avocat.
2 (*for wills, property*)
le *notaire* ◇ *She's a solicitor.* Elle est notaire.

solid ADJECTIVE
1 (*not hollow*)
massif MASC
massive FEM
◇ *solid gold* l'or massif
2 *solide* ◇ *a solid wall* un mur solide
◆ **for three hours solid** pendant trois heures entières

solo NOUN
le *solo* ◇ *a guitar solo* un solo de guitare

solution NOUN
la *solution*

solve VERB
résoudre

some ADJECTIVE, PRONOUN

When **some** *means "a certain amount of", use* **du**, **de la** *or* **des** *according to the gender of the French noun that follows it.* **du** *and* **de la** *become* **de l'** *when they are followed by a noun starting with a vowel.*

1 *du* ◇ *Would you like some bread?* Voulez-vous du pain?
de la ◇ *Would you like some beer?* Voulez-vous de la bière?
de l' ◇ *Have you got some mineral water?* Avez-vous de l'eau minérale?
des ◇ *I've got some Blur albums.* J'ai des albums de Blur.
◆ **Some people say that...** Il y a des gens qui disent que...
◆ **some day** un de ces jours
◆ **some day next week** un jour la semaine prochaine
2 *certains* (*some but not all*) ◇ *Are these mushrooms poisonous?–Only some.* Est-ce que ces champignons sont vénéneux?–Certains le sont.
◆ **some of them** quelques-uns ◇ *I only sold some of them.* J'en ai seulement vendu quelques-uns.
◆ **I only took some of it.** J'en ai seulement pris un peu.
◆ **I'm going to buy some stamps. Do you want some too?** Je vais acheter des timbres. Tu en veux aussi?
◆ **Would you like some coffee?–No thanks, I've got some.** Tu veux du café?–Non merci, j'en ai déjà.

somebody PRONOUN
quelqu'un ◇ *Somebody stole my bag.* Quelqu'un a volé mon sac.

somehow ADVERB
◆ **I'll do it somehow.** Je trouverai le moyen de le faire.
◆ **Somehow I don't think he believed me.** Quelque chose me dit qu'il ne m'a pas cru.

someone PRONOUN
quelqu'un ◇ *Someone stole my bag.* Quelqu'un a volé mon sac.

something PRONOUN
quelque chose ◇ *something special* quelque chose de spécial ◇ *Wear something warm.* Mets quelque chose de chaud. ◇ *That's really something!* C'est vraiment quelque chose! ◇ *It cost £100, or something like that.* Ça a coûté cent livres, ou quelque chose comme ça.
◆ **His name is Pierre or something.** Il s'appelle Pierre, ou quelque chose comme ça.

sometime ADVERB
un de ces jours ◇ *You must come and see us sometime.* Passez donc nous voir un de ces jours.
◆ **sometime last month** dans le courant du mois dernier

sometimes ADVERB
quelquefois ◇ *Sometimes I think she hates me.* Quelquefois j'ai l'impression qu'elle me déteste.

somewhere ADVERB
quelque part ◇ *I left my keys somewhere.* J'ai laissé mes clés quelque part. ◇ *I'd like to go on holiday, somewhere sunny.* J'aimerais aller en vacances, quelque part où il fait du soleil.

son NOUN
le *fils*

song NOUN
la *chanson*

son-in-law NOUN
le *gendre*

soon ADVERB
bientôt ◇ *very soon* très bientôt

- **soon afterwards** peu après
- **as soon as possible** aussitôt que possible

sooner ADVERB
plus tôt ◇ *Can't you come a bit sooner?* Tu ne peux pas venir un peu plus tôt?
- **sooner or later** tôt ou tard

soppy ADJECTIVE
sentimental
(*sentimentaux* MASC PL)

soprano NOUN (*singer*)
le/la *soprano*

sorcerer NOUN
le *sorcier*

sore ADJECTIVE
see also sore NOUN
- **My feet are sore.** J'ai mal aux pieds.
- **It's sore.** Ça fait mal.
- **That's a sore point.** C'est un point sensible.

sore NOUN
see also sore ADJECTIVE
la *plaie*

sorry ADJECTIVE
désolé ◇ *I'm really sorry.* Je suis vraiment désolé. ◇ *I'm sorry, I haven't got any change.* Je suis désolé, je n'ai pas de monnaie. ◇ *I'm sorry I'm late.* Je suis désolé d'être en retard.
- **Sorry!** Pardon!
- **Sorry?** Pardon?
- **I'm sorry about the noise.** Je m'excuse pour le bruit.
- **You'll be sorry!** Tu le regretteras!
- **to feel sorry for somebody** plaindre quelqu'un

sort NOUN
la *sorte* ◇ *What sort of bike have you got?* Quelle sorte de vélo as-tu?

to **sort out** VERB
1 *ranger* (*objects*)
2 *résoudre* (*problems*)

so-so ADVERB
comme ci comme ça ◇ *How are you feeling?–So-so.* Comment est-ce que tu te sens?–Comme ci comme ça.

soul NOUN
1 l' *âme* FEM (*spirit*)
2 la *soul* (*music*)

sound NOUN
see also sound VERB, ADJECTIVE
1 le *bruit* (*noise*) ◇ *Don't make a sound!* Pas un bruit! ◇ *the sound of footsteps* des bruits de pas
2 le *son* ◇ *Can I turn the sound down?* Je peux baisser le son?

to **sound** VERB
see also sound NOUN, ADJECTIVE
- **That sounds interesting.** Ça a l'air intéressant.
- **It sounds as if she's doing well at school.** Elle a l'air de bien travailler à l'école.
- **That sounds like a good idea.** C'est une bonne idée.

sound ADJECTIVE, ADVERB
see also sound NOUN, VERB
bon MASC
bonne FEM
◇ *That's sound advice.* C'est un bon conseil.
- **sound asleep** profondément endormi

soundtrack NOUN
la *bande sonore*

soup NOUN
la *soupe* ◇ *vegetable soup* la soupe aux légumes

sour ADJECTIVE
aigre

south ADJECTIVE, ADVERB
see also south NOUN
1 *sud* MASC, FEM, PL ◇ *the south coast* la côte sud
2 *vers le sud* ◇ *We were travelling south.* Nous allions vers le sud.
- **south of** au sud de ◇ *It's south of London.* C'est au sud de Londres.

south NOUN
see also south ADJECTIVE
le *sud* ◇ *in the south* dans le sud ◇ *the South of France* le sud de la France

South Africa NOUN
l' *Afrique du Sud* FEM
- **in South Africa** en Afrique du Sud
- **to South Africa** en Afrique du Sud

South America NOUN
l' *Amérique du Sud* FEM
- **in South America** en Amérique du Sud
- **to South America** en Amérique du Sud

southeast NOUN
le *sud-est* ◇ *southeast England* le sud-est de l'Angleterre

southern ADJECTIVE
- **the southern part of the island** la partie sud de l'île
- **Southern England** le sud de l'Angleterre

South Pole NOUN
le *pôle Sud*

South Wales NOUN
le *sud du Pays de Galles*

southwest NOUN
le *sud-ouest* ◇ *southwest France* le sud-ouest de la France

souvenir NOUN
le *souvenir*
- **a souvenir shop** une boutique de souvenirs

soya NOUN

le *soja*

soy sauce NOUN
la *sauce de soja*

space NOUN
1 la *place* ◇ *There isn't enough space.* Il n'y a pas suffisamment de place.
◆ **a parking space** une place de parking
2 l' *espace* MASC (*universe, gap*) ◇ *Leave a space after your answer.* Laissez un espace après votre réponse.

spacecraft NOUN
l' *engin spatial* MASC

spade NOUN
la *pelle*
◆ **spades** (*in cards*) le pique SING ◇ *the ace of spades* l'as de pique

Spain NOUN
l' *Espagne* FEM
◆ **in Spain** en Espagne
◆ **to Spain** en Espagne

Spaniard NOUN
l' *Espagnol* MASC
l' *Espagnole* FEM

spaniel NOUN
l' *épagneul* MASC

Spanish ADJECTIVE
see also Spanish NOUN
espagnol ◇ *She's Spanish.* Elle est espagnole.

Spanish NOUN
see also Spanish ADJECTIVE
l' *espagnol* MASC (*language*)
◆ **the Spanish** les Espagnols

to **spank** VERB
◆ **to spank somebody** donner une fessée à quelqu'un

spanner NOUN
la *clé anglaise*

spare ADJECTIVE
see also spare VERB, NOUN
de rechange ◇ *spare batteries* des piles de rechange ◇ *a spare part* une pièce de rechange
◆ **a spare room** une chambre d'amis
◆ **spare time** le temps libre ◇ *What do you do in your spare time?* Qu'est-ce que tu fais pendant ton temps libre?
◆ **spare wheel** une roue de secours

to **spare** VERB
see also spare ADJECTIVE, NOUN
◆ **Can you spare a moment?** Vous pouvez m'accorder un instant?
◆ **I can't spare the time.** Je n'ai pas le temps.
◆ **There's no room to spare.** Il n'y a plus de place.
◆ **We arrived with time to spare.** Nous sommes arrivés en avance.

spare NOUN
see also spare ADJECTIVE, VERB
◆ **a spare** un autre ◇ *I've lost my key.–Have you got a spare?* J'ai perdu ma clé.–Tu en as une autre?

sparkling ADJECTIVE
pétillant (*water*)
◆ **sparkling wine** le mousseux

sparrow NOUN
le *moineau*
(les *moineaux* PL)

spat VERB *see* **spit**

to **speak** VERB
parler ◇ *Do you speak English?* Est-ce que vous parlez anglais?
◆ **to speak to somebody** parler à quelqu'un ◇ *Have you spoken to him?* Tu lui as parlé? ◇ *She spoke to him about it.* Elle lui en a parlé.
◆ **spoken French** le français parlé

speaker NOUN
1 l' *enceinte* FEM (*loudspeaker*)
2 l' *intervenant* MASC (*in debate*)

special ADJECTIVE
spécial
(*spéciaux* MASC PL)

specialist NOUN
le/la *spécialiste*

speciality NOUN
la *spécialité*

to **specialize** VERB
se spécialiser ◇ *We specialize in skiing equipment.* Nous nous spécialisons dans les articles de ski.

specially ADVERB
1 *spécialement* ◇ *It's specially designed for teenagers.* C'est spécialement conçu pour les adolescents.
◆ **not specially** pas spécialement ◇ *Do you like opera?–Not specially.* Tu aimes l'opéra?–Pas spécialement.
2 *surtout* ◇ *It can be very cold here, specially in winter.* Il peut faire très froid ici, surtout en hiver.

species NOUN
l' *espèce* FEM

specific ADJECTIVE
1 (*particular*)
particulier MASC
particulière FEM
◇ *certain specific issues* certains problèmes particuliers
2 (*precise*)
précis ◇ *Could you be more specific?* Est-ce que vous pourriez être plus précis?

specifically ADVERB
1 *spécialement* ◇ *It's specifically designed for teenagers.* C'est spécialement conçu pour les adolescents.
2 *particulièrement* ◇ *in Britain, or*

PTO

more specifically in England en Grande-Bretagne, ou plus particulièrement en Angleterre
- **I specifically said that...** J'ai clairement dit que...

specs, spectacles PL NOUN
les *lunettes* FEM PL

spectacular ADJECTIVE
spectaculaire

spectator NOUN
le *spectateur*
la *spectatrice*

speech NOUN
le *discours* ◇ *to make a speech* faire un discours

speechless ADJECTIVE
muet MASC
muette FEM
◇ *speechless with admiration* muet d'admiration
- **I was speechless.** Je suis resté sans voix.

speed NOUN
la *vitesse* ◇ *a three-speed bike* un vélo à trois vitesses ◇ *at top speed* à toute vitesse

to **speed up** VERB
accélérer

speedboat NOUN
la *vedette*

speeding NOUN
l' *excès de vitesse* MASC ◇ *He was fined for speeding.* Il a reçu une contravention pour excès de vitesse.

speed limit NOUN
la *limitation de vitesse*
- **to break the speed limit** faire un excès de vitesse

speedometer NOUN
le *compteur*

to **spell** VERB
see also spell NOUN
1 *écrire* (*in writing*) ◇ *How do you spell that?* Comment est-ce que ça s'écrit?
2 *épeler* (*out loud*) ◇ *Can you spell that please?* Est-ce que vous pouvez épeler, s'il vous plaît?
- **I can't spell.** Je fais des fautes d'orthographe.

spell NOUN
see also spell VERB
- **to cast a spell on somebody** jeter un sort à quelqu'un
- **to be under somebody's spell** être sous le charme de quelqu'un

spelling NOUN
l' *orthographe* FEM ◇ *My spelling is terrible.* Je fais beaucoup de fautes d'orthographe.
- **a spelling mistake** une faute d'orthographe

to **spend** VERB
1 *dépenser* (*money*)
2 *passer* (*time*) ◇ *He spent a month in France.* Il a passé un mois en France.

spice NOUN
l' *épice* FEM

spicy ADJECTIVE
épicé

spider NOUN
l' *araignée* FEM

to **spill** VERB
1 *renverser* (*tip over*) ◇ *He spilled his coffee over his trousers.* Il a renversé son café sur son pantalon.
2 *se répandre* (*get spilt*) ◇ *The soup spilled all over the table.* La soupe s'est répandue sur la table.

spinach NOUN
les *épinards* MASC PL

spine NOUN
la *colonne vertébrale*

spinster NOUN
la *célibataire*

spire NOUN
la *flèche*

spirit NOUN
1 le *courage* (*courage*)
- **to be in good spirits** être de bonne humeur

2 l' *énergie* FEM (*energy*)

spirits PL NOUN
les *alcools forts* MASC PL ◇ *I don't drink spirits.* Je ne bois pas d'alcools forts.

spiritual ADJECTIVE
religieux MASC
religieuse FEM
◇ *the spiritual leader of Tibet* le chef religieux du Tibet

spit NOUN
see also spit VERB
la *salive*

to **spit** VERB
see also spit NOUN
cracher
- **to spit something out** cracher quelque chose

spite NOUN
see also spite VERB
- **in spite of** malgré
- **out of spite** par méchanceté

to **spite** VERB
see also spite NOUN
contrarier ◇ *He just did it to spite me.* Il a fait ça juste pour me contrarier.

spiteful ADJECTIVE
1 (*action*)
méchant

2 (*person*)
rancunier MASC
rancunière FEM

splash VERB
see also splash NOUN
éclabousser ◇ *Careful! Don't splash me!* Attention! Ne m'éclabousse pas!

splash NOUN
see also splash VERB
le *plouf* ◇ *I heard a splash.* J'ai entendu un plouf.
◆ **a splash of colour** une touche de couleur

splendid ADJECTIVE
splendide

splint NOUN
l' *attelle* FEM

splinter NOUN
l' *écharde* FEM

split VERB
1 *fendre* (*break apart*) ◇ *He split the wood with an axe.* Il a fendu le bois avec une hache.
2 *se fendre* ◇ *The ship hit a rock and split in two.* Le bateau a percuté un rocher et s'est fendu en deux.
3 *partager* (*divide up*) ◇ *They decided to split the profits.* Ils ont décidé de partager les bénéfices.
◆ **to split up (1)** (*couple*) rompre
◆ **to split up (2)** (*group*) se disperser

spoil VERB
1 *abîmer* (*object*)
2 *gâcher* (*occasion*)
3 *gâter* (*child*)

spoiled ADJECTIVE
gâté ◇ *a spoiled child* un enfant gâté

spoilsport NOUN
le/la *trouble-fête*

spoke VERB *see* **speak**

spoke NOUN
le *rayon* (*of wheel*)

spoken VERB *see* **speak**

spokesman NOUN
le *porte-parole*
(les *porte-parole* PL)

spokeswoman NOUN
le *porte-parole*
(les *porte-parole* PL)

sponge NOUN
l' *éponge* FEM
◆ **a sponge bag** une trousse de toilette
◆ **a sponge cake** un biscuit de Savoie

sponsor NOUN
see also sponsor VERB
le *donateur*
la *donatrice*

sponsor VERB
see also sponsor NOUN
parrainer ◇ *The festival was sponsored by...* Le festival a été parrainé par...

spontaneous ADJECTIVE
spontané

spooky ADJECTIVE
1 *sinistre* (*eerie*)
◆ **a spooky story** une histoire qui fait froid dans le dos
2 *étrange* (*strange*) ◇ *a spooky coincidence* une étrange coïncidence

spoon NOUN
la *cuiller*
◆ **a spoonful** une cuillerée

sport NOUN
le *sport* ◇ *What's your favourite sport?* Quel est ton sport préféré?
◆ **a sports bag** un sac de sport
◆ **a sports car** une voiture de sport
◆ **a sports jacket** une veste sport
◆ **Go on, be a sport!** Allez, sois sympa!

sportsman NOUN
le *sportif*

sportswear NOUN
les *vêtements de sport* MASC PL

sportswoman NOUN
la *sportive*

sporty ADJECTIVE
sportif MASC
sportive FEM
◇ *I'm not very sporty.* Je ne suis pas très sportif.

spot NOUN
see also spot VERB
1 la *tache* (*mark*) ◇ *There's a spot on your shirt.* Il y a une tache sur ta chemise.
2 le *pois* (*in pattern*) ◇ *a red dress with white spots* une robe rouge à pois blancs
3 le *bouton* (*pimple*) ◇ *He's covered in spots.* Il est couvert de boutons.
4 le *coin* (*place*) ◇ *It's a lovely spot for a picnic.* C'est un coin agréable pour un pique-nique.
◆ **on the spot (1)** (*immediately*) sur-le-champ ◇ *They gave her the job on the spot.* Ils lui ont offert le poste sur-le-champ.
◆ **on the spot (2)** (*at the same place*) sur place ◇ *Luckily they were able to mend the car on the spot.* Heureusement ils ont pu réparer la voiture sur place.

to **spot** VERB
see also spot NOUN
repérer ◇ *I spotted a mistake.* J'ai repéré une faute.

spotless ADJECTIVE
immaculé

spotty ADJECTIVE
(*pimply*)
boutonneux MASC

PTO

boutonneuse FEM

spouse NOUN
l' *époux* MASC
l' *épouse* FEM

to **sprain** VERB
see also sprain NOUN
- **to sprain one's ankle** se faire une entorse à la cheville

sprain NOUN
see also sprain VERB
l' *entorse* FEM ◇ *It's just a sprain.* C'est juste une entorse.

spray NOUN
see also spray VERB
la *bombe* (*spray can*)

to **spray** VERB
see also spray NOUN
1 *vaporiser* ◇ *to spray perfume on one's hand* se vaporiser du parfum sur la main
2 *traiter* (*crops*)
3 *peindre avec une bombe* (*graffiti*)
◇ *Somebody had sprayed graffiti on the wall.* Quelqu'un avait peint des graffitis avec une bombe sur le mur.

spread NOUN
see also spread VERB
- **cheese spread** le fromage à tartiner
- **chocolate spread** le chocolat à tartiner

to **spread** VERB
see also spread NOUN
1 *étaler* ◇ *to spread butter on a slice of bread* étaler du beurre sur une tranche de pain
2 *se propager* (*disease, news*) ◇ *The news spread rapidly.* La nouvelle s'est propagée rapidement.
- **to spread out** (*people*) se disperser
◇ *The soldiers spread out across the field.* Les soldats se sont dispersés dans le champ.

spreadsheet NOUN
le *tableur* (*computer program*)

spring NOUN
1 le *printemps* (*season*)
- **in spring** au printemps
2 le *ressort* (*metal coil*)
3 la *source* (*water hole*)

spring-cleaning NOUN
le *grand nettoyage de printemps*

springtime NOUN
le *printemps*
- **in springtime** au printemps

sprinkler NOUN
l' *arroseur* MASC (*for lawn*)

sprint NOUN
see also sprint VERB
le *sprint*

to **sprint** VERB
see also sprint NOUN
courir à toute vitesse ◇ *She sprinted for the bus.* Elle a couru à toute vitesse pour attraper le bus.

sprinter NOUN
le *sprinteur*
la *sprinteuse*

sprouts PL NOUN
- **Brussels sprouts** les choux de Bruxelles MASC PL

spy NOUN
see also spy VERB
l' *espion* MASC
l' *espionne* FEM

to **spy** VERB
see also spy NOUN
- **to spy on somebody** espionner quelqu'un

spying NOUN
l' *espionnage* MASC

to **squabble** VERB
se chamailler ◇ *Stop squabbling!* Arrêtez de vous chamailler!

square NOUN
see also square ADJECTIVE
1 le *carré* ◇ *a square and a triangle* un carré et un triangle
2 la *place* ◇ *the town square* la place de l'hôtel de ville

square ADJECTIVE
see also square NOUN
carré ◇ *two square metres* deux mètres carrés
- **It's 2 metres square.** Ça fait deux mètres sur deux.

squash NOUN
see also squash VERB
le *squash* (*sport*) ◇ *I play squash.* Je joue au squash.
- **a squash court** un court de squash
- **a squash racket** une raquette de squash
- **orange squash** l' orangeade FEM
- **lemon squash** la citronnade

to **squash** VERB
see also squash NOUN
écraser ◇ *You're squashing me.* Tu m'écrases.

to **squeak** VERB
1 *pousser un petit cri* (*mouse, child*)
2 *grincer* (*creak*)

to **squeeze** VERB
1 *presser* (*fruit, toothpaste*)
2 *serrer* (*hand, arm*)
- **to squeeze into some tight jeans** rentrer tout juste dans un jean serré

to **squint** VERB
see also squint NOUN
loucher

squint NOUN

see also squint VERB
- **He has a squint.** Il louche.

squirrel NOUN
l' *écureuil* MASC

stab VERB
poignarder

stable NOUN
see also stable ADJECTIVE
l' *écurie* FEM

stable ADJECTIVE
see also stable NOUN
stable ◇ *a stable relationship* une relation stable

stack NOUN
le *pile* ◇ *a stack of books* une pile de livres

stadium NOUN
le *stade*

staff NOUN
1 le *personnel* (*in company*)
2 les *professeurs* MASC PL (*in school*)

stage NOUN
1 la *scène* (*in plays*)
2 l' *estrade* FEM (*for speeches, lectures*)
- **at this stage (1)** à ce stade ◇ *at this stage in the negotiations* à ce stade des négociations
- **at this stage (2)** pour l'instant ◇ *At this stage, it's too early to comment.* Pour l'instant, il est trop tôt pour se prononcer.
- **to do something in stages** faire quelque chose étape par étape

stagger VERB
chanceler

stain NOUN
see also stain VERB
la *tache*

stain VERB
see also stain NOUN
tacher

stainless steel NOUN
l' *inox* MASC

stain remover NOUN
le *détachant*

stair NOUN
la *marche* (*step*)

staircase NOUN
l' *escalier* MASC

stairs PL NOUN
l' *escalier* MASC SING

stale ADJECTIVE
rassis (*bread*)

stalemate NOUN
le *pat* (*in chess*)

stall NOUN
le *stand* MASC ◇ *He's got a market stall.* Il a un stand au marché.
- **the stalls** (*in cinema, theatre*) l'orchestre MASC

stammer NOUN
le *bégaiement*
- **He's got a stammer.** Il bégaie.

to **stamp** VERB
see also stamp NOUN
affranchir (*letter*)
- **to stamp one's foot** taper du pied

stamp NOUN
see also stamp VERB
1 le *timbre* ◇ *My hobby is stamp collecting.* Je collectionne les timbres.
- **a stamp album** un album de timbres
- **a stamp collection** une collection de timbres

2 le *tampon* (*rubber stamp*)

to **stand** VERB
1 *être debout* (*be standing*) ◇ *He was standing by the door.* Il était debout à la porte.
2 *se lever* (*stand up*)
3 *supporter* (*tolerate, withstand*) ◇ *I can't stand all this noise.* Je ne supporte pas tout ce bruit.
- **to stand for (1)** (*be short for*) être l'abréviation de ◇ *"BT" stands for "British Telecom".* "BT" est l'abréviation de "British Telecom".
- **to stand for (2)** (*tolerate*) supporter ◇ *I won't stand for it!* Je ne supporterai pas ça!
- **to stand in for somebody** remplacer quelqu'un
- **to stand up** (*get up*) se lever

standard ADJECTIVE
see also standard NOUN
1 *courant* ◇ *standard French* le français courant
2 *ordinaire* (*equipment*)
- **the standard procedure** la procédure normale

standard NOUN
see also standard ADJECTIVE
le *niveau*
(les *niveaux* PL)
◇ *The standard is very high.* Le niveau est très haut.
- **the standard of living** le niveau de vie
- **She's got high standards.** Elle est très exigeante.

stand-by ticket NOUN
le *billet stand-by*

standpoint NOUN
le *point de vue*

stands PL NOUN
la *tribune* FEM (*at sports ground*)

stank VERB *see* **stink**

staple NOUN
see also staple VERB

S

PTO

l' *agrafe* FEM

to **staple** VERB

see also staple NOUN

agrafer

stapler NOUN

l' *agrafeuse* FEM

star NOUN

see also star VERB

1 l' *étoile* FEM (*in sky*)

2 la *vedette* (*celebrity*) ◇ *He's a TV star.* C'est une vedette de la télé.

- **the stars** (*horoscope*) l' horoscope MASC

to **star** VERB

see also star NOUN

être la vedette ◇ *to star in a film* être la vedette d'un film

- **The film stars Glenda Jackson.** Le film a pour vedette Glenda Jackson.
- **...starring Johnny Depp** ...avec Johnny Depp

to **stare** VERB

- **to stare at something** fixer quelque chose

stark ADVERB

- **stark naked** complètement nu

start NOUN

see also start VERB

1 le *début* ◇ *It's not much, but it's a start.* Ce n'est pas grand chose, mais c'est un début.

- **Shall we make a start on the washing-up?** On commence à faire la vaisselle?

2 le *départ* (*of race*)

to **start** VERB

see also start NOUN

1 *commencer* ◇ *What time does it start?* À quelle heure est-ce que ça commence?

- **to start doing something** commencer à faire quelque chose ◇ *I started learning French three years ago.* J'ai commencé à apprendre le français il y a trois ans.

2 *créer* (*organization*) ◇ *He wants to start his own business.* Il veut créer sa propre entreprise.

3 *organiser* (*campaign*) ◇ *She started a campaign against drugs.* Elle a organisé une campagne contre la drogue.

4 *démarrer* (*car*) ◇ *He couldn't start the car.* Il n'a pas réussi à démarrer la voiture. ◇ *The car wouldn't start.* La voiture ne voulait pas démarrer.

- **to start off** (*leave*) partir ◇ *We started off first thing in the morning.* Nous sommes partis en début de matinée.

starter NOUN

l' *entrée* FEM (*first course*)

to **starve** VERB

mourir de faim ◇ *People were literally starving.* Les gens mouraient littéralement de faim.

- **I'm starving!** Je meurs de faim!

state NOUN

see also state VERB

l' *état* MASC

- **he was in a real state** il était dans tous ses états
- **the state** (*government*) l'État
- **the States** (*USA*) les États-Unis MASC

to **state** VERB

see also state NOUN

1 *déclarer* (*say*) ◇ *He stated his intention to resign.* Il a déclaré son intention de démissionner.

2 *donner* (*give*) ◇ *Please state your name and address.* Veuillez donner vos nom et adresse.

stately home NOUN

le *château*

(les *châteaux* PL)

statement NOUN

la *déclaration*

station NOUN

la *gare* (*railway*)

- **the bus station** la gare routière
- **a police station** un poste de police
- **a radio station** une station de radio

stationer's NOUN

la *papeterie*

statue NOUN

la *statue*

to **stay** VERB

see also stay NOUN

1 *rester* (*remain*) ◇ *Stay here!* Reste ici!

- **to stay in** (*not go out*) rester à la maison
- **to stay up** rester debout ◇ *We stayed up till midnight.* Nous sommes restés debout jusqu'à minuit.

2 *loger* (*spend the night*) ◇ *to stay with friends* loger chez des amis ◇ *Where are you staying?* Où est-ce que vous logez?

- **to stay the night** passer la nuit
- **We stayed in Belgium for a few days.** Nous avons passé quelques jours en Belgique.

stay NOUN

see also stay VERB

le *séjour* ◇ *my stay in France* mon séjour en France

steady ADJECTIVE

1 *régulier* MASC

régulière FEM

◇ *steady progress* des progrès réguliers

2 *stable* ◇ *a steady job* un emploi stable

3 *ferme* (*voice, hand*)

4 *calme* (*person*)

- **a steady boyfriend** un copain
- **a steady girlfriend** une copine
- **Steady on!** Doucement!

steak NOUN (*beef*)
le *steak* ◇ *steak and chips* un steak frites

steal VERB
voler

steam NOUN
la *vapeur* ◇ *a steam engine* une locomotive à vapeur

steel NOUN
l' *acier* MASC ◇ *a steel door* une porte en acier

steep ADJECTIVE
raide (*slope*)

steeple NOUN
le *clocher*

steering wheel NOUN
le *volant*

step NOUN
see also step VERB
1 le *pas* (*pace*) ◇ *He took a step forward.* Il a fait un pas en avant.
2 la *marche* (*stair*) ◇ *She tripped over the step.* Elle a trébuché sur la marche.

step VERB
see also step NOUN
- **to step aside** faire un pas de côté
- **to step back** faire un pas en arrière

stepbrother NOUN
le *demi-frère*

stepdaughter NOUN
la *belle-fille*
(les *belles-filles* PL)

stepfather NOUN
le *beau-père*
(les *beaux-pères* PL)

stepladder NOUN
l' *escabeau* MASC
(les *escabeaux* PL)

stepmother NOUN
la *belle-mère*
(les *belles-mères* PL)

stepsister NOUN
la *demi-sœur*

stepson NOUN
le *beau-fils*
(les *beaux-fils* PL)

stereo NOUN
la *chaîne stéréo*
(les *chaînes stéréo* PL)

sterling ADJECTIVE
- **£5 sterling** cinq livres sterling

stew NOUN
le *ragoût*

steward NOUN
le *steward*

stick NOUN
see also stick VERB
1 le *bâton*
2 la *canne* (*walking stick*)

to **stick** VERB
see also stick NOUN
coller (*with adhesive*) ◇ *Stick the stamps on the envelope.* Collez les timbres sur l'enveloppe.
- **I can't stick it any longer.** Je n'en peux plus.

sticker NOUN
l' *autocollant* MASC

sticky ADJECTIVE
1 *poisseux* MASC
poisseuse FEM
◇ *to have sticky hands* avoir les mains poisseuses
2 *adhésif* MASC
adhésive FEM
◇ *a sticky label* une étiquette adhésive

stiff ADJECTIVE, ADVERB
rigide (*rigid*)
- **to have a stiff back** avoir mal au dos
- **to feel stiff** avoir des courbatures
- **to be bored stiff** s'ennuyer à mourir
- **to be frozen stiff** être mort de froid
- **to be scared stiff** être mort de peur

still ADVERB
see also still ADJECTIVE
1 *encore* ◇ *I still haven't finished.* Je n'ai pas encore fini. ◇ *Are you still in bed?* Tu es encore au lit?
- **better still** encore mieux

2 *quand même* (*even so*) ◇ *She knows I don't like it, but she still does it.* Elle sait que je n'aime pas ça, mais elle le fait quand même.
3 *enfin* (*after all*) ◇ *Still, it's the thought that counts.* Enfin, c'est l'intention qui compte.

still ADJECTIVE
see also still ADVERB
- **Keep still!** Ne bouge pas!
- **Sit still!** Reste tranquille!

sting NOUN
see also sting VERB
la *piqûre* ◇ *a bee sting* une piqûre d'abeille

to **sting** VERB
see also sting NOUN
piquer ◇ *I've been stung.* J'ai été piqué.

stingy ADJECTIVE
pingre

to **stink** VERB
see also stink NOUN
puer ◇ *It stinks!* Ça pue!

stink NOUN
see also stink VERB

S

la *puanteur*

to **stir** VERB
remuer

to **stitch** VERB
see also stitch NOUN
coudre (*cloth*)

stitch NOUN
see also stitch VERB
1 le *point* (*in sewing*)
2 le *point de suture* (*in wound*) ◇ *I had five stitches.* J'ai eu cinq points de suture.

stock NOUN
see also stock VERB
1 la *réserve* (*supply*)
2 le *stock* (*in shop*) ◇ *in stock* en stock
◆ **out of stock** épuisé
3 le *bouillon* ◇ *chicken stock* du bouillon de volaille

to **stock** VERB
see also stock NOUN
avoir (*have in stock*) ◇ *Do you stock camping stoves?* Vous avez des camping-gaz?
◆ **to stock up** s'approvisionner ◇ *to stock up with something* s'approvisionner en quelque chose

stock cube NOUN
le *cube de bouillon*

stocking NOUN
le *bas*

stole, stolen VERB *see* **steal**

stomach NOUN
l' *estomac* MASC

stomachache NOUN
◆ **to have a stomachache** avoir mal au ventre

stone NOUN
1 (*rock*)
la *pierre* ◇ *a stone wall* un mur en pierre
2 (*in fruit*)
le *noyau*
(les *noyaux* PL)
◇ *a peach stone* un noyau de pêche

In France, weight is expressed in kilos. A stone is about 6.3 kg.

◆ **I weigh eight stone.** Je pèse cinquante kilos.

stood VERB *see* **stand**

stool NOUN
le *tabouret*

to **stop** VERB
see also stop NOUN
1 *arrêter* ◇ *a campaign to stop whaling* une campagne pour arrêter la chasse à la baleine
2 *s'arrêter* ◇ *The bus doesn't stop there.* Le bus ne s'arrête pas là. ◇ *I think the rain's going to stop.* Je pense qu'il va s'arrêter de pleuvoir.
◆ **to stop doing something** arrêter de faire quelque chose ◇ *to stop smoking* arrêter de fumer
◆ **to stop somebody doing something** empêcher quelqu'un de faire quelque chose
◆ **Stop!** Stop!

stop NOUN
see also stop VERB
l' *arrêt* MASC ◇ *a bus stop* un arrêt de bus
◆ **This is my stop.** Je descends ici.

stopwatch NOUN
le *chronomètre*

store NOUN
see also store VERB
1 le *magasin* (*shop*) ◇ *a furniture store* un magasin de meubles
2 la *réserve* (*stock, storeroom*)

to **store** VERB
see also store NOUN
1 *garder* ◇ *They store potatoes in the cellar.* Ils gardent des pommes de terre dans la cave.
2 *enregistrer* (*information*)

storey NOUN
l' *étage* MASC ◇ *a three-storey building* un immeuble à trois étages

storm NOUN
1 la *tempête* (*gale*)
2 l' *orage* MASC (*thunderstorm*)

stormy ADJECTIVE
orageux MASC
orageuse FEM

story NOUN
l' *histoire* FEM

stove NOUN
1 la *cuisinière* (*in kitchen*)
2 le *réchaud* (*camping stove*)

straight ADJECTIVE
1 *droit* ◇ *a straight line* une ligne droite
2 *raide* ◇ *straight hair* les cheveux raides
3 *hétéro* (*heterosexual*)
◆ **straight away** tout de suite
◆ **straight on** tout droit

straightforward ADJECTIVE
simple

strain NOUN
see also strain VERB
le *stress*
◆ **It was a strain.** C'était éprouvant.

to **strain** VERB
see also strain NOUN
se faire mal à ◇ *I strained my back.* Je me suis fait mal au dos.

to strain a muscle se froisser un muscle

trained ADJECTIVE
froissé (*muscle*)

tranded ADJECTIVE
We were stranded. Nous étions coincés.

trange ADJECTIVE
bizarre ◇ *That's strange!* C'est bizarre!

tranger NOUN
l' *inconnu* MASC
l' *inconnue* FEM
◇ *Don't talk to strangers.* Ne parle pas aux inconnus.
I'm a stranger here. Je ne suis pas d'ici.

trangle VERB
étrangler

trap NOUN
1 la *courroie* (*of bag, camera, suitcase*)
2 la *bretelle* (*of bra, dress*)
3 la *lanière* (*on shoe*)
4 le *bracelet* (*of watch*)

traw NOUN
la *paille*
That's the last straw! Ça, c'est le comble!

trawberry NOUN
la *fraise* ◇ *strawberry jam* la confiture de fraises ◇ *a strawberry ice cream* une glace à la fraise

tray NOUN
a stray cat un chat perdu

tream NOUN
le *ruisseau*
(les *ruisseaux* PL)

treet NOUN
la *rue* ◇ *in the street* dans la rue

treetlamp NOUN
le *réverbère*

treet plan NOUN
le *plan de la ville*

treetwise ADJECTIVE
dégourdi

trength NOUN
la *force*

stress VERB
see also stress NOUN
souligner ◇ *I would like to stress that...* J'aimerais souligner que...

stress NOUN
see also stress VERB
le *stress*

stretch VERB
1 *s'étirer* (*person, animal*) ◇ *The dog woke up and stretched.* Le chien s'est réveillé et s'est étiré.
2 *se détendre* (*get bigger*) ◇ *My sweater stretched when I washed it.* Mon pull s'est détendu au lavage.
3 *tendre* (*stretch out*) ◇ *They stretched a rope between two trees.* Ils ont tendu une corde entre deux arbres.
to stretch out one's arms tendre les bras

stretcher NOUN
le *brancard*

stretchy ADJECTIVE
élastique

strict ADJECTIVE
strict

strike NOUN
see also strike VERB
la *grève*
to be on strike être en grève
to go on strike faire grève

to **strike** VERB
see also strike NOUN
1 *sonner* (*clock*) ◇ *The clock struck three.* L'horloge a sonné trois heures.
2 *faire grève* (*go on strike*)
3 *frapper* (*hit*)
to strike a match frotter une allumette

striker NOUN
1 le/la *gréviste* (*person on strike*)
2 le *buteur* (*footballer*)

striking ADJECTIVE
1 *en grève* (*on strike*) ◇ *striking miners* les mineurs en grève
2 *frappant* (*noticeable*) ◇ *a striking difference* une différence frappante

string NOUN
1 la *ficelle* ◇ *a piece of string* un bout de ficelle
2 la *corde* (*of violin, guitar*)

to **strip** VERB
see also strip NOUN
se déshabiller (*get undressed*)

strip NOUN
see also strip VERB
la *bande*
a strip cartoon une bande dessinée

stripe NOUN
la *rayure*

striped ADJECTIVE
à rayures ◇ *a striped skirt* une jupe à rayures

stripper NOUN
le *strip-teaseur*
la *strip-teaseuse*

stripy ADJECTIVE
rayé ◇ *a stripy shirt* une chemise rayée

to **stroke** VERB
see also stroke NOUN
caresser

stroke NOUN
see also stroke VERB
l' *attaque* FEM ◇ *to have a stroke* avoir une attaque

stroll NOUN
to go for a stroll aller faire une petite

PTO

promenade

strong ADJECTIVE
1 *fort* ◇ *She's very strong.* Elle est très forte.
2 *résistant* (*material*)

strongly ADVERB
fortement ◇ *We recommend strongly that...* Nous recommandons fortement que...
◆ **He smelt strongly of tobacco.** Il sentait fort le tabac.
◆ **strongly built** solidement bâti
◆ **I don't feel strongly about it.** Ça m'est égal.

to **struggle** VERB
see also struggle NOUN
se débattre (*physically*) ◇ *He struggled, but he couldn't escape.* Il s'est débattu, mais il n'a pas pu s'échapper.
◆ **to struggle to do something (1)** (*fight*) se battre pour faire quelque chose ◇ *He struggled to get custody of his daughter.* Il s'est battu pour obtenir la garde de sa fille.
◆ **to struggle to do something (2)** (*have difficulty*) avoir du mal à faire quelque chose

struggle NOUN
see also struggle VERB
la *lutte* (*for independence, equality*)
◆ **It was a struggle.** Ça a été laborieux.

stub NOUN
le *mégot* (*of cigarette*)

stubborn ADJECTIVE
têtu

to **stub out** VERB
écraser (*cigarette*)

stuck VERB *see* **stick**

stuck ADJECTIVE
coincé (*jammed*) ◇ *It's stuck.* C'est coincé.
◆ **to get stuck** rester coincé ◇ *We got stuck in a traffic jam.* Nous sommes restés coincés dans un embouteillage.

stuck-up ADJECTIVE
coincé (*informal*)

stud NOUN
1 la *boucle d'oreille* (*earring*)
2 le *clou* (*on football boots*)

student NOUN
l' *étudiant* MASC
l' *étudiante* FEM

studio NOUN
le *studio* ◇ *a TV studio* un studio de télévision
◆ **a studio flat** un studio

to **study** VERB
1 *faire des études* (*at university*) ◇ *I plan to study biology.* J'ai l'intention de faire des études de biologie.
2 *travailler* (*do homework*) ◇ *I've got to study tonight.* Je dois travailler ce soir.

stuff NOUN
1 le *truc* (*substance*) ◇ *I need some stuff for hay fever.* J'ai besoin d'un truc contre le rhume des foins.
2 les *trucs* MASC PL (*things*) ◇ *There's some stuff on the table for you.* Il y a des trucs sur la table pour toi.
3 les *affaires* FEM PL (*possessions*) ◇ *Have you got all your stuff?* Est-ce que tu as toutes tes affaires?

stuffy ADJECTIVE
mal aéré (*room*)
◆ **It's really stuffy in here.** On étouffe ici.

to **stumble** VERB
trébucher

stung VERB *see* **sting**

stunk VERB *see* **stink**

stunned ADJECTIVE
sidéré (*amazed*) ◇ *I was stunned.* J'étais sidéré.

stunning ADJECTIVE
superbe

stunt NOUN
la *cascade* (*in film*)

stuntman NOUN
le *cascadeur*

stupid ADJECTIVE
stupide ◇ *a stupid joke* une plaisanterie stupide
◆ **Me, go jogging? Don't be stupid!** Moi, faire du footing? Ne dis pas de bêtises!

to **stutter** VERB
see also stutter NOUN
bégayer

stutter NOUN
see also stutter VERB
◆ **He's got a stutter.** Il bégaie.

style NOUN
le *style* ◇ *That's not his style.* Ça n'est pas son style.

subject NOUN
1 le *sujet* ◇ *The subject of my project was the Internet.* Le sujet de mon projet était l'Internet.
2 la *matière* (*at school*) ◇ *What's your favourite subject?* Quelle est ta matière préférée?

submarine NOUN
le *sous-marin*

subscription NOUN
l' *abonnement* MASC (*to paper, magazine*)
◆ **to take out a subscription to** s'abonner à

to **subsidize** VERB
subventionner

subsidy NOUN

la *subvention*

substance NOUN
la *substance*

substitute NOUN
see also substitute VERB
(*person*)
le *remplaçant*
la *remplaçante*

substitute VERB
see also substitute NOUN
substituer ◇ *to substitute A for B* substituer A à B

subtitled ADJECTIVE
sous-titré

subtitles PL NOUN
les *sous-titres* MASC PL ◇ *a French film with English subtitles* un film français avec des sous-titres en anglais

subtle ADJECTIVE
subtil

subtract VERB
retrancher ◇ *to subtract 3 from 5* retrancher trois de cinq

suburb NOUN
la *banlieue* ◇ *a suburb of Paris* une banlieue de Paris ◇ *They live in the suburbs.* Ils habitent en banlieue.

suburban ADJECTIVE
de banlieue ◇ *a suburban train* un train de banlieue

subway NOUN
le *passage souterrain* (*underpass*)

succeed VERB
réussir ◇ *to succeed in doing something* réussir à faire quelque chose

success NOUN
le *succès* ◇ *The play was a great success.* La pièce a eu beaucoup de succès.

successful ADJECTIVE
réussi ◇ *a successful attempt* une tentative réussie
- **to be successful in doing something** réussir à faire quelque chose
- **He's a successful businessman.** Ses affaires marchent bien.

successfully ADVERB
avec succès

successive ADJECTIVE
- **on four successive occasions** quatre fois de suite

such ADJECTIVE, ADVERB
si ◇ *such nice people* des gens si gentils ◇ *such a long journey* un voyage si long
- **such a lot of** tellement de ◇ *such a lot of work* tellement de travail
- **such as** (*like*) comme ◇ *hot countries, such as India* les pays chauds, comme l'Inde
- **not as such** pas exactement ◇ *He's not an expert as such, but...* Ce n'est pas exactement un expert, mais...
- **There's no such thing.** Ça n'existe pas. ◇ *There's no such thing as the yeti.* Le yéti n'existe pas.

such-and-such ADJECTIVE
tel ou tel MASC
telle ou telle FEM
◇ *such-and-such a place* tel ou tel endroit

to **suck** VERB
sucer ◇ *to suck one's thumb* sucer son pouce

sudden ADJECTIVE
soudain ◇ *a sudden change* un changement soudain
- **all of a sudden** tout à coup

suddenly ADVERB
1 *brusquement* (*stop, leave, change*)
2 *subitement* (*die*)
3 *soudain* (*at beginning of sentence*)
◇ *Suddenly, the door opened.* Soudain, la porte s'est ouverte.

suede NOUN
le *daim* ◇ *a suede jacket* une veste en daim

to **suffer** VERB
souffrir ◇ *She was really suffering.* Elle souffrait beaucoup.
- **to suffer from a disease** avoir une maladie ◇ *I suffer from hay fever.* J'ai le rhume des foins.

to **suffocate** VERB
suffoquer

sugar NOUN
le *sucre* ◇ *Do you take sugar?* Est-ce que vous prenez du sucre?

to **suggest** VERB
suggérer ◇ *I suggested they set off early.* Je leur ai suggéré de partir de bonne heure.

suggestion NOUN
la *suggestion* ◇ *to make a suggestion* faire une suggestion

suicide NOUN
le *suicide*
- **to commit suicide** se suicider

suit NOUN
see also suit VERB
1 le *costume* (*man's*)
2 le *tailleur* (*woman's*)

to **suit** VERB
see also suit NOUN
1 *convenir à* (*be convenient for*) ◇ *What time would suit you?* Quelle heure vous conviendrait?
- **That suits me fine.** Ça m'arrange.

PTO

- **Suit yourself!** Comme tu veux!

2 *aller bien à* (*look good on*) ◇ *That dress really suits you.* Cette robe te va vraiment bien.

suitable ADJECTIVE
1 *convenable* ◇ *a suitable time* une heure convenable
2 *approprié* (*clothes*) ◇ *suitable clothing* des vêtements appropriés

suitcase NOUN
la *valise*

suite NOUN
la *suite* (*of rooms*)
- **a bedroom suite** une chambre à coucher

to **sulk** VERB
bouder

sulky ADJECTIVE
boudeur MASC
boudeuse FEM

sum NOUN
1 le *calcul* (*calculation*) ◇ *She's good at sums.* Elle est bonne en calcul.
2 la *somme* (*amount*) ◇ *a sum of money* une somme d'argent

to **summarize** VERB
résumer

summary NOUN
le *résumé*

summer NOUN
l' *été* MASC
- **in summer** en été
- **summer clothes** les vêtements d'été
- **the summer holidays** les vacances d'été

summertime NOUN
l' *été* MASC
- **in summertime** en été

summit NOUN
le *sommet*

to **sum up** VERB
résumer

sun NOUN
le *soleil* ◇ *in the sun* au soleil

to **sunbathe** VERB
se bronzer

sunblock NOUN
l' *écran total* MASC

sunburn NOUN
le *coup de soleil*

sunburnt ADJECTIVE
- **I got sunburnt.** J'ai attrapé un coup de soleil.

Sunday NOUN
le *dimanche* ◇ *on Sunday* dimanche ◇ *on Sundays* le dimanche ◇ *every Sunday* tous les dimanches ◇ *last Sunday* dimanche dernier ◇ *next Sunday* dimanche prochain

Sunday school NOUN
le *catéchisme*

le catéchisme, *the French equivalent of* Sunday school, *takes place during the week after school rather than on a Sunday.*

◇ *to go to Sunday school* aller au catéchisme

sunflower NOUN
le *tournesol*

sung VERB *see* **sing**

sunglasses PL NOUN
les *lunettes de soleil* FEM PL

sunk VERB *see* **sink**

sunlight NOUN
le *soleil*

sunny ADJECTIVE
ensoleillé ◇ *a sunny morning* une matinée ensoleillée
- **It's sunny.** Il fait du soleil.
- **a sunny day** une belle journée

sunrise NOUN
le *lever du soleil*

sunroof NOUN
le *toit ouvrant*

sunscreen NOUN
la *crème solaire*

sunset NOUN
le *coucher du soleil*

sunshine NOUN
le *soleil*

sunstroke NOUN
l' *insolation* FEM ◇ *to get sunstroke* attraper une insolation

suntan NOUN
le *bronzage*
- **suntan lotion** le lait solaire
- **suntan oil** l'huile solaire FEM

super ADJECTIVE
formidable

superb ADJECTIVE
superbe

supermarket NOUN
le *supermarché*

supernatural ADJECTIVE
surnaturel MASC
surnaturelle FEM

superstitious ADJECTIVE
superstitieux MASC
superstitieuse FEM

to **supervise** VERB
surveiller

supervisor NOUN
1 (*in factory*)
le *surveillant*
la *surveillante*
2 (*in department store*)
le *chef de rayon*

supper NOUN
le *dîner*

supplement NOUN

le *supplément*

supplies PL NOUN
les *vivres* MASC PL (*food*)

supply VERB
see also supply NOUN
fournir (*provide*)
- **to supply somebody with something** fournir quelque chose à quelqu'un
◇ *The centre supplied us with all the equipment.* Le centre nous a fourni tout l'équipement.

supply NOUN
see also supply VERB
la *provision* ◇ *a supply of paper* une provision de papier
- **the water supply** (*to town*) l'approvisionnement en eau MASC

supply teacher NOUN
le *suppléant*
la *suppléante*

support VERB
see also support NOUN
1 *soutenir* ◇ *My mum has always supported me.* Ma mère m'a toujours soutenu.
2 *être supporter de* ◇ *What team do you support?* Tu es supporter de quelle équipe?
3 *subvenir aux besoins de* (*financially*) ◇ *She had to support five children on her own.* Elle a dû subvenir toute seule aux besoins de cinq enfants.

support NOUN
see also support VERB
le *soutien* (*backing*)

supporter NOUN
1 le *supporter* ◇ *a Liverpool supporter* un supporter de Liverpool
2 le *sympathisant*
la *sympathisante*
◇ *a supporter of the Labour Party* un sympathisant du parti travailliste

suppose VERB
imaginer ◇ *I suppose he's late.* J'imagine qu'il est en retard. ◇ *Suppose you won the lottery.* Imaginez que vous gagniez à la loterie.
- **I suppose so.** J'imagine.
- **to be supposed to do something** être censé faire quelque chose ◇ *You're supposed to show your passport.* On est censé montrer son passeport.

supposing CONJUNCTION
si ◇ *Supposing you won the lottery...* Si tu gagnais à la loterie...

surcharge NOUN
la *surcharge*

sure ADJECTIVE
sûr ◇ *Are you sure?* Tu es sûr?
- **Sure!** Bien sûr!
- **to make sure that...** vérifier que...
◇ *I'm going to make sure the door's locked.* Je vais vérifier que la porte est fermée à clé.

surely ADVERB
- **Surely you've been to London?** J'imagine que tu es allé à Londres, non?
- **The shops are closed on Sundays, surely?** J'imagine que les magasins sont fermés le dimanche, non?

surf NOUN
le *ressac*

surface NOUN
la *surface*

surfboard NOUN
la *planche de surf*
(les *planches de surf* PL)

surfing NOUN
le *surf* ◇ *to go surfing* faire du surf

surgeon NOUN
le *chirurgien* ◇ *She's a surgeon.* Elle est chirurgien.

surgery NOUN
le *cabinet médical* (*doctor's surgery*)
- **surgery hours** les heures de consultation FEM

surname NOUN
le *nom de famille*
(les *noms de famille* PL)

surprise NOUN
la *surprise*

surprised ADJECTIVE
surpris ◇ *I was surprised to see him.* J'ai été surpris de le voir.

surprising ADJECTIVE
surprenant

to **surrender** VERB
capituler

surrogate mother NOUN
la *mère porteuse*

to **surround** VERB
encercler ◇ *The police surrounded the house.* La police a encerclé la maison.
◇ *You're surrounded!* Vous êtes encerclé!
- **surrounded by** entouré de ◇ *The house is surrounded by trees.* La maison est entourée d'arbres.

survey NOUN
l' *enquête* FEM (*research*)

surveyor NOUN
1 l' *expert en bâtiment* MASC (*of buildings*)
2 le/la *géomètre* (*of land*)

survivor NOUN
le *survivant*
la *survivante*
◇ *There were no survivors.* Il n'y a pas eu de survivants.

S

to **suspect** VERB
see also suspect NOUN
soupçonner

suspect NOUN
see also suspect VERB
le *suspect*
la *suspecte*

to **suspend** VERB
1 *exclure* (*from school, team*) ◇ *He's been suspended.* Il s'est fait exclure.
2 *suspendre* (*from job*)

suspense NOUN
1 l' *attente* FEM (*waiting*) ◇ *The suspense was terrible.* L'attente a été terrible.
2 le *suspense* (*in story*) ◇ *a film with lots of suspense* un film avec beaucoup de suspense

suspension NOUN
1 l' *exclusion* FEM (*from school, team*)
2 la *suspension* (*from job*)

suspicious ADJECTIVE
1 *méfiant* ◇ *He was suspicious at first.* Il était méfiant au début.
2 *louche* (*suspicious-looking*) ◇ *a suspicious person* un individu louche

to **swallow** VERB
avaler

swam VERB *see* **swim**

swan NOUN
le *cygne*

to **swap** VERB
échanger ◇ *Do you want to swap?* Tu veux échanger? ◇ *to swap A for B* échanger A contre B

to **swat** VERB
écraser

to **sway** VERB
osciller

to **swear** VERB
jurer (*make an oath, curse*)

swearword NOUN
le *gros mot*

sweat NOUN
see also sweat VERB
la *transpiration*

to **sweat** VERB
see also sweat NOUN
transpirer

sweater NOUN
le *pull*

sweaty ADJECTIVE
1 *en sueur* (*person, face*) ◇ *I'm all sweaty.* Je suis en sueur.
2 *moite* (*hands*)

Swede NOUN
(*person*)
le *Suédois*
la *Suédoise*

swede NOUN
le *rutabaga* (*vegetable*)

Sweden NOUN
la *Suède*
◆ **in Sweden** en Suède
◆ **to Sweden** en Suède

Swedish ADJECTIVE
see also Swedish NOUN
suédois ◇ *She's Swedish.* Elle est suédoise.

Swedish NOUN
see also Swedish ADJECTIVE
le *suédois* (*language*)

to **sweep** VERB
balayer
◆ **to sweep the floor** balayer

sweet NOUN
see also sweet ADJECTIVE
1 le *bonbon* (*candy*) ◇ *a bag of sweets* un paquet de bonbons
2 le *dessert* (*pudding*) ◇ *What sweet did you have?* Qu'est-ce que vous avez mangé comme dessert?

sweet ADJECTIVE
see also sweet NOUN
1 (*not savoury*)
sucré
2 (*kind*)
gentil MASC
gentille FEM
◇ *That was really sweet of you.* C'était vraiment gentil de ta part.
3 (*cute*)
mignon MASC
mignonne FEM
◇ *Isn't she sweet?* Comme elle est mignonne!
◆ **sweet and sour pork** le porc à la sauce aigre-douce

sweetcorn NOUN
le *maïs doux*

sweltering ADJECTIVE
◆ **It was sweltering.** Il faisait une chaleur étouffante.

swept VERB *see* **sweep**

to **swerve** VERB
faire une embardée ◇ *He swerved to avoid the cyclist.* Il a fait une embardée pour éviter le cycliste.

swim NOUN
see also swim VERB
◆ **to go for a swim** aller se baigner

to **swim** VERB
see also swim NOUN
nager ◇ *Can you swim?* Tu sais nager?
◆ **She swam across the river.** Elle a traversé la rivière à la nage.

swimmer NOUN
le *nageur*

la *nageuse*
◇ *She's a good swimmer.* C'est une bonne nageuse.

swimming NOUN
la *natation* ◇ *Do you like swimming?* Tu aimes la natation?
◆ **to go swimming** (*in a pool*) aller à la piscine
◆ **a swimming cap** un bonnet de bain
◆ **a swimming costume** un maillot de bain
◆ **a swimming pool** une piscine
◆ **swimming trunks** le maillot de bain

swimsuit NOUN
le *maillot de bain*

swing NOUN
la *balançoire* (*in playground, garden*)

Swiss ADJECTIVE
see also **Swiss** NOUN
suisse ◇ *Sabine's Swiss.* Sabine est suisse.

Swiss NOUN
see also **Swiss** ADJECTIVE
le/la *Suisse* (*person*)
◆ **the Swiss** les Suisses

switch NOUN
see also **switch** VERB
le *bouton* (*for light, radio etc*)

switch VERB
see also **switch** NOUN
changer de ◇ *We switched partners.* Nous avons changé de partenaire.

switch off VERB
1 *éteindre* (*electrical appliance*)
2 *arrêter* (*engine, machine*)

to **switch on** VERB
1 *allumer* (*electrical appliance*)
2 *mettre en marche* (*engine, machine*)

Switzerland NOUN
la *Suisse*
◆ **in Switzerland** en Suisse

swollen ADJECTIVE
enflé (*arm, leg*)

to **swop** VERB
échanger ◇ *Do you want to swop?* Tu veux échanger? ◇ *to swop A for B* échanger A contre B

sword NOUN
l' *épée* FEM

swore, sworn VERB *see* **swear**

swum VERB *see* **swim**

swung VERB *see* **swing**

syllabus NOUN
le *programme* ◇ *on the syllabus* au programme

symbol NOUN
le *symbole*

sympathetic ADJECTIVE
compréhensif MASC
compréhensive FEM

to **sympathize** VERB
◆ **to sympathize with somebody** comprendre quelqu'un

sympathy NOUN
la *compassion*

syringe NOUN
la *seringue*

system NOUN
le *système*

T

table NOUN
la *table* ◇ *to lay the table* mettre la table

tablecloth NOUN
la *nappe*

tablespoon NOUN
la *grande cuillère*
◆ **a tablespoonful of sugar** une cuillerée à soupe de sucre

tablet NOUN
le *comprimé*

table tennis NOUN
le *ping-pong* ◇ *to play table tennis* jouer au ping-pong

tabloid NOUN
le *quotidien populaire*

tackle NOUN
see also tackle VERB
1 le *tacle* (*in football*)
2 le *plaquage* (*in rugby*)
◆ **fishing tackle** le matériel de pêche

to **tackle** VERB
see also tackle NOUN
1 *tacler* (*in football*)
2 *plaquer* (*in rugby*)
◆ **to tackle a problem** s'attaquer à un problème

tact NOUN
le *tact*

tactful ADJECTIVE
plein de tact

tactics PL NOUN
la *tactique* SING

tactless ADJECTIVE
◆ **to be tactless** manquer de tact ◇ *a tactless remark* une remarque qui manque de tact

tadpole NOUN
le *têtard*

tag NOUN
l' *étiquette* FEM (*label*)

tail NOUN
la *queue*
◆ **Heads or tails?** Pile ou face?

tailor NOUN
le *tailleur*

to **take** VERB
1 *prendre* ◇ *Are you taking your new camera?* Tu prends ton nouvel appareil photo? ◇ *He took a plate from the cupboard.* Il a pris une assiette dans le placard. ◇ *It takes about an hour.* Ça prend environ une heure.
2 *emmener* (*person*) ◇ *He goes to London every week, but he never takes me.* Il va à Londres toutes les semaines, mais il ne m'emmène jamais.
◆ **to take something somewhere** emporter quelque chose quelque part ◇ *Do you take your exercise books home?* Vous emportez vos cahiers chez vous? ◇ *Don't take anything valuable with you.* N'emportez pas d'objets de valeur.
◆ **I'm going to take my coat to the cleaner's.** Je vais donner mon manteau à nettoyer.
3 *demander* (*effort, skill*) ◇ *that takes a lot of courage* cela demande beaucoup de courage
◆ **It takes a lot of money to do that.** Il faut beaucoup d'argent pour faire ça.
4 *supporter* (*tolerate*) ◇ *He can't take being criticized.* Il ne supporte pas d'être critiqué.
5 *passer* (*exam, test*) ◇ *Have you taken your driving test yet?* Est-ce que tu as déjà passé ton permis de conduire?
6 *faire* (*subject*) ◇ *I decided to take French instead of German.* J'ai décidé de faire du français au lieu de l'allemand.

to **take after** VERB
ressembler à ◇ *She takes after her mother.* Elle ressemble à sa mère.

to **take apart** VERB
◆ **to take something apart** démonter quelque chose

to **take away** VERB
1 *emporter* (*object*)
2 *emmener* (*person*)
◆ **to take something away** (*confiscate*) confisquer quelque chose
◆ **hot meals to take away** des plats chauds à emporter

takeaway NOUN
1 le *plat à emporter* (*meal*)
2 le *restaurant qui vend des plats à emporter* (*shop*) ◇ *a Chinese takeaway* un restaurant chinois qui vend des plats à emporter

to **take back** VERB
rapporter ◇ *I took it back to the shop.* Je l'ai rapporté au magasin.
◆ **I take it all back!** Je n'ai rien dit!

to **take in** VERB
comprendre (*understand*) ◇ *I didn't really take it in.* Je n'ai pas bien compris.

to **take off** VERB
1 *décoller* (*plane*) ◇ *The plane took off twenty minutes late.* L'avion a décollé avec vingt minutes de retard.
2 *enlever* (*clothes*) ◇ *Take your coat off.* Enlevez votre manteau.

akeoff NOUN
le *décollage* (*of plane*)

ake out VERB
sortir (*from container, pocket*)
He took her out to the theatre. Il l'a emmenée au théâtre.

ake over VERB
prendre la relève ◇ *I'll take over now.* Je vais prendre la relève.
to take over from somebody remplacer quelqu'un

alcum powder NOUN
le *talc*

ale NOUN
le *conte* FEM (*story*)

alent NOUN
le *talent* ◇ *She's got lots of talent.* Elle a beaucoup de talent.
to have a talent for something être doué pour quelque chose ◇ *He's got a real talent for languages.* Il est vraiment doué pour les langues.

alented ADJECTIVE
She's a talented pianist. C'est une pianiste de talent.

alk NOUN
see also talk VERB
1 l' *exposé* MASC (*speech*) ◇ *She gave a talk on rock climbing.* Elle a fait un exposé sur la varappe.
2 la *conversation* (*conversation*) ◇ *I had a talk with my Mum about it.* J'ai eu une petite conversation avec ma mère à ce sujet.
3 les *racontars* MASC (*gossip*) ◇ *It's just talk.* Ce sont des racontars.

alk VERB
see also talk NOUN
parler ◇ *to talk about something* parler de quelque chose
to talk something over with somebody discuter de quelque chose avec quelqu'un

alkative ADJECTIVE
bavard

all ADJECTIVE
1 *grand* (*person, tree*)
to be 2 metres tall mesurer deux mètres
2 *haut* (*building*)

ampon NOUN
le *tampon*

an NOUN
le *bronzage* ◇ *She's got an amazing tan.* Elle a un bronzage superbe.

angerine NOUN
la *mandarine*

ank NOUN
1 le *réservoir* (*for water, petrol*)
2 le *char d'assaut* (*military*)
a fish tank un aquarium

tanker NOUN
1 le *pétrolier* (*ship*)
an oil tanker un pétrolier
2 le *camion-citerne* (*truck*)
a petrol tanker un camion-citerne

tap NOUN
1 le *robinet* (*water tap*)
2 la *petite tape* (*gentle blow*)

tap-dancing NOUN
les *claquettes* FEM PL ◇ *I do tap-dancing.* Je fais des claquettes.

to **tape** VERB
see also tape NOUN
enregistrer (*record*) ◇ *Did you tape that film last night?* As-tu enregistré le film hier soir?

tape NOUN
see also tape VERB
1 la *cassette* ◇ *a tape of Sinead O'Connor* une cassette de Sinead O'Connor
2 le *scotch* ® (*sticky tape*)

tape deck NOUN
le *magnétophone*

tape measure NOUN
le *mètre à ruban*

tape recorder NOUN
le *magnétophone*

target NOUN
la *cible*

tarmac NOUN
le *macadam* (*on road*)

tart NOUN
la *tarte* ◇ *an apple tart* une tarte aux pommes

tartan ADJECTIVE
écossais ◇ *a tartan scarf* une écharpe écossaise

task NOUN
la *tâche*

taste NOUN
see also taste VERB
le *goût* ◇ *It's got a really strange taste.* Ça a un goût vraiment bizarre. ◇ *a joke in bad taste* une plaisanterie de mauvais goût
Would you like a taste? Tu veux goûter?

to **taste** VERB
see also taste NOUN
goûter ◇ *Would you like to taste it?* Vous voulez y goûter?
to taste of something avoir un goût de quelque chose ◇ *It tastes of fish.* Ça a un goût de poisson.
You can taste the garlic in it. Ça a bien le goût d'ail.

tasteful ADJECTIVE

T

PTO

de bon goût

tasteless ADJECTIVE
1 fade (*food*)
2 de mauvais goût (*in bad taste*) ◇ *a tasteless remark* une remarque de mauvais goût

tasty ADJECTIVE
savoureux MASC
savoureuse FEM

tattoo NOUN
le tatouage

taught VERB *see* **teach**

Taurus NOUN
le Taureau ◇ *I'm Taurus.* Je suis Taureau.

tax NOUN
1 les impôts MASC PL (*on income*)
2 la taxe (*on goods, alcohol*)

taxi NOUN
le taxi
◆ **a taxi driver** un chauffeur de taxi

taxi rank NOUN
la station de taxis

TB NOUN
la tuberculose

tea NOUN
1 le thé ◇ *a cup of tea* une tasse de thé
◆ **a tea bag** un sachet de thé
2 le dîner (*evening meal*)
◆ **We were having tea.** Nous étions en train de dîner.

to **teach** VERB
1 apprendre ◇ *My sister taught me to swim.* Ma sœur m'a appris à nager. ◇ *That'll teach you!* Ça t'apprendra!
2 enseigner (*in school*) ◇ *She teaches physics.* Elle enseigne la physique.

teacher NOUN
1 (*in secondary school*)
le professeur ◇ *a maths teacher* un professeur de maths ◇ *She's a teacher.* Elle est professeur.
2 (*in primary school*)
l' instituteur MASC
l' institutrice FEM
◇ *He's a primary school teacher.* Il est instituteur.

teacher's pet NOUN
le chouchou
la chouchoute

tea cloth NOUN
le torchon

team NOUN
l' équipe FEM ◇ *a football team* une équipe de football ◇ *She was in my team.* Elle était dans mon équipe.

teapot NOUN
la théière

tear NOUN
see also tear VERB
la larme ◇ *She was in tears.* Elle était en larmes.

to **tear** VERB
see also tear NOUN
1 déchirer ◇ *Be careful or you'll tear the page.* Fais attention, tu vas déchirer la page.
2 se déchirer ◇ *It won't tear, it's very strong.* Ça ne se déchire pas, c'est très solide.
◆ **to tear up** déchirer ◇ *He tore up the letter.* Il a déchiré la lettre.

tear gas NOUN
le gaz lacrymogène

to **tease** VERB
1 tourmenter (*unkindly*) ◇ *Stop teasing that poor animal!* Arrête de tourmenter cette pauvre bête!
2 taquiner (*jokingly*) ◇ *He's teasing you.* Il te taquine.
◆ **I was only teasing.** Je plaisantais.

teaspoon NOUN
la petite cuillère
◆ **a teaspoonful of sugar** une cuillerée à café de sucre

teatime NOUN
l' heure du dîner FEM (*in evening*) ◇ *It was nearly teatime.* C'était presque l'heure du dîner.
◆ **Teatime!** À table!

tea towel NOUN
le torchon

technical ADJECTIVE
technique
◆ **a technical college** un lycée technique

technician NOUN
1 le technicien
2 la technicienne

technique NOUN
la technique

techno NOUN
la techno (*music*)

technological ADJECTIVE
technologique

technology NOUN
la technologie

teddy bear NOUN
le nounours

teenage ADJECTIVE
1 pour les jeunes ◇ *a teenage magazine* un magazine pour les jeunes
2 adolescent (*boys, girls*) ◇ *She has two teenage daughters.* Elle a deux filles adolescentes.

teenager NOUN
l' adolescent MASC
l' adolescente FEM

teens PL NOUN

She's in her teens. C'est une adolescente.

e-shirt NOUN
le *tee-shirt*

eth PL NOUN
les *dents*

ethe VERB
faire ses dents

etotal ADJECTIVE
I'm teetotal. Je ne bois jamais d'alcool.

lecommunications PL NOUN
les *télécommunications* FEM PL

lephone NOUN
see also phone NOUN *and* VERB
le *téléphone* ◇ *on the telephone* au téléphone
a telephone box une cabine téléphonique
a telephone call un coup de téléphone
the telephone directory l'annuaire MASC
a telephone number un numéro de téléphone

lescope NOUN
le *télescope*

levision NOUN
la *télévision*
on television à la télévision
a television licence une redevance de télévision
a television programme une émission de télévision

ell VERB
dire
to tell somebody something dire quelque chose à quelqu'un ◇ *Did you tell your mother?* Tu l'as dit à ta mère? ◇ *I told him that I was going on holiday.* Je lui ai dit que je partais en vacances.
to tell somebody to do something dire à quelqu'un de faire quelque chose ◇ *He told me to wait a moment.* Il m'a dit d'attendre un moment.
to tell lies dire des mensonges
to tell a story raconter une histoire
I can't tell the difference between them. Je n'arrive pas à les distinguer.

ell off VERB
gronder

elly NOUN
la *télé* ◇ *to watch telly* regarder la télé
on telly à la télé

emper NOUN
le *caractère* ◇ *He's got a terrible temper.* Il a un sale caractère
to be in a temper être en colère
to lose one's temper se mettre en colère ◇ *I lost my temper.* Je me suis mis en colère.

emperature NOUN
la *température* (*of oven, water, person*)
The temperature was 30 degrees. Il faisait trente degrés.
to have a temperature avoir de la fièvre

temple NOUN
le *temple*

temporary ADJECTIVE
temporaire

to **tempt** VERB
tenter ◇ *I'm very tempted!* Je suis très tenté!
to tempt somebody to do something persuader quelqu'un de faire quelque chose

temptation NOUN
la *tentation*

tempting ADJECTIVE
tentant

ten NUMBER
dix ◇ *She's ten.* Elle a dix ans.

to **tend to** VERB
to tend to do something avoir tendance à faire quelque chose ◇ *He tends to arrive late.* Il a tendance à arriver en retard.

tennis NOUN
le *tennis* ◇ *Do you play tennis?* Vous jouez au tennis?
a tennis ball une balle de tennis
a tennis court un court de tennis
a tennis racket une raquette de tennis

tennis player NOUN
le *joueur de tennis*
la *joueuse de tennis*
◇ *He's a tennis player.* Il est joueur de tennis.

tenor NOUN
le *ténor*

tenpin bowling NOUN
le *bowling* ◇ *to go tenpin bowling* jouer au bowling

tense ADJECTIVE
see also tense NOUN
tendu

tense NOUN
see also tense ADJECTIVE
the present tense le présent
the future tense le futur

tension NOUN
la *tension*

tent NOUN
la *tente*
a tent peg un piquet de tente
a tent pole un montant de tente

tenth ADJECTIVE
dixième ◇ *the tenth floor* le dixième étage
the tenth of August le dix août

term NOUN

T

PTO

1 le *trimestre* (*at school*)
2 le *terme* ◇ *a short-term solution* une solution à court terme
- **to come to terms with something** accepter quelque chose

terminal ADJECTIVE
see also terminal NOUN
incurable (*illness, patient*)

terminal NOUN
see also terminal ADJECTIVE
un terminal (*of computer*)
- **an oil terminal** un terminal pétrolier
- **an air terminal** une aérogare

terminally ADVERB
- **to be terminally ill** être condamné

terrace NOUN
1 la *terrasse* (*patio*)
2 la *rangée de maisons* (*row of houses*)
- **the terraces** (*at stadium*) les gradins MASC

terraced ADJECTIVE
- **a terraced house** une maison mitoyenne

terrible ADJECTIVE
épouvantable ◇ *My French is terrible.* Mon français est épouvantable.

terrier NOUN
le *terrier*

terrific ADJECTIVE
super (*wonderful*) ◇ *That's terrific!* C'est super!
- **You look terrific!** Tu es superbe!

terrified ADJECTIVE
terrifié ◇ *I was terrified!* J'étais terrifié!

terrorism NOUN
le *terrorisme*

terrorist NOUN
le/la *terroriste*
- **a terrorist attack** un attentat terroriste

test NOUN
see also test VERB
1 l' *interrogation* FEM (*at school*) ◇ *I've got a test tomorrow.* J'ai une interrogation demain.
2 l' *essai* MASC (*trial, check*) ◇ *nuclear tests* les essais nucléaires
3 l' *analyse* FEM (*medical*) ◇ *a blood test* une analyse de sang ◇ *They're going to do some more tests.* Ils vont faire d'autres analyses.
- **driving test** l'examen du permis de conduire ◇ *He's got his driving test tomorrow.* Il passe son permis de conduire demain.

to **test** VERB
see also test NOUN
1 *essayer* ◇ *to test something out* essayer quelque chose
2 *interroger* (*class*) ◇ *He tested us on the new vocabulary.* Il nous a interrogés sur le nouveau vocabulaire.
- **She was tested for drugs.** On lui a fait subir un contrôle antidopage.

test match NOUN
le *match international*

test tube NOUN
l' *éprouvette* FEM

tetanus NOUN
le *tétanos* ◇ *a tetanus injection* un vaccin contre le tétanos

textbook NOUN
le *manuel* ◇ *a French textbook* un manuel de français

textiles NOUN
les *textiles* MASC PL ◇ *a textiles factory* une usine textile

Thames NOUN
la *Tamise*

than CONJUNCTION
que ◇ *She's taller than me.* Elle est plus grande que moi. ◇ *I've got more books than him.* J'ai plus de livres que lui.
- **more than ten years** plus de dix ans
- **more than once** plus d'une fois

to **thank** VERB
remercier ◇ *Don't forget to write and thank them.* N'oublie pas de leur écrire pour les remercier.
- **thank you** merci
- **thank you very much** merci beaucoup

thanks EXCLAMATION
merci!
- **thanks to** grâce à ◇ *Thanks to him, everything went OK.* Grâce à lui, tout s'est bien passé.

that ADJECTIVE, PRONOUN, CONJUNCTION
Use **ce** *when* that *is followed by a masculine noun, and* **cette** *when* that *is followed by a feminine noun.* **ce** *changes to* **cet** *before a vowel and before most words beginning with "h".*
1 *ce* ◇ *that book* ce livre
cet ◇ *that man* cet homme
cette ◇ *that woman* cette femme
- **that road** cette route
- **THAT road** cette route-là
- **that one (1)** celui-là (*masculine*) ◇ *This man?–No, that one.* Cet homme-ci?–Non, celui-là.
- **that one (2)** celle-là (*feminine*) ◇ *Do you like this photo?–No, I prefer that one.* Tu aimes cette photo?–Non, je préfère celle-là.

2 *ça* ◇ *You see that?* Tu vois ça?
- **What's that?** Qu'est-ce que c'est?
- **Who's that?** Qui est-ce?
- **Is that you?** C'est toi?
- **That's...** C'est... ◇ *That's my French teacher.* C'est mon prof de français. ◇ *That's what he said.* C'est ce qu'il a dit.

In relative phrases use **qui** *when* that *refers to the subject of the sentence, and* **que** *when it refers to the object.*

3 *qui* ◇ *the man that saw us* l'homme qui nous a vus ◇ *the man that spoke to us* l'homme qui nous a parlé ◇ *the dog that bit her* le chien qui l'a mordue

4 *que* ◇ *the man that we saw* l'homme que nous avons vu ◇ *the man that we spoke to* l'homme à qui nous avons parlé

que *changes to* **qu'** *before a vowel and before most words beginning with "h".*

◇ *the dog that she bought* le chien qu'elle a acheté ◇ *He thought that Henri was ill.* Il pensait qu'Henri était malade. ◇ *I know that she likes chocolate.* Je sais qu'elle aime le chocolat.

It was that big. Il était grand comme ça.

It's about that high. Il est à peu près haut comme ça.

It's not that difficult. Ça n'est pas si difficile que ça.

hatched ADJECTIVE

a thatched cottage une chaumière

the ARTICLE

Use **le** *with a masculine noun, and* **la** *with a feminine noun. Use* **l'** *before a vowel and most words beginning with "h". For plural nouns always use* **les**.

le ◇ *the boy* le garçon

l' ◇ *the man* l'homme MASC ◇ *the orange* l'orange FEM ◇ *the habit* l'habitude FEM

la ◇ *the girl* la fille

les ◇ *the children* les enfants

theatre NOUN

le *théâtre*

theft NOUN

le *vol*

their ADJECTIVE

leur (*leurs* PL)

◇ *their house* leur maison ◇ *their parents* leurs parents

theirs PRONOUN

le leur + MASC NOUN ◇ *It's not our garage, it's theirs.* Ce n'est pas notre garage, c'est le leur.

la leur + FEM NOUN ◇ *It's not our car, it's theirs.* Ce n'est pas notre voiture, c'est la leur.

les leurs + PL NOUN ◇ *They're not our ideas, they're theirs.* Ce ne sont pas nos idées, ce sont les leurs.

Is this theirs? (1) C'est à eux? (*masculine owners*)

Is this theirs? (2) C'est à elles? (*feminine owners*) ◇ *This car is theirs.* Cette voiture est à eux. ◇ *Whose is this?–It's theirs.* C'est à qui?–À eux.

them PRONOUN

1 *les* ◇ *I didn't see them.* Je ne les ai pas vus.

Use **leur** *when* them *means* to them.

2 *leur* ◇ *I gave them some brochures.* Je leur ai donné des brochures. ◇ *I told them the truth.* Je leur ai dit la vérité.

Use **eux** *or* **elles** *after a preposition.*

3 *eux* MASC ◇ *It's for them.* C'est pour eux.

elles FEM ◇ *Ann and Sophie came–Graham was with them.* Ann et Sophie sont venues–Graham était avec elles.

theme NOUN

le *thème*

themselves PRONOUN

1 *se* ◇ *Did they hurt themselves?* Est-ce qu'ils se sont fait mal?

2 *eux-mêmes* MASC

elles-mêmes FEM

◇ *They did it themselves.* Ils l'ont fait eux-mêmes.

then ADVERB, CONJUNCTION

1 *ensuite* (*next*) ◇ *I get dressed. Then I have breakfast.* Je m'habille. Ensuite je prends mon petit déjeuner.

2 *alors* (*in that case*) ◇ *My pen's run out.–Use a pencil then!* Il n'y a plus d'encre dans mon stylo.–Alors utilise un crayon!

3 *à l'époque* (*at that time*) ◇ *There was no electricity then.* Il n'y avait pas l'électricité à l'époque.

- **now and then** de temps en temps ◇ *Do you play chess?–Now and then.* Vous jouez aux échecs?–De temps en temps.
- **By then it was too late.** Il était déjà trop tard.

therapy NOUN

la *thérapie*

there ADVERB

1 *là* ◇ *Put it there, on the table.* Mets-le là, sur la table.

- **over there** là-bas
- **in there** là
- **on there** là
- **up there** là-haut
- **down there** là-bas
- **There he is!** Le voilà!

2 *y* ◇ *He went there on Friday.* Il y est allé vendredi. ◇ *Paris? I've never been there.* Paris? Je n'y suis jamais allé.

- **There is...** Il y a... ◇ *There's a factory near my house.* Il y a une usine près de

T

PTO

chez moi.

- **There are...** Il y a... ◇ *There are five people in my family.* Il y a cinq personnes dans ma famille.
- **There has been an accident.** Il y a eu un accident.

therefore ADVERB
donc

there's = **there is, there has**

thermometer NOUN
le *thermomètre*

Thermos ® NOUN
le *thermos* ®

these ADJECTIVE, PRONOUN
1 *ces* ◇ *these shoes* ces chaussures
- **THESE shoes** ces chaussures-là

2 *ceux-ci* MASC ◇ *I want these!* Je veux ceux-ci!
celles-ci FEM ◇ *I'm looking for some sandals. Can I try these?* Je cherche des sandales. Je peux essayer celles-ci?

they PRONOUN
Check if they *stands for a masculine or feminine noun.*
ils ◇ *Are there any tickets left?–No, they're all sold.* Est-ce qu'il reste des billets?–Non, ils sont tous vendus.
elles ◇ *Do you like those shoes?–No, they're horrible.* Tu aimes ces chaussures?–Non, elles sont affreuses.
- **They say that...** On dit que...

they'd = **they had, they would**

they'll = **they will**

they're = **they are**

they've = **they have**

thick ADJECTIVE
1 (*not thin*)
épais MASC
épaisse FEM
- **The walls are one metre thick.** Les murs font un mètre d'épaisseur.

2 (*stupid*)
bête

thief NOUN
le *voleur*
la *voleuse*

thigh NOUN
la *cuisse*

thin ADJECTIVE
1 *mince* (*person, slice*)
2 *maigre* (*skinny*)

thing NOUN
1 la *chose* ◇ *beautiful things* de belles choses
2 le *truc* (*thingy*) ◇ *What's that thing called?* Comment s'appelle ce truc?
- **my things** (*belongings*) mes affaires FEM
- **You poor thing!** Mon pauvre!

to think VERB
1 *penser* (*believe*) ◇ *I think you're wrong.* Je pense que vous avez tort. ◇ *What do you think about the death penalty?* Que pensez-vous de la peine de mort?
2 *réfléchir* (*spend time thinking*) ◇ *Think carefully before you reply.* Réfléchis bien avant de répondre. ◇ *What are you thinking about?* À quoi tu penses? ◇ *I'll think about it.* Je vais y réfléchir.
3 *imaginer* (*imagine*) ◇ *Think what life would be like without cars.* Imaginez la vie sans voitures.
- **I think so.** Oui, je crois.
- **I don't think so.** Je ne crois pas.
- **I'll think it over.** Je vais y réfléchir.

third ADJECTIVE
see also third NOUN
troisième ◇ *the third day* le troisième jour ◇ *the third time* la troisième fois ◇ *came third.* Je suis arrivé troisième.
- **the third of March** le trois mars

third NOUN
see also third ADJECTIVE
le *tiers* ◇ *a third of the population* un tiers de la population

thirdly ADVERB
troisièmement

Third World NOUN
le *tiers monde*

thirst NOUN
la *soif*

thirsty ADJECTIVE
- **to be thirsty** avoir soif

thirteen NUMBER
treize ◇ *I'm thirteen.* J'ai treize ans.

thirty NUMBER
trente

this ADJECTIVE, PRONOUN
Use **ce** *when* this *is followed by a masculine noun, and* **cette** *when* this *is followed by a feminine noun.* **ce** *changes to* **cet** *before a vowel and before most words beginning with "h".*
1 *ce* ◇ *this book* ce livre
cet ◇ *this man* cet homme
cette ◇ *this woman* cette femme
- **this road** cette route
- **THIS road** cette route-ci
- **this one (1)** celui-ci (*masculine*) ◇ *Pass me that pen.–This one?* Passe-moi ce stylo.–Celui-ci?
- **this one (2)** celle-ci (*feminine*) ◇ *Of the two photos, I prefer this one.* Des deux photos, c'est celle-ci que je préfère.

2 *ça* ◇ *You see this?* Tu vois ça?
- **What's this?** Qu'est-ce que c'est?
- **This is my mother.** (*introduction*) Je te présente ma mère.
- **This is Gavin speaking.** (*on the phone*)

C'est Gavin à l'appareil.

thistle NOUN
le *chardon*

thorough ADJECTIVE
minutieux MASC
minutieuse FEM
◇ *She's very thorough.* Elle est très minutieuse.

thoroughly ADVERB
à fond (*examine*)

those ADJECTIVE, PRONOUN
1 *ces* ◇ *those shoes* ces chaussures
- **THOSE shoes** ces chaussures-là

2 *ceux-là* MASC ◇ *I want those!* Je veux ceux-là!
celles-là FEM ◇ *I'm looking for some sandals. Can I try those?* Je cherche des sandales. Je peux essayer celles-là?

though CONJUNCTION, ADVERB
bien que
bien que *has to be followed by a verb in the subjunctive.*
◇ *Though it's raining...* Bien qu'il pleuve...
- **He's a nice person, though he's not very clever.** Il est sympa, mais pas très malin.

thought VERB *see* **think**

thought NOUN
l' *idée* FEM (*idea*) ◇ *I've just had a thought.* Je viens d'avoir une idée.
- **It was a nice thought, thank you.** C'est gentil de ta part, merci.

thoughtful ADJECTIVE
1 (*deep in thought*)
pensif MASC
pensive FEM
◇ *You look thoughtful.* Tu as l'air pensif.
2 (*considerate*)
prévenant ◇ *She's very thoughtful.* Elle est très prévenante.

thoughtless ADJECTIVE
- **He's completely thoughtless.** Il ne pense absolument pas aux autres.

thousand NUMBER
- **a thousand** mille ◇ *a thousand francs* mille francs
- **£2000** deux mille livres
- **thousands of people** des milliers de personnes

thread NOUN
le *fil*

threat NOUN
la *menace*

to **threaten** VERB
menacer ◇ *to threaten to do something* menacer de faire quelque chose

three NUMBER
trois ◇ *She's three.* Elle a trois ans.

three-dimensional ADJECTIVE
à trois dimensions

threw VERB *see* **throw**

thrifty ADJECTIVE
économe

thrill NOUN
l' *émotion* FEM (*excitement*)

thrilled ADJECTIVE
- **I was thrilled.** (*pleased*) J'étais absolument ravi.

thriller NOUN
le *thriller*

thrilling ADJECTIVE
palpitant

throat NOUN
la *gorge* ◇ *to have a sore throat* avoir mal à la gorge

to **throb** VERB
- **a throbbing pain** un élancement
- **My arm's throbbing.** J'ai des élancements dans le bras.

throne NOUN
le *trône*

through PREPOSITION, ADJECTIVE, ADVERB
1 *par* ◇ *through the window* par la fenêtre ◇ *I know her through my sister.* Je la connais par ma sœur. ◇ *to go through Birmingham* passer par Birmingham
- **to go through a tunnel** traverser un tunnel

2 *à travers* ◇ *through the mist* à travers la brume ◇ *through the crowd* à travers la foule ◇ *The window was dirty and I couldn't see through.* La fenêtre était sale et je n'arrivais pas à voir à travers.
- **a through train** un train direct
- **"no through road"** "impasse"

throughout PREPOSITION
- **throughout Britain** dans toute la Grande-Bretagne
- **throughout the year** pendant toute l'année

to **throw** VERB
lancer ◇ *He threw the ball to me.* Il m'a lancé le ballon.
- **to throw a party** organiser une soirée
- **That really threw him.** Ça l'a décontenancé.
- **to throw away (1)** (*rubbish*) jeter
- **to throw away (2)** (*chance*) perdre
- **to throw out (1)** (*throw away*) jeter
- **to throw out (2)** (*person*) mettre à la porte ◇ *I threw him out.* Je l'ai mis à la porte.
- **to throw up** vomir

thug NOUN
le *voyou*

thumb NOUN
le *pouce*

to **thump** VERB
- **to thump somebody** donner un coup de poing à quelqu'un

thunder NOUN
le *tonnerre*

thunderstorm NOUN
l' *orage* MASC

thundery ADJECTIVE
orageux MASC
orageuse FEM

Thursday NOUN
le *jeudi* ◇ *on Thursday* jeudi ◇ *on Thursdays* le jeudi ◇ *every Thursday* tous les jeudis ◇ *last Thursday* jeudi dernier ◇ *next Thursday* jeudi prochain

thyme NOUN
le *thym*

tick NOUN
1 la *coche* (*mark*)
2 le *tic-tac* (*of clock*)
- **I'll be back in a tick.** J'en ai pour une seconde.

ticket NOUN
Be careful to choose correctly between **le ticket** *and* **le billet**.
1 le *ticket* (*for bus, tube, cinema, museum*) ◇ *an underground ticket* un ticket de métro
2 le *billet* (*for plane, train, theatre, concert*)
- **a parking ticket** Un p.-v.

ticket inspector NOUN
le *contrôleur*
la *contrôleuse*

ticket office NOUN
le *guichet*

to **tickle** VERB
chatouiller

ticklish ADJECTIVE
chatouilleux MASC
chatouilleuse FEM
◇ *Are you ticklish?* Tu es chatouilleux?

to **tick off** VERB
- **to tick something off** cocher quelque chose
- **to tick somebody off** enguirlander quelqu'un

tide NOUN
la *marée*
- **high tide** la marée haute
- **low tide** la marée basse

tidy ADJECTIVE
see also tidy VERB
1 *bien rangé* (*room*) ◇ *Your room's very tidy.* Ta chambre est bien rangée.
2 *ordonné* (*person*) ◇ *She's very tidy.* Elle est très ordonnée.

to **tidy** VERB
see also tidy ADJECTIVE
ranger ◇ *Go and tidy your room.* Va ranger ta chambre.
- **to tidy up** ranger ◇ *Don't forget to tidy up afterwards.* N'oubliez pas de ranger après.

tie NOUN
see also tie VERB
la *cravate* (*necktie*)
- **It was a tie.** (*in sport*) Ils ont fait match nul.

to **tie** VERB
see also tie NOUN
1 *nouer* (*ribbon, shoelaces*)
- **to tie a knot in something** faire un nœud à quelque chose

2 *faire match nul* (*in sport*) ◇ *They tied three all.* Ils ont fait match nul, trois à trois.
- **to tie up (1)** (*parcel*) ficeler
- **to tie up (2)** (*dog, boat*) attacher
- **to tie up (3)** (*prisoner*) ligoter

tiger NOUN
le *tigre*

tight ADJECTIVE
1 *moulant* (*tight-fitting*) ◇ *tight clothes* les vêtements moulants
2 *juste* (*too tight*) ◇ *This dress is a bit tight.* Cette robe est un peu juste.

to **tighten** VERB
1 *tendre* (*rope*)
2 *resserrer* (*screw*)

tightly ADVERB
fort (*hold*)

tights PL NOUN
le *collant* SING

tile NOUN
1 (*on roof*)
la *tuile*
2 (*on wall, floor*)
le *carreau*
(les *carreaux* PL)

tiled ADJECTIVE
1 *en tuiles* (*roof*)
2 *carrelé* (*wall, floor, room*)

till NOUN
see also till PREPOSITION
la *caisse*

till PREPOSITION, CONJUNCTION
see also till NOUN
1 *jusqu'à* ◇ *I waited till ten o'clock.* J'ai attendu jusqu'à dix heures.
- **till now** jusqu'à présent
- **till then** jusque-là

Use **avant** *if the sentence you want to translate contains a negative, such as "not" or "never".*
2 *avant* ◇ *It won't be ready till next week.* Ça ne sera pas prêt avant la semaine prochaine. ◇ *Till last year I'd never been to France.* Avant l'année dernière, je n'étais jamais allé en France.

time NOUN
1 l' *heure* FEM (*on clock*) ◇ *What time is it?* Quelle heure est-il? ◇ *What time do you get up?* À quelle heure tu te lèves? ◇ *It was two o'clock, French time.* Il était deux heures, heure française.
- **on time** à l'heure ◇ *He never arrives on time.* Il n'arrive jamais à l'heure.

2 le *temps* (*amount of time*) ◇ *I'm sorry, I haven't got time.* Je suis désolé, je n'ai pas le temps.
- **from time to time** de temps en temps
- **in time** à temps ◇ *We arrived in time for lunch.* Nous sommes arrivés à temps pour le déjeuner.
- **just in time** juste à temps
- **in no time** en un rien de temps ◇ *It was ready in no time.* Ça a été prêt en un rien de temps.
- **It's time to go.** Il est temps de partir.

3 le *moment* (*moment*) ◇ *This isn't a good time to ask him.* Ce n'est pas le bon moment pour lui demander.
- **for the time being** pour le moment

4 la *fois* (*occasion*) ◇ *this time* cette fois-ci ◇ *next time* la prochaine fois ◇ *two at a time* deux à la fois
- **How many times?** Combien de fois?
- **at times** parfois
- **a long time** longtemps ◇ *Have you lived here for a long time?* Vous habitez ici depuis longtemps?
- **in a week's time** dans une semaine ◇ *I'll come back in a month's time.* Je reviendrai dans un mois.
- **Come and see us any time.** Venez nous voir quand vous voulez.
- **to have a good time** bien s'amuser ◇ *Did you have a good time?* Vous vous êtes bien amusés?
- **2 times 2 is 4** deux fois deux égalent quatre

time bomb NOUN
la *bombe à retardement*

time off NOUN
le *temps libre*

timer NOUN
le *minuteur*

time-share NOUN
l' *appartement en multipropriété* MASC

timetable NOUN
1 l' *horaire* MASC (*for train, bus*)
2 l' *emploi du temps* MASC (*at school*)

time zone NOUN
le *fuseau horaire*

tin NOUN
1 la *boîte* ◇ *a tin of soup* une boîte de soupe ◇ *a biscuit tin* une boîte à biscuits
2 la *boîte de conserve* ◇ *The bin was full of tins.* La poubelle était pleine de boîtes de conserve.
3 l' *étain* MASC (*type of metal*)

tinned ADJECTIVE
en boîte (*food*) ◇ *tinned peaches* des pêches en boîte

tin opener NOUN
l' *ouvre-boîte* MASC

tinsel NOUN
les *guirlandes de Noël* FEM PL

tinted ADJECTIVE
teinté (*spectacles, glass*)

tiny ADJECTIVE
minuscule

tip NOUN
see also tip VERB
1 (*money*)
le *pourboire* ◇ *Shall I give him a tip?* Je lui donne un pourboire?
2 (*advice*)
le *tuyau*
(les *tuyaux* PL)
◇ *a useful tip* un bon tuyau (*informal*)
3 (*end*)
le *bout* ◇ *It's on the tip of my tongue.* Je l'ai sur le bout de la langue.
- **a rubbish tip** une décharge
- **This place is a complete tip!** Quel fouillis!

to tip VERB
see also tip NOUN
donner un pourboire à ◇ *Don't forget to tip the taxi driver.* N'oubliez pas de donner un pourboire au chauffeur de taxi.

tiptoe NOUN
- **on tiptoe** sur la pointe des pieds

tired ADJECTIVE
fatigué ◇ *I'm tired.* Je suis fatigué.
- **to be tired of something** en avoir assez de quelque chose

tiring ADJECTIVE
fatigant

tissue NOUN
le *kleenex* ® ◇ *Have you got a tissue?* Tu as un kleenex? ®

title NOUN
le *titre*

title role NOUN
le *rôle principal*

to PREPOSITION
à + **le** *changes to* **au**. **à** + **les** *changes to* **aux**.
1 *à* ◇ *to go to Paris* aller à Paris ◇ *to go to school* aller à l'école ◇ *a letter to his mother* une lettre à sa mère ◇ *the answer to the question* la réponse à la question
au ◇ *to go to the theatre* aller au théâtre
aux ◇ *We said goodbye to the*

T

PTO

neighbours. Nous avons dit au revoir aux voisins.

- **ready to go** prêt à partir
- **ready to eat** prêt à manger
- **It's easy to do.** C'est facile à faire.
- **something to drink** quelque chose à boire
- **I've got things to do.** J'ai des choses à faire.
- **from...to...** de...à... ◇ *from nine o'clock to half past three* de neuf heures à trois heures et demie

2 *de* ◇ *the train to London* le train de Londres ◇ *the road to Edinburgh* la route d'Édimbourg ◇ *the key to the front door* la clé de la porte d'entrée

- **It's difficult to say.** C'est difficile à dire.
- **It's easy to criticize.** C'est facile de critiquer.

When referring to someone's house, shop or office, use **chez**.

3 *chez* ◇ *to go to the doctor's* aller chez le docteur ◇ *to go to the butcher's* aller chez le boucher ◇ *Let's go to Anne's house.* Si on allait chez Anne?

When to *refers to a country which is feminine, use* **en**; *when the country is masculine, use* **au**.

4 *en* ◇ *to go to France* aller en France *au* ◇ *to go to Portugal* aller au Portugal

5 *jusqu'à* (*up to*) ◇ *to count to ten* compter jusqu'à dix

6 *pour* (*in order to*) ◇ *I did it to help you.* Je l'ai fait pour vous aider. ◇ *She's too young to go to school.* Elle est trop jeune pour aller à l'école.

toad NOUN
le *crapaud*

toadstool NOUN
le *champignon vénéneux*

toast NOUN
1 le *pain grillé* ◇ *a piece of toast* une tranche de pain grillé
2 le *toast* (*speech*) ◇ *to drink a toast to somebody* porter un toast à quelqu'un

toaster NOUN
le *grille-pain*
(les *grille-pain* PL)

tobacco NOUN
le *tabac*

tobacconist's NOUN
le *bureau de tabac*
(les *bureaux de tabac* PL)

toboggan NOUN
la *luge*

tobogganing NOUN
- **to go tobogganing** faire de la luge

today ADVERB
aujourd'hui ◇ *What did you do today?* Qu'est-ce tu as fait aujourd'hui?

toddler NOUN
le *bambin*

toe NOUN
le *doigt de pied*

toffee NOUN
le *caramel*

together ADVERB
1 *ensemble* ◇ *Are they still together?* Ils sont toujours ensemble?
2 *en même temps* (*at the same time*) ◇ *Don't all speak together!* Ne parlez pas tous en même temps!

- **together with** (*with person*) avec

toilet NOUN
les *toilettes* FEM PL

toilet paper NOUN
le *papier hygiénique*

toiletries PL NOUN
les *articles de toilette* MASC PL

toilet roll NOUN
le *rouleau de papier hygiénique*
(les *rouleaux de papier hygiénique* PL)

token NOUN
- **a gift token** un bon-cadeau

told VERB *see* **tell**

tolerant ADJECTIVE
tolérant

toll NOUN
le *péage* (*on bridge, motorway*)

tomato NOUN
la *tomate* ◇ *tomato soup* la soupe à la tomate

tomboy NOUN
le *garçon manqué* ◇ *She's a real tomboy.* C'est un vrai garçon manqué.

tomorrow ADVERB
demain ◇ *tomorrow morning* demain matin ◇ *tomorrow night* demain soir

- **the day after tomorrow** après-demain

ton NOUN
la *tonne* ◇ *That old bike weighs a ton.* Ce vieux vélo pèse une tonne.

tongue NOUN
la *langue*

- **to say something tongue in cheek** dire quelque chose en plaisantant

tonic NOUN
le *Schweppes* ® (*tonic water*)

- **a gin and tonic** un gin tonic

tonight ADVERB
1 *ce soir* (*this evening*) ◇ *Are you going out tonight?* Tu sors ce soir?
2 *cette nuit* (*during the night*) ◇ *I'll sleep well tonight.* Je dormirai bien cette nuit.

tonsillitis NOUN
l' *angine* FEM

tonsils PL NOUN
les *amygdales* FEM PL

too ADVERB, ADJECTIVE

1 *aussi* (*as well*) ◇ *My sister came too.* Ma sœur est venue aussi.
2 *trop* (*excessively*) ◇ *The water's too hot.* L'eau est trop chaude. ◇ *We arrived too late.* Nous sommes arrivés trop tard.
- **too much (1)** (*with noun*) trop de ◇ *too much noise* trop de bruit
- **too much (2)** (*with verb*) trop ◇ *At Christmas we always eat too much.* À Noël nous mangeons toujours trop.
- **too much (3)** (*too expensive*) trop cher ◇ *Fifty francs? That's too much.* Cinquante francs? C'est trop cher.
- **too many** trop de ◇ *too many hamburgers* trop de hamburgers
- **Too bad!** Tant pis!

took VERB *see* **take**

tool NOUN
l' *outil* MASC
- **a tool box** une boîte à outils

tooth NOUN
la *dent*

toothache NOUN
le *mal de dents* ◇ *to have toothache* avoir mal aux dents

toothbrush NOUN
la *brosse à dents*

toothpaste NOUN
le *dentifrice*

top NOUN
see also top ADJECTIVE
1 le *haut* (*of page, ladder, garment*) ◇ *at the top of the page* en haut de la page
- **a bikini top** un haut de bikini

2 le *sommet* (*of mountain*)
3 le *dessus* (*of table*)
- **on top of** (*on*) sur ◇ *on top of the fridge* sur le frigo
- **There's a surcharge on top of that.** Il a un supplément en plus.
- **from top to bottom** de fond en comble ◇ *I searched the house from top to bottom.* J'ai fouillé la maison de fond en comble.

4 le *couvercle* (*of box, jar*)
5 le *bouchon* (*of bottle*)

top ADJECTIVE
see also top NOUN
grand (*first-class*) ◇ *a top surgeon* un grand chirurgien
- **a top model** un top model
- **He always gets top marks in French.** Il a toujours d'excellentes notes en français.
- **the top floor** le dernier étage ◇ *on the top floor* au dernier étage

topic NOUN
le *sujet* ◇ *The essay can be on any topic.* Cette dissertation peut être sur n'importe quel sujet.

topical ADJECTIVE
d'actualité ◇ *a topical issue* un sujet d'actualité

topless ADJECTIVE
aux seins nus (*model*)
- **to go topless** enlever le haut

top-secret ADJECTIVE
top secret MASC
top secrète FEM
◇ *top-secret documents* des documents top secrets

torch NOUN
la *lampe de poche*

tore, torn VERB *see* **tear**

tortoise NOUN
la *tortue*

torture NOUN
see also torture VERB
la *torture* ◇ *It was pure torture.* C'était une vraie torture.

to **torture** VERB
see also torture NOUN
torturer ◇ *Stop torturing that poor animal!* Arrête de torturer cette pauvre bête!

Tory ADJECTIVE
see also Tory NOUN
conservateur MASC
conservatrice FEM
◇ *the Tory government* le gouvernement conservateur

Tory NOUN
see also Tory ADJECTIVE
le *conservateur*
la *conservatrice*
- **the Tories** les conservateurs

to **toss** VERB
- **to toss pancakes** faire sauter les crêpes
- **Shall we toss for it?** On joue à pile ou face?

total ADJECTIVE
see also total NOUN
total
(*totaux* MASC PL)
- **the total amount** le total

total NOUN
see also total ADJECTIVE
le *total*
(les *totaux* PL)
- **the grand total** le total

totally ADVERB
complètement ◇ *He's totally useless.* Il est complètement nul.

touch NOUN
see also touch VERB
- **to get in touch with somebody** prendre contact avec quelqu'un
- **to keep in touch with somebody** ne pas perdre contact avec quelqu'un

T

PTO

- **Keep in touch!** Donne-moi de tes nouvelles!
- **to lose touch** se perdre de vue
- **to lose touch with somebody** perdre quelqu'un de vue

to **touch** VERB
see also touch NOUN
toucher
- **Don't touch that!** N'y touche pas!

touchdown NOUN
l' *atterrissage* MASC

touched ADJECTIVE
touché ◇ *I was really touched.* Ça m'a beaucoup touché.

touching ADJECTIVE
touchant

touchline NOUN
la *ligne de touche*

touchy ADJECTIVE
susceptible ◇ *She's a bit touchy.* Elle est susceptible.

tough ADJECTIVE
1 *dur* ◇ *It was tough, but I managed OK.* C'était dur, mais je m'en suis tiré. ◇ *It's a tough job.* C'est dur.
- **The meat's tough.** La viande est coriace.

2 (*strong*)
solide ◇ *tough leather gloves* de solides gants en cuir ◇ *She's tough. She can take it.* Elle est solide. Elle tiendra le coup.
3 (*rough, violent*)
dangereux MASC
dangereuse FEM
- **He thinks he's a tough guy.** Il se prend pour un gros dur.
- **Tough luck!** C'est comme ça!

toupee NOUN
le *postiche*

tour NOUN
see also tour VERB
1 la *visite* (*of town, museum*) ◇ *We went on a tour of the city.* Nous avons visité la ville.
- **a package tour** un voyage organisé

2 la *tournée* (*by singer, group*) ◇ *on tour* en tournée
- **to go on tour** faire une tournée

to **tour** VERB
see also tour NOUN
- **Paul Weller's touring Europe.** (*singer, artiste*) Paul Weller est en tournée en Europe.

tour guide NOUN
le/la *guide*

tourism NOUN
le *tourisme*

tourist NOUN
le/la *touriste*
- **tourist information office** l'office du tourisme MASC

tournament NOUN
le *tournoi*

towards PREPOSITION
1 *vers* (*in the direction of*) ◇ *He came towards me.* Il est venu vers moi.
2 *envers* (*of attitude*) ◇ *my feelings towards him* mes sentiments envers lui

towel NOUN
la *serviette*

tower NOUN
la *tour*
- **a tower block** une tour

town NOUN
la *ville* ◇ *a town plan* un plan de ville
- **the town centre** le centre-ville
- **the town hall** la mairie

toy NOUN
le *jouet* ◇ *a toy shop* un magasin de jouets
- **a toy car** une petite voiture

trace NOUN
see also trace VERB
la *trace* ◇ *There was no trace of the robbers.* Il n'y avait pas de trace des voleurs.

to **trace** VERB
see also trace NOUN
décalquer (*draw*)

tracing paper NOUN
le *papier calque*

track NOUN
1 le *chemin* (*dirt road*)
2 la *voie ferrée* (*railway line*)
3 la *piste* (*in sport*) ◇ *two laps of the track* deux tours de piste
4 la *chanson* (*song*) ◇ *This is my favourite track.* C'est ma chanson préférée.
5 les *traces* FEM PL (*trail*) ◇ *They followed the tracks for miles.* Ils ont suivi les traces pendant des kilomètres.

to **track down** VERB
- **to track somebody down** retrouver quelqu'un ◇ *The police never tracked down the killer.* La police n'a jamais retrouvé l'assassin.

tracksuit NOUN
le *survêtement*

tractor NOUN
le *tracteur*

trade NOUN
le *métier* (*skill, job*) ◇ *to learn a trade* apprendre un métier

trade union NOUN
le *syndicat*

trade unionist NOUN
le/la *syndicaliste*

tradition NOUN
la *tradition*

traditional ADJECTIVE
traditionnel MASC
traditionnelle FEM

traffic NOUN
la *circulation* ◇ *The traffic was terrible.* Il y avait une circulation épouvantable.

traffic jam NOUN
l' *embouteillage* MASC

traffic lights PL NOUN
les *feux* MASC

traffic warden NOUN
le *contractuel*
la *contractuelle*

tragedy NOUN
la *tragédie*

tragic ADJECTIVE
tragique

trailer NOUN
1 la *remorque* (*vehicle*)
2 la *bande-annonce* (*film advert*)

train NOUN
see also train VERB
1 le *train*
2 la *rame* (*on underground*)

train VERB
see also train NOUN
s'entraîner (*sport*) ◇ *to train for a race* s'entraîner pour une course
◆ **to train as a teacher** suivre une formation d'enseignant
◆ **to train an animal to do something** dresser un animal à faire quelque chose

trained ADJECTIVE
◆ **She's a trained nurse.** Elle est infirmière diplômée.

trainee NOUN
1 (*in profession*)
le/la *stagiaire* ◇ *She's a trainee.* Elle est stagiaire.
2 (*apprentice*)
l' *apprenti* MASC
l' *apprentie* FEM
◇ *a trainee plumber* un apprenti plombier

trainer NOUN
1 (*sports coach*)
l' *entraîneur* MASC
2 (*of animals*)
le *dompteur*
la *dompteuse*

trainers PL NOUN
les *baskets* FEM PL ◇ *a pair of trainers* une paire de baskets

training NOUN
1 la *formation* ◇ *a training course* un stage de formation
2 l' *entraînement* MASC (*sport*)

tram NOUN
le *tramway*

tramp NOUN
le *clochard*
la *clocharde*

trampoline NOUN
le *trampoline*

tranquillizer NOUN
le *tranquillisant* ◇ *She's on tranquillizers.* Elle prend des tranquillisants.

transfer NOUN
la *décalcomanie* (*sticker*)

transfusion NOUN
la *transfusion*

transistor NOUN
le *transistor*

transit lounge NOUN
la *salle de transit*

to **translate** VERB
traduire ◇ *to translate something into English* traduire quelque chose en anglais

translation NOUN
la *traduction*

translator NOUN
le *traducteur*
la *traductrice*
◇ *Anita's a translator.* Anita est traductrice.

transparent ADJECTIVE
transparent

transplant NOUN
la *greffe* ◇ *a heart transplant* une greffe du cardiaque

transport NOUN
see also transport VERB
le *transport* ◇ *public transport* les transports en commun

to **transport** VERB
see also transport NOUN
transporter

trap NOUN
le *piège*

trashy ADJECTIVE
nul MASC
nulle FEM
◇ *a really trashy film* un film vraiment nul

traumatic ADJECTIVE
traumatisant ◇ *It was a traumatic experience.* Ça a été une expérience traumatisante.

travel NOUN
see also travel VERB
les *voyages* MASC PL

to **travel** VERB
see also travel NOUN
voyager ◇ *I prefer to travel by train.* Je

PTO

préfère voyager en train.
- **I'd like to travel round the world.** J'aimerais faire le tour du monde.
- **We travelled over 800 kilometres.** Nous avons fait plus de huit cents kilomètres.
- **News travels fast!** Les nouvelles circulent vite!

travel agency NOUN
l' *agence de voyages* FEM

travel agent NOUN
- **She's a travel agent.** Elle travaille dans une agence de voyages.

traveller NOUN
1 (*on bus, train, plane*)
le *voyageur*
la *voyageuse*
2 (*gypsy*)
le/la *nomade*

traveller's cheque NOUN
le *chèque de voyage*

travelling NOUN
- **I love travelling.** J'adore les voyages.

travel sickness NOUN
le *mal des transports*

tray NOUN
le *plateau*
(les *plateaux* PL)

to **tread** VERB
marcher ◇ *to tread on something* marcher sur quelque chose

treasure NOUN
le *trésor*

treat NOUN
see also treat VERB
1 le *petit cadeau* (*present*)
2 la *gâterie* (*food*)
- **to give somebody a treat** faire plaisir à quelqu'un

to **treat** VERB
see also treat NOUN
traiter (*well, badly*)
- **to treat somebody to something** offrir quelque chose à quelqu'un ◇ *He treated us to an ice cream.* Il nous a offert une glace.

treatment NOUN
le *traitement*

to **treble** VERB
tripler ◇ *The cost of living there has trebled.* Le coût de la vie y a triplé.

tree NOUN
l' *arbre* MASC

to **tremble** VERB
trembler

trend NOUN
la *mode* (*fashion*)

trendy ADJECTIVE
branché

trial NOUN
le *procès* (*in court*)

triangle NOUN
le *triangle*

tribe NOUN
la *tribu*

trick NOUN
see also trick VERB
1 le *tour* ◇ *to play a trick on somebody* jouer un tour à quelqu'un
2 le *truc* FEM (*knack*) ◇ *It's not easy: there's a trick to it.* Ce n'est pas facile: il y a un truc.

to **trick** VERB
see also trick NOUN
- **to trick somebody** rouler quelqu'un

tricky ADJECTIVE
délicat

tricycle NOUN
le *tricycle*

trifle NOUN
le *diplomate* (*dessert*)

to **trim** VERB
see also trim NOUN
1 *égaliser* (*hair*)
2 *tondre* (*grass*)

trim NOUN
see also trim VERB
la *coupe d'entretien* (*haircut*) ◇ *to have a trim* se faire faire une coupe d'entretien

trip NOUN
see also trip VERB
le *voyage* ◇ *to go on a trip* faire un voyage ◇ *Have a good trip!* Bon voyage!
- **a day trip** une excursion d'une journée

to **trip** VERB
see also trip NOUN
trébucher (*stumble*)

triple ADJECTIVE
triple

triplets PL NOUN
les *triplés* MASC PL (*boys*)
(les *triplées* FEM PL) (*girls*)

trivial ADJECTIVE
insignifiant

trolley NOUN
le *chariot*

trombone NOUN
le *trombone* ◇ *I play the trombone.* Je joue du trombone.

troops PL NOUN
les *troupes* MASC PL ◇ *British troops* les troupes britanniques

trophy NOUN
le *trophée* ◇ *to win a trophy* gagner un trophée

tropical ADJECTIVE
tropical ◇ *The weather was tropical.* Il faisait une chaleur tropicale.

to **trot** VERB
trotter

trouble NOUN
le *problème* ◇ *The trouble is, it's too expensive.* Le problème, c'est que c'est trop cher.
- **to be in trouble** avoir des ennuis
- **What's the trouble?** Qu'est-ce qui ne va pas?
- **stomach trouble** troubles gastriques
- **to take a lot of trouble over something** se donner beaucoup de mal pour quelque chose
- **Don't worry, it's no trouble.** Mais non, ça ne me dérange pas du tout.

troublemaker NOUN
l' *élément perturbateur* MASC

trousers PL NOUN
le *pantalon* SING

trout NOUN
la *truite*

truant NOUN
- **to play truant** faire l'école buissonnière

truck NOUN
le *camion*
- **a truck driver** un camionneur ◇ *He's a truck driver.* Il est camionneur.

true ADJECTIVE
vrai
- **That's true.** C'est vrai.
- **to come true** se réaliser ◇ *I hope my dream will come true.* J'espère que mon rêve se réalisera.
- **true love** le grand amour

trumpet NOUN
la *trompette* ◇ *She plays the trumpet.* Elle joue de la trompette.

trunk NOUN
1 le *tronc* (*of tree*)
2 la *trompe* (*of elephant*)
3 la *malle* (*luggage*)

trunks PL NOUN
- **swimming trunks** le maillot de bain

trust NOUN
see also trust VERB
la *confiance* ◇ *to have trust in somebody* avoir confiance en quelqu'un

to **trust** VERB
see also trust NOUN
- **to trust somebody** faire confiance à quelqu'un ◇ *Don't you trust me?* Tu ne me fais pas confiance? ◇ *Trust me!* Fais-moi confiance!

trusting ADJECTIVE
confiant

truth NOUN
la *vérité*

truthful ADJECTIVE
- **She's a very truthful person.** Elle dit toujours la vérité.

try NOUN
see also try VERB
l' *essai* MASC ◇ *his third try* son troisième essai
- **to have a try** essayer
- **It's worth a try.** Ça vaut la peine d'essayer.
- **to give something a try** essayer quelque chose

to **try** VERB
see also try NOUN
1 *essayer* (*attempt*) ◇ *to try to do something* essayer de faire quelque chose
- **to try again** refaire un essai

2 *goûter* (*taste*) ◇ *Would you like to try some?* Voulez-vous goûter?
- **to try on** essayer (*clothes*)
- **to try something out** essayer quelque chose

T-shirt NOUN
le *tee-shirt*

tube NOUN
le *tube*
- **the Tube** (*underground*) le métro

tuberculosis NOUN
la *tuberculose*

Tuesday NOUN
le *mardi* ◇ *on Tuesday* mardi ◇ *on Tuesdays* le mardi ◇ *every Tuesday* tous les mardis ◇ *last Tuesday* mardi dernier ◇ *next Tuesday* mardi prochain
- **Shrove Tuesday, Pancake Tuesday** le mardi gras

tug-of-war NOUN
la *lutte à la corde*

tuition NOUN
les *cours* MASC PL
- **private tuition** les cours particuliers

tulip NOUN
la *tulipe*

tumble dryer NOUN
le *sèche-linge*
(les *sèche-linge* PL)

tummy NOUN
le *ventre*

tuna NOUN
le *thon*

tune NOUN
l' *air* MASC (*melody*)
- **to play in tune** jouer juste
- **to sing out of tune** chanter faux

Tunisia NOUN
la *Tunisie*
- **in Tunisia** en Tunisie

tunnel NOUN
le *tunnel*
- **the Tunnel** (*Chunnel*) le tunnel sous la Manche

Turk NOUN
le *Turc*
la *Turque*

Turkey NOUN
la *Turquie*
- **in Turkey** en Turquie
- **to Turkey** en Turquie

turkey NOUN
1 la *dinde* (*meat*)
2 le *dindon* (*live bird*)

Turkish ADJECTIVE
see also Turkish NOUN
turc MASC
turque FEM

Turkish NOUN
see also Turkish ADJECTIVE
le *turc* (*language*)

turn NOUN
see also turn VERB
1 le *tournant* (*bend in road*)
- **"no left turn"** "défense de tourner à gauche"

2 le *tour* (*go*) ◇ *It's my turn!* C'est mon tour!

to **turn** VERB
see also turn NOUN
1 *tourner* ◇ *Turn right at the lights.* Tournez à droite aux feux.
2 *devenir* (*become*) ◇ *to turn red* devenir rouge
- **to turn into something** se transformer en quelque chose ◇ *The frog turned into a prince.* La grenouille s'est transformée en prince.

to **turn back** VERB
faire demi-tour ◇ *We turned back.* Nous avons fait demi-tour.

to **turn down** VERB
1 *refuser* (*offer*)
2 *baisser* (*radio, TV, heating*) ◇ *Shall I turn the heating down?* Je baisse le chauffage?

to **turn off** VERB
1 *éteindre* (*light, radio*)
2 *fermer* (*tap*)
3 *arrêter* (*engine*)

to **turn on** VERB
1 *allumer* (*light, radio*)
2 *ouvrir* (*tap*)
3 *mettre en marche* (*engine*)

to **turn out** VERB
- **It turned out to be a mistake.** Il s'est avéré que c'était une erreur.
- **It turned out that she was right.** Il s'est avéré qu'elle avait raison.

to **turn round** VERB
1 *faire demi-tour* (*car*)
2 *se retourner* (*person*)

to **turn up** VERB
1 *arriver* (*arrive*)
2 *monter* (*heater*)
- **Could you turn up the radio?** Tu peux monter le son de la radio?

turning NOUN
- **It's the third turning on the left.** C'est la troisième à gauche.
- **We took the wrong turning.** Nous n'avons pas tourné au bon endroit.

turnip NOUN
le *navet*

turquoise ADJECTIVE
turquoise MASC, FEM, PL (*colour*)

turtle NOUN
la *tortue*

tutor NOUN
le *professeur particulier* (*private teacher*)

TV NOUN
la *télé*

tweezers PL NOUN
la *pince à épiler* SING

twelfth ADJECTIVE
douzième ◇ *the twelfth floor* le douzième étage
- **the twelfth of August** le douze août

twelve NUMBER
douze ◇ *She's twelve.* Elle a douze ans.
- **twelve o'clock (1)** (*midday*) midi
- **twelve o'clock (2)** (*midnight*) minuit

twenty NUMBER
vingt ◇ *He's twenty.* Il a vingt ans.

twice ADVERB
deux fois
- **twice as much** deux fois plus ◇ *He gets twice as much pocket money as me.* Il a deux fois plus d'argent de poche que moi.

twin NOUN
le *jumeau* (*boy*)
la *jumelle* (*girl*)
(les *jumeaux* PL)
(les *jumelles* FEM PL)
- **my twin brother** mon frère jumeau
- **her twin sister** sa sœur jumelle
- **identical twins** les vrais jumeaux
- **a twin room** une chambre à deux lits

twinned ADJECTIVE
jumelé ◇ *Stroud is twinned with Châteaubriant.* Stroud est jumelée avec Châteaubriant.

to **twist** VERB
1 *tordre* (*bend*)
2 *déformer* (*distort*) ◇ *You're twisting my words.* Tu déformes ce que j'ai dit.

twit NOUN
le *crétin*
la *crétine*

two NUMBER
deux ◇ *She's two.* Elle a deux ans.

type NOUN
see also type VERB
le *type* ◇ *What type of camera have you got?* Quel type d'appareil photo as-tu?

to type VERB
see also type NOUN
taper à la machine ◇ *Can you type?* Tu sais taper à la machine?
◆ **to type a letter** taper une lettre

typewriter NOUN
la *machine à écrire*

typical ADJECTIVE
typique ◇ *That's just typical!* C'est typique!

tyre NOUN
le *pneu*
◆ **the tyre pressure** la pression des pneus

U

UFO NOUN
l' *OVNI* MASC (= objet volant non identifié)

ugh EXCLAMATION
pouah!

ugly ADJECTIVE
laid

ulcer NOUN
l' *ulcère* MASC
- **a mouth ulcer** un aphte

Ulster NOUN
l' *Irlande du Nord* FEM
- **in Ulster** en Irlande du Nord

ultimate ADJECTIVE
suprême ◇ *the ultimate challenge* le défi suprême
- **It was the ultimate adventure.** C'était la grande aventure.

ultimately ADVERB
au bout du compte ◇ *Ultimately, it's your decision.* Au bout du compte, c'est votre décision.

umbrella NOUN
1 le *parapluie*
2 le *parasol* (*for sun*)

umpire NOUN
1 l' *arbitre* MASC (*in cricket*)
2 le *juge de chaise* (*in tennis*)

UN NOUN
l' *ONU* FEM (= Organisation des Nations unies)

unable ADJECTIVE
- **to be unable to do something** ne pas pouvoir faire quelque chose ◇ *I was unable to come.* Je n'ai pas pu venir.

unacceptable ADJECTIVE
inacceptable

unanimous ADJECTIVE
unanime ◇ *a unanimous decision* une décision unanime

unavoidable ADJECTIVE
inévitable

unaware ADJECTIVE
- **to be unaware (1)** (*not know about*) ignorer ◇ *I was unaware of the regulations.* J'ignorais le règlement.
- **to be unaware (2)** (*not notice*) ne pas se rendre compte ◇ *She was unaware that she was being filmed.* Elle ne s'était pas rendu compte qu'on la filmait.

unbearable ADJECTIVE
insupportable

unbeatable ADJECTIVE
imbattable

unbelievable ADJECTIVE
incroyable

unborn ADJECTIVE
- **the unborn child** le fœtus

unbreakable ADJECTIVE
incassable

uncanny ADJECTIVE
étrange ◇ *That's uncanny!* C'est étrange!
- **an uncanny resemblance** une ressemblance troublante

uncertain ADJECTIVE
incertain ◇ *The future is uncertain.* L'avenir est incertain.
- **to be uncertain about something** ne pas être sûr de quelque chose

uncivilized ADJECTIVE
barbare

uncle NOUN
l' *oncle* MASC ◇ *my uncle* mon oncle

uncomfortable ADJECTIVE
pas confortable ◇ *The seats are rather uncomfortable.* Les sièges ne sont pas très confortables.

unconscious ADJECTIVE
sans connaissance

unconventional ADJECTIVE
peu conventionnel MASC
peu conventionnelle FEM

under PREPOSITION
1 *sous* ◇ *The cat's under the table.* Le chat est sous la table. ◇ *The tunnel goes under the Channel.* Le tunnel passe sous la Manche.
- **under there** là-dessous ◇ *What's under there?* Qu'est-ce qu'il y a là-dessous?

2 *moins de* (*less than*) ◇ *under 20 people* moins de vingt personnes ◇ *children under 10* les enfants de moins de dix ans

underage ADJECTIVE
- **He's underage.** Il n'a pas l'âge réglementaire.

undercover ADJECTIVE, ADVERB
secret MASC
secrète FEM
◇ *an undercover agent* un agent secret
- **She was working undercover.** Elle travaillait sous une fausse identité.

underestimate VERB
sous-estimer ◇ *I underestimated her.* Je l'ai sous-estimée.

underground ADJECTIVE, ADVERB
see also underground NOUN
1 *souterrain* ◇ *an underground car park* un parking souterrain
2 *sous terre* ◇ *Moles live underground.* Les taupes vivent sous terre.

underground NOUN
see also underground ADJECTIVE
le *métro* ◇ *Is there an underground in Lille?* Est-ce qu'il y a un métro à Lille?

underline VERB
souligner

underneath PREPOSITION, ADVERB
1 *sous* ◇ *underneath the carpet* sous la moquette
2 *dessous* ◇ *I got out of the car and looked underneath.* Je suis descendu de la voiture et j'ai regardé dessous.

underpaid ADJECTIVE
sous-payé ◇ *I'm underpaid.* Je suis sous-payé.

underpants PL NOUN
le *slip* SING

underpass NOUN
1 le *passage souterrain* (*for people*)
2 le *passage inférieur* (*for cars*)

understand VERB
comprendre ◇ *Do you understand?* Vous comprenez? ◇ *I don't understand this word.* Je ne comprends pas ce mot. ◇ *Is that understood?* C'est compris?

understanding ADJECTIVE
compréhensif MASC
compréhensive FEM
◇ *She's very understanding.* Elle est très compréhensive.

undertaker NOUN
l' *entrepreneur des pompes funèbres* MASC

underwater ADJECTIVE, ADVERB
sous l'eau ◇ *This sequence was filmed underwater.* Cette séquence a été filmée sous l'eau.
◆ **an underwater camera** un appareil photographique de plongée
◆ **underwater photography** la photographie subaquatique

underwear NOUN
les *sous-vêtements* MASC PL

undo VERB
1 *défaire* (*buttons, knot*)
2 *déballer* (*parcel*)

undress VERB
se déshabiller (*get undressed*) ◇ *The doctor told me to undress.* Le médecin m'a dit de me déshabiller.

uneconomic ADJECTIVE
pas rentable

unemployed ADJECTIVE
au chômage ◇ *He's unemployed.* Il est au chômage. ◇ *He's been unemployed for a year.* Ça fait un an qu'il est au chômage.
◆ **the unemployed** les chômeurs MASC

unemployment NOUN
le *chômage*

unexpected ADJECTIVE
inattendu ◇ *an unexpected visitor* un visiteur inattendu

unexpectedly ADVERB
à l'improviste ◇ *They arrived unexpectedly.* Ils sont arrivés à l'improviste.

unfair ADJECTIVE
injuste ◇ *It's unfair to girls.* C'est injuste pour les filles.

unfamiliar ADJECTIVE
◆ **I heard an unfamiliar voice.** J'ai entendu une voix que je ne connaissais pas.

unfashionable ADJECTIVE
démodé

unfit ADJECTIVE
◆ **I'm rather unfit at the moment.** Je ne suis pas en très bonne condition physique en ce moment.

to **unfold** VERB
déplier ◇ *She unfolded the map.* Elle a déplié la carte.

unforgettable ADJECTIVE
inoubliable

unfortunately ADVERB
malheureusement ◇ *Unfortunately, I arrived late.* Malheureusement, je suis arrivé en retard.

unfriendly ADJECTIVE
pas aimable ◇ *The waiters are a bit unfriendly.* Les serveurs ne sont pas très aimables.

ungrateful ADJECTIVE
ingrat

unhappy ADJECTIVE
malheureux MASC
malheureuse FEM
◇ *He was very unhappy as a child.* Il était très malheureux quand il était petit.
◆ **to look unhappy** avoir l'air triste

unhealthy ADJECTIVE
1 (*person*)
maladif MASC
maladive FEM
2 (*place, habit*)
malsain
3 (*food*)
pas sain

uniform NOUN
l' *uniforme* MASC ◇ *the school uniform* l'uniforme scolaire

uninhabited ADJECTIVE
inhabité

union NOUN
le *syndicat* (*trade union*)

Union Jack NOUN
le *drapeau du Royaume-Uni*

unique ADJECTIVE
unique

unit NOUN
1 l' *unité* FEM ◇ *a unit of measurement* une unité de mesure
2 l' *élément* MASC (*piece of furniture*) ◇ *a kitchen unit* un élément de cuisine

United Kingdom NOUN
le *Royaume-Uni*

United Nations NOUN
l' *O.N.U.* FEM (= Organisation des Nations Unies)

United States NOUN
les *États-Unis* MASC PL
➔ **in the United States** aux États-Unis
➔ **to the United States** aux États-Unis

universe NOUN
l' *univers* MASC

university NOUN
l' *université* FEM ◇ *She's at university.* Elle va à l'université. ◇ *Do you want to go to university?* Tu veux aller à l'université? ◇ *Lancaster University* l'université de Lancaster

unleaded petrol NOUN
l' *essence sans plomb* FEM

unless CONJUNCTION
➔ **unless he leaves** à moins qu'il ne parte ◇ *I won't come unless you phone me.* Je ne viendrai pas à moins que tu ne me téléphones.

unlike PREPOSITION
contrairement à ◇ *Unlike him, I really enjoy flying.* Contrairement à lui, j'adore prendre l'avion.

unlikely ADJECTIVE
peu probable ◇ *It's possible, but unlikely.* C'est possible, mais peu probable.

to **unload** VERB
décharger ◇ *We unloaded the car.* Nous avons déchargé la voiture. ◇ *The lorries go there to unload.* Les camions y vont pour être déchargés.

to **unlock** VERB
ouvrir ◇ *He unlocked the door of the car.* Il a ouvert la portière de la voiture.

unlucky ADJECTIVE
➔ **to be unlucky (1)** (*number, object*) porter malheur ◇ *They say thirteen is an unlucky number.* On dit que le nombre treize porte malheur.
➔ **to be unlucky (2)** (*person*) ne pas avoir de chance ◇ *Did you win?–No, I was unlucky.* Vous avez gagné?–Non, je n'ai pas eu de chance.

unmarried ADJECTIVE
célibataire (*person*) ◇ *an unmarried mother* une mère célibataire
➔ **an unmarried couple** un couple non marié

unnatural ADJECTIVE
pas naturel MASC
pas naturelle FEM

unnecessary ADJECTIVE
inutile

unofficial ADJECTIVE
1 (*meeting, leader*)
non officiel MASC
non officielle FEM
2 (*strike*)
sauvage

to **unpack** VERB
1 *défaire* ◇ *I unpacked my suitcase.* J'ai défait ma valise.
2 *déballer ses affaires* ◇ *I went to my room to unpack.* Je suis allé dans ma chambre pour déballer mes affaires. ◇ *I haven't unpacked my clothes yet.* Je n'ai pas encore déballé mes affaires.

unpleasant ADJECTIVE
désagréable

to **unplug** VERB
débrancher

unpopular ADJECTIVE
impopulaire

unpredictable ADJECTIVE
imprévisible

unreal ADJECTIVE
incroyable (*incredible*) ◇ *It was unreal!* C'était incroyable!

unrealistic ADJECTIVE
peu réaliste

unreasonable ADJECTIVE
pas raisonnable ◇ *Her attitude was completely unreasonable.* Son attitude n'était pas du tout raisonnable.

unreliable ADJECTIVE
pas fiable (*car, machine*) ◇ *It's a nice car, but a bit unreliable.* C'est une belle voiture, mais elle n'est pas très fiable.
➔ **He's completely unreliable.** On ne peut pas du tout compter sur lui.

to **unroll** VERB
dérouler

unsatisfactory ADJECTIVE
insatisfaisant

to **unscrew** VERB
dévisser ◇ *She unscrewed the top of the bottle.* Elle a dévissé le bouchon de la bouteille.

unshaven ADJECTIVE
mal rasé

unskilled worker ADJECTIVE
le *manœuvre*

unstable ADJECTIVE
instable

unsteady ADJECTIVE

mal assuré (*walk, voice*)
- **He was unsteady on his feet.** Il marchait d'un pas mal assuré.

unsuccessful ADJECTIVE
vain (*attempt*)
- **to be unsuccessful in doing something** ne pas réussir à faire quelque chose ◇ *an unsuccessful artist* un artiste qui n'a pas réussi

unsuitable ADJECTIVE
inapproprié (*clothes, equipment*)

untidy ADJECTIVE
1 *en désordre* ◇ *My bedroom's always untidy.* Ma chambre est toujours en désordre.
2 *débraillé* (*appearance, person*) ◇ *He's always untidy.* Il est toujours débraillé.
3 *désordonné* (*in character*) ◇ *He's a very untidy person.* Il est très désordonné.

untie VERB
1 *défaire* (*knot, parcel*)
2 *détacher* (*animal*)

until PREPOSITION, CONJUNCTION
1 *jusqu'à* ◇ *I waited until ten o'clock.* J'ai attendu jusqu'à dix heures.
- **until now** jusqu'à présent ◇ *It's never been a problem until now.* Ça n'a jamais été un problème jusqu'à présent.
- **until then** jusque-là ◇ *Until then I'd never been to France.* Jusque-là je n'étais jamais allé en France.

Use **avant** *if the sentence you want to translate contains a negative, such as "not" or "never".*

2 *avant* ◇ *It won't be ready until next week.* Ça ne sera pas prêt avant la semaine prochaine. ◇ *Until last year I'd never been to France.* Avant l'année dernière, je n'étais jamais allé en France.

unusual ADJECTIVE
1 *insolite* ◇ *an unusual shape* une forme insolite
2 *rare* ◇ *It's unusual to get snow at this time of year.* Il est rare qu'il neige à cette époque de l'année.

unwilling ADJECTIVE
- **to be unwilling to do something** ne pas être disposé à faire quelque chose ◇ *He was unwilling to help me.* Il n'était pas disposé à m'aider.

unwind VERB
se détendre (*relax*)

unwise ADJECTIVE
imprudent (*person*) ◇ *That was rather unwise of you.* C'était plutôt imprudent de votre part.

unwrap VERB
déballer ◇ *After the meal we unwrapped the presents.* Après le repas nous avons déballé les cadeaux.

up PREPOSITION, ADVERB
For other expressions with up, *see the verbs* go, come, put, turn *etc.*
en haut ◇ *up on the hill* en haut de la colline
- **up here** ici
- **up there** là-haut
- **up north** dans le nord
- **to be up** être levé (*out of bed*) ◇ *We were up at 6.* Nous étions levés à six heures. ◇ *He's not up yet.* Il n'est pas encore levé.
- **What's up?** Qu'est-ce qu'il y a? ◇ *What's up with her?* Qu'est-ce qu'elle a?
- **to get up** (*in the morning*) se lever ◇ *What time do you get up?* À quelle heure est-ce que tu te lèves?
- **to go up** monter ◇ *The bus went up the hill.* Le bus a monté la colline.
- **to go up to somebody** s'approcher de quelqu'un ◇ *She came up to me.* Elle s'est approchée de moi.
- **up to** (*as far as*) jusqu'à ◇ *to count up to fifty* compter jusqu'à cinquante ◇ *up to three hours* jusqu'à trois heures ◇ *up to now* jusqu'à présent
- **It's up to you.** C'est à vous de décider.

upbringing NOUN
l' *éducation* FEM

uphill ADVERB
- **to go uphill** monter

upper sixth NOUN
- **the upper sixth** la terminale ◇ *She's in the upper sixth.* Elle est en terminale.

upright ADJECTIVE
- **to stand upright** se tenir droit

upset NOUN
see also upset ADJECTIVE, VERB
- **a stomach upset** une indigestion

upset ADJECTIVE
see also upset NOUN, VERB
contrarié ◇ *She's still a bit upset.* Elle est encore un peu contrariée.
- **I had an upset stomach.** J'avais l'estomac dérangé.

to **upset** VERB
see also upset NOUN, ADJECTIVE
- **to upset somebody** contrarier quelqu'un

upside down ADVERB
à l'envers ◇ *That painting is upside down.* Ce tableau est à l'envers.

upstairs ADVERB
en haut ◇ *Where's your coat?–It's upstairs.* Où est ton manteau?–Il est en haut.
- **to go upstairs** monter

uptight ADJECTIVE

U

PTO

tendu ◇ *She's really uptight.* Elle est très tendue.

up-to-date ADJECTIVE
1 *moderne* (*car, stereo*)
2 *à jour* (*information*) ◇ *an up-to-date timetable* un horaire à jour
- **to bring something up to date** moderniser quelque chose

upwards ADVERB
vers le haut ◇ *to look upwards* regarder vers le haut

urgent ADJECTIVE
urgent ◇ *Is it urgent?* C'est urgent?

urine NOUN
l' *urine* FEM

US NOUN
les *USA* MASC PL

us PRONOUN
nous ◇ *They helped us.* Ils nous ont aidés. ◇ *They gave us a map.* Ils nous ont donné une carte.

USA NOUN
les *USA* MASC PL

use NOUN
see also use VERB
- **It's no use.** Ça ne sert à rien. ◇ *It's no use shouting, she's deaf.* Ça ne sert à rien de crier, elle est sourde.
- **It's no use, I can't do it.** Il n'y a rien à faire, je n'y arrive pas.
- **to make use of something** utiliser quelque chose

to **use** VERB
see also use NOUN
utiliser ◇ *Can we use a dictionary in the exam?* Est-ce qu'on peut utiliser un dictionnaire à l'examen?
- **Can I use your phone?** Je peux téléphoner?
- **to use the toilet** aller aux W.C.
- **to use up (1)** finir ◇ *We've used up all the paint.* Nous avons fini la peinture.
- **to use up (2)** (*money*) dépenser
- **I used to live in London.** J'habitais à Londres autrefois.
- **I used not to like maths, but now...** Avant, je n'aimais pas les maths, mais maintenant...
- **to be used to something** avoir l'habitude de quelque chose ◇ *He wasn't used to driving on the right.* Il n'avait pas l'habitude de conduire à droite. ◇ *Don't worry, I'm used to it.* Ne t'inquiète pas, j'ai l'habitude.
- **a used car** une voiture d'occasion

useful ADJECTIVE
utile

useless ADJECTIVE
nul MASC
nulle FEM
◇ *This map is just useless.* Cette carte est vraiment nulle. ◇ *You're useless!* Tu es nul!
- **It's useless!** Ça ne sert à rien!

usual ADJECTIVE
habituel MASC
habituelle FEM
- **as usual** comme d'habitude

usually ADVERB
1 *en général* (*generally*) ◇ *I usually get to school at about half past eight.* En général, j'arrive à l'école vers huit heures et demie.
2 *d'habitude* (*when making a contrast*) ◇ *Usually I don't wear make-up, but today is a special occasion.* D'habitude je ne me maquille pas, mais aujourd'hui c'est spécial.

utility room NOUN
la *buanderie*

U-turn NOUN
le *demi-tour* ◇ *to do a U-turn* faire demi-tour

V

vacancy NOUN
1 le *poste vacant* (*job*)
2 la *chambre disponible* (*room in hotel*)
◆ **"no vacancies"** (*on sign*) "complet"

vacant ADJECTIVE
libre

vaccinate VERB
vacciner

vacuum VERB
passer l'aspirateur ◇ *to vacuum the hall* passer l'aspirateur dans le couloir

vacuum cleaner NOUN
l' *aspirateur* MASC

vagina NOUN
le *vagin*

vague ADJECTIVE
vague

vain ADJECTIVE
vaniteux MASC
vaniteuse FEM
◇ *He's so vain!* Qu'est-ce qu'il est vaniteux!
◆ **in vain** en vain

Valentine card NOUN
la *carte de la Saint-Valentin*

Valentine's Day NOUN
la *Saint-Valentin*

valid ADJECTIVE
valable ◇ *This ticket is valid for three months.* Ce billet est valable trois mois.

valley NOUN
la *vallée*

valuable ADJECTIVE
1 *de valeur* ◇ *a valuable picture* un tableau de valeur
2 *précieux* MASC
précieuse FEM
◇ *valuable help* une aide précieuse

valuables PL NOUN
les *objets de valeur* MASC PL ◇ *Don't take any valuables with you.* N'emportez pas d'objets de valeur.

value NOUN
la *valeur*

van NOUN
la *camionnette*

vandal NOUN
le/la *vandale*

vandalism NOUN
le *vandalisme*

vandalize VERB
saccager

vanilla NOUN
la *vanille*
◆ **vanilla ice cream** la glace à la vanille

vanish VERB
disparaître

variable ADJECTIVE
variable

varied ADJECTIVE
varié

variety NOUN
la *variété*

various ADJECTIVE
plusieurs ◇ *We visited various villages in the area.* Nous avons visité plusieurs villages de la région.

to **vary** VERB
varier

vase NOUN
le *vase*

VAT NOUN (= *value added tax*)
la *TVA* (= taxe sur la valeur ajoutée)

VCR NOUN (= *video cassette recorder*)
le *magnétoscope*

VDU NOUN (= *visual display unit*)
la *console*

veal NOUN
le *veau*

vegan NOUN
le *végétalien*
la *végétalienne*
◇ *I'm a vegan.* Je suis végétalien.

vegetable NOUN
le *légume* ◇ *vegetable soup* la soupe aux légumes

vegetarian ADJECTIVE
see also vegetarian NOUN
végétarien MASC
végétarienne FEM
◇ *I'm vegetarian.* Je suis végétarien.
◇ *vegetarian lasagne* les lasagnes végétariennes

vegetarian NOUN
see also vegetarian ADJECTIVE
le *végétarien*
la *végétarienne*
◇ *I'm a vegetarian.* Je suis végétarien.

vehicle NOUN
le *véhicule*

vein NOUN
la *veine*

velvet NOUN
le *velours*

vending machine NOUN
le *distributeur automatique*

Venetian blind NOUN
le *store vénitien*

verb NOUN
le *verbe*

verdict NOUN
le *verdict*

vertical ADJECTIVE
vertical
(*verticaux* MASC PL)

vertigo NOUN
le *vertige* ◇ *I get vertigo.* J'ai le vertige.

very ADVERB
très ◇ *very tall* très grand ◇ *not very interesting* pas très intéressant
➔ **very much** beaucoup

vest NOUN
le *maillot de corps*

vet NOUN
le/la *vétérinaire* ◇ *She's a vet.* Elle est vétérinaire.

via PREPOSITION
en passant par ◇ *We went to Paris via Boulogne.* Nous sommes allés à Paris en passant par Boulogne.

vicar NOUN
le *pasteur* ◇ *He's a vicar.* Il est pasteur.

vice NOUN
l' *étau* (*for holding things*) MASC

vice versa ADVERB
vice versa

vicious ADJECTIVE
1 *brutal*
(*brutaux* MASC PL)
◇ *a vicious attack* une agression brutale
2 *méchant* (*dog, person*)
➔ **a vicious circle** un cercle vicieux

victim NOUN
la *victime* ◇ *He was the victim of a mugging.* Il a été victime d'une agression.

victory NOUN
la *victoire*

to **video** VERB
see also video NOUN
1 *enregistrer* (*from TV*)
2 *filmer* (*with video camera*)

video NOUN
see also video VERB
1 la *vidéo* (*film*) ◇ *to watch a video* regarder une vidéo ◇ *a video of my family on holiday* une vidéo de ma famille en vacances ◇ *It's out on video.* C'est sorti en vidéo.
2 la *cassette vidéo* (*video cassette*)
◇ *She lent me a video.* Elle m'a prêté une cassette vidéo.
3 le *magnétoscope* (*video recorder*)
◇ *Have you got a video?* Tu as un magnétoscope?
➔ **a video camera** une caméra vidéo
➔ **a video cassette** une cassette vidéo
➔ **a video game** un jeu vidéo ◇ *He likes playing video games.* Il aime les jeux vidéo.
➔ **a video recorder** un magnétoscope
➔ **a video shop** un vidéoclub

Vietnam NOUN
le *Viêt-Nam*
➔ **in Vietnam** au Viêt-Nam

Vietnamese ADJECTIVE
vietnamien MASC
vietnamienne FEM

view NOUN
1 la *vue* ◇ *There's an amazing view.* Il y a une vue extraordinaire.
2 l' *avis* MASC (*opinion*) ◇ *in my view* à mon avis

viewer NOUN
le *téléspectateur*
la *téléspectatrice*

viewpoint NOUN
le *point de vue*

vile ADJECTIVE
dégoûtant (*smell, food*)

villa NOUN
la *villa*

village NOUN
le *village*

villain NOUN
1 le *malfrat* (*criminal*)
2 le *méchant* (*in film*)

vine NOUN
la *vigne*

vinegar NOUN
le *vinaigre*

vineyard NOUN
le *vignoble*

viola NOUN
l' *alto* MASC ◇ *I play the viola.* Je joue de l'alto.

violence NOUN
la *violence*

violent ADJECTIVE
violent

violin NOUN
le *violon* ◇ *I play the violin.* Je joue du violon.

violinist NOUN
le/la *violoniste*

virgin NOUN
la *vierge* ◇ *to be a virgin* être vierge

Virgo NOUN
la *Vierge* ◇ *I'm Virgo.* Je suis Vierge.

virtual reality NOUN
la *réalité virtuelle*

virus NOUN
le *virus*

visa NOUN
le *visa*

visible ADJECTIVE
visible

visit NOUN
see also visit VERB
1 la *visite* (*to museum*)

2 le *séjour* (*to country*) ◇ *Did you enjoy your visit to France?* Ton séjour en France s'est bien passé?

➤ **my last visit to my grandmother** la dernière fois que je suis allé voir ma grand-mère

visit VERB

see also visit NOUN

1 *rendre visite à* (*person*) ◇ *to visit somebody* rendre visite à quelqu'un

2 *visiter* (*place*) ◇ *We'd like to visit the castle.* Nous voudrions visiter le château.

visitor NOUN

1 (*tourist*)
le *visiteur*
la *visiteuse*

2 (*guest*)
l' *invité* MASC
l' *invitée* FEM

➤ **to have a visitor** avoir de la visite

visual ADJECTIVE
visuel MASC
visuelle FEM

visualize VERB
imaginer

vital ADJECTIVE
vital
(*vitaux* MASC PL)

vitamin NOUN
la *vitamine*

vivid ADJECTIVE
(*colour*)
vif MASC
vive FEM

➤ **to have a vivid imagination** avoir une imagination débordante

vocabulary NOUN
le *vocabulaire*

vocational ADJECTIVE
professionnel MASC
professionnelle FEM

➤ **a vocational course** un stage de formation professionnelle

vodka NOUN
la *vodka*

voice NOUN
la *voix*
(les *voix* PL)

volcano NOUN
le *volcan*

volleyball NOUN
le *volley-ball* ◇ *to play volleyball* jouer au volley-ball

volt NOUN
le *volt*

voltage NOUN
le *voltage*

voluntary ADJECTIVE
volontaire (*contribution, statement*)

➤ **to do voluntary work** travailler bénévolement

volunteer NOUN

see also volunteer VERB

le/la *volontaire*

to **volunteer** VERB

see also volunteer NOUN

➤ **to volunteer to do something** se proposer pour faire quelque chose

to **vomit** VERB
vomir

to **vote** VERB
voter

voucher NOUN
le *bon* ◇ *a gift voucher* un bon d'achat

vowel NOUN
la *voyelle*

vulgar ADJECTIVE
vulgaire

W

wafer NOUN
la *gaufrette*

wage NOUN
le *salaire* ◇ *He collected his wages.* Il a retiré son salaire.

waist NOUN
la *taille*

waistcoat NOUN
le *gilet*

to **wait** VERB
attendre
- **to wait for something** attendre quelque chose
- **to wait for somebody** attendre quelqu'un ◇ *I'll wait for you.* Je t'attendrai.
- **Wait for me!** Attends-moi!
- **Wait a minute!** Attends!
- **to keep somebody waiting** faire attendre quelqu'un ◇ *They kept us waiting for hours.* Ils nous ont fait attendre pendant des heures.
- **I can't wait for the holidays.** J'ai hâte d'être en vacances.
- **I can't wait to see him again.** J'ai hâte de le revoir.

waiter NOUN
le *serveur*

waiting list NOUN
la *liste d'attente*

waiting room NOUN
la *salle d'attente*

waitress NOUN
la *serveuse*

to **wake up** VERB
se réveiller ◇ *I woke up at six o'clock.* Je me suis réveillé à six heures.
- **to wake somebody up** réveiller quelqu'un ◇ *Please would you wake me up at seven o'clock?* Pourriez-vous me réveiller à sept heures?

Wales NOUN
le *pays de Galles*
- **in Wales** au pays de Galles
- **to Wales** au pays de Galles
- **I'm from Wales.** Je suis gallois.
- **the Prince of Wales** le prince de Galles

to **walk** VERB
see also walk NOUN
1 *marcher* ◇ *He walks fast.* Il marche vite.
2 *aller à pied* (*go on foot*) ◇ *Are you walking or going by bus?* Tu y vas à pied ou en bus? ◇ *We walked 10 kilometres.* Nous avons fait dix kilomètres à pied.
- **to walk the dog** promener le chien

walk NOUN
see also walk VERB
la *promenade* ◇ *to go for a walk* faire une promenade
- **It's 10 minutes' walk from here.** C'est à dix minutes d'ici à pied.

walkie-talkie NOUN
le *talkie-walkie*

walking NOUN
la *randonnée* ◇ *I did some walking in the Alps last summer.* J'ai fait de la randonnée dans les Alpes l'été dernier.

walking stick NOUN
la *canne*

Walkman® NOUN
le *baladeur*

wall NOUN
le *mur*

wallet NOUN
le *portefeuille*

wallpaper NOUN
le *papier peint*

walnut NOUN
la *noix*
(les *noix* PL)

to **wander** VERB
- **to wander around** flâner ◇ *I just wandered around for a while.* J'ai flâné un peu.

to **want** VERB
vouloir ◇ *Do you want some cake?* Tu veux du gâteau?
- **to want to do something** vouloir faire quelque chose ◇ *I want to go to the cinema.* Je veux aller au cinéma. ◇ *What do you want to do tomorrow?* Qu'est-ce que tu veux faire demain?

war NOUN
la *guerre*

ward NOUN
la *salle* (*room in hospital*)

warden NOUN
(*of youth hostel*)
le *directeur*
la *directrice*

wardrobe NOUN
l' *armoire* FEM (*piece of furniture*)

warehouse NOUN
l' *entrepôt* MASC

warm ADJECTIVE
1 *chaud* ◇ *warm water* l'eau chaude
- **It's warm in here.** Il fait chaud ici.
- **to be warm** (*person*) avoir chaud ◇ *I'm too warm.* J'ai trop chaud.

2 *chaleureux* MASC
chaleureuse FEM

◇ *a warm welcome* un accueil chaleureux
- **to warm up (1)** (*for sport*) s'échauffer
- **to warm up (2)** (*food*) réchauffer ◇ *I'll warm up some lasagne for you.* Je vais te réchauffer des lasagnes.

warn VERB
prévenir ◇ *Well, I warned you!* Je t'avais prévenu!
- **to warn somebody to do something** conseiller à quelqu'un de faire quelque chose

warning NOUN
l' *avertissement* MASC

Warsaw NOUN
Varsovie

wart NOUN
la *verrue*

was VERB *see* **be**

wash NOUN
see also wash VERB
- **to have a wash** se laver ◇ *I had a wash.* Je me suis lavé.
- **to give something a wash** laver quelque chose ◇ *He gave the car a wash.* Il a lavé la voiture.

wash VERB
see also wash NOUN
1 *laver* ◇ *to wash something* laver quelque chose
2 *se laver* (*have a wash*) ◇ *Every morning I get up, wash and get dressed.* Tous les matins je me lève, je me lave et je m'habille.
- **to wash one's hands** se laver les mains
- **to wash one's hair** se laver les cheveux
- **to wash up** faire la vaisselle

washbasin NOUN
le *lavabo*

washing NOUN
le *linge* ◇ *dirty washing* du linge sale
- **Have you got any washing?** Tu as du linge à laver?
- **to do the washing** faire la lessive

washing machine NOUN
la *machine à laver*

washing powder NOUN
la *lessive*

washing-up NOUN
- **to do the washing-up** faire la vaisselle

washing-up liquid NOUN
le *produit à vaisselle*

wasn't = **was not**

wasp NOUN
la *guêpe*

waste NOUN
see also waste VERB
1 le *gaspillage* ◇ *It's such a waste!* C'est vraiment du gaspillage!
- **It's a waste of time.** C'est une perte de temps.

2 les *déchets* MASC (*rubbish*) ◇ *nuclear waste* les déchets nucléaires

to **waste** VERB
see also waste NOUN
gaspiller ◇ *I don't like wasting money.* Je n'aime pas gaspiller de l'argent.
- **to waste time** perdre du temps ◇ *There's no time to waste.* Il n'y a pas de temps à perdre.

wastepaper basket NOUN
la *corbeille à papier*

watch NOUN
see also watch VERB
la *montre*

to **watch** VERB
see also watch NOUN
1 *regarder* ◇ *to watch television* regarder la télévision ◇ *Watch me!* Regarde-moi!
2 *surveiller* (*keep a watch on*) ◇ *The police were watching the house.* La police surveillait la maison.
- **to watch out** faire attention
- **Watch out!** Attention!

water NOUN
see also water VERB
l' *eau* FEM

to **water** VERB
see also water NOUN
arroser ◇ *He was watering his tulips.* Il arrosait ses tulipes.

waterfall NOUN
la *cascade*

watering can NOUN
l' *arrosoir* MASC

watermelon NOUN
la *pastèque*

waterproof ADJECTIVE
imperméable ◇ *Is this jacket waterproof?* Ce blouson est-il imperméable?
- **a waterproof watch** une montre étanche

water-skiing NOUN
le *ski nautique* ◇ *to go water-skiing* faire du ski nautique

wave NOUN
see also wave VERB
1 la *vague* (*in water*)
2 le *signe* (*of hand*) ◇ *We gave him a wave.* Nous lui avons fait signe.

to **wave** VERB
see also wave NOUN
faire un signe de la main ◇ *to wave at somebody* faire un signe de la main à quelqu'un
- **to wave goodbye** faire au revoir de la main ◇ *I waved her goodbye.* Je lui ai

fait au revoir de la main.

wavy ADJECTIVE
ondulé ◇ *wavy hair* les cheveux ondulés

wax NOUN
la *cire*

way NOUN
1 la *façon* (*manner*) ◇ *She looked at me in a strange way.* Elle m'a regardé d'une façon étrange.
- **This book tells you the right way to do it.** Ce livre explique comment il faut faire.
- **You're doing it the wrong way.** Ce n'est pas comme ça qu'il faut faire.
- **in a way...** dans un sens...
- **a way of life** un mode de vie

2 le *chemin* (*route*) ◇ *I don't know the way.* Je ne connais pas le chemin.
- **on the way** en chemin ◇ *We stopped for lunch on the way.* Nous nous sommes arrêtés pour déjeuner en chemin.
- **It's a long way.** C'est loin. ◇ *Paris is a long way from London.* Paris est loin de Londres.
- **Which way is it?** C'est par où?
- **The supermarket is this way.** Le supermarché est par ici.
- **Do you know the way to the station?** Est-ce que vous savez comment aller à la gare?
- **He's on his way.** Il arrive.
- **"way in"** "entrée"
- **"way out"** "sortie"
- **by the way...** au fait...

we PRONOUN
nous ◇ *We're staying here for a week.* Nous restons une semaine ici.

weak ADJECTIVE
faible

wealthy ADJECTIVE
riche

weapon NOUN
l' *arme* FEM

to **wear** VERB
porter (*clothes*) ◇ *She was wearing a hat.* Elle portait un chapeau.
- **She was wearing black.** Elle était en noir.

weather NOUN
le *temps* ◇ *What was the weather like?* Quel temps a-t-il fait? ◇ *The weather was lovely.* Il a fait un temps magnifique.

weather forecast NOUN
la *météo*

we'd = **we had, we would**

wedding NOUN
le *mariage*
- **wedding anniversary** l'anniversaire de mariage MASC
- **wedding dress** la robe de mariée

Wednesday NOUN
le *mercredi* ◇ *on Wednesday* mercredi ◇ *on Wednesdays* le mercredi ◇ *every Wednesday* tous les mercredis ◇ *last Wednesday* mercredi dernier ◇ *next Wednesday* mercredi prochain

weed NOUN
la *mauvaise herbe* ◇ *The garden's full of weeds.* Le jardin est plein de mauvaises herbes.

week NOUN
la *semaine* ◇ *last week* la semaine dernière ◇ *every week* toutes les semaines ◇ *next week* la semaine prochaine ◇ *in a week's time* dans une semaine
- **a week on Friday** vendredi en huit

weekday NOUN
- **on weekdays** en semaine

weekend NOUN
le *week-end* ◇ *at weekends* le week-end ◇ *last weekend* le week-end dernier ◇ *next weekend* le week-end prochain

to **weigh** VERB
peser ◇ *How much do you weigh?* Combien est-ce que tu pèses? ◇ *First, weigh the flour.* Tout d'abord, pesez la farine.
- **to weigh oneself** se peser

weight NOUN
le *poids*
- **to lose weight** maigrir
- **to put on weight** grossir

weightlifter NOUN
l' *haltérophile* MASC

weightlifting NOUN
l' *haltérophilie* FEM

weird ADJECTIVE
bizarre

welcome NOUN
see also welcome VERB
l' *accueil* MASC ◇ *They gave her a warm welcome.* Ils lui ont fait un accueil chaleureux.
- **Welcome!** Bienvenue! ◇ *Welcome to France!* Bienvenue en France!

to **welcome** VERB
see also welcome NOUN
- **to welcome somebody** accueillir quelqu'un
- **Thank you! – You're welcome!** Merci! – De rien!

well ADJECTIVE, ADVERB
see also well NOUN
1 *bien* ◇ *You did that really well.* Tu as

très bien fait ça.
to do well réussir bien ◇ *She's doing really well at school.* Elle réussit vraiment bien à l'école.
to be well (*in good health*) aller bien ◇ *I'm not very well at the moment.* Je ne vais pas très bien en ce moment.
Get well soon! Remets-toi vite!
Well done! Bravo!
2 *enfin* ◇ *It's enormous! Well, quite big anyway.* C'est énorme! Enfin, c'est assez grand.
as well aussi ◇ *We worked hard, but we had some fun as well.* Nous avons travaillé dur, mais nous nous sommes bien amusés aussi. ◇ *We went to Chartres as well as Paris.* Nous sommes allés à Paris et à Chartres aussi.

well NOUN
see also well ADJECTIVE
le *puits*
(les *puits* PL)

we'll = **we will**

well-behaved ADJECTIVE
sage

well-dressed ADJECTIVE
bien habillé

wellingtons PL NOUN
les *bottes en caoutchouc* FEM PL

well-known ADJECTIVE
célèbre ◇ *a well-known film star* une vedette de cinéma célèbre

well-off ADJECTIVE
aisé

Welsh ADJECTIVE
see also Welsh NOUN
gallois ◇ *She's Welsh.* Elle est galloise.
Welsh people les Gallois MASC

Welsh NOUN
see also Welsh ADJECTIVE
le *gallois* (*language*)

Welshman NOUN
le *Gallois*

Welshwoman NOUN
la *Galloise*

went VERB *see* **go**

were VERB *see* **be**

we're = **we are**

weren't = **were not**

west NOUN
see also west ADJECTIVE
l' *ouest* MASC ◇ *in the west* dans l'ouest

west ADJECTIVE, ADVERB
see also west NOUN
1 *ouest* MASC, FEM, PL ◇ *the west coast* la côte ouest
west of à l'ouest de ◇ *Stroud is west of Oxford.* Stroud est à l'ouest d'Oxford.
2 *vers l'ouest* ◇ *We were travelling west.* Nous allions vers l'ouest.
the West Country le sud-ouest de l'Angleterre

western NOUN
see also western ADJECTIVE
le *western* (*film*)

western ADJECTIVE
see also western NOUN
the western part of the island la partie ouest de l'île
Western Europe l'Europe de l'Ouest

West Indian ADJECTIVE
see also West Indian NOUN
antillais ◇ *She's West Indian.* Elle est antillaise.

West Indian NOUN
see also West Indian ADJECTIVE
1 l' *Antillais* MASC
2 l' *Antillaise* FEM (*person*)

West Indies PL NOUN
les *Antilles* FEM PL
in the West Indies aux Antilles

wet ADJECTIVE
mouillé ◇ *wet clothes* les vêtements mouillés
to get wet se faire mouiller
dripping wet trempé
wet weather le temps pluvieux
It was wet all week. Il a plu toute la semaine.

wetsuit NOUN
la *combinaison de plongée*
(les *combinaisons de plongée* PL)

we've = **we have**

whale NOUN
la *baleine*

what ADJECTIVE, PRONOUN
1 (*which*)
quel MASC
quelle FEM
◇ *What subjects are you studying?* Quelles matières est-ce que tu fais? ◇ *What colour is it?* C'est de quelle couleur? ◇ *What's the capital of Finland?* Quelle est la capitale de la Finlande? ◇ *What a mess!* Quel fouillis!
2 *qu'est-ce que* ◇ *What are you doing?* Qu'est-ce que vous faites? ◇ *What did you say?* Qu'est-ce que vous avez dit? ◇ *What is it?* Qu'est-ce que c'est? ◇ *What's the matter?* Qu'est-ce qu'il y a?
3 *qu'est-ce qui* ◇ *What happened?* Qu'est-ce qui s'est passé? ◇ *What's bothering you?* Qu'est-ce qui te préoccupe?

In relative phrases use **ce qui** *or* **ce que** *depending on whether* what *refers to the subject or the object of the sentence.*

PTO

4 (*subject*)
ce qui ◇ *I saw what happened.* J'ai vu ce qui est arrivé. ◇ *I know what's bothering you.* Je sais ce qui te préoccupe.
5 (*object*)
ce que ◇ *Tell me what you did.* Dites-moi ce que vous avez fait. ◇ *I heard what he said.* J'ai entendu ce qu'il a dit.
- **What?** (*what did you say*) Comment?
- **What!** (*shocked*) Quoi!

wheat NOUN
le *blé*

wheel NOUN
la *roue*
- **the steering wheel** le volant

wheelchair NOUN
le *fauteuil roulant*

when ADVERB, CONJUNCTION
quand ◇ *When did he go?* Quand est-ce qu'il est parti? ◇ *She was reading when I came in.* Elle lisait quand je suis entré.

where ADVERB, CONJUNCTION
où ◇ *Where's Emma today?* Où est Emma aujourd'hui? ◇ *Where do you live?* Où habites-tu? ◇ *Where are you going?* Où vas-tu? ◇ *a shop where you can buy croissants* un magasin où l'on peut acheter des croissants

whether CONJUNCTION
si ◇ *I don't know whether to go or not.* Je ne sais pas si y aller ou non.

which ADJECTIVE, PRONOUN
1 *quel* MASC
quelle FEM
◇ *Which flavour do you want?* Quel parfum est-ce que tu veux?

When asking which one *use* **lequel** *or* **laquelle**, *depending on whether the noun is masculine or feminine.*

- **I know his brother.–Which one?** Je connais son frère.–Lequel?
- **I know his sister.–Which one?** Je connais sa sœur.–Laquelle?
- **Which would you like?** Lequel est-ce que vous voulez?
- **Which of these are yours?** Lesquels sont à vous?

In relative phrases use **qui** *or* **que** *depending on whether* which *refers to the subject or the object of the sentence.*

2 *qui* (*subject*) ◇ *the CD which is playing now* le CD qui passe maintenant
3 *que* (*object*) ◇ *the CD which I bought today* le CD que j'ai acheté hier

while CONJUNCTION
see also while NOUN
1 *pendant que* ◇ *You hold the torch while I look inside.* Tiens la lampe électrique pendant que je regarde à l'intérieur.
2 *alors que* ◇ *Isobel is very dynamic, while Kay is more laid-back.* Isobel est très dynamique, alors que Kay est plus relax.

while NOUN
see also while CONJUNCTION
le *moment* ◇ *after a while* au bout d'un moment
- **a while ago** il y a un moment ◇ *He was here a while ago.* Il était là il y a un moment.
- **for a while** pendant quelque temps ◇ *I lived in London for a while.* J'ai vécu à Londres pendant quelque temps.
- **quite a while** longtemps ◇ *quite a while ago* il y a longtemps ◇ *I haven't seen him for quite a while.* Ça fait longtemps que je ne l'ai pas vu.

whip NOUN
see also whip VERB
le *fouet*

to **whip** VERB
see also whip NOUN
1 *fouetter* (*person, animal*)
2 *battre* (*eggs*)

whipped cream NOUN
la *crème fouettée*

whisk NOUN
le *fouet*

whiskers PL NOUN
les *moustaches* FEM PL

whisky NOUN
le *whisky*
(les *whiskies* PL)

to **whisper** VERB
chuchoter

whistle NOUN
see also whistle VERB
le *sifflet*
- **The referee blew his whistle.** L'arbitre a sifflé.

to **whistle** VERB
see also whistle NOUN
siffler

white ADJECTIVE
blanc MASC
blanche FEM
◇ *He's got white hair.* Il a les cheveux blancs.
- **white wine** le vin blanc
- **white bread** le pain blanc
- **white coffee** le café au lait
- **a white man** un Blanc
- **a white woman** une Blanche
- **white people** les Blancs

Whitsun NOUN

la *Pentecôte*

who PRONOUN

1 *qui* ◇ *Who said that?* Qui a dit ça? ◇ *Who is Jacques Chirac?* Qui est Jacques Chirac?

In relative phrases use **qui** *or* **que** *depending on whether* who *refers to the subject or the object of the verb.*

2 *qui* (*subject*) ◇ *the man who saw us* l'homme qui nous a vus ◇ *the man who spoke to us* l'homme qui nous a parlé

3 *que* (*object*) ◇ *the man who we saw* l'homme que nous avons vu ◇ *the man who she married* l'homme qu'elle a épousé

whole ADJECTIVE

see also whole NOUN

tout ◇ *the whole class* toute la classe ◇ *the whole afternoon* tout l'après-midi

- **a whole box of chocolates** toute une boîte de chocolats
- **the whole world** le monde entier

whole NOUN

see also whole ADJECTIVE

- **The whole of Wales was affected.** Le pays de Galles tout entier a été touché.
- **on the whole** dans l'ensemble

wholemeal ADJECTIVE

complet MASC
complète FEM

- **wholemeal bread** le pain complet

whom PRONOUN

qui ◇ *Whom did you see?* Qui avez-vous vu? ◇ *the man to whom I spoke* l'homme à qui j'ai parlé

whose PRONOUN, ADJECTIVE

1 *à qui* ◇ *Whose is this?* À qui est-ce? ◇ *I know whose it is.* Je sais à qui c'est. ◇ *Whose book is this?* À qui est ce livre?

2 *dont* (*after noun*) ◇ *the girl whose picture was in the paper* la jeune fille dont la photo était dans le journal

why ADVERB

pourquoi ◇ *Why did you do that?* Pourquoi avez-vous fait ça? ◇ *That's why he did it.* Voilà pourquoi il a fait ça. ◇ *Tell me why.* Dis-moi pourquoi.

- **I've never been to France.–Why not?** Je ne suis jamais allé en France.–Pourquoi?
- **All right, why not?** D'accord, pourquoi pas?

wicked ADJECTIVE

1 (*evil*)
méchant

2 (*really great*)
génial
(*géniaux* MASC PL)

wicket NOUN

le *guichet* (*stumps*)

wide ADJECTIVE, ADVERB

large ◇ *a wide road* une route large

- **wide open** grand ouvert ◇ *The door was wide open.* La porte était grande ouverte. ◇ *The windows were wide open.* Les fenêtres étaient grandes ouvertes.
- **wide awake** complètement réveillé

widow NOUN

la *veuve* ◇ *She's a widow.* Elle est veuve.

widower NOUN

le *veuf* ◇ *He's a widower.* Il est veuf.

width NOUN

la *largeur*

wife NOUN

la *femme* ◇ *She's his wife.* C'est sa femme.

wig NOUN

la *perruque*

wild ADJECTIVE

1 (*not tame*)
sauvage ◇ *a wild animal* un animal sauvage

2 (*crazy*)
fou MASC
folle FEM
◇ *She's a bit wild.* Elle est un peu folle.

wildlife NOUN

la *nature* ◇ *I'm interested in wildlife.* Je m'intéresse à la nature.

will NOUN

see also will VERB

le *testament* ◇ *He left me some money in his will.* Il m'a laissé de l'argent dans son testament.

will VERB

see also will NOUN

- **I'll show you your room.** Je vais te montrer ta chambre.
- **I'll give you a hand.** Je vais t'aider.

Use the French future tense when referring to the more distant future.

- **I will finish it tomorrow.** Je le finirai demain.
- **It won't take long.** Ça ne prendra pas longtemps.
- **Will you wash up?–No, I won't.** Est-ce que tu peux faire la vaisselle?–Non.
- **Will you help me?** Est-ce que tu peux m'aider?
- **Will you be quiet!** Voulez-vous bien vous taire!
- **That will be the postman.** Ça doit être le facteur.

willing ADJECTIVE

- **to be willing to do something** être prêt à faire quelque chose

to **win** VERB

PTO

see also win NOUN
gagner ◇ *Did you win?* Est-ce que tu as gagné?
◆ **to win a prize** remporter un prix

win NOUN
see also win VERB
la *victoire*

to **wind** VERB
see also wind NOUN
1 *enrouler* (*rope, wool, wire*)
2 *serpenter* (*river, path*) ◇ *The road winds through the valley.* La route serpente à travers la vallée.

wind NOUN
see also wind VERB
le *vent* ◇ *There was a strong wind.* Il y avait beaucoup de vent.
◆ **a wind instrument** un instrument à vent
◆ **wind power** l'énergie éolienne FEM

windmill NOUN
le *moulin à vent*
(les *moulins à vent* PL)

window NOUN
1 (*of building*)
la *fenêtre*
2 (*in car, train*)
la *vitre*
◆ **a shop window** une vitrine
3 (*window pane*)
le *carreau*
(les *carreaux* PL)
◇ *to break a window* casser un carreau
◇ *a broken window* un carreau cassé

windscreen NOUN
le *pare-brise*
(les *pare-brise* PL)

windscreen wiper NOUN
l' *essuie-glace* MASC
(les *essuie-glace* PL)

windy ADJECTIVE
(*place*)
venteux MASC
venteuse FEM
◆ **It's windy.** Il y a du vent.

wine NOUN
le *vin* ◇ *a bottle of wine* une bouteille de vin ◇ *a glass of wine* un verre de vin
◆ **white wine** le vin blanc
◆ **red wine** le vin rouge
◆ **a wine bar** un bar à vin
◆ **a wine glass** un verre à vin
◆ **the wine list** la carte des vins

wing NOUN
l' *aile* FEM

to **wink** VERB
◆ **to wink at somebody** faire un clin d'œil à quelqu'un ◇ *He winked at me.* Il m'a fait un clin d'œil.

winner NOUN
le *gagnant*
la *gagnante*

winning ADJECTIVE
◆ **the winning team** l'équipe gagnante
◆ **the winning goal** le but décisif

winter NOUN
l' *hiver* MASC
◆ **in winter** en hiver

winter sports PL NOUN
les *sports d'hiver* MASC PL

to **wipe** VERB
essuyer
◆ **to wipe one's feet** s'essuyer les pieds
◇ *Wipe your feet!* Essuie-toi les pieds!
◆ **to wipe up** essuyer

wire NOUN
le *fil de fer*

wisdom tooth NOUN
la *dent de sagesse*
(les *dents de sagesse* PL)

wise ADJECTIVE
sage

to **wish** VERB
see also wish NOUN
◆ **to wish for something** souhaiter quelque chose ◇ *What more could you wish for?* Que pourrais-tu souhaiter de plus?
◆ **to wish to do something** désirer faire quelque chose ◇ *I wish to make a complaint.* Je désire porter plainte.
◆ **I wish you were here!** Si seulement tu étais ici!
◆ **I wish you'd told me!** Si seulement tu m'en avais parlé!

wish NOUN
see also wish VERB
le *vœu*
(les *vœux* PL)
◇ *to make a wish* faire un vœu
◆ **"best wishes"** (*on greetings card*) "meilleurs vœux"
◆ **"with best wishes, Kathy"** "bien amicalement, Kathy"

wit NOUN
l' *esprit* MASC (*humour*)

with PREPOSITION
1 *avec* ◇ *Come with me.* Venez avec moi. ◇ *He walks with a stick.* Il marche avec une canne.
◆ **a woman with blue eyes** une femme aux yeux bleus
2 *chez* (*at the home of*) ◇ *We stayed with friends.* Nous avons logé chez des amis.
3 *de* ◇ *green with envy* vert de jalousie
◇ *to shake with fear* trembler de peur
◇ *Fill the jug with water.* Remplis la carafe d'eau.

within PREPOSITION

- **The shops are within easy reach.** Les magasins sont à proximité.
- **within the week** avant la fin de la semaine

vithout PREPOSITION
sans ◇ *without a coat* sans manteau ◇ *without speaking* sans parler

vitness NOUN
le *témoin* ◇ *There were no witnesses.* Il n'a pas eu de témoins.

vitty ADJECTIVE
spirituel MASC
spirituelle FEM

vives PL NOUN *see* **wife**

voke up, woken up VERB *see* **wake up**

volf NOUN
le *loup*

voman NOUN
la *femme* ◇ *a woman doctor* une femme médecin

von VERB *see* **win**

vonder VERB
se demander ◇ *I wonder why she said that.* Je me demande pourquoi elle a dit ça. ◇ *I wonder what that means.* Je me demande ce que ça veut dire. ◇ *I wonder where Caroline is.* Je me demande où est Caroline.

vonderful ADJECTIVE
formidable

von't = **will not**

vood NOUN
le *bois* (*timber, forest*) ◇ *It's made of wood.* C'est en bois. ◇ *We went for a walk in the wood.* Nous sommes allés nous promener dans le bois.

vooden ADJECTIVE
en bois ◇ *a wooden chair* une chaise en bois

voodwork NOUN
la *menuiserie* ◇ *My hobby is woodwork.* Je fais de la menuiserie.

vool NOUN
la *laine* ◇ *It's made of wool.* C'est en laine.

vord NOUN
le *mot* ◇ *a difficult word* un mot difficile

- **What's the word for "shop" in German?** Comment dit-on "magasin" en allemand?
- **in other words** en d'autres termes
- **to have a word with somebody** parler avec quelqu'un
- **the words** (*lyrics*) les paroles ◇ *I really like the words of this song.* J'adore les paroles de cette chanson.

word processing NOUN
le *traitement de texte*

word processor NOUN
la *machine de traitement de texte*

wore VERB *see* **wear**

work NOUN
see also **work** VERB
le *travail*
(les *travaux* PL)
◇ *She's looking for work.* Elle cherche du travail. ◇ *He's at work at the moment.* Il est au travail en ce moment.

- **It's hard work.** C'est dur.
- **to be off work** (*sick*) être malade ◇ *He's been off work for a week.* Il est malade depuis une semaine.
- **He's out of work.** Il est sans emploi.

to **work** VERB
see also **work** NOUN
1 *travailler* (*person*) ◇ *She works in a shop.* Elle travaille dans un magasin. ◇ *to work hard* travailler dur
2 *marcher* (*machine, plan*) ◇ *The heating isn't working.* Le chauffage ne marche pas. ◇ *My plan worked perfectly.* Mon plan a marché impeccablement.

- **to work out (1)** (*exercise*) faire de l'exercice ◇ *I work out twice a week.* Je fais de l'exercice deux fois par semaine.
- **to work out (2)** (*turn out*) marcher ◇ *In the end it worked out really well.* Au bout du compte, ça a très bien marché.
- **to work out (3)** (*figure out*) arriver à comprendre ◇ *I just couldn't work it out.* Je n'arrivais pas du tout à comprendre.
- **It works out at £10 each.** Ça fait dix livres chacun.

worker NOUN
(*in factory*)
l' *ouvrier* MASC
l' *ouvrière* FEM

- **He's a factory worker.** Il est ouvrier.
- **She's a good worker.** Elle travaille bien.

work experience NOUN
le *stage* ◇ *I'm going to do work experience in a factory.* Je vais faire un stage dans une usine.

working-class ADJECTIVE
ouvrier MASC
ouvrière FEM
◇ *a working-class family* une famille ouvrière

works NOUN
l' *usine* FEM (*factory*)

worksheet NOUN
la *feuille d'exercices*

workshop NOUN
l' *atelier* MASC ◇ *a drama workshop* un atelier de théâtre

workstation NOUN
le *poste de travail*

PTO

(les *postes de travail* PL)

world NOUN
le *monde*
- **He's the world champion.** Il est champion du monde.

worm NOUN
le *ver*

worn VERB *see* **wear**

worn ADJECTIVE
usé ◇ *The carpet is a bit worn.* La moquette est un peu usée.
- **worn out** (*tired*) épuisé

worried ADJECTIVE
inquiet MASC
inquiète FEM
◇ *She's very worried.* Elle est très inquiète.
- **to be worried about something** s'inquiéter pour quelque chose ◇ *I'm worried about the exams.* Je m'inquiète pour les examens.
- **to look worried** avoir l'air inquiet ◇ *She looks a bit worried.* Elle a l'air un peu inquiète.

to **worry** VERB
s'inquiéter
- **Don't worry!** Ne t'inquiète pas!

worse ADJECTIVE, ADVERB
1 *pire* ◇ *It was even worse than that.* C'était encore pire que ça. ◇ *My results were bad, but his were even worse.* Mes notes étaient mauvaises, mais les siennes étaient encore pires.
2 *plus mal* ◇ *I'm feeling worse.* Je me sens plus mal.

to **worship** VERB
vénérer (*God*)
- **He really worships her.** Il est en adoration devant elle.

worst ADJECTIVE
see also worst NOUN
- **the worst** le plus mauvais ◇ *the worst student in the class* le plus mauvais élève de la classe ◇ *He got the worst mark in the whole class.* Il a eu la plus mauvaise note de toute la classe.
- **my worst enemy** mon pire ennemi
- **Maths is my worst subject.** Je suis vraiment nul en maths.

worst NOUN
see also worst ADJECTIVE
le *pire* ◇ *The worst of it is that...* Le pire c'est que...
- **at worst** au pire
- **if the worst comes to the worst** au pire

worth ADJECTIVE
- **to be worth** valoir ◇ *It's worth a lot of money.* Ça vaut très cher. ◇ *How much is it worth?* Ça vaut combien?
- **It's worth it.** Ça vaut la peine. ◇ *Is it worth it?* Est-ce que ça vaut la peine? ◇ *It's not worth it.* Ça ne vaut pas la peine.

would VERB
- **Would you like a biscuit?** Vous voulez un biscuit?
- **Would you like to go and see a film?** Est-ce que tu veux aller voir un film?
- **Would you close the door please?** Vous pouvez fermer la porte, s'il vous plaît?
- **I'd like...** J'aimerais... ◇ *I'd like to go to America.* J'aimerais aller en Amérique. ◇ *Shall we go and see a film?–Yes, I'd like that.* Si on allait voir un film?–Oui, j'aimerais bien.
- **I said I would do it.** J'ai dit que je le ferais.
- **If you asked him he'd do it.** Si vous le lui demandiez, il le ferait.
- **If you had asked him he would have done it.** Si vous le lui aviez demandé, il l'aurait fait.

wouldn't = **would not**

wound NOUN
see also wound VERB
la *blessure*

to **wound** VERB
see also wound NOUN
blesser ◇ *He was wounded in the leg.* Il a été blessé à la jambe.

to **wrap** VERB
emballer ◇ *She's wrapping her Christmas presents.* Elle est en train d'emballer ses cadeaux de Noël.
- **Can you wrap it for me please?** (*in shop*) Vous pouvez me faire un papier cadeau, s'il vous plaît?
- **to wrap up** emballer

wrapping paper NOUN
le *papier cadeau*

wreck NOUN
see also wreck VERB
1 le *tas de ferraille* (*vehicle, machine*) ◇ *That car is a wreck!* Cette voiture est un tas de ferraille!
2 la *loque* (*person*) ◇ *After the exams I was a complete wreck.* Après les examens j'étais une véritable loque.

to **wreck** VERB
see also wreck NOUN
1 *démolir* (*building, vehicle*) ◇ *The explosion wrecked the whole house.* L'explosion a démoli toute la maison.
2 *ruiner* (*plan, holiday*) ◇ *The trip was wrecked by bad weather.* Le voyage a été ruiné par le mauvais temps.

wreckage NOUN

1 les *débris* MASC PL (*of vehicle*)
2 les *décombres* MASC PL (*of building*)

estler NOUN
le *lutteur*
la *lutteuse*

estling NOUN
la *lutte*

inkled ADJECTIVE
ridé

ist NOUN
le *poignet*

ite VERB
écrire ◇ *to write a letter* écrire une lettre
to write to somebody écrire à quelqu'un ◇ *I'm going to write to her in French.* Je vais lui écrire en français.
to write down noter ◇ *I wrote down the address.* J'ai noté l'adresse.
Can you write it down for me, please? Vous pouvez me l'écrire, s'il vous plaît?

iter NOUN
l' *écrivain* MASC ◇ *She's a writer.* Elle est écrivain.

iting NOUN
l' *écriture* FEM ◇ *I can't read your writing.* Je n'arrive pas à lire ton écriture.
◆ **in writing** par écrit

written VERB *see* **write**

wrong ADJECTIVE, ADVERB
1 (*incorrect*)
faux MASC
fausse FEM
◇ *The information they gave us was wrong.* Les renseignements qu'ils nous ont donnés étaient faux.
◆ **the wrong answer** la mauvaise réponse
◆ **You've got the wrong number.** Vous vous êtes trompé de numéro.
2 (*morally bad*)
mal ◇ *I think hunting is wrong.* Je trouve que c'est mal de chasser.
◆ **to be wrong** (*mistaken*) se tromper ◇ *You're wrong about that.* Tu te trompes.
◆ **to do something wrong** se tromper ◇ *You've done it wrong.* Tu t'es trompé.
◆ **to go wrong** (*plan*) mal tourner ◇ *The robbery went wrong and they got caught.* Le cambriolage a mal tourné et ils ont été pris.
◆ **What's wrong?** Qu'est-ce qu'il y a?
◆ **What's wrong with her?** Qu'est-ce qu'elle a?

wrote VERB *see* **write**

X

to **X-ray** VERB
- **to X-ray something** faire une radio de quelque chose ◇ *They X-rayed my arm.* Ils ont fait une radio de mon bras.

X-ray NOUN
la *radio* ◇ *to have an X-ray* passer une radio

Y

yacht NOUN
1 le *voilier* (*sailing boat*)
2 le *yacht* (*luxury motorboat*)

yard NOUN
la *cour* (*of building*) ◇ *in the yard* dans la cour

to **yawn** VERB
bâiller

year NOUN
l' *an* MASC ◇ *last year* l'an dernier ◇ *next year* l'an prochain
- **to be 15 years old** avoir quinze ans
- **an eight-year-old child** un enfant de huit ans

In French secondary schools, years are counted from the sixième *(youngest) to* première *and* terminale *(oldest).*

◇ *the first year* la sixième ◇ *the second year* la cinquième ◇ *the third year* la quatrième ◇ *the fourth year* la troisième ◇ *the fifth year* la seconde
- **She's in the fifth year.** Elle est en seconde.
- **He's a first-year.** Il est en sixième.

to **yell** VERB
hurler

yellow ADJECTIVE
jaune

yes ADVERB
1 *oui* ◇ *Do you like it?–Yes.* Tu aimes ça?–Oui.
- **Would you like a cup of tea?–Yes please.** Voulez-vous une tasse de thé?–Je veux bien.

Use **si** *when answering negative questions.*

2 *si* ◇ *Don't you like it?–Yes!* Tu n'aimes pas ça?–Si! ◇ *You're not Swiss, are you?–Yes I am!* Tu n'es pas suisse, si?–Si!

yesterday ADVERB
hier ◇ *yesterday morning* hier matin ◇ *yesterday afternoon* hier après-midi ◇ *yesterday evening* hier soir ◇ *all day yesterday* toute la journée d'hier

yet ADVERB
encore
- **not yet** pas encore ◇ *It's not finished yet.* Ce n'est pas encore fini.
- **not as yet** pas encore ◇ *There's no news as yet.* Nous n'avons pas encore de nouvelles.
- **Have you finished yet?** Vous avez fini?

yob NOUN
le *loubard*

yoghurt NOUN
le *yaourt*

yolk NOUN
le *jaune d'œuf*
(les *jaunes d'œuf* PL)

you PRONOUN

Only use **tu** *when speaking to one person of your own age or younger. If in doubt use* **vous**.

1 *vous* (*polite form or plural*) ◇ *Do you like football?* Est-ce que vous aimez le football? ◇ *Can I help you?* Est-ce que je peux vous aider? ◇ *It's for you.* C'est pour vous.
2 *tu* (*familiar singular*) ◇ *Do you like football?* Tu aimes le football?

vous *never changes, but* **tu** *has different forms. When* you *is the object of the sentence use* **te** *not* **tu**. **t'** *becomes* **t'** *before a vowel sound.*

3 *te* ◇ *I know you.* Je te connais. ◇ *I gave it you.* Je te l'ai donné.
t' ◇ *I saw you.* Je t'ai vu. ◇ *I'll help you* Je vais t'aider.

toi *is used instead of* **tu** *after a preposition and in comparisons.*

4 *toi* ◇ *It's for you.* C'est pour toi. ◇ *I'll come with you.* Je viens avec toi. ◇ *She's younger than you.* Elle est plus jeune que toi.

young ADJECTIVE
jeune
- **young people** les jeunes

younger ADJECTIVE
plus jeune ◇ *He's younger than me.* Il est plus jeune que moi.
- **my younger brother** mon frère cadet
- **my younger sister** ma sœur cadette

your ADJECTIVE

Only use **ton/ta/tes** *when speaking to one person of your own age or younger. If in doubt use* **votre/vos**.

1 (*polite form or plural*)
votre ◇ *your house* votre maison

vos PL ◇ *your seats* vos places
2 (*familiar singular*)
ton MASC ◇ *your brother* ton frère
ta FEM ◇ *your sister* ta sœur
tes PL ◇ *your parents* tes parents
ta *becomes* **ton** *before a vowel sound.*
your friend (1) (*male*) ton ami
your friend (2) (*female*) ton amie
Do not use **votre/vos** *or* **ton/ta/tes** *with parts of the body.*
◇ *Would you like to wash your hands?* Est-ce que vous voulez vous laver les mains? ◇ *Do you want to wash your hair?* Tu veux te laver les cheveux?

yours PRONOUN
Only use **le tien/la tienne/les tiens/les tiennes** *when talking to one person of your own age or younger. If in doubt use* **le vôtre/la vôtre/les vôtres**. *The same applies to* **à toi** *and* **à vous**.
1 *le vôtre* + MASC NOUN ◇ *I've lost my pen. Can I use yours?* J'ai perdu mon stylo. Je peux utiliser le vôtre?
la vôtre + FEM NOUN ◇ *I like that car. Is it yours?* J'aime cette voiture-là. C'est la vôtre?
les vôtres + PL NOUN ◇ *my parents and yours* mes parents et les vôtres
Is this yours? C'est à vous? ◇ *This book is yours.* Ce livre est à vous. ◇ *Whose is this?–It's yours.* C'est à qui?–À vous.
Yours sincerely... Veuillez agréer l'expression de mes sentiments les meilleurs...
2 *le tien* + MASC NOUN ◇ *I've lost my pen. Can I use yours?* J'ai perdu mon stylo. Je peux utiliser le tien?
la tienne + FEM NOUN ◇ *I like that car. Is it yours?* J'aime cette voiture-là. C'est la tienne?
les tiens + MASC PL NOUN ◇ *my parents and yours* mes parents et les tiens
les tiennes + FEM PL NOUN ◇ *My hands are dirty, yours are clean.* Mes mains sont sales, les tiennes sont propres.
→ **Is this yours?** C'est à toi? ◇ *This book is yours.* Ce livre est à toi. ◇ *Whose is this?–It's yours.* C'est à qui?–À toi.

yourself PRONOUN
Only use **te** *when talking to one person of your own age or younger; use* **vous** *to everyone else. If in doubt use* **vous**.
1 *vous* (*polite form*) ◇ *Have you hurt yourself?* Est-ce que vous vous êtes fait mal? ◇ *Tell me about yourself!* Parlez-moi de vous!
2 *te* (*familiar form*) ◇ *Have you hurt yourself?* Est-ce que tu t'es fait mal?
After a preposition, use **toi** *instead of* **te**.
3 *toi* (*familiar form*) ◇ *Tell me about yourself!* Parle-moi de toi!
4 *toi-même* ◇ *Do it yourself!* Fais-le toi-même!
5 *vous-même* ◇ *Do it yourself!* Faites-le vous-même!

yourselves PRONOUN
1 *vous* ◇ *Did you enjoy yourselves?* Vous vous êtes bien amusés?
2 *vous-mêmes* ◇ *Did you make it yourselves?* Vous l'avez fait vous-mêmes?

youth club NOUN
le *centre de jeunes*

youth hostel NOUN
l' *auberge de jeunesse* FEM
(les *auberges de jeunesse* PL)

Yugoslavia NOUN
la *Yougoslavie*
→ **in the former Yugoslavia** en ex-Yougoslavie

Z

zany ADJECTIVE
loufoque

zebra NOUN
le *zèbre*

zebra crossing NOUN
le *passage clouté*

zero NOUN
le *zéro*

Zimbabwe NOUN
le *Zimbabwe*
in Zimbabwe au Zimbabwe

zimmer frame ® NOUN
le *déambulateur*

zip NOUN
la *fermeture éclair* ®
(les *fermetures éclair* PL)

zit NOUN
le *bouton*

zodiac NOUN
le *zodiaque* ◇ *the signs of the zodiac* les signes du zodiaque

zone NOUN
la *zone*

zoo NOUN
le *zoo*

zoom lens NOUN
le *zoom*

DEVELOPING DICTIONARY SKILLS IN FRENCH

The National Curriculum states that students "should be taught to use dictionaries and reference materials" and students are now entitled to take a dictionary into examinations. Thus, the need for students to use (and not misuse!) a bilingual dictionary has never been more pressing.

- This pack of photocopiable masters provides you with ready-to-use and "fun" activities to develop your students' dictionary skills.
- Examples are taken from Collins Pocket French Dictionary but the materials can be used alongside any reputable bilingual dictionary.
- The easy way to meet the new NC requirements for dictionary usage
- Crosses age ranges and abilities: KS3 and KS4, less able and more able
- Fully photocopiable
- Ideal for use in the classroom or at home

0 00 320194-5 48pp

Contents

The activities contained in the pack cover a wide range of topic areas and help students to develop a variety of dictionary skills including: learning how a dictionary is organized - finding meanings - mastering phonetics - when not to use a dictionary - using a dictionary in an exam.